6级轻过书课包

单词之间

大学英语6级核心词汇单词书

主编 马天艺 启航大学生考试研究中心

版权专有　侵权必究

图书在版编目（CIP）数据

单词之间：大学英语 6 级核心词汇单词书 / 马天艺，启航大学生考试研究中心主编 . — 北京：北京理工大学出版社 , 2022.3

（6 级轻过书课包）

ISBN 978 – 7 – 5763 – 1134 – 1

Ⅰ.①单… Ⅱ.①马… ②启… Ⅲ.①大学英语水平考试 – 词汇 – 自学参考资料　Ⅳ.① H319.34

中国版本图书馆 CIP 数据核字（2022）第 040774 号

出版发行 / 北京理工大学出版社有限责任公司

社　　址 / 北京市海淀区中关村南大街 5 号

邮　　编 / 100081

电　　话 /（010）68914775（总编室）

　　　　　（010）82562903（教材售后服务热线）

　　　　　（010）68944723（其他图书服务热线）

网　　址 / http://www.bitpress.com.cn

经　　销 / 全国各地新华书店

印　　刷 / 天津市蓟县宏图印务有限公司

开　　本 / 710 毫米 ×1000 毫米　1/16

印　　张 / 15.5　　　　　　　　　　　　　　责任编辑 / 武丽娟

字　　数 / 387 千字　　　　　　　　　　　　文案编辑 / 武丽娟

版　　次 / 2022 年 3 月第 1 版　2022 年 3 月第 1 次印刷　　责任校对 / 刘亚男

定　　价 / 149.60 元（全 2 册）　　　　　　　　　　　　　责任印制 / 李志强

图书出现印装质量问题，请拨打售后服务热线，本社负责调换

它从来不只是一本单词书

自 2009 年正式进入英语四六级、考研培训行业,如今本人已投身英语教学事业 10 年有余。我深感学生在背单词时的痛苦和无奈,有多少同学背了忘、忘了背、背了再忘、忘了再背?有多少同学在背与忘的过程中开始怀疑自己的智商,甚至怀疑人生?

背单词绝对没有错,错是错在背单词的方法和思路上。那么什么是科学与正确的背单词方法呢?有太多的同学问我:我是应该买本词汇书或者跟着背单词的 APP"刷词"吗?还是我要在语境和句子中学习和背诵单词?我心中的想法是,难道不应该将这两种方式结合吗?为什么要分开呢?试想我们学汉语的时候,难道不是先记"忙"这个字,然后才在句子乃至文章中理解,甚至自己造句学习及应用"忙碌"这个词语吗?难道不是先记"难"这个字,再通过句子和语境去理解"艰难"一词吗?所以我一直坚信学习英语单词既离不开对这个单词本身的理解和识记,也少不了在语境和句子中应用这个单词。这二者缺一不可,没有前者,英语单词就变成了无本之木;没有后者,英语单词就失去了秀丽之彩。

2018 年,《单词之间:考研英语核心词汇单词书》正式出版,3 年期间历经 5 次迭代,凭借着科学的记词体系与真题的紧密结合成为考研词汇书中的畅销书,被数十万考研学子所选择,得到了他们的好评。通过对原有体系的精进,我编成了这本《6 级轻过书课包——单词之间:大学英语 6 级核心词汇单词书》,现将本书的科学体系与特征介绍如下:

选词全面,重点突出

本书共收录 2 033 个单词和 739 条六级真句,所收录单词皆为大学英语六级考试中的核心词汇。

本书将大学英语六级大纲词汇分为三类:

高、中频词 在六级真题中的出现频率≥2(必背)

基础词 在六级真题中的出现频率很高但难度较低的中小学词汇(必背)

零频词和低频词 在六级真题中的出现频率<2(要求过线即可的考生可以不背)

科学体系,高效背诵

本书主要用科学的构词法及词源拆分法完成对词汇的理解和速记,辅之以联想记忆法,穿插希腊罗马神话故事,并配以全套的视频讲解。先从词根理解开始,让考生清楚词根的意义以及如何记忆;在了解词根的基础上,串出一组单词,形成群组式、"撸串"式记忆,告别传统的逐个字母死记硬背法、自然拼读法、重复拼写记忆法等，用科学的词根词源法完成词汇的高效记忆，再配以详解课程科学有效地记忆单词。同时，每个主词都配以考频，而不是简单地将其标记为传统的高频词、中频词、低频词或超纲词。如此一来，各个单词的重要程度一目了然，这也让笔者做的在真题中逐个查找每个词的准确考频这项庞大的工程有了价值。

紧跟真题，精确考点

基本上，每个主词都配备记法、派生词、形近词、近义词、考法、真句及参考译文等，将真题考点一网打尽。本书以最新几年的真题为蓝本，内容更精准有效，基本所有考点均来自 2019 年 12 月至 2021 年 12 月的共 15 套真题。在选取真题的过程中，笔者剔除了早年的大学英语六级真题，筛除了过旧的考点，从而极大地帮助考生提高学习效率，顺利通关大学英语六级考试。

三轮背词，辅助 APP

本书遵循三轮复习法，旨在帮助考生减少选择忧虑，克服学习方向上的障碍，解决多少天背完、每天背完哪些词、多少天复习完毕、怎么复习等问题。本书复习手段多样化，可以提高考生学习的热情，再配以"启航背单词"的配套小程序，让考生随时随地想背就背。纸质书籍与小程序相结合，达到最好的学习效果（详见使用说明）。另外，我的微博（@考研英语马天艺）和英语学习微信公众号（马天艺英语）这两个平台会推送大学英语六级相关的干货内容，也欢迎大家在微博上与我交流学习问题。

最后，我想和大家分享一句话：方向永远比努力更重要。你要记住：原地踏步、不愿向前奔跑的人是可恨的，而摸不清方向只顾向前奔跑的人是可怜的。愿你们成为聪明睿智的人，选择正确的方向努力奔跑。愿这本集结了我 13 年英语单词讲解精华并耗时 3 年之久编撰而成的用心之作——《6级轻过书课包——单词之间：大学英语6级核心词汇单词书》能成为让所有考生一往无前的指南针。

马天艺

45天三轮复习法使用说明

第一轮 精学全书28个单元及配套详解视频

▶ 适用于六级核心词汇的全面背诵与掌握。

核心词汇详解视频可通过扫描书中每个单元第一页的二维码获取,配合本书完成每个单元单词第一轮的记忆与背诵。基本上,所有主词都包括考频、词义、速记方法、引申词、派生词、近义词、形近词、考法、真句及参考译文等内容,紧贴考点,紧跟真题,紧追考试,真正做到科学高效、有的放矢学习大纲词汇。

▶ 时间:30天(28个单元,1天1个单元,空余两天可间隔休息)
▶ 频次:1遍

第二轮 利用附录部分"单词索引"强化记忆

▶ 适用于六级核心词汇的速记与巩固。

正文部分按照词根进行编写,让考生形成群组式、"撸串"式记忆;而附录部分的"单词索引"按照字母表顺序将收录词进行重新排列,词后标注的页码是该单词在正文所处的页码。"单词索引"部分无中文释义,让考生看英文想中文。看英文想中文本身是一种很好的记忆和复习单词的手段,相当于去掉了"拐杖"完全靠自己前行,也更能帮助考生检测自身真正的词汇水平,避免"伪熟悉"的假象。

使用过程中,已掌握词汇可直接划掉或者画对勾进行标记区分,未掌握词汇可用记号笔或者画问号进行标记区分,按照标注页码回到正文对应位置查找完整内容,并"复看"配套课程。

▶ 时间:15天(每7天快速过完1遍,中间间隔一天休息)
▶ 频次:2遍

第三轮 结合"启航背单词"小程序,活用"单词索引"

▶ 适用于六级核心词汇的"快速排雷+查漏补缺"。

本轮运用无纸化便携学习模式,旨在帮助完成前两轮学习的考生利用碎片时间对核心词汇进行快速且高效的自测和反复记忆。运用"背词模式",考生可以通过"辨意"来检验自己对于核心词汇的掌握程度，确保自己真正掌握了某一单词的准确释义。运用"浏览模式"，考生则可以通过"快速阅读"来全面复习所有核心词汇。排队打饭的时候、排队打水的时候……不用拿书，就用随身携带的手机，你就可以把握好等候的每分每秒，让你的等待有价值、有意义。

此外，到了第三轮背词的时候，大部分考生应该都开始了真题的训练，这个时候附录部分的"单词索引"就可配合正文内容充当做题时的专属"词典"。遇到不会的单词时，通过"单词索引"来定位正文内容进行再次学习和学习配套课程。真题中出现但没有收录到本书的词汇相对没有那么重要，词汇的重要性在背诵过程中一目了然，考生就可以给自己适当减负，不需要去学习那些有难度但偏僻的生词。

▶ 时间/频次：考生可根据自身的复习进度而定

目录

Day 01

-ab- 否定,不 001
-academy- 学院 001
-act-、-ag- 行动,作用 002
-alter- 改变 003
-ann-、-enn- 年 003
-astr-、-aster- 星星 004
-aud-、-audi- 听见 004
-auth- 作者,权威 004
-a-、-a 辅-(除了-ab-)=to 加强,强调 005

Day 02

非成组词(A 字母)........................ 009
-bas- 基础 011
-bat- 打 011
-be- 是,成为 012
-board- 板 -broad- 宽广 012
-boast- 自夸,吹嘘 013
-bound- 束缚,约束 013
非成组词(B 字母)........................ 013

Day 03

-camp- 营地,露营 016
-cap-、-capt-、-cip-、-cup- 头;抓 016
-car- 汽车 018
-car-、-care-、-cer-、-cher- 关心,担忧 018
-ceed-、-cede-、-cess- 走 019
-ceive-、-cept- 抓,拿 021
-centr- 中心,中央 022

Day 04

-cid-、-cis-、-cas- 切,切开;落下,跌落 024
-circ- 圆,圆圈,圆环 025
-civi- 文明 026
-clar- 清楚,清晰 026
-class- 等级,类别 026
-cline- 爬,攀登 027
-clud-、-clus- 关闭 027
-com-、-con-、-col-、-cor- 全部,共同,一起;加强 028

001

Day 05

- -commun- 共同 032
- -contr-、-counter- 反,相反 032
- -cord- 心,核心 033
- -count- 计算 034
- -cover- 覆盖 034
- -creat-、-creas- 产生,创造 035
- -cred- 相信,信用 036
- -crim- 罪 036
- -crit- 批评,评论 037
- -cult- 耕种 037
- -cur- 跑;流 038

Day 06

- -cure- 治疗 040
- 非成组词（C 字母）....................... 040
- -de- 下,向下 043
- -dem- 民众 044
- -dent- 相同 045
- -dic-、-dict- 说 045

Day 07

- -di-、-dis-、-dif- 散,分散;否定,不 047
- -divid-、-divis- 分 048
- -dom- 房子,家;统治,支配 048
- -duc-、-duce-、-duct- 引导 049
- -dur- 持续 050

- -dyn- 动力,力量 051
- 非成组词（D 字母）....................... 051
- -econom- 经济 052

Day 08

- -electr- 电,电流 054
- -empt- 空,空虚 054
- -em-、-en- 使动 055
- -equ- 相等 056
- -e-、-e 辅-（除了 -em-、-en-）= out 外,向外,出去 057
- 非成组词（E 字母）....................... 060

Day 09

- -fac-、-fec-、-fic-、-feat- 做;脸,面 062
- -fenc-、-fend-、-fens-=fence 篱笆,栅栏,围墙 065
- -fer- 拿 066
- -fess- 说 068
- -fid- 相信,忠诚 068
- -fil-、-fill- 填充,填满 069

Day 10

- -fin- 限制,极限 070
- -firm- 坚固,坚定,确定 071
- -flect-、-flex-、-flict- 弯曲,折 071
- -flu-、-fuse- 流 072

–fore– 前，以前，提前 073
–form– 形式 074
–found– 建立，创立 075
–fract–、–frag– 破，打破 075
–fund– 资本，资金，资助 076

Day 11

非成组词（F 字母）................... 077
–gen–、–gn–、–gene– 基因 080
–geo– 大地，土地 082
–gl– 光线，光明 082
–gn(o)– 知道，认识 082

Day 12

–grad–、–grat–、–gret–、–gress– 走 ... 084
非成组词（G 字母）................... 086
–hand– 手 086
–heir–、–heri–、–herit– 继承 087
–hum– 人类，土 087
非成组词（H 字母）................... 088
–imag– 想象 089

Day 13

–im–、–in–、–il– 里，里面 090
–ject– 送，投掷 092
–just– 刚才的，刚好的，正好的；公平的，正义的 093
非成组词（I 字母和 J 字母）......... 093

–labor– 努力，劳动 094
–lect–、–leg–、–lig– 选择；法律 ... 095

Day 14

–lev– 举起，抬起；轻的 098
–liber– 自由 099
–light– 轻的；灯，光 100
–liter– 文字 101
–loc– 地点，地方 101
–log– 说话 102
–logy– 学科 102
–lum–、–lus–、–lux– 光线，光明 ... 103
非成组词（L 字母）................... 103

Day 15

–man–、–manu– 手 105
–mark– 标记 105
–med–、–mid– 中间 106
–mod– 样式，模式 106
–mem– 记忆 107
–ment– 思想，想法 107
–mer– 经商，商业 109
–minis– 管理，经营 109
–mis– 否定，不 110
–max–、–maj– 大 –min– 小 110
–mis–、–mit– 思念，错过；送，扔 ... 111

003

Day 16

-mob-、-mot-、-mat-、-mov- 移动，运动 114

-mult-、-multi- 多 116

非成组词（M 字母） 116

-nat-、-nas- 生，出生 118

-norm- 标准，正常 119

-not- 表示，注意 119

-nov- 新 120

Day 17

-num- 数，数字 121

非成组词（N 字母） 121

-opt- 选择 122

-ord- 顺序，秩序 123

-ori- 开始，起初 124

-out- 出去，向外 125

-over- 上，上面 125

非成组词（O 字母） 126

Day 18

-par-、-part- 部分；分离，分开 128

-pas-、-pass- 经过，放弃；感情，情绪 129

-pel-、-pul- 拉 130

-pend-、-pens- 悬挂；花费 131

-per- 贯穿 132

-pet- 喜爱，追求 132

-phys- 身体，肉体，物质 133

-ple-、-pli-、-plo- 填充，填满 133

-plea- 请求；高兴 135

Day 19

-ply-、-pli- 折 137

-poli- 政治 138

-port- 港口；扛，运输 138

-pos-、-pon- 放置 139

-post- 作单词；作前缀时表示"后，向后" 142

-prec- 价值 143

-press- 压 143

-pre-、-pro-、-pri- 前，以前，向前 144

Day 20

-prim-、-prin- 第一 146

-priv- 私人，个人 146

-prov- 证明 147

-pub- 公开 147

-put- 想，思考 148

非成组词（P 字母） 148

-que-、-quire- 求 150

-re- 向回，向反，向后 =back、return；反复，再一次 =again and again 151

Day 21

-rect-、-ract- 正，直 153
-reg-、-rig-、-rog- 管理，统治 154
-riv- 河流 155
-rout- 路，道路 155
非成组词（R 字母）................................ 156
-sect-、-seg- 部分 158
-sens-、-sent- 送，派遣；感觉，情绪 158
-sert- 塞，放 160

Day 22

-serv- 服务；保持，保留 161
-sid- 坐 162
-sign- 签，符号 163
-sim-、-sem-、-sym-、-syn- 相同 164
-soci- 社会 165
-sol- 单独 166
-solv-、-solu- 解决，溶解 166
-soph- 智慧，思考 167
-spec- 专门的 167

Day 23

-spec-、-spect-、-spic- 看 169
-st-、-sist-、-stitute- 站立 171

Day 24

-st-、-sist-、-stitute- 站立 178

-sti-、-stinct-、-sting- 刺，叮 178
-spir- 呼吸，吹气 179
-str- 拖，拉 180
-stru-、-struct- 建筑，建造 181
-sult- 说 183
-sum- 拿 183
-sur- 上，上面 184
-sure- 确定，确信 184

Day 25

非成组词（S 字母）................................ 186
-tach-、-tact- 接触 190
-tain- 保持，保留 191
-tect- 盖 192

Day 26

-tend-、-tent-、-tens- 倾向 193
-tire- 疲倦，疲劳 194
-tract-、-trag- 拖，拉 195
-tribute- 给，给予 196
-tric-、-trig- 阴谋，诡计 196
-tern- 转动，翻转 197
-tut-、-tuit- 教，教授 197
非成组词（T 字母）................................ 198

Day 27

-ult- 老 201
-uni- 一 201

非成组词（U字母）.................................. 202

-vac-、-ves-、-val-、-void- 空，空虚
.... 204

-val-、-vail- 价值 205

-var-、-vary- 变化 206

-van-、-ven-、-vent-、-ves- 走，来；风 207

Day 28

-vers-、-vert- 转，转变 210

-vey- 道路 212

-vi-、-vid-、-vis- 看见 212

-view- 看，看见，观点，意见 214

-voc-、-vok- 声音，呼喊 214

-vi-、-viv-、-vit- 活命，生活 215

-vol-、-volv-、-volu- 旋转，卷；意愿，自愿 215

非成组词（V字母）.................................. 217

-ward- 向 218

非成组词（W字母和Z字母）............. 218

单词索引 221

Day 01

扫码即刻听课

–ab– 否定，不

abolish[2] [əˈbɒlɪʃ] *v.* 废除；取消

[记] ab+ol（无义）+ish（*v.*）→ "不要，否定的动作" → *v.* 废除；取消

[助] a（一）+bo（谐音"破"）+lish（谐音"历史"）→ "一部破历史"；曾经的三妻四妾，曾经的裹足，曾经的男尊女卑，都是一部部破历史，所以需要→ *v.* 废除；取消

absurd[2] [əbˈsɜːd] *a.* 不合理的，荒谬的

[记] ab+surd（改写自 sound；合理的）→ "不合理的" → *a.* 不合理的，荒谬的

[派] absurdity [əbˈsɜːdəti] *n.* 荒谬，荒谬的事／行为

–academy– 学院

academy[2] [əˈkædəmi] *n.* 学院，专科院校

[记] 柏拉图曾在雅典城外的 Academus 建立学院，这所学院是欧洲历史上第一所综合性传授知识、进行学术研究、提供政治咨询、培养学者和政治人才的学校，直至东罗马皇帝下令关闭为止，持续存在达 900 年之久，以后西方各国的主要学术研究院都沿袭它的名称，叫 Academy → *n.* 学院，专科院校

academic[22] [ˌækəˈdemɪk] *a.* 学术的；学院的　*n.* 大学教师；高校科研人员；学者

[记] 上词 academy 的形容词；academ（简写自 academy）+ic（*a.*）→ *a.* 学术的；学院的 → "与学术、学院相关的人员" → *n.* 大学教师；高校科研人员；学者

[派] academics [ˌækəˈdemɪks] *n.* 学习；学术；学者

academically [ˌækəˈdemɪkli] *ad.* 从学术观点上

[真] It isn't a school subject or an **academic** discipline, but it can be learned.【2021 年 6 月 仔细阅读】

［译］它不是一门学校课程，也不是一门学术科目，但它可以被习得。

-act-、-ag- 行动，作用

active [7]
['æktɪv] a. 起作用的，活跃的，积极的
［记］act+ive（a.）→词根"行动"+形容词后缀→a. 起作用的→小男孩"动来动去"→a. 活跃的→遇到问题总是"行动"而不是抱怨→a. 积极的
［派］actively ['æktɪvli] ad. 积极地
［真］[C] Energy usage devoted to **active** learning accounts for a big part of it.【2020年12月 听力 20题 C选项】
［译］放在自主学习上的精力占了很大比例。

activate [2]
['æktɪveɪt] v. 使起作用；刺激；激活
［记］act+iv（无义）+ate（v.）→"act（作用）加个 ate 动词后缀"→v. 使起作用→"使之起相应的作用"→v. 刺激；激活

react [4]
[rɪ'ækt] v. 作出反应，起反作用
［记］re（back）+act→v. 作出反应，起反作用
［派］reaction [rɪ'ækʃn] n. 反应，反作用
［考］react to... 对……有反应，对……有反作用
［真］There's an even darker side to how people **react** to jargon.【2021年6月 听力原文】
［译］人们对术语的反应还有更隐秘的一面。

exact [10]
[ɪɡ'zækt] a. 真实的；精确的，准确的
［记］ex（out）+act→"行动，实践"出真知→a. 真实的→何为真实数据？→a. 精确的，准确的
［派］exactly [ɪɡ'zæktli] ad. 精确地，确切地；恰恰
［真］You can't see it, smell it, or hear it, and people disagree on how precisely to define it, or where **exactly** it comes from.【2021年6月 仔细阅读】
［译］你看不见它，闻不到它，听不到它，人们对如何准确地定义它各持己见，对它的确切来源也有分歧。

interact [20]
[ˌɪntər'ækt] v. 相互作用；互动，交流
［记］inter（between；彼此，互相）+act→v. 相互作用；互动，交流
［派］interaction [ˌɪntər'ækʃn] n. 相互影响，相互作用；互动
   interactive [ˌɪntər'æktɪv] a. 相互影响的，相互作用的；互动的
［考］interact with... 与……相互作用/相互影响
［真］Another consideration is the risks when humans **interact** with large machinery.【2021年6月 听力原文】

[译] 另一个考量是人类操作大型机械时的风险。

agency [6] ['eɪdʒənsi] *n.* 服务/代理/经销机构；代理处

[记] ag+ency（*n.*）→给钱之后"行动，做事，起作用的人"，比如代理某种产品→ *n.* 服务/代理/经销机构；代理处

[真] [C] Its **agencies** in charge of drafting the guidelines have the expertise.【2020年12月仔细阅读52题C选项】

[译] 其负责起草这些准则的机构具有专业知识。

–alter– 改变

alter [7] ['ɔːltə(r)] *v.* 改变，更改，改动

六级基础词汇

[派] alterable ['ɔːltərəbl] *a.* 可改变的，可改动的

alternate [6] ['ɔːltəneɪt] *v.*（使）交替，（使）轮流 *a.* 交替的，轮流的

[记] alter+n（无义）+ate（*v.&a.*）→次序或顺序"改变"→ *v.*（使）交替，（使）轮流→ *a.* 交替的，轮流的

[派] alternation [ˌɔːltə'neɪʃn] *n.* 交替，轮流
　　alternative [ɔːl'tɜːnətɪv] *a.* 替代的，备选的　*n.* 可供选择的事物

[真] I'm here to suggest an **alternative** that having less might actually be a preferable decision.【2020年12月听力原文】

[译] 我在这里提议一个可替代方案——精简物品，这实际上可能是更可取的决定。

–ann–、–enn– 年

annual [7] ['ænjuəl] *a.* 每年的；一年一次的　*n.* 年刊

[记] ann+u（无义）+al（*a.&n.*）→"一年一次"→ *a.* 每年的；一年一次的　*n.* 年刊

[派] annually ['ænjuəli] *ad.* 每年一次，一年一度

[真] According to official statistics, Thailand's **annual** road death rate is almost double the global average.【2021年6月听力原文】

[译] 据官方统计，泰国每年的道路交通死亡率几乎是全球平均水平的两倍。

anniversary [2] [ˌænɪ'vɜːsəri] *n.* 周年纪念（日）

[记] ann+i（无义）+词根 vers（转，转变）+ary（*n.*）→"一年转至一回的日子"→ *n.* 周年纪念（日）

–astr–、–aster– 星星

disaster [18] [dɪˈzɑːstə(r)] *n.* 灾难，灾祸

[记] dis（散）+aster → "星星四散"，预示着人间出现→ *n.* 灾难，灾祸

[派] disastrous [dɪˈzɑːstrəs] *a.* 灾难性的；损失惨重的

[真] Many people get the idea from the massive bones in the pit wall that some **disaster**, such as a volcanic explosion or a sudden flood, killed a whole herd of dinosaurs in this area.【2020 年 7 月 听力原文】

[译] 很多人看到化石坑壁的众多恐龙骨架会产生这样的想法：一些诸如火山爆发或突发洪水的自然灾难，杀死了该地区的整个恐龙种群。

catastrophe [7] [kəˈtæstrəfi] *n.* 大灾难，横祸

[记] cata（下）+str（简写自 astr）+o（无义）+phe（谐音"飞"）→ "星星不但向下落，还到处乱飞"；有假说指出，恐龙的灭绝就与 6 500 万年前一颗大陨星坠落地球有关→ *n.* 大灾难，横祸

[派] catastrophic [ˌkætəˈstrɒfɪk] *a.* 灾难性的

[真] News of Notre Dame Cathedral **catastrophe** instantly caught media attention throughout the world.【2021 年 6 月 长篇阅读 45 题】

[译] 巴黎圣母院大灾难的消息立即引起了全世界媒体的关注。

–aud–、–audi– 听见

audience [4] [ˈɔːdiəns] *n.* 听众，观众

[记] audi+ence（*n.*）→ "听……的人"→ *n.* 听众，观众

[真] [B] They want to avoid offending any of their **audience**.【2020 年 12 月 仔细阅读 47 题 B 选项】

[译] 他们不想冒犯任何一个观众。

audio [2] [ˈɔːdiəʊ] *n.* 音频 *a.* 声音的，音频的

[记] audi+o（*n.*&*a.*）→ "听见的东西"→ *n.* 音频 *a.* 声音的，音频的

–auth– 作者，权威

author [46] [ˈɔːθə(r)] *n.* 作者，著作人

六级基础词汇

authority [5] [ɔːˈθɒrəti] *n.* 权威，权力；官方，当局

[记] author（*n.* 作者）+ity（*n.*）→作者对自己的书最有发言权，在这方面有→ *n.* 权威，权力→ "最有权威的是"→ *n.* 官方，当局

Day 01

[真] France's tax on overnight stays was introduced to assist thermal spa towns to develop, and around half of French local **authorities** use it today.【2021 年 6 月 仔细阅读】

[译] 法国实施了"暂住税"以支持温泉小镇的发展，现如今，法国大约一半的地方政府都在采用这项税收。

authorize/ise [²] [ˈɔːθəraɪz] *v.* 授权；批准

[记] 上词 authority 的动词；author+ize/ise（使动）→ "使某事有官方权威、权力"，那必是得到→ *v.* 授权；批准

authentic [⁵] [ɔːˈθentɪk] *a.* 真的，真正的；可信的

[记] auth+ent（*a.*）+ic（*a.*）→ "作者权威的观点"→ *a.* 真的，真正的；可信的

[派] inauthentic [ˌɪnɔːˈθentɪk] *a.* 不真实的，假的

[真] [D] It may render us vulnerable and **inauthentic**.【2020 年 12 月 仔细阅读 46 题 D 选项】

[译] 它可能使我们变得脆弱和不真实。

–a–、–a 辅–（除了 –ab–）=to 加强，强调

abandon [⁴] [əˈbændən] *v.* 放弃；抛弃，丢弃

[记] 六级基础词汇；a（to）+ban（*v.* 禁止）+don（无义）→因为"禁止"，所以要→ *v.* 放弃；抛弃，丢弃

[派] abandonment [əˈbændənmənt] *n.* 放弃；抛弃，丢弃

accelerate [¹⁴] [əkˈseləreɪt] *v.* （使）加快，加速

[记] ac（to）+ celer+ate（*v.*）→ "去有速度，去加速"→ *v.* （使）加快，加速

[派] acceleration [əkˌseləˈreɪʃn] *n.* 加速

[真] I'm always baffled when I walk into a pharmacy and see shelves bursting with various vitamins, extracts and other supplements, all promising to **accelerate** or promote weight loss.【2021 年 6 月 选词填空】

[译] 当我走进药店，看到货架上摆满了各种承诺能加速或促进减肥的维生素、萃取物和其他补品时，我总是很困惑。

accompany [⁴] [əˈkʌmpəni] *v.* 陪伴，伴随

[记] ac（to）+company（*n.&v.* 陪伴，伴随）→ *v.* 陪伴，伴随

[真] [C] It is frequently **accompanied** by singing.【2019 年 12 月 听力 3 题 C 选项】

[译] 它经常伴随着歌声。

accuse [⁵] [əˈkjuːz] *v.* 指责；控告

[记] ac（to）+cuse（简写自 cause；原因）→ "就是因为某人"→ *v.* 指责（某人）；控告（某人）

005

[助] ac（to）+cuse（谐音"哭死"）→ "快哭死了"，因为被人→ v. 指责；控告

[派] accusation [ˌækjuˈzeɪʃn] n. 指责，谴责；控告

[考] accuse sb. of sth. 指责/控告某人某事
be accused of 被控告，被起诉

[真] But as the emergency services picked through the burnt debris, a row was resurfacing over **accusations** that the beloved cathedral, immortalised in Victor Hugo's novel, was already crumbling before the fire. 【2021年6月 长篇阅读C选项】

[译] 但是当紧急救援人员在废墟中搜寻时，一场争论又重新出现，因为有人指控，维克多·雨果的小说中描写的不朽的、深受人们喜爱的大教堂，在大火之前就已经摇摇欲坠了。

accustomed [2]

[əˈkʌstəmd] a. 习惯的，适应的

[记] ac（to）+custom（n. 习惯）+ed（a.）→ "去变得习惯"→ a. 习惯的，适应的

[考] be accustomed to... 习惯于……，适应于……

acquaint [2]

[əˈkweɪnt] v. 使熟悉，使了解

[记] ac（to）+qu（谐音"去"）+ai（谐音"爱"）+ nt（无义）→ "很爱去"；去的次数多，所以很熟→ v. 使熟悉，使了解

[派] acquaintance [əˈkweɪntəns] n. 熟悉；熟人

[考] acquaint with... 对……了解/熟悉

address [10]

[əˈdres] n. 地址 v. 解决；表达；演讲（熟词僻义，重点关注）

六级基础词汇

[真] [D] It welcomes them as a tool to **address** chronic hunger and malnutrition. 【2020年12月 仔细阅读50题D选项】

[译] 它乐于将它们作为解决长期饥饿和营养不良问题的工具。

admire [2]

[ədˈmaɪə(r)] v. 称赞；羡慕

[记] ad（to）+mire（简写自 miracle；奇迹，惊奇）→ "出于惊奇，感叹奇迹"→ v. 称赞；羡慕

[助] ad（to）+mire（谐音"买啊"）→土豪天天"买啊买啊买啊"，我也想过这样的生活→ v. 称赞；羡慕

[派] admiration [ˌædməˈreɪʃn] n. 钦佩，赞美

afford [7]

[əˈfɔːd] v. 负担，买得起

[记] af（to）+ford（"福特"汽车）→ "去开Ford，去买福特"→ v. 负担，买得起

[派] affordable [əˈfɔːdəbl] a. 买得起的，负担得起的

[真] [B] They can **afford** to choose easier majors in order to enjoy themselves. 【2020年7月 仔细阅读54题B选项】

Day 01

[译] 他们可以选择更容易的专业让自己轻松一些。

announce³   [əˈnaʊns] *v.* 宣布，宣告

[记] an (to) +noun (*n.* 名词) +ce (*v.*) → "去说个名词" → *v.* 宣布，宣告

[派] announcement [əˈnaʊnsmənt] *n.* 宣告，通告

[真] Late in 2019, it was **announced** that US actor James Dean, who died in 1955, will star in a Vietnam War film scheduled for release later this year.【2021年6月 长篇阅读B选项】

[译] 2019年年末，有消息宣布，1955年去世的美国演员詹姆斯·迪恩将主演一部有关越南战争的电影，该片定于今年年末上映。

annoy³   [əˈnɔɪ] *v.* 打扰；使烦恼

[记] an (to) +noy (简写自 noise；噪声) → "有噪声"；烦死了→ *v.* 打扰；使烦恼

[派] annoying [əˈnɔɪɪŋ] *a.* 令人生气的，令人烦恼的
　　annoyance [əˈnɔɪəns] *n.* 生气，烦恼

[真] But the best available science also has a lot to say about what those food choices do to the environment, and some researchers are **annoyed** that new dietary recommendations of the USDA (United States Department of Agriculture) released yesterday seem to utterly ignore that fact.【2020年12月 仔细阅读】

[译] 但是现有的最佳科学就食物选择对环境的影响也有很多论述。昨天美国农业部 (USDA) 发布的新饮食建议似乎完全忽略了这个事实，一些研究人员为此十分恼火。

approach⁵   [əˈprəʊtʃ] *v.&n.* 接近，靠近；方法，途径　*v.* 解决，处理

[记] ap (to) + 词根 proach (接近，靠近) → "去接近，去靠近" → *v.&n.* 接近，靠近；方法，途径　*v.* 解决，处理

[真] Halfway through the trip, we received news that a hurricane was **approaching**.【2021年6月 听力原文】

[译] 在旅程进行到一半时，我们收到消息说飓风即将来临。

appropriate⁶   [əˈprəʊpriət] [əˈprəʊprieɪt] *a.* 合适的，恰当的

[记] ap (to) +propri (改写自 proper；合适的，恰当的) +ate (*a.*) → "去变得 proper" → *a.* 合适的，恰当的

[派] appropriately [əˈprəʊpriətli] *ad.* 合适地，适当地
　　inappropriate [ˌɪnəˈprəʊpriət] *a.* 不合适的，不恰当的

[形] approximate [əˈprɒksɪmət] *a.* 大约的，近似的
　　approximately [əˈprɒksɪmətli] *ad.* 大约地，近似地

[真] [A] Find **appropriate** topics.【2021年6月 听力11题A选项】

[译] 找到适当的话题。

astonish [4]

[əˈstɒnɪʃ] v. 使惊讶，使吃惊

［记］as（to）+ton（改写自 thunder；雷）+ish（v.）→ "晴天惊雷" → v. 使惊讶，使吃惊

［助］谐音"啊，倒你身" → "啊，倒在你的身上" → v. 使惊讶，使吃惊

［派］astonishment [əˈstɒnɪʃmənt] n. 惊吓
astonishing [əˈstɒnɪʃɪŋ] a. 令人吃惊的，惊人的

［真］It's an **astonishing** but statistical fact, a primary cause of employees' dissatisfaction, according to fresh research, is that many believe they have terrible managers.【2021 年 6 月 听力原文】

［译］这是一个令人惊讶但有统计依据的事实，根据最新研究，员工不满的主要原因是许多人认为他们的经理很糟糕。

扫码快速学习

Day 02

扫码即刻听课

非成组词（A 字母）

alien [6] ['eɪliən] *n.* 外侨，外国人 *a.* 外国的，陌生的

[助] 谐音"艾琳"；外国人名→ *n.* 外侨，外国人 *a.* 外国的，陌生的
[派] alienate ['eɪliəneɪt] *v.* 使疏远，离间
[真] Despite his autonomy, Marconi felt **alienated** and suffered from a lack of acceptance.【2021 年 6 月 长篇阅读 45 题】
[译] 尽管他有自主权，马可尼还是感到被疏远，不被接受。

ambition [6] [æmˈbɪʃn] *n.* 雄心，抱负；野心

[记] 源自拉丁语 ambitio（四处走），其中 amb 后来成了英语词根，表示"走"，如救护车 ambulance 本意就是四处走的医院。ambition 本来仅仅指以前的政客四处奔走发表演说拉选票的行为。在古罗马时期，谋求官职的人就像今天参加竞选活动的人一样，到处发表演说争取选票。政客拉选票自然是为了实现自己的政治抱负，所以 ambition 从"四处走"的基本意义中又引申出"野心，政治抱负"的含义，原本含有贬义，但现在已经变成中性词，既可以指"野心"，也可以指"雄心，抱负"→ *n.* 雄心，抱负；野心
[助] 谐音"俺必胜"→"俺一定会胜的"→ *n.* 雄心，抱负；野心
[派] ambitious [æmˈbɪʃəs] *a.* 有雄心的；有野心的
[真] [C] They are **ambitious**.【2021 年 6 月 听力 2 题 C 选项】
[译] 他们有雄心抱负。

analyse/yze [16] ['ænəlaɪz] *v.* 分析，分解

[记] 词根 ana（相同）+lyse/lyze（使动）→"使之成为相同的规律"→使之相同，使之有共性→ *v.* 分析，分解
[派] analysis [əˈnæləsɪs] *n.* 分析，分解
　　analytic [ˌænəˈlɪtɪk] *a.* 分析的
　　analytical [ˌænəˈlɪtɪkl] *a.* 分析的，分解的
[真] [B] It should be carefully **analyzed**.【2021 年 6 月 听力 2 题 B 选项】
[译] 它应该被仔细分析。

009

animate [4]

[ˈænɪmeɪt] [ˈænɪmət] *v.* 使有生气 *a.* 有生命的；有活力的

[记] 词根 anim（生命；呼吸）+ate（*v.&a.*）→ "有生命的，有生气的" → *v.* 使有生气 *a.* 有生命的；有活力的

[派] animated [ˈænɪmeɪtɪd] *a.* 活泼的，生气勃勃的
animation [ˌænɪˈmeɪʃn] *n.* 动画片（制作）；生气
inanimate [ɪnˈænɪmət] *a.* 无生命的，无生气的

[真] Now, a person can be **animated** from scratch.【2021年6月长篇阅读 E 选项】

[译] 现在，一个人可以从零开始被制作成动画了。

apparent [4]

[əˈpærənt] *a.* 出现的；表面的；明显的

[记] appar（简写自 appear；出现，显现）+ent（*a.*）；appear（出现，显现）的形容词 → *a.* 出现的 → 乍出现的人或物只能看到表面，只看一两次不可能看到其内在 → *a.* 表面的；明显的

[派] apparently [əˈpærəntli] *ad.* 看来，显然

[真] The discrepancy is startlingly **apparent**.【2019年12月仔细阅读】

[译] 这种差异非常明显。

autonomy [16]

[ɔːˈtɒnəmi] *n.* 自治，自治权

[记] auto（self；自己）+ 词根 nom（改写自 name；名字）+y（*n.*）→ "有自己的名字" "自己能给自己起名字"，说明有 → *n.* 自治，自治权

[派] autonomous [ɔːˈtɒnəməs] *a.* 自治的，自治权的

[真] [B] They present a false picture of the **autonomy** cars provide.【2021年6月仔细阅读 51 题 B 选项】

[译] 它们错误描述了汽车提供的自主性。

award [3]

[əˈwɔːd] *n.* 奖，奖赏 *v.* 授予，奖给

[助] 谐音"啊，我的？！"；得奖之后兴奋的话语 → *n.* 奖，奖赏 → *v.* 授予，奖给

[真] [A] He won an **award** from the US government for his work.【2021年6月听力 15 题 A 选项】

[译] 他因为工作获得了美国政府颁发的奖项。

asset [2]

[ˈæset] *n.* 资产，财产

[记] as（to）+set（*n.* 一套）→ "一套房产" → *n.* 资产，财产

assess [10]

[əˈses] *v.* 评价，估价

[记] 可以看成上词 asset 的动词 → *v.* 评价，估价

[派] assessment [əˈsesmənt] *n.* 评估，评价

[形] access [ˈækses] *n.* 通道，机会 *v.* 到达，进入

[真] [A] Its consequences are usually difficult to **assess**.【2021年6月仔细阅读 54 题 A 选项】

[译] 其后果通常难以评估。

Day 02

-bas- 基础

base [5]
[beɪs] *n.* 基础　*v.* 以……为基础

[记] bas+e（无义）→ *n.* 基础　*v.* 以……为基础
[派] database ['deɪtəbeɪs] *n.* 数据库
[考] be based on... 以……为基础
[真] A point worth making is that the study was **based** only on the perspective of employees.【2021年6月 听力原文】
[译] 值得一提的是，该研究仅基于员工的观点。

basis [4]
['beɪsɪs] *n.* 基础，底部

[记] bas+is（*n.*）→ *n.* 基础，底部
[考] on the basis of... 根据……
[真] While there's an undoubted genetic **basis** to individual difference, it is wrong to think that socially defined groups can be genetically accounted for.【2021年6月 仔细阅读】
[译] 虽然个体差异具有无可置疑的遗传基础，但认为可以通过遗传来解释社会群体的界定是错误的。

basic [8]
['beɪsɪk] *a.* 基本的，基础的

[记] bas+ic（*a.*）→ *a.* 基本的，基础的
[派] basics ['beɪsɪks] *n.* 基本要素，基础
　　 basically ['beɪsɪkli] *ad.* 基本上；从本质上来说
[真] How can we live more **basically**?【2020年12月 听力原文】
[译] 我们怎样才能更基本地生活呢？

-bat- 打

battle [2]
['bætl] *n.* 战役；战斗　*v.* 奋斗

[记] bat+t（无义）+le（*n.*&*v.*）→ "打斗" → *n.* 战役；战斗　*v.* 奋斗

debate [13]
[dɪ'beɪt] *v.*&*n.* 辩论，争论

[记] de（下）+bat+e（无义）→ "打下去"，只不过是用嘴 → *v.*&*n.* 辩论，争论
[考] debate about/over... 关于……的争论/辩论
[真] There is an ongoing **debate** among the public as to whether the images of deceased celebrities should be recreated.【2021年6月 长篇阅读36题】
[译] 关于是否应该重现已故名人的形象，公众正在进行一场争论。

011

–be– 是，成为

beneath [bɪˈniːθ] *prep.* 在……下边，低于 *ad.* 在下方

[记] be+n（无义）+eath（简写自 earth；地，土地）→ "土地不就在下面嘛" → *prep.* 在……下边，低于 *ad.* 在下方

[真] [A] It may be freezing fast **beneath** the glacier.【2020 年 9 月 听力 10 题 A 选项】

[译] 它可能会在冰川下面迅速结冰。

betray [bɪˈtreɪ] *v.* 对……不忠，背叛，出卖，暴露

[记] be+tray（改写自法语 trair；背叛）→ *v.* 对……不忠，背叛，出卖，暴露

[助] 谐音"必啐"→遇到背叛者、出卖者、泄密者，必啐其一脸

[派] betrayal [bɪˈtreɪəl] *n.* 背叛，出卖

[真] As for the hazards of friendship, more than a few relationships have been shattered because of cut-throat competition and feelings of **betrayal**.【2020 年 7 月 听力原文】

[译] 提到什么会危害友谊，残酷的竞争和背叛感让很多关系破裂。

–board– 板 –broad– 宽广

board [bɔːd] *n.* 板，甲板；董事会（熟词僻义，重点关注）

[记] blackboard（*n.* 黑板）→ *n.* 板，甲板→站在黑板前面指挥的是→ *n.* 董事会

[真] Both absent-minded doodling and copying from life have been shown to positively affect your memory and visual perception, so complain loudly the next time your school **board** slashes the art department's budget.【2021 年 6 月 仔细阅读】

[译] 心不在焉的涂鸦和对生活的复现都会积极地影响你的记忆力和视觉感知，所以下次学校董事会削减艺术系的预算时，你可以大声抱怨。

broad [brɔːd] *a.* 宽广的

[记] 核心词为 road（道路）→"有路就为广"→ *a.* 宽广的

[派] broadly [ˈbrɔːdli] *ad.* 宽广地；大体上
broaden [ˈbrɔːdn] *v.* 变宽，扩展，加宽
abroad [əˈbrɔːd] *ad.* 到国外，到海外 *a.* 国外的
broadcast [ˈbrɔːdkɑːst] *n.* 广播，电视节目 *v.* 播出（节目）

[真] [D] To identify a **broad** general strength to elaborate on.【2020 年 12 月 听力 24 题 D 选项】

[译] 为了确定要详细说明的宽泛的、综合的实力。

Day 02

-boast- 自夸，吹嘘

boast [2]
[bəʊst] *v.&n.* 自夸，夸耀，吹嘘
［助］谐音"喷他"→"喝点小酒，就开始喷"→ *v.&n.* 自夸，夸耀，吹嘘

boost [10]
[buːst] *v.&n.* 提升，增加；抬高（价格）
［记］来自 boast（自夸，夸耀）→"自夸是为了提升自己，也是为了抬价"→ *v.&n.* 提升，增加；抬高（价格）
［真］[C] The UK will take new measures to **boost** tourism.【2021 年 6 月 仔细阅读 51 题 C 选项】
［译］英国将采取新的措施来促进旅游业的发展。

-bound- 束缚，约束

boundary [6]
[ˈbaʊndri] *n.* 边界，分界线
［记］bound+ary（*n.*）→束缚、约束人的→ *n.* 边界，分界线
［真］[C] It breaks the **boundary** of hierarchy.【2020 年 7 月 听力 9 题 C 选项】
［译］它打破了等级界限。

abound [2]
[əˈbaʊnd] *v.* 富于，大量存在
［记］ab（否定）+（b）ound→数量上"不限制、不束缚"；要多少给多少→ *v.* 富于，大量存在

abundant [6]
[əˈbʌndənt] *a.* 大量的，充足的
［记］上词 abound 的形容词→ *a.* 大量的，充足的
［派］abundance [əˈbʌndəns] *n.* 丰富，大量
［考］be abundant in 充足，丰富
［真］Fear of better options offers little benefit. It's an ailment of **abundance**.【2021 年 6 月 听力原文】
［译］对更好选择的恐惧并没有带来什么好处。这是选择过多导致的苦恼。

非成组词（B 字母）

barrier [3]
[ˈbæriə(r)] *n.* 栅栏；屏障；障碍（物）
［记］bar（*n.* 障碍）+ri(无义)+er（表示物的后缀）→ *n.* 障碍（物）→什么能成为障碍物？→ *n.* 栅栏；屏障
［真］[D] Policymakers help remove the **barriers** to people's choice of food.【2020 年 12 月 仔细阅读 48 题 D 选项】
［译］政策制定者有助于消除人们选择食物的障碍。

013

bias [6]

[ˈbaɪəs] *n.* 偏见，偏向　*v.* 使倾向于，使对……有偏见

[记] 改写自 balance（平衡），取其反义"不平衡"→"不平衡"就是"偏"→ *n.* 偏见，偏向　*v.* 使倾向于，使对……有偏见

[真] [D] Most recruiters are unable to control their racial **biases**.【2020年7月 仔细阅读48题D选项】

[译] 大多数招聘人员都无法控制自己的种族偏见。

bill [5]

[bɪl] *n.* 账单；钞票；法案（熟词僻义，重点关注）

[记] 发音很像钞票的"票"→ *n.* 账单；钞票→使一张纸成为钞票，需要"法案"→ *n.* 法案

[真] Controversy continues to surround the true value of the dollar **bill**.【2020年9月 听力原文】

[译] 围绕美元纸币真实价值的争论一直存在。

bizarre [6]

[bɪˈzɑː(r)] *a.* 奇特的，奇异的，离奇的

[记] 英语单词 bizarre 来自法语，意为"奇异的，怪异的"→ *a.* 奇特的，奇异的，离奇的

[助] 谐音"比萨"→比萨斜塔就是因为造型奇特、奇异而闻名于世，而且这个词的拼写本身就挺怪的→ *a.* 奇特的，奇异的，离奇的

[真] Ms. Wilson, according to the notes on your account, the **bizarre** technical detail that you mentioned refers to the fact that you hadn't paid house insurance the month before the incident.【2020年12月 听力原文】

[译] 威尔逊女士，根据您的账户记录，您刚才提到的奇怪的技术细节指的是在事发前一个月您没有缴纳房屋保险。

biography

[baɪˈɒɡrəfi] *n.* 传记，个人简介

[记] 词根 bio（life；生命，生活；比如 biology 是生物学）+graph+y（*n.*）→"描写、描绘某人的生平、生活"→ *n.* 传记，个人简介

[派] autobiography [ˌɔːtəbaɪˈɒɡrəfi] *n.* 自传

[真] Marconi's **biography** is also a story about choices and the motivations behind them.【2021年6月 长篇阅读H选项】

[译] 马可尼的传记也是一个关于选择及其背后动机的故事。

blame [6]

[bleɪm] *v.&n.* 指责，责备

[助] b（谐音"不"）+la（谐音"拉"）+me（我）→"我说拉我一下，你说不拉，不拉就不拉"；会受到别人的→ *v.&n.* 指责，责备

[真] Leniaud told *La Croix* newspaper: "This is not about looking for people to **blame**."【2021年6月 长篇阅读K选项】

[译] 莱尼奥告诉《拉克罗伊报》："这不是要寻找应受责备的人。"

Day 02

blunt [2] [blʌnt] *a.* 钝的，不锋利的；呆板的，迟钝的

[助] 谐音 "不烂它" → "刀切不烂" → *a.* 钝的，不锋利的 → 脑子 "钝，不锋利" → *a.* 呆板的，迟钝的

boom [2] [bu:m] *n.* 迅速发展；激增 *v.* 发出隆隆声；繁荣，快速发展

[助] 谐音 "bong" → *v.* 发出隆隆声，引申出人们在工地上干得热火朝天，一座座高楼大厦拔地而起→ *n.* 迅速发展；激增 *v.* 繁荣，快速发展

botany [3] [ˈbɒtəni] *n.* 植物，植物学

[记] 来自希腊语 botane（植物，草）→ *n.* 植物，植物学
[助] 谐音 "包点泥" → 种植花草 → *n.* 植物，植物学
[派] botanist [ˈbɒtənɪst] *n.* 植物学家
[真] [D] Her career as a **botanist**.【2021 年 6 月 听力 5 题 D 选项】
[译] 她作为一名植物学家的职业生涯。

branch [3] [brɑ:ntʃ] *n.* 分支（机构），部门

[记] 改写自 break（打破，破碎）→ 把整体 "打破"，形成一个个 → *n.* 分支（机构），部门
[真] [C] It has several **branches** in London.【2019 年 12 月 听力 1 题 C 选项】
[译] 它在伦敦有几家分支机构。

budget [8] [ˈbʌdʒɪt] *n.* 预算

[记] bud（改写自 bag；书包，钱包）+get（*v.* 获得，得到）→ "从钱包里获得的" → *n.* 预算
[真] Both absent-minded doodling and copying from life have been shown to positively affect your memory and visual perception, so complain loudly the next time your school board slashes the art department's **budget**.【2021 年 6 月 仔细阅读】
[译] 心不在焉的涂鸦和对生活的复现都会积极地影响你的记忆力和视觉感知，所以下次学校董事会削减艺术系的预算时，你可以大声抱怨。

burden [12] [ˈbɜ:dn] *n.* 重担，负担 *v.* 使负担

[记] 谐音 "别担" → 别担什么？→ *n.* 重担，负担 *v.* 使负担
[派] overburden [ˌəʊvəˈbɜ:dn] *v.* 负担过重，装载过多
　　 unburden [ˌʌnˈbɜ:dn] *v.* 卸掉负担，消除负担
[真] [D] ease its financial **burden** of providing local services.【2021 年 6 月 仔细阅读 53 题 D 选项】
[译] 减轻其提供当地服务的财政负担。

扫码快速学习

扫码即刻听课

-camp- 营地，露营

camp [2]
[kæmp] *v.&n.* 宿营，露营；营地
六级基础词汇

campaign [9]
[kæmˈpeɪn] *n.* 战役　*v.&n.* （发起）政治或商业运动
[记] cam（简写自 camp）+paign（结合"pain；疼痛，痛苦"加深记忆）→ "疼痛、痛苦的营地"→ *n.* 战役→"无硝烟的战役"，正所谓商场如战场→ *v.&n.* （发起）政治或商业运动
[真] [D] Showing its sense of responsibility by leading the global **campaign**. 【2019 年 12 月 仔细阅读 53 题 D 选项】
[译] 通过领导全球运动来展示责任感。

campus [4]
[ˈkæmpəs] *n.* （大学）校园
[记] camp+us（我们）→ "我们大学生的营地"→ *n.* （大学）校园
[真] Universities, now emptying their **campuses**, have never tried online learning on this scale. 【2020 年 12 月 选词填空】
[译] 现在已经清空校园的大学从未尝试过如此大规模的在线学习。

-cap-、-capt-、-cip-、-cup-

①头

capital [5]
[ˈkæpɪtl] *n.* 首都；资本，资金
[记] cap+it（它）+al（*n.*）→ "它是头"→国家的"头等"城市→ *n.* 首都→现代社会什么"头等"重要？→ *n.* 资本，资金
[派] capitalism [ˈkæpɪtəlɪzəm] *n.* 资本主义
[真] "You have to spend substantial **capital** in creating awareness around their likeness and making sure people are familiar with who they are," says Cloyd. 【2021

年 6 月长篇阅读 K 选项】

[译] 克洛伊德说："你必须花费大量资金，提高人们对其相貌的认知度，确保人们熟悉它们是谁。"

captain ²

[ˈkæptɪn] *n.* 首领，队长（考过含义），船长，机长

[记] cap+t（无义）+ain（表示人的后缀）→ "带头人" → *n.* 首领，队长，船长，机长

②抓

capture ²

[ˈkæptɪ(r)] *v.* 捕获，抓捕；引起（注意、想象、兴趣）

[记] capt+ure（*v.*）→ "抓"小偷，"抓"坏人，"抓"强盗 → *v.* 捕获，抓捕 → "抓住"注意力 → *v.* 引起（注意、想象、兴趣）

capacity ⁸

[kəˈpæsəti] *n.* 能力；容量

[记] cap+ac（无义）+ity（*n.*）→ "抓住"多少东西 → *n.* 容量 → 人的"容量" → *n.* 能力（取"能力"的意思时与 capability 是同义词）

[真] [A] Everybody is born with the **capacity** to draw.【2021 年 6 月仔细阅读 48 题 A 选项】

[译] 每个人天生就有画画的能力。

participate ¹⁵

[pɑːˈtɪsɪpeɪt] *v.* 参加，参与

[记] part（部分）+i（无义）+cip+ate（*v.*）→ "把这部分抓进来"的动作 → *v.* 参加，参与

[派] participation [pɑːˌtɪsɪˈpeɪʃn] *n.* 参加，参与
participant [pɑːˈtɪsɪpənt] *n.* 参加者，参与者

[考] participate in 参加，参与

[真] Yet the same state's lawyers don't require continuing legal education, although most lawyers do **participate** in it informally.【2020 年 12 月长篇阅读 N 选项】

[译] 然而，同一州的律师不需要接受法律继续教育，尽管大多数律师确实非正式地参加了法律继续教育。

anticipate ⁴

[ænˈtɪsɪpeɪt] *v.* 预料，期待

[记] anti（前，提前）+cip+ate（*v.*）→ "提前抓住"事情的结果，此事早在我"预料、期待"之中 → *v.* 预料，期待

[派] anticipation [ænˌtɪsɪˈpeɪʃn] *n.* 预料，期待，预期

[真] There are obvious benefits, though I don't seem to have the freedom I **anticipated**, as I just don't seem able to decline work offers.【2020 年 12 月听力原文】

[译] 还是有一些明显好处的，虽然我看起来并没有得到预期的自由，因为我似乎来"单"不拒。

occupy [4]

[ˈɒkjupaɪ] *v.* 占用，占据；使忙碌

[记] oc（加强）+cup+y（无义）→"抓住这一动作，比如把一个人的所有时间全部抓住"，就是→ *v.* 占用，占据→"时间都被占了"→ *v.* 使忙碌

[派] occupation [ˌɒkjuˈpeɪʃn] *n.* 占有，占据；职业，工作
preoccupy [priˈɒkjupaɪ] *v.* 占据（某人）思想，使对……全神贯注，使专心于

[真] They also work in more than 1,000 different **occupations**.【2020 年 12 月 选词填空】

[译] 他们还从事 1 000 多种不同的职业。

-car- 汽车

carbon [9]

[ˈkɑːbən] *n.* 碳

[记] car+bon（改写自 burn；燃烧）→"汽车烧汽油"排出的是碳

[助] 化学元素周期表中的 C → *n.* 碳

[真] In reality, **carbon** taxes alone won't be enough to halt global warming, but they would be a useful part of any climate plan.【2020 年 12 月 选词填空】

[译] 事实上，仅仅靠征收碳税不足以阻止全球变暖，但它们对任何气候计划都有所裨益。

career [16]

[kəˈrɪə(r)] *n.* 职业，生涯

[记] car+eer（表示人的后缀）→根据开的"车"判断"人"的→ *n.* 职业，生涯

[真] [D] Her **career** as a botanist.【2021 年 6 月 听力 5 题 D 选项】

[译] 她作为一名植物学家的职业生涯。

cargo [5]

[ˈkɑːgəʊ] *n.* 货物

[记] car+go（走）→跟着"车走"的东西→ *n.* 货物

[真] [D] **Cargo** logistics.【2020 年 12 月 听力 1 题 D 选项】

[译] 货物物流。

-car-、-care-、-cer-、-cher- 关心，担忧

care [62]

[keə(r)] *v.&n.* 关心，担心，照顾

六级基础词汇

[派] careful [ˈkeəfl] *a.* 小心的，仔细的
carefully [ˈkeəfəli] *ad.* 小心地，仔细地
careless [ˈkeələs] *a.* 粗心的，漫不经心的

[考] take care of 照顾，照料；处理，应付
care about 关心，在乎

Day 03

scare [5]
[skeə(r)] v. 使惊吓，使恐惧

[记] s（谐音"死"）+care → "死人关心你，照顾你"；天哪，吓死宝宝了！→ v. 使惊吓，使恐惧

[派] scary ['skeəri] a. 容易受惊的；可怕的，吓人的

[形] scarce [skeəs] a. 缺乏的，缺少的

[真] It looked at positive emotions such as being excited or interested and negative emotions including being **scared** or distressed.【2020 年 12 月 听力原文】

[译] 它研究了积极情绪，如兴奋或感兴趣，以及消极情绪，如害怕或忧虑。

cherish [4]
['tʃerɪʃ] v. 珍爱，珍惜，爱护

[记] cher+ish（v.）→ "关心、照顾别人的方式" → v. 珍爱，珍惜，爱护

[真] [C] The ever-growing commercial value of long-**cherished** artistic works.【2020 年 12 月 仔细阅读 46 题 C 选项】

[译] 长期珍视的艺术作品不断增长的商业价值。

concern [22]
[kənˈsɜːn] v.&n. 关心，关注；担心

[记] con（加强）+cer+n（无义）→ v.&n. 关心，关注；担心

[派] concerning [kənˈsɜːnɪŋ] prep. 关于
　　concerned [kənˈsɜːnd] a. 关注的；担心的

[考] be concerned about 关心，挂念
　　be concerned with... 关心……；与……相关

[真] Some actors are **concerned** that they may lose jobs because of the CGI technology.【2021 年 6 月 长篇阅读 45 题】

[译] 一些演员担心，他们可能会因为 CGI 技术而失去工作。

–ceed–、–cede–、–cess– 走

proceed [2]
[prəˈsiːd] v. 前进，前行；继续进行

[记] pro（前）+ceed → "向前走" → v. 前进，前行；继续进行

[派] proceeding [prəˈsiːdɪŋ] n. 进行，进程，行动

process [18]
['prəʊses] [prəˈses] n. 过程　v. 处理，加工（熟词僻义，重点关注）

[记] 上词 proceed 的名词；pro（前）+cess → "向前走"；备考时"向前走"的各种经历 → n. 过程

[助] 想想电脑里的 CPU（central processing unit；中央处理器），所以本词还有"v. 处理，加工"的意思

[考] in/during the process of... 在……过程中

[真] [A] It ignores the harmful effect of red meat and **processed** food on health.【2020 年 12 月 仔细阅读 51 题 A 选项】

[译] 它忽略了红肉和加工食品对健康的有害影响。

precede [6]

[prɪˈsiːd] v. 在……之前，领先

[记] pre（前）+cede → "走在……之前" → v. 在……之前，领先

[派] precedent [ˈpresɪdənt] n. 先例
　　unprecedented [ʌnˈpresɪdentɪd] a. 前所未有的，无前例的

[真] [C] It is yielding an **unprecedented** profit.【2021年6月 听力 19题 C 选项】

[译] 它正在产生前所未有的利润。

recession [4]

[rɪˈseʃn] n. 后退，衰退；经济衰退，不景气

[记] re（back）+cess+ion（n.）→ n. 后退，衰退；经济衰退，不景气

[派] recede [rɪˈsiːd] v. 后退，倒退

[真] There is another explanation that Twenge and her colleagues wanted to address: the impact of the great **recession** of 2007−2009, which hit a great number of American families and might be affecting adolescents.【2019年12月 长篇阅读 I 选项】

[译] Twenge 和她的同事们想要表达的另一种解释是 2007 至 2009 年的经济大衰退的影响，这次大衰退打击了许多美国家庭，而且可能会影响青少年。

exceed [3]

[ɪkˈsiːd] v. 超越，超过，胜过

[记] ex（out）+ceed → "走出去"，见世面，长见识，丰富阅历 → v. 超越，超过，胜过

[真] We cut food into bite-sized pieces, we wear seatbelts, and we take care not to **exceed** the speed limit.【2020年12月 选词填空】

[译] 我们把食物切成一口就能吃下去的大小，我们系安全带，同时也会注意不超速。

excess [5]

[ɪkˈses] [ˈekses] n. 超过，过多

[记] 上词 exceed 的名词；ex（out）+cess → n. 超过，过多

[派] excessive [ɪkˈsesɪv] a. 过多的，过度的
　　excessively [ɪkˈsesɪvli] ad. 过度地，过分地

[真] But in the state sector the **excessive** focus on English, maths and science threatens to crush arts subjects; meanwhile, reduced school budgets mean diminishing extracurricular activities.【2021年6月 仔细阅读】

[译] 但在公立学校，对英语、数学和科学这些科目的过度关注可能会压垮艺术学科的发展；同时，学校预算的减少意味着课外活动的不断减少。

excel [5]

[ɪkˈsel] v. 优于，胜过

[记] exceed 的同源词；ex（out）+cel（改写自 ceed）→ "走出去" → v. 优于，胜过

[真] Pollio conducted a study that proved humour can help workers **excel** at routine production tasks.【2020年7月 听力原文】

[译] 波利奥做了一项研究，证明幽默可以帮助员工在日常工作任务中有杰出表现。

excellent [2]

[ˈeksələnt] a. 卓越的，优秀的，出色的

Day 03

[记] excell（改写自 excel；优于，胜过）+ent (*a.*) → "优于，胜过"其他人→ *a.* 卓越的，优秀的，出色的
[派] excellence [ˈeksələns] *n.* 优秀，卓越

concede ²

[kənˈsiːd] *v.* 退让，让步；承认（熟词僻义，重点关注）

[记] con（共同，全部）+cede → "全走了"；遇到极不讲理之人大家都走了，惹不起还躲不起吗？→ *v.* 退让，让步；承认

access ¹⁷

[ˈækses] *n.* 通道；机会 *v.* 到达，进入

[记] ac（to）+cess → "去走过去" → *v.* 到达，进入→为此需要→ *n.* 通道；机会
[派] accessible [əkˈsesəbl] *a.* 可接近的，能靠近的；可获得的，可得到的
[形] assess [əˈses] *v.* 评价，估价
[考] the access to... ……的方法／途径
[真] [C] Providing all children with equal **access** to arts education.【2021 年 6 月 仔细阅读 50 题 C 选项】
[译] 为所有儿童提供平等接受艺术教育的机会。

–ceive–、-cept- 抓，拿

receive ¹⁶

[rɪˈsiːv] *v.* 收到，接收；接待，招待

[记] re（back）+ceive → "拿回来" →别人给我的，我拿回来→ *v.* 收到，接收→去车站把人"拿"回来→ *v.* 接待，招待
[真] [A] She has not **received** any letter from the man.【2020 年 12 月 听力 1 题 A 选项】
[译] 她还没有收到那个男人的任何信件。

accept ¹⁷

[əkˈsept] *v.* 接受；同意

[记] ac（to）+cept → "我送礼物，你拿了"，表示→ *v.* 接受；同意
[派] acceptance [əkˈseptəns] *n.* 接受；同意，认可
acceptable [əkˈseptəbl] *a.* 能接受的，可接受的
unacceptable [ˌʌnəkˈseptəbl] *a.* 不可接受的，无法接受的
[真] Workers' union have **accepted** the inevitability of the introduction of new technology.【2021 年 6 月 听力原文】
[译] 工会已经接受了引进新技术的必然性。

concept ⁹

[ˈkɒnsept] *n.* 概念，想法

[记] 新概念英语 New Concept English → *n.* 概念，想法
[派] conception [kənˈsepʃn] *n.* 概念，想法
conceptual [kənˈseptʃuəl] *a.* 概念（上）的，观念（上）的
[真] [C] They pursue individuality and originality in design **concept**.【2021 年 6 月

仔细阅读 51 题 C 选项〗
［译］他们追求设计理念中的个性和原创性。

perceive¹²
[pəˈsiːv] *v.* 察觉，发觉；领悟，理解

［记］per（贯穿）+ceive → "贯穿表面并抓住事物本质的过程" → *v.* 察觉，发觉；领悟，理解

［派］perception [pəˈsepʃn] *n.* 觉察（力），知觉；领悟，悟性
misperception [ˌmɪspəˈsepʃn] *n.* 误解

［真］There's also evidence that drawing talent is based on how accurately someone **perceives** the world.【2021 年 6 月 仔细阅读】

［译］也有证据表明，绘画天分是以一个人怎样精确地感知世界为基础的。

deceive²
[dɪˈsiːv] *v.* 欺骗，误导

［记］de（下）+ceive → "往下拿，往下抓"，使别人放下心理防线，不就是→ *v.* 欺骗，误导

［派］deception [dɪˈsepʃn] *n.* 欺骗，欺诈

except⁴
[ɪkˈsept] *v.&prep.* 除……之外

［记］ex（out）+cept → "拿了出去"，把某物从整体中"拿了出去" → *v.&prep.* 除……之外

［派］exception [ɪkˈsepʃn] *n.* 例外
exceptional [ɪkˈsepʃənl] *a.* 例外的，特殊的；优越的，杰出的
exceptionally [ɪkˈsepʃənəli] *ad.* 例外地，异常地，特殊地

［形］expect [ɪkˈspekt] *v.* 期待，期盼

［真］The team identified 39 of these traditions that are practiced by some communities but not others—a pattern that, at the time, hadn't been seen in any animal **except** humans.【2020 年 12 月 仔细阅读】

［译］研究小组鉴定了其中 39 种传统，其中一些只存在于某些群体，而在其他群体没有——除了人类，在其他的动物群体中都未见过这种模式。

susceptible³
[səˈseptəbl] *a.* 易受影响的，易遭受……

［记］sus（下）+cept+ible（*a.* 能……）→ "抓到下面的，拿到下面的"；我在上，你在下，自然是遭受啦→ *a.* 易受影响的，易遭受……

［派］susceptibility [səˌseptəˈbɪləti] *n.* 易受影响（或伤害等）的特性

［考］be susceptible to... 易受……影响，易遭受……

［真］[A] They are quite **susceptible** to suicide.【2020 年 9 月 听力 21 题 A 选项】

［译］他们很容易自杀。

–centr– 中心，中央

central¹³
[ˈsentrəl] *a.* 中心的，中央的

Day 03

[记] centr+al（*a.*）→ *a.* 中心的，中央的

[真] **Central** control and collective organisation can produce smoother and fairer outcomes, though even that much is never guaranteed.【2021 年 6 月 仔细阅读】

[译] 集中控制系统和集体组织可以产生更平稳、更公平的结果，尽管这一点也从来无法保证。

concentrate³ [ˈkɒnsntreɪt] *v.* 集中，全神贯注

[记] con（加强）+centr+ate（*v.*）→ *v.* 集中，全神贯注

[派] concentration [ˌkɒnsnˈtreɪʃn] *n.* 集中，关注

[考] concentrate on... 集中/专注于……

[真] [D] It helps improve **concentration** and memory.【2021 年 6 月 仔细阅读 49 题 D 选项】

[译] 它有助于提高注意力和记忆力。

扫码快速学习

Day 04

扫码即刻听课

-cid-、-cis-、-cas-

①切，切开

suicide[2] ['su:ɪsaɪd] *n.* 自杀

[记] sui（self）+cid+e（无义）→ "切自己" → *n.* 自杀

precise[8] [prɪ'saɪs] *a.* 精确的，准确的

[记] pre（前）+cis+e（无义）→ "提前切"；来自英国的宝石工业，在手工业时代，宝石戒指并非成品，而是买块宝石，然后找工匠根据宝石外沿切出底座，这个底座必须切得精准从而保证宝石能够完美镶嵌其中，太大太小都不行，所以"提前切出来的"要是→ *a.* 精确的，准确的

[派] precisely [prɪ'saɪsli] *ad.* 准确地，精确地
　　precision [prɪ'sɪʒn] *n.* 精确，准确，精度

[真] [D] **Precision** in visual perception.【2021年6月 仔细阅读50题 D选项】

[译] 视觉感知力精确。

casualty[5] ['kæʒuəlti] *n.* 伤亡人员，伤亡人数；受害者

[记] cas+u（无义）+al（*n.*）+ty（*n.*）→ "被切死的人" → *n.* 伤亡人员，伤亡人数；受害者

[真] One **casualty** of this was The Great Organ constructed in the 1730s, which was said to have escaped the flames but been significantly damaged by water.【2021年6月 长篇阅读J选项】

[译] 建于18世纪30年代的大风琴就是其中一个牺牲品，据说它躲过了大火，却因灭火的水遭到严重损坏。

②落下，跌落

accident[8] ['æksɪdənt] *n.* 事故，交通事故

[记] ac（to）+cid+ent（*n.*）→ 车落下悬崖，人跌落出来→ *n.* 事故，交通事故

Day 04

[派] accidental [ˌæksɪˈdentl] *a.* 偶然的，意外的
[考] by accident 碰巧，偶然
[真] [C] It sharply reduces the incidence of traffic **accidents**.【2021 年 6 月 仔细阅读 53 题 C 选项】
[译] 它大大降低了交通事故的发生率。

occasion [6]
[əˈkeɪʒn] *n.* 时机，机会，场合

[记] oc（加强）+cas+ion（*n.*）→ "从天而降的" → *n.* 时机，机会；后引申为 → *n.* 场合（场合就是一种机会）
[派] occasional [əˈkeɪʒnl] *a.* 偶然的，临时的
　　 occasionally [əˈkeɪʒnəli] *ad.* 偶尔，偶然
[真] On many **occasions**, the entrepreneurs reported not paying themselves a wage at all initially in order to cover salaries and expenses.【2021 年 6 月 听力原文】
[译] 在许多情况下，创业者报告说，为了支付工资和开销，他们最初根本不给自己发工资。

incident [6]
[ˈɪnsɪdənt] *n.* 事件

[记] in（里）+cid+ent（*n.*）→ "落在里面"；从天而降的喜事或从天而降的灾祸，"落在生活里面"，产生→ *n.* 事件
[派] incidence [ˈɪnsɪdəns] *n.*（事件）发生，发生率
[真] [C] It sharply reduces the **incidence** of traffic accidents.【2021 年 6 月 仔细阅读 53 题 C 选项】
[译] 它大大降低了交通事故的发生率。

coincidence [2]
[kəʊˈɪnsɪdəns] *n.* 一致，巧合

[记] co（共同，全部）+incidence → "共同、同时发生"，实在是太→ *n.* 一致，巧合
[派] coincidental [kəʊˌɪnsɪˈdentl] *a.* 巧合的，同时发生的

◀ -circ- 圆，圆圈，圆环 ▶

circle [4]
[ˈsɜːkl] *n.* 圆，圆圈

六级基础词汇

circuit [2]
[ˈsɜːkɪt] *n.* 电路，回路；巡回

[记] circ+u（无义）+ 词根 it（go；想想 exit 出口）→ "走了一个圈"；电流走了一个圈，形成→ *n.* 电路，回路→歌手办演唱会在各国走了一圈→ *n.* 巡回
[考] integrated circuit 集成电路

circulate [2]
[ˈsɜːkjəleɪt] *v.* 循环，流通

[记] circ+ul（中缀）+ate（*v.*）→使之成为一个"圆环、圆圈"；周而复始→ *v.* 循

环，流通

[派] circulation [ˌsɜːkjəˈleɪʃn] n. 循环，流通；发行量（熟词僻义，重点关注）

–civi– 文明

civil [2]
[ˈsɪvl] a. 文明的；公民的，市民的

[记] 本意是"文明的"，来自文明 civilization；具有现代文明意识的人才能称得上是"公民"，所以引申为→ a. 公民的，市民的

civilization/isation [2]
[ˌsɪvəlaɪˈzeɪʃn] n. 文明，文化

[记] 上词 civil 的名词；civil+iz/is（ize/ise）+ation（n.）→ n. 文明，文化

[派] civilize/ise [ˈsɪvəlaɪz] v. 使文明，使开化

–clar– 清楚，清晰

clarify [5]
[ˈklærəfaɪ] v. 使清楚，澄清

[记] clar+ify（使动）→ "使之清楚、清晰" → v. 使清楚，澄清

[派] clarity [ˈklærəti] n. 清楚，清晰

[真] [D] Persuade them to **clarify** the confusion they have caused.【2020 年 12 月 仔细阅读 53 题 D 选项】

[译] 说服他们来澄清他们所造成的混乱。

declare [2]
[dɪˈkleə(r)] v. 宣布，声明

[记] de（下）+clar+e（无义）→ "让下面的人很清楚" → v. 宣布，声明

[派] declaration [ˌdekləˈreɪʃn] n. 宣言，公告，声明

–class– 等级，类别

class [16]
[klɑːs] n. 班级；等级，阶级；种类（熟词僻义，重点关注）

六级基础词汇

[考] middle class 中产阶级
　　 social class 社会阶层

[真] [C] Gather gene data from people of all social **classes**.【2021 年 6 月 仔细阅读 49 题 C 选项】

[译] 从所有社会阶层的人那里收集基因数据。

classify [2]
[ˈklæsɪfaɪ] v. 分类

[记] class+ify（使动）→ "使之成为不同等级、类别" → v. 分类

[派] classification [ˌklæsɪfɪˈkeɪʃn] n. 分类，归类

Day 04

classic [5]
[ˈklæsɪk] *a.* 经典的，第一流的　*n.* 经典作品

[记] class+ic（*a.&n.*）→ "等级很高，很好的事物"，便是→ *a.* 经典的，第一流的　*n.* 经典作品

[真] [D] Wear **classic** pieces to impress their clients.【2020 年 12 月听力 15 题 D 选项】
[译] 穿经典单品给客户留下深刻印象。

classical [4]
[ˈklæsɪkl] *a.* 古典的，经典的

[记] class+ic（*a.*）+al（*a.*）→ "等级很高，很好的事物"，便是→ *a.* 古典的，经典的

[真] Because universities and curricula are designed along the three unities of French **classical** tragedy: time, action, and place.【2020 年 12 月长篇阅读 B 选项】
[译] 因为大学及其课程根据法国古典悲剧的三一律设计而成：时间、情节和地点。

–cline– 爬，攀登

decline [19]
[dɪˈklaɪn] *v.&n.* 下降，衰落；拒绝

[记] de（下）+ cline → "往下爬"→ *v.&n.* 下降，衰落→ "使别人热情下降"→ *v.&n.* 拒绝
[考] decline by 下降了
[真] [A] They are **declining** gradually in number.【2021 年 6 月仔细阅读 47 题 A 选项】
[译] 它们的数量正在逐渐减少。

incline [2]
[ɪnˈklaɪn] *v.&n.* 倾斜，倾向

[记] in（里）+cline → "向内部爬，向里爬"→ *v.&n.* 倾斜→ "心里向某事或某人倾斜"→ *v.&n.* 倾向
[派] inclination [ˌɪnklɪˈneɪʃn] *n.* 倾向，偏好

–clud–、–clus– 关闭

conclude [10]
[kənˈkluːd] *v.* 终止，结束；做总结，下结论

[记] con（全部，共同）+clud+e（无义）→ "全都关闭了"→ *v.* 终止，结束→ 行将结束时才需要 "做总结，下结论"→ *v.* 做总结，下结论
[派] conclusion [kənˈkluːʒn] *n.* 终止，结束；总结，结论
　　 conclusive [kənˈkluːsɪv] *a.* 确定的，结论性的
[考] conclude that... 结论是……
[真] Which might explain why, as the researchers **conclude**, those same middle managers are usually unaware that they are a bad manager.【2021 年 6 月听力原文】

027

[译] 正如研究人员得出的结论所言，这或许可以解释为什么这些中层管理人员通常不知道他们是一个糟糕的经理。

include [26]

[ɪnˈkluːd] v. 包含，包括

[记] in（里）+clud+e（无义）→ "关在里面"，这里面有你→ v. 包含，包括

[派] including [ɪnˈkluːdɪŋ] prep. 包含，包括
inclusive [ɪnˈkluːsɪv] a. 兼收并蓄的；范围广泛的

[真] These **include** better processes, greater team cohesion, reduced conflict and sharper alertness.【2021年6月 听力原文】

[译] 这些结果包括流程得到优化、团队凝聚力增强、冲突减少以及警觉性变得更加敏锐。

exclude [6]

[ɪkˈskluːd] v. 排斥，排除

[记] ex（out）+clud+e（无义）→ "关在外面"，不让其进来→ v. 排斥，排除

[派] exclusion [ɪkˈskluːʒn] n. 排斥，排除
exclusive [ɪkˈskluːsɪv] a. 排斥的，排除的；专门的（熟词僻义，重点关注）
exclusively [ɪkˈskluːsɪvli] ad. 唯一地，专门地

[真] Sometimes **excluded** from these arguments is the fact that we already produce enough food to more than feed the world's 7.4 billion people but do not provide adequate access to all individuals.【2020年9月 仔细阅读】

[译] 有时候，这些争论忽略了这样一个事实：我们生产的粮食已经足够养活全世界74亿人，但并没有为所有人提供充足的获取粮食的机会。

disclose [4]

[dɪsˈkləʊz] v. 泄露，暴露，显露

[记] dis（否定）+close（关）→ "不关门"→ v. 泄露，暴露，显露

[派] disclosure [dɪsˈkləʊʒə(r)] n. 披露，暴露，泄露

[真] Now you've got me rethinking what I'll **disclose** in the interview.【2021年6月 听力原文】

[译] 现在你让我想要重新思考我要在面谈中披露的内容了。

-com-、-con-、-col-、-cor-

①全部，共同，一起

cohere [3]

[kəʊˈhɪə(r)] v. 黏合，凝聚；团结一致

[记] co（简写自com）+her+e（无义）→ "全部黏在一起"→ v. 黏合，凝聚；团结一致

[派] coherent [kəʊˈhɪərənt] a. 一致的，连贯的
cohesion [kəʊˈhiːʒn] n. 团结，凝聚力

[真] These include better processes, greater team **cohesion**, reduced conflict and

sharper alertness.【2021年6月听力原文】
[译] 这些结果包括流程得到优化、团队凝聚力增强、冲突减少以及警觉性变得更加敏锐。

accumulate [7]

[əˈkjuːmjəleɪt] v. 堆积，积累

[记] ac（to）+cum（改写自com）+ul（中缀）+ate（v.）→ "共同放在一起的动作" → v. 堆积，积累

[派] accumulation [əˌkjuːmjəˈleɪʃn] n. 积累；堆积物
accumulative [əˈkjuːmjələtɪv] a. 累计的

[真] [A] Their failure to **accumulate** wealth.【2020年12月听力16题A选项】
[译] 他们没有积累财富。

combine [7]

[kəmˈbaɪn] [ˈkɒmbaɪn] v. 联合，结合

[记] com+bine（谐音"绑"）→ "全部绑在一起" → v. 联合，结合

[派] combination [ˌkɒmbɪˈneɪʃn] n. 结合（体），联合（体）

[考] combine A with B A与B联合/结合

[真] For the next nine days until the well was capped, the well poured out more oil than all the wells in America **combined**.【2021年6月听力原文】
[译] 在接下来的9天里，直到油井封顶，这口油井喷出的石油比美国所有油井涌出的石油总和还多。

compact [4]

[kəmˈpækt] [ˈkɒmpækt] v. 压紧 a. 紧凑的；简洁的 n. 协议

[记] com+ 词根 pact（简写自 package；包裹）→ "把全部东西包在一起"，表示"挤，挤压"→ v. 压紧 a. 紧凑的；简洁的 n. 协议

[真] To date, 17 states have joined a **compact** that will allow a doctor licensed in one member state to quickly obtain a license in another.【2020年9月长篇阅读O选项】
[译] 迄今为止，已有17个州加入一项协议，允许在一个成员州获得执照的医生快速获得另一个成员州的执照。

confront [3]

[kənˈfrʌnt] v. 面对；遭遇

[记] con+front（n. 面前，前面）→ "在所有人的面前、前面" → v. 面对；遭遇

[派] confrontation [ˌkɒnfrʌnˈteɪʃn] n. 面对；遭遇

[考] be confronted with 面对，面临

[真] [C] People are often at a loss when **confronted** with a number of choices.
【2020年12月仔细阅读52题C选项】
[译] 当面对许多选择时，人们往往不知所措。

conscious [10]

[ˈkɒnʃəs] a. 有意识的，清醒的

[记] con+ 词根 sci（know；知道）+ous（a.）→ "全都知道"；醒来后什么都知道 → a. 有意识的，清醒的

[派] consciousness [ˈkɒnʃəsnəs] n. 意识；知觉

consciously [ˈkɒnʃəsli] ad. 有意识地
unconscious [ʌnˈkɒnʃəs] a. 无意识的
subconscious [ˌsʌbˈkɒnʃəs] a. 潜意识的
conscience [ˈkɒnʃəns] n. 良心，良知

[真] A lot of that activity is unrelated to **conscious** activities like learning how to sing or play the guitar.【2020年12月听力原文】
[译] 很多活动都与有意识的活动无关，比如学习唱歌或弹吉他。

contemporary [2] [kənˈtemprəri] *a.* 同时代的，当代的

[记] con+ 词根 temp（改写自 time；时间）+or（表示人的后缀）+ary（*a.*）→"共同时间的人"→ *a.* 同时代的，当代的

collapse [6] [kəˈlæps] *v.&n.* 倒塌；崩溃

[记] col+lapse（*n.* 小错，疏忽）→"全部的小错汇成大错"→ *v.&n.* 倒塌；崩溃

[真] Once again people began to argue whether Notre Dame Cathedral was going to **collapse** even without the fire.【2021年6月长篇阅读37题】
[译] 人们又一次开始争论，即使没有火灾，巴黎圣母院是否也会倒塌。

colleague [12] [ˈkɒliːg] *n.* 同事

[记] col+league（联盟，同盟）→ 大家"全部在一个同盟中"，彼此就是 → *n.* 同事

[真] [D] They responded to **colleagues**' suspicion.【2020年12月听力20题D选项】
[译] 他们对同事们的怀疑做出了回应。

context [2] [ˈkɒntekst] *n.* 上下文，语境；环境，背景

[记] con+text（文章）→ *n.* 上下文，语境；进一步引申出→ *n.* 环境，背景

②加强

complacent [2] [kəmˈpleɪsnt] *a.* 自满的，自鸣得意的

[记] com+plac（改写自 please；满意）+ent（*a.*）→ *a.* 自满的，自鸣得意的
[派] complacency [kəmˈpleɪsnsi] *n.* 自满

connect [18] [kəˈnekt] *v.* 连接；联系

[记] con+nect（改写自 net；网络）→ "网络是干什么用的？人为什么上网？"为了→ *v.* 连接；联系
[派] connection [kəˈnekʃn] *n.* 连接；联系
[考] connect A to/with B 连接 A 与 B/ 联系 A 与 B
[真] What **connected** the 19th century and our present time was the development of

wireless communication.【2021 年 6 月 长篇阅读 44 题】
［译］连接 19 世纪和我们当前时代的是无线通信的发展。

contaminate²
[kənˈtæmɪneɪt] v. 污染，弄脏

［助］con+tamin（谐音"踏泥"）+ate（v.）→ "踏了一脚泥巴"→ v. 污染，弄脏
［派］contamination [kənˌtæmɪˈneɪʃn] n. 污染，弄脏

convince⁷
[kənˈvɪns] v. 使相信，使信服

［记］con+ 词根 vin（改写自 win；赢）+ce（v.）→ "赢了"才能→ v. 使相信，使信服
［派］convincing [kənˈvɪnsɪŋ] a. 令人信服的，有信服力的
　　 convincingly [kənˈvɪnsɪŋli] ad. 信服地
［考］be convinced that... 相信……
［真］Patillo Higgins, a disreputable local businessman, became **convinced** that there was oil below the gassy hill.【2021 年 6 月 听力原文】
［译］当地声名狼藉的商人帕蒂罗·希金斯确信，在充满气体的山下有石油。

扫码快速学习

扫码即刻听课

◀ –commun– 共同 ▶

common [10] [ˈkɒmən] *a.* 常见的，普通的，共同的

六级基础词汇

[派] commonly [ˈkɒmənli] *ad.* 常见地，通常地，普遍地
uncommon [ʌnˈkɒmən] *a.* 不常见的，非同寻常的
commonplace [ˈkɒmənpleɪs] *a.* 普遍的，平常的　*n.* 平常的事

community [22] [kəˈmju:nəti] *n.* 社区，团体，共同体

[记] commun+ity（*n.*）→ "共同生活的地方"→ *n.* 社区，团体，共同体
[真] [A] It is beneficial to poor as well as rich **communities**.【2021 年 6 月 听力 9 题 A 选项】
[译] 它对穷人和富人都是有益的。

communicate [48] [kəˈmju:nɪkeɪt] *v.* 沟通，交流；通讯，通信

[记] commun+ic（*a.*）+ate（*v.*）→ 本来是我的想法，要想 "使之成为共同的想法"，要靠→ *v.* 沟通，交流→ "设备之间信息的沟通与交流"→ *v.* 通讯，通信
[派] communication [kəˌmju:nɪˈkeɪʃn] *n.* 沟通，交流；通讯，通信
[考] communicate with... 与……沟通 / 交流 / 通话
[真] But scientists who want to **communicate** with the general public need to modify their language.【2021 年 6 月 听力原文】
[译] 但是想要与公众交流的科学家需要修改他们的语言。

◀ –contr–、–counter– 反，相反 ▶

contrast [3] [ˈkɒntrɑ:st] *v.&n.*（形成）对比，（形成）对照

[记] contr+ast（改写自 est；最）→ "最相反"→ *v.&n.*（形成）对比，（形成）对照
[考] by contrast 对比之下，相比之下
　　in contrast 相反地
[真] In many rich countries, by **contrast**, roads are becoming even safer.【2021 年 6

Day 05

月 听力原文】
[译] 相比之下，许多富裕国家的道路交通变得更加安全了。

contrary [5]

['kɒntrəri] [kən'treəri] *a.* 相反的

[记] contr+ary（*a.*）→ *a.* 相反的
[考] on the contrary 相反地
　　　be contrary to... 与……相反
[真] On the **contrary**, the personal storage business is now a growing industry.【2020年12月 听力原文】
[译] 相反，私人物品存储业务现在是一个不断发展的行业。

counterpart [2]

['kaʊntəpɑːt] *n.* 相对物，对应的人或物

[记] counter+part（*n.* 部分）→ 与主物"相对、相对应的那一部分"→ *n.* 相对物，对应的人或物

encounter [4]

[ɪn'kaʊntə(r)] *v.* 面对；相遇；遭遇

[记] en（使动）+counter → "使方向相反"，必然是面对面坐着或站着→ *v.* 面对；相遇；遭遇
[真] After **encountering** several setbacks, Captain Lucas decided to use a drill, and his innovations created the modern oil drilling industry.【2021年6月 听力原文】
[译] 遇到几次挫折后，卢卡斯队长决定使用钻头，他的革新创造了现代石油钻探工业。

–cord– 心，核心

core [4]

[kɔː(r)] *n.* 中心，核心；果核　*a.* 最重要的，主要的

[记] 改写自 cord → *n.* 中心，核心；果核　*a.* 最重要的，主要的
[助] 处理器是计算机最核心的部件，英特尔的处理器名字就叫 core（酷睿）
[真] However, at its **core** is love.【2020年12月 选词填空】
[译] 然而，它的核心是爱。

record [6]

[rɪ'kɔːd] ['rekɔːd] *v.* 记录，录音　*n.*（文字或影像）记录；录音，唱片；（体育运动或活动的）纪录

[记] re（反复）+cord → "反复用心"，是为了 → *v.&n.* 记录，录音→记录下来的东西→ *n.* 唱片；（体育运动或活动的）纪录
[真] The world is seeing sports **records** being broken that could only be broken with the aid of technology, whether this be the speed of a tennis serve or the fastest time in a 100-meter dash or a 200-meter swimming race.【2020年7月听力原文】
[译] 世界一直在见证一项项体育纪录被打破，但是只有在科技的辅助下，这些纪录才能被打破，不管是网球的发球速度，还是100米短跑或者200米游泳的最短用时。

–count– 计算

count [kaʊnt] v. 数；计算

六级基础词汇

[派] counter [ˈkaʊntə(r)] n. 计算器 v. 抵制；反驳
[考] count on 依靠，依赖

account [əˈkaʊnt] n. 账户，账目；解释，说明 v. 解释，说明；认为是；报账；（在数量、比例方面）占

[记] ac（to）+count → "去算" → 去算什么？→ n. 账目，账户 v. 报账；（在数量、比例方面）占 → "计算的过程" 就是 → v.&n. 解释，说明；认为是
[派] accounting [əˈkaʊntɪŋ] n. 会计，会计学
　　accountant [əˈkaʊntənt] n. 会计
　　accountable [əˈkaʊntəbl] a. 可解释的；有责任的
　　accountability [əˌkaʊntəˈbɪləti] n. 责任；问责制
[考] take sth. into account 考虑某事
　　account for... 对……负责；占有，占据；解释，说明
　　on account of 由于
[真] [A] Take all relevant factors into **account** in interpreting their data.【2021年6月 仔细阅读49题 A选项】
[译] 在解释他们的数据时，应考虑所有相关因素。

discount [ˈdɪskaʊnt] [dɪsˈkaʊnt] n. 折扣 v. 打折

[记] dis（否定）+count → 老板，这10块钱"别算了"，这是要求老板给→ n. 折扣 v. 打折

–cover– 覆盖

cover [ˈkʌvə(r)] v. 覆盖；采访，报道；掩护；负担，承担（成本）n. 封面，封皮

六级基础词汇

[派] coverage [ˈkʌvərɪdʒ] n. 覆盖；采访，报道；范围，程度
[真] On many occasions, the entrepreneurs reported not paying themselves a wage at all initially in order to **cover** salaries and expenses.【2021年6月 听力原文】
[译] 在许多情况下，创业者报告说，为了支付工资和开销，他们最初根本不给自己发工资。

discover [dɪˈskʌvə(r)] v. 发现，发觉

[记] dis（否定）+cover → "没有覆盖" → v. 发现，发觉
[派] discovery [dɪˈskʌvəri] n. 发现，发觉
[真] "They **discovered** the uncanny valley."【2021年6月 长篇阅读 I 选项】

Day 05

[译]"他们发现了这个恐怖谷。"

recover³
[rɪˈkʌvə(r)] *v.* 愈合；恢复，痊愈

[记] re（反复）+cover → "再一次覆盖" → 摔伤了，过几天，生长出的皮肤组织"再一次覆盖"伤口，使伤口→ *v.* 愈合；恢复，痊愈

[派] recovery [rɪˈkʌvəri] *n.* 愈合；恢复，痊愈

[考] recover from... 从……中痊愈/恢复

[真] They have to operate for long periods of time before the costs of development have been **recovered**.【2020 年 7 月长篇阅读 J 选项】

[译] 收回开发成本前，它们必须长时间运作。

uncover²
[ʌnˈkʌvə(r)] *v.* 揭露，揭发

[记] un（否定）+cover → "不要盖盖儿"；让丑事大白于天下 → *v.* 揭露，揭发

–creat–、–creas– 产生，创造

create⁸⁴
[kriˈeɪt] *v.* 产生，创造

六级基础词汇

[派] creative [kriˈeɪtɪv] *a.* 有创造力的
creativity [ˌkriːeɪˈtɪvəti] *n.* 创造力
creation [kriˈeɪʃn] *n.* 创造
creator [kriˈeɪtə(r)] *n.* 创造者，创作者
recreate [ˌriːkriˈeɪt] *v.* 重现，重建
recreation [ˌriːkriˈeɪʃn] *n.* 重现，重建；娱乐，游戏

concrete²
[ˈkɒŋkriːt] *a.* 具体的，有形的 *n.* 混凝土

[记] con（全部，共同）+cret（简写自 creat）+e（无义）→ "所有东西全部产生在一起""小零件放在一起产生成品" → *a.* 具体的，有形的 → 水泥、沙子、水"全部产生在一起"，形成 → *n.* 混凝土

increase⁶²
[ɪnˈkriːs] [ˈɪnkriːs] *v.&n.* 增加，增长

[记] in（里）+creas+e（无义）→ "向里产生/创造"，数量自然增多了 → *v.&n.* 增加，增长

[派] increasingly [ɪnˈkriːsɪŋli] *ad.* 愈加，日益

[真] [A] Many of them have **increasing** numbers of cars on the road.【2021 年 6 月听力 24 题 A 选项】

[译] 其中许多国家在路上行驶的汽车数量越来越多。

decrease⁴
[dɪˈkriːs] [ˈdiːkriːs] *v.&n.* 减小，减少

[记] 上词 increase 的反义词；de（下）+creas+e（无义）→ "产生/创造下去

了"；数量自然变少了 → *v.&n.* 减小，减少

[真] [C] It will sharply **decrease** work efficiency.【2020 年 12 月 听力 14 题 C 选项】
[译] 它会大大降低工作效率。

–cred– 相信，信用

credit [7]　['kredɪt] *n.* 信用；赞扬，荣誉；学分（熟词僻义，重点关注）

[记] cred+it（*n.*）→ *n.* 信用 → 说一个人讲"信用"，对于 TA 来说是 → *n.* 赞扬，荣誉；进而引申出 → *n.* 学分

[考] credit card 信用卡

[真] This phenomenon has resulted in significant credit **card** debt.【2020 年 12 月 听力原文】
[译] 这种现象造成了巨额的信用卡债务。

credible [3]　['kredəbl] *a.* 可信的，可靠的

[记] cred+ible（*a.*）→ "能相信的" → *a.* 可信的，可靠的

[派] incredible [ɪn'kredəbl] *a.* 难以置信的，不可思议的
　　incredibly [ɪn'kredəbli] *ad.* 令人难以置信地；极其

[真] Not so much the form of variety one obtains from a university but the informal variety that comes from **credible** work experience and professional accomplishments.【2021 年 6 月 听力原文】
[译] 与其说是从大学获得的多样性形式，不如说是来自可靠的工作经验和专业成就的非正式多样性。

credential [2]　[krə'denʃl] *n.* 凭证，证书

[记] cred+ent（*n.*）+ial（*n.*）→ 让别人"相信"的东西 → *n.* 凭证，证书

grant [6]　[grɑːnt] *v.* 承认；授予；同意　*n.* 拨款，资金

[记] 改写自 cred → "相信"某人才会 → *v.* 承认；授予；同意　*n.* 拨款，资金

[助] 谐音"哥让他"；哥让着他，这个让给他吧，哥哥"同意"不争了

[真] He was **granted** over 200 patents and continued to pioneer rocket technology until his death in 1945.【2021 年 6 月 听力原文】
[译] 他获得了 200 多项专利，并持续开拓火箭技术，直到他在 1945 年去世为止。

–crim– 罪

crime [2]　[kraɪm] *n.* 罪；犯罪活动

[记] crim+e（无义）→ *n.* 罪；犯罪活动

[派] criminal ['krɪmɪnl] *n.* 罪犯，犯人　*a.* 犯罪的

Day 05

discriminate [4]
[dɪˈskrɪmɪneɪt] *v.* 歧视,区别对待

[记] dis(散)+crim+in(无义)+ate(*v.*)→与"犯罪或有罪之人"保持"分散、离开"的动作,是一种→*v.* 区别对待→*v.* 歧视

[派] discrimination [dɪˌskrɪmɪˈneɪʃn] *n.* 歧视,区别对待

[真] [D] Promoting **discrimination** in the name of science.【2021年6月 仔细阅读50题 D 选项】

[译] 以科学的名义促进歧视。

–crit– 批评,评论

criticize/ise [9]
[ˈkrɪtɪsaɪz] *v.* 批评;评论

[记] crit+ic(*a.*)+ize/ise(使动)→*v.* 批评;评论

[派] criticism [ˈkrɪtɪsɪzəm] *n.* 批评;评论

[真] Mix with critical people and we learn to **criticize**.【2020年9月 听力原文】

[译] 和挑剔的人在一起,我们也学会了挑剔。

critic [11]
[ˈkrɪtɪk] *n.* 批评家,评论家

[记] crit+ic(*n.*)→"进行批评、评论的人"→*n.* 批评家,评论家

[真] What do **critics** think of the Coral Sea plan?【2020年9月 仔细阅读55题 题干】

[译] 批评者对珊瑚海的计划有何看法?

critical [10]
[ˈkrɪtɪkl] *a.* 批评的;关键的,重要的

[记] crit+ic(*a.*)+al(*a.*)→*a.* 批评的→此事重要,做不好就得受批评,由此引申出→*a.* 关键的,重要的

[派] critically [ˈkrɪtɪkli] *ad.* 批判性地;严重地

[真] [D] It is conductive to **critical** thinking.【2021年6月 听力4题 D 选项】

[译] 它有利于形成批判性思维。

crucial [2]
[ˈkruːʃl] *a.* 关键的,重要的

[记] 上词 critical 的同源词;cruc(改写自 crit)+ial(*a.*)→*a.* 关键的,重要的

–cult– 耕种

culture [57]
[ˈkʌltʃə(r)] *n.* 文化,文明

六级基础词汇

[派] cultural [ˈkʌltʃərəl] *a.* 文化的
　　culturally [ˈkʌltʃərəli] *ad.* 从文化角度,文化意义上

037

multicultural [ˌmʌltiˈkʌltʃərəl] a. 多元文化的

cultivate⁹ [ˈkʌltɪveɪt] v. 耕种；培养

[记] cult+iv（无义）+ate（v.）→ v. 耕种；培养

[派] cultivation [ˌkʌltɪˈveɪʃn] n. 耕种；培养

[真] [D] It is an ability everyone should **cultivate**.【2021年6月 仔细阅读46题D选项】

[译] 这是一种每个人都应该培养的能力。

colony⁸ [ˈkɒləni] n. 殖民地

[记] col（改写自 cult）+on（在……之上）+y（n.）→ "在……之上耕种"；本义是去新地方开发、耕作，后指殖民占领别人的土地→ n. 殖民地

[助] 谐音 "占了你" → n. 殖民地

[派] colonial [kəˈləʊniəl] a. 殖民的，殖民地的

[真] When the Constitution was signed, people had little regard for paper money because of its steadily decreasing value during the **colonial** era.【2020年9月 听力原文】

[译] 签署宪法的时候，人们并不重视纸币，因为在殖民时期它不断贬值。

①跑

accurate¹² [ˈækjərət] a. 精确的，准确的

[记] ac（to）+cur+ate（a.）→ 来自跑步；本身是终点线的一种仪器名称，通过运动员最后的撞线提供精确、准确的结果，后来变成普通化和社会化的单词 → a. 精确的，准确的

[派] accurately [ˈækjərətli] ad. 精确地，准确地
accuracy [ˈækjərəsi] n. 精确，准确
inaccurate [ɪnˈækjərət] a. 不准确的，不正确的

[真] [B] The woman's **inaccurate** description of the whole incident.【2020年12月 听力3题B选项】

[译] 那个女人对整个事件的描述并不准确。

occur¹⁸ [əˈkɜː(r)] v. 发生；出现

[记] oc（在……之前）+cur → "事情在眼前跑" → v. 发生；出现

[派] occurrence [əˈkʌrəns] n. 发生；出现

[真] [C] Deliberate the consequences that may **occur**.【2021年6月 听力6题C选项】

[译] 考虑一下可能出现的后果。

Day 05

curriculum [7]

[kəˈrɪkjələm] *n.*（*pl.* curriculums 或 curricula）课程，（学校等的）全部课程

[记] curr（改写自 cur）+ic（无义）+ul（中缀）+um（*n.*）→ "上完一门课跑到另外一门课；从一间教室跑到另外一间教室" → *n.* 课程，（学校等的）全部课程

[助] 谐音 "课轮课" → "一轮又一轮课" → *n.* 课程，（学校等的）全部课程

[真] [B] Cultivation of creativity should permeate the entire school **curriculum**. 【2021 年 6 月 仔细阅读 47 题 B 选项】

[译] 创造力的培养应该渗透到学校的整个课程中。

②流

current [18]

[ˈkʌrənt] *n.*（水、气、电）流；趋势 *a.* 流通的；现在的，当前的

[记] curr（改写自 cur）+ent（*n.&a.*）→ *n.*（水、气、电）流；趋势→ *a.* 流通的→ "流在当下" → *a.* 现在的，当前的

[派] currently [ˈkʌrəntli] *ad.* 现在，当前

[真] [C] Only some can be put to use under **current** traffic conditions.【2021 年 6 月 仔细阅读 52 题 C 选项】

[译] 只有一些设备可以在当前的交通条件下使用。

currency [8]

[ˈkʌrənsi] *n.* 流通，流行；货币

[记] curr（改写自 cur）+ency（*n.*）→ *n.* 流通，流行→ "什么东西最具有流通性？" 当然是→ *n.* 货币

[真] American history has seen generations of politicians argue in favor of a gold standard for American **currency**.【2020 年 9 月 听力原文】

[译] 为了支持美国货币的黄金标准，美国历史已经见证了几代政客的争论。

扫码快速学习

扫码即刻听课

-cure- 治疗

cure [2]
[kjʊə(r)] *v.& n.* 治疗，治愈

六级基础词汇
[近] heal [hi:l] *v.* 治疗，治愈

secure [18]
[sɪˈkjʊə(r)] *a.* 安全的；安心的

[记] se（away）+cure → "治愈而使疾病远离（away）" → *a.* 安全的；安心的
[派] security [sɪˈkjʊərəti] *n.* 安全，安全性；保险，保障（熟词僻义，重点关注）
　　insecurity [ˌɪnsɪˈkjʊərəti] *n.* 不安全
[真] Police and fire services will spend the next 48 hours assessing the "**security** and safety" of the 850-year-old structure.【2021年6月 长篇阅读 H 选项】
[译] 警方和消防部门将在接下来的48小时里，对这座有850年历史的建筑进行"安全和安保"评估。

非成组词（C 字母）

calculate [2]
[ˈkælkjuleɪt] *v.* 计算

[记] 词根 calc（计算）+ul（中缀）+ ate（*v.*）→ *v.* 计算
[派] calculation [ˌkælkjuˈleɪʃn] *n.* 计算，估算

candidate [9]
[ˈkændɪdət] *n.* 候选者，候选人

[记] can（能）+did（do 的过去式；做）+ate（*n.*）→ "能做这份工作的人"，就是→ *n.* 候选者，候选人
[真] Secondly, **candidates** should know what's at stake for the company with this job opening.【2020年12月 听力原文】
[译] 第二，求职者应该了解这个职位空缺对公司有什么成败攸关的影响。

category [6]
[ˈkætəɡəri] *n.* 种类，分类

[助] 谐音"快点归类" → *n.* 种类，分类

Day 06

[派] categorize/ise [ˈkætəɡəraɪz] v. 把……归类，把……分门别类
categorization/isation [ˌkætəɡəraɪˈzeɪʃn] n. 分类；分门别类
[真] [C] Accuracy in **categorization**.【2021 年 6 月 仔细阅读 50 题 C 选项】
[译] 分类的准确性。

cater 2

[ˈkeɪtə(r)] v. 满足，迎合

[记] cat（猫）+er（表示人的后缀）→ "猫对人"；猫很温柔，会围着主人温柔地喵喵叫 → v. 满足，迎合
[考] cater to 满足，迎合

chain 5

[tʃeɪn] n. 链子，链条；连锁，连锁店

[助] 谐音 "抻" → "用力抻，断不了"，因为有 → n. 链子，链条；进而引申为 → n. 连锁，连锁店
[考] food chain 食物链
supply chain 供应链
[真] Penguins, like other seabirds and marine mammals, occupy higher levels in the food **chain** and they are what we call bio-indicators of their ecosystems.【2019 年 12 月 仔细阅读】
[译] 企鹅和其他海鸟以及海洋哺乳动物一样，在食物链中有着更高等级，它们就是我们所说的它们生态系统的生物指标。

challenge 30

[ˈtʃælɪndʒ] v.&n. 挑战；怀疑

[助] 改写自 change（变化）→ "变化" 带来 "挑战、怀疑"；两词同时记忆 → v.&n. 挑战，怀疑
[派] challenging [ˈtʃælɪndʒɪŋ] a. 艰巨的，有挑战性的
[真] It can sometimes make recruiting staff a **challenge**.【2021 年 6 月 听力原文】
[译] 这有时会使招聘员工成为一大困难。

charge 10

[tʃɑːdʒ] v.&n. 控诉；收费；负责；充电（量）

[助] char（谐音 "叉" 或 "插"）+ge（谐音 "哥"）→ 一个 "大哥" 被 "叉" 了；我要控诉你 → v.&n. 控诉→不能白被 "叉"，赔我的身体和精神损失费 → v.&n. 收费→你得照顾我一辈子 → v.&n. 负责→插上充电器 → v.&n. 充电（量）
[真] [C] Its agencies in **charge** of drafting the guidelines have the expertise.【2020 年 12 月 仔细阅读 52 题 C 选项】
[译] 其负责起草这些准则的机构具有专业知识。

chronic 11

[ˈkrɒnɪk] a. 长期的；（疾病）慢性的

[记] chron+ic（a.）→ a. 长期的 → "长期的病" → a.（疾病）慢性的
[派] chronically [ˈkrɒnɪkli] ad. 长期地
[真] How can one stop being a **chronic** complainer according to the author?【2020 年 12 月 仔细阅读 55 题题干】

041

[译] 根据作者的说法，人们如何才能停止长期地抱怨呢？

cite [4]

[saɪt] *v.* 引用，采用

[助] 谐音"采他"→"采用他的说法"就是→ *v.* 引用，采用

[派] citation [saɪˈteɪʃn] *n.* 引用，引述

[真] Edwards **cites** widespread backlash to the digital recreation of Carrie Fisher as a young Princess Leia in *Rogue One,* a trick later repeated in the recent *Star Wars: The Rise of Skywalker*, which was filmed after Fisher's death in 2016.【2021 年 6 月 长篇阅读 I 选项】

[译] 爱德华兹指出，凯丽·费雪通过数字化方式在《侠盗一号》中出演年轻的莱娅公主，这一做法遭到了广泛反对，后来同样的操作又出现在《星球大战：天行者崛起》中，而这部电影是在 2016 年费雪去世后拍摄的。

citizen [2]

[ˈsɪtɪzn] *n.* 公民，市民

[记] citi（改写自 city；城市）+zen（谐音"人"）→"城市里的人"→ *n.* 公民，市民

[派] citizenship [ˈsɪtɪzənʃɪp] *n.* 公民身份，公民权

clash [2]

[klæʃ] *v.&n.* 碰撞（声）

[记] 拟声词，两物相撞发出巨大的声音；cla（咔啦）+sh（嘶）→ *v.&n.* 碰撞（声）

clash 的引申词

crash [6]

[kræʃ] *v.* 撞击，坠毁；崩溃 *n.* 猛撞，崩溃

[记] 改写自上词 clash（使用了辅音字母 r 和 l 的替换）→ *v.* 撞击，坠毁 *n.* 猛撞；进而引申为→ *v.&n.* 崩溃

[真] Had the bell towers' wooden frames burned down, the heavy bells would have **crashed** down.【2021 年 6 月 长篇阅读 41 题】

[译] 如果钟楼的木制框架被烧毁，沉重的钟就会倒塌。

corporation [5]

[ˌkɔːpəˈreɪʃn] *n.* 公司

[记] corpor（改写自 compan=company）+ation（*n.*）→ *n.* 公司；其实就是 company 的变体

[派] corporate [ˈkɔːpərət] *a.* 公司的，法人的
incorporate [ɪnˈkɔːpəreɪt] *v.* 包含；使并入

[真] The ongoing push by the mining **corporations** to be more productive and more efficient is another powerful driver in embracing automation technology.【2021 年 6 月 听力原文】

[译] 矿业公司不断提高产量和效率是采用自动化技术的另一个强大驱动力。

Day 06

curse [2]　[kɜːs] *v.&n.* 诅咒，咒骂

[助] 谐音"克死"→"克死"对方→ *v.&n.* 诅咒，咒骂

-de- 下，向下

decay [2]　[dɪˈkeɪ] *v.&n.* 腐朽，腐烂；衰退

[记] de+cay（=cad=cid；落下）→"往下落"→ *v.&n.* 腐朽，腐烂；衰退

delay [2]　[dɪˈleɪ] *v.&n.* 延迟，拖延

[记] de+lay（*v.* 放，放置）→"把这件事往下放放"→ *v.&n.* 延迟，拖延

deliver [9]　[dɪˈlɪvə(r)] *v.* 分娩；交付，传递；发表

[记] de+live（生命，活物）+r（无义）→"下来一个生命、活物"→ *v.* 分娩；后引申出→ *v.* 交付，传递；发表

[派] delivery [dɪˈlɪvəri] *n.* 分娩；交付，传递；发表

[真] [B] It seldom **delivers** all the benefits as promised.【2021 年 6 月 仔细阅读 54 题 B 选项】

[译] 它很少像承诺的那样提供所有的好处。

depict [5]　[dɪˈpɪkt] *v.* 描绘，描写，描述

[记] de+pict（简写自 picture；图画，图片）→"把它画了下来"→ *v.* 描绘，描写，描述

[派] depiction [dɪˈpɪkʃn] *n.* 描绘，描写，描述

[真] [A] It proved hard to **depict** objectively.【2020 年 12 月 听力 18 题 A 选项】

[译] 事实证明，很难客观地描述它。

deploy [3]　[dɪˈplɔɪ] *v.* 部署；有效利用

[记] de+ploy（改写自 play；起作用）→"在下面起作用"→ *v.* 部署；有效利用

[派] deployment [dɪˈplɔɪmənt] *n.* 部署，调集；有效利用

[真] This is because the more technology is put into the field, the more people are needed to **deploy**, maintain and improve it.【2021 年 6 月 听力原文】

[译] 这是因为该领域使用的技术越多，需要部署、维护和改进它的人就越多。

descend [2]　[dɪˈsend] *v.* 下来，下降；遗传

[记] de+ 词根 scend（改写自 send；送）→"送下来"；高度就会→ *v.* 下来，下降→父辈的特征"往下送"→ *v.* 遗传

[派] descent [dɪˈsent] *n.* 下降；血统

detail [12]　[ˈdiːteɪl] *n.* 细节　*v.* 详述

[记] de+tail（尾巴）→"向下直到尾部"；从头到尾什么都管→ *n.* 细节→"每

043

个细节都不放过"→ v. 详述
[派] detailed ['di:teɪld] a. 详细的，细节的
[真] But I really appreciate all the **details** that go into the game. 【2020 年 12 月听力原文】
[译] 但是我真的很欣赏游戏中涉及的所有细节。

deteriorate [6]

[dɪ'tɪərɪəreɪt] v. 恶化，变坏

[记] de+ter（谐音"他"）+i（无义）+or（表示人的后缀）+ate（v.）→"他这个人不停地向下"，有点自甘堕落的感觉→ v. 恶化，变坏
[派] deterioration [dɪˌtɪərɪə'reɪʃn] n. 恶化，变坏
[真] [D] **Deterioration** in the quality of new music. 【2020 年 12 月听力 22 题 D 选项】
[译] 新音乐的质量在下降。

determine [15]

[dɪ'tɜ:mɪn] v. 决定，决心；确定，断定

[记] de+ 词根 term（end；结束）+in（v.）+e（无义）→事态"一直往下发展到了结束之时"，必须要→ v. 决定，决心；确定，断定
[派] determination [dɪˌtɜ:mɪ'neɪʃn] n. 决定，决心
[考] determine to do... 决定 / 决心做……
be determined to do... 决定 / 决心做……
[真] [D] Students' academic performance is **determined** by their genes. 【2021 年 6 月仔细阅读 46 题 D 选项】
[译] 学生的学习成绩是由他们的基因决定的。

detriment [2]

['detrɪmənt] n. 损害，伤害

[记] de+tri（改写自 try；尝试）+ment（n.）→ n. 损害，伤害
[派] detrimental [ˌdetrɪ'mentl] a. 有害的，不利的

–dem– 民众

democracy [2]

[dɪ'mɒkrəsi] n. 民主，民主制；民主国家

[记] dem+o（无义）+ 词根 crac（统治）+y（n.）→"人民统治，人民当家做主"→ n. 民主，民主制；民主国家
[派] democratic [ˌdemə'krætɪk] a. 民主的

demonstrate [12]

['demənstreɪt] v. 示威，游行；证明，证实；显示

[记] dem+on（上，上面）+str（简写自 street；大街，街道）+ate（v.）→"人们在大街上的动作"→ v. 示威，游行→"示威是为了证明自己的要求是对的"→ v. 证明，证实；显示
[派] demonstration [ˌdemən'streɪʃn] n. 示威，游行；证明；显示
[真] [A] Chimps **demonstrate** highly developed skills of communication. 【2020 年 12 月仔细阅读 52 题 A 选项】
[译] 黑猩猩表现出高度发达的沟通能力。

Day 06

-dent- 相同

identity [aɪˈdentəti] *n.* 身份

[记] identity card 简称 ID card（身份证）
[考] identity card 身份证
[真] As it becomes easier to digitally recreate celebrities and to entirely manufacture on-screen **identities**, could this kind of technology put actors out of jobs?【2021 年 6 月 长篇阅读 I 选项】
[译] 随着用数字技术重现名人和完整地制作屏幕上的人物变得越来越容易，这种技术会让演员失业吗？

identify [aɪˈdentɪfaɪ] *v.* 识别，认出；确认

[记] 上词 identity 的动词；ident（改写自 dent）+ify（使动）→你好，请出示身份证！"使其亮出身份" → *v.* 识别，认出；确认
[派] identifiable [aɪˌdentɪˈfaɪəbl] *a.* 可辨认的，可视为相同的
[真] [D] To **identify** a broad general strength to elaborate on.【2020 年 12 月 听力 24 题 D 选项】
[译] 为了确定要详细说明的宽泛的、综合的实力。

-dic-、-dict- 说

predict [prɪˈdɪkt] *v.* 预报，预测

[记] pre（前）+dict →"提前说出来" → *v.* 预报，预测
[派] prediction [prɪˈdɪkʃn] *n.* 预报，预测
predictable [prɪˈdɪktəbl] *a.* 可预测的
predictably [prɪˈdɪktəbli] *ad.* 可预见地
predictability [prɪˌdɪktəˈbɪləti] *n.* 可预测性；可预言性
unpredictable [ˌʌnprɪˈdɪktəbl] *a.* 不可预测的
unpredictability [ˌʌnprɪˌdɪktəˈbɪləti] *n.* 不可预测性，不可预知性
[真] [C] It **predicted** their value would increase.【2020 年 9 月 听力 24 题 C 选项】
[译] 它预测它们的价值将会增加。

indicate [ˈɪndɪkeɪt] *v.* 暗示，指示

[记] in（里）+dic+ate（*v.*）→"在里面，关上门说"；不是明示，而是→ *v.* 暗示，指示
[派] indication [ˌɪndɪˈkeɪʃn] *n.* 表明，指示
indicative [ɪnˈdɪkətɪv] *a.* 指示的，表示的
indicator [ˈɪndɪkeɪtə(r)] *n.* 指示剂，指示器
[真] The Paris prosecutor's office has opened an inquiry into "involuntary

045

destruction by fire", **indicating** they believe the cause of the blaze was accidental rather than criminal.【2021 年 6 月 长篇阅读 K 选项】

[译] 巴黎检察官办公室已经针对这次"意外的火灾破坏"进行了调查，这一说法表明他们认为火灾的发生是意外事件，而非人为纵火。

contradict ²

[ˌkɒntrəˈdɪkt] *v.* 反驳，与……说反话；与……矛盾

[记] contr（相反）+a（无义）+dict → "反着说" → *v.* 反驳，与……说反话 → "一个人总和你反着说，说明你们之间有矛盾" → *v.* 与……矛盾

[派] contradiction [ˌkɒntrəˈdɪkʃn] *n.* 矛盾，抵触

addict ²

[ˈædɪkt] *v.* 上瘾

[记] add（增加）+ict → "用量不断地增加"；说明已经→ *v.* 上瘾

[派] addiction [əˈdɪkʃn] *n.* 上瘾，着迷

[考] be addicted to... 对……上瘾

dedicate ⁴

[ˈdedɪkeɪt] *v.* 宣誓，致力于；贡献，献身

[记] de（下）+dic+ate（*v.*）→ "在党旗下说话的动作" → *v.* 宣誓；后引申为→ *v.* 致力于；贡献，献身

[形] delicate [ˈdelɪkət] *a.* 微妙的；精致的；纤弱的

[考] be dedicated to 致力于……，献身于……

[真] It increased employees' perception of the likelihood of success in the attainment of job goals, and therefore fostered a willingness to **dedicate** their effort and ability to their work.【2021 年 6 月 听力原文】

[译] 它增强了员工对成功实现工作目标的可能性的感知，从而让他们形成了将自己的努力和能力奉献给工作的意愿。

扫码快速学习

Day 07

扫码即刻听课

–di–、–dis–、–dif–

①散，分散

dilemma [2] [dɪˈlemə] *n.* 困境，进退两难

[记] di+lemma（谐音"来嘛"）→"和前女友分了，对方打电话说'来嘛'"；去还是不去呢？→ *n.* 困境，进退两难

divorce [2] [dɪˈvɔːs] *v.&n.* 离婚；分离

[记] di+vorce（改写自 voice；声音）→"两个人的声音分开"；你不想听到我的声音，我也不想听到你的声音→ *v.&n.* 离婚；分离

disrupt [2] [dɪsˈrʌpt] *v.* 扰乱，打断

[记] dis+ 词根 rupt（破，打破）→对话"四散打破"→ *v.* 扰乱，打断

[派] disruption [dɪsˈrʌpʃn] *n.* 扰乱，打断

②否定，不

discourage [3] [dɪsˈkʌrɪdʒ] *v.* 使气馁；阻止

[记] dis+courage（*n.* 勇气）→"否定某人的勇气，使之没有勇气"，就是→ *v.* 使气馁；阻止

[考] discourage sb. from doing sth. 劝某人不要做某事

[真] The problem is that the mere presence of jargon sends a **discouraging** message to readers.【2021 年 6 月 听力原文】

[译] 问题在于，只要出现术语就会向读者发出令其感到沮丧的信息。

disguise [2] [dɪsˈɡaɪz] *v.&n.* 伪装，掩饰

[记] dis+gui（谐音"鬼"）+se（谐音"色"）→"不是人，是色鬼"→ *v.&n.* 伪装，掩饰

–divid–、–divis– 分

divide [10]
[dɪˈvaɪd] *v.* 分割；分离
六级基础词汇
[考] divide... into... 把……分成……
[派] divided [dɪˈvaɪdɪd] *a.* 分裂的，有分歧的　*v.* divide 的过去分词和过去式

division [2]
[dɪˈvɪʒn] *n.* 分开；分歧；部门
[记] divis+ion（*n.*）→ *n.* 分开；分歧→"公司里被分开的部分"→ *n.* 部门

dividend [2]
[ˈdɪvɪdend] *n.* 分红，股息
[记] divid+end（结束）→上市公司在"一年结束时分"什么？→ *n.* 分红，股息

individual [32]
[ˌɪndɪˈvɪdʒuəl] *n.* 个人，个体　*a.* 个别的
[记] in（否定）+divid+u（you）+al（*n.&a.*）→"不能分给你"；个人的为什么要分给你？→ *n.* 个人，个体　*a.* 个别的
[派] individuality [ˌɪndɪˌvɪdʒuˈæləti] *n.* 个别；个性
[真] But that disguises a lot of changes in **individual** countries.【2021 年 6 月 听力原文】
[译] 但这掩盖了个别国家的许多变化。

–dom–

①房子，家

domestic [3]
[dəˈmestɪk] *a.* 家里的，家庭的；本国的，国家的
[记] dom+est（无义）+ic（*a.*）→"家的"→ *a.* 家里的，家庭的→引申出"所有人民的家"→ *a.* 本国的，国家的
[真] Both international and **domestic** visitors in the UK should pay tourist tax so as to...【2021 年 6 月 仔细阅读 53 题题干】
[译] 在英国的国际和国内游客都应缴纳旅游税，以便……

②统治，支配

domain [2]
[dəˈmeɪn] *n.* 领域，范围
[记] dom+ain（*n.*）→"统治的地方"；这是我的地盘→ *n.* 领域，范围

Day 07

dominate [6] [ˈdɒmɪneɪt] *v.* 统治，支配

[记] dom+in（无义）+ate（*v.*）→ *v.* 统治，支配

[派] dominance [ˈdɒmɪnəns] *n.* 支配，统治
　　dominant [ˈdɒmɪnənt] *a.* 占支配地位的；显著的

[真] How did the foreign-language **dominant** speakers manage this feat?【2020 年 9 月 长篇阅读 L 选项】

[译] 以说外语为主的人是如何做到这一壮举的？

random [3] [ˈrændəm] *a.* 随机的　*n.* 随机数

六级基础词汇

[派] randomize/ise [ˈrændəmaɪz] *v.* 使随机化，完全打乱

[真] Consulting a **random** doctor patients will never meet, they say, further fragments the health-care system, and even minor issues such as upper respiratory（上呼吸道的）infections can't be thoroughly evaluated by a doctor who can't listen to your heart or feel your swollen glands.【2020 年 9 月 长篇阅读 I 选项】

[译] 他们说，随机咨询一位病人见不到的医生，会进一步分解医疗保健系统。即使是上呼吸道感染这样的小毛病，也不能让一个听不见心率或摸不到你肿胀腺体的医生充分评估。

–duc–、–duce–、–duct– 引导

introduce [10] [ˌɪntrəˈdjuːs] *v.* 提出，介绍；引入，引进

[记] intro（里）+duce →"向里面引导"；把客户"向里面引导"→ *v.* 提出，介绍→把这项高科技"向国家里面引导"→ *v.* 引入，引进

[派] introduction [ˌɪntrəˈdʌkʃn] *n.* 介绍，引言；引入，引进
　　introductory [ˌɪntrəˈdʌktəri] *a.* 介绍的；入门的

[考] introduce A to B　把 A 介绍给 B
　　introduce A into B　把 A 引入 B

[真] Workers' union have accepted the inevitability of the **introduction** of new technology.【2021 年 6 月 听力原文】

[译] 工会已经接受了引进新技术的必然性。

conduct [16] [kənˈdʌkt] [ˈkɒndʌkt] *v.* 引导，领导，带领；指挥；进行，实施　*n.* 行为

[记] con（加强）+duct →"引导的动作"→ *v.* 引导，领导，带领→"在乐队里引导演奏的动作"→ *v.* 指挥→"引导事情进行的动作"→ *v.* 进行，实施→"引导孩子的"→ *n.* 行为

[派] conductive [kənˈdʌktɪv] *a.* 传导的

[真] [B] It was **conducted** from frontline managers' point of view.【2021 年 6 月 听力 18 题 B 选项】

[译] 它是从一线管理人员的观点出发的。

049

produce [40]

[prəˈdjuːs] *v.* 生产，产生

[记] pro（前）+duce → "向前引导"；工厂中的流水线向前引导，经过各个工序得到成品的过程 → *v.* 生产，产生

[派] product [ˈprɒdʌkt] *n.* 产品
byproduct [ˈbaɪˌprɒdʌkt] *n.* 副产品
producer [prəˈdjuːsə(r)] *n.* 制造商；制片人
production [prəˈdʌkʃn] *n.* 生产；产量；产品
reproduce [ˌriːprəˈdjuːs] *v.* 繁殖，生殖，复制，再现
reproduction [ˌriːprəˈdʌkʃn] *n.* 繁殖，生殖；复制，复制品
reproductive [ˌriːprəˈdʌktɪv] *a.* 生殖的；再生产的；复制的

[真] Central control and collective organisation can **produce** smoother and fairer outcomes, though even that much is never guaranteed.【2021年6月 仔细阅读】

[译] 集中控制系统和集体组织可以产生更平稳、更公平的结果，尽管这一点也从来无法保证。

productive [10]

[prəˈdʌktɪv] *a.* 高产的，多产的；富有成效的

[记] product（*n.* 产品）+ ive（*a.*）→ "产品很多的" → *a.* 高产的，多产的；富有成效的

[派] productivity [ˌprɒdʌkˈtɪvəti] *n.* 生产率，生产力

[真] Researchers conducted a review of all studies relating to air-conditioning and **productivity**.【2020年12月 听力原文】

[译] 研究人员对空调和生产力的所有相关研究进行了综述研究。

induce [3]

[ɪnˈdjuːs] *v.* 引诱，引起

[记] in（里）+duce → "向里引导，引进去" → *v.* 引诱，引起

[派] inducement [ɪnˈdjuːsmənt] *n.* 引诱，引起

[真] And the water is muddied by lobbying from the industries that profit from consumption of obesity-**inducing** products.【2020年9月 仔细阅读】

[译] 此外，从诱发肥胖产品的消费中获利的行业的游说，也让情况变得更加棘手。

◀ -dur- 持续 ▶

durable [2]

[ˈdjʊərəbl] *a.* 持久的，耐久的

[记] dur+able（*a.*）→ "能够持续的" → *a.* 持久的，耐久的

endure [6]

[ɪnˈdjʊə(r)] *v.* 持久，持续；忍受

[记] en（使动）+dur+e（无义）→ "使之持续下去" → *v.* 持久，持续；忍受

[派] endurance [ɪnˈdjʊərəns] *n.* 耐久（力），持久（力）

[真] [C] She had to **endure** many hardships.【2021年6月 听力6题C选项】

[译] 她不得不忍受许多苦难。

Day 07

◆ –dyn– 动力，力量 ▶

dynamic [6] [daɪˈnæmɪk] *a.* 精力充沛的；动力的

[记] dyn+am（无义）+ic（*a.*）→有动力的，有力量的→ *a.* 精力充沛的；动力的
[派] dynamics [daɪˈnæmɪks] *n.* 动力；动态
[真] A mixed student body may change the classroom **dynamics** and benefit learning.【2020 年 12 月 长篇阅读 42 题】
[译] 一个混合的学生群体可能会改变课堂的动态，有利于学习。

dynasty [2] [ˈdɪnəsti] *n.* 王朝，朝代

[记] dyn+ast（改写自最高级后缀 est）+y（*n.*）→"最有力量的时候"；形成了→ *n.* 王朝，朝代

◆ 非成组词（D 字母）▶

debt [4] [det] *n.* 欠债，债务

[助] 谐音"打他"，因为他欠债不还→ *n.* 欠债，债务
[真] [A] Pay a **debt** long overdue.【2019 年 12 月 听力 7 题 A 选项】
[译] 偿还逾期已久的债务。

decorate [2] [ˈdekəreɪt] *v.* 装饰，布置

[记] dec（简写自 deck；装饰）+or（表示人或物的后缀）+ate（*v.*）→"装饰人或物的动作"→ *v.* 装饰，布置
[派] decoration [ˌdekəˈreɪʃn] *n.* 装饰，布置

destine [4] [ˈdestɪn] *v.* 注定，命定

[助] 谐音"得死定"→"得定死"，不能改了→ *v.* 注定，命定
[派] destiny [ˈdestəni] *n.* 命运，天命
[真] Genetic selection is a way of exerting influence over others, "the ultimate collective control of human **destinies**", as writer H.G.Wells put it.【2021 年 6 月 仔细阅读】
[译] 正如作家 H.G. 威尔斯所言，基因选择是对他人施加影响的一种方式，"是对人类命运的最终集体控制"。

dignity [2] [ˈdɪɡnəti] *n.* 尊严，自尊

[记] 词根 dign（尊严）+ity（*n.*）→ *n.* 尊严，自尊
[助] dig（挖）+ ni（谐音"你"）+ty（*n.*）→"挖苦你"；让你失去→ *n.* 尊严，自尊

digital [18] [ˈdɪdʒɪtl] *a.* 数字的，数位的；手指的

[记] digit（n. 数字；手指）+al（a.）→ a. 数字的，数位的；手指的
[派] digitally [ˈdɪdʒɪtəli] ad. 数字化地
　　 digitalize/ise [ˈdɪdʒɪtəlaɪz] v. 使数字化
[真] The use of **digital** technology can bring images of deceased celebrities back to the screen.【2021 年 6 月 长篇阅读 39 题】
[译] 数字技术的使用可以将已故名人的图像带回屏幕上。

dramatic [5]
[drəˈmætɪk] a. 戏剧的，戏剧性的；剧烈的；引人注目的

[记] drama 的形容词；drama（n. 戏剧）+t（无义）+ic（a.）→ a. 戏剧的，戏剧性的；剧烈的；引人注目的
[派] dramatically [drəˈmætɪkli] ad. 戏剧地；引人注目地；急剧地
[真] [C] It has experienced **dramatic** changes in recent years.【2020 年 7 月 仔细阅读 51 题 C 选项】
[译] 近年来，它经历了巨大的变化。

drown [3]
[draʊn] v. 溺死；淹没

[记] r（辅音字母表示"人"）+down（向下）→"人不停向下"→ v. 溺死；淹没
[真] Sheep, cattle, deer are often trapped by rising waters and often **drown**.【2020 年 7 月 听力原文】
[译] 水位上升，羊、牛和鹿经常受困于水中并溺水而亡。

dual [9]
[ˈdjuːəl] a. 两部分的；双重的

[记] 词根 du（=bi=2）+al（a.）→ a. 两部分的；双重的
[真] According to a researcher, **dual**-language experiences exert a lifelong influence on one's brain.【2020 年 9 月 长篇阅读 42 题】
[译] 据一名研究人员说，双语经历会对一个人的大脑产生一生的影响。

dwelling [3]
[ˈdwelɪŋ] n. 住宅，住所

[记] dwell（v. 居住）+ing（n.）→"居住的地方"→ n. 住宅，住所
[派] dweller [ˈdwelə(r)] n. 居民，居住者
　　 dwell [dwel] v. 居住；栖身
[真] [A] It tends to **dwell** upon their joyous experiences.【2019 年 12 月 听力 12 题 A 选项】
[译] 它往往停留于他们的快乐经历。

—econom— 经济

economy [13]
[ɪˈkɒnəmi] n. 经济

六级基础词汇

Day 07

economics [2] [ˌiːkəˈnɒmɪks] [ˌekəˈnɒmɪks] *n.* 经济学

［记］econom+ics（表示学科的后缀）→ *n.* 经济学

economist [2] [ɪˈkɒnəmɪst] *n.* 经济学家

［记］econom+ist（表示专家的后缀）→ *n.* 经济学家

economic [16] [ˌiːkəˈnɒmɪk] *a.* 经济的，经济学的

［记］econom+ic（*a.*）→ *a.* 经济的，经济学的

［真］What the research revealed was the rather less surprising result: the educational benefits of selective schools largely disappear once pupils' inborn ability and socio-**economic** background were taken into account.【2021 年 6 月 仔细阅读】

［译］这项研究揭示了一个反而不太令人惊讶的结果：一旦考虑到学生与生俱来的能力和社会经济背景，精英学校的教育优势在很大程度上就消失了。

economical [3] [ˌiːkəˈnɒmɪkl] *a.* 节约的，节俭的

［记］econom+ic（*a.*）+al（*a.*）→ 指人过日子过得很"经济" → *a.* 节约的，节俭的

［派］economically [ˌiːkəˈnɒmɪkli] *ad.* 经济上；节俭地

［真］Ethnically and **economically** balanced bilingual classrooms are found to be helpful for kids to get used to social and cultural diversity.【2020 年 9 月 长篇阅读 40 题】

［译］种族和经济平衡的双语教室被发现有助于孩子们适应社会和文化的多样性。

扫码快速学习

扫码即刻听课

–electr– 电，电流

electricity [5] [ɪˌlekˈtrɪsəti] *n.* 电，电流

六级基础词汇

[记] electr+ic（*a.*）+ity（*n.*）→ *n.* 电，电流

electric [4] [ɪˈlektrɪk] *a.* 电的，导电的

[记] electr+ic（*a.*）→ *a.* 电的，导电的

[派] electrical [ɪˈlektrɪkl] *a.* 用电的

[真] We fear the breakdown of the **electric** grid, the end of non-renewable resources, the expansion of deserts, the loss of islands, and the pollution of our air and water.【2020年12月 长篇阅读 C 选项】

[译] 我们担心电网崩溃，不可再生资源枯竭，沙漠扩张，岛屿消失，以及空气和水污染。

electronic [12] [ɪˌlekˈtrɒnɪk] *a.* 电子的

[记] electr+on（简写自 ion：离子）+ic（*a.*）→ *a.* 电子的

[派] electronics [ɪˌlekˈtrɒnɪks] *n.* 电子学；电子器件
electronically [ɪˌlekˈtrɒnɪkli] *ad.* 用电子方法，用电子装置

[真] Between 1896, when he applied for his first patent in England at the age of 22, and his death in Italy in 1937, Marconi was at the center of every major innovation in **electronic** communication.【2021年6月 长篇阅读 C 选项】

[译] 1896 年，22 岁的马可尼在英国申请了他的第一项专利。1937 年，他在意大利去世。在此期间，马可尼一直处于电子通信领域每一项重大创新的中心。

–empt– 空，空虚

tempt [2] [tempt] *v.* 诱惑，引诱

[记] t（无义）+empt →人感到"空虚"时可能会→ *v.* 诱惑，引诱

[派] temptation [tempˈteɪʃn] *n.* 诱惑，引诱

[考] tempt sb. to do sth. 诱惑/引诱某人做某事

Day 08

contempt [2]
[kənˈtempt] *n.* 轻视，蔑视

[记] con（全部，共同）+tempt（诱惑）→想想身边某个人，"所有人都诱惑，上到九十九，下到刚会走"，你会怎么看待这个人 → *n.* 轻视，蔑视

[派] contemptible [kənˈtemptəbl] *a.* 受人鄙视的，可鄙的

attempt [4]
[əˈtempt] *v.* 尝试，试图　*n.* 企图，尝试

[记] at（to）+tempt（诱惑）→"想要引诱"，就得试→ *v.* 尝试，试图　*n.* 企图，尝试

[考] attempt to do sth. 尝试做某事

[真] The sand under the hill defeated several **attempts** by Higgins' workers to make a proper hole.【2021年6月 听力原文】

[译] 山下的沙子数次挫败了希金斯的工人挖出一个合适的洞的尝试。

exempt [2]
[ɪɡˈzempt] *n.* 免除，豁免　*a.* 免除的，豁免的

[记] ex（out）+empt → *n.* 免除，豁免　*a.* 免除的，豁免的

[派] exemption [ɪɡˈzempʃn] *n.* 免除，豁免

-em-、-en- 使动

embrace [4]
[ɪmˈbreɪs] *v.* 包含，包括　*v.&n.* 拥抱（熟词僻义，重点关注）

[记] em+brace（*n.* 大括号）→ "使之像被大括号包起来一样" → *v.* 包含，包括 →接受就是一种包含、包括，进一步引申为 → *v.&n.* 拥抱

[真] The most controversial aspect of Marconi's life—and the reason why there has been no satisfying biography of Marconi until now—was his uncritical **embrace** of Benito Mussolini.【2021年6月 长篇阅读 K 选项】

[译] 马可尼一生中最具争议的方面——也是直到现在还没有令人满意的马可尼传记的原因——是他对贝尼托·墨索里尼不加批判的拥护。

enable [12]
[ɪˈneɪbl] *v.* 使能够，使成为可能

[记] en+able（*a.* 能……的）→ *v.* 使能够，使成为可能

[考] enable sb. to do sth. 使某人能够做某事

[真] [D] It **enables** one to write intriguing sequels to famous stories.【2021年6月 仔细阅读 54题 D 选项】

[译] 它使一个人能够为著名的故事写出有趣的续集。

encourage [13]
[ɪnˈkʌrɪdʒ] *v.* 鼓励，激励；促进，促成

[记] en+courage（*n.* 勇气）→ "使人有了勇气" → *v.* 鼓励，激励→ "使事有了勇气" → *v.* 促进，促成

[派] encouragement [ɪnˈkʌrɪdʒmənt] *n.* 鼓励，激励；起促进作用的事物
encouraging [ɪnˈkʌrɪdʒɪŋ] *v.* encourage 的现在分词　*a.* 鼓舞人心的

［考］encourage sb. to do sth. 鼓励某人做某事
　　　be encouraged to do sth. 被鼓励做某事
［真］[A] It **encourages** people to imitate.【2021 年 6 月 仔细阅读 53 题 A 选项】
［译］它鼓励人们去模仿。

endanger ³

[ɪnˈdeɪndʒə(r)] v. 使危险，危及

［记］en+danger（n. 危险）→ "使之危险" → v. 使危险，危及
［派］endangered [ɪnˈdeɪndʒəd] a.（动植物）濒危的，濒临灭绝的
［真］[C] The erupting gas might **endanger** local children.【2021 年 6 月 听力 12 题 C 选项】
［译］喷发的气体可能危及当地儿童。

endow ²

[ɪnˈdaʊ] v. 资助，捐赠；给予，赋予

［记］en + 词根 dow（给予）→ "使之给予" → v. 资助，捐赠；给予，赋予

engage ⁹

[ɪnˈgeɪdʒ] v. 参与，从事；吸引

［记］en+gage（改写自 gate；大门）→ "使之进了这个门"，进了这行 → v. 参与，从事；吸引
［派］engagement [ɪnˈgeɪdʒmənt] n. 参加，参与；约会
［考］engage in 参与，从事；忙于
　　　engage with 与……建立关系
［真］What do people tend to do while **engaging** in a conversation?【2021 年 6 月 仔细阅读 51 题题干】
［译］人们在交谈时往往会做些什么？

enhance ⁴

[ɪnˈhɑːns] v. 提高，增加，加强

［记］en+ 词根 hanc（改写自 high；高）+e（无义）→ "使之高" → v. 提高，增加，加强
［派］enhancement [ɪnˈhɑːnsmənt] n. 提高，增加，加强
［真］Will looking smarter **enhance** my ability to do my job?【2020 年 12 月 听力原文】
［译］看起来衣冠楚楚会提高我的工作能力吗？

enrol(l) ²

[ɪnˈrəʊl] v. 招收，登记，加入，成为会员

［记］en+roll（n. 名单，名册）→ "使之进入名单、名册" → v. 招收，登记，加入，成为会员
［派］enrol(l)ment [ɪnˈrəʊlmənt] n. 登记，注册，入会

-equ- 相等

equal ¹⁷

[ˈiːkwəl] v. 等于，使相等　　a. 相等的，平等的

[记] equ+al（a.）→ v. 等于，使相等　a. 相等的，平等的
[派] equally [ˈiːkwəli] ad. 平等地，同样地
　　 equality [iˈkwɒləti] n. 平等，相等
　　 inequality [ˌɪnɪˈkwɒləti] n. 不平等，不平衡
　　 unequal [ʌnˈiːkwəl] a. 不相等的，不平等的
　　 unequally [ʌnˈiːkwəli] ad. 不平等地
[考] equal（v.）to 使相等，等于
　　 be equal（a.）to 等于
[真] [C] Providing all children with **equal** access to arts education.【2021 年 6 月仔细阅读 50 题 C 选项】
[译] 为所有儿童提供平等接受艺术教育的机会。

equip⁶

[ɪˈkwɪp] v. 装备，配备

[记] equ+i（无义）+p（谐音"配"）→"为了同一目的，往一起配"→ v. 装备，配备
[派] equipment [ɪˈkwɪpmənt] n. 装备，设备
[考] be equipped with... 装备／配备……
[真] The best seek to alleviate the external pressures on their pupils while **equipping** them better to understand and handle the world outside—at once sheltering them and broadening their horizons.【2019 年 12 月仔细阅读】
[译] 最好的办法是减轻学生所面临的外部压力，同时让他们更好地理解和处理外部世界——同时庇护他们，拓宽他们的视野。

adequate⁸

[ˈædɪkwət] a. 足够的；胜任的

[记] ad（to）+equ+ate（a.）→"去相等"→数量上"去相等"，要多少都能相等→ a. 足够的→能力上"去相等"→ a. 胜任的
[派] adequately [ˈædɪkwətli] ad. 充分地，足够地
　　 inadequate [ɪnˈædɪkwət] a. 不充足的；不胜任的，不合格的
　　 inadequately [ɪnˈædɪkwətli] ad. 不充足地；不胜任地
[考] be adequate for... 对于……是足够的
　　 be adequate to... 胜任……
[真] It is impossible to know for sure, because official statistics are so **inadequate**.【2021 年 6 月听力原文】
[译] 不可能确切知道具体的情况，因为官方统计数据严重不足。

-e-、-e 辅-（除了 -em-、-en-）=out 外，向外，出去

elicit²

[iˈlɪsɪt] v. 引出

[记] e+ 词根 lic（吸引）+it（它）→"把它吸引出来"→ v. 引出
[形] elite [eɪˈliːt] [ɪˈliːt] n. 精英　a. 精英的，杰出的

eliminate [6]

[ɪˈlɪmɪneɪt] *v.* 排除，消除

[记] e+limin（改写自 limit；限制，界限）+ate（*v.*）→"超出限制、界限了"；超出极限太过分，必须要→ *v.* 排除，消除

[派] elimination [ɪˌlɪmɪˈneɪʃn] *n.* 排除，消除

[真] They need to **eliminate** jargon.【2021 年 6 月 听力原文】

[译] 他们需要做到不使用行业术语。

emerge [14]

[iˈmɜːdʒ] *v.* 出现，浮现；冒出

[记] e+merge（*v.* 沉没）→"沉没下去又出来"→ *v.* 出现，浮现；冒出

[派] emergence [iˈmɜːdʒəns] *n.* 出现，浮现
emergency [iˈmɜːdʒənsi] *n.* 紧急情况；急诊
emerging [ɪˈmɜːdʒɪŋ] *a.*（用作定语）新兴的

[真] The revelation of how close France came to losing its most famous cathedral **emerged** as police investigators questioned workers involved in the restoration of the monument to try to establish the cause of the devastating blaze.【2021 年 6 月 长篇阅读 B 选项】

[译] 当警方调查人员询问参与修复建筑的工作人员，试图确定这场毁灭性大火的起因时，法国最著名的大教堂差点被烧毁的真相浮出了水面。

estimate [8]

[ˈestɪmeɪt] [ˈestɪmət] *v.&n.* 估计，评价

[记] es+tim（简写自 time；时间）+ate（*v.*）→"向外看时间的动作"；古代通过观察太阳看时间，把头伸出去看时间往往是不够准确的，没有分，也没有秒，所以只能→ *v.&n.* 估计，评价

[派] estimation [ˌestɪˈmeɪʃn] *n.* 估计，评价
underestimate [ˌʌndərˈestɪmeɪt] [ˌʌndərˈestɪmət] *v.&n.* 低估；对……估计不足
overestimate [ˌəʊvərˈestɪmeɪt] [ˌəʊvərˈestɪmət] *v.&n.* 对……做过高的评价；对……估计过高

[真] [C] The value of drawing tends to be **overestimated**.【2021 年 6 月 仔细阅读 48 题 C 选项】

[译] 绘画的价值往往被高估。

exaggerate [8]

[ɪɡˈzædʒəreɪt] *v.* 扩大；夸大，夸张

[记] ex+ag（to）+gerat（改写自 great；大的）+e（无义）→"向外并且变大"→ *v.* 扩大；夸大，夸张

[派] exaggeration [ɪɡˌzædʒəˈreɪʃn] *n.* 夸张，夸大

[真] [A] The consequences of technological innovation need not be **exaggerated**.【2021 年 6 月 仔细阅读 55 题 A 选项】

[译] 技术创新的结果不必被夸大。

exchange [6]

[ɪksˈtʃeɪndʒ] *v.&n.* 交换，交易

[记] ex+change（*v.&n.* 变化，变换）→"变了出去，换了出去"；我的变到你

Day 08

手上，你的变到我手上→ *v.&n.* 交换，交易
[考] exchange A for B 把 A 换成 B
[真] [C] promote its cultural **exchange** with other nations.【2021 年 6 月 仔细阅读 53 题 C 选项】
[译] 促进与其他国家的文化交流。

exotic [5]
[ɪɡˈzɒtɪk] *a.* 异国情调的；奇异的
[记] ex+ot(表示人的后缀)+ic（*a.*）→ "外国人的" → *a.* 异国情调的；奇异的
[真] You certainly get to travel to some very **exotic** locations.【2021 年 6 月 听力原文】
[译] 那你肯定要去一些非常有异国情调的地方旅行。

expand [14]
[ɪkˈspænd] *v.* （使）膨胀，（使）扩张
[记] ex+pand（谐音"胖的"）→ "向外变胖" → *v.* （使）膨胀，（使）扩张
[派] expansion [ɪkˈspænʃn] *n.* 膨胀，扩张
expansive [ɪkˈspænsɪv] *a.* 开阔的；全面的
expanding [ɪksˈpændɪŋ] *a.* 展开的，扩大的 *v.* expand 的现在分词
[真] [D] It is **expanding** at an accelerating speed.【2021 年 6 月 听力 19 题 D 选项】
[译] 它正在加速扩张。

expedition [3]
[ˌekspəˈdɪʃn] *n.* 短途旅行；远征
[记] ex+ 词根 ped（改写自 feet；脚）+ition（*n.*）→ "把脚伸出去，放出去" → *n.* 短途旅行；远征
[真] Why did you cut the **expedition** short?【2021 年 6 月 听力原文】
[译] 你为什么缩短了考察时间呢？

exploit [3]
[ɪkˈsplɔɪt] *v.* 开发；利用
[记] ex+p（谐音"喷"）+loi（改写自 oil；油）+t（无义）→ "向外喷出石油" → *v.* 开发；进一步引申为→ *v.* 利用
[派] exploitation [ˌeksplɔɪˈteɪʃn] *n.* 开发；利用
[真] [B] Organic farming may be **exploited** to solve the global food problem.【2020 年 9 月仔细阅读 51 题 B 选项】
[译] 有机农业可以被用来解决全球粮食问题。

explosion [4]
[ɪkˈspləʊʒn] *n.* 爆炸，爆发；激增
[记] ex+plo（谐音"bong"）+sion（*n.*）→ "bong 的一下崩出来" → *n.* 爆炸，爆发；激增
[真] A hundred years before iconic figures like Bill Gates and Steve Jobs permeated our lives, an Irish-Italian inventor laid the foundation of the communication **explosion** of the 21st century.【2021 年 6 月 长篇阅读 A 选项】
[译] 在比尔·盖茨和史蒂夫·乔布斯等标志性人物全面影响我们生活的一百年前，一位爱尔兰裔意大利发明家奠定了 21 世纪通信产业呈爆发式增长的基础。

非成组词（E 字母）

eager [4] ['i:gə(r)] *a.* 渴望的，热切的
[助] 谐音 "一哥" → 每个人都想当行业里的 "一哥" → *a.* 渴望的，热切的
[考] be eager to do sth. 渴望做某事
　　　be eager for... 渴望……
[真] [D] They are **eager** to boost their popularity.【2020 年 12 月 仔细阅读 47 题 D 选项】
[译] 他们渴望提高自己的声望。

enterprise [10] ['entəpraɪz] *n.* 企（事）业单位；事业心，进取心；事业
[记] enter+pri（前）+se（*n.*）→ "进入后就要不停前进" 的地方 → *n.* 企（事）业单位；→ 不停前进表示有 → *n.* 事业心，进取心；事业
[派] entrepreneur [ˌɒntrəprə'nɜ:(r)] *n.* 企业家
　　　entrepreneurial [ˌɒntrəprə'nɜ:riəl] *a.* 具有企业家素质的，富于企业家精神的
[真] [B] It is most often wielded by scientists and **entrepreneurs**.【2021 年 6 月 仔细阅读 46 题 B 选项】
[译] 它最常被科学家和企业家使用。

entity [5] ['entəti] *n.* 实体，存在（物）
[记] ent（简写自 enter；进入）+ity（*n.*）→ "能够进入的东西"；不是抽象的 → *n.* 实体，存在（物）
[真] [A] Focus entirely on culturally-based **entities** rather than genetically-based ones.【2020 年 12 月 仔细阅读 55 题 A 选项】
[译] 完全关注基于文化的实体，而不是基于基因的实体。

essence [8] ['esns] *n.* 本质，实质；精华
[记] "精华液" 的英文 → *n.* 精华 → 只有本质、实质好的东西才是精华 → *n.* 本质，实质
[派] essential [ɪ'senʃl] *a.* 本质的，基本的；必不可少的
　　　essentially [ɪ'senʃəli] *ad.* 本质上，根本上
[考] in essence 本质上；其实
　　　be essential to/for... 对于……是必不可少的，对于……是必要的
[真] [A] Prioritize what is **essential** to their best advantage.【2021 年 6 月 听力 6 题 A 选项】
[译] 优先考虑对他们最有利的事情。

esteem [3] [ɪ'sti:m] *v.&n.* 尊敬，尊重
[记] est（最高级的后缀）+eem（简写自 seem；看起来，似乎）→ "看起来最高，最大"，所以要 → *v.&n.* 尊敬，尊重

Day 08

[派] esteemed [ɪˈstiːmd] *a.* 受人尊敬的
[考] self-esteem [ˌself ɪˈstiːm] *n.* 自尊
[真] [D] It hurts laymen's dignity and self-**esteem**.【2021 年 6 月听力 9 题 D 选项】
[译] 它损害了外行人的尊严和自尊。

evil ²

[ˈiːvl] *n.* 邪恶，罪恶 *a.* 邪恶的，罪恶的

[记] 改写自 live → 正常的"live 生活"颠倒过来就是"evil 邪恶，罪恶"→ *n.* 邪恶，罪恶 *a.* 邪恶的，罪恶的

executive ⁴

[ɪɡˈzekjətɪv] *n.* 执行者；管理人员 *a.* 执行的；经理的

[记] exe 表示执行（电脑里后缀名为".exe"的文件为可执行文件，双击可安装）；首席执行官 CEO：chief executive officer → *n.* 执行者；管理人员 *a.* 执行的；经理的
[真] Well, Luk found, they also scored higher on tests of **executive** functioning.【2020 年 9 月长篇阅读 L 选项】
[译] 卢克发现，他们在执行功能测试中的得分也更高。

exhaust ⁶

[ɪɡˈzɔːst] *v.* 耗尽，使筋疲力尽

[助] 谐音"一个早死（的）他"→ *v.* 耗尽，使筋疲力尽
[派] exhausted [ɪɡˈzɔːstɪd] *a.* 耗尽的，筋疲力尽的
　　exhausting [ɪɡˈzɔːstɪŋ] *a.* 使耗尽的，使人筋疲力尽的
[真] [A] It **exhausts** resources sooner.【2021 年 6 月听力 20 题 A 选项】
[译] 它更快耗尽了资源。

扫码快速学习

扫码即刻听课

–fac–、–fec–、–fic–、–feat–

① 做

fact [16]

[fækt] *n.* 事实

六级基础词汇

[派] factual [ˈfæktʃuəl] *a.* 事实的，真实的

[考] in fact 事实上

　　as a matter of fact 事实上

affect [20]

[əˈfekt] *v.* 影响

[记] af（to）+fect（改写自 fec）→"去做"；事物之间具有普遍联系，"去做"一件事必然会影响另一件事→ *v.* 影响

[考] be affected by... 受……影响

[真] There is always a chance that it could **affect** my reputation and my ability to network in the industry.【2021 年 6 月 听力原文】

[译] 这很有可能影响我的声誉以及我在行业内建立工作关系的能力。

effect [39]

[ɪˈfekt] *n.* 影响，效果

[记] ef（out）+fect（改写自 fec）→事情"做出来"所产生的→ *n.* 影响，效果

[考] in effect 实际上；生效

　　have a(n)... effect on... 对……有着……的影响

[真] [B] They will wait to see its **effect**.【2021 年 6 月 听力 21 题 B 选项】

[译] 他们等着看其效果。

effective [18]

[ɪˈfektɪv] *a.* 有效的

[记] 上词 effect 的形容词；effect+ive（*a.*）→ *a.* 有效的

[派] effectiveness [ɪˌfekˈtɪvnəs] *n.* 有效，有效性；效益

　　effectively [ɪˈfektɪvli] *ad.* 有效地；实际上

　　ineffective [ˌɪnɪˈfektɪv] *a.* 无效果的，不起作用的

Day 09

[真] [B] Most of them are as **effective** as advertised.【2021年6月 仔细阅读 52题 B 选项】
[译] 大多数都和广告中所说的一样有效。

efficient [14]
[ɪˈfɪʃnt] *a.* 效率高的；有能力的

[记] effective 的同源词；ef（out）+fic+ i（无义）+ent（*a.*）→ *a.* 效率高的；有能力的
[派] efficiently [ɪˈfɪʃntli] *ad.* 高效地
efficiency [ɪˈfɪʃnsi] *n.* 效率
inefficient [ˌɪnɪˈfɪʃnt] *a.* 效率低的；能力差的
[真] And it's more energy-**efficient** because it doesn't rely on synthetic fertilizers or pesticides.【2020年9月 仔细阅读】
[译] 除此之外，它更节能，因为它不依赖合成肥料或杀虫剂。

infect [4]
[ɪnˈfekt] *v.* 传染，感染

[记] in（里）+fect（改写自 fec）→病毒在"里面起作用"→ *v.* 传染，感染
[派] infection [ɪnˈfekʃn] *n.* 传染，感染；传染病
infectious [ɪnˈfekʃəs] *a.* 传染的，感染的
[真] There's something about the founder's energy and enthusiasm that **infects** the rest of the team.【2021年6月 听力原文】
[译] 创始人的能量和热情会感染到团队的其他成员。

infect 的引申词

virus [2]
[ˈvaɪrəs] *n.* 病毒

[助] vi（形似罗马数字"六"）+ru（谐音"蠕"）+s（弯曲像"虫"）→"六个小蠕虫"→ *n.* 病毒

immune [4]
[ɪˈmjuːn] *a.* 免疫的，有免疫力的

[助] 谐音"疫苗"；为什么打疫苗？增强身体免疫力啊！→ *a.* 免疫的，有免疫力的
[派] immunity [ɪˈmjuːnəti] *n.* 免疫，免疫力
[考] be immune to... 对……免疫；不受……的影响
[真] None of us are **immune** to the influences of our own world.【2020年9月 听力原文】
[译] 我们之中没有一个人不受我们身处的世界的影响。

perfect [14]
[ˈpɜːfɪkt] [pəˈfekt] *a.* 完美的 *v.* 使完美

[记] per（全，都）+fect（改写自 fec）→"全部都做好"→ *a.* 完美的 *v.* 使完美
[派] perfection [pəˈfekʃn] *n.* 完美，完善

063

perfectly [ˈpɜːfɪktli] ad. 完美地

[真] But I found myself moving from one accommodation to another, trying to find the **perfect** place.【2021年6月 听力原文】

[译] 但我发现自己总是在从一个住处搬到另一个住处，试图找到一个完美的地方。

facilitate [6]

[fəˈsɪlɪteɪt] v. 使容易，使便利

[记] facil（简写自 facile；容易做的，轻易可得的）+it（无义）+ate（v.）→ v. 使容易，使便利

[派] facilitation [fəˌsɪlɪˈteɪʃn] n. 促进，便利
facility [fəˈsɪləti] n. 天赋；设备

[真] [A] It **facilitates** the creation of one's own writing style.【2021年6月 仔细阅读54题A选项】

[译] 它促进了创造自己的写作风格。

sufficient [9]

[səˈfɪʃnt] a. 足够的，充足的，充分的

[记] suf（下）+fic+i（无义）+ent（a.）→"下面做"；要想考试分数"充足"，要"在下面做足"功夫，正所谓"台上一分钟，台下十年功"→ a. 足够的，充足的，充分的

[派] insufficient [ˌɪnsəˈfɪʃnt] a. 不足的，不够的

[考] be sufficient for... 对于……是充足的/足够的

[真] [D] It is not based on **sufficient** investigations into the ecological system.【2020年9月 仔细阅读53题D选项】

[译] 它不是基于对生态系统的充分调查。

artificial [10]

[ˌɑːtɪˈfɪʃl] a. 人工的，人造的；虚假的

[记] art（n. 艺术，技巧）+i（无义）+fic+ial（a.）→"做得很有艺术感，很有技巧"；不是天然的、自然的→ a. 人工的，人造的；虚假的

[派] artificially [ˌɑːtɪˈfɪʃəli] ad. 人工地，人为地；不自然地

[考] AI=artificial intelligence 人工智能

[真] I think **artificial** intelligence will actually help create new kinds of jobs, which would require less of our time and allow us to be centered on creative tasks.【2020年12月 听力原文】

[译] 我认为，实际上人工智能会有助于创造新的工种，这样可以节省人类的时间，让我们专注于创造性的任务。

sacrifice [8]

[ˈsækrɪfaɪs] v.&n. 牺牲

[记] sacr（简写自 sacred；神圣的）+i（无义）+fic+e（无义）→"为神圣的事情而做出的"；想想建立中华人民共和国过程中无数烈士的英勇行为→ v.&n. 牺牲

[真] [B] It inspires willingness to make **sacrifices**.【2021年6月 听力17题B选项】

[译] 它会激发人们做出牺牲的意愿。

Day 09

deficiency ³
[dɪˈfɪʃnsi] **n.** 缺点，缺陷；缺乏，不足

[记] de（下）+fic+i（无义）+ency（n.）→ "做事做得低下"，当然是这个人的 → n. 缺点，缺陷；缺乏，不足

[派] deficient [dɪˈfɪʃnt] a. 不足的，有缺陷的

[真] The third cause of poor management was associated with their **deficiency** of qualifications.【2021 年 6 月 听力原文】

[译] 管理不善的第三个原因与他们的资质不足有关。

fiction ⁴
[ˈfɪkʃn] **n.** 虚构，编造；小说

[记] fict+ion（n.）→ 矫揉造"作"；不是真实的，是人为"做"出来的 → n. 虚构，编造；小说

[真] [D] Life will become like a science **fiction** film.【2020 年 12 月 听力 8 题 D 选项】

[译] 生活将变成一部科幻电影。

feature ¹²
[ˈfiːtʃə(r)] **n.** 特征，特点　**v.** 以……为特征；起重要作用

[记] feat（改写自 fec）+ure（n.）→ "做出来的"；企业为了区别于同行，做出来的 → n. 特征，特点　v. 以……为特征；起重要作用

[真] [C] Insights into the **features** of good music.【2020 年 12 月 听力 22 题 C 选项】

[译] 洞察到好音乐的特点。

② 脸，面

surface ⁵
[ˈsɜːfɪs] **n.** 表面

[记] sur（上）+face（改写自 fac）→ n. 表面

[派] resurface [ˌriːˈsɜːfɪs] v. 重铺路面；重新露面；浮上水面

[真] Recently, close-up pictures of Jupiter's moon Europa showed signs of water beneath its icy **surface**.【2020 年 9 月 听力原文】

[译] 最近，木星的卫星欧罗巴的特写照片显示出其冰川表面之下存在水的迹象。

superficial ²
[ˌsuːpəˈfɪʃl] **a.** 表面的；肤浅的

[记] super（上）+fic+ial（a.）→ a. 表面的 → "此人很表面" → a. 肤浅的

–fenc–、–fend–、–fens–＝fence 篱笆，栅栏，围墙

fence
[fens] **n.** 篱笆，栅栏

注意：本词不重要，是为了帮助理解下面的六级单词

defense/ce [dɪˈfens] *n.* 防卫，防御

[记] de（下）+fence → "下面安个栅栏"；干吗用？防贼、防盗、防偷袭嘛→ *n.* 防卫，防御

[派] defend [dɪˈfend] *v.* 防御，保卫

offend [əˈfend] *v.* 攻击；冒犯，得罪

[记] 与 defend 互为反义词；of（off）+fend →使"栅栏""离开"→地下安个栅栏，起防卫作用，是 defend；相反，把栅栏撞开、使栅栏离开，是干吗呢？→ *v.* 攻击→言语上的"攻击"→ *v.* 冒犯，得罪

[派] offense/ce [əˈfens] *n.* 攻击；冒犯
offensive [əˈfensɪv] *a.* 攻击的；冒犯的，无礼的

[真] [B] They want to avoid **offending** any of their audience.【2020 年 12 月 仔细阅读 47 题 B 选项】

[译] 他们不想冒犯任何一个观众。

-fer- 拿

differ [ˈdɪfə(r)] *v.* 与……不同，与……意见不同

[记] different（不同的）的动词→ *v.* 与……不同，与……意见不同

[考] differ from... 与……不同
differ with... 与……意见不同

[真] [B] They **differ** greatly in their knowledge of modern technology.【2020 年 12 月 听力 5 题 B 选项】

[译] 他们对现代技术的认识有很大的不同。

confer [kənˈfɜː(r)] *v.* 商议，商量；授予

[记] con（共同，全部）+fer → "把所有问题全部拿到一起" → *v.* 商议，商量 → "把所有东西都拿给某人" → *v.* 授予

[派] conference [ˈkɒnfərəns] *n.* 会议，讨论

inferior [ɪnˈfɪəriə(r)] *a.* （人）次的，下等的；（质量等）低劣的

[记] in（里）+fer+i（无义）+or（表示人或物的后缀）→ "某个人从里面拿东西"；顺手牵羊的行为→ *a.* （人）次的，下等的；（质量等）低劣的

[形] interior [ɪnˈtɪəriə(r)] *a.* 内部的，内地的 *n.* 内部

[考] be inferior to... 比……次 / 差；不如……

inferior 的引申词

superior [suːˈpɪəriə(r)] *n.* 上级，领导 *a.* 上级的；优秀的

[记] super（上）+i（我）+or（表示人或物的后缀）→ "此人在我之上" → *n.* 上级，领导 *a.* 上级的；优秀的
[派] superiority [suːˌpɪəriˈɒrəti] [sjuːˌpɪəriˈɒrəti] *n.* 优越（性），优等
[考] be superior to... 比……好/优质
[真] [C] It may displease his immediate **superiors**.【2021年6月 听力3题C选项】
[译] 这可能会使他的直接上级不高兴。

prefer ¹⁶

[prɪˈfɜː(r)] *v.* 更喜欢，倾向

[记] pre（前）+fer → "提前拿"；提前拿哪个，表示→ *v.* 更喜欢，倾向
[派] preference [ˈprefrəns] *n.* 喜爱，偏好
　　preferable [ˈprefrəbl] *a.* 更好的，更可取的
[考] prefer A to B 相对于B更喜欢A
　　prefer to do sth. 更倾向于做某事
[真] If they are used to the environment which is air conditioned, they tend to **prefer** lower temperatures.【2020年12月 听力原文】
[译] 如果人们习惯了空调环境，他们往往偏爱较低的温度。

refer ¹²

[rɪˈfɜː(r)] *v.* 参考，查阅；涉及；提及

[记] re（反复）+fer → "反复拿"一本书→ *v.* 参考，查阅；涉及；提及
[派] reference [ˈrefrəns] *n.* 参考；涉及；提及
[考] refer to 参考，查阅；涉及；指的是
[真] This **refers** to the idea that when objects trying to resemble humans aren't quite perfect, they can make viewers feel uneasy because they fall somewhere between obviously non-human and fully human.【2021年6月 长篇阅读J选项】
[译] 这（"诡异谷"效应）指的是，物体试图模仿人类，但效果并不完美时，就会让观众感到不适，因为它们介于显而易见的非人类和真正的人类之间。

suffer ¹¹

[ˈsʌfə(r)] *v.* 受痛苦，受折磨；遭受

[记] suf（下）+fer → 被人从上面"拿到下面"；从天堂跌至地狱，从身居高位到锒铛入狱，就是→ *v.* 受痛苦，受折磨；遭受
[派] suffering [ˈsʌfərɪŋ] *n.* 疼痛，痛苦
[考] suffer from 患病；遭受
[真] [B] They **suffer** from rapid temperature changes.【2020年12月 听力15题B选项】
[译] 它们忍受剧烈的温度变化。

interfere ²

[ˌɪntəˈfɪə(r)] *v.* 干扰，妨碍

[记] inter（middle；between）+fer+e（无义）→ "拿到彼此中间" → *v.* 干扰，妨碍
[派] interference [ˌɪntəˈfɪərəns] *n.* 干涉，干扰，介入

transfer [2]

[trænsˈfɜː(r)] [ˈtrænsfɜː(r)] *v.&n.* 转移；调动；（飞机）换乘

[记] trans（across）+fer → "穿梭着拿"过去→把某物从 A 地穿梭着拿到 B 地 → *v.&n.* 转移→把某人从 A 公司穿梭着拿到 B 公司 → *v.&n.* 调动→从一个航班穿梭着到另一个航班 → *v.&n.*（飞机）换乘

[派] transferable [trænsˈfɜːrəbl] *a.* 可转移的；可调动的

–fess– 说

profession [14]

[prəˈfeʃn] *n.* 职业，专业

[记] pro（向前）+fess+ion（*n.*）→ "走到前面说话"，这是一种→ *n.* 职业，专业

[派] professional [prəˈfeʃnl] *a.* 职业的，专业的 *n.* 专业人士

[真] Psychiatrists have a higher incidence of suicide in their **profession** for related reasons.【2020 年 9 月 听力原文】

[译] 出于职业相关原因，精神病医生自杀概率会更高。

emphasize/ise [6]

[ˈemfəsaɪz] *v.* 强调，突出

[记] em（使动）+phas（改写自 fess）+ize/ise（使动）→ "加强语气说出来"→ *v.* 强调，突出

[派] emphasis [ˈemfəsɪs] *n.* 强调，重点

[考] place emphasis on... 强调/注重……

[真] [B] Too much **emphasis** is given to eating less meat and buying local food.【2020 年 12 月 仔细阅读 51 题 B 选项】

[译] 人们过于强调少吃肉和购买当地的食物。

–fid– 相信，忠诚

faith [2]

[feɪθ] *n.* 信仰；信任；忠诚

[助] 谐音"非死" → "为了 faith（信仰）非死不可" → *n.* 信仰；信任；忠诚

[派] faithful [ˈfeɪθfl] *a.* 忠实的，忠诚的

confident [6]

[ˈkɒnfɪdənt] *a.* 有信心的，自信的

[记] con（加强）+fid+ent（*a.*）→ *a.* 有信心的，自信的

[派] confidence [ˈkɒnfɪdəns] *n.* 信心，自信
　　 self-confident [ˌself ˈkɒnfɪdənt] *a.* 自信的

[考] be confident of... 相信……
　　 sb. be confident that... 某人相信……

[真] They asked the workers a range of procedure related questions, such as whether they found the procedures useful, how **confident** they felt in their job, how comfortable they were to speak up in the workplace, and how closely they followed

any new procedures set by their managers.【2021 年 6 月 听力原文】
[译] 他们向工人们提出了一系列与程序有关的问题，例如，他们是否认为程序有用，他们对自己的工作有多大的信心，他们在工作场所有多大的发言权，以及他们在多大程度上遵守了他们的管理人员制定的每一个新程序。

confidential [2] [ˌkɒnfɪˈdenʃl] *a.* 秘密的，机密的

[记] con（加强）+fid+ent（*a.*）+ial（*a.*）→ 只有"相信、信任"才会告诉→ *a.* 秘密的，机密的

federal [8] [ˈfedərəl] *a.* 联邦（制）的

[记] fed（改写自 fid）+er（表示人的后缀）+al（*a.*）→ "彼此信任、相信的人"才能组成→ *a.* 联邦（制）的
[助] 好莱坞电影中经常提到的 FBI（美国联邦调查局，英文全称 Federal Bureau of Investigation）的首字母 F 就是 federal 的缩写，表示→ *a.* 联邦（制）的
[派] federation [ˌfedəˈreɪʃn] *n.* 联邦，同盟
[真] The guidelines drive billions of dollars of food production through **federal** programs like school lunches and nutrition assistance for the needy.【2020 年 12 月 仔细阅读】
[译] 这些指南通过学校午餐和向贫困人口提供营养援助等联邦项目，推动了高达数十亿美元的食品生产。

◀ –fil–、–fill– 填充，填满 ▶

affiliate [2] [əˈfɪlieɪt] *v.* 使隶属（或附属）于，使并入　*n.* 附属机构，分公司

[记] af（to）+fil+i（无义）+ate（*v.*）→ "把人填充进公司或组织"→ *v.* 使隶属（或附属）于，使并入→ *n.* 附属机构，分公司
[派] affiliation [əˌfɪliˈeɪʃn] *n.* 隶属（关系）；联系

fulfil(l) [3] [fʊlˈfɪl] *v.* 履行；实现；完成

[记] ful（简写自 full；满）+fil(l) → "把某项工作填满了，把某事填满了" → *v.* 履行；实现；完成
[派] fulfil(l)ment [fʊlˈfɪlmənt] *n.* 完成，实现，满足
[真] [C] **Fulfill** its mission by closely cooperating with the industries.【2020 年 12 月 仔细阅读 55 题 C 选项】
[译] 与各行业密切合作，完成其使命。

扫码快速学习

069

扫码即刻听课

–fin– 限制，极限

finite [2]

['faɪnaɪt] *a.* 有限的，限定的

[记] fin+ite（*a.*）→有"限制"的→ *a.* 有限的，限定的

[派] infinite ['ɪnfɪnət] *a.* 无限的

define [16]

[dɪ'faɪn] *v.* 下定义，解释；限定，界定

[记] de（下）+fin+e（无义）→给某个事物"设下限制、界限"→ *v.* 下定义，解释；限定，界定

[派] definition [ˌdefɪ'nɪʃn] *n.* 定义，规定
　　redefine [ˌri:dɪ'faɪn] *v.* 重新定义，再定义

[真] [D] Drawing should be **redefined** as a realistic illusion.【2021 年 6 月 仔细阅读 48 题 D 选项】

[译] 绘画应该被重新定义为一种现实的幻想。

definite [2]

['defɪnət] *a.* 明确的，清楚的

[记] 上词 define 的形容词；defin（简写自 define）+ite（*a.*）→"有了定义"，理解起来就是→ *a.* 明确的，清楚的

[派] definitely ['defɪnətli] *ad.* 确定地，明确地

confine [2]

[kən'faɪn] *v.* 限制，局限

[记] con（加强）+fin+e（无义）→"加强限制"→ *v.* 限制，局限

[考] be confined to 局限于

refine [4]

[rɪ'faɪn] *v.* 提炼；改善

[记] re（反复）+fine（*a.* 好的）→"反复更好"→ *v.* 提炼；改善

[派] refinement [rɪ'faɪnmənt] *n.* 提炼；改善；提纯

[真] What can contribute to the **refinement** of one's attitude, according to the passage?【2019 年 12 月 仔细阅读 47 题题干】

[译] 根据文章，什么有助于改善一个人的态度呢？

Day 10

finance [21] [ˈfaɪnæns] [faɪˈnæns] [fəˈnæns] *n.* 财政；金融，金融学 *v.* 为……提供资金（熟词僻义，重点关注）

[记] 谐音"犯难死"→一文钱难倒英雄好汉，干着急就是没钱，真是犯难啊→ *n.* 财政，金融，金融学→财政分配和金融投资就是→ *v.* 为……提供资金

[派] financial [faɪˈnænʃl] [fəˈnænʃl] *a.* 财政的，金融的
financially [faɪˈnænʃəli] [fəˈnænʃəli] *ad.* 财政上，金融上

[真] [D] ease its **financial** burden of providing local services.【2021年6月 仔细阅读 53题D选项】

[译] 减轻其提供当地服务的财政负担。

–firm– 坚固，坚定，确定

firm [7] [fɜːm] *n.* 公司 *a.* 坚固的；坚定的；确定的

六级基础词汇

[派] firmly [ˈfɜːmli] *ad.* 坚固地；坚定地

confirm [6] [kənˈfɜːm] *v.* 确认；批准

[记] con（加强）+firm→"加强语气地坚定"；因为经过→ *v.* 确认；批准

[派] confirmation [ˌkɒnfəˈmeɪʃn] *n.* 确认；认可；批准

[真] Nicola Sturgeon's speech last Tuesday setting out the Scottish government's legislative programme for the year ahead **confirmed** what was already pretty clear.【2021年6月 仔细阅读】

[译] 上周二，尼古拉·斯特金在其演说中阐明了苏格兰政府未来一年的立法方案，证实了一个已然相当清晰的事实。

–flect–、–flex–、–flict– 弯曲，折

reflect [15] [rɪˈflekt] *v.&n.* 反射；反映；思考，考虑

[记] re（back）+flect→光线"向反方向折"→ *v.&n.* 反射；反映→"反射、反映"出来的问题值得→ *v.* 思考，考虑

[派] reflection [rɪˈflekʃn] *n.* 反射；反映
reflective [rɪˈflektɪv] *a.* 反射的；反映的

[考] reflect on 考虑，回想

[真] [B] They don't **reflect** the changes in individual countries.【2021年6月 听力23题B选项】

[译] 它们并不能反映个别国家的变化。

flexible [4] [ˈfleksəbl] *a.* 易弯曲的；灵活的

[记] flex+ible（*a.*）→"能被折，能弯曲的"→ *a.* 易弯曲的；灵活的

[派] flexibility [ˌfleksəˈbɪləti] *n.* 灵活性，机动性

inflexible [ɪnˈfleksəbl] *a.* 僵硬的，不可弯曲的

[真] [D] They can work **flexible** hours. 【2021 年 6 月 听力 3 题 D 选项】
[译] 他们可以有灵活的工作时间。

conflict [5]

[kənˈflɪkt]　[ˈkɒnflɪkt] *v.&n.* 冲突；抵触

[记] con（共同，全部）+flict → "共同折来折去" → *v.&n.* 冲突；抵触
[派] conflicting [kənˈflɪktɪŋ] *a.* 冲突的，矛盾的
[真] [C] It causes **conflicts** between employers and employees. 【2021 年 6 月 听力 20 题 C 选项】
[译] 这会导致雇主和雇员之间的冲突。

–flu–、–fuse– 流

flu [2]

[flu:] *n.* 流感

六级基础词汇

flaw [2]

[flɔ:] *n.* 裂缝；缺陷

[记] 改写自 flow（流动）→ 因为有了 "flaw" 才会 "flow" → *n.* 裂缝；缺陷
[派] flawed [flɔ:d] *a.* 有缺点的，有错误的

fuel [5]

[ˈfju:əl] *n.* 燃料；食物　*v.* 给……加燃料；刺激

[记] 改写自 flu → "燃料" 就是 "流进去的" → 供给人的生命的 "燃料"，就是食物 → *n.* 燃料；食物　*v.* 给……加燃料；刺激
[派] fossil-fuel [ˈfɒsl fju:əl] *n.* 化石燃料
[真] [B] Activities that help to **fuel** students' ingenuity. 【2019 年 12 月 仔细阅读 48 题 B 选项】
[译] 有助于激发学生创造力的活动。

affluent [3]

[ˈæfluənt] *a.* 富裕的，有钱的

[记] af（to）+flu+ent（*a.*）→ 花钱如 "流水" 一般 → *a.* 富裕的，有钱的
[派] affluence [ˈæfluəns] *n.* 富裕，充足
[真] A Stanford study in 2014 suggested the same was true for students in California's **affluent** communities. 【2021 年 6 月 听力原文】
[译] 2014 年，美国斯坦福大学的一项研究表明，加利福尼亚州富裕社区的学生情况也是如此。

fluid [3]

[ˈflu:ɪd] *a.* 流动的，液体的　*n.* 液体

[记] flu+id（*a.&n.*）→ *a.* 流动的，液体的　*n.* 液体
[真] According to a report from the Harvard School of Public Health, many everyday products, including some bug sprays and cleaning **fluids**, could lead to an increased risk of brain and behavioral disorders in children. 【2020 年 7 月 选词填空】

[译] 哈佛大学公共卫生学院的一份报告指出，包括一些驱虫喷雾剂和清洁液在内的许多日常用品，可能会增加儿童大脑和行为紊乱的风险。

influence [24]

['ɪnfluəns] v.&n. 影响

[记] in（里）+flu+ence（v.&n.）→ "流入"；思想、精神、道德如涓涓细流般 "流入" 大脑，产生的就是→ v.&n. 影响

[派] influential [ˌɪnfluˈenʃl] a. 有影响的，有影响力的　　n. 有影响力的人或物

[考] be influenced by... 受……的影响
　　　have an influence on... 对……有影响

[真] They might not have even reflected on what good management looks like and how it would **influence** their own management style.【2021 年 6 月 听力原文】

[译] 他们甚至可能没有考虑过什么是好的管理，以及它将如何影响他们自己的管理风格。

fluctuate [2]

[ˈflʌktʃueɪt] v. 波动，改变

[记] flu+ctu（无义）+ate（v.）→ "流水发出的动作" → v. 波动，改变

[派] fluctuation [ˌflʌktʃuˈeɪʃn] n. 波动，改变

confuse [3]

[kənˈfjuːz] v. 使困惑，使糊涂

[记] con（全部，共同）+fuse → "全部流在一起"；你在背单词时有没有发现背着背着，很多长得很像的单词流在一起，把你彻底搞糊涂了→ v. 使困惑，使糊涂

[派] confusion [kənˈfjuːʒn] n. 困惑
　　　confusing [kənˈfjuːzɪŋ] a. 困惑的

[考] be confused about... 对……感到困惑/迷惑

[真] They're famously **confusing**, which is why so many TV shows and movies revolve around high school turmoil.【2020 年 12 月 听力原文】

[译] 那时候是出了名的困惑期，这就是为什么那么多的电视节目和电影都围绕着高中风波展开。

◀ –fore– 前，以前，提前 ▶

foresee [5]

[fɔːˈsiː] v. 预见，预知

[记] fore+see（v. 看见）→ "提前看见" → v. 预见，预知

[派] foreseeable [fɔːˈsiːəbl] a. 可预见的

[真] Similar limits can be **foreseen** for the much greater advances promised by self-driving cars.【2021 年 6 月 仔细阅读】

[译] 对承诺会做出更多改进的无人驾驶汽车领域，也可以预见类似的限制。

forecast [2]

[ˈfɔːkɑːst] v.&n. 预测，预报

[记] fore+cast（v. 投射）→ 信息的 "提前投射" → v.&n. 预测，预报

–form– 形式

form [18]
[fɔ:m] *n.* 形式，样式　*v.* 形成，构成

六级基础词汇
[派] formation [fɔ:ˈmeɪʃn] *n.* 形成，构成；结构

formal [4]
[ˈfɔ:ml] *a.* 形式上的；正式的

[记] form 的形容词；form+al（*a.*）→ *a.* 形式上的；正式的
[派] informal [ɪnˈfɔ:ml] *a.* 不正式的，非正式的
　　 informally [ɪnˈfɔ:məli] *ad.* 不正式地，非正式地
[真] Smith says he'll provide services ranging from **formal** seminars to on-farm workshops on holistic（整体的）management, to one-on-one hand-holding and an almost 24/7 phone hotline for farmers who are converting.【2019 年 12 月　长篇阅读 H 选项】
[译] 史密斯说，他将提供各种服务，从正式的研讨会到整体管理的农场研讨会，到一对一的牵手，以及为正在转变的农民提供近全天候的电话热线。

format [2]
[ˈfɔ:mæt] *v.* 格式化

[记] form+at（无义）→经过这个动作后电脑硬盘的"形式"发生剧烈变化→ *v.* 格式化

formula [4]
[ˈfɔ:mjələ] *n.* 公式，方程式

[记] form+ul（中缀）+a（很像数学符号 α）→"形式上有很多 α"→ *n.* 公式，方程式
[助] 函数 f(x) 中的 f 就是 formula 的首字母
[派] formulate [ˈfɔ:mjuleɪt] *v.* 用公式表达；确切地阐述
[真] Online sellers often use complex mathematical **formulas** to determine what products to feature and how to price these products.【2020 年 12 月 听力原文】
[译] 网络卖家通常使用复杂的数学公式来确定招牌产品以及如何为这些产品定价。

perform [26]
[pəˈfɔ:m] *v.* 表演，表现；执行（熟词僻义，重点关注）

[记] per（贯穿）+form →"形式"上有一个"贯穿始终"的主题→ *v.* 表演，表现；执行
[派] performance [pəˈfɔ:məns] *n.* 表演，表现；执行
　　 performer [pəˈfɔ:mə(r)] *n.* 执行者；演奏者
　　 outperform [ˌaʊtpəˈfɔ:m] *v.* 做得比……更好，胜过
[真] It's quite possible, they are content with how the individuals they promoted are now **performing**, merrily ignorant of the damage they're actually causing.【2021 年 6 月 听力原文】

Day 10

[译] 他们很有可能对提拔的个人现在的表现感到满意，而对他们实际造成的损害一无所知。

inform 5
[ɪnˈfɔːm] v. 通知

[记] information（n. 信息）的动词→"信息传递"的动作→v. 通知
[派] informed [ɪnˈfɔːmd] a. 了解情况的，见多识广的，消息灵通的
[考] inform sb. of sth. 通知某人某事
[真] They also felt less **informed** about science and less qualified to discuss science topics.【2021年6月 听力原文】
[译] 他们还觉得自己对科学的了解较少，也不太有资格讨论有关科学的话题。

transform 10
[trænsˈfɔːm] v. 使改变，使变形

[记] trans（across）+form →"形式、样式的穿梭"；一会儿这个形式，一会儿那个形式→ v. 使改变，使变形
[派] transformation [ˌtrænsfəˈmeɪʃn] n. 改变，变化
[真] [A] It radically **transformed** the state's economy.【2021年6月 听力15题A选项】
[译] 它从根本上改变了这个州的经济。

–found– 建立，创立

found 6
[faʊnd] v. 建立，创立

六级基础词汇
[派] founder [ˈfaʊndə(r)] n. 创始人，建立者

foundation 10
[faʊnˈdeɪʃn] n. 基础；基金会

[记] 上词 found 的名词；found+ation（n.）→首先"建立，创立"什么？→ n. 基础→做慈善的基础形式可以是成立→ n. 基金会
[派] foundational [faʊnˈdeɪʃənəl] a. 基本的，基础的
[真] Cotton and beef were the **foundation** of the economy.【2021年6月 听力原文】
[译] 棉花和牛肉是经济的基础。

–fract–、–frag– 破，打破

fragile 2
[ˈfrædʒaɪl] a. 易碎的；脆弱的

[记] frag+ile（a.）→容易被"打破"的→ a. 易碎的；脆弱的
[派] fragility [frəˈdʒɪləti] n. 脆弱，虚弱；易碎

fragment 3
[ˈfrægmənt] [frægˈment] n. 碎片，片段　v.（使）破碎

075

[记] frag+ment（n.&v.）→"打破"的结果和动作→ n.碎片，片段 v.（使）破碎
[真] These **fragments** got the smooth, round shape by rolling along the stream bottom.【2020年7月 听力原文】
[译] 这些碎片通过沿河底漂流，变得光滑圆润。

–fund– 资本，资金，资助

fund [10]

[fʌnd] n. 基金，资金 v. 资助

[记] 本词核心为 fun（喜悦，快乐），基金、资金是不是可以给人带来喜悦？fund 能够给人带来 fun，所以这个词表示→ n. 基金，资金 v. 资助
[派] fundraising [ˈfʌndˌreɪzɪŋ] n. 筹款，募款 a. 筹款的
[真] Other rocket enthusiasts also raised **funds** for him.【2021年6月 听力原文】
[译] 其他火箭爱好者也为他筹集资金。

fundamental [6]

[ˌfʌndəˈmentl] a. 根本的，基本的

[记] fund+a（无义）+ment（n.）+al（a.）→ 对个人、组织、企业或社会来说，fund is fundamental → a. 根本的，基本的
[派] fundamentally [ˌfʌndəˈmentəli] ad. 根本地，根本上，基本地
[真] Many public health policymakers believe that the resolution of age-associated disease will tell us something **fundamental** about the aging process.【2021年6月 听力原文】
[译] 许多公共卫生政策制定者认为，解决与年龄相关的疾病会让我们了解关于衰老过程的一些基本情况。

fond [2]

[fɒnd] a. 喜爱的，喜欢的

[记] fond（改写自 fund；资本，资金）→"对于 fund（资金）谁不 fond（喜欢，喜爱）！"→ a. 喜爱的，喜欢的
[考] be fond of... 喜爱……，喜欢……

扫码快速学习

扫码即刻听课

非成组词（F字母）

fade [2]　[feɪd] *v.* 褪色；衰减，逐渐消逝

［助］谐音"废的"→"慢慢被废，慢慢无用，慢慢消失"→ *v.* 褪色；衰减，逐渐消逝

fatal [2]　[ˈfeɪtl] *a.* 致命的，毁灭性的

［记］fat（简写自 fate；命，命运）+（t）al（谐音"头"）→"命到头了"→ *a.* 致命的，毁灭性的
［派］fatality [fəˈtæləti] *n.* 死亡；致命性

familiar [10]　[fəˈmɪliə(r)] *a.* 熟悉的，亲近的

［记］famili（改写自 family；家庭）+ar（表示人的后缀）→"家里人的"→ *a.* 熟悉的，亲近的
［派］unfamiliar [ˌʌnfəˈmɪliə(r)] *a.* 不熟悉的
　　　familiarity [fəˌmiliˈærəti] *n.* 熟悉，通晓
［考］be familiar with　熟悉
［真］That would become a **familiar** pattern of the boom-or-bust Texas economy.【2021年6月 听力原文】
［译］这将成为得克萨斯州经济繁荣或萧条的常见模式。

fascinate [10]　[ˈfæsɪneɪt] *v.* 使着迷

［记］fasc（改写自 fans；粉丝）+in（无义）+ate（*v.*）→"让粉丝着迷的动作"，当然是→ *v.* 使着迷
［派］fascination [ˌfæsɪˈneɪʃn] *n.* 着迷，入迷
　　　fascinating [ˈfæsɪneɪtɪŋ] *a.* 有吸引力的，迷人的
［真］Humans are **fascinated** by the source of their failings and virtues.【2021年6月 仔细阅读】
［译］人类着迷于他们的失败和美德的根源。

fertile [10]　[ˈfɜːtaɪl] *a.* 肥沃的，富饶的

[记] fert（改写自 fat；肥）+ile（a.）→ 土地"很肥的"→ a. 肥沃的，富饶的
[助] 谐音"富田儿"→ a. 肥沃的，富饶的
[派] fertility [fəˈtɪləti] n. 富饶，肥沃
　　 fertilizer/iser [ˈfɜːtəlaɪzə(r)] n. 肥料
[真] [D] It is **fertile** and productive.【2019 年 12 月 听力 9 题 D 选项】
[译] 它肥沃而多产。

favo(u)r [12]

[ˈfeɪvə(r)] *n.* 好感，喜爱；关心；支持　*v.* 支持，赞成

[记] 来自拉丁语 favere（好感）→ n. 好感，喜爱；关心；支持　v. 支持，赞成
[助] 谐音"飞吻"→"送你个飞吻"，对你当然有→ n. 好感，喜爱；关心；支持 → v. 支持，赞成
[派] favo(u)rite [ˈfeɪvərɪt] n. 喜爱的人或物　a. 喜爱的
　　 favo(u)rable [ˈfeɪvərəbl] a. 赞成的；有利的
[形] flavo(u)r [ˈfleɪvə] n. 风味，滋味　v. 给……调味
[考] in favor of 赞同，支持
[真] Your **favorite** songs and artists become familiar, comforting parts of your routine.【2020 年 12 月 听力原文】
[译] 你最喜欢的歌曲和艺术家已经变成你生活中熟悉且令人舒适的一部分。

fatigue [3]

[fəˈtiːɡ] *v.&n.* 疲劳，疲乏

[记] fat（a. 胖的）+i（无义）+gue（谐音"哥"）→"哥很胖"，容易→ v.&n. 疲劳，疲乏
[真] Other researchers say too much protein can cause cramps, headaches, and **fatigue**.【2019 年 12 月 长篇阅读 L 选项】
[译] 其他研究人员说，过多的蛋白质会导致痉挛、头痛和疲劳。

fee [3]

[fiː] *n.* 费用，酬金

[助] 谐音"费"→ n. 费用，酬金
[真] The Himalayan Kingdom of Bhutan has a longstanding policy of charging visitors a daily **fee**.【2021 年 6 月 仔细阅读】
[译] 喜马拉雅不丹王国长久以来有每日向游客收费的政策。

fellow [2]

[ˈfeləʊ] *n.* 伙伴，同事　*a.* 伙伴的，同类的

[记] 改写自 follow（跟随）→"跟在后面的"是→ n. 伙伴；后引申出→ n. 同事→ a. 伙伴的，同类的
[派] fellowship [ˈfeləʊʃɪp] n. 伙伴关系

fierce [2]

[fɪəs] *a.* 凶猛的，残忍的；狂热的，猛烈的

[助] 谐音"fear 死"→"吓死我了，怕死我了"→ a. 凶猛的，残忍的；狂热的，猛烈的
[派] fiercely [fɪəsli] ad. 凶猛地；残酷地；猛烈地，激烈地

Day 11

figure [12]
[ˈfɪɡə(r)] *n.* 人物；数字 *v.* 计算；认为

[记] 改写自 finger（手指）→在计算工具未出现之前，手指的一个作用就是"计数、计算"→*n.* 数字 *v.* 计算；认为→手指长在人身上→*n.* 人物

[考] figure out 计算出；解决；想出

[真] Higgins had forecast oil at 1,000 feet, a totally made-up **figure**.【2021 年 6 月听力原文】

[译] 希金斯曾预测，地下 1 000 英尺处有石油，这是一个完全虚构的数字。

flourish [4]
[ˈflʌrɪʃ] *v.* 繁荣，兴旺

[记] 词根 flour（改写自 flower；花，花朵）+ish（*v.*）→"像花一样绽放"→*v.* 繁荣，兴旺

[真] Where we **flourish**, their cultures wither.【2020 年 12 月仔细阅读】

[译] 在我们繁荣的地方，他们的文化就会枯萎。

fortune [5]
[ˈfɔːtʃuːn] *n.* 幸运；财富

[记] 来源于罗马神话中的女神 Fortuna（福尔图娜）。作为幸运女神，她掌管着人间的幸福和机遇。在西方神像中，Fortuna 一手拿着象征丰饶和富裕的羊角，一手拿着主宰人们时运的方向舵，站在旋转的飞轮之上。西方人认为，Fortuna 手中的方向舵和脚下的飞轮转到哪里，就把人们的时运带到哪里→*n.* 幸运；财富

[派] fortunate [ˈfɔːtʃənət] *a.* 幸运的
unfortunate [ʌnˈfɔːtʃənət] *a.* 不幸的
unfortunately [ʌnˈfɔːtʃənətli] *ad.* 不幸地

[真] Nicole admitted she was **fortunate**.【2021 年 6 月选词填空】

[译] 妮可承认她很幸运。

fossil [2]
[ˈfɒsl] *n.* 化石；老顽固

[助] 谐音"发馊"→时间长了，"发馊了"→*n.* 化石；老顽固

foster [8]
[ˈfɒstə(r)] *v.* 养育，抚育，收养；促进；培养

[记] fos（改写自 food；食品，食物）+t（无义）+er（表示人的后缀）→"给人 food"→*v.* 养育，抚育，收养；促进；培养

[真] [A] **Foster** better driving behavior.【2021 年 6 月听力 25 题 A 选项】

[译] 培养更好的驾驶行为。

frame [3]
[freɪm] *n.* 相框，框架；身材，体格（熟词僻义，重点关注）

[记] fame（*n.* 名声，名气）+r（辅音字母表示"人"）→"有名声、名气的人"能够被画进→*n.* 相框，框架；引申出人外在的框架→*n.* 身材，体格

[派] framework [ˈfreɪmwɜːk] *n.* 框架，构架

[真] Had the bell towers' wooden **frames** burned down, the heavy bells would have crashed down.【2021 年 6 月长篇阅读 41 题】

[译] 如果钟楼的木制框架被烧毁，沉重的钟就会倒塌。

frank [2]　[fræŋk] *a.* 坦白的，直率的

［记］改写自 friend→你我是"friend"，彼此应该"frank"→ *a.* 坦白的，直率的
［派］frankness [ˈfræŋknəs] *n.* 坦白，直率

frustrate [4]　[frʌˈstreɪt] *v.* 挫败，使灰心

［记］frus（改写自 froz=frozen；冷冻的）+tr（无义）+ate（*v.*）→"心被冻住了"；遇到重大挫败，心都凉了→ *v.* 挫败，使灰心
［派］frustration [frʌˈstreɪʃn] *n.* 挫败，失败
　　frustrating [frʌˈstreɪtɪŋ] *a.* 令人沮丧的
［真］[D] Pour out his **frustrations** on a rate-your-employer website.【2021年6月 听力4题D选项】
［译］把他的沮丧发泄在一个"给雇主评分"的网站上。

–gen–、–gn–、–gene–　基因

gene [9]　[dʒiːn] *n.* 基因

六级基础词汇

genetic [19]　[dʒəˈnetɪk] *a.* 基因的；遗传的

［记］gene+t（无义）+ic（*a.*）→ *a.* 基因的；遗传的
［派］genetically [dʒəˈnetɪkli] *ad.* 基因地；遗传地
　　genetics [dʒəˈnetɪks] *n.* 遗传学
　　geneticist [dʒəˈnetɪsɪst] *n.* 遗传学家
［真］[B] **Genetic** differences between students are far greater than supposed.【2021年6月 仔细阅读46题B选项】
［译］学生之间的基因差异远比预期的要大得多。

generate [6]　[ˈdʒenəreɪt] *v.* 繁殖，生殖；使形成，产生

［记］gene+rat（*n.* 老鼠）+e（无义）→"老鼠的基因"；其特点就是繁殖能力极强→ *v.* 繁殖，生殖→ *v.* 使形成，产生
［派］regenerate [rɪˈdʒenəreɪt] *v.* 使再生
［真］The notion that they're utterly powerless suddenly seems unrealistic—not to mention rather annoying—so they're prompted instead to **generate** ideas about how they might change things.【2020年12月 仔细阅读】
［译］（之前持有的）他们完全无能为力的想法突然看起来不切实际，更不用提让人讨厌了，因此他们被鼓励去思考如何针对现状做出改变。

generation [13]　[ˌdʒenəˈreɪʃn] *n.* 代，一代人

［记］上词 generate 的名词；generat（简写自 generate；繁殖，生殖）+ion（*n.*）→"生出来的一批人"→ *n.* 代，一代人

Day 11

［派］generational [ˌdʒenəˈreɪʃnl] *a.* 世代的

［真］[C] Study the unique characteristics of each **generation** of chimps.【2020 年 12 月 仔细阅读 54 题 C 选项】

［译］研究每一代黑猩猩的独特特征。

genius [5]

[ˈdʒiːniəs] *n.* 天才；天赋

［助］gen（谐音"真"）+（n）iu（谐音"牛"）+s（无义）→此人"真牛"→ *n.* 天才；天赋

［真］That was visionary **genius**.【2021 年 6 月 长篇阅读 D 选项】

［译］那是有远见的天才见解。

genius 的引申词

gift [2]

[ɡɪft] *n.* 礼物；天才；天赋

［记］我们肯定记得"礼物"的含义 →上帝送给一个人最大的"礼物"，就是→ *n.* 天才；天赋

［派］gifted [ˈɡɪftɪd] *a.* 有天赋的

［考］have a gift for... 对于……有天赋

talent [12]

[ˈtælənt] *n.* 才能；人才

［记］tal（简写自 tall；高）+ent（表示人的后缀）→此乃"高人"→ *n.* 才能；人才

［派］talented [ˈtæləntɪd] *a.* 有才能的，能干的

［真］What is characteristic of people with drawing **talent**?【2021 年 6 月 仔细阅读 50 题题干】

［译］有绘画才能的人的特点是什么？

ingenious [9]

[ɪnˈdʒiːniəs] *a.* 心灵手巧的；精巧的

［记］in（里）+genious（改写自 genius；天才）→ "里面是天才"→ *a.* 心灵手巧的；精巧的

［派］ingenuity [ˌɪndʒəˈnjuːəti] *n.* 足智多谋；善于创新

［形］indigenous [ɪnˈdɪdʒənəs] *a.* 土生土长的，本地的

［真］[A] They are motivated to find **ingenious** ways to persuade their interlocutor.【2020 年 12 月 仔细阅读 54 题 A 选项】

［译］他们想要找到巧妙的方法来说服他们的对话者。

gender [3]

[ˈdʒendə(r)] *n.* 性别

［记］gen+d（谐音"弟"）+er（表示人或物）→ "基因"决定"人"是弟弟还是妹妹→ *n.* 性别

［真］[C] Their contact with the opposite **gender**.【2020 年 12 月 仔细阅读 47 题 C

081

选项】
［译］他们与异性的接触。

-geo- 大地，土地

geography [2] [dʒiˈɒgrəfi] *n.* 地理（学）；地形
［记］geo+graph（*v.* 描写，描绘）+y（*n.*）→"描绘土地、大地"的学科；这里是北京，这里是上海，这里是天津→ *n.* 地理（学）；地形
［派］geographical [ˌdʒi:əˈgræfɪkl] *a.* 地理的，地理学的

geology [3] [dʒiˈɒlədʒi] *n.* 地质学
［记］geo+logy（表示学科的后缀）→直接和"土地、大地相关的学科"→ *n.* 地质学
［派］geologist [dʒiˈɒlədʒɪst] *n.* 地质学家
　　geological [ˌdʒi:əˈlɒdʒɪkl] *a.* 地质的，地质学的
［真］What does marine **geologist** Robin Beaman say about the Coral Sea plan?【2020年9月 仔细阅读 54题题干】
［译］海洋地质学家罗宾·比曼对珊瑚海计划有什么看法？

-gl- 光线，光明

glimpse [3] [glɪmps] *v.&n.* 一瞥，扫视
［记］gl+im（里）+p（无义）+se（*v.&n.*）→"眼里发出光线"→ *v.&n.* 一瞥，扫视
［真］It is a **glimpse** of the blindingly obvious—and there's nothing to back strongly either a hereditary or environmental argument.【2021年6月 仔细阅读】
［译］可以初步感受一个显而易见的事实——无论是遗传决定论还是环境决定论，都没有得到任何证据的有力支持。

glamo(u)r [5] [ˈglæmə] *n.* 魅力，魔法
［助］谐音"格莱美"→"格莱美大奖最能体现出音乐的 glamo(u)r"→ *n.* 魅力，魔法
［派］glamo(u)rous [ˈglæmərəs] *a.* 富有魅力的，迷人的
［真］Being a graduate from Harvard Law School carries that extra **glamour**, doesn't it?【2020年12月 长篇阅读 A选项】
［译］成为哈佛大学法学院的毕业生有着额外的魅力，难道不是吗？

-gn(o)- 知道，认识

recognize/ise [10] [ˈrekəgnaɪz] *v.* 认出，识别；承认

Day 11

六级基础词汇

［派］ recognition [ˌrekəɡˈnɪʃn] *n.* 认出，识别；承认
　　 recognizable/sable [ˈrekəɡnaɪzəbl] [ˌrekəɡˈnaɪzəbl] *a.* 可识别的，可辨认的

cognitive[16] [ˈkɒɡnətɪv] *a.* 认知的，认识的

［记］ co（加强）+gn +it（无义）+ive（*a.*）→ "知道的，认识的" → *a.* 认知的，认识的

［派］ cognition [kɒɡˈnɪʃn] *n.* 认知，认识
　　 cognitively [ˈkɒɡnətɪvli] *ad.* 认知地

［真］ [A] Sensitivity to **cognitive** stimulation.【2021 年 6 月 仔细阅读 50 题 A 选项】
［译］ 对认知刺激的敏感性。

扫码快速学习

扫码即刻听课

–grad–、–grat–、–gret–、–gress– 走

grade [6]
[greɪd] *n.* 年级；等级；成绩，分数（熟词僻义，重点关注）
六级基础词汇

gradual [6]
[ˈɡrædʒuəl] *a.* 逐渐的，慢慢的
[记] grad+u（无义）+al（*a.*）→ 聚会分别时，人们总喜欢说"慢走啊，慢点啊"→ *a.* 逐渐的，慢慢的
[派] gradually [ˈɡrædʒuəli] *ad.* 逐渐地，渐渐地
[真] [A] They are declining **gradually** in number.【2021年6月 仔细阅读47题 A选项】
[译] 它们的数量正在逐渐减少。

graduate [10]
[ˈɡrædʒueɪt] [ˈɡrædʒuət] *v.* 毕业，授予学位或毕业证书 *n.* 毕业生
[记] grad+u（无义）+ate（*v.&n.*）→ "毕业"就是要"走了"；"毕业生"就是要"走"的人→ *v.* 毕业，授予学位或毕业证书 *n.* 毕业生
[派] graduation [ˌɡrædʒuˈeɪʃn] *n.* 毕业（典礼）
undergraduate [ˌʌndəˈɡrædʒuət] *n.* 大学生，在校生
[考] graduate from... 从……毕业
[真] For instance, **graduates** from the year 2000 would have to come back in 2005.【2020年12月 长篇阅读 L选项】
[译] 例如，2000年的毕业生将不得不在2005年回来。

degrade [6]
[dɪˈɡreɪd] *v.* 降低，降级
[记] de（下）+grad+e（无义）→ "往下走"；人往低处走→ *v.* 降低，降级
[派] degradation [ˌdeɡrəˈdeɪʃn] *n.* 堕落，恶化，衰退
[真] A few factors that could impact on variation would typically include the measurement of rain per unit of a crop planted, soil type, patterns of soil **degradation**, daylight hours, temperature and so forth.【2020年12月 长篇阅读 M选项】
[译] 一些可能影响变化的因素通常包括每单位种植作物的降雨量、土壤类型、土壤退化模式、日照时间和温度等。

084

Day 12

upgrade [3]
[ˌʌpˈɡreɪd] *v.* 升级，提升

[记] up（上）+grad+e（无义）→"往上走"；人往高处走→ *v.* 升级，提升

[真] [D] They are constantly **upgraded** to make driving easier and safer.【2021 年 6 月 仔细阅读 52 题 D 选项】

[译] 它们不断被升级，使驾驶更容易、更安全。

ingredient [4]
[ɪnˈɡriːdiənt] *n.* （混合物的）组成部分；（烹调的）原料；（构成）要素，因素

[记] in（里）+gred（改写自 gret）+i（无义）+ent（*n.*）→"走到物品里面的东西"→ *n.* （混合物的）组成部分；（烹调的）原料→"走到事情里面的东西"→ *n.* （构成）要素，因素

[真] The EAT report presumes that "traditional diets" in countries like India include little red meat, which might be consumed only on special occasions or as minor **ingredients** in mixed dishes.【2020 年 12 月 仔细阅读】

[译] EAT 报告推测，诸如印度等国家的"传统饮食"中含有的红肉量较少，红肉可能只在一些特殊场合食用，或作为混合菜肴的配菜。

progress [16]
[ˈprəʊɡres] [prəˈɡres] *n.* 前进，进步 *v.* 进步，发展

[记] pro（前）+gress→"向前走"→ *n.* 前进，进步 *v.* 进步，发展

[派] progressive [prəˈɡresɪv] *a.* 不断前进的，进步的

[真] But undeniably, there would simply be no **progress** without radicals.【2020 年 9 月 听力原文】

[译] 但是，无可否认的是，没有"激进分子"，确实就没有进步。

aggressive [2]
[əˈɡresɪv] *a.* 侵略的，好斗的；有进取心的，上进的

[记] aggress 的形容词；aggress（*v.* 攻击，侵犯）+ive（*a.*）→ *a.* 侵略的，好斗的→向目标"慢慢走过去"，不达目的誓不罢休→ *a.* 有进取心的，上进的

[派] aggressively [əˈɡresɪvli] *ad.* 侵略地，攻击地

congress [2]
[ˈkɒŋɡres] *n.* 会议，国会

[记] con（共同，全部）+gress →"所有人全部走在一起"；干什么呢？当然是开会啦！→ *n.* 会议，国会

integrate [6]
[ˈɪntɪɡreɪt] *v.* 合并，使成为一体

[记] inte（简写自 inter；彼此，互相）+grat+e（无义）→"彼此走在一起"→ *v.* 合并，使成为一体

[派] integration [ˌɪntɪˈɡreɪʃn] *n.* 结合，整合，一体化

[真] There is huge potential for artificial intelligence and machine learning to revolutionize agriculture by **integrating** these technologies into critical markets on a global scale.【2020 年 12 月 长篇阅读 R 选项】

[译] 人工智能和机器学习具有巨大的潜力，可以将这些技术整合到全球范围内的关键市场，从而实现农业革命。

integrity ⁴

[ɪnˈteɡrəti] *n.* 完整；正直，诚实

[记] 上词 integrate 的名词→ *n.* 完整→"人格完整"→ *n.* 正直，诚实

[派] integral [ˈɪntɪɡrəl] *a.* 完整的；必需的

[真] This usually results in a failure of a product, which leads to skepticism from the market and delivers a blow to the **integrity** of Machine Learning technology.【2020年12月 长篇阅读 Q 选项】

[译] 这通常会导致某种产品的失败，从而导致市场的怀疑，并对机器学习技术的完整性带来沉重的打击。

非成组词（G 字母）

giant ²

[ˈdʒaɪənt] *n.* 巨人；巨头，大公司 *a.* 巨大的

六级基础词汇

[派] gigantic [dʒaɪˈɡæntɪk] *a.* 巨大的，庞大的

global ⁴²

[ˈɡləʊbl] *a.* 全球的，全世界的

六级基础词汇

[派] globalize/ise [ˈɡləʊbəlaɪz] *v.*（使）全球化

grave ⁴

[ɡreɪv] [ɡrɑːv] *n.* 坟墓 *a.* 严肃的，沉重的

[助] 谐音"鬼屋"→ *n.* 坟墓→走进坟墓，心情变得→ *a.* 严肃的，沉重的

[派] graveyard [ˈɡreɪvjɑːd] *n.* 墓地

[真] [C] Dinosaurs went to their **grave** before they died.【2020年7月 听力21题 C 选项】

[译] 恐龙在它们死前就进了坟墓。

guarantee ⁹

[ˌɡærənˈtiː] *v.* 保证，担保 *n.* 保证，保证书

[记] guar（简写自 guard；保卫，守护）+ant（表示人的后缀）+ee（表示人的后缀）→中国军人说"国家有我保卫"，放心！→ *v.* 保证，担保→ *n.* 保证，保证书

[真] [D] Its benefits are **guaranteed** by collective wisdom.【2021年6月 仔细阅读 54题 D 选项】

[译] 它的利益得到了集体智慧的保证。

–hand– 手

handicap ²

[ˈhændikæp] *n.* 障碍；缺陷；不利条件 *v.* 妨碍

[记] hand+i（无义）+cap（帽子）→"手里拿着帽子"，多不方便！→ *n.* 障碍；缺陷；不利条件 *v.* 妨碍

Day 12

handle [5]
['hændl] *v.* 处理；操纵
[记] hand+le（*v.*）→ "用手" → *v.* 处理；操纵
[真] [D] They are better able to survive or **handle** disease.【2021 年 6 月 听力 19 题 D 选项】
[译] 他们能更好地生存或处理疾病。

–heir–、–heri–、–herit– 继承

heir [2]
[eə(r)] *n.* 继承人
[助] he（他）+i（我）+（he）r（她）→ 爸爸他（he）和妈妈她（her）的中间夹着我（i），我在爸爸（he）和妈妈（her）的中间，所以我就是父母的→ *n.* 继承人

inherit [5]
[ɪnˈherɪt] *v.* 继承，继任
[记] in（里）+herit → *v.* 继承，继任
[派] inherent [ɪnˈhɪərənt] *a.* 天生的；内在的
　　inherently [ɪnˈhɪərəntli] *ad.* 固有地；天生地；内在地
　　inheritability [ɪnˌherɪtəˈbɪlɪti] *n.* 继承性
[真] Unlike-minded academics say the **inheritability** of human traits is scientifically unsound.【2021 年 6 月 仔细阅读】
[译] 持不同观点的学者说，人类特征的可遗传性在科学上是不可靠的。

–hum– 人类，土

human [39]
['hju:mən] *n.* 人，人类
六级基础词汇

humanity [4]
[hju:ˈmænəti] *n.* 人类，人性，人道
[记] human+ity（*n.*）→ *n.* 人类，人性，人道
[真] [A] Natural sciences should be learned the way **humanities** courses are.【2021 年 6 月 仔细阅读 47 题 A 选项】
[译] 学习自然科学的方式应该像学习人文学科一样。

humid [3]
['hju:mɪd] *a.* 潮湿的，湿气重的
[记] hum+id（*a.*）→ "（泥）土中有水分" → *a.* 潮湿的，湿气重的
[派] humidity [hju:ˈmɪdəti] *n.* 湿度，潮湿
[真] [D] They could no longer bear the **humidity**.【2021 年 6 月 听力 7 题 D 选项】
[译] 他们再也不能忍受潮湿了。

humo(u)r [8]
['hju:mə(r)] *n.* 幽默；精神状态；心情

087

［助］谐音"幽默"→ n. 幽默；精神状态；心情

［派］humorous [ˈhjuːmərəs] a. 幽默的

［真］Pollio conducted a study that proved **humour** can help workers excel at routine production tasks.【2020 年 7 月 听力原文】

［译］波利奥做了一项研究，证明幽默可以帮助员工在日常工作任务中有杰出表现。

非成组词（H 字母）

habitat [10]

[ˈhæbɪtæt] *n.* 栖息地，住所

［记］词根 habit（习惯）+at（在……）→"习惯待在这里"，这里就是→ n. 栖息地，住所

［真］[D] Endeavor to restore chimp **habitats** to expand its total population.【2020 年 12 月 仔细阅读 54 题 D 选项】

［译］努力恢复黑猩猩的栖息地，以扩大其种群总数。

harmony [6]

[ˈhɑːməni] *n.* 和谐，融洽

［记］harm（v. 伤害，损害）+ony（改写自 one；一个）→"伤害任何一个人"，都会影响→ n. 和谐，融洽

［派］harmonious [hɑːˈməʊniəs] a. 和谐的，融洽的，协调的

［真］[A] Wood was **harmonious** with nature.【2019 年 12 月 听力 18 题 A 选项】

［译］木材与自然是和谐的。

harsh [3]

[hɑːʃ] *a.* 粗糙的；苛刻的，严酷的

［记］改写自 hard（艰难的，困难的）→因为此人"harsh"所以相处"hard"→ a. 粗糙的；苛刻的，严酷的

［真］[B] Allow us to escape the **harsh** reality.【2020 年 12 月 仔细阅读 50 题 B 选项】

［译］让我们逃离残酷的现实。

hinder [2]

[ˈhɪndə(r)] *v.* 阻碍

［记］hind（简写自 behind；后面）+er（表示人或物的后缀）→"把人往后拉的动作"；你给我上后面待着去→ v. 阻碍

［派］hindrance [ˈhɪndrəns] n. 阻碍，妨碍；障碍物，起妨碍作用的人

honest [13]

[ˈɒnɪst] *a.* 诚实的，老实的

六级基础词汇

［派］honestly [ˈɒnɪstli] ad. 诚实地，老实地

honesty [ˈɒnəsti] n. 诚实，正直

dishonest [dɪsˈɒnɪst] a. 不诚实的，不老实的

dishonesty [dɪsˈɒnɪsti] n. 不正直，不诚实

Day 12

hono(u)r [2] [ˈɒnə] *n.* 荣耀，光荣；尊敬，敬意 *v.* 使光荣，荣耀；尊敬

[记]"荣耀"手机的正面或背面就写着 honor 这个单词→ *n.* 荣耀，光荣，尊敬，敬意 *v.* 使光荣，荣耀；尊敬

[派] hono(u)rable [ˈɒnərəbl] *a.* 光荣的，可敬的

huge [23] [hju:dʒ] *a.* 巨大的，庞大的

[助] hu（谐音"虎"）+ge（谐音"哥"）→"老虎大哥的身体"→ *a.* 巨大的，庞大的

[派] hugely [ˈhju:dʒli] *ad.* 非常

[真] [A] The local gassy hill might start a **huge** fire.【2021 年 6 月听力 12 题 A 选项】

[译] 当地充满气体的山可能会引发一场大火。

hypothesis [8] [haɪˈpɒθəsɪs] *n.* 假设

[记] hypo（下）+thesis（*n.* 论点，论文）→"论点之下"；还没有真正成为论点→ *n.* 假设

[派] hypothetical [ˌhaɪpəˈθetɪkl] *a.* 假定的，假设的
　　hypothetically [ˌhaɪpəˈθetɪkli] *ad.* 假设地，假想地

[真] Now, this **hypothesis** is new and some skeptics argue that this isn't a whole new category of lie, but the findings seem intuitive to me.【2020 年 12 月听力原文】

[译] 现在这个假设是新提出来的，一些怀疑论者争论说这不是一个全新的谎言种类，但是在我看来，这些发现似乎凭直觉就可以得出。

–imag– 想象

imagine [10] [ɪˈmædʒɪn] *v.* 想象

[记] imag+in（里）+e（无义）→ *v.* 想象

[派] imagination [ɪˌmædʒɪˈneɪʃn] *n.* 想象力
　　imaginative [ɪˈmædʒɪnətɪv] *a.* 富于想象力的，创新的

[真] Dangerous driving is not a fixed cultural trait as some **imagine**.【2021 年 6 月听力原文】

[译] 和一些人想象的不同，危险驾驶不是一种固定的文化特征。

image [26] [ˈɪmɪdʒ] *n.* 形象，肖像，图片

[记] 来自上词 imagine（想象）→"想象出来的"→ *n.* 形象，肖像，图片

[真] However advanced the CGI technology is, the recreated **image** will differ in a way from the real actor.【2021 年 6 月长篇阅读 43 题】

[译] 无论 CGI 技术多么先进，重建的图像都会在某种程度上不同于真正的演员。

扫码即刻听课

–im–、–in–、–il– 里，里面

impact [38]
['ɪmpækt] [ɪm'pækt] *n.* 影响，冲击 *v.* 对……有影响/有冲击
[记] im+ 词根 pact（挤，挤压）→ "挤入，压入"，产生→ *n.* 影响，冲击 *v.* 对……有影响/有冲击
[考] have an impact on... 对……产生影响
[真][D] Study the long-term **impact** of climate change on food production.【2020年12月仔细阅读55题D选项】
[译] 研究气候变化对粮食生产的长期影响。

inborn [2]
[,ɪn'bɔːn] *a.* 天生的，固有的
[记] in+born（*a.* 出生的）→ *a.* 天生的，固有的

incentive [6]
[ɪn'sentɪv] *n.*（金钱方面的）鼓励，刺激
[记] in+cent（*n.* 美分）+ive（*n.*）→ "进入一分钱里"，特别像掉钱眼儿里了→ *n.*（金钱方面的）鼓励，刺激
[真] The solution lies not just in better infrastructure, but in better social **incentives**.【2021年6月听力原文】
[译] 解决方案不仅在于更好的基础设施，还在于更好的社会激励措施。

income [20]
['ɪnkʌm] *n.* 收入，收益
[记] in+come（*v.* 进来）→ 钱哗啦哗啦地"进入口袋"，产生→ *n.* 收入，收益
[真] But the most important and intriguing changes are taking place in middle **income** countries, which contain most of the world's people and have some of the most dangerous roads.【2021年6月听力原文】
[译] 但最重要和最有趣的变化发生在中等收入国家，这些国家拥有世界上大多数的人口，并有着一些最危险的道路交通。

infant [3]
['ɪnfənt] *n.* 婴儿，幼儿
[记] in+fant（改写自 fat；胖）→ "里面胖胖的"→ *n.* 婴儿，幼儿
[助] 谐音"婴儿肥"
[真][A] **Infants**' facial expressions.【2019年12月听力21题A选项】

[译] 婴儿的面部表情。

initial [7]

[ɪˈnɪʃl] *a.* 最初的，开始的

[记] in+it（它）+i（很像数字 1）+al（*a.*）→ "刚一进入它" → *a.* 最初的，开始的

[派] initially [ɪˈnɪʃəli] *ad.* 开始，最初

[真] On many occasions, the entrepreneurs reported not paying themselves a wage at all **initially** in order to cover salaries and expenses.【2021 年 6 月听力原文】

[译] 在许多情况下，创业者报告说，为了支付工资和开销，他们最初根本不给自己发工资。

initiate [4]

[ɪˈnɪʃieɪt] *v.* 开始，发起，创始

[记] 上词 initial 的同源词 → *v.* 开始，发起，创始

[派] initiation [ɪˌnɪʃiˈeɪʃn] *n.* 开始，创始
initiative [ɪˈnɪʃətɪv] *n.* 倡议；主动权
initiator [ɪˈnɪʃieɪtə(r)] *n.* 创始人，发起人

[真] There's no one around to offer praise or **initiate** collaboration, no one to make greater use of our interests and talents.【2020 年 12 月听力原文】

[译] 身边没人赞扬，没人发起合作，也没有人能更好地利用我们的兴趣和才能。

insight [6]

[ˈɪnsaɪt] *n.* 洞察力，洞悉

[记] in+sight（*n.* 看见；景色）→ "看进去"；看得深入 → *n.* 洞察力，洞悉

[派] insightful [ˈɪnsaɪtfl] *a.* 富有洞察力的，有深刻见解的

[真] [C] **Insights** into the features of good music.【2020 年 12 月 听力 22 题 C 选项】

[译] 洞察到好音乐的特点。

intake [2]

[ˈɪnteɪk] *n.* 吸入；摄入，摄取

[记] 短词 take in 的反写词；in+take（*v.* 食用；饮用）→ *n.* 吸入；摄入，摄取

interior [2]

[ɪnˈtɪəriə(r)] *a.* 内部的，里面的 *n.* 内部

[记] in+ter（无义）+ior（*a.*）→ *a.* 内部的，里面的 *n.* 内部

intimidate [2]

[ɪnˈtɪmɪdeɪt] *v.* 恐吓，威胁

[记] in+timid（*a.* 胆小的）+ate（*v.*）→ "内心胆小的人容易害怕" → *v.* 恐吓，威胁

[派] intimidatory [ɪnˌtɪmɪˈdeɪtəri] *a.* 恐吓的，威胁的

invest [16]

[ɪnˈvest] *v.* 投资

[记] in+vest（改写自 west；西部）→ "进入西部"，想想美国和中国都曾有过西部大开发，资本、人才、技术统统进入西部 → *v.* 投资

[派] investment [ɪnˈvestmənt] n. 投资，投资物
investor [ɪnˈvestə(r)] n. 投资者

[真] He said, on her income, with some changes, she would be able to buy an **investment** unit within two years, which she did.【2021 年 6 月 选词填空】

[译] 他说，根据她的收入，再做一些改变，她将能够在两年内购买一套投资公寓，她也确实做到了这一点。

investigate [6]

[ɪnˈvestɪɡeɪt] v. 调查，研究

[记] 上词 invest 的同源词；invest+ig（无义）+ate（v.）→ "投资"需要"调查"和"研究"→ v. 调查，研究

[派] investigation [ɪnˌvestɪˈɡeɪʃn] n. 调查，研究
investigator [ɪnˈvestɪɡeɪtə(r)] n. 调查者，研究者

[真] [D] It is not based on sufficient **investigations** into the ecological system.【2020 年 9 月 仔细阅读 53 题 D 选项】

[译] 它不是基于对生态系统的充分调查。

◀ –ject– 送，投掷 ▶

subject [28]

[ˈsʌbdʒɪkt] [ˈsʌbdʒekt] [səbˈdʒekt] n. 主题；主观；科目；（批评、学习、调查、实验的）对象；主题　a. 易遭受……的；易服从……的　v. 使臣服；使顺从

[记] sub（下）+ject → "扔到下面，送到下面"；把他扔到下面，想怎么欺负就怎么欺负，不就是→ a. 易遭受……的；易服从……的　v. 使臣服；使顺从 ["n. 主题；主观；科目；（批评、学习、调查、实验的）对象；主题"是基础含义，在六级中重点关注 subject 作为形容词的含义]

[派] subjective [səbˈdʒektɪv] a. 主观的

[考] be subject to... 易遭受……；易服从……

[真] [C] It is **subject** to interpretation of statistics.【2021 年 6 月 仔细阅读 48 题 C 选项】

[译] 它取决于对于数据的解释。

[真] [C] They prioritize arts **subjects** over maths and sciences.【2021 年 6 月 仔细阅读 49 题 C 选项】

[译] 他们优先考虑艺术学科，而不是数学和科学。

object [20]

[ˈɒbdʒɪkt] [əbˈdʒekt] n. 物体；客观；目的（基础含义）　v. 反对

[记] ob（反对）+ject → v. 反对

[派] objection [əbˈdʒekʃn] n. 反对
objective [əbˈdʒektɪv] a. 客观的　n. 目标，任务
objectively [əbˈdʒektɪvli] ad. 客观地

[真] Firstly, we must ruthlessly cut the unnecessary **objects** out of our lives.【2020 年 12 月 听力原文】

[译] 首先，我们必须无情地减少生活中的非必需品。

Day 13

project [32]

['prɒdʒekt] **n.** 计划；工程，项目

[记] pro（前）+ject → "投掷到前方" → **n.** 计划；工程，项目

[真] Students should develop the key skills before they start a **project**.【2020 年 12 月 长篇阅读 36 题】

[译] 学生们在开始一个项目前应培养这些关键技能。

–just–

① 刚才的，刚好的，正好的

adjust [4]

[əˈdʒʌst] **v.** 调节，调整；适应

[记] ad（to）+just → "去变得刚好、正好"；本来不是刚好，怎么变刚好呢？调一下呗！→ **v.** 调节，调整；适应

[派] adjustment [əˈdʒʌstmənt] **n.** 调节，调整；适应

[考] adjust to... 调整以适应……

[真] [A] The UK is set to **adjust** its policy on taxation.【2021 年 6 月 仔细阅读 51 题 A 选项】

[译] 英国将调整其税收政策。

② 公平的，正义的

justice [2]

[ˈdʒʌstɪs] **n.** 公平，正义；法官

[记] just+ice（**n.**）→ **n.** 公平，正义 → "守护公平、正义的人" → **n.** 法官

[派] injustice [ɪnˈdʒʌstɪs] **n.** 不公正，不公平

justify [5]

[ˈdʒʌstɪfaɪ] **v.** 证明……合理；为……辩护

[记] just+ify（使动）→ "使之公平、合理" → **v.** 证明……合理；为……辩护

[派] justification [ˌdʒʌstɪfɪˈkeɪʃn] **n.** 正当理由，辩解
　　justifiable [ˈdʒʌstɪfaɪəbl] **a.** 有理由的，可证明是正当的
　　unjustifiable [ʌnˈdʒʌstɪfaɪəbl] **a.** 不合理的，无法辩解的

[真] [D] To **justify** government intervention in solving the obesity problem.【2020 年 9 月 仔细阅读 49 题 D 选项】

[译] 为了证明政府通过干预来解决肥胖问题是合理的。

非成组词（I 字母和 J 字母）

interpret [16]

[ɪnˈtɜːprət] **v.** 翻译；解释

[记] inter（between；彼此，互相）+pret（谐音"破译它"）→ "语言之间彼此

破译"→ *v.* 翻译；解释

[派] interpretation [ɪnˌtɜːprəˈteɪʃn] *n.* 解释；翻译
interpreter [ɪnˈtɜːprətə(r)] *n.* 解释者；口译员
misinterpret [ˌmɪsɪnˈtɜːprɪt] *v.* 误解，曲解

[真] [C] It fosters correct **interpretation** of professional writing.【2021 年 6 月 仔细阅读 54 题 C 选项】

[译] 它促进了对专业写作的正确解释。

irony³

[ˈaɪrəni] *n.* 讽刺，反语

[助] i（谐音"爱"）+ro（谐音"wrong"）+ny（谐音"你"）→"爱上你是 wrong 的"；"爱上你是错误的"→ *n.* 讽刺，反语

[派] ironic [aɪˈrɒnɪk] *a.* 讽刺的
ironical [aɪˈrɒnɪkl] *a.* 讽刺的
ironically [aɪˈrɒnɪkli] *ad.* 嘲讽地，挖苦地

[真] Which illustrates the **irony** of the responsibility/fault fallacy: evading responsibility feels comfortable, but turns out to be a prison; whereas assuming responsibility feels unpleasant, but ends up being freeing.【2020 年 12 月 仔细阅读】

[译] 这说明了责任/过错谬误的讽刺之处：逃避责任让人感觉舒服，但结果证明那是一座牢笼；而承担责任让人不开心，但最终可以获得解脱。

issue²⁴

[ˈɪʃuː] *v.* 发行；流出 *n.* 发行（物）；问题

[助] 谐音"印出"→ *v.* 发行；流出 *n.* 发行（物）；问题

[真] My company's managers tend to be accommodating and kind, overlooking mistakes or **issues** so as not to hurt feelings.【2021 年 6 月 听力原文】

[译] 我们公司的管理者往往比较随和、友好，为了不伤感情而忽略错误或问题。

journal²

[ˈdʒɜːnl] *n.* 日志，日记；杂志，期刊

[记] jour（改写自 tour；旅行）+n（无义）+al（*n.*）→最早表示"旅行"时写的→ *n.* 日志，日记；后引申为→ *n.* 杂志，期刊

–labor– 努力，劳动

labo(u)r⁸

[ˈleɪbə] *v.&n.* 劳动，劳作

[助] 谐音"累不"→"干了这么多活，累不累啊？"→ *v.&n.* 劳动，劳作

[派] laborious [ləˈbɔːriəs] *a.* 费力的，辛苦的

[真] Leisure, thus conceived, is hard **labour**, and returning to work becomes a well-earned break from the ordeal.【2020 年 12 月 仔细阅读】

[译] 因此，休闲被认为是一种艰苦的劳动，而重返工作岗位则成为一种摆脱苦难的理所应当的休息。

Day 13

laboratory [2] [ləˈbɒrətri] *n.* 实验室（简称 lab）

［记］labor+at（无义）+ory（表示地点）→ "劳动、努力的地方" → *n.* 实验室

collaborate [4] [kəˈlæbəreɪt] *v.* 合作，协作；勾结

［记］col（共同，全部）+labor+ate（*v.*）→ "共同劳动"，彼此之间需要→ *v.* 合作，协作 → "与坏人合作"，就是→ *v.* 勾结

［派］collaboration [kəˌlæbəˈreɪʃn] *n.* 合作，协作；勾结
collaborative [kəˈlæbərətɪv] *a.* 合作的，协作的

［考］collaborate with... 与……合作/协作/勾结
collaborate on... 就……合作/协作/勾结

［真］It seems to help us to course correct, improve and meet challenges while also building teams that **collaborate** and care for one another.【2021 年 6 月 听力原文】

［译］这样似乎可以帮助我们纠正错误、提升自我并迎接挑战，同时也使团队成员之间互相协作、互相关心。

elaborate [2] [ɪˈlæbərət] [ɪˈlæbəreɪt] *a.* 精心制作的，详尽的 *v.* 详尽说明

［记］e（out）+labor+ate（*a.&v.*）→ "从劳动中出来的"；费了好大劲出来的→ *a.* 精心制作的，详尽的 *v.* 详尽说明

［派］elaboration [ɪˌlæbəˈreɪʃn] *n.* 精心制作；详尽描述

-lect-、-leg-、-lig-

①选择

select [16] [sɪˈlekt] *v.* 选择，挑选

［记］se（away；离开）+lect → "选择后，剩下的离开" → *v.* 选择，挑选

［派］selection [sɪˈlekʃn] *n.* 挑选，可供选择的人或物
selective [sɪˈlektɪv] *a.* 挑选的，选择的
selectively [sɪˈlektɪvli] *ad.* 有选择地

［真］Yet the paper does say children are "unintentionally genetically **selected**" by the school system.【2021 年 6 月 仔细阅读】

［译］然而，该论文确实说明孩子们被学校系统 "无意中进行了基因选择"。

neglect [4] [nɪˈɡlekt] *v.&n.* 忽略，忽视

［记］neg（否定）+lect → "不选" 是对被选举人的→ *v.* 忽略，忽视

［派］negligible [ˈneɡlɪdʒəbl] *a.* 可以忽略的，无足轻重的

［真］What may account for the **neglect** of sustainability in the USDA's Dietary Guidelines according to the author?【2020 年 12 月 仔细阅读 54 题题干】

［译］根据作者，什么可以解释美国农业部的饮食指南中对可持续性的忽视呢？

095

collect [16]

[kəˈlekt] *v.* 收集，收藏

[记] col（全部，共同）+lect → "喜欢的全选" → *v.* 收集，收藏

[派] collection [kəˈlekʃn] *n.* 收集，收藏品
collective [kəˈlektɪv] *a.* 共有的，集体的

[真] [A] It **collected** feedback from both employers and employees.【2021 年 6 月听力 18 题 A 选项】

[译] 它收集了来自雇主和员工的反馈。

intellect [10]

[ˈɪntəlekt] *n.* 智力；有才智的人，知识分子

[记] intel（联想成 Intel，英特尔）+lect → "英特尔选人才"；选什么人？当然是→ *n.* 有才智的人，知识分子→ *n.* 智力

[派] intellectual [ˌɪntəˈlektʃuəl] *a.* 智力的；有才智的 *n.* 知识分子
intelligence [ɪnˈtelɪdʒəns] *n.* 智力；智能
intelligent [ɪnˈtelɪdʒənt] *a.* 聪明的，明智的

[真] Something as complex as **intellect** is likely to be affected by many factors beyond genes.【2021 年 6 月 仔细阅读】

[译] 像智力这样复杂的东西可能受到基因以外的许多因素的影响。

elegant [4]

[ˈelɪɡənt] *a.* 有气质的；优雅的，优美的

[记] e（out）+leg+ant（表示人的后缀）→ "此人可以被选出来"，因为此人是 → *a.* 有气质的；优雅的，优美的

[派] elegance [ˈelɪɡəns] *n.* 高雅，优雅；简练

[真] Marconi's career was devoted to making wireless communication happen cheaply, efficiently, smoothly, and with an **elegance** that would appear to be intuitive and uncomplicated to the user—user-friendly, if you will.【2021 年 6 月 长篇阅读 E 选项】

[译] 马可尼在其职业生涯中一直致力于使无线通信变得便宜、高效、流畅，且对用户而言具有直观和简明的优点——或者说做到对用户友好。

②法律

legal [4]

[ˈliːɡl] *a.* 法律的，合法的

[记] leg+al（*a.*）→ *a.* 法律的，合法的

[派] legally [ˈliːɡəli] *ad.* 法律上，合法地
illegal [ɪˈliːɡl] *a.* 不合法的，非法的

[真] **Legally**, a person's rights to control the commercial use of their name and image beyond their death differ between and even within countries.【2021 年 6 月 长篇阅读 G 选项】

[译] 从法律上讲，在不同的国家，甚至是同一国家里，一个人在死亡后对其姓名和肖像的商业使用控制权都是不同的。

Day 13

legislate ³

[ˈledʒɪsleɪt] *v.* 立法，制定法律

[记] leg+is（是，成为）+l（无义）+ate（*v.*）→ "使之是法律、成为法律" → *v.* 立法，制定法律

[派] legislation [ˌledʒɪsˈleɪʃn] *n.* 立法，制定法律
legislative [ˈledʒɪslətɪv] *a.* 立法的

[真] Nicola Sturgeon's speech last Tuesday setting out the Scottish government's **legislative** programme for the year ahead confirmed what was already pretty clear.【2021 年 6 月 仔细阅读】

[译] 上周二，尼古拉·斯特金在其演说中阐明了苏格兰政府未来一年的立法方案，证实了一个已然相当清晰的事实。

oblige ⁸

[əˈblaɪdʒ] *v.* 强迫，强制

[记] ob（相反）+lig+e（无义）→ "与法律相反，与法律相对"；法律具有强制性→ *v.* 强迫，强制

[派] obligation [ˌɒblɪˈɡeɪʃn] *n.* 义务，责任
obligatory [əˈblɪɡətri] *a.* 义务的，强制的

[考] oblige sb. to do sth. 强迫某人做某事

[真] When you're feeling hard done by—taken for granted by your partner, say, or **obliged** to work for a half-witted boss—it's easy to become attached to the position that it's not your job to address the matter, and that doing so would be an admission of fault.【2020 年 12 月 仔细阅读】

[译] 当你认为自己受到不公正待遇时，如被你的伴侣视为理所当然，或者被迫为一个愚蠢的老板工作，你很容易就对这个情境产生了依恋：解决这个问题不是你的工作，否则就是承认自己错了。

扫码快速学习

扫码即刻听课

① 举起，抬起

lift [2]

[lɪft] *v.* 举起，抬起　*n.* 电梯

六级基础词汇

level [23]

[ˈlevl] *n.* 标准，水平

[记] lev+el（*n.*）→ "举起的高度" → *n.* 标准，水平

[真] [A] It is a must for maintaining a base **level** of brain activity.【2021 年 6 月 仔细阅读 49 题 A 选项】

[译] 这是维持大脑活动基本水平的必要条件。

elevate [3]

[ˈelɪveɪt] *v.* 举起；提高，提升

[记] e（out）+lev+ate（*v.*）→ *v.* 举起 → "把职位举起、抬起" → *v.* 提高，提升

[派] elevation [ˌelɪˈveɪʃn] *n.* 高处；升级；上进
　　elevator [ˈelɪveɪtə(r)] *n.* 电梯

[真] [A] **elevate** its tourism to international standards.【2021 年 6 月 仔细阅读 53 题 A 选项】

[译] 将其旅游业提升到国际标准。

levy [3]

[ˈlevi] *v.* 征收　*n.* 征兵，征税

[记] lev+y（无义）→ *v.* 征收　*n.* 征兵，征税

[真] What are UK people's opinions about the **levy** of tourist tax?【2021 年 6 月 仔细阅读 55 题题干】

[译] 英国人民对征收旅游税有什么看法？

relevant [8]

[ˈreləvənt] *a.* 有关的，相关的

[记] re（反复）+lev+ant（*a.*）→ 说 A 的时候，"反复提起" B，说明 A 与 B 一

定是 → *a.* 有关的，相关的

[派] relevance [ˈreləvəns] *n.* 意义；相关性
　　　irrelevant [ɪˈreləvənt] *a.* 不相关的，无关的

[考] be relevant to... 与……有关/相关

[真] [A] Take all **relevant** factors into account in interpreting their data.【2021年6月 仔细阅读49题A选项】

[译] 在解释他们的数据时，应考虑所有相关因素。

② 轻的

alleviate [6]
[əˈliːvieɪt] *v.* 减轻；缓和

[记] al（to）+lev+i（无义）+ate（*v.*）→ "去变得轻" → *v.* 减轻；缓和

[派] alleviation [əˌliːviˈeɪʃn] *n.* 减轻；缓解

[真] [A] They can help to **alleviate** traffic jams.【2021年6月 仔细阅读52题A选项】

[译] 它们有助于缓解交通堵塞。

relieve [4]
[rɪˈliːv] *v.* 减轻；缓解，宽慰

[记] re（反复）+liev（改写自lev）+e（无义）→ "反复变轻" → *v.* 减轻 → "压力、痛苦的减轻" → *v.* 缓解，宽慰

[派] relief [rɪˈliːf] *n.* 减轻；缓解；解除

[真] [C] It is conducive to **relieving** mental exhaustion.【2020年12月 听力21题C选项】

[译] 它有利于缓解精神衰竭。

–liber– 自由

liberate [3]
[ˈlɪbəreɪt] *v.* 使自由，解放，释放

[记] liber+ate（*v.*）→ *v.* 使自由，解放，释放

[派] liberation [ˌlɪbəˈreɪʃn] *n.* 解放，释放

[真] [B] She proved we could **liberate** ourselves from sleep.【2020年9月 仔细阅读47题B选项】

[译] 她证明了我们可以把自己从睡眠中解放出来。

liberty [2]
[ˈlɪbəti] *n.* 自由

[记] liber+ty（*n.*）→ *n.* 自由

deliberate [3]
[dɪˈlɪbərət] [dɪˈlɪbəreɪt] *a.* 故意的；从容谨慎的　*v.* 仔细考虑

[记] de（下）+liber+ate（*a.*&*v.*）→ "自由度下降，不能随心所欲"，说话需要 → *a.* 故意的；从容谨慎的　*v.* 仔细考虑

［派］deliberately [dɪˈlɪbərətli] *ad.* 故意地
deliberation [dɪˌlɪbəˈreɪʃn] *n.* 考虑，深思熟虑
［真］[C] **Deliberate** the consequences that may occur.【2021 年 6 月 听力 6 题 C 选项】
［译］考虑一下可能出现的后果。

–light–

①轻的

flight [6]

[flaɪt] *n.* 飞行；航班

［记］fl（简写自 fly；飞）+ight（简写自 light）→"轻轻地飞起来"→ *n.* 飞行；航班

［真］Can you guess what she did? She didn't take that **flight**.【2020 年 9 月 听力原文】
［译］你猜她做了什么？她没有乘坐那架飞机。

slight [3]

[slaɪt] *a.* 轻微的；不足道的；瘦小的

［记］s（谐音"死"）+light →惩罚"死轻的"→ *a.* 轻微的；不足道的→体重"死轻的"→ *a.* 瘦小的

［派］slightly [ˈslaɪtli] *ad.* 轻微地；苗条地
［真］The research of Gigi Luk at Harvard offers a **slightly** different explanation.【2020 年 9 月 长篇阅读 K 选项】
［译］哈佛大学吉吉·卢克的研究提供了一个略有不同的解释。

delight [2]

[dɪˈlaɪt] *v.&n.*（使）高兴，快乐

［记］de（下）+light →"向下变轻"；减肥时体重向下变得很轻，会是什么心情？→ *v.&n.*（使）高兴，快乐
［派］delightful [dɪˈlaɪtfl] *a.* 使人快乐的

②灯，光

plight [3]

[plaɪt] *n.* 困境；誓约

［记］p（谐音"扑"）+light →"扑灭灯光，一片黑暗"；陷入→ *n.* 困境→"人在困境下喜欢发誓"→ *n.* 誓约
［真］Le Bohec said: "The **plight** of the king penguin should serve as a warning about the future of the entire marine environment in the Antarctic."【2019 年 12 月 仔细阅读】
［译］勒波赫克说："帝企鹅的困境应该作为对南极整个海洋环境未来的一个警告。"

Day 14

highlight [3]
[ˈhaɪlaɪt] *v.* 突出，强调

[记] high（*a.* 高的）+light → "高处的灯光"；舞台剧里，为了凸显某个场景，会突然全场黑灯，然后从高处打出一束追光灯，照在主持人或嘉宾身上，所以"高处的灯光"表示→ *v.* 突出，强调

[真] [C] To **highlight** the area deserving the most attention from the public.【2020年9月仔细阅读49题C选项】

[译] 为了突出这个最值得公众关注的地区。

bright [2]
[braɪt] *a.* 明亮的，辉煌的；聪明的

[记] br（简写自 bring；带来）+ight（简写自 light）→ "带来了光亮、光明"→ *a.* 明亮的，辉煌的→ "头脑很亮，很辉煌"→ *a.* 聪明的

–liter– 文字

literature [4]
[ˈlɪtrətʃə(r)] *n.* 文学；文献

[记] liter+a（无义）+ture（谐音"扯"）→ "能扯出很多文字"的人，不仅仅是识字，还能写出→ *n.* 文学；文献

[真] A new study had drawn a bleak picture of cultural inclusiveness reflected in the children's **literature** available in Australia.【2021年6月选词填空】

[译] 一项新研究描绘了澳大利亚儿童文学中反映的文化包容性较弱的状况。

literary [2]
[ˈlɪtərəri] *a.* 文学的，文学上的

[记] 上词 literature 的形容词→ *a.* 文学的，文学上的

–loc– 地点，地方

allocate [2]
[ˈæləkeɪt] *v.* 分配，分派

[记] al（to）+loc+ate（*v.*）→ "去……地方"；让东西去……地方→ *v.* 分配→ 让人去……地方→ *v.* 分派

[派] allocation [ˌæləˈkeɪʃn] *n.* 分配，分派

local [22]
[ˈləʊkl] *a.* 本地的，当地的 *n.* 本地人

[记] loc+al（*a.*&*n.*）→ "就是这个地方的人"→ *a.* 本地的，当地的 *n.* 本地人

[派] locally [ˈləʊkəli] *ad.* 在附近，在本地
　　locality [ləʊˈkæləti] *n.* 位置，地区

[真] Patillo Higgins, a disreputable **local** businessman, became convinced that there was oil below the gassy hill.【2021年6月听力原文】

[译] 当地声名狼藉的商人帕蒂罗·希金斯确信，在充满气体的山下有石油。

locate [12]

[ləʊˈkeɪt] *v.* 位于；定位，查找

[记] loc+ate（*v.*）→ 查看"地点"的动作 → *v.* 位于；定位，查找

[派] location [ləʊˈkeɪʃn] *n.* 位置，场所

relocate [ˌriːləʊˈkeɪt] *v.* 迁徙；重新安置

[考] be located in... 坐落于……，位于……

[真] Currently, doctors must have a valid license in the state where the patient is **located** to provide medical care, which means virtual-visit companies can match users only with locally licensed clinicians.【2020 年 9 月 长篇阅读 N 选项】

[译] 目前，医生必须拥有患者所在州的有效许可证才可以提供医疗服务，这意味着网络医疗公司只能将用户与获得当地许可证的临床医生进行匹配。

–log– 说话

logic [2]

[ˈlɒdʒɪk] *n.* 逻辑，逻辑学

[记] 音译词

[派] logical [ˈlɒdʒɪkl] *a.* 逻辑的，符合逻辑的

apology [2]

[əˈpɒlədʒi] *n.* 道歉，认错

[记] ap（谐音"挨批"）+o（无义）+ log+y（*n.*）→ "挨批时说的话"→ *n.* 道歉，认错

[派] apologize/ise [əˈpɒlədʒaɪz] *v.* 道歉，认错

[考] apologize to sb. for sth. 因为某事向某人道歉

lobby [4]

[ˈlɒbi] *v.* 游说，陈情 *n.* 游说团

[记] lob（改写自 log）+by（无义）→ "说话"就是→ *v.* 游说，陈情 *n.* 游说团

[真] Some UK cities have **lobbied** without success for the power to levy a charge on visitors.【2021 年 6 月 仔细阅读】

[译] 一些英国城市曾游说，要求有权对游客收费，但没有成功。

–logy– 学科

ideology [6]

[ˌaɪdiˈɒlədʒi] *n.* 思想体系，意识形态

[记] ideo（改写自 idea；思想，想法）+logy → "每个人思想、想法的学科"，个人独立的思想、想法的学科，在这样的想法下形成自身判断事物的标准→ *n.* 思想体系，意识形态

[派] ideological [ˌaɪdiəˈlɒdʒɪkl] *a.* 思想的，意识形态的

[真] [B] When **ideological** differences are resolved.【2020 年 9 月 仔细阅读 50 题 B 选项】

[译] 当意识形态上的分歧得到解决时。

Day 14

psychology [24] [saɪˈkɒlədʒi] *n.* 心理学

[记] 词根 psycho（心灵，精神；来自希腊罗马神话里的心灵和智慧女神 Psyche）+logy → *n.* 心理学
[派] psychologist [saɪˈkɒlədʒɪst] *n.* 心理学家，心理医生
psychological [ˌsaɪkəˈlɒdʒɪkl] *a.* 心理的，精神的
[真] **Psychology** research has shown that the emotions that we experience as teens seem more intense than those that come later.【2020 年 12 月 听力原文】
[译] 心理学研究表明，我们青少年时期经历的情感似乎比之后的更强烈。

psychology 的引申词

psychiatry [3] [saɪˈkaɪətri] *n.* 精神病学

[记] psych（简写自 psycho；心灵，精神）+ia（表示病的后缀）+try（*v.* 尝试）→ "在精神疾病方面的尝试" → *n.* 精神病学
[派] psychiatrist [saɪˈkaɪətrɪst] *n.* 精神病学家；精神科医生
[真] **Psychiatrists** have a higher incidence of suicide in their profession for related reasons.【2020 年 9 月 听力原文】
[译] 出于职业相关原因，精神病医生自杀概率会更高。

–lum–、–lus–、–lux– 光线，光明

illusion [2] [ɪˈluːʒn] *n.* 幻觉，错觉

[记] il（否定）+lus+ion（*n.*）→ "没有光线、光明"，看不清楚，所以产生 → *n.* 幻觉，错觉
[派] illusory [ɪˈluːsəri] *a.* 幻觉的；迷惑人的

illustrate [6] [ˈɪləstreɪt] *v.* 说明，表明

[记] il（改写自 in；里）+lus+tr（无义）+ate（*v.*）→ "使之进入光线、光明里"；本来一片黑暗看不清方向，我三言两语就让你看到光明，豁然开朗 → *v.* 说明，表明
[派] illustration [ˌɪləˈstreɪʃn] *n.* 说明，表明，例证
[真] What does the author try to **illustrate** with the example of the newborn on one's doorstep?【2020 年 12 月 仔细阅读 52 题题干】
[译] 作者试图用新生儿站在一个人家门口的例子来说明什么？

非成组词（L 字母）

launch [12] [lɔːntʃ] *v.&n.* 发射；发起，发动

［记］laun（改写自 lance；长矛）+ch（发音）→ 原指掷出长矛，后引申为 → *v.&n.* 发射；发起，发动

［真］Goddard later consulted with a weather expert and determined that the climate of New Mexico was ideal for year-round rocket **launches**.【2021 年 6 月 听力原文】

［译］戈达德后来咨询了气象专家，确定新墨西哥州的气候全年都适合发射火箭。

leak [2]

[li:k] *v.&n.* 泄露；（有）漏洞

［助］谐音"力磕"→ 用力磕，"露出来了"→ *v.&n.* 泄露；（有）漏洞

［派］leakage [ˈli:kɪdʒ] *n.* 泄露

legacy [4]

[ˈlegəsi] *n.* 遗产

［记］leg（改写自 leave；留）+acy（*n.*）→ "留下来的东西"→ *n.* 遗产

［真］And what is in the best interest of a deceased person's **legacy** may conflict with the desires of their family or the public, says Edwards.【2021 年 6 月 长篇阅读 G 选项】

［译］爱德华兹说，逝者遗产的最大利益可能会与其家人或公众的愿望相冲突。

load [4]

[ləʊd] *v.* 装载，负载 *n.* 负载，装载量

［记］改写自 road（路，道路）→ "路上"的车→ *v.* 装载，负载 *n.* 负载，装载量

［派］download [ˌdaʊnˈləʊd] [ˈdaʊnləʊd] *v.* 下载 *n.* 已下载的数据资料
　　 unload [ˌʌnˈləʊd] *v.* 卸货；清除负担

［真］The 240 giant autonomous trucks in use, in the Western Australian mines, can weigh 400 tons, fully **loaded**, and travel at speeds of up to sixty kilometers per hour.【2021 年 6 月 听力原文】

［译］在西澳大利亚矿山使用的 240 辆巨型自动驾驶卡车，满载时可重达 400 吨，并以高达每小时 60 千米的速度行驶。

lucrative [2]

[ˈlu:krətɪv] *a.* 获利多的，赚钱的

［记］lucra（改写自 lucre；金钱，利润）+tive（*a.*）→ *a.* 获利多的，赚钱的

［助］谐音"掳可多"→ "掳掠了很多钱"

扫码快速学习

Day 15

扫码即刻听课

–man–、–manu– 手

manufacture [2] [ˌmænjuˈfæktʃə(r)] *v.&n.* 制造，加工

[记] manu+fact（做）+ure（*v.&n.*）→ "用手做的动作"；用手做出设备、产品→ *v.&n.* 制造，加工

[派] manufacturer [ˌmænjuˈfæktʃərə(r)] *n.* 制造商，制造厂

manipulate [6] [məˈnɪpjuleɪt] *v.* 操作，控制

[记] man+i（无义）+pul（简写自 pull；拉）+ate（*v.*）→ "用手拉的动作"；用手推拉仪器、设备→ *v.* 操作，控制

[派] manipulation [məˌnɪpjuˈleɪʃn] *n.* 操作，控制
manipulative [məˈnɪpjələtɪv] *a.* 操作的

[真] We don't have the strength of chimpanzees because we've given up animal strength to **manipulate** subtle instruments, like hammers, spears, and—later—pens and pencils.【2021 年 6 月 仔细阅读】

[译] 我们没有大猩猩的力量，因为我们已经放弃了动物的野蛮力量，选择去操纵精密仪器，例如锤子、长矛，还有后来的钢笔和铅笔。

–mark– 标记

mark [10] [mɑːk] *v.* 标记 *n.* 记号；分数

六级基础词汇

[助] 谐音 "马克" → "马克" 笔有什么用？→ *v.* 标记 *n.* 记号；分数

remark [4] [rɪˈmɑːk] *v.&n.* 评论

[记] re（反复）+mark → "反复标记之后" → *v.&n.* 评论

[派] remarkable [rɪˈmɑːkəbl] *a.* 值得评论的；异常的；引人注目的
remarkably [rɪˈmɑːkəbli] *ad.* 引人注目地；非常地

[真] That last statement was the most instructive because, as the researchers found, there was a **remarkably** strong correlation between how helpful supervisors were perceived to be, and how likely their employees were to follow their directors.【2021年6月 听力原文】

[译] 研究人员发现，最后一项最有启发性，因为员工认为的得到上司的帮助程度与他们听从上司指示的可能性之间存在显著的强相关性。

–med–、–mid– 中间

media 26　['miːdiə] *n.* 媒体；媒介

[记] med+ia（*n.*）→ "中间的东西"→夹在明星与老百姓中间的→ *n.* 媒体→上课时能听见老师讲话，是因为有空气在中间作为→ *n.* 媒介

[考] social media 社交媒体

[真] News of Notre Dame Cathedral catastrophe instantly caught **media** attention throughout the world.【2021年6月 长篇阅读45题】

[译] 巴黎圣母院大灾难的消息立即引起了全世界媒体的关注。

immediate 13　[ɪ'miːdiət] *a.* 立即的；直接的

[记] im（否定）+med+i（无义）+ate（*a.*）→ "没有中间过程的"→ *a.* 立即的；直接的

[派] immediately [ɪ'miːdiətli] *ad.* 立即，马上；直接地

[真] [C] It may displease his **immediate** superiors.【2021年6月 听力3题C选项】

[译] 这可能会使他的直接上级不高兴。

intermediate 2　[ˌɪntə'miːdiət] *a.* 中间的，中级的

[记] inter（between）+med+i（无义）+ate（*a.*）→ *a.* 中间的，中级的

[派] intermediary [ˌɪntə'miːdiəri] *n.* 中间人；媒介

amid 2　[ə'mɪd] *prep.* 在……中间，在……之中

[记] a（to）+mid → *prep.* 在……中间，在……之中

–mod– 样式，模式

mode 2　[məʊd] *n.* 方式；模式

[记] mod+e（无义）→ *n.* 方式；模式

accommodate 6　[ə'kɒmədeɪt] *v.* 使适应；容纳

[记] ac（to）+com（共同，全部）+mod+ate（*v.*）→ "去让所有人接受这种模式"→ *v.* 使适应→ "去让所有人进入这种模式"→ *v.* 容纳

[派] accommodation [əˌkɒmə'deɪʃn] *n.* 适应；住处

[真] But I found myself moving from one **accommodation** to another, trying to find the perfect place.【2021年6月 听力原文】

Day 15

[译] 但我发现自己总是在从一个住处搬到另一个住处，试图找到一个完美的地方。

commodity [3] [kəˈmɒdəti] *n.* 商品，日用品

[记] com（共同，全部）+mod+ity（*n.*）→ "大家共同买的样式" → *n.* 商品，日用品

[真] In this oversubscribed society, experience becomes a **commodity** like any other.【2020 年 12 月 仔细阅读】

[译] 在这个供不应求的社会里，体验和其他东西一样变成了商品。

–mem– 记忆

remember [6] [rɪˈmembə(r)] *v.* 记得

六级基础词汇

[记] re（反复）+mem+ber（无义）→ "反复记忆" → *v.* 记得

memory [16] [ˈmeməri] *n.* 记忆，记忆力；[计] 存储器，内存

[记] mem+ory（表示地点）→ 人 "记忆数据的地方" → *n.* 记忆，记忆力→计算机 "记忆数据的地方" → *n.* [计] 存储器，内存

[真] [D] It helps improve concentration and **memory**.【2021 年 6 月 仔细阅读 49 题 D 选项】

[译] 它有助于提高注意力和记忆力。

memorable [3] [ˈmemərəbl] *a.* 值得纪念的，难忘的

[记] mem+or（表示人或物的后缀）+able（*a.* 能……的）→ "能够记住的" → *a.* 值得纪念的，难忘的

[真] [A] It was **memorable**.【2021 年 6 月 听力 8 题 A 选项】

[译] 它令人难忘。

monument [6] [ˈmɒnjumənt] *n.* 纪念碑，纪念馆

[记] mon（改写自 mem）+u（无义）+ment（*n.*）→ "记忆某个人的东西" → *n.* 纪念碑，纪念馆

[派] monumental [ˌmɒnjuˈmentl] *a.* 纪念碑上的；不朽的

[真] "We've been saying for years that the budget for maintaining historic **monuments** is too low," Gady said.【2021 年 6 月 长篇阅读 K 选项】

[译] 加迪表示："多年来，我们一直强调维护这座历史纪念馆的预算太低了。"

–ment– 思想，想法

mental [26] [ˈmentl] *a.* 思想的，智力的；精神的，内心的

[记] ment+al（*a.*）→ *a.* 思想的，智力的→ "思想上想太多"；精神上容易出问

题 → *a.* 精神的，内心的

[派] mentally [ˈmentəli] *ad.* 智力上；心理上，精神上
mentality [menˈtæləti] *n.* 心态

[考] mental health 心理健康

[真] All of us benefit from it and we thrive **mentally** and spiritually when we are able to wield it.【2021 年 6 月 仔细阅读】

[译] 我们所有人都因它受益，当我们能够驾驭它时，我们在智力上和精神上都会茁壮成长。

mention ⁶   [ˈmenʃn] *v.&n.* 提及，提到

[记] ment+ion（*n.&v.*）→ "想起某个人或某件事了"，就会 → *v.&n.* 提及，提到

[派] mentioned [ˈmenʃnd] *a.* 被提及的
unmentioned [ʌnˈmenʃnd] *a.* 未被提及的

[真] Ms. Wilson, according to the notes on your account, the bizarre technical detail that you **mentioned** refers to the fact that you hadn't paid house insurance the month before the incident.【2020 年 12 月 听力原文】

[译] 威尔逊女士，根据您的账户记录，您刚才提到的奇怪的技术细节指的是在事发前一个月您没有缴纳房屋保险。

comment ⁹   [ˈkɒment] *v.&n.* 评论

[记] com（加强）+ment → "加强地想"；通俗说法就是想好了，想仔细了，之后才会 → *v.&n.* 评论

[派] commentary [ˈkɒməntri] *n.* 评论性文章；评论
commentator [ˈkɒmənteɪtə(r)] *n.* 评论员

[考] comment on... 就……评论

[真] Why do people post **comments** selectively on social media?【2020 年 12 月 仔细阅读 47 题题干】

[译] 为什么人们会在社交媒体上有选择性地发表评论？

recommend ¹⁶   [ˌrekəˈmend] *v.* 推荐，建议

[记] re（反复）+commend（*v.* 推荐）→ "反复推荐" → *v.* 推荐，建议

[派] recommendation [ˌrekəmenˈdeɪʃn] *n.* 推荐，建议；推荐信

[考] recommend sth. to sb. 向某人推荐某物

[真] [C] The dietary **recommendations** are not based on medical science.【2020 年 12 月 仔细阅读 51 题 C 选项】

[译] 这些饮食建议并不是基于医学科学而提出的。

recommend 的引申词

remind ¹⁰   [rɪˈmaɪnd] *v.* 提醒，使想起

[记] re（back）+mind → "思考回去；想起来，想到过去的事" → *v.* 提醒，使

Day 15

想起

[派] reminder [rɪˈmaɪndə(r)] *n.* 令人回忆起……的东西；提醒……的东西；（告知该做某事的）通知单；提示信

[考] remind sb. to do sth. 提醒某人做某事
remind sb. of sth. 提醒某人某事

[真] I was **reminded** of this again recently listening to an interview with Nicole Haddow, the author of *Smashed Avocado*, explaining how she cracked the property market at 31.【2021年6月 选词填空】

[译] 最近在听《牛油果泥》的作者妮可·哈多的采访时，我再次想起了这一点，她解释了她如何在31岁时进入房地产市场。

–mer– 经商，商业

commerce [9] [ˈkɒmɜːs] *n.* 商业，贸易

[记] com（加强）+mer+ce（*n.*）→ *n.* 商业，贸易

[派] commercial [kəˈmɜːʃl] *a.* 商业（化）的 *n.* 商业广告

[真] Legally, a person's rights to control the **commercial** use of their name and image beyond their death differ between and even within countries.【2021年6月 长篇阅读G选项】

[译] 从法律上讲，在不同的国家，甚至是同一国家里，一个人在死亡后对其姓名和肖像的商业使用控制权都是不同的。

merit [2] [ˈmerɪt] *n.* 优点；价值 *v.* 值得

[助] 谐音"marry他" → "嫁给他"，因为他有→ *n.* 优点；价值 *v.* 值得

–minis– 管理，经营

minister [4] [ˈmɪnɪstə(r)] *n.* 大臣，部长

[记] minis+t（无义）+er（表示人的后缀）→ "管理人员"；国家的管理人员→ *n.* 大臣，部长

[派] ministry [ˈmɪnɪstri] *n.*（政府的）部门

[真] The interior **minister**, Christophe Castaner, visited the cathedral on Tuesday afternoon to see the extent of the devastation.【2021年6月 长篇阅读I选项】

[译] 内政部部长克里斯托夫·卡斯塔纳于周二下午视察了大教堂，了解其损毁的情况。

administration [4] [ədˌmɪnɪˈstreɪʃn] *n.* 管理（部门），行政（部门）

[记] ad（to）+minis+tr（无义）+ation（*n.*）→ *n.* 管理（部门），行政（部门）

[派] administrative [ədˈmɪnɪstrətɪv] *a.* 管理的，行政的

[真] A time-determined revalidation would ease **administration** for everybody.【2020 年 12 月 长篇阅读 L 选项】
[译] 在一段时间内重新验证将会简化每个人的管理。

–mis– 否定，不

mislead [2]
[ˌmɪsˈliːd] v. 误导，使……误入歧途

[记] mis+lead（v. 引领，引导）→ "被人否定地引领、引导，或者不好地引导" → v. 误导，使……误入歧途

[派] misleading [ˌmɪsˈliːdɪŋ] a. 误导性的，骗人的

misery [2]
[ˈmɪzəri] n. 痛苦，悲惨，不幸

[记] mis+er（表示人的后缀）+y（n.）→ "不是人"；过着不是人的生活→ n. 痛苦，悲惨，不幸

[派] miserable [ˈmɪzrəbl] a. 痛苦的，悲惨的

–max–、–maj– 大 –min– 小

maximum [2]
[ˈmæksɪməm] a. 最大的，最大值的　n. 最大值

[记] max+im（无义）+um（n.）→ a. 最大的，最大值的　n. 最大值

[派] maximize/ise [ˈmæksɪmaɪz] v. 使最大，最大化

major [20]
[ˈmeɪdʒə(r)] a. 较大的，较多的；主要的　n. 专业　v. 以……为专业

[记] maj+or（比较级后缀）→ a. 较大的，较多的；主要的→ n. 专业　v. 以……为专业

[派] majority [məˈdʒɒrəti] n. 大多数

[考] major in...　以……为专业
　　　the majority of　大多数

[真] [B] It gives the **majority** of students ready access to their teachers.【2021 年 6 月 听力 10 题 B 选项】
[译] 它让大多数学生随时都可以接触到他们的老师。

minimal [2]
[ˈmɪnɪməl] a. 最小的，极少的

[记] min+im（无义）+al（a.）→ a. 最小的，极少的

[派] minimize/ise [ˈmɪnɪmaɪz] v. 使最小，使达到最小值；贬低

[真] It was specifically stressful work environments, **minimal** training, and a lack of accountability that were found to be the most blame worthy.【2021 年 6 月 听力原文】
[译] 尤其是压力大的工作环境、最简单的培训和问责制的缺失被认为是最应受到指责的。

Day 15

minor [10]
[ˈmaɪnə(r)] *a.* 较小的，较少的；次要的

[记] min+or（比较级后缀）→ *a.* 较小的，较少的；次要的

[派] minority [maɪˈnɒrəti] *n.* 少数，少数人

[真] The EAT report presumes that "traditional diets" in countries like India include little red meat, which might be consumed only on special occasions or as **minor** ingredients in mixed dishes.【2020 年 12 月 仔细阅读】

[译] EAT 报告推测，诸如印度等国家的"传统饮食"中含有的红肉量较少，红肉可能只在一些特殊场合食用，或作为混合菜肴的配菜。

diminish [3]
[dɪˈmɪnɪʃ] *v.* 减小，缩小

[记] di（散）+min+ish（*v.*）→ "分散、变小的动作" → *v.* 减小，缩小

[真] [A] It **diminishes** laymen's interest in science.【2021 年 6 月 听力 9 题 A 选项】

[译] 它降低了外行人对科学的兴趣。

①思念，错过

miss [10]
[mɪs] *n.*（用于姓名或姓之前，对未婚女子的称呼）小姐；女士 *v.* 思念；错过

六级基础词汇

[派] missing [ˈmɪsɪŋ] *a.* 丢失的；漏掉的

dismiss [3]
[dɪsˈmɪs] *v.* 解雇；解散；不受理，不理会

[记] dis（否定）+miss（*v.* 思念）→公司、企业"不再思念你了"→ *v.* 解雇；解散→法官"不再思念你了"→ *v.* 不受理，不理会

[派] dismissal [dɪsˈmɪsl] *n.* 解雇；解散；不受理，不理会

[真] [C] They constantly **dismiss** others' proposals while taking no responsibility for tackling the problem.【2020 年 12 月 仔细阅读 51 题 C 选项】

[译] 他们经常拒绝别人的建议，而不承担解决这个问题的责任。

imitate [10]
[ˈɪmɪteɪt] *v.* 模仿，仿效

[记] 来自拉丁语 imitari（复制，模仿）→ *v.* 模仿，仿效

[助] im（当成 I'm）+it（它）+ate（*v.*）→我和它做一样的动作→ *v.* 模仿，仿效

[派] imitation [ˌɪmɪˈteɪʃn] *n.* 模仿，仿效

[近] emulate [ˈemjuleɪt] *v.* 模仿，仿效

[真] [A] It encourages people to **imitate**.【2021 年 6 月 仔细阅读 53 题 A 选项】

[译] 它鼓励人们去模仿。

②送，扔

mission [6]
['mɪʃn] *n.* 任务，使命

[记] mis+sion (*n.*) →"把东西送过去就是任务；把人派遣过去就是完成任务"→ *n.* 任务→"高尚的任务"→ *n.* 使命

[真] [C] A weather expert invited him to go there for his **mission**.【2021年6月听力14题C选项】

[译] 一位气象专家邀请他去那里执行任务。

emit [8]
[iˈmɪt] *v.* 发出，发射；散发（光、热等）

[记] e (out)+mit →"送出去，扔出去"→ *v.* 发出，发射；散发（光、热等）

[派] emission [iˈmɪʃn] *n.* 排放，辐射；排放物；散发物（尤指气体）
emitter [ɪˈmɪtə(r)] *n.* 发出者；发射体

[真] Red meats are among the biggest and most notorious **emitters**, but trucking a salad from California to Minnesota in January also carries a significant burden.【2020年12月仔细阅读】

[译] 红肉是其中一种最大、最臭名昭著的排放源，但1月份时，用卡车将沙拉从加利福尼亚州运输到明尼苏达州也给环境带来了沉重的负担。

commit [8]
[kəˈmɪt] *v.* 犯（罪）；做（坏事）；委托；承诺

[记] com（加强语气）+mit →加重语气说"帮我把某物送过去"→ *v.* 委托；承诺

[助] co（谐音"靠"）+mm（谐音"美眉"）+it（它）→"靠mm"；在公交、地铁上，用身体靠美眉，这不就是→ *v.* 犯（罪）；做（坏事）

[派] committee [kəˈmɪti] *n.* 委员会
commitment [kəˈmɪtmənt] *n.* 委托，承诺

[真] So if you want to compliment someone on the work they have done and imitate it, just make sure you do it the right way to avoid **committing** plagiarism.【2021年6月仔细阅读】

[译] 所以，如果你想称赞别人的作品并模仿它，只要确保你以正确的方式去做，从而避免抄袭即可。

commission [8]
[kəˈmɪʃn] *v.* 正式委托 *n.* 委员会

[记] 上词commit的同源词；commis（改写自commit）+sion (*n.*) → *v.* 正式委托→受人委托产生的组织→ *n.* 委员会

[真] One suggestion from the **commission** is a network of teacher-led "creativity collaboratives", along the lines of existing maths hubs（中心）, with the aim of supporting teaching for creativity through the school curriculum.【2021年6月仔细阅读】

[译] 该委员会的一项建议是，按照现有以数学为中心的思路，建立一个由教师主导的"创造力协作"网络，旨在通过学校课程支持创造力教学。

Day 15

submit [6]

[səbˈmɪt] *v.* 上交；服从

[记] sub（下）+mit → "从下面送"上去→ *v.* 上交；服从
[派] submission [səbˈmɪʃn] *n.* 提交；服从
[考] submit sth. to sb. 向某人上交某物
[真] [B] Its researchers have already **submitted** relevant proposals.【2020 年 12 月 仔细阅读 52 题 B 选项】
[译] 研究人员已经提交了相关的建议。

promise [12]

[ˈprɒmɪs] *v.&n.* 许诺，承诺

[助] 谐音 "只要没死" → "只要我不死，我一定会……" → *v.&n.* 许诺，承诺
[派] promising [ˈprɒmɪsɪŋ] *a.* 有前途的，有希望的
[考] promise to do sth. 承诺做某事
　　 make a promise 做出承诺
[真] [B] It seldom delivers all the benefits as **promised**.【2021 年 6 月 仔细阅读 54 题 B 选项】
[译] 它很少像承诺的那样提供所有的好处。

compromise [2]

[ˈkɒmprəmaɪz] *v.&n.* 妥协，让步

[记] com（共同，全部）+promise（*v.&n.* 承诺）→ "共同给出承诺"；彼此做出→ *v.&n.* 妥协，让步
[派] uncompromising [ʌnˈkɒmprəmaɪzɪŋ] *a.* 不妥协的
[考] compromise to sb. for sth. 因为某事向某人妥协

扫码快速学习

扫码即刻听课

-mob-、-mot-、-mat-、-mov- 移动，运动

mobile [4]

[ˈməʊbaɪl] *a.* 可移动的，活动的

[记] mob+ile（*a.*）→ *a.* 可移动的，活动的
[派] mobility [məʊˈbɪləti] *n.* 流动性，移动性
[考] mobile phone　手机
[真] Marconi invented the idea of global communication—or, more straightforwardly, globally networked, **mobile**, wireless communication.【2021 年 6 月长篇阅读 F 选项】
[译] 马可尼发明了全球通信的概念——或者更直接地说，是全球联网的移动无线通信。

motion [4]

[ˈməʊʃn] *n.* 运动

[记] mot+ion（*n.*）→ *n.* 运动
[考] in motion　运动中；兴奋中
[真] Energy systems, like an aircraft carrier set in **motion**, have huge momentum.【2020 年 7 月长篇阅读 41 题】
[译] 能源系统，就像正在启动的航空母舰一样，有巨大的动力。

motivate [22]

[ˈməʊtɪveɪt] *v.* 使有动机，激发

[记] motiv（简写自 motive；动机）+ate（*v.*）→ *v.* 使有动机，激发
[派] motivation [ˌməʊtɪˈveɪʃn] *n.* 动力；积极性
　　motivational [ˌməʊtɪˈveɪʃənəl] *a.* 动机的
[考] motivate sb. to do sth.　激发某人做某事
[真] [D] When they are financially **motivated**.【2021 年 6 月听力 24 题 D 选项】
[译] 当他们有经济动机时。

promote [12]

[prəˈməʊt] *v.* 推动，促进；提升，提拔；促销

[记] pro（前）+mot+e（无义）→ "向前移动、运动" → *v.* 推动，促进 → "推动职位" → *v.* 提升，提拔 → "推动销量" → *v.* 促销
[派] promotion [prəˈməʊʃn] *n.* 推动，促进；提升，提拔；促销
　　promoter [prəˈməʊtə(r)] *n.* 发起人；促进者

Day 16

[真] The fourth cause concerned managers who've been **promoted** for reasons other than potential.【2021 年 6 月 听力原文】
[译] 第四个原因涉及因潜力以外的因素而晋升的管理人员。

emotion [42]
[ɪˈməʊʃn] *n.* 情绪，情感
[记] e（out）+mot+ion（*n.*）→ "移动出来的东西"；从心中和胸腔中"移动出来的东西"→ *n.* 情绪，情感
[派] emotional [ɪˈməʊʃnəl] *a.* 情绪的，情感的
[真] Psychology research has shown that the **emotions** that we experience as teens seem more intense than those that come later.【2020 年 12 月 听力原文】
[译] 心理学研究表明，我们青少年时期经历的情感似乎比之后的更强烈。

remote [15]
[rɪˈməʊt] *a.* 遥远的，远程的
[记] re（反复）+mot+e（无义）→ "反复移动"；越来越远→ *a.* 遥远的，远程的
[派] remotely [rɪˈməʊtli] *ad.* 遥远地，远程地
[真] In 1930, Goddard and his family relocated there to a **remote** valley in the southwest of the country.【2021 年 6 月 听力原文】
[译] 1930 年，戈达德和他的家人搬到了该地区西南部的一个偏远山谷。

automate [16]
[ˈɔːtəmeɪt] *v.*（使）自动，（使）自动化
[记] auto（self；自己）+mat+e（无义）→ "自己就能移动、运动"→ *v.*（使）自动，（使）自动化
[派] automation [ˌɔːtəˈmeɪʃn] *n.* 自动，自动化
automatic [ˌɔːtəˈmætɪk] *a.* 自动的，自动化的
automatically [ˌɔːtəˈmætɪkli] *ad.* 自动地；无意识地
[真] But they still have reservations about the rise of **automation** technology.【2021 年 6 月 听力原文】
[译] 但他们对自动化技术的发展仍持保留态度。

mutual [3]
[ˈmjuːtʃuəl] *a.* 相互的，彼此的；共有的
[记] mutu（改写自 commute；经常往返）+al（*a.*）→ "有来有往的，彼此的"→ *a.* 相互的，彼此的；共有的
[派] mutually [ˈmjuːtʃuəli] *ad.* 相互地，彼此地
[真] [B] Focus as much as possible on topics of **mutual** interest.【2021 年 6 月 仔细阅读 51 题 B 选项】
[译] 尽可能多地关注双方共同感兴趣的话题。

momentum [20]
[məˈmentəm] *n.* 动力；动量；势头
[记] mom（改写自 mov）+en（使动）+t（无义）+um（*n.*）→ *n.* 动力；动量；势头
[真] Energy systems, like an aircraft carrier set in motion, have huge **momentum**.

【2020 年 7 月长篇阅读 41 题】
[译] 能源系统，就像正在启动的航空母舰一样，有巨大的动力。

remove [6]

[rɪˈmuːv] *v.* 迁移；离开；去除；脱掉

[记] re（反复）+mov+e（无义）→"反复移动"，就是不在原地的意思 → *v.* 迁移；离开；去除；脱掉

[派] removal [rɪˈmuːvl] *n.* 迁移；离开；去除；免职

–mult–、–multi– 多

multiple [6]

[ˈmʌltɪpl] *a.* 多重的，多样的

[记] multi+ple（*a.*）→ *a.* 多重的，多样的

[真] [C] They serve **multiple** purposes.【2020 年 12 月听力 18 题 C 选项】
[译] 它们有多种用途。

multiply [3]

[ˈmʌltɪplaɪ] *v.* 繁殖；增加；乘

[记] multi+ 词根 ply（折）→"折成很多份、很多人"→ *v.* 繁殖；增加；乘

[真] Stories of accelerated catastrophe **multiply**.【2020 年 12 月长篇阅读 C 选项】
[译] 灾难加速的报道大量增多。

非成组词（M 字母）

massive [5]

[ˈmæsɪv] *a.* 大的；大规模的

[记] mass（*n.* 巨大，大量）+ive（*a.*）→ *a.* 大的；大规模的

[真] We gathered a **massive** amount of data about the local plant life.【2021 年 6 月听力原文】
[译] 我们收集了大量有关当地植物的数据。

match [2]

[mætʃ] *n.* 比赛；配偶　*v.* 匹配，配对（熟词僻义，重点关注）

六级基础词汇

mature [2]

[məˈtʃʊə(r)] *a.* 成熟的　*v.* 成熟

[记] mat（简写自 mate；伙伴，交配）+ure（*v.*）→"到了能够交配的时候"→ *a.* 成熟的　*v.* 成熟

[派] premature [ˈpremətʃə(r)] *a.* 过早的，提前的；早产的

melody [2]

[ˈmelədi] *n.* 旋律，曲调；悦耳的音乐

[助] 谐音"麦乐迪"→唱歌的地方啊→ *n.* 旋律，曲调；悦耳的音乐

melt [2]

[melt] *v.* 熔化；融化

[助] 谐音"没有它"→"它没有了"，即→ v. 熔化；融化

method [10]

['meθəd] *n.* 方法

[记] 词根 meth（改写自 math；数学）+od（无义）→ 做 math 题时需要 method → *n.* 方法

[真] Using scientific **methods**, some of them can define authorship with 85% accuracy.【2021 年 6 月 仔细阅读】

[译] 通过使用科学的方法，其中一些方法可以以 85% 的准确率来明确作者身份。

migrate [3]

[maɪˈɡreɪt] *v.* 迁移，迁徙；移动

[记] 词根 migr（移动）+ate（*v.*）→ "移动的动作" → *v.* 迁移，迁徙；移动

[派] migration [maɪˈɡreɪʃn] *n.* 迁移，迁徙；移动

[真] [B] Many of them will have to **migrate** to isolated islands in the Southern Ocean.【2019 年 12 月 仔细阅读 53 题 B 选项】

[译] 许多帝企鹅将不得不迁徙到南大洋的孤立岛屿上。

military [2]

[ˈmɪlətri] *a.* 军事的，军用的

[记] 词根 milit（军队，战斗）+ary（*a.*）→ *a.* 军事的，军用的

moral [3]

[ˈmɒrəl] *n.* 道德　*a.* 道德上的；精神上的

[记] mor（简写自 more；更）+al（简写自 all；全部，所有）→ "所有中更重要的"，在一个人的所有特性中道德是否是更重要的？大到一个国家，小到一个组织，道德是否更为重要？中国现如今的很多社会问题是不是由于我们这 20 年只关注 GDP，而忽视了 moral 导致的呢？→ *n.* 道德　*a.* 道德上的；精神上的

[派] morality [məˈræləti] *n.* 道德，美德
morally [ˈmɒrəli] *ad.* 道德上

[真] It feels **morally** questionable, yet claims of genetic selection by intelligence are making headlines.【2021 年 6 月 仔细阅读】

[译] 在道德层面上是值得怀疑的，然而最近按照智力进行基因选择的主张成了头条新闻。

mortal [3]

[ˈmɔːtl] *a.* 致命的；终有一死的　*n.* 凡人

[记] mort（表示"死亡"；改写自罗马神话中的死神墨尔斯 Mors）+al（*a.*）→ *a.* 致命的；终有一死的→人终有一死→ *n.* 凡人

[派] mortality [mɔːˈtæləti] *n.* 死亡数；死亡率；生命的有限
immortal [ɪˈmɔːtl] *a.* 不死的，不朽的

[真] A diet directed at the affluent West fails to recognize that in low-income countries undernourished children are known to benefit from the consumption of milk and other animal source foods, improving cognitive functions, while reducing the prevalence of nutritional deficiencies as well as **mortality**.【2020 年 12 月 仔细阅读】

[译] 适用于富裕的西方的饮食没有意识到，在低收入国家，营养不良的儿童可以通过牛奶和其他动物源食品获益，改善认知功能，同时降低营养不良的概率和死亡率。

mortgage [2]

[ˈmɔːgɪdʒ] *n. & v.* 抵押（借款）

[记] 在古代西方，家庭中的长子在法律上拥有继承父亲遗产的权利。如果长子需要一大笔钱，而又无法从其父亲那里获得，他往往会找其他人借款。而其他人之所以愿意借钱给他，看中的是他的长子继承权，相信他将来继承遗产后可以偿还债务。借钱的时候，借款人会立下誓言，等他父亲过世，他继承遗产后就会偿还债务及利息。这就是英语单词 mortgage 的来源。mortgage 由 mort 和 gage 组成，mort 表示"死亡"，gage 表示"誓言，保证"，所以 mortgage 一词的字面含义就是"死亡保证"，即以其父亲的死亡（等于遗产）为保证的贷款→ *n. & v.* 抵押（借款）

[助] 谐音"猫给之"→把猫先给你→ *n. & v.* 抵押（借款）

◂ –nat–、–nas– 生，出生 ▸

nation [25]

[ˈneɪʃn] *n.* 国家；民族

六级基础词汇

[记] nat+ion（*n.*）→"出生的地方"→ *n.* 国家；民族

[派] national [ˈnæʃnəl] *a.* 国家的；民族的
nationwide [ˌneɪʃnˈwaɪd] *a.* 全国性的
international [ˌɪntəˈnæʃnəl] *a.* 国际的
internationally [ˌɪntəˈnæʃnəli] *ad.* 国际地

native [8]

[ˈneɪtɪv] *a.* 本地的，本国的；天生的 *n.* 本地人，本国人

[记] nat+ive（*a. & n.*）→"生在此处"→ *a.* 本地的，本国的；天生的 *n.* 本地人，本国人

[真] Goddard lunched his first rocket from an aunt's farm in his **native** Massachusetts in March 1926.【2021 年 6 月听力原文】

[译] 1926 年 3 月，戈达德从家乡马萨诸塞州他姑姑家的农场发射了他的第一枚火箭。

nature [40]

[ˈneɪtʃə(r)] *n.* 自然，大自然；天性，本性（熟词僻义，重点关注）

[记] nat+ure（*n.*）→"生来就如此"→ *n.* 天性，本性→ *n.* 自然，大自然

[派] natural [ˈnætʃrəl] *a.* 自然的；天生的
naturally [ˈnætʃrəli] *ad.* 自然地；天生地
unnatural [ʌnˈnætʃrəl] *a.* 不自然的；不真诚的；做作的

[真] [A] **Natural** sciences should be learned the way humanities courses are.【2021 年 6 月仔细阅读 47 题 A 选项】

Day 16

[译] 学习自然科学应该像学习人文课程一样。

nature 的形近词

nurture [2] ['nɜːtʃə(r)] *v.&n.* 养育，培育

[记] nurt（简写自 nurse；护士，保姆；培育）+ure（*v.&n.*）→ *v.&n.* 养育，培育

–norm– 标准，正常

normal [7] ['nɔːml] *a.* 标准的，正常的

[记] norm+al（*a.*）→ *a.* 标准的，正常的

[派] normally ['nɔːməli] *ad.* 一般地，通常地
abnormal [æb'nɔːml] *a.* 不正常的，异常的

[真] Online "friends" made through social media do not follow the **normal** psychological progression of an interpersonal relationship.【2020 年 12 月 仔细阅读】

[译] 通过社交媒体结交的网上"朋友"并不遵循人际关系的正常心理发展过程。

enormous [7] [ɪ'nɔːməs] *a.* 巨大的，庞大的

[记] e（out）+norm+ous（*a.*）→ "大得超出了标准" → *a.* 巨大的，庞大的

[派] enormously [ɪ'nɔːməsli] *ad.* 巨大地，庞大地

[真] [A] The **enormous** appeal of a great piece of artistic work to tourists.【2020 年 12 月 仔细阅读 46 题 A 选项】

[译] 一件伟大的艺术作品对游客有着巨大的吸引力。

–not– 表示，注意

note [12] [nəʊt] *n.* 笔记　*v.* 记录；注意；表示，表达（熟词僻义，重点关注）

[记] notebook *n.* 笔记本→ note *n.* 笔记　*v.* 记录；后引申出→ *v.* 注意；表示，表达

[派] noteworthy ['nəʊtwɜːði] *a.* 值得注意的；显著的

[考] sb. note that... 某人表示……

[真] French political commentators **noted** the devastating fire had succeeded where Macron had failed in uniting the country.【2021 年 6 月 长篇阅读 K 选项】

[译] 法国政治评论家指出，马克龙未能促进国家团结，但这场毁灭性的火灾使该目标得以实现。

notion [3] ['nəʊʃn] *n.* 概念；观念；意见

[记] not+ion（*n.*）→ "表示的东西，表示什么呢？" → *n.* 概念；观念；意见

[真] Tim Joseph was fascinated by the **notion** that sunlight brings energy and wealth to mankind.【2019 年 12 月 长篇阅读 41 题】

［译］蒂姆·约瑟夫被阳光为人类带来能量和财富的概念所吸引。

notice [8]
[ˈnəʊtɪs] *v. & n.* 注意；通知

[记] not+ice（*n.*）→ *n.* 注意；通知 → *v.* 注意；通知
[派] noticeable [ˈnəʊtɪsəbl] *a.* 值得注意的；明显的，显而易见的
noticeably [ˈnəʊtɪsəbli] *ad.* 显著地，明显地
[真] We had to evacuate on very short **notice**.【2021年6月 听力原文】
[译] 我们不得不在很短的时间内撤离。

notorious [2]
[nəʊˈtɔːriəs] *a.* 臭名昭著的

[记] not+or（表示人的后缀）+i（无义）+ous（*a.*）→ "不是人的"，天哪，你就不是个人！→ *a.* 臭名昭著的
[派] notoriously [nəʊˈtɔːriəsli] *ad.* 臭名昭著地

connotation [2]
[ˌkɒnəˈteɪʃn] *n.* 含义

[记] con（加强）+not+ation（*n.*）→ "表达"什么？→ *n.* 含义

–nov– 新

novel [12]
[ˈnɒvl] *n.* 小说 *a.* 新奇的，新颖的

[记] nov+el（*n.*）→ *a.* 新奇的，新颖的 → "充满新奇元素的" → *n.* 小说
[派] novelty [ˈnɒvlti] *n.* 创新；新奇，新颖
novelist [ˈnɒvəlɪst] *n.* 小说家
[真] [C] Conserve animal species in a **novel** and all-round way.【2020年12月 仔细阅读55题 C 选项】
[译] 以一种新颖而全面的方式保护动物物种。

innovate [10]
[ˈɪnəveɪt] *v.* 创新，引入（新事物、思想或方法）

[记] in（里）+nov+ate（*v.*）→ *v.* 创新，引入（新事物、思想或方法）
[派] innovation [ˌɪnəˈveɪʃn] *n.* 创新，新想法
innovative [ˈɪnəvətɪv] [ˈɪnəvətɪv] *a.* 创新的
innovator [ˈɪnəveɪtə(r)] *n.* 改革者；创新者
[真] After encountering several setbacks, Captain Lucas decided to use a drill, and his **innovations** created the modern oil drilling industry.【2021年6月 听力原文】
[译] 遇到几次挫折后，卢卡斯队长决定使用钻头，他的革新创造了现代石油钻探工业。

renovate [2]
[ˈrenəveɪt] *v.* 更新，革新

[记] re（反复）+nov+ate（*v.*）→ "反复使之变新" → *v.* 更新，革新
[派] renovation [ˌrenəˈveɪʃn] *n.* 更新，革新

扫码快速学习

扫码即刻听课

–num– 数，数字

numerous [7]
['nju:mərəs] *a.* 许多的，很多的
[记] num+er（表示人或物的后缀）+ous（*a.*）→ *a.* 许多的，很多的
[真] When you study an author's writing style, don't stop on a single one, but explore **numerous** styles instead.【2021 年 6 月 仔细阅读】
[译] 当你研究作家的写作风格时，不要只停留在一种风格上，而要探索多种风格。

amount [24]
[əˈmaʊnt] *n.* 数量；总量 *v.* 总计
[记] a（to）+moun（改写自 num）+t（无义）→ "去达到相应数字；去达到某个数值"→ *n.* 数量；总量 *v.* 总计
[考] the amount of+ 不可数名词 ……的总量
　　 amount to　 总计，共达
[真] We gathered a massive **amount** of data about the local plant life.【2021 年 6 月 听力原文】
[译] 我们收集了大量有关当地植物的数据。

非成组词（N 字母）

narrate [5]
[nəˈreɪt] *v.* 讲，叙述，讲述
[记] 来自拉丁语 narrare（讲述）→ *v.* 讲，叙述，讲述
[助] 谐音 "那说他"→那就说说他吧→ *v.* 讲，叙述，讲述
[派] narration [nəˈreɪʃn] *n.* 叙述；故事
　　 narrative [ˈnærətɪv] *a.* 叙述性的，叙述的 *n.* 故事；叙述
[真] [B] Strive to take control of their **narrative**.【2020 年 12 月听力 23 题 B 选项】
[译] 努力控制他们的叙述。

navigate [4]
[ˈnævɪɡeɪt] *v.* 航行；导航
[记] 词根 nav（简写自 navy；船，航行）+ig（无义）+ate（*v.*）→ "开船，航行的动作"→ *v.* 航行；导航

121

[派] navigation [ˌnævɪˈɡeɪʃn] n. 航行；导航；驾驶

[真] What does the author say about the use of **navigation** apps?【2021 年 6 月 仔细阅读 53 题题干】

[译] 作者对导航应用程序的使用有什么看法？

nutrition [16]

[njuˈtrɪʃn] n. 营养，营养品

[记] 词根 nutr（营养）+ition（n.）→ n. 营养，营养品

[助] 发音、拼写都很像"纽崔莱"→ n. 营养，营养品

[派] nutrient [ˈnjuːtriənt] n. 营养物，营养品 a. 营养的
nutritional [njuˈtrɪʃnl] a. 营养的，营养品的

[真] [A] Give top priority to things like **nutrition** and food security.【2020 年 12 月 仔细阅读 55 题 A 选项】

[译] 优先考虑营养和食品安全等问题。

nourish [5]

[ˈnʌrɪʃ] v. 抚养，滋养；施肥

[记] 词根 nour（营养）+ish（v.）→ "使人有营养" → v. 抚养，滋养 → "使地有营养" → v. 施肥

[派] nourishment [ˈnʌrɪʃmənt] n. 食物，营养品
undernourished [ˌʌndəˈnʌrɪʃt] a. 营养不良的

[真] [D] It may worsen the **nourishment** problem in low-income countries.【2020 年 12 月 仔细阅读 49 题 D 选项】

[译] 它可能会使低收入国家的营养问题恶化。

nuclear [8]

[ˈnjuːkliə(r)] a. 原子能的，核能的

[记] nu（简写自 new；新的）+clear（改写自 clean；清洁的）→ "新式的清洁能源" → a. 原子能的，核能的

[真] Shortly after Marconi's death, the **nuclear** physicist Enrico Fermi—soon to be the developer of the Manhattan Project—wrote that Marconi proved that theory and experimentation were complementary features of progress.【2021 年 6 月 长篇阅读 J 选项】

[译] 马可尼去世后不久，即将成为曼哈顿计划的制订者的核物理学家恩利克·费米写到，马可尼证明了理论和实验是互补的，两者共同促成了进步。

-opt- 选择

opt [20]

[ɒpt] v. 选择，挑选

六级基础词汇

[派] option [ˈɒpʃn] n. 选择，可选择的事物
optional [ˈɒpʃənl] a. 可选的，任选的

[考] opt to do sth. 选择做某事
opt for... 选择……

Day 17

adopt [3]
[əˈdɒpt] v. 采用，采纳；收养，领养

[记] ad（to）+opt → "去选"什么？选的东西不一样，意思就不一样 → "选择某个方法或建议" → v. 采用，采纳 → "去选孩子" → v. 收养，领养

[派] adoption [əˈdɒpʃn] n. 采用；收养

[真] [A] One should not **adopt** it without consulting a sleep expert.【2020 年 9 月仔细阅读 50 题 A 选项】

[译] 没有咨询睡眠专家就不应该采用它。

adopt 的形近词

adapt [8]
[əˈdæpt] v. 适应，使适合

[记] ad（to）+apt（a. 恰当的，合适的）→ "去变得恰当、合适"；本来不合适，慢慢觉得合适，说明已经 → v. 适应，使适合

[派] adaptation [ˌædæpˈteɪʃn] n. 适应

[考] adapt to 适应

[真] [C] Chimps alter their culture to quickly **adapt** to the changed environment.【2020 年 12 月仔细阅读 53 题 C 选项】

[译] 黑猩猩改变了它们的文化，以迅速适应不断变化的环境。

optimistic [9]
[ˌɒptɪˈmɪstɪk] a. 乐观的

[记] opt+im（里）+ist（无义）+ic（a.）→ 无论遇到多难的事情，"里面还有的选，还有别的选择" → a. 乐观的

[派] optimism [ˈɒptɪmɪzəm] n. 乐观主义

[形] optimal [ˈɒptɪməl] a. 最佳的

[真] AI? I'm not so **optimistic** actually.【2020 年 12 月听力原文】

[译] 人工智能？说实话，我感觉并不乐观。

-ord- 顺序，秩序

order [12]
[ˈɔːdə(r)] n. 顺序，秩序；命令；预订，订单 v. 命令，订购（熟词僻义，重点关注）

六级基础词汇

[派] orderly [ˈɔːdəli] a. 有顺序的，整齐的，有条理的

[考] in order to... 为了……

[真] As an adult, Marconi had an intuition that he had to be loyal to politicians in **order** to be influential.【2021 年 6 月长篇阅读 37 题】

[译] 成年后，马可尼有一种直觉，即他必须忠于政客才能有影响力。

disorder [2]
[dɪsˈɔːdə(r)] n. 混乱，杂乱

[记] dis（否定）+order（n. 顺序，秩序）→ 这个地方"无秩序" → n. 混乱，杂乱

border ²

[ˈbɔːdə(r)] *n.* 边境，边界

[记] b（谐音"不"）+order（*n.* 顺序，秩序）→"不秩序，无秩序"的地方→*n.* 边境，边界

coordinate ⁶

[kəʊˈɔːdɪneɪt] *v.* 协调

[记] co（共同，全部）+ord+in（里）+ate（*v.*）→"所有人在里面的顺序"，谁在第一排，谁在最后一排，需要有人→*v.* 协调

[派] coordination [kəʊˌɔːdɪˈneɪʃn] *n.* 协调
　　coordinator [kəʊˈɔːdɪneɪtə(r)] *n.* 协调者

[真] [A] **Coordinating** various disaster-relief efforts.【2019年12月 仔细阅读 54 题 A 选项】

[译] 协调各种救灾工作。

–ori– 开始，起初

horizon ⁴

[həˈraɪzn] *n.* 地平线；眼界，视野

[记] h（无义）+ori+zon（改写自 sun；太阳）→"太阳开始的地方"→*n.* 地平线→沿着地平线极目远眺，开阔→*n.* 眼界，视野

[真] Picture yourself at a college graduation day, with a fresh cohort of students about to set sail for new **horizons**.【2020年12月 长篇阅读 A 选项】

[译] 想象一下自己在大学毕业那天，和一群学生即将向新愿景启航。

origin ²

[ˈɒrɪdʒɪn] *n.* 起源；出身

[记] ori+gin（无义）→物种从哪"开始"？→*n.* 起源→人从哪"开始"？→*n.* 出身

original ⁵

[əˈrɪdʒənl] *a.* 起源的，最初的；独创的

[记] origin+al（*a.*）→*a.* 起源的，最初的；独创的

[派] originally [əˈrɪdʒənəli] *ad.* 起初，原来
　　originality [əˌrɪdʒəˈnæləti] *n.* 独创性，创造性

[真] But criticism over the **original** state of the building is likely to intensify over coming days.【2021年6月 长篇阅读 K 选项】

[译] 但在未来几天，人们对火灾前该建筑起初状态的批评可能会加剧。

originate ²

[əˈrɪdʒɪneɪt] *v.* 起源，起源于

[记] 上词 origin 的动词；origin（起源）+ate（*v.*）→*v.* 起源，起源于

[考] originate from... 起源于……，源于……

Day 17

-out- 出去，向外

outcome [8]　['aʊtkʌm] *n.* 结果，成果

[记] 短语 come out 的反写词；out+come（*v.* 来）→ "走了出来" → 事情 "走了出来"，形成 → *n.* 结果，成果

[真] The same seed and fertilizer program may yield completely different **outcomes** in different places.【2020 年 12 月 长篇阅读 45 题】

[译] 相同的种子和肥料计划可能会在不同的地方产生完全不同的结果。

outdated [4]　[,aʊt'deɪtɪd] *a.* 过时的，不流行的

[记] out+date（*n.* 日期）+ed（*a.*）→ "出了日期，出了日子" → *a.* 过时的，不流行的

[真] [C] Abolish all **outdated** traffic rules.【2021 年 6 月 听力 25 题 C 选项】

[译] 废除所有过时的交通规则。

outer [2]　['aʊtə(r)] *a.* 外表的；远离中心的

[记] out+er（表示人或物的后缀）→ "人或物的外面" → *a.* 外表的；远离中心的

outfit [5]　['aʊtfɪt] *n.* 装备，衣服

[记] out+fit（*a.* 适合的）→ "适合身体外形的" → *n.* 装备，衣服

[真] But no one can be unique with their **outfit** every day.【2020 年 12 月 听力原文】

[译] 但没有人每天穿的衣服都是独特的。

outline [2]　['aʊtlaɪn] *n.* 轮廓；大纲　*v.* 概述；描绘……轮廓

[记] out+line（*n.* 线）→ 物体 "外面的线" → *n.* 轮廓；大纲 → *v.* 概述；描绘……轮廓

-over- 上，上面

overall [12]　[,əʊvər'ɔːl] *a.&ad.* 全面的（地），全体的（地）

[记] over+all（全部的，一切的）→ "在所有之上还有" → *a.&ad.* 全面的（地），全体的（地）

[真] The brain is able to allocate blood and thus energy to particular regions that are being active at that point, but the **overall** energy availability in the brain is thought to be constant.【2020 年 12 月 听力原文】

[译] 大脑能够指挥运输血液，进而将能量分配给当时活跃的特定区域，但大脑整体能量的可用性被认为是恒定的。

overcome [3]　[,əʊvə'kʌm] *v.* 战胜，克服

[记] over+come（*v.* 来）→ "从上面走过来"；从敌人的尸体上走过来 → *v.* 战

125

胜，克服

[真]"The fire at Notre Dame reminds us that we will always have challenges to **overcome**," Macron said.【2021年6月 长篇阅读E选项】
[译]"巴黎圣母院的火灾提醒我们，我们总是要克服挑战。"马克龙说道。

overseas ²
[ˌəʊvəˈsiːz] *a.* 海外的，国外的　*ad.* 在海外，在国外

[记] over+seas（*n.* 海）→"超过海洋"；漂洋过海→ *a.* 海外的，国外的　*ad.* 在海外，在国外

overlook ⁴
[ˌəʊvəˈlʊk] *v.* 俯瞰，俯视；忽略，不理会

[记] over+look（*v.* 看）→"从上面看"→ *v.* 俯瞰，俯视→站在20层的高楼上往下看，只能看到整体，看不到细节，就是对细节的→ *v.* 忽略，不理会

[真] My company's managers tend to be accommodating and kind, **overlooking** mistakes or issues so as not to hurt feelings.【2021年6月 听力原文】
[译] 我们公司的管理者往往比较随和、友好，为了不伤害感情而忽略错误或问题。

overwhelm ³
[ˌəʊvəˈwelm] *v.* 压倒，制服，击败

[记] over+ 词根 whelm（=press；压）→"从上面压下去"→ *v.* 压倒，制服，击败

[派] overwhelming [ˌəʊvəˈwelmɪŋ] *a.* 势不可挡的，压倒一切的；巨大的

[真] An **overwhelming** majority of family physicians are willing to use telemedicine if they are duly paid.【2020年9月 长篇阅读36题】
[译] 如果可以得到适当的报酬，绝大多数的家庭医生都愿意使用远程医疗。

非成组词（O 字母）

obese ²⁶
[əʊˈbiːs] *a.* 肥胖的

[记] ob（加强）+es（改写自 eat；吃）+e（无义）→"加强地吃，不停地吃"→ *a.* 肥胖的
[助] 谐音"饿不死"→ *a.* 肥胖的
[派] obesity [əʊˈbiːsəti] *n.* 肥胖
[真] [D] To justify government intervention in solving the **obesity** problem.【2020年9月 仔细阅读49题D选项】
[译] 为了证明政府通过干预来解决肥胖问题是合理的。

obey ²
[əˈbeɪ] *v.* 服从，顺从

[助] 谐音"哦，背"→"哦，让我背我就背"→ *v.* 服从，顺从
[派] disobey [ˌdɪsəˈbeɪ] *v.* 不服从，不顺从

obscure ²
[əbˈskjʊə(r)] *a.* 昏暗的；朦胧的；晦涩的

Day 17

[记] ob（相反，反对）+scu（改写自 see；看）+re（无义）→ "看不清的，看不明白的" → *a.* 昏暗的；朦胧的；晦涩的

[派] obscurity [əbˈskjʊərəti] *n.* 朦胧；晦涩

oral[2] [ˈɔːrəl] *a.* 口头的

[记] 词根 or（说话）+al（*a.*）→ "说的" → *a.* 口头的

扫码快速学习

扫码即刻听课

‹ –par–、–part– ›

① 部分

compare [28]   [kəmˈpeə(r)] v. 比较，对比

［记］com（全部，共同）+par+e（无义）→ "把各个部分全部放在一起"，进行 → v. 比较，对比

［派］comparison [kəmˈpærɪsn] n. 比较，对比
　　　comparable [ˈkɒmpərəbl] a. 可比较的，比得上的
　　　comparative [kəmˈpærətɪv] a. 比较的，相当的

［考］compare A with B　比较 A 和 B
　　　compare A to B　把 A 比作 B

［真］Europe has many scenarios, but the French and Swiss ones are interesting to **compare**.【2020 年 12 月 长篇阅读 O 选项】

［译］欧洲各国的情况各异，但法国和瑞士的情况比较起来就有趣了。

partial [2]   [ˈpɑːʃl] a. 部分的；偏爱的，偏袒的

［记］part+i（谐音"爱"）+al（a.）→ "只爱这一部分" → a. 部分的；偏爱的，偏袒的

［派］partially [ˈpɑːʃəli] ad. 部分地；偏袒地

［考］be partial to...　对……偏爱

particle [2]   [ˈpɑːtɪkl] n. 颗粒，微粒

［记］part+ic（a.）+le（n.）→ "一小部分" → n. 颗粒，微粒

department [5]   [dɪˈpɑːtmənt] n. 系；部门

［记］de（向下）+part+ment（n.）→ "部分" → 大学里最小的一部分 → n. 系 → 公司里分成各个部分 → n. 部门

［真］Both absent-minded doodling and copying from life have been shown to positively affect your memory and visual perception, so complain loudly the next time your school board slashes the art **department**'s budget.【2021 年 6 月 仔细阅读】

Day 18

[译] 心不在焉的涂鸦和对生活的复现都会积极地影响你的记忆力和视觉感知，所以下次学校董事会削减艺术系的预算时，你可以大声抱怨。

particular [12] [pəˈtɪkjələ(r)] *a.* 特别的，特定的

[记] part+i（无义）+cu（谐音"酷"）+l（无义）+ar（*a.*）→"很酷的一部分"，真是好特别→*a.* 特别的，特定的

[派] particularly [pəˈtɪkjələli] *ad.* 特别地，尤其地

[考] in particular 特别，尤其

[真] One reason in **particular** why these people had been promoted was that they had been around the longest.【2021年6月 听力原文】

[译] 这些人被提拔的一个特别原因是他们待的时间最长。

proportion [2] [prəˈpɔːʃn] *n.* 比例；部分

[记] pro（前）+portion（*n.* 部分）→"向前伸出的部分"；占整体的→*n.* 比例；部分

② 分离，分开

apart [7] [əˈpɑːt] *a.* 分离的；隔离的 *ad.* 分离地；分开地

[记] a（to）+part → *a.* 分离的；隔离的 *ad.* 分离地；分开地

[派] apartment [əˈpɑːtmənt] *n.* 公寓，房间

[考] apart from... 除……之外

[真] **Apart** from the fire, the water used to extinguish it also caused a lot of damage to Notre Dame Cathedral.【2021年6月 长篇阅读43题】

[译] 除了火灾，用来灭火的水也对巴黎圣母院造成了很大的破坏。

separate [8] [ˈsepəreɪt] [ˈseprət] *v.* 分离，分开 *a.* 单独的，分开的

[记] se（away）+par+ate（*v.&a.*）→ *v.* 分离，分开 *a.* 单独的，分开的

[派] separation [ˌsepəˈreɪʃn] *n.* 分离，分开；间隔

[考] separate from... 从……分离/分开

[真] The research scholars surveyed 152 blue-collar workers from two **separate** sites in the mining industry.【2021年6月 听力原文】

[译] 研究学者们调查了采矿业中两个不同地点的152名蓝领工人。

-pas-、-pass-

① 经过，放弃

pace [5] [peɪs] *n.* 步速，步伐；节奏

[记] pac（改写自pas；经过）+e（无义）→"经过时迈的步子"→ *n.* 步速，步

伐；节奏

[真] Those projects are then interwoven with modules fast-**paced** technical learned "on-the-fly" and "at will" depending on the nature of project.【2020 年 12 月 长篇阅读 H 选项】

[译] 然后，根据课题的性质，将这些课题与"即时"和"随意"学习的快节奏技术模块交织在一起。

②感情，情绪

passion [10] [ˈpæʃn] *n.* 激情，热情

[记] pass+ion（*n.*）→ "富有感情" → *n.* 激情，热情

[派] passionate [ˈpæʃənət] *a.* 有激情的，热情的

[真] [A] She can devote all her life to pursuing her **passion**.【2020 年 9 月 听力 1 题 A 选项】

[译] 她可以奉献一生去追求自己的热爱。

compassion [5] [kəmˈpæʃn] *n.* 同情，怜悯

[记] com（全部，共同）+pass+ion（*n.*）→ "相同、共同的感情"，简称 → *n.* 同情，怜悯

[派] compassionate [kəmˈpæʃənət] *a.* 有同情心的，表示同情的

[真] My new company seems to employ a feedback policy that combines **compassion** and directness.【2021 年 6 月 听力原文】

[译] 我的新公司似乎采用了一种有爱心而又直接的反馈政策。

-pel-、-pul- 拉

compel [6] [kəmˈpel] *v.* 强迫，迫使

[记] com（全部，共同）+pel → "所有人都拉"；我不想去，他们都拉我去，我被 → *v.* 强迫，迫使

[派] compulsory [kəmˈpʌlsəri] *a.* 强制的，义务的，必须做的
compulsion [kəmˈpʌlʃn] *n.* 强迫，强制

[考] compel sb. to do sth.　强迫某人做某事
be compelled by...　被……强迫
compulsory course　必修课

[真] On the contrary, **compelling** tourists to make a financial contribution to the places they visit beyond their personal consumption should be part of a wider cultural shift.【2021 年 6 月 仔细阅读】

[译] 相反，迫使游客在自身消费外还要对观光地做出经济贡献，这应该成为更大范围内文化转型的一部分。

Day 18

propel [2] [prə'pel] *v.* 推进，推动

[记] pro（前）+pel → "向前拖、拉" → *v.* 推进，推动

–pend–、–pens–

① 悬挂

depend [13] [dɪ'pend] *v.* 依靠，依赖

[记] de（下）+pend → "挂靠在下面" → *v.* 依靠，依赖
[派] dependent [dɪ'pendənt] *a.* 依靠的，依赖的
　　dependence [dɪ'pendəns] *n.* 依靠，依赖
[考] depend on/upon　依靠，依赖；取决于
　　be dependent on　依靠，依赖；取决于
[真] [C] It **depends** on the required knowledge for application.【2021年6月 仔细阅读54题C选项】
[译] 这取决于申请所需的知识。

independent [19] [ˌɪndɪ'pendənt] *a.* 独立的，自主的

[记] in（否定）+depend（*v.* 依靠，依赖）+ent（*a.*）→ "不依靠别人的" → *a.* 独立的，自主的
[派] independence [ˌɪndɪ'pendəns] *n.* 独立，自主
　　independently [ˌɪndɪ'pendəntli] *ad.* 独立地
[考] be independent of...　与……无关；脱离……而独立
[真] [D] **Independent** learning.【2021年6月 仔细阅读48题D选项】
[译] 独立学习。

② 花费

expend [20] [ɪk'spend] *v.* 花费，消耗

[记] ex（out）+pend → "花费出去" → *v.* 花费，消耗
[派] expense [ɪk'spens] *n.* 费用，消耗
　　expensive [ɪk'spensɪv] *a.* 昂贵的
　　inexpensive [ˌɪnɪk'spensɪv] *a.* 不贵的，便宜的
[真] On many occasions, the entrepreneurs reported not paying themselves a wage at all initially in order to cover salaries and **expenses**.【2021年6月 听力原文】
[译] 在许多情况下，创业者报告说，为了支付工资和开销，他们最初根本不给自己发工资。

131

compensate [5]

['kɒmpenseɪt] v. 赔偿，补偿

[记] com（加强）+pens（谐音"赔"）+ate（v.）→ v. 赔偿，补偿

[派] compensation [ˌkɒmpenˈseɪʃn] n. 赔偿，补偿
compensatory [ˌkɒmpenˈseɪtəri] a. 赔偿的，补偿的

[真] [C] Most of the respondents got **compensated** for driving 384 miles.【2020年12月 听力 19题 C 选项】

[译] 大多数受访者因开车驾驶 384 英里而得到了补偿。

–per– 贯穿

permanent [6]

[ˈpɜːmənənt] a. 永久的，固定的

[记] per+man（男人）+ent（a.）→ "贯穿一生只有一个 man 而不是一群 men" → a. 永久的，固定的

[派] permanently [ˈpɜːmənəntli] ad. 永久地，长远地
permanence [ˈpɜːmənəns] n. 永久，持久

[真] Marconi placed a **permanent** stamp on the way we live.【2021年6月 长篇阅读 I 选项】

[译] 马可尼对我们的生活方式产生了永久的影响。

permeate [3]

[ˈpɜːmieɪt] v. 弥漫，遍布

[记] per+me（无义）+ate（v.）→ "贯穿整个房间" → v. 弥漫，遍布

[派] permeation [ˌpɜːmɪˈeɪʃn] n. 弥漫，遍布

[真] [B] Cultivation of creativity should **permeate** the entire school curriculum.【2021年12月 仔细阅读 47题 B 选项】

[译] 创造力的培养应该渗透到整个学校的课程中。

–pet– 喜爱，追求

compete [14]

[kəmˈpiːt] v. 竞争，比赛

[记] com（共同，全部）+pet+e（无义）→ "所有人都喜欢或者所有人都想追求这个人或物"，那怎么办？那就争呗，谁强归谁→ v. 竞争，比赛

[派] competition [ˌkɒmpəˈtɪʃn] n. 竞争，比赛
competitive [kəmˈpetətɪv] a. 竞争的，比赛的
competitiveness [kəmˈpetətɪvnəs] n. 竞争，竞争性
uncompetitive [ˌʌnkəmˈpetətɪv] a. 无竞争力的
competitor [kəmˈpetɪtə(r)] n. 竞争者，对手

[考] compete with... 与……竞争，抗争
compete for... 为……而竞争

[真] [D] Fierce **competition**.【2021年6月 听力 7题 D 选项】

Day 18

[译] 激烈的竞争。

competent [5] [ˈkɒmpɪtənt] *a.* 有能力的；能胜任的；称职的

[记] compet（简写自 compete；竞争）+ent（*a.*）→ 想要 "compete"，自己得是 "competent" → *a.* 有能力的；能胜任的；称职的

[派] competence [ˈkɒmpɪtəns] *n.* 能力，技能
　　incompetent [ɪnˈkɒmpɪtənt] *a.* 无能力的，不胜任的

[真] [C] It may make us feel isolated and **incompetent**.【2020 年 12 月 仔细阅读 46 题 C 选项】

[译] 它可能会让我们感到孤立和无能。

–phys– 身体，肉体，物质

physical [22] [ˈfɪzɪkl] *a.* 肉体的，身体的；物质的，物理的

[记] phys+ic（*a.*）+al（*a.*）→ *a.* 肉体的，身体的；物质的，物理的

[助] 体育课 Physical Education (PE)

[派] physically [ˈfɪzɪkli] *ad.* 身体上

[真] "A performance is a lot more than a **physical** resemblance."【2021 年 6 月 长篇阅读 H 选项】

[译] "表演不仅仅是外表上的相似。"

physician [6] [fɪˈzɪʃn] *n.* 内科医生

[记] phys+ic（*a.*）+ian（表示人的后缀）→ "医治人身体、肉体的人" → *n.* 内科医生

[真] "If not, the patient should talk to his primary-care **physician** about it," says Steve Ommen, who runs Mayo's Connected Care program.【2020 年 9 月 长篇阅读 N 选项】

[译] "如果没有执照，病人应该和他的初级保健医生谈，"梅奥联网护理项目的运营者史蒂夫·奥门说。

–ple–、–pli–、–plo– 填充，填满

complete [24] [kəmˈpliːt] *v.* 完成　*a.* 完成的；完整的；完全的

[记] com（全部，共同）+ple+te（无义）→ "全部填满"，表示工作已经 → *v.* 完成　*a.* 完成的；完整的；完全的

[派] completely [kəmˈpliːtli] *ad.* 完全地；完整地

[真] However, fire officers have said a **complete** inventory of the damage will not be possible until the cathedral structure has been deemed safe.【2021 年 6 月 长篇阅读 I 选项】

[译] 然而，消防官员表示，在确认大教堂结构安全之前，无法对火灾造成的损失进行完整清点。

accomplish [10]

[əˈkʌmplɪʃ] *v.* 完成，达到（目的），实现

[记] 和上词 complete 前缀、词根一样，是同源同义词；ac（to）+com（全部，共同）+pli+sh（*v.*）→ *v.* 完成，达到（目的），实现

[派] accomplishment [əˈkʌmplɪʃmənt] *n.* 完成，成就

[真]【A】Exaggerate their life's **accomplishments**.【2020 年 12 月 仔细阅读 48 题 A 选项】

[译] 夸大他们一生的成就。

deplete [4]

[dɪˈpliːt] *v.* 减少，消耗

[记] de（下）+ple+te（无义）→ "向下填充"，"填充，填满" 的反向，越填充越向下→ *v.* 减少，消耗

[派] depletion [dɪˈpliːʃn] *n.* 减少，消耗

[真]【A】Government health budgets are **depleted**.【2020 年 9 月 仔细阅读 46 题 A 选项】

[译] 政府的卫生预算已经耗尽。

complement [2]

[ˈkɒmplɪment] [ˈkɒmplɪmənt] *v.&n.* 补充，补足

[记] com（全部，共同）+ple+ment（*v.&n.*）→ "全部填充" → *v.&n.* 补充，补足

[派] complementary [ˌkɒmplɪˈmentri] *a.* 补充的，互补的

supplement [13]

[ˈsʌplɪment] [ˈsʌplɪmənt] *v.&n.* 补充，增补

[记] sup（下）+ple+ment（*v.&n.*）→ "从下面填充、补充" → *v.&n.* 补充，增补

[真] I'm always baffled when I walk into a pharmacy and see shelves bursting with various vitamins, extracts and other **supplements**, all promising to accelerate or promote weight loss.【2021 年 6 月 选词填空】

[译] 当我走进药店，看到货架上摆满了各种承诺能加速或促进减肥的维生素、萃取物和其他补品时，我总是很困惑。

implement [6]

[ˈɪmplɪmənt] [ˈɪmplɪment] *n.* 工具，器具　*v.* 实施；实现

[记] im（里）+ple+ment（*v.&n.*）→ "往里填充"；所谓工具就是向里填充，例如杯子就是往里填充水变成喝水的工具，钢笔或水笔就是往里填充墨水变成写字的工具→ *n.* 工具，器具→ "工具" 用来实现人类仅用双手完成不了的任务→ *v.* 实施；实现

[派] implementation [ˌɪmplɪmenˈteɪʃn] *n.* 实施，执行

complex [11]

[ˈkɒmpleks] *a.* 难的，复杂的

[记] com（全部，共同）+ple+x（未知数 x）→ 来自数学，"一道题充满了 x"；这道题实在是→ *a.* 难的，复杂的

[派] complexity [kəmˈpleksəti] *n.* 复杂性

[真] Something as **complex** as intellect is likely to be affected by many factors

Day 18

beyond genes.【2021 年 6 月 仔细阅读】
[译] 像智力这样复杂的东西可能受到基因以外的许多因素的影响。

complicated [8] ['kɒmplɪkeɪtɪd] *a.* 复杂的

[记] 上词 complex 的近义词→ *a.* 复杂的
[派] uncomplicated [ʌnˈkɒmplɪkeɪtɪd] *a.* 简单的，不复杂的
　　　complication [ˌkɒmplɪˈkeɪʃn] *n.* 复杂的难题（或困难）
[真] The topic gets more **complicated** when we talk about the divide between rural and urban communities.【2021 年 6 月 听力原文】
[译] 当我们谈及农村和城市社区之间的鸿沟时，这个话题就变得更加复杂。

explore [9] [ɪkˈsplɔː(r)] *v.* 探索，探究

[记] ex（out）+plo+re（无义）→"向外填充"→ *v.* 探索，探究
[助] IE 浏览器 Internet Explorer
[派] exploration [ˌekspləˈreɪʃn] *n.* 探索，探究
[真] When you study an author's writing style, don't stop on a single one, but **explore** numerous styles instead.【2021 年 6 月 仔细阅读】
[译] 当你研究作家的写作风格时，不要只停留在一种风格上，而要探索多种风格。

①请求

appeal [5] [əˈpiːl] *v.&n.* 呼吁；恳求；上诉

[记] ap（to）+peal（改写自 plea）→"去求"；求你了，帮帮忙→ *v.&n.* 呼吁；恳求→"恳求不听，来硬的，我告你"→ *v.&n.* 上诉
[考] appeal to... 向……呼吁；对……有吸引力
[真] [B] It **appeals** mostly to big names.【2021 年 6 月 仔细阅读 53 题 B 选项】
[译] 它主要吸引名人。

pledge [2] [pledʒ] *v.* 保证，发誓，承诺　*n.* 保证，誓言，承诺

[记] pled（改写自 plea）+ge（无义）→"求别人的时候进一步就要保证、发誓、承诺了"，人们经常说，我求求你了，我保证，我发誓，我承诺→ *v.* 保证，发誓，承诺→ *n.* 保证，誓言，承诺

②高兴

pleasant [8] ['pleznt] *a.* 令人愉快的，高兴的；舒适的

六级基础词汇

［记］pleas（改写自 plea）+ant（*a.*）→ *a.* 令人愉快的，高兴的；舒适的

［派］unpleasant [ʌnˈpleznt] *a.* 令人不愉快的；不友善的

pleasure 6　[ˈpleʒə(r)] *n.* 愉快，快乐

六级基础词汇

［记］pleas（改写自 plea）+ure（*n.*）→ *n.* 愉快，快乐

扫码快速学习

扫码即刻听课

-ply-、-pli- 折

apply [20]

[əˈplaɪ] v. 申请，请求；应用，运用

[记] ap（to）+ply → "去折向什么" → v. 申请，请求；应用，运用
[派] appliance [əˈplaɪəns] n. 应用；（家用）电器
application [ˌæplɪˈkeɪʃn] n. 申请，请求；应用，运用
applicant [ˈæplɪkənt] n. 申请人
[考] apply to 适用于，运用于；致力于
apply for 申请
[真] [A] By **applying** the latest research methods.【2020年9月 听力4题A选项】
[译] 通过应用最新的研究方法。

imply [4]

[ɪmˈplaɪ] v. 暗示

[记] im（里）+ply → "折在里面"；把真正的意思折在话语里，自己悟；把真正的意思折在句子里，自己读出来 → v. 暗示
[派] implication [ˌɪmplɪˈkeɪʃn] n. 含意，言外之意
[真] What does the author **imply** about the various gadgets on cars?【2021年6月 仔细阅读52题题干】
[译] 作者对于汽车上的各种小工具有什么暗示？

comply [3]

[kəmˈplaɪ] v. 遵从，顺从

[记] com（共同，全部）+ply → "任所有人折来折去"；任人摆布 → v. 遵从，顺从
[派] compliance [kəmˈplaɪəns] n. 服从，听从
[考] comply with 服从，遵从
[真] Much to their frustration, managers often struggle to get their staff to **comply** with even simple instructions.【2021年6月 听力原文】
[译] 令管理人员感到沮丧的是，他们往往很难让他们的员工遵守哪怕非常简单的指示。

supply [12]

[səˈplaɪ] v.&n. 提供，供给   n. 供给物

137

六级基础词汇
[派] supplier [səˈplaɪə(r)] n. 供应商，供应者

–poli– 政治

politics [18]　[ˈpɒlətɪks] n. 政治，政治学

[记] poli+t（无义）+ics（表示学科的后缀）→ n. 政治，政治学
[派] political [pəˈlɪtɪkl] a. 政治的
politically [pəˈlɪtɪkli] ad. 政治上
politician [ˌpɒləˈtɪʃn] n. 政治家，政客
[真] French **political** commentators noted the devastating fire had succeeded where Macron had failed in uniting the country.【2021年6月 长篇阅读 K选项】
[译] 法国政治评论家指出，马克龙未能促进国家团结，但这场毁灭性的火灾使该目标得以实现。

policy [14]　[ˈpɒləsi] n. 政策，方针

[记] poli+cy（n.）→ "具体的政治" → n. 政策，方针
[派] policymaker [ˈpɒləsimeɪkə(r)] n. 政策制定者，决策人
[真] [A] The UK is set to adjust its **policy** on taxation.【2021年6月 仔细阅读 51题 A选项】
[译] 英国将调整其税收政策。

①港口

import [6]　[ɪmˈpɔːt] [ˈɪmpɔːt] v.&n. 进口，引进

[记] im（里）+port → "进入港口" → v.&n. 进口，引进
[真] [C] It has **imported** some exotic foods from overseas.【2019年12月 听力 12题 C选项】
[译] 它从海外进口了一些外来食品。

transport [8]　[trænˈspɔːt] [ˈtrænspɔːt] v.&n. 运输，运送　n. 交通工具

[记] trans（across；穿越，穿梭）+port → "穿梭于港口之间"；大的集装箱运输车穿梭于各大港口之间，后面跟货物，就是→ v.&n. 运输，运送 n. 交通工具
[派] transportation [ˌtrænspɔːˈteɪʃn] n. 运送，运输；交通工具
[真] Just as the environmental harm caused by aviation and other **transport** must come under far greater scrutiny, the social cost of tourism must also be confronted.【2021年6月 仔细阅读】

138

Day 19

[译] 正如必须要严格监管航空和其他交通带来的环境危害，我们也必须面对旅游业的社会成本。

report [40]

[rɪˈpɔːt] *v.* 报道，公布 *n.* 报告

六级基础词汇

[记] re（反复）+port → "reporter 表示记者"；记者常常各地跑，所以就是常去各个港口的人，其所做的工作就是→ *v.* 报道，公布 *n.* 报告

[派] reporter [rɪˈpɔːtə(r)] *n.* 记者
　　reportedly [rɪˈpɔːtɪdli] *ad.* 据报道

passport [4]

[ˈpɑːspɔːt] *n.* 护照

[记] pass（*n.&v.* 通过，经过）+port → "经过港口"，出示→ *n.* 护照

[真] If lifelong learning were to become a priority and the new norm, diplomas, just like **passports**, could be revalidated periodically. 【2020 年 12 月 长篇阅读 L 选项】

[译] 如果终身学习成为一个优先事项和新规范，文凭就可以像护照一样，定期重新验证。

② 扛，运输

support [16]

[səˈpɔːt] *v.&n.* 支持，支撑；赡养，供养

[记] sup（下）+port → "出什么事有我在下面支撑、扛着" → *v.&n.* 支持，支撑 → "子女对父母的支撑" → *v.&n.* 赡养，供养

[派] supportive [səˈpɔːtɪv] *a.* 支持的，拥护的
　　supporter [səˈpɔːtə(r)] *n.* 支持者，拥护者

[真] [D] It will win little **support** from environmental organisations. 【2020 年 9 月 仔细阅读 55 题 D 选项】

[译] 它几乎不会得到环保组织的支持。

-pos-、-pon- 放置

pose [4]

[pəʊz] *n.* 姿势，造型　*v.* 摆姿势；提出（问题）；造成（问题或危险）

[记] "摆 pose"；照相时摆什么? → *n.* 姿势，造型　*v.* 摆姿势→简写自 oppose（反对）→ "反对"时可能会进行质问，从而引申为→ *v.* 提出（问题）；造成（问题或危险）

[考] pose a threat to/pose threats to... 对……造成威胁
　　pose a risk to... 对……构成危险

[真] [D] It **posed** an unprecedented threat to the wildlife around Antarctica. 【2019 年 12 月 仔细阅读 51 题 D 选项】

[译] 它对南极洲周围的野生动物构成了前所未有的威胁。

puzzle [2]

[ˈpʌzl] *n.* 难题，谜　*v.*（使）迷惑，（使）为难

[记] puzz［改写自 pose；提出（问题）］+le（*n.&v.*）→ "提出问题" → *n.* 难题，谜　*v.*（使）迷惑，（使）为难

[助] pu（谐音"趴"）+zz（表示睡觉）+le（*n.&v.*）→ 遇到"puzzle"解不出来，只能"趴在那儿睡觉" → *n.* 难题，谜　*v.*（使）迷惑，（使）为难

[派] puzzlement [ˈpʌzlmənt] *n.* 迷惑，费解

position [8]

[pəˈzɪʃn] *n.* 位置；职位；立场，见解

[记] pos+it（它）+ion（*n.*）→ "把它放在那里"，就是它所处的 → *n.* 位置 → "在公司和企业中所处的位置" → *n.* 职位 → "每个人思想的位置" → *n.* 立场，见解

[真] [B] It is easy to become attached to the **position** of overlooking one's own fault.【2020 年 12 月 仔细阅读 52 题 B 选项】

[译] 人们很容易忽视自己的过错。

positive [28]

[ˈpɒzətɪv] *a.* 积极的，肯定的

[记] posit（改写自 pos）+ive（*a.*）→ 从主观心理和客观实际上"放下来了、确定下来了" → *a.* 积极的，肯定的

[派] positively [ˈpɒzətɪvli] *ad.* 积极地，肯定地

[反] negative [ˈneɡətɪv] *a.* 消极的，否定的
　　negatively [ˈneɡətɪvli] *ad.* 消极地，否定地

[真] Researchers, teachers, and artists are starting to see how drawing can **positively** impact a wide variety of skills and disciplines.【2021 年 6 月 仔细阅读】

[译] 研究人员、教师和艺术家们正开始了解绘画如何能够积极地影响多种技能和学科。

compose [5]

[kəmˈpəʊz] *v.* 组成，构成；创作（诗歌等），作曲

[记] com（全部，共同）+pos+e（无义）→ "把所有东西全部放在一起" → *v.* 组成，构成；创作（诗歌等），作曲

[派] composition [ˌkɒmpəˈzɪʃn] *n.* 组成；作品；作文
　　component [kəmˈpəʊnənt] *n.* 组成部分；成分

[考] be composed of...　由……组成

[真] Because they are **composed** of native English speakers deliberately placed together with recent immigrants, they tend to be more ethnically and economically balanced.【2020 年 9 月 长篇阅读 M 选项】

[译] 因为这是故意将当地的英语母语者和新移民放置一处，他们在种族上和经济上都更趋于平衡。

deposit [7]

[dɪˈpɒzɪt] *n.* 存款；沉积物　*v.* 存放；使沉淀

[记] de（下）+pos+it → "把它往下放"；挖个坑，把钱往下放到坑里 → *n.* 存款　*v.* 存放 → 在水里，往下放、往下沉 → *n.* 沉积物　*v.* 使沉淀

Day 19

[真] [D] There were oil **deposits** below a local gassy hill.【2021 年 6 月 听力 12 题 D 选项】
[译] 在当地充满气体的山下有石油储量。

dispose [2]
[dɪˈspəʊz] *v.* 处理，处置；布置，安排

[记] dis（散）+pos+e（无义）→ "四散摆放"，等待→ *v.* 处理，处置；布置，安排
[派] disposal [dɪˈspəʊzl] *n.* 处理；清除

expose [8]
[ɪkˈspəʊz] *v.* 暴露，揭露；接触

[记] ex（out）+pos+e（无义）→ "放在外面"，都能看到→ *v.* 暴露，揭露 → "暴露于"空气中，就是与空气→ *v.* 接触
[派] exposure [ɪkˈspəʊʒə(r)] *n.* 暴露，揭发
[考] be exposed to... 遭受……；暴露于……；接触……
[真] In a new study, people **exposed** to jargon when reading about subjects like autonomous vehicles and surgical robots later said they were less interested in science than others who read about the same topics, but without the use of specialized terms.【2021 年 6 月 听力原文】
[译] 在一项新研究中，人们在阅读有关自动驾驶汽车和外科手术机器人等主题时会遇到专业术语。这些人随后表示，他们对科学的兴趣不如其他阅读相同主题的人，而那些主题没有使用专业术语。

oppose [9]
[əˈpəʊz] *v.* 反对，反抗

[记] op（反对，相反）+pos+e（无义）→ *v.* 反对，反抗
[派] opposite [ˈɒpəzɪt] [ˈɒpəsɪt] *a.* 对面的；相反的
opposition [ˌɒpəˈzɪʃn] *n.* 反对，敌对，反抗
opponent [əˈpəʊnənt] *n.* 对手，反对者
[考] be opposed to... 与……相反/相对，不同于……
[真] [C] They are strongly **opposed** to it.【2021 年 6 月 听力 21 题 C 选项】
[译] 他们强烈反对它。

impose [6]
[ɪmˈpəʊz] *v.* 强加，强制实行

[记] im（里）+pos+e（无义）→ "把……放在里面"；硬往里放→ *v.* 强加，强制实行
[考] impose sth. on sb. 把某事强加于某人
[真] [D] **Impose** heavier penalties on speeding.【2021 年 6 月 听力 25 题 D 选项】
[译] 对超速驾驶处以更重的处罚。

suppose [6]
[səˈpəʊz] *v.* 假设，猜想

[记] sup（下）+pos+e（无义）→ "放下来；把前提条件放下来"→ *v.* 假设，猜想
[派] supposedly [səˈpəʊzɪdli] *ad.* 据认为，据猜测

[考] be supposed to do... 应该做……
[真] An exit interview is **supposed** to be private, but often isn't.【2021 年 6 月 听力原文】
[译] 离职面谈应该是私密的,但通常并非如此。

propose²⁴ [prəˈpəʊz] v. 求婚;建议,提议

[记] pro(前)+pose(v. 摆姿势)→"在恋人前摆个单膝跪地的姿势"→v. 求婚→求婚不是命令,而是一种→v. 建议,提议
[派] proposal [prəˈpəʊzl] n. 求婚;建议,提议
    proposition [ˌprɒpəˈzɪʃn] n. 建议;主张
[考] propose to do sth.=propose doing sth. 建议/打算做某事
[真] [B] Its researchers have already submitted relevant **proposals**.【2020 年 12 月 仔细阅读 52 题 B 选项】
[译] 研究人员已经提交了相关的建议。

possess⁶ [pəˈzes] v. 占有,拥有

[记] pos+sess(谐音"塞死")→"使劲放,塞到死";听上去就有种全部充满、拥有的感觉→v. 占有,拥有
[派] possession [pəˈzeʃn] n. 拥有;所有权;财产
[真] Obviously, we should **possess** some great stuff, but we want belongings that we're going to love for years.【2020 年 12 月 听力原文】
[译] 显然,我们应该拥有一些很棒的物品,但我们想要的是能够持续热爱多年的东西。

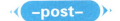

–post–

①作单词

post⁶ [pəʊst] n. 邮寄;邮件;邮政;职位,岗位;帖子 v. 贴出;公告;投寄

六级基础词汇,重点关注"帖子;贴出;公告"的含义
[派] postage [ˈpəʊstɪdʒ] n. 邮费
[真] The so-called "ghostwriting" can take various forms: books, articles, autobiographies, and even social media **posts**.【2021 年 6 月 仔细阅读】
[译] 所谓的"代写"形式多种多样:书籍、文章、自传,甚至是社交媒体上的帖子。

②作前缀时表示"后,向后"

postpone² [pəˈspəʊn] v. 推迟,延期

[记] post+pon(改写自 put;放,放置)+e(无义)→"往后放,往后

搁"→ v. 推迟，延期

[考] postpone sth. to... 把某事推迟／延期到……

–prec– 价值

precious [2]
[ˈpreʃəs] *a.* 珍贵的，宝贵的

[记] prec+ious（*a.*）→ "有价值的" → *a.* 珍贵的，宝贵的

appreciate [14]
[əˈpriːʃieɪt] *v.* 升值；欣赏；感激，感谢

[记] ap（to）+prec+i（无义）+ate（*v.*）→ "去变得有价值"；价值在上涨→ *v.* 升值 → "有没有价值除了自身，还取决于有没有人" → *v.* 欣赏→ "别人欣赏你，难道不应回馈？ → *v.* 感激，感谢

[派] appreciation [əˌpriːʃiˈeɪʃn] *n.* 升值；欣赏；感激，感谢
　　 appreciative [əˈpriːʃətɪv] *a.* 欣赏的；感激的，感谢的

[真] [C] It is an art form that is **appreciated** by all.【2021年6月 仔细阅读46题C选项】

[译] 这是一种人人都能欣赏的艺术形式。

–press– 压

press [2]
[pres] *v.* 压，按　*n.* 出版社；新闻记者（熟词僻义，重点关注）

六级基础词汇

express [6]
[ɪkˈspres] *v.* 表示，表达

[记] ex（out）+press → "压了出去"；把情感、情绪压出去→ *v.* 表示，表达

[派] expression [ɪkˈspreʃn] *n.* 表现，表达；表情

[真] [C] It makes their **expressions** more explicit.【2021年6月 听力9题C选项】

[译] 这使他们的表达更加清楚。

impress [10]
[ɪmˈpres] *v.* 给……留下印象

[记] im（里）+press →在"心里压压压"，时间长了留下很深的印象→ *v.* 给……留下印象

[派] impression [ɪmˈpreʃn] *n.* 印象
　　 impressive [ɪmˈpresɪv] *a.* 印象深刻的；感人的

[真] [D] Wear classic pieces to **impress** their clients.【2020年12月 听力15题D选项】

[译] 穿经典单品给客户留下深刻印象。

depress [6]
[dɪˈpres] *v.* 压下，压低；使沮丧

[记] de（下）+press → "压下去" → *v.* 压下，压低→把人往下压→ *v.* 使沮丧

［派］depression [dɪˈpreʃn] *n.* 萧条，经济衰退；抑郁，抑郁症

［真］Fred may say, "I'm always broke, frequently **depressed**."【2020 年 9 月 听力原文】

［译］弗莱德可能会说："我总是不断崩溃，经常灰心丧气。"

oppress 5

[əˈpres] *v.* 压迫，压制；使烦恼

［记］op（against）+press → "基于反对去压"别人→ *v.* 压迫，压制；使烦恼

［派］oppression [əˈpreʃn] *n.* 压迫；苦闷
　　 oppressive [əˈpresɪv] *a.* 压迫的，沉重的

［真］[C] One who acts in the interests of the **oppressed**.【2020 年 9 月 听力 17 题 C 选项】

［译］一个为被压迫者的利益而行事的人。

–pre–、–pro–、–pri– 前，以前，向前

previous 2

[ˈpriːviəs] *a.* 先前的，以前的

［记］pre+vi（无义）+ous（*a.*）→ *a.* 先前的，以前的

［派］previously [ˈpriːviəsli] *ad.* 事先，以前

prohibit 2

[prəˈhɪbɪt] *v.* 禁止，不准，阻止

［助］谐音"不要黑他"→ *v.* 禁止，不准，阻止

［派］prohibition [ˌprəʊɪˈbɪʃn] *n.* 禁令，禁律

prompt 9

[prɒmpt] *a.* 敏捷的，迅速的　*v.* 促进，推动

［记］pro+m（谐音"猛"）+p（谐音"跑"）+t（谐音"他"）→"他向前猛跑"，跑得真快！→ *a.* 敏捷的，迅速的→ *v.* 促进，推动

［派］promptly [ˈprɒmptli] *ad.* 敏捷地，迅速地，立即地

［考］prompt sb. to do sth. 促使 / 激励某人做某事

［真］[B] They are **prompted** to come up with ideas for making possible changes.【2020 年 12 月 仔细阅读 54 题 B 选项】

［译］他们被激励去思考出一些可能的改变。

prosecute 3

[ˈprɒsɪkjuːt] *v.* 告发，控告，起诉

［记］pro+ 词根 secu（跟随）+te（无义）→"跟紧前面的人"→ *v.* 告发，控告，起诉

［派］prosecution [ˌprɒsɪˈkjuːʃn] *n.* 控告，起诉
　　 prosecutor [ˈprɒsɪkjuːtə(r)] *n.* 公诉人；检察官

［真］He was also a skilled and sophisticated organizer, an entrepreneurial innovator, who mastered the use of corporate strategy, media relations, government lobbying, international diplomacy, patents, and **prosecution**.【2021 年 6 月 长篇阅读 C 选项】

［译］他还是一位技术娴熟、经验丰富的组织者、企业创新者，并精通企业战

略、媒体关系、政府游说、国际外交、专利和起诉的运用。

prosper [6]

[ˈprɒspə(r)] *v.* 繁荣，昌盛

[记] pro+sper → "充满希望向前" → *v.* 繁荣，昌盛
[派] prosperity [prɒˈsperəti] *n.* 繁荣，昌盛
　　 prosperous [ˈprɒspərəs] *a.* 繁荣的，昌盛的
[真] [B] It is bringing **prosperity** to the region.【2021 年 6 月 听力 19 题 B 选项】
[译] 它给该地区带来了繁荣。

prior [12]

[ˈpraɪə(r)] *a.* 优先的；在前的

[记] pri+or（表示人的后缀）→ "在前面的" → *a.* 优先的；在前的
[派] priority [praɪˈɒrəti] *n.* 优先，优先权
　　 prioritize/ise [praɪˈɒrətaɪz] *v.* 按重要性排列，划分优先顺序；优先处理
[考] be prior to... 比……优先
[真] [C] They **prioritize** arts subjects over maths and sciences.【2021 年 6 月 仔细阅读 49 题 C 选项】
[译] 他们优先考虑艺术学科，而不是数学和科学。

扫码快速学习

扫码即刻听课

-prim-、-prin- 第一

prime [praɪm] *a.* 首要的；最好的

[记] prim+e（无义）→ *a.* 首要的；最好的

primary [ˈpraɪməri] *a.* 主要的，首要的；最早的，最初的

[记] prim+ary（*a.*）→ "第一的" → "地位上第一的" → *a.* 主要的，首要的 → "时间上第一的" → *a.* 最早的，最初的

[派] primarily [praɪˈmerəli] [ˈpraɪmərəli] *ad.* 主要地，首要地

[真] It's an astonishing but statistical fact, a **primary** cause of employees' dissatisfaction, according to fresh research, is that many believe they have terrible managers. 【2021年6月 听力原文】

[译] 这是一个令人惊讶但有统计依据的事实，根据最新研究，员工不满的主要原因是许多人认为他们的经理很糟糕。

principle [ˈprɪnsəpl] *n.* 原则，准则；原理

[记] prin+ 词根 cip（抓）+le（*n.*）→ "第一位要抓住的" → 做人"第一位要抓住的" → *n.* 原则，准则→学习"第一位要抓住的" → *n.* 原理

[真] In *The Principle of Hope* (1954–1959), Ernst Bloch, one of the leading philosophers of the future, wrote that "the most tragic form of loss... is the loss of the capacity to imagine that things could be different". 【2020年12月 长篇阅读 I 选项】

[译] 在《希望的原理》（1954—1959）一书中，一位主要的未来哲学家恩斯特·布洛赫写道："最悲惨的损失……是无法想象事物可能会有所不同。"

principal [ˈprɪnsəpl] *n.* 校长；负责人 *a.* 主要的；最重要的

[记] prin+ 词根 cip（抓）+al（简写自 all；所有）→ "第一人，主抓所有事的人" → *n.* 校长；负责人→ *a.* 主要的；最重要的

-priv- 私人，个人

private [ˈpraɪvət] *a.* 私人的，个人的

六级基础词汇
[记] priv+ate（a.）→ a. 私人的，个人的
[派] privacy ['prɪvəsi] n. 隐私

deprive [10]
[dɪ'praɪv] v. 剥夺；使丧失

[记] de（否定）+priv+e（无义）→ "私人权利不断被否定" → v. 剥夺；使丧失
[派] deprivation [ˌdeprɪ'veɪʃn] n. 剥夺；丧失
[真] [A] To demonstrate the dilemma of people living in **deprived** areas.【2020 年 9 月仔细阅读 49 题 A 选项】
[译] 来展示贫困地区人们的困境。

-prov- 证明

prove [6]
[pru:v] v. 证明，证实

六级基础词汇

approve [4]
[ə'pru:v] v. 批准；赞同，同意

[记] ap（to）+prove（v. 证明）→ "去证明"；任何提拔都需要先证明自己的能力，领导才会→ v. 批准；赞同，同意
[派] approval [ə'pru:vl] n. 批准；赞同，同意
　　 disapprove [ˌdɪsə'pru:v] v. 不赞成，反对
　　 disapproval [ˌdɪsə'pru:vl] n. 不赞成，反对
[真] [C] It gives them **approval** regardless of opposition from nutrition experts.【2020 年 12 月仔细阅读 50 题 C 选项】
[译] 它不顾营养专家的反对，批准了这些建议。

improve [36]
[ɪm'pru:v] v. 提高，改善

[记] im（里）+prove（v. 证明）→ "心里的证明"；自己与自己较劲→ v. 提高，改善
[派] improvement [ɪm'pru:vmənt] n. 提高，改善
[真] This is because the more technology is put into the field, the more people are needed to deploy, maintain and **improve** it.【2021 年 6 月听力原文】
[译] 这是因为该领域使用的技术越多，需要部署、维护和改进它的人就越多。

-pub- 公开

public [30]
['pʌblɪk] a. 公共的，公开的　n. 公众

六级基础词汇
[派] publication [ˌpʌblɪ'keɪʃn] n. 出版；公布，发表

publish [10]

[ˈpʌblɪʃ] v. 出版；发行，发表

[记] pub+l（无义）+ish（v.）→ "使之成为公众的、公开的"→ v. 出版；发行，发表

[派] publisher [ˈpʌblɪʃə(r)] n. 出版者，出版商

[真] What is the conclusion of a recently-**published** report?【2021年6月 仔细阅读 47题题干】

[译] 最近发表的一份报告的结论是什么？

–put– 想，思考

reputation [8]

[ˌrepjuˈteɪʃn] n. 名声，名誉

[记] re（back）+put+ation（n.）→ "想起来，回想起"；若干年后，让别人想起来的印象，就是在他人心中的→ n. 名声，名誉

[真] There is always a chance that it could affect my **reputation** and my ability to network in the industry.【2021年6月 听力原文】

[译] 这很可能影响我的声誉以及我在行业内建立工作关系的能力。

dispute [4]

[dɪˈspjuːt] v.&n. 争论，争吵

[记] dis（散）+put+e（无义）→ "想法分散了，不往一个方向想了"；出现了→ v.&n. 争论，争吵

[派] disputable [dɪˈspjuːtəbl] a. 可争辩的，有争议的

[真] The cathedral is owned by the French state and has been at the centre of a years-long **dispute** over who should finance restoration work of the collapsing staircases, crumbling statues and cracked walls.【2021年6月 长篇阅读 D 选项】

[译] 这座大教堂为法国政府所有，多年来一直处于争论的中心，争论的焦点是谁应该资助倒塌的楼梯、摇摇欲坠的雕像和破碎的墙壁的修复工作。

非成组词（P 字母）

panic [2]

[ˈpænɪk] v.&n. 惊慌，恐慌

[助] pa（谐音"怕"）+ni（谐音"你"）+c（谐音"可"）→ "你可怕，可怕你了"→ v.&n. 惊慌，恐慌

patent [4]

[ˈpætnt] [ˈpeɪtnt] n. 专利，专利权 v. 获得……专利

[记] pa（简写自 pay；支付，付钱）+t（谐音"他"）+ent（n.&v.）→ "支付给他钱"，因为使用了别人的→ n. 专利，专利权 v. 获得……专利

[真] He was granted over 200 **patents** and continued to pioneer rocket technology until his death in 1945.【2021年6月 听力原文】

[译] 他获得了200多项专利，并持续开拓火箭技术，直到他在1945年去世为止。

peculiar [2]

[pɪˈkju:liə(r)] *a.* 奇怪的，古怪的；特有的，特殊的

[助] pe（谐音"皮"）+cu（谐音"酷"）+li（无义）+ar（表示人的后缀）→"此人长着很酷的皮"→ *a.* 奇怪的，古怪的；特有的，特殊的

[派] peculiarity [pɪˌkju:liˈærəti] *n.* 特性，特质；怪癖；奇怪

peer [8]

[pɪə(r)] *n.* 同等地位的人；同辈 *v.* 凝视

[助] p（谐音"趴"）+ee（两只眼睛）+r（人）→"趴在某地瞪着两只眼睛悄悄盯着其他人"；这是不是"同辈"经常干的事啊？→ *n.* 同等地位的人；同辈 →"瞪着两只眼睛看其他人"，本身就是→ *v.* 凝视

[真] A study showed that dual-language students did significantly better than their **peers** in reading English texts.【2020年9月 长篇阅读38题】

[译] 一项研究表明，双语学生在阅读英语文本方面的表现明显优于同龄人。

penalty [2]

[ˈpenəlti] *n.* 惩罚；罚款，罚金

[记] pen（改写自 punish；惩罚）+al（*n.*）+ty（*n.*）→惩罚；罚款，罚金

plausible [5]

[ˈplɔ:zəbl] *a.* 貌似真实的，貌似可信的

[记] plaus（简写自 applaud；鼓掌）+ible（*a.*）→"能鼓掌的"→ *a.* 貌似真实的，貌似可信的

[派] plausibly [ˌplɔ:zəbli] *ad.* 貌似真实地

[真] [B] It is difficult to sound natural or **plausible**.【2019年12月 仔细阅读47题B选项】

[译] 听起来自然或可信很难。

pollute [12]

[pəˈlu:t] *v.* 弄脏，污染

[记] 来自拉丁语动词 polluere（弄脏）→ *v.* 弄脏，污染

[助] 谐音"泼路"→"脏东西泼一路"→ *v.* 弄脏，污染

[派] pollution [pəˈlu:ʃn] *n.* 污染；污染物
    pollutant [pəˈlu:tənt] *n.* 污染物

[真] They suggest that geoengineering, cold fusion or faster-than-light spaceships might transcend once and for all the terrestrial constraints of rising temperatures, lack of energy, scarcity of food, lack of space, mountains of waste, **polluted** water—you name it.【2020年12月 长篇阅读E选项】

[译] 他们认为，地球工程、冷聚变或超光速宇宙飞船可能会彻底冲破你能想到的地球上的种种限制——气温上升、能源匮乏、食物短缺、空间不足、垃圾成山、水污染等。

potential [22]

[pəˈtenʃl] *n.* 潜力，潜能 *a.* 潜在的，可能的

[记] 词根 pot（改写自 pos=poss=possibility；可能，可能性）+ent（*n.&a.*）+ial（*n.&a.*）→有无限"可能"→ *n.* 潜力，潜能 *a.* 潜在的，可能的

[派] potentially [pəˈtenʃəli] *ad.* 潜在地

potentiality [pəˌtenʃiˈæləti] *n.* 潜力，潜能

[真] [D] They overestimate the **potential** market of autonomous cars.【2021 年 6 月 仔细阅读 51 题 D 选项】

[译] 他们高估了自动驾驶汽车的潜在市场。

pour [4]

[pɔː(r)] *v.* 涌出；倾泻；倒

[助] 谐音 "泼" → "水泼出去" → *v.* 涌出；倾泻；倒

[派] outpouring [ˈaʊtpɔːrɪŋ] *n.* 倾泻，流出

[考] pour A into B   把 A 倒入 B 中

[真] [D] **Pour** out his frustrations on a rate-your-employer website.【2021 年 6 月 听力 4 题 D 选项】

[译] 把他的沮丧发泄在一个"给雇主评分"的网站上。

poverty [4]

[ˈpɒvəti] *n.* 贫穷

[记] poor（*a.* 贫穷的）的名词 → *n.* 贫穷

[真] You should start your essay with a brief description of the chart and comment on China's achievements in **poverty** alleviation.【2021 年 6 月 作文题目】

[译] 首先，你应该简要描述一下图表，并评论中国在扶贫方面的成就。

-que-、-quire- 求

quest [3]

[kwest] *v.&n.* 追求；探索，寻找

[记] que+st（无义）→ *v.&n.* 追求 → "不停地去追求"，就是一种 → *v.&n.* 探索，寻找

[考] quest for   追求；探索

[真] [D] They should keep people from the unhealthy **quest** for perfection.【2020 年 12 月 仔细阅读 49 题 D 选项】

[译] 他们应该阻止人们对完美的一种不健康追求。

acquire [6]

[əˈkwaɪə(r)] *v.* 获得，得到

[记] ac（to）+quire → "去寻求"，不停地去寻求，就会 → *v.* 获得，得到

[派] acquisition [ˌækwɪˈzɪʃn] *n.* 获得；收购

[真] [B] It is a skill that is **acquired** with practice.【2021 年 6 月 仔细阅读 46 题 B 选项】

[译] 这是一种通过练习获得的技能。

require [50]

[rɪˈkwaɪə(r)] *v.* 需要，要求

[记] re（反复）+quire → "反复求" → *v.* 需要，要求

[派] requirement [rɪˈkwaɪəmənt] *n.* 需要，要求

[真] [C] It depends on the **required** knowledge for application.【2021 年 6 月 仔细阅读 54 题 C 选项】

[译] 这取决于申请所需的知识。

enquire/inquire [2]
[ɪnˈkwaɪə(r)] *v.* 询问,打听

[记] en/in(里)+quire → "在内部进行寻求、探索" → *v.* 询问,打听
[派] enquiry/inquiry [ɪnˈkwaɪəri] *n.* 询问;调查

①向回,向反,向后 =back、return

respond [16]
[rɪˈspɒnd] *v.* 回复,回答

[记] re+ 词根 spond(=spons;说)→ "话说回来";问一句,回一句 → *v.* 回复,回答
[派] response [rɪˈspɒns] *n.* 反应,回答
responsive [rɪˈspɒnsɪv] *a.* 应答的,响应的
[考] respond to... 对……回复,对……回答
in response to... 作为对……的回复/反应
in response 作为回复
[真] People **respond** to incentives such as traffic laws that are actually enforced.【2021年6月 听力原文】
[译] 人们会对实际执行的交通法规等激励措施有所反应。

reveal [10]
[rɪˈviːl] *v.&n.* 显示,揭露

[记] re+veal(改写自 veil;面纱)→ "面纱向后";露出容貌 → *v.&n.* 显示,揭露
[派] revelation [ˌrevəˈleɪʃn] *n.* 揭发,暴露;被揭露出来的事物
[真] Notre Dame Cathedral in the heart of Paris was within "15 to 30 minutes" of complete destruction as firefighters battled to stop flames reaching its bell towers on Monday evening, French authorities have **revealed**.【2021年6月 长篇阅读A选项】
[译] 法国当局透露,周一晚上,消防员奋力阻止火势蔓延到巴黎市中心的巴黎圣母院钟楼,避免了该教堂在 "15 至 30 分钟内" 完全被毁的悲剧。

reward [6]
[rɪˈwɔːd] *v.* 酬谢;奖赏 *n.* 酬金,报酬

[记] re+ward(谐音 "我的")→ 本来是 "我的",需要 "给回去";是给你的→ *v.* 酬谢;奖赏 *n.* 酬金,报酬
[派] rewarding [rɪˈwɔːdɪŋ] *a.* 值得的;有报酬的
[真] [B] It is usually financially **rewarding**.【2021年6月 听力16题B选项】
[译] 这通常有经济上的回报。

②反复，再一次 =again and again

relay [2]
[ˈriːleɪ] [ɪˈleɪ] *v.* 转播；转述；转送

[记] re+lay（*v.* 放）→ "反复放"→ *v.* 转播；转述；转送

reluctant [6]
[ɪˈlʌktənt] *a.* 不情愿的，勉强的

[记] re+luc（谐音"拉"）+t（谐音"他"）+ant（*a.*）→ "反复拉他"，他都不去，因为人家不情愿啊→ *a.* 不情愿的，勉强的

[派] reluctance [ɪˈlʌktəns] *n.* 不情愿，勉强

[考] be reluctant to do sth.　不情愿做某事

[真] [A] They are **reluctant** to follow instructions.【2021年6月 听力22题A选项】

[译] 他们不愿意听从指示。

recruit [4]
[ɪˈkruːt] *v.* 招聘　*n.* 新兵；新员工；新学生

[记] re+ 词根 cru（改写自 grow；生长，增长）+it（无义）→ 数量"反复增长"，就是招人，增人手→ *v.* 招聘　*n.* 新兵；新员工；新学生

[派] recruitment [ɪˈkruːtmənt] *n.* 招聘，招募
　　recruiter [ɪˈkruːtə(r)] *n.* 招聘人员

[真] [D] Most **recruiters** are unable to control their racial biases.【2020年7月 仔细阅读48题D选项】

[译] 大多数招聘人员都无法控制自己的种族偏见。

rehearse [2]
[ɪˈhɜːs] *v.* 排练，排演

[记] re+hear（*v.* 听）+se（*v.*）→ "反复听"节目→ *v.* 排练，排演

[派] rehearsal [ɪˈhɜːsl] *n.* 排练，排演

relax [6]
[ɪˈlæks] *v.*（使）放松，（使）松弛

[记] re+lax（*a.* 松的）→ 心情"反复松"→ *v.*（使）放松，（使）松弛

[派] relaxation [ˌriːlækˈseɪʃn] *n.* 放松，松弛

[真] [C] He had a great time sightseeing and **relaxing**.【2021年6月 听力5题C选项】

[译] 他在观光和放松时玩得很开心。

replace [8]
[ɪˈpleɪs] *v.* 替换，代替

[记] re+place（*n.* 地点，方）→ "反复的位置；人再一次到了一个位置"→ *v.* 替换，代替

[派] replacement [ɪˈpleɪsmənt] *n.* 代替

[考] replace A with B　用B代替A

[真] There's a risk that human civilization could be **replaced** by a superior type of digital life.【2020年12月 听力原文】

[译] 人类文明面临着有可能被一种更高级的数字生活取代的风险。

扫码快速学习

Day 21

扫码即刻听课

–rect–、–ract– 正,直

correct [6] [kəˈrekt] *a.* 正确的 *v.* 纠正

[记] cor(加强)+rect → *a.* 正确的 *v.* 纠正
[派] correction [kəˈrekʃn] *n.* 纠正,改正
correctly [kəˈrektli] *ad.* 正确地
[真] [C] It fosters **correct** interpretation of professional writing.【2021 年 6 月 仔细阅读 54 题 C 选项】
[译] 它促进了对专业写作的正确解释。

direct [16] [dəˈrekt] [dɪˈrekt] [daɪˈrekt] *v.* 指导,指引 *a.* 直接的

[记] di(无义)+rect → "给别人正确的方向" → *v.* 指导,指引→ "说话、做事很直" → *a.* 直接的
[派] direction [dəˈrekʃn] [dɪˈrekʃn] [daɪˈrekʃn] *n.* 方向;指导
director [dəˈrektə(r)] [dɪˈrektə(r)] [daɪˈrektə(r)] *n.* 主管;主人;导演;负责人
directness [dəˈrektnəs] [dɪˈrektnəs] [daɪˈrektnəs] *n.* 直接,率直
indirect [ˌɪndəˈrekt] [ˌɪndaɪˈrekt] *a.* 间接的
[真] There was a remarkably strong correlation between how helpful supervisors were perceived to be, and how likely their employees were to follow their **directors**.【2021 年 6 月 听力原文】
[译] 员工认为的得到上司的帮助程度与他们听从上司指示的可能性之间存在显著的相关性。

character [18] [ˈkærəktə(r)] *n.* 人物;性格;特点,特征

[记] cha(无义)+ract+er(表示人的后缀)→ "这个人很正直",这是在说→ *n.* 人物;性格→ "事物的性格" → *n.* 特点,特征
[派] characterize/ise [ˈkærəktəraɪz] *v.* 描绘……的特性;以……为特征
characteristic [ˌkærəktəˈrɪstɪk] *n.* 特性,特征,特色
[真] Increasingly, even Silicon Valley has to acknowledge the costs of the intoxicating(令人陶醉的) hurry that **characterises** its culture.【2021 年 6 月 仔细阅读】
[译] 渐渐地,就连硅谷也不得不承认其文化特点——这种令人陶醉的速度——

需要付出的代价。

–reg–、–rig–、–rog– 管理，统治

region [28]
['ri:dʒən] *n.* 地区，地域
[记] reg+ion（*n.*）→"管理、统治的地方"→ *n.* 地区，地域
[派] regional ['ri:dʒənl] *a.* 地区的，区域的
[真] A range of factors has pushed Western Australia's desert **region** to the lead of this automation revolution.【2021年6月 听力原文】
[译] 一系列因素促使西澳大利亚州的沙漠地区引领了这场自动化革命。

register [2]
['redʒɪstə(r)] *v.&n.* 登记，注册
[记] reg+ist（无义）+er（表示物的后缀）→"登记，注册"是一种"管理"的手段；比如外来人员出入中小学需要"登记"，这就是一种管理的手段→ *v.&n.* 登记，注册
[派] registration [ˌredʒɪ'streɪʃn] *n.* 登记，注册

regulate [28]
['regjuleɪt] *v.* 管理，控制；调节，调整
[记] reg+ul（中缀）+ate（*v.*）→ *v.* 管理，控制；调节，调整
[派] regulation [ˌregju'leɪʃn] *n.* 管理，控制；规章；制度
regulatory ['regjələtəri] *a.* 调整的；监管的
regulator ['regjuleɪtə(r)] *n.* 管理者；监管机构
[真] [C] Technological innovation should be properly **regulated**.【2021年6月 仔细阅读55题C选项】
[译] 应该适当地管控技术创新。

regular [8]
['regjələ(r)] *a.* 有规律的；普通的，平凡的
[记] reg+ul（中缀）+ar（*a.*）→ 有人"管理、控制"，又有"规章、制度"；人们的行为自然变得→ *a.* 有规律的→"循规蹈矩的"→ *a.* 普通的，平凡的
[派] regularly ['regjələli] *ad.* 有规律地
irregular [ɪ'regjələ(r)] *a.* 不规则的，无规律的
[真] [C] Lack of **regular** evaluation.【2021年6月 听力17题C选项】
[译] 缺乏定期评估。

rigorous [3]
['rɪgərəs] *a.* 严格的，严厉的；严密的
[记] rig+or（表示人的后缀）+ous（*a.*）→"管理人的方式"→ *a.* 严格的，严厉的；严密的
[派] rigorously ['rɪgərəsli] *ad.* 严厉地；残酷地
[真] [C] The absence of **rigorous** discipline.【2020年7月 仔细阅读52题C选项】

Day 21

[译] 缺乏严格的纪律。

arrogant [2] ['ærəgənt] *a.* 傲慢的，自大的

[记] ar（to）+rog+ant（*a.*）→ "对于傲慢、自大的员工要加强管理" → *a.* 傲慢的，自大的

[助] 谐音"俺要搞他"，因为他太傲慢自大了→ *a.* 傲慢的，自大的

[派] arrogance ['ærəgəns] *n.* 傲慢，自大

-riv- 河流

derive [2] [dɪˈraɪv] *v.* 源于，起源

[记] de（下）+riv+e（无义）→ "河流往下流"；源头在哪里？→ *v.* 源于，起源

[考] derive from　源于，起源于

thrive [5] [θraɪv] *v.* 繁荣，兴盛

[记] 沿着河流，两岸人类越来越多，人类几乎所有的早期文明都是河流文明，所以引申为→ *v.* 繁荣，兴盛

[派] thriving [ˈθraɪvɪŋ] *a.* 繁荣的，兴盛的

[真] All of us benefit from it and we **thrive** mentally and spiritually when we are able to wield it.【2021 年 6 月 仔细阅读】

[译] 我们所有人都因它受益，当我们能够驾驭它时，我们在智力上和精神上都会茁壮成长。

-rout- 路，道路

route [6] [ru:t] *n.* 路线

[记] rout+e（无义）→抽象的"路" → *n.* 路线

[真] They are a technological leap, transporting iron ore along **routes** which run for hundreds of kilometers from mines to their destinations.【2021 年 6 月 听力原文】

[译] 它们是一项技术飞跃，沿着从矿山到目的地的数百公里路线运输铁矿石。

routine [8] [ru:ˈti:n] *n.* 例行公事，常规　*a.* 常规的，日常的

[记] rout+in（里）+e（无义）→ "天天都在这条 route 里"，每天都一样→ *n.* 例行公事，常规　*a.* 常规的，日常的

[派] routinely [ru:ˈti:nli] *ad.* 例行公事地，常规地

[真] Pollio conducted a study that proved humour can help workers excel at **routine** production tasks.【2020 年 7 月 听力原文】

[译] 波利奥做了一项研究，证明幽默可以帮助员工在日常工作任务中有杰出表现。

非成组词（R 字母）

race [10]
[reɪs] *n.* 人种，种族；赛跑 *v.* 赛跑
[记] r（辅音字母表示"人"）+ace（无义）→ *n.* 人种，种族；进而引申为→ *n.&v.* 赛跑
[派] racial [ˈreɪʃl] *a.* 人种的，种族的
[真] American public school classrooms as a whole are becoming more segregated by **race** and class.【2020 年 9 月 长篇阅读 M 选项】
[译] 整体上，美国公立学校的班级由于种族和阶级变得越来越分离。

radical [18]
[ˈrædɪkl] *a.* 根本的；激进的 *n.* 激进分子
[记] 词根 rad（改写自 root；根）+ic（*a.*）+al（*a.*）→ *a.* 根本的→"从根本上相信某个理念"的人→ *a.* 激进的 *n.* 激进分子
[真] To me, a **radical** is simply someone who rebels against the norm while advocates a change in the existing state of affairs.【2020 年 9 月 听力原文】
[译] 对我来说，激进分子只不过是反抗常规，同时倡导改变现状的人。

rapid [18]
[ˈræpɪd] *a.* 快速的
[记] 改写自 rabbit（兔子）→"跑得像兔子一样快"→ *a.* 快速的
[派] rapidly [ˈræpɪdli] *ad.* 很快地，快速地
[真] [A] It contributes to **rapid** business expansion.【2021 年 6 月 听力 17 题 A 选项】
[译] 它有助于业务的快速扩张。

rational [12]
[ˈræʃnəl] *a.* 理性的；合理的
[记] rat（简写自 rate；评估，评价）+ion（*n.*）+al（*a.*）→经过评估、评价的→ *a.* 理性的；合理的
[派] rationalise/ize [ˈræʃənəlaɪz] *v.* 使合理化
　　irrational [ɪˈræʃnəl] *a.* 不理性的，不合理的
[真] But even if we think they are ridiculous, emotions can be just as powerful as **rational** thinking.【2020 年 9 月 听力原文】
[译] 但是即使我们认为情感很荒谬，它们也可以和理性思考一样强大。

realize/ise [25]
[ˈriːəlaɪz] *v.* 实现；意识到
[记] real 的动词；real（*a.* 真实的）+ ize/ise（使动）→"使之成为真的"，就是→ *v.* 实现；意识到
[派] realization/sation [ˌriːəlaɪˈzeɪʃn] [ˌrɪəlaɪˈzeɪʃn] *n.* 实现；领会
　　reality [riˈæləti] *n.* 现实，事实
　　realistic [ˌriːəˈlɪstɪk] [ˌrɪəˈlɪstɪk] *a.* 现实的，现实主义的
　　unrealistic [ˌʌnrɪəˈlɪstɪk] *a.* 不现实的，不切实际的
[真] Most of them don't **realize** the harmful effects of this practice.【2021 年 6 月

Day 21

听力原文】
［译］他们中的大多数都没有意识到这种做法带来的负面影响。

release 15
[rɪˈliːs] *v.&n.* 释放；发布，发行（熟词僻义，重点关注）

六级基础词汇

［真］Recently, Jane, you've become quite a celebrity, since the **release** of your latest documentary.【2021 年 6 月 听力原文】
［译］简，最近自从你的最新纪录片上映后，你就成了一个名人。

ridiculous 6
[rɪˈdɪkjələs] *a.* 荒谬的，可笑的

［助］谐音"真的可乐死"→"这事可乐死我了"，实在是太→ *a.* 荒谬的，可笑的
［派］ridicule [ˈrɪdɪkjuːl] *v.&n.* 嘲笑，嘲弄
［真］But even if we think they are **ridiculous**, emotions can be just as powerful as rational thinking.【2020 年 9 月 听力原文】
［译］但是即使我们认为情感很荒谬，它们也可以和理性思考一样强大。

robot 12
[ˈrəʊbɒt] *n.* 机器人

六级科技类文章高频词

［派］robotic [rəʊˈbɒtɪk] *a.* 机器人的；自动的
［真］It may only be five years before the use of automation technology leads to a fully **robotic** mine.【2021 年 6 月 听力原文】
［译］使用自动化技术可能只需要五年时间就可以让矿山实现完全自动化操作。

royal 2
[ˈrɔɪəl] *a.* 皇室的；高贵的 *n.* 皇室，皇室成员

［助］谐音"荣耀"→"无限光荣与荣耀"→ *a.* 皇室的；高贵的 *n.* 皇室，皇室成员
［派］royalty [ˈrɔɪəlti] *n.* 王位，王权

royal 的引申词

loyal 3
[ˈlɔɪəl] *a.* 忠诚的，忠贞的 *n.* 效忠的臣民

［记］loyal 模仿 royal（*n.* 皇室，皇室成员）→对于"royal"要"loyal"→ *a.* 忠诚的，忠贞的 *n.* 效忠的臣民
［派］loyalty [ˈlɔɪəlti] *n.* 忠诚
［真］As an adult, Marconi had an intuition that he had to be **loyal** to politicians in order to be influential.【2021 年 6 月 长篇阅读 37 题】
［译］成年后，马可尼有一种直觉，即他必须忠于政客才能有影响力。

-sect-、-seg- 部分

sector [5]
['sektə(r)] *n.* 部分；部门；区域

[记] sect+or（表示物的后缀）→ "一部分，一部分的东西" → *n.* 部分；部门；区域

[考] public sector 公共部门
　　private sector 私营部门
　　state sector 国营部门
　　education sector 教育部门

[真] But in the state **sector** the excessive focus on English, maths and science threatens to crush arts subjects; meanwhile, reduced school budgets mean diminishing extracurricular activities.【2021 年 6 月 仔细阅读】

[译] 但在公立学校，对英语、数学和科学这些科目的过度关注可能会压垮艺术学科的发展；同时，学校预算的减少意味着课外活动的不断减少。

insect [3]
['ɪnsekt] *n.* 昆虫

[记] in（里）+sect → "里面一部分一部分的生物"，节支类动物 → *n.* 昆虫

[真] [D] It has joined hands with Sainsbury's to sell pet **insects**.【2019 年 12 月 听力 12 题 D 选项】

[译] 它已经与塞恩斯伯里公司联手出售宠物昆虫。

-sens-、-sent-

①送，派遣

absent [4]
['æbsənt] *a.* 缺席的，不到场的

[记] ab（否定）+sent → "不把自己送到……面前"，就是不来了 → *a.* 缺席的，不到场的

[派] absence ['æbsəns] *n.* 缺席，缺勤；不存在，缺失

[考] be absent from 缺席
　　in the absence of... 缺乏 / 没有……

[真] Both **absent**-minded doodling and copying from life have been shown to positively affect your memory and visual perception, so complain loudly the next time your school board slashes the art department's budget.【2021 年 6 月 仔细阅读】

[译] 心不在焉的涂鸦和对生活的复现都会积极地影响你的记忆力和视觉感知，所以下次学校董事会削减艺术系的预算时，你可以大声抱怨。

present [28]
['preznt] [prɪ'zent] *n.* 礼物；现在 *a.* 出席的；当前的 *v.* 提供，呈现

Day 21

[记] pre（前）+sent → "送到面前" → n. 礼物；现在 v. 提供，呈现→把自己"送到……面前" → a. 出席的；当前的

[派] presence ['prezns] n. 出席；存在
presently ['prezntli] ad. 目前，现在

[真] [B] They **present** a false picture of the autonomy cars provide.【2021年6月仔细阅读 51 题 B 选项】

[译] 它们错误描述了汽车提供的自主性。

represent [16]

[ˌreprɪ'zent] v. 代表；象征

[记] re（反复）+present（v. 出席，到场）→ "与之相关的活动总是出席、到场" → v. 代表；象征

[派] representation [ˌreprɪzen'teɪʃn] n. 表现，陈述
representative [ˌreprɪ'zentətɪv] n. 代表 a. 典型的；有代表性的

[真] [B] Subtlety of **representation**.【2021年6月长篇阅读 50 题 B 选项】

[译] 陈述的微妙之处。

②感觉，情绪

sense [23]

[sens] v.&n. 感觉，意识

六级基础词汇

sentiment [3]

['sentɪmənt] n. 感情；情绪

[记] sent+i（无义）+ment（n.）→ n. 感情；情绪

[派] sentimental [ˌsentɪ'mentl] a. 伤感的；多愁善感的

[真] [B] Teenagers are much more **sentimental**.【2020年12月听力 25 题 B 选项】

[译] 青少年更多愁善感。

sensitive [7]

['sensətɪv] a. 敏感的；灵敏的

[记] sens+itive（a.）→ "感觉多的"；人感觉多，情绪多→ a. 敏感的→仪器能感觉细微的事物→ a. 灵敏的

[派] sensitivity [ˌsensə'tɪvəti] n. 敏感；灵敏

[考] be sensitive to... 对……敏感；对……灵敏

[真] [A] Teenagers are much more **sensitive**.【2020年12月听力 25 题 A 选项】

[译] 青少年更敏感。

consensus [2]

[kən'sensəs] n. 一致，一致同意

[记] con（共同，全部）+sens+us（我们）→ "我们有同感" → n. 一致，一致同意

resent [4]

[rɪ'zent] v. 憎恨，讨厌

［记］re（back）+sent → "反感"；连在一起很像人们说的"此事我很反感"→ *v.* 憎恨，讨厌

［派］resentment [rɪˈzentmənt] *n.* 愤恨，不满

［真］[A] They only feel angry about their ill treatment and **resent** whoever tries to help.【2020 年 12 月 仔细阅读 51 题 A 选项】

［译］他们只对自己受到的虐待感到愤怒，怨恨任何试图帮助他们的人。

–sert– 塞，放

assert⁵

[əˈsɜːt] *v.* 声称，断言，主张

［记］as（加强）+sert → "把话放在这儿"；我今天把话放在这儿→ *v.* 声称，断言，主张

［派］assertion [əˈsɜːʃn] *n.* 声称，主张

［考］assert that... 声称 / 主张……

［真］Experts **assert** homework requiring the Internet isn't fair.【2021 年 6 月 听力原文】

［译］专家认为，需要使用互联网完成的家庭作业是不公平的。

exert⁵

[ɪɡˈzɜːt] *v.* 发挥，运用；努力

［记］ex（out）+ert（简写自 sert）→ "放出去"；把能力、力气放出去→ *v.* 发挥，运用；努力

［真］Genetic selection is a way of **exerting** influence over others, "the ultimate collective control of human destinies", as writer H.G.Wells put it.【2021 年 6 月 仔细阅读】

［译］正如作家 H.G. 威尔斯所言，基因选择是对他人施加影响的一种方式，"是对人类命运的最终集体控制"。

desert⁴

[ˈdezət] [dɪˈzɜːt] *n.* 沙漠 *v.* 抛弃，遗弃

［记］de（下）+sert → "放在下面"；人们不要的、讨厌的东西，扔在下面→ *v.* 抛弃，遗弃→ "被遗弃的土地"→ *n.* 沙漠

［派］deserted [dɪˈzɜːtɪd] *a.* 无人居住的；被抛弃的

［形］dessert [dɪˈzɜːt] *n.* 正餐后的水果或甜食

［真］[A] In the **deserted** fields.【2020 年 7 月 听力 19 题 A 选项】

［译］在荒野。

扫码快速学习

扫码即刻听课

① 服务

service [38] [ˈsɜːvɪs] *n.* 服务

六级基础词汇
[记] serv+ice（*n.*）→ *n.* 服务

② 保持，保留

conserve [16] [kənˈsɜːv] *v.* 保护；保存

[记] con（共同，全部）+serv+e（无义）→ "把所有的都保持下来" → *v.* 保护；保存
[派] conservative [kənˈsɜːvətɪv] *a.* 保守的
　　conservation [ˌkɒnsəˈveɪʃn] *n.* 保护；保存
[真] [C] **Conserve** animal species in a novel and all-round way.【2020 年 12 月 仔细阅读 55 题 C 选项】
[译] 以一种新颖而全面的方式保护动物物种。

preserve [6] [prɪˈzɜːv] *v.* 保持；保存；保鲜

[记] pre（前）+serv+e（无义）→ "提前保留在冰箱" → *v.* 保持；保存；保鲜
[派] preservation [ˌprezəˈveɪʃn] *n.* 保持；保存；保鲜
[真] [B] Make efforts to **preserve** each individual chimp community.【2020 年 12 月仔细阅读 54 题 B 选项】
[译] 努力保护每个黑猩猩的群落。

deserve [4] [dɪˈzɜːv] *v.* 应受，应得

[记] de（下）+serv+e（无义）→ "留下来"；别客气，留下吧，因为你→ *v.* 应受，应得
[真] [C] To highlight the area **deserving** the most attention from the public.【2020

161

年 9 月 仔细阅读 49 题 C 选项】
[译] 为了突出这个最值得公众关注的地区。

reserve²⁵

[rɪˈzɜːv] v. 储备；保留；预约

[记] re（反复）+serv+e（无义）→ "再一次保留下来" → v. 储备；保留→ "把包间先留下来" → v. 预约

[派] reservation [ˌrezəˈveɪʃn] n. 保留；预约

[真] [C] They should be **reserved** for urgent communication.【2021 年 6 月 听力 25 题 C 选项】

[译] 它们应该被保留下来，用于紧急沟通。

observe⁷

[əbˈzɜːv] v. 观察；遵守

[记] ob（加强）+serv+e（无义）→ "保留在眼前" → v. 观察 → "保持规则" → v. 遵守

[派] observation [ˌɒbzəˈveɪʃn] n. 观察，观察力；遵守
observer [əbˈzɜːvə(r)] n. 观察者，观察员

[真] [D] **Observe** carefully how their partners make use of gestures.【2021 年 6 月 仔细阅读 51 题 D 选项】

[译] 仔细观察对方是如何使用手势的。

–sid– 坐

consider⁴⁰

[kənˈsɪdə(r)] v. 考虑；认为

六级基础词汇

[记] con（全部，共同）+sid+er（表示人的后缀）→ "所有人坐在一起" → v. 考虑；认为

[派] consideration [kənˌsɪdəˈreɪʃn] n. 考虑
considering [kənˈsɪdərɪŋ] prep. 考虑到，鉴于
considerate [kənˈsɪdərət] a. 考虑周到的，体贴的
considerable [kənˈsɪdərəbl] a. 相当大的，相当多的
considerably [kənˈsɪdərəbli] ad. 相当，非常

[考] consider A as B   把 A 认为是 / 当作 B
be considered (as)...   被认为是……
take sth. into consideration   考虑……

site⁹

[saɪt] n. 地点；遗址；场所；网站

[记] sit（v. 坐）+e（无义）→ "坐落" 在某地，就是→ n. 地点；遗址；场所；网站

[派] website [ˈwebsaɪt] n. 网站

[真] [B] **Sites** of cultural pilgrimage are always flooded with visitors.【2020 年 12 月 仔细阅读 48 题 B 选项】

[译] 文化朝圣的地点总是充满着游客。

Day 22

resident [8]
[ˈrezɪdənt] *n.* 居民　*a.* 居住的

[记] re（反复）+sid+ent（表示人的后缀）→ "长期反复坐在某个城市里的人"，就是这个城市的→ *n.* 居民→ *a.* 居住的

[派] reside [rɪˈzaɪd] *v.* 居住
residence [ˈrezɪdəns] *n.* 住处，住宅

[真] This includes the impact of short-term lets on housing costs and quality of life for **residents**.【2021 年 6 月 仔细阅读】

[译] 其中包括短期租房对当地居民住房成本以及生活质量造成的影响。

obsess [4]
[əbˈses] *v.* 使着迷，迷住

[记] ob（加强）+sess（改写自 sid）→ "坐上去的"，指传说中鬼神附体或着魔，引申为→ *v.* 使着迷，迷住

[助] 谐音 "哦，不，塞死"→肚子里塞得好满，快塞死了，好喜欢→ *v.* 使着迷，迷住

[派] obsession [əbˈseʃn] *n.* 痴迷；使人痴迷的人或物

[真] [B] Their **obsession** with consumption.【2020 年 12 月 听力 16 题 B 选项】

[译] 他们对消费的痴迷。

–sign– 签，符号

sign [10]
[saɪn] *v.* 签　*n.* 符号；标志；迹象（熟词僻义，重点关注）

六级基础词汇

[派] signature [ˈsɪɡnətʃə(r)] *n.* 签名，署名

[真] [A] Clearer road **signs**.【2020 年 12 月 听力 4 题 A 选项】

[译] 道路标志更清晰。

design [36]
[dɪˈzaɪn] *v.&n.* 设计，构思

[记] de（下）+sign → "在下面签字"；古代的文人、诗人会在其作品下面签字、署名以表示是自己创作的，引申为在科学、仪器、发明的下面签字，表示由自己→ *v.&n.* 设计，构思

[派] designer [dɪˈzaɪnə(r)] *n.* 设计师，设计者

[近] devise [dɪˈvaɪz] *v.* 设计，发明

[真] [C] They pursue individuality and originality in **design** concept.【2021 年 6 月 仔细阅读 51 题 C 选项】

[译] 他们追求设计理念中的个性和原创性。

designate [4]
[ˈdezɪɡneɪt] *v.* 指明，指出；指派

[记] de（下）+sign+ate（*v.*）→ "签到下面去了"；从中央到了地方→ *v.* 指明，指出；指派

[真] The remaining 30% is for recreation and entertainment, but for many young people, it'll be difficult to **designate** such a large proportion of their income for savings.【2020 年 12 月 听力原文】

[译] 剩下的 30% 用于休闲和娱乐，但对很多年轻人来说，很难存储这么大比例的收入。

assign [7]

[əˈsaɪn] *v.* 分配；分派

[记] as（to）+sign → "去签字"；古时签军令状，签完就表示这个任务是你的，就是把任务给你了 → *v.* 分配；分派

[派] assignment [əˈsaɪnmənt] *n.* 分配；任务，工作

[真] Studies found that in remote areas, the poor quality or lack of Internet access can put students at a disadvantage because 70% of teachers in these areas **assign** homework that requires Internet access.【2021 年 6 月 听力原文】

[译] 研究发现，在偏远地区，网络质量差或缺乏网络连接会使学生处于不利地位，因为这些地区 70% 的教师布置的家庭作业需要借助网络完成。

–sim–、–sem–、–sym–、–syn– 相同

simplify [2]

[ˈsɪmplɪfaɪ] *v.* 简化，使简单

[记] simpl（简写自 simple；简单的）+ify（使动）→ "使之简单" → *v.* 简化，使简单

[派] simplification [ˌsɪmplɪfɪˈkeɪʃn] *n.* 简化，简单

simulate [6]

[ˈsɪmjuleɪt] *v.* 模仿，模拟

[记] sim+ul（中缀）+ate（*v.*）→ "做相同"的事；你怎么做，我就怎么做 → *v.* 模仿，模拟

[派] simulation [ˌsɪmjuˈleɪʃn] *n.* 模仿，模拟
　　simulator [ˈsɪmjuleɪtə(r)] *n.* 模拟装置，模拟器

[真] AI will be able to completely **simulate** a person in every way possible.【2020 年 12 月 听力原文】

[译] 人工智能可以用尽一切可能的方式完全模拟一个人。

resemble [4]

[rɪˈzembl] *v.* 像，类似于

[记] re（反复）+sem+ble（无义）→ "反复相同，各方面都相同" → *v.* 像，类似于

[派] resemblance [rɪˈzembləns] *n.* 相似，形似

[真] This refers to the idea that when objects trying to **resemble** humans aren't quite perfect, they can make viewers feel uneasy because they fall somewhere between obviously non-human and fully human.【2021 年 6 月 长篇阅读 J 选项】

[译] "诡异谷"效应指的是，物体试图模仿人类，但效果并不完美时，就会让观众感到不适，因为它们介于显而易见的非人类和真正的人类之间。

sympathy [3]

[ˈsɪmpəθi] *n.* 同情，同情心；赞同

Day 22

[记] sym+ 词根 path（=feeling；感情，情绪）+y（n.）→ "相同的感情"，简称 → n. 同情，同情心 → "相同的感情"，必然彼此 → n. 赞同

[派] sympathetic [ˌsɪmpəˈθetɪk] a. 同情的

[考] in sympathy with 同情，赞成

[真] [A] When both sides are **sympathetic** with each other.【2021年6月 仔细阅读 52题A选项】

[译] 当双方都互相同情时。

symbol 9 [ˈsɪmbl] n. 象征，标志，符号

[派] symbolic [sɪmˈbɒlɪk] a. 象征的，象征性的
symbolize/ise [ˈsɪmbəlaɪz] v. 象征；用符号表达

[真] There is something almost delightful in the detachment from reality of advertisements showing mass-produced cars marketed as **symbols** of individuality and of freedom when most of their lives will be spent making short journeys on choked roads.【2021年6月 仔细阅读】

[译] 汽车大规模量产，被营销成为个性和自由的象征，这种广告呈现美妙得无以复加但脱离了现实，购车后人们的大部分时间都在拥挤不堪的道路上做短途旅行。

synonym 2 [ˈsɪnənɪm] n. 同义词

[记] syn+o（无义）+ 词根 nym（改写自 name；名字）→ "相同名字"的词 → n. 同义词

[派] synonymous [sɪˈnɒnɪməs] a. 同义的，同义词的

–soci– 社会

socialize/ise 3 [ˈsəʊʃəlaɪz] v. 与……交往，参与社交

[记] social（a. 社会的）+ize/ise（使动）→ "使之社会" → v. 与……交往，参与社交

[派] sociality [ˌsəʊʃɪˈælɪti] n. 社会性

[真] [C] They are born with a stronger ability to **socialize**.【2021年6月 听力19题C选项】

[译] 他们天生就有更强的社交能力。

associate 27 [əˈsəʊsieɪt] [əˈsəʊʃieɪt] [əˈsəʊʃiət] v. 交往，联系 n. 伙伴

[记] as（to）+soci+ate（v.&n.）→ "去社会，进入社会"；进入社会后就免不了与别人 → v. 交往，联系 → 经常和我们"交往，联系"的人 → n. 伙伴

[派] association [əˌsəʊsiˈeɪʃn] [əˌsəʊʃiˈeɪʃn] n. 联合；协会，社团

[考] associate A with B   把A和B联系起来
be associated with... 与……有关

[真] Many public health policymakers believe that the resolution of age-**associated** disease will tell us something fundamental about the aging process.【2021 年 6 月 听力原文】

[译] 许多公共卫生政策制定者认为，解决与年龄相关的疾病会让我们了解关于衰老过程的一些基本情况。

–sol– 单独

sole [3]
[səʊl] *a.* 单独的，唯一的
[记] sol+e（无义）→ *a.* 单独的，唯一的
[派] solely [ˈsəʊlli] *ad.* 单独地；仅仅地
[真] [B] Its **sole** responsibility for providing dietary advice.【2020 年 12 月 仔细阅读 54 题 B 选项】
[译] 它的唯一责任是提供饮食建议。

solitude [13]
[ˈsɒlɪtjuːd] *n.* 独处，独居
[记] sol+it（它）+ude → "它是单独的" → *n.* 独处，独居
[真] A second study measured the effects of **solitude** on low-arousal emotions.【2020 年 12 月 听力原文】
[译] 第二项研究评估了独处对低唤醒情绪的影响。

isolate [6]
[ˈaɪsəleɪt] *v.* （使）隔离；（使）孤立
[记] i（我）+sol+ate（*v.*）→ "使我孤身一人的动作" → *v.* （使）隔离；（使）孤立
[派] isolation [ˌaɪsəˈleɪʃn] *n.* 隔离；孤立
[真] [C] It may make us feel **isolated** and incompetent.【2020 年 12 月 仔细阅读 46 题 C 选项】
[译] 它可能会让我们感到孤立和无能。

insulate
[ˈɪnsjuleɪt] *v.* 隔离；使免除
[记] in（里）+sul（改写自 sol）+ate（*v.*）→ "使其进入单独、孤独里面" → *v.* 隔离；使免除
[派] insulation [ˌɪnsjuˈleɪʃn] *n.* 隔热材料；隔音

–solv–、–solu– 解决，溶解

solve [15]
[sɒlv] *v.* 解决；溶解
六级基础词汇
[记] solv+e（无义）→ *v.* 解决；溶解
[派] solution [səˈluːʃn] *n.* 解决，解决方案；溶解；溶液

resolve [5]
[rɪˈzɒlv] *v.* 解决；决心，决定

Day 22

［记］re（反复）+solv+e（无义）→ "反复解决" → v. 解决→ "反复解决" 表示你已经下了→ v. 决心，决定
［派］resolution [ˌrezəˈluːʃn] n. 解决；决心
［考］resolve to do sth.　决心/决定做某事
［真］[B] When ideological differences are **resolved**.【2020 年 12 月 仔细阅读 50 题 B 选项】
［译］当意识形态不同的问题得到解决时。

absolute [4]

[ˈæbsəluːt] a. 绝对的，完全的

［记］ab（否定）+solu+te（无义）→ "不能解决的"；这个世界上真正不好解决的或者不能解决的都是世间的绝对真理，比如一加一等于二，人人都知道，但是你无法证明为什么。再比如，怎么能过英语四六级和考研英语？我说，把单词背完，长难句搞定，可是这两件事都需要日积月累，都不好解决→ a. 绝对的，完全的
［派］absolutely [ˈæbsəluːtli] ad. 绝对地，完全地
［真］**Absolutely** not.【2021 年 6 月 听力原文】
［译］当然不是。

-soph- 智慧，思考

philosophy [3]

[fəˈlɒsəfi] n. 哲学

［记］词根 philo（爱，爱好）+soph+y（n.）→ "热爱" 知识，追求 "智慧" → n. 哲学
［派］philosopher [fəˈlɒsəfə(r)] n. 哲学家
　　　philosophical [ˌfɪləˈsɒfɪkl] a. 哲学的
［真］Why did the late **philosopher** Richard Wollheim spend four hours before a picture?【2020 年 12 月 仔细阅读 47 题题干】
［译］为什么已故的哲学家理查德·沃尔海姆要在一幅画前待四个小时？

sophisticated [9]

[səˈfɪstɪkeɪtɪd] a. 先进的；老练的；复杂的

［记］soph+（h）is（他的）+t（无义）+ic（a.）+ate（a.）+(e)d（a.）→ "他的智慧"，他很有智慧→ a. 老练的→ "一个东西很有智慧" → a. 先进的；复杂的
［真］[B] Conduct their research using more **sophisticated** technology.【2021 年 6 月 仔细阅读 49 题 B 选项】
［译］使用更先进的技术进行他们的研究。

-spec- 专门的

special [8]

[ˈspeʃl] a. 特殊的；专门的

［记］spec+ial（a.）→ a. 特殊的；专门的

[真] [B] Drawing is a skill that requires **special** training.【2021 年 6 月 仔细阅读 48 题 B 选项】
[译] 绘画是一种需要特殊训练的技能。

specialize/ise [8]

[ˈspeʃəlaɪz] *v.* 专门从事；专攻

[记] special（*a.* 专门的）+ize/ise（使动）→ "使之专门研究一个领域" → *v.* 专门从事；专攻
[派] specialist [ˈspeʃəlɪst] *n.* 专家
[考] specialize in 专攻
specialist in... 某方面的专家
[真] In a new study, people exposed to jargon when reading about subjects like autonomous vehicles and surgical robots later said they were less interested in science than others who read about the same topics, but without the use of **specialized** terms.【2021 年 6 月 听力原文】
[译] 在一项新研究中，人们在阅读有关自动驾驶汽车和外科手术机器人等主题时会遇到专业术语。这些人随后表示，他们对科学的兴趣不如其他阅读相同主题的人，而那些主题没有使用专业术语。

specific [6]

[spəˈsɪfɪk] *a.* 明确的；具体的；特殊的

[记] spec+if（无义）+ic（*a.*）→ "专门说明的" → *a.* 明确的；具体的；特殊的
[派] specifically [spəˈsɪfɪkli] *ad.* 明确地；具体地；特殊地
[真] As *Nature* went to press, the Australian government had not responded to **specific** criticisms of the plan.【2020 年 9 月 仔细阅读】
[译] 在《自然》杂志付印之际，澳大利亚政府并没有对这个计划的具体批评做出回应。

species [20]

[ˈspiːʃiːz] *n.* 物种，种类

[记] spec+ies（*n.*）→ "专门的种类" → *n.* 物种，种类
[真] [D] Explore the cultures of **species** before they vanish.【2020 年 12 月 仔细阅读 55 题 D 选项】
[译] 在物种消失之前探索物种文化。

扫码快速学习

Day 23

–spec–、–spect–、–spic– 看

aspect [6]

[ˈæspekt] *n.* 外貌，外表；方面

[记] a（to）+spect→"去看一看，看一眼"→看人"看一看"，只能看见"外貌、外表"→*n.* 外貌，外表→看事情"看一看"，只能看见某个"方面"→*n.* 方面

[真] The most controversial **aspect** of Marconi's life—and the reason why there has been no satisfying biography of Marconi until now—was his uncritical embrace of Benito Mussolini.【2021 年 6 月 长篇阅读 K 选项】

[译] 马可尼一生中最具争议的方面——也是直到现在还没有令人满意的马可尼传记的原因——是他对贝尼托·墨索里尼不加批判的拥护。

expect [33]

[ɪkˈspekt] *v.* 期待，期盼

[记] ex（out）+pect（简写自 spect）→"往外看"；焦急地等人时，不停地往外看→*v.* 期待，期盼

[派] expectation [ˌekspekˈteɪʃn] *n.* 期待；盼望
　　expectancy [ɪkˈspektənsi] *n.* 期待；预料
　　unexpected [ˌʌnɪkˈspektɪd] *a.* 意想不到的，意外的
　　unexpectedly [ˌʌnɪkˈspektɪdli] *ad.* 出乎意料地

[形] except [ɪkˈsept] *v.* 把……除外　*prep.* 除……之外

[真] More CGI-recreated images of deceased celebrities are **expected** to appear on screen.【2021 年 6 月 长篇阅读 41 题】

[译] 更多已故名人的 CGI 重建图像有望出现在屏幕上。

inspect [2]

[ɪnˈspekt] *v.* 检查；监督

[记] in（里）+spect→"往里看"；打开门缝朝里看，不放心→*v.* 检查；监督

[派] inspection [ɪnˈspekʃn] *n.* 检查，检验

prospect [8]

[ˈprɒspekt] *n.* 前途，前景；风景，景色

[记] pro（前）+spect→"向前看"；往前看，看什么？→*n.* 前途，前景；风景，景色

[派] prospective [prəˈspektɪv] *a.* 预期的；即将发生的

169

prospector [prəˈspektə(r)] n. 勘探者；探矿者

[真] [B] It may adversely affect his future career **prospects**.【2021 年 6 月 听力 3 题 B 选项】

[译] 这可能会对他未来的职业前景产生不利影响。

respect⁹

[rɪˈspekt] v.&n. 尊敬，尊重　n. 方面

[记] re（反复）+spect → "反复看人"，看不够 → v.&n. 尊敬，尊重 → "反复地看事物"，看到了各个 → n. 方面

[派] respectable [rɪˈspektəbl] a. 值得尊敬的，可敬的
respectful [rɪˈspektfl] a. 表示敬意的，尊敬的
respected [rɪˈspektɪd] v. 尊重（respect 的过去式和过去分词）a. 受尊敬的
respective [rɪˈspektɪv] a. 各自的，分别的
irrespective [ɪrɪˈspektɪv] a. 不考虑的，不管的

[真] [C] They feel great **respect** towards scientists.【2021 年 6 月 听力 10 题 C 选项】

[译] 他们非常尊敬科学家。

suspect⁶

[səˈspekt] v. 怀疑，猜想　n. 犯罪嫌疑人

[记] su（上下）+spect → "上下看，上下打量"；这就是怀疑的动作 → v. 怀疑，猜想　n. 犯罪嫌疑人

[派] suspicion [səˈspɪʃn] n. 怀疑
suspicious [səˈspɪʃəs] a. 怀疑的；可疑的

[真] The scientists **suspect** that micro-organisms may be living in Lake Vostok, closed off from the outside world for more than two million years.【2020 年 9 月 听力原文】

[译] 科学家猜想，与外部世界隔绝长达二百万年以上的沃斯托克湖中，可能生活着微生物。

suspect 的引申词

s(c)keptical¹⁰

[ˈskeptɪkl] a. 怀疑的

[派] skeptically [ˈskeptɪkəli] ad. 怀疑地
skepticism [ˈskeptɪsɪzəm] n. 怀疑态度；怀疑论
skeptic [ˈskeptɪk] n. 怀疑者

[考] be skeptical of... 怀疑……

[真] I'm really **skeptical** about this claim.【2020 年 12 月 听力原文】

[译] 对于这种说辞，我深感怀疑。

perspective⁶

[pəˈspektɪv] n. 透镜；透视；视角；观点，看法

[记] per（贯穿）+spect+ive (n.) → "贯穿某物看到" → n. 透镜；透视；视角 → "看透了"，产生 → n. 观点，看法

Day 23

[真] A point worth making is that the study was based only on the **perspective** of employees.【2021 年 6 月 听力原文】
[译] 值得一提的是，该研究仅基于员工的观点。

conspicuous [2] [kənˈspɪkjuəs] *a.* 显眼的，明显的

[记] con（全部，共同）+spic+u（无义）+ous（*a.*）→ "所有人都能看到的"→ *a.* 显眼的，明显的
[派] conspicuously [kənˈspɪkjuəsli] *ad.* 显眼地；引人注目地

spectacular [2] [spekˈtækjələ(r)] *a.* 壮观的，引人注目的

[记] spec+tacular（谐音"太酷了"）→"看起来太酷了"→ *a.* 壮观的，引人注目的

spectrum [2] [ˈspektrəm] *n.* 光谱，波谱

[记] spect+r（无义）+um（*n.*）→"光谱，波谱"也和看有关系→ *n.* 光谱，波谱

-st-、-sist-、-stitute- 站立

stand [9] [stænd] *v.* 站立；忍受 *n.* 立场；地位（熟词僻义，重点关注）

六级基础词汇

[派] standing [ˈstændɪŋ] *n.* 起立，站立；身份；地位
[真] [D] One's professional **standing** and income are related to their educational background.【2020 年 7 月 仔细阅读 49 题 D 选项】
[译] 一个人的职业地位和收入与他们的教育背景有关。

standard [16] [ˈstændəd] *n.* 标准；军旗 *a.* 标准的，合格的

[记] 在 12 世纪时，standard 指的是打仗时指示集合地点的军旗，一般是国王或军队最高统帅的旗帜。这种旗帜系在旗杆或长矛上，牢固地竖立在地面上，充当醒目的标识，因此被叫作 stand-hard（稳稳站立），后来缩写成 standard。由于 standard 是国王或军队最高统帅的旗帜，代表了权威。因此，在古代度量衡制度中，国王所确定的度量衡单位就被称为 standard（标准）→ *n.* 标准；军旗 → *a.* 标准的，合格的
[派] standardize/ise [ˈstændədaɪz] *v.* 使标准化
[真] American history has seen generations of politicians argue in favor of a gold **standard** for American currency.【2020 年 9 月 听力原文】
[译] 为了支持美国货币的黄金标准，美国历史已经见证了几代政客的争论。

state [88] [steɪt] *n.* 国，州；状态，情况 *v.* 陈述，说明（熟词僻义，重点关注）

六级基础词汇

[派] statement [ˈsteɪtmənt] *n.* 声明，陈述

statesman [ˈsteɪtsmən] *n.* 政治家

[真] They asked participants to spend 15 minutes sitting alone without engaging in any activity and measured how this solitude influencing their emotional **state**.【2020 年 12 月 听力原文】

[译] 他们要求参与者独自坐 15 分钟，不做任何活动，同时测量这种独处如何影响他们的情绪状态。

statue [4]

[ˈstætʃuː] *n.* 雕像，塑像

[记] st+at（在）+u（无义）+e（眼睛）→ 一堆石头"站在那儿一动不动地瞪着眼"；表示→ *n.* 雕像，塑像

[真] And Brandston knows a thing or two about lighting, being the man who illuminated the **Statue** of Liberty.【2020 年 7 月 长篇阅读 H 选项】

[译] 布兰斯顿设计了自由女神像的照明，所以他很精通照明。

status [6]

[ˈsteɪtəs] *n.* 地位；身份

[记] st+at（在）+us（无义）→ 一个人"在社会上站立的位置"，就是所处的→ *n.* 地位；身份

[助] S 联想成 $（美元），一个人有 $ 才能有→ *n.* 地位；身份

[真] [B] Black people's socioeconomic **status** in America remains low.【2020 年 7 月 仔细阅读 49 题 B 选项】

[译] 黑人在美国的社会经济地位仍然很低。

store [8]

[stɔː(r)] *n.* 商店；存货 *v.* 存储

[助] *n.* 商店→商店里面肯定有→ *n.* 存货→ *v.* 存储

[派] storage [ˈstɔːrɪdʒ] *n.* 储藏，存储

[真] The culture minister, Franck Riester, said religious relics saved from the cathedral were being securely held at the Hotel de Ville, and works of art that sustained smoke damage were being taken to the Louvre, the world's largest art museum, where they would be dried out, repaired and **stored**.【2021 年 6 月 长篇阅读 J 选项】

[译] 文化部部长弗兰克·里斯特表示，从大教堂抢救出的宗教文物正被妥善安置在巴黎市政厅，而遭受烟熏的艺术品正被送往世界最大的艺术博物馆卢浮宫，在那里它们将被烘干、修复，然后保存起来。

restore [10]

[rɪˈstɔː(r)] *v.* 恢复，复原

[记] re（反复）+store（*v.* 存储）→ "反复存储"体力、精力、战斗力→ *v.* 恢复，复原

[派] restoration [ˌrestəˈreɪʃn] *n.* （规章制度等的）恢复，复原

[真] [D] Endeavor to **restore** chimp habitats to expand its total population.【2020 年 12 月 仔细阅读 54 题 D 选项】

[译] 努力恢复黑猩猩的栖息地，以扩大其种群总数。

Day 23

stock [2]
[stɒk] *n.* 股票，股份；库存　*v.* 储存
[记] 改写自 store（存货；存储）→ *v.* 储存→ *n.* 股票，股份；库存
[考] stock market 股票市场

stake [3]
[steɪk] *n.* 股票，股份；（在公司、计划等中的）重大利益
[记] 上词 stock 的同源词；改写自 stock（股票，股份）→ *n.* 股票，股份；（在公司、计划等中的）重大利益
[派] stakeholder [ˈsteɪkhəʊldə(r)] *n.* 股东；利益相关者
[考] at stake 处于成败关头
[真] Secondly, candidates should know what's at **stake** for the company with this job opening.【2020 年 12 月 听力原文】
[译] 第二，求职者应该了解这个职位空缺对公司有什么成败攸关的影响。

stable [10]
[ˈsteɪbl] *a.* 稳定的，稳固的
[记] st+able（*a.*）→"能够站立的"；table（桌子）能够站立的→ *a.* 稳定的，稳固的
[派] stability [stəˈbɪləti] *n.* 稳定，稳固
　　 instability [ˌɪnstəˈbɪləti] *n.* 不稳定，不稳固
　　 unstable [ʌnˈsteɪbl] *a.* 不稳定的，不稳固的
[真] She had no **stable** income, $12,000 in credit-card debt and no plan, but to her astonishment , her father, an accountant, told her that her financial plight wasn't as bad as she thought.【2021 年 6 月 选词填空】
[译] 她没有稳定的收入，只有 12 000 美元的信用卡债务，也没有任何计划，但令她惊讶的是，她从事会计的父亲告诉她，她的财务困境并没有她想象的那么糟糕。

steady [4]
[ˈstedi] *a.* 稳定的；不变的
[记] st+eady（简写自 ready；准备好的）→"准备好站立的"→ *a.* 稳定的；不变的
[派] steadily [ˈstedɪli] *ad.* 稳定地；持续地
[真] [D] A **steady** appreciation of the U.S. dollar.【2020 年 9 月 听力 25 题 D 选项】
[译] 美元的稳步升值。

circumstance [3]
[ˈsɜːkəmstəns] *n.* 环境；情况
[记] circum（改写自 circle；圆，圈）+st+ance（*n.*）→"环绕房子一圈而站立的地方"，就是你所处的→ *n.* 环境；情况
[真] This is ambitious in any **circumstances**, and in a divided and unequal society the two ideals can clash outright.【2019 年 12 月 仔细阅读】
[译] 这在任何情况下都是雄心勃勃的，在一个分裂和不平等的社会中，这两种理想会发生直接冲突。

173

obstacle [2]

[ˈɒbstəkl] *n.* 障碍（物），妨碍

[记] ob（相反，反对）+st+acle（*n.*）→ "反对你站立、站稳的东西" → *n.* 障碍（物），妨碍

statistic [14]

[stəˈtɪstɪk] *n.* 统计，统计学

[记] stat（简写自 state；国家，州）+ist（*n.*）+ic（表示学科的后缀）→ "统计学就是从国家角度考虑数字的学科" → *n.* 统计，统计学

[派] statistical [stəˈtɪstɪkl] *a.* 统计的，统计学的
statistically [stəˈtɪstɪkli] *ad.* 统计上地

[真] According to official **statistics**, Thailand's annual road death rate is almost double the global average.【2021 年 6 月 听力原文】

[译] 据官方统计，泰国每年的道路交通死亡率几乎是全球平均水平的两倍。

constant [12]

[ˈkɒnstənt] *a.* 永恒的，持续的

[记] con（全部，共同）+st+ant（*a.*）→ "全部站在一起，不分离"；我们永远在一起 → *a.* 永恒的，持续的

[派] constantly [ˈkɒnstəntli] *ad.* 不断地，持续地

[真] The question of who will bear the cost of lifelong learning is a topic of **constant** debate.【2020 年 12 月 长篇阅读 43 题】

[译] 谁将承担终身学习的开销是一个不断被争论的话题。

distant [14]

[ˈdɪstənt] *a.* 遥远的；冷漠的

[记] di（散）+st+ant（*a.*）→ "分散站立，分散站开" → *a.* 遥远的 → "关系的遥远" → *a.* 冷漠的

[派] distance [ˈdɪstəns] *n.* 距离

[真] [D] Over 10% of the respondents lied about the **distance** they drove.【2020 年 12 月 听力 19 题 D 选项】

[译] 超过 10% 的受访者谎报了他们的驾车里程。

instant [6]

[ˈɪnstənt] *a.* 立即的；方便的

[记] in（否）+st+ant（*a.*）→ "不站"；连站都不站，立即就走 → *a.* 立即的 → "立即就走" → *a.* 方便的

[派] instantly [ˈɪnstəntli] *ad.* 立即

[真] News of Notre Dame Cathedral catastrophe **instantly** caught media attention throughout the world.【2021 年 6 月 长篇阅读 45 题】

[译] 巴黎圣母院大灾难的消息立即引起了全世界媒体的关注。

substance [3]

[ˈsʌbstəns] *n.* 物质；材料；本质

[记] sub（下）+st+ance（*n.*）→ "站在人类之下"；几千年来，站在人类之下的具体物质支撑着人类社会从低级到高级、从愚昧到文明的发展 → *n.* 物质；材料；本质

Day 23

[派] substantial [səbˈstænʃl] *a.* 结实的，牢固的；大量的，重大的
substantially [səbˈstænʃəli] *ad.* 本质上，实质上；大体上
[真] [D] **Substantially** reduce their food choice.【2020 年 12 月 仔细阅读 47 题 D 选项】
[译] 大大减少了他们的食物选择。

superstition [2]

[ˌsuːpəˈstɪʃn] *n.* 迷信

[记] super（上）+st+ition（*n.*）→ "站在人类之上的"；人类、科学无法解释的，超过人们现有认知的，站在人类之上的→ *n.* 迷信

estate [3]

[ɪˈsteɪt] *n.* 房地产，不动产

[记] e（out）+st+ate（*n.*）→ "楼房站立出来"，形成→ *n.* 房地产，不动产
[考] real estate 房地产
[真] Other actors have been revived, with the permission of their **estates**, for advertising purposes: for example, a 2011 advertisement for Dior featured contemporary actress Charlize Theron alongside iconic 20th-century stars Marilyn Monroe, Grace Kelly and Marlene Dietrich.【2021 年 6 月 长篇阅读 D 选项】
[译] 在获得其他演员的遗产许可后，这些演员也被"复活"用于广告目的：例如，2011 年，迪奥的一支广告中，当代女演员查理兹·塞隆与 20 世纪的标志性明星玛丽莲·梦露、格蕾丝·凯利和玛琳·黛德丽在一起。

stage [8]

[steɪdʒ] *n.* 舞台；戏剧；阶段，时期

[记] st+age（*n.*）→ "站在哪个位置？站在哪个时间点？"→演员站在"舞台"表演"戏剧"→ *n.* 舞台；戏剧→人生站在哪个时间点？→ *n.* 阶段，时期
[真] At 43, I've reached the **stage** where women are warned to watch out for the creeping sadness of middle age.【2021 年 6 月 选词填空】
[译] 43 岁的时候，我已经到了一个人生阶段，在这个阶段里，女人们被警告要提防人到中年带来的令人毛骨悚然的悲伤。

consist [6]

[kənˈsɪst] *v.* 由……组成

[记] con（全部，共同）+sist → "全部站在一起"；组成班，组成排，组成连 → *v.* 由……组成
[派] consistent [kənˈsɪstənt] *a.* 一致的；连续的；坚持的
consistently [kənˈsɪstəntli] *ad.* 坚持地；一致地
[考] consist of... 由……组成
[真] It turns out that, in many ways, the real trick to speaking two languages **consists** in managing not to speak one of those languages at a given moment—which is fundamentally a feat of paying attention.【2020 年 9 月 长篇阅读 F 选项】
[译] 事实证明，在很多方面，能说两种语言的真正诀窍在于在一个给定的时间点设法不去说另外一种语言，从根本上说，这是集中注意力的一种技巧。

assist [4]

[əˈsɪst] *v.&n.* 帮助，协助

[记] as（to）+sist → "去站起来"；遇到挫折一蹶不振，使其能够重新站起来 → *v.&n.* 帮助，协助

[派] assistant [əˈsɪstənt] *n.* 助手；助教　*a.* 助理的；副的
　　 assistance [əˈsɪstəns] *n.* 帮助，协助

[真] France's tax on overnight stays was introduced to **assist** thermal spa towns to develop, and around half of French local authorities use it today.【2021 年 6 月 仔细阅读】

[译] 法国实施了"暂住税"以支持温泉小镇的发展，现如今，法国大约一半的地方政府都在采用这项税收。

exist [18]

[ɪɡˈzɪst] *v.* 存在

[记] ex（out）+ist（简写自 sist）→ "站在外面，露在外面"；别人看得见，摸得着 → *v.* 存在

[派] existing [ɪɡˈzɪstɪŋ] *a.* 现存的；目前的
　　 existence [ɪɡˈzɪstəns] *n.* 存在
　　 existent [ɪɡˈzɪstənt] *a.* 存在的，现存的

[真] [B] Narrowing the **existing** gap between the rich and the poor.【2021 年 6 月 仔细阅读 50 题 B 选项】

[译] 缩小贫富之间现有的差距。

insist [2]

[ɪnˈsɪst] *v.* 坚持；坚持要求

[记] in（里）+sist → "站在里面不出来" → *v.* 坚持；坚持要求

[派] insistence [ɪnˈsɪstəns] *n.* 坚持；极力主张

[考] insist on 坚持
　　 insist that... 坚持（认为）……

persist [3]

[pəˈsɪst] *v.* 坚持；持续

[记] per（贯穿）+sist → "从头到尾一直站着" → *v.* 坚持；持续

[派] persistence [pəˈsɪstəns] *n.* 坚持；毅力；持续；存留
　　 persistent [pəˈsɪstənt] *a.* 坚持不懈的，执着的

[考] persist in 坚持

[真] Experience can rarely, unless guided by a theoretical concept, arrive at results of any great significance... on the other hand, an excessive trust in theoretical conviction would have prevented Marconi from **persisting** in experiments which were destined to bring about a revolution in the technique of radio-communications.【2021 年 6 月 长篇阅读 J 选项】

[译] 除非以理论概念为指导，否则单靠经验很少能得出任何具有重大意义的结果……另一方面，过度依赖理论概念则可能会阻止马可尼坚持进行实验，而这些实验注定会为无线电通信技术带来变革。

resist[6] [rɪˈzɪst] *v.* 抵抗，抵制；反对

［记］re（back）+sist → "反着站"；站都反着站，不站在一起→ *v.* 抵抗，抵制；反对

［派］resistance [rɪˈzɪstəns] *n.* 抵抗，阻力
　　　resistable [rɪˈzɪstəbl] *a.* 可抵抗的
　　　irresistible [ˌɪrɪˈzɪstəbl] *a.* 不可阻挡的，无法抗拒的

［真］Historical precedent suggests that science and politics can overcome **resistance** from businesses that pollute and poison but it takes time, and success often starts small.【2020 年 9 月 仔细阅读】

［译］历史先例表明，科学和政治可以应对来自排放污染、有毒物质的企业的阻力，但这需要时间，而且成功都是从小事开始积累的。

扫码快速学习

扫码即刻听课

-st-、-sist-、-stitute- 站立

constitute² [ˈkɒnstɪtjuːt] v. 组成，构成

[记] con（全部，全部）+stitute → "全部站在一起"；组成班，组成排，组成连 → v. 组成，构成

[派] constitution [ˌkɒnstɪˈtjuːʃn] n. 组成，构成；宪法

institute³ [ˈɪnstɪtjuːt] n. 学院，（教育、专业等）机构 v. 建立，创立

[助] 麻省理工学院 Massachusetts Institute of Technology（MIT）→ n. 学院，（教育、专业等）机构 → "学院、机构"怎么来的？→ v. 建立，创立

[真] Researchers at the **Institute** for Health Metrics and Evaluation in America put the death toll in 2017 at 1.24 million.【2021年6月 听力原文】

[译] 美国卫生计量与评价研究所的研究人员估计，2017年的道路交通事故死亡人数为124万。

-sti-、-stinct-、-sting- 刺，叮

sting² [stɪŋ] v.&n. 叮，刺，刺痛

[助] 谐音"死叮" → v.&n. 叮，刺，刺痛

stick⁷ [stɪk] n. 棍，棒 v. 刺；粘贴；坚持

[记] sti+ck（无义）→ "棍棒是放大版的刺" → n. 棍，棒 v. 刺；后引申为 → v. 粘贴；坚持

[考] stick to 粘住；坚持

[真] [C] Try to **stick** to their initial plan.【2020年12月 听力10题C选项】

[译] 试着坚持他们最初的计划。

instinct⁴ [ˈɪnstɪŋkt] n. 本能；天性

[记] in（里）+stinct → "刺入内心，扎根于内心的"，就是人的 → n. 本能；天性

[派] instinctive [ɪnˈstɪŋktɪv] a. 天生的；本能的；直觉的

Day 24

[真] [D] Trust their gut **instinct**.【2021 年 6 月 听力 8 题 D 选项】
[译] 相信他们的直觉。

extinct ⁹
[ɪkˈstɪŋkt] *a.* 灭绝的，绝种的

[记] ex（out）+tinct（简写自 stinct）→蜜蜂的刺"刺出了身体"，会连带着部分内脏，所以蜜蜂叮人，刺出了身体后，自己也会死→ *a.* 灭绝的，绝种的
[派] extinction [ɪkˈstɪŋkʃn] *n.* 熄灭；灭绝
extinguish [ɪkˈstɪŋgwɪʃ] *v.* 熄灭；使破灭
[真] [A] They will turn out to be the second-largest species of birds to become **extinct**.【2019 年 12 月 仔细阅读 53 题 A 选项】
[译] 它们将会成为即将灭绝的第二大鸟类物种。

distinct ²
[dɪˈstɪŋkt] *a.* 明显的，清楚的

[记] di（散）+stinct（谐音"死盯着他"）→同志们，"散开，给我死死盯着犯罪嫌疑人"，自然看得→ *a.* 明显的，清楚的
[派] distinctive [dɪˈstɪŋktɪv] *a.* 有特色的，与众不同的

distinction ³
[dɪˈstɪŋkʃn] *n.* 区别，差别；荣誉；卓越

[记] 上词 distinct 的名词；distinct+ion（*n.*）→"什么东西很明显？"→ *n.* 区别，差别→有别于一般，就是→ *n.* 荣誉；卓越
[真] [B] They can make subtle **distinctions** about music.【2020 年 12 月 听力 23 题 B 选项】
[译] 他们可以对音乐做出微妙的区分。

distinguish ³
[dɪˈstɪŋgwɪʃ] *v.* 区别，辨别

[记] 上词 distinction 的动词→ *v.* 区别，辨别
[派] distinguishable [dɪˈstɪŋgwɪʃəbl] *a.* 可区别的，可辨别的
indistinguishable [ˌɪndɪˈstɪŋgwɪʃəbl] *a.* 难区分的，不能分辨的
[真] [B] It **distinguishes** offices from prisons.【2020 年 7 月 听力 9 题 B 选项】
[译] 它将办公室和监狱区分开来。

stimulate ¹²
[ˈstɪmjuleɪt] *v.* 刺激，使兴奋

[记] sti+m（无义）+ul（中缀）+ate（*v.*）→ *v.* 刺激，使兴奋
[派] stimulation [ˌstɪmjuˈleɪʃən] *n.* 刺激，激励
stimulus [ˈstɪmjələs] *n.* 刺激，刺激物；促进因素
[真] [B] **Stimulate** their interest.【2021 年 6 月 听力 11 题 B 选项】
[译] 激起他们的兴趣。

–spir– 呼吸，吹气

spirit ¹²
[ˈspɪrɪt] *n.* 精神；灵魂

六级基础词汇

［记］spir+it（n.）→有"呼吸"，就有→ n. 精神；灵魂
［派］spiritual [ˈspɪrɪtʃuəl] a. 精神上的

inspire [8]

[ɪnˈspaɪə(r)] v. 吸，吸入；鼓舞，激励

［记］in（里）+spir+e（无义）→"向里吸气"→ v. 吸，吸入→"深吸一口气，心中想着我一定可以"→ v. 鼓舞，激励
［派］inspiration [ˌɪnspəˈreɪʃn] n. 灵感；启发灵感的人或事物
［真］[B] It **inspires** willingness to make sacrifices.【2021年6月听力17题B选项】
［译］它会激发人们做出牺牲的意愿。

–str– 拖，拉

stress [20]

[stres] n. 压力 v. 强调；给……加压力

［记］本词与本组其余词略有不同；str（简写自 strong；强壮，强烈）+ess（简写自 press；压）→"强烈地压"，产生→ n. 压力→ v. 强调；给……加压力
［派］stressed [strest] a. 有压力的
　　stressful [ˈstresfl] a. 有压力的
　　distressed [dɪˈstrest] a. 痛苦的，烦恼的
　　distressful [dɪsˈtresfl] a. 使人苦恼的
［真］[B] Place more **stress** on animal traditions than on their physical conservation.【2020年12月仔细阅读55题B选项】
［译］更强调动物的传统，而不是它们的物理保护。

straight [3]

[streɪt] a. 直的；直率的　ad. 直接地；坦率地

［记］str+aight（a.）→"拉"直→ a. 直的；直率的→说话"直"→ ad. 直接地；坦率地
［派］straightforward [ˌstreɪtˈfɔːwəd] a. 直率的，坦率的
［真］This seems to be one of the few areas where the benefit of sharing personal information comes **straight** back to the sharer: because these apps know where almost all the users are, and how fast they are moving almost all the time, they can spot traffic congestion very quickly and suggest ways round it.【2021年6月仔细阅读】
［译］这好像是分享者从分享个人信息中直接受益的为数不多的领域：因为这些应用程序可以知道几乎全部司机在什么路段，以及他们的实时移动速度有多快，所以它们可以快速发现交通堵塞，并提出绕道方案。

constrain [2]

[kənˈstreɪn] v. 强迫，迫使；限制

［记］con（全部）+str+ain（v.）→"所有人都拉"；我不想去，他们都拉我去，我被→ v. 强迫，迫使→"所有人都拉着我"，放不开手脚→ v. 限制
［派］constraint [kənˈstreɪnt] n. 强制；约束；限制

Day 24

restrain [2]
[rɪˈstreɪn] *v.* 禁止，阻止；抑制，制止

[记] re（back）+str+ain（*v.*）→ "拉了回来"；你刚要去，我把你拉了回来，别去→ *v.* 禁止，阻止；抑制，制止

[派] restraint [rɪˈstreɪnt] *n.* 禁止；抑制，制止

restrict [2]
[rɪˈstrɪkt] *v.* 限制，约束

[记] re（反复）+strict（*a.* 严格的，严厉的）→ "对某人反复严格、严厉"；外在表现形式就是→ *v.* 限制，约束

[派] restriction [rɪˈstrɪkʃn] *n.* 限制，约束

[考] restrict A to B 把 A 限制于 B

stretch [3]
[stretʃ] *v.* 伸展，延伸

[记] str+etch（发音符号）→困了，在桌子前"拉拉身体，拉拉筋骨"→ *v.* 伸展，延伸

[真] Essentially, we have this tendency to keep **stretching** out the decision-making process.【2021 年 6 月 听力原文】

[译] 从本质上说，我们有这种持续延长决策过程的倾向。

strength [15]
[streŋθ] *n.* 力气，力量

[记] str+ength（*n.*）→ "拖、拉"都需要→ *n.* 力气，力量

[派] strengthen [ˈstreŋθn] *v.* 加强，巩固

[真] We don't have the **strength** of chimpanzees because we've given up animal **strength** to manipulate subtle instruments, like hammers, spears, and—later—pens and pencils.【2021 年 6 月 仔细阅读】

[译] 我们没有大猩猩的力量，因为我们已经放弃了动物的野蛮力量，选择去操纵精密仪器，例如锤子、长矛，还有后来的钢笔和铅笔。

-stru-、-struct- 建筑，建造

structure [15]
[ˈstrʌktʃə(r)] *n.* 结构，构造；建筑物

[记] struct+ure（*n.*）→ *n.* 结构，构造；建筑物

[派] structural [ˈstrʌktʃərəl] *a.* 结构（上）的，构架（上）的；建筑的

[真] The total amount of damage to Notre Dame Cathedral can be assessed only when its **structure** is considered safe.【2021 年 6 月 长篇阅读 36 题】

[译] 巴黎圣母院的总损失数额只有在其结构被认为是安全的情况下才能进行评估。

infrastructure [6]
[ˈɪnfrəstrʌktʃə(r)] *n.* 基础设施

[记] infra（在下）+structure（*n.* 结构；建筑）→ "下面的结构、建筑"→ *n.* 基础设施

［真］The solution lies not just in better **infrastructure**, but in better social incentives.【2021 年 6 月 听力原文】
［译］解决方案不仅在于更好的基础设施，还在于更好的社会激励措施。

construct ⁹ [kənˈstrʌkt] v. 建筑，建造

［记］con（加强）+struct → v. 建筑，建造
［派］construction [kənˈstrʌkʃn] n. 建造；建筑物
　　 constructive [kənˈstrʌktɪv] a. 建设性的；有益的
［真］One casualty of this was The Great Organ **constructed** in the 1730s, which was said to have escaped the flames but been significantly damaged by water.【2021 年 6 月 长篇阅读 J 选项】
［译］建于 18 世纪 30 年代的大风琴就是其中一个牺牲品，据说它躲过了大火，却因灭火的水遭到严重损坏。

destruct ¹² [dɪsˈtrʌkt] v. 破坏

［记］de（下）+struct → 上词 construct 的反义词，"向下修建"，越建越低，越建越矮，不是建造，而是破坏 → v. 破坏
［派］destruction [dɪˈstrʌkʃn] n. 破坏，毁坏
　　 destructive [dɪˈstrʌktɪv] a. 破坏的，毁坏的
［真］The Paris prosecutor's office has opened an inquiry into "involuntary **destruction** by fire", indicating they believe the cause of the blaze was accidental rather than criminal.【2021 年 6 月 长篇阅读 K 选项】
［译］巴黎检察官办公室已经针对这次"意外的火灾破坏"进行了调查，这一说法表明他们认为火灾的发生是意外事件，而非人为纵火。

instruct ⁹ [ɪnˈstrʌkt] v. 教，教授；指导，指示

［记］in（里）+struct → "里面修建"；父母或者老师帮助孩子在内心修建一堵无形的墙来抵御外来的诱惑 → v. 教，教授；指导，指示
［派］instruction [ɪnˈstrʌkʃn] n. 教授；指导；说明书
　　 instructive [ɪnˈstrʌktɪv] a. 教育性的；有益的
　　 instructor [ɪnˈstrʌktə(r)] n. 教练，导师
［真］Much to their frustration, managers often struggle to get their staff to comply with even simple **instructions**.【2021 年 6 月 听力原文】
［译］令管理人员感到沮丧的是，他们往往很难让他们的员工遵守哪怕非常简单的指示。

instrument ⁴ [ˈɪnstrəmənt] n. 工具，仪器；乐器

［记］in（里）+stru+ment（n.）→ "建筑里修建"用的东西；→ n. 工具，仪器 → stru 谐音 "丝竹"；丝竹不就是一种 → n. 乐器
［派］instrumental [ˌɪnstrəˈmentl] a. 仪器的，乐器的；起作用的，有帮助的
［真］We don't have the strength of chimpanzees because we've given up animal

strength to manipulate subtle **instruments**, like hammers, spears, and—later—pens and pencils.【2021年6月 仔细阅读】

[译] 我们没有大猩猩的力量，因为我们已经放弃了动物的野蛮力量，选择去操纵精密仪器，例如锤子、长矛，还有后来的钢笔和铅笔。

–sult– 说

result [28]

[rɪˈzʌlt] *n.* 结果　*v.* 导致，引起（熟词僻义，重点关注）

六级基础词汇

[考] as a result 因此，表示"结果"
　　　as a result of 由于，表示"原因"
　　　result in 导致，引起
　　　result from... 由……引起

[真] [B] It **resulted** in an oil surplus all over the world.【2021年6月 听力15题B选项】

[译] 它导致了世界各地的石油过剩。

consult [12]

[kənˈsʌlt] *v.* 咨询；商量，商议

[记] con（共同，全部）+sult → "共同说话"，你一句，我一句，彼此在→ *v.* 咨询；商量，商议

[派] consultant [kənˈsʌltənt] *n.* 顾问
　　 consultation [ˌkɒnslˈteɪʃn] *n.* 咨询；商讨

[真] Goddard later **consulted** with a weather expert and determined that the climate of New Mexico was ideal for year-round rocket launches.【2021年6月 听力原文】

[译] 戈达德后来咨询了气象专家，确定新墨西哥州的气候全年都适合发射火箭。

–sum– 拿

assume [6]

[əˈsjuːm] *v.* 承担；假定；认为

[记] as（to）+sum+e（无义）→ "去拿着"；拿着压力、责任→ *v.* 承担→拿着想法、观点→ *v.* 假定；认为

[派] assumption [əˈsʌmpʃn] *n.* 承担；假定，假设

[考] sb. assume that 某人认为……

[真] [C] **Assuming** responsibility to free oneself.【2020年12月 仔细阅读55题C选项】

[译] 承担着解放自己的责任。

consume [40]

[kənˈsjuːm] *v.* 消耗；消费

[记] con（共同，全部）+sum+e（无义）→ "共同拿"，你拿一个，我拿一个→

v. 消耗；消费

[派] consumer [kənˈsju:mə(r)] *n.* 消费者
consumption [kənˈsʌmpʃn] *n.* 消费；消耗

[真] At other times, they may disagree with the spirit of the procedure—the effort demanded, the time **consumed**, the lack of potential effectiveness. 【2021 年 6 月 听力原文】

[译] 或者有时候，他们可能不认同这个程序所传递的精神——所需要的努力、所消耗的时间以及潜在效能的缺失。

resume [4]

[rɪˈzju:m] *v.* 重新开始；继续　*n.* 简历

[记] re（反复）+sum+e（无义）→ "再一次拿起来"；有点重操旧业的感觉 → *v.* 重新开始；继续 → "失业了，重新拿起" → *n.* 简历

[真] But that's what most people will do, as it's their instinct to recite things that are already on the **resume**. 【2020 年 12 月 听力原文】

[译] 但大多数人还是会这么做，因为背诵简历上的已有信息是他们的本能。

-sur- 上，上面

surplus [3]

[ˈsɜ:pləs] *a.* 过剩的，剩余的　*n.* 过剩，剩余

[记] sur+plus（加和）→ "在加和、总和上还有"，用不完了 → *a.* 过剩的，剩余的　*n.* 过剩，剩余

[真] [B] It resulted in an oil **surplus** all over the world. 【2021 年 6 月 听力 15 题 B 选项】

[译] 它导致了世界各地的石油过剩。

surround [2]

[səˈraʊnd] *v.* 包围，环绕

[记] sur+round（圆，圆环）→ "成一个圆环" → *v.* 包围，环绕

[派] surrounding [səˈraʊndɪŋ] *n.* 周围的事物；环境　*a.* 周围的，附近的

-sure- 确定，确信

measure [22]

[ˈmeʒə(r)] *v.* 测量，衡量　*n.* 尺度；措施，办法

[记] me（我）+a（无义）+sure → "我想确定一下，自己测一下呗" → *v.* 测量，衡量 → "怎么测量" → *n.* 尺度；措施，方法

[派] measurement [ˈmeʒəmənt] *n.* 测量；尺寸
measurable [ˈmeʒərəbl] *a.* 可测量的

[真] [C] The UK will take new **measures** to boost tourism. 【2021 年 6 月 仔细阅读 51 题 C 选项】

[译] 英国将采取新的措施来促进旅游业的发展。

[真] It is the standard by which we **measure** our distances.【2021 年 6 月 长篇阅读 E 选项】
[译] 它是我们测量自己差距的标准。

measure 的引申词

tremendous [6]

[trəˈmendəs] *a.* 巨大的，极大的

[记] tre（谐音"超"）+mend（改写自 mens；测量）+ous（*a.*）→ "超越测量的"，无法测量的→ *a.* 巨大的，极大的
[派] tremendously [trəˈmendəsli] *ad.* 极大地；极其，非常
[真] In his later years, Marconi exerted a **tremendous** influence on all aspects of people's life.【2021 年 6 月 长篇阅读 43 题】
[译] 在他的晚年，马可尼对人们生活的各个方面都产生了巨大的影响。

ensure [6]

[ɪnˈʃʊə(r)] *v.* 保证，确保

[记] en（使动）+sure → "使之确定、确信" → *v.* 保证，确保
[考] ensure sb. sth. 保证某人某事
[真] [B] It **ensures** the accuracy of their arguments.【2021 年 6 月 听力 9 题 B 选项】
[译] 它确保了他们论点的准确性。

insure [16]

[ɪnˈʃʊə(r)] *v.* 保证，确保；为……上保险

[记] in（里）+sure → "使之进入确定、确信里面" → *v.* 保证，确保；为……上保险
[派] insurance [ɪnˈʃʊərəns] *n.* 保险，保险费
　　insurer [ɪnˈʃʊərə(r)] [ɪnˈʃɔːrə(r)] *n.* 承保人；保险公司
[考] insure A against B 给 A 上保险以防 B
[真] [B] Consult her lawyer about the **insurance** policy.【2020 年 12 月 听力 4 题 B 选项】
[译] 向律师咨询她的保险单。

扫码快速学习

扫码即刻听课

非成组词（S 字母）

scale [13]
[skeɪl] *n.* 刻度；比例；等级；规模 *v.* 攀登

[记] s（无义）+cal（改写自 carve；切，切开；雕刻）+e（无义）→"刻出来，切出来"→ *n.* 刻度；比例→"把人分成不同比例"→ *n.* 等级→"把事分成不同比例"→ *n.* 规模→"达到相应的比例"→ *v.* 攀登

[真] It **scaled** an altitude of only 12 meters.【2021 年 6 月 听力原文】
[译] 它所到达的高度只有 12 米。

scene [8]
[si:n] *n.* 场景，情景；景色

[记] sce（改写自 see；看见）+ne（无义）→"看见的东西"→ *n.* 场景，情景；景色

[派] scenery [ˈsi:nəri] *n.* 风景，景色
　　scenic [ˈsi:nɪk] *a.* 风景优美的

[真] What does the **scene** at the Louvre demonstrate according to the author?【2020 年 12 月 仔细阅读 46 题题干】
[译] 据作者所说，卢浮宫的场景展示了什么？

scheme [2]
[ski:m] *n.* 计划，方案；阴谋 *v.* 计划，策划；密谋

[记] sche（简写自 schedule；时间表，时刻表；安排，计划）+me（无义）；schedule 的近义词→ *n.* 计划，方案　 *v.* 计划，策划→计划不好的事情→ *n.* 阴谋　 *v.* 密谋

scholar [3]
[ˈskɒlə(r)] *n.* 学者

[记] schol（简写自 school；学校）+ar（表示人的后缀）→"学校里的人"→ *n.* 学者

[派] scholarship [ˈskɒləʃɪp] *n.* 奖学金；学术

[真] The research **scholars** surveyed 152 blue-collar workers from two separate sites in the mining industry.【2021 年 6 月 听力原文】
[译] 研究学者们调查了采矿业中两个不同地点的 152 名蓝领工人。

Day 25

scrutiny [2] ['skru:təni] ***n.*** 周密的调查；监视

[助] 谐音"死扣太细"→"扣得很细"→ *n.* 周密的调查；监视
[派] scrutinize/ise ['skru:tənaɪz] *v.* 仔细检查

setback [3] ['setbæk] ***n.*** 挫折；阻碍

[记] set（放，放置）+back →"往后放"；影响了前进→ *n.* 挫折；阻碍
[真] After encountering several **setbacks**, Captain Lucas decided to use a drill, and his innovations created the modern oil drilling industry.【2021年6月 听力原文】
[译] 遇到几次挫折后，卢卡斯队长决定使用钻头，他的革新创造了现代石油钻探工业。

senior [8] ['si:niə(r)] ***a.*** 高级的；年长的；资深的　***n.*** 毕业班学生

[记] sen+i（无义）+or（表示人的后缀）→"年老、年长之人"；自然是→ *a.* 高级的；年长的；资深的　*n.* 毕业班学生
[真] [C] It can be quite useful to **senior** managers.【2021年6月 听力2题C选项】
[译] 这对高级管理人员非常有用。

shape [15] [ʃeɪp] ***n.*** 形状，外形　***v.*** 成型；塑造（熟词僻义，重点关注）

六级基础词汇
[派] reshape [ˌri:'ʃeɪp] *v.* 重塑，重造
[真] As technology progresses, we all have a duty to make sure that we **shape** a future that we would want to find ourselves in.【2021年6月 仔细阅读】
[译] 随着技术的进步，我们都有责任去塑造一个我们希望自己身处其中的未来。

shabby [2] ['ʃæbi] ***a.*** 破旧的；卑鄙的

[助] 谐音"沙闭"→地方"有沙又封闭"→ *a.* 破旧的→"杀baby"的人是→ *a.* 卑鄙的

share [10] [ʃeə(r)] ***v.*** 分享，共有　***n.*** 股，（参与、得到等的）份（熟词僻义，重点关注）

六级基础词汇
[真] You **share** neither physical time nor emotional conversations over the Internet.【2020年12月 仔细阅读】
[译] 通过网络，你们彼此不会当面共度时光，也不会进行情感交流。

shatter [2] ['ʃætə(r)] ***v.*** 破碎；损害

[助] 谐音"扇他"→ *v.* 破碎；损害

shed [3] [ʃed] ***v.*** 流出，流下；脱皮，脱落

[助] 谐音"晒得"→"晒得脱皮"→ *v.* 脱皮，脱落→"晒得流泪"→ *v.* 流出，流下
[考] shed light on... 清楚地显出……；阐明……

[真] The scientists hope their discoveries will **shed** light on life in outer space, which might exist in similar dark and airless conditions.【2020 年 9 月 听力原文】
[译] 科学家希望他们的发现能证明外太空是有生物的，它们可能也在相似的黑暗和无空气的环境下生存。

shelter [2]

['ʃeltə(r)] *n.* 避难所，收容所　*v.* 避难；庇护

[记] shelt（改写自 shell；贝壳；坚果壳）+er（表示人的后缀）→ "人进了这个壳" → *n.* 避难所，收容所　*v.* 避难；庇护

shift [10]

[ʃɪft] *v.&n.* 转换；替换

[记] 键盘最左一列从下至上第二个键 Shift（换档键），功能就是在中英文输入法之间进行→ *v.&n.* 转换；替换

[真] On the contrary, compelling tourists to make a financial contribution to the places they visit beyond their personal consumption should be part of a wider cultural **shift**.【2021 年 6 月 仔细阅读】
[译] 相反，迫使游客在自身消费外还要对观光地做出经济贡献，这应该成为更大范围内文化转型的一部分。

shrewd [2]

[ʃruːd] *a.* 精明的；敏锐的

[助] 谐音"鼠的"→"像老鼠一样的"→ *a.* 精明的；敏锐的

[派] shrewdly [ʃruːdli] *ad.* 精明地，机灵地

spark [2]

[spɑːk] *n.* 火花，火星　*v.* 冒火花；引发，触发（熟词僻义，重点关注）

[记] 拟声词，源自火花喷出时发出的"嘶啪"声→ *n.* 火花；火星　*v.* 冒火花；引发，触发

spread [14]

[spred] *v.&n.* 散布，传播；伸开，伸展

[助] 谐音"死铺开的"→"照死里铺开"，铺得越大越好→ *v.&n.* 散布，传播；伸开，伸展

[派] widespread ['waɪdspred] *a.* 分布广泛的，普遍的

[真] But when everyone has perfect information, traffic jams simply **spread** onto the side roads that seem to offer a way round them.【2021 年 6 月 仔细阅读】
[译] 但是，如果每个人都消息灵通，交通堵塞可能就蔓延到那些本可以让司机绕过拥堵的辅路上。

startle [2]

['stɑːtl] *v.* 惊吓，使吃惊

[助] 谐音"厮打头"→"这厮突然打我头"，吓我一跳啊→ *v.* 惊吓，使吃惊

[派] startling ['stɑːtlɪŋ] *a.* 惊吓的，令人吃惊的

stem [3]

[stem] *v.* 起源于，来自

[助] 谐音"随他们"→这孩子随谁啊？随父母啊→ *v.* 起源于，来自

[考] stem from 来自，起源于

Day 25

[真] We often think of drawing as something that takes inborn talent, but this kind of thinking **stems** from our misclassification of drawing as, primarily, an art form rather than a tool for learning.【2021 年 6 月 仔细阅读】
[译] 我们通常认为绘画需要天赋异禀，但是这种想法主要源于对绘画的错误归类——把它归为一种艺术形式，而不是一种学习工具。

stereotype³

['steriətaɪp] *n.* 刻板印象，老套，模式化 *v.* 使定型，使模式化

[记] stereo（谐音"死呆肉"）+type（*n.* 类型）→"死呆肉的类型"→ *n.* 刻板印象，老套，模式化 *v.* 使定型，使模式化
[派] stereotypical [ˌsteriə'tɪpɪkl] *a.* 老一套的，刻板化的，模式化的
[真] Minority cultures were often featured in **stereotypical** or tokenistic ways, for example, by portraying Asian culture with chopsticks and traditional dress.【2021 年 6 月 选词填空】
[译] 少数民族文化通常以刻板印象或象征性的方式得以呈现，例如，用筷子和传统服饰来描绘亚洲文化。

strategy⁶

['strætədʒi] *n.* 战略，策略

[助] 谐音"别追太急"→"追敌别太急"；得讲究→ *n.* 战略，策略
[派] strategic [strə'ti:dʒɪk] *a.* 战略（上）的
[真] He was also a skilled and sophisticated organizer, an entrepreneurial innovator, who mastered the use of corporate **strategy**, media relations, government lobbying, international diplomacy, patents, and prosecution.【2021 年 6 月 长篇阅读 C 选项】
[译] 他还是一位技术娴熟、经验丰富的组织者、企业创新者，并善于运用企业战略、媒体关系、政府游说、国际外交、专利和起诉。

strike³

[straɪk] *v.&n.* 打，打击；攻击；罢工

[助] s（谐音"死"）+tr（谐音"踹"）+i（谐音"挨"）+k（无义）+e（无义）→"被人死踹，挨了一顿 K"→显然是挨打了呗→ *v.&n.* 打，打击；攻击→被打后不想工作→ *v.* 罢工
[派] striking ['straɪkɪŋ] *a.* 引人注目的，异乎寻常的
[真] The New York transit **strike** of 1980 is credited with prompting several long-term changes in the city, including bus and bike lanes, and women wearing sports shoes to work.【2020 年 12 月 选词填空】
[译] 1980 年的纽约公交系统罢工被认为是促使纽约市发生一些长期变化的原因，包括公共汽车车道和自行车车道，以及女性穿运动鞋上班。

struggle²

['strʌgl] *v.&n.* 打斗，搏斗；奋斗，努力

[记] strugg（改写自 strike；打，打击）+le（无义）→ *v.&n.* 打斗，搏斗→ *v.&n.* 奋斗，努力

strive²

[straɪv] *v.* 努力，奋斗

189

［记］s（无义）+tri（改写自 try；尝试）+v（辅音字母表示"胜利"）+e（无义）
→拼命"尝试"并取得"胜利"的过程→ v. 努力，奋斗

［考］strive to do sth. 努力做某事
　　　strive for... 为……而努力／奋斗

subtle [5]

[ˈsʌtl] a. 精巧的，巧妙的；微妙的

［记］来自拉丁语 subtilis（精细的，精致的）→ a. 精巧的，巧妙的；微妙的
［助］谐音"三头"→"此人有着三个人的智慧，就像长着三个人的头脑"，所思所想皆是→ a. 精巧的，巧妙的；微妙的
［派］subtlety [ˈsʌtlti] n. 精巧，巧妙
［真］[B] They can make **subtle** distinctions about music.【2020 年 12 月 听力 23 题 B 选项】
［译］他们可以对音乐做出微妙的区分。

surgery [4]

[ˈsɜːdʒəri] n. 外科，外科手术

［记］s（无义）+urger（改写自 organ；器官）+y（n.）→ n. 外科，外科手术
［派］surgeon [ˈsɜːdʒən] n. 外科医生
　　　surgical [ˈsɜːdʒɪkl] a. 外科（手术）的
［真］In a new study, people exposed to jargon when reading about subjects like autonomous vehicles and **surgical** robots later said they were less interested in science than others who read about the same topics, but without the use of specialized terms.
【2021 年 6 月 听力原文】
［译］在一项新研究中，人们在阅读有关自动驾驶汽车和外科手术机器人等主题时会遇到专业术语。这些人随后表示，他们对科学的兴趣不如其他阅读相同主题的人，而那些主题没有使用专业术语。

switch [9]

[swɪtʃ] n. 开关；转换 v. 转变，转换

六级基础词汇
［考］switch to 转变为，转换成
［真］"Bilinguals can pay focused attention without being distracted and also improve in the ability to **switch** from one task to another," says Sorace.【2020 年 9 月 长篇阅读 G 选项】
［译］索瑞斯说："双语者通常注意力集中，不会分心，也能提高任务转换的能力。"

-tach-、-tact- 接触

attach [5]

[əˈtætʃ] v. 系，贴，装，连接

［记］at（to）+tach → "去接触" → "系、贴、装、连接"这些动作全都是"一物去亲密接触另一物" → v. 系，贴，装，连接

Day 25

[派] attachment [əˈtætʃmənt] *n.* 依恋，爱慕
[考] attach importance to... 重视……
　　　attach... to... 把……系/贴到……
[真] [B] They **attach** great importance to arts education.【2021年6月 仔细阅读 49题B选项】
[译] 他们非常重视艺术教育。

detach ²
[dɪˈtætʃ] *v.* 分开，分离，拆开

[记] 上词 attach 的反义词；de（下）+ tach →"不去接触，不去挨着"→ *v.* 分开，分离，拆开
[派] detachment [dɪˈtætʃmənt] *n.* 拆卸；超脱

contact ⁸
[ˈkɒntækt] *v.&n.* 联系；接触

[记] con（共同，全部）+tact →"共同接触，彼此接触"→ *v.&n.* 联系；接触
[形] contract [ˈkɒntrækt] *v.* 缩小，收缩；签合同　*n.* 合同
[真] [C] His **contact** with a social worker had greatly aroused his interest in the tribe.
【2020年9月 听力12题C选项】
[译] 他与一名社会工作者的接触极大地引起了他对这个部落的兴趣。

◀ –tain– 保持，保留 ▶

maintain ¹⁸
[meɪnˈteɪn] *v.* 维持，保持；维护，保养（熟词僻义，重点关注）

[记] main（*a.* 主要的）+tain → *v.* 维持，保持→"维持机器、设备、厂房"→ *v.* 维护，保养
[派] maintenance [ˈmeɪntənəns] *n.* 保持，维持；保养
[真] This is because the more technology is put into the field, the more people are needed to deploy, **maintain** and improve it.【2021年6月 听力原文】
[译] 这是因为该领域使用的技术越多，需要部署、维护和改进它的人就越多。

sustain ¹⁸
[səˈsteɪn] *v.* 维持；支撑，支持

[记] sus（下）+tain →"保持下来"→ *v.* 维持；支撑，支持
[派] sustainable [səˈsteɪnəbl] *a.* 可持续的；可以忍受的；可支撑的
　　sustainably [səˈsteɪnəbli] *ad.* 支撑得住地；能保持住地
　　sustainability [səˌsteɪnəˈbɪləti] *n.* 持久性，耐久性
[真] The culture minister, Franck Riester, said religious relics saved from the cathedral were being securely held at the Hotel de Ville, and works of art that **sustained** smoke damage were being taken to the Louvre, the world's largest art museum, where they would be dried out, repaired and stored.【2021年6月 长篇阅读 J选项】
[译] 文化部部长弗兰克·里斯特表示，从大教堂抢救出的宗教文物正被妥善安

置在巴黎市政厅，而遭受烟熏的艺术品正被送往世界最大的艺术博物馆卢浮宫，在那里它们将被烘干、修复，然后保存起来。

attain [2]

[əˈteɪn] *v.* 达到；获得

[记] at（to）+tain → "去保持，去维持"；时间长了→ *v.* 达到；获得

[派] attainment [əˈteɪnmənt] *n.* 达到；成就

obtain [6]

[əbˈteɪn] *v.* 获得，得到

[记] 本词核心为 tain → *v.* 获得，得到

[派] obtainment [əbˈteɪnmənt] *n.* 获得，得到

[真] The agronomist is sure that he will **obtain** a near accurate count of plant population with his software.【2020 年 12 月 长篇阅读 38 题】

[译] 这位农学家确信用他的软件可以获得一个基本准确的植物种群数量。

entertain [6]

[ˌentəˈteɪn] *v.* 使娱乐；招待，款待

[记] enter（进入）+tain → "进入后留了下来"；因为太有意思了→ *v.* 使娱乐 → "使娱乐、快乐" → *v.* 招待，款待

[派] entertainment [ˌentəˈteɪnmənt] *n.* 娱乐；娱乐活动；招待，款待
entertaining [ˌentəˈteɪnɪŋ] *a.* 有趣的，令人愉快的

[真] [B] It is possible to combine **entertainment** with appreciation of serious art.【2020 年 12 月 仔细阅读 49 题 B 选项】

[译] 将娱乐与严肃艺术的欣赏相结合是可能的。

–tect– 盖

protect [38]

[prəˈtekt] *v.* 保护

六级基础词汇

[记] pro（前）+tect → "打仗时面前放个盖子（盾牌）" → *v.* 保护

[派] protection [prəˈtekʃn] *n.* 保护；保护措施
protective [prəˈtektɪv] *a.* 保护的，防护的
overprotective [ˌəʊvəprəˈtektɪv] *a.* 过分保护的

[考] protect... from... 保护……不受……

architect [2]

[ˈɑːkɪtekt] *n.* 建筑师，设计师

[记] arch（弧形，拱形）+i（无义）+ tect → "修建弧形、拱形盖的人"；西式的建筑很多是弧顶→ *n.* 建筑师，设计师

[派] architecture [ˈɑːkɪtektʃə(r)] *n.* 建筑学；建筑风格

扫码快速学习

–tend–、–tent–、–tens– 倾向

tend [35]

[tend] *v.* 趋向，倾向；照顾，照料

六级基础词汇
[考] tend to do sth. 倾向于做某事，往往会做某事

tendency [6]

[ˈtendənsi] *n.* 趋势，趋向

[记] 上词 tend 的名词；tend+ency（*n.*）→ *n.* 趋势，趋向
[真] Essentially, we have this **tendency** to keep stretching out the decision-making process.【2021 年 6 月 听力原文】
[译] 从本质上说，我们有这种持续延长决策过程的倾向。

trend [13]

[trend] *n.* 趋势，趋向

[记] r（辅音字母表示"人"）+tend →"人都有的倾向"→ *n.* 趋势，趋向
[真] [B] Fight the ever-changing **trends** in fashion.【2020 年 12 月 听力 15 题 B 选项】
[译] 与不断变化的时尚趋势作斗争。

attend [8]

[əˈtend] *v.* 照顾，照料；出席，参加

[记] at（to）+tend →"有某种倾向"→"对生病的人有倾向"→ *v.* 照顾，照料 →"对某个活动或者会议有倾向"→ *v.* 出席，参加
[派] attendance [əˈtendəns] *n.* 出席，参加
[真] [C] He is going to **attend** a job interview.【2021 年 6 月 听力 1 题 C 选项】
[译] 他要去参加一场工作面试。

intend [12]

[ɪnˈtend] *v.* 打算，想要

[记] in（里）+tend →"里面、心里有某种倾向"；外在行动上→ *v.* 打算，想要
[派] intention [ɪnˈtenʃn] *n.* 意图，目的
　　unintended [ˌʌnɪnˈtendɪd] *a.* 非故意的，无意识的
　　intentional [ɪnˈtenʃənl] *a.* 有意的，故意的
　　unintentional [ˌʌnɪnˈtenʃənl] *a.* 无意的，无意识的
[考] intend to do sth. 打算/想要做某事

［真］[B] It **intends** them to spark conversations among all Indian stakeholders.【2020年12月 仔细阅读50题B选项】
［译］它打算用它们引发所有印度利益相关者之间的对话。

intense¹²　[ɪnˈtens] *a.* 热情的；强烈的

［记］in（里）+tense（谐音"烫死"）→"心里好烫"→ *a.* 热情的；强烈的
［派］intensity [ɪnˈtensəti] *n.* 强烈，强度
　　　intensify [ɪnˈtensɪfaɪ] *v.* 增强，增加
　　　intensive [ɪnˈtensɪv] *a.* 加强的，强烈的

extend¹²　[ɪkˈstend] *v.* 延伸，扩展

［记］ex（out）+tend →"向外的倾向"→ *v.* 延伸，扩展
［派］extension [ɪkˈstenʃn] *n.* 延伸，延期
　　　extensive [ɪkˈstensɪv] *a.* 广大的，广阔的
　　　extent [ɪkˈstent] *n.* 广度，宽度，程度
［真］[B] There have been **extended** families in most parts of the world.【2020年7月 听力24题B选项】
［译］世界上的大部分地区都有大家庭。

contend⁹　[kənˈtend] *v.* 竞争，斗争；坚决主张，认为

［记］con（共同，全部）+tend →"大家有着共同的倾向"；你也想要，我也想要，怎么办？→ *v.* 竞争，斗争；坚决主张，认为
［派］contention [kənˈtenʃn] *n.* 竞争，争论
　　　contentious [kənˈtenʃəs] *a.* 有竞争的，有争论的
［形］content [ˈkɒntent] *n.* 内容；满意，满足　 *a.* 满意的，满足的　 *v.* 使满足，使满意
［考］sb. contend that... 某人主张……
［真］Advocates **contend** that the environmental advantages of organic agriculture far outweigh the lower yields, and that increasing research and breeding resources for organic systems would reduce the yield gap.【2020年9月 仔细阅读】
［译］倡导者认为，有机农业的环境优势远远超过了较低的产量，增加相关有机系统的研究和育种资源将缩小产量差距。

–tire– 疲倦，疲劳

retire⁶　[rɪˈtaɪə(r)] *v.* 退休；离开

［记］re（反复）+tire →"反复疲劳"，干什么都疲劳，干不动了，最终选择→ *v.* 退休；离开
［派］retirement [rɪˈtaɪəmənt] *n.* 退休；离开
［真］[D] They keep themselves busy even after **retirement**.【2019年12月 听力10题D选项】
［译］即使退休后他们也会忙。

Day 26

entire [16] [ɪnˈtaɪə(r)] *a.* 全部的，全体的，完全的

[记] en（使动）+tire → "使之很疲倦"；因为他干了全部的工作→ *a.* 全部的，全体的，完全的

[派] entirely [ɪnˈtaɪəli] *ad.* 完全地，全部地

[真] [B] Cultivation of creativity should permeate the **entire** school curriculum.【2021 年 6 月 仔细阅读 47 题 B 选项】

[译] 创造力的培养应该渗透到学校的整个课程中。

–tract–、–trag– 拖，拉

attract [16] [əˈtrækt] *v.* 吸引，引人注目

[记] at（to）+tract → "去拖，去拉"；把别人的目光、注意力拉到这里→ *v.* 吸引，引人注目

[派] attraction [əˈtrækʃn] *n.* 吸引（力），魅力
attractive [əˈtræktɪv] *a.* 有吸引力的，迷人的，有魅力的
attractiveness [əˈtræktɪvnəs] *n.* 吸引力
unattractive [ˌʌnəˈtræktɪv] *a.* 没有吸引力的

[真] [A] Its government wants to **attract** more tourists.【2021 年 6 月 仔细阅读 52 题 A 选项】

[译] 英国政府希望吸引更多的游客。

distract [2] [dɪˈstrækt] *v.* 使分心，使分神；打扰

[记] 上词 attract 的反义词；dis（散）+tract → "把注意力拉得分散了，拉到别处了" → *v.* 使分心，使分神；打扰

[派] distraction [dɪˈstrækʃn] *n.* 分散注意力的事

contract [7] [ˈkɒntrækt] *v.* 缩小，收缩；签合同 *n.* 合同

[记] con（全部，共同）+tract → "把所有东西拖走、拉走"；由大变小的过程 → *v.* 缩小，收缩→ "把甲乙双方拉到一起"；达成共识→ *v.* 签合同 *n.* 合同

[派] contraction [kənˈtrækʃn] *n.* 收缩，缩小；（肌肉的）收缩
contractor [kənˈtræktə(r)] *n.* 承包人，承包商

[形] contact [ˈkɒntækt] *v.&n.* 联系；接触

[真] [A] Revise the terms and conditions of the **contract**.【2020 年 12 月 听力 4 题 A 选项】

[译] 修改本合同的条款和条件。

trigger [4] [ˈtrɪɡə(r)] *n.* 扳机；引发反应的事（或行动） *v.* 引起，触发

[记] trig（改写自 trag）+g（无义）+er（表示人或物的后缀）→ "拉的东西" → *n.* 扳机→ "一拉扳机" → *v.* 引起，触发→ *n.* 引发反应的事（或行动）

[真] Why does social media **trigger** feelings of loneliness and inadequacy?【2020 年

12月 仔细阅读】

［译］为什么社交媒体会引发孤独感和自卑感？

retreat [2]　[rɪˈtri:t] *v. & n.* 撤退，退却，撤回

［记］re（back）+treat（改写自 tract）→ "向后、向回拉"，把兄弟们都拉回来 → *v. & n.* 撤退，退却，撤回

◀ –tribute– 给，给予 ▶

attribute [2]　[əˈtrɪbju:t] *v.* 把……归（因）于

［记］at（to）+tribute → "去给"；"把原因都给你；都是因为你" → *v.* 把……归（因）于

［派］attributable [əˈtrɪbjətəbl] *a.* 可归因于……的

［考］attribute A to B　把 A 归因于 B

contribute [20]　[kənˈtrɪbju:t] *v.* 贡献；捐赠

［记］con（全部，共同）+ tribute → "所有人都在给"；地震之后，无数中国人都在给，有钱给钱，没钱给物资 → *v.* 贡献；捐赠

［派］contribution [ˌkɒntrɪˈbju:ʃn] *n.* 贡献；捐赠
　　contributor [kənˈtrɪbjətə(r)] *n.* 贡献者；捐赠者

［考］contribute A to B　把 A 贡献给 B
　　contribute to　促成，有助于；捐献

［真］[D] It **contributes** to intellectual growth but can easily be killed.【2021 年 6 月仔细阅读 46 题 D 选项】

［译］它有助于智力的增长，但也很容易被扼杀。

distribute [3]　[dɪˈstrɪbju:t] *v.* 分发，散发

［记］dis（散）+tribute → "四散地给"，你一个，他一个 → *v.* 分发，散发

［派］distribution [ˌdɪstrɪˈbju:ʃn] *n.* 分发，分配

［真］[C] Inequality in food **distribution**.【2020 年 9 月仔细阅读 53 题 C 选项】

［译］食品分配不均。

◀ –tric–、–trig– 阴谋，诡计 ▶

intrigue [5]　[ɪnˈtri:g] [ˈɪntri:g] *n.* 阴谋，诡计　*v.* 密谋，私通

［记］in（里）+trig+ue（无义）→ "里面有很多诡计、把戏" → *n.* 阴谋，诡计 → *v.* 密谋，私通

［派］intriguing [ɪnˈtri:gɪŋ] *a.* 有趣的，迷人的

［真］[D] It enables one to write **intriguing** sequels to famous stories.【2021 年 6 月

仔细阅读 54 题 D 选项】

[译] 它使一个人能够为著名的故事写出有趣的续集。

intricate [2]

['ɪntrɪkət] *a.* 错综的，复杂的

[记] in（里）+tric+ate（*a.*）→ "里面有很多诡计、把戏" → *a.* 错综的，复杂的

–tern– 转动，翻转

external [4]

[ɪkˈstɜːnl] *a.* 外部的；外用的

[记] ex（out）+tern+al（*a.*）→ "转到外面" → *a.* 外部的；外用的
[真] A teacher could not seriously tell a parent their child has a low genetic tendency to study when **external** factors clearly exist.【2021 年 6 月 仔细阅读】
[译] 当明显存在外部因素时，老师不能认真地告诉家长，他们的孩子具有较低的学习遗传倾向。

internal [3]

[ɪnˈtɜːnl] *a.* 内部的，内在的

[记] in（里）+tern+al（*a.*）→ "转到里面" → *a.* 内部的，内在的
[派] internally [ɪnˈtɜːnəli] *ad.* 内部地，内心地
[真] Protein supplements may overburden some **internal** organ, thus leading to its malfunctioning.【2019 年 12 月 长篇阅读 40 题】
[译] 蛋白质补充剂可能会使某些内部器官负担过重，从而导致其功能障碍。

disturb [2]

[dɪˈstɜːb] *v.* 扰乱，妨碍；使不安

[记] dis（散）+turb（改写自 tern）→ "四散地翻转"；不安定因素 → *v.* 扰乱，妨碍；使不安
[派] undisturbed [ˌʌndɪˈstɜːbd] *a.* 未被打搅的；镇定的

–tut–、–tuit– 教，教授

tuition [6]

[tjuˈɪʃ(ə)n] *n.* 教学，教授；学费

[记] tuit+ion（*n.*）→ 词根是教，这个单词必然和"教，教授"有直接关系 → *n.* 教学，教授；学费
[真] For students who have been coasting through college, and for American universities that have been demanding less work, offering more attractions and charging higher **tuition**, the party may soon be over.【2020 年 7 月 仔细阅读】
[译] 对那些顺利读完大学的学生，以及那些学习要求更低、提供更多吸引力、收取更高学费的美国大学来说，这种狂欢可能很快就要结束了。

intuition [6]

[ˌɪntjuˈɪʃn] *n.* 直觉

[记] in（否定）+tuit+ion（n.）→ "不用教就会，靠什么呢？ → n. 直觉
[派] intuitive [ɪnˈtjuːɪtɪv] a. 直觉的，直观的
　　 intuitively [ɪnˈtjuːɪtɪvli] ad. 直觉地
[真] As an adult, Marconi had an **intuition** that he had to be loyal to politicians in order to be influential.【2021年6月长篇阅读37题题干】
[译] 成年后，马可尼有一种直觉，即他必须忠于政客才能有影响力。

非成组词（T 字母）

tackle³

[ˈtækl] v. 解决，处理

[记] tack（改写自 take；拿起）+le（无义）→ take 工具 tackle 问题 → v. 解决，处理

[助] 谐音"太抠"→老婆"太抠"，不给我零花钱，这个问题需要→ v. 解决，处理

[真] [C] They constantly dismiss others' proposals while taking no responsibility for **tackling** the problem.【2020年12月仔细阅读51题C选项】
[译] 他们经常拒绝别人的建议，而不承担解决这个问题的责任。

temper²

[ˈtempə(r)] n. 脾气，性情 v. 调和，缓和

[记] 来自拉丁语 temperare（混合；使温和）→ v. 调和，缓和

[助] 谐音"太泼"→ n. 脾气，性情→"此人太泼"；动不动就发"脾气"，需要→ v. 调和，缓和

[派] temperament [ˈtemprəmənt] n. 性格，性情，气质

testify⁴

[ˈtestɪfaɪ] v. 证明，证实

[记] test+ify（使动）→ "使之参加考试"；很多同学讨厌 test，为什么还要考研，因为要证明自己的实力、能力→ v. 证明，证实

[派] testimony [ˈtestɪməni] n. 证据，证词

[真] "I can **testify** to the huge effort that government agencies and other organisations have put into trying to understand the ecological values of this vast area," he says.【2020年9月仔细阅读】
[译] "我可以证实，政府机构和其他组织付出了很多努力，他们试图理解这片广阔区域的生态价值。"他说。

tolerate³

[ˈtɒləreɪt] v. 容忍，忍受；（对药物、毒品等）有耐受性

[记] 词根 toler（忍受，忍耐）+ate（v.）→ v. 容忍，忍受；（对药物、毒品等）有耐受性

[助] 谐音"疼了忍着"→ v. 容忍，忍受；（对药物、毒品等）有耐受性

[派] tolerance [ˈtɒlərəns] n. 容忍，忍受
　　 tolerant [ˈtɒlərənt] a. 宽容的，容忍的

[真] [C] **Tolerant**.【2021年6月1题C选项】

[译] 宽容的。

tough [5]

[tʌf] *a.* 困难的；难对付的；艰苦的；强壮的；粗暴的

[记] 来自古英语 toh（结实的，坚硬的）→ *a.* 困难的；难对付的；艰苦的；强壮的；粗暴的

[助] 谐音"Ta 服"→"让 Ta 服了"→ *a.* 困难的；难对付的；艰苦的；强壮的；粗暴的

[派] toughness [tʌfnəs] *n.* 坚韧，韧性

[真] [D] **Tough** regulations.【2021 年 6 月听力 16 题 D 选项】

[译] 严格的规定。

toxic [7]

[ˈtɒksɪk] *a.* 有毒的，中毒的

[记] 古希腊人用水松木（拉丁语为 taxus）制造弓箭，并根据水松木的名称将弓箭称为 toxon。希腊语 toxon 的形容词是 toxikon，意思是"与 toxon（弓箭）相关的"。由于水松木有毒，用水松木制造的弓箭也有毒，因此 toxikon 一词衍生出"有毒的"含义。该词经由拉丁语进入英语后，产生了英语单词 toxic，原本与弓箭有关的含义已经消失，光剩下"有毒的"含义。→ *a.* 有毒的，中毒的

[助] 谐音"投毒"→ *a.* 有毒的，中毒的

[真] Such workplaces are sometimes described as **toxic**.【2021 年 6 月听力原文】

[译] 这种工作场所有时被描述为有毒的。

track [11]

[træk] *v.* 追踪，跟踪 *n.* 痕迹，踪迹

[助] 谐音"追客"→ *v.* 追踪，跟踪 *n.* 痕迹，踪迹

[近] trail [treɪl] *n.* 踪迹，痕迹；小路 *v.* 追踪，跟踪

[真] Anything you initially gained from the instant satisfaction of telling it like it is, you might lose down the **track** by injuring your future career prospects.【2021 年 6 月 听力原文】

[译] 最初你从如实讲述的即时满足中获得的任何东西，可能都会因为损害你未来的职业前景而逐渐消失。

tragedy [4]

[ˈtrædʒədi] *n.* 悲剧，悲惨

[助] 谐音"踹弟弟"→"我弟弟被踹了一脚"；再惨也莫过于此吧→ *n.* 悲剧，悲惨

[派] tragic [ˈtrædʒɪk] *a.* 悲剧的，悲惨的

[真] Because universities and curricula are designed along the three unities of French classical **tragedy**: time, action, and place.【2020 年 12 月 长篇阅读 B 选项】

[译] 因为大学及其课程根据法国古典悲剧的三一律设计而成：时间、情节和地点。

transition [10]

[trænˈzɪʃn] *n.* 转变；变迁

[记] trans（across；穿越，穿梭）+ 词根 it（go；想想 exit 出口）+ion（*n.*）

→"穿梭着快速走过去",中国人说的时过境迁,物是人非→ *n.* 转变;变迁

[派] transit [ˈtrænzɪt] *n.* 交通运输系统;运输,运送

[真] Or that public **transit** won't go broke without federal assistance.【2020年12月 选词填空】

[译] 也不清楚没有联邦政府的援助,公共交通会不会破产。

trap³

[træp] *n.* 圈套 *v.* 诱骗;困住

[助] 谐音"踹吧"→一脚踹进坑里,进了→ *n.* 圈套→ *v.* 诱骗;困住

[真] [B] Avoiding hazardous **traps** in everyday social life.【2020年12月 仔细阅读55题B选项】

[译] 避免日常社交生活中的危险圈套。

treasure²

[ˈtreʒə(r)] *n.* 财宝,珍宝 *v.* 珍藏,珍视

[记] 来自拉丁语 thesaurus(宝库)→ *n.* 财宝,珍宝 *v.* 珍藏,珍视

[助] 谐音"揣着"→"财宝、珍宝"当然要好好揣着→ *n.* 财宝,珍宝→既然是财宝,那么需要→ *v.* 珍藏,珍视

typical¹⁰

[ˈtɪpɪkl] *a.* 典型的;特有的

[记] typ(简写自 type;类型)+ic(*a.*)+al(*a.*)→"要的就是这种类型"→ *a.* 典型的;特有的

[派] typically [ˈtɪpɪkli] *ad.* 通常,一般;典型地

[真] Repeating someone's behavior is **typical** of talented communicators, not always because the person is sympathetic, but because there is a goal to be achieved.【2021年6月 仔细阅读】

[译] 重复某人的行为是天赋沟通者的典型特征,这并不总是因为这个人富有同情心,而是因为他有目标要实现。

扫码快速学习

Day 27

扫码即刻听课

◀ -ult- 老 ▶

adult [19]　['ædʌlt] *n.* 成年人

六级基础词汇
[记] ad（to）+ult → "去变老" → *n.* 成年人
[派] adulthood ['ædʌlthʊd] *n.* 成年，成年期

adolescent [8]　[ˌædə'lesnt] *n.* 青少年　*a.* 青少年的，青春期的

[记] adol（简写自 adult；成年人）+(l) esc（改写自 less；更少的，更小的）+ent（表示人的后缀）→ "比成年人小的人" → *n.* 青少年　*a.* 青少年的，青春期的
[派] adolescence [ˌædə'lesns] *n.* 青春期
[真] Marconi needed to achieve the goal that was set in his mind as an **adolescent**; by the time he reached adulthood, he understood, intuitively, that in order to have an impact he had to both develop an independent economic base and align himself with political power.【2021 年 6 月 长篇阅读 I 选项】
[译] 马可尼需要实现他青少年时期设定的目标；到成年时，他从直觉上明白，为了产生一定的影响，他必须具有独立的经济基础，并且与政治权力结盟。

ultimate [8]　['ʌltɪmət] *a.* 最终的，最后的

[记] ult+im（最）+ate（*a.*）→ "事物发展到最末期的时候" → *a.* 最终的，最后的
[派] ultimately ['ʌltɪmətli] *ad.* 最后，最终
[真] Genetic selection is a way of exerting influence over others, "the **ultimate** collective control of human destinies", as writer H.G.Wells put it.【2021 年 6 月 仔细阅读】
[译] 正如作家 H.G. 威尔斯所言，基因选择是对他人施加影响的一种方式，"是对人类命运的最终集体控制"。

◀ -uni- 一 ▶

unite [7]　[juˈnaɪt] *v.* 联合，合并

201

[记] uni+te（无义）→"使之成为一个"→ v. 联合，合并
[派] reunite [ˌri:juˈnaɪt] v. 使再次联合
　　 unity [ˈju:nəti] n. 联合，统一
[真] The Notre Dame Cathedral catastrophe was said to have helped **unite** the French nation.【2021年6月长篇阅读38题】
[译] 据说巴黎圣母院的灾难有助于联合法国民族。

union ³ [ˈju:niən] *n.* 联盟；工会（熟词僻义，重点关注）

[记] 上词 unite 的间接名词→"联合在一起"；组成→ *n.* 联盟；工会
[考] European Union 欧盟
[真] Workers' **union** have accepted the inevitability of the introduction of new technology.【2021年6月听力原文】
[译] 工会已经接受了引进新技术的必然性。

unique ¹² [juˈni:k] *a.* 唯一的，独一无二的

[记] uni+que（谐音"缺"）→"只有一个，而且很缺乏"→ *a.* 唯一的，独一无二的
[派] uniqueness [juˈni:knəs] *n.* 唯一性，独特性
[真] But no one can be **unique** with their outfit every day.【2020年12月听力原文】
[译] 但没有人每天穿的衣服都是独特的。

uniform ³ [ˈju:nɪfɔ:m] *n.* 校服，制服，（某一群体的）特种服式　*a.* 相同的，同样的

[记] uni+form（*n.* 形式，样式）→"同一个形式、样式"；穿上了→ *n.* 校服，制服，（某一群体的）特种服式→穿上"校服或制服"；看起来→ *a.* 相同的，同样的
[真] [A] Design their own **uniform** to appear unique.【2020年12月听力15题A选项】
[译] 设计出他们自己的制服，让他们看起来很独特。

非成组词（U字母）

underground ² [ˌʌndəˈgraʊnd] *n.* 地铁　*a.* 地下的；秘密的

[记] under+ground（*n.* 地面，土地）→"地面、土地之下的"→ *a.* 地下的
　　 n. 地铁→"地下恋情"→ *a.* 秘密的

urban ⁶ [ˈɜ:bən] *a.* 城市的

[记] 来自拉丁语 urbanus（城市）→ *a.* 城市的
[助] 谐音"墨尔本"→澳大利亚的著名"城市"→ *a.* 城市的
[派] urbanize/ise [ˈɜ:bənaɪz] *v.* 使都市化
　　 urbanization/sation [ˌɜ:bənaɪˈzeɪʃn] *n.* 都市化
[真] The topic gets more complicated when we talk about the divide between rural

and **urban** communities.【2021 年 6 月 听力原文】
［译］当我们谈及农村和城市社区之间的鸿沟时，这个话题就变得更加复杂。

urban 的引申词

rural [5]
[ˈrʊərəl] *a.* 乡村的，农村的
［记］来自拉丁语 ruralis（乡村的）→ *a.* 乡村的，农村的
［助］上词 urban 的反义词；谐音"路远"→离城市远的，在边缘的，就是→ *a.* 乡村的，农村的
［真］[C] It totally destroyed the state's **rural** landscape.【2021 年 6 月 听力 15 题 C 选项】
［译］它彻底摧毁了该州的乡村景观。

urgent [6]
[ˈɜːdʒənt] *a.* 急迫的，催促的
［记］urg（简写自 urge；催促）+ent（*a.*）→"不停催促的"→ *a.* 急迫的，催促的
［助］谐音"饿，真的"→"真的饿，快点做饭"→ *a.* 急迫的，催促的
［派］urgency [ˈɜːdʒənsi] *n.* 紧迫，急迫
［真］[C] They should be reserved for **urgent** communication.【2021 年 6 月 听力 25 题 C 选项】
［译］它们应该被保留下来，用于紧急沟通。

urge [4]
[ɜːdʒ] *v.* 催促；敦促；力劝 *n.* 冲动
［记］上词 urgent 的动词和名词→ *v.* 催促；敦促；力劝 *n.* 冲动
［考］urge sb. to do sth. 催促 / 力劝某人做某事
［真］[D] **Urge** us to explore the unknown domain of the universe.【2020 年 12 月 仔细阅读 50 题 D 选项】
［译］敦促我们探索宇宙的未知领域。

utilize/ise [6]
[ˈjuːtəlaɪz] *v.* 利用，使用
［记］uti（改写自 use；使用，利用）+l（无义）+ize/ise（使动）→ *v.* 利用，使用
［派］utilization/sation [ˌjuːtəlaɪˈzeɪʃn] *n.* 利用，使用
utility [juːˈtɪləti] *n.* 功用，效用
［真］For guests, I can relocate the movable wall and **utilize** the foldable guest beds I installed.【2020 年 12 月 听力原文】
［译］如果有客人，我可以重新安置活动墙并使用我安装的可折叠客人床。

utter [3]
[ˈʌtə(r)] *v.* 说，出声 *a.* 完全的，彻底的
［记］utt（改写自 out；出来，外面；完全，彻底）+er（表示人的后缀）→话从口里"出来"→ *v.* 说，出声→ *a.* 完全的，彻底的

[派] utterly [ˈʌtəli] ad. 完全地，彻底地

[真] When people **uttered** a falsehood, the scientists noticed a burst of activity in their amygdala.【2019年12月 仔细阅读】

[译] 当人们说谎时，科学家们注意到他们的扁桃体有大量活动。

–vac–、–ves–、–val–、–void– 空，空虚

evacuate [4]
[ɪˈvækjueɪt] v. 撤离，疏散

[记] e（out）+vac+u（无义）+ate（v.）→"出去然后使之空"；楼里有炸弹，使所有人出去，然后大楼空无一人→ v. 撤离，疏散

[派] evacuation [ɪˌvækjuˈeɪʃn] n. 疏散，撤离

[真] We had to **evacuate** on very short notice.【2021年6月 听力原文】

[译] 我们不得不在很短的时间内撤离。

vessel [2]
[ˈvesl] n. 管道；血管；容器

[记] ves+se（n.）+l（形状像管子）→"管道中间就是空的，而且字母l的形状很像长长的管道"→ n. 管道；血管；容器

valley [6]
[ˈvæli] n. 山谷，溪谷，峡谷

[记] vall（简写自 val）+ey（n.）→"空旷的地方"→ n. 山谷，溪谷，峡谷

[考] Silicon Valley 美国硅谷

[真] [D] The culture of Silicon **Valley** ought not to be emulated.【2021年6月 仔细阅读55题 D选项】

[译] 不应该效仿硅谷文化。

avoid [19]
[əˈvɔɪd] v. 避免，防止

[记] a（简写自 ab；否定）+void →"不要空白、空虚的生活"→ v. 避免，防止

[派] avoidance [əˈvɔɪdəns] n. 避免
　　avoidable [əˈvɔɪdəbl] a. 能避免的，可回避的

[真] Traffic jams often appear where no one has enough information to **avoid** them.【2021年6月 仔细阅读】

[译] 在人们得不到充足信息的时候，交通堵塞经常出现。

vanish [4]
[ˈvænɪʃ] v. 消失，突然不见

[记] van（改写自 val）+ish（v.）→"使之空"；屋里空了→ v. 消失，突然不见

[真] [D] Explore the cultures of species before they **vanish**.【2020年12月 仔细阅读55题 D选项】

[译] 在物种消失之前探索物种文化。

Day 27

–val–、–vail– 价值

value [25]
[ˈvælju:] *n.* 价值 *v.* 重视；评估（熟词僻义，重点关注）
[助] 谐音"我留"，我们会把什么留下？当然是有"价值"的，没价值的谁留啊！→ *n.* 价值 → "有价值的"，人们才会 → *v.* 重视；评估
[派] valuable [ˈvæljuəbl] *a.* 有价值的，贵重的
valueless [ˈvælju:ləs] *a.* 无价值的；不足道的
devalue [ˌdi:ˈvælju:] *v.* （货币）贬值，降低（某事物的）价值；贬低
[真] [C] The **value** of drawing tends to be overestimated.【2021 年 6 月 仔细阅读 48 题 C 选项】
[译] 绘画的价值往往被高估。

evaluate [4]
[ɪˈvæljueɪt] *v.* 估价，评价
[记] e（out）+valu（改写自 val）+ate（*v.*）→ "使其价值出来"；对于物来说 → *v.* 估价 → 对于人来说 → *v.* 评价
[派] evaluation [ɪˌvæljuˈeɪʃn] *n.* 估价，评价
[真] [C] Lack of regular **evaluation**.【2021 年 6 月 听力 17 题 C 选项】
[译] 缺乏定期评估。

valid [11]
[ˈvælɪd] *a.* 有效的
[记] val+id（*a.*）→ "依然有价值"；就是在有效期内 → *a.* 有效的
[派] invalid [ɪnˈvælɪd] *a.* 无效的，不能成立的
validate [ˈvælɪdeɪt] *v.* 使合法化；使生效
validation [ˌvælɪˈdeɪʃn] *n.* 确认，生效
revalidate [ri:ˈvælɪdeɪt] *v.* 使重新生效，使重新有法律效力
revalidation [ri:vælɪˈdeʃən] *n.* 重新生效
[真] Some supporters of telemedicine hope states will accept each other's medical practice licenses as **valid**.【2020 年 9 月 长篇阅读 41 题】
[译] 一些远程医疗的支持者希望各州能认可彼此的医疗执照。

available [9]
[əˈveɪləbl] *a.* 可获得的，可利用的；有空的
[记] a（to）+vail+able（*a.*）→ "有价值"才会希望它是 → *a.* 可获得的，可利用的 → Are you available tonight? 字面含义是"今晚可获得吗？"，实际上表示"今晚有空吗？" → *a.* 有空的
[派] availability [əˌveɪləˈbɪləti] *n.* 有效；可利用性；获得，得到
[真] A new study had drawn a bleak picture of cultural inclusiveness reflected in the children's literature **available** in Australia.【2021 年 6 月 选词填空】
[译] 一项新研究描绘了澳大利亚儿童文学中反映的文化包容性较弱的状况。

worth [22]
[wɜːθ] *n.* 价值 *a.* 值得的；等值的

[记] wor（改写自 val；价值）+th（无义）→ n. 价值→ a. 值得的；等值的
[派] worthwhile [ˌwɜːθˈwaɪl] a. 有价值的；值得花时间的；值得做的
worthy [ˈwɜːði] a. 值得的；配得上的
trustworthy [ˈtrʌstwɜːði] a. 值得信赖的，可靠的
newsworthy [ˈnjuːzwɜːði] a. 有报道价值的
[考] it is worth doing sth. 做某事是值得的
[真] A point **worth** making is that the study was based only on the perspective of employees.【2021 年 6 月 听力原文】
[译] 值得一提的是，该研究仅基于员工的观点。

–var–、–vary– 变化

vary [8]
[ˈveəri] v. 变化；不同

六级基础词汇

various [12]
[ˈveəriəs] a. 各种各样的，许多的
[记] 上词 vary 的形容词；var+ious（a.）→"变来变去，各种变"→ a. 各种各样的，许多的
[真] What does the author imply about the **various** gadgets on cars?【2021 年 6 月 仔细阅读 52 题题干】
[译] 作者对汽车上的各种小工具有什么暗示？

variation [3]
[ˌveəriˈeɪʃn] n. 变化，变动
[记] 上词 vary 的名词；var+i（无义）+ation（n.）→ n. 变化，变动
[真] Central to hereditarian science is a tall claim: that identifiable **variations** in genetic sequences can predict an individual's aptness to learn, reason and solve problems.【2021 年 6 月 仔细阅读】
[译] 遗传科学的核心是一个夸张的论断：基因序列中可识别的差异可以预测一个人学习、推理和解决问题的能力。

variety [10]
[vəˈraɪəti] n. 多样，多样性；种类
[记] 上词 vary 的名词；var+i（无义）+ety（n.）→"变来变去，各种变"→ n. 多样，多样性；种类
[考] a variety of 种种的，各种各样的
[真] [D] Helping them advertise a greater **variety** of products.【2020 年 12 月 听力 11 题 D 选项】
[译] 帮助他们宣传更多种类的产品。

variable [4]
[ˈveəriəbl] a. 变化的，可变的　n. 变量
[记] 上词 vary 的形容词；var+i（无义）+able（a.）→"能变化的"→ a. 变化

的，可变的　　*n.* 变量

[真] First, they explain that if a given **variable** is playing a role in affecting wellbeing, then we should expect any change in that variable to correlate with the observed changes in wellbeing.【2019 年 12 月 长篇阅读 E 选项】

[译] 首先，他们解释说，如果一个给定的变量在影响幸福感方面发挥了作用，那么我们应该期望该变量的任何变化都与观察到的幸福感变化相关。

–van–、–ven–、–vent–、–ves–

① 走，来

advance [13]　[ədˈvɑːns] *v.&n.* 前进，发展；(数量) 增加，上涨

[记] ad (to) +van+ce (*v.&n.*) →"去往前走"→ *v.&n.* 前进，发展；(数量) 增加，上涨

[派] advanced [ədˈvɑːnst] *a.* 先进的，高等的
　　　advancement [ədˈvɑːnsmənt] *n.* 前进，发展

[真] Similar limits can be foreseen for the much greater **advances** promised by self-driving cars.【2021 年 6 月 仔细阅读】

[译] 对承诺会做出更多改进的无人驾驶汽车领域，也可以预见类似的限制。

eventually [6]　[ɪˈventʃuəli] *ad.* 终于，最终

[记] event+ (t) ual (谐音 "头") +ly (*ad.*) →"此事到头了"→ *ad.* 终于，最终

[真] [C] It will **eventually** give way to organic farming.【2020 年 9 月 仔细阅读 54 题 C 选项】

[译] 它最终将让位于有机农业。

venture [4]　[ˈventʃə(r)] *v.* 冒险　*n.* 企业；风险项目；冒险活动

[记] vent+ure (*v.&n.*) →"走来走去"；在未知领域探索和行走本身就是→ *v.* 冒险→创业本身就是一种"冒险"→ *n.* 企业；风险项目；冒险活动

[真] Likewise, the second—a passion for founding the **venture**—doesn't necessarily translate into great success.【2021 年 6 月 听力原文】

[译] 同样地，第二阶段——对创办企业的热情——也不一定能转化为巨大的成功。

convention [21]　[kənˈvenʃn] *n.* 会议；惯例，习俗

[记] con (全部，共同) +vent+ion (*n.*) →"所有人全部走在一起"→ *n.* 会议→过年时，中国人无论在哪里，"都会和家人走在一起"→ *n.* 惯例，习俗

[派] conventional [kənˈvenʃnl] *a.* 传统的，依照惯例的
　　　unconventional [ˌʌnkənˈvenʃnl] *a.* 非传统的，不按常规的

［真］[C] They can break **conventions**.【2021 年 6 月 听力 3 题 C 选项】
［译］他们可以打破惯例。

convenient [6]

[kənˈviːniənt] *a.* 方便的，便利的

［记］con（全部，共同）+ven+i（谐音"爱"）+ent（*a.*）→ "所有人都爱来这里"买东西；因为→ *a.* 方便的，便利的

［派］convenience [kənˈviːniəns] *n.* 便利，方便
conveniently [kənˈviːniəntli] *ad.* 方便地，便利地

［考］convenient store 便利店

［真］However, after a lifetime of moving within the circles of power, he was unable to break with authority, and served Mussolini faithfully (as president of Italy's national research council and royal academy, as well as a member of the Fascist Grand Council) until the day he died—**conveniently**—in 1937, shortly before he would have had to take a stand in the conflict that consumed a world that he had, in part, created.【2021 年 6 月 长篇阅读 K 选项】

［译］然而，由于他一生都在不同的权势圈中活动，他无法与权势决裂，于是忠实地为墨索里尼服务（担任意大利国家研究委员会和皇家科学院的主席，并且一直是法西斯大委员会的成员），直到他在 1937 年凑巧离世的那一天。因为如果他还没有去世，他很快就不得不在一场冲突中表明立场，而这场冲突最终摧毁了他参与构建的世界。

intervene [5]

[ˌɪntəˈviːn] *v.* 干预，介入

［记］inter（middle；between）+ven+e（无义）→ "走到彼此中间"；很像第三者→ *v.* 干预，介入

［派］intervention [ˌɪntəˈvenʃn] *n.* 干预，介入

［真］[D] To justify government **intervention** in solving the obesity problem.【2020 年 9 月 仔细阅读 49 题 D 选项】

［译］为了证明政府通过干预来解决肥胖问题是合理的。

revenue [8]

[ˈrevənjuː] *n.* 税收，收入

［记］re（back）+ven+ue（无义）→ "走回来，向回走"；收入中的这一部分将以 revenue 的形式"走回国家，走回国库"→ *n.* 税收，收入

［真］[B] The tax is unlikely to add much to its **revenue**.【2021 年 6 月 仔细阅读 52 题 B 选项】

［译］这项税收不可能大大增加其收入。

evade [2]

[ɪˈveɪd] *v.* 逃避，逃脱

［记］e（out）+vad（改写自 vent）+e（无义）→ 这里有危险，"走出去"→ *v.* 逃避，逃脱

［派］evasion [ɪˈveɪʒn] *n.* 逃避，回避

Day 27

inevitable [2] [ɪnˈevɪtəbl] *a.* 不可避免的，必然的

[记] in（否）+evit（改写自 evade；逃避）+able（*a.*）→ "无法逃避的，无法躲避的"，通俗说法就是躲不过去了，只能如此→ *a.* 不可避免的，必然的
[派] inevitably [ɪnˈevɪtəbli] *ad.* 不可避免地，必然地

②风

ventilate [3] [ˈventɪleɪt] *v.* （使）通风

[记] vent+il（无义）+ate（*v.*）→（使）通风
[派] ventilation [ˌventɪˈleɪʃn] *n.* 通风（设备）
[真] [A] A naturally **ventilated** office is more comfortable.【2020 年 12 月 听力 12 题 A 选项】
[译] 一个自然通风的办公室更舒适。

扫码快速学习

–vers–、–vert– 转，转变

version [4] ['vɜːʃn] **n.** 版本；译文

[记] vers+ion（n.）→ "转变来转变去"；形成了不同的→ n. 版本；译文
[真] [C] He was really drawn to its other **versions**.【2020 年 12 月 听力 2 题 C 选项】
[译] 他真的被其他版本所吸引。

avert [5] [ə'vɜːt] **v.** 转移（目光、话题等）；避免

[记] a（to）+vert→遇到敏感话题，"去转一下"→ v. 转移（目光、话题等）→ 转移话题是"避免"尴尬→ v. 避免
[派] aversion [ə'vɜːʃn] n. 厌恶，反感
[真] A greater disaster was **averted** by members of the Paris fire brigade, who risked their lives to remain inside the burning monument to create a wall of water between the raging fire and the two towers on the west of the building.【2021 年 6 月 长篇阅读 A 选项】
[译] 巴黎消防队队员避免了一场更大的灾难，他们冒着生命危险留在燃烧的建筑物内，在熊熊大火和巴黎圣母院西边的两座钟楼之间筑起了一道水墙。

adverse [6] ['ædvɜːs] **a.** 反面的；不利的

[记] ad（to）+vers+e（无义）→ "去转，转过去"→ a. 反面的；不利的
[派] adversely [æd'vɜːsli] ad. 反对地；不利地
adversarial [ˌædvə'seəriəl] a. 敌对的；对抗（性）的
[真] [B] It may **adversely** affect his future career prospects.【2021 年 6 月 听力 3 题 B 选项】
[译] 这可能会对他未来的职业前景产生不利影响。

convert [8] [kən'vɜːt] **v.** 转变，转化

[记] con（加强）+vert → v. 转变，转化
[派] conversion [kən'vɜːʃn] n. 转变，转化
[真] Another grass-fed booster spurring farmers to **convert** is EPIC, which makes

Day 28

meat-based protein bars.【2019 年 12 月 长篇阅读 K 选项】
[译] 另一种促使农民思想改变的草饲促进剂是 EPIC，它生产肉基蛋白棒。

reverse [5]

[rɪˈvɜːs] *v.* 翻转，倒转　*a.* 反面的；颠倒的

[记] re（back）+vers+e（无义）→ "向反方向转，向回转" → *v.* 翻转，倒转　*a.* 反面的；颠倒的

[真] Yet the **reverse** compulsion is hidden in the proposals for a new plant-based "planetary diet".【2020 年 12 月 仔细阅读】

[译] 然而，在一项新的以植物为基准的"星球饮食"提议中隐含了强迫人们吃素的信息。

controversy [3]

[ˈkɒntrəvɜːsi] *n.* 争论，辩论

[记] contr（相反）+o（无义）+vers+y（*n.*）→ 话题"相反"，话语权"转来转去"；双方在→ *n.* 争论，辩论

[派] controversial [ˌkɒntrəˈvɜːʃl] *a.* 有争议的，引起争论的

[真] The most **controversial** aspect of Marconi's life—and the reason why there has been no satisfying biography of Marconi until now—was his uncritical embrace of Benito Mussolini.【2021 年 6 月 长篇阅读 K 选项】

[译] 马可尼一生中最具争议的方面——也是直到现在还没有令人满意的马可尼传记的原因——是他对贝尼托·墨索里尼不加批判的拥护。

diverse [18]

[daɪˈvɜːs] *a.* 多种多样的，不同的

[记] di（散）+vers+e（无义）→ "四散地转变"；转变来转变去 → *a.* 多种多样的，不同的

[派] diversity [daɪˈvɜːsəti] *n.* 多样化，多样性
　　biodiversity [ˌbaɪəʊdaɪˈvɜːsəti] *n.* 生物多样性

[真] You simply communicate photographs and catchy posts to a **diverse** group of people whom you have "friended" or "followed" based on an accidental interaction.【2020 年 12 月 仔细阅读】

[译] 你只需要将照片和有吸引力的帖子发给不同的群组，群组成员都是基于偶然互成为你的好友或者你关注的人。

universal [4]

[ˌjuːnɪˈvɜːsl] *a.* 宇宙的；全体的，通用的

[记] univers（简写自 universe；宇宙）+al（*a.*）→ *a.* 宇宙的 → "宇宙包罗万象" → *a.* 全体的，通用的

[派] universally [ˌjuːnɪˈvɜːsəli] *ad.* 普遍地，全体地

converge [2]

[kənˈvɜːdʒ] *v.* 汇集，聚集；（路线）相交

[记] con（共同，全部）+verg（改写自 vers）+e（无义）→ "全部转到一起" → *v.* 汇集，聚集；（路线）相交

–vey– 道路

convey [2]
[kənˈveɪ] *v.* 传达，传递；运送，输送

[记] con（加强）+vey → "货在道路上" → *v.* 传达，传递；运送，输送

survey [6]
[ˈsɜːveɪ] *v.&n.* 调查；俯瞰；勘测

[记] sur（上）+vey → "站在路上到处看" → *v.&n.* 调查；俯瞰；勘测
[真] The research scholars **surveyed** 152 blue-collar workers from two separate sites in the mining industry.【2021 年 6 月 听力原文】
[译] 研究学者们调查了采矿业中两个不同地点的 152 名蓝领工人。

–vi–、–vid–、–vis– 看见

video [9]
[ˈvɪdiəʊ] *n.* 视频，录像 *a.* 视频的，录像的

[记] vid+eo（无义）→ "视频、录像" 都和看有直接关系 → *n.* 视频，录像 *a.* 视频的，录像的
[真] A collection of dramatic **videos** and photos quickly spread across social media, showing the horrifying destruction, and attracting emotional responses from people all over the world.【2021 年 6 月 长篇阅读 G 选项】
[译] 一系列戏剧性的视频和照片在社交媒体上迅速传播，展示了可怕的毁坏过程，引起了全世界人们的情感共鸣。

obvious [14]
[ˈɒbviəs] *a.* 明显的

[记] o（谐音"哦"）+b（谐音"不"）+vi+ous（*a.*）→ "哦，看不到吗？" → *a.* 明显的
[派] obviously [ˈɒbviəsli] *ad.* 明显地
[真] [D] Students should learn more **obviously** creative subjects.【2021 年 6 月 仔细阅读 47 题 D 选项】
[译] 学生应该学习更明显的创造性科目。

evident [14]
[ˈevɪdənt] *a.* 明显的，清楚的

[记] e（out）+vid+ent（*a.*）→ "露在外面，能被看见" → *a.* 明显的，清楚的
[派] evidence [ˈevɪdəns] *n.* 证据
[真] It is **evident** by their selections that when women speak of close friendships, they are referring to emotional factors, while men emphasize the pleasure they find in a friend's company.【2020 年 7 月 听力原文】
[译] 受访者的选择可以证明，当女性谈及亲密关系时，她们多偏向情感因素，然而男性则看重在朋友的陪伴下，他们能得到的快乐。

Day 28

vision [10]
['vɪʒn] *n.* 视力，视野；想象，设想
[记] vis+ion（*n.*）→ *n.* 视力，视野 → "脑海里能看到"的景象 → *n.* 想象，设想
[派] visionary ['vɪʒənri] *n.* 有远见的人　*a.* 幻想的；有远见的
[真] In a sense, Marconi's **vision** jumped from his time to our own.【2021年6月长篇阅读E选项】
[译] 从某种意义上来说，马可尼的愿景从他的时代直接跨越到了我们目前的时代。

visible [4]
['vɪzəbl] *a.* 看得见的，明显的
[记] vis+ible（*a.*）→ "能看得见的" → *a.* 看得见的，明显的
[派] invisible [ɪnˈvɪzəbl] *a.* 看不见的
[真] What is more **visible** in India than anywhere else according to the passage?【2020年12月仔细阅读46题题干】
[译] 根据这篇文章，印度有什么比其他任何地方都更明显的东西呢？

visual [13]
['vɪʒuəl] *a.* 视觉的
[记] vis+u（无义）+al（*a.*）→ *a.* 视觉的
[派] visualize/ise ['vɪʒuəlaɪz] *v.* 使形象化；构思
[真] [D] Precision in **visual** perception.【2021年6月仔细阅读50题D选项】
[译] 视觉感知力精确。

envisage [2]
[ɪnˈvɪzɪdʒ] *v.* 想象，展望
[记] en（使动）+vis+age（*n.*）→ *v.* 想象，展望

revise [3]
[rɪˈvaɪz] *v.&n.* 复习；修订，校对
[记] re（反复）+vis+e（无义）→ "反复地看"，看的东西不一样，意思也就不一样 → "考试前反复看书"，就是 → *v.&n.* 复习 → "编辑时反复看书"，就是 → *v.&n.* 修订，校对
[派] revision [rɪˈvɪʒn] *n.* 复习；修订，校对
[真] [A] **Revise** the terms and conditions of the contract.【2020年12月听力4题A选项】
[译] 修改本合同的条款和条件。

supervise [4]
['suːpəvaɪz] *v.* 监督，管理；调查
[记] super（上）+vis+e（无义）→ "领导在上面看的动作" → *v.* 监督，管理；调查
[派] supervision [ˌsjuːpəˈvɪʒn] *n.* 监督，管理
supervisor ['suːpəvaɪzə(r)] *n.* 监督者，指导者
[真] **Supervisors**' helping behavior was found to be motivational in nature.【2021年6月听力原文】
[译] 研究发现，上司的帮助行为在本质上是一种激励。

–view– 看，看见，观点，意见

view [10]　[vju:] *n.* 看法，观点；风景　*v.* 看，看待（熟词僻义，重点关注）

六级基础词汇
［派］viewpoint [ˈvjuːpɔɪnt] *n.* 观点
［考］view A as B　把 A 看作 B
［真］[B] It was conducted from frontline managers' point of **view**.【2021 年 6 月 听力 18 题 B 选项】
［译］它是从一线管理人员的观点出发的。

interview [28]　[ˈɪntəvjuː] *v.&n.* 面试；采访

［记］inter（between）+view → "彼此交换观点" → *v.&n.* 面试；采访
［派］interviewer [ˈɪntəvjuːə(r)] *n.* 面试官
　　　interviewee [ˌɪntəvjuːˈiː] *n.* 面试者
［真］Now you've got me rethinking what I'll disclose in the **interview**.【2021 年 6 月 听力原文】
［译］现在你让我想要重新思考我要在面谈中披露的内容了。

review [6]　[rɪˈvjuː] *v.&n.* 复习，回顾；评论

［记］re（反复）+view → "反复看" → *v.&n.* 复习，回顾；评论
［派］reviewer [rɪˈvjuːə(r)] *n.* 评论家，评论者
［真］Researchers conducted a **review** of all studies relating to air-conditioning and productivity.【2020 年 12 月 听力原文】
［译］研究人员对空调和生产力的所有相关研究进行了综述研究。

–voc–、–vok– 声音，呼喊

vocal [2]　[ˈvəʊkl] *a.* 声音的，有声的

［记］voc+al（*a.*）→ *a.* 声音的，有声的

advocate [19]　[ˈædvəkeɪt] *v.* 支持；提倡，主张　*n.* 提倡者，支持者

［记］ad（to）+voc+ate（*v.&n.*）→ "通过大声呼喊表示对某人或某事的支持"；比如演唱会上疯狂喊歌星的名字 → *v.* 支持 → "支持某个观点、想法" → *v.* 提倡，主张 → "提倡、主张某观点的人" → *n.* 提倡者，支持者
［派］advocacy [ˈædvəkəsi] *n.* 支持，拥护
［真］To me, a radical is simply someone who rebels against the norm while **advocates** a change in the existing state of affairs.【2020 年 9 月 听力原文】
［译］对我来说，激进分子只不过是反抗常规，同时倡导改变现状的人。

Day 28

–vi–、–viv–、–vit– 活命，生活

viable [2]
['vaɪəbl] *a.* 能活的，能生存的；能行得通的
[记] vi+able（*a.* 能……的）→ *a.* 能活的，能生存的；能行得通的
[派] unviable [ʌnˈvaɪəb(ə)l] *a.* 不能独立生存的；不可行的

revive [2]
[rɪˈvaɪv] *v.* 复活，再生；复苏，振兴
[记] re（反复）+viv+e（无义）→"再一次活过来"→ *v.* 复活，再生→经济"再一次活过来"→ *v.* 复苏，振兴
[派] revival [rɪˈvaɪvl] *n.* 复活，再生；复兴

survive [10]
[səˈvaɪv] *v.* 幸存，存活；比……活得长
[记] sur（上）+viv+e（无义）→"上面有活人"；上面还有人活着→ *v.* 幸存，存活→"活的时间在你之上"→ *v.* 比……活得长
[派] survival [səˈvaɪvl] *n.* 幸存，存活
[考] survive from... 从……幸存/存活下来
[真] No one is really certain of the reason for this, although the speculation centers around the idea that women are more capable of **surviving** or handling disease than men.【2021年6月 听力原文】
[译] 没有人确切地知道这其中的原因，尽管人们的猜测集中在女性比男性更有能力生存或应对疾病这一观点上。

vital [3]
['vaɪtl] *a.* 性命攸关的，至关重要的
[记] vit+al（*a.*）→"与生命、活命有关的"→ *a.* 性命攸关的，至关重要的
[派] vitality [vaɪˈtæləti] *n.* 活力，生命力
　　revitalize/ise [ˌriːˈvaɪtəlaɪz] *v.* 使更强壮，使恢复生机
[考] be vital to... 对……至关重要
[真] There is no reason why visitors to the UK, or domestic tourists on holiday in hotspots such as Cornwall, should be exempt from taxation—particularly when **vital** local services including waste collection, park maintenance and arts and culture spending are under unprecedented strain.【2021年6月 仔细阅读】
[译] 尤其是在垃圾回收、公园维护以及艺术文化开销等重要的当地服务面临前所未有的压力时，来英国旅游的国外游客又或是在诸如康沃尔等热门景区度假的国内游客，没有理由不交旅游税。

–vol–、–volv–、–volu–

①旋转，卷

involve [22]
[ɪnˈvɒlv] *v.* 卷入；包含，涉及

［记］in（里）+volv+e（无义）→"卷到里面，卷进去"→ v. 卷入；包含，涉及

［派］involvement [ɪnˈvɒlvmənt] n. 牵连，参与，加入

［考］be involved in 卷入，涉及

［真］But if your job **involves** interacting with other people, the answer to this is often yes.【2020 年 12 月 听力原文】

［译］但是如果你的工作涉及与他人互动交流，那么答案通常是肯定的。

evolve ³　　[iˈvɒlv] v. 进化；发展

［记］e（out）+volv+e（无义）→"向外卷"；想想生物进化图，是不是一圈一圈往外卷或转→ v. 进化→进化的过程就是生物发展的过程→ v. 发展

［派］evolution [ˌi:vəˈlu:ʃn] [ˌevəˈlu:ʃn] n. 进化；发展

［考］evolve into... 逐渐发展成……

［真］Well, one thing is for sure, technology is **evolving** faster than our ability to understand it.【2020 年 12 月 听力原文】

［译］嗯，有一点是肯定的，技术发展的速度超过了我们能理解它的速度。

revolution ⁷　　[ˌrevəˈlu:ʃn] n. 旋转；革命

［记］re（反复）+volu+tion（n.）→"反复旋转"→ n. 旋转→"社会大旋转"→ n. 革命

［派］revolutionary [ˌrevəˈlu:ʃənəri] a. 革命的
　　　revolutionize/ise [ˌrevəˈlu:ʃənaɪz] v. 发动革命

［真］[A] It is seeing an automation **revolution**.【2021 年 6 月 听力 19 题 A 选项】

［译］它正在见证一场自动化革命。

vehicle ⁸　　[ˈvi:əkl] n. 车辆；工具

［记］vehi（改写自 volv）+cle（n.）→"车辆"是不是在不停地旋转啊！→ n. 车辆→"车辆"理所当然是一种→ n. 工具

［真］In a new study, people exposed to jargon when reading about subjects like autonomous **vehicles** and surgical robots later said they were less interested in science than others who read about the same topics, but without the use of specialized terms. 【2021 年 6 月 听力原文】

［译］在一项新研究中，人们在阅读有关自动驾驶汽车和外科手术机器人等主题时会遇到专业术语。这些人随后表示，他们对科学的兴趣不如其他阅读相同主题的人，而那些主题没有使用专业术语。

②意愿，自愿

will ²⁵⁹　　[wɪl] v. 将要　n. 愿意，意愿（熟词僻义，重点关注）

六级基础词汇

［派］willing [ˈwɪlɪŋ] a. 自愿的，乐意的

216

Day 28

willingness [ˈwɪlɪŋnəs] *n.* 自愿，乐意
unwilling [ʌnˈwɪlɪŋ] *a.* 不愿意的，不情愿的

volunteer [ˌvɒlənˈtɪə(r)] *n.* 义务工作者，志愿者

［记］vol+unt（改写自 ent=ant；表示人的后缀）+eer（表示人的后缀）→ "有意愿做某事的人" → *n.* 义务工作者，志愿者

voluntary [ˈvɒləntri] *a.* 自愿的，自发的

［记］vol+unt（改写自 ent=ant；表示人的后缀）+ary（*a.*）→ "此人是愿意的、自愿的、有意愿的" → *a.* 自愿的，自发的
［派］involuntary [ɪnˈvɒləntri] *a.* 非自愿的，不是故意的

非成组词（V 字母）

violate [ˈvaɪəleɪt] *v.* 违背；冒犯；侵犯；妨碍

［记］viol（简写自 violence；暴力）+ ate（*v.*）→ "暴力的动作" 就会违背法律，冒犯或妨碍他人→ *v.* 违背；冒犯；侵犯；妨碍
［派］violation [ˌvaɪəˈleɪʃn] *n.* 违背；侵犯；破坏

virtue [ˈvɜːtʃuː] *n.* 贞操，美德

［记］来自 virgin（处女）→ 在古代女性守身如玉被视为一种美德→ *n.* 贞操，美德

virtual [ˈvɜːtʃuəl] *a.* 实际上的，事实上的；虚拟的

［记］virtu（简写自 virtue；美德）+al（*a.*）→ 何为美德？做人的美德就是实事求是→ *a.* 实际上的，事实上的
［助］VR=virtual reality 虚拟现实→ *a.* 虚拟的
［派］virtually [ˈvɜːtʃuəli] *ad.* 实际上，事实上
［真］"I think we're a long way away from having **virtual** beings that have the ability to pre-sell content."【2021 年 6 月 长篇阅读 K 选项】
［译］"我认为，要制作出有能力支撑预售电影的虚拟人物，我们还有很长的路要走。"

devote [dɪˈvəʊt] *v.* 奉献，致力

［记］de（下）+vote → "把选票向下投入箱子"，从此就要为自己的选择→ *v.* 奉献，致力
［派］devotion [dɪˈvəʊʃn] *n.* 奉献，献身
［考］devote... to... 把……贡献于/用于……
be devoted to 致力于
［真］Marconi's career was **devoted** to making wireless communication happen cheaply, efficiently, smoothly, and with an elegance that would appear to be intuitive and uncomplicated to the user—user-friendly, if you will.【2021 年 6 月 长篇阅读 E

选项】

[译] 马可尼在其职业生涯中一直致力于使无线通信变得便宜、高效、流畅，且对用户而言具有直观和简明的优点——或者说做到对用户友好。

vulnerable [10] [ˈvʌlnərəbl] *a.* 脆弱的，易受攻击的

[助] 谐音"我特弱吧"→ *a.* 脆弱的，易受攻击的

[派] vulnerability [ˌvʌlnərəˈbɪləti] *n.* 弱点；致命性

[考] be vulnerable to... 易受……的伤害

[真] [D] It may render us **vulnerable** and inauthentic.【2020 年 12 月 仔细阅读 46 题 D 选项】

[译] 它可能使我们变得脆弱和不真实。

–ward– 向

forward [2] [ˈfɔːwəd] *a.&ad.* 向前（的）

[记] for（简写自 fore；前）+ward → *a.&ad.* 向前（的）

upward [2] [ˈʌpwəd] *a.&ad.* 向上（的）

[记] up（上）+ward → *a.&ad.* 向上（的）

非成组词（W 字母和 Z 字母）

weigh [31] [weɪ] *v.* 称重

[记] weight 的动词→ *v.* 称重

[派] weight [weɪt] *n.* 体重
　　overweight [ˌəʊvəˈweɪt] *a.&n.* 超重（的）

[考] lose weight 减肥

[真] The 240 giant autonomous trucks in use, in the Western Australian mines, can **weigh** 400 tons, fully loaded, and travel at speeds of up to sixty kilometers per hour.【2021 年 6 月 听力原文】

[译] 在西澳大利亚矿山使用的 240 辆巨型自动驾驶卡车，满载时可重达 400 吨，并以高达每小时 60 千米的速度行驶。

welfare [3] [ˈwelfeə(r)] *n.* 福利；幸福

[记] wel（简写自 well；好）+fare（无义）→ "进入了好的状态"→ *n.* 福利；幸福

[真] [B] improve the **welfare** of its maintenance workers.【2021 年 6 月 仔细阅读 53 题 B 选项】

[译] 提高其维修工人的福利水平。

Day 28

worsen[4]   ['wɜ:sn] v. 使恶化，使变得更坏

[记] worse（a. 更坏的，恶化的）+en（使动）→"使之变得更坏"→ v. 使恶化，使变得更坏

[真] [D] It may **worsen** the nourishment problem in low-income countries.【2020 年 12 月 仔细阅读 49 题 D 选项】

[译] 它可能会使低收入国家的营养问题恶化。

扫码快速学习

单词索引

abandon / 005
abandonment / 005
abnormal / 119
abolish / 001
abound / 013
abroad / 012
absence / 158
absent / 158
absolute / 167
absolutely / 167
absurd / 001
absurdity / 001
abundance / 013
abundant / 013
academic / 001
academically / 001
academics / 001
academy / 001
accelerate / 005
acceleration / 005
accept / 021
acceptable / 021
acceptance / 021
access / 010, 021
accessible / 021
accident / 024
accidental / 025
accommodate / 106
accommodation / 106

accompany / 005
accomplish / 134
accomplishment / 134
account / 034
accountability / 034
accountable / 034
accountant / 034
accounting / 034
accumulate / 029
accumulation / 029
accumulative / 029
accuracy / 038
accurate / 038
accurately / 038
accusation / 006
accuse / 005
accustomed / 006
acquaint / 006
acquaintance / 006
acquire / 150
acquisition / 150
activate / 002
active / 002
actively / 002
adapt / 123
adaptation / 123
addict / 046
addiction / 046
address / 006

adequate / 057
adequately / 057
adjust / 093
adjustment / 093
administration / 109
administrative / 109
admiration / 006
admire / 006
adolescence / 201
adolescent / 201
adopt / 123
adoption / 123
adult / 201
adulthood / 201
advance / 207
advanced / 207
advancement / 207
adversarial / 210
adverse / 210
adversely / 210
advocacy / 214
advocate / 214
affect / 062
affiliate / 069
affiliation / 069
affluence / 072
affluent / 072
afford / 006
affordable / 006

agency / 003
aggressive / 085
aggressively / 085
alien / 009
alienate / 009
alleviate / 099
alleviation / 099
allocate / 101
allocation / 101
alter / 003
alterable / 003
alternate / 003
alternation / 003
alternative / 003
ambition / 009
ambitious / 009
amid / 106
amount / 121
analyse/yze / 009
analysis / 009
analytic / 009
analytical / 009
animate / 010
animated / 010
animation / 010
anniversary / 003
announce / 007
announcement / 007
annoy / 007

annoyance / 007
annoying / 007
annual / 003
annually / 003
anticipate / 017
anticipation / 017
apart / 129
apartment / 129
apologize/ise / 102
apology / 102
apparent / 010
apparently / 010
appeal / 135
appliance / 137
applicant / 137
application / 137
apply / 137
appreciate / 143
appreciation / 143
appreciative / 143
approach / 007
appropriate / 007
appropriately / 007
approval / 147
approve / 147
approximate / 007
approximately / 007
architect / 192
architecture / 192
arrogance / 155
arrogant / 155
artificial / 064

artificially / 064
aspect / 169
assert / 160
assertion / 160
assess / 010, 021
assessment / 010
asset / 010
assign / 164
assignment / 164
assist / 176
assistance / 176
assistant / 176
associate / 165
association / 165
assume / 183
assumption / 183
astonish / 008
astonishing / 008
astonishment / 008
attach / 190
attachment / 191
attain / 192
attainment / 192
attempt / 055
attend / 193
attendance / 193
attract / 195
attraction / 195
attractive / 195
attractiveness / 195
attributable / 196
attribute / 196

audience / 004
audio / 004
authentic / 005
author / 004
authority / 004
authorize/ise / 005
autobiography / 014
automate / 115
automatic / 115
automatically / 115
automation / 115
autonomous / 010
autonomy / 010
availability / 205
available / 205
aversion / 210
avert / 210
avoid / 204
avoidable / 204
avoidance / 204
award / 010
barrier / 013
base / 011
basic / 011
basically / 011
basics / 011
basis / 011
battle / 011
beneath / 012
betray / 012
betrayal / 012
bias / 014

bill / 014
biodiversity / 211
biography / 014
bizarre / 014
blame / 014
blunt / 015
board / 012
boast / 013
boom / 015
boost / 013
border / 124
botanist / 015
botany / 015
boundary / 013
branch / 015
bright / 101
broad / 012
broadcast / 012
broaden / 012
broadly / 012
budget / 015
burden / 015
byproduct / 050
calculate / 040
calculation / 040
camp / 016
campaign / 016
campus / 016
candidate / 040
capacity / 017
capital / 016
capitalism / 016

captain / 017
capture / 017
carbon / 018
care / 018
career / 018
careful / 018
carefully / 018
careless / 018
cargo / 018
casualty / 024
catastrophe / 004
catastrophic / 004
categorization/isation / 041
categorize/ise / 041
category / 040
cater / 041
central / 022
chain / 041
challenge / 041
challenging / 041
character / 153
characteristic / 153
characterize/ise / 153
charge / 041
cherish / 019
chronic / 041
chronically / 041
circle / 025
circuit / 025
circulate / 025
circulation / 026

circumstance / 173
citation / 042
cite / 042
citizen / 042
citizenship / 042
civil / 026
civilization/isation / 026
civilize/ise / 026
clarify / 026
clarity / 026
clash / 042
class / 026
classic / 027
classical / 027
classification / 026
classify / 026
cognition / 083
cognitive / 083
cognitively / 083
cohere / 028
coherent / 028
cohesion / 028
coincidence / 025
coincidental / 025
collaborate / 095
collaboration / 095
collaborative / 095
collapse / 030
colleague / 030
collect / 096
collection / 096
collective / 096

colonial / 038
colony / 038
combination / 029
combine / 029
comment / 108
commentary / 108
commentator / 108
commerce / 109
commercial / 109
commission / 112
commit / 112
commitment / 112
committee / 112
commodity / 107
common / 032
commonly / 032
commonplace / 032
communicate / 032
communication / 032
community / 032
compact / 029
comparable / 128
comparative / 128
compare / 128
comparison / 128
compassion / 130
compassionate / 130
compel / 130
compensate / 132
compensation / 132
compensatory / 132
compete / 132

competence / 133
competent / 133
competition / 132
competitive / 132
competitiveness / 132
competitor / 132
complacency / 030
complacent / 030
complement / 134
complementary / 134
complete / 133
completely / 133
complex / 134
complexity / 134
compliance / 137
complicated / 135
complication / 135
comply / 137
component / 140
compose / 140
composition / 140
compromise / 113
compulsion / 130
compulsory / 130
concede / 021
concentrate / 023
concentration / 023
concept / 021
conception / 021
conceptual / 021
concern / 019
concerned / 019

223

concerning / 019	conservative / 161	contempt / 055	coordination / 124
conclude / 027	conserve / 161	contemptible / 055	coordinator / 124
conclusion / 027	consider / 162	contend / 194	core / 033
conclusive / 027	considerable / 162	content / 194	corporate / 042
concrete / 035	considerably / 162	contention / 194	corporation / 042
conduct / 049	considerate / 162	contentious / 194	correct / 153
conductive / 049	consideration / 162	context / 030	correction / 153
confer / 066	considering / 162	contract / 191, 195	correctly / 153
conference / 066	consist / 175	contraction / 195	count / 034
confidence / 068	consistent / 175	contractor / 195	counter / 034
confident / 068	consistently / 175	contradict / 046	counterpart / 033
confidential / 069	conspicuous / 171	contradiction / 046	cover / 034
confine / 070	conspicuously / 171	contrary / 033	coverage / 034
confirm / 071	constant / 174	contrast / 032	crash / 042
confirmation / 071	constantly / 174	contribute / 196	create / 035
conflict / 072	constitute / 178	contribution / 196	creation / 035
conflicting / 072	constitution / 178	contributor / 196	creative / 035
confront / 029	constrain / 180	controversial / 211	creativity / 035
confrontation / 029	constraint / 180	controversy / 211	creator / 035
confuse / 073	construct / 182	convenience / 208	credential / 036
confusing / 073	construction / 182	convenient / 208	credible / 036
confusion / 073	constructive / 182	conveniently / 208	credit / 036
congress / 085	consult / 183	convention / 207	crime / 036
connect / 030	consultant / 183	conventional / 207	criminal / 036
connection / 030	consultation / 183	converge / 211	critic / 037
connotation / 120	consume / 183	conversion / 210	critical / 037
conscience / 030	consumer / 184	convert / 210	critically / 037
conscious / 029	consumption / 184	convey / 212	criticism / 037
consciously / 030	contact / 191, 195	convince / 031	criticize/ise / 037
consciousness / 029	contaminate / 031	convincing / 031	crucial / 037
consensus / 159	contamination / 031	convincingly / 031	cultivate / 038
conservation / 161	contemporary / 030	coordinate / 124	cultivation / 038

cultural / 037
culturally / 037
culture / 037
cure / 040
currency / 039
current / 039
currently / 039
curriculum / 039
curse / 043
database / 011
debate / 011
debt / 051
decay / 043
deceive / 022
deception / 022
declaration / 026
declare / 026
decline / 027
decorate / 051
decoration / 051
decrease / 035
dedicate / 046
defend / 066
defense/ce / 066
deficiency / 065
deficient / 065
define / 070
definite / 070
definitely / 070
definition / 070
degradation / 084
degrade / 084

delay / 043
deliberate / 099
deliberately / 100
deliberation / 100
delicate / 046
delight / 100
delightful / 100
deliver / 043
delivery / 043
democracy / 044
democratic / 044
demonstrate / 044
demonstration / 044
department / 128
depend / 131
dependence / 131
dependent / 131
depict / 043
depiction / 043
deplete / 134
depletion / 134
deploy / 043
deployment / 043
deposit / 140
depress / 143
depression / 144
deprivation / 147
deprive / 147
derive / 155
descend / 043
descent / 043
desert / 160

deserted / 160
deserve / 161
design / 163
designate / 163
designer / 163
dessert / 160
destine / 051
destiny / 051
destruct / 182
destruction / 182
destructive / 182
detach / 191
detachment / 191
detail / 043
detailed / 044
deteriorate / 044
deterioration / 044
determination / 044
determine / 044
detriment / 044
detrimental / 044
devalue / 205
devise / 163
devote / 217
devotion / 217
differ / 066
digital / 051
digitalize/ise / 052
digitally / 052
dignity / 051
dilemma / 047
diminish / 111

direct / 153
direction / 153
directness / 153
director / 153
disapproval / 147
disapprove / 147
disaster / 004
disastrous / 004
disclose / 028
disclosure / 028
discount / 034
discourage / 047
discover / 034
discovery / 034
discriminate / 037
discrimination / 037
disguise / 047
dishonest / 088
dishonesty / 088
dismiss / 111
dismissal / 111
disobey / 127
disorder / 123
disposal / 141
dispose / 141
disputable / 148
dispute / 148
disrupt / 047
disruption / 047
distance / 174
distant / 174
distinct / 179

225

distinction / 179	dynamic / 051	elimination / 058	enquiry/inquiry / 151
distinctive / 179	dynamics / 051	elite / 057	enrol(l) / 056
distinguish / 179	dynasty / 051	embrace / 055	enrol(l)ment / 056
distinguishable / 179	eager / 060	emerge / 058	ensure / 185
distract / 195	economic / 053	emergence / 058	enterprise / 060
distraction / 195	economical / 053	emergency / 058	entertain / 192
distressed / 180	economically / 053	emerging / 058	entertaining / 192
distressful / 180	economics / 053	emission / 112	entertainment / 192
distribute / 196	economist / 053	emit / 112	entire / 195
distribution / 196	economy / 052	emitter / 112	entirely / 195
disturb / 197	effect / 062	emotion / 115	entity / 060
diverse / 211	effective / 062	emotional / 115	entrepreneur / 060
diversity / 211	effectively / 062	emphasis / 068	entrepreneurial / 060
divide / 048	effectiveness / 062	emphasize/ise / 068	envisage / 213
divided / 048	efficiency / 063	emulate / 111	equal / 056
dividend / 048	efficient / 063	enable / 055	equality / 057
division / 048	efficiently / 063	encounter / 033	equally / 057
divorce / 047	elaborate / 095	encourage / 055	equip / 057
domain / 048	elaboration / 095	encouragement / 055	equipment / 057
domestic / 048	electric / 054	encouraging / 055	essence / 060
dominance / 049	electrical / 054	endanger / 056	essential / 060
dominant / 049	electricity / 054	endangered / 056	essentially / 060
dominate / 049	electronic / 054	endow / 056	estate / 175
download / 104	electronically / 054	endurance / 050	esteem / 060
dramatic / 052	electronics / 054	endure / 050	esteemed / 061
dramatically / 052	elegance / 096	engage / 056	estimate / 058
drown / 052	elegant / 096	engagement / 056	estimation / 058
dual / 052	elevate / 098	enhance / 056	evacuate / 204
durable / 050	elevation / 098	enhancement / 056	evacuation / 204
dwell / 052	elevator / 098	enormous / 119	evade / 208
dweller / 052	elicit / 057	enormously / 119	evaluate / 205
dwelling / 052	eliminate / 058	enquire/inquire / 151	evaluation / 205

evasion / 208
eventually / 207
evidence / 212
evident / 212
evil / 061
evolution / 216
evolve / 216
exact / 002
exactly / 002
exaggerate / 058
exaggeration / 058
exceed / 020
excel / 020
excellence / 021
excellent / 020
except / 022, 169
exception / 022
exceptional / 022
exceptionally / 022
excess / 020
excessive / 020
excessively / 020
exchange / 058
exclude / 028
exclusion / 028
exclusive / 028
exclusively / 028
executive / 061
exempt / 055
exemption / 055
exert / 160
exhaust / 061

exhausted / 061
exhausting / 061
exist / 176
existence / 176
existent / 176
existing / 176
exotic / 059
expand / 059
expanding / 059
expansion / 059
expansive / 059
expect / 022, 169
expectancy / 169
expectation / 169
expedition / 059
expend / 131
expense / 131
expensive / 131
exploit / 059
exploitation / 059
exploration / 135
explore / 135
explosion / 059
expose / 141
exposure / 141
express / 143
expression / 143
extend / 194
extension / 194
extensive / 194
extent / 194
external / 197

extinct / 179
extinction / 179
extinguish / 179
facilitate / 064
facilitation / 064
facility / 064
fact / 062
factual / 062
fade / 077
faith / 068
faithful / 068
familiar / 077
familiarity / 077
fascinate / 077
fascinating / 077
fascination / 077
fatal / 077
fatality / 077
fatigue / 078
favo(u)r / 078
favo(u)rable / 078
favo(u)rite / 078
feature / 065
federal / 069
federation / 069
fee / 078
fellow / 078
fellowship / 078
fence / 065
fertile / 077
fertility / 078
fertilizer/iser / 078

fiction / 065
fierce / 078
fiercely / 078
figure / 079
finance / 071
financial / 071
financially / 071
finite / 070
firm / 071
firmly / 071
flavo(u)r / 078
flaw / 072
flawed / 072
flexibility / 071
flexible / 071
flight / 100
flourish / 079
flu / 072
fluctuate / 073
fluctuation / 073
fluid / 072
fond / 076
forecast / 073
foresee / 073
foreseeable / 073
form / 074
formal / 074
format / 074
formation / 074
formula / 074
formulate / 074
fortunate / 079

fortune / 079	genetically / 080	harsh / 088	illustration / 103
forward / 218	geneticist / 080	heal / 040	image / 089
fossil / 079	genetics / 080	heir / 087	imagination / 089
fossil-fuel / 072	genius / 081	highlight / 101	imaginative / 089
foster / 079	geographical / 082	hinder / 088	imagine / 089
found / 075	geography / 082	hindrance / 088	imitate / 111
foundation / 075	geological / 082	honest / 088	imitation / 111
foundational / 075	geologist / 082	honestly / 088	immediate / 106
founder / 075	geology / 082	honesty / 088	immediately / 106
fragile / 075	giant / 086	hono(u)r / 089	immortal / 117
fragility / 075	gift / 081	hono(u)rable / 089	immune / 063
fragment / 075	gifted / 081	horizon / 124	immunity / 063
frame / 079	gigantic / 086	huge / 089	impact / 090
framework / 079	glamo(u)r / 082	hugely / 089	implement / 134
frank / 080	glamo(u)rous / 082	human / 087	implementation / 134
frankness / 080	glimpse / 082	humanity / 087	implication / 137
frustrate / 080	global / 086	humid / 087	imply / 137
frustrating / 080	globalize/ise / 086	humidity / 087	import / 138
frustration / 080	grade / 084	humo(u)r / 087	impose / 141
fuel / 072	gradual / 084	humorous / 088	impress / 143
fulfil(l) / 069	gradually / 084	hypothesis / 089	impression / 143
fulfil(l)ment / 069	graduate / 084	hypothetical / 089	impressive / 143
fund / 076	graduation / 084	hypothetically / 089	improve / 147
fundamental / 076	grant / 036	identifiable / 045	improvement / 147
fundamentally / 076	grave / 086	identify / 045	inaccurate / 038
fundraising / 076	graveyard / 086	identity / 045	inadequate / 057
gender / 081	guarantee / 086	ideological / 102	inadequately / 057
gene / 080	habitat / 088	ideology / 102	inanimate / 010
generate / 080	handicap / 086	illegal / 096	inappropriate / 007
generation / 080	handle / 087	illusion / 103	inauthentic / 005
generational / 081	harmonious / 088	illusory / 103	inborn / 090
genetic / 080	harmony / 088	illustrate / 103	incentive / 090

incidence / 025
incident / 025
inclination / 027
incline / 027
include / 028
including / 028
inclusive / 028
income / 090
incompetent / 133
incorporate / 042
increase / 035
increasingly / 035
incredible / 036
incredibly / 036
independence / 131
independent / 131
independently / 131
indicate / 045
indication / 045
indicative / 045
indicator / 045
indigenous / 081
indirect / 153
indistinguishable / 179
individual / 048
individuality / 048
induce / 050
inducement / 050
ineffective / 062
inefficient / 063
inequality / 057
inevitable / 209

inevitably / 209
inexpensive / 131
infant / 090
infect / 063
infection / 063
infectious / 063
inferior / 066
infinite / 070
inflexible / 072
influence / 073
influential / 073
inform / 075
informal / 074
informally / 074
informed / 075
infrastructure / 181
ingenious / 081
ingenuity / 081
ingredient / 085
inherent / 087
inherently / 087
inherit / 087
inheritability / 087
initial / 091
initially / 091
initiate / 091
initiation / 091
initiative / 091
initiator / 091
injustice / 093
innovate / 120
innovation / 120

innovative / 120
innovator / 120
insect / 158
insecurity / 040
insight / 091
insightful / 091
insist / 176
insistence / 176
inspect / 169
inspection / 169
inspiration / 180
inspire / 180
instability / 173
instant / 174
instantly / 174
instinct / 178
instinctive / 178
institute / 178
instruct / 182
instruction / 182
instructive / 182
instructor / 182
instrument / 182
instrumental / 182
insufficient / 064
insulate / 166
insulation / 166
insurance / 185
insure / 185
insurer / 185
intake / 091
integral / 086

integrate / 085
integration / 085
integrity / 086
intellect / 096
intellectual / 096
intelligence / 096
intelligent / 096
intend / 193
intense / 194
intensify / 194
intensity / 194
intensive / 194
intention / 193
intentional / 193
interact / 002
interaction / 002
interactive / 002
interfere / 067
interference / 067
interior / 066, 091
intermediary / 106
intermediate / 106
internal / 197
internally / 197
international / 118
internationally / 118
interpret / 093
interpretation / 094
interpreter / 094
intervene / 208
intervention / 208
interview / 214

interviewee / 214	irrespective / 170	locality / 101	mental / 107
interviewer / 214	isolate / 166	locally / 101	mentality / 108
intimidate / 091	isolation / 166	locate / 102	mentally / 108
intimidatory / 091	issue / 094	location / 102	mention / 108
intricate / 197	journal / 094	logic / 102	mentioned / 108
intrigue / 196	justice / 093	logical / 102	merit / 109
intriguing / 196	justifiable / 093	loyal / 157	method / 117
introduce / 049	justification / 093	loyalty / 157	migrate / 117
introduction / 049	justify / 093	lucrative / 104	migration / 117
introductory / 049	labo(u)r / 094	maintain / 191	military / 117
intuition / 197	laboratory / 095	maintenance / 191	minimal / 110
intuitive / 198	laborious / 094	major / 110	minimize/ise / 110
intuitively / 198	launch / 103	majority / 110	minister / 109
invalid / 205	leak / 104	manipulate / 105	ministry / 109
invest / 091	leakage / 104	manipulation / 105	minor / 111
investigate / 092	legacy / 104	manipulative / 105	minority / 111
investigation / 092	legal / 096	manufacture / 105	miserable / 110
investigator / 092	legally / 096	manufacturer / 105	misery / 110
investment / 092	legislate / 097	mark / 105	misinterpret / 094
investor / 092	legislation / 097	massive / 116	mislead / 110
invisible / 213	legislative / 097	match / 116	misleading / 110
involuntary / 217	level / 098	mature / 116	misperception / 022
involve / 215	levy / 098	maximize/ise / 110	miss / 111
involvement / 216	liberate / 099	maximum / 110	missing / 111
ironic / 094	liberation / 099	measurable / 184	mission / 112
ironical / 094	liberty / 099	measure / 184	mobile / 114
ironically / 094	lift / 098	measurement / 184	mobility / 114
irony / 094	literary / 101	media / 106	mode / 106
irrational / 156	literature / 101	melody / 116	momentum / 115
irregular / 154	load / 104	melt / 116	monument / 107
irrelevant / 099	lobby / 102	memorable / 107	monumental / 107
irresistible / 177	local / 101	memory / 107	moral / 117

morality / 117
morally / 117
mortal / 117
mortality / 117
mortgage / 118
motion / 114
motivate / 114
motivation / 114
motivational / 114
multicultural / 038
multiple / 116
multiply / 116
mutual / 115
mutually / 115
narrate / 121
narration / 121
narrative / 121
nation / 118
national / 118
nationwide / 118
native / 118
natural / 118
naturally / 118
nature / 118
navigate / 121
navigation / 122
negative / 140
negatively / 140
neglect / 095
negligible / 095
newsworthy / 206
normal / 119

normally / 119
note / 119
noteworthy / 119
notice / 120
noticeable / 120
noticeably / 120
notion / 119
notorious / 120
notoriously / 120
nourish / 122
nourishment / 122
novel / 120
novelist / 120
novelty / 120
nuclear / 122
numerous / 121
nurture / 119
nutrient / 122
nutrition / 122
nutritional / 122
obese / 126
obesity / 126
obey / 126
object / 092
objection / 092
objective / 092
objectively / 092
obligation / 097
obligatory / 097
oblige / 097
obscure / 126
obscurity / 127

observation / 162
observe / 162
observer / 162
obsess / 163
obsession / 163
obstacle / 174
obtain / 192
obtainment / 192
obvious / 212
obviously / 212
occasion / 025
occasional / 025
occasionally / 025
occupation / 018
occupy / 018
occur / 038
occurrence / 038
offend / 066
offense/ce / 066
offensive / 066
opponent / 141
oppose / 141
opposite / 141
opposition / 141
oppress / 144
oppression / 144
oppressive / 144
opt / 122
optimal / 123
optimism / 123
optimistic / 123
option / 122

optional / 122
oral / 127
order / 123
orderly / 123
origin / 124
original / 124
originality / 124
originally / 124
originate / 124
outcome / 125
outdated / 125
outer / 125
outfit / 125
outline / 125
outperform / 074
outpouring / 150
overall / 125
overburden / 015
overcome / 125
overestimate / 058
overlook / 126
overprotective / 192
overseas / 126
overweight / 218
overwhelm / 126
overwhelming / 126
pace / 129
panic / 148
partial / 128
partially / 128
participant / 017
participate / 017

231

participation / 017	physical / 133	precede / 020	privacy / 147
particle / 128	physically / 133	precedent / 020	private / 146
particular / 129	physician / 133	precious / 143	proceed / 019
particularly / 129	plausible / 149	precise / 024	proceeding / 019
passion / 130	plausibly / 149	precisely / 024	process / 019
passionate / 130	pleasant / 135	precision / 024	produce / 050
passport / 139	pleasure / 136	predict / 045	producer / 050
patent / 148	pledge / 135	predictability / 045	product / 050
peculiar / 149	plight / 100	predictable / 045	production / 050
peculiarity / 149	policy / 138	predictably / 045	productive / 050
peer / 149	policymaker / 138	prediction / 045	productivity / 050
penalty / 149	political / 138	prefer / 067	profession / 068
perceive / 022	politically / 138	preferable / 067	professional / 068
perception / 022	politician / 138	preference / 067	progress / 085
perfect / 063	politics / 138	premature / 116	progressive / 085
perfection / 063	pollutant / 149	preoccupy / 018	prohibit / 144
perfectly / 064	pollute / 149	presence / 159	prohibition / 144
perform / 074	pollution / 149	present / 158	project / 093
performance / 074	pose / 139	presently / 159	promise / 113
performer / 074	position / 140	preservation / 161	promising / 113
permanence / 132	positive / 140	preserve / 161	promote / 114
permanent / 132	positively / 140	press / 143	promoter / 114
permanently / 132	possess / 142	previous / 144	promotion / 114
permeate / 132	possession / 142	previously / 144	prompt / 144
permeation / 132	post / 142	primarily / 146	promptly / 144
persist / 176	postage / 142	primary / 146	propel / 131
persistence / 176	postpone / 142	prime / 146	proportion / 129
persistent / 176	potential / 149	principal / 146	proposal / 142
perspective / 170	potentiality / 150	principle / 146	propose / 142
philosopher / 167	potentially / 149	prior / 145	proposition / 142
philosophical / 167	pour / 150	prioritize/ise / 145	prosecute / 144
philosophy / 167	poverty / 150	priority / 145	prosecution / 144

prosecutor / 144
prospect / 169
prospective / 169
prospector / 170
prosper / 145
prosperity / 145
prosperous / 145
protect / 192
protection / 192
protective / 192
prove / 147
psychiatrist / 103
psychiatry / 103
psychological / 103
psychologist / 103
psychology / 103
public / 147
publication / 147
publish / 148
publisher / 148
puzzle / 140
puzzlement / 140
quest / 150
race / 156
racial / 156
radical / 156
random / 049
randomize/ise / 049
rapid / 156
rapidly / 156
rational / 156
rationalise/ize / 156

react / 002
reaction / 002
realistic / 156
reality / 156
realization/sation / 156
realize/ise / 156
recede / 020
receive / 021
recession / 020
recognition / 083
recognizable/sable / 083
recognize/ise / 082
recommend / 108
recommendation / 108
record / 033
recover / 035
recovery / 035
recreate / 035
recreation / 035
recruit / 152
recruiter / 152
recruitment / 152
redefine / 070
refer / 067
reference / 067
refine / 070
refinement / 070
reflect / 071
reflection / 071
reflective / 071
regenerate / 080

region / 154
regional / 154
register / 154
registration / 154
regular / 154
regularly / 154
regulate / 154
regulation / 154
regulator / 154
regulatory / 154
rehearsal / 152
rehearse / 152
relax / 152
relaxation / 152
relay / 152
release / 157
relevance / 099
relevant / 098
relief / 099
relieve / 099
relocate / 102
reluctance / 152
reluctant / 152
remark / 105
remarkable / 105
remarkably / 105
remember / 107
remind / 108
reminder / 109
remote / 115
remotely / 115
removal / 116

remove / 116
renovate / 120
renovation / 120
replace / 152
replacement / 152
report / 139
reportedly / 139
reporter / 139
represent / 159
representation / 159
representative / 159
reproduce / 050
reproduction / 050
reproductive / 050
reputation / 148
require / 150
requirement / 150
resemblance / 164
resemble / 164
resent / 159
resentment / 160
reservation / 162
reserve / 162
reshape / 187
reside / 163
residence / 163
resident / 163
resist / 177
resistable / 177
resistance / 177
resolution / 167
resolve / 166

respect / 170	revival / 215	scrutiny / 187	simplify / 164
respectable / 170	revive / 215	sector / 158	simulate / 164
respected / 170	revolution / 216	secure / 040	simulation / 164
respectful / 170	revolutionary / 216	security / 040	simulator / 164
respective / 170	revolutionize/ise / 216	select / 095	site / 162
respond / 151	reward / 151	selection / 095	skeptic / 170
response / 151	rewarding / 151	selective / 095	skeptically / 170
responsive / 151	ridicule / 157	selectively / 095	skepticism / 170
restoration / 172	ridiculous / 157	self-confident / 068	slight / 100
restore / 172	rigorous / 154	self-esteem / 061	slightly / 100
restrain / 181	rigorously / 154	senior / 187	sociality / 165
restraint / 181	robot / 157	sense / 159	socialize/ise / 165
restrict / 181	robotic / 157	sensitive / 159	sole / 166
restriction / 181	route / 155	sensitivity / 159	solely / 166
result / 183	routine / 155	sentiment / 159	solitude / 166
resume / 184	routinely / 155	sentimental / 159	solution / 166
resurface / 065	royal / 157	separate / 129	solve / 166
retire / 194	royalty / 157	separation / 129	sophisticated / 167
retirement / 194	rural / 203	service / 161	spark / 188
retreat / 196	s(c)keptical / 170	setback / 187	special / 167
reunite / 202	sacrifice / 064	shabby / 187	specialist / 168
revalidate / 205	scale / 186	shape / 187	specialize/ise / 168
revalidation / 205	scarce / 019	share / 187	species / 168
reveal / 151	scare / 019	shatter / 187	specific / 168
revelation / 151	scary / 019	shed / 187	specifically / 168
revenue / 208	scene / 186	shelter / 188	spectacular / 171
reverse / 211	scenery / 186	shift / 188	spectrum / 171
review / 214	scenic / 186	shrewd / 188	spirit / 179
reviewer / 214	scheme / 186	shrewdly / 188	spiritual / 180
revise / 213	scholar / 186	sign / 163	spread / 188
revision / 213	scholarship / 186	signature / 163	stability / 173
revitalize/ise / 215	scrutinize/ise / 187	simplification / 164	stable / 173

stage / 175
stake / 173
stakeholder / 173
stand / 171
standard / 171
standardize/ise / 171
standing / 171
startle / 188
startling / 188
state / 171
statement / 171
statesman / 172
statistic / 174
statistical / 174
statistically / 174
statue / 172
status / 172
steadily / 173
steady / 173
stem / 188
stereotype / 189
stereotypical / 189
stick / 178
stimulate / 179
stimulation / 179
stimulus / 179
sting / 178
stock / 173
storage / 172
store / 172
straight / 180
straightforward / 180

strategic / 189
strategy / 189
strength / 181
strengthen / 181
stress / 180
stressed / 180
stressful / 180
stretch / 181
strike / 189
striking / 189
strive / 189
structural / 181
structure / 181
struggle / 189
subconscious / 030
subject / 092
subjective / 092
submission / 113
submit / 113
substance / 174
substantial / 175
substantially / 175
subtle / 190
subtlety / 190
suffer / 067
suffering / 067
sufficient / 064
suicide / 024
superficial / 065
superior / 066
superiority / 067
superstition / 175

supervise / 213
supervision / 213
supervisor / 213
supplement / 134
supplier / 138
supply / 137
support / 139
supporter / 139
supportive / 139
suppose / 141
supposedly / 141
surface / 065
surgeon / 124
surgery / 124
surgical / 124
surplus / 184
surround / 184
surrounding / 184
survey / 212
survival / 215
survive / 215
susceptibility / 022
susceptible / 022
suspect / 170
suspicion / 170
suspicious / 170
sustain / 191
sustainability / 191
sustainable / 191
sustainably / 191
switch / 190
symbol / 165

symbolic / 165
symbolize/ise / 165
sympathetic / 165
sympathy / 164
synonym / 165
synonymous / 165
tackle / 198
talent / 081
talented / 081
temper / 198
temperament / 198
tempt / 054
temptation / 054
tend / 193
tendency / 193
testify / 198
testimony / 198
thrive / 155
thriving / 155
tolerance / 198
tolerant / 198
tolerate / 198
tough / 199
toughness / 199
toxic / 199
track / 199
tragedy / 199
tragic / 199
trail / 199
transfer / 068
transferable / 068
transform / 075

transformation / 075
transit / 200
transition / 199
transport / 138
transportation / 138
trap / 200
treasure / 200
tremendous / 185
tremendously / 185
trend / 193
trigger / 195
trustworthy / 206
tuition / 197
typical / 200
typically / 200
ultimate / 201
ultimately / 201
unacceptable / 021
unattractive / 195
unburden / 015
uncommon / 032
uncompetitive / 132
uncomplicated / 135
uncompromising / 113
unconscious / 030
unconventional / 207
uncover / 035
underestimate / 058
undergraduate / 084
underground / 202
undernourished / 122
undisturbed / 197

unequal / 057
unequally / 057
unexpected / 169
unexpectedly / 169
unfamiliar / 077
unfortunate / 079
unfortunately / 079
uniform / 202
unintended / 193
unintentional / 193
union / 202
unique / 202
uniqueness / 202
unite / 201
unity / 202
universal / 211
universally / 211
unjustifiable / 093
unload / 104
unmentioned / 108
unnatural / 118
unpleasant / 136
unprecedented / 020
unpredictability / 045
unpredictable / 045
unrealistic / 156
unstable / 173
unviable / 215
unwilling / 217
upgrade / 085
upward / 218
urban / 202

urbanization/sation / 202
urbanize/ise / 202
urge / 203
urgency / 203
urgent / 203
utility / 203
utilization/sation / 203
utilize/ise / 203
utter / 203
utterly / 204
valid / 205
validate / 205
validation / 205
valley / 204
valuable / 205
value / 205
valueless / 205
vanish / 204
variable / 206
variation / 206
variety / 206
various / 206
vary / 206
vehicle / 216
ventilate / 209
ventilation / 209
venture / 207
version / 210
vessel / 204
viable / 215
video / 212

view / 214
viewpoint / 214
violate / 217
violation / 217
virtual / 217
virtually / 217
virtue / 217
virus / 063
visible / 213
vision / 213
visionary / 213
visual / 213
visualize/ise / 213
vital / 215
vitality / 215
vocal / 214
voluntary / 217
volunteer / 217
vulnerability / 218
vulnerable / 218
website / 162
weigh / 218
weight / 218
welfare / 218
widespread / 188
will / 216
willing / 216
willingness / 217
worsen / 219
worth / 205
worthwhile / 206
worthy / 206

听力专项突破

主讲：邹寅老师

一、六级听力必备语音知识

1. 连读

规则：结尾辅音 + 开头元音

　　如果相邻两词的前一个词以辅音结尾，后一个词以元音开头，通常要将辅音与元音连起来读。

练习

an apple	/ə-næpl/	take off
pick up	find out	turn around
check in / out	fill in / out	look in / out
not at all	/nɒ-tæ-tɒl/	think about it
tired of it	cut it out	rest of it
check it out	get it over	get over it

整体练习：

例1 W: It's really cold in this apartment. Can we _____ the heat a little bit?

　　　M: Sorry, I've _____ money and can hardly pay the fuel bill. Maybe you'd better put on a sweater.

例2 M: I think you ought to see a doctor _____ about that cough.

　　　W: Well, I'll wait a few more days, I'm sure I'll _____ soon.

例3 If we ask Americans why they eat with knives and forks, or why their men wear pants _____ skirts, or why they may be married to only one person at a time.

例4　　1. A fight scene has to look real. Punches must _____ enemies' jaws.

　　　　2. If a movie scene is dangerous, stunt people usually _____ the stars.

目 录

听力专项突破 1

 一、六级听力必备语音知识 2

 二、六级听力概况 + 读选项技巧 + 长对话题型解题技巧 4

 三、长对话重点场景讲解 11

 四、长对话次重点场景讲解 21

 五、篇章听力题型概述 + 解题技巧 + 重点话题 28

 六、篇章听力重点话题讲解 34

 七、Section C 题型概述 + 解题技巧 + 重点话题 39

 八、Section C 听力重点提示词技巧 47

 九、讲座类题型强化练习 54

阅读专项突破 61

 一、大学英语六级考试题型 62

 二、2021 年大学英语六级考试阅读真题 62

翻译专项突破 107

 一、题型概况 108

 二、定语翻译 109

三、状语 + 插入语翻译 111

四、多动句 112

五、无主句 + there be 句型 113

六、真题带练 114

写作专项突破 121

一、如何快速获得写作高分 122

二、雅词 123

三、佳句 124

四、点睛 125

五、谋篇 126

六、历年真题 127

3. Canutt also _____ a new way to make a punch look real. He was the only stunt man ever to get an Oscar.

连音条件：

例5 I'm no doctor, but it's not _____.

例6 He's also told me _____ he wished to study for some profession _____ going into business.

2. 失去爆破

规则：爆破音 + 非元音

如果前一个单词以爆破音结尾，后一个单词不是以元音开头，通常需要对爆破音进行轻读或略读。

✏ **六大爆破音：** /p/ /b/ /t/ /d/ /k/ /g/

例1

15. A) He understands the woman's feelings.
    B) He has gone through a similar experience.
    C) The woman should have gone on the field trip.
    D) The teacher is just following the regulations.   答案：(   )

The Listening Scripts:

W: I was so angry yesterday! My biology teacher did not even let me explain why I missed the field trip. He just wouldn't let me pass!

M: That doesn't seem fair. I'd feel that way too if I were you.

15. What does the man imply?

例2

W: Well, I guess I'd sell my watch or computer or do some _____ till I _____ return plane ticket.

3. 轻音浊化

浊化规则： 当清辅音 /s/ 后面跟 /p/、/k/、/t/、/tr/ 时，通常需要将其依次浊化成 /b/、/g/、/d/、/dr/。

- 3 -

规则：/s/ + /p/=/b/　　　spy
　　　/s/ + /k/=/g/　　　scope
　　　/s/ + /t/ =/d/　　　store
　　　/s/ + /tr/=/dr/　　　street

练习

strike	extend	station	space	straight
Australia	experience	studio	discover	expensive
ski	skate	spring	spirit	discuss

整体练习：

例1

M: Excuse me. Where's your rock music section?

W: Rock music? I'm sorry. We're a jazz store. We don't have any rock and roll.

例2

M: Do you mind taking my photo with the statue over there? I think it will make a great shot.

M: I am, completely. I just got the idea a few months ago after posting some holiday photos on my social media accounts. A lot of people liked my photos and started asking me for travel tips. So I figured I'd give it a go. I post a lot on social media anyway. So I've got nothing to lose.

例3

W: What you need to do is research, have a process, invest time exploring your options, and eliminate as many things as you can. The most toxic part of decision making is going over the same options, time and time again.

二、六级听力概况 + 读选项技巧 + 长对话题型解题技巧

1. 六级听力概况

题型：长对话 + 篇章听力 + 讲座 / 讲话 / 报道

时间：30 分钟

语速：140～160 词 / 分钟

答题时间：13 秒 / 题

词汇难点：Unorthodox/Upbringing/Eminent scholars/Satire/Unprecedented 等

2. 读选项技巧

扫读主干

求同

存异

3. 长对话题型解题技巧

大纲针对长对话题型的要求：要求考生能听懂就熟悉话题展开的多话轮英语会话。

长对话：2 篇，每篇 280～320 词，每篇 4 题，共 8 题。

长对话题型解题技巧可总结为以下几点：

| 题文同序 | 同义替换 | 视听一致 |
| 问句出题 | 首三尾三 | 重复出题 |

长对话场景之工作场景：

例 1

19. A) An accountant of a computer firm.
    B) A director of a sales department.
    C) A sales clerk at a shopping center.
    D) A manager at a computer store.   答案：（   ）

20. A) Handling customer complaints.
    B) Recruiting and training new staff.
    C) Developing computer programs.
    D) Dispatching ordered goods on time.   答案：（   ）

21. A) She likes something more challenging.
    B) She likes to be nearer to her parents.
    C) She wants to be with her husband.
    D) She wants to have a better-paid job.   答案：（   ）

— 5 —

22. A) In a couple of days.
    B) Right away.
    C) In two months.
    D) Early next month.   答案:(   )

工作场景——重点场景词:

例2

5. A) Give a presentation.
   B) Raise some questions.
   C) Start a new company.
   D) Attend a board meeting.   答案:(   )

6. A) It will cut production costs.
   B) It will raise productivity.
   C) No staff will be dismissed.
   D) No new staff will be hired.   答案:(   )

7. A) The timeline of restructuring.
   B) The reasons for restructuring.
   C) The communication channels.
   D) The company's new missions.   答案:(   )

8. A) By consulting their own department managers.
   B) By emailing questions to the man or the woman.
   C) By exploring various channels of communication.
   D) By visiting the company's own computer network. 答案:(   )

练习1

1. A) Project organizer.

B) Public relations officer.

C) Marketing manager.

D) Market research consultant.   答案：(   )

2. A) Quantitative advertising research.

   B) Questionnaire design.

   C) Research methodology.

   D) Interviewer training.   答案：(   )

3. A) They are intensive studies of people's spending habits.

   B) They examine relations between producers and customers.

   C) They look for new and effective ways to promote products.

   D) They study trends or customer satisfaction over a long period.   答案：(   )

4. A) The lack of promotion opportunity.

   B) Checking charts and tables.

   C) Designing questionnaires.

   D) The persistent intensity.   答案：(   )

练习 2

23. A) Transferring to another department.

    B) Studying accounting at a university.

    C) Thinking about doing a different job.

    D) Making preparations for her wedding.   答案：(   )

24. A) She has finally got a promotion and a pay raise.

    B) She has got a satisfactory job in another company.

    C) She could at last leave the accounting department.

    D) She managed to keep her position in the company. 答案：(   )

25. A) He and Andrea have proved to be a perfect match.

    B) He changed his mind about marriage unexpectedly.

    C) He declared that he would remain single all his life.

D) He would marry Andrea even without meeting her.   答案：(   )

The Listening Scripts

例1

M: I see on your resume that you worked as a manager of store called "Computer Country". Could you tell me a little more about your responsibilities there?

W: Sure. I was responsible for overseeing about 30 employees. I did all of the orderings for the store and I kept track of the inventory.

M: What was the most difficult part of your job?

W: Probably handling angry customers. We didn't have them very often, but when we did, I needed to make sure they were well taken good care of. After all, the customer is always right.

M: That's how we feel here, too. How long did you work there?

W: I was there for three and a half years. I left the company last month.

M: And why did you leave?

W: My husband has been transferred to Boston. And I understand your company has an opening there, too.

M: Yes, that's right. We do. But the position won't start until early next month. Would that be a problem for you?

W: No, not at all. My husband's new job doesn't begin for a few weeks, so we thought we would spend some time driving to Boston and stop to see my parents.

M: That sounds nice. So, tell me, why are you interested in this particular position?

W: I know that your company has a great reputation, and a wonderful product. I've thought many times that I would like to be a part of it. When I heard about the opening in Boston, I jumped to the opportunity.

M: Well, I'm glad you did.

19. What was the woman's previous job?
20. What does the woman say with the most difficult part of her job?
21. Why is the woman looking for a job in Boston?
22. When can the woman start to work if she gets the job?

例2

W: So how's our presentation about the restructuring of the company coming along?

M: Fine. I'm putting the finishing touches to it now, but we'll have to be prepared for questions.

W: Yes, there is already a feeling that this is a top-down change. We really need to get everyone on board.

M: Well, there's been an extensive consultation period.

W: I know, but there's always the feeling that if it isn't broke, don't fix it.

M: People are worried about their jobs, too. I think we need to stress that while there will be some job changes, there won't be anyone getting dismissed. In fact, we're looking to take on more staff,

W: Agreed. You can hardly blame people for worrying though. We need to make it clear that it's not just change for change's sake. In other words, we really must make the case for why we're doing it. So what's the outline of the presentation?

M: I'll start with a brief review of the reasons for the change that we really need to make a clean break to restart growth. After that, I'll outline the new company structures and who's going where. Then I'll hand it over to you to discuss the timeline and summarize. And we'll take questions together at the end. Anything else?

W: Oh, yeah. We should let the staff know the channels of communication, you know, who they can contact or direct questions to about these changes.

M: Yes. And we can collect some frequently asked questions and present some general answers.

W: Mm, and we'll make the presentation and the questions available via the company's own computer network, right?

M: Yes. We'll make a page on the network where staff can download all the details.

W: All right. Perhaps we should do a practice run of the presentation first.

M: You bet.

5. What is the man going to do?

6. What does the man say about the restructuring?

7. What will the man explain first?

8. How can the staff learn more about the company's restructuring?

练习1

M: So, how long have you been a market research consultant?

W: Well, I started straight after finishing university.

M: Did you study market research?

W: Yeah, and it really helped me to get into the industry, but I have to say that it's more important to get experience in different types of market research to find out exactly what you're interested in.

M: So what are you interested in?

W: Well, at the moment, I specialize in quantitative advertising research, which means that I do two types of projects. Trackers, which are ongoing projects that look at trends or customer satisfaction over a long period of time. The only problem with trackers is that it takes up a lot of your time. But you do build up a good relationship with the client. I also do a couple of ad hoc jobs which are much shorter projects.

M: What exactly do you mean by ad hoc jobs?

W: It's basically when companies need quick answers to their questions about their consumers' habits. They just ask for one questionnaire to be sent out, for example, so the time you spend on an ad hoc project tends to be fairly short.

M: Which do you prefer, trackers or ad hoc?

W: I like doing both and in fact I need to do both at the same time to keep me from going crazy. I need the variety.

M: Can you just explain what process you go through with a new client?

W: Well, together we decide on the methodology and the objectives of the research. I then design a questionnaire. Once the interviewers have been briefed, I send the client a schedule and then they get back to me with deadlines. Once the final charts and tables are ready, I have to check them and organize a presentation.

M: Hmm, one last question, what do you like and dislike about your job?

W: As I said, variety is important, and as for what I don't like, it has to be the checking of charts and tables.

1. What position does the woman hold in the company?
2. What does the woman specialize in at the moment?
3. What does the woman say about trackers?
4. What does the woman dislike about her job?

练习 2

W: Hi, Kevin!

M: Hi, Laura. long time no see! What have you been up to lately?

W: Not much. I can assure you. And you?

M: Much the same, except I do have some big news.

W: Come on. This suspense is killing me.

M: No, really, what have you been doing these past few weeks? The last time I saw you, you were looking for a new job.

W: Well, that's not exactly true. I was thinking about changing jobs. Luckily, they offered me a new position in the accounting department.

M: A step up in the big business world.

W: I wouldn't exaggerate, but I am pleased. I had been hoping to get a promotion for a while. So when it finally came through, I was relieved. Actually, that's why I was looking for a new job. I just didn't want to work there anymore if they weren't going to recognize my efforts.

M: Right, sometimes you can do your best and it seems like the others don't know you exist. I hope the money's better.

W: I got a reasonable raise, now enough about me. I'm dying to hear your news.

M: I am getting married.

W: No, you said you'd never get married.

M: That was then and this is now. You've got to meet Andrea, she's great!

W: This is all news to me. I didn't even know you were dating.

M: We weren't. We've just been dating for two weeks now.

W: And you getting married?

M: I know. I can't help it. I just know she's the one.

W: Well, congratulations! That's fantastic!

M: Thanks, I'm glad to hear you feel that way.

23. What was the woman doing when the man last saw her?
24. Why does the woman say she was relieved?
25. Why is the woman surprised at the man's news?

三、长对话重点场景讲解

1. 长对话场景之校园场景

例1

5. A) They have to spend more time studying.
   B) They have to participate in club activities.

C) They have to be more responsible for what they do.

D) They have to choose a specific academic discipline.　　　答案:(　　)

6. A) Get ready for a career.

   B) Make a lot of friends.

   C) Set a long-term goal.

   D) Behave like adults.　　　答案:(　　)

7. A) Those who share her academic interests.

   B) Those who respect her student commitments.

   C) Those who can help her when she is in need.

   D) Those who go to the same clubs as she does.　　　答案:(　　)

8. A) Those helpful for tapping their potential.

   B) Those conducive to improving their social skills.

   C) Those helpful for cultivating individual interests.

   D) Those conducive to their academic studies.　　　答案:(　　)

校园场景——重点场景词:

例2

5. A) His view on Canadian universities.

   B) His understanding of higher education.

   C) His suggestions for improvements in higher education.

   D) His complaint about bureaucracy in American universities.　　　答案:(　　)

6. A) It is well designed.
   B) It is rather inflexible.
   C) It varies among universities.
   D) It has undergone great changes.   答案:(   )

7. A) The United States and Canada can learn from each other.
   B) Public universities are often superior to private universities.
   C) Everyone should be given equal access to higher education.
   D) Private schools work more efficiently than public institutions.   答案:(   )

8. A) University systems vary from country to country.
   B) Efficiency is essential to university management.
   C) It is hard to say which is better, a public university or a private one.
   D) Many private universities in the U.S. are actually large bureaucracies.   答案:(   )

2. 长对话场景之演播室场景

例3

19. A) In a studio.
    B) In a clothing store.
    C) At a beach resort
    D) At a fashion show.   答案:(   )

20. A) To live there permanently.
    B) To stay there for half a year.
    C) To find a better job to support herself.
    D) To sell leather goods for a British company.   答案:(   )

21. A) Designing fashion items for several companies.
    B) Modeling for a world-famous Italian company.
    C) Working as an employee for Ferragamo.
    D) Serving as a sales agent for Burberrys.   答案:(   )

22. A) It has seen a steady decline in its profits.

B) It has become much more competitive.

C) It has lost many customers to foreign companies.

D) It has attracted lot more designers from abroad.   答案:(   )

演播室场景——重点场景词:

例4

5. A) A journal reporting the latest progress in physics.

   B) An introductory course of modern physics.

   C) An occasion for physicists to exchange ideas.

   D) A series of interviews with outstanding physicists.   答案:(   )

6. A) The future of the physical world.

   B) the origin of the universe.

   C) Sources of radiation.

   D) Particle theory.   答案:(   )

7. A) How matter collides with anti-matter.

   B) Whether the universe will turn barren.

   C) Why there exists anti-matter.

   D) Why there is a universe at all.   答案:(   )

8. A) Matter and anti-matter are opposites of each other.

   B) Anti-matter allowed humans to come into existence.

   C) The universe formed due to a sufficient amount of matter.

D) Anti-matter exists in very high-temperature environments.　　　　答案:(　　)

练习1

5. A) He is too busy to finish his assignment in time.
   B) He does not know what kind of topic to write on.
   C) He does not understand the professor's instructions.
   D) He has no idea how to proceed with his dissertation.　　　　答案:(　　)

6. A) It is too broad.
   B) It is a bit outdated.
   C) It is challenging.
   D) It is interesting.　　　　答案:(　　)

7. A) Biography.
   B) Nature.
   C) Philosophy.
   D) Beauty.　　　　答案:(　　)

8. A) Improve his cumulative grade.
   B) Develop his reading ability.
   C) Stick to the topic assigned.
   D) List the parameters first.　　　　答案:(　　)

练习2

19. A) Current trends in economic development.
    B) Domestic issues of general social concern.
    C) Stories about Britain's relations with other nations.
    D) Conflicts and compromises among political parties.　　　　答案:(　　)

20. A) Based on the poll of public opinions.
    B) By interviewing people who file complaints.
    C) By analyzing the domestic and international situation.
    D) Based on public expectations and editors' judgment.　　　　答案:(　　)

21. A) Underlying rules of editing.
    B) Practical experience.
    C) Audience's feedback.
    D) Professional qualifications.   答案:(   )

The Listening Scripts

例 1

M: You are heading for a completely different world now that you are about to graduate from high school.

W: I know it's the end of high school, but many of my classmates are going on to the same university and we are still required to study hard. So what's the difference?

M: Many aspects are different here at university. The most important one is that you have to take more individual responsibility for your actions. It's up to your own self-discipline how much effort you put into study. Living in college dormitories, there are no parents to tell you to study harder or stop wasting time. Lecturers have hundreds of students, and they are not going to follow you up or question you if you miss their lectures.

W: Nobody cares, you mean?

M: It's not that nobody is concerned about you. It's just that suddenly at university you are expected to behave like an adult. That means concentrating on the direction of your life in general and your own academic performance specifically.

W: For example?

M: Well, like you need to manage your daily, weekly and monthly schedules so that you will study regularly. Be sure to attend all classes and leave enough time to finish assignments and prepare well for examinations.

W: Okay, and what else is different?

M: Well, in college, there are lots of distractions and you need to control yourself. You will make interesting friends, but you need only keep the friends who respect your student commitments. Also, there are a lot of wonderful clubs, but you shouldn't allocate too much time to club activities, unless they are directly related to your study. It's also your choice if you want to go out at night, but you will be foolish to let that affect your class performance during the day.

W: Well, I'm determined to do well at university and I guess I am going to have to grow up fast.

5. What does the man say about college students as compared with high schoolers?
6. What are college students expected to do according to the man?
7. What kind of friends does the man suggest the woman make as a college student?
8. What kind of club activities should college students engage in according to the man?

例2

W: Hello, I'm here with Frederick. Now Fred, you went to university in Canada?

M: Yeah, that's right.

W: OK, and you have very strong views about universities in Canada. Could you please explain?

M: Well, we don't have private universities in Canada. They're all public. All the universities are owned by the government, so there is the Ministry of Education in charge of creating the curriculum for the universities and so there is not much room for flexibility. Since it's a government operated institution, things don't move very fast. If you want something to be done, then their staff do not have so much incentive to help you because he's a worker for the government. So I don't think it's very efficient. However, there are certain advantages of public universities, such as the fees being free. You don't have to pay for your education. But the system isn't efficient, and it does not work that well.

W: Yeah, I can see your point, but in the United States we have many private universities, and I think they are large bureaucracies also. Maybe people don't act that much differently, because it's the same thing working for a private university. They get paid for their job. I don't know if they're that much more motivated to help people. Also, we have a problem in the United States that usually only wealthy kids go to the best schools and it's kind of a problem actually.

M: I agree with you. I think it's a problem because you're not giving equal access to education to everybody. It's not easy, but having only public universities also might not be the best solution. Perhaps we can learn from Japan where they have a system of private and public universities. Now, in Japan, public universities are considered to be the best.

W: Right. It's the exact opposite in the United States.

M: So, as you see, it's very hard to say which one is better.

W: Right, a good point.

5. What does the woman want Frederick to talk about?
6. What does the man say about the curriculum in Canadian universities?

7. On what point do the speakers agree?

8. What point does the man make at the end of the conversation?

例 3

M: Hello and welcome to our program "Working Abroad". Our guest this evening is a Londoner who lives and works in Italy. Her name is Susan Hill. Susan, welcome to the program. You live in Florence. How long have you been living there?

W: Since 1982, but when I went there in 1982, I planned to stay for only 6 months.

M: Why did you change your mind?

W: Well, I'm a designer. I design leather goods, mainly shoes and handbags. Soon after I arrived in Florence, I got a job with one of Italy's top fashion houses, Ferragamo. So I decided to stay.

M: How lucky! Do you still work for Ferragamo?

W: No, I've been a freelance designer for quite a long time now. Since 1988, in fact.

M: So, does that mean you design for several different companies now?

W: Yes, that's right. I've designed many fashion items for a number of Italian companies. And in the last 4 years, I've also been designing for the British company, Burberrys.

M: What have you been designing for them?

W: Mostly handbags and small leather goods.

M: How has fashion industry in Italy changed since 1982?

W: Oh, yes, it has become a lot more competitive, because the quality of products from other countries has improved a lot, but Italian quality and design is still world famous.

M: And do you ever think of returning to live in England?

W: No, not really. Working in Italy is more interesting, I also love the Mediterranean sun and the Italian life style.

M: Well, thank you for talking to us, Susan.

W: It was a pleasure.

19. Where does this talk most probably take place?

20. What was the woman's original plan when she went to Florence?

21. What has the woman been doing for a living since 1988?

22. What do we learn about the change in Italy's fashion industry?

例4

M: Good evening and welcome to Physics Today. Here we interview some of the greatest minds in physics as they help us to understand some of the most complicated theories. Today, I'm very pleased to welcome Dr. Melissa Phillips, professor of theoretical physics. She's here to tell us a little about what it is she studies. Dr. Phillips, you seem to study everything

W: I guess that would be fair to say I spent most of my time studying the Big Bang theory and where our universe came from.

M: Can you tell us a little about that?

W: Well, I'm very interested in why the universe exists at all. That may sound odd, but the fact is at the moment of the Big Bang, both matter and anti-matter were created for a short time, and I mean just a fraction of a second. The whole universe was a super-hot soup of radiation filled with these particles. So what's baffled scientists for so long is "why is there a universe at all"?

M: That's because matter and anti-matter are basically opposites of each other. They are exactly alike except that they have opposite electrical charges. So when they collide, they destroy each other?

W: Exactly. So during the first few moments of the Big Bang, the universe was extremely hot and very small Matter and the now more exotic anti-matter would have had little space to avoid each other. This means that they should have totally wiped each other out, leaving the universe completely barren.

M: But a recent study seems to point to the fact that when matter and anti-matter were first created, there were slightly more particles of matter, which allowed the universe we all live in to form?

W: Exactly. Because there was slightly more matter, the collisions quickly depleted all the anti-matter and left just enough matter to create stars, planets and eventually us.

5. What does the man say is Physics Today?
6. What is the woman physicist's main research area?
7. What is the woman interested in?
8. What seems to be the finding of the recent study?

练习1

M: Hi, professor. I was hoping I could have a moment of your time if you're not too busy. I'm having some problems getting started on my dissertation, and I was hoping you could give me some advice on how to begin.

W: Sure. I have quite a few students, though. So can you remind me what your topic is?

M: The general topic I chose is aesthetics, but that's as far as I've got. I don't really know where to go from there.

W: Yeah. That's much too large a topic. You really need to narrow it down in order to make it more accessible. Otherwise, you'll be writing a book.

M: Exactly. That's what I wanted to ask you about. I was hoping it would be possible for me to change topics. I'm really more interested in nature than beauty.

W: I'm afraid you have to adhere to the assigned topic. Still, if you're interested in nature, then that certainly can be worked into your dissertation. We've talked about Hume before in class, right?

M: Oh, yeah. He's the philosopher who wrote about where our ideas of beauty come from.

W: Exactly. I suggest you go to the library and get a copy of his biography. Start from there, but remember to stick to the parameters of the assignment. This paper is a large part of your cumulative grade, so make sure to follow the instructions. If you take a look at his biography, you can get a good idea of how his life experiences manifest themselves in his theories of beauty, specifically the way he looked towards nature as the origin of what we find beautiful.

M: Great. Thanks for taking the time to answer my questions, professor. I'll let you get back to class now.

W: If there's anything else you need, please come see me in my office anytime.

5. What is the man's problem?
6. What does the professor think of the man's topic?
7. What is the man really more interested in?
8. What does the professor say the man has to do?

练习2

W: You're the editor of *Public Eye*. What kind of topics does your program cover?

M: Well, there are essentially domestic stories. We don't cover international stories. We don't cover party politics or economics. We do issues of general social concern to our British audience. They can be anything from the future of the health service to the way the environment is going downhill.

W: How do you choose the topic? Do you choose one because it's what the public wants to know about or because it's what you feel the public ought to know about?

M: I think it's a mixture of both. Sometimes you have a strong feeling that something is important and you want to see it examined and you want to contribute to a public debate. Sometimes people come to you with things they are worried about and they can be quite small things. They can be a story about corruption in local government, something they cannot quite understand, why it doesn't seem to be working out properly, like they are not having their litter collected properly or the dustbins emptied.

W: How do you know that you've got a really successful program? One that is just right for the time?

M: I think you get a sense about it after working in it in a number of years. You know which stories are going to get the attention. They are going to be published just the point when the public are concerned about that.

19. What kind of topics does Public Eye cover?
20. How does Public Eye choose its topics?
21. What factor plays an important role in running a successful program?

四、长对话次重点场景讲解

1. 长对话场景之餐饮场景

例1

1. A) They were proud of their cuisine.
   B) They were particular about food.
   C) They were all good at cooking.
   D) They were fond of bacon and eggs.

   答案：(   )

2. A) His parents.
   B) His parents' friends.
   C) His friends.
   D) His schoolmates.

   答案：(   )

3. A) No one of the group ate it.
   B) It was a little overcooked.
   C) No tea was served with the meal.
   D) It was the real English breakfast.   答案：(   )

4. A) It was full of excitement.
   B) It was rather disappointing.
   C) It was a risky experience.
   D) It was really extraordinary.   答案：(   )

餐饮场景——重点场景词：

2. 长对话场景之交通场景

例 2

19. A) To go sightseeing.
    B) To have meetings.
    C) To promote a new champagne.
    D) To join in a training program.   答案：(   )

20. A) It can reduce the number of passenger complaints.
    B) It can make air travel more entertaining.
    C) It can cut down the expenses for air travel.
    D) It can lessen the discomfort caused by air travel.   答案：(   )

21. A) Took balanced meals with champagne.
    B) Ate vegetables and fruit only.
    C) Refrained from fish or meat.
    D) Avoided eating rich food.   答案：(   )

22. A) Many of them found it difficult to exercise on a plane.

B) Many of them were concerned with their well-being.

C) Not many of them chose to do what she did.

D) Not many of them understood the program.   答案：(   )

交通场景——重点场景词：

练习1

1. A) It is a typical salad.

   B) It is a Spanish soup.

   C) It is a weird vegetable.

   D) It is a kind of spicy food.   答案：(   )

2. A) To make it thicker.

   B) To make it more nutritious.

   C) To add to its appeal.

   D) To replace an ingredient.   答案：(   )

3. A) It contains very little fat.

   B) It uses olive oil in cooking.

   C) It uses no artificial additives.

   D) It is mainly made of vegetables.   答案：(   )

4. A) It does not go stale for two years.

   B) It takes no special skill to prepare.

   C) It comes from a special kind of pig.

   D) It is a delicacy blended with bread.   答案：(   )

练习2

1. A) A driving test.

   B) A video game.

   C) Traffic routes.

D) Cargo logistics.   答案：(   )

2. A) He found it instructive and realistic.
   B) He bought it when touring Europe.
   C) He was really drawn to its other versions.
   D) He introduced it to his brother last year.   答案：(   )

3. A) Traveling all over the country.
   B) Driving from one city to another.
   C) The details in the driving simulator.
   D) The key role of the logistics industry.   答案：(   )

4. A) Clearer road signs.
   B) More people driving safely.
   C) Stricter traffic rules.
   D) More self-driving trucks on the road.   答案：(   )

The Listening Scripts

例 1

M: Guess what? The worst food I've ever had was in France.

W: Really? That's odd. I thought the French were all good cooks.

M: Yes, that's right. I suppose it's really like anywhere else, though. You know, some places are good. Some bad. But it's really all our own fault.

W: What do you mean?

M: Well, it was the first time I'd been to France. This was years ago when I was at school. I went there with my parents' friends, from my father's school. They'd hired a coach to take them to Switzerland.

W: A school trip?

M: Right. Most of them had never been abroad before. We'd crossed the English Channel at night, and we set off through France, and breakfast time arrived, and the coach driver had arranged for us to stop at this little café. There we all were, tired and hungry, and then we made the great discovery.

W: What was that?

M: Bacon and eggs.

W: Fantastic! The real English breakfast.

M: Yes, anyway, we didn't know any better—so we had it, and ugh...!

W: What was it like? Disgusting?

M: Oh, it was incredible! They just got a bowl and put some fat in it. And then they put some bacon in the fat, broke an egg over the top and put the whole lot in the oven for about ten minutes.

W: In the oven! You're joking. You can't cook bacon and eggs in the oven!

M: Well, they must have done it that way. It was hot, but it wasn't cooked. There was just this egg floating about in gallons of fat and raw bacon.

W: Did you actually eat it?

M: No, nobody did. They all wanted to turn round and go home. You know, back to teabags and fish and chips. You can't blame them really. Anyway, the next night we were all given another foreign specialty.

W: What was that?

M: Snails. That really finished them off. Lovely holiday that was!

1. What did the woman think of the French?
2. Who did the man travel with on his first trip to Switzerland?
3. What does the man say about the breakfast at the little French café?
4. What did the man think of his holiday in France?

例2

M: Hi, Anna! Welcome back! How's your trip to the States?

W: Very busy. I had a lot of meetings, so, of course, I didn't have much time to see New York.

M: What a pity! Actually, I have a trip there myself next week.

W: Do you? Then take my advice, do the well-being in the air program. It really works.

M: Oh, I read about that in a magazine. You say it works?

W: Yes, I did the program on the flight to the States, and when I arrived at New York, I didn't have any problem, no jet lag at all. On the way back, I didn't do it, and I felt terrible.

M: You're joking!

W: Not at all, it really meant a lot of difference.

M: En. So what did you do?

W: Well, I didn't drink an alcohol or coffee, and I didn't eat any meat or rich food. I drink a lot of water, and fresh juice, and I ate the noodles on the well-being menu. They're lighter. They have fish, vegetables, and noodles, for example, and I did some of the exercises of the program.

M: Exercises? On a plane?

W: Yes. I didn't do many, of course, there isn't much space on a plane.

M: How many passengers do the exercises?

W: Not many.

M: Then how much champagne did they drink?

W: A lot! It was more popular than mineral water.

M: So, basically, it's a choice. Mineral water and exercises, or champagne and jet lag.

W: That's right! It's a difficult choice.

19. Why did the woman go to New York?
20. What does the woman say about the well-being in the air program?
21. What did the woman do to follow the well-being menu?
22. What did the woman say about other passengers?

练习 1

M: What's all that? Are you going to make a salad?

W: No, I'm going to make a gazpacho.

M: What's that?

W: Gazpacho is a cold soup from Spain. It's mostly vegetables. I guess you could call it a liquid salad.

M: Cold soup? Sounds weird.

W: It's delicious. Trust me. I tried it for the first time during my summer vacation in Spain. You see, in the south of Spain, it gets very hot in the summer, up to 40℃. So a cold gazpacho is very refreshing. The main ingredients are tomato, cucumber, bell peppers, olive oil and stale bread.

M: Stale bread? Surely you mean bread for dipping into the soup?

W: No. Bread is crushed and blended in like everything else. It adds texture and thickness to the soup.

M: Mm. And is it healthy?

W: Sure. As I said earlier, it's mostly vegetables. You can also add different things if you like, such as hard-boiled egg or cured ham.

M: Cured ham? What's that?

W: That's another Spanish delicacy. Have you never heard of it? It is quite famous.

M: No. Is it good too?

W: Oh, yeah, definitely. It's amazing. It's a little dry and salty. And it's very expensive because it comes from a special type of pig that only eats a special type of food. The ham is covered in salt to dry and preserve it, and left to hang for up to two years. It has a very distinct flavor.

M: Mm. Sounds interesting. Where can I find some?

W: It used to be difficult to get Spanish produce here. But it's now a lot more common. Most large supermarket chains have cured ham in little packets, but in Spain you can buy a whole leg.

M: A whole pig leg? Why would anybody want so much ham?

W: In Spain, many people buy a whole leg for special group events, such as Christmas. They cut it themselves into very thin slices with a long flat knife.

1. What do we learn about gazpacho?
2. For what purpose is stale bread mixed into gazpacho?
3. Why does the woman think gazpacho is healthy?
4. What does the woman say about cured ham?

练习 2

W: This is unbelievable, unlike any video game I've ever played before. It's so boring yet so relaxing at the same time. How did you hear about this driving simulator?

M: My brother introduced it to me last year. I was surprised to find how educational and realistic it was. It is called Euro Truck Simulator but they have other versions as well for American and so on. I was really drawn to the scenery. The routes go through parts of the country you don't normally see as a tourist.

W: Yeah, I can see that. It seems so simple, just transporting cargo from point A to point B, driving from one city to another. But I really appreciate all the details that go into the game. It's even giving me a new appreciation for the logistics industry and traffic on the road.

M: I completely agree. My brother also introduced me to some videos of someone that streams the games online. It was fascinating to watch really. This guy drove very carefully, obeyed all the road signs and traffic rules, such a contrast to most violent games.

W: Honestly, playing has inspired me to look into the industry more. I've read articles about how self-driving trucks may soon be available and could greatly impact cargo logistics. Considering all that goes into driving these larger vehicles, it's amazing that we could soon have that kind of technology.

M: Ah, I've gone one step further. I registered to take a safe driving course to improve my real-life driving skills. In a way, I feel like I have a head start compared to other students in the class. Playing this video game has given me some maneuvering practice already.

W: I am not sure how accurate the video game is compared to real life situations. But if it results in more drivers looking both ways before entering an intersection, I'd say that's a positive outcome.

1. What are the speakers mainly talking about?
2. What does the man say about the driving simulator?
3. What does the woman say she really appreciates?
4. What outcome did this woman expect from the driving simulator?

五、篇章听力题型概述＋解题技巧＋重点话题

1. 篇章听力题型概述

篇章听力：2篇，每篇240～260词，每篇3～4题，共7题。

2. 解题技巧

题文同序　　　　　同义替换　　　　　视听一致
问句出题　　　　　首三尾三　　　　　重复出题

3. 重点话题——工作类

例 1

32. A) Germany.

B) Japan.

C) The U.S.

D) The U.K.   答案：(   )

33. A) By doing odd jobs at weekends.

    B) By working long hours every day.

    C) By putting in more hours each week.

    D) By taking shorter vacations each year.   答案：(   )

34. A) To combat competition and raise productivity.

    B) To provide them with more job opportunities.

    C) To help them maintain their living standard.

    D) To prevent them from holding a second job.   答案：(   )

35. A) Change their jobs.

    B) Earn more money.

    C) Reduce their working hours.

    D) Strengthen the government's role.   答案：(   )

例2

12. A) All services will be personalized.

    B) A lot of knowledge-intensive jobs will be replaced.

    C) Technology will revolutionize all sectors of industry.

    D) More information will be available.   答案：(   )

13. A) In the robotics industry.

    B) In the information service.

    C) In the personal care sector.

    D) In high-end manufacturing.   答案：(   )

14. A) They charge high prices.

    B) They need lots of training.

    C) They cater to the needs of young people.

D) They focus on customers' specific needs. 答案：(   )

15. A) The rising demand in education and healthcare in the next 20 years.
    B) The disruption caused by technology in traditionally well-paid jobs.
    C) The tremendous changes new technology will bring to people's lives.
    D) The amazing amount of personal attention people would like to have. 答案：(   )

4. 重点话题——校园类

例 3

33. A) It may produce an increasing number of idle youngsters.
    B) It may affect the quality of higher education in America.
    C) It may cause many schools to go out of operation.
    D) It may lead to a lack of properly educated workers. 答案：(   )

34. A) It is less serious in cities than in rural areas.
    B) It affects both junior and senior high schools.
    C) It results from a worsening economic climate.
    D) It is a new challenge facing American educators. 答案：(   )

35. A) Allowing them to choose their favorite teachers.
    B) Creating a more relaxed learning environment.
    C) Rewarding excellent academic performance.
    D) Helping them to develop better study habits. 答案：(   )

5. 重点话题——新闻类

大纲要求：能听懂语速中等、题材熟悉、篇幅较长的英语广播。

例 4

26. A) It carried passengers leaving an island.
    B) A terrorist forced it to land on Tenerife.
    C) It crashed when it was circling to land.
    D) 18 of its passengers survived the crash. 答案：(   )

27. A) He was kidnapped eight months ago.
    B) He failed in his negotiations with the Africans.
    C) He was assassinated in Central Africa.
    D) He lost lots of money in his African business.   答案：(   )

28. A) The management and union representatives reached an agreement.
    B) The workers' pay was raised and their working hours were shortened.
    C) The trade union gave up its demand.
    D) The workers on strike were all fired.   答案：(   )

29. A) Sunny.
    B) Rainy.
    C) Windy.
    D) Cloudy.   答案：(   )

The Listening Scripts

例1

Americans suffer from an overdose of work. Regardless of who they are or what they do. Americans spend more time at work than that any time since World War II. In 1950, the US had fewer working hours than any other industrialized country. Today, it exceeds every country but Japan where industrialized employees log 2,155 hours a year compared with 1,951 in the US and 1,603 in the former West Germany. Between 1969 and 1989, employed Americans add an average of 138 hours to their yearly work schedules. The workweek has remained above 40 hours. But people are working more weeks each year. Specifically pay time off holidays, vacations, sick leave shrink by 50% in the 1980s. As corporations have experienced stiff competitions and slow in growth of productivity, they have pressed employees to work longer. Cost-cutting lay-offs in the 1980s reduced the professional and managerial runs, leaving fewer people to get the job done. In lower paid occupations where wages have been reduced, workers have added hours in overtime or extra jobs to preserve their living standards. The government estimates that more than 7 million people hold a second job. For the first time, large numbers of people say they want to cut back on working hours even it means earning less money. But most employers are unwilling to let them do so. The government which has stepped back from its traditional role as a regulator of work time should take steps to make shorter hours possible.

32. In which country do industrial employees work the longest hours?

33. How do employed Americans manage to work more hours?

34. Why do corporations press their employees to work longer hours according to the speaker?

35. What does the speaker say many Americans prefer to do?

例 2

If you are young and thinking about your career, you'll want to know where you can make a living. Well, there's going to be a technological replacement of a lot of knowledge-intensive jobs in the next twenty years, particularly in the two largest sectors of the labor force with professional skills. One is teaching, and the other, healthcare. You have so many applications and software and platforms that are going to come in and provide information and service in these two fields, which means a lot of healthcare and education sectors will be radically changed and a lot of jobs will be lost. Now, where will the new jobs be found? Well, the one sector of the economy that can't be easily duplicated by even smart technologies is the caring sector, the personal care sector. That is, you can't really get a robot to do a great massage or physical therapy, or you can't get the kind of personal attention you need with regard to therapy or any other personal service. There could be very high-end personal services. Therapists do charge a lot of money. I think there's no limit to the amount of personal attention and personal care people would like if they could afford it. But the real question in the future is how come people afford these things if they don't have money, because they can't get a job that pays enough. That's why I wrote this book, which is about how to reorganize the economy for the future when technology brings about destructive changes to what we used to consider high-income work.

12. What does the speaker say will happen in the next twenty years?

13. Where will young people have more chances to find jobs?

14. What does the speaker say about therapists?

15. What is the speaker's book about?

例 3

Articles in magazines and newspapers and special reports on radio and television reflect the concern of many Americans about the increasing dropout rate in our junior and senior high schools. Coupled with this fact is the warning that soon we will no longer have workforce to fill the many jobs that require properly-educated personnel. The highest student dropout rate is not a recent development. Ten years ago, many urban schools were reporting dropout rates between 35 and 50 percent. Some administrators maintain that dropouts remain the single greatest problem in their schools. Consequently, much effort has been spent on identifying students with problems in order to give them more attention before they become failures.

Since the dropout problem doesn't start in senior high school, special programs in junior high school focus on students who show promise but have a record of truancy, that is, staying away from school without permission. Under the guidance of counselors, these students are placed in classes with teachers who have had success in working with similar young people. Strategies to motivate students in high school include rewarding academic excellence by designating scholars of the month, or by issuing articles of clothing, such as school letter jackets formally given only to athletes. No one working with these students claims to know how to keep all students in school. Counselors, teachers, and administrators are in the frontlines of what seems at times to be a losing battle. Actually, this problem should be everyone's concern, since uneducated, unemployed citizens affect us all.

33. Why are many Americans concerned with the increasing dropout rate in school?
34. What do we learn about the student dropout problem in America?
35. What is mentioned as one of the strategies used to motivate students?

例 4

The time is 9 o'clock and this is Marian Snow with the news.

The German authorities are sending investigators to discover the cause of the plane crash late yesterday on the island of Tenerife. The plane, a Boeing 737, taking German holiday-makers to the island crashed into a hillside as it circled while preparing to land. The plane was carrying 180 passengers. It's thought there are no survivors. Rescue workers are at the scene.

The British industrialist James Louis, held by kidnappers in Central Africa for the past 8 months, was released unharmed yesterday. The kidnappers had been demanding one million pounds for the release of Mr. Louis. The London Bank and their agents who have been negotiating with the kidnappers have not said whether any amount of money has been paid.

The 500 UK motors workers who had been on strike in High Town for the past three weeks went back to work this morning. This follows successful talks between management and union representatives, which resulted in a new agreement on working hours and conditions. A spokesman for the management said that they'd hope they could now get back to producing cars, and that they lost a lot of money and orders over this dispute.

　　And finally the weather. After a cold start, most of the country should be warm and sunny. But towards late afternoon, rain will spread from Scotland to cover most parts by midnight.

26. What does the news say about the Boeing 737 plane?

27. What happened to British industrialist James Louis?

28. How did the 3-week strike in High Town end?

29. What kind of weather will be expected by midnight in most parts of the country?

六、篇章听力重点话题讲解

1. 篇章听力重点话题讲解——实验研究型文章

例 1

9. A) It makes claims in conflict with the existing research.
　 B) It focuses on the link between bedtime and nutrition.
　 C) It cautions against the overuse of coffee and alcohol.
　 D) It shows that "night owls" work much less efficiently.　　　　答案：（　　）

10. A) They pay greater attention to food choice.
　　B) They tend to achieve less than their peers.
　　C) They run a higher risk of gaining weight.
　　D) They stand a greater chance to fall sick.　　　　答案：（　　）

11. A) Get up late.
　　B) Sleep 8 hours a day.
　　C) Exercise more.
　　D) Go to bed earlier.　　　　答案：（　　）

例 2

9. A) They are on the verge of extinction because of pollution.

B) They carry plant seeds and spread them to faraway places.

C) They deliver pollutants from the ocean to their nesting sites.

D) They can be used to deliver messages in times of emergency.   答案:(   )

10. A) They originate from Devon Island in the Arctic area.

    B) They migrate to the Arctic Circle during the summer.

    C) They have the ability to survive in extreme weathers.

    D) They travel as far as 400 kilometers in search of food.   答案:(   )

11. A) They had become more poisonous.

    B) They were carried by the wind.

    C) They poisoned some of the fulmars.

    D) They were less than on the continent.   答案:(   )

12. A) The effects of the changing climate on Arctic seabirds.

    B) The harm Arctic seabirds may cause to humans.

    C) The diminishing colonies for Arctic seabirds.

    D) The threats humans pose to Arctic seabirds.   答案:(   )

例3

12. A) They appear restless.

    B) They lose consciousness.

    C) They become upset.

    D) They die almost instantly.   答案:(   )

13. A) It has an instant effect on your body chemistry.

    B) It keeps returning to you every now and then.

    C) It leaves you with a long lasting impression.

    D) It contributes to the shaping of you mind.   答案:(   )

14. A) To succeed while feeling irritated.

    B) To feel happy without good health.

    C) To be free from frustration and failure.

    D) To enjoy good health while in dark moods.   答案:(   )

15. A) They are closely connected.
    B) They function in a similar way.
    C) They are too complex to understand.
    D) They reinforce each other constantly.　　　　　　　　　　答案：(   )

练习 1

32. A) A goods train hit a bus carrying many passengers.
    B) Two passenger trains crashed into each other.
    C) A passenger train collided with a goods train.
    D) An express train was derailed when hit by a bomb.　　　答案：(   )

33. A) The rescue operations have not been very effective.
    B) More than 300 injured passengers were hospitalized.
    C) The cause of the tragic accident remains unknown.
    D) The exact casualty figures are not yet available.　　　　答案：(   )

34. A) There was a bomb scare.
    B) There was a terrorist attack.
    C) A fire alarm was set off by mistake.
    D) 50 pounds of explosives were found.　　　　　　　　　答案：(   )

35. A) Follow policemen's directions.
    B) Keep an eye on the weather.
    C) Avoid snow-covered roads.
    D) Drive with special care.　　　　　　　　　　　　　　答案：(   )

The Listening Scripts

例 1

A report on sleep and nutrition released this month found that people who consistently went to bed earlier than 11 p.m. took in fewer calories and ate more healthy food. In contrast, "night owls" who go to bed between 11 p.m and 3 a.m. tend to consume more coffee, alcohol, refined sugars and processed meats than early risers.

This report corresponds with the existing scientific literature on bedtime and wellness. The relationship between getting more sleep and making better food choices is well-documented. A study published last year in *The American Journal of Clinical Nutrition* found that people who sleep more tend to eat less unhealthy food than their peers who don't get as much rest. And a 2015 study from the University of California, Berkeley, found that teens who go to bed late are more likely to gain weight over a five-year period.

As a group, "night owl" types tend to eat less healthy food and take in more calories overall than early risers. The later one goes to bed, the more calories one records the next day. As yet a challenge to explain the cause-and-effect relationship between sleep and nutrition, there may be a third factor that impacts both of them. Or the relationship could be reversed, that is, people who eat less fall asleep earlier. Still, if late sleepers want to lose a few pounds, they can go to bed earlier than they usually do, thereby reducing their chances of taking snacks before bedtime.

9. What do we learn about the report released this month?
10. What does the study from the University of California, Berkeley, find about teens who go to bed late?
11. What should "night owls" do to reduce their consumption of unhealthy food?

例2

Birds are famous for carrying things around. Some, like homing pigeons, can be trained to deliver messages and packages. Other birds unknowingly carry seeds that cling to them for the ride. Canadian scientists have found a worrisome, new example of the power that birds have to spread stuff around. Way up north in the Canadian Arctic, seabirds are picking up dangerous chemicals in the ocean and delivering them to ponds near where the birds live.

Some 10,000 pairs of the birds, called fulmars, a kind of Arctic seabird, make their nests on Devon Island, north of the Arctic Circle. The fulmars travel some 400 kilometers over the sea to find food. When they return home, their droppings end up all around their nesting sites, including in nearby ponds.

Previously, scientists noticed pollutants arriving in the Arctic with the wind. Salmon also carry dangerous chemicals, as the fish migrate between rivers and the sea. The bodies of fish and other meat-eaters can build up high levels of the chemicals.

To test the polluting power of fulmars, researchers collected samples of deposits from 11 ponds on Devon Island. In ponds closest to the colony, the results showed that there were far more pollutants than in ponds less affected by the birds. The pollutants in the ponds appear to come from fish that fulmars eat when they're out on the ocean. People who live, hunt, or fish near bird colonies need to be careful, the researchers say. The birds don't mean to cause harm, but the chemicals they carry can cause major problems.

9. What have the Canadian scientists found about some seabirds?
10. What does the speaker say about the seabirds called fulmars?
11. What did scientists previously notice about pollutants in the Arctic?
12. What does the speaker warn about at the end of the talk?

例3

Scientific experiments have demonstrated incredible ways to kill a guinea pig, a small furry animal. Emotional upsets generate powerful and deadly toxic substances. Blood samples taken from persons experiencing intense fear or anger when injected into guinea pigs have killed them in less than two minutes. Imagine what these poisonous substances can do to your own body. Every thought that you have affects your body chemistry within a split second. Remember how you feel when you're speeding down the highway and a big truck suddenly brakes twenty meters in front of you. A shock wave shoots through your whole system. Your mind produces instant reactions in your body. The toxic substances that fear, anger, frustration and stress produce not only kill guinea pigs but kill us off in a similar manner. It is impossible to be fearful, anxious, irritated and healthy at the same time. It is not just difficult; it is impossible. Simply put, your body's health is a reflection of your mental health. Sickness will often then be a result of unresolved inner conflicts which in time show up in the body. It is also fascinating how our subconscious mind shapes our health. Do you recall falling sick on a day when you didn't want to go to school? Headaches brought on by fear? The mind-body connection is such that if, for example, we want to avoid something, very often our subconscious mind will arrange it. Once we recognize that these things happen to us, we are halfway to doing something about them.

12. What happens to guinea pigs when blood samples of angry people are injected into them?
13. What does the speaker say about every thought you have?
14. What does the speaker say is impossible?
15. What does the passage say about out mind and body?

> 练习 1

This is Ray McCarthy with the news. Reports are coming in of a major train crash in Japan. A passenger train carrying hundreds of workers home from the center of Tokyo is reported to have hit an oncoming goods train. Both were traveling at high speed. Figures are not yet available but it is believed that the death toll could be as high as 300, with hundreds more injured. Emergency and rescue services rushed to the scene. But our reporter says it will take days to clear the track and to establish the numbers of the dead and injured. There was a similar accident on the same stretch of track four years ago.

There was another bomb scare in a large London store last night during late night shopping. Following a telephone call to the police from an anonymous caller, hundreds of shoppers were shepherded out of the store while roads in the area were sealed off. Police dogs spent hours searching the store for a bag which the caller claimed contained 50 pounds of explosives. Nothing was found and the store was given the all-clear by opening time this morning. A police spokesman said that this was the third bomb scare within a week and that we should all be on our guard.

And finally, the motoring organizations have issued a warning to drivers following the recent falls of snow in many parts of the country. Although the falls may be slight, they say extra care is needed.

32. What accident happened recently in Japan?
33. What do the reports say about the recent accident in Japan?
34. Why did people have to leave the London store last night?
35. What did motoring organizations advise drivers to do?

七、Section C 题型概述 + 解题技巧 + 重点话题

1. Section C 题型概述

大纲要求：能听懂语速中等、题材熟悉的讲话、报道和内容浅显的学术讲座。

讲座 / 讲话 / 报道：3 篇，总共约 1 200 词，每篇 3 ~ 4 题，共 10 题。

题型特征：

- In last week's lecture, we discussed..., but in today's lecture, we'll look at three very interesting studies.

- Today I am going to talk about poverty.
- Welcome to the third lecture in our series on the future of small businesses in Europe.
- Today we are going to be talking about becoming a social worker.

2. 解题技巧

题文同序	同义替换	视听一致
问句出题	首三尾三	重复出题

例 1

16. A) They investigate the retirement homes in America.
    B) They are on issues facing senior citizens in America.
    C) They describe the great pleasures of the golden years.
    D) They are filled with fond memories of his grandparents.　　答案：(　　)

17. A) The loss of the ability to take care of himself.
    B) The feeling of not being important any more.
    C) Being unable to find a good retirement home.
    D) Leaving the home he had lived in for 60 years.　　答案：(　　)

18. A) The loss of identity and self-worth.
    B) Fear of being replaced or discarded.
    C) Freedom from pressure and worldly cares.
    D) The possession of wealth and high respect.　　答案：(　　)

19. A) The urgency of pension reform.
    B) Medical care for senior citizens.
    C) Finding meaningful roles for the elderly in society.
    D) The development of public facilities for senior citizens.　　答案：(　　)

3. 重点话题——工作类

例 2

16. A) They get bored after working for a period of time.
    B) They spend an average of one year finding a job.

C) They become stuck in the same job for decades.
D) They choose a job without thinking it through. 答案:(   )

17. A) See if there will be chances for promotion.
    B) Find out what job choices are available.
    C) Watch a film about ways of job hunting.
    D) Decide which job is most attractive to you. 答案:(   )

18. A) The qualifications you have.
    B) The pay you are going to get.
    C) The culture of your target company.
    D) The work environment you will be in. 答案:(   )

4. 重点话题——校园类

例3

16. A) It improves students' ability to think.
    B) It is accessible only to the talented.
    C) It starts a lifelong learning process.
    D) It gives birth to many eminent scholars. 答案:(   )

17. A) They protect students' rights.
    B) They promote globalization.
    C) They uphold the presidents' authority.
    D) They encourage academic democracy. 答案:(   )

18. A) His eagerness to find a job.
    B) His thirst for knowledge.
    C) His potential for leadership.
    D) His contempt for authority. 答案:(   )

例4

16. A) They encourage international cooperation.
    B) They lay stress on basic scientific research.

C) They place great emphasis on empirical studies.

D) They favour scientists from its member countries.   答案：(   )

17. A) Many of them wish to win international recognition.

    B) They believe that more hands will make light work.

    C) They want to follow closely the international trend.

    D) Many of their projects have become complicated.   答案：(   )

18. A) It requires mathematicians to work independently.

    B) It is faced with many unprecedented challenges.

    C) It lags behind other disciplines in collaboration.

    D) It calls for more research funding to catch up.   答案：(   )

练习 1

16. A) About half of current jobs might be automated.

    B) The jobs of doctors and lawyers would be threatened.

    C) The job market is becoming somewhat unpredictable.

    D) Machine learning would prove disruptive by 2013.   答案：(   )

17. A) They are widely applicable for massive open online courses.

    B) They are now being used by numerous high school teachers.

    C) They could read as many as 10,000 essays in a single minute.

    D) They could grade high-school essays just like human teachers.   答案：(   )

18. A) It needs instructions throughout the process.

    B) It does poorly on frequent, high-volume tasks.

    C) It has to rely on huge amounts of previous data.

    D) It is slow when it comes to tracking novel things.   答案：(   )

The Listening Scripts

例 1

Moderator:

Hello Ladies and Gentleman, it gives me great pleasure to introduce our keynote speaker for today's session, Dr. Howard Miller. Dr. Miller, Professor of Sociology at Washington University, has written numerous articles and books on the issues facing older Americans in our graying society for the past 15 years. Dr. Miller:

Dr. Miller:

Thank you for that introduction. Today, I'd like to preface my remarks with a story from my own life which I feel highlights the common concerns that bring us here together. Several years ago when my grandparents were well into their eighties, they were faced with the reality of no longer being able to adequately care for themselves. My grandfather spoke of his greatest fear, that of leaving the only home they had known for the past 60 years. Fighting back the tears, he spoke proudly of the fact that he had built their home from the ground up, and that he had pounded every nail and laid every brick in the process. The prospect of having to sell their home and give up their independence, and move into a retirement home was an extremely painful experience for them. It was, in my grandfather's own words, like having a limb cut off. He exclaimed in a forceful manner that he felt he wasn't important anymore.

For them and some older Americans, their so-called "golden years" are at times not so pleasant, for this period can mean the decline of not only one's health but the loss of identity and self-worth. In many societies, this self-identity is closely related with our social status, occupation, material possessions, or independence. Furthermore, we often live in societies that value what is "new" or in fashion, and our own usage of words in the English language is often a sign of bad news for older Americans. I mean how would your family react if you came home tonight exclaiming, "Hey, come to the living room and see the OLD black and white TV I brought!" Unfortunately, the word "old" calls to mind images of the need to replace or discard.

Now, many of the lectures given at this conference have focused on the issues of pension reform, medical care, and the development of public facilities for senior citizens. And while these are vital issues that must be addressed, I'd like to focus my comments on an important issue that will affect the overall success of the other programs mentioned. This has to do with changing our perspectives on what it means to be a part of this group, and finding meaningful roles the elderly can play and should play in our societies.

First of all, I'd like to talk about...

16. What does the introduction say about Dr. Howard Miller's articles and books?
17. What is the greatest fear of Dr. Miller's grandfather?
18. What does Dr. Miller say the "golden years" can often mean?

19. What is the focus of Dr. Miller's speech?

例 2

You dream about being a movie star. You'll live in a big house in Hollywood, go to the Oscars every year—and win! You will be rich and famous. Wait a minute. You also hate having your photo taken, and you are very shy. So how could you ever become a movie star? Choosing the right career can be hard. Many people graduate from school or college not knowing what to do with their lives and get a job without really thinking about it. For some, things work out fine. But others often find themselves stuck in a job they hate. Your working life lasts an average of 40 years, so it's important to find a job you like and feel enthusiastic about.

Luckily, there are many ways you can get help to do this. The Australian website, www. careersonline. com, compares choosing a career with going to the movies. Before you see a movie, you find out what films are showing. The site suggests you should do the same with your career—find out what jobs are available and what your options are. Next, decide which movie you like best. If you are not a romantic person, you won't want to see a love story. In other words, with your career, you should decide which job will suit your personality. Finally, decide how to get movie ticket, and find out where the theater is before you go. With your career, you need to find information about where you can work, and how to get a job in that profession.

So, how do you start? Begin by asking yourself some questions. Some jobs require you to have certain life experiences: Have you travelled overseas? Do you have any extra certificates besides your degree? Such as a first aid license, for example. Your physical state and build can also affect which jobs you can do. A person, for example, who is allergic to cats, would probably never become an animal doctor. Flight attendants, firefighters and police officers have to be over a certain height, and be physically fit. Your personality matters too. Are you outgoing or shy? If you like working alone, a job that requires lots of teamwork might not suit you.

Choosing a career can take time and a lot of thought. However, when you know you can look forward to working in your dream job, you will be glad you thought it through.

16. What does the speaker say about many college graduates?
17. What does the Australia website suggest you do first to find a suitable job?
18. What should you think about when you look for the right job according to the Australian website?

例 3

This is the reason you are here in a university. You are here to be educated. You are here to understand thinking better and to think better yourself. It's not a chance you're going to have throughout your lifetime. For the next few years, you have a chance to focus on thinking. I think about some of the students who took advantage of their opportunities in a university. One of the stories I always like to tell is of a freshman seminar that I had a chance to teach at Harvard when I was president of the university. I taught a seminar on globalization, and I assigned a reading that I had written about global capital flows. And as I did each week, I asked one of the students to introduce the readings.

And this young man, in October of his freshman year, said something like the following. "The reading by President Summers on the flow of capital across countries, it was kind of interesting, but the data did not come close to supporting the conclusions." And I thought to myself, "what a fantastic thing this was. How could somebody who had been there for five weeks, tell the person who had the title 'President' that he didn't really know what he was talking about." And it was a special moment. Now, I don't want to be misunderstood. I explained to my student that I actually thought he was rather more confused than I was and I argued back, but what was really important about that was the universities stand out as places that really are about the authority of ideas. You see it in faculty members who are pleased when their students make a discovery that undermines a cherished theory that they had put forward.

I think of another student I had who came to me one morning, one evening actually, walked into my office and said that I had written a pretty good paper, but that it had five important mistakes and that he wanted a job. You could debate whether they actually were mistakes, but you couldn't debate that young man's hunger to learn. You could not debate that that young man was someone who wanted to make a difference in economics and he is today a professor of economics. And his works are more cited as an economist than any other economist in the world.

16. What does the speaker say about a university?
17. What do we learn from the speaker's stories about universities?
18. What does the speaker see in the young man who challenged his paper?

例 4

Good afternoon, class. Today I want to discuss with you a new approach to empirical research. In the past, scientists often worked alone. They were confined to the university or research center where they worked. Today, though, we are seeing mergers of some of the greatest scientific minds regardless of their location. There has never been a better time for collaborations with foreign scientists. In fact, the European Union is taking the lead. Spurred on by funding policies, half of European research articles and international co-authors in 2007. This is more than twice the level of two decades ago. The European Union's level of international co-authorship is about twice that of the United States, Japan and India. Even so, the levels in these countries are also rising. This is a sign of the continued allure of creating scientific coalitions across boarders. Andrew Schubert, a researcher at the Institute for Science Policy Research, says that the rising collaboration is partly out of necessity. This necessity comes with the rise of "big science." Many scientific endeavors have become more complicated. These new complications require the money and labor of many nations. But he says collaborations have also emerged because of increased possibilities: the Internet allows like-minded scientists to find each other. Simultaneously, dramatic drops in communication costs ease long-distance interactions. And there is a reward: studies of citation counts show that internationally co-authored papers have better visibility. Schubert says international collaboration is a way to spread ideas in wider and wider circles. Caroline Wagner, a research scientist at George Washington University, notes that international collaborations offer additional flexibility. Whereas local collaborations sometimes persist past the point of usefulness because of social or academic obligations, international ones can be cultivated and dropped more freely. The collaborative trend is true across scientific disciplines. Some fields, though, have a greater tendency for it. Particle physicists and astronomers collaborate often. This is because they must share expensive facilities.

Mathematicians, by contrast, tend historically towards solitude. As a consequence, they lag behind other disciplines. However, Wagner says partnerships are rising there too. The level of collaboration also varies from country to country. "There are historical and political reasons as to why collaborations emerge," says Wagner. This rise is also apparently boosted by policies embedded in European framework funding schemes. These policies underlie funding requirements that often require teamwork.

16. What do we learn about the research funding policies in the European Union?
17. Why do researchers today favour international collaboration?
18. What do we learn about the field of mathematics?

练习 1

Here is my baby niece Sarah. Her mom is a doctor and her dad is a lawyer. By the time Sarah goes to college, the jobs her parents do are going to look dramatically different. In 2013, researchers at Oxford University did a study on the future of work. They concluded that almost one in every two jobs has a high risk of being automated by machines. Machine learning is the technology that's responsible for most of this disruption. It's the most powerful branch of artificial intelligence. It allows machines to learn from data and copy some of the things that humans can do.

My company, Kaggle, operates on the cutting edge of machine learning. We bring together hundreds of thousands of experts to solve important problems for industry and academia. This gives us a unique perspective on what machines can do, what they can't do and what jobs they might automate or threaten. Machine learning started making its way into industry in the early 90s. It started with relatively simple tasks. It started with things like assessing credit risk from loan applications, sorting the mail by reading handwritten zip codes. Over the past few years, we have made dramatic breakthroughs. Machine learning is now capable of far, far more complex tasks. In 2012, Kaggle challenged its community to build a program that could grade high-school essays. The winning programs were able to match the grades given by human teachers. Now, given the right data, machines are going to outperform humans at tasks like this. A teacher might read 10,000 essays over a 40-year career. A machine can read millions of essays within minutes. We have no chance of competing against machines on frequent, high-volume tasks.

But there are things we can do that machines cannot. Where machines have made very little progress is in tackling novel situations. Machines can't handle things they haven't seen many times before. The fundamental limitation of machine learning is that it needs to learn from large volumes of past data. But humans don't. We have the ability to connect seemingly different threads to solve problems we've never seen before.

16. What did the researchers at Oxford University conclude?
17. What do we learn about Kaggle company's winning programs?
18. What is the fundamental limitation of machine learning?

八、Section C 听力重点提示词技巧

1. Section C 听力重点提示词技巧

重点逻辑提示词：but，however，yet，though，whereas，actually，in fact，instead of， nonetheless（转折）

since，as，because，so，that's why...（因果）

if，when，only，unless，otherwise（条件）

for example，such as，in other words，for instance（举例）

信息比较提示词：more，most，-er，-est

结论信息提示词：show，indicate，find，believe，conclude，identify，reveal，discover，suggest，argue，report，it turns out that...

数字时间提示词：年代（10 years=a decade），价格（20%=one fifth），倍数（half=50%）

态度情绪提示词：sadly，unfortunately，fortunately，must，have to，had better...

顺序线索提示词：first，for the first time，first of all，on top of all，second，finally，eventually

例 1

23. A) It is one of the world's most healthy diets.

　　B) It contains large amounts of dairy products.

　　C) It began to impact the world in recent years.

　　D) It consists mainly of various kinds of seafood.　　　　　　　　答案：(　　)

24. A) It involved 13,000 researchers from Asia, Europe and America.

　　B) It was conducted in seven Mid-Eastern countries in the 1950s.

　　C) It is regarded as one of the greatest researches of its kind.

　　D) It has drawn the attention of medical doctors the world over.　　答案：(　　)

25. A) They care much about their health.

　　B) They eat foods with little fat.

　　C) They use little oil in cooking.

　　D) They have lower mortality rates.　　　　　　　　　　　　　　答案：(　　)

例 2

19. A) It is likely to give up paper money in the near future.

　　B) It is the first country to use credit cards in the world.

　　C) It is trying hard to do away with dirty money.

　　D) It is helping its banks to improve efficiency.　　　　　　　　　答案：(　　)

20. A) Whether it is possible to travel without carrying any physical currency.
    B) Whether it is possible to predict how much money one is going to spend.
    C) Whether the absence of physical currency is going to affect everyday life.
    D) Whether the absence of physical currency causes a person to spend more. 答案: (   )

21. A) The cash in her handbag was missing.
    B) The service on the train was not good.
    C) The restaurant car accepted cash only.
    D) There was no food service on the train. 答案: (   )

22. A) By drawing money week by week.
    B) By putting money into envelopes.
    C) By limiting their day-to-day spending.
    D) By refusing to buy anything on credit. 答案: (   )

例3

16. A) They form the basis on which he builds his theory of love.
    B) They were carried out over a period of some thirty years.
    C) They were done by his former colleague at Yale.
    D) They are focused more on attraction than love. 答案: (   )

17. A) The relationship cannot last long if no passion is involved.
    B) It is not love if you don't wish to maintain the relationship.
    C) Romance is just impossible without mutual understanding.
    D) Intimacy is essential but not absolutely indispensable to love. 答案: (   )

18. A) Whether it is true love without commitment.
    B) Which of them is considered most important.
    C) How the relationship is to be defined if any one is missing.
    D) When the absence of any one doesn't affect the relationship. 答案: (   )

练习 1

19. A) Similarities between human babies and baby animals.
    B) Cognitive features of different newly born mammals.
    C) Adults' influence on children.
    D) Abilities of human babies.   答案:(   )

20. A) They can distinguish a happy tune from a sad one.
    B) They love happy melodies more than sad ones.
    C) They fall asleep easily while listening to music.
    D) They are already sensitive to beats and rhythms.   答案:(   )

21. A) Infants' facial expressions.
    B) Babies' emotions.
    C) Babies' interaction with adults.
    D) Infants' behaviors.   答案:(   )

The Listening Scripts

例 1

The Mediterranean diet is based upon the eating patterns of traditional cultures in the Mediterranean region. Several noted nutritionists and research projects have concluded that this diet is one of the most healthful in the world in terms of preventing such illnesses as heart disease and cancer, and increasing life expectancy. The countries that have inspired the Mediterranean diet all surround the Mediterranean Sea. These cultures have eating habits that developed over thousands of years. In Europe, parts of Italy, Greece, Portugal, Spain and southern France adhere to principles of the Mediterranean diet, as do Morocco and Tunisia in North Africa. Parts of the Balkan region and Turkey follow the diet, as well as middle Eastern countries like Lebanon and Syria. The Mediterranean region is warm and sunny, and produces large supplies of fresh fruits and vegetables almost a year round that people eat many times a day. Wine, bread, olive oil and nuts are other staples of the region, and the Mediterranean sea has historically yielded abundant quantities of fish. International interest in the therapeutic qualities of the Mediterranean diet began back in the late 1950s. When medical researchers started to link the occurrence of heart disease with diet, Doctor Ancel Keys performed the epidemiological analysis of diets around the world. Entitled the Seven Countries Study, it is considered one of the greatest studies of its kind ever performed. In it, Keys gathered data on heart disease and its potential causes from nearly 13,000 men in Greece, Italy, Croatia, Serbia, Japan, Finland, the Netherlands and the United States. The study was conducted over period of decades. It concluded that the Mediterranean people in the study enjoyed some significant health advantages. The Mediterranean groups had lower mortality rates in all age brackets and from all causes, particularly from heart disease. The study also showed that the Mediterranean diet is as high as or higher in fat than other diets, obtaining up to forty percent of all its calories from fat. It has, however, different patterns of fat intake. Mediterranean cooking use smaller amounts of saturated fat and higher amounts of unsaturated fat, mostly in the form of olive oil. Saturated fats are fats that are found principally in meat and dairy products, although some nuts and vegetable oils also contain them. Saturated fats are used by the body to make cholesterol, and high levels of cholesterol have since been directly related to heart disease.

23. What has research concluded about the Mediterranean diet?
24. What do we learn about the Seven Countries Study?
25. What do we learn about the Mediterranean people from the Seven Countries Study?

例2

Sweden was the first European country to print and use paper money, but it may soon do away with physical currencies. Banks can save a lot of money and avoid regulatory headaches by moving to a cash-free system, and they can also avoid bank robberies, theft and dirty money. Claer Barrett, the editor of *Financial Times Money*, says the Western world is headed toward a world without physical currency. Andy Holder, the chief economist at The Bank of England, suggested that the UK move towards a government-backed digital currency. But does a cashless society really make good economic sense?

The fact that cash is being drawn out of society, is less a feature of our everyday lives, and the ease of electronic payments is actually making us spend more money without realizing it. Barrett wanted to find out if the absence of physical currency does indeed cause a person to spend more, so she decided to conduct an experiment a few months ago. She decided that she was going to try to just use cash for two weeks to make all of her essential purchases and see what that would do to her spending. She found she did spend a lot less money because it is incredibly hard to predict how much cash one is going to need. She was forever drawing money out of cash points. Months later, she was still finding cash stuffed in her trouser pockets and the pockets of her handbags. During the experiment, Barrett took a train ride. On the way, there was an announcement that the restaurant car was not currently accepting credit cards. The train cars were filled with groans because many of the passengers were traveling without cash. "It underlines just how much things have changed in the last generation," Barrett says. "My parents, when they were younger, used to budget by putting money into envelopes. They'd get paid and they'd immediately separate the cash into piles and put them in envelopes, so they knew what they had to spend week by week. It was a very effective way for them to keep track of their spending." Nowadays, we're all on credit cards, we're doing online purchases, and money is kind of becoming a less physical and more imaginary type of thing that we can't get our heads around.

19. What do we learn about Sweden?
20. What did Claer Barrett want to find out with her experiment?
21. What did Claer Barrett find on her train ride?
22. How did people of the last generation budget their spending?

例 3

Okay. So let's get started. And to start things off I think what we need to do is consider a definition. I'm going to define what love is but the most of the experiments I'm going to talk about are really focused more on attraction than love. And I'm going to pick a definition from a former colleague, Robert Sternberg, who is now the dean at Tufts University but was here on our faculty at Yale for nearly thirty years. And he has a theory of love that argues that it's made up of three components: intimacy, passion, and commitment, or what is sometimes called decision commitment. And these are relatively straightforward. He argued that you don't have love if you don't have all three of these elements.

Intimacy is the feeling of closeness, of connectedness with someone, of bonding. Operationally, you could think of intimacy as you share secrets, you share information with this person that you don't share with anybody else. Okay. That's really what intimacy is, the bond that comes from sharing information that isn't shared with other people. The second element is passion. Passion is the drive that leads to romance. You can think of it as physical attraction. And Sternberg argues that this is a required component of a love relationship. The third element of love in Sternberg's theory is what he calls decision commitment, the decision that one is in a love relationship, the willingness to label it as such, and a commitment to maintain that relationship at least for some period of time. Sternberg would argue it's not love if you don't call it love and if you don't have some desire to maintain the relationship. So if you have all three of these, intimacy, passion and commitment, in Sternberg's theory you have love. Now what's interesting about the theory is what do you have if you only have one out of three or two out of three. What do you have and how is it different if you have a different two out of three? What's interesting about this kind of theorizing is it gives rise to many different combinations that can be quite interesting when you break them down and start to look them carefully. So what I've done is I've taken Sternberg's three elements of love, intimacy, passion and commitment, and I've listed out the different kinds of relationships you would have if you had zero, one, two or three out of the three elements.

16. What does the speaker say about most of the experiments mentioned in his talk?
17. What does Robert Sternberg argue about love?
18. What question does the speaker think is interesting about Sternberg's three elements of love?

练习 1

In last week's lecture, we discussed the characteristics of the newly born offspring of several mammals. You probably remember that human infants are less developed physically than other mammals of the same age. But in today's lecture, we'll look at three very interesting studies that hint at the surprising abilities of human babies. In the first study, three-year-olds watched two videos shown side by side, each featuring a different researcher, one of whom they'd met once two years earlier. The children spent longer watching the video showing the researcher they hadn't met. This is consistent with young children's usual tendency to look longer at things that aren't familiar. And really, this is amazing. It suggests the children remembered the researcher they'd met just one time when they were only one-year-olds. Of course, as most of us forget memories from our first few years as we grow older, these early long-term memories will likely be lost in subsequent years.

Our second study is about music. For this study, researchers played music to babies through speakers located on either side of a human face. They waited until the babies got bored and averted their gaze from the face. And then they changed the mood of the music, either from sad to happy or the other way around. This mood switch made no difference to the three-year-olds. But for the nine-month-olds, it was enough to renew their interest and they started looking again in the direction of the face. This suggests that babies of that age can tell the difference between a happy melody and a sad tune.

Our final study is from 1980, but is still relevant today. In fact, it's one of the most famous pieces of research about infant emotion ever published. The study involved ordinary adults watching video clips of babies (nine months or younger). In the video clips, the babies made various facial expressions in response to real-life events, including playful interactions and painful ones. The adult observers were able to reliably discern an assortment of emotions on the babies' faces. These emotions included interest, joy, surprise, sadness, anger, disgust, contempt and fear. Next week, we'll be looking at this last study more closely. In fact, we will be viewing some of the video clips from that study and together see how well we do in discerning the babies' emotions.

19. What are the three interesting studies about?
20. What does the second study find about nine-month-old babies?
21. What is the 1980 study about?

九、讲座类题型强化练习

练习1

19. A) Respect their traditional culture.
    B) Attend their business seminars.
    C) Research their specific demands.
    D) Adopt the right business strategies.   答案:(   )

20. A) Showing them your palm.
    B) Giving them gifts of great value.
    C) Drinking alcohol on certain days of a month.
    D) Clicking your fingers loudly in their presence.   答案:(   )

21. A) They are very easy to satisfy.
    B) They have a strong sense of worth.
    C) They trend to be friendly and enthusiastic.
    D) They have a break from 2:00 to 5:30 p.m.   答案:(   )

练习2

19. A) They do more harm than good.
    B) They have often been ignored.
    C) They do not help build friendship.
    D) They may not always be negative.   答案:(   )

20. A) Biased sources of information.
    B) Ignorance of cultural differences.
    C) Misinterpretation of Shakespeare.
    D) Tendency to jump to conclusions.   答案:(   )

21. A) They are hard to dismiss once attached to a certain group.
    B) They may have a negative impact on people they apply to.
    C) They persist even when circumstances have changed.
    D) They are often applied to minorities and ethnic people.   答案:(   )

22. A) They impact people more or less in the same way.
    B) Some people are more sensitive to them than others.
    C) A positive stereotype may help one achieve better results.
    D) A negative stereotype sticks while a positive one does not.   答案:(   )

练习3

22. A) Its middle-class is disappearing.
    B) Its wealth is rationally distributed.
    C) Its population is rapidly growing.
    D) Its cherished dream is coming true.   答案:(   )

23. A) Success was but a dream without conscientious effort.
    B) They could realize their dreams through hard work.
    C) A few dollars could go a long way.
    D) Wealth was shared by all citizens.   答案:(   )

24. A) Better working conditions.
    B) Better-paying jobs.

C) High social status.

D) Full employment.   答案:(   )

25. A) Reduce the administrative costs.

    B) Adopt effective business models.

    C) Hire part-time employees only.

    D) Make use of the latest technology.   答案:(   )

练习 4

22. A) They were on the verge of breaking up.

    B) They were compatible despite differences.

    C) They quarreled a lot and never resolved their arguments.

    D) They argued persistently about whether to have children.   答案:(   )

23. A) Neither of them has any brothers or sisters.

    B) Neither of them won their parents' favor.

    C) They weren't spoiled in their childhood.

    D) They didn't like to be the apple of their parents' eyes.   答案:(   )

24. A) They are usually good at making friends.

    B) They tend to be adventurous and creative.

    C) They are often content with what they have.

    D) They tend to be self-assured and responsible.   答案:(   )

25. A) They enjoy making friends.

    B) They tend to be well adjusted.

    C) They are least likely to take initiative.

    D) They usually have successful marriages.   答案:(   )

The Listening Scripts

练习 1

Good morning, ladies and gentlemen! And welcome to the third in our series of business seminars in the program—Doing Business Abroad. Today we are going to look at intercultural awareness, that is, the fact that not everyone is British, not everyone speaks English, and not everyone does business in the British way. And why should they? If overseas business people are selling to us, then they will make every effort to speak English and to respect our traditions and methods. It is only polite for us to do the same when we visit them. It is not only polite. It is essential if we want to sell British products overseas.

First, a short quiz. Let's see how interculturally aware you are.

Question 1: Where must you not drink alcohol on the first and seventh of every month?

Question 2: Where should you never admire your host's possessions?

Question 3: How should you attract the waiter during a business lunch in Bangkok?

And Question 4: Where should you try to make all your appointments either before 2: 00 or after 5: 30 p. m.? OK. Everyone had a chance to make some notes? Right. Here are the answers—although I am sure that the information could equally well apply to countries other than those I have chosen. So No. 1, you must not drink alcohol on the first and seventh of the month in India. In international hotels you may find it served, but if you are having a meal with an Indian colleague, remember to avoid asking for a beer if your arrival coincides with one of those dates. No. 2: In Arab countries, the politeness and generosity of the people is without parallel. If you admire your colleague's beautiful golden bowls, you may well find yourself being presented with them as a present. This is not a cheap way to do your shopping, however, as your host will, quite correctly, expect you to respond by presenting him with a gift of equal worth and beauty. In Thailand, clicking the fingers, clapping your hands, or just shouting "Waiter" will embarrass your hosts, fellow diners, the waiter himself, and most of all, you! Place your palm downward and make an inconspicuous waving gesture, which will produce instant and satisfying results. And finally, in Spain, some businessmen maintain the pattern of working until about 2 o'clock and then returning to the office from 5: 30 to 8: 00, 9: 00 or 10: 00 in the evening.

19. What should you do when doing business with foreigners?
20. What must you avoid doing with your Indian colleague?
21. What do we learn about some Spanish business people?

练习 2

Stereotype may sounds like a bad word. but there's nothing bad about it. For one thing. stereotypes are often accurate. When you ask people about their concept of stereotypes, they get it pretty much right. Also, stereotypes are often positive, particularly of groups that we ourselves belong to. Some of the statistical generalizations may be positive as some groups have reputations for being smart, for being loyal, for being brave, for all sorts of things that are not at all negative. And so there's nothing inherently wrong about stereotypes.

But there are problems with stereotypes. For one thing, they're reliable insofar as they're based on unbiased samples. But a lot of the information we get about human groups is through biased sources like how they're represented in the media. And if these sources don't give you an accurate depiction, your stereotype won't be accurate.

For example, many Jews have been troubled by Shakespeare's depiction of Shylock. If the only Jew you know is Shakespeare's Shylock, it's going to be a very bad impression. So one problem with stereotypes is while we are good at drawing conclusions from them, often our information isn't reliable.

A second problem is that stereotypes, regardless of whether or not they're accurate, can have a negative effect on the people that they apply to. And this is what psychologist, Claude Steele, described as stereotype threat. He has a vivid example of this. Here's how to make African-Americans do worse on a math test. You have the test and you put on the test that they have to identify their race. The very act of acknowledging that they are African-Americans when given a test ignites in them thoughts of their own stereotype which is negative regarding academics and that makes them do worse. Want to know how to make a woman do worse on a math test? Same thing, get her to write down her sex.

One recent study found a sort of clever twist on this. When Asian American women are given a test and they're asked to mark down their race, they do better than they would otherwise do. They're reminded of a positive stereotype that boosts their morale. You ask them, on the other hand, to mark down their sex, they do worse because they're reminded of a negative stereotype. That's an example of how stereotypes have a potentially damaging effect on people.

19. What does the speaker say about stereotypes?
20. What leads to the bias of stereotypes?
21. What does the speaker say is a problem with stereotypes?
22. What did one recent study find about stereotypes?

练习3

We often hear people say that America is a land of opportunity, a country built on hope to aspire the greatness on the American dream. But is the dream as we once knew it dying?

Today's demographics show that the middle-class is disappearing and now the richest 1% of the population has mastered more wealth than the bottom 90%. Once upon a time, Americans thought that if they worked hard enough, even in the phase of adversity, they would be rewarded with success. These days, though, the divide between rich and poor is greater than it has ever been.

The question is, what is it going to take to change things? Maybe one day soon, real change will actually be made in our nation and the gap will be eradicated. But what happens in the meantime? Is there something that we can do to close the gap? Is there something that we can do to prove that a little compassion goes a long way?

If we want to fix the problem of the income gap, first, we have to understand it. It is a grim reality that you can have one person who only makes around $13,000 a year, or across town, another is making millions. For me, it is kind of astonishing. And if you ask low-income people what's the one thing that will change their life, they'll say "a full-time job." That's all they aspire to. So why is it so difficult for so many people to find employment? It partly comes down to profit-driven business models that are built around low-wage work and part-time jobs that don't provide benefits. Businessmen, in order to boost profits, hire employees as part time workers only. This means they are paid the lowest legal wage and receive no health care or other benefits provided to full-time employees.

Simultaneously, technological advancement and a global economy has reduced the demand for well-paying blue-collar jobs here in the United Sates. The cumulative effect of these two factors is that many Americans are forced to take two or more part-time jobs, just to make ends meet. What has become obvious to me when it comes to the income gap is that there needs to be an opportunity for the people at the bottom to push them back up and push them into the middle-class to give them hope in their lives.

22. What do the surveys show about America according to the speaker?
23. What did Americans used to believe?
24. What do low-income people aspire to?
25. What do businessmen do to increase their revenues?

练习4

Ronald and Lois, married for two decades, consider themselves a happy couple. But in the early years of their marriage, both were disturbed by persistent arguments that seemed to fade away without ever being truly resolved. They uncovered clues to what was going wrong by researching a fascinating subject: how birth order affects not only your personality, but also how compatible you are with your mate. Ronald and Lois are only children, and "onlies" grow up accustomed to being the apple of their parents' eyes. Match two onlies and you have partners who subconsciously expect each other to continue fulfilling this expectation, while neither has much experience in the "giving" end. Here's a list of common birth-order characteristics—and some thoughts on the best and worst marital matches for each. The oldest tends to be self-assured, responsible, a high achiever, and relatively serious and reserved. He may be slow to make friends, perhaps content with only one companion. The best matches are with a youngest, an "only", or a mate raised in a large family. The worst match is with another oldest, since the two will be too sovereign to share a household comfortably. The youngest child of the family thrives on attention and tends to be outgoing, adventurous, optimistic, creative and less ambitious than others in the family. He may lack self-discipline and have difficulty making decisions on his own. A youngest brother of brothers, often unpredictable and romantic, will match best with an oldest sister of brothers. The youngest sister of brothers is best matched with an oldest brother of sisters, who will happily indulge these traits. The middle child is influenced by many variables; however, middles are less likely to take initiative and more anxious and self-critical than others. Middles often successfully marry other middles, since both are strong on tact, not so strong on the aggressiveness and tend to crave affection. The only child is often most comfortable when alone. But since an "only" tends to be a well-adjusted individual, she'll eventually learn to relate to any chosen spouse. The male only child expects his wife to make life easier without getting much in return. He is sometimes best matched with a younger sister of brothers. The female only child, who tends to be slightly more flexible, is well matched with an older man, who will indulge her tendency to test his love. Her worst match? Another "only", of course.

22. what does the speaker say about Ronald and Lois's early years of married life?
23. What do we learn about Ronald and Lois?
24. What does the speaker say about the oldest child in a family?
25. What does the speaker say about the only children?

阅读专项突破

主讲：田静老师

微信公众号：田静老师

微博/B 站：考研英语田静

一、大学英语六级考试题型

六级笔试试卷构成

试卷结构	测试内容	测试题型	题目数量	分值比例	考试时间
写作	写作	短文写作	1	15%	30 分钟
听力理解	长对话	选择题（单选题）	8	8%	30 分钟
	听力篇章	选择题（单选题）	7	7%	
	讲话/报道/讲座	选择题（单选题）	10	20%	
阅读理解	词汇理解	选词填空	10	5%	40 分钟
	长篇阅读	匹配	10	10%	
	仔细阅读	选择题（单选题）	10	20%	
翻译	汉译英	段落翻译	1	15%	30 分钟
总计			57	100%	130 分钟

二、2021 年大学英语六级考试阅读真题

2021 年 12 月大学英语六级考试阅读真题（第 1 套）

（本套试题中的 Section A 对应主书第 2 套 Section A）

Part Ⅲ　　　　　　　　Reading Comprehension　　　　　　　（40 minutes）

Section A

Directions: In this section, there is a passage with ten blanks. You are required to select one word for each blank from a list of choices given in a word bank following the passage. Read the passage through carefully before making your choices. Each choice in the bank is identified by a letter. Please mark the corresponding letter for each item on *Answer Sheet 2* with a single line through the centre. You may not use any of the *words in the bank more than once.*

If you think life is wonderful and expect it to stay that way, then you may have a good chance of living to a ripe old age, at least that is what the findings of a new study suggest. That study found that participants who reported the highest levels of optimism were far more likely to live to age 85 or __26__. This was compared to those participants who reported the lowest levels of optimism. It is __27__ that the findings held even after the researchers considered factors that could __28__ the link, including whether participants had health conditions such as heart disease or cancer, or whether they experienced depression. The results add to a growing body of evidence that certain psychological factors may predict a longer life __29__. For example, previous studies have found that more optimistic people have a lower risk of developing chronic diseases, and a lower risk of __30__ death. However, the new study appears to be the first to __31__ look at the relationship between optimism and longevity. The researchers __32__ that the link found in the new study was not as strong when they factored in the effects of certain health behaviors, including exercise levels, sleep habits and diet. This suggests that these behaviors may, at least in part, explain the link. In other words, optimism may __33__ good habits that bolster health. It is also important to note that the study found only a __34__, as researchers did not prove for certain that optimism leads to a longer life. However, if the findings are true, they suggest that optimism could serve as a psychological __35__ that promotes health and a longer life.

A) affect	I) plausibly
B) beyond	J) premature
C) conceded	K) reconciled
D) correlation	L) span
E) foster	M) specifically
F) henceforth	N) spiral
G) lofty	O) trait
H) noteworthy	

选词填空解题步骤

1. _____选项：把选项按照_____进行_____。

例如，上面的选项中有
动词：

名词：
_____

形容词：
_____

副词：
_____

2. 阅读原文：通过本句和上下文综合判断填空中的_____和_____。

例如，上面的原文中：

- That study found that participants who reported the highest levels of optimism were far more likely to live to age 85 or ___26___.
- The researchers ___32___ that the link found in the new study was not as strong when they factored in the effects of certain health behaviors, including exercise levels, sleep habits and diet.
- In other words, optimism may ___33___ good habits that bolster health.
- It is also important to note that the study found only a ___34___, as researchers did not prove for certain that optimism leads to a longer life.

Section B

Directions: *In this section, you are going to read a passage with ten statements attached to it. Each statement contains information given in one of the paragraphs. Identify the paragraph from which the information is derived. You may choose a paragraph more than once. Each paragraph is marked with a letter. Answer the questions by marking the corresponding letter on **Answer Sheet 2**.*

No one in fashion is surprised that Burberry burnt £28 million of stock

[A] Last week, Burberry's annual report revealed that £28.6 million worth of stock was burnt last year. The news has left investors and consumers outraged but comes as little surprise to those in the fashion industry.

[B] The practice of destroying unsold stock, and even rolls of unused fabric, is commonplace for luxury labels. Becoming too widely available at a cheaper price through discount stores discourages full-price sales. Sending products for recycling leaves them vulnerable to being stolen and sold on the black market. Jasmine Bina, CEO of brand strategy agency Concept

Bureau explains, "Typically, luxury brands rally around exclusivity to protect their business interests, namely intellectual property and preservation of brand *equity* (资产)." She stated she had heard rumors of stock burning but not specific cases until this week.

[C] Another reason for the commonplace practice is a financial incentive for brands exporting goods to America. United States Customs states that if imported merchandise is unused and destroyed under their supervision, 99% of the duties, taxes or fees paid on the merchandise may be recovered. It is incredibly difficult to calculate how much dead stock currently goes to waste. While there are incentives to do it, there's no legal obligation to report it.

[D] A source, who chose to remain anonymous, shared her experience working in a Burberry store in New York in October 2016. "My job was to toss items in boxes so they could be sent to be burned. It was killing me inside because all that leather and fur went to waste and animals had died for nothing. I couldn't stay there any longer, their business practices threw me off the roof." In May this year, Burberry announced it was taking fur out of its catwalk shows and reviewing its use elsewhere in the business. "Even though we asked the management, they refused to give us detailed answers as to why they would do this with their collection," continued the source, who left her role within two weeks. She has since worked with another high-profile, luxury label.

[E] In an online forum post, which asked if it's true that Louis Vuitton burned its bags, Ahmed Bouchfaa, who claimed to work for Louis Vuitton, responded that the brand holds sales of old stock for staff members twice a year. Items which have still not sold after several sales are destroyed. "Louis Vuitton doesn't have public sales. They either sell a product at a given price or discontinue it. This is to make sure that everybody pays the same price for an item," he says. He goes on to disclose the strict guidelines around the employee sales: "You may buy gifts for someone, but they track each item, and if your gift ends up online they know who to ask." One investor commenting on the Burberry figures was reportedly outraged that the unsold goods were not even offered to investors before they were destroyed.

[F] Richemont, who owns several luxury brands, hit the headlines in May for taking back £437 million of watches for destruction in the last two years to avoid marked-down prices. It's not just luxury brands either. In October last year, a Danish TV show exposed H&M for burning 12 tonnes of unsold clothing since 2013. In a statement, the high street retailer defended itself by saying that the burnt clothing had failed safety tests: "The products to which the media are referring have been tested in external laboratories. The test results show that one of the products is mold infested and the other product contains levels of lead that are too high.

Those products have rightly been stopped in accordance with our safety routines." In March, a report revealed that H&M was struggling with $4.3 billion worth of unsold stock. The brand told *The New York Times* that the plan was to reduce prices to move the stock, arguably encouraging consumers to buy and throw away with little thought.

[G] Over-production is perhaps the biggest concern for Burberry. While there has been much outrage at the elitist connotation of burning goods rather than making them affordable, executives at the British fashion house are no doubt struggling to defend how they miscalculated production. The waste has been put down to burning old cosmetic stock to make way for their new beauty range. However, while the value of destroyed stock is up from £26.9 million last year, it's an even more significant increase from 2016's figure of £18.8 million, highlighting that this is an ongoing issue.

[H] In September 2016, Burberry switched to a "see now, buy now" catwalk show format. The move was a switch to leverage on the coverage of their fashion week show to make stock available immediately to consumers. This is opposed to the traditional format of presenting to the industry, taking orders for production and becoming available in six months' time. While Burberry announced "record-breaking" online reach and engagement, there has been little evidence to suggest that the strategy has had a significant effect on sales, particularly as the *hype* (炒作) slows across the season. In February they made adjustments to the format, dropping some catwalk items immediately and promising that others would launch in the coming months.

[I] In a statement, Burberry denied that switching to "see now, buy now" has had an impact on waste. A Burberry spokesperson further said, "On the occasions when disposal of products is necessary, we do so in a responsible manner. We are always seeking ways to reduce and revalue our waste. This is a core part of our strategy and we have forged partnerships and committed support to innovative organizations to help reach this goal."

[J] One such partnership is with Elvis & Kresse, an accessories brand working with reclaimed materials. Co-founder Kresse Wesling said, "Late last year we launched an ambitious five-year partnership with the Burberry Foundation. The main aim of this is to scale our leather rescue project, starting with off-cuts from the production of Burberry leather goods. We are working tirelessly to expand our solutions and would love to welcome anyone to our workshop to come and see what we are doing." At the moment, the partnership only addresses waste at the production stage and not unsold goods.

[K] While these are honorable schemes, it makes it harder for Burberry to defend these latest figures. Fifteen years ago, Burberry was at crisis point as their signature check pattern was widely imitated by cheap, imitation brands. It deterred luxury consumers who found their expensive clothing more closely associated with working-class youth culture than a prestigious heritage fashion house. In the year 2004, at the height of over-exposure of the Burberry check, the brand's turnover was £715.5 million. Under Christopher Bailey as creative director they turned the brand around and this past year revenue hit £2.73 billion.

[L] Bina believes that brands need to readdress their exclusivity tactic. "Exclusivity is starting to be challenged," she says, "I think that goes hand in hand with how luxury itself is being challenged. Access to fashion, and the brands who police it, are becoming less and less relevant. Things like health, enlightenment, and social and environmental responsibility are the new luxuries. These all come from within, not without. That's the challenge that traditional luxury brands will have to contend with in the mid- to long-term future."

36. Burberry's executives are trying hard to attribute their practice of destroying old products to miscalculated production.
37. Selling products at a discount will do greater harm to luxury brands than destroying them.
38. Imitated Burberry products discouraged luxury consumers from buying its genuine products.
39. Staff members of a luxury brand may buy its old stock at cheaper prices, but they are not allowed to resell them.
40. In future traditional luxury brands will have to adapt their business strategies to the changing concepts of luxury.
41. One luxury brand employee quit her job because she simply couldn't bear to see the destruction of unsold products.
42. Destroying old stock is a practice not just of luxury brands but of less prestigious fashion brands.
43. Burberry is working with a partner to make full use of leather materials to reduce waste.
44. Burberry's plan to destroy its unsold products worth millions of dollars aroused public indignation.
45. Burberry's change of marketing strategy to make a product available as soon as consumers see it on the fashion show did not turn out to be as effective as expected.

长篇阅读解题步骤

1. 先看_____：找出其中的可以用来_____的_____；

注意避开_____。

2. 再看_____：根据_____定位，注意_____。

例如，上面的题目中，

36. Burberry's executives are trying hard to attribute their practice of destroying old products to miscalculated production.

其中的_____是_____，检索原文之后定位段落_____。

37. Selling products at a discount will do greater harm to luxury brands than destroying them.

其中的_____是_____，检索原文之后定位段落_____。

44. Burberry's plan to destroy its unsold products worth millions of dollars aroused public indignation.

其中的_____是_____，检索原文之后定位段落_____。

Section C

Directions: *There are 2 passages in this section. Each passage is followed by some questions or unfinished statements. For each of them there are four choices marked A), B), C) and D). You should decide on the best choice and mark the corresponding letter on **Answer Sheet 2** with a single line through the centre.*

Passage One

Questions 46 to 50 are based on the following passage.

Social media is absolutely everywhere. Billions of people use social media on a daily basis to create, share, and exchange ideas, messages, and information. Both individuals and businesses post regularly to engage and interact with people from around the world. It is a powerful communication medium that simultaneously provides immediate, frequent, permanent, and wide-reaching information across the globe.

People post their lives on social media for the world to see. Facebook, Twitter, LinkedIn, and countless other social channels provide a quick and simple way to glimpse into a job candidate's personal life—both the positive and negative sides of it. Social media screening is tempting to use as part of the hiring process, but should employers make use of it when researching a potential candidate's background?

Incorporating the use of social media to screen job candidates is not an uncommon practice. A 2018 survey found that almost 70% of employers use social media to screen candidates before hiring them. But there are consequences and potential legal risks involved too. When done inappropriately, social media screening can be considered unethical or even illegal.

Social media screening is essentially scrutinising a job candidate's private life. It can reveal information about protected characteristics like age, race, nationality, disability, gender, religion, etc., and that could bias a hiring decision. Pictures or comments on a private page that are taken out of context could ruin a perfectly good candidate's chances of getting hired. This process could potentially give an unfair advantage to one candidate over another. It creates an unequal playing field and potentially provides hiring managers with information that can impact their hiring decision in a negative way.

It's hard to ignore social media as a screening tool. While there are things that you shouldn't see, there are some things that can be lawfully considered—making it a valuable source of relevant information too. Using social media screening appropriately can help ensure that you don't hire a toxic employee who will cost you money or stain your company's reputation. Consider the lawful side of this process and you may be able to hire the best employee ever. There is a delicate balance.

Screening job candidates on social media must be done professionally and responsibly. Companies should stipulate that they will never ask for passwords, be consistent, document decisions, consider the source used and be aware that other laws may apply. In light of this it is probably best to look later in the process and ask human resources for help in navigating it. Social media is here to stay. But before using social media to screen job candidates, consulting with management and legal teams beforehand is essential in order to comply with all laws.

46. What does the author mainly discuss in the passage?

　　A) The advantage of using social media in screening job candidates.

　　B) The potentially invasive nature of social media in everyday life.

　　C) Whether the benefits of social media outweigh the drawbacks.

　　D) Whether social media should be used to screen job candidates.

47. What might happen when social media is used to screen job candidates?

　　A) Moral or legal issues might arise.

　　B) Company reputation might suffer.

　　C) Sensational information might surface.

　　D) Hiring decisions might be complicated.

48. When could online personal information be detrimental to candidates?

　　A) When it is separated from context.

B) When it is scrutinised by an employer.

C) When it is magnified to a ruinous degree.

D) When it is revealed to the human resources.

49. How can employers use social media information to their advantage while avoiding unnecessary risks?

A) By tipping the delicate balance.

B) By using it in a legitimate way.

C) By keeping personal information on record.

D) By separating relevant from irrelevant data.

50. What does the author suggest doing before screening job candidates on social media?

A) Hiring professionals to navigate the whole process.

B) Anticipating potential risks involved in the process.

C) Seeking advice from management and legal experts.

D) Stipulating a set of rules for asking specific questions.

仔细阅读解题步骤

1. 先看_____: 找出其中的可以用来_____的_____。
2. 再看_____: 重点看其中的_____和_____。
   遇到_____，拿_____比对原文。

常见错误选项的"挖坑陷阱"：

46. What does the author mainly discuss in the passage?

    A) The advantage of using social media in screening job candidates.

    B) The potentially invasive nature of social media in everyday life.

    C) Whether the benefits of social media outweigh the drawbacks.

    如上，常见错误的"坑点"：_____。

47. What might happen when social media is used to screen job candidates?

    B) Company reputation might suffer.

    D) Hiring decisions might be complicated.

    如上，常见错误的"坑点"：_____。

49. How can employers use social media information to their advantage while avoiding

unnecessary risks?

C) By keeping personal information on record.

D) By separating relevant from irrelevant data.

如上，常见错误的"坑点"：_____。

50. What does the author suggest doing before screening job candidates on social media?

B) Anticipating potential risks involved in the process.

D) Stipulating a set of rules for asking specific questions.

如上，常见错误的"坑点"：_____。

Passage Two
Questions 51 to 55 are based on the following passage.

In recent years, the food industry has increased its use of labels. Whether the labels say 'non-GMO (非转基因的)' or 'no sugar,' or 'zero carbohydrates', consumers are increasingly demanding more information about what's in their food. One report found that 39 percent of consumers would switch from the brands they currently buy to others that provide clearer, more accurate product information. Food manufacturers are responding to the report with new labels to meet that demand, and they're doing so with an eye towards giving their products an advantage over the competition, and bolstering profits.

This strategy makes intuitive sense. If consumers say they want transparency, tell them exactly what is in your product. That is simply supplying a certain demand. But the marketing strategy in response to this consumer demand has gone beyond articulating what is in a product, to labeling what is NOT in the food. These labels are known as "absence claims" labels, and they represent an emerging labeling trend that is detrimental both to the consumers who purchase the products and the industry that supplies them.

For example, Hunt's put a "non-GMO" label on its canned crushed tomatoes a few years ago—despite the fact that at the time there was no such thing as a GMO tomato on the market. Some dairy companies are using the "non-GMO" label on their milk, despite the fact that all milk is naturally GMO-free, another label that creates unnecessary fear around food.

While creating labels that play on consumer fears and misconceptions about their food may give a company a temporary marketing advantage over competing products on the grocery aisle, in the long term this strategy will have just the opposite effect: by injecting fear into the discourse about our food, we run the risk of eroding consumer trust in not just a single product, but the entire food business.

Eventually, it becomes a question in consumers' minds: Were these foods ever safe? By purchasing and consuming these types of products, have I already done some kind of harm to my family or the planet? For food manufacturers, it will mean damaged consumer trust and lower sales for everyone. And this isn't just supposition. A recent study found that absence claims labels can create a stigma around foods even when there is no scientific evidence that they cause harm.

It's clear that food manufacturers must tread carefully when it comes to using absence claims. In addition to the likely negative long-term impact on sales, this verbal trick sends a message that innovations in farming and food processing are unwelcome, eventually leading to less efficiency, fewer choices for consumers, and ultimately, more costly food products. If we allow this kind of labeling to continue, we will all lose.

51. What trend has been observed in a report?

    A) Food manufacturers' rising awareness of product safety.

    B) Food manufacturers' changing strategies to bolster profits.

    C) Consumers' growing demand for eye-catching food labels.

    D) Consumers' increasing desire for clear product information.

52. What does the author say is manufacturers' new marketing strategy?

    A) Stressing the absence of certain elements in their products.

    B) Articulating the unique nutritional value of their products.

    C) Supplying detailed information of their products.

    D) Designing transparent labels for their products.

53. What point does the author make about non-GMO labels?

    A) They are increasingly attracting customers' attention.

    B) They create lots of trouble for GMO food producers.

    C) They should be used more for vegetables and milk.

    D) They cause anxiety about food among consumers.

54. What does the author say absence claims labels will do to food manufacturers?

    A) Cause changes in their marketing strategies.

    B) Help remove stigma around their products.

    C) Erode consumer trust and reduce sales.

    D) Decrease support from food scientists.

55. What does the author suggest food manufacturers do?

A) Take measures to lower the cost of food products.
B) Exercise caution about the use of absence claims.
C) Welcome new innovations in food processing.
D) Promote efficiency and increase food variety.

2021年12月大学英语六级考试阅读真题（第2套）

（本套试题中的 Section A 对应主书第1套，Section B 和 Section C 对应主书第3套）

Part Ⅲ　　　　　　　**Reading Comprehension**　　　　（40 minutes）

Section A

Directions: *In this section, there is a passage with ten blanks. You are required to select one word for each blank from a list of choices given in a word bank following the passage. Read the passage through carefully before making your choices. Each choice in the bank is identified by a letter. Please mark the corresponding letter for each item on* ***Answer Sheet 2*** *with a single line through the centre. You may not use any of the words in the bank more than once.*

According to psychologist Sharon Draper, our clothing choices can absolutely affect our well-being. When we wear ill-fitting clothes, or feel over- or under-dressed for an event, it's natural to feel self-conscious or even stressed. Conversely, she says, opting for clothes that fit well and __26__ with your sense of style can improve your confidence.

But can you improve your health through your __27__ clothing, without having to dash out and buy a whole new __28__? "Absolutely," says Draper. If your goal is to improve your thinking, she recommends picking clothes that fit well and are unlikely to encourage restlessness, so, avoid bows, ties and unnecessary __29__. It also helps to opt for clothes you __30__ as tying in with your goals, so, if you want to perform better at work, select pieces you view as professional. Draper says this fits in with the concept of behavioral activation, whereby __31__ in a behavior (in this case, selecting clothes) can set you on the path to then achieving your goals (working harder).

Another way to improve your __32__ of mind is to mix things up. Draper says we often feel stuck in a *rut*（常规）if we wear the same clothes—even if they're our favorites—thus opting for an item you don't wear often, or adding something different to an outfit, such as a hat, can __33__ shift your mood. On days when you're really __34__ to brave the world, Draper suggests selecting sentimental items of clothing, such as ones you wore on a special day, or given to you by a loved one, as clothes with __35__ associations can help you tap into constructive emotions.

A) accessories	I) perceive
B) align	J) positively
C) concurrently	K) profile
D) current	L) prospering
E) engaging	M) reluctant
F) fond	N) showcase
G) frame	O) wardrobe
H) locations	

Section B

Directions: *In this section, you are going to read a passage with ten statements attached to it. Each statement contains information given in one of the paragraphs. Identify the paragraph from which the information is derived. You may choose a paragraph more than once. Each paragraph is marked with a letter. Answer the questions by marking the corresponding letter on **Answer Sheet 2**.*

Do music lessons really make children smarter?

[A] A recent analysis found that most research mischaracterizes the relationship between music and skills enhancement.

[B] In 2004, a paper appeared in the journal *Psychological Science*, titled "Music Lessons Enhance IQ." The author, composer and psychologist Glenn Schellenberg had conducted an experiment with 144 children randomly assigned to four groups: one learned the keyboard for a year, one took singing lessons, one joined an acting class, and a control group had no extracurricular training. The IQ of the children in the two musical groups rose by an average of seven points in the course of a year; those in the other two groups gained an average of 4.3 points.

[C] Schellenberg had long been skeptical of the science supporting claims that music education enhances children's abstract reasoning, math, or language skills. If children who play the piano are smarter, he says, it doesn't necessarily mean they are smarter because they play the piano. It could be that the youngsters who play the piano also happen to be more ambitious or better at focusing on a task. Correlation, after all, does not prove causation.

[D] The 2004 paper was specifically designed to address those concerns. And as a passionate musician, Schellenberg was delighted when he turned up credible evidence that music has transfer effects on general intelligence. But nearly a decade later, in 2013, the Education Endowment Foundation funded a bigger study with more than 900 students. That study failed to confirm Schellenberg's findings, producing no evidence that music lessons improved math and literacy skills.

[E] Schellenberg took that news in stride while continuing to cast a skeptical eye on the research in his field. Recently, he decided to formally investigate just how often his fellow researchers in psychology and neuroscience make what he believes are erroneous—or at least premature—causal connections between music and intelligence. His results, published in May, suggest that many of his peers do just that.

[F] For his recent study, Schellenberg asked two research assistants to look for correlational studies on the effects of music education. They found a total of 114 papers published since 2000. To assess whether the authors claimed any causation, researchers then looked for telltale verbs in each paper's title and abstract, verbs like "enhance," "promote," "facilitate," and "strengthen." The papers were categorized as neuroscience if the study employed a brain imaging method like magnetic resonance, or if the study appeared in a journal that had "brain," "neuroscience," or a related term in its title. Otherwise the papers were categorized as psychology. Schellenberg, didn't tell his assistants what exactly he was trying to prove.

[G] After computing their assessments, Schellenberg concluded that the majority of the articles erroneously claimed that music training had a causal effect. The overselling, he also found, was more prevalent among neuroscience studies, three quarters of which mischaracterized a mere association between music training and skills enhancement as a cause-and-effect relationship. This may come as a surprise to some. Psychologists have been battling charges that they don't do "real" science for some time—in large part because many findings from classic experiments have proved unreproducible. Neuroscientists, on the other hand, armed with brain scans and *EEGs* (脑电图), have not been subject to the same degree of critique.

[H] To argue for a cause-and-effect relationship, scientists must attempt to explain why and how a connection could occur. When it comes to transfer effects of music, scientists frequently point to brain plasticity—the fact that the brain changes according to how we use it. When a child learns to play the violin, for example, several studies have shown that the brain region responsible for the fine motor skills of the left hand's fingers is likely to grow. And many experiments have shown that musical training improves certain hearing capabilities, like filtering voices from background noise or distinguishing the difference between the *consonants* (辅音) 'b' and 'g'.

[I] But Schellenberg remains highly critical of how the concept of plasticity has been applied in his field. "Plasticity has become an industry of its own," he wrote in his May paper. Practice does change the brain, he allows, but what is questionable is the assertion that these changes affect other brain regions, such as those responsible for spatial reasoning or math problems.

[J] Neuropsychologist Lutz Jäncke agrees. "Most of these studies don't allow for causal inferences," he said. For over two decades, Jancke has researched the effects of music lessons, and like Schellenberg, he believes that the only way to truly understand their effects is to run longitudinal studies. In such studies, researchers would need to follow groups of children with and without music lessons over a long period of time—even if the assignments are not completely random. Then they could compare outcomes for each group.

[K] Some researchers are starting to do just that. The neuroscientist Peter Schneider from Heidelberg University in Germany, for example, has been following a group of children for ten years now. Some of them were handed musical instruments and given lessons through a school-based program in the Ruhr region of Germany called Jedem Kind ein Instrument, or "an instrument for every child," which was carried out with government funding. Among these children, Schneider has found that those who were enthusiastic about music and who practiced voluntarily showed improvements in hearing ability, as well as in more general competencies, such as the ability to concentrate.

[L] To establish whether effects such as improved concentration are caused by music participation itself, and not by investing time in an extracurricular activity of any kind, Assal Habibi, a psychology professor at the University of Southern California, is conducting a five-year longitudinal study with children from low-income communities in Los Angeles. The youngsters fall into three groups: those who take after-school music, those who do after-school sports, and those with no structured afterschool program at all. After two years, Habibi and her colleagues reported seeing structural changes in the brains of the musically trained children, both locally and in the pathways connecting different parts of the brain.

[M] That may seem compelling, but Habibi's children were not selected randomly. Did the children who were drawn to music perhaps have something in them from the start that made them different but eluded the brain scanners? "As somebody who started taking piano lessons at the age of five and got up every morning at seven to practice, that experience changed me and made me part of who I am today," Schellenberg said. "The question is whether those kinds of experiences do so systematically across individuals and create exactly the same changes. And I think that is that huge leap of faith."

[N] Did he have a hidden talent that others didn't have? Or more endurance than his peers? Music researchers tend, like Schellenberg, to be musicians themselves, and as he noted in his recent paper, "the idea of positive cognitive and neural side effects from music training (and other pleasurable activities) is inherently appealing." He also admits that if he had children of his own, he would encourage them to take music lessons and go to university. "I would think that it makes them better people, more critical, just wiser in general," he said.

[O] But those convictions should be checked at the entrance to the lab, he added. Otherwise, the work becomes religion or faith. "You have to let go of your faith if you want to be a scientist."

36. Glenn Schellenberg's latest research suggests many psychologists and neuroscientists wrongly believe in the causal relationship between music and IQ.

37. The belief in the positive effects of music training appeals to many researchers who are musicians themselves.

38. Glenn Schellenberg was doubtful about the claim that music education helps enhance children's intelligence.

39. Glenn Schellenberg came to the conclusion that most of the papers assessed made the wrong claim regarding music's effect on intelligence.

40. You must abandon your unverified beliefs before you become a scientist.

41. Lots of experiments have demonstrated that people with music training can better differentiate certain sounds.

42. Glenn Schellenberg's findings at the beginning of this century were not supported by a larger study carried out some ten years later.

43. One researcher shares Glenn Schellenberg's view that it is necessary to conduct long-term developmental studies to understand the effects of music training.

44. Glenn Schellenberg's research assistants had no idea what he was trying to prove in his new study.

45. Glenn Schellenberg admits that practice can change certain areas of the brain but doubts that the change can affect other areas.

Section C

Directions: *There are 2 passages in this section. Each passage is followed by some questions or unfinished statements. For each of them there are four choices marked A), B), C) and D). You should decide on the best choice and mark the corresponding letter on* **Answer Sheet 2** *with a single line through the centre.*

Passage One

Questions 46 to 50 are based on the following passage.

The trend toward rationality and enlightenment was endangered long before the advent of the World Wide Web. As Neil Postman noted in his 1985 book *Amusing Ourselves to Death*, the rise of television introduced not just a new medium but a new discourse: a gradual shift from a *typographic* (印刷的) culture to a photographic one, which in turn meant a shift from rationality to emotions, exposition to entertainment. In an image-centered and pleasure-driven world, Postman noted, there is no place for rational thinking, because you simply cannot think with images. It is text that enables us to "uncover lies, confusions and overgeneralizations, and to detect abuses of logic and common sense. It also means to weigh ideas, to compare and contrast assertions, to connect one generalization to another."

The dominance of television was not confined to our living rooms. It overturned all of those habits of mind, fundamentally changing our experience of the world, affecting the conduct of politics, religion, business, and culture. It reduced many aspects of modern life to entertainment, sensationalism, and commerce. "Americans don't talk to each other, we entertain each other," Postman wrote. "They don't exchange ideas, they exchange images. They do not argue with propositions, they argue with good looks, celebrities and commercials."

At first, the web seemed to push against this trend. When it emerged towards the end of the 1980s as a purely text-based medium, it was seen as a tool to pursue knowledge, not pleasure. Reason and thought were most valued in this garden—all derived from the project of the Enlightenment. Universities around the world were among the first to connect to this new medium, which hosted discussion groups, informative personal or group blogs, electronic magazines, and academic mailing lists and forums. It was an intellectual project, not about commerce or control, created in a scientific research center in Switzerland. And for more than a decade, the web created an alternative space that threatened television's grip on society.

Social networks, though, have since colonized the web for television's values. From Facebook to Instagram, the medium refocuses our attention on videos and images, rewarding emotional appeals—'like' buttons—over rational ones. Instead of a quest for knowledge, it engages us in an endless *zest* (热情) for instant approval from an audience, for which we are constantly but unconsciously performing. (It's telling that, while Google began life as a PhD thesis, Facebook started as a tool to judge classmates' appearances.) It reduces our curiosity by showing us exactly what we already want and think, based on our profiles and preferences. The Enlightenment's *motto* (座右铭) of 'Dare to know' has become 'Dare not to care to know.'

46. What did Neil Postman say about the rise of television?

   A) It initiated a change from dominance of reason to supremacy of pleasure.

   B) It brought about a gradual shift from cinema going to home entertainment.

   C) It started a revolution in photographic technology.

   D) It marked a new age in the entertainment industry.

47. According to the passage, what is the advantage of text reading?

   A) It gives one access to huge amounts of information.

   B) It allows more information to be processed quickly.

   C) It is capable of enriching one's life.

   D) It is conducive to critical thinking.

48. How has television impacted Americans?

   A) It has given them a lot more to argue about.

   B) It has brought celebrities closer to their lives.

   C) It has made them care more about what they say.

   D) It has rendered their interactions more superficial.

49. What does the passage say about the World Wide Web?

   A) It was developed primarily for universities worldwide.

   B) It was created to connect people in different countries.

   C) It was viewed as a means to quest for knowledge.

   D) It was designed as a discussion forum for university students.

50. What do we learn about users of social media?

   A) They are bent on looking for an alternative space for escape.

   B) They are constantly seeking approval from their audience.

   C) They are forever engaged in hunting for new information.

   D) They are unable to focus their attention on tasks for long.

Passage Two
Questions 51 to 55 are based on the following passage.

   According to a recent study, a small but growing proportion of the workforce is affected to some degree by a sense of entitlement. Work is less about what they can contribute but more about what they can take. It can lead to workplace dysfunction and diminish their own job satisfaction. I'm not referring to employees who are legitimately dissatisfied with their employment conditions due to, say, being denied fair pay or flexible work practices. I'm talking about those who consistently believe they deserve special treatment and generous rewards. It's an expectation that exists irrespective of their abilities or levels of performance.

As a result of that discrepancy between the privileges they feel they're owed and their inflated sense of self-worth, they don't work as hard for their employer. They prefer instead to slack off. It's a tendency which many scholars believe begins in childhood due to parents who overindulge their kids. This thereby leads them to expect the same kind of spoilt treatment throughout their adult lives. And yet despite how these employees feel, it's obviously important for their manager to nonetheless find out how to keep them motivated. And, by virtue of that heightened motivation, to perform well.

The research team from several American universities surveyed more than 240 individuals. They sampled managers as well as team members. Employee entitlement was measured by statements such as "I honestly feel I'm just more deserving than others." The respondents had to rate the extent of their agreement. Employee engagement, meanwhile, was assessed with statements like "I really throw myself into my work." The findings revealed ethical leadership is precisely what alleviates the negative effects of employee entitlement. That's because rather than indulging employees or neglecting them, ethical leaders communicate very direct and clear expectations. They also hold employees accountable for their behaviors and are genuinely committed to doing the right thing. Additionally, these leaders are consistent in their standards. They're also less likely to deviate in how they treat employees.

This means, when confronted by an entitled team member, an ethical leader is significantly disinclined to accommodate their demands. He or she will instead point out, constructively and tactfully, exactly how their inflated sense of deservingness is somewhat distorted. They'd then go further to explain the specific, and objective, criteria the employee must meet to receive their desired rewards. This shift away from unrealistic expectations is successful because entitled employees feel more confident that ethical leaders will deliver on their promises. This occurs because they're perceived to be fair and trustworthy. The researchers, however, exercise caution by warning no one single response is the perfect remedy. But there's no denying ethical leadership is at least a critical step in the right direction.

51. What does a recent study find about a growing number of workers?

    A) They attempt to make more contributions.

B) They feel they deserve more than they get.

C) They attach importance to job satisfaction.

D) They try to diminish workplace dysfunction.

52. Why don't some employees work hard according to many scholars?

A) They lack a strong sense of self-worth.

B) They were spoiled when growing up.

C) They have received unfair treatment.

D) They are overindulged by their boss.

53. What is a manager supposed to do to enable workers to do a better job?

A) Be aware of their emotions.

B) Give them timely promotions.

C) Keep a record of their performance.

D) Seek ways to sustain their motivation.

54. What do the research findings reveal about ethical leaders?

A) They are held accountable by their employees.

B) They are always transparent in their likes and dislikes.

C) They convey their requirements in a straightforward way.

D) They make it a point to be on good terms with their employees.

55. What kind of leaders are viewed as ethical by entitled employees?

A) Those who can be counted on to fulfill commitments.

B) Those who can do things beyond normal expectations.

C) Those who exercise caution in making major decisions.

D) Those who know how to satisfy their employees' needs.

2021年12月大学英语六级考试阅读真题（第3套）

（本套试题中的 Section B 和 Section C 对应主书第2套）

Part Ⅲ　　　　　　　　Reading Comprehension　　　　　（40 minutes）

Section B

Directions: *In this section, you are going to read a passage with ten statements attached to it. Each statement contains information given in one of the paragraphs. Identify the paragraph from which the information is derived. You may choose a paragraph more* than once. Each paragraph is marked with a letter. Answer the questions by marking the corresponding letter on **Answer Sheet 2**.

Why facts don't change our minds

[A] The economist J. K. Galbraith once wrote, "Faced with a choice between changing one's mind and proving there is no need to do so, almost everyone gets busy with the proof."

[B] Leo Tolstoy was even bolder: "The most difficult subjects can be explained to the most slow-witted man if he has not formed any idea of them already; but the simplest thing cannot be made clear to the most intelligent man if he is firmly persuaded that he knows already, without a shadow of a doubt, what is laid before him."

[C] What's going on here? Why don't facts change our minds? And why would someone continue to believe a false or inaccurate idea anyway? How do such behaviors serve us? Humans need a reasonably accurate view of the world in order to survive. If your model of reality is wildly different from the actual world, then you struggle to take effective actions each day. However, truth and accuracy are not the only things that matter to the human mind. Humans also seem to have a deep desire to belong.

[D] In *Atomic Habits*, I wrote, "Humans are herd animals. We want to fit in, to bond with others, and to earn the respect and approval of our peers. Such inclinations are essential to our survival. For most of our evolutionary history, our ancestors lived in tribes. Becoming separated from the tribe—or worse, being cast out—was a death sentence."

[E] Understanding the truth of a situation is important, but so is remaining part of a tribe. While these two desires often work well together, they occasionally come into conflict. In many circumstances, social connection is actually more helpful to your daily life than understanding the truth of a particular fact or idea. The Harvard psychologist Steven Pinker put it this way, "People are embraced or condemned according to their beliefs, so one function of the mind may be to hold beliefs that bring the belief-holder the greatest number of allies, protectors, or *disciples* (信徒), rather than beliefs that are most likely to be true."

[F] We don't always believe things because they are correct. Sometimes we believe things because they make us look good to the people we care about. I thought Kevin Simler put it well when he wrote, "if a brain anticipates that it will be rewarded for adopting a particular belief, it's perfectly happy to do so, and doesn't much care where the reward comes from—whether it's *pragmatic* (实用主义的) (better outcomes resulting from better decisions), social (better treatment from one's peers), or some mix of the two."

[G] False beliefs can be useful in a social sense even if they are not useful in a factual sense. For lack of a better phrase, we might call this approach "factually false, but socially accurate." When we have to choose between the two, people often select friends and family over facts. This insight not only explains why we might hold our tongue at a dinner party or look the other way when our parents say something offensive, but also reveals a better way to change the minds of others.

[H] Convincing someone to change their mind is really the process of convincing them to change their tribe. If they abandon their beliefs, they run the risk of losing social ties. You can't expect someone to change their mind if you take away their community too. You have to give them somewhere to go. Nobody wants their worldview torn apart if loneliness is the outcome.

[I] The way to change people's minds is to become friends with them, to integrate them into your tribe, to bring them into your circle. Now, they can change their beliefs without the risk of being abandoned socially.

[J] Perhaps it is not difference, but distance, that breeds tribalism and hostility. As proximity increases, so does understanding. I am reminded of Abraham Lincoln's quote, "I don't like that man. I must get to know him better."

[K] Facts don't change our minds. Friendship does. Years ago, Ben Casnocha mentioned an idea to me that I haven't been able to shake: The people who are most likely to change our minds are the ones we agree with on 98 percent of topics. If someone you know, like, and trust believes a radical idea, you are more likely to give it merit, weight, or consideration. You already agree with them in most areas of life. Maybe you should change your mind on this one too. But if someone wildly different than you proposes the same radical idea, well, it's easy to dismiss them as nuts.

[L] One way to visualize this distinction is by mapping beliefs on a spectrum. If you divide this spectrum into 10 units and you find yourself at Position 7, then there is little sense in trying to convince someone at Position 1. The gap is too wide. When you're at Position 7, your time is better spent connecting with people who are at Positions 6 and 8, gradually pulling them in your direction.

[M] The most heated arguments often occur between people on opposite ends of the spectrum, but the most frequent learning occurs from people who are nearby. The closer you are to someone, the more likely it becomes that the one or two beliefs you don't share will bleed over into your own mind and shape your thinking. The further away an idea is from your current position, the more likely you are to reject it outright. When it comes to changing people's minds, it is very difficult to jump from one side to another. You can't jump down the spectrum. You have to slide down it.

[N] Any idea that is sufficiently different from your current worldview will feel threatening. And the best place to ponder a threatening idea is in a non-threatening environment. As a result, books are often a better vehicle for transforming beliefs than conversations or debates. In conversation, people have to carefully consider their status and appearance. They want to save face and avoid looking stupid. When confronted with an uncomfortable set of facts, the tendency is often to double down on their current position rather than publicly admit to being wrong. Books resolve this tension. With a book, the conversation takes place inside someone's head and without the risk of being judged by others. It's easier to be open-minded when you aren't feeling defensive.

[O] There is another reason bad ideas continue to live on, which is that people continue to talk about them. Silence is death for any idea. An idea that is never spoken or written down dies with the person who conceived it. Ideas can only be remembered when they are repeated. They can only be believed when they are repeated. I have already pointed out that people repeat ideas to signal they are part of the same social group. But here's a crucial point most people miss: People also repeat bad ideas when they complain about them. Before you can criticize an idea, you have to reference that idea. You end up repeating the ideas you're hoping people will forget—but, of course, people can't forget them because you keep talking about them. The more you repeat a bad idea, the more likely people are to believe it.

[P] Let's call this phenomenon Clear's Law of Recurrence: The number of people who believe an idea is directly proportional to the number of times it has been repeated during the last year—even if the idea is false.

36. According to the author, humans can hardly survive if separated from their community.

37. People often accept false beliefs because they prioritize social bonds rather than facts.

38. Most often people learn from those close to them.

39. Sometimes people adopt certain beliefs in order to leave a favorable impression on those dear to them.

40. Compared with face-to-face communication, books often provide a better medium for changing people's beliefs.

41. On many occasions in daily life, people benefit more from their social bonds than from knowing the truth.

42. If you want to change somebody's beliefs, you should first establish social connection with them.

43. Humans cannot survive without a fair knowledge of the actual world.

44. Repetition of bad ideas increases their chances of being accepted.

45. Nobody is willing to give up their beliefs at the risk of getting isolated.

Section C

Directions: *There are 2 passages in this section. Each passage is followed by some questions or unfinished statements. For each of them there are four choices marked A), B), C) and D). You should decide on the best choice and mark the corresponding letter on **Answer Sheet 2** with a single line through the centre.*

Passage One

Questions 46 to 50 are based on the following passage.

The subject of automation and its role in our economy has taken hold in American public discourse. Technology broadly and automation specifically are dramatically reshaping the way we work. And we need to have a plan for what's still to come.

We don't have to look further than our own communities to see the devastating impact of automation. From automated warehouses to cashierless grocery stores to neighborhood libraries that offer self-checkout lanes instead of employing real people—automation is increasingly replacing jobs and leaving too few good new jobs behind.

The statistics in manufacturing are staggering. Despite the widespread fears about trade, a recent report showed that just 13 percent of jobs lost in manufacturing are due to trade—the rest of the losses have been due to advances in technology.

That is why more people are criticizing the ever-increasing role of technology in our economy. Our country is manufacturing more than ever before, but we are doing it with fewer workers. However, it's not just factories that are seeing losses—software and information technology are also having a dramatic impact on jobs most people think are secure from the forces of a rapidly-changing economy. Something transformative is happening in America that is having an adverse effect on American families. Whether policymakers and politicians admit it or not, workers have made clear their feelings about their economic insecurity and desire to keep good jobs in America.

So why are people so insistent on ignoring the perils of automation? They are failing to look ahead at a time when planning for the future is more important than ever. Resisting automation is futile: it is as inevitable as industrialization was before it. I sincerely hope that those who assert that automation will make us more effective and pave the way for new occupations are right, but the reality of automation's detrimental effects on workers makes me skeptical. No one can currently say where the new jobs are coming from or when, and any sensible company or country should prepare for all alternatives.

I'm not overstating the danger: look at what's happened to the labor force. According to economic research, one in six working-age men, 25-54, doesn't have a job. Fifty years ago, nearly 100 percent of men that age were working. Women's labor force participation, meanwhile, has slipped back to the level it was at in the late 1980s.

American families and prominent business leaders are aware that there's a big problem with automation. The value of a college degree is diminishing, and our upward mobility is declining. If we want an economy that allows everyone to be economically secure, we need to start thinking about how we can rightfully address automation.

46. What can we observe from the author's description of our communities?

  A) The growing passion for automation.

  B) The shift from manual jobs to IT ones.

  C) Their changing views on employment.

  D) Their fading employment opportunities.

47. What do we learn from a recent report?

  A) The manufacturing sector is declining at a fast rate.

  B) The concerns about the effect of trade are exaggerated.

  C) The fears about trade have been spreading far and wide.

  D) The impact of trade on employment has been staggering.

48. What does the passage tell us about American workers in an era of transformation?

  A) They feel ignored by politicians.

  B) They feel increasingly vulnerable.

  C) They keep adapting to the changes.

  D) They keep complaining but to no avail.

49. What does the author think of automation?

  A) It will have the same impact as industrialization.

  B) It provides sensible companies with alternatives.

  C) Its alleged positive effects are doubtful.

D) Its detrimental effects are unavoidable

50. What should we attach importance to when dealing with automation?

A) College graduates' job prospects.

B) Women's access to employment.

C) People's economic security.

D) People's social mobility.

Passage Two

Questions 51 to 55 are based on the following passage.

Look at the people around you. Some are passive, others more aggressive. Some work best alone, others crave companionship. We easily recognize that there is great variation among the individuals who live near us. Yet, when we speak of people from elsewhere, we seem to inevitably characterize them based on their country of origin.

Statistics specialists, when they speak of national averages, often make the same mistake.

Newly published research shows how erroneous such overviews are. Three researchers analyzed decades of values-based surveys and found that only between 16% and 21% of the variation in cultural values could be explained by differences between countries. In other words, the vast majority of what makes us culturally distinct from one another has nothing to do with our homeland.

To determine what factors really are associated with culture, the authors combined data from 558 prior surveys that each measured one or more of Hofstede's cultural dimensions. These are traits, such as individualism and masculinity, that describe work-related cultural values. (They are not a measure of visible cultural traits, such as food or dress.) Though the validity of Hofstede's dimensions has been questioned, they have the singular benefit of having been in use for decades, which allows for historical and international comparisons.

The researchers found that both demographic factors, such as age, and environmental factors, such as long-term unemployment rates, were more correlated with cultural values than nationality. Occupation and social economic status were the most strongly correlated, suggesting that our values are more economically driven than we usually give them credit for.

The evidence implies that people with similar jobs and incomes are more culturally alike, regardless of where they live. Vas Taras, the lead author of the study, puts it this way: "Tell me how much you make and I will make a pretty accurate prediction about your cultural values. Tell me what your nationality is and I probably will make a wrong prediction."

Taras says our erroneous belief that countries are cultures has caused businesses to teach their employees useless or even harmful ways of interacting with their international peers. Chinese and American lawyers might be trained to interact based on the assumption that the Chinese person is less individualistic, even though their similar social economic situations make it probable they are actually quite alike in that regard.

The country, as the unit of authority, is often a convenient way of generalizing about a population. However, our focus on countries can mask broad variations within them. In the majority of cases we would be better off identifying people by the factors that constrain their lives, like income, rather than by the lines surrounding them on a map.

51. What error do experts often make when describing people from other places?

   A) They tend to overly rely on nationality.

   B) They often exaggerate their differences.

   C) They often misunderstand their cultures.

   D) They tend to dwell on national averages.

52. What do we learn about Hofstede's cultural dimensions?

   A) They are useful in comparing cultural values across time and space.

   B) They have brought unusual benefits to people of different cultures.

   C) They are widely used to identify people's individual traits.

   D) They provide valuable questions for researchers to study.

53. What did researchers find about previous studies on factors determining people's values?

   A) Environmental factors were prioritized over other factors.

   B) An individual's financial status was often underestimated.

   C) Too much emphasis had been placed on one's occupation.

   D) The impact of social progress on one's values was ignored.

54. What is the impact on employees when cultures are identified with countries?

   A) They may fail to see the cultural biases of their business partners.

   B) They may fail to attach sufficient importance to cultural diversity.

   C) They may not be taught how to properly interact with overseas partners.

   D) They may not be able to learn the legal procedures for business transactions.

55. What does the author suggest at the end of the passage?

   A) There is sufficient reason to generalize about a country's population.

   B) The majority of people are still constrained by their national identity.

C) It is arguable that the country should be regarded as the unit of authority.

D) Nationality is less useful than socio-economic status as an indicator of one's values.

2021年6月大学英语六级考试阅读真题（第1套）
（本套试题对应主书第2套）

Part Ⅲ　　　　　　Reading Comprehension　　　　（40 minutes）

Section A

Directions: *In this section, there is a passage with ten blanks. You are required to select one word for each blank from a list of choices given in a word bank following the passage. Read the passage through carefully before making your choices. Each choice in the bank is identified by a letter. Please mark the corresponding letter for each item on **Answer Sheet 2** with a single line through the centre. You may not use any of the words in the bank more than once.*

A new study has drawn a bleak picture of cultural inclusiveness reflected in the children's literature available in Australia. Dr. Helen Adam from Edith Cowan University's School of Education __26__ the cultural diversity of children's books. She examined the books __27__ in the kindergarten rooms of four day-care centers in Western Australia. Just 18 percent of 2,413 books in the total collection contained any __28__ of non-white people. Minority cultures were often featured in stereotypical or tokenistic ways, for example, by __29__ Asian culture with chopsticks and traditional dress. Characters that did represent a minority culture usually had __30__ roles in the books. The main characters were mostly Caucasian. This causes concern as it can lead to an impression that whiteness is of greater value.

Dr. Adam said children formed impressions about "difference" and identity from a very young age. Evidence has shown they develop own-race __31__ from as young as three months of age. The books we share with young children can be a valuable opportunity to develop children's understanding of themselves and others. Books can also allow children to see diversity. They discover both similarities and differences between themselves and others. This can help develop understanding, acceptance and __32__ of diversity.

Census data has shown Australians come from more than 200 countries. They speak over 300 languages at home. Additionally, Australians belong to more than 100 different religious groups. They also work in more than 1,000 different occupations. "Australia is a multicultural society. The current __33__ promotion of white middle-class ideas and lifestyles risks __34__ children from minority groups. This can give white middle-class children a sense of __35__ or privilege," Dr. Adam said.

A) alienating	I) representation
B) appreciation	J) safeguarded
C) bias	K) secondary
D) fraud	L) superiority
E) housed	M) temperament
F) investigated	N) tentative
G) overwhelming	O) threshold
H) portraying	

Section B

Directions: *In this section, you are going to read a passage with ten statements attached to it. Each statement contains information given in one of the paragraphs. Identify the paragraph from which the information is derived. You may choose a paragraph more than once. Each paragraph is marked with a letter. Answer the questions by marking the corresponding letter on* **Answer Sheet 2**.

How Marconi Gave Us the Wireless World

[A] A hundred years before iconic figures like Bill Gates and Steve Jobs permeated our lives, an Irish-Italian inventor laid the foundation of the communication explosion of the 21st century. Guglielmo Marconi was arguably the first truly global figure in modern communication. Not only was he the first to communicate globally, he was the first to think globally about communication. Marconi may not have been the greatest inventor of his time, but more than anyone else, he brought about a fundamental shift in the way we communicate.

[B] Today's globally networked media and communication system has its origins in the 19th century, when, for the first time, messages were sent electronically across great distances. The telegraph, the telephone, and radio were the obvious predecessors of the Internet, iPods, and mobile phones. What made the link from then to now was the development of wireless communication. Marconi was the first to develop and perfect this system, using the recently-discovered "air waves" that make up the electromagnetic spectrum.

[C] Between 1896, when he applied for his first patent in England at the age of 22, and his death in Italy in 1937, Marconi was at the center of every major innovation in electronic communication. He was also a skilled and sophisticated organizer, an entrepreneurial innovator, who mastered the use of corporate strategy, media relations, government lobbying, international diplomacy, patents, and prosecution. Marconi was really interested in only one thing: the extension of mobile, personal, long-distance communication to the ends of the earth (and beyond, if we can believe some reports). Some like to refer to him as a genius, but if there was any genius to Marconi it was this vision.

[D] In 1901 he succeeded in signaling across the Atlantic, from the west coast of England to Newfoundland, despite the claims of science that it could not be done. In 1924 he convinced the British government to encircle the world with a chain of wireless stations using the latest technology that he had devised, shortwave radio. There are some who say Marconi lost his edge when commercial broadcasting came along; he didn't see that radio could or should be used to *frivolous*（无聊的）ends. In one of his last public speeches, a radio broadcast to the United States in March 1937, he deplored that broadcasting had become a one-way means of communication and foresaw it moving in another direction, toward communication as a means of exchange. That was visionary genius.

[E] Marconi's career was devoted to making wireless communication happen cheaply, efficiently, smoothly, and with an elegance that would appear to be intuitive and uncomplicated to the user—user-friendly, if you will. There is a direct connection from Marconi to today's social media, search engines, and program streaming that can best be summed up by an admittedly provocative exclamation: the 20th century did not exist. In a sense, Marconi's vision jumped from his time to our own.

[F] Marconi invented the idea of global communication—or, more straightforwardly, globally networked, mobile, wireless communication. Initially, this was wireless Morse code *telegraphy*（电报通讯）, the principal communication technology of his day. Marconi was the first to develop a practical method for wireless telegraphy using radio waves. He borrowed technical details from many sources, but what set him apart was a self-confident vision of the paradigm-shifting power of communication technology on the one hand, and, on the other, of the steps that needed to be taken to consolidate his own position as a player in that field. Tracing Marconi's lifeline leads us into the story of modern communication itself. There were other important figures, but Marconi towered over them all in reach, power, and influence, as well as in the grip he had on the popular imagination of his time. Marconi was quite simply the central figure in the emergence of a modern understanding of communication.

[G] In his lifetime, Marconi foresaw the development of television and the fax machine, GPS, radar, and the portable hand-held telephone. Two months before he died, newspapers were reporting that he was working on a "death ray," and that he had "killed a rat with an intricate device at a distance of three feet." By then, anything Marconi said or did was newsworthy. Stock prices rose or sank according to his pronouncements. If Marconi said he thought it might rain, there was likely to be a run on umbrellas.

[H] Marconi's biography is also a story about choices and the motivations behind them. At one level, Marconi could be fiercely autonomous and independent of the constraints of his own social class. On another scale, he was a perpetual outsider. Wherever he went, he was never "of" the group; he was always the "other," considered foreign in Britain, British in Italy, and "not American" in the United States. At the same time, he also suffered tremendously from a need for acceptance that drove, and sometimes tarnished, every one of his relationships.

[I] Marconi placed a permanent stamp on the way we live. He was the first person to imagine a practical application for the wireless spectrum, and to develop it successfully into a *global communication system*—in both terms of the word; that is, worldwide and all-inclusive. He was able to do this because of a combination of factors—most important, timing and opportunity—but the single-mindedness and determination with which he carried out his self-imposed mission was fundamentally character-based; millions of Marconi's contemporaries had the same class, gender, race, and colonial privilege as he, but only a handful did anything with it. Marconi needed to achieve the goal that was set in his mind as an adolescent; by the time he reached adulthood, he understood, intuitively, that in order to have an impact he had to both develop an independent economic base and align himself with political power. Disciplined, uncritical loyalty to political power became his compass for the choices he had to make.

[J] At the same time, Marconi was uncompromisingly independent intellectually. Shortly after Marconi's death, the nuclear physicist Enrico Fermi—soon to be the developer of the Manhattan Project—wrote that Marconi proved that theory and experimentation were complementary features of progress. "Experience can rarely, unless guided by a theoretical concept, arrive at results of any great significance... on the other hand, an excessive trust in theoretical conviction would have prevented Marconi from persisting in experiments which were destined to bring about a revolution in the technique of radio-communications." In other words, Marconi had the advantage of not being burdened by preconceived assumptions.

[K] The most controversial aspect of Marconi's life—and the reason why there has been no satisfying biography of Marconi until now—was his uncritical embrace of Benito Mussolini. At first this was not problematic for him. But as the *regressive*（倒退的）nature of Mussolini's regime became clear, he began to suffer a crisis of conscience. However, after a lifetime of moving within the circles of power, he was unable to break with authority, and served Mussolini faithfully (as president of Italy's national research council and royal academy, as well as a member of the Fascist Grand Council) until the day he died—conveniently—in 1937, shortly before he would have had to take a stand in the conflict that consumed a world that he had, in part, created.

36. Marconi was central to our present-day understanding of communication.
37. As an adult, Marconi had an intuition that he had to be loyal to politicians in order to be influential.
38. Marconi disapproved of the use of wireless communication for commercial broadcasting.
39. Marconi's example demonstrates that theoretical concepts and experiments complement each other in making progress in science and technology.
40. Marconi's real interest lay in the development of worldwide wireless communication.
41. Marconi spent his whole life making wireless communication simple to use.
42. Because of his long-time connection with people in power, Marconi was unable to cut himself off from the fascist regime in Italy.
43. In his later years, Marconi exerted a tremendous influence on all aspects of people's life.
44. What connected the 19th century and our present time was the development of wireless communication.
45. Despite his autonomy, Marconi felt alienated and suffered from a lack of acceptance.

Section C

Directions: *There are 2 passages in this section. Each passage is followed by some questions or unfinished statements. For each of them there are four choices marked A), B), C) and D). You should decide on the best choice and mark the corresponding letter on **Answer Sheet 2** with a single line through the centre.*

Passage One

Questions 46 to 50 are based on the following passage.

Humans are fascinated by the source of their failings and virtues. This preoccupation inevitably leads to an old debate: whether nature or nurture moulds us more. A revolution in genetics has poised this as a modern political question about the character of our society: if personalities are hard-wired into our genes, what can governments do to help us? It feels morally questionable, yet claims of genetic selection by intelligence are making headlines.

This is down to "*hereditarian*" (遗传论的) science and a recent paper claimed "differences in exam performance between pupils attending selective and non-selective schools mirror the genetic differences between them". With such an assertion, the work was predictably greeted by a lot of absurd claims about "genetics determining academic success". What the research revealed was the rather less surprising result: the educational benefits of selective schools largely disappear once pupils' inborn ability and socio-economic background were taken into account. It is a glimpse of the blindingly obvious—and there's nothing to back strongly either a hereditary or environmental argument.

Yet the paper does say children are "unintentionally genetically selected" by the school system. Central to hereditarian science is a tall claim: that identifiable variations in genetic sequences can predict an individual's aptness to learn, reason and solve problems. This is problematic on many levels. A teacher could not seriously tell a parent their child has a low genetic tendency to study when external factors clearly exits. Unlike-minded academics say the inheritability of human traits is scientifically unsound. At best there is a weak statistical association and not a causal link between DNA and intelligence. Yet sophisticated statistics are used to create an intimidatory atmosphere of scientific certainty.

While there's an undoubted genetic basis to individual difference, it is wrong to think that socially defined groups can be genetically accounted for. The fixation on genes as destiny is surely false too. Medical predictability can rarely be based on DNA alone; the environment maters too. Something as complex as intellect is likely to be affected by many factors beyond genes. If hereditarians want to advance their cause it will require more balanced interpretation and not just acts of advocacy.

Genetic selection is a way of exerting influence over others, "the ultimate collective control of human destinies", as writer H. G. Wells put it. Knowledge becomes power and power requires a sense of responsibility. In understanding cognitive ability, we must not elevate discrimination to a science; allowing people to climb the ladder of life only as far as their cells might suggest. This will need a more sceptical eye on the science. As technology progresses, we all have a duty to make sure that we shape a future that we would want to find ourselves in.

46. What did a recent research paper claim?

A) The type of school students attend makes a difference to their future.

B) Genetic differences between students are far greater than supposed.

C) The advantages of selective schools are too obvious to ignore.

D) Students' academic performance is determined by their genes.

47. What does the author think of the recent research?

    A) Its result was questionable.

    B) Its implication was positive.

    C) Its influence was rather negligible.

    D) Its conclusions were enlightening.

48. What does the author say about the relationship between DNA and intelligence?

    A) It is one of scientific certainty.

    B) It is not one of cause and effect.

    C) It is subject to interpretation of statistics.

    D) It is not fully examined by gene scientists.

49. What do hereditarians need to do to make their claims convincing?

    A) Take all relevant factors into account in interpreting their data.

    B) Conduct their research using more sophisticated technology.

    C) Gather gene data from people of all social classes.

    D) Cooperate with social scientists in their research.

50. What does the author warn against in the passage?

    A) Exaggerating the power of technology in shaping the world.

    B) Losing sight of professional ethics in conducting research.

    C) Misunderstanding the findings of human cognition research.

    D) Promoting discrimination in the name of science.

Passage Two

Questions 51 to 55 are based on the following passage.

　　Nicola Sturgeon's speech last Tuesday setting out the Scottish government's legislative programme for the year ahead confirmed what was already pretty clear. Scottish councils are set to be the first in the UK with the power to levy charges on visitors, with Edinburgh likely to lead the way.

　　Tourist taxes are not new. The Himalayan kingdom of Bhutan has a longstanding policy of charging visitors a daily fee. France's tax on overnight stays was introduced to assist *thermal spa* (温泉) towns to develop, and around half of French local authorities use it today.

　　But such levies are on the rise. Moves by Barcelona and Venice to deal with the phenomenon of "over-tourism" through the use of charges have recently gained prominence. Japan and Greece are among the countries to have recently introduced tourist taxes.

That the UK lags behind is due to our weak, by international standards, local government, as well as the opposition to taxes and regulation of our aggressively pro-market ruling party. Some UK cities have lobbied without success for the power to levy a charge on visitors. Such levies are no universal remedy as the amounts raised would be tiny compared with what has been taken away by central government since 2010. Still, it is to be hoped that the Scottish government's bold move will prompt others to act. There is no reason why visitors to the UK, or domestic tourists on holiday in hotspots such as Cornwall, should be exempt from taxation—particularly when vital local services including waste collection, park maintenance and arts and culture spending are under unprecedented strain.

On the contrary, compelling tourists to make a financial contribution to the places they visit beyond their personal consumption should be part of a wider cultural shift. Westerners with disposable incomes have often behaved as if they have a right to go wherever they choose with little regard for the consequences. Just as the environmental harm caused by aviation and other transport must come under far greater scrutiny, the social cost of tourism must also be confronted. This includes the impact of short-term lets on housing costs and quality of life for residents. Several European capitals, including Paris and Berlin, are leading a campaign for tougher regulation by the European Union. It also includes the impact of overcrowding, litter and the kinds of behaviour associated with noisy parties.

There is no "one size fits all" solution to this problem. The existence of new revenue streams for some but not all councils is complicated, and businesses are often opposed, fearing higher costs will make them uncompetitive. But those places that want them must be given the chance to make tourist taxes work.

51. What do we learn from Nicola Sturgeon's speech?

    A) The UK is set to adjust its policy on taxation.

    B) Tourists will have to pay a tax to visit Scotland.

    C) The UK will take new measures to boost tourism.

    D) Edinburgh contributes most to Scotland's tourism.

52. How come the UK has been slow in imposing the tourist tax?

    A) Its government wants to attract more tourists.

    B) The tax is unlikely to add much to its revenue.

C) Its ruling party is opposed to taxes and regulation.

D) It takes time for local governments to reach consensus.

53. Both international and domestic visitors in the UK should pay tourist tax so as to _____.

    A) elevate its tourism to international standards

    B) improve the welfare of its maintenance workers

    C) promote its cultural exchange with other nations

    D) ease its financial burden of providing local services

54. What does the author say about Western tourists?

    A) They don't seem to care about the social cost of tourism.

    B) They don't seem to mind paying for additional services.

    C) They deem travel an important part of their life.

    D) They subject the effects of tourism to scrutiny.

55. What are UK people's opinions about the levy of tourist tax?

    A) Supportive.

    B) Skeptical.

    C) Divided.

    D) Unclear.

2021年6月大学英语六级考试阅读真题（第2套）

（本套试题对应主书第1套）

Part III　　　　Reading Comprehension　　　　（40 minutes）

Section A

Directions: *In this section, there is a passage with ten blanks. You are required to select one word for each blank from a list of choices given in a word bank following the passage. Read the passage through carefully before making your choices. Each choice in the bank is identified by a letter. Please mark the corresponding letter for each item on **Answer Sheet 2** with a single line through the centre. You may not use any of the words in the bank more than once.*

　　I'm always baffled when I walk into a pharmacy and see shelves bursting with various vitamins, extracts and other supplements, all promising to accelerate or promote weight loss.

Aisles of marketing genius *belie* (掩饰) the fact that, 26 , weight loss is dictated by the laws of arithmetic. Economist Jessica Irvine wrote a book about how she used math to help her lose more than 18 kilograms. If calories taken in are less than calories 27 , weight shall be lost, and so it is with money.

Despite the 28 of financial products, services and solutions geared towards accumulating wealth, it all begins with the same 29 : getting ahead financially requires a reduction of spending, so that income is greater than expenses. I was reminded of this again recently listening to an interview with Nicole Haddow, the author of *Smashed Avocado*, explaining how she cracked the property market at 31. It was quite a 30 , given where she had been two years earlier.

Nicole didn't celebrate her 30th birthday as she had 31 . She was sobbing at the dinner table with her parents, with whom she had just moved back in. She had no stable income, $12,000 in credit-card debt and no plan, but to her 32 , her father, an accountant, told her that her financial 33 wasn't as bad as she thought. He said, on her income, with some changes, she would be able to buy an investment unit within two years, which she did.

Nicole admitted she was fortunate, as she was able to live with her parents and 34 her spending—and life—to get herself on track financially. Creating a gap between her income and spending required a paradigm shift and 35 sacrifice and commitment, but by going into financial lockdown, Nicole gained financial independence.

A) abundance	I) impetus
B) astonishment	J) overhaul
C) entailed	K) permanently
D) envisaged	L) plight
E) equation	M) prosper
F) expended	N) shatter
G) feat	O) ultimately
H) fiscally	

Section B

Directions: *In this section, you are going to read a passage with ten statements attached to it. Each statement contains information given in one of the paragraphs. Identify the paragraph from which the information is derived. You may choose a paragraph more than once. Each paragraph is marked with a letter. Answer the questions by marking the corresponding letter on **Answer Sheet 2**.*

France's Beloved Cathedral Only Minutes Away from Complete Destruction

[A] Notre Dame Cathedral in the heart of Paris was within "15 to 30 minutes" of complete destruction as firefighters battled to stop flames reaching its bell towers on Monday evening, French authorities have revealed. A greater disaster was averted by members of the Paris fire brigade, who risked their lives to remain inside the burning monument to create a wall of water between the raging fire and the two towers on the west of the building.

[B] The revelation of how close France came to losing its most famous cathedral emerged as police investigators questioned workers involved in the restoration of the monument to try to establish the cause of the devastating blaze. Paris prosecutor Remy Heitz said that an initial fire alert was sounded at 6:20 pm on Monday evening but no fire was found. The second alert was sounded at 6:43 pm, and the blaze was discovered on the roof.

[C] More than $650 million was raised in a few hours on Tuesday as French business leaders and global corporations announced they would donate to a restoration campaign launched by the president, Emmanuel Macron. But as the emergency services picked through the burnt debris, a row was resurfacing over accusations that the beloved cathedral, immortalised in Victor Hugo's novel, was already crumbling before the fire.

[D] The cathedral is owned by the French state and has been at the centre of a years-long dispute over who should finance restoration work of the collapsing staircases, crumbling statues and cracked walls. Jean-Michel Leniaud, the president of the scientific council at the National Heritage Institute, said: "What happened was bound to happen. The lack of adequate maintenance and daily attention to such a majestic building is the cause of this catastrophe." After the blaze was declared completely extinguished, 15 hours after it started, the junior interior minister, Laurent Nunez, said the structure had been saved but remained vulnerable. He praised the actions of the firefighters but admitted the fate of the cathedral had been uncertain. "They saved the main structure, but it all came down to 15-30 minutes," Nunez said.

[E] In a surprise televised address on Tuesday evening, Macron said he wanted to see the cathedral rebuilt within five years. "The fire at Notre Dame reminds us that we will always have challenges to overcome," Macron said, "Notre Dame is our history, our literature, the centre of our life. It is the standard by which we measure our distances. It's so many books, so many paintings. It's the cathedral of every French person, even those who have never visited it. This history is ours and so we will rebuild Notre Dame. It is what the French people expect; it is what our history deserves. It is our deep destiny. We will rebuild Notre Dame so it is even more beautiful than before. I want it done in the next five years. We can do it. After the time of testing comes a time of reflection and then of action."

[F] The fire, which had started at the base of the 93-metre *spire* (尖塔) at about 6:40 pm on Monday, spread through the cathedral's roof, made up of hundreds of oak beams, some dating back to the 13th century. These beams, known as la forêt (the forest) because of their density, formed the cross-shaped roof that ran the length of the central part of the cathedral. As hundreds of tourists and Parisians stood and watched the flames leaping from the roof, there was shock and tears as the cathedral spire caught fire, burned and then collapsed into itself.

[G] A collection of dramatic videos and photos quickly spread across social media, showing the horrifying destruction, and attracting emotional responses from people all over the world. Indeed, within minutes the fire occupied headlines of every major global newspaper and television network. This is not surprising given Notre Dame Cathedral, meaning "Our Lady", is one of the most recognised symbols of the city of Paris attracting millions of tourists every year.

[H] While the world looked on, the 500 firefighters at the scene then battled to prevent the flames from reaching the two main towers, where the cathedral bells hang. If the wooden frame of the towers had caught fire, it could have sent the bells—the largest of which, the Emmanuel Bell, weighs 13 tons—crashing down, potentially causing the collapse of both towers. Police and fire services will spend the next 48 hours assessing the "security and safety" of the 850-year-old structure. Nunez said: "We have identified vulnerabilities throughout the structure, all of which still need securing." As a result, residents of five buildings around the northern side of the cathedral were being temporarily evacuated, he added. Architects have identified three main holes in the structure, in the locations of the spire, the main hall and the upper rooms to the north of the central aisle. Most of the wooden roof beams have been burned, and parts of the concrete holding up the roof have collapsed.

[I] The interior minister, Christophe Castaner, visited the cathedral on Tuesday afternoon to see the extent of the devastation. Ash covered the marble diamond-patterned floor and floated in large pools of grey water from the fire hoses. Behind a heap of blackened oak beams that lay piled up where they had fallen, daylight from vast holes in the cathedral roof lit a golden cross over a statue by Nicolas Coustou, which appeared to have escaped damage. Preliminary inspections also suggested the three *ornate* (装饰华丽的) stained glass "rose" windows appeared to have survived the fire, officials said. However, fire officers have said a complete inventory of the damage will not be possible until the cathedral structure has been deemed safe.

[J] The culture minister, Franck Riester, said religious relics saved from the cathedral were being securely held at the Hotel de Ville, and works of art that sustained smoke damage were being taken to the Louvre, the world's largest art museum, where they would be dried out, repaired and stored. Sixteen copper statues that decorated the spire had been removed for restoration only a few days before the fire. Relics at the top of the spire are believed lost as the spire was destroyed. As well as damage from the heat, which firefighters said reached more than 800 ℃, experts also need to assess damage from the vast quantities of water firefighters poured into the cathedral. One casualty of this was The Great Organ constructed in the 1730s, which was said to have escaped the flames but been significantly damaged by water.

[K] French political commentators noted the devastating fire had succeeded where Macron had failed in uniting the country. But criticism over the original state of the building is likely to intensify over coming days. Leniaud told *La Croix* newspaper: "This is not about looking for people to blame. The responsibility is collective because this is the most loved monument in the country." Alexandre Gady, an art historian, agreed. "We've been saying for years that the budget for maintaining historic monuments is too low," Gady said. The Paris prosecutor's office has opened an inquiry into "involuntary destruction by fire", indicating they believe the cause of the blaze was accidental rather than criminal.

36. The total amount of damage to Notre Dame Cathedral can be assessed only when its structure is considered safe.

37. Once again people began to argue whether Notre Dame Cathedral was going to collapse even without the fire.

38. The Notre Dame Cathedral catastrophe was said to have helped unite the French nation.

39. The roof of Notre Dame Cathedral was built with large numbers of densely laid-out wood beams.

40. Renovation workers of Notre Dame Cathedral were questioned to find out the cause of the accident.

41. Had the bell towers' wooden frames burned down, the heavy bells would have crashed down.

42. The timely action of the firefighters prevented the fire from reaching the Cathedral's bell towers.

43. Apart from the fire, the water used to extinguish it also caused a lot of damage to Notre Dame Cathedral.

44. There has been argument over the years as to who should pay for the restoration of Notre Dame Cathedral.
45. News of Notre Dame Cathedral catastrophe instantly caught media attention throughout the world.

Section C

Directions: *There are 2 passages in this section. Each passage is followed by some questions or unfinished statements. For each of them there are four choices marked A), B), C) and D). You should decide on the best choice and mark the corresponding letter on* ***Answer Sheet 2*** *with a single line through the centre.*

Passage One

Questions 46 to 50 are based on the following passage.

We often think of drawing as something that takes inborn talent, but this kind of thinking stems from our misclassification of drawing as, primarily, an art form rather than a tool for learning.

Researchers, teachers, and artists are starting to see how drawing can positively impact a wide variety of skills and disciplines.

Most of us have spent some time drawing before, but at some point, most of us stop drawing. There are people who don't, obviously, and thank god for that: a world without designers and artists would be a very shabby one indeed.

Some argue that so many adults have abandoned drawing because we've miscategorized it and given it a very narrow definition. In his book, *Stick Figures: Drawing as a Human Practice,* Professor D. B. Dowd argues that we have misfiled the significance of drawing because we see it as a professional skill instead of a personal capacity. We mistakenly think of "good" drawings as those which work as recreations of the real world, as realistic illusions. Rather, drawing should be recategorized as a symbolic tool.

Human beings have been drawing for 73,000 years. It's part of what it means to be human. We don't have the strength of *chimpanzees* (大猩猩) because we've given up animal strength to manipulate subtle instruments, like hammers, spears, and—later—pens and pencils. The human hand is an extremely dense network of nerve endings. In many ways, human beings are built to draw.

Some researchers argue that *doodling* (涂画) activates the brain's so-called default circuit—essentially, the areas of the brain responsible for maintaining a baseline level of activity in the absence of other stimuli. Because of this, some believe that doodling during a boring lecture can help students pay attention. In one study, participants were asked to listen to a list of names while either doodling or sitting still. Those who doodled remembered 29 percent more of the names than those who did not.

There's also evidence that drawing talent is based on how accurately someone perceives the world. The human visual system tends to misjudge size, shape, color, and angles but artists perceive these qualities more accurately than non-artists. Cultivating drawing talent can become an essential tool to improve people's observational skills in fields where the visual is important.

Rather than think of drawing as a talent that some creative people are gifted in, we should consider it as a tool for seeing and understanding the world better—one that just so happens to double as an art form. Both absent-minded doodling and copying from life have been shown to positively affect your memory and visual perception, so complain loudly the next time your school board slashes the art department's budget.

46. What do people generally think about drawing?

    A) It is a gift creative people are endowed with.

    B) It is a skill that is acquired with practice.

    C) It is an art form that is appreciated by all.

    D) It is an ability everyone should cultivate.

47. What do we learn about designers and artists?

    A) They are declining gradually in number.

    B) They are keen on changing shabby surroundings.

    C) They add beauty and charm to the world.

    D) They spend most of their lives drawing.

48. What does Professor D. B. Dowd argue in his book?

    A) Everybody is born with the capacity to draw.

    B) Drawing is a skill that requires special training.

    C) The value of drawing tends to be overestimated.

    D) Drawing should be redefined as a realistic illusion.

49. What have some researchers found from one study about doodling?

    A) It is a must for maintaining a base level of brain activity.

    B) It can turn something boring into something interesting.

    C) It is the most reliable stimulant to activate the brain.

D) It helps improve concentration and memory.

50. What is characteristic of people with drawing talent?

A) Sensitivity to cognitive stimulation.

B) Subtlety of representation.

C) Accuracy in categorization.

D) Precision in visual perception.

Passage Two

Questions 51 to 55 are based on the following passage.

The car has reshaped our cities. It seems to offer autonomy for everyone. There is something almost delightful in the detachment from reality of advertisements showing mass-produced cars marketed as symbols of individuality and of freedom when most of their lives will be spent making short journeys on choked roads.

For all the fuss made about top speeds, cornering ability and acceleration, the most useful gadgets on a modern car are those which work when you're going very slowly: parking sensors, sound systems, and navigation apps which will show a way around upcoming traffic jams. This seems to be one of the few areas where the benefit of sharing personal information comes straight back to the sharer: because these apps know where almost all the users are, and how fast they are moving almost all the time, they can spot traffic *congestion* (堵塞) very quickly and suggest ways round it.

The problem comes when everyone is using a navigation app which tells them to avoid everyone else using the same gadget. Traffic jams often appear where no one has enough information to avoid them. When a lucky few have access to the knowledge, they will benefit greatly. But when everyone has perfect information, traffic jams simply spread onto the side roads that seem to offer a way round them.

This new congestion teaches us two things. The first is that the promises of technology will never be realised as fully as we hope; they will be limited by their unforeseen and unintended consequences. Sitting in a more comfortable car in a different traffic jam is pleasant but hardly the liberation that once seemed to be promised. The second is that self-organisation will not get us where we want to go. The efforts of millions of drivers to get ahead do not miraculously produce a situation in which everyone does better than before, but one in which almost everyone does rather worse. Central control and collective organisation can produce smoother and fairer outcomes, though even that much is never guaranteed.

Similar limits can be foreseen for the much greater advances promised by self-driving cars. Last week, one operated by the taxi company Uber struck and killed a woman pushing her bicycle across a wide road in Arizona. This was the first recorded death involving a car which was supposed to be fully autonomous. Experts have said that it suggests a "catastrophic failure" of technology.

Increasingly, even Silicon Valley has to acknowledge the costs of the *intoxicating* (令人陶醉的) hurry that characterises its culture. What traffic teaches us is that reckless and uncontrolled change is as likely to harm us as it is to benefit us, and that thoughtful regulation is necessary for a better future.

51. What does the author say about car advertisements?

    A) They portray drivers who enjoy speed on the road.

    B) They present a false picture of the autonomy cars provide.

    C) They pursue individuality and originality in design concept.

    D) They overestimate the potential market of autonomous cars.

52. What does the author imply about the various gadgets on cars?

    A) They can help to alleviate traffic jams.

    B) Most of them are as effective as advertised.

    C) Only some can be put to use under current traffic conditions.

    D) They are constantly upgraded to make driving easier and safer.

53. What does the author say about the use of navigation apps?

    A) It is likely to create traffic jams in other places.

    B) It helps a great deal in easing traffic congestion.

    C) It sharply reduces the incidence of traffic accidents.

    D) It benefits those who are learning to drive.

54. What does the author say about technology?

    A) Its consequences are usually difficult to assess.

    B) It seldom delivers all the benefits as promised.

    C) It depends on the required knowledge for application.

    D) Its benefits are guaranteed by collective wisdom.

55. What key message does the author try to convey in the passage?

    A) The consequences of technological innovation need not be exaggerated.

    B) There is always a price to pay to develop technology for a better world.

C) Technological innovation should be properly regulated.
D) The culture of Silicon Valley ought not to be emulated.

感谢大家的陪伴和支持！

预祝大家跟六级"分手"快乐！

翻译专项突破

主讲：邹寅老师

一、题型概况

1. 题型介绍

要求：将题材熟悉，语言难度中等的汉语段落译成英语

内容：涉及中国的文化、历史及社会发展（不含生僻的专业词汇或习语）

长度：180～200个汉字（四级140～160个汉字）

难度：试题内容的难度略高于四级

时间：30分钟

分值：15%

2. 评分标准

六级翻译评分标准

档 次	档次描述
14分档	译文准确表达了原文的意思。译文流畅，结构清晰，用词贴切，基本无语言错误，仅有个别小错。
11分档	译文基本表达了原文的意思。结构较清晰，语言通顺，但有少量语言错误。
8分档	译文勉强表达了原文的意思。译文勉强连贯，语言错误相当多，其中有一些是严重错误。
5分档	译文仅表达了小部分原文的意思。译文连贯性差，有相当多的严重语言错误。
2分档	除个别词语或句子，译文基本没有表达原文的意思。

3. 翻译方法

（1）通读全句，判断句型

（2）去掉修饰，找准主干

（3）梳理词汇时态语态，理清动词主次

（4）定语围绕名词前后，状语短前长后

二、定语翻译

1. 定语前置

公认的文学名著

勤劳和富有创造性的中国农民

安全、清洁和经济型交通系统

2. 定语后置——介词短语作定语后置

一部中国著名的历史小说

经济的发展与生活水平的提高

博物馆展览次数和参观人数

三国时期的历史

中国许多地方的湖泊和池塘

体育馆建设投资

通信网络的快速发展

中国智能手机用户数量

移动支付市场的最大群体

3. 定语后置——分词短语作定语后置

剪纸用的材料和工具

学汉语的人数

使用移动支付的顾客

新公布的统计数字

选择乘飞机外出旅游的人的数量

做兼职工作的学生数量

从农村搬到城市的人口数量

4. 定语后置——定语从句

狮子是兽中之王，象征幸福和好运，所以人们通常在春节和其他节日期间表演狮子舞。

唐朝始于618年，终于907年，是中国历史上最灿烂的时期。

经过近三百年的发展，唐代中国成为世界上最繁荣的强国，其首都长安是当时世界上最大的城市。

李白和杜甫是以作品简洁自然著称的诗人。

三、状语 + 插入语翻译

1. 介词短语作状语后置

近年来，节假日期间选择乘飞机外出旅游的人数在不断增加。

政府官员均通过竞争性选拔考试任用。

人们通常在春节和其他节日期间表演狮子舞。

许多体育馆通过应用现代信息技术大大提高了服务质量。

2. 插入语

如今，随着经济的发展和生活水平的提高，越来越多的中国人包括农民和外出务工人员都能乘飞机出行。

大量商品，包括酒和丝绸，都在市场销售。同时，还进口许多外国产品，如时钟和烟草。

《三国演义》写于14世纪，是中国著名的历史小说。

舞狮作为中国传统民间表演已有 2 000 多年历史。

在中国传统文化中，红灯笼象征生活美满和生意兴隆，通常在春节、元宵节和国庆节等节日期间悬挂。

四、多动句

人们兴高采烈，庆祝丰收。

2011 年 3 月日本核电站事故后，中国的核能开发停了下来，中止审批新的核电站，并开展全国性的核安全检查。

这些资金用于改善教学设施、购买书籍，使 16 万多所中小学收益。

随着中国经济的蓬勃发展，学汉语的人数迅速增加，使汉语成了世界上人们最爱学的语言之一。

来自 87 个国家共计 126 位选手聚集在湖南省省会参加了从 7 月 6 日到 8 月 5 日进行的半决赛和决赛。

五、无主句 + there be 句型

1. 无主句

要欣赏大山的宏伟壮丽，通常得向上看。但要欣赏黄山美景，就得向下看。

整个义务教育阶段，要求学生在每学期期末参加期末考试。

因此，强烈建议大学生在课余时间做一些兼职工作，以积累相关的工作经验。

自上世纪 90 年代安装缆车以来，参观人数大大增加。

核能是可以安全开发和利用的。

2. there be 句型

目前,世界上大约有 1 000 只大熊猫。

中国有不少这样的特殊购物日。

丽江到处都是美丽的自然风光。

(黄山)这里还有很多温泉,其泉水有助于防治皮肤病。

六、真题带练

1. 2020 年 9 月六级真题——《西游记》

《西游记》(*Journey to the West*)也许是中国文学四大经典小说中最具影响力的一部,当然也是在国外最广为人知的一部小说。

这部小说描绘了著名僧侣玄奘在三个随从的陪同下穿越中国西部地区前往印度取经（Buddhist scripture）的艰难历程。

虽然故事的主题基于佛教，但这部小说采用了大量中国民间故事和神话的素材，创造了各种栩栩如生的人物和动物形象。

其中最著名的是孙悟空，他与各种各样的妖魔作斗争的故事几乎为每个中国孩子所熟知。

2. 2020年9月六级真题——《水浒传》

《水浒传》（*Water Margin*）是中国文学四大经典小说之一。

这部小说基于历史人物宋江及其伙伴反抗封建帝王的故事，数百年来一直深受中国读者的喜爱。

毫不夸张地说，几乎每个中国人都熟悉小说中的一些主要人物。

这部小说中的精彩故事在茶馆、戏剧舞台、广播电视、电影屏幕和无数家庭中反复讲述。

事实上，这部小说的影响已经远远超出了国界。

越来越多的外国读者也感到这部小说里的故事生动感人、趣味盎然。

3. 2020年12月六级真题——北京大兴国际机场

北京大兴国际机场位于天安门广场以南46公里处，于2019年9月30日投入使用。

该巨型工程于2014年开工建设,高峰时工地上有4万多工人。

航站楼设计紧凑,可以允许最大数量的飞机直接停靠在最靠近航站楼中心的位置,这给乘客提供了极大的方便。

航站楼共有82个登机口,但乘客通过安检后,只需不到8分钟就能抵达任何一个登机口。

机场的设计可确保每小时300架次起降。

机场年客运量2040年将达到1亿人次,有望成为世界上最繁忙的机场。

4. 2020年12月六级真题——港珠澳大桥

港珠澳大桥(Hong Kong-Zhuhai-Macau Bridge)全长55公里,是我国一项不同寻常的工程壮举。

大桥将三个城市连接起来，是世界上最长的跨海桥梁和隧道系统。

大桥将三个城市之间的旅行时间从3小时缩短到30分钟。

这座跨度巨大的钢筋混凝土大桥充分证明中国有能力建造创纪录的巨型建筑。

它将助推区域一体化，促进经济增长。

大桥是中国发展自己的大湾区总体规划的关键。

中国希望将大湾区建成在技术创新和经济繁荣上能与旧金山、纽约和东京的湾区相媲美的地区。

5. 2021年6月六级真题——青海

青海是中国西北部的一个省份，平均海拔3 000米以上，大部分地区为高山和高原。

青海省得名于全国最大的咸水湖青海湖。

青海湖被誉为"中国最美的湖泊"，是最受欢迎的旅游景点之一，也是摄影师和艺术家的天堂。

青海山川壮丽，地大物博。

石油和天然气储量丰富，省内许多城市的经济在石油和天然气工业带动下得到了长足发展。

青海尤以水资源丰富而闻名，是中国三大河流长江、黄河和澜沧江的发源地，在中国的水生态中发挥着重要作用。

6. 2021年6月六级真题——云南

云南是位于中国西南的一个省，平均海拔1 500米。

云南历史悠久，风景秀丽，气候宜人。

云南生态环境优越，生物多种多样，被誉为野生动植物的天堂。

云南还有多种矿藏和充足的水资源，为全省经济的可持续发展提供了有利条件。

云南居住着25个少数民族，他们大多有自己的语言、习俗和宗教。

云南独特的自然景色和丰富的民族文化使其成为中国最受欢迎的旅游目的地之一，每年都吸引着大批国内外游客前往观光旅游。

写作专项突破

主讲：陈锦斌老师

一、如何快速获得写作高分

二、雅词

三、佳句

四、点睛

五、谋篇

六、历年真题

① Directions: For this part, you are allowed 30 minutes to write an essay titled "Is technology making people lazy?" You should write at least **120** words but no more than **180** words.【2021 年 6 月英语四级】

② Directions: For this part, you are allowed 30 minutes to write an essay titled "Do violent video games lead to violence?" You should write at least **120** words but no more than **180** words.【2021 年 6 月英语四级】

③ For this part, you are allowed 30 minutes to write an essay commenting on the saying "Never go out there to see what happens, go out there to make something happen." You can cite examples to illustrate the importance of being creative rather than the mere onlookers in life. You should write at least **120** words, no more than **180** words.【2015 年 12 月英语四级】

④ Directions: For this part, you are allowed 30 minutes to write an essay based on the chart below. You should start your essay with a brief description of the graph and comment on China's achievements in urbanization. You should write at least **150** words but no more than **200** words.【2021 年 6 月英语六级】

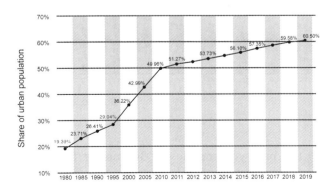
Degree of urbanization in China from 1980 to 2019

⑤ Directions: For this part, you are allowed 30 minutes to write an essay based on the chart below. You should start your essay with a brief description of the chart and comment on China's achievements in poverty alleviation. You should write at least **150** words but no more than **200** words.【2021年6月英语六级】

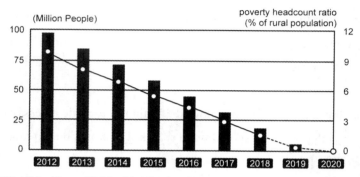

⑥ Directions: For this part, you are allowed 30 minutes to write an essay based on the chart below. You should start your essay with a brief description of the chart and comment on China's achievements in higher education. You should write at least **150** words but no more than **200** words.【2021年6月英语六级】

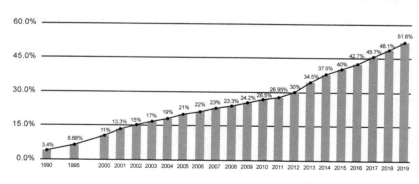

⑦ Directions: For this part, you are allowed 30 minutes to write an essay related to the short passage given below. In your essay, you are to comment on the phenomenon described in the passage and suggest measures to address the issue. You should write at least **150** words but no more than **200** words. <u>Some parents in China are overprotective of their children. They plan everything for their children, make all the decisions for them, and do not allow them to explore on their own in case they make mistakes or get hurt.</u>【2021 年 12 月英语六级】

⑧ For this part, you are allowed 30 minutes to write an essay on <u>why students should be encouraged to develop effective</u> communication skills. You should write at least **150** words but no more than **200** words.【2020 年 12 月英语六级】

⑨ From this part, you are allowed 30 minutes to write a short essay about <u>a campus activity that has benefited you most</u>. You should state the reasons and write at least **120** words but no more than **180** words.【2014 年 12 月英语四级】

⑩ For this part, you are allowed 30 minutes to write an essay on <u>why students should be encouraged to develop creativity</u>. You should write at least **150** words but no more than **200** words.【2020 年 12 月英语六级】

⑪ For this part, you are allowed 30 minutes to write an essay on <u>the importance of having a sense of social responsibility</u>. You should write at least **150** words but no more than **200** words.【2019 年 12 月英语六级】

⑫ For this part, you are allowed 30 minutes to write an essay on <u>the importance of having a sense of family responsibility</u>. You should write at least **150** words but no more than **200** words.【2019 年 12 月英语六级】

⑬ For this part, you are allowed 30 minutes to write an essay. <u>Suppose you have two options upon graduation: one is to find a job somewhere and the other to start a business of your own. You are to make a decision.</u> Write an essay to explain the reasons for your decision. You should write at least **120** words but no more than **180** words.【2016 年 12 月英语四级】

⑭ For this part, you are allowed 30 minutes to write a letter to <u>express your thanks to your parents or any other family member upon making a memorable achievement</u>. You should write at least **120** words but no more than **180** words.【2016 年 6 月英语四级】

⑮ For this part, you are allowed 30 minutes to write a short essay on <u>the challenges of living in a big city</u>. You should write at least **120** words but no more than **180** words.【2018 年 12 月英语四级】

⑯ Directions: For this part, you are allowed 30 minutes to write an essay on the saying "The best preparation for tomorrow is doing your best today." You can give an example or two to illustrate your point of view. You should write at least **150** words but no more than **200** words.【2020 年 7 月英语六级】

⑰ Directions: For this part, you are allowed 30 minutes to write a short essay based on the picture below. <u>You should focus on the harm caused by misleading information online</u>. You are required to write at least **150** words but no more than **200** words.【2015 年 12 月英语六级】

"I just feel unfortunate to live in a world with so much misleading information!"

⑱ Directions: For this part, you are allowed 30 minutes to write an essay based on the picture below. You should start your essay with a brief description of the picture and then discuss <u>what qualities an employer should look for in a job applicant</u>. You should give sound arguments to support your views and write at least **150** words but no more than **200** words.【2014 年 12 月英语六级】

⑲ Directions: For this part, you are allowed 30 minutes to write an essay based on the picture below. You should start your essay with a brief description of the picture and then discuss whether there is a shortcut to learning. You should give sound arguments to support your views and write at least **150** words but no more than **200** words.【2014 年 12 月英语六级】

"'How To Do Well In School Without Studying' is over there in the fiction section."

⑳ Directions: For this part, you are allowed 30 minutes to write a short essay entitled <u>The Impact of the Internet on Interpersonal Communication</u>. Your essay should start with a brief description of the picture. You should write at least **150** words but no more than **200** words.【2012年6月英语六级】

2021年12月大学英语六级考试真题（第一套）

Part I　　　　　　　　　Writing　　　　　　　　(30 minutes)
（请于正式开考后半小时内完成该部分，之后将进行听力考试）

Directions: *For this part, you are allowed 30 minutes to write an essay related to the short passage given below. In your essay, you are to comment on the phenomenon described in the passage and suggest measures to address the issue. You should write at least <u>150</u> words but no more than <u>200</u> words.*

Nowadays star chasing is prevalent among many teenagers. They take pop stars as their idols, imitating their way of talking, following their style of dressing, and seeking every chance to meet them in person at great expenses.

Part II　　　　　Listening Comprehension　　　　(30 minutes)

Section A

Directions: *In this section, you will hear two long conversations. At the end of each conversation, you will hear four questions. Both the conversation and the questions will be spoken only once. After you hear a question, you must choose the best answer from the four choices marked A), B), C) and D). Then mark the corresponding letter on **Answer Sheet 1** with a single line through the centre.*

Questions 1 to 4 are based on the conversation you have just heard.

1. A) It has given rise to much controversy.　　C) It was primarily written for vegetarians.
   B) It has been very favorably received.　　　D) It offends many environmentalists.
2. A) She neglects people's efforts in animal protection.
   B) She tries to force people to accept her radical ideas.
   C) She ignores the various benefits of public transport.
   D) She insists vegetarians are harming the environment.
3. A) They are significant.　　C) They are rational.
   B) They are revolutionary.　　D) They are modest.
4. A) It would help to protect the environment.　　C) It would need support from the general public.
   B) It would generate money for public health.　　D) It would force poor people to change their diet.

Questions 5 to 8 are based on the conversation you have just heard.

5. A) Where successful people's strengths come from.　　C) How she achieved her life's goal.
   B) Why many people fight so hard for success.　　　　D) What makes people successful.
6. A) Having someone who has confidence in them.　　C) Having a firm belief in their own ability.
   B) Having someone who is ready to help them.　　　D) Having a realistic attitude towards life.
7. A) They adjust their goals accordingly.　　C) They stay positive.
   B) They try hard to appear optimistic.　　　D) They remain calm.
8. A) An understanding leadership.　　C) Mutual respect among colleagues.
   B) A nurturing environment.　　　　D) Highly cooperative teammates.

Section B

Directions: *In this section, you will hear two passages. At the end of each passage, you will hear three or four questions. Both the passage and the questions will be spoken only once. After you hear a question, you must choose the best answer from the four choices marked A), B), C) and D). Then mark the corresponding letter on **Answer Sheet 1** with a single line through the centre.*

Questions 9 to 11 are based on the passage you have just heard.

9. A) They use their sense of hearing to capture their prey.
   B) Their food mainly consists of small animals and fish.
   C) They have big eyes and distinctive visual centers.
   D) Their ancestor is different from that of micro bats.
10. A) With the help of moonlight.   C) With the aid of daylight vision.
    B) By means of echolocation.   D) By means of vision and smell.
11. A) To make up for their natural absence of vision.   C) To facilitate their travel over long distances.
    B) To adapt themselves to a particular lifestyle.   D) To survive in the ever-changing weather.

Questions 12 to 15 are based on the passage you have just heard.

12. A) They acquire knowledge not found in books.   C) They become more emotionally aggressive.
    B) They learn how to interact with their peers. D) They get much better prepared for school.
13. A) They are far from emotionally prepared.   C) They can't follow the conflicts in the show.
    B) They tend to be more attracted by images.   D) They lack the cognitive and memory skills.
14. A) Choose appropriate programs for their children.
    B) Help their children understand the program's plot.
    C) Outline the program's plot for their children first.
    D) Monitor their children's watching of TV programs.
15. A) Explain its message to their children.   C) Encourage their children to retell the story.
    B) Check if their children have enjoyed it.   D) Ask their children to describe its characters.

Section C

Directions: *In this section, you will hear three recordings of lectures or talks followed by three or four questions. The recordings will be played only once. After you hear a question, you must choose the best answer from the four choices marked A), B), C) and D). Then mark the corresponding letter on **Answer Sheet 1** with a single line through the centre.*

Questions 16 to 18 are based on the recording you have just heard.

16. A) They are afraid of injuring their feet.   C) They believe a little dirt harms no one.
    B) They have never developed the habit.   D) They find it rather troublesome to do so.
17. A) Different types of bacteria existed on public-toilet floors.
    B) There were more bacteria on sidewalks than in the home.
    C) Office carpets collected more bacteria than elsewhere.
    D) A large number of bacteria collected on a single shoe.
18. A) The chemicals on shoes can deteriorate air quality.
    B) Shoes can upset family members with their noise.
    C) The marks left by shoes are hard to erase.
    D) Shoes can leave scratches on the floor.

Questions 19 to 21 are based on the recording you have just heard.

19. A) It is sinful and immoral.   C) It is an uncontrollable behavior.
    B) It is deemed uncivilized.   D) It is a violation of faith and trust.
20. A) Assess their consequences.   C) Accept them as normal.
    B) Guard against their harm.   D) Find out their causes.

21. A) Try to understand what messages they convey. C) Consider them from different perspectives.
    B) Pay attention to their possible consequences. D) Make sure they are brought under control.

Questions 22 to 25 are based on the recording you have just heard.

22. A) Cultivation of new varieties of crops.   C) Development of more effective pesticides.
    B) Measures to cope with climate change.   D) Application of more nitrogen-rich fertilizers.
23. A) The expansion of farmland in developing countries.
    B) The research on crop rotation in developing countries.
    C) The cooperation of the world's agricultural scientists.
    D) The improvement of agricultural infrastructure.
24. A) For encouraging farmers to embrace new farming techniques.
    B) For aligning their research with advances in farming technology.
    C) For turning their focus to the needs of farmers in poorer countries.
    D) For cooperating closely with policymakers in developing countries.
25. A) Rapid transition to become a food exporter.   C) Quick rise to become a leading grain producer.
    B) Substantial funding in agricultural research. D) Assumption of humanitarian responsibilities.

Part III Reading Comprehension (40 minutes)

Section A

Directions: *In this section, there is a passage with ten blanks. You are required to select one word for each blank from a list of choices given in a word bank following the passage. Read the passage through carefully before making your choices. Each choice in the bank is identified by a letter. Please mark the corresponding letter for each item on **Answer Sheet 2** with a single line through the centre. You may not use any of the words in the bank more than once.*

According to psychologist Sharon Draper, our clothing choices can absolutely affect our well-being. When we wear ill-fitting clothes, or feel over- or under-dressed for an event, it's natural to feel self-conscious or even stressed. Conversely, she says, opting for clothes that fit well and __26__ with your sense of style can improve your confidence.

But can you improve your health through your __27__ clothing, without having to dash out and buy a whole new __28__? "Absolutely," says Draper. If your goal is to improve your thinking, she recommends picking clothes that fit well and are unlikely to encourage restlessness, so, avoid bows, ties and unnecessary __29__. It also helps to opt for clothes you __30__ as tying in with your goals, so, if you want to perform better at work, select pieces you view as professional. Draper says this fits in with the concept of behavioral activation, whereby __31__ in a behavior (in this case, selecting clothes) can set you on the path to then achieving your goals (working harder).

Another way to improve your __32__ of mind is to mix things up. Draper says we often feel stuck in a *rut* (常规) if we wear the same clothes — even if they're our favorites — thus opting for an item you don't wear often, or adding something different to an outfit, such as a hat, can __33__ shift your mood. On days when you're really __34__ to brave the world, Draper suggests selecting sentimental items of clothing, such as ones you wore on a special day, or given to you by a loved one, as clothes with __35__ associations can help you tap into constructive emotions.

A) accessories	F) fond	K) profile
B) align	G) frame	L) prospering
C) concurrently	H) locations	M) reluctant
D) current	I) perceive	N) showcase
E) engaging	J) positively	O) wardrobe

Section B

Directions: *In this section, you are going to read a passage with ten statements attached to it. Each statement contains information given in one of the paragraphs. Identify the paragraph from which the information is derived. You may choose a paragraph more than once. Each paragraph is marked with a letter. Answer the questions by marking the corresponding letter on* **Answer Sheet 2**.

No one in fashion is surprised that Burberry burnt £28 million of stock

[A] Last week, Burberry's annual report revealed that £28.6 million worth of stock was burnt last year. The news has left investors and consumers outraged but comes as little surprise to those in the fashion industry.

[B] The practice of destroying unsold stock, and even rolls of unused fabric, is commonplace for luxury labels. Becoming too widely available at a cheaper price through discount stores discourages full-price sales. Sending products for recycling leaves them vulnerable to being stolen and sold on the black market. Jasmine Bina, CEO of brand strategy agency Concept Bureau explains, "Typically, luxury brands rally around exclusivity to protect their business interests, namely intellectual property and preservation of brand *equity* (资产)." She stated she had heard rumors of stock burning but not specific cases until this week.

[C] Another reason for the commonplace practice is a financial incentive for brands exporting goods to America. United States Customs states that if imported merchandise is unused and destroyed under their supervision, 99% of the duties, taxes or fees paid on the merchandise may be recovered. It is incredibly difficult to calculate how much dead stock currently goes to waste. While there are incentives to do it, there's no legal obligation to report it.

[D] A source, who chose to remain anonymous, shared her experience working in a Burberry store in New York in October 2016. "My job was to toss items in boxes so they could be sent to be burned. It was killing me inside because all that leather and fur went to waste and animals had died for nothing. I couldn't stay there any longer, their business practices threw me off the roof." In May this year, Burberry announced it was taking fur out of its catwalk shows and reviewing its use elsewhere in the business. "Even though we asked the management, they refused to give us detailed answers as to why they would do this with their collection," continued the source, who left her role within two weeks. She has since worked with another high-profile, luxury label.

[E] In an online forum post, which asked if it's true that Louis Vuitton burned its bags, Ahmed Bouchfaa, who claimed to work for Louis Vuitton, responded that the brand holds sales of old stock for staff members twice a year. Items which have still not sold after several sales are destroyed. "Louis Vuitton doesn't have public sales. They either sell a product at a given price or discontinue it. This is to make sure that everybody pays the same price for an item," he says. He goes on to disclose the strict guidelines around the employee sales: "You may buy gifts for someone, but they track each item, and if your gift ends up online they know who to ask." One investor commenting on the Burberry figures was reportedly outraged that the unsold goods were not even offered to investors before they were destroyed.

[F] Richemont, who owns several luxury brands, hit the headlines in May for taking back £437 million of watches for destruction in the last two years to avoid marked-down prices. It's not just luxury brands either. In October last year, a Danish TV show exposed H&M for burning 12 tonnes of unsold clothing since 2013. In a statement, the high street retailer defended itself by saying that the burnt clothing had failed safety tests: "The products to which the media are referring have been tested in external laboratories. The test results show that one of the products is mold infested and the other product contains levels of lead that are too high. Those products have rightly been stopped in accordance with our safety routines." In March, a report revealed that H&M was struggling with $4.3 billion worth of unsold stock. The brand told *The New York Times* that the plan was to reduce prices to move the stock, arguably encouraging consumers to buy and throw away with little thought.

[G] Over-production is perhaps the biggest concern for Burberry. While there has been much outrage at the elitist connotation of burning goods rather than making them affordable, executives at the British fashion house are no doubt struggling to defend how they miscalculated production. The waste has been put down to burning old cosmetic stock to make way for their new beauty range. However, while the value of destroyed stock is up from £26.9 million last year, it's an even more significant increase from 2016's figure of £18.8 million, highlighting that this is an ongoing issue.

[H] In September 2016, Burberry switched to a "see now, buy now" catwalk show format. The move was a switch to leverage on the coverage of their fashion week show to make stock available immediately to consumers. This is opposed to the traditional format of presenting to the industry, taking orders for production and becoming available in six months' time. While Burberry announced "record-breaking" online reach and engagement, there has been little evidence to suggest that the strategy has had a significant effect on sales, particularly as the *hype* (炒作) slows across the season. In February they made adjustments to the format, dropping some catwalk items immediately and promising that others would launch in the coming months.

[I] In a statement, Burberry denied that switching to "see now, buy now" has had an impact on waste. A Burberry spokesperson further said, "On the occasions when disposal of products is necessary, we do so in a responsible manner. We are always seeking ways to reduce and revalue our waste. This is a core part of our strategy and we have forged partnerships and committed support to innovative organizations to help reach this goal."

[J] One such partership is with Elvis & Kresse, an accessories brand working with reclaimed materials. Co-founder Kresse Wesling said, "Late last year we launched an ambitious five-year partnership with the Burberry Foundation. The main aim of this is to scale our leather rescue project, starting with off-cuts from the production of Burberry leather goods. We are working tirelessly to expand our solutions and would love to welcome anyone to our workshop to come and see what we are doing." At the moment, the partnership only addresses waste at the production stage and not unsold goods.

[K] While these are honorable schemes, it makes it harder for Burberry to defend these latest figures. Fifteen years ago, Burberry was at crisis point as their signature check pattern was widely imitated by cheap, imitation brands. It deterred luxury consumers who found their expensive clothing more closely associated with working-class youth culture than a prestigious heritage fashion house. In the year 2004, at the height of over-exposure of the Burberry check, the brand's turnover was £715.5 million. Under Christopher Bailey as creative director they turned the brand around and this past year revenue hit £2.73 billion.

[L] Bina believes that brands need to readdress their exclusivity tactic. "Exclusivity is starting to be challenged," she says. "I think that goes hand in hand with how luxury itself is being challenged. Access to fashion, and the brands who police it, are becoming less and less relevant. Things like health, enlightenment, and social and environmental responsibility are the new luxuries. These all come from within, not without. That's the challenge that traditional luxury brands will have to contend with in the mid- to long-term future."

36. Burberry's executives are trying hard to attribute their practice of destroying old products to miscalculated production.
37. Selling products at a discount will do greater harm to luxury brands than destroying them.

38. Imitated Burberry products discouraged luxury consumers from buying its genuine products.
39. Staff members of a luxury brand may buy its old stock at cheaper prices, but they are not allowed to resell them.
40. In future traditional luxury brands will have to adapt their business strategies to the changing concepts of luxury.
41. One luxury brand employee quit her job because she simply couldn't bear to see the destruction of unsold products.
42. Destroying old stock is a practice not just of luxury brands but of less prestigious fashion brands.
43. Burberry is working with a partner to make full use of leather materials to reduce waste.
44. Burberry's plan to destroy its unsold products worth millions of dollars aroused public indignation.
45. Burberry's change of marketing strategy to make a product available as soon as consumers see it on the fashion show did not turn out to be as effective as expected.

Section C

Directions: *There are 2 passages in this section. Each passage is followed by some questions or unfinished statements. For each of them there are four choices marked A), B), C) and D). You should decide on the best choice and mark the corresponding letter on **Answer Sheet 2** with a single line through the centre.*

Passage One

Questions 46 to 50 are based on the following passage.

Social media is absolutely everywhere. Billions of people use social media on a daily basis to create, share, and exchange ideas, messages, and information. Both individuals and businesses post regularly to engage and interact with people from around the world. It is a powerful communication medium that simultaneously provides immediate, frequent, permanent, and wide-reaching information across the globe.

People post their lives on social media for the world to see. Facebook, Twitter, LinkedIn, and countless other social channels provide a quick and simple way to glimpse into a job candidate's personal life — both the positive and negative sides of it. Social media screening is tempting to use as part of the hiring process, but should employers make use of it when researching a potential candidate's background?

Incorporating the use of social media to screen job candidates is not an uncommon practice. A 2018 survey found that almost 70% of employers use social media to screen candidates before hiring them. But there are consequences and potential legal risks involved too. When done inappropriately, social media screening can be considered unethical or even illegal.

Social media screening is essentially scrutinising a job candidate's private life. It can reveal information about protected characteristics like age, race, nationality, disability, gender, religion, etc., and that could bias a hiring decision. Pictures or comments on a private page that are taken out of context could ruin a perfectly good candidate's chances of getting hired. This process could potentially give an unfair advantage to one candidate over another. It creates an unequal playing field and potentially provides hiring managers with information that can impact their hiring decision in a negative way.

It's hard to ignore social media as a screening tool. While there are things that you shouldn't see, there are some things that can be lawfully considered — making it a valuable source of relevant information too. Using social media screening appropriately can help ensure that you don't hire a toxic employee who will cost you money or stain your company's reputation. Consider the lawful side of this process and you may be able to hire the best employee ever. There is a delicate balance.

Screening job candidates on social media must be done professionally and responsibly. Companies should stipulate that they will never ask for passwords, be consistent, document decisions, consider the source used and be aware that other laws may apply. In light of this it is probably best to look later in the process and ask human resources for help in navigating it. Social media is here to stay. But before using social media to screen job candidates, consulting with management and legal teams beforehand is essential in order to comply with all laws.

46. What does the author mainly discuss in the passage?
    A) The advantage of using social media in screening job candidates.
    B) The potentially invasive nature of social media in everyday life.
    C) Whether the benefits of social media outweigh the drawbacks.
    D) Whether social media should be used to screen job candidates.
47. What might happen when social media is used to screen job candidates?
    A) Moral or legal issues might arise.   C) Sensational information might surface.
    B) Company reputation might suffer.   D) Hiring decisions might be complicated.
48. When could online personal information be detrimental to candidates?
    A) When it is separated from context.   C) When it is magnified to a ruinous degree.
    B) When it is scrutinised by an employer.   D) When it is revealed to the human resources.
49. How can employers use social media information to their advantage while avoiding unnecessary risks?
    A) By tipping the delicate balance.   C) By keeping personal information on record.
    B) By using it in a legitimate way.   D) By separating relevant from irrelevant data.
50. What does the author suggest doing before screening job candidates on social media?
    A) Hiring professionals to navigate the whole process.
    B) Anticipating potential risks involved in the process.
    C) Seeking advice from management and legal experts.
    D) Stipulating a set of rules for asking specific questions.

Passage Two

Questions 51 to 55 are based on the following passage.

In recent years, the food industry has increased its use of labels. Whether the labels say "non-GMO (非转基因的)" or "no sugar," or "zero carbohydrates", consumers are increasingly demanding more information about what's in their food. One report found that 39 percent of consumers would switch from the brands they currently buy to others that provide clearer, more accurate product information. Food manufacturers are responding to the report with new labels to meet that demand, and they're doing so with an eye towards giving their products an advantage over the competition, and bolstering profits.

This strategy makes intuitive sense. If consumers say they want transparency, tell them exactly what is in your product. That is simply supplying a certain demand. But the marketing strategy in response to this consumer demand has gone beyond articulating what is in a product, to labeling what is NOT in the food. These labels are known as "absence claims" labels, and they represent an emerging labeling trend that is detrimental both to the consumers who purchase the products and the industry that supplies them.

For example, Hunt's put a "non-GMO" label on its canned crushed tomatoes a few years ago — despite the fact that at the time there was no such thing as a GMO tomato on the market. Some dairy companies are using the "non-GMO" label on their milk, despite the fact that all milk is naturally GMO-free, another label that creates unnecessary fear around food.

While creating labels that play on consumer fears and misconceptions about their food may give a company a temporary marketing advantage over competing products on the grocery aisle, in the long term this strategy will have just the opposite effect: by injecting fear into the discourse about our food, we run the risk of eroding consumer trust in not just a single product, but the entire food business.

   Eventually, it becomes a question in consumers' minds: Were these foods ever safe? By purchasing and consuming these types of products, have I already done some kind of harm to my family or the planet? For food manufacturers, it will mean damaged consumer trust and lower sales for everyone. And this isn't just supposition. A recent study found that absence claims labels can create a stigma around foods even when there is no scientific evidence that they cause harm.

   It's clear that food manufacturers must tread carefully when it comes to using absence claims. In addition to the likely negative long-term impact on sales, this verbal trick sends a message that innovations in farming and food processing are unwelcome, eventually leading to less efficiency, fewer choices for consumers, and ultimately, more costly food products. If we allow this kind of labeling to continue, we will all lose.

51. What trend has been observed in a report?
    A) Food manufacturers' rising awareness of product safety.
    B) Food manufacturers' changing strategies to bolster profits.
    C) Consumers' growing demand for eye-catching food labels.
    D) Consumers' increasing desire for clear product information.
52. What does the author say is manufacturers' new marketing strategy?
    A) Stressing the absence of certain elements in their products.
    B) Articulating the unique nutritional value of their products.
    C) Supplying detailed information of their products.
    D) Designing transparent labels for their products.
53. What point does the author make about non-GMO labels?
    A) They are increasingly attracting customers' attention.
    B) They create lots of trouble for GMO food producers.
    C) They should be used more for vegetables and milk.
    D) They cause anxiety about food among consumers.
54. What does the author say absence claims labels will do to food manufacturers?
    A) Cause changes in their marketing strategies.   C) Erode consumer trust and reduce sales.
    B) Help remove stigma around their products.   D) Decrease support from food scientists.
55. What does the author suggest food manufacturers do?
    A) Take measures to lower the cost of food products.   C) Welcome new innovations in food processing.
    B) Exercise caution about the use of absence claims.   D) Promote efficiency and increase food variety.

Part Ⅳ　　　　　　　　Translation　　　　　　　　(30 minutes)

Directions: *For this part, you are allowed 30 minutes to translate a passage from Chinese into English. You should write your answer on **Answer Sheet 2**.*

中国共产党第一次全国代表大会会址位于上海兴业路76号，是一栋典型的上海式住宅，建于1920年秋。1921年7月23日，中国共产党第一次全国代表大会在此召开，大会通过了中国共产党的第一个纲领和第一个决议，选举产生了中央领导机构，宣告了中国共产党的诞生。1952年9月，中共一大会址修复，建立纪念馆并对外开放。纪念馆除了介绍参加一大的代表之外，还介绍党的历史发展进程，现已成为了解党史、缅怀革命先烈的爱国主义教育基地。

2021年12月大学英语六级考试真题解析
（第一套）

Part Ⅰ Writing

成文构思

本文是一篇议论文，话题是"年轻人追星"，可按照以下思路进行写作。
第一段：引出话题，提出"年轻人追星的现象很普遍"这一观点。
第二段：分析"年轻人追星"的原因，可从经济原因和作用两个方面进行分析。本段是全文的中心段落。
第三段：总结，针对现象提出建议。

参考范文及译文

　　It is widely acknowledged that an increasing number of individuals, especially teenagers, are keen on star-chasing in this constantly changing society, which has **aroused** great concern among their parents. As teenagers would like to **imitate** their idols in every aspect, such as ways of talking, styles of dressing, their parents worry that this behavior would affect their physical and mental health and result in bad academic performance.

　　As far as I am concerned, several factors could **account for** this phenomenon. Firstly, with the rapid development of the national economy, people's living standard, both materially and spiritually, has improved greatly, which enables teenagers to have the time and ability to keep up with the fashion, such as star-chasing. What's more, as a kind of social relationship, although it has all kinds of **shortcomings**, it can at least partially meet our basic needs for social relationships and a sense of belonging.

　　All in all, star-chasing is a trend, and what is more important is to take reasonable measures to guide teenagers to do it more rationally. The authorities concerned can **formulate** more relevant laws and regulations. And it is better for parents to provide **appropriate** guidance to their children on this issue.

　　众所周知，在这个不断变化的社会中，越来越多的人——尤其是青少年——都热衷于追星，这引起了他们父母的极大关切。由于青少年喜欢在各个方面模仿他们的偶像，比如说话方式、着装风格，他们的父母担心此举会影响他们的身心健康，导致糟糕的学习成绩。

　　在我看来，有几个原因可以解释这一现象。首先，随着国家经济的快速发展，人们的生活水平，不论是在物质上还是精神上，都有了很大的提升，这使得青少年有时间和精力紧跟时尚潮流，如追星。此外，追星作为一种社会关系，虽然存在种种不足，却至少能部分满足我们对于社交关系和归属感的基本需求。

　　总而言之，追星是一种趋势，更重要的是采取合理的措施来引导青少年更理智地追星。有关当局可以制定更多的相关法律法规。且父母最好在这个问题上给孩子提供适当的指导。

词句点拨

arouse /əˈraʊz/ v. 引起，激起
account for 说明……的原因
formulate /ˈfɔːmjuleɪt/ v. 制定，规划

imitate /ˈɪmɪteɪt/ v. 模仿，仿效
shortcoming /ˈʃɔːtkʌmɪŋ/ n. 缺点，短处
appropriate /əˈprəʊpriət/ a. 合适的，相称的

1. It is widely acknowledged that...
   众所周知……

2. As far as I am concerned, several factors could account for this phenomenon. Firstly, ...
   在我看来，有几个原因可以解释这一现象。首先，……

3. All in all, ... is a trend, and what is more important is to take reasonable measures to...
   总而言之，……是一种趋势，更重要的是采取合理的措施来……

Part II　Listening Comprehension

Section A

Questions 1 to 4 are based on the conversation you have just heard.

听力原文及译文

M: Good morning and welcome to *People in the News*. With me today is Megan Brown, (1) <u>an environmental activist whose controversial new book *Beyond Recycling* is making headlines.</u>

W: Hi Brian. Thanks for having me today. I'm excited to explain to the audience what my book is really about.

M: (2) <u>Critics of your book asserted that you're trying to force radical changes on the entire country.</u> Some claim that you want to force everyone to eat a vegetarian diet and make private transport illegal.

W: I'm aware of those claims. But they simply aren't true. People who haven't read the book are making assumptions about my arguments. They know I am a vegetarian, that I don't wear leather or fur, and that I always use public transportation. So they're depicting me as a radical animal rights activist and environmentalist determined to force my beliefs on others.

M: But don't you want others to adopt your practices? You've campaigned for animal rights and the environment for decades.

W: I'd love it if people choose to live as I do. But my life choices are based on my personal convictions. They aren't my recommendations for others who don't share those convictions.

M: Well. In this excerpt from your book, you argue that meat consumption and private transport are devastating the environment and that the best choices for the planet are vegetarians diets and public transport.

W: I did write that. But those are examples of what I called "Best Practices", not what I'm actually suggesting. In my guidelines for saving the environment, (3) <u>I suggest modest changes, like eating vegetarian meals two days a week.</u>

M: You also endorse high taxes on meat and other animal products and increased taxes on gasoline. Those taxes could force poor people to adopt your life choices.

W: But the taxes I suggest aren't that high — less than three percent only. (4) <u>Plus, the money generated would be allocated to environmental protection which benefits everyone.</u>

男：早上好，欢迎收看《新闻人物》。今天和我一起主持节目的是梅根·布朗，（1）<u>她是一位环保人士，她的新书《超越回收利用》备受争议，正占据着新闻头条。</u>

女：嗨，布莱恩，感谢你今天邀请我来节目做客。能向观众解释书中的真正内容，我很兴奋。

男：（2）<u>这本书的批评者断言你正试图强迫整个国家发生巨大改变。</u>有人声称，你想强迫每个人都吃素，并将私人交通定为非法。

女：我知道这些说法。但这些根本都不是真的。没读过我这本书的人正臆断我的论点。他们知道我是素食主义者，不穿皮革或毛皮外套，而且我总是乘坐公共交通工具。因此他们正把我描绘成一个激进的动物权利活动家和环保主义者，下定决心强行施加自己的信仰给他人。

男：但是难道你不想让别人接受你的做法吗？几十年来，你一直在倡导动物权利和环境保护。

女：如果人们选择像我这样生活，我是很乐意的。但我基于个人信念做人生选择。这些选择不是我给那些不持有这些信念的人提出的建议。

男：嗯。在你书中的这段摘录中，你认为肉类消费和私人交通正毁坏环境，对于地球来说，素食和公共交通是最佳选择。

女：我确实写了这个。但这些是我叫作"最佳实践"的案例，而不是我实际上的建议。在我的环保指南中，（3）<u>我建议做一些适度改变，比如每周吃两天素食。</u>

男：你也赞同对肉类和其他动物制品征收高额税，并增加汽油税。这些税收可以强迫穷人接受你的人生选择。

女：但是我建议的税率并没那么高——仅不到百分之三。（4）<u>而且，所产生的资金将用于惠及所有人的环境保护。</u>

难词总结

controversial /ˌkɒntrəˈvɜːʃl/ *a.* 有争议的
conviction /kənˈvɪkʃn/ *n.* 信念

claim /kleɪm/ *v.* 声称；断言
endorse /ɪnˈdɔːs/ *v.* 赞同；认可

题目精析

1. What do we learn about the woman's new book?
   A) It has given rise to much controversy.
   B) It has been very favorably received.
   C) It was primarily written for vegetarians.
   D) It offends many environmentalists.

1. 关于女士的新书，我们可以了解到什么？
   A）它已引起很多争议。
   B）它已被广泛接受。
   C）它主要是为素食主义者撰写。
   D）它冒犯了许多环保主义者。

【答案及分析】A。本题问女士新书的相关内容。音频中提到，an environmental activist whose controversial new book *Beyond Recycling* is making headlines（她是一位环保人士，她的新书《超越回收利用》备受争议，正占据着新闻头条）。A 项与音频内容相符，其中 controversy 对应音频中的 controversial，故选 A 项。

2. What do some critics say about the author of the book?

   A) She neglects people's efforts in animal protection.

   B) She tries to force people to accept her radical ideas.

   C) She ignores the various benefits of public transport.

   D) She insists vegetarians are harming the environment.

2. 一些批评者对这本书的作者有何评价？

   A）她忽视了人们在动物保护方面的努力。

   B）她设法强迫人们接受她的激进思想。

   C）她忽视了公共交通的各种好处。

   D）她坚持认为素食主义者正在危害环境。

   【答案及分析】B。本题问批评者对女士的评价。音频中提到，Critics of your book asserted that you're trying to force radical changes on the entire country.（这本书的批评者断言你正试图强迫整个国家发生巨大改变。）B 项与音频内容相符，其中 tries to force people to accept her radical ideas 是音频中 trying to force radical changes on the entire country 的同义表达，tries to force 和 radical 为原词复现，故选 B 项。

3. What does the woman claim about the diet changes she suggested?

   A) They are significant.   C) They are rational.

   B) They are revolutionary.   D) They are modest.

3. 这位女士对于她建议的饮食改变有何说法？

   A）它们意义重大。   C）它们是理性的。

   B）它们具有突破性。   D）它们是适度的。

   【答案及分析】D。本题问女士对饮食改变的看法。音频中提到，I suggest modest changes, like eating vegetarian meals two days a week.（我建议做一些适度改变，比如每周吃两天素食。）D 项与音频内容相符，其中 modest 为原词复现，故选 D 项。

4. What does the woman say about her suggested tax increase?

   A) It would help to protect the environment.

   B) It would generate money for public health.

   C) It would need support from the general public.

   D) It would force poor people to change their diet.

4. 这位女士对她提出的增税建议有何说法？

   A）它将有助于保护环境。   C）它将需要公众支持。

   B）它将为公共卫生创造收入。   D）它将迫使穷人改变饮食。

   【答案及分析】A。本题问女士对增税建议的看法。音频中提到，Plus, the money generated would be allocated to environmental protection which benefits everyone.（而且，所产生的资金将用于惠及所有人的环境保护。）A 项与音频内容相符，其中 protect the environment 是音频中 environmental protection 的同义表达，故选 A 项。

Questions 5 to 8 are based on the conversation you have just heard.

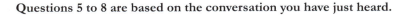

M: With me in the studio today is Miss Jane Logan, author of a new book *Secrets to Success*. (5) She claims to have uncovered how people achieve success. So, Miss Logan, in your book, you claim that successful people have many things in common. For instance, they know their strengths when pursuing a goal.

W: That's right. They also tend to be motivated by a negative or positive life event. (6) They credit their success to having someone in their life who believes in them.

M: You also write that there are a number of different factors related to success. And while successful people are driven to achieve their goals, the ultra successful have even greater ambition.

W: Yes, greater ambition as well as a burning desire to be the best of the best is also a common characteristic.

M: Right. So those who are determined don't see obstacles as something that prevents success, but mere inconveniences that need to be overcome.

W: Absolutely. (7) Successful people are also optimistic as it is important to stay positive while being aware of obstacles that can deter us from achieving our goals.

M: That's a good point. All too often, people give up at the first hurdle. Would you say then that most successful people make it all by themselves?

W: Not exactly. They are usually good at cooperating with people and understanding the needs of others.

M: So people will be willing to help them, I guess.

W: That's correct. And this often leads to a great deal of mutual respect, whether it's with a colleague, an assistant or even a receptionist.

M: Most successful people I know are very passionate about their work. Would you say that passion is the single biggest key to success?

W: Not entirely. (8) There's a prerequisite, that is, you have to work in an environment that nurtures passion. If that exists, success will follow.

男：今天和我一起在演播室的是新书《成功的秘诀》的作者——简·洛根小姐。（5）她声称已经揭开了人们获得成功的奥秘。所以，洛根小姐，你在书中提到了成功人士有很多共同点。比如，他们了解自己在追求目标时的优势。

女：没错。他们往往会被生活中消极或积极的事件激励。（6）他们把成功归功于生活中有人相信他们。

男：你同样也写到，有很多因素和成功相关。当成功人士被驱使实现目标时，超级成功者的野心甚至更大。

女：是的，野心更大以及成为强中最强的强烈愿望也是成功者的一个共同特征。

男：对。因此那些意志坚定的人不会认为障碍会阻碍我们实现目标，只是把它们看作需要克服的不便。

女：当然。（7）成功人士也很乐观，因为意识到障碍会阻止我们实现目标时，保持积极的态度很重要。

男：这个观点很好。人们经常在第一关就放弃了。那么，你会说大多数成功人士都是靠自己取得成功的吗？

女：不完全是。通常他们善于与人合作，能够理解他人的需求。

男：我猜，因此人们会乐意帮助他们。

女：没错。不管是与同事、助理，或者甚至是接待员共事，通常这都会带来极大的相互尊重。

男：我认识的绝大多数成功人士都对他们的工作充满激情。你会说激情是获得成功的唯一的最关键因素吗？

女：不完全是这样。（8）有一个前提，那就是你必须在可以培养激情的环境中工作。如果存在这种情况，成功就会随之而来。

难词总结

uncover /ʌnˈkʌvə(r)/ v. 揭露；发现

obstacle /ˈɒbstəkl/ n. 障碍；阻碍

credit /ˈkredɪt/ v. 认为是……的功劳

prerequisite /ˌpriːˈrekwəzɪt/ n. 前提

题目精析

5. What has the woman revealed in her book?

A) Where successful people's strengths come from.
B) Why many people fight so hard for success.
C) How she achieved her life's goal.
D) What makes people successful.

5. 女士在她的书中揭示了什么？

A）成功人士的优势来源。
B）为什么很多人为了成功努力奋斗。
C）她是怎样实现人生目标的。
D）什么可以让人获得成功。

【答案及分析】D。本题问女士的新书内容。音频中提到，She claims to have uncovered how people achieve success.（她声称已经揭开了人们获得成功的奥秘。）D 项 What makes people successful 是音频中 uncovered how people achieve success 的同义表达，故选 D 项。

6. What do successful people attribute their achievements to?

A) Having someone who has confidence in them.
B) Having someone who is ready to help them.
C) Having a firm belief in their own ability.
D) Having a realistic attitude towards life.

6. 成功人士把自身成就归功于什么？

A）有人信任他们。
B）有人乐意帮助他们。
C）对自己的能力有坚定信念。
D）用现实的态度面对生活。

【答案及分析】A。本题问成功人士认为自己获得成功的原因。音频中提到，They credit their success to having someone in their life who believes in them.（他们把成功归功于生活中有人相信他们。）A 项与音频内容相符，其中 someone who has confidence in them 是音频中 someone in their life who believes in them 的同义表达，故选 A 项。

7. What do successful people do when faced with difficulties?

A) They adjust their goals accordingly.
B) They try hard to appear optimistic.
C) They stay positive.
D) They remain calm.

7. 成功人士在面对困难时会做什么？

A）他们对自己的目标做出相应调整。
B）他们努力让自己看起来乐观。
C）他们保持乐观。
D）他们保持冷静。

【答案及分析】C。本题问成功人士在面对困难时会做什么。音频中提到，Successful people are also

optimistic as it is important to stay positive while being aware of obstacles that can deter us from achieving our goals.（成功人士也很乐观，因为意识到障碍会阻止我们实现目标时，保持积极的态度很重要。）C 项是音频内容的同义表达，其中 stay positive 为原词复现，故选 C 项。

8. What is one prerequisite for passion at work according to the woman?

A) An understanding leadership.
B) A nurturing environment.
C) Mutual respect among colleagues.
D) Highly cooperative teammates.

8. 根据这位女士的说法，热情工作的前提是什么？

A）宽容的领导。
B）培养人才的环境。
C）同事之间的相互尊重。
D）高度合作的队友。

【答案及分析】B。本题问热情工作的前提。音频中提到，There's a prerequisite, that is, you have to work in an environment that nurtures passion.（有一个前提，那就是你必须在可以培养激情的环境中工作。）B 项是音频内容的同义表达，故选 B 项。

Section B

Questions 9 to 11 are based on the passage you have just heard.

听力原文及译文

The saying "blind as a bat" simply isn't correct. The truth is that all 1,100 bat species can see and often their vision is pretty good, although not as excellent as other-night hunting animals.

There are two main groups of bats, which are believed to have evolved independently of each other, but both from a common ancestor. The first group, known as the mega bats, are mostly medium-sized or large bats who eat fruits, flowers, and sometimes small animals or fish. (9) These species have distinctive visual centers and big eyes. They use senses of vision and smell to capture their prey. For example, Flying Foxes not only see well during daylight, but can also distinguish colors. They actually rely on their daylight vision and cannot fly during the nights with no moonlight.

The second group, called micro bats, are smaller in size and mostly eat insects. (10) These species use echolocation to find their way and identify food. Scientists have proven that despite their poorly developed small eyes, these bats still can see during the day. When we consider the nightly lifestyle of these bats, we will see they have to be sensitive to the changing light levels because this is how they sense when to start hunting. Moreover, vision is used by micro bats to travel over long distances, beyond the range of echolocation.

So the truth is, there are no bats which are naturally blind. (11) Some species use their sense of hearing more than their eyes as a matter of adaptation to a particular lifestyle, but their eyes are still functional.

"像蝙蝠一样瞎"的谚语简直就不正确。事实是，所有的 1 100 种蝙蝠都可以看得见，并且它们的视力通常都相当好，尽管不如其他夜间狩猎动物的视力那样出色。

蝙蝠有两大类，人们认为它们分别独立进化，但都来自同一个祖先。第一类蝙蝠被称为巨型蝙蝠，多半是中型或大型蝙蝠，它们吃水果和花朵，有时也吃小动物或鱼类。（9）这些蝙蝠物种有与众不同的视觉中枢和大眼睛。它们利用视觉和嗅觉捕捉猎物。例如，飞狐不仅能在白天看得很清楚，还能分辨颜色。实际上，它们只能依靠昼视觉，在没有月光的夜晚无法飞行。

第二类叫作微型蝙蝠，体型较小，主食昆虫。（10）这些物种利用回声定位辨别方向和识别食物。科学家已证明，尽管这些蝙蝠的眼睛小、发育不良，但在白天它们依然可以看得见。当我们考虑蝙蝠的夜间生活方式时，我们会发现它们必须对光的变化水平敏感，因为这就是它们感知何时开始狩猎的方式。此外，微型蝙蝠利用视觉进行长距离飞行，飞行距离超出了回声定位的范围。

因此，事实是，蝙蝠不是天生眼盲。（11）一些物种利用听觉而不是视觉来适应特定的生活方式，但它们的眼睛仍然有功能。

难词总结

distinctive /dɪˈstɪŋktɪv/ a. 独特的；与众不同的
sensitive /ˈsensətɪv/ a. 灵敏的；敏感的
echolocation /ˌekəʊləʊˈkeɪʃn/ n. 回声定位能力
adaptation /ˌædæpˈteɪʃn/ n. 适应

题目精析

9. What do we learn about mega bats?

    A) They use their sense of hearing to capture their prey.
    B) Their food mainly consists of small animals and fish.
    C) They have big eyes and distinctive visual centers.
    D) Their ancestor is different from that of micro bats.

9. 关于巨型蝙蝠，我们可以了解到什么？

    A）它们利用自身听觉捕捉猎物。
    B）它们主食小动物和鱼。
    C）它们的眼睛大，视觉中枢独特。
    D）它们的祖先不同于微型蝙蝠。

【答案及分析】C。本题问关于巨型蝙蝠的信息。音频中提到，These species have distinctive visual centers and big eyes.（这些蝙蝠物种有与众不同的视觉中枢和大眼睛。）C 项与音频相符，其中 big eyes 和 distinctive visual centers 为原词复现。B 项中的 mainly 和音频中的 sometimes 不符，音频中提到巨型蝙蝠有时也吃小动物和鱼，但并不能推断出它们以此为主食。故选 C 项。

10. How do micro bats find their way and identify food?

    A) With the help of moonlight.
    B) By means of echolocation.
    C) With the aid of daylight vision.
    D) By means of vision and smell.

10. 微型蝙蝠如何辨别方向和识别食物？

    A）借助月光。
    C）借助昼视觉。
    B）通过回声定位。
    D）通过视觉和嗅觉。

【答案及分析】B。本题问微型蝙蝠辨别方向和识别食物的方式。音频中提到，These species use echolocation to find their way and identify food.（这些物种利用回声定位辨别方向和识别食物。）B 项 By means of echolocation 是音频中 use echolocation 的同义表达，故选 B 项。

11. Why do some species of bats use their sense of hearing more than their eyes?

　　A) To make up for their natural absence of vision.　　C) To facilitate their travel over long distances.

　　B) To adapt themselves to a particular lifestyle.　　D) To survive in the ever-changing weather.

11. 为什么某些种类的蝙蝠使用听觉多于视觉？

　　A）来弥补它们天生缺乏的视力。　　C）方便它们长途飞行。

　　B）让自己适应特定的生活方式。　　D）在不断变化的天气下生存。

【答案及分析】B。本题问某些蝙蝠使用听觉多过视觉的原因。音频中提到，Some species use their sense of hearing more than their eyes as a matter of adaptation to a particular lifestyle（一些物种利用听觉而不是视觉来适应特定的生活方式）。B 项中的 adapt themselves to a particular lifestyle 对应音频中的 adaptation to a particular lifestyle，故选 B 项。

Questions 12 to 15 are based on the passage you have just heard.

【听力原文及译文】

　　A study has found that educational TV shows come with an added lesson that influences the child's behavior. (12) Children spending more time watching educational programs increase their emotional aggression toward other children. This shows that children can learn the educational lesson that was intended. However, they're also learning other things along the way. The unintended impact has to do with the portrayal of conflict in media and how preschool-age children comprehend that conflict. TV and movie producers often incorporate an element of bad behavior. This is to teach children a lesson at the end of the program.

　　Educational shows have pre-education and pro-social goals. However, conflict between characters is often depicted with characters being unkind to each other, or they may use emotionally aggressive tactics with each other. (13) Preschool children really don't get the moral of the story. That's because it requires that they understand how all the parts of the show fit together. You need pretty complicated cognitive skills and memory skills to be able to do that. These are still developing in young children.

　　However, parents shouldn't completely constrain children's viewing. (14) Parents should instead watch with their kids and help them to understand the plot. (15) Parents can comment along the way and then explain the message at the end. They should explain how certain type of behavior was not appropriate. This will help children interpret and get the message and help them to watch the show for those messages.

　　一项研究已发现，教育电视节目附带着影响孩子行为的额外课程。（12）花更多时间观看教育节目的孩子会增加对其他孩子的情感侵犯。这表明孩子们可以学到预期中的教育课程。然而，他们同时也正学习着其他内容。这种预期外的影响与"媒体对冲突的描述"以及"学龄前儿童如何理解这种冲突"有关。电视和电影制作人通常会加入不良行为要素。这是为了在节目最后给孩子们上一课。

　　教育节目的目的是学前教育和亲社会。但是，人物角色之间的冲突通常被描绘成彼此不友好，又或者可能会在情感上相互攻击。（13）学龄前儿童确实不能理解这个故事的寓意。因为这要求他们理解节目中的各部分是怎样结合一起的。你需要相当复杂的认知和记忆技能才能做到这一点。幼儿仍在发展这种技能。

然而，父母不应该完全限制孩子观看这种节目。（14）相反，父母应该和孩子一块儿观看，帮助他们理解故事情节。（15）父母可以同时进行评论，然后在节目最后解释信息。他们应该解释某种类型的行为是怎样不合适的。这将有助于孩子们解释、明白信息，并帮助他们观看传达这些信息的电视节目。

难词总结

aggression /əˈgreʃn/ n. 好斗性；攻击性
incorporate /ɪnˈkɔːpəreɪt/ v. 包含；使并入
constrain /kənˈstreɪn/ v. 限制；约束

unintended /ˌʌnɪnˈtendɪd/ a. 非计划的；无意识的
cognitive /ˈkɒgnətɪv/ a. 认知的；认识的

题目精析

12. What does the passage say about children watching educational programs?

A) They acquire knowledge not found in books.
B) They learn how to interact with their peers.
C) They become more emotionally aggressive.
D) They get much better prepared for school.

12. 这篇文章对于观看教育节目的孩子有何说法？

A）他们能掌握书本上学不到的知识。
B）他们学习怎样与同龄人互动。
C）他们变得更具情感侵犯性。
D）他们为上学做更好的准备。

【答案及分析】C。本题问观看教育节目对孩子的影响。音频中提到，Children spending more time watching educational programs increase their emotional aggression toward other children.（花更多时间观看教育节目的孩子会增加对其他孩子的情感侵犯。）C项中的 more emotionally aggressive 是音频中 increase their emotional aggression 的同义表达，故选C项。

13. Why can't preschool children get the moral conveyed in the TV programs?

A) They are far from emotionally prepared.
B) They tend to be more attracted by images.
C) They can't follow the conflicts in the show.
D) They lack the cognitive and memory skills.

13. 为什么学龄前儿童不能理解电视节目传达的寓意？

A）他们在情感上还远没有做好准备。
B）他们更容易被图像吸引。
C）他们无法理解节目里的冲突。
D）他们缺乏认知和记忆技能。

【答案及分析】D。本题问学龄前儿童无法理解节目传达的寓意的原因。音频中提到，Preschool children really don't get the moral of the story.（学龄前儿童确实不能理解这个故事的寓意。）之后又提到原因，You need pretty complicated cognitive skills and memory skills to be able to do that. These are still developing in young children.（你需要相当复杂的认知和记忆技能才能做到这一点。幼儿仍在发展这种技能。）D项为音频内容的同义表达，cognitive and memory skills 为原词复现，故选D项。

14. What does the passage suggest parents do?

A) Choose appropriate programs for their children.
B) Help their children understand the program's plot.
C) Outline the program's plot for their children first.

D) Monitor their children's watching of TV programs.

14. 文章建议父母应该做什么？

A）为他们的孩子选择合适的节目。

B）帮他们的孩子理解节目情节。

C）首先为他们的孩子概述节目情节。

D）对他们的孩子看电视节目进行监控。

【答案及分析】B。本题问对父母的建议。音频中提到，Parents should instead watch with their kids and help them to understand the plot.（相反，父母应该和孩子一块儿观看，帮助他们理解故事情节。）可知 B 项是音频内容的同义表达，故选 B 项。

15. What should parents do right after watching the TV program?

A) Explain its message to their children.
B) Check if their children have enjoyed it.
C) Encourage their children to retell the story.
D) Ask their children to describe its characters.

15. 看完电视节目后，父母应该做什么？

A）向他们的孩子解释节目传递的信息。
B）核实他们的孩子是否喜欢看这个节目。
C）鼓励他们的孩子复述这个故事。
D）让他们的孩子描述节目中的人物角色。

【答案及分析】A。本题问父母在看完电视节目后应该做什么。音频中提到，Parents can comment along the way and then explain the message at the end.（父母可以同时进行评论，然后在节目最后解释信息。）A 项为音频内容的同义表达，故选 A 项。

Section C

Questions 16 to 18 are based on the recording you have just heard.

听力原文及译文

　　While it has long been at practice in Asian countries, many people in Western countries have yet to embrace the no-shoes-in-the-house rule. For many in those countries, wiping their shoes before going inside is regarded as sufficient. (16) After all, they may think a little dirt doesn't hurt anyone. But I can give you several good reasons why people should remove their shoes before going inside their homes.

　　Bacteria are everywhere. They collect on your shoes when you walk along sidewalks, public toilet floors and even office carpets. In one study conducted at an American university, researchers collected microscopic germs from footwear. (17) They found that up to 421,000 units of bacteria can collect on the outside of a single shoe and it only takes a little bit of dirt to damage your timber floors. The more dirt you track in, the more it scratches and the more often you'd have to clean. The extra scrubbing will harm your floors over time.

　　Shoes can also leave marks and scratches on floors, especially high heels or shoes with pointed or hard parts. These can dent and scratch your floor. And if you live in an apartment building, removing your noisy shoes is the polite thing to do out of consideration for your downstairs neighbors. Walking around with bare feet is actually better for your feet. It strengthens the muscles in your feet. Though many people are accustomed to wearing shoes during all their waking hours, the more time you spend wearing shoes, the more likely you are to incur foot injuries as a result.

(18) And if people aren't yet convinced by my arguments, I can give one final reason. The dust and toxic chemicals you bring into your house via your shoes can deteriorate the air quality in your home. Toxic chemicals are everywhere in our lives: insect-killing chemicals used on public grass areas, cleaning chemicals on the floors of public areas. By kicking off your shoes before you enter the home, you are denying entry to these harmful chemicals. Given the amount of time we spend in classrooms and the number of shoes that pass through them every day, you may well understand me if I were to propose a no-shoes-in-the-classroom rule.

虽然这在亚洲国家已经实践了很长时间，但许多西方国家的人还没有接受室内不穿鞋的规定。对这些国家的许多人来说，进屋前擦鞋就足够了。(16) 毕竟，他们可能认为一点污垢不会伤害任何人。但我可以给你几个充分的理由来说明为什么人们进屋前应该脱鞋。

细菌无处不在。当你走在人行道、公共厕所的地板，甚至办公室的地毯上时，它们会在你的鞋子上聚集。在美国一所大学进行的一项研究中，研究人员从鞋子上收集了微小的细菌。(17) 他们发现，一只鞋的表面可以收集多达42.1万个细菌，而且只需要一点点灰尘就能损坏木制地板。你踩进去的灰尘越多，刮破的地方就越多，你需要清理的次数也就越多。长时间的擦洗会随着时间的推移损害你的地板。

鞋子也会在地板上留下痕迹和划痕，尤其是高跟鞋和带有尖头或硬质部位的鞋子。这些会使你的地板凹陷并刮破你的地板。如果你住在公寓楼里，脱掉发出噪声的鞋子是礼貌的做法，这是为你楼下的邻居着想。光脚走来走去实际上对你的脚更好。它可以增强脚部的肌肉。虽然许多人习惯于在醒着的时候一直穿着鞋，但你穿鞋的时间越长，就越有可能导致脚部受伤。

（18）如果人们还没有被我的论点说服，我可以给出最后一个理由，即你通过鞋子带入家中的灰尘和有毒化学物质会恶化你的空气质量。有毒化学物质在我们的生活中无处不在，如用于公共草坪区域的杀虫化学制品和公共区域地板上的清洁类化学制品。在进入家中之前脱掉鞋子，就是拒绝这些有害化学物质进入。考虑到我们在教室里度过的时间以及每天经过教室的鞋子数量，如果我提出一个在课堂上不穿鞋的规定，你很可能会理解我。

难词总结

embrace /ɪmˈbreɪs/ v. 欣然接受，乐意采纳
scratch /skrætʃ/ v. 划出，刮出（痕迹）
dent /dent/ v. 使产生凹痕；损害

microscopic /ˌmaɪkrəˈskɒpɪk/ a. 微小的；显微镜的
pointed /ˈpɔɪntɪd/ a. 尖的；有尖头的
deteriorate /dɪˈtɪəriəreɪt/ v. 恶化，变坏

题目精析

16. Why don't many Westerners take off shoes before entering a house?
    A) They are afraid of injuring their feet.
    B) They have never developed the habit.
    C) They believe a little dirt harms no one.
    D) They find it rather troublesome to do so.

16. 为什么很多西方人在进屋前不脱鞋呢？
    A）他们害怕伤到自己的脚。
    B）他们从来没有养成这种习惯。
    C）他们认为一点污垢不会伤害任何人。
    D）他们觉得这样做很麻烦。

【答案及分析】C. 本题问很多西方人在进屋前不脱鞋的原因。音频中提到，After all, they may think a little dirt doesn't hurt anyone.（毕竟，他们可能认为一点污垢不会伤害任何人。）C 项中的 believe a little dirt harms no one 是音频中 think a little dirt doesn't hurt anyone 的同义表达，故选 C 项。

17. What is the finding of one study by researchers at an American university?

   A) Different types of bacteria existed on public-toilet floors.

   B) There were more bacteria on sidewalks than in the home.

   C) Office carpets collected more bacteria than elsewhere.

   D) A large number of bacteria collected on a single shoe.

17. 美国一所大学的研究人员的一项研究有什么发现？

   A）公共厕所地板上存在不同类型的细菌。

   B）人行道上的细菌比家里的细菌要多。

   C）在办公室地毯上收集的细菌比其他地方多。

   D）在一只鞋上收集了大量的细菌。

   【答案及分析】D。本题问研究人员的发现。音频中提到，They found that up to 421,000 units of bacteria can collect on the outside of a single shoe and it only takes a little bit of dirt to damage your timber floors.（他们发现，一只鞋的表面可以收集多达 42.1 万个细菌，而且只需要一点点灰尘就能损坏木制地板。）D 项是音频中 up to 421,000 units of bacteria can collect on the outside of a single shoe 的同义表达，故选 D 项。

18. What is the final reason the speaker gives for removing shoes before entering a house?

   A) The chemicals on shoes can deteriorate air quality.

   B) Shoes can upset family members with their noise.

   C) The marks left by shoes are hard to erase.

   D) Shoes can leave scratches on the floor.

18. 说话者给出的进屋前脱鞋的最后一个理由是什么？

   A）鞋子上的化学物质会恶化空气质量。

   B）鞋子发出的噪声会使家人心烦意乱。

   C）鞋印很难擦去。

   D）鞋子会在地板上留下划痕。

   【答案及分析】A。本题问进屋前脱鞋的最后一个理由。音频中提到，And if people aren't yet convinced by my arguments, I can give one final reason. The dust and toxic chemicals you bring into your house via your shoes can deteriorate the air quality in your home.（如果人们还没有被我的论点说服，我可以给出最后一个理由，即你通过鞋子带入家中的灰尘和有毒化学物质会恶化你家的空气质量。）A 项是音频中 dust and toxic chemicals you bring into your house via your shoes can deteriorate the air quality 的同义表达，故选 A 项。

Questions 19 to 21 are based on the recording you have just heard.

听力原文及译文

   Emotions are an essential and inseparable part of our consciousness. They are part of a built-in mechanism which allows us to cope with the ups and downs of our lives both physically and mentally. When we hide our emotions and our true feelings, we stop being genuine, spontaneous and authentic in our relationships. When we put on cultivated and polished faces in the company of others, we stop being true to ourselves. (19) Socially, it may be a good tactic to hide our true emotions, but morally it is also a breach of faith and trust.

Although humans are more advanced and intelligent, animals are more genuine and authentic in their behavior and responses than human beings. The more educated we are, the less transparent and reliable we become. We are drawn to our pets because pets do not lie.

(20) One of the first steps in dealing with emotions such as anger or fear is to acknowledge them as normal and human. There is nothing sinful or immoral about being emotional, unless your emotions make you inhuman, insensitive and cruel to others. Feelings of guilt associated with emotions are more devastating and damaging than the experience of emotion itself. So when you deal with the problem of emotions, you should learn not only how to control them, but also how to accept them and manage the guilt and anguish arising from them.

Our brains are made up of a primitive inner core and a more evolved and rational outer core. Most of the time, the rational part of the mind controls the information coming from the primitive core and makes its own decisions as to what to do and how to respond. However, during critical situations, especially when a threat is perceived, the outer core loses control and fails to regulate the impulses and instinctual responses coming from the primitive brain. As a result, we let disturbing thoughts and emotions arise in our consciousness and surrender to our primitive behavior.

In times of emotional turmoil, remember that emotions arise because your senses are wired to the primitive part of your mind which is self-regulated, autonomous and spontaneous. Your rational mind does not always deal with the messages coming from it effectively. These messages are part of your survival mechanism and should not be stifled simply because emotions are unhealthy and betray your weakness. (21) When emotions arise, instead of stifling them, pay attention to them and try to understand the messages they are trying to deliver. This way, you make use of your emotions without losing your balance and inner stability.

情绪是我们意识中必不可少的、不可分割的一部分。它们是内在机制的一部分，让我们能够应对生活中生理和心理上的起起落落。当我们隐藏自己的情绪和真实感受时，我们在人际关系中就不再是真正的、自发的和真实的了。当我们在别人面前摆出一副有教养、圆滑的面孔时，我们就不再对自己真实。（19）在社会上，隐藏我们的真实情感可能是一个很好的策略，但在道德上，这也是一种对信仰和信任的违背。

虽然人类更先进、更聪明，但动物的行为和反应却比人类更真实、更可信。我们受教育的程度越高，就越不容易被人所知、越不可靠。我们被宠物吸引，因为宠物不会说谎。

（20）应对愤怒或恐惧等情绪的第一步是承认它们是人之常情。情绪化并不是罪恶或不道德的，除非你的情绪让你失去人性，变得麻木不仁和对他人残忍。与情绪相关的内疚感比情感体验本身更具破坏性和伤害性。所以当你处理情绪问题时，你不仅要学会如何控制它们，还要学会如何接受它们，并应对由此产生的内疚和痛苦。

我们的大脑由一个原始的内在核心和一个更高级和理性的外在核心组成。大多数时候，大脑的理性部分控制着来自原始核心的信息，并就该做什么和如何应对做出自己的决定。然而，在危急情况下，特别是当感知到威胁时，外核失去控制，无法调节来自原始大脑的冲动和本能反应。结果，我们让烦恼的想法和情绪在我们的意识中出现，并屈服于我们的原始行为。

在情绪混乱的时候，请记住，情绪的产生是因为你的感觉连接到你大脑的原始部分，这是自我调节的、自主的和自发的。你的理性思维并不总是有效地处理来自它的信息。这些信息是你生存机制的一部分，不应该仅仅因为情绪不健康或暴露了你的弱点而被扼杀。(21) 当情绪出现时，与其扼杀它们，不如关注它们，并尝试理解它们试图传递的信息。通过这种方式，你可以利用你的情绪，而不会失去平衡和内在的稳定性。

难词总结

inseparable /ɪnˈseprəbl/ a. 分不开的，不可分离的
authentic /ɔːˈθentɪk/ a. 真实的，可靠的
transparent /trænsˈpærənt/ a. 易被人所知的
primitive /ˈprɪmɪtɪv/ a. 原始的；远古的
turmoil /ˈtɜːmɔɪl/ n. 混乱，骚动

spontaneous /spɒnˈteɪnɪəs/ a. 自发的
polished /ˈpɒlɪʃt/ a. 圆滑的；优美的
anguish /ˈæŋɡwɪʃ/ n. 剧痛，极度痛苦
surrender /səˈrendə(r)/ v. 投降；任凭摆布
stifle /ˈstaɪfl/ v. 扼杀；抑制

题目精析

19. What does the speaker say about hiding one's emotions?

   A) It is sinful and immoral.　　　　　C) It is an uncontrollable behavior.
   B) It is deemed uncivilized.　　　　　D) It is a violation of faith and trust.

19. 关于隐藏情绪，说话者说了什么？

   A）这是罪恶和不道德的。　　　　　C）这是一种无法控制的行为。
   B）这被认为是不文明的。　　　　　D）这是对信仰和信任的违背。

【答案及分析】D。本题问说话者对于隐藏情绪的看法。音频中提到，Socially, it may be a good tactic to hide our true emotions, but morally it is also a breach of faith and trust.（在社会上，隐藏我们的真实情感可能是一个很好的策略，但在道德上，这也是一种对信仰和信任的违背。）D 项中的 a violation of faith and trust 是音频中 a breach of faith and trust 的同义表达，故选 D 项。

20. What should we do first in dealing with emotions?

   A) Assess their consequences.　　　　C) Accept them as normal.
   B) Guard against their harm.　　　　 D) Find out their causes.

20. 在处理情绪时，我们首先应该做什么？

   A）评估其后果。　　　　　C）将其视作正常的。
   B）防范其伤害。　　　　　D）找到其原因。

【答案及分析】C。本题问处理情绪的第一步。音频中提到，One of the first steps in dealing with emotions such as anger or fear is to acknowledge them as normal and human.（应对愤怒或恐惧等情绪的第一步是承认它们是人之常情。）C 项是音频中 acknowledge them as normal and human 的同义表达，故选 C 项。

21. What are we advised to do when emotions arise?

    A) Try to understand what messages they convey.   C) Consider them from different perspectives.

    B) Pay attention to their possible consequences.   D) Make sure they are brought under control.

21. 当情绪出现时，我们该怎么做？

    A）试着理解它们所传达的信息。   C）从不同的角度考虑它们。

    B）注意它们可能带来的后果。   D）确保它们得到了控制。

【答案及分析】A。本题问情绪出现时应采取的做法。音频中提到，When emotions arise, instead of stifling them, pay attention to them and try to understand the messages they are trying to deliver.（当情绪出现时，与其扼杀它们，不如关注它们，并尝试理解它们试图传递的信息。）A 项是音频中 try to understand the messages they are trying to deliver 的同义表达，故选 A 项。

Questions 22 to 25 are based on the recording you have just heard.

听力原文及译文

    Good morning, class. My topic today is how to feed a hungry world. The world's population is expected to grow from 6.8 billion today to 9.1 billion by 2050. Meanwhile, the world's population more than doubled from 3 billion between 1961 and 2007.

    Simultaneously, food production has been constrained by a lack of scientific research. Still, the task of feeding the world's population in 2050 seems easily possible. What is needed is a second green revolution. This is an approach that is described as the sustainable growth of global agriculture. Such a revolution will require a wholesale shift of priorities in agricultural research. (22) <u>There is an urgent need for new crop varieties.</u> They must offer higher yields but use less water, nitrogen-rich fertilizer or other inputs. These new crops must also be more resistant to drought, heat and pests. Equally crucial is lower-tech research into basics such as crop rotation and mixed farming of animals and plants on small farms.

    Developing nations could score substantial gains in productivity by making better use of modern technologies and practices. But that requires money. It is estimated that to meet the 2050 challenge, investment must double to 83 billion US dollars a year. (23) <u>Most of that money needs to go towards improving agricultural infrastructure.</u> Everything from production to storage and processing must improve. However, research agendas need to be focused on the needs of the poorest and most resource-limited countries. It is there that most of the world's population lives and it is there that population growth over the next decades will be the greatest.

    (24) <u>To their credit, the world's agricultural scientists are embracing such a broad view. In March, for example, they came together at the first Global Conference on Agricultural Research to begin working out how to change research agendas to help meet the needs of farmers in poorer nations.</u> But these plans will not bear fruit unless they get considerably more support from policymakers.

    The growth in public agricultural-research spending peaked in the 1970s and has been shrinking ever since. (25) <u>The big exception is China, where spending has far surpassed other countries over the past decade.</u> China seems set to transition to become the key supplier of relevant science and technology to poorer countries.

But developed countries have a humanitarian responsibility too. Calls by scientists for large increases in the appropriation of funds for public spending on agricultural research are more than justified.

同学们，早上好。我今天的主题是如何养活一个饥饿的世界。预计到2050年，世界人口将从目前的68亿增长到91亿。与此同时，世界人口由1961年的30亿到2007年增加了一倍多。

同时，由于缺乏科学研究，粮食生产受到了限制。尽管如此，在2050年养活世界人口的任务似乎仍然很容易实现。我们需要的是第二次绿色革命。这种方法被称为全球农业的可持续增长。这样的革命将需要农业研究中优先事项的大规模转变。（22）迫切需要新的作物品种。这些品种必须有更高的产量，但水、富氮肥料或其他投入更少。这些新作物还必须更能抵抗干旱、高温和害虫。同样重要的是对基本要素进行技术含量低的研究，例如作物轮作和小型农场中种植业和畜牧业的结合。

发展中国家可以通过更好地利用现代技术和实践，在生产力方面取得重大进展。但这需要资金。据估计，要应对2050年的挑战，每年的投资必须翻一番，达到每年830亿美元。（23）其中大部分资金需要用于改善农业基础设施。从生产到储存，以及加工的方方面面都必须得到改善。然而，研究议程需要集中于最贫穷和资源最有限的国家的需求。那里是世界上大多数人口居住的地方，也是未来几十年内人口增长最快的地方。

（24）值得赞扬的是，世界农业科学家正在接受这样一种广泛的观点。例如，今年3月，他们齐聚一堂，参加了第一届全球农业研究会议，开始研究如何改变研究议程，以帮助满足较贫穷国家农民的需求。但这些计划不会取得成果，除非它们得到政策制定者的更多支持。

公共农业研究支出的增长在20世纪70年代达到顶峰，此后一直处于低迷状态。（25）最大的例外是中国，在过去十年中，中国的支出远远超过了其他国家。中国似乎准备转型，成为向较贫穷国家提供相关科学技术的主要国家。但发达国家也负有人道主义责任。科学家呼吁大幅增加农业研究公共支出资金的拨款，这是非常合理的。

难词总结

wholesale /ˈhəʊlseɪl/ a. 大规模的，大批的
resistant /rɪˈzɪstənt/ a. 有抵抗力的；抵制的，反抗的
to one's credit 值得赞扬的是
humanitarian /hjuːˌmænɪˈteəriən/ a. 人道主义的

nitrogen /ˈnaɪtrədʒən/ n. [化学] 氮
rotation /rəʊˈteɪʃn/ n. 轮作，轮耕
surpass /səˈpɑːs/ v. 超过，胜过，优于

题目精析

22. What is an urgent need for feeding the world's population in 2050 according to the speaker?
    A) Cultivation of new varieties of crops.
    B) Measures to cope with climate change.
    C) Development of more effective pesticides.
    D) Application of more nitrogen-rich fertilizers.

22. 说话者认为到2050年养活世界人口迫切需要什么？
    A）培育农作物新品种。
    B）应对气候变化的措施。
    C）开发更有效的农药。
    D）施用更多的富氮肥料。

【答案及分析】A。本题问2050年养活世界人口的条件。音频中提到，There is an urgent need for new crop varieties.（迫切需要新的作物品种。）A项是音频内容的同义表达，故选A项。

23. Where should most of money be invested to feed the ever-growing population?

　　A) The expansion of farmland in developing countries.

　　B) The research on crop rotation in developing countries.

　　C) The cooperation of the world's agricultural scientists.

　　D) The improvement of agricultural infrastructure.

23. 为了养活不断增长的人口，大部分资金应该投向哪里？

　　A）发展中国家耕地的扩张。

　　B）发展中国家作物轮作的研究。

　　C）世界农业科学家的合作。

　　D）改善农业基础设施。

【答案及分析】D。本题问大部分资金的投放领域。音频中提到，Most of that money needs to go towards improving agricultural infrastructure.（其中大部分资金需要用于改善农业基础设施。）D 项是音频中 improving agricultural infrastructure 的同义表达，故选 D 项。

24. Why does the speaker give credit to the world's agricultural scientists?

　　A) For encouraging farmers to embrace new farming techniques.

　　B) For aligning their research with advances in farming technology.

　　C) For turning their focus to the needs of farmers in poorer countries.

　　D) For cooperating closely with policymakers in developing countries.

24. 为什么说话者把功劳归于世界农业科学家？

　　A）因为他们鼓励农民接受新的农业技术。

　　B）因为他们的研究与农业技术的进步相结合。

　　C）因为他们将重点转向较贫穷国家农民的需求。

　　D）因为他们与发展中国家的决策者密切合作。

【答案及分析】C。本题问把功劳归于世界农业科学家的原因。音频中提到，To their credit, the world's agricultural scientists are embracing such a broad view. In March, for example, they came together at the first Global Conference on Agricultural Research to begin working out how to change research agendas to help meet the needs of farmers in poorer nations.（值得赞扬的是，世界农业科学家正在接受这样一种广泛的观点。例如，今年 3 月，他们齐聚一堂，参加了第一届全球农业研究会议，开始研究如何改变研究议程，以帮助满足较贫穷国家农民的需求。）C 项中的 turning their focus to the needs of farmers in poorer countries 是音频中 help meet the needs of farmers in poorer nations 的同义表达，故选 C 项。

25. What makes China exceptional in comparison with the rest of the world?

　　A) Rapid transition to become a food exporter.　　C) Quick rise to become a leading grain producer.

　　B) Substantial funding in agricultural research.　　D) Assumption of humanitarian responsibilities.

25. 与世界其他国家相比，是什么让中国与众不同？

　　A）迅速转型成为粮食出口国。　　C）快速崛起成为粮食生产大国。

　　B）为农业研究提供大量资金。　　D）承担人道主义责任。

【答案及分析】B。本题问中国不同于其他国家的原因。音频中提到，The big exception is China, where spending has far surpassed other countries over the past decade.（最大的例外是中国，在过去十年中，中国的支出远远超过了其他国家。）音频中的 spending 指上文提到的公共农业研究支出。B 项是音频内容的同义表达，故选 B 项。

Part Ⅲ Reading Comprehension

Section A

【全文翻译】

根据心理学家莎伦·德雷珀的说法，我们的着装选择绝对会影响我们的健康。当我们穿着不合身的衣服，或者觉得在某个活动上穿得过于夸张或不得体时，很自然地会感到难为情，甚至有压力。相反，她说，选择得体、符合自己风格的衣服可以增强你的自信。

但是你能通过你现在的衣服来改善你的健康，而不必冲出去买全新的衣服吗？"当然可以。"德雷珀说。如果你的目标是提高你的思维能力，她建议你选择合适的而且不太可能让你不安的衣服，所以要避免蝴蝶结、领带和不必要的配饰。选择你认为与你的目标相匹配的衣服也很有帮助，所以，如果你想在工作中表现得更好，就选择你认为专业的衣服。德雷珀说，这符合行为激活的概念，即投入一种行为（此处指选择衣服）可以让你走上实现目标的道路（更努力地工作）。

另一种改善你的心态的方法是混搭。德雷珀说，如果我们穿同样的衣服——即使它们是我们的最爱，我们经常会感到拘泥于常规，因此选择一件你不经常穿的衣服，或者给衣服添加一些不同的东西，比如帽子，可以积极地改变你的情绪。在你真的不愿意勇敢面对世界的日子里，德雷珀建议选择有感情意义的衣服，比如你在特殊的日子穿的，或者你爱的人送给你的，因为有美好联想的衣服可以帮助你挖掘有积极助益的情感。

【难词总结】

ill-fitting /ˌɪlˈfɪtɪŋ/ a. 不合适的
restlessness /ˈrestləsnəs/ n. 坐立不安；不安定
outfit /ˈaʊtfɪt/ n.（尤指在某一场合穿的）全套服装

under-dressed /ˌʌndəˈdrest/ a.（衣着）不够正式的
activation /ˌæktɪˈveɪʃn/ n. 激活；活化作用
tap into 挖掘

【题目精析】

26. B。根据句子结构可知，空格位于 that 引导的定语从句中，从句修饰名词 clothes，该从句缺少谓语动词，因此空格处需填入动词原形，且动词可以与介词 with 搭配，B 项 align（使一致；使对齐）可以与 with 搭配，align with 表示"和……一致"，符合此处语境及语法要求，故选 B 项。

27. D。根据句子结构可知，空格处需填入形容词，修饰 clothing，且下文提到 without having to dash out and buy a whole new...（不必冲出去买全新的……），不用买新的，反之就是用当前有的，D 项 current（目前的，现在的）符合此处语境及语法要求，故选 D 项。

28. O。根据句子结构可知，空格处需填入名词，本文的关键词是"衣服"，本句中"现在的衣服"与"全新的……"构成对应，因此所填名词应含有"衣服"的意思，O 项 wardrobe（全部衣物）符合此处语境及语法要求，故选 O 项。

29. A。根据句子结构可知，空格处需填入名词，与 bows 和 ties 并列。根据句意可知，蝴蝶结和领带可能让你感到不安，且蝴蝶结和领带本身就属于配饰，因此此处指的是不必要的配饰。A 项 accessories（配饰，配件）符合此处语境及语法要求，故选 A 项。

30. I。根据句子结构可知，空格位于省略了引导词的定语从句（you... with your goals）中，修饰 clothes，该定语从句缺少谓语动词，主语为 you，时态为一般现在时，因此空格处需填入动词原形，且可以与 as 搭配，I 项 perceive（认为，理解）与 as 搭配表示"视为；当作"，符合语境及语法要求，故选 I 项。

31. E。根据句子结构可知，____ in a behavior 作主语，空格处需填入动名词，且动名词可以与介词 in 搭配，E 项 engaging（参与，参加）与介词 in 搭配表示"从事于（参加）"，可以与 a behavior 构成合理搭配，符合语境及语法要求，故选 E 项。

32. G。根据句子结构可知，空格位于 your 之后，且后面跟着 of 介词短语，因此空格处需填入名词。根据句首的 Another way to improve... 可知该段承接上文，接着讲有助于改善健康的另一个方法，因此所填词与 of mind 搭配应表示与"健康"相关的内容。G 项 frame（框架；边框）与 of mind 可构成固定搭配，表示"心情；心境"，符合语境及语法要求，故选 G 项。

33. J。根据句子结构可知，空格所在句主干齐全，因此空格处需填入副词。所给选项中只有 C 项 concurrently（同时发生地）和 J 项 positively（积极地；肯定地）符合语法要求。J 项代入原文后符合语境，故选 J 项。

34. M。根据句子结构可知，空格处需要填入一个形容词，且可以构成 be... to do sth. 的搭配。M 项 reluctant（不情愿的；勉强的）可构成 be reluctant to do sth. 的搭配，表示"不情愿做某事"，符合语境及语法要求，故选 M 项。

35. F。根据句子结构可知，空格位于 with 介词短语中，空格后为名词 associations，因此空格处需填入一个形容词，修饰 associations，根据下文 can help you tap into constructive emotions（可以帮助你挖掘有积极助益的情感）可知，所填形容词应带有积极正向的感情色彩，F 项 fond（喜爱的，喜欢的）代入原文后符合语境及语法要求，故选 F 项。

Section B

全文翻译

时尚界没有人对巴宝莉烧毁了 2 800 万英镑的库存感到惊讶

[A] 上周，巴宝莉的年度报告显示，去年烧毁了价值 2 860 万英镑的库存。这一消息让投资者和消费者感到愤怒，但对时尚界人士来说，这并不奇怪。

[B] 对于奢侈品品牌来说，销毁未售出的库存，甚至是未用过的一卷一卷的布料，是司空见惯的事。

通过折扣店以更低的价格买到太多商品会阻碍全价销售。把产品送去回收会让它们很容易被偷并在黑市上出售。品牌战略机构概念局首席执行官贾斯敏·比娜解释说："通常，奢侈品品牌团结在一起，支持专有权，以保护其商业利益，即知识产权和品牌资产保护。"她表示，她听说过烧库存的谣言，但直到本周才听到具体事例。

[C] 这种司空见惯的做法的另一个原因是，对出口到美国的品牌来说，这是一种经济激励。美国海关声明，如果进口商品在其监督下未使用并被销毁，则可收回为商品支付的99%的关税、税收或费用。很难计算出目前有多少积压存货被浪费了。虽然有对这种做法的激励措施，但没有法律义务对此进行报告。

[D] 一位不愿透露姓名的消息人士分享了她于2016年10月在纽约一家巴宝莉商店工作的经历。"我的工作是把物品扔进箱子里，这样它们就可以被送去烧掉。我心里很难受，因为所有的皮革和皮毛都被浪费了，动物们白白牺牲了。我不能再待在那里了，他们的商业行为让我无法忍受。"今年5月，巴宝莉宣布将从T台秀中剔除皮草，并评估其在商业领域的其他用途。"尽管我们询问了管理层，但他们拒绝向我们详细回答这样做的原因。"消息人士继续说道，她在两周内离职了。此后，她为另一家知名奢侈品品牌工作。

[E] 在一篇在线论坛帖子中，当被问及路易威登烧毁其包包一事是否属实时，声称为路易威登工作的艾哈迈德·布夏法回应说，该品牌每年会为员工进行两次旧货促销。经过多次销售后仍未售出的物品将被销毁。"路易威登没有公开销售。他们要么以一定的价格出售产品，要么停止销售。这是为了确保每个人都为同一件物品支付相同的价格。"他说。他接着透露了员工销售的严格准则："你可能会给别人买礼物，但他们会跟踪每一件物品，如果你的礼物最终出现在网上，那么他们知道该问谁。"据报道，一位投资者在评论巴宝莉的数据时感到非常愤怒，因为未售出的商品在被销毁之前甚至没有提供给投资者。

[F] 拥有多个奢侈品品牌的历峰集团在5月登上了新闻头条，原因是它在过去两年收回了价值4.37亿英镑的手表并进行销毁，以避免降价。这种做法不仅限于奢侈品品牌。去年10月，一档丹麦电视节目揭露H&M自2013年以来烧毁了12吨未售出的衣服。在一份声明中，这家商业街零售商为自己辩护说，被烧毁的衣服没有通过安全测试："媒体所提及的产品已在外部实验室进行了测试。检测结果显示，其中一件产品霉变，另一件产品含铅量过高。这些产品已经按照我们的安全程序正当地停止生产。"今年3月，一份报告显示，H&M正在努力处理其价值43亿美元的库存。该品牌在接受《纽约时报》采访时表示，其计划是通过降低价格来推动库存流通，可以说是鼓励消费者不加思索地购买和丢弃。

[G] 生产过剩或许是巴宝莉最大的担忧。尽管人们对于宁愿焚烧商品也不让商品变得平价的精英主义内涵感到愤怒，但这家英国时尚品牌的高管们无疑在竭力为自己误判产量进行辩护。这些废弃物被用来焚烧旧的化妆品原料，为新的美妆产品系列让路。然而，尽管被销毁的存货价值与去年的2 690万英镑相比有所上升，但与2016年的1 880万英镑相比，增长幅度更大，突出表明这是一个持续存在的问题。

[H] 2016年9月，巴宝莉转向了一种"即看即买"的时装秀模式。此举是为了利用其时装周的报道，让消费者可以立即获得库存商品。这与传统的向业界展示产品的方式背道而驰，即接受

生产订单，并在六个月内提供产品。虽然巴宝莉宣布了"破纪录"的在线访问量和用户参与度，但几乎没有证据表明，该战略对销售额产生了重大影响，尤其是在整个季度的宣传力度放缓之际。2月份，他们对模式做了调整，立即放弃了一些T台产品，并承诺将在未来几个月内推出其他服装。

[I] 在一份声明中，巴宝莉否认改用"即看即买"对浪费有影响。巴宝莉的一位发言人进一步表示："在有必要处理产品的情况下，我们会以负责任的方式进行。我们一直在寻找方法来减少和重新评估我们的废弃物。这是我们战略的核心部分，我们已经建立了伙伴关系，并致力于支持创新组织，以帮助实现这一目标。"

[J] 其中一个合作伙伴是 Elvis & Kresse，一个使用再生材料的配饰品牌。联合创始人克雷斯·韦斯林说："去年年底，我们与巴宝莉基金会启动了一项雄心勃勃的五年合作计划。这样做的主要目的是扩大我们皮革救援项目的规模，从巴宝莉皮革制品生产的下脚料开始。我们正在不懈努力，扩展我们的解决方案，并欢迎任何人来到我们的工作室，看看我们正在做什么。"目前，该合作伙伴关系仅解决生产阶段的浪费问题，而非未售出的货物。

[K] 虽然这些计划值得赞誉，但这使得巴宝莉更难为这些最新数据辩护。15年前，巴宝莉正处于危机之中，因为其标志性格纹图案被廉价的仿冒品牌广泛模仿。这让奢侈品消费者望而却步，他们发现自己昂贵的服装与工薪阶层青年文化的联系比与著名的传统时尚品牌的联系更紧密。2004年，在巴宝莉格纹过度曝光的高峰期，该品牌的营业额为7.155亿英镑。在创意总监克里斯托弗·贝利的带领下，他们扭转了品牌的局面，去年的收入达到27.3亿英镑。

[L] 比娜认为品牌需要重新调整他们的专有权策略。"专有权正开始受到挑战，"她表示，"我认为这与奢侈品本身受到的挑战密切相关。接触时尚以及管理时尚的品牌正变得越来越无关紧要。像健康、启蒙、社会和环境责任这类事物都是新的奢侈品。这些都是内在的，而不是外在的。这是传统奢侈品品牌在未来中长期内必须应对的挑战。"

难词总结

outraged /ˈaʊtreɪdʒd/ a. 愤慨的，气愤的
rally around 团结在一起
incentive /ɪnˈsentɪv/ n. 激励；刺激
obligation /ˌɒblɪˈɡeɪʃn/ n. 义务，责任
anonymous /əˈnɒnɪməs/ a. 匿名的
disclose /dɪsˈkləʊz/ v. 透露，公开；揭开
cosmetic /kɒzˈmetɪk/ a. 化妆用的，美容的
coverage /ˈkʌvərɪdʒ/ n. 媒体报道
reclaimed /rɪˈkleɪmd/ a. 回收的，再生的
deter /dɪˈtɜː(r)/ v. 使打消念头，防止
turnover /ˈtɜːnəʊvə(r)/ n. 营业额，成交量
police /pəˈliːs/ v. 管理；监督

vulnerable /ˈvʌlnərəbl/ a. 脆弱的，易受伤的
exclusivity /ˌekskluːˈsɪvəti/ n. 专有权；独特性
merchandise /ˈmɜːtʃəndaɪs/ n. 商品，货品
source /sɔːs/ n. 提供信息的人
high-profile /ˌhaɪˈprəʊfaɪl/ a. 知名度高的
in accordance with 依照；与……一致
leverage /ˈliːvərɪdʒ/ n. 影响力
disposal /dɪˈspəʊzl/ n. 处理，清除
off-cut n. 下脚料
prestigious /preˈstɪdʒəs/ a. 有威望的，有声望的
readdress /ˌriːəˈdres/ v. 重新审视
contend with 对付；与……作斗争

题目精析

36. Burberry's executives are trying hard to attribute their practice of destroying old products to miscalculated production.

36. 巴宝莉的高管们正极力将他们销毁旧产品的做法归咎于生产失算。

【答案及分析】G。根据题干中的 Burberry's executives、are trying hard to 和 miscalculated production 定位到 G 段。定位句指出，While there has been much outrage at the elitist connotation of burning goods rather than making them affordable, executives at the British fashion house are no doubt struggling to defend how they miscalculated production.（尽管人们对于宁愿焚烧商品也不让商品变得平价的精英主义内涵感到愤怒，但这家英国时尚品牌的高管们无疑在竭力为自己误判产量进行辩护。）其中，are trying hard to 是原文中 are no doubt struggling to 的同义表达，miscalculated production 为原词复现，题干是原文的同义表达，故选 G 项。

37. Selling products at a discount will do greater harm to luxury brands than destroying them.

37. 打折销售产品对奢侈品品牌的伤害比毁掉它们更大。

【答案及分析】B。根据题干中的 at a discount 和 will do greater harm 定位到 B 段。定位句指出，Becoming too widely available at a cheaper price through discount stores discourages full-price sales.（通过折扣店以更低的价格买到太多商品会阻碍全价销售。）其中，Selling products at a discount 是原文中 too widely available at a cheaper price 的同义表达，will do greater harm 是原文中 discourages full-price sales 的同义表达。B 段第一句指出，销毁库存在奢侈品行业很普遍，因此题干是对原文的归纳，故选 B 项。

38. Imitated Burberry products discouraged luxury consumers from buying its genuine products.

38. 仿制的巴宝莉产品阻止了奢侈品消费者购买其正品。

【答案及分析】K。根据题干中的 Imitated Burberry products 和 discouraged luxury consumers 定位到 K 段。定位句指出，Fifteen years ago, Burberry was at crisis point as their signature check pattern was widely imitated by cheap, imitation brands. It deterred luxury consumers（15 年前，巴宝莉正处于危机之中，因为其标志性格纹图案被廉价的仿冒品牌广泛模仿。这让奢侈品消费者望而却步）。其中，Imitated Burberry products 是原文中 imitated by cheap, imitation brands 的同义表达，discouraged luxury consumers 是原文中 deterred luxury consumers 的同义表达，题干是原文的同义表达，故选 K 项。

39. Staff members of a luxury brand may buy its old stock at cheaper prices, but they are not allowed to resell them.

39. 奢侈品品牌的职员可以以更低的价格购买旧库存，但不允许转售。

【答案及分析】E。根据题干中的 Staff members 和 not allowed to resell 定位到 E 段。定位句指出，He goes on to disclose the strict guidelines around the employee sales: "You may buy gifts for someone, but they track each item, and if your gift ends up online they know who to ask."（他接着透露了员工销售的严格准则："你可能会给别人买礼物，但他们会跟踪每一件物品，如果你的礼物最终出现在网上，那么他们知道该问谁。"）其中，Staff members 是原文中 the employee 的同义表达。根据原文可知，职员购买的旧库存不允许转售，题干是原文的同义表达，故选 E 项。

40. In future traditional luxury brands will have to adapt their business strategies to the changing concepts of luxury.

40. 在未来，传统奢侈品品牌将不得不调整他们的经营策略，以适应不断变化的奢侈品概念。

【答案及分析】L。根据题干中的 traditional luxury brands、adapt their business strategies 和 the changing concepts of luxury 定位到 L 段。定位句指出，Bina believes that brands need to readdress their exclusivity tactic... Things like health, enlightenment, and social and environmental responsibility are the new luxuries... That's the challenge that traditional luxury brands will have to contend with in the mid- to long-term future.（比娜认为品牌需要重新调整他们的专有权策略……像健康、启蒙、社会和环境责任这类事物都是新的奢侈品……这是传统奢侈品品牌在未来中长期内必须应对的挑战。）其中，traditional luxury brands 为原词复现，have to adapt their business strategies 是原文中 need to readdress their exclusivity tactic 的同义表达，the changing concepts of luxury 是原文中 Things like health, enlightenment, and social and environmental responsibility are the new luxuries 的同义表达，故选 L 项。

41. One luxury brand employee quit her job because she simply couldn't bear to see the destruction of unsold products.

41. 一位奢侈品品牌员工辞职的原因是她根本无法忍受看到未售出的产品被销毁。

【答案及分析】D。根据题干中的 quit her job 和 couldn't bear to see the destruction 定位到 D 段。定位句指出，I couldn't stay there any longer, their business practices threw me off the roof... continued the source, who left her role within two weeks.（我不能再待在那里了，他们的商业行为让我无法忍受……消息人士继续说道，她在两周内离职了。）其中，quit her job 是原文中 left her role 的同义表达，couldn't bear to see the destruction of unsold products 是原文中 their business practices threw me off the roof 的同义表达，题干是原文的同义表达，故选 D 项。

42. Destroying old stock is a practice not just of luxury brands but of less prestigious fashion brands.

42. 销毁旧库存不仅是奢侈品品牌的做法，也是不太知名的时尚品牌的做法。

【答案及分析】F。根据题干中的 a practice not just of luxury brands 定位到 F 段。定位句指出，It's not just luxury brands either. In October last year, a Danish TV show exposed H&M for burning 12 tonnes of unsold clothing since 2013.（这种做法不仅限于奢侈品品牌。去年 10 月，一档丹麦电视节目揭露 H&M 自 2013 年以来烧毁了 12 吨未售出的衣服。）其中，not just 和 luxury brands 为原词复现，题干中的 less prestigious fashion brands 对应原文中 H&M 的例子，题干是原文的同义表达，故选 F 项。

43. Burberry is working with a partner to make full use of leather materials to reduce waste.

43. 巴宝莉正在与一个合作伙伴合作，充分利用皮革材料来减少浪费。

【答案及分析】J。根据题干中的 a partner 和 leather materials 定位到 J 段。定位句指出，Late last year we launched an ambitious five-year partnership with the Burberry Foundation. The main aim of this is to scale our leather rescue project, starting with off-cuts from the production of Burberry leather goods.（去年年底，我们与巴宝莉基金会启动了一项雄心勃勃的五年合作计划。这样做的主要目的是扩大我们皮革救援项目的规模，从巴宝莉皮革制品生产的下脚料开始。）其中，make full use of leather materials 是原文中 scale our leather rescue project 的同义表达，题干是原文的同义表达，故选 J 项。

44. Burberry's plan to destroy its unsold products worth millions of dollars aroused public indignation.

44. 巴宝莉计划销毁其价值数百万美元的未售出产品，这引起了公众的愤慨。

【答案及分析】A。根据题干中的 destroy its unsold products worth millions of dollars 和 aroused public indignation 定位到 A 段。定位句指出，Last week, Burberry's annual report revealed that £28.6 million worth of stock was burnt last year. The news has left investors and consumers outraged but comes as little surprise to those in the fashion industry.（上周，巴宝莉的年度报告显示，去年烧毁了价值 2 860 万英镑的库存。这一消息让投资者和消费者感到愤怒，但对时尚界人士来说，这并不奇怪。）其中，destroy its unsold products worth millions of dollars 是原文中 £28.6 million worth of stock was burnt 的同义表达，aroused public indignation 是原文中 left investors and consumers outraged 的同义表达，题干是原文的同义表达，故选 A 项。

45. Burberry's change of marketing strategy to make a product available as soon as consumers see it on the fashion show did not turn out to be as effective as expected.

45. 巴宝莉改变营销策略，让消费者在时装秀上一看到产品就能买到，结果并没有像预期的那样有效。

【答案及分析】H。根据题干中的 to make a product available as soon as consumers see it on the fashion show 定位到 H 段。定位句指出，In September 2016, Burberry switched to a "see now, buy now" catwalk show format... there has been little evidence to suggest that the strategy has had a significant effect on sales（2016 年 9 月，巴宝莉转向了一种"即看即买"的时装秀模式……但几乎没有证据表明，该战略对销售额产生了重大影响）。其中，Burberry's change of marketing strategy to make a product available as soon as consumers see it on the fashion show 是原文中 Burberry switched to a "see now, buy now" catwalk show format 的同义表达，did not turn out to be as effective as expected 是原文中 there has been little evidence to suggest that the strategy has had a significant effect 的同义表达，题干是原文的同义表达，故选 H 项。

Section C

Passage One

全文翻译

社交媒体绝对是无处不在。数十亿人每天都在使用社交媒体来创建、分享和交流想法、信息和资料。个人和企业都定期发帖，与来自世界各地的人们互动交流。它是一个强大的通信媒介，同时在全球范围内提供即时、频繁、永久和广泛的信息。

人们在社交媒体上发布自己的生活状态，让全世界都得以看到。脸书、推特、领英以及无数其他社交网站都提供了一种快速而简单的方式来了解求职者的个人生活——包括它的积极和消极方面。作为招聘过程的一部分，社交媒体筛选很有吸引力，但是雇主在研究潜在候选人的背景时是否应该利用它呢？

利用社交媒体来筛选求职者并不罕见。2018 年的一项调查发现，近 70% 的雇主在雇用应聘者之前会使用社交媒体对他们进行筛选。但这一做法也有其后果和潜在的法律风险。如果使用不当，社交媒体筛选便会被视为不道德的，甚至是非法的。

社交媒体筛选实质上是在审查求职者的私生活。它可以透露受保护的特征的相关信息，比如年龄、种族、国籍、残疾、性别、宗教等，这可能会使招聘出现决策偏见。在私人页面上被断章取义的图片或评论可能会毁掉一个完美的求职者被录用的机会。这个过程可能会给某个候选人带来不公平的优势。它创造了一个不平等的竞争环境，并且潜在地为招聘经理提供可能对他们的招聘决定产生负面影响的信息。

很难忽视社交媒体作为筛选工具的作用。虽然有些东西是你不应该看到的，但有些东西是可以合法地考虑在内的——这也使它成为相关信息的宝贵来源。适当地使用社交媒体筛选可以帮助你确保不会雇用一个会让你损失金钱或玷污公司声誉的"有毒员工"。考虑这个过程的合法方面，你也许能够雇用有史以来最好的员工。这里有一种微妙的平衡。

在社交媒体上筛选求职者时必须专业而负责。公司应该规定，他们永远不会（向求职者）索要密码，前后要保持一致，记录（招聘）决策，考虑所用（信息）的来源，并意识到其他法律也可能适用。有鉴于此，最好的办法可能是在后面的过程中寻求人力资源的帮助，（在网上）浏览相关信息。社交媒体将继续存在。但在使用社交媒体筛选求职者之前，事先咨询管理层和法律团队对于遵守所有法律至关重要。

难词总结

wide-reaching *a.* 涉及面很广的；影响深远的
screen /skri:n/ *v.* 审查，甄别
scrutinise /ˈskru:tɪnaɪz/ *v.* 仔细查看
playing field 竞争环境
delicate /ˈdelɪkət/ *a.* 微妙的
comply with 遵守

incorporate /ɪnˈkɔ:pəreɪt/ *v.* 包含；加上
inappropriately /ˌɪnəˈprəʊpriətli/ *ad.* 不适当地
take out of context 断章取义
stain /steɪn/ *v.* （被）玷污；留下污渍
stipulate /ˈstɪpjuleɪt/ *v.* 规定，明确要求

题目精析

46. What does the author mainly discuss in the passage?

   A) The advantage of using social media in screening job candidates.

   B) The potentially invasive nature of social media in everyday life.

   C) Whether the benefits of social media outweigh the drawbacks.

   D) Whether social media should be used to screen job candidates.

46. 作者在文章中主要讨论了什么？

   A）使用社交媒体筛选求职者的优势。

   B）社交媒体在日常生活中的潜在入侵性。

   C）社交媒体是否利大于弊。

   D）是否应该使用社交媒体来筛选求职者。

【答案及分析】D。文章首段指出社交媒体无处不在，即本文关键词为"社交媒体"，接着第二段末尾用疑问句指出，should employers make use of it when researching a potential candidate's background?（雇主在研究潜在候选人的背景时是否应该利用它呢？），紧接着下文围绕这一现象及其利弊方面展开讨论，因此文章主要讨论了是否应该使用社交媒体来筛选求职者，D 项符合文章大意，故选 D 项。

47. What might happen when social media is used to screen job candidates?

　　A) Moral or legal issues might arise.　　C) Sensational information might surface.

　　B) Company reputation might suffer.　　D) Hiring decisions might be complicated.

47. 当社交媒体被用来筛选求职者时，会发生什么？

　　A）可能会引发道德或法律问题。　　C）可能会有耸人听闻的消息。

　　B）公司声誉可能受损。　　D）招聘决定可能很复杂。

【答案及分析】A。根据题干关键词 when social media is used to screen job candidates 定位到原文第三段最后一句。该句指出，When done inappropriately, social media screening can be considered unethical or even illegal.（如果使用不当，社交媒体筛选便会被视为不道德的，甚至是非法的。）A 项是原文中 can be considered unethical or even illegal 的同义表达，故选 A 项。

48. When could online personal information be detrimental to candidates?

　　A) When it is separated from context.　　C) When it is magnified to a ruinous degree.

　　B) When it is scrutinised by an employer.　　D) When it is revealed to the human resources.

48. 在线个人信息何时可能对候选人有害？

　　A）当它被断章取义时。　　C）当它被放大到毁灭性的程度时。

　　B）当它被雇主审查时。　　D）当它被披露给人力资源时。

【答案及分析】A。根据题干关键词 online personal information 和 be detrimental to candidates 定位到原文第四段第三句。该句指出，Pictures or comments on a private page that are taken out of context could ruin a perfectly good candidate's chances of getting hired.（在私人页面上被断章取义的图片或评论可能会毁掉一个完美的求职者被录用的机会。）A 项是该句的同义表达，故选 A 项。

49. How can employers use social media information to their advantage while avoiding unnecessary risks?

　　A) By tipping the delicate balance.　　C) By keeping personal information on record.

　　B) By using it in a legitimate way.　　D) By separating relevant from irrelevant data.

49. 雇主可以如何在利用社交媒体信息的同时避免不必要的风险？

　　A）通过打破微妙的平衡。　　C）通过记录个人信息。

　　B）通过以一种合法的方式使用它。　　D）通过分离相关数据和无关数据。

【答案及分析】B。根据题干关键词 How can employers use social media information 定位到原文第五段。该段指出，Using social media screening appropriately can help ensure that you don't hire a toxic employee...Consider the lawful side of this process and you may be able to hire the best employee ever.（适当地使用社交媒体筛选可以帮助你确保不会雇用一个……"有毒员工"。考虑这个过程的合法方面，你也许能够雇用有史以来最好的员工。）由此可知雇主应该以合法的方式利用社交媒体信息来筛选求职者，B 项与原文相符，故选 B 项。

50. What does the author suggest doing before screening job candidates on social media?

　　A) Hiring professionals to navigate the whole process.

　　B) Anticipating potential risks involved in the process.

　　C) Seeking advice from management and legal experts.

　　D) Stipulating a set of rules for asking specific questions.

50. 作者建议在社交媒体上筛选求职者之前做什么？
   A）雇用专业人士来掌控整个过程。
   B）预测该过程中涉及的潜在风险。
   C）寻求管理层和法律专家的意见。
   D）制定一套提出特定问题的规则。

【答案及分析】C。根据题干关键词before screening job candidates on social media定位到原文最后一段最后一句。该句指出，But before using social media to screen job candidates, consulting with management and legal teams beforehand is essential in order to comply with all laws.（但在使用社交媒体筛选求职者之前，事先咨询管理层和法律团队对于遵守所有法律至关重要。）可知C项是原文中consulting with management and legal teams 的同义表达，故选C项。

Passage Two

全文翻译

近年来，食品工业增加了标签的使用。无论标签上写的是"非转基因"还是"无糖"，或者"零碳水化合物"，消费者越来越多地要求了解食品中所含成分。一份报告发现，39%的消费者会从目前购买的品牌转向其他提供更清晰、更准确产品信息的品牌。食品制造商对这份报告的回应便是使用新的标签以满足这一要求，试图让自己的产品在竞争中占有优势，并提高利润。

这个策略在直觉上说得通。如果消费者说他们想要透明度，那就确切地告诉他们你的产品里到底有什么。这只是为了满足某种需求。但是，针对消费者这种需求的营销策略已经不仅仅是明确说明产品中的成分，而是给食品中不含有的成分贴上标签。这些标签被称为"缺席声明"标签，它们呈现了一种新兴的标签趋势，这对购买产品的消费者和供应产品的行业都是有害的。

例如，几年前，Hunt's公司在其罐装番茄酱上贴上了"非转基因"的标签——尽管当时市场上没有转基因番茄这种东西。一些乳制品公司在其牛奶上贴上了"非转基因"的标签，尽管事实上所有牛奶都是天然非转基因的，这是另一个制造不必要恐惧的食品标签。

虽然利用消费者对食物的恐惧和误解制作标签可能会让公司在与杂货店货架上的竞争产品相比时获得暂时的营销优势，但从长远来看，这种策略只会产生逆反效果：通过在关于食物的说明中注入恐惧感，我们面临的风险是，消费者不是仅对某一种产品，而是对整个食品行业都失去了信任。

最终，消费者开始思考：这些食物安全吗？通过购买和消费这些类型的产品，我是否已经对我的家庭或地球造成了某种伤害？对于食品制造商来说，这将意味着消费者的信任受损以及销售额下降。这不仅仅是推测。最近的一项研究发现，即使没有科学证据证明食品会造成伤害，"缺席声明"标签也会使人们对食品产生偏见。

很明显，食品制造商在使用"缺席声明"标签时必须谨慎行事。除了可能对销售产生长期的负面影响，这种文字伎俩还传递出了一条信息，即农业和食品加工领域的创新是不受欢迎的，最终导致效率下降、消费者的选择减少，并最终导致食品价格更高。如果我们允许这种标签继续下去，我们都将失败。

难词总结

bolster /ˈbəʊlstə(r)/ v. 加强；支持

transparency /trænsˈpærənsi/ n. 透明性

detrimental /ˌdetrɪˈmentl/ *a.* 有害的，不利的
discourse /ˈdɪskɔːs/ *n.* 谈话，谈论
supposition /ˌsʌpəˈzɪʃn/ *n.* 推测，假定
tread carefully 小心翼翼地做

misconception /ˌmɪskənˈsepʃn/ *n.* 错误想法，误解
run the risk of 冒着……的危险
stigma /ˈstɪɡmə/ *n.* 污名；耻辱
verbal /ˈvɜːbl/ *a.* 文字的；口头的

题目精析

51. What trend has been observed in a report?

A) Food manufacturers' rising awareness of product safety.
B) Food manufacturers' changing strategies to bolster profits.
C) Consumers' growing demand for eye-catching food labels.
D) Consumers' increasing desire for clear product information.

51. 在一份报告中观察到了什么趋势？
A）食品制造商对产品安全意识的提高。
B）食品制造商改变策略以提高利润。
C）消费者对醒目的食品标签的需求不断增长。
D）消费者对清晰产品信息的渴望日益增加。

【答案及分析】D。根据题干关键词 a report 定位到原文第一段第三句。该句指出，One report found that 39 percent of consumers would switch from the brands they currently buy to others that provide clearer, more accurate product information.（一份报告发现，39% 的消费者会从目前购买的品牌转向其他提供更清晰、更准确产品信息的品牌。）D 项是原文中 provide clearer, more accurate product information 的同义表达，故选 D 项。

52. What does the author say is manufacturers' new marketing strategy?

A) Stressing the absence of certain elements in their products.
B) Articulating the unique nutritional value of their products.
C) Supplying detailed information of their products.
D) Designing transparent labels for their products.

52. 作者说制造商的新营销策略是什么？
A）强调其产品中不含某些成分。
B）阐明其产品独特的营养价值。
C）提供其产品的详细信息。
D）为其产品设计透明标签。

【答案及分析】A。根据题干关键词 manufacturers' new marketing strategy 定位到原文第二段第四句。该句指出，But the marketing strategy in response to this consumer demand has gone beyond articulating what is in a product, to labeling what is NOT in the food.（但是，针对消费者这种需求的营销策略已经不仅仅是明确说明产品中的成分，而是给食品中不含有的成分贴上标签。）A 项是原文中 to labeling what is NOT in the food 的同义表达，故选 A 项。

53. What point does the author make about non-GMO labels?

A) They are increasingly attracting customers' attention.

B) They create lots of trouble for GMO food producers.

C) They should be used more for vegetables and milk.

D) They cause anxiety about food among consumers.

53. 作者对非转基因标签有什么看法？

A）它们越来越吸引客户的注意力。

B）它们给转基因食品生产商带来了很多麻烦。

C）它们应该更多地用于蔬菜和牛奶。

D）它们引起消费者对食物的焦虑。

【答案及分析】D。根据题干定位到原文第四段。该段指出，…in the long term this strategy will have just the opposite effect: by injecting fear into the discourse about our food, we run the risk of eroding consumer trust in not just a single product, but the entire food business.（……但从长远来看，这种策略只会产生逆反效果：通过在关于食物的说明中注入恐惧感，我们面临的风险是，消费者不是仅对某一种产品，而是对整个食品行业都失去了信任。）D项是原文的同义表达，故选D项。

54. What does the author say absence claims labels will do to food manufacturers?

A) Cause changes in their marketing strategies.　　C) Erode consumer trust and reduce sales.

B) Help remove stigma around their products.　　D) Decrease support from food scientists.

54. 作者说"缺席声明"标签会对食品制造商产生什么影响？

A）改变他们的营销策略。　　C）破坏消费者的信任，降低销售额。

B）帮助他们消除产品的污名。　　D）减少食品科学家的支持。

【答案及分析】C。根据题干关键词to food manufacturers定位到原文第五段第三句。该句指出，For food manufacturers, it will mean damaged consumer trust and lower sales for everyone.（对于食品制造商来说，这将意味着消费者的信任受损以及销售额下降。）C项是原文中damaged consumer trust and lower sales的同义表达，故选C项。

55. What does the author suggest food manufacturers do?

A) Take measures to lower the cost of food products.

B) Exercise caution about the use of absence claims.

C) Welcome new innovations in food processing.

D) Promote efficiency and increase food variety.

55. 作者建议食品制造商做什么？

A）采取措施来降低食品的成本。

B）在使用"缺席声明"标签时要谨慎行事。

C）接受食品加工领域的新创新。

D）提高效率，增加食品种类。

【答案及分析】B。根据题干定位到原文最后一段。该段首句指出，It's clear that food manufacturers must tread carefully when it comes to using absence claims.（很明显，食品制造商在使用"缺席声明"标签时必须谨慎行事。）B项是原文中tread carefully when it comes to using absence claims的同义表达，故选B项。

Part Ⅳ Translation

参考译文

The site of the First National Congress of the Communist Party of China (CPC), built in the autumn of 1920 and sited at No. 76 Xingye Road in Shanghai, is a typical Shanghai-style residence. On July 23, 1921, the First National Congress of the CPC was held here, which adopted the first guiding principle and the first resolution of the CPC, elected the central leadership, and declared the birth of the CPC. In September 1952, the site of the First National Congress of the CPC was restored, and a memorial hall was established and opened to the public. In addition to introducing the delegates who attended the first meeting of the CPC, the memorial hall also introduces the historical development process of the CPC, and it has become a patriotic education base for knowing the history of the CPC and commemorating our revolutionary martyrs.

难词总结

residence /ˈrezɪdəns/ n. 住宅，住所
resolution /ˌrezəˈluːʃn/ n. 决议，正式决定
restore /rɪˈstɔː(r)/ v. 修复（建筑物、艺术品、车辆等）
delegate /ˈdelɪɡət/ n. 代表
commemorate /kəˈmeməreɪt/ v. 纪念
martyr /ˈmɑːtə(r)/ n. 烈士

guiding principle 指导原则；纲领
declare /dɪˈkleə(r)/ v. 宣布，声明
memorial /məˈmɔːriəl/ a. 纪念的
patriotic /ˌpeɪtriˈɒtɪk/ a. 爱国的，有爱国心的
revolutionary /ˌrevəˈluːʃənəri/ a. 革命的

译点释义

1. 第一句中包含三个动词"位于""是"和"建于"，翻译时需要将其中两个动词处理成非谓语，仅保留一个谓语动词。如参考译文将"位于上海兴业路76号"和"建于1920年秋"译成了 built in the autumn of 1920 and sited at No. 76 Xingye Road in Shanghai；"典型的上海式住宅"译为 a typical Shanghai-style residence。

2. 第二句中的"大会通过了……，选举产生了……，宣告了……"可译为非限制性定语从句 which adopted the first guiding principle and the first resolution of the CPC, elected the central leadership, and declared the birth of the CPC。

3. 第三句中有两个主语，"中共一大会址"和"纪念馆"，因此译为两个独立的句子，用 and 连接，译为 the site of the first National Congress of the CPC was restored, and a memorial hall was established and opened to the public。

4. 最后一句中的"除……之外"译为介词短语 In addition to...，"参加一大的"译为 who 引导的定语从句，修饰"代表"；"现已成为……教育基地"译为并列句，用 and 连接，it 指代"纪念馆"。

版权专有　侵权必究

图书在版编目（CIP）数据

大学英语6级真题详解及速刷狂练 / 马天艺，启航大学生考试研究中心主编. — 北京：北京理工大学出版社，2022.3

（6级轻过书课包）

ISBN 978 – 7 – 5763 – 1134 – 1

Ⅰ. ①大… Ⅱ. ①马… ②启… Ⅲ. ①大学英语水平考试–解题　Ⅳ. ①H310.421-44

中国版本图书馆CIP数据核字（2022）第042563号

出版发行 / 北京理工大学出版社有限责任公司
社　　址 / 北京市海淀区中关村南大街5号
邮　　编 / 100081
电　　话 /（010）68914775（总编室）
　　　　　（010）82562903（教材售后服务热线）
　　　　　（010）68944723（其他图书服务热线）
网　　址 / http://www.bitpress.com.cn
经　　销 / 全国各地新华书店
印　　刷 / 天津市蓟县宏图印务有限公司
开　　本 / 787毫米 × 1092毫米　1/16　　　　　　　　　　　责任编辑 / 武丽娟
印　　张 / 23　　　　　　　　　　　　　　　　　　　　　　文案编辑 / 武丽娟
字　　数 / 574千字
版　　次 / 2022年3月第1版　2022年3月第1次印刷　　　　　　责任校对 / 刘亚男
定　　价 / 149.60元（全2册）　　　　　　　　　　　　　　　责任印制 / 李志强

图书出现印装质量问题，请拨打售后服务热线，本社负责调换

未得到监考教师指令前，不得翻阅该试题册！

2021年12月大学英语六级考试真题（第二套）

Part I Writing (30 minutes)

（请于正式开考后半小时内完成该部分，之后将进行听力考试）

Directions: *For this part, you are allowed 30 minutes to write an essay related to the short passage given below. In your essay, you are to comment on the phenomenon described in the passage and suggest measures to address the issue. You should write at least **150** words but no more than **200** words.*

Some parents in China are overprotective of their children. They plan everything for their children, make all the decisions for them, and do not allow them to explore on their own in case they make mistakes or get hurt.

Part II Listening Comprehension (30 minutes)

Section A

Directions: *In this section, you will hear two long conversations. At the end of each conversation, you will hear four questions. Both the conversation and the questions will be spoken only once. After you hear a question, you must choose the best answer from the four choices marked A), B), C) and D). Then mark the corresponding letter on **Answer Sheet 1** with a single line through the centre.*

Questions 1 to 4 are based on the conversation you have just heard.

1. A) He was enjoying his holiday.
   B) He was recovering in hospital.
   C) He was busy writing his essays.
   D) He was fighting a throat infection.
2. A) He broke his wrist.
   B) He lost his antibiotics.
   C) He slipped on ice and fell.
   D) He was laughed at by some girls.
3. A) Turn to her father for help.
   B) Call the repair shop to fix it.
   C) Ask the manufacturer for repairs.
   D) Replace it with a brand-new one.
4. A) Help David retrieve his essays.
   B) Introduce David to her parents.
   C) Offer David some refreshments.
   D) Accompany David to his home.

Questions 5 to 8 are based on the conversation you have just heard.

5. A) She is a critic of works on military affairs.
   B) She is an acclaimed hostess of *Book Talk*.
   C) She is a researcher of literary genres.
   D) She is a historian of military history.
6. A) It is about the military history of Europe.
   B) It is set in the 18th and 19th centuries.
   C) It is her fifth book of military history.
   D) It is a war novel set in the future.
7. A) She visited soldiers' wives and mothers.
   B) She conducted surveys of many soldiers.
   C) She met a large number of soldiers in person.
   D) She looked into the personal lives of soldiers.
8. A) She doesn't have much freedom for imagination.
   B) It is not easy to make her readers believe in her.
   C) It is difficult to attract young readers.
   D) She has to combine fact with fiction.

Section B

Directions: *In this section, you will hear two passages. At the end of each passage, you will hear three or four questions. Both the passage and the questions will be spoken only once. After you hear a question, you must choose the best answer from the four choices marked A), B), C) and D). Then mark the corresponding letter on **Answer Sheet 1** with a single line through the centre.*

Questions 9 to 11 are based on the passage you have just heard.

9. A) Santa Claus.
   B) A polar bear.
   C) Cocoa seeds.
   D) A glass bottle.
10. A) To attract customer attention.
    B) To keep up with the times.
    C) To combat counterfeits.
    D) To promote its sales.
11. A) It resembles a picture in the encyclopedia.
    B) It appears in the shape of a cocoa seed.
    C) It has the drink's logo in the middle.
    D) It displays the image of Santa Claus.

Questions 12 to 15 are based on the passage you have just heard.

12. A) It often occurs among commuters.
    B) It promotes mutual understanding.
    C) It improves their mood considerably.
    D) It takes a great deal of effort to sustain.
13. A) Social anxiety.
    B) Excessive caution.
    C) Lack of social skills.
    D) Preference for solitude.
14. A) People usually regard it as an unforgettable lesson.
    B) Human brains tend to dwell on negative events.
    C) Negative events often hurt people deeply.
    D) People generally resent being rejected.
15. A) Contagious.
    B) Temporary.
    C) Unpredictable.
    D) Measurable.

Section C

Directions: *In this section, you will hear three recordings of lectures or talks followed by three or four questions. The recordings will be played only once. After you hear a question, you must choose the best answer from the four choices marked A), B), C) and D). Then mark the corresponding letter on **Answer Sheet 1** with a single line through the centre.*

Questions 16 to 18 are based on the recording you have just heard.

16. A) It depends heavily on tourism.
    B) It is flourishing in foreign trade.
    C) It is mainly based on agriculture.
    D) It relies chiefly on mineral export.
17. A) Tobacco.
    B) Bananas.
    C) Coffee.
    D) Sugar.
18. A) They toil on farms.
    B) They live a poor life.
    C) They live in Spanish-style houses.
    D) They hire people to do housework.

Questions 19 to 21 are based on the recording you have just heard.

19. A) They will be more demanding of their next generation.
    B) They will end up lonely, dependent and dissatisfied.
    C) They will experience more setbacks than successes.
    D) They will find it difficult to get along with others.
20. A) Failure to pay due attention to their behavior.
    B) Unwillingness to allow them to play with toys.
    C) Unwillingness to satisfy their wishes immediately.
    D) Failure to spend sufficient quality time with them.
21. A) It will enable them to learn from mistakes.
    B) It will help them to handle disappointment.

C) It will do much good to their mental health.
D) It will build their ability to endure hardships.

Questions 22 to 25 are based on the recording you have just heard.

22. A) Failing to make sufficient preparations.
    B) Looking away from the hiring manager.
    C) Saying the wrong thing at the wrong time.
    D) Making a wrong judgment of the interview.
23. A) Complaining about their previous job.
    B) Inquiring about their salary to be paid.
    C) Exaggerating their academic background.
    D) Understating their previous achievements.
24. A) Those who have both skill and experience.
    B) Those who get along well with colleagues.
    C) Those who take initiative in their work.
    D) Those who are loyal to their managers.
25. A) Ability to shoulder new responsibilities.
    B) Experience of performing multiple roles.
    C) Readiness to work to flexible schedules.
    D) Skills to communicate with colleagues.

Part Ⅲ　　　　　Reading Comprehension　　　（40 minutes）

Section A

Directions: *In this section, there is a passage with ten blanks. You are required to select one word for each blank from a list of choices given in a word bank following the passage. Read the passage through carefully before making your choices. Each choice in the bank is identified by a letter. Please mark the corresponding letter for each item on **Answer Sheet 2** with a single line through the centre. You may not use any of the words in the bank more than once.*

　　If you think life is wonderful and expect it to stay that way, then you may have a good chance of living to a ripe old age, at least that is what the findings of a new study suggest. That study found that participants who reported the highest levels of optimism were far more likely to live to age 85 or __26__. This was compared to those participants who reported the lowest levels of optimism. It is __27__ that the findings held even after the researchers considered factors that could __28__ the link, including whether participants had health conditions such as heart disease or cancer, or whether they experienced depression. The results add to a growing body of evidence that certain psychological factors may predict a longer life __29__. For example, previous studies have found that more optimistic people have a lower risk of developing chronic diseases, and a lower risk of __30__ death. However, the new study appears to be the first to __31__ look at the relationship between optimism and longevity. The researchers __32__ that the link found in the new study was not as strong when they factored in the effects of certain health behaviors, including exercise levels, sleep habits and diet. This suggests that these behaviors may, at least in part, explain the link. In other words, optimism may __33__ good habits that bolster health. It is also important to note that the study found only a __34__, as researchers did not prove for certain that optimism leads to a longer life. However, if the findings are true, they suggest that optimism could serve as a psychological __35__ that promotes health and a longer life.

A) affect	I) plausibly
B) beyond	J) premature
C) conceded	K) reconciled
D) correlation	L) span
E) foster	M) specifically
F) henceforth	N) spiral
G) lofty	O) trait
H) noteworthy	

3

Section B

Directions: *In this section, you are going to read a passage with ten statements attached to it. Each statement contains information given in one of the paragraphs. Identify the paragraph from which the information is derived. You may choose a paragraph more than once. Each paragraph is marked with a letter. Answer the questions by marking the corresponding letter on **Answer Sheet 2**.*

Why facts don't change our minds

[A] The economist J. K. Galbraith once wrote, "Faced with a choice between changing one's mind and proving there is no need to do so, almost everyone gets busy with the proof."

[B] Leo Tolstoy was even bolder: "The most difficult subjects can be explained to the most slow-witted man if he has not formed any idea of them already; but the simplest thing cannot be made clear to the most intelligent man if he is firmly persuaded that he knows already, without a shadow of a doubt, what is laid before him."

[C] What's going on here? Why don't facts change our minds? And why would someone continue to believe a false or inaccurate idea anyway? How do such behaviors serve us? Humans need a reasonably accurate view of the world in order to survive. If your model of reality is wildly different from the actual world, then you struggle to take effective actions each day. However, truth and accuracy are not the only things that matter to the human mind. Humans also seem to have a deep desire to belong.

[D] In *Atomic Habits*, I wrote, "Humans are herd animals. We want to fit in, to bond with others, and to earn the respect and approval of our peers. Such inclinations are essential to our survival. For most of our evolutionary history, our ancestors lived in tribes. Becoming separated from the tribe — or worse, being cast out — was a death sentence."

[E] Understanding the truth of a situation is important, but so is remaining part of a tribe. While these two desires often work well together, they occasionally come into conflict. In many circumstances, social connection is actually more helpful to your daily life than understanding the truth of a particular fact or idea. The Harvard psychologist Steven Pinker put it this way, "People are embraced or condemned according to their beliefs, so one function of the mind may be to hold beliefs that bring the belief-holder the greatest number of allies, protectors, or *disciples* (信徒), rather than beliefs that are most likely to be true."

[F] We don't always believe things because they are correct. Sometimes we believe things because they make us look good to the people we care about. I thought Kevin Simler put it well when he wrote, "If a brain anticipates that it will be rewarded for adopting a particular belief, it's perfectly happy to do so, and doesn't much care where the reward comes from — whether it's *pragmatic* (实用主义的) (better outcomes resulting from better decisions), social (better treatment from one's peers), or some mix of the two."

[G] False beliefs can be useful in a social sense even if they are not useful in a factual sense. For lack of a better phrase, we might call this approach "factually false, but socially accurate." When we have to choose between the two, people often select friends and family over facts. This insight not only explains why we might hold our tongue at a dinner party or look the other way when our parents say something offensive, but also reveals a better way to change the minds of others.

[H] Convincing someone to change their mind is really the process of convincing them to change their tribe. If they abandon their beliefs, they run the risk of losing social ties. You can't expect someone to change their mind if you take away their community too. You have to give them somewhere to go. Nobody wants their worldview torn apart if loneliness is the outcome.

[I] The way to change people's minds is to become friends with them, to integrate them into your tribe, to bring them into your circle. Now, they can change their beliefs without the risk of being abandoned socially.

[J] Perhaps it is not difference, but distance, that breeds tribalism and hostility. As proximity increases, so does understanding. I am reminded of Abraham Lincoln's quote, "I don't like that man. I must get to know him better."

[K] Facts don't change our minds. Friendship does. Years ago, Ben Casnocha mentioned an idea to me that I haven't been able to shake: The people who are most likely to change our minds are the ones we agree with on 98 percent of topics. If someone you know, like, and trust believes a radical idea, you are more likely to give it merit, weight, or consideration. You already agree with them in most areas of life. Maybe you should change your mind on this one too. But if someone wildly different than you proposes the same radical idea, well, it's easy to dismiss them as nuts.

[L] One way to visualize this distinction is by mapping beliefs on a spectrum. If you divide this spectrum into 10 units and you find yourself at Position 7, then there is little sense in trying to convince someone at Position 1. The gap is too wide. When you're at Position 7, your time is better spent connecting with people who are at Positions 6 and 8, gradually pulling them in your direction.

[M] The most heated arguments often occur between people on opposite ends of the spectrum, but the most frequent learning occurs from people who are nearby. The closer you are to someone, the more likely it becomes that the one or two beliefs you don't share will bleed over into your own mind and shape your thinking. The further away an idea is from your current position, the more likely you are to reject it outright. When it comes to changing people's minds, it is very difficult to jump from one side to another. You can't jump down the spectrum. You have to slide down it.

[N] Any idea that is sufficiently different from your current worldview will feel threatening. And the best place to ponder a threatening idea is in a non-threatening environment. As a result, books are often a better vehicle for transforming beliefs than conversations or debates. In conversation, people have to carefully consider their status and appearance. They want to save face and avoid looking stupid. When confronted with an uncomfortable set of facts, the tendency is often to double down on their current position rather than publicly admit to being wrong. Books resolve this tension. With a book, the conversation takes place inside someone's head and without the risk of being judged by others. It's easier to be open-minded when you aren't feeling defensive.

[O] There is another reason bad ideas continue to live on, which is that people continue to talk about them. Silence is death for any idea. An idea that is never spoken or written down dies with the person who conceived it. Ideas can only be remembered when they are repeated. They can only be believed when they are repeated. I have already pointed out that people repeat ideas to signal they are part of the same social group. But here's a crucial point most people miss: People also repeat bad ideas when they complain about them. Before you can criticize an idea, you have to reference that idea. You end up repeating the ideas you're hoping people will forget — but, of course, people can't forget them because you keep talking about them. The more you repeat a bad idea, the more likely people are to believe it.

[P] Let's call this phenomenon Clear's Law of Recurrence: The number of people who believe an idea is directly proportional to the number of times it has been repeated during the last year — even if the idea is false.

36. According to the author, humans can hardly survive if separated from their community.
37. People often accept false beliefs because they prioritize social bonds rather than facts.
38. Most often people learn from those close to them.
39. Sometimes people adopt certain beliefs in order to leave a favorable impression on those dear to them.
40. Compared with face-to-face communication, books often provide a better medium for changing people's beliefs.
41. On many occasions in daily life, people benefit more from their social bonds than from knowing the truth.
42. If you want to change somebody's beliefs, you should first establish social connection with them.

43. Humans cannot survive without a fair knowledge of the actual world.
44. Repetition of bad ideas increases their chances of being accepted.
45. Nobody is willing to give up their beliefs at the risk of getting isolated.

Section C

Directions: *There are 2 passages in this section. Each passage is followed by some questions or unfinished statements. For each of them there are four choices marked A), B), C) and D). You should decide on the best choice and mark the corresponding letter on **Answer Sheet 2** with a single line through the centre.*

Passage One

Questions 46 to 50 are based on the following passage.

The subject of automation and its role in our economy has taken hold in American public discourse. Technology broadly and automation specifically are dramatically reshaping the way we work. And we need to have a plan for what's still to come.

We don't have to look further than our own communities to see the devastating impact of automation. From automated warehouses to cashierless grocery stores to neighborhood libraries that offer self-checkout lanes instead of employing real people — automation is increasingly replacing jobs and leaving too few good new jobs behind.

The statistics in manufacturing are staggering. Despite the widespread fears about trade, a recent report showed that just 13 percent of jobs lost in manufacturing are due to trade — the rest of the losses have been due to advances in technology.

That is why more people are criticizing the ever-increasing role of technology in our economy. Our country is manufacturing more than ever before, but we are doing it with fewer workers. However, it's not just factories that are seeing losses — software and information technology are also having a dramatic impact on jobs most people think are secure from the forces of a rapidly-changing economy. Something transformative is happening in America that is having an adverse effect on American families. Whether policymakers and politicians admit it or not, workers have made clear their feelings about their economic insecurity and desire to keep good jobs in America.

So why are people so insistent on ignoring the perils of automation? They are failing to look ahead at a time when planning for the future is more important than ever. Resisting automation is futile: it is as inevitable as industrialization was before it. I sincerely hope that those who assert that automation will make us more effective and pave the way for new occupations are right, but the reality of automation's detrimental effects on workers makes me skeptical. No one can currently say where the new jobs are coming from or when, and any sensible company or country should prepare for all alternatives.

I'm not overstating the danger: look at what's happened to the labor force. According to economic research, one in six working-age men, 25-54, doesn't have a job. Fifty years ago, nearly 100 percent of men that age were working. Women's labor force participation, meanwhile, has slipped back to the level it was at in the late 1980s.

American families and prominent business leaders are aware that there's a big problem with automation. The value of a college degree is diminishing, and our upward mobility is declining. If we want an economy that allows everyone to be economically secure, we need to start thinking about how we can rightfully address automation.

46. What can we observe from the author's description of our communities?
    A) The growing passion for automation.
    B) The shift from manual jobs to IT ones.
    C) Their changing views on employment.
    D) Their fading employment opportunities.
47. What do we learn from a recent report?
    A) The manufacturing sector is declining at a fast rate.
    B) The concerns about the effect of trade are exaggerated.
    C) The fears about trade have been spreading far and wide.
    D) The impact of trade on employment has been staggering.
48. What does the passage tell us about American workers in an era of transformation?
    A) They feel ignored by politicians.
    B) They feel increasingly vulnerable.
    C) They keep adapting to the changes.
    D) They keep complaining but to no avail.
49. What does the author think of automation?
    A) It will have the same impact as industrialization.
    B) It provides sensible companies with alternatives.
    C) Its alleged positive effects are doubtful.
    D) Its detrimental effects are unavoidable.
50. What should we attach importance to when dealing with automation?
    A) College graduates' job prospects.
    B) Women's access to employment.
    C) People's economic security.
    D) People's social mobility.

Passage Two

Questions 51 to 55 are based on the following passage.

Look at the people around you. Some are passive, others more aggressive. Some work best alone, others crave companionship. We easily recognize that there is great variation among the individuals who live near us. Yet, when we speak of people from elsewhere, we seem to inevitably characterize them based on their country of origin.

Statistics specialists, when they speak of national averages, often make the same mistake.

Newly published research shows how erroneous such overviews are. Three researchers analyzed decades of values-based surveys and found that only between 16% and 21% of the variation in cultural values could be explained by differences between countries. In other words, the vast majority of what makes us culturally distinct from one another has nothing to do with our homeland.

To determine what factors really are associated with culture, the authors combined data from 558 prior surveys that each measured one or more of Hofstede's cultural dimensions. These are traits, such as individualism and masculinity, that describe work-related cultural values. (They are not a measure of visible cultural traits, such as food or dress.) Though the validity of Hofstede's dimensions has been questioned, they have the singular benefit of having been in use for decades, which allows for historical and international comparisons.

The researchers found that both demographic factors, such as age, and environmental factors, such as long-term unemployment rates, were more correlated with cultural values than nationality. Occupation and social economic status were the most strongly correlated, suggesting that our values are more economically driven than we usually give them credit for.

The evidence implies that people with similar jobs and incomes are more culturally alike, regardless of where they live. Vas Taras, the lead author of the study, puts it this way: "Tell me how much you make and

I will make a pretty accurate prediction about your cultural values. Tell me what your nationality is and I probably will make a wrong prediction."

Taras says our erroneous belief that countries are cultures has caused businesses to teach their employees useless or even harmful ways of interacting with their international peers. Chinese and American lawyers might be trained to interact based on the assumption that the Chinese person is less individualistic, even though their similar social economic situations make it probable they are actually quite alike in that regard.

The country, as the unit of authority, is often a convenient way of generalizing about a population. However, our focus on countries can mask broad variations within them. In the majority of cases we would be better off identifying people by the factors that constrain their lives, like income, rather than by the lines surrounding them on a map.

51. What error do experts often make when describing people from other places?
    A) They tend to overly rely on nationality.
    B) They often exaggerate their differences.
    C) They often misunderstand their cultures.
    D) They tend to dwell on national averages.

52. What do we learn about Hofstede's cultural dimensions?
    A) They are useful in comparing cultural values across time and space.
    B) They have brought unusual benefits to people of different cultures.
    C) They are widely used to identify people's individual traits.
    D) They provide valuable questions for researchers to study.

53. What did researchers find about previous studies on factors determining people's values?
    A) Environmental factors were prioritized over other factors.
    B) An individual's financial status was often underestimated.
    C) Too much emphasis had been placed on one's occupation.
    D) The impact of social progress on one's values was ignored.

54. What is the impact on employees when cultures are identified with countries?
    A) They may fail to see the cultural biases of their business partners.
    B) They may fail to attach sufficient importance to cultural diversity.
    C) They may not be taught how to properly interact with overseas partners.
    D) They may not be able to learn the legal procedures for business transactions.

55. What does the author suggest at the end of the passage?
    A) There is sufficient reason to generalize about a country's population.
    B) The majority of people are still constrained by their national identity.
    C) It is arguable that the country should be regarded as the unit of authority.
    D) Nationality is less useful than socio-economic status as an indicator of one's values.

Part Ⅳ Translation (30 minutes)

Directions: *For this part, you are allowed 30 minutes to translate a passage from Chinese into English. You should write your answer on* **Answer Sheet 2**.

井冈山地处湖南江西两省交界处，因其辉煌的革命历史被誉为"中国革命红色摇篮"。1927年10月，毛泽东、朱德等老一辈革命家率领中国工农红军来到这里，开展了艰苦卓绝的斗争，创建了第一个农村革命根据地，点燃了中国革命的星星之火，开辟了"农村包围（besiege）城市，武装夺取政权"这一具有中国特色的革命道路，中国革命从这里迈向胜利。井冈山现有100多处革命旧址，成为一个"没有围墙的革命历史博物馆"，是爱国主义和革命传统教育的重要基地。

2021年12月大学英语六级考试真题解析
（第二套）

Part Ⅰ　Writing

成文构思

本文是一篇议论文，话题是"父母过度保护孩子"，可按照以下思路进行写作。
第一段：**引出话题**，提出"父母对孩子过度保护"这一现象具有负面影响。
第二段：**具体分析**"父母对孩子过度保护"对孩子产生的负面影响，可从缺乏独立性和意志力两个方面进行分析。本段是全文的中心段落。
第三段：**总结段**，可进一步呼应文章主题。

参考范文及译文

　　Overprotective parents control their children's actions and make all the decisions for them. Although they want to ensure children's well-being, their efforts might be unnecessary and even **detrimental**.

　　In such a society full of challenges and frustrations, it is of absolute necessity to realize that overprotection will **take a heavy toll on** children. For one thing, children who get overprotection are more likely to be less independent. According to a report released by *China Daily*, those being overprotected in all likelihood rely so heavily on their parents and fail to overcome difficulties and solve problems on their own. For another thing, overprotective parenting would make children less **determined**. A distinguished psychologist in China once noted that if parents protect their children so much, children would tend to be less **persistent** when suffering hardship or setbacks.

　　Given the analysis above, it can be indisputable that overprotective parenting can not be instrumental when it comes to developing children's independence and perseverance. Therefore, it is highly **recommended** that parents shouldn't be overprotective and moderately divert their attention from children.

　　对孩子过度保护的父母控制孩子的行为，为孩子做所有决定。虽然他们希望确保孩子能够幸福，但这些努力可能是不必要的，甚至是有害的。

　　现在的社会充满挑战和挫折，意识到过度保护将给孩子带来巨大负面影响是非常必要的。一方面，受到过度保护的儿童更有可能缺乏独立性。《中国日报》发布的一份报告显示，正受到过度保护的孩子很可能会对父母产生严重依赖，且无法独自克服困难和解决问题。另一方面，父母过度保护会使孩子们意志力不坚定。中国一位著名的心理学家曾经指出，如果父母过于保护孩子，那么孩子在遇到困难或挫折时往往不会坚持到底。

　　鉴于上述分析，毫无疑问，父母过度保护孩子不会有助于培养孩子的独立性和意志力。因此，强烈建议父母不要对孩子过度保护，适度地转移一下对孩子的关注。

词句点拨

overprotective /ˌəʊvəprəˈtektɪv/ a. 过分保护的
take a heavy toll on 给……造成重大负面影响
persistent /pəˈsɪstənt/ a. 坚持不懈的

detrimental /ˌdetrɪˈment(ə)l/ a. 有害的
determined /dɪˈtɜːmɪnd/ a. 坚定的
recommend /ˌrekəˈmend/ v. 建议；劝告

1. In such a society full of challenges and frustrations, it is of absolute necessity to realize that...
   现在的社会充满挑战和挫折，意识到……是非常必要的。

2. A distinguished psychologist in China once noted that...
   中国一位著名的心理学家曾经指出……

3. Given the analysis above, it can be indisputable that... can not be instrumental when it comes to developing...
   鉴于上述分析，毫无疑问，……不会有助于培养……

Part II Listening Comprehension

Section A

Questions 1 to 4 are based on the conversation you have just heard.

听力原文及译文

W: Hi, David, I haven't seen you in class for almost two weeks. (1) <u>We thought you had disappeared on holiday early or something.</u>

M: Hi, Sarah. Well, it's a bit of a long story, I'm afraid. I got a throat infection last week and had to go to the hospital to get some antibiotics as I really wasn't getting any better.

W: Oh, yeah. There have been so many viruses going around this winter. The weather has been so awful for the last few weeks.

M: (2) <u>And on the way back from the hospital, I slipped on some ice and fell</u>, and then had to go to the hospital to get an X-ray because I basically thought I broke my wrist, although, thankfully, it's not broken. But I need to be careful with it for the next few weeks.

W: Oh, that's too bad. How unfortunate!

M: To make things worse, I managed to fall right in front of four girls from the ninth grade. So, it was utterly humiliated. Plus, the laptop in my bag was broken too.

W: No! What a complete catastrophe! Is the laptop still under warranty? If it is, then you can easily send it back to the manufacturer and they'll send you a brand-new one for free surely.

M: The warranty ran out three days before I broke it. And all my essays are in there, and I need to hand them in before we break for the Christmas holidays.

W: Listen, I have the number of a really good, affordable computer repair shop at home. My dad has used this guy before and he can work miracles. (3—4) Let's go back to my house and we can call the repair shop, and you could have some tea and cookies too.

M: Wow. Thanks, Sarah. That would be great. Let me just call my mom and let her know I'll be home a little bit later.

女：嗨，大卫，我已经快两周没看见你上课了。（1）我们还以为你提前去度假或是去做别的事了呢。

男：你好，萨拉。好吧，恐怕说来话长。上周我的喉咙感染了，由于实在是没有好转，不得不去医院打抗生素。

女：哦，是的。这个冬天到处都是病毒。过去几周天气一直很糟糕。

男：（2）而且从医院回来的路上，我在冰上滑倒了，然后不得不去医院照 X 光，因为我以为我的手腕摔断了。不过还好没摔断。但接下来几周我得小心点。

女：哦，那太糟糕了。多么不幸啊！

男：更糟糕的是，我竟然摔倒在四个九年级女生面前了。所以，这真是太丢脸了。另外，我包里的笔记本电脑也坏了。

女：不！真是个大灾难！这台笔记本电脑还在保修期内吗？如果在的话，你可以很容易地把它寄回给制造商，他们肯定会免费寄给你一台全新的。

男：我把它弄坏的时候保修期就过了三天了。我的所有论文都在里面，我得在圣诞节放假前提交。

女：听着，我家那边有一家很好的、价格适中的电脑维修店，我有这家店的电话号码。我爸以前用过这个人，他能创造奇迹。（3—4）我们回我家去，给修理店打个电话，你也可以喝点茶，吃点饼干。

男：哇。谢谢你，萨拉。那太好了。我给我妈打个电话，告诉她我晚点回。

难词总结

infection /ɪnˈfekʃn/ n. 感染；传染病
awful /ˈɔːfl/ a. 让人讨厌的，糟糕的
humiliated /hjuːˈmɪlieɪtɪd/ a. 蒙羞的；感到自惭的
warranty /ˈwɒrənti/ n.（商品的）保修单
antibiotics /ˌæntibaɪˈɒtɪks/ n. [药] 抗生素；抗生学
wrist /rɪst/ n. 手腕；腕关节
catastrophe /kəˈtæstrəfi/ n. 灾难；麻烦
run out 到期；用完；耗尽；跑出

题目精析

1. What does Sarah think David was doing for the last two weeks?

    A) He was enjoying his holiday.
    B) He was recovering in hospital.
    C) He was busy writing his essays.
    D) He was fighting a throat infection.

1. 萨拉认为大卫在过去的两周里在做什么？

    A）他在享受假期。
    B）他正在医院休养康复。
    C）他忙着写他的论文。
    D）他在治疗喉咙感染。

【答案及分析】A。本题问萨拉对大卫的看法。音频中提到，We thought you had disappeared on holiday early or something.（我们还以为你提前去度假或是去做别的事了呢。）A 项与音频内容相符，其中 enjoying his holiday 是音频中 on holiday 的同义表达，故选 A 项。

2. What happened to David on his way back from the hospital?

A) He broke his wrist.　　　　　　　　　C) He slipped on ice and fell.

B) He lost his antibiotics.　　　　　　　D) He was laughed at by some girls.

2. 大卫在从医院回来的路上发生了什么？

A）他摔断了手腕。　　　　　　　　　　C）他在冰上滑倒了。

B）他弄丢了抗生素。　　　　　　　　　D）他被一些女孩嘲笑。

【答案及分析】C。本题问大卫在从医院回来的路上遇到的状况。音频中提到，And on the way back from the hospital, I slipped on some ice and fell（而且从医院回来的路上，我在冰上滑倒了）。C项与音频内容相符，其中 slipped on ice and fell 是原词复现，故选 C 项。

3. What does Sarah say they should do with the damaged computer?

A) Turn to her father for help.　　　　　C) Ask the manufacturer for repairs.

B) Call the repair shop to fix it.　　　　D) Replace it with a brand-new one.

3. 萨拉说他们应该怎么处理损坏的电脑？

A）寻求她父亲的帮助。　　　　　　　　C）要求制造商进行修理。

B）打电话给修理店去修理它。　　　　　D）换一台全新的。

【答案及分析】B。本题问萨拉提出的解决方法。音频中提到，Let's go back to my house and we can call the repair shop, and you could have some tea and cookies too.（我们回我家去，给修理店打个电话，你也可以喝点茶，吃点饼干。）B项与音频内容相符，其中 Call the repair shop 是原词复现，故选 B 项。

4. What does Sarah say she is going to do?

A) Help David retrieve his essays.　　　C) Offer David some refreshments.

B) Introduce David to her parents.　　　D) Accompany David to his home.

4. 萨拉说她要做什么？

A）帮助大卫找回他的论文。　　　　　　C）给大卫一些茶点。

B）把大卫介绍给她的父母。　　　　　　D）陪大卫回家。

【答案及分析】C。本题问萨拉要做什么。音频中提到，Let's go back to my house and we can call the repair shop, and you could have some tea and cookies too.（我们回我家去，给修理店打个电话，你也可以喝点茶，吃点饼干。）C项是音频中 you could have some tea and cookies too 的同义表达，故选 C 项。

Questions 5 to 8 are based on the conversation you have just heard.

听力原文及译文

M: Welcome to this week's episode of *Book Talk*. (5) With me today is Heidi Brown, a historian who has written five critically acclaimed books about military history.

W: Thanks for having me, John. I'm so excited to talk about my latest book, which was published last month.

M: So this book is a novel, your first attempt at that genre. I thought it was a bit of a departure for you.

W: I'd say it's a major departure as it's not just a work of fiction. (6) It's set 200 years in the future.

M: Right. So how did that happen? You spent three decades writing about the past and focusing on the 18th and

19th centuries. And now you're speculating about the future.

W: Well, after years of researching soldiers and chronicling their lives during battle, I just started wondering about other facets of their lives, especially their personal lives.

M: I can see that. Your novel is about soldiers, but it focuses on their relationships, especially the bonds between sons and mothers, and men and their wives.

W: Yes. (7) That focus came about when I still intended to write another book of history, I started by researching soldier's actual personal lives, studying their letters home.

M: So how did that history book become a novel?

W: Well, I realized that the historical record was incomplete. So I'd either have to leave a lot of gaps or make a lot more assumptions than a historian should.

M: But why write a novel set in the future when your credentials are perfect for a historical novel? As a historian, any historical novel you write would have a lot of credibility.

W: (8-1) I felt too constrained working with the past, like what I wrote needed to be fact as opposed to fiction. (8-2) But writing about the future gave me more freedom to imagine, to invent.

M: Well, having read your book, I'm glad you made that choice to move into fiction.

男：欢迎来到本周的《书友会》。（5）今天和我一起的是海蒂·布朗，一位历史学家，她写了五本关于军事史的书，广受好评。

女：谢谢你邀请我，约翰。我很高兴能谈谈我上个月出版的新书。

男：所以这本书是一部小说，你第一次尝试这种体裁。我觉得这对你来说有点不同。

女：我想说这是一个重大的转变，因为它不仅仅是一部虚构的作品。（6）它发生于200年后。

男：是的。那么，这是怎么发生的呢？你花了三十年的时间写过去，专注于18世纪和19世纪。而现在你正在推测未来。

女：在多年研究士兵并记录他们在战场上的生活之后，我开始想知道他们生活的其他方面，尤其是他们的个人生活。

男：我看得出来。你的小说是关于士兵的，但它侧重于写他们的关系，尤其是儿子和母亲之间的关系，男人和他们的妻子之间的关系。

女：是的。（7）当我还打算写另一本历史书的时候，我的关注点是开始研究士兵的实际生活，研究他们的家书。

男：那么，这本历史书是如何成为小说的呢？

女：嗯，我意识到历史记录是不完整的。所以，我要么留下很多空白，要么比历史学家做出更多的假设。

男：但是，当你的资历非常适合写历史小说时，为什么要写一部以未来为背景的小说呢？作为一名历史学家，你写的任何历史小说都会有很大的可信度。

女：(8-1) 和过去打交道让我觉得太拘束了，好像我写的东西必须是事实，而不能是虚构的。（8-2) 但是关于未来的写作给了我更多的自由去想象，去创造。

男：哦，读了你的书后，我很高兴你选择了小说领域。

难词总结

episode /ˈepɪsəʊd/ n.（电视剧或广播剧的）集
speculate /ˈspekjuleɪt/ v. 猜测，推测
facet /ˈfæsɪt/ n. 方面
credential /krəˈdenʃl/ n. 资格，证明

acclaimed /əˈkleɪmd/ a. 受到赞扬的；广受欢迎的
chronicle /ˈkrɒnɪkl/ v. 按事件顺序记载
assumption /əˈsʌmpʃn/ n. 假定，假设

题目精析

5. What does the man say about the woman?

   A) She is a critic of works on military affairs.
   B) She is an acclaimed hostess of *Book Talk*.
   C) She is a researcher of literary genres.
   D) She is a historian of military history.

5. 关于女士，男士说了些什么？

   A）她是军事著作的评论家。
   B）《书友会》备受赞誉的主持人。
   C）她是文学体裁的研究者。
   D）她是一位研究军事史的历史学家。

【答案及分析】D。本题问男士对女士的介绍。音频中男士提到，With me today is Heidi Brown, a historian who has written five critically acclaimed books about military history.（今天和我一起的是海蒂·布朗，一位历史学家，她写了五本关于军事史的书，广受好评。）D 项与音频内容相符，其中 a historian of military history 是音频中 a historian who has written five critically acclaimed books about military history 的同义表达，故选 D 项。

6. What does the woman say about her newly published book?

   A) It is about the military history of Europe.
   B) It is set in the 18th and 19th centuries.
   C) It is her fifth book of military history.
   D) It is a war novel set in the future.

6. 关于她新出版的书，女士说了什么？

   A）它是关于欧洲军事史的。
   B）它发生在 18 世纪和 19 世纪。
   C）这是她写的第五本关于军事史的书。
   D）这是一部发生在未来的战争小说。

【答案及分析】D。本题问女士新书的相关信息。音频中女士提到，It's set 200 years in the future.（它发生于 200 年后。）D 项与音频内容相符，其中 set in the future 是原词复现，故选 D 项。

7. What did the woman do before writing her new book?

   A) She visited soldiers' wives and mothers.
   B) She conducted surveys of many soldiers.
   C) She met a large number of soldiers in person.
   D) She looked into the personal lives of soldiers.

7. 女士在写新书之前做了什么？

   A）她去拜访了士兵们的妻子和母亲。
   B）她对许多士兵进行了调查。

C）她亲自会见了一大批士兵。

D）她研究了士兵们的个人生活。

【答案及分析】D。本题问女士在写新书之前所做的准备。音频中女士提到，That focus came about when I still intended to write another book of history, I started by researching soldier's actual personal lives, studying their letters home.（当我还打算写另一本历史书的时候，我的关注点是开始研究士兵的实际生活，研究他们的家书。）D 项与音频内容相符，其中 looked into the personal lives of soldiers 是音频中 researching soldier's actual personal lives 的同义表达，故选 D 项。

8. What does the woman say about her writing history books?

A) She doesn't have much freedom for imagination.

B) It is not easy to make her readers believe in her.

C) It is difficult to attract young readers.

D) She has to combine fact with fiction.

8. 关于她写历史书一事，女士说了什么？

A）她没有太多想象的自由。

B）要使她的读者相信她是不容易的。

C）很难吸引年轻读者。

D）她必须把事实与虚构结合起来。

【答案及分析】A。本题问女士对于她写历史书一事的看法。音频中提到，I felt too constrained working with the past... But writing about the future gave me more freedom to imagine, to invent.（和过去打交道让我觉得太拘束了……但是关于未来的写作给了我更多的自由去想象，去创造。）A 项与音频内容相符，其中 doesn't have much freedom for imagination 对应音频中的 felt too constrained 和 gave me more freedom to imagine, to invent，故选 A 项。

Section B

Questions 9 to 11 are based on the passage you have just heard.

听力原文及译文

(9) Whether it's in the hands of animated polar bears or Santa Claus, there's one thing you'll find in nearly all ads for Coca-Cola: the characteristic glass bottle.

Most Americans don't drink soda out of the glass bottles seen in Coke's ads anymore. But this week, the company is celebrating a century of the bottle that's been sold in more than 200 countries.

Flash back to 1915, when a bottle of Coca-Cola cost just a nickel. (10) As the soft drink gained in popularity, it faced a growing number of competitors — counterfeits even trying to copy Coke's logo. So according to Coca-Cola historian, Ted Ryan, the company decided to come up with packaging that couldn't be duplicated.

A product request was sent to eight different glass makers. Workers at the Root Glass Company got the request and began flipping through the encyclopedia at the local library, landing on cocoa seed. (11) Though cocoa seed is not an ingredient of the soda, they designed their bottle based on the seeds' shape and large middle. It won over Coke executives in Atlanta and would go on to receive its own trademark, spur collections and earn Coca-Cola an iconic image that made it part of American culture for a century.

It was 100 years ago this week that the bottle earned a package. By World War II, Coke bottle sales had ballooned into billions. Americans mostly consumed Coke out of aluminum or plastic today, but the glass bottle remains a symbol of America that's readily recognized around the world.

（9）无论是卡通北极熊还是圣诞老人，你在所有可口可乐的广告中几乎都能找到一件东西，那就是可口可乐特有的玻璃瓶。

大多数美国人不再用可口可乐广告里的玻璃瓶喝汽水了。但本周，该公司正在庆祝这款已在200多个国家销售的瓶子诞生一个世纪。

回溯到1915年，那时候一瓶可口可乐只卖五分钱。（10）随着这种软饮料越来越受欢迎，它面临着越来越多的竞争对手——仿冒品甚至试图复制可口可乐的商标。因此，根据可口可乐历史学家泰德·瑞恩的说法，该公司决定推出一种不可复制的包装。

8家不同的玻璃制造商收到了产品要求。鲁特玻璃公司的员工收到了要求，开始在当地图书馆翻阅百科全书，结果发现了可可种子。（11）虽然可可种子不是苏打汽水的成分，但是他们根据种子的形状和中间部分比较大的特点来设计瓶子。它赢得了可口可乐在亚特兰大的高管的支持，并持续作为商标，刺激了系列产品，为可口可乐赢得了一个标志性的形象，使其成为一个世纪以来美国文化的一部分。

100年前的这个星期，这个瓶子获得了一个包装。到第二次世界大战时，可口可乐瓶的销量已飙升至数十亿瓶。如今，美国人喝的可乐的包装大多是铝制或塑料制的，但玻璃瓶仍然是美国的象征，这在全世界都是公认的。

难词总结

animated /ˈænɪmeɪtɪd/ a. 动画（片）的
counterfeit /ˈkaʊntəfɪt/ n. 伪造物
encyclopedia /ɪnˌsaɪkləˈpiːdiə/ n. 百科全书
readily /ˈredɪli/ ad. 乐意地；迅速地

nickel /ˈnɪkl/ n. 五分硬币
duplicate /ˈdjuːplɪkeɪt/ v. 复制
iconic /aɪˈkɒnɪk/ a. 象征性的；图符的

题目精析

9. What does the passage say appears in almost all ads for Coca-Cola?

   A) Santa Claus.
   B) A polar bear.
   C) Cocoa seeds.
   D) A glass bottle.

9. 这篇文章说什么几乎出现在可口可乐的所有广告中？

   A）圣诞老人。
   B）一只北极熊。
   C）可可种子。
   D）一个玻璃瓶。

【答案及分析】D. 本题问出现在可口可乐所有广告中的是什么。音频中提到，Whether it's in the hands of animated polar bears or Santa Claus, there's one thing you'll find in nearly all ads for Coca-Cola: the characteristic glass bottle.（无论是卡通北极熊还是圣诞老人，你在所有可口可乐的广告中几乎都能找到一件东西，那就是可口可乐特有的玻璃瓶。）D 项中的 glass bottle 是原词复现，故选 D 项。

10. Why did the Coca-Cola company decide to have special packaging designed?
    A) To attract customer attention. C) To combat counterfeits.
    B) To keep up with the times.   D) To promote its sales.

10. 为什么可口可乐公司决定设计特殊的包装？
    A）吸引客户关注。   C）打击假冒产品。
    B）与时俱进。   D）提升销量。

【答案及分析】C。本题问可口可乐公司决定设计特殊包装的原因。音频中提到，As the soft drink gained in popularity, it faced a growing number of competitors — counterfeits even trying to copy Coke's logo. So according to Coca-Cola historian, Ted Ryan, the company decided to come up with packaging that couldn't be duplicated.（随着这种软饮料越来越受欢迎，它面临着越来越多的竞争对手——仿冒品甚至试图复制可口可乐的商标。因此，根据可口可乐历史学家泰德·瑞恩的说法，该公司决定推出一种不可复制的包装。）C 项是对音频内容的概括总结，counterfeits 为原词复现，故选 C 项。

11. What do we learn about the Coca-Cola bottle designed by the Root Glass Company?
    A) It resembles a picture in the encyclopedia.   C) It has the drink's logo in the middle.
    B) It appears in the shape of a cocoa seed.   D) It displays the image of Santa Claus.

11. 关于鲁特玻璃公司设计的可口可乐瓶，我们了解到什么？
    A）它类似于百科全书中的一张图片。   C）它的中间有这种饮料的标志。
    B）它呈可可种子的形状。   D）它显示了圣诞老人的形象。

【答案及分析】B。本题问鲁特玻璃公司给可口可乐瓶的设计。音频中提到，Though cocoa seed is not an ingredient of the soda, they designed their bottle based on the seeds' shape and large middle.（虽然可可种子不是苏打汽水的成分，但是他们根据种子的形状和中间部分比较大的特点来设计瓶子。）B 项中的 appears in the shape of a cocoa seed 是音频中 based on the seeds' shape and large middle 的同义表达，故选 B 项。

Questions 12 to 15 are based on the passage you have just heard.

听力原文及译文

(12) Research shows that a few moments of conversation with a stranger create a measurable improvement in mood. But most of us are reluctant to start these conversations because we presume the opposite.

In an experiment, commuters who talked to nearby strangers found their commute more enjoyable than those who didn't. They were asked to predict whether they'd enjoy the commute more if they conversed with other people. Intriguingly, most expected the more solitary experience to be more pleasurable.

(13) Why is this? Social anxiety appears to be the problem. People's reluctance to start conversations with nearby strangers comes partly from underestimating others' interest in connecting. The sad thing is that people

presume that a nearby stranger doesn't want to converse and don't start a conversation. Only those who forced themselves to chat because it was required by the experiment found out what a pleasant experience it could be.

Human beings are social animals. Those who misunderstand the impact of social interactions may not, in some contexts, be social enough for their own well-being.

You should be chatting with the strangers you encounter. You may occasionally have a negative encounter that might stick in your memory. (14) <u>This is because the human brain is biased to dwell on negative events.</u> But starting conversations with strangers is still well worth the risk of rejection.

It may surprise you that conversing with strangers will make them happier too. (15) <u>The pleasure of connection seems contagious.</u> People who were talked to have equally positive experiences as those who initiate a conversation.

（12）研究表明，与陌生人交谈片刻可以显著改善情绪。但我们大多数人都不愿意开始这些对话，因为我们的假设恰恰相反。

在一项实验中，那些与附近的陌生人交谈的通勤者发现，他们的通勤过程比没有参与交谈的人更愉快。他们被要求预测，如果他们与他人交谈，他们是否会更享受通勤过程。有趣的是，大多数人认为越孤独的体验越愉快。

（13）这是为什么呢？社交焦虑似乎是问题所在。人们不愿意与附近的陌生人开始对话，部分原因是低估了他人对交流的兴趣。可悲的是，人们认为附近的陌生人不想交谈，也不会开启一段对话。只有那些因为实验要求而强迫自己聊天的人才发现这可能是一种多么愉快的体验。

人类是群居性动物。在某些情况下，就幸福感而言，那些误解了社交互动的影响的人可能不够社会化。

你应该和你遇到的陌生人聊天。你可能偶尔会有一次负面的遭遇，这可能会留在你的记忆中。（14）这是因为人类的大脑偏向于关注负面事件。但是，与陌生人开始对话仍然值得冒着被拒绝的风险。

你可能会惊讶地发现，与陌生人交谈也会让对方更快乐。（15）这种交谈的快乐似乎具有传染性。被交谈的人与主动交谈的人有着同样积极的体验。

难词总结

reluctant /rɪˈlʌktənt/ *a.* 不情愿的
intriguingly /ɪnˈtriːɡɪŋli/ *ad.* 有趣地；有魅力地
contagious /kənˈteɪdʒəs/ *a.* （情感）具有感染力的；（疾病）接触性传染的
commuter /kəˈmjuːtə(r)/ *n.* 上下班往返的人
encounter /ɪnˈkaʊntə(r)/ *v. & n.* 偶遇；遭遇

题目精析

12. What does research show about a conversation between strangers?
   A) It often occurs among commuters.
   B) It promotes mutual understanding.
   C) It improves their mood considerably.
   D) It takes a great deal of effort to sustain.

12. 关于陌生人之间的对话，研究表明了什么？
   A）它经常发生在通勤者之间。
   C）它大大地改善了他们的情绪。

B）它能促进相互理解。 D）它需要付出大量的努力才能维持下去。

【答案及分析】C。本题问关于陌生人之间的对话的研究结果。音频中提到，Research shows that a few moments of conversation with a stranger create a measurable improvement in mood.（研究表明，与陌生人交谈片刻可以显著改善情绪。）C项是音频中 create a measurable improvement in mood 的同义表达，故选 C 项。

13. What prevents people from starting a conversation with strangers?

    A) Social anxiety.   C) Lack of social skills.
    B) Excessive caution.   D) Preference for solitude.

13. 什么阻止了人们与陌生人开始对话？

    A）社交焦虑。   C）缺乏社交技能。
    B）过度谨慎。   D）对孤独的偏好。

【答案及分析】A。本题问人们不愿意与陌生人交谈的原因。音频中提到，Why is this? Social anxiety appears to be the problem.（这是为什么呢？社交焦虑似乎是问题所在。）A 项 Social anxiety 为原词复现，故选 A 项。

14. Why does a negative encounter with strangers stick in one's memory?

    A) People usually regard it as an unforgettable lesson.
    B) Human brains tend to dwell on negative events.
    C) Negative events often hurt people deeply.
    D) People generally resent being rejected.

14. 为什么与陌生人的消极邂逅会留在人的记忆中？

    A）人们通常认为这是一个令人难忘的教训。
    B）人类的大脑倾向于关注消极的事件。
    C）负面的事件往往会深深地伤害到人们。
    D）人们通常会憎恨被拒绝。

【答案及分析】B。本题问与陌生人的消极邂逅会留在人的记忆中的原因。音频中提到，This is because the human brain is biased to dwell on negative events.（这是因为人类的大脑偏向于关注负面事件。）B 项是音频中 the human brain is biased to dwell on negative events 的同义表达，故选 B 项。

15. What does the passage say the pleasure of connection seems to be?

    A) Contagious.   C) Unpredictable.
    B) Temporary.   D) Measurable.

15. 这篇文章说，交谈的乐趣似乎是什么？

    A）具有传染性的。   C）不可预测的。
    B）暂时的。   D）显著的。

【答案及分析】A。本题问交谈的乐趣是什么。音频中提到，The pleasure of connection seems contagious.（这种交谈的快乐似乎具有传染性。）A 项 Contagious 为原词复现，故选 A 项。

Section C

Questions 16 to 18 are based on the recording you have just heard.

听力原文及译文

The Caribbean islands are divided into two worlds, a rich one, and a poor one. (16) This tropical region's economy is based mainly on farming. Farmers are of two types. One is the plantation owner who may have hundreds of thousands of acres. In contrast, the small cultivator is working only a few acres of land. Most visitors to the Caribbean are rich, like the plantation owner. They do not realize or do not want to realize that many farm families barely managed to get by on what they grow.

(17) The Caribbean produces many things. Sugar is the main product. Other export crops are tobacco, coffee, bananas, spices, and citrus fruits, such as orange, lemon or grapefruit. From the West Indies also come oil, mineral pitch, and many forest products. Jamaica's aluminum or supplies are the world's largest. Oil comes from Trinidad, Aruba and Curacao, but for many of the smaller islands, sugar is the only export. Rum, a strong alcoholic drink, which is distilled from sugar cane, is also an export. The world's best rum comes from this area. Local kinds vary from the light rums of Puerto Rico to the heavier, darker rums of Barbados and Jamaica. American tourists enjoy stocking up on inexpensive high-quality Caribbean rum while they're on vacation. In Curacao, the well-known liquor of that name is made from the thick outer skin of a native orange.

Ever since America's colonial days, the Caribbean islands have been favorite places to visit. Since World War II, tourism has increased rapidly because great numbers of people go there. The islanders have built elaborate resorts, developed harbors and airfields, improved beaches and have expanded sea and air routes. Everything is at the resort — hotel, beach, shopping and recreation. The vacationer never has any reason to explore the island.

As in most places, those who have money live well, indeed; (18) those who don't have money live at various levels of poverty, but here the poor greatly outnumber the wealthy. A visitor will find rich people living in apartments or Spanish houses at the seaside or in the countryside. Their servants might include a cook, a maid and a nurse for the children. Most of the people live well below the poverty level. In towns, they live crowded together in tiny houses. Islanders make the best they can of what they have. Their homes are quite shabby. Sadly, most tourists never see this side of the Caribbean.

加勒比海群岛被分为两个世界：一个富裕，一个贫穷。（16）这片热带地区的经济主要以农业为基础。这里有两种农民。一种是拥有数十万英亩土地的种植园园主。相比之下，小型种植者只能耕种几英亩土地。大多数来加勒比海群岛的游客像种植园园主一样富有。他们没有意识到，或者不想意识到，许多农户仅靠自己种植的农作物勉强过活。

（17）加勒比海地区出产许多东西。糖是主要产品。其他出口作物有烟草、咖啡、香蕉、香料和柑橘类水果，比如橙子、柠檬或葡萄柚。西印度群岛还出产石油、柏油和许多林业产品。牙买加的铝或铝供应量位居世界第一。石油产自特立尼达拉岛、阿鲁巴岛和库拉索岛，但是就很多较小的岛屿而言，糖是唯一的出口物。朗姆酒是一种烈性酒，由甘蔗蒸馏而成，也是出口物。世界上最好的朗姆酒就产自于此。当地的朗姆酒种类繁多，有波多黎各的清淡型朗姆酒，也有巴巴多斯和牙买加的浓香型、颜色较深的朗姆酒等。在度假时，美国游客喜欢囤积廉价优质的加勒比朗姆酒。在库拉索岛，有一种用当地的橙子厚厚的外皮制成的名酒，这种酒名叫库拉索。

　　自美国殖民时代以来，加勒比海群岛一直是最受欢迎的旅游观赏地。第二次世界大战之后，由于大量游客来到此地，旅游业得以迅速发展。岛上居民精心打造了度假胜地，建设了港口和机场，改善了海滩环境，扩展了海空航线。酒店、海滩、购物和娱乐设施在这个度假地一应俱全。度假者没有理由不去探索这个岛屿。

　　和大多数地方相似，实际上有钱人生活得很好；(18)那些没有钱的人处于不同的贫困程度，但在这里，穷人的数量远超富人。游客会发现富人住在海边或乡村的公寓或西班牙住宅。他们的仆人可能包括一名厨师、一名女佣和一名儿童护士。大多数人生活在贫困线以下。在城镇里，他们住在拥挤的小房子里。岛上居民尽可能地利用他们所拥有的一切。他们的房子相当破旧。可悲的是，大多数游客从未见过加勒比海地区的这一面。

难词总结

Caribbean /ˌkærɪˈbiːən/ *a.* 加勒比海地区的
cultivator /ˈkʌltɪveɪtə(r)/ *n.* 耕者；栽培者
pitch /pɪtʃ/ *n.* 沥青；柏油
outnumber /ˌaʊtˈnʌmbə(r)/ *v.* 数目超过；比……多

plantation /plɑːnˈteɪʃn/ *n.* 种植地；农园
produce /prəˈdjuːs/ *v.* 生产
rum /rʌm/ *n.* 朗姆酒

题目精析

16. What does the speaker say about the economy of the Caribbean islands?
    A) It depends heavily on tourism.　　　　C) It is mainly based on agriculture.
    B) It is flourishing in foreign trade.　　　　D) It relies chiefly on mineral export.

16. 说话者对加勒比海群岛的经济有何评价？
    A）很大程度上依赖旅游业。　　　　C）主要以农业为主。
    B）对外贸易蓬勃发展。　　　　D）主要依赖矿产出口。

【答案及分析】C。本题问说话者对加勒比海群岛经济的评价。音频中提到，This tropical region's economy is based mainly on farming.（这片热带地区的经济主要以农业为基础。）C项是音频中 economy is based mainly on farming 的同义表达，故选C项。

17. What is the main product of the Caribbean islands?
    A) Tobacco.　　　　C) Coffee.
    B) Bananas.　　　　D) Sugar.

17. 加勒比海群岛主产什么？
    A）烟草。　　　　C）咖啡。
    B）香蕉。　　　　D）糖。

【答案及分析】D。本题问加勒比海群岛的主要产品。音频中提到，The Caribbean produces many

things. Sugar is the main product.（加勒比海地区出产许多东西。糖是主要产品。）D 项 Sugar 属于原词复现，故选 D 项。

18. What do we learn about the majority of people in the Caribbean islands?

    A) They toil on farms.　　　　　　　　C) They live in Spanish-style houses.

    B) They live a poor life.　　　　　　　D) They hire people to do housework.

18. 我们可以了解到关于大多数加勒比海群岛人的什么信息？

    A）他们在农场劳作。　　　　　　　　C）他们住在西班牙风格的房子里。

    B）他们生活贫穷。　　　　　　　　　D）他们雇人做家务。

【答案及分析】B。本题问大多数加勒比海群岛居民的相关信息。音频中提到，those who don't have money live at various levels of poverty, but here the poor greatly outnumber the wealthy（那些没有钱的人处于不同的贫困程度，但在这里，穷人的数量远超富人）。B 项是音频中 live at various levels of poverty 的同义表达，故选 B 项。

Questions 19 to 21 are based on the recording you have just heard.

听力原文及译文

　　Talk to anyone who is a generation not too older, and they would most likely comment that children are most spoiled these days. No one wants to have — or be around — demanding, selfish and spoiled children, those who get bad-tempered or silently-brute when they're not given everything they want immediately.

　　Paradoxically, the parents of such children encourage this demanding behavior in the mistaken belief that by giving that children everything they can their children will be happy.

　　In the short term, perhaps they are right. (19) But in the longer term, such children end up lonely, dependent, chronically dissatisfied and resentful of the parents who tried so hard to please them.

　　Undoubtedly, parents want to raise happy children who are confident, capable, and likable rather than spoiled and miserable. (20) One factor hindering this is that parents can't, or don't spend enough quality time with their kids and substitute this deficit with toys, games, gadgets, and the like. Rather than getting material things, children need parents' devoted attention. The quantity of time spent together is less important than the content of that time.

　　Instead of instantly satisfying their wishes, parents should help them work out a plan to earn things they'd like to have. This teaches them to value the effort as well as what it achieves.

　　Allow them to enjoy anticipation. Numerous psychological studies have demonstrated that children who learn to wait for things they desire are more likely to succeed in a number of ways later in life. One famous experiment in the 1960s involved 3- to 6-year-old children. They were given a choice between receiving a small reward, such as a cookie immediately, or if they waited 15 minutes, they could have two. Follow-up studies have found that those who chose to delay satisfaction are now more academically successful, have greater self-worth, and even tend to be healthier.

　　If they fail, children should be encouraged to keep trying, rather than to give up, if they really want the desired result. (21) This teaches them how to handle and recover from disappointment, which is associated with greater success and satisfaction academically, financially, and in personal relationships.

And lastly, parents should encourage their children to look at life from other points of view as well as their own. This teaches them to be understanding of and sympathetic towards others — qualities sure to take them a long way in life.

和比我们稍稍年长的人交谈，他们很有可能评论说，现在的孩子几乎被宠坏了。没有人想拥有——或者身边是——苛求、自私和被宠坏的孩子，在没有被立即给予想要的一切时，那些孩子便会发脾气或默默地使用蛮劲。

自相矛盾的是，这些孩子的父母鼓励这种苛求的行为，错误地认为给孩子他们所能给予的一切，孩子就会快乐。

从短期来看，也许他们是正确的。（19）但从长远来看，这些孩子最终会变得孤独和依赖他人，对竭力取悦他们的父母长期心存不满和怨恨。

毋庸置疑，父母希望培养出有幸福感的孩子，他们自信、有能力、讨人喜欢，而不是被宠坏的、差劲的孩子。（20）阻碍这一点的一个因素是，父母不能或没有花足够的黄金时光陪伴孩子，而是用玩具、游戏、小玩意等来弥补这一块缺失。孩子们需要父母全神贯注的关注，而不是物质上的东西。一起度过的时间的多少不如在这一段时间做了些什么重要。

父母不应该即刻满足孩子们的愿望，而应该帮助他们制订一个计划，来获取他们想要的物品。这教会他们重视努力以及因努力获得的成果。

让孩子们享受期待。大量心理学研究表明，学会等待期待物品的孩子在之后的生活中更有可能在多方面取得成功。20世纪60年代的一个著名实验研究了一些3到6岁的儿童：孩子们可以选择接受一个小奖励，比如立即得到一块饼干，又或者如果他们选择等待15分钟，便可得到两块饼干。后续研究发现，那些选择延迟满足感的孩子如今在学业上更成功，自我价值更高，甚至更健康。

如果孩子们失败了，应该鼓励他们继续尝试，而不是放弃，如果他们真的想得到预期的结果。（21）这教会孩子们如何处理失望以及如何从失望中恢复，这与取得学业、经济和人际关系方面的更大的成功和满足感有关。

最后，父母应鼓励他们的孩子从其他及自己的角度看待生活。这教会他们理解和同情他人——这些品质肯定会让他们在生活中走得更长远。

难词总结

spoil /spɔɪl/ v. 溺爱；宠坏
chronically /ˈkrɒnɪkli/ ad. 长期地；慢性地
miserable /ˈmɪzrəbl/ a. 糟糕的；差劲的
anticipation /ænˌtɪsɪˈpeɪʃn/ n. 期盼；期望

demanding /dɪˈmɑːndɪŋ/ a. 苛刻的；难以满足的
resentful /rɪˈzentfl/ a. 气愤的；憎恨的
substitute /ˈsʌbstɪtjuːt/ v. 替代；取代
involve /ɪnˈvɒlv/ v.（使）参加；加入

题目精析

19. What will happen to children if they always get immediate satisfaction?

A) They will be more demanding of their next generation.

B) They will end up lonely, dependent and dissatisfied.

C) They will experience more setbacks than successes.

D) They will find it difficult to get along with others.

19. 如果孩子们总能立即得到满足，他们会怎么样？

A）他们将对自己的下一代更苛刻。

B）他们最终会变得孤独、依赖他人和不满。

C）他们将经历更多的挫折，而不是成功。

D）他们会发现很难与他人相处。

【答案及分析】B。本题问孩子立即得到满足后面临的后果。音频中提到，But in the longer term, such children end up lonely, dependent, chronically dissatisfied and resentful of the parents who tried so hard to please them.（但从长远来看，这些孩子最终会变得孤独和依赖他人，对竭力取悦他们的父母长期心存不满和怨恨。）音频中的 such children 即总能立即得到满足的孩子，B 项中的 lonely, dependent and dissatisfied 是原词复现，故选 B 项。

20. What may prevent parents from raising confident and capable children?

A) Failure to pay due attention to their behavior.

B) Unwillingness to allow them to play with toys.

C) Unwillingness to satisfy their wishes immediately.

D) Failure to spend sufficient quality time with them.

20. 什么可能阻碍父母养育自信和有能力的孩子？

A）没能对他们的行为给予应有的关注。

B）不愿意让他们玩玩具。

C）不愿意立即满足他们的愿望。

D）没有花足够的黄金时光陪伴孩子。

【答案及分析】D。本题问阻碍父母培养自信、有能力的孩子的因素。音频中提到，One factor hindering this is that parents can't, or don't spend enough quality time with their kids（阻碍这一点的一个因素是，父母不能或没有花足够的黄金时光陪伴孩子）。D 项是音频内容的同义表达，故选 D 项。

21. Why should children be encouraged to keep trying when they fail?

A) It will enable them to learn from mistakes.   C) It will do much good to their mental health.

B) It will help them to handle disappointment.   D) It will build their ability to endure hardships.

21. 为什么要鼓励孩子失败后继续尝试？

A）这将使他们能从错误中汲取教训。   C）这对他们的心理健康大有裨益。

B）这将帮助他们应对失望情绪。   D）这将培养他们忍受艰难困苦的能力。

【答案及分析】B。本题问鼓励孩子失败后继续尝试的原因。音频中提到，This teaches them how to handle and recover from disappointment（这教会孩子们如何处理失望以及如何从失望中恢复）。B 项中的 handle disappointment 是原词复现，故选 B 项。

Questions 22 to 25 are based on the recording you have just heard.

It's not hard to mess up an interview. Most people feel nervous sitting across from a hiring manager, answering questions that effectively opened themselves up for judgment. (22) And your chances of being more carefully considered for the job can quickly go downhill just by saying the wrong thing at the wrong time.

(23) The most obvious thing not to do is complain. Employers want to hire positive people. Talking about a previous job negatively raises concerns that you might be difficult to manage, or you might be someone that blames management for your own poor performance. Don't say that you've moved around in jobs because you haven't found the right fit or feel that you were not challenged enough. Statements like these will make you sound aimless and lost. An interviewer may well think, why would this role be any different for you? You will probably leave here in six months.

It also begs the question of what type of relationship you had with your manager. It doesn't sound like you had open communication with him or her. (24) Managers usually love people who can self-sustain and enable growth through taking initiative, who are strong at following through their work and who bring ideas and solutions to the table.

If you were in a management or leadership position when discussing your current role, never take all the credit for accomplishments or achievements. Emphasize your team and how through their talents your vision was realized. Most successful leaders know that they are only as good as their team. And acknowledging this in an interview will go a long way towards suggesting that you might be the right person for the position you are applying for.

Lastly, have a good idea of what your role will be and try and convey the idea that you're flexible. Asking what your role will be suggests you will limit yourself purely to what is expected of you. In reality, your role is whatever you make of it. (25) This is especially true in small companies, where the ability to adapt and take on new responsibilities is highly valued. And this is equally important, if you're just starting out. Entry level interviewees would do well to demonstrate a broad set of skills in most interviews. It's important to have a wide skill set, as many startups and small companies are moving really fast. Employers are looking for candidates that are intelligent and can quickly adapt and excel in a growing company.

搞砸一次面试并不难。坐在招聘经理对面，回答那些能有效打开自己心扉，让他人评判自己的问题，大部分人都会感到紧张。（22）并且，只要你在错误的时间节点说错了话，你被仔细考虑获得工作机会的概率可能会急剧下降。

（23）当然，最理所当然的是不要抱怨。雇主希望雇用积极的员工。消极谈论之前的工作会让人担心你可能难以管理，或者你可能会因个人糟糕的工作表现去指责管理层。不要说你因为没有找到合适的工作或者觉得自己没有面临更多的挑战而游走于各个工作岗位中。类似这样的言论听起来会让人觉得你漫无目的、不知所措。面试官也可能会想，为什么这份工作对你来说会有所不同呢？你可能将在六个月后就离职。

这也引起关于你和经理之间的关系类型的疑问。听起来你和经理并没有开诚布公的交流。（24）管理者通常喜欢那些可以采取主动措施实现自足和成长的人，那些善于跟进工作的人，那些能够把想法和解决方案摆到台面上的人。

如果你是处在管理层或领导层讨论你当前的角色，那么千万不要把所有功劳或成就都揽在自己身上。要强调你的团队以及如何通过团队的才能实现你的愿景。大多数成功的领导者都知道他们和每一位团队成员是一样的。在面试中承认这一点对表明你是所申请职位的合适人选大有裨益。

最后，对你的应聘岗位有一个良好认知，并试着表达你的灵活性。问你将起着什么样的作用意味着你完全将自己局限在别人对你的期望上。实际上，你的作用即关于这个工作你所能够做的一切。（25）在小公司尤其如此，因为这些公司高度重视适应和承担新责任的能力。如果你刚开始着手准备面试，这也同样重要。入门级面试者最好在大多数面试中表现出广泛的技能。因为许多初创公司和小公司都在快速发展，所以拥有广泛的技能很重要。雇主们正在寻找那些有智慧、可快速适应并在成长型企业中脱颖而出的候选人。

难词总结

mess up 把……弄乱；陷入困境
take initiative 积极主动
value /ˈvæljuː/ v. 重视；评价
downhill /ˌdaʊnˈhɪl/ ad. 向下；每况愈下
acknowledge /əkˈnɒlɪdʒ/ v. 承认；认可

题目精析

22. What does the speaker say can easily prevent an interviewee from getting a job?
    A) Failing to make sufficient preparations.　　C) Saying the wrong thing at the wrong time.
    B) Looking away from the hiring manager.　　D) Making a wrong judgment of the interview.

22. 说话者说什么能轻易阻碍面试者找到工作？
    A）没能做好充足准备。　　C）在不适宜的时间说错话。
    B）把目光从招聘经理身上移开。　　D）对面试做错误的判断。

【答案及分析】C。本题问导致面试失败的原因。音频中提到，And your chances of being more carefully considered for the job can quickly go downhill just by saying the wrong thing at the wrong time.（并且，只要你在错误的时间节点说错了话，你被仔细考虑获得工作机会的概率可能会急剧下降。）C项是音频内容的同义表达，Saying the wrong thing at the wrong time 为原词复现，故选C项。

23. What should the interviewee avoid doing in an interview?
    A) Complaining about their previous job.　　C) Exaggerating their academic background.
    B) Inquiring about their salary to be paid.　　D) Understating their previous achievements.

23. 面试者在面试中应避免做什么？
    A）抱怨他们之前的工作。　　C）夸大他们的教育背景。
    B）询问他们被支付多少薪酬。　　D）低估他们之前的成就。

【答案及分析】A。本题问面试者在面试中应该避免做什么。音频中提到，The most obvious thing not to do is complain.（当然，最理所当然的是不要抱怨。）A项是音频内容的同义表达，故选A项。

24. What kind of employees do companies like to recruit?

A) Those who have both skill and experience.
B) Those who get along well with colleagues.
C) Those who take initiative in their work.
D) Those who are loyal to their managers.

24. 公司喜欢招聘什么类型的员工？

A）有技能和经验的员工。
B）与同事相处融洽的员工。
C）那些在工作中积极主动的员工。
D）那些对经理忠诚的员工。

【答案及分析】C。本题问公司喜欢的员工类型。音频中提到，Managers usually love people who can self-sustain and enable growth through taking initiative（管理者通常喜欢那些可以采取主动措施实现自足和成长的人）。C项为音频内容的同义表达，take initiative 为原词复现，故选C项。

25. What is especially important for those working in a small company?

A) Ability to shoulder new responsibilities.
B) Experience of performing multiple roles.
C) Readiness to work to flexible schedules.
D) Skills to communicate with colleagues.

25. 对于在小公司工作的人而言，什么是特别重要的？

A）承担新责任的能力。
B）具有担任多重角色的经验。
C）愿意按照灵活的时间表工作。
D）与同事沟通的技巧。

【答案及分析】A。本题问小公司的员工需要具备的工作能力。音频中提到，This is especially true in small companies, where the ability to adapt and take on new responsibilities is highly valued.（在小公司尤其如此，因为这些公司高度重视适应能力和承担新责任的能力。）A项与音频内容相符，Ability to shoulder new responsibilities 是 the ability to adapt and take on new responsibilities 的同义表达，故选A项。

Part Ⅲ Reading Comprehension

Section A

【全文翻译】

如果你认为生活是美好的，并期望一直保持这种美好，那么你很有可能享有高寿，至少一项新的研究发现表明如此。这项研究发现，相较于那些乐观程度最低的研究对象，乐观程度最高的研究对象更有可能活至85岁或更久。值得注意的是，即使研究人员将可能影响这种关联的因素考虑在内，包括参与者是否患有心脏病或癌症等健康状况，又或者他们是否患有抑郁症，这个研究结论仍然成立。这一结果为"某些心理因素可以预言更长的寿命"这一论断提供了越来越多的证据。例如，之前的研究发现更乐观的人患有慢性病和过早死亡的风险更低。尽管如此，这项新研究似乎开启了专门研究乐观与长寿之间的关联的先河。研究人员承认，如果将运动水平、睡眠习惯和饮食等某些健康行为的影响考虑在内，新研究中发现的联系就没有那么密切了。这表明这些行为至少能够在某种程度上解释这种联系。换言之，乐观可能会养成有益健康的好习惯。注意到这项研究只发现了一种相关性也同样重要，因为研究人员并没有肯定地证明乐观会延长寿命。然而，如果研究结果属实，他们认为乐观可以作为一种心理特征，促进健康和长寿。

难词总结

optimism /ˈɒptɪmɪzəm/ n. 乐观；乐观主义
longevity /lɒnˈdʒevəti/ n. 寿命；长寿
promote /prəˈməʊt/ v. 促进；提倡

chronic /ˈkrɒnɪk/ a.（疾病）慢性的；长期的
bolster /ˈbəʊlstə(r)/ v. 增强；改善

题目精析

26. B。根据句子结构可知，空格处应填入一个副词或者不及物动词原形。所给选项中只有 B 项 beyond（以远；更远处）、F 项 henceforth（从今以后）、I 项 plausibly（合理地）、M 项 specifically（专门地；明确地）和 N 项 spiral（螺旋式上升或下降）符合语法要求。结合语境可知，此处讲的是乐观程度最高的参与者更有可能活到 85 岁或更久，故只有 beyond 符合语境，故选 B 项。

27. H。根据句子结构可知，空格处需要填入一个形容词或者过去分词。所给选项中只有 C 项 conceded（承认）、G 项 lofty（崇高的）、H 项 noteworthy（值得注意的）、J 项 premature（过早的）、K 项 reconciled（和解；和好）和 N 项 spiral（螺旋式的）符合语法要求。结合上文可知 noteworthy 符合语境，代入文中意为"值得注意的是……这个研究结论仍然成立"。故选 H 项。

28. A。根据句子结构可知，空格处需要填入一个动词原形，所给选项中只有 A 项 affect（影响）、E 项 foster（促进）、L 项 span（持续；贯穿）和 N 项 spiral（螺旋式上升或下降）符合语法要求。结合语境以及空格前的 factors（因素）可知，此处讲的是"影响这种关联"，affect 符合语境，故选 A 项。

29. L。根据句子结构可知，空格处需要填入一个名词，所给选项中只有 D 项 correlation（关联）、L 项 span（跨度）、N 项 spiral（螺旋式）和 O 项 trait（特征）符合语法要求。结合上文提到的寿命相关内容，life span 意为"寿命"，符合语境，故选 L 项。

30. J。根据句子结构可知，空格处需要填入一个形容词。所给选项中只有 G 项 lofty（崇高的）、J 项 premature（过早的）和 N 项 spiral（螺旋式的）符合语法要求。premature death 意为"过早死亡"，符合语境，故选 J 项。

31. M。根据句子结构可知，空格处需要填入一个副词。所给选项中只有 F 项 henceforth（从今以后）、I 项 plausibly（合理地）和 M 项 specifically（专门地；明确地）符合语法要求。结合语境可知，此处讲的是专门研究乐观与长寿之间的关联，故 M 项符合语境，故选 M 项。

32. C。根据句子结构可知，空格处需要填入一个谓语动词，由下文 was 以及 factored 可知应填入动词的过去式。所给选项中，C 项 conceded（承认）和 K 项 reconciled（和解；和好）符合语法要求。conceded 代入原文后意为"研究人员承认……"，符合语境，故选 C 项。

33. E。根据句子结构可知，空格处需要填入一个动词原形。所给选项中只剩 E 项 foster（促进）符合语法要求和语境，故选 E 项。

34. D。根据句子结构可知，空格处需要填入一个可数名词单数，跟在冠词 a 之后。所给选项中只剩

D 项 correlation（关联）、N 项 spiral（螺旋式）和 O 项 trait（特征）符合语法要求。结合上下文可知，这项研究发现了乐观与寿命之间的关联，D 项 correlation 代入原文后符合语境，故选 D 项。

35. O。根据句子结构可知，空格处需要填入一个名词，所给选项中只剩 N 项 spiral（螺旋式）和 O 项 trait（特征）符合语法要求，psychological trait 意为"心理特征"，符合语境，故选 O 项。

Section B

全文翻译

事实为何没有改变我们的想法

[A] 经济学家 J. K. 加尔布雷斯曾经写道："面临着改变想法和证明没有必要改变想法的选择时，几乎全部的人都忙于证明没必要改变想法。"

[B] 列夫·托尔斯泰甚至更大胆："可以向头脑最迟钝的人解释最难的课题，如果他们对这些课题还没有任何概念；但是，如果最有智慧的人已经毫无疑问地了解摆在其面前的东西，那么连最简单的事情都无法向其说清。"

[C] 这是怎么回事？为什么事实没有改变我们的想法？为什么有人会继续相信一个错误或不准确的想法？这些行为如何服务于我们？为了生存，人类需要一个合理而准确的世界观。如果你的现实模型与真实世界截然不同，那么每一天你都在努力采取有效的行动。然而，对人类思想来说，真相和准确性并不是唯一重要的事情。人类看起来也有强烈的归属感。

[D] 我在《原子习惯》一书中写道："人类是群居动物。我们想融入他人，想与他人建立联系，想获得同龄人的尊重和认可。这种倾向对我们的生存极其重要。在人类进化史的大部分时间里，我们的祖先以部落形式生存。与部落分离——又或更糟，被部落驱逐——是一种死刑。"

[E] 了解事情的真相很重要，但一直隶属于部落也很重要。尽管通常来说这两种欲望合作融洽，但偶尔两者会发生冲突。在许多情况下，相较于了解某个特定事实或想法，实际上社交联系对你的日常生活更有帮助。哈佛大学心理学家史蒂文·平克这样说道："人们由于自身的信仰被接受或谴责，因此心智的一个功能有可能是持有能够为信仰持有者带来最多盟友、保护者或门徒的信仰，而不是最有可能为真理的信仰。"

[F] 我们并不总是因为事物是正确的就选择相信。有时我们选择对其相信，是因为它们让我们在关心的人面前看起来表现不错。我认为凯文·西姆勒在写作时把这一点表述得很好，"如果大脑预期到会因接受特定信念而获得奖励，那么它绝对会非常高兴这样做，而且不太在意奖励的来源——它是否务实（更好的结果源于更好的决定）、社交（同龄人对自己更好）或两者的某种结合"。

[G] 错误信仰即使在事实意义上无用，但是在某种社会意义上可能有用。由于没有更好的措辞，我们可以称这种方法为"事实上为假，社会意义上是真"。当我们不得不在两者之间做出选择时，人们通常会选择朋友和家人，而非事实。这一观点不仅解释了为什么我们可能会在晚宴上保持沉默或在父母说一些不快的事情时不以为然，而且揭示了一种改变别人看法的更好的方式。

[H] 劝某人改变思想实际上是说服他们改变自己部落的过程。如果他们放弃自身的信仰，他们就面临失去社会联系的风险。如果你夺走了他们的团体，那么你也就不能期待他们改变想法。你必须给他们一个去处。如果孤独是最后的结局，那么没有人希望自己的世界观被撕裂。

[I] 改变人们思想的方式是与他们为友，将他们融入你的部落，将他们带进你的朋友圈。现在，他们可以改变自身的信仰，并且不会面临被社会抛弃的风险。

[J] 也许是距离而不是差异滋生了部落主义和敌意。随着亲密度的增加，互相理解也会加深。我想起了亚伯拉罕·林肯的一句名言："我不喜欢那个人。我必须更好地了解他。"

[K] 事实无法改变我们的想法，但友情可以。几年前，本·卡斯诺查向我提及一个我一直无法动摇的想法：最有可能改变我们想法的人是我们在98%的话题上都能达成一致的人。如果你认识、喜欢并信任的人相信一种激进的思想，你更有可能给予它价值、重要性或考虑。你已经在生活中的大部分领域与他们的观点保持一致。可能这一次你也应该改变想法。但是，如果有一个与你截然不同的人提出了同样的激进思想，那么你很容易将他们看作疯子。

[L] 将信念映射到光谱上可以可视化这种信念。如果你把这个光谱分成10个单位，并且发现自己处于第7位，那么试图说服处于第1位的人没有任何意义。思想的差距太大了。当你处于第7位时，你最好把时间花在与处于第6位和第8位的人建立联系，慢慢将他们拉向你的阵营。

[M] 处于光谱两端的人之间往往发生最激烈的争论，但附近的人则频繁出现互相学习的情况。你与某人越亲密，你不认同的一两个观点就越有可能渗透你的思想并影响你的想法。一个想法距离你目前的光谱位置越远，你就越有可能将其直接拒绝。当谈到改变人们的想法时，从一端跳到另一端是非常困难的。你不能直接从这个光谱跳下。你必须慢慢"滑"下来。

[N] 任何与你目前的世界观截然不同的想法都会让人感到威胁。没有威胁性的环境是思考让人感到威胁的想法的最佳场所。因此，相比于对话或辩论，书籍往往是转变信念的更好的工具。在交谈中，人们必须仔细考虑自己的地位和外表。他们想要保住面子，避免显得愚蠢。在面对一系列令人不快的事实时，人们通常更加坚定他们目前的立场，而不是公开承认自己错了。书籍解决了这种矛盾。有了书籍，对话便可在脑海中进行，避免了被他人评判的风险。当你没有心存戒心时，就很容易保持思想开明。

[O] 人们不断谈论坏的想法是它们继续存在的另一个原因。沉默可以让任何思想销声匿迹。一个从未被说出来或写下来的想法会随着构思它的人而消亡。想法只有在被重复时才能被记住。只有在被重复时这种想法才能被相信。我已经指出，人们重复想法是为了表明他属于某个社会团体。但是大多数人都忽视了这一关键要点：人们在抱怨这些糟糕的想法时，其实也是在重复它们。在批判一种想法时，你必须提到它。最终，你重复了你希望人们忘记的想法——但是，人们当然无法忘记，因为你一直在谈论它们。你越是重复一种糟糕的想法，人们就越有可能相信它。

[P] 让我们把这种现象称为"克里尔重复定律"：相信某种想法的人数与该想法在过去一年中被重复的次数成正比——即使该想法有误。

难词总结

bond /bɒnd/ v.（使）建立亲密关系
condemn /kənˈdem/ v. 谴责
proportional /prəˈpɔːʃnl/ a. 成比例的；相称的
sentence /ˈsentəns/ n. 判刑，判决
proximity /prɒkˈsɪməti/ n. 靠近，亲近

题目精析

36. According to the author, humans can hardly survive if separated from their community.

36. 根据作者所说，如果人类脱离团体，便几乎无法生存。

【答案及分析】D。根据题干中的 hardly survive、separated from their community 定位到 D 段。定位句指出，For most of our evolutionary history, our ancestors lived in tribes. Becoming separated from the tribe — or worse, being cast out — was a death sentence.（在人类进化史的大部分时间里，我们的祖先以部落形式生存。与部落分离——又或更糟，被部落驱逐——是一种死刑。）题干是原文的同义表达，其中 separated from their community 是 separated from the tribe 的同义表达，humans can hardly survive 是 a death sentence 的同义表达，故选 D 项。

37. People often accept false beliefs because they prioritize social bonds rather than facts.

37. 因为人们优先考虑社会关系而不是事实，所以人们通常接受错误的信仰。

【答案及分析】G。根据题干中的 false beliefs 和 social bonds 定位到 G 段。定位句指出，False beliefs can be useful in a social sense even if they are not useful in a factual sense.（错误信仰即使在事实意义上无用，但是在某种社会意义上可能有用。）紧接着下文指出，When we have to choose between the two, people often select friends and family over facts.（当我们不得不在两者之间做出选择时，人们通常会选择朋友和家人，而非事实。）题干是原文的同义表达，false beliefs 为原词复现，故选 G 项。

38. Most often people learn from those close to them.

38. 大多数情况下，人们向自己附近的人学习。

【答案及分析】M。根据题干中的 learn from those close to them 定位到 M 段。定位句指出，the most frequent learning occurs from people who are nearby（但附近的人则频繁出现互相学习的情况）。题干是原文的同义表达，其中 Most often 是原文中 most frequent 的同义表达，learn from those close to them 是 learning occurs from people who are nearby 的同义表达，故选 M 项。

39. Sometimes people adopt certain beliefs in order to leave a favorable impression on those dear to them.

39. 有时人们接受某种信仰是为了给亲近的人留下好印象。

【答案及分析】F。根据题干中的 adopt certain beliefs、leave a favorable impression on those dear to them 定位到 F 段。定位句指出，Sometimes we believe things because they make us look good to the people we care about.（有时我们选择对其相信，是因为它们让我们在关心的人面前看起来表现不错。）题干是原文的同义表达，其中 adopt certain beliefs 是原文中 believe things 的同义表达，leave a favorable impression on those dear to them 是原文中 make us look good to the people we care about 的同义表达，

故选 F 项。

40. Compared with face-to-face communication, books often provide a better medium for changing people's beliefs.

40. 与面对面交流相比，书籍通常提供了改变人们信仰的更好媒介。

【答案及分析】N。根据题干中的 communication、books 和 changing people's beliefs 定位到 N 段。定位句指出，As a result, books are often a better vehicle for transforming beliefs than conversations or debates.（因此，相比于对话或辩论，书籍往往是转变信念的更好的工具。）题干是原文的同义表达，books 为原词复现，communication 为 conversations or debates 的同义表达，provide a better medium for changing people's beliefs 为 a better vehicle for transforming beliefs 的同义表达，故选 N 项。

41. On many occasions in daily life, people benefit more from their social bonds than from knowing the truth.

41. 在日常生活中的许多场合中，社会联系比了解事情真相更能让人获益。

【答案及分析】E。根据题干中的 On many occasions、benefit more from their social bonds 和 knowing the truth 定位到 E 段。定位句指出，In many circumstances, social connection is actually more helpful to your daily life than understanding the truth of a particular fact or idea.（在许多情况下，相较于了解某个特定事实或想法，实际上社交联系对你的日常生活更有帮助。）题干是原文的同义表达，其中 On many occasions 是原文中 In many circumstances 的同义表达，benefit more from their social bonds than from knowing the truth 是 social connection is actually more helpful... than understanding the truth 的同义表达，故选 E 项。

42. If you want to change somebody's beliefs, you should first establish social connection with them.

42. 如果想改变某人的信仰，你应该首先和他们建立社交关系。

【答案及分析】I。根据题干中的 change somebody's beliefs 和 establish social connection with them 定位到 I 段。定位句指出，The way to change people's minds is to become friends with them, to integrate them into your tribe, to bring them into your circle.（改变人们思想的方式是与他们为友，将他们融入你的部落，将他们带进你的朋友圈。）题干是原文的同义表达，其中 change somebody's beliefs 是原文中 change people's minds 的同义表达，establish social connection 是原文中 to become friends with them... to bring them into your circle 的同义表达，故选 I 项。

43. Humans cannot survive without a fair knowledge of the actual world.

43. 如果不熟悉现实世界，人类就无法生存。

【答案及分析】C。根据题干中的 cannot survive 和 without a fair knowledge of the actual world 定位到 C 段。定位句指出，Humans need a reasonably accurate view of the world in order to survive.（为了生存，人类需要一个合理而准确的世界观。）题干是原文的同义表达，其中 survive 为原词复现，a fair knowledge of the actual world 是 a reasonably accurate view of the world 的同义表达，故选 C 项。

44. Repetition of bad ideas increases their chances of being accepted.

44. 重复坏想法会增加它们被接受的概率。

【答案及分析】O。根据题干中的 Repetition of bad ideas 定位到 O 段。定位句指出，There is another reason bad ideas continue to live on, which is that people continue to talk about them... Ideas can only be remembered when they are repeated. They can only be believed when they are repeated. （人们不断谈论坏的想法是它们继续存在的另一个原因……想法只有在被重复时才能被记住。只有在被重复时这种想法才能被相信。）题干是原文的同义表达，故选 O 项。

45. Nobody is willing to give up their beliefs at the risk of getting isolated.
45. 没有人愿意冒着被孤立的风险放弃自身信仰。

【答案及分析】H。根据题干中的 Nobody、willing to give up their beliefs 和 getting isolated 定位到 H 段。定位句指出，If they abandon their beliefs, they run the risk of losing social ties... Nobody wants their worldview torn apart if loneliness is the outcome.（如果他们放弃自身的信仰，他们就面临失去社会联系的风险……如果孤独是最后的结局，那么没有人希望自己的世界观被撕裂。）题干是原文的同义表达，故选 H 项。

Section C

Passage One

全文翻译

　　自动化这门学科及其在经济中的作用已占据美国公众话题。广泛的技术，特别是自动化正剧烈地改变我们的工作方式，我们还需要为即将到来的事情制订一个计划。

　　要看到自动化的毁灭性影响，我们无须比自己的群体看得更长远。从自动化仓库到无人收银杂货店，再到提供自助结账通道而不是雇用真人的社区图书馆，自动化正在越来越多地取代人类工作，几乎没有留下好的新工作。

　　制造业的统计数字令人感到震惊。尽管人们普遍对贸易感到担忧，但最近的一份报告显示，制造业只有 13% 的失业是由贸易造成的，其他的损失则由技术进步导致。

　　这就是越来越多的人批评技术在我们的经济中愈发重要的原因。我们国家正在制造比以往任何时候都要多的产品，但是我们完成这件事需要的工人越来越少。但是，不仅仅工厂正遭受失业，软件和信息技术还对一些工作产生巨大影响，而大多数人原以为在快速变化的经济力量下这些工作是安全的。美国正在发生一些变革，这对美国家庭正产生不利影响。不管政策制定者和政治家承不承认，工人们已明确表达了对经济不安全的感受，以及在美国保住好工作的愿望。

　　那么，为什么人们还要如此坚持忽视自动化的危险性呢？当规划未来比以往任何时候都要更加重要的时候，人们没有展望未来。抵制自动化徒劳无用：自动化与之前的工业化一样不可避免。一些人断言自动化使我们工作更有效率，给新职业铺平道路，我真诚地希望他们是正确的，但自动化对工人产生有害影响这个现实让我产生了怀疑。目前没有人可以说出新的工作岗位来自何处或何时到来，任何明智的公司或国家都应该准备好所有替代方案。

　　我并没有夸大这种风险：看看在劳动力群体身上发生了什么。由经济研究可知，在 25～54 岁的适龄男性劳动力中，有六分之一的人没有工作。五十年前，这个年龄段的男性的就业率几乎为100%。与此同时，女性劳动力参与率已倒退至20世纪80年代后期的水平。

美国家庭和杰出的商业领袖意识到自动化存在一个大问题。大学学位的价值正在减弱，我们的向上流动性正在下降。如果我们想拥有让每个人都有经济保障的经济体，就需要开始思考怎样能正确地解决自动化问题。

难词总结

automation /ˌɔːtəˈmeɪʃn/ n. 自动化
staggering /ˈstæɡərɪŋ/ a. 惊人的，令人震惊的
transformative /trænsˈfɔːmətɪv/ a. 有改革能力的
dramatically /drəˈmætɪkli/ ad. 剧烈地；明显地
manufacture /ˌmænjuˈfæktʃə(r)/ v.（用机器大量）生产
diminish /dɪˈmɪnɪʃ/ v. 减弱；降低

题目精析

46. What can we observe from the author's description of our communities?

A) The growing passion for automation.
B) The shift from manual jobs to IT ones.
C) Their changing views on employment.
D) Their fading employment opportunities.

46. 通过作者对我们群体的描述，我们可以了解到什么？

A）对自动化的热情不断增长。
B）从手工工作到信息技术工作的转变。
C）他们一直改变对就业的看法。
D）他们的就业机会日益减少。

【答案及分析】D。根据题干关键词 the author's description of our communities 定位到原文第二段第一句。作者在第一句提到自动化的毁灭性影响，第二句提到，automation is increasingly replacing jobs and leaving too few good new jobs behind（自动化正在越来越多地取代人类工作，几乎没有留下好的新工作）。D 项中的 fading employment opportunities 是 increasingly replacing jobs and leaving too few good new jobs behind 的同义表达，故选 D 项。

47. What do we learn from a recent report?

A) The manufacturing sector is declining at a fast rate.
B) The concerns about the effect of trade are exaggerated.
C) The fears about trade have been spreading far and wide.
D) The impact of trade on employment has been staggering.

47. 我们可以从最近的报告中了解到什么？

A）制造业正快速衰退。
B）对贸易影响的担忧被夸大了。
C）对贸易的担忧一直在广泛传播。
D）贸易对就业的影响一直让人震惊。

【答案及分析】B。根据题干关键词 a recent report 定位到原文第三段第二句。该句提到，Despite the widespread fears about trade, a recent report showed that just 13 percent of jobs lost in manufacturing are due to trade — the rest of the losses have been due to advances in technology. （尽管人们普遍对贸易感到担忧，但最近的一份报告显示，制造业只有 13% 的失业是由贸易造成的，其他的损失则由技术进步导致。）B 项是对该句的总结概括，故选 B 项。

48. What does the passage tell us about American workers in an era of transformation?

   A) They feel ignored by politicians.　　　　C) They keep adapting to the changes.

   B) They feel increasingly vulnerable.　　　　D) They keep complaining but to no avail.

48. 关于处于变革时代的美国工人，这篇文章向我们讲述了他们的哪些情况？

   A）他们觉得自己被政客忽视了。　　　　C）他们不断适应变化。

   B）他们感到越来越脆弱。　　　　D）他们不断抱怨但无济于事。

   【答案及分析】B。根据题干关键词 American workers in an era of transformation 定位到原文第四段第四句，该句指出，Something transformative is happening in America（美国正在发生一些变革），下一句承接说明，workers have made clear their feelings about their economic insecurity and desire to keep good jobs in America（工人们已明确表达了对经济不安全的感受，以及在美国保住好工作的愿望）。由此可推断出美国工人感到越来越脆弱，故选 B 项。

49. What does the author think of automation?

   A) It will have the same impact as industrialization.　　　　C) Its alleged positive effects are doubtful.

   B) It provides sensible companies with alternatives.　　　　D) Its detrimental effects are unavoidable.

49. 作者对自动化有何看法？

   A）它将产生与工业化相同的影响。　　　　C）它的所谓积极影响值得怀疑。

   B）它为明智的公司提供了替代方案。　　　　D）它的有害影响不可避免。

   【答案及分析】C。根据题干关键词 author think of automation 定位到原文第五段第四句，该句前半句指出，I sincerely hope that those who assert that automation will make us more effective... are right（一些人断言自动化使我们工作更有效率……我真诚地希望他们是正确的），后半句转折指出，but the reality of automation's detrimental effects on workers makes me skeptical（但自动化对工人产生有害影响这个现实让我产生了怀疑），因此作者的看法是自动化的所谓积极影响被夸大了，C 项符合原文，故选 C 项。

50. What should we attach importance to when dealing with automation?

   A) College graduates' job prospects.　　　　C) People's economic security.

   B) Women's access to employment.　　　　D) People's social mobility.

50. 在处理自动化问题时，我们应该重视什么？

   A）大学毕业生的工作前景。　　　　C）人们的经济安全。

   B）女性就业途径。　　　　D）人们的社会流动性。

   【答案及分析】C。根据题干关键词 attach importance to 和 when dealing with automation 定位到原文最后一段最后一句。该句指出，If we want an economy that allows everyone to be economically secure, we need to start thinking about how we can rightfully address automation. （如果我们想拥有让每个人都有经济保障的经济体，就需要开始思考怎样能正确地解决自动化问题。）C 项符合原文内容，C 项

中的 economic security 是原文中 economically secure 的同义表达，故选 C 项。

Passage Two

全文翻译

看一看你身边的人。有些人是被动的，有些人是好斗的。有些人独自工作时状态最佳，有些人渴望陪伴。我们很容易意识到，在我们附近居住的人之间存在着很大差异。然而，当我们谈及来自其他地方的人时，我们似乎会不可避免地根据国籍描述他们的特征。

统计学专家在谈到国家平均水平时，通常也会犯同样的错误。

最新发表的研究表明这样的概述是极大的谬误。三位研究员分析了数十年来基于价值观的调查，发现国家之间的差异只可以解释 16% 到 21% 的文化价值观差异。换句话说，让我们在文化上看起来与他人与众不同的主要原因与我们的祖国无关。

为了查明什么因素与文化真正相关，作者结合了 558 项之前的调查数据，每项调查都对霍夫斯泰德的一个或多个文化维度进行了评估。诸如个人主义和男子气概之类的特征是描述与工作相关的文化价值观。（它们不能衡量可见的文化特征，例如食物或服饰。）虽然霍夫斯泰德维度的有效性一直备受质疑，但它们的独特好处是已被使用数十年，允许进行历史和国际比较。

研究人员发现，相比于国籍，人口因素（如年龄）和环境因素（如长期失业率）与文化价值观的相关性更高。职业和社会经济地位的相关性最强，这表明我们的价值观所受的经济驱动比我们通常所认为的更强。

证据表明，不管居住地在哪，工作和收入相似的人在文化上更相似。这项研究的首席作者瓦斯·塔拉斯如此说："告诉我你挣多少钱，我会对你的文化价值观做出相当准确的预测。但是告诉我你的国籍，我可能会预测出错。"

塔拉斯说，"国籍就是文化"这种错误看法已导致企业教员工用无用甚至有害的方式与国际同行互动交流。中国和美国律师可能基于"中国人不那么个人主义"的假设进行培训互动交流，尽管他们相似的社会经济状况实际上使得他们在这方面很可能非常相似。

国家代表着权威性，通常是概括一国人特点的便捷方式。然而，我们对国家的关注可能掩盖它们内部的广泛差异。在大多数情况下，我们最好通过限制人们生活的因素（如收入）识人，而不是通过地图上包围他们的线条。

难词总结

characterize /ˈkærəktəraɪz/ v. 描述，刻画
determine /dɪˈtɜːmɪn/ v. 查明，确定
question /ˈkwestʃən/ v. 对……提出质疑（异议）；向……提出问题
constrain /kənˈstreɪn/ v. 约束；迫使

erroneous /ɪˈrəʊniəs/ a. 错误的，不正确的

51. What error do experts often make when describing people from other places?

A) They tend to overly rely on nationality.
B) They often exaggerate their differences.
C) They often misunderstand their cultures.
D) They tend to dwell on national averages.

51. 专家在描述来自其他地方的人时通常会犯什么错误？

A）他们往往过分依赖国籍。
B）他们往往夸大这些人的不同。
C）他们经常误解这些人的文化。
D）他们往往关注全国平均水平。

【答案及分析】A。根据题干关键词 describing people from other places 定位到第一段最后一句。该句提到，Yet, when we speak of people from elsewhere, we seem to inevitably characterize them based on their country of origin.（然而，当我们谈及来自其他地方的人时，我们似乎会不可避免地根据国籍描述他们的特征。）第二段接着指出，专家也会犯同样的错误，即依赖国籍描述来自其他地方的人，A 项与原文相符，故选 A 项。

52. What do we learn about Hofstede's cultural dimensions?

A) They are useful in comparing cultural values across time and space.
B) They have brought unusual benefits to people of different cultures.
C) They are widely used to identify people's individual traits.
D) They provide valuable questions for researchers to study.

52. 关于霍夫斯泰德的文化维度，我们能了解到什么？

A）它们益于进行跨时空维度的文化价值观比较。
B）它们已给不同文化背景的人带来非同寻常的好处。
C）它们被广泛用于识别人们的个人特征。
D）它们为研究人员的研究提供了有价值的问题。

【答案及分析】A。根据题干关键词 Hofstede's cultural dimensions 定位到原文第四段第一句。该句首先引出霍夫斯泰德的文化维度。该段最后一句对霍夫斯泰德的文化维度进行了评价，Though the validity of Hofstede's dimensions has been questioned, they have the singular benefit of having been in use for decades, which allows for historical and international comparisons.（虽然霍夫斯泰德维度的有效性一直备受质疑，但它们的独特好处是已被使用数十年，允许进行历史和国际比较。）A 项符合原文，故选 A 项。

53. What did researchers find about previous studies on factors determining people's values?

A) Environmental factors were prioritized over other factors.
B) An individual's financial status was often underestimated.
C) Too much emphasis had been placed on one's occupation.
D) The impact of social progress on one's values was ignored.

53. 从之前关于决定人们价值观的因素的研究中，研究人员发现了什么？

A）环境因素的重要性大于其他因素。

B）个人的财务状况通常被低估。

C）个人职业被过分强调。

D）社会进步对个人价值观的影响被忽视了。

【答案及分析】B。根据题干关键词 previous studies on factors determining people's values 定位到原文第五段第一句，该句指出一个研究发现，The researchers found that both demographic factors... and environmental factors... were more correlated with cultural values than nationality.（研究人员发现，相比于国籍，人口因素……和环境因素……与文化价值观的相关性更高。）下一句介绍另一个研究发现，Occupation and social economic status were the most strongly correlated, suggesting that our values are more economically driven than we usually give them credit for.（职业和社会经济地位的相关性最强，这表明我们的价值观所受的经济驱动比我们通常所认为的更强。）B项与第五段内容相符，故选 B 项。

54. What is the impact on employees when cultures are identified with countries?

    A) They may fail to see the cultural biases of their business partners.

    B) They may fail to attach sufficient importance to cultural diversity.

    C) They may not be taught how to properly interact with overseas partners.

    D) They may not be able to learn the legal procedures for business transactions.

54. 当用国家来识别文化时，员工会受到什么影响？

    A）他们可能无法发现商业伙伴的文化偏见。

    B）他们可能不能充分重视文化多样性。

    C）他们可能不会被教授怎样和海外伙伴正确互动。

    D）他们可能无法学习商业交易的法律程序。

【答案及分析】C。根据题干关键词 impact on employees 和 when cultures are identified with countries 定位到原文第七段第一句。该句指出，Taras says our erroneous belief that countries are cultures has caused businesses to teach their employees useless or even harmful ways of interacting with their international peers.（塔拉斯说，"国籍就是文化"这种错误看法已导致企业教员工用无用甚至有害的方式与国际同行互动交流。）C 项为该句的同义表达，故选 C 项。

55. What does the author suggest at the end of the passage?

    A) There is sufficient reason to generalize about a country's population.

    B) The majority of people are still constrained by their national identity.

    C) It is arguable that the country should be regarded as the unit of authority.

    D) Nationality is less useful than socio-economic status as an indicator of one's values.

55. 作者在文章结尾提出什么建议？

    A）有充分的理由去概括一国人的特点。

    B）大多数人仍然被其民族身份限制。

C）国家应被视为权威性的代表一事具有争议。
D）在衡量一个人的价值观时，国籍不如社会经济地位有用。

【答案及分析】D。根据题干关键词 at the end of the passage 定位到最后一段。该段最后一句为作者提出的建议，In the majority of cases we would be better off identifying people by the factors that constrain their lives, like income, rather than by the lines surrounding them on a map. [在大多数情况下，我们最好通过限制人们生活的因素（如收入）识人，而不是通过地图上包围他们的线条。] the lines surrounding them on a map 指代国籍，D 项符合原文，故选 D 项。

Part IV　Translation

参考译文

　　Jinggangshan on the border of Hunan and Jiangxi provinces is acclaimed as the "red cradle of Chinese revolution" because of its glorious revolutionary history. In October 1927, Mao Zedong, Zhu De and other revolutionaries of the older generation led the Chinese Workers' and Peasants' Red Army here to launch an arduous struggle. They established the first rural revolutionary base, ignited the sparks of the Chinese revolution, and cleared a revolutionary path with Chinese characteristics of "besieging cities from rural areas and seizing the state power with armed forces". From here, the Chinese revolution marched towards victory. There are more than 100 revolutionary sites at Jinggangshan and it has become a fenceless museum of the Chinese revolutionary history and an important base for patriotism and revolutionary tradition education.

难词总结

acclaim /əˈkleɪm/ v. 赞扬；称赞
revolutionary /ˌrevəˈluːʃənəri/ a. 革命的；突破性的
rural revolutionary base 农村革命根据地
armed force 武装力量

revolution /ˌrevəˈluːʃn/ n. 革命
Chinese Workers' and Peasants' Red Army 中国工农红军
besiege /bɪˈsiːdʒ/ v. 包围

译点释义

1. 第一句中包含两个动词"地处"和"被誉为"，翻译时仅保留一个谓语动词，可将"地处"处理成后置定语。如参考译文将"井冈山地处湖南江西两省交界处"译成了介词短语 on the border of Hunan and Jiangxi provinces。
2. 第二句中的"开展了艰苦卓绝的斗争"译为 to launch an arduous struggle，作目的状语。第二句内容较长，可以将"创建了……，点燃了……，开辟了……"归结为一个意群，翻译为 3 个并列的动宾短语 established..., ignited..., cleared...。"中国革命从这里迈向胜利"可单独成句，"迈向胜利"可翻译为 marched towards victory。

3. 第三句中的"井冈山现有100多处革命旧址，成为一个……"可以翻译成两个并列句，如参考译文中的 There are more than 100 revolutionary sites at Jinggangshan and it has become...，也可以将"井冈山现有100多处革命旧址"翻译成伴随状语 with more than 100 revolutionary sites。

未得到监考教师指令前，不得翻阅该试题册！

2021年12月大学英语六级考试真题（第三套）

Part Ⅰ　　　　　　　　　Writing　　　　　　　　　(30 minutes)
（请于正式开考后半小时内完成该部分，之后将进行听力考试）

Directions: *For this part, you are allowed 30 minutes to write an essay related to the short passage given below. In your essay, you are to comment on the phenomenon described in the passage and suggest measures to address the issue. You should write at least **150** words but no more than **200** words.*

Young people spend a lot of time on the internet. However, they are sometimes unable to recognize false information on the internet, judge the reliability of online information sources, or tell real news stories from fake ones.

Part Ⅱ　　　　　　Listening Comprehension　　　　　　(30 minutes)

说明：由于2021年12月六级考试全国共考了两套听力，本套真题听力与前两套内容完全一样，只是顺序不一样，因此在本套真题中不再重复出现。

Part Ⅲ　　　　　　Reading Comprehension　　　　　　(40 minutes)

Section A

说明：据统计，2021年12月六级考试共考了两套阅读词汇理解，本套阅读词汇理解与前两套内容完全一样，因此在本套真题中不再重复出现。

Section B

Directions: *In this section, you are going to read a passage with ten statements attached to it. Each statement contains information given in one of the paragraphs. Identify the paragraph from which the information is derived. You may choose a paragraph more than once. Each paragraph is marked with a letter. Answer the questions by marking the corresponding letter on **Answer Sheet 2**.*

Do music lessons really make children smarter?

[A] A recent analysis found that most research mischaracterizes the relationship between music and skills enhancement.

[B] In 2004, a paper appeared in the journal *Psychological Science*, titled "Music Lessons Enhance IQ." The author, composer and psychologist Glenn Schellenberg had conducted an experiment with 144 children randomly assigned to four groups: one learned the keyboard for a year, one took singing lessons, one joined an acting class, and a control group had no extracurricular training. The IQ of the children in the two musical groups rose by an average of seven points in the course of a year; those in the other two groups gained an average of 4.3 points.

[C] Schellenberg had long been skeptical of the science supporting claims that music education enhances children's abstract reasoning, math, or language skills. If children who play the piano are smarter, he says, it doesn't necessarily mean they are smarter because they play the piano. It could be that the youngsters who play the piano also happen to be more ambitious or better at focusing on a task. Correlation, after all, does not prove causation.

[D] The 2004 paper was specifically designed to address those concerns. And as a passionate musician, Schellenberg was delighted when he turned up credible evidence that music has transfer effects on general intelligence. But nearly a decade later, in 2013, the Education Endowment Foundation funded a bigger study with more than 900 students. That study failed to confirm Schellenberg's findings, producing no evidence that music lessons improved math and literacy skills.

[E] Schellenberg took that news in stride while continuing to cast a skeptical eye on the research in his field. Recently, he decided to formally investigate just how often his fellow researchers in psychology and neuroscience make what he believes are erroneous — or at least premature — causal connections between music and intelligence. His results, published in May, suggest that many of his peers do just that.

[F] For his recent study, Schellenberg asked two research assistants to look for correlational studies on the effects of music education. They found a total of 114 papers published since 2000. To assess whether the authors claimed any causation, researchers then looked for telltale verbs in each paper's title and abstract, verbs like "enhance," "promote," "facilitate," and "strengthen." The papers were categorized as neuroscience if the study employed a brain imaging method like magnetic resonance, or if the study appeared in a journal that had "brain," "neuroscience," or a related term in its title. Otherwise the papers were categorized as psychology. Schellenberg didn't tell his assistants what exactly he was trying to prove.

[G] After computing their assessments, Schellenberg concluded that the majority of the articles erroneously claimed that music training had a causal effect. The overselling, he also found, was more prevalent among neuroscience studies, three quarters of which mischaracterized a mere association between music training and skills enhancement as a cause-and-effect relationship. This may come as a surprise to some. Psychologists have been battling charges that they don't do "real" science for some time — in large part because many findings from classic experiments have proved unreproducible. Neuroscientists, on the other hand, armed with brain scans and *EEGs* (脑电图), have not been subject to the same degree of critique.

[H] To argue for a cause-and-effect relationship, scientists must attempt to explain why and how a connection could occur. When it comes to transfer effects of music, scientists frequently point to brain plasticity — the fact that the brain changes according to how we use it. When a child learns to play the violin, for example, several studies have shown that the brain region responsible for the fine motor skills of the left hand's fingers is likely to grow. And many experiments have shown that musical training improves certain hearing capabilities, like filtering voices from background noise or distinguishing the difference between the *consonants* (辅音) "b" and "g".

[I] But Schellenberg remains highly critical of how the concept of plasticity has been applied in his field. "Plasticity has become an industry of its own," he wrote in his May paper. Practice does change the brain, he allows, but what is questionable is the assertion that these changes affect other brain regions, such as those responsible for spatial reasoning or math problems.

[J] Neuropsychologist Lutz Jäncke agrees. "Most of these studies don't allow for causal inferences," he said. For over two decades, Jäncke has researched the effects of music lessons, and like Schellenberg, he believes that the only way to truly understand their effects is to run longitudinal studies. In such studies, researchers would need to follow groups of children with and without music lessons over a long period of time — even if the assignments are not completely random. Then they could compare outcomes for each group.

[K] Some researchers are starting to do just that. The neuroscientist Peter Schneider from Heidelberg University in Germany, for example, has been following a group of children for ten years now. Some of them were handed musical instruments and given lessons through a school-based program in the Ruhr region of Germany called Jedem Kind ein Instrument, or "an instrument for every child," which was carried out with government funding. Among these children, Schneider has found that those who were enthusiastic about music and who practiced voluntarily showed improvements in hearing ability, as well as in more general competencies, such as the ability to concentrate.

[L] To establish whether effects such as improved concentration are caused by music participation itself, and not by investing time in an extracurricular activity of any kind, Assal Habibi, a psychology professor at the University of Southern California, is conducting a five-year longitudinal study with children from low-income communities in Los Angeles. The youngsters fall into three groups: those who take after-school music, those who do after-school sports, and those with no structured after-school program at all. After two years, Habibi and her colleagues reported seeing structural changes in the brains of the musically trained children, both locally and in the pathways connecting different parts of the brain.

[M] That may seem compelling, but Habibi's children were not selected randomly. Did the children who were drawn to music perhaps have something in them from the start that made them different but eluded the brain scanners? "As somebody who started taking piano lessons at the age of five and got up every morning at seven to practice, that experience changed me and made me part of who I am today," Schellenberg said. "The question is whether those kinds of experiences do so systematically across individuals and create exactly the same changes. And I think that is that huge leap of faith."

[N] Did he have a hidden talent that others didn't have? Or more endurance than his peers? Music researchers tend, like Schellenberg, to be musicians themselves, and as he noted in his recent paper, "the idea of positive cognitive and neural side effects from music training (and other pleasurable activities) is inherently appealing." He also admits that if he had children of his own, he would encourage them to take music lessons and go to university. "I would think that it makes them better people, more critical, just wiser in general," he said.

[O] But those convictions should be checked at the entrance to the lab, he added. Otherwise, the work becomes religion or faith. "You have to let go of your faith if you want to be a scientist."

36. Glenn Schellenberg's latest research suggests many psychologists and neuroscientists wrongly believe in the causal relationship between music and IQ.
37. The belief in the positive effects of music training appeals to many researchers who are musicians themselves.
38. Glenn Schellenberg was doubtful about the claim that music education helps enhance children's intelligence.
39. Glenn Schellenberg came to the conclusion that most of the papers assessed made the wrong claim regarding music's effect on intelligence.
40. You must abandon your unverified beliefs before you become a scientist.
41. Lots of experiments have demonstrated that people with music training can better differentiate certain sounds.
42. Glenn Schellenberg's findings at the beginning of this century were not supported by a larger study carried out some ten years later.
43. One researcher shares Glenn Schellenberg's view that it is necessary to conduct long-term developmental studies to understand the effects of music training.
44. Glenn Schellenberg's research assistants had no idea what he was trying to prove in his new study.
45. Glenn Schellenberg admits that practice can change certain areas of the brain but doubts that the change can affect other areas.

Section C

Directions: *There are 2 passages in this section. Each passage is followed by some questions or unfinished statements. For each of them there are four choices marked A), B), C) and D). You should decide on the best choice and mark the corresponding letter on **Answer Sheet 2** with a single line through the centre.*

Passage One

Questions 46 to 50 are based on the following passage.

The trend toward rationality and enlightenment was endangered long before the advent of the World Wide Web. As Neil Postman noted in his 1985 book *Amusing Ourselves to Death*, the rise of television introduced not just a new medium but a new discourse: a gradual shift from a *typographic* (印刷的) culture to a photographic one, which in turn meant a shift from rationality to emotions, exposition to entertainment. In an image-centered and pleasure-driven world, Postman noted, there is no place for rational thinking, because you simply cannot think with images. It is text that enables us to "uncover lies, confusions and overgeneralizations, and to detect abuses of logic and common sense. It also means to weigh ideas, to compare and contrast assertions, to connect one generalization to another."

The dominance of television was not confined to our living rooms. It overturned all of those habits of mind, fundamentally changing our experience of the world, affecting the conduct of politics, religion, business, and culture. It reduced many aspects of modern life to entertainment, sensationalism, and commerce. "Americans don't talk to each other, we entertain each other," Postman wrote. "They don't exchange ideas, they exchange images. They do not argue with propositions, they argue with good looks, celebrities and commercials."

At first, the web seemed to push against this trend. When it emerged towards the end of the 1980s as a purely text-based medium, it was seen as a tool to pursue knowledge, not pleasure. Reason and thought were most valued in this garden — all derived from the project of the Enlightenment. Universities around the world were among the first to connect to this new medium, which hosted discussion groups, informative personal or group blogs, electronic magazines, and academic mailing lists and forums. It was an intellectual project, not about commerce or control, created in a scientific research center in Switzerland. And for more than a decade, the web created an alternative space that threatened television's grip on society.

Social networks, though, have since colonized the web for television's values. From Facebook to Instagram, the medium refocuses our attention on videos and images, rewarding emotional appeals — "like" buttons — over rational ones. Instead of a quest for knowledge, it engages us in an endless *zest* (热情) for instant approval from an audience, for which we are constantly but unconsciously performing. (It's telling that, while Google began life as a PhD thesis, Facebook started as a tool to judge classmates' appearances.) It reduces our curiosity by showing us exactly what we already want and think, based on our profiles and preferences. The Enlightenment's *motto* (座右铭) of "Dare to know" has become "Dare not to care to know."

46. What did Neil Postman say about the rise of television?

    A) It initiated a change from dominance of reason to supremacy of pleasure.

    B) It brought about a gradual shift from cinema going to home entertainment.

    C) It started a revolution in photographic technology.

    D) It marked a new age in the entertainment industry.

47. According to the passage, what is the advantage of text reading?

    A) It gives one access to huge amounts of information.

    B) It allows more information to be processed quickly.

    C) It is capable of enriching one's life.

    D) It is conducive to critical thinking.

48. How has television impacted Americans?

    A) It has given them a lot more to argue about.

    B) It has brought celebrities closer to their lives.

    C) It has made them care more about what they say.

    D) It has rendered their interactions more superficial.

49. What does the passage say about the World Wide Web?

    A) It was developed primarily for universities worldwide.

    B) It was created to connect people in different countries.

    C) It was viewed as a means to quest for knowledge.

    D) It was designed as a discussion forum for university students.

50. What do we learn about users of social media?

   A) They are bent on looking for an alternative space for escape.

   B) They are constantly seeking approval from their audience.

   C) They are forever engaged in hunting for new information.

   D) They are unable to focus their attention on tasks for long.

Passage Two

Questions 51 to 55 are based on the following passage.

According to a recent study, a small but growing proportion of the workforce is affected to some degree by a sense of entitlement. Work is less about what they can contribute but more about what they can take. It can lead to workplace dysfunction and diminish their own job satisfaction. I'm not referring to employees who are legitimately dissatisfied with their employment conditions due to, say, being denied fair pay or flexible work practices. I'm talking about those who consistently believe they deserve special treatment and generous rewards. It's an expectation that exists irrespective of their abilities or levels of performance.

As a result of that discrepancy between the privileges they feel they're owed and their inflated sense of self-worth, they don't work as hard for their employer. They prefer instead to slack off. It's a tendency which many scholars believe begins in childhood due to parents who overindulge their kids. This thereby leads them to expect the same kind of spoilt treatment throughout their adult lives. And yet despite how these employees feel, it's obviously important for their manager to nonetheless find out how to keep them motivated. And, by virtue of that heightened motivation, to perform well.

The research team from several American universities surveyed more than 240 individuals. They sampled managers as well as team members. Employee entitlement was measured by statements such as "I honestly feel I'm just more deserving than others." The respondents had to rate the extent of their agreement. Employee engagement, meanwhile, was assessed with statements like "I really throw myself into my work." The findings revealed ethical leadership is precisely what alleviates the negative effects of employee entitlement. That's because rather than indulging employees or neglecting them, ethical leaders communicate very direct and clear expectations. They also hold employees accountable for their behaviors and are genuinely committed to doing the right thing. Additionally, these leaders are consistent in their standards. They're also less likely to deviate in how they treat employees.

This means, when confronted by an entitled team member, an ethical leader is significantly disinclined to accommodate their demands. He or she will instead point out, constructively and tactfully, exactly how their inflated sense of deservingness is somewhat distorted. They'd then go further to explain the specific, and objective, criteria the employee must meet to receive their desired rewards. This shift away from unrealistic expectations is successful because entitled employees feel more confident that ethical leaders will deliver on their promises. This occurs because they're perceived to be fair and trustworthy. The researchers, however, exercise caution by warning no one single response is the perfect remedy. But there's no denying ethical leadership is at least a critical step in the right direction.

51. What does a recent study find about a growing number of workers?
    A) They attempt to make more contributions.
    B) They feel they deserve more than they get.
    C) They attach importance to job satisfaction.
    D) They try to diminish workplace dysfunction.

52. Why don't some employees work hard according to many scholars?
    A) They lack a strong sense of self-worth.
    B) They were spoiled when growing up.
    C) They have received unfair treatment.
    D) They are overindulged by their boss.

53. What is a manager supposed to do to enable workers to do a better job?
    A) Be aware of their emotions.
    B) Give them timely promotions.
    C) Keep a record of their performance.
    D) Seek ways to sustain their motivation.

54. What do the research findings reveal about ethical leaders?
    A) They are held accountable by their employees.
    B) They are always transparent in their likes and dislikes.
    C) They convey their requirements in a straightforward way.
    D) They make it a point to be on good terms with their employees.

55. What kind of leaders are viewed as ethical by entitled employees?
    A) Those who can be counted on to fulfill commitments.
    B) Those who can do things beyond normal expectations.
    C) Those who exercise caution in making major decisions.
    D) Those who know how to satisfy their employees' needs.

Part IV   Translation   (30 minutes)

Directions: *For this part, you are allowed 30 minutes to translate a passage from Chinese into English. You should write your answer on **Answer Sheet 2**.*

延安位于陕西省北部,地处黄河中游,是中国革命的圣地。毛泽东等老一辈革命家曾在这里生活战斗了十三个春秋,领导了抗日战争和解放战争,培育了延安精神,为中国革命做出了巨大贡献。延安的革命旧址全国数量最大、分布最广、级别最高。延安是全国爱国主义、革命传统和延安精神教育基地。延安有9个革命纪念馆,珍藏着中共中央和老一辈革命家在延安时期留存下来的大量重要物品,因此享有"中国革命博物馆城"的美誉。

2021年12月大学英语六级考试真题解析
（第三套）

Part Ⅰ　Writing

成文构思

本文是一篇议论文，话题是"网络虚假信息"，可按照以下思路进行写作。
第一段：引出话题，提出"年轻人可能无法识别网上的虚假信息"这一观点。
第二段：针对问题，提出建议。本段是全文的中心段落。
第三段：进行总结。

参考范文及译文

　　Nowadays, it is well known that young people spend lots of time on the internet. However, they are sometimes unable to identify false information on the internet, judge the **reliability** of online information sources, which may lead to negative effects. Thus, there is a growing concern about the **authenticity** and reliability of online information.

　　Serious and timely actions must be taken to avoid this phenomenon. To begin with, authorities concerned should strengthen the supervision on the news media to reduce the spread of misinformation. What's more, legal departments can **formulate** relevant laws and rules to punish those who publish fake news online. Last but not least, family and school education in this respect also play a vital role in building young people's ability to think both critically and independently.

　　All in all, the development of the internet is an **inevitable** trend, and what is more important is to take reasonable measures to guide teenagers to use it more rationally. All quarters of society should strive to address the problem. Only in this way will our society be more harmonious.

　　如今，众所周知，年轻人花很多时间在互联网上。然而，他们有时无法识别互联网上的虚假信息，无法判断网络信息来源的可靠性，这可能会带来不好的影响。因此，人们越来越关注网络信息的真实性和可靠性。

　　必须采取严肃和及时的行动，以避免这种现象。首先，有关当局应加强对新闻媒体的监督，以减少虚假信息的传播。此外，法律部门可制定相关法律法规，对发布虚假新闻的人实施相应的惩罚。最后但同样重要的是，在这方面的家庭和学校教育在培养年轻人辩证思考和独立思考的能力方面也发挥着重要作用。

　　总而言之，网络的发展是一种不可避免的趋势。更重要的是采取合理的措施，引导青少年更合理地使用它。社会各方都应该努力解决这个问题。只有这样，我们的社会才能更加和谐。

词句点拨

reliability /rɪˌlaɪəˈbɪləti/ *n.* 可靠性；可信度
formulate /ˈfɔːmjuleɪt/ *v.* 制定
authenticity /ˌɔːθenˈtɪsəti/ *n.* 真实性
inevitable /ɪnˈevɪtəbl/ *a.* 不可避免的

1. Serious and timely actions must be taken to avoid this phenomenon. To begin with, ...
   必须采取严肃和及时的行动，以避免这种现象。首先，……

2. All in all, ... is an inevitable trend, and what is more important is to take reasonable measures to...
   总而言之，……是一种不可避免的趋势。更重要的是采取合理的措施，……

3. All quarters of society should strive to address the problem.
   社会各方都应该努力解决这个问题。

4. Only in this way will our society be more harmonious.
   只有这样，我们的社会才能更加和谐。

Part Ⅱ　Listening Comprehension

说明：由于 2021 年 12 月六级考试全国共考了两套听力，本套真题听力与前两套内容完全一样，只是顺序不一样，因此在本套真题中不再重复出现。

Part Ⅲ　Reading Comprehension

Section A

说明：据统计，2021 年 12 月六级考试共考了两套阅读词汇理解，本套阅读词汇理解与前两套内容完全一样，因此在本套真题中不再重复出现。

Section B

全文翻译

音乐课真的会让孩子更聪明吗？

[A] 最近一项分析发现，大多数研究都曲解了音乐与技能提升之间的关系。

[B] 2004 年，一篇题为"音乐课提高智商"的论文发表在期刊《心理科学》上。论文作者是作曲家兼心理学家格伦·谢伦伯格，他对 144 名儿童进行了一项实验，这些儿童被随机分为四组：一组学

习一年键盘，一组上声乐课，一组参加表演课，对照组没有课外培训。一年内，两个声乐组孩子们的智商平均提高了 7 分；其他两组孩子们的智商则平均提高了 4.3 分。

[C] 长期以来，对于支持音乐教育提高儿童抽象推理、数学或语言技能论断的科学，谢伦伯格一直持怀疑态度。他说，如果弹钢琴的孩子更聪明，这并不一定意味着会弹钢琴让他们更聪明。这可能是因为弹钢琴的少年碰巧更具雄心壮志或更善于专注一项任务。毕竟，相关性并不能证明因果关联。

[D] 2004 年发表的论文旨在专门解决这些疑虑。作为一位充满激情的音乐家，当谢伦伯格找到证明音乐对一般智力有转移效应的可靠证据时，他非常高兴。但近十年后，也就是 2013 年，教育捐赠基金会资助了一项有 900 多名学生参与的更大规模的研究。该研究未能证实谢伦伯格的研究发现，没有证据表明音乐课提高了数学和识字技能。

[E] 谢伦伯格从容地接受了这个消息，同时继续对他所在领域的研究持怀疑态度。最近，他决定正式调查心理学和神经科学领域的同行在音乐和智力之间建立他认为是错误的——或者至少是仓促的——因果关系的频率。他在 5 月份发表的结果中表明，许多同行就是这样做的。

[F] 在他最近的研究中，谢伦伯格要求两名研究助理寻找关于音乐教育效果相关性的研究。他们共找到 2000 年以来发表的 114 篇论文。为了评估作者是否在其论文中宣称了任何因果关联，研究人员随后在每篇论文的标题和摘要中寻找了能说明问题的动词，如"增强""促进""推动"和"加强"等。如果该研究采用了磁共振等脑成像方法，或者该研究发表在了标题中包含"大脑""神经科学"或相关术语的期刊中，那么这些论文被归类为神经科学。否则，论文则被归类为心理学。谢伦伯格没有告诉助手他究竟想证明什么。

[G] 对他们的评估做了计算后，谢伦伯格得出结论，大多数文章都错误地宣称音乐训练具有因果效应。他还发现，在神经科学研究中，过度宣传更为普遍，其中四分之三的研究将音乐训练和技能提高之间的单纯关联误解成因果关系。这可能会让一些人感到惊讶。一段时间以来，心理学家一直和他们没有做"真正"科学的指控作斗争——这在很大程度上是因为经典实验的许多发现已被证明不能复制。另一方面，有脑部扫描和脑电图辅助的神经科学家并没有受到同样程度的批判。

[H] 为了论证一种因果关系，科学家必须尝试解释这种联系为什么发生、如何发生。当谈到音乐的传递效应时，科学家们频繁地指出大脑的可塑性——即大脑根据我们怎样使用它而产生变化。例如，少数研究表明，当孩子学习小提琴时，负责左手手指精细运动技能的大脑区域可能会发育。许多实验已表明，音乐训练能提高某些听力能力，比如从背景噪声中过滤声音或区分辅音"b"和"g"之间的差异。

[I] 但谢伦伯格对可塑性概念在他所在的领域中的应用仍然持高度批判态度。他在 5 月份发表的论文中写道："可塑性已成为一门独立领域。"他承认，练习确实能改变大脑，但声称这些变化会影响比如负责空间推理或数学问题的其他大脑区域就值得怀疑了。

[J] 神经心理学家卢茨·詹克同意这种观点。他说:"这些研究中的大多数不能够做因果推断。"二十多年来,詹克一直在研究音乐课的效果,与谢伦伯格一样,他认为进行纵向研究是真正理解音乐课效果的唯一途径。在这类研究中,研究人员需要长期跟踪上音乐课和不上音乐课的儿童——即使不是完全随机分配任务。然后他们可以对每组的结果进行比较。

[K] 一些研究人员正开始这样做。例如,德国海德堡大学的神经科学家彼得·施奈德已经跟踪调查一群儿童十年了。德国鲁尔地区一个名为"每个孩子的乐器"的学校项目为一些儿童提供了乐器和音乐课程,这些都在政府资助下进行。在这些孩子中,施奈德发现那些对音乐充满热情并且自愿练习的孩子在听力和更综合的能力(比如集中注意力的能力)上有所提高。

[L] 为了确定诸如提高注意力等效果是由参与音乐本身而不是在任意类型的课外活动中投入时间引起的,南加州大学的心理学教授阿萨尔·哈比比正对洛杉矶低收入社区的儿童进行一项为期5年的纵向研究。这些儿童被分成了三类:参加课外音乐培训的人、参加课外运动的人以及根本没有安排课外活动的人。两年后,哈比比和她的同事宣布,接受音乐训练的儿童的大脑结构发生了变化,包括局部变化和连接大脑不同部分的神经通路变化。

[M] 这看起来可能很有说服力,但哈比比并没有随机选择研究对象。那些被音乐吸引的孩子是否一开始就具有使他们与众不同的某种因素,但脑部扫描仪没有发现呢?谢伦伯格说:"作为一个从5岁开始学习钢琴并每天早上7点起床练习的人,这种经历改变了我,让我成为今天的我。问题在于,这种经历是否会在个体之间系统地发生,并产生完全相同的变化。我认为这是信仰的巨大飞跃。"

[N] 他有没有其他人没有的隐藏才能?又或者比他的同龄人更有耐力?像谢伦伯格一样,音乐研究人员往往自己也是音乐家,正如谢伦伯格在最近的论文中指出的那样,"音乐训练(和其他令人愉悦的活动)产生积极认知和神经副作用的这种想法在本质上很有吸引力。"他还承认,如果他有自己的孩子,他会鼓励他们上音乐课,上大学。"我认为这会让他们成为更好的人,更具有批判思维,总体上来说更聪明。"他说道。

[O] 但他补充说,应该在实验前对这种坚定的看法进行检查。否则,这项工作就会变成宗教或信仰。"如果你想成为一名科学家,你就必须放弃你的信仰。"

难词总结

correlation /ˌkɒrəˈleɪʃn/ n. 关联;相互关系
confirm /kənˈfɜːm/ v. 证实;确定
compute /kəmˈpjuːt/ v. 计算;估算
conviction /kənˈvɪkʃn/ n. 坚定的看法(或信念)

causation /kɔːˈzeɪʃn/ n. 因果关系
telltale /ˈtelteɪl/ a. 能说明问题的
longitudinal /ˌlɒŋɡɪˈtjuːdɪnl/ a. 纵向的;经度的

题目精析

36. Glenn Schellenberg's latest research suggests many psychologists and neuroscientists wrongly believe in the causal relationship between music and IQ.

36. 格伦·谢伦伯格的最新研究表明，许多心理学家和神经科学家错误地认为音乐与智力之间存在因果关系。

【答案及分析】E。根据题干中的 psychologists and neuroscientists、wrongly believe 和 the causal relationship between music and IQ 定位到 E 段。定位句指出，Recently, he decided to formally investigate just how often his fellow researchers in psychology and neuroscience make what he believes are erroneous... causal connections between music and intelligence.（最近，他决定正式调查心理学和神经科学领域的同行在音乐和智力之间建立他认为是错误的……因果关系的频率。）题干是原文的同义表达，其中 psychologists and neuroscientists 是原文中 researchers in psychology and neuroscience 的同义表达，wrongly believe 是原文中 he believes are erroneous 的同义表达，the causal relationship between music and IQ 对应原文中的 causal connections between music and intelligence，故选 E 项。

37. The belief in the positive effects of music training appeals to many researchers who are musicians themselves.

37. 对许多本身就是音乐家的研究者来说，音乐训练具有积极作用这种看法很有吸引力。

【答案及分析】N。根据题干中的 positive effects of music training 和 appeals to many researchers 定位到 N 段。定位句指出，Music researchers tend... to be musicians themselves（音乐研究人员往往自己也是音乐家），下文接着指出，the idea of positive cognitive and neural side effects from music training... is inherently appealing（音乐训练……产生积极认知和神经副作用的这种想法在本质上很有吸引力）。题干是原文的同义表达，positive effects of music training 是 positive... effects from music training 的同义表达，musicians themselves 为原词复现，故选 N 项。

38. Glenn Schellenberg was doubtful about the claim that music education helps enhance children's intelligence.

38. 格伦·谢伦伯格对音乐教育有助于提高儿童智力的说法持怀疑态度。

【答案及分析】C。根据题干中的 Glenn Schellenberg 和 doubtful about the claim 定位到 C 段。定位句指出，Schellenberg had long been skeptical of the science supporting claims that music education enhances children's abstract reasoning, math, or language skills.（长期以来，对于支持音乐教育提高儿童抽象推理、数学或语言技能论断的科学，谢伦伯格一直持怀疑态度。）题干是原文的同义表达，其中 Glenn Schellenberg was doubtful 是原文中 Schellenberg had long been skeptical 的同义表达，music education 为原词复现，故选 C 项。

39. Glenn Schellenberg came to the conclusion that most of the papers assessed made the wrong claim regarding music's effect on intelligence.

39. 格伦·谢伦伯格得出结论，大多数被评估的论文就音乐对智力的影响做了错误论断。

【答案及分析】G。根据题干中的 papers assessed 和 made the wrong claim 定位到 G 段。定位句指出，After computing their assessments, Schellenberg concluded that the majority of the articles erroneously claimed that music training had a causal effect.（对他们的评估做了计算后，谢伦伯格得出结论，大多数文章都错误地宣称音乐训练具有因果效应。）题干是原文的同义表达，assessed 对应 assessments，most of the papers... made the wrong claim 是 the majority of the articles erroneously claimed 的同义表达，故选 G 项。

40. You must abandon your unverified beliefs before you become a scientist.

40. 在成为科学家之前，你必须放弃你未经证实的信仰。

【答案及分析】O。根据题干中的 abandon your unverified beliefs 和 before you become a scientist 定位到 O 段。定位句指出，You have to let go of your faith if you want to be a scientist.（如果你想成为一名科学家，你就必须放弃你的信仰。）题干是原文的同义表达，其中 abandon your unverified beliefs 是原文中 have to let go of your faith 的同义表达，before you become a scientist 是原文中 if you want to be a scientist 的同义表达，故选 O 项。

41. Lots of experiments have demonstrated that people with music training can better differentiate certain sounds.

41. 大量实验表明，接受过音乐训练的人能更好地辨别某些声音。

【答案及分析】H。根据题干中的 better differentiate certain sounds 定位到 H 段。定位句指出，And many experiments have shown that musical training improves certain hearing capabilities, like filtering voices from background noise or distinguishing the difference between the consonants "b" and "g".（许多实验已表明，音乐训练能提高某些听力能力，比如从背景噪声中过滤声音或区分辅音"b"和"g"之间的差异。）题干是原文的同义表达，其中 Lots of experiments have demonstrated that 是原文中 many experiments have shown that 的同义表达，better differentiate certain sounds 是 improves certain hearing capabilities 的同义表达，故选 H 项。

42. Glenn Schellenberg's findings at the beginning of this century were not supported by a larger study carried out some ten years later.

42. 格伦·谢伦伯格本世纪初的研究发现没有得到大约十年后开展的更大规模研究的支持。

【答案及分析】D。根据题干中的 were not supported by a larger study 和 ten years later 定位到 D 段。定位句指出，But nearly a decade later, in 2013, the Education Endowment Foundation funded a bigger study with more than 900 students.（但近十年后，也就是 2013 年，教育捐赠基金会资助了一项有 900 多名学生参与的更大规模的研究。）下句接着指出，That study failed to confirm Schellenberg's findings（该研究未能证实谢伦伯格的研究发现）。题干是原文的同义表达，其中 a larger study 是原文中 a bigger study 的同义表达，were not supported 是原文中 failed to confirm 的同义表达，故选 D 项。

43. One researcher shares Glenn Schellenberg's view that it is necessary to conduct long-term developmental studies to understand the effects of music training.

43. 一位研究人员与格伦·谢伦伯格的观点一致，即为了了解音乐训练效果，有必要进行长期的发展研究。

【答案及分析】J。根据题干中的 shares Glenn Schellenberg's view 和 long-term developmental studies 定位到 J 段。定位句指出，For over two decades, Jäncke has researched the effects of music lessons, and like

Schellenberg, he believes that the only way to truly understand their effects is to run longitudinal studies.（二十多年来，詹克一直在研究音乐课的效果，与谢伦伯格一样，他认为进行纵向研究是真正理解音乐课效果的唯一途径。）题干是原文的同义表达，其中 shares Glenn Schellenberg's view 是原文中 like Schellenberg, he believes that 的同义表达，it is necessary to conduct... music training 是原文中 the only way... is to run longitudinal studies 的同义表达，故选 J 项。

44. Glenn Schellenberg's research assistants had no idea what he was trying to prove in his new study.

44. 格伦·谢伦伯格的研究助理不知道他试图在新研究中证明什么。

【答案及分析】F。根据题干中的 Schellenberg's research assistants 和 trying to prove 定位到 F 段。定位句指出，Schellenberg didn't tell his assistants what exactly he was trying to prove.（谢伦伯格没有告诉助手他究竟想证明什么。）题干是原文的同义表达，Schellenberg's research assistants 和 trying to prove 为原词复现，故选 F 项。

45. Glenn Schellenberg admits that practice can change certain areas of the brain but doubts that the change can affect other areas.

45. 格伦·谢伦伯格承认，练习可以改变大脑的某些区域，但他对这种改变是否会影响其他区域持怀疑态度。

【答案及分析】I。根据题干中的 Glenn Schellenberg admits、change、doubts 和 affect，定位到 I 段。定位句指出，Practice does change the brain, he allows, but what is questionable is the assertion that these changes affect other brain regions（他承认，练习确实能改变大脑，但声称这些变化会影响其他大脑区域就值得怀疑了）。题干是原文的同义表达，admits 是 allows 的同义表达，practice、change the brain 为原词复现，doubts... affect other areas 是 what is questionable... affect other brain regions 的同义表达，故选 I 项。

Section C

Passage One

全文翻译

早在万维网出现之前，理性和启蒙的趋势就已受到威胁。正如尼尔·波兹曼在他1985年发行的《娱乐至死》一书中指出的那样，电视的兴起不仅带来了一种新媒介，而且带来了一种新的话语方式：印刷文化逐渐向摄影文化转变，这反过来意味着从理性到情感、从阐述到娱乐的转变。波兹曼指出，在一个以图像为中心、以快乐为导向的世界里，没有理性思考的空间，因为你根本无法用图像思考。正是文本让我们"发现谎言、迷惑和过度概括，并找出滥用逻辑和常识的地方。它还意味着权衡思想，比较和对比断言，将一种概括与另一种概括联系起来。"

电视的主导地位并不局限于我们的客厅。它颠覆了所有这些思维习惯，从根本上改变了我们对世界的体验，影响了政治、宗教、商业和文化行为。它把现代生活的许多方面降格为娱乐、哗众取宠和商业。"美国人彼此不交谈，我们互相娱乐。"波兹曼写道，"他们不交流想法，他们交换图像。他们不与主张争论，而是与美貌、名人和商业广告争论。"

　　一开始，网络似乎是在逆潮流而动。20世纪80年代末，网络在作为一种纯粹的文本媒介出现时被视为一种追求知识而非快乐的工具。理性和思想在这座"花园"里最受重视——这些都源于启蒙运动。世界各地的大学是第一批连接到这种新媒介的，该媒介主办了讨论小组、信息丰富的个人或团体博客、电子杂志、学术邮件列表和论坛。这是瑞士一个科学研究中心创建的智力项目，与商业或控制无关。十多年来，网络创造了一个威胁到电视对社会的控制的替代空间。

　　然而，自那以后，社交网络为了电视的价值将网络殖民化了。从Facebook到Instagram，社交媒体让我们的注意力重新集中在视频和图片上，奖励情感上的诉求——如"点赞"按键——而不是理性的诉求。它让我们对观众的即时认可产生无穷无尽的兴趣，而不是追求知识，为此我们不断地、无意识地表演。（很明显，谷歌最初是以博士论文起家的，而Facebook最初是用来评价同学外表的工具。）它会根据我们的个人资料和偏好，准确地向我们展示我们已经想要的东西和我们已有的想法，从而减少我们的好奇心。启蒙运动的座右铭"敢于求知"变成了"不敢在乎求知"。

难词总结

rationality /ˌræʃəˈnæləti/ *n.* 理性
exposition /ˌekspəˈzɪʃn/ *n.* 解释，阐述
assertion /əˈsɜːʃn/ *n.* 断言；主张
sensationalism /senˈseɪʃənəlɪzəm/ *n.* 哗众取宠
grip /ɡrɪp/ *n.* 控制；理解

enlightenment /ɪnˈlaɪtnmənt/ *n.* 启迪，指导
overgeneralization /ˌəʊvədʒenrəlaɪˈzeɪʃn/ *n.* 过度泛化
overturn /ˌəʊvəˈtɜːn/ *v.* 推翻
proposition /ˌprɒpəˈzɪʃn/ *n.* 主张，观点

题目精析

46. What did Neil Postman say about the rise of television?

　　A) It initiated a change from dominance of reason to supremacy of pleasure.

　　B) It brought about a gradual shift from cinema going to home entertainment.

　　C) It started a revolution in photographic technology.

　　D) It marked a new age in the entertainment industry.

46. 关于电视的崛起，尼尔·波兹曼说了些什么？

　　A）它引发了一种从理性支配到快乐至上的转变。

　　B）它带来了从电影向家庭娱乐的逐渐转变。

　　C）它开创了摄影技术的革命。

D）它标志着娱乐业的一个新时代。

【答案及分析】A。根据题干关键词 Neil Postman 和 the rise of television 定位到原文第一段第二句。该句指出，As Neil Postman noted in his 1985 book *Amusing Ourselves to Death*, the rise of television introduced not just a new medium but a new discourse: a gradual shift from a typographic culture to a photographic one, which in turn meant a shift from rationality to emotions, exposition to entertainment.（正如尼尔·波兹曼在他 1985 年发行的《娱乐至死》一书中指出的那样，电视的兴起不仅带来了一种新媒介，而且带来了一种新话语方式：印刷文化逐渐向摄影文化转变，这反过来意味着从理性到情感、从阐述到娱乐的转变。）A 项是原文中 a shift from rationality to emotions, exposition to entertainment 的同义表达，故选 A 项。

47. According to the passage, what is the advantage of text reading?

    A) It gives one access to huge amounts of information.
    C) It is capable of enriching one's life.

    B) It allows more information to be processed quickly.
    D) It is conducive to critical thinking.

47. 根据这篇文章，文本阅读的好处是什么？

    A）它让人们获得大量的信息。
    C）它可以丰富一个人的生活。

    B）它可以使更多的信息被快速处理。
    D）它有助于批判性思维。

【答案及分析】D。根据题干关键词 the advantage of text reading 定位到原文第一段第四句。该句指出，It is text that enables us to "uncover lies, confusions and overgeneralizations, and to detect abuses of logic and common sense…"（正是文本让我们"发现谎言、迷惑和过度概括，并找出滥用逻辑和常识的地方……"）D 项是对原文的概括表达，故选 D 项。

48. How has television impacted Americans?

    A) It has given them a lot more to argue about.

    B) It has brought celebrities closer to their lives.

    C) It has made them care more about what they say.

    D) It has rendered their interactions more superficial.

48. 电视是如何影响美国人的？

    A）它提供了更多值得争论的内容。

    B）它使名人更接近他们的生活。

    C）这让他们更关心自己说了些什么。

    D）这使得他们之间的互动更加肤浅。

【答案及分析】D。根据题干定位到原文第二段第三句。该句指出，It reduced many aspects of modern life to entertainment, sensationalism, and commerce.（它把现代生活的许多方面降格为娱乐、哗众取宠和商业。）D 项中的 more superficial 是对原文的概括表达，故选 D 项。

49. What does the passage say about the World Wide Web?

A) It was developed primarily for universities worldwide.

B) It was created to connect people in different countries.

C) It was viewed as a means to quest for knowledge.

D) It was designed as a discussion forum for university students.

49. 关于万维网，这篇文章说了什么？

A）它主要是为世界各地的大学开发的。

B）它的创建是为了连接不同国家的人们。

C）它被视为一种追求知识的手段。

D）它是为大学生设计的一个论坛。

【答案及分析】C。根据题干关键词 the World Wide Web 定位到原文第三段第一句。其后一句指出，When it emerged towards the end of the 1980s as a purely text-based medium, it was seen as a tool to pursue knowledge, not pleasure.（20 世纪 80 年代末，网络在作为一种纯粹的文本媒介出现时被视为一种追求知识而非快乐的工具。）句中的 it 指代的就是 the World Wide Web。C 项中的 as a means to quest for knowledge 是原文中 as a tool to pursue knowledge 的同义表达，故选 C 项。

50. What do we learn about users of social media?

A) They are bent on looking for an alternative space for escape.

B) They are constantly seeking approval from their audience.

C) They are forever engaged in hunting for new information.

D) They are unable to focus their attention on tasks for long.

50. 关于社交媒体用户，我们了解到什么？

A）他们一心想寻找另一个逃生空间。

B）他们不断地寻求观众的认可。

C）他们永远致力于寻找新的信息。

D）他们无法长时间地把注意力集中在任务上。

【答案及分析】B。根据题干关键词 users of social media 定位到原文最后一段第三句。该句指出，Instead of a quest for knowledge, it engages us in an endless zest for instant approval from an audience, for which we are constantly but unconsciously performing.（它让我们对观众的即时认可产生无穷无尽的兴趣，而不是追求知识，为此我们不断地、无意识地表演。）B 项中的 seeking approval from their audience 是原文中 for instant approval from an audience 的同义表达，故选 B 项。

Passage Two

全文翻译

根据最近的一项研究，一群占比很小但人数越来越多的劳动力在一定程度上受到了权益感的影响。工作不在于他们能做出什么贡献，而在于他们能得到什么。这会导致职场功能失衡，降低他们自己的工作满意度。我指的不是那些因为被剥夺了公平薪酬或弹性工作方式而对雇佣条件不满的员工。我说的是那些一直认为自己应该得到特殊待遇和丰厚奖励的人。不管他们的能力和表现水平如何，这种期望都是存在的。

由于他们认为自己应得的特权和他们膨胀的自我价值感之间存在差异，他们不会为雇主努力工作。相反，他们更喜欢偷懒。许多学者认为，由于父母过度溺爱孩子，这种趋势从儿童时期就开始了。这就导致了他们在成年后期待着同样被宠坏的待遇。然而，不管这些员工的感受如何，对于他们的经理来说，弄清如何让他们保持积极性且由于强烈的积极性而表现出色显然是很重要的。

来自美国几所大学的研究团队调查了240多人。他们抽样调查了管理人员和团队成员。衡量员工权益感的标准是诸如"我真的觉得自己比其他人更有资格"之类的话。被调查者必须对他们的认同程度进行评分。与此同时，员工参与度的评估标准是诸如"我真的全身心投入到工作中"之类的话。调查结果显示，正是道德领导力减轻了员工权益感的负面影响。这是因为有道德的领导者不会纵容或忽视员工，而是直接而明确地传达他们的期望。他们还要求员工对自己的行为负责，并真诚地致力于做正确的事情。此外，这些领导者的标准是一致的。他们对待员工的方式也不太可能有偏差。

这意味着，当面对一个争取权益的团队成员时，一个有道德的领导者明显不愿意满足他们的要求。相反，他或她会积极而巧妙地指出，他们膨胀的应得感究竟是如何在某种程度上被扭曲的。然后他们会进一步解释员工为了得到想要的奖励而必须达到的具体和客观的标准。这种远离不切实际的期望的做法是成功的，因为想要争取权益的员工更相信有道德的领导者会兑现他们的承诺。这是因为他们认为领导是公平和值得信赖的。然而，研究人员警告我们要谨慎地实践，任何单一的反应都不是完美的补救方法。但不可否认的是，道德领导力至少是朝着正确方向迈出的关键一步。

难词总结

sense of entitlement 权益感

generous /ˈdʒenərəs/ a. 慷慨的；大量的

privilege /ˈprɪvəlɪdʒ/ n. 特权，特殊待遇

overindulge /ˌəʊvərɪnˈdʌldʒ/ v. 过分放任

alleviate /əˈliːvieɪt/ v. 减轻，缓和

dysfunction /dɪsˈfʌŋkʃn/ n. 功能紊乱

discrepancy /dɪsˈkrepənsi/ n. 差异，不符

slack off 偷懒；懈怠

by virtue of 由于；凭借

deviate /ˈdiːvieɪt/ v. 偏离，违背

disincline /ˌdɪsɪnˈklaɪn/ v. 使不愿，使不欲

exercise /ˈeksəsaɪz/ v. 行使；使用；运用

accommodate /əˈkɒmədeɪt/ v. 考虑到；顾及

题目精析

51. What does a recent study find about a growing number of workers?

   A) They attempt to make more contributions.

   B) They feel they deserve more than they get.

   C) They attach importance to job satisfaction.

   D) They try to diminish workplace dysfunction.

51. 关于越来越多的员工，最近的一项研究有什么发现？

   A）他们试图做出更多的贡献。

   B）他们觉得自己应该得到的更多。

   C）他们很重视工作满意度。

   D）他们试图减轻职场的功能失衡。

   【答案及分析】B。根据题干关键词 a growing number of workers 定位到原文第一段第一句和第二句。定位句指出，According to a recent study, a small but growing proportion of the workforce is affected to some degree by a sense of entitlement. Work is less about what they can contribute but more about what they can take.（根据最近的一项研究，一群占比很小但人数越来越多的劳动力在一定程度上受到了权益感的影响。工作不在于他们能做出什么贡献，而在于他们能得到什么。）定位句中的 growing proportion of the workforce 对应题干关键词；B 项是原文中 Work is less about what they can contribute but more about what they can take 的同义表达，故选 B 项。

52. Why don't some employees work hard according to many scholars?

   A) They lack a strong sense of self-worth.   C) They have received unfair treatment.

   B) They were spoiled when growing up.   D) They are overindulged by their boss.

52. 据许多学者所说，为什么有些员工不努力工作呢？

   A）他们缺乏强烈的自我价值感。   C）他们受到了不公平的待遇。

   B）他们在成长过程中被宠坏了。   D）他们被老板过分纵容了。

   【答案及分析】B。根据题干关键词 many scholars 定位到原文第二段第三句。定位句指出，It's a tendency which many scholars believe begins in childhood due to parents who overindulge their kids.（许多学者认为，由于父母过度溺爱孩子，这种趋势从儿童时期就开始了。）B 项是原文中 due to parents who overindulge their kids 的同义表达，故选 B 项。

53. What is a manager supposed to do to enable workers to do a better job?

   A) Be aware of their emotions.   C) Keep a record of their performance.

   B) Give them timely promotions.   D) Seek ways to sustain their motivation.

53. 一个经理应该做些什么来让员工们做得更好呢?

　　A) 要注意他们的情绪。　　　　　　　C) 记录下他们的表现。

　　B) 及时给他们晋升。　　　　　　　　D) 寻找维持他们动力的方法。

【答案及分析】D。根据题干关键词 a manager 定位到原文第二段最后两句。定位句指出，And yet despite how these employees feel, it's obviously important for their manager to nonetheless find out how to keep them motivated. And, by virtue of that heightened motivation, to perform well.（然而，不管这些员工的感受如何，对于他们的经理来说，弄清如何让他们保持积极性且由于强烈的积极性而表现出色显然是很重要的。）D 项是原文中 find out how to keep them motivated 的同义表达，故选 D 项。

54. What do the research findings reveal about ethical leaders?

　　A) They are held accountable by their employees.

　　B) They are always transparent in their likes and dislikes.

　　C) They convey their requirements in a straightforward way.

　　D) They make it a point to be on good terms with their employees.

54. 研究结果揭示了关于有道德的领导者的什么?

　　A）他们被员工追究责任。

　　B）他们的喜好和厌恶总是显而易见的。

　　C）他们以一种直接的方式传达他们的需求。

　　D）他们强调要与员工保持良好的关系。

【答案及分析】C。根据题干关键词 the research findings reveal about ethical leaders 定位到原文第三段第六句和第七句。定位句指出，The findings revealed ethical leadership is precisely what alleviates the negative effects of employee entitlement. That's because rather than indulging employees or neglecting them, ethical leaders communicate very direct and clear expectations.（调查结果显示，正是道德领导力减轻了员工权益感的负面影响。这是因为有道德的领导者不会纵容或忽视员工，而是直接而明确地传达他们的期望。）C 项是原文中 communicate very direct and clear expectations 的同义表达，故选 C 项。

55. What kind of leaders are viewed as ethical by entitled employees?

　　A) Those who can be counted on to fulfill commitments.

　　B) Those who can do things beyond normal expectations.

　　C) Those who exercise caution in making major decisions.

　　D) Those who know how to satisfy their employees' needs.

55. 什么样的领导者才会被想要争取权益的员工认为是有道德的?

　　A）那些可以指望会履行承诺的人。

　　B）那些能做超乎寻常的事的人。

C）那些在做重大决定时谨慎行事的人。

D）那些知道如何满足员工需求的人。

【答案及分析】A。根据题干关键词 entitled employees 定位到原文最后一段第四句。定位句指出，This shift away from unrealistic expectations is successful because entitled employees feel more confident that ethical leaders will deliver on their promises.（这种远离不切实际的期望的做法是成功的，因为想要争取权益的员工更相信有道德的领导者会兑现他们的承诺。）A 项是原文中 feel more confident that ethical leaders will deliver on their promises 的同义表达，故选 A 项。

Part Ⅳ Translation

参考译文

　　Yan'an, located in the northern part of Shaanxi Province and in the middle reaches of the Yellow River, is the sacred land of the Chinese revolution. Mao Zedong and other revolutionaries of the older generation lived and battled here for 13 years, leading the War of Resistance Against Japanese Aggression and the War of Liberation, cultivating the Yan'an spirit and making tremendous contributions to the Chinese revolution. With the largest number of revolutionary sites distributed widest and ranked highest in the country, Yan'an is a national education base for patriotism, revolutionary traditions and the Yan'an spirit. There are nine revolutionary memorial halls in Yan'an, which treasure a huge number of significant items left by the Central Committee of the Communist Party of China and the revolutionaries of the older generation during the Yan'an period. Therefore, it has maintained its reputation as "the museum city of the Chinese revolution".

难词总结

the War of Resistance Against Japanese Aggression 抗日战争　　　　the War of Liberation 解放战争

memorial /məˈmɔːriəl/ a. 纪念的；记忆的　　　　treasure /ˈtreʒə(r)/ v. 珍藏；珍视

the Communist Party of China 中国共产党

译点释义

1. 第一句中包含三个谓语动词"位于""地处"和"是"，翻译时需要将其中两个处理成非谓语，仅保留一个谓语动词。如参考译文将"位于陕西省北部，地处黄河中游"译成了 located in the northern part of Shaanxi Province and in the middle reaches of the Yellow River。

2. 第二句中包含多个谓语动词，可将"生活战斗"作为整个句子的谓语动词；"领导了……，培育了……，为中国革命做出了……"可译为并列的非谓语动词 doing 的词组，作伴随状语，比如参考译文中的 leading..., cultivating... and making...。

3. 第三句和第四句逻辑关系紧密，翻译时可合并为一句，同时可将第三句"延安的革命旧址全国数量最大、分布最广、级别最高"翻译成 with 独立主格结构，即 With the largest number of revolutionary sites distributed widest and ranked highest in the country。

4. 第五句中的"延安有9个革命纪念馆，珍藏着……"和"因此享有'中国革命博物馆城'的美誉"为因果关系，可将"因此享有……美誉"独立成句翻译。"中共中央和老一辈革命家在延安时期留存下来的大量重要物品"可译成 a huge number of significant items left by the Central Committee of the Communist Party of China and the revolutionaries of the older generation during the Yan'an period，其中非谓语动词词组 left by... period 作后置定语，修饰 items。

未得到监考教师指令前，不得翻阅该试题册！

2021年6月大学英语六级考试真题（第一套）

Part I   Writing   (30 minutes)

（请于正式开考后半小时内完成该部分，之后将进行听力考试）

Directions: *For this part, you are allowed 30 minutes to write an essay based on the chart below. You should start your essay with a brief description of the chart and comment on* **China's achievements in poverty alleviation**. *You should write at least* **150** *words but no more than* **200** *words.*

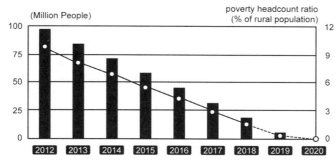

Part II   Listening Comprehension   (30 minutes)

Section A

Directions: *In this section, you will hear two long conversations. At the end of each conversation, you will hear four questions. Both the conversation and the questions will be spoken only once. After you hear a question, you must choose the best answer from the four choices marked A), B), C) and D). Then mark the corresponding letter on* **Answer Sheet 1** *with a single line through the centre.*

APP 扫码，听音频

Questions 1 to 4 are based on the conversation you have just heard.

1. A) He will tell the management how he really feels.
   B) He will meet his new manager in two weeks.
   C) He is going to attend a job interview.
   D) He is going to leave his present job.

2. A) It should be kept private.
   B) It should be carefully analyzed.
   C) It can be quite useful to senior managers.
   D) It can improve interviewees' job prospects.

3. A) It may leave a negative impression on the interviewer.
   B) It may adversely affect his future career prospects.
   C) It may displease his immediate superiors.
   D) It may do harm to his fellow employees.

4. A) Prepare a comprehensive exit report.
   B) Do some practice for the exit interview.
   C) Network with his close friends to find a better employer.
   D) Pour out his frustrations on a rate-your-employer website.

Questions 5 to 8 are based on the conversation you have just heard.

5. A) Her unsuccessful journey.
   B) Her month-long expedition.
   C) Her latest documentary.
   D) Her career as a botanist.
6. A) She had to live like a vegetarian.
   B) She was caught in a hurricane.
   C) She had to endure many hardships.
   D) She suffered from water shortage.
7. A) A hurricane was coming.
   B) A flood was approaching.
   C) They had no more food in the canoe.
   D) They could no longer bear the humidity.
8. A) It was memorable.
   B) It was unbearable.
   C) It was uneventful.
   D) It was fruitful.

Section B

Directions: *In this section, you will hear two passages. At the end of each passage, you will hear three or four questions. Both the passage and the questions will be spoken only once. After you hear a question, you must choose the best answer from the four choices marked A), B), C) and D). Then mark the corresponding letter on **Answer Sheet 1** with a single line through the centre.*

Questions 9 to 11 are based on the passage you have just heard.

9. A) It diminishes laymen's interest in science.
   B) It ensures the accuracy of their arguments.
   C) It makes their expressions more explicit.
   D) It hurts laymen's dignity and self-esteem.
10. A) They can learn to communicate with scientists.
    B) They tend to disbelieve the actual science.
    C) They feel great respect towards scientists.
    D) They will see the complexity of science.
11. A) Find appropriate topics.
    B) Stimulate their interest.
    C) Explain all the jargon terms.
    D) Do away with jargon terms.

Questions 12 to 15 are based on the passage you have just heard.

12. A) The local gassy hill might start a huge fire.
    B) There was oil leakage along the Gulf Coast.
    C) The erupting gas might endanger local children.
    D) There were oil deposits below a local gassy hill.
13. A) The massive gas underground.
    B) Their lack of the needed skill.
    C) The sand under the hill.
    D) Their lack of suitable tools.
14. A) It rendered many oil workers jobless.
    B) It was not as effective as he claimed.
    C) It gave birth to the oil drilling industry.
    D) It was not popularized until years later.
15. A) It radically transformed the state's economy.
    B) It resulted in an oil surplus all over the world.
    C) It totally destroyed the state's rural landscape.
    D) It ruined the state's cotton and beef industries.

Section C

Directions: *In this section, you will hear three recordings of lectures or talks followed by three or four questions. The recordings will be played only once. After you hear a question, you must choose the best answer from the four choices marked A), B), C) and D). Then mark the corresponding letter on **Answer Sheet 1** with a single line through the centre.*

Questions 16 to 18 are based on the recording you have just heard.

16. A) Unsuitable jobs.
    B) Bad managers.
    C) Insufficient motivation.
    D) Tough regulations.
17. A) Ineffective training.
    B) Toxic company culture.
    C) Lack of regular evaluation.
    D) Overburdening of managers.
18. A) It collected feedback from both employers and employees.

B) It was conducted from frontline managers' point of view.
C) It provided meaningful clues to solving the problem.
D) It was based only on the perspective of employees.

Questions 19 to 21 are based on the recording you have just heard.

19. A) It is seeing an automation revolution.
    B) It is bringing prosperity to the region.
    C) It is yielding an unprecedented profit.
    D) It is expanding at an accelerating speed.
20. A) It exhausts resources sooner.
    B) It creates a lot of new jobs.
    C) It causes conflicts between employers and employees.
    D) It calls for the retraining of unskilled mining workers.
21. A) They welcome it with open arms.
    B) They will wait to see its effect.
    C) They are strongly opposed to it.
    D) They accept it with reservations.

Questions 22 to 25 are based on the recording you have just heard.

22. A) Their cost to the nation's economy is incalculable.
    B) They kill more people than any infectious disease.
    C) Their annual death rate is about twice that of the global average.
    D) They have experienced a gradual decline since the year of 2017.
23. A) They show a difference between rich and poor nations.
    B) They don't reflect the changes in individual countries.
    C) They rise and fall from year to year.
    D) They are not as reliable as claimed.
24. A) Many of them have increasing numbers of cars on the road.
    B) Many of them are following the example set by Thailand.
    C) Many of them have seen a decline in road-death rates.
    D) Many of them are investing heavily in infrastructure.
25. A) Foster better driving behavior.
    B) Provide better training for drivers.
    C) Abolish all outdated traffic rules.
    D) Impose heavier penalties on speeding.

Part Ⅲ　　　　　　Reading Comprehension　　　　　　(40 minutes)

Section A

Directions: *In this section, there is a passage with ten blanks. You are required to select one word for each blank from a list of choices given in a word bank following the passage. Read the passage through carefully before making your choices. Each choice in the bank is identified by a letter. Please mark the corresponding letter for each item on* **Answer Sheet 2** *with a single line through the centre. You may not use any of the words in the bank more than once.*

　　I'm always baffled when I walk into a pharmacy and see shelves bursting with various vitamins, extracts and other supplements, all promising to accelerate or promote weight loss. Aisles of marketing genius *belie* (掩饰) the fact that, __26__, weight loss is dictated by the laws of arithmetic. Economist Jessica Irvine wrote a book about how she used math to help her lose more than 18 kilograms. If calories taken in are less than calories __27__, weight shall be lost, and so it is with money.

　　Despite the __28__ of financial products, services and solutions geared towards accumulating wealth, it all begins with the same __29__: getting ahead financially requires a reduction of spending, so that income is greater than expenses. I was reminded of this again recently listening to an interview with Nicole Haddow, the author of *Smashed Avocado*, explaining how she cracked the property market at 31. It was quite a __30__, given where she had been two years earlier.

　　Nicole didn't celebrate her 30th birthday as she had __31__. She was sobbing at the dinner table with her parents, with whom she had just moved back in. She had no stable income, $12,000 in credit-card debt and no plan, but to her   32 , her father, an accountant, told her that her financial   33   wasn't as bad as she thought. He said, on her income, with some changes, she would be able to buy an investment unit within two years, which she did.

Nicole admitted she was fortunate, as she was able to live with her parents and   34   her spending — and life — to get herself on track financially. Creating a gap between her income and spending required a paradigm shift and   35   sacrifice and commitment, but by going into financial lockdown, Nicole gained financial independence.

A) abundance	I) impetus
B) astonishment	J) overhaul
C) entailed	K) permanently
D) envisaged	L) plight
E) equation	M) prosper
F) expended	N) shatter
G) feat	O) ultimately
H) fiscally	

Section B

Directions: *In this section, you are going to read a passage with ten statements attached to it. Each statement contains information given in one of the paragraphs. Identify the paragraph from which the information is derived. You may choose a paragraph more than once. Each paragraph is marked with a letter. Answer the questions by marking the corresponding letter on **Answer Sheet 2**.*

France's Beloved Cathedral Only Minutes Away from Complete Destruction

[A] Notre Dame Cathedral in the heart of Paris was within "15 to 30 minutes" of complete destruction as firefighters battled to stop flames reaching its bell towers on Monday evening, French authorities have revealed. A greater disaster was averted by members of the Paris fire brigade, who risked their lives to remain inside the burning monument to create a wall of water between the raging fire and the two towers on the west of the building.

[B] The revelation of how close France came to losing its most famous cathedral emerged as police investigators questioned workers involved in the restoration of the monument to try to establish the cause of the devastating blaze. Paris prosecutor Remy Heitz said that an initial fire alert was sounded at 6:20 pm on Monday evening but no fire was found. The second alert was sounded at 6:43 pm, and the blaze was discovered on the roof.

[C] More than €650 million was raised in a few hours on Tuesday as French business leaders and global corporations announced they would donate to a restoration campaign launched by the president, Emmanuel Macron. But as the emergency services picked through the burnt debris, a row was resurfacing over accusations that the beloved cathedral, immortalised in Victor Hugo's novel, was already crumbling before the fire.

[D] The cathedral is owned by the French state and has been at the centre of a years-long dispute over who should finance restoration work of the collapsing staircases, crumbling statues and cracked walls. Jean-Michel Leniaud, the president of the scientific council at the National Heritage Institute, said: "What happened was bound to happen. The lack of adequate maintenance and daily attention to such a majestic building is the cause of this catastrophe." After the blaze was declared completely extinguished, 15 hours after it started, the junior interior minister, Laurent Nunez, said the structure had been saved but remained vulnerable. He praised the actions of the firefighters but admitted the fate of the cathedral had been uncertain. "They saved the main structure, but it all came down to 15-30 minutes," Nunez said.

[E] In a surprise televised address on Tuesday evening, Macron said he wanted to see the cathedral rebuilt within five years. "The fire at Notre Dame reminds us that we will always have challenges to overcome,"

Macron said. "Notre Dame is our history, our literature, the centre of our life. It is the standard by which we measure our distances. It's so many books, so many paintings. It's the cathedral of every French person, even those who have never visited it. This history is ours and so we will rebuild Notre Dame. It is what the French people expect; it is what our history deserves. It is our deep destiny. We will rebuild Notre Dame so it is even more beautiful than before. I want it done in the next five years. We can do it. After the time of testing comes a time of reflection and then of action."

[F] The fire, which had started at the base of the 93-metre *spire* (尖塔) at about 6:40 pm on Monday, spread through the cathedral's roof, made up of hundreds of oak beams, some dating back to the 13th century. These beams, known as la forêt (the forest) because of their density, formed the cross-shaped roof that ran the length of the central part of the cathedral. As hundreds of tourists and Parisians stood and watched the flames leaping from the roof, there was shock and tears as the cathedral spire caught fire, burned and then collapsed into itself.

[G] A collection of dramatic videos and photos quickly spread across social media, showing the horrifying destruction, and attracting emotional responses from people all over the world. Indeed, within minutes the fire occupied headlines of every major global newspaper and television network. This is not surprising given Notre Dame Cathedral, meaning "Our Lady", is one of the most recognised symbols of the city of Paris attracting millions of tourists every year.

[H] While the world looked on, the 500 firefighters at the scene then battled to prevent the flames from reaching the two main towers, where the cathedral bells hang. If the wooden frame of the towers had caught fire, it could have sent the bells—the largest of which, the Emmanuel Bell, weighs 13 tons — crashing down, potentially causing the collapse of both towers. Police and fire services will spend the next 48 hours assessing the "security and safety" of the 850-year-old structure. Nunez said: "We have identified vulnerabilities throughout the structure, all of which still need securing." As a result, residents of five buildings around the northern side of the cathedral were being temporarily evacuated, he added. Architects have identified three main holes in the structure, in the locations of the spire, the main hall and the upper rooms to the north of the central aisle. Most of the wooden roof beams have been burned, and parts of the concrete holding up the roof have collapsed.

[I] The interior minister, Christophe Castaner, visited the cathedral on Tuesday afternoon to see the extent of the devastation. Ash covered the marble diamond-patterned floor and floated in large pools of grey water from the fire hoses. Behind a heap of blackened oak beams that lay piled up where they had fallen, daylight from vast holes in the cathedral roof lit a golden cross over a statue by Nicolas Coustou, which appeared to have escaped damage. Preliminary inspections also suggested the three *ornate* (装饰华丽的) stained glass "rose" windows appeared to have survived the fire, officials said. However, fire officers have said a complete inventory of the damage will not be possible until the cathedral structure has been deemed safe.

[J] The culture minister, Franck Riester, said religious relics saved from the cathedral were being securely held at the Hotel de Ville, and works of art that sustained smoke damage were being taken to the Louvre, the world's largest art museum, where they would be dried out, repaired and stored. Sixteen copper statues that decorated the spire had been removed for restoration only a few days before the fire. Relics at the top of the spire are believed lost as the spire was destroyed. As well as damage from the heat, which firefighters said reached more than 800℃, experts also need to assess damage from the vast quantities of water firefighters poured into the cathedral. One casualty of this was The Great Organ constructed in the 1730s, which was said to have escaped the flames but been significantly damaged by water.

[K] French political commentators noted the devastating fire had succeeded where Macron had failed in uniting the country. But criticism over the original state of the building is likely to intensify over coming days. Leniaud told *La Croix* newspaper: "This is not about looking for people to blame. The responsibility is collective because this is the most loved monument in the country." Alexandre Gady, an art historian, agreed. "We've been saying for years that the budget for maintaining historic monuments is too low," Gady said. The Paris prosecutor's office has opened an inquiry into "involuntary destruction by fire", indicating they believe the cause of the blaze was accidental rather than criminal.

36. The total amount of damage to Notre Dame Cathedral can be assessed only when its structure is considered safe.
37. Once again people began to argue whether Notre Dame Cathedral was going to collapse even without the fire.
38. The Notre Dame Cathedral catastrophe was said to have helped unite the French nation.
39. The roof of Notre Dame Cathedral was built with large numbers of densely laid-out wood beams.
40. Renovation workers of Notre Dame Cathedral were questioned to find out the cause of the accident.
41. Had the bell towers' wooden frames burned down, the heavy bells would have crashed down.
42. The timely action of the firefighters prevented the fire from reaching the Cathedral's bell towers.
43. Apart from the fire, the water used to extinguish it also caused a lot of damage to Notre Dame Cathedral.
44. There has been argument over the years as to who should pay for the restoration of Notre Dame Cathedral.
45. News of Notre Dame Cathedral catastrophe instantly caught media attention throughout the world.

Section C

Directions: *There are 2 passages in this section. Each passage is followed by some questions or unfinished statements. For each of them there are four choices marked A), B), C) and D). You should decide on the best choice and mark the corresponding letter on* **Answer Sheet 2** *with a single line through the centre.*

Passage One

Questions 46 to 50 are based on the following passage.

We often think of drawing as something that takes inborn talent, but this kind of thinking stems from our misclassification of drawing as, primarily, an art form rather than a tool for learning.

Researchers, teachers, and artists are starting to see how drawing can positively impact a wide variety of skills and disciplines.

Most of us have spent some time drawing before, but at some point, most of us stop drawing. There are people who don't, obviously, and thank god for that: a world without designers and artists would be a very shabby one indeed.

Some argue that so many adults have abandoned drawing because we've miscategorized it and given it a very narrow definition. In his book, *Stick Figures: Drawing as a Human Practice*, Professor D. B. Dowd argues that we have misfiled the significance of drawing because we see it as a professional skill instead of a personal capacity. We mistakenly think of "good" drawings as those which work as recreations of the real world, as realistic illusions. Rather, drawing should be recategorized as a symbolic tool.

Human beings have been drawing for 73,000 years. It's part of what it means to be human. We don't have the strength of *chimpanzees* (大猩猩) because we've given up animal strength to manipulate subtle instruments, like hammers, spears, and — later — pens and pencils. The human hand is an extremely dense network of nerve endings. In many ways, human beings are built to draw.

Some researchers argue that *doodling* (涂画) activates the brain's so-called default circuit — essentially, the areas of the brain responsible for maintaining a baseline level of activity in the absence of other stimuli. Because of this, some believe that doodling during a boring lecture can help students pay attention. In one study, participants were asked to listen to a list of names while either doodling or sitting still. Those who doodled remembered 29 percent more of the names than those who did not.

There's also evidence that drawing talent is based on how accurately someone perceives the world.

The human visual system tends to misjudge size, shape, color, and angles but artists perceive these qualities more accurately than non-artists. Cultivating drawing talent can become an essential tool to improve people's observational skills in fields where the visual is important.

Rather than think of drawing as a talent that some creative people are gifted in, we should consider it as a tool for seeing and understanding the world better — one that just so happens to double as an art form. Both absent-minded doodling and copying from life have been shown to positively affect your memory and visual perception, so complain loudly the next time your school board slashes the art department's budget.

46. What do people generally think about drawing?
    A) It is a gift creative people are endowed with.
    B) It is a skill that is acquired with practice.
    C) It is an art form that is appreciated by all.
    D) It is an ability everyone should cultivate.
47. What do we learn about designers and artists?
    A) They are declining gradually in number.
    B) They are keen on changing shabby surroundings.
    C) They add beauty and charm to the world.
    D) They spend most of their lives drawing.
48. What does Professor D. B. Dowd argue in his book?
    A) Everybody is born with the capacity to draw.
    B) Drawing is a skill that requires special training.
    C) The value of drawing tends to be overestimated.
    D) Drawing should be redefined as a realistic illusion.
49. What have some researchers found from one study about doodling?
    A) It is a must for maintaining a base level of brain activity.
    B) It can turn something boring into something interesting.
    C) It is the most reliable stimulant to activate the brain.
    D) It helps improve concentration and memory.
50. What is characteristic of people with drawing talent?
    A) Sensitivity to cognitive stimulation.
    B) Subtlety of representation.
    C) Accuracy in categorization.
    D) Precision in visual perception.

Passage Two

Questions 51 to 55 are based on the following passage.

The car has reshaped our cities. It seems to offer autonomy for everyone. There is something almost delightful in the detachment from reality of advertisements showing mass-produced cars marketed as symbols of individuality and of freedom when most of their lives will be spent making short journeys on choked roads.

For all the fuss made about top speeds, cornering ability and acceleration, the most useful gadgets on a modern car are those which work when you're going very slowly: parking sensors, sound systems, and navigation apps which will show a way around upcoming traffic jams. This seems to be one of the few areas where the benefit of sharing personal information comes straight back to the sharer: because these apps know where almost all the users are, and how fast they are moving almost all the time, they can spot traffic *congestion* (堵塞) very quickly and suggest ways round it.

The problems comes when everyone is using a navigation app which tells them to avoid everyone else using the same gadget. Traffic jams often appear where no one has enough information to avoid them. When a lucky few have access to the knowledge, they will benefit greatly. But when everyone has perfect information, traffic jams simply spread onto the side roads that seem to offer a way round them.

This new congestion teaches us two things. The first is that the promises of technology will never be realised as fully as we hope; they will be limited by their unforeseen and unintended consequences. Sitting in a more comfortable car in a different traffic jam is pleasant but hardly the liberation that once seemed to be promised. The second is that self-organisation will not get us where we want to go. The efforts of millions of drivers to get ahead do not miraculously produce a situation in which everyone does better than before, but one in which almost everyone does rather worse. Central control and collective organisation can produce smoother and fairer outcomes, though even that much is never guaranteed.

　　Similar limits can be foreseen for the much greater advances promised by self-driving cars. Last week, one operated by the taxi company Uber struck and killed a woman pushing her bicycle across a wide road in Arizona. This was the first recorded death involving a car which was supposed to be fully autonomous. Experts have said that it suggests a "catastrophic failure" of technology.

　　Increasingly, even Silicon Valley has to acknowledge the costs of the *intoxicating* (令人陶醉的) hurry that characterises its culture. What traffic teaches us is that reckless and uncontrolled change is as likely to harm us as it is to benefit us, and that thoughtful regulation is necessary for a better future.

51. What does the author say about car advertisements?
　　A) They portray drivers who enjoy speed on the road.
　　B) They present a false picture of the autonomy cars provide.
　　C) They pursue individuality and originality in design concept.
　　D) They overestimate the potential market of autonomous cars.
52. What does the author imply about the various gadgets on cars?
　　A) They can help to alleviate traffic jams.
　　B) Most of them are as effective as advertised.
　　C) Only some can be put to use under current traffic conditions.
　　D) They are constantly upgraded to make driving easier and safer.
53. What does the author say about the use of navigation apps?
　　A) It is likely to create traffic jams in other places.
　　B) It helps a great deal in easing traffic congestion.
　　C) It sharply reduces the incidence of traffic accidents.
　　D) It benefits those who are learning to drive.
54. What does the author say about technology?
　　A) Its consequences are usually difficult to assess.
　　B) It seldom delivers all the benefits as promised.
　　C) It depends on the required knowledge for application.
　　D) Its benefits are guaranteed by collective wisdom.
55. What key message does the author try to convey in the passage?
　　A) The consequences of technological innovation need not be exaggerated.
　　B) There is always a price to pay to develop technology for a better world.
　　C) Technological innovation should be properly regulated.
　　D) The culture of Silicon Valley ought not to be emulated.

Part Ⅳ　　　　　　　　Translation　　　　　　　　(30 minutes)

Directions: *For this part, you are allowed 30 minutes to translate a passage from Chinese into English. You should write your answer on **Answer Sheet 2**.*

　　青海是中国西北部的一个省份，平均海拔3 000米以上，大部分地区为高山和高原。青海省得名于全国最大的咸水湖青海湖。青海湖被誉为"中国最美的湖泊"，是最受欢迎的旅游景点之一，也是摄影师和艺术家的天堂。

　　青海山川壮丽，地大物博。石油和天然气储量丰富，省内许多城市的经济在石油和天然气工业带动下得到了长足发展。青海尤以水资源丰富而闻名，是中国三大河流长江、黄河和澜沧江的发源地，在中国的水生态中发挥着重要作用。

2021年6月大学英语六级考试真题解析
（第一套）

Part Ⅰ　Writing

成文构思

本文是一篇议论文，主题是"中国脱贫攻坚取得显著成果"，可按照以下思路进行写作。
第一段：描述图表，指出主题"中国脱贫攻坚取得显著成果"。
第二段：分析原因，可以从中国政府采取的诸多措施出发，选择几点进行说明。
第三段：总结，可进一步强调中国政府在脱贫攻坚中的重要作用。

参考范文及译文

　　In the past few years, China has achieved great success in poverty **alleviation**, and the rural population in poverty has witnessed a gradual decrease **year on year**, so has the poverty headcount ratio. According to the chart, the total number of rural people in poverty decreased from nearly 100 million in 2012 to 0 in 2020 and during the same period of time, the poverty headcount ratio descended from about 10% to 0.

　　Obviously, the biggest **credit** for these achievements should be given to the Chinese government which has **implemented** countless policies and carried out so many projects to reduce poverty in rural areas. One of the most important measures the government took was that more financial budget was **allocated** to projects about alleviating poverty. They have built roads in remote areas to make the traffic more convenient, promoting the communication between rural areas and urban cities. They also designed specific programs to promote economic development in different places, like establishing factories to **facilitate** local employment.

　　There is no doubt that if there had been no efforts from the Chinese government, it would be impossible to achieve such remarkable success within just a few years.

　　过去几年，中国脱贫攻坚取得了巨大成功，农村贫困人口逐年减少，贫困人口比例也逐年下降。从图表上看，农村贫困人口总数从2012年的近1亿人下降到2020年的0人，同期，贫困人口比例从10%左右下降到0。

　　显然，这些成就最应该归功于中国政府，中国政府实施了无数政策，进行了诸多农村扶贫项目。政府采取的最重要的措施之一是将更多的财政预算用于扶贫项目。他们在偏远地区修路，使交通更加便利，促进了农村与城市的交流。他们还设计了一些具体的项目来帮助各地的经济发展，比如建立工厂以促进当地就业。

　　毫无疑问，如果没有中国政府的努力，就不可能在短短几年内取得如此显著的成功。

词句点拨

alleviation /əˌliːviˈeɪʃn/ *n.* 减轻；缓和
obviously /ˈɒbviəsli/ *ad.* 显然，显而易见
implement /ˈɪmplɪment/ *v.* 执行，贯彻
facilitate /fəˈsɪlɪteɪt/ *v.* 促进，推动

year on year 逐年
credit /ˈkredɪt/ *n.* 称赞，认可；学分
allocate /ˈæləkeɪt/ *v.* 分配

1. ...has witnessed a gradual decrease year on year, so has...
   ……逐年减少，……也逐年下降。

2. According to the chart, the total number of... decreased from... in... to... in... and during the same period of time, ... descended from... to...
   从图表上看，……总数从……年的……下降到……年的……，同期，……从……下降到……

3. Obviously, the biggest credit for... should be given to...
   显然，……最应该归功于……

4. If there had been no efforts from..., it would be impossible to... within just a few years.
   如果没有……的努力，就不可能在短短几年内……

Part II Listening Comprehension

Section A

Questions 1 to 4 are based on the conversation you have just heard.

听力原文及译文

M: (1) It's my last day at work tomorrow. I'll start my new job in two weeks. My human resources manager wants to conduct an interview with me before I leave.

W: Ah, an exit interview. Are you looking forward to it?

M: I'm not sure how I feel about it. I resigned because I've been unhappy at that company for a long time, but I'm not sure if I should tell them how I really feel.

W: To my way of thinking, there are two main potential benefits that come from unleashing and agitated stream of truth during an exit interview. The first is release. Unburdening yourself of frustration, and perhaps even anger to someone who isn't a friend or close colleague can be wonderfully free.

M: Let me guess. The second is that the criticism will, theoretically, help the organization I'm leaving to improve, making sure employees of the future are less likely to encounter what I did?

W: That's right. But the problem with the company improvement part is that very often it doesn't happen. (2) An exit interview is supposed to be private, but often isn't. In my company, the information gained from these interviews is often not confidential. The information is used as dirt against another manager, or can be traded among senior managers.

M: Now you've got me rethinking what I'll disclose in the interview. (3) There is always a chance that it could affect my reputation and my ability to network in the industry. It is a pretty small industry after all.

W: Anything you initially gained from the instant satisfaction of telling it like it is, you might lose down the track by injuring your future career prospects.

M: Right. (4) <u>Perhaps it'll be better getting things off my chest by going to one of those rate-your-employer websites.</u>

W: You could. And don't do the interview at all. Exit interviews are not mandatory.

男：（1）<u>明天是我最后一天上班，两周后我就要开始一份新工作了。</u>我的人事经理想在我离职前和我谈话。

女：啊，离职面谈。你期待这次面谈吗？

男：我不知道自己对此有何感受。我辞职是因为我在公司老早就待得不开心了，但我不知道是否应该说出我的真实感受。

女：在我看来，离职面谈时无拘无束地大胆吐露真相有两大潜在好处。第一个好处是释放。向一个不是朋友或亲密同事的人吐露自己的沮丧和愤怒会让人感觉极度自由。

男：让我猜一下。第二个好处是，理论上来说，批评意见有助于我即将离开的组织改善自身缺陷，降低未来员工和我有相同境遇的可能性，对吗？

女：没错。但关于公司自我改善这一点的问题是，这通常不会发生。（2）<u>离职面谈理应保密</u>，但公司通常做不到。在我们企业，从这些离职面谈中获得的信息通常无法保密，而是被用作攻击另一位管理者的丑闻，或者被高层领导人用来进行交易。

男：现在你让我觉得我得重新思考一下我要在离职面谈中透漏的信息了。（3）<u>这很有可能影响我的声誉以及我在行业内建立工作关系的能力。</u>毕竟这个行业的圈子很小。

女：最初你从如实讲述的即时满足感中获得的一切，可能都会因为破坏自己未来的职业前景而逐渐消失。

男：没错。（4）<u>也许去一个给雇主打分的网站吐露自己的不满会更好。</u>

女：你可以这么做。根本就不要进行离职面谈，这并非强制性的。

难词总结

human resources manager 人事经理
resign /rɪˈzaɪn/ v. 辞职
disclose /dɪsˈkloʊz/ v. 透露；揭开

look forward to 期待
unburden /ˌʌnˈbɜːdn/ v. 吐露；卸下……的负担
mandatory /ˈmændətəri/ a. 强制性的

题目精析

1. What do we learn about the man from the conversation?

   A) He will tell the management how he really feels.

   B) He will meet his new manager in two weeks.

   C) He is going to attend a job interview.

   D) He is going to leave his present job.

1. 关于这位男士，我们可以从对话中知道什么？
   A）他将告诉经理他的真实感受。
   B）两周后他将与新经理见面。
   C）他要去参加一场求职面试。
   D）他要辞去现在的工作。

   【答案及分析】D。本题问从对话中获得的关于男士的信息。音频中提到，It's my last day at work tomorrow. I'll start my new job in two weeks.（明天是我最后一天上班，两周后我就要开始一份新工作了。）D 项与音频内容相符，其中 leave his present job 是音频中 last day at work 的同义表达，故选 D 项。

2. What does the woman think of the information gained from an exit interview?
   A) It should be kept private.
   B) It should be carefully analyzed.
   C) It can be quite useful to senior managers.
   D) It can improve interviewees' job prospects.

2. 女士怎么看从离职面谈中获得的信息？
   A）它应该被保密。
   B）它应该被仔细分析。
   C）它可能对高层领导很有用。
   D）它可以改善被面谈者的职业前景。

   【答案及分析】A。本题问女士怎么看从离职面谈中获得的信息。音频中提到，An exit interview is supposed to be private（离职面谈理应保密），A 项与音频内容相符，其中 should be kept private 是音频中 is supposed to be private 的同义表达，故选 A 项。

3. Why does the man want to rethink what he will say in the coming exit interview?
   A) It may leave a negative impression on the interviewer.
   B) It may adversely affect his future career prospects.
   C) It may displease his immediate superiors.
   D) It may do harm to his fellow employees.

3. 男士为什么要重新思考他在即将到来的离职面试中要说的话？
   A）它可能会给面谈者留下一个负面印象。
   B）它可能会对他未来的职业前景有负面影响。
   C）它可能会使他的直系领导不快。
   D）它可能会伤害他的同事。

   【答案及分析】B。本题问男士重新思考自己要在离职面谈中所说的话的原因。音频中提到，There is always a chance that it could affect my reputation and my ability to network in the industry.（这很有可能影响我的声誉以及我在行业内建立工作关系的能力。）B 项与音频内容相符，其中 adversely affect his future career prospects 是音频中 affect my reputation and my ability to network in the industry 的总结。故选 B 项。

4. What does the man think he had better do?
   A) Prepare a comprehensive exit report.
   B) Do some practice for the exit interview.
   C) Network with his close friends to find a better employer.
   D) Pour out his frustrations on a rate-your-employer website.

4. 男士认为他最好做什么?

A) 准备一份全面的离职报告。

B) 做一些离职面谈练习。

C) 和他的密友联系，寻找更好的雇主。

D) 在一个给雇主打分的网站上发泄他的挫败感。

【答案及分析】D。本题问男士认为自己应该采取的做法。音频中提到，Perhaps it'll be better getting things off my chest by going to one of those rate-your-employer websites.（也许去一个给雇主打分的网站吐露自己的不满会更好。）D 项与音频内容相符，其中 Pour out his frustrations 是音频中 getting things off my chest 的同义表达，a rate-your-employer website 与音频中的 those rate-your-employer websites 对应。故选 D 项。

Questions 5 to 8 are based on the conversation you have just heard.

听力原文及译文

M: Today, I'm talking to the renowned botanist, Jane Forster.

W: Thank you for inviting me to join you on the show, Henry.

M: (5) Recently, Jane, you've become quite a celebrity, since the release of your latest documentary. Can you tell us a little about it?

W: Well, it follows my expedition to study the vegetation indigenous to the rain forest in equatorial areas of southeast Asia.

M: You certainly get to travel to some very exotic locations.

W: (6) It was far from glamorous, to be honest. The area we visited was accessible only by canoe and the living conditions in the hut were primitive, to say the least. There was no electricity. Our water supply was a nearby stream.

M: How were the weather conditions while you were there?

W: The weather was not conducive to our work at all, since the humidity was almost unbearable. At midday, we stayed in the hut and did nothing. It was too humid to either work or sleep.

M: How long did your team spend in the jungle?

W: Originally, we planned to be there for a month. But in the end, we stayed for only two weeks.

M: Why did you cut the expedition short?

W: (7) Halfway through the trip, we received news that a hurricane was approaching. We had to evacuate on very short notice.

M: That sounds like a fascinating anecdote.

W: It was frightening. The fastest evacuation route was through river rapids. We had to navigate them carrying all of our equipment.

M: So overall was the journey unsuccessful?

W: Absolutely not. (8) We gathered a massive amount of data about the local plant life.

M: Why do you put up with such adverse conditions?

W: Botany is an obsession for me. Many of the destinations I visit have a stunning scenery. I get to meet a variety of people from all over the world.

M: So where will your next destination be?

W: I haven't decided yet.

M: Then we can leave it for another vacation. Thanks.

男：今天，我将对话著名植物学家简·福斯特。

女：感谢你邀请我来参加你的节目，亨利。

男：（5）最近，简，自你的最新纪录片发布以来，你就成了一个大红人。你可以向我们介绍一下你的纪录片吗？

女：嗯，这部纪录片记录了我去东南亚赤道地区研究热带雨林中的原生植被的考察过程。

男：那你肯定要参观一些非常有异国风情的地方。

女：（6）说实话，这一点儿都不吸引人。我们参观的地方只能乘独木舟到达，毫不夸张地说，我们临时住所的生活条件非常简陋。那里没有电，水源就是附近的一条小溪。

男：你们在那儿时，天气怎么样呢？

女：那里的天气非常不利于我们工作，因为空气中的湿度令人根本无法忍受。中午，我们待在临时住所，什么事都不能做。天气太潮湿了，既不能工作，也无法睡觉。

男：你们的团队在丛林里面待了多久呢？

女：我们原本计划待一个月，但是最后我们只待了两周。

男：你们为什么缩短了考察的时间呢？

女：（7）旅程中途，我们收到消息说一场飓风即将来临。我们必须在短时间内撤离。

男：那听起来像是一个令人着迷的故事。

女：那很吓人。最快的撤离路线要通过河中急流。我们不得不带着所有设备在急流中航行。

男：那么，总的来说，这次旅行没有成功吗？

女：当然不是。（8）我们收集了大量有关当地植物生命的数据。

男：你为什么要忍受如此艰苦的条件呢？

女：我对植物学很痴迷。我去过的许多地方都有着令人惊奇的风景。我还能结识来自世界各地的各种各样的人。

男：那么，你下一个目的地是哪里呢？

女：我还没有决定呢。

男：那我们就下一次休假再揭晓吧。谢谢。

难词总结

renowned /rɪˈnaʊnd/ a. 著名的，有名望的
celebrity /səˈlebrəti/ n. 名人，明星
indigenous /ɪnˈdɪdʒənəs/ a. 本土的，固有的
primitive /ˈprɪmɪtɪv/ a. 简陋的；原始的
evacuate /ɪˈvækjueɪt/ v. 撤离，疏散

题目精析

5. What does the man want Jane Foster to talk about?

A) Her unsuccessful journey. C) Her latest documentary.
B) Her month-long expedition. D) Her career as a botanist.

5. 男士想要简·福斯特谈论一下什么？

A）她的失败旅行。 C）她最新的纪录片。
B）她长达一个月的考察。 D）她作为植物学家的职业。

【答案及分析】C。本题问男士想让简·福斯特谈论的内容。音频中男士提到，Recently, Jane, you've become quite a celebrity, since the release of your latest documentary. Can you tell us a little about it?（最近，简，自你的最新纪录片发布以来，你就成了一个大红人。你可以向我们介绍一下你的纪录片吗？）C项与音频内容相符，其中 latest documentary 是原词复现，故选 C 项。

6. Why does the woman describe her experience as far from glamorous?

A) She had to live like a vegetarian. C) She had to endure many hardships.
B) She was caught in a hurricane. D) She suffered from water shortage.

6. 女士为什么将其经历描述为一点都不吸引人？

A）她必须像素食主义者一样生活。 C）她不得不忍受许多艰难。
B）她遇到了飓风。 D）她遭受了缺水之苦。

【答案及分析】C。本题问女士认为自己的经历不吸引人的原因。音频中提到，It was far from glamorous, to be honest. The area we visited was accessible only by canoe and the living conditions in the hut were primitive, to say the least. There was no electricity. Our water supply was a nearby stream.（说实话，这一点儿都不吸引人。我们参观的地方只能乘独木舟到达，毫不夸张地说，我们临时住所的生活条件非常简陋。那里没有电，水源就是附近的一条小溪。）C项与音频内容相符，其中 many hardship 概括了音频中提到的各种困难，故选 C 项。

7. Why did the woman and those who went with her end their trip halfway?

A) A hurricane was coming. C) They had no more food in the canoe.
B) A flood was approaching. D) They could no longer bear the humidity.

7. 女士和跟她一起前往的人为什么中途结束了他们的旅程？

A）一场飓风即将来临。 C）独木舟里面没有食物了。
B）一场洪水即将来临。 D）他们无法再忍受潮湿的天气了。

【答案及分析】A。本题问女士和其团队中途结束旅程的原因。音频中提到，Halfway through the trip, we received news that a hurricane was approaching. We had to evacuate on very short notice.（旅程中途，我们收到消息说一场飓风即将来临。我们必须在短时间内撤离。）A项是音频内容的同义表达，故选 A 项。

8. What does the woman think of the journey?

A) It was memorable. C) It was uneventful.
B) It was unbearable. D) It was fruitful.

8. 女士认为这次旅程如何？
   A）它令人记忆深刻。　　　　　　C）它很平淡无奇。
   B）它令人无法忍受。　　　　　　D）它收获颇丰。

【答案及分析】D。本题问女士对此次旅程的看法。音频中提到，We gathered a massive amount of data about the local plant life.（我们收集了大量有关当地植物生命的数据。）D项中的 fruitful 是对音频内容的准确概括，故选 D 项。

Section B

Questions 9 to 11 are based on the passage you have just heard.

听力原文及译文

Scientists often use specialized jargon terms while communicating with laymen. Most of them don't realize the harmful effects of this practice. (9) In a new study, people exposed to jargon when reading about subjects like autonomous vehicles and surgical robots later said they were less interested in science than others who read about the same topics, but without the use of specialized terms. They also felt less informed about science and less qualified to discuss science topics. It's noteworthy that it made no difference if the jargon terms were defined in the text. Even when the terms were defined, readers still felt the same lack of engagement as readers who read jargon that wasn't explained.

The problem is that the mere presence of jargon sends a discouraging message to readers. Hillary Schulman, the author of the study, asserts that specialized words are a signal. Jargon tells people that the message isn't for them. There's an even darker side to how people react to jargon. (10) In another study, researchers found that reading scientific articles containing jargon led people to doubt the actual science. They found the opposite, when a text is easier to read, then people are more persuaded. Thus, it's important to communicate clearly when talking about complex science subjects. This is especially true with issues related to public health, like the safety of new medications and the benefits of vaccines. Schulman concedes that the use of jargon is appropriate with scientific audiences. (11) But scientists who want to communicate with the general public need to modify their language. They need to eliminate jargon.

科学家经常在与非专业人士交流时使用特殊的行业术语。他们中的大多数人都没有意识到这种做法带来的负面影响。（9）在一项新的研究中，阅读诸如自动驾驶汽车和外科手术机器人这类主题时，遇到行业术语的读者随后表示他们对科学的兴趣小于那些阅读同样主题但没有遇到行业术语的人。他们还感觉自己更不了解科学，更没有资格谈论科学主题。值得注意的是，在文中对行业术语进行注释也没有什么不同。即便对行业术语进行注释，读者感到缺乏了解的程度也并不比读到没有注释的行业术语的读者低。

问题在于仅仅是行业术语的出现就给读者传达了一种令人沮丧的信息。该研究的作者希拉里·舒尔曼坚称，特殊的词汇是一种信号。行业术语告诉人们这条信息不是给他们看的。关于人们对于行业术语的反应还有更黑暗的一面。（10）在另一项研究中，研究人员发现阅读包含行业术语的科学类文章会让人怀疑真正的科学。当文本容易阅读时，他们发现情况相反，人们更容易被说服。因此，谈论复杂的科学主题时，清楚地交流非常重要。当涉及公共卫生问题时，如新药物的安全性和疫苗的益处，这一点尤为准确。舒尔曼承认对科学领域的受众使用行业术语无可厚非。(11)<u>但是，想要和公众交流的科学家需要修改他们的语言。他们需要消除行业术语。</u>

难词总结

jargon /ˈdʒɑːgən/ n. 行业术语
qualified /ˈkwɒlɪfaɪd/ a. 有资格的，胜任的
persuade /pəˈsweɪd/ v. 说服；使相信
surgical /ˈsɜːdʒɪkl/ a. 外科手术的；外科的
engagement /ɪnˈɡeɪdʒmənt/ n. 对……的了解
vaccine /ˈvæksiːn/ n. 疫苗

题目精析

9. What does the passage say about the use of jargon terms by experts?
   A) It diminishes laymen's interest in science.　　C) It makes their expressions more explicit.
   B) It ensures the accuracy of their arguments.　　D) It hurts laymen's dignity and self-esteem.

9. 文章对于专家使用行业术语一事有何说法？
   A）这降低了非专业人士对科学的兴趣。　　C）这使他们的表述更加清楚。
   B）这保证了他们观点的准确性。　　D）这会伤害非专业人士的尊严和自尊。

【答案及分析】A。本题问音频中对于专家使用行业术语一事的说法。音频中提到，In a new study, people exposed to jargon when reading about subjects like autonomous vehicles and surgical robots later said they were less interested in science than others who read about the same topics, but without the use of specialized terms.（在一项新的研究中，阅读诸如自动驾驶汽车和外科手术机器人这类主题时，遇到行业术语的读者随后表示他们对科学的兴趣小于那些阅读同样主题但没有遇到行业术语的人。）A 项中的 diminishes laymen's interest in science 是音频中 less interested in science 的同义表达，故选 A 项。

10. What do researchers find about people reading scientific articles containing jargon terms?
    A) They can learn to communicate with scientists.　　C) They feel great respect towards scientists.
    B) They tend to disbelieve the actual science.　　D) They will see the complexity of science.

10. 研究人员发现阅读包含行业术语的科学类文章的人会如何？
    A）他们可以学会与科学家交流。　　C）他们对科学家充满敬意。
    B）他们倾向于怀疑真正的科学。　　D）他们将看到科学的复杂性。

【答案及分析】B。本题问阅读包含行业术语的科学类文章的人会如何。音频中提到，In another study, researchers found that reading scientific articles containing jargon led people to doubt the actual science.（在另一项研究中，研究人员发现阅读包含行业术语的科学类文章会让人怀疑真正的科学。）B 项中的 disbelieve the actual science 是音频中 doubt the actual science 的同义表达，故选 B 项。

11. What does Schulman suggest scientists do when communicating with the general public?
    A) Find appropriate topics.　　C) Explain all the jargon terms.
    B) Stimulate their interest.　　D) Do away with jargon terms.

11. 舒尔曼建议科学家在与公众交流时做什么？

A）找到合适的主题。　　　　　　　C）解释所有的行业术语。

B）激发他们的兴趣。　　　　　　　D）不要提及行业术语。

【答案及分析】D。本题问舒尔曼建议科学家在与公众交流时应该怎么做。音频中提到，But scientists who want to communicate with the general public need to modify their language. They need to eliminate jargon.（但是，想要和公众交流的科学家需要修改他们的语言。他们需要消除行业术语。）D 项 Do away with jargon terms 是音频中 eliminate jargon 的同义表达，故选 D 项。

Questions 12 to 15 are based on the passage you have just heard.

听力原文及译文

At the beginning of the twentieth century, on the Gulf Coast in the US state of Texas, there was a hill where gas leakage was so noticeable that schoolboys would sometimes set the hill on fire.

(12) Patillo Higgins, a disreputable local businessman, became convinced that there was oil below the gassy hill. Oil wells weren't drilled back then. They were essentially dug. (13) The sand under the hill defeated several attempts by Higgins' workers to make a proper hole. Higgins had forecast oil at 1,000 feet, a totally made-up figure. Higgins subsequently hired a mining engineer, Captain Anthony Lucas. (14) After encountering several setbacks, Captain Lucas decided to use a drill, and his innovations created the modern oil drilling industry. In January 1901, at 1,020 feet, almost precisely the depth predicted by Higgins' wild guess, the well roared and suddenly ejected mud and six tons of drilling pipe out of the ground, terrifying those present. For the next nine days until the well was capped, the well poured out more oil than all the wells in America combined.

In those days, Texas was almost entirely rural, with no large cities and practically no industry. (15) Cotton and beef were the foundation of the economy. Higgins' well changed that. The boom made some prospectors millionaires, but the sudden surplus of petroleum was not entirely a blessing for Taxes. In the 1930s, prices crashed to the point that in some parts of the country, oil was cheaper than water. That would become a familiar pattern of the boom-or-bust Texas economy.

20 世纪初，在美国得克萨斯州的墨西哥湾，有一座山的气体泄漏非常明显，以至于学校的男孩子有时会把小山点燃。

（12）当地一位声名狼藉的商人帕蒂罗·希金相信充满气体的山下有石油。当时的油井不是钻出来的，基本上是挖出来的。（13）山下的沙子多次阻碍了希金雇用的工人挖出一个合适的洞的尝试。希金预测石油在地下 1 000 英尺的地方，这个数字完全是他编造的。后来，希金雇用了一位采矿工程师——安东尼·卢卡斯队长。（14）在经历了数次失败后，卢卡斯队长决定使用钻头，他的这一发明创造了现代石油钻探工业。1901 年 1 月，在地下 1 020 英尺处，几乎正好是希金大胆预测的深度，油井轰鸣，突然喷射出泥土和 6 吨钻杆，在场的人都受到了惊吓。在接下来的 9 天里，直到油井封顶，从中喷出的石油比美国所有油井加在一起喷出的石油还要多。

那时，得克萨斯州几乎完全是农村，没有大城市，也几乎没有工业。（15）棉花和牛肉是经济基础。希金的油井改变了这一点。这一繁荣使得一些探矿者成为百万富翁，但是突然的石油过剩对于得克萨斯州来说不完全是福音。20世纪30年代，美国部分地区的石油价格暴跌，出现石油比水还便宜的局面。那将成为得克萨斯州经济繁荣或萧条的常见模式。

难词总结

leakage /ˈliːkɪdʒ/ n. 泄漏（量）
subsequently /ˈsʌbsɪkwəntli/ ad. 后来，随后
surplus /ˈsɜːpləs/ n. 过剩

disreputable /dɪsˈrepjətəbl/ a. 声名狼藉的
eject /ɪˈdʒekt/ v. 喷射，排出
boom-or-bust 繁荣或萧条

题目精析

12. What did Texas businessmen Patillo Higgins believe?
    A) The local gassy hill might start a huge fire.
    B) There was oil leakage along the Gulf Coast.
    C) The erupting gas might endanger local children.
    D) There were oil deposits below a local gassy hill.

12. 得克萨斯州商人帕蒂罗·希金相信什么？
    A）当地充满气体的小山可能会引发一场大火。
    B）墨西哥湾沿岸有石油泄漏。
    C）喷出的气体可能会危及当地的孩子。
    D）当地一座充满气体的小山下面有油田。

【答案及分析】D。本题问商人希金相信什么。音频中提到，Patillo Higgins, a disreputable local businessman, became convinced that there was oil below the gassy hill.（当地一位声名狼藉的商人帕蒂罗·希金相信充满气体的山下有石油。）D项是音频的同义表达，故选D项。

13. What prevented Higgins' workers from digging a proper hole to get the oil?
    A) The massive gas underground.   C) The sand under the hill.
    B) Their lack of the needed skill.   D) Their lack of suitable tools.

13. 什么阻碍了希金雇用的工人挖出一个合适的洞来获取石油？
    A）地下大量的石油。   C）山下的沙子。
    B）他们缺乏所需的技术。   D）他们缺少合适的工具。

【答案及分析】C。本题问阻碍希金雇用的工人挖出合适的洞的原因。音频中提到，The sand under the hill defeated several attempts by Higgins' workers to make a proper hole.（山下的沙子多次阻碍了希金雇用的工人挖出一个合适的洞的尝试。）C项是原词复现，故选C项。

14. What does the passage say about Captain Lucas' drilling method?
    A) It rendered many oil workers jobless.   C) It gave birth to the oil drilling industry.
    B) It was not as effective as he claimed.   D) It was not popularized until years later.

14. 文章对卢卡斯队长的钻井方法有何说法？
    A）它使许多石油工人失业了。   C）它催生了石油钻探工业。
    B）它没有他所说的那样有效。   D）它直到多年后才流行起来。

【答案及分析】C。本题问卢卡斯队长的钻井方法的相关信息。音频中提到，After encountering several setbacks, Captain Lucas decided to use a drill, and his innovations created the modern oil drilling industry.（在经历了数次失败后，卢卡斯队长决定使用钻头，他的这一发明创造了现代石油钻探工业。）C 项中的 gave birth to the oil drilling industry 是音频中 created the modern oil drilling industry 的同义表达，故选 C 项。

15. What do we learn about Texas's oil industry boom?
    A) It radically transformed the state's economy.　　C) It totally destroyed the state's rural landscape.
    B) It resulted in an oil surplus all over the world.　　D) It ruined the state's cotton and beef industries.
15. 我们对得克萨斯州石油行业的繁荣有何了解？
    A）它彻底改变了该州的经济。　　C）它彻底破坏了该州的乡村景观。
    B）它造成了全世界的石油过剩。　　D）它破坏了该州的棉花和牛肉产业。

【答案及分析】A。本题问得克萨斯州石油行业的繁荣带来的影响。音频中提到，Cotton and beef were the foundation of the economy. Higgins' well changed that.（棉花和牛肉是经济基础。希金的油井改变了这一点。）A 项中的 transformed the state's economy 是音频内容的同义表达，故选 A 项。

Section C

Questions 16 to 18 are based on the recording you have just heard.

听力原文及译文

　　Most people dislike their jobs. (16) It's an astonishing but statistical fact, a primary cause of employees' dissatisfaction, according to fresh research, is that many believe they have terrible managers. Few describe their managers as malicious or manipulative, though, while those types certainly exist, they are minority. The majority of managers seemingly just don't know any better. They're often emulating bad managers they've had in the past. It's likely they've never read a management book or attended a management course. They might not have even reflected on what good management looks like and how it would influence their own management style. The researchers interviewed employees about their managers. Beginning with a question about the worst manager they had ever had. From this, the researchers came up with four main causes of why some managers are perceived as being simply awful at their jobs. (17-1) The first cause was company culture, which was seen by employees as enabling poor management practices. It was specifically stressful work environments, minimal training, and a lack of accountability that were found to be the most blame worthy.

　　Often a manager's superiors can effectively encourage a manager's distasteful behavior when they fail to discipline the person's wrong doings. (17-2) Such workplaces are sometimes described as toxic. The second cause was attributed to the managers' characteristics: those deemed to be most destructive were odd people, those who without drive, those allow personal problems into the workplace, and those with an unpleasant temperament or personality in general. The third cause of poor management was associated with their deficiency of qualifications. Not so much the form of variety one obtains from a university but the informal variety that comes from credible work experience and professional accomplishments. The fourth cause concerned managers who've been promoted for reasons other than potential. One reason in particular why these people had been promoted was that they had been around the longest. It wasn't their skill set, or other merits that got them the job, it was their tenure. (18) A point worth making is that the study was based only on the perspective of employees. The researchers didn't ask senior leaders what they thought of their front-line managers. It's quite possible, they are content with how the individuals they promoted are now performing, merrily ignorant of the damage they're actually causing, which might explain why, as the researchers conclude, those same middle managers are usually unaware that they are a bad manager.

大多数人都讨厌自己的工作。（16）这是一个令人震惊但源于统计的事实，根据最新研究，员工产生不满的一个主要原因是他们认为自己的经理很糟糕。但很少有人将他们的经理描述为恶毒或善于摆布他人，虽然这种人确实存在，但只是少数。大多数经理似乎只是不知道如何做得更好。他们经常仿效自己以前遇到过的糟糕的经理。他们很有可能从未阅读过一本管理类书籍或参加过一门管理类课程。他们可能从未思考过好的管理是什么样子，以及这将如何影响他们自己的管理风格。就对经理的看法，研究人员采访了一些员工。第一个问题就是关于他们遇到过的最糟糕的经理。据此，研究人员提出了经理被认为不擅长管理工作的四个原因。（17-1）第一个原因是公司文化，员工认为这会导致糟糕的管理行为。最应该受到指责的就是充满压力的工作环境、极少的培训和缺少问责制。

通常，当管理者的上级没能惩罚一个人的错误行为时，就是在有效地鼓励管理者令人反感的行为。（17-2）这样的工作场所有时被描述为有毒的。第二个原因归咎于管理者的性格特点：被认为最具破坏性的是那些奇怪的人、没有动力的人、将私人问题带到工作场所的人，以及那些脾气或性格令人不快的人。管理不善的第三个原因与资质不足有关。与其说是从大学里面学到的多样性的形式，不如说是来自可靠的工作经验和专业成就的非正式的多样性。第四大原因与因潜力以外的原因晋升的管理者有关。这些人晋升的一个特别原因是他们在公司待的时间最长。他们获得管理岗位不是因为他们的技能或其他优点，而是他们的任职时间。（18）值得一提的是，该研究仅基于雇员的观点。研究人员没有询问高层领导对他们的一线管理者的看法。很有可能，他们对于自己提拔的管理者现在的表现很满意，毫无顾忌地忽视他们实际造成的破坏。研究人员总结道，这可能就解释了为什么相似的中层管理者通常没有意识到自己是一个糟糕的经理。

难词总结

statistical /stəˈtɪstɪk(ə)l/ *a.* 统计的；统计学的
manipulative /məˈnɪpjələtɪv/ *a.* 善于摆布（他人）的
reflect /rɪˈflekt/ *v.* 深思，反省
accountability /əˌkaʊntəˈbɪləti/ *n.* 责任
destructive /dɪˈstrʌktɪv/ *a.* 破坏性的

malicious /məˈlɪʃəs/ *a.* 恶毒的，恶意的
emulate /ˈemjuleɪt/ *v.* 效仿，模仿
minimal /ˈmɪnɪml/ *a.* 极少的
discipline /ˈdɪsəplɪn/ *v.* 惩罚，处分
temperament /ˈtemprəmənt/ *n.* 脾气，性格

题目精析

16. What is a primary cause of employee dissatisfaction according to recent research?

    A) Unsuitable jobs.　　　　　　　　C) Insufficient motivation.

    B) Bad managers.　　　　　　　　　D) Tough regulations.

16. 根据最近的研究，员工不满的一个主要原因是什么？

　　A）不合适的工作。　　　　　　　　C）缺乏动力。

　　B）糟糕的经理。　　　　　　　　　D）严厉的规则。

　　【答案及分析】B。本题问员工不满的一个主要原因。音频中提到，It's an astonishing but statistical fact, a primary cause of employees' dissatisfaction, according to fresh research, is that many believe they have terrible managers.（这是一个令人震惊但源于统计的事实，根据最新研究，员工产生不满的一个主要原因是他们认为自己的经理很糟糕。）B项 Bad managers 是音频中 terrible managers 的同义表达，故选 B 项。

17. What is one of the causes for poor management practices?

　　A) Ineffective training.　　　　　　C) Lack of regular evaluation.

　　B) Toxic company culture.　　　　　D) Overburdening of managers.

17. 导致糟糕的管理行为的一大原因是什么？

　　A）缺少培训。　　　　　　　　　　C）缺少例行考评。

　　B）有毒的公司文化。　　　　　　　D）经理压力过大。

　　【答案及分析】B。本题问导致糟糕的管理行为的原因。音频中提到，The first cause was company culture, which was seen by employees as enabling poor management practices.（第一个原因是公司文化，员工认为这会导致糟糕的管理行为。）后面又提到，Such workplaces are sometimes described as toxic.（这样的工作场所有时被描述为有毒的。）B项中的 Toxic 和 company culture 均是原词复现，故选 B 项。

18. What do we learn about the study on job dissatisfaction?

　　A) It collected feedback from both employers and employees.

　　B) It was conducted from frontline managers' point of view.

　　C) It provided meaningful clues to solving the problem.

　　D) It was based only on the perspective of employees.

18. 关于对工作不满的研究，我们知道什么？

　　A）它收集了来自雇主和雇员双方的反馈。

　　B）它是站在一线经理的立场上进行的。

　　C）它提供了有意义的线索来解决问题。

　　D）它仅基于雇员的观点。

　　【答案及分析】D。本题问有关工作不满的研究的信息。音频中提到，A point worth making is that the study was based only on the perspective of employees.（值得一提的是，该研究仅基于雇员的观点。）D 项是原词复现，故选 D 项。

Questions 19 to 21 are based on the recording you have just heard.

听力原文及译文

　　With the use of driverless vehicles seemingly inevitable, mining companies in the vast Australian desert state of Western Australia are definitely taking the lead. Iron ore is a key ingredient in steel-making. The mining companies here produce almost 300 million tons of iron ore a year. The 240 giant autonomous trucks in use, in the Western Australian mines, can weigh 400 tons, fully loaded, and travel at speeds of up to sixty kilometers per hour. They are a technological leap, transporting iron ore along routes which run for hundreds of kilometers from mines to their destinations. Here when the truck arrives at its destination, staff in the operation center direct it precisely where to unload. Vast quantities of iron ore are then transported by autonomous trains to ocean ports. Advocates argue these automated vehicles will change mining forever. (19) It may only be five years before the use of automation technology leads to a fully robotic mine. A range of factors has pushed Western Australia's desert region to the lead of this automation revolution. These include the huge size of the mines, the scale of equipment and the repetitive nature of some of the work. Then there's the area's remoteness, at 502,000 square kilometers. It can sometimes make recruiting staff a challenge. Another consideration is the risks when humans interact with large machinery. There are also the financial imperatives. The ongoing push by the mining corporations to be more productive and more efficient is another powerful driver in embracing automation technology. The concept of a fully autonomous mine is a bit of a misleading term, however. (20) This is because the more technology is put into the field, the more people are needed to deploy, maintain and improve it. The automation and digitization of the industry is creating a need for different jobs. These include data scientists and engineers in automation and artificial intelligence. The mining companies claim automation and robotics present opportunities to make mining more sustainable and safer. Employees will be offered a career that is even more fulfilling and more rewarding. (21) Workers' unions have accepted the inevitability of the introduction of new technology. But they still have reservations about the rise of automation technology. Their main concern is the potential impact on remote communities. As automation spreads further, the question is how these remote communities will survive when the old jobs are eliminated. And this may well prove to be the most significant impact of robotic technology in many places around the world.

使用无人驾驶汽车似乎不可避免，而西澳大利亚州广袤沙漠地区的矿业公司无疑是此举的领头羊。铁矿石是炼钢的关键原料。这里的矿业公司每年生产近3亿吨铁矿石。西澳大利亚矿区正在使用的240辆大型自动卡车满载时重达400吨，并以高达每小时60千米的速度行驶。这是一次技术飞跃，沿着从矿区到目的地数百千米的路径运输铁矿石。当卡车到达目的地时，操控中心的工作人员准确地指导在哪里卸货。然后，大量的铁矿石被自动列车运送至海洋港口。倡导者认为这些自动汽车将永远改变采矿业。(19) 可能只需要5年时间，自动驾驶技术的使用就会使矿山完全自动化。一系列因素促使西澳大利亚州的沙漠地区成为这场自动化革命的领头羊。这些因素包括矿山和采矿装备的巨大规模，以及一些工作重复的本质。其次是矿区所处之处偏远，有502 000平方千米。这有时会使得招聘员工成为一大困难。另一个考虑因素是人与大型机器互动时可能产生的风险。还有财务方面的要求。矿业公司对提高生产力和生产效率的持续要求是欣然接受自动化技术的另一大有力驱动。但是，完全自动化的矿山这一概念有点误导性。(20) 这是因为矿区使用的科技越多，就需要越多人来部署、维护和改善它们。该产业的自动化和数字化正在创造对不同工作的需求。其中包括自动化和人工智能领域的数据科学家和工程师。矿业公司声称自动化和机器人技术提供了使采矿业更加可持续和更安全的机会。员工将获得成就感更高和回报更好的工作。(21) 工会已经接受了引进新技术的必然性。但是他们对自动化技术的兴起仍有所保留。他们的主要担忧是对偏远地区产生的潜在影响。

自动化技术进一步扩张带来的问题是，当旧时的工作岗位消失时，偏远地区将如何生存。这可能是机器人技术对世界上许多地方造成的最严重的影响。

难词总结

inevitable /ɪnˈevɪtəbl/ a. 不可避免的
ingredient /ɪnˈɡriːdiənt/ n. 原料，成分
recruit /rɪˈkruːt/ v. 招聘
deploy /dɪˈplɔɪ/ v. 部署
eliminate /ɪˈlɪmɪneɪt/ v. 消除，根除

take the lead 带头，领先
precisely /prɪˈsaɪsli/ ad. 准确地
productive /prəˈdʌktɪv/ a. 多产的；有效益的
fulfilling /fʊlˈfɪlɪŋ/ a. 令人满意的

题目精析

19. What does the passage say about the mining industry in Western Australia?

 A) It is seeing an automation revolution.
 B) It is bringing prosperity to the region.
 C) It is yielding an unprecedented profit.
 D) It is expanding at an accelerating speed.

19. 文章对于西澳大利亚州的采矿业有何说法？

 A）它正在见证一场自动化革命。
 B）它正在为该地区带来繁荣。
 C）它正在产生前所未有的利润。
 D）它正在以前所未有的速度扩张。

【答案及分析】A。本题问西澳大利亚州采矿业的相关信息。音频中提到，It may only be five years before the use of automation technology leads to a fully robotic mine. A range of factors has pushed Western Australia's desert region to the lead of this automation revolution.（可能只需要 5 年时间，自动驾驶技术的使用就会使矿山完全自动化。一系列因素促使西澳大利亚州的沙漠地区成为这场自动化革命的领头羊。）A 项中的 automation revolution 是原词复现，故选 A 项。

20. What is the impact of the digitization of the mining industry?

 A) It exhausts resources sooner.
 B) It creates a lot of new jobs.
 C) It causes conflicts between employers and employees.
 D) It calls for the retraining of unskilled mining workers.

20. 采矿业数字化的影响是什么？

 A）它会更早耗尽资源。
 B）它会创造许多新的工作。
 C）它会引发雇主和雇员之间的冲突。
 D）它要求重新培训没有技术的采矿工人。

【答案及分析】B。本题问采矿业数字化的影响。音频中提到，This is because the more technology is put into the field, the more people are needed to deploy, maintain and improve it. The automation and digitization of the industry is creating a need for different jobs.（这是因为矿区使用的科技越多，就需要越多人来部署、维护和改善它们。该产业的自动化和数字化正在创造对不同工作的需求。）B 项是对音频内容的概括，故选 B 项。

21. What is the attitude of workers' unions towards the introduction of new technology?

A) They welcome it with open arms.　　C) They are strongly opposed to it.

B) They will wait to see its effect.　　D) They accept it with reservations.

21. 工会对于引进新技术的态度是什么？

A）他们敞开怀抱欢迎它。　　C）他们强烈地反对它。

B）他们等着看它的效果。　　D）他们有所保留地接受它。

【答案及分析】D。本题问工会对引进新技术的态度。音频中提到，Workers' unions have accepted the inevitability of the introduction of new technology. But they still have reservations about the rise of automation technology.（工会已经接受了引进新技术的必然性。但是他们对自动化技术的兴起仍有所保留。）D项是对音频内容的总结，其中accept和reservations是原词复现，故选D项。

Questions 22 to 25 are based on the recording you have just heard.

听力原文及译文

　　(22) According to official statistics, Thailand's annual road death rate is almost double the global average. Thai people know that their roads are dangerous, but they don't know this could easily be changed. Globally, road accidents kill more people every year than any infectious disease. Researchers at the Institute for Health Metrics and Evaluation in America put the death toll in 2017 at 1.24 million. (23) According to the institute, the overall number of deaths has been more or less static since the turn of the century. But that disguises a lot of changes in individual countries. In many poor countries, road accidents are killing more people than ever before. Those countries have swelling young populations of fast-growing fleet of cars and motorbikes and a limited supply of surgeons. It is impossible to know for sure, because official statistics are so inadequate. But deaths are thought to have risen by 40% since 1990 in many low income countries. In many rich countries, by contrast, roads are becoming even safer. In Estonia and Ireland, for example, the number of deaths has fallen by about two thirds since the late 1990s. (24) But the most important and intriguing changes are taking place in middle income countries, which contain most of the world's people and have some of the most dangerous roads. According to researchers in China and South Africa, traffic deaths have been falling since 2000. And in India since 2012, and the Philippines reached its peak four years ago. The question is whether Thailand can soon follow suit. Rob Mckinney, head of the International Road Assessment Program, says that all countries tend to go through three phases. They begin with poor, slow roads. In the second phase, as they grow wealthier, they pave the roads, allowing traffic to move faster and pushing up the death rate. Lastly, in the third phase, countries act to make their roads safer. The trick, then, is to reach the third stage sooner by focusing earlier and more closely on fatal accidents. How to do that? (25) The solution lies not just in better infrastructure, but in better social incentives. Safe driving habits are practices which people know they should follow but often don't. Dangerous driving is not a fixed cultural trait as some imagine. People respond to incentives such as traffic laws that are actually enforced.

　　（22）根据官方数据，泰国每年的道路死亡率几乎是全球平均水平的两倍。泰国人民知道他们的道路很危险，但是他们不知道这很容易改变。在全球范围内，道路交通事故每年致死的人数比任传染病都多。美国卫生计量与评价研究所的研究人员估计，2017年的道路交通死亡人数为124万。（23）根据该研究所，道路交通死亡总人数自世纪之交以来保持不变。但是这掩盖了个别国家发生的许多变化。在许多贫穷国家，道路交通事故致死的人数比以前更多。那些国家拥有小汽车和摩托车的年轻人数量迅速增加，而外科医生却数量不足。想要知道确切数字是不可能的，因为官方统计数据不足。但是人们认为一些低收入国家的道路交通死亡人数自1990年开始上升了40%。许多富裕国家的情况相反，道路正在变得越来越安全。例如，在爱沙尼亚和爱尔兰，死亡人数自20世纪90年代以来大约下降了2/3。（24）但是，最重要且最有趣的变化正发生在中等收入国家，这些国家容纳了世界上大多数人口，且拥有一些最危险的道路交通。根据中国和南非的研究人员所说，他们的道路交通死亡人数自2000年开始下降，印度的道路交通死亡人数从2012年开始下降，菲律宾的道路交通死亡人数在4年前达到顶峰。问题是泰国能否很快跟进。国际道路评估项目负责人罗伯·麦金尼说，所有国家都倾向于经历三个阶段。他们的道路交通一开始又差又慢。在第二个阶段，随着他们变得富有，他们开始铺路，使得交通更加快速，同时也提高了死亡率。最后，在第三个阶段，国家开始行动，使其道路更加安全。于是，诀窍就是通过更早、更紧密地关注致命的事故来更快地达到第三阶段。怎么做呢？（25）解决办法不仅在于更好的基础设施，还在于更好的社会激励。人们知道应该遵守安全驾驶的习惯，却又不去遵守。危险驾驶不像一些人所想象的那样是一种固定的文化特征。人们会对实际执行的激励措施有所反应，如交通规则。

难词总结

infectious /ɪnˈfekʃəs/ a. 传染性的
death toll 死亡人数
follow suit 跟着做；学样

evaluation /ɪˌvæljuˈeɪʃn/ n. 评估，评价
disguise /dɪsˈɡaɪz/ v. 掩饰，隐瞒
incentive /ɪnˈsentɪv/ n. 激励，刺激

题目精析

22. What does the speaker say about traffic accidents in Thailand?

A) Their cost to the nation's economy is incalculable.
B) They kill more people than any infectious disease.
C) Their annual death rate is about twice that of the global average.
D) They have experienced a gradual decline since the year of 2017.

22. 说话者对泰国的交通事故有何说法？

A）它们对该国经济造成的损失不可估量。
B）它们致死的人数比任何传染病都多。
C）它们每年的死亡率大约是全球平均水平的两倍。
D）它们从2017年开始逐渐下降。

【答案及分析】C。本题问说话者对泰国交通事故的说法。音频第一句便提到，According to official statistics, Thailand's annual road death rate is almost double the global average.（根据官方数据，泰国每年的道路死亡率几乎是全球平均水平的两倍。）C项中的 twice that of the global average 是音频中 double the global average 的同义表达，故选C项。

23. What do we learn from an American institute's statistics regarding road deaths?

   A) They show a difference between rich and poor nations.

   B) They don't reflect the changes in individual countries.

   C) They rise and fall from year to year.

   D) They are not as reliable as claimed.

23. 我们可以从美国一家研究所有关道路交通死亡的数据中知道什么？

   A）它们显示了富裕国家和贫穷国家之间的差异。

   B）它们没有反映出个别国家发生的变化。

   C）它们每年都有升有降。

   D）它们不像声称的那样可靠。

   【答案及分析】B。本题问美国一家研究所有关道路交通死亡的数据的信息。音频中提到，According to the institute, the overall number of deaths has been more or less static since the turn of the century. But that disguises a lot of changes in individual countries.（根据该研究所，道路交通死亡总人数自世纪之交以来保持不变。但是这掩盖了个别国家发生的许多变化。）B 项中的 don't reflect the changes in individual countries 是音频中 disguises a lot of changes in individual countries 的同义表达，故选 B 项。

24. What is said about middle income countries?

   A) Many of them have increasing numbers of cars on the road.

   B) Many of them are following the example set by Thailand.

   C) Many of them have seen a decline in road-death rates.

   D) Many of them are investing heavily in infrastructure.

24. 有关中等收入国家，音频中说了什么？

   A）许多国家道路上的车越来越多。

   B）许多国家效仿泰国的例子。

   C）许多国家见证了道路交通死亡率的下降。

   D）许多国家在基础设施上进行了大量投资。

   【答案及分析】C。本题问中等收入国家的相关情况。音频中提到，But the most important and intriguing changes are taking place in middle income countries, which contain most of the world's people and have some of the most dangerous roads. According to researchers in China and South Africa, traffic deaths have been falling since 2000. And in India since 2012, and the Philippines reached its peak four years ago.（但是，最重要且最有趣的变化正发生在中等收入国家，这些国家容纳了世界上大多数人口，且拥有一些最危险的道路交通。根据中国和南非的研究人员所说，他们的道路交通死亡人数自 2000 年开始下降，印度的道路交通死亡人数从 2012 年开始下降，菲律宾的道路交通死亡人数在 4 年前达到顶峰。）C 项是对音频内容的概括总结，故选 C 项。

25. What else could be done to reduce fatal road accidents in addition to safer roads?

   A) Foster better driving behavior.   C) Abolish all outdated traffic rules.

   B) Provide better training for drivers.   D) Impose heavier penalties on speeding.

25. 除了更加安全的道路，还可以做什么来减少致命的道路交通事故？

A）养成更好的驾驶行为。　　C）取消所有过时的交通规则。
B）为驾驶员提供更好的训练。　　D）向超速驾驶实施更重的惩罚。

【答案及分析】A。本题问减少道路交通事故的方法。音频中提到，The solution lies not just in better infrastructure, but in better social incentives. Safe driving habits are practices which people know they should follow but often don't. Dangerous driving is not a fixed cultural trait as some imagine. People respond to incentives such as traffic laws that are actually enforced.（解决办法不仅在于更好的基础设施，还在于更好的社会激励。人们知道应该遵守安全驾驶的习惯，却又不去遵守。危险驾驶不像一些人所想象的那样是一种固定的文化特征。人们会对实际执行的激励措施有所反应，如交通规则。）A 项中的 better driving behavior 是音频中 Safe driving habits 的同义表达，故选 A 项。

Part Ⅲ　Reading Comprehension

Section A

全文翻译

当我走进药店，看到架子上塞满各种承诺有助于促进减肥的维生素、萃取物和其他补品时，我总是很疑惑。药店货架营销天才掩饰了一个事实——归根结底，减肥是由算数法则决定的。经济学家杰西卡·欧文写了一本书，这本书讲述了她如何利用数学帮助自己减掉 18 公斤的体重。如果摄入的卡路里比消耗的卡路里少，体重就会减少。关于金钱，也是如此。

尽管有大量旨在积累财富的金融产品、服务和方法，但这些都始于同样一个等式：获得经济方面的成功需要减少开支，这样收入才会高于开销。我再次想到这点是因为近期听了妮可·哈多的访谈，她是《牛油果泥》的作者，她在访谈中解释了自己是如何在 31 岁时打入房地产市场的。与她两年前的状态相比，这确实是一项伟大的成就。

妮可没有像她所设想的那样庆祝她的 30 岁生日。她在与父母共进晚餐时啜泣起来，当时她刚搬回父母家。她没有稳定的收入，信用卡负债 12 000 美元，也没有什么计划，但令她惊奇的是，她的会计师父亲告诉她，她的经济困境没有她想的那么糟糕。他说，对她的收入做出一点改变，她就能够在两年之内购买一套投资公寓，她也确实这么做了。

妮可承认她很幸运，因为她可以和她的父母住在一起，并彻底改变她的开销——还有生活——让自己在经济上步入正轨。使她的收入多于开销需要范式转变以及牺牲和决心，但是通过限制经济活动，妮可获得了经济独立。

难词总结

baffle /ˈbæfl/ v. 使困惑　　　　　　　　　burst with 充满
arithmetic /əˈrɪθmətɪk/ n. 算数　　　　　paradigm /ˈpærədaɪm/ n. 典范，范例
feat /fi:t/ n. 功绩　　　　　　　　　　　overhaul /ˌəʊvəˈhɔ:l/ v. 彻底改变
plight /plaɪt/ n. 困境

题目精析

26. O。根据句子结构可知，空格处需要填入一个副词，修饰整个句子。所给选项中 H 项 fiscally（财政上）、K 项 permanently（永久地）和 O 项 ultimately（根本上；最终）符合语法要求，空格所在部分意为：_____，减肥是由算数法则决定的。三个选项中 ultimately 代入后最符合语义，故选 O 项。

27. F。根据句子结构可知，空格处需要填入一个过去分词，修饰 calories。所给选项中只有 C 项 entailed（需要）、D 项 envisaged（设想）和 F 项 expended（消耗）符合语法要求。根据常识可知，当摄入的卡路里低于消耗的卡路里时，体重会减少，expended 代入后符合语义，故选 F 项。

28. A。根据句子结构可知，空格处需要填入一个名词，所给选项中 A 项 abundance（大量）、B 项 astonishment（惊奇）、E 项 equation（等式）、G 项 feat（功绩，壮举）、I 项 impetus（动力；促进）和 L 项 plight（困境）符合语法要求。根据空格所在句开头的 Despite 可知，前半句与后半句之间是转折的关系，由后面的 all begins with the same 可知，前面应表示"大量的金融产品……"，A 项填入后符合语义逻辑，故选 A 项。

29. E。根据句子结构可知，空格处需要填入一个名词，B 项 astonishment（惊奇）、E 项 equation（等式）、G 项 feat（功绩，壮举）、I 项 impetus（动力；促进）和 L 项 plight（困境）符合语法要求。根据语义可知，equation 代入后最符合语境，故选 E 项。

30. G。根据句子结构可知，空格处需要填入一个可数名词单数，且以辅音音素开头，G 项 feat（功绩，壮举）和 L 项 plight（困境）符合语法要求。结合上文提到的她打入房地产市场可知，此处指她取得的成就，feat 符合语义，故选 G 项。

31. D。根据句子结构可知，空格处需要填入一个过去分词，与 had 构成过去完成时态。所给选项中只有 C 项 entailed（需要）和 D 项 envisaged（设想）符合语法要求。envisaged 代入原文后意为"没有像她所设想的那样庆祝她的 30 岁生日"，符合语境，故选 D 项。

32. B。根据句子结构可知，空格处需要填入一个名词。所给选项中还剩 B 项 astonishment（惊奇）、I 项 impetus（动力；促进）和 L 项 plight（困境）符合语法要求。根据前面提到的她没钱且负债和后面提到的她的经济没有所想的那么糟糕，可知上下文在语义上为对比关系，astonishment 代入后意为"令她惊奇的是"，符合上下文的逻辑，故选 B 项。

33. L。根据句子结构可知，空格处需要填入一个名词。所给选项中还剩 I 项 impetus（动力；促进）和 L 项 plight（困境）符合语法要求。根据前面提到的她没钱且负债，可知她陷入了经济困境，plight 代入后符合语境，故选 L 项。

34. J。根据句子结构可知，空格处需要填入一个及物动词，与 her spending — and life 构成动宾搭配。且空格处所填的动词与 live 并列，故也应该填动词原形。所给选项中 J 项 overhaul（彻底改变）、M 项 prosper（使繁荣）和 N 项 shatter（使破碎）符合语法要求。overhaul 代入原文后意为"彻底改变她的开销——还有生活"，符合语境，故选 J 项。

35. C。根据句子结构可知，空格处需要填入一个动词，该动词与前面的 required 并列，因此应填动词的过去式。剩下的选项中只有 C 项 entailed（需要）符合语法要求，代入后意为"需要牺牲和决心"，符合语境，故选 C 项。

Section B

全文翻译

法国人民钟爱的大教堂只差几分钟就被完全毁灭了

[A] 法国当局透露,周一晚上,当消防员奋力阻止火势蔓延至巴黎中心的巴黎圣母院钟楼时,该大教堂避免了在"15~30分钟"内被彻底毁坏的命运。巴黎消防队冒着生命危险,留在被大火吞噬的建筑内,在熊熊烈火与建筑西侧的两座钟楼之间筑起一道水墙,避免了一场更大的灾难。

[B] 当警方调查人员询问参与巴黎圣母院修缮的工作人员,试着确认这场毁灭性火灾的原因时,法国差一点就失去其最著名的大教堂的真相浮出水面。巴黎检察官雷米·海茨说,首次火灾警报在周一下午6点20分响起,但是没有发现起火点。第二次警报在下午6点43分响起,并在屋顶发现了火光。

[C] 当法国企业领导者和跨国公司宣布他们将向总统埃马纽埃尔·马克龙发起的修复运动捐款时,星期二几个小时内就筹集了6.5亿欧元。但是当紧急救援人员清理被烧坏的残骸时,一场争论再次出现,有人指控这座在维克多·雨果的小说中不朽的、人们钟爱的大教堂在起火之前就已经摇摇欲坠了。

[D] 巴黎圣母院归法国国家所有,数年来一直处于谁来支付修复坍塌的楼梯、摇摇欲坠的雕塑和破裂的墙壁的费用的争议中心。国家遗产研究所科学委员会主席让-米歇尔·勒尼奥表示:"已发生的事情必然会发生。对该伟大建筑维护和日常关注的不足导致了这次灾难。"火灾开始15小时后,(消防队)宣布火势被完全扑灭,内政部初级部长劳伦特·努涅斯表示,该建筑被救了下来,但是仍然很脆弱。他表扬了消防员的举动,但是也承认该建筑的命运还不确定。"他们救下了建筑的主体架构,但归根结底在于那15~30分钟的时间。"努涅斯表示。

[E] 周二晚上,在一场令人惊讶的电视讲话中,马克龙表示他希望在5年之内看到巴黎圣母院被重建。"巴黎圣母院的火灾提醒我们挑战无时不在,"马克龙说,"巴黎圣母院是我们的历史,我们的文学,是我们生活的中心。它是我们测量自己差距的标准。这里收藏了如此多的书籍和画作。它是每个法国人的大教堂,甚至包括那些从未参观过该教堂的人。这个历史是我们的,所以我们将重建巴黎圣母院。这是法国人民所期待的,这也是我们的历史所值得的。这是我们深深扎根的命运。我们将重建巴黎圣母院,所以它会比以前更加美丽。我希望它的重建能在未来5年之内完成。我们能够做到。考验降临后,我们便需要反思,然后采取行动。"

[F] 这场大火在周一下午6点40分左右开始,起火点在93米高的尖塔底部,随后蔓延至教堂屋顶,该屋顶是由数百根橡木梁建成的,其中有些橡木梁可追溯至13世纪。这些横梁被称为"森林",因为它们排列非常紧密,它们构成贯穿大教堂中心部分的十字形屋顶。数百名游客和巴黎人站在那里,看着火焰从屋顶窜出,当尖塔着火、被烧毁并倒塌时,人们震惊不已,还流下了眼泪。

[G] 许多令人印象深刻的视频和照片很快在社交媒体上传播,展示了令人震惊的毁坏(场景),触动了全世界人民的感情。事实上,在几分钟之内,这场大火就成了全球所有大型报纸和电视广播公司的头条新闻。这并不令人惊奇,因为巴黎圣母院——意为"我们的女士"——是巴黎每年吸引数百万名游客的最著名的城市标志之一。

[H] 当全世界都在关注时,现场的 500 名消防员在努力阻止火势蔓延至两座主楼,大教堂的钟就挂在那里。如果钟楼的木质结构着火了,那些钟可能会坠毁,其中最大的是重达 13 吨的艾曼纽钟,这可能会导致两座钟楼的倒塌。警察和消防将在接下来的 48 个小时评估这座有着 850 年历史的建筑的安全性。努涅斯表示:"我们已经找出整个建筑的弱点,这些都还需要保护。"因此,大教堂北面五栋建筑中的居民都暂时撤离了,他补充说。建筑学家检测到了建筑中的 3 个漏洞,分别在尖塔、主厅和中央通道北面高层房间的位置。绝大多数木质屋顶横梁都被烧毁了,部分支撑屋顶的混凝土也坍塌了。

[I] 内政部部长克里斯托夫·卡斯塔纳于周二下午去查看了大教堂的毁坏程度。灰尘覆盖了菱形图案的大理石地板,并漂浮在从消防水龙带中喷洒出的大滩灰水中。在一堆掉落的被烧黑的橡木梁后面,从大教堂屋顶的巨大洞口投下的阳光照亮了尼古拉·库斯图制作的雕塑上一个金色的十字架,这座雕塑似乎未被大火损坏。初步检查也显示三扇装饰华丽的玻璃"玫瑰"窗户似乎在大火中幸存来了下来,官员表示。然而,消防官员也表示,在确认大教堂结构安全之前,不可能给出被破坏物品的完整清单。

[J] 文化部部长弗兰克·里斯特表示,从大教堂中被救出的宗教文物被安全地保存在巴黎市政厅,遭受烟雾破坏的艺术作品被送往世界上最大的艺术博物馆卢浮宫,它们将在那里被烘干、修复及保存。16 尊装饰尖塔的铜像在大火发生的前几天被送去修复了。尖塔的遗迹被认为已经失去了,因为尖塔被破坏了。除了高温造成的破坏——消防员说温度达到了 800℃以上,专家还需要评估大量由消防员洒进大教堂的水所造成的损失。其中的一大受损物是于 18 世纪 30 年代制作的大风琴,据说它未被火焰破坏,却被水严重毁坏了。

[K] 法国政治评论家指出,这场毁灭性的大火做到了马克龙没能做到的事情——使国家团结一致。但是,在接下来的几天,有关火灾前该建筑本身状态的批评可能会加重。勒尼奥在接受《十字架报》采访时表示:"这并非是要找到应该受责备的人,大家应该共同承担责任,因为这是法国最受喜爱的历史遗迹。"艺术历史学家亚历山大·加迪对此表示赞同。他说:"数年来,我们一直说维护历史遗迹的预算太低。"巴黎检察官办公室展开了一项关于"火灾导致的无意识破坏"的调查,表明他们认为火灾是意外,而非人为纵火。

难词总结

avert /əˈvɜːt/ v. 防止,避免
prosecutor /ˈprɒsɪkjuːtə(r)/ n. 检察官;公诉人
row /rəʊ; raʊ/ n. 争吵;纠纷
extinguish /ɪkˈstɪŋgwɪʃ/ v. 熄灭;消灭
preliminary /prɪˈlɪmɪnəri/ a. 初步的;预备性的

monument /ˈmɒnjumənt/ n. 历史遗迹
debris /ˈdebriː; ˈdeɪbriː/ n. 残骸;碎片
immortalise /ɪˈmɔːtəlaɪz/ v. 使不朽
crash down 朝下猛撞

题目精析

36. The total amount of damage to Notre Dame Cathedral can be assessed only when its structure is considered safe.

36. 巴黎圣母院遭受的全部破坏只有当确认其结构安全后才能被评估。

【答案及分析】I。根据题干中的 total amount of damage 和 only when... considered safe 定位到 I 段。定位句指出，However, fire officers have said a complete inventory of the damage will not be possible until the cathedral structure has been deemed safe.（然而，消防官员也表示，在确认大教堂结构安全之前，不可能给出被破坏物品的完整清单。）题干是原文的同义表达，故选 I 项。

37. Once again people began to argue whether Notre Dame Cathedral was going to collapse even without the fire.

37. 人们又开始争论，是不是没有这场火灾，巴黎圣母院也会倒塌。

【答案及分析】C。根据题干中的 again、argue 和 collapse even without the fire 定位到 C 段。定位句指出，...a row was resurfacing over accusations that the beloved cathedral, immortalised in Victor Hugo's novel, was already crumbling before the fire.（……一场争论再次出现，有人指控这座在维克多·雨果的小说中不朽的、人们钟爱的大教堂在起火之前就已经摇摇欲坠了。）题干是原文的同义表达，其中题干中的 argue 对应 row，collapse even without the fire 对应 already crumbling before the fire，故选 C 项。

38. The Notre Dame Cathedral catastrophe was said to have helped unite the French nation.

38. 据说，巴黎圣母院的灾难促进了法国团结一致。

【答案及分析】K。根据题干中的 helped unite the French nation 定位到 K 段。定位句指出，French political commentators noted the devastating fire had succeeded where Macron had failed in uniting the country.（法国政治评论家指出，这场毁灭性的大火做到了马克龙没能做到的事情——使国家团结一致。）题干中的 helped unite the French nation 是原文中 succeeded... in uniting the country 的同义表达，故选 K 项。

39. The roof of Notre Dame Cathedral was built with large numbers of densely laid-out wood beams.

39. 巴黎圣母院的屋顶是由密集排列的木横梁建成的。

【答案及分析】F。根据题干中的 roof 和 large numbers of densely laid-out wood beams 定位到 F 段。定位句指出，the cathedral's roof, made up of hundreds of oak beams... These beams, known as la forêt (the forest) because of their density（该屋顶是由数百根橡木梁建成的……这些横梁被称为"森林"，因为它们排列非常紧密）。题干是对定位句的概括，故选 F 项。

40. Renovation workers of Notre Dame Cathedral were questioned to find out the cause of the accident.

40. 巴黎圣母院的维修工人接受了询问，以找到这场事故的原因。

【答案及分析】B。根据题干中的 find out the cause of the accident 定位到 B 段。定位句指出，police investigators questioned workers involved in the restoration of the monument to try to establish the cause of the devastating blaze（警方调查人员询问参与巴黎圣母院修缮的工作人员，试着确认这场毁灭性火灾的原因）。题干中的 find out the cause of the accident 是原文中 establish the cause of the devastating blaze 的同义表达，故选 B 项。

41. Had the bell towers' wooden frames burned down, the heavy bells would have crashed down.

41. 如果钟楼的木质结构被烧坏，沉重的钟就会坠落。

【答案及分析】H。根据题干中的 wooden frames 和 bells... crashed down 定位到 H 段。定位句指出，If the wooden frame of the towers had caught fire, it could have sent the bells — the largest of which, the

Emmanuel Bell, weighs 13 tons — crashing down（如果钟楼的木质结构着火了，那些钟可能会坠毁，其中最大的是重达13吨的艾曼纽钟）。题干是对H段该句的总结，故选H项。

42. The timely action of the firefighters prevented the fire from reaching the Cathedral's bell towers.
42. 消防员的及时行动阻止了火势蔓延至大教堂的钟楼。

【答案及分析】A。根据题干中的firefighters和prevented the fire定位到A段。定位句指出，firefighters battled to stop flames reaching its bell towers（消防员奋力阻止火势蔓延至巴黎圣母院钟楼）。题干是原文的同义表达，故选A项。

43. Apart from the fire, the water used to extinguish it also caused a lot of damage to Notre Dame Cathedral.
43. 除了大火，用来灭火的水也对巴黎圣母院造成了很大的破坏。

【答案及分析】J。根据题干中的the water和caused a lot of damage定位到J段。定位句指出，As well as damage from the heat, which firefighters said reached more than 800℃, experts also need to assess damage from the vast quantities of water firefighters poured into the cathedral.（除了高温造成的破坏——消防员说温度达到了800℃以上，专家还需要评估大量由消防员洒进大教堂的水所造成的损失。）题干是该句的同义表达，故选J项。

44. There has been argument over the years as to who should pay for the restoration of Notre Dame Cathedral.
44. 近年来，存在关于谁应该支付修缮巴黎圣母院费用的争议。

【答案及分析】D。根据题干中的argument和pay for the restoration定位到D段。定位句指出，The cathedral... has been at the centre of a years-long dispute over who should finance restoration work...（巴黎圣母院……数年来一直处于谁来支付修复……费用的争议中心）。题干中的argument是原文中dispute的同义表达，pay for the restoration是finance restoration work的同义表达，故选D项。

45. News of Notre Dame Cathedral catastrophe instantly caught media attention throughout the world.
45. 巴黎圣母院发生灾难的消息立即引起了全世界媒体的关注。

【答案及分析】G。根据题干中的caught media attention定位到G段。定位句指出，Indeed, within minutes the fire occupied headlines of every major global newspaper and television network.（事实上，在几分钟之内，这场大火就成了全球所有大型报纸和电视广播公司的头条新闻。）题干是原文的同义表达，故选G项。

Section C

Passage One

全文翻译

　　我们通常认为绘画需要与生俱来的天赋，但是这种想法源于我们对绘画的错误分类，我们主要将其视为一种艺术形式，而非一项学习的工具。

　　研究人员、教师和艺术家正开始观察绘画将如何积极地影响一系列的技能和科目。

　　我们中的绝大多数人以前都画过画，但是在某些时刻，我们大多数人都停止了绘画。当然，有一些人没有停止绘画，为此我们要感谢上帝：没有设计师和艺术家的世界确实会十分破败。

一些人认为如此多成年人放弃绘画是因为我们对它的分类不当，给它下了一个非常狭隘的定义。D. B. 多德教授在他撰写的《简笔画：绘画是一种人类实践》一书中指出，我们弄错了绘画的意义，因为我们将其视为一项专业技能，而非个人能力。我们错误地认为好的绘画作品是真实世界的重现，是现实的幻想。恰恰相反，绘画应该被归为象征性的工具。

人类拥有 73 000 年的绘画历史。这是人之所以为人的部分意义。我们不具备大猩猩的力气，因为我们放弃了动物的力量，从而可以操作更小的工具，例如锤子、矛，以及后来的钢笔和铅笔。人类的手是由神经末梢构成的极其密集的网络。在诸多方面，人类生来就是要绘画的。

一些研究人员认为涂画可以活跃所谓的默认脑回路——从本质上来说，即大脑中负责在缺少其他刺激的情况下维持活动基本水平的区域。因此，一些人认为在无聊的讲座上涂画可以帮助学生集中注意力。在一项研究中，参与者在听一组名字时被要求涂画或者坐着不动。那些涂画的人记住的名字比坐着不动的人多29%。

还有证据表明，绘画天赋取决于一个人能够多么准确地感知世界。人类的视觉系统倾向于对尺寸、形状、颜色和角度做出错误判断，但是艺术家在感知这些特征时比非艺术家更加准确。在视觉发挥重要作用的领域，培养绘画才能可以成为一项重要的工具，有助于提高人们的观察能力。

与其将绘画视为一些有创造力的人具有的天赋，不如将其视为更好地观察和理解世界的工具——它恰好也是一种艺术形式。心不在焉地涂画和复现生活都能积极地影响你的记忆和视觉感知，所以，下次你的学校董事会削减美术系的预算时，就大声抱怨吧。

难词总结

inborn /ˌɪnˈbɔːn/ a. 天生的
discipline /ˈdɪsəplɪn/ n. 学科
misfile /ˌmɪsˈfaɪl/ v. 把……归错档案
default /dɪˈfɔːlt/ n. 默认；系统设定值
slash /slæʃ/ v. 削减

stem from 来自，起源于
shabby /ˈʃæbi/ a. 破败的
manipulate /məˈnɪpjuleɪt/ v. 操作，操控
perceive /pəˈsiːv/ v. 感知到；认为

题目精析

46. What do people generally think about drawing?

   A) It is a gift creative people are endowed with.
   B) It is a skill that is acquired with practice.
   C) It is an art form that is appreciated by all.
   D) It is an ability everyone should cultivate.

46. 人们通常怎么看待绘画？

   A）它是有创造力的人赋有的天赋。
   B）它是一项通过练习获得的技能。
   C）它是一项所有人都欣赏的艺术形式。
   D）它是所有人都应该培养的能力。

   【答案及分析】A。根据题干关键词generally think about drawing定位到原文第一段第一句。该句提到，We often think of drawing as something that takes inborn talent（我们通常认为绘画需要与生俱来的天赋）。A项是原文的同义表达，故选A项。

47. What do we learn about designers and artists?

   A) They are declining gradually in number.

B) They are keen on changing shabby surroundings.

C) They add beauty and charm to the world.

D) They spend most of their lives drawing.

47. 我们对设计师和艺术家有何认识？

A）他们的数量正在逐渐减少。

B）他们热衷于改变破败的周围环境。

C）他们为世界增加了美感与魅力。

D）他们生活中大多数时间都在画画。

【答案及分析】C。根据题干关键词 designers and artists 定位到原文第三段第二句。该句提到，a world without designers and artists would be a very shabby one indeed（没有设计师和艺术家的世界确实会十分破败），由此可知设计师和艺术家为世界增加了美感，C 项符合原文，故选 C 项。

48. What does Professor D. B. Dowd argue in his book?

A) Everybody is born with the capacity to draw.

B) Drawing is a skill that requires special training.

C) The value of drawing tends to be overestimated.

D) Drawing should be redefined as a realistic illusion.

48. D. B. 多德教授在他的书中提到了什么？

A）每个人生来就具备绘画的能力。

B）绘画是一项需要特殊训练的技能。

C）绘画的价值往往被高估。

D）绘画应该被重新定义为一种现实的幻想。

【答案及分析】A。根据题干关键词 Professor D. B. Dowd 和 his book 定位到原文第四段第二至四句，其中提到，In his book, *Stick Figures: Drawing as a Human Practice*, Professor D. B. Dowd argues that we have misfiled the significance of drawing because we see it as a professional skill instead of a personal capacity. We mistakenly think of "good" drawings as those which work as recreations of the real world, as realistic illusions. Rather, drawing should be recategorized as a symbolic tool.（D. B. 多德教授在他撰写的《简笔画：绘画是一种人类实践》一书中指出，我们弄错了绘画的意义，因为我们将其视为一项专业技能，而非个人能力。我们错误地认为好的绘画作品是真实世界的重现，是现实的幻想。恰恰相反，绘画应该被归为象征性的工具。）A 项符合原文；B 项中的 special training 文中未提；C 项利用文中的 misfiled 设置陷阱，但与文意不符；D 项与文意相反。故选 A 项。

49. What have some researchers found from one study about doodling?

A) It is a must for maintaining a base level of brain activity.

B) It can turn something boring into something interesting.

C) It is the most reliable stimulant to activate the brain.

D) It helps improve concentration and memory.

49. 关于涂画，一些研究人员通过一项研究发现了什么？

A）它是维持大脑活动基本水平的必需品。

B）它可以将无聊的事情转变为有趣的事情。

C）它是使大脑活跃的最可靠的刺激因素。

D）它有助于改善注意力和记忆。

【答案及分析】D。根据题干关键词researchers found 和 doodling 定位到原文第六段，该段提到，涂画可以帮助学生集中注意力，边涂画边听名字可以记住更多名字，由此可知D项符合文意，故选D项。

50. What is characteristic of people with drawing talent?

　　A) Sensitivity to cognitive stimulation.　　C) Accuracy in categorization.

　　B) Subtlety of representation.　　D) Precision in visual perception.

50. 具有绘画天赋的人有什么特点？

　　A）对认知刺激敏感。　　C）分类准确。

　　B）描绘细腻。　　D）视觉感知准确。

【答案及分析】D。根据题干关键词 characteristic 和 drawing talent 定位到原文倒数第二段第二句。该句指出，The human visual system tends to misjudge size, shape, color, and angles but artists perceive these qualities more accurately than non-artists.（人类的视觉系统倾向于对尺寸、形状、颜色和角度做出错误判断，但是艺术家在感知这些特征时比非艺术家更加准确。）根据该句的后半句可知，有绘画天赋的人在视觉感知方面更准确，D项符合文意，故选D项。

Passage Two

全文翻译

　　汽车重塑了我们的城市。它似乎为每个人提供了自主权。在脱离现实的广告中存在一些几乎令人愉快的事情，这些广告显示，大规模生产的汽车被营销为个性和自由的象征，而购车后人们的大部分时间都花在了短途旅程的拥挤道路上。

　　虽然人们过度关注最快速度、转弯能力和加速能力，但现代汽车上最实用的是那些当你开得很慢时起作用的小工具：停车感测器、音响系统和在即将到来的交通拥堵前指出其他路线的导航应用。这似乎是为数不多的分享个人信息给分享者带来的好处之一：因为这些应用几乎知道所有使用者的位置以及他们几乎每时每刻的驾驶速度，所以它们可以非常快速地发现交通拥堵，并指出绕过拥堵的路线。

　　当每个人都使用导航应用时，该应用会告知车主避开其他使用相同应用的司机，问题就出现了。交通拥堵经常发生在没有足够信息的时候。当少数幸运的人可以获得信息时，他们将大大受益于此。但是当每个人都有充足的信息时，交通拥堵便会延伸至那些本可以让司机绕过拥堵的辅路上。

　　这种新型的交通拥堵告诉我们两件事。第一，科技的承诺永远不会像我们所期待的那样完全实现；它们将受限于不可预测和意外的结果。在不同的交通拥堵情况下，坐在更加舒适的汽车里是令人愉快的，但是这几乎并不是技术曾经许诺过的自由。第二，自我安排无法使我们到达想去的地方。数百万名司机想要前进的努力没有奇迹般地产生每个人都做得比以前更好的局面，而是每个人都做得更差了。中央控制和集体组织可以产生更加顺利和更加公平的结果，即使这一点也不能保证。

在自动驾驶汽车承诺的更大进步中也可以预测到相同的局限性。上周，优步出租车公司操作的一辆无人驾驶汽车在亚利桑那州撞死了一名推着自行车穿过一条宽阔马路的女性。这是首次记录的全自动化驾驶汽车的致死事件。专家表示这显示了科技的"灾难性的失败"。

逐渐地，连硅谷也不得不承认其追求令人陶醉的速度的文化特点需要付出代价。交通现状告诉我们，莽撞和不加控制的改变在给我们带来好处的同时也会带来伤害，经过深思熟虑的监管对于更美好的未来十分必要。

难词总结

autonomy /ɔːˈtɒnəmi/ n. 自主权；自治
have access to 可以获得；使用
reckless /ˈrekləs/ a. 莽撞的

detachment /dɪˈtætʃmənt/ n. 超脱；分离
miraculously /mɪˈrækjələsli/ ad. 奇迹般地

题目精析

51. What does the author say about car advertisements?
 A) They portray drivers who enjoy speed on the road.
 B) They present a false picture of the autonomy cars provide.
 C) They pursue individuality and originality in design concept.
 D) They overestimate the potential market of autonomous cars.

51. 作者对于汽车广告有何说法？
 A）它们描述了在路上享受高速驾驶乐趣的司机。
 B）它们展示了汽车提供的自主权的假象。
 C）它们在设计概念上追求个性和原创性。
 D）它们高估了自动驾驶汽车的潜在市场。

【答案及分析】B。根据题干关键词 car advertisements 定位到原文第一段第三句。该句指出，There is something almost delightful in the detachment from reality of advertisements showing mass-produced cars marketed as symbols of individuality and of freedom when most of their lives will be spent making short journeys on choked roads.（在脱离现实的广告中存在一些几乎令人愉快的事情，这些广告显示，大规模生产的汽车被营销为个性和自由的象征，而购车后人们的大部分时间都花在了短途旅程的拥挤道路上。）B 项是对原文的总结，故选 B 项。

52. What does the author imply about the various gadgets on cars?
 A) They can help to alleviate traffic jams.
 B) Most of them are as effective as advertised.
 C) Only some can be put to use under current traffic conditions.
 D) They are constantly upgraded to make driving easier and safer.

52. 关于汽车上的各种小工具，作者暗示了什么？
 A）它们有助于缓解交通拥堵。
 B）它们中的绝大多数都像广告中所说的一样有效。

C) 在现在的交通条件下，只有一些可以被使用。

D) 为了使驾驶更加容易和安全，它们经常被升级。

【答案及分析】C。根据题干关键词 gadgets on cars 定位到原文第二段第一句。该句提到，For all the fuss made about top speeds, cornering ability and acceleration, the most useful gadgets on a modern car are those which work when you're going very slowly（虽然人们过度关注最快速度、转弯能力和加速能力，但现代汽车上最实用的是那些当你开得很慢时起作用的小工具），由此可知，汽车上的小工具只有部分有作用，C 项符合文意，故选 C 项。

53. What does the author say about the use of navigation apps?

    A) It is likely to create traffic jams in other places.

    B) It helps a great deal in easing traffic congestion.

    C) It sharply reduces the incidence of traffic accidents.

    D) It benefits those who are learning to drive.

53. 关于导航应用的使用，作者说了什么？

    A) 它可能导致其他地方出现交通拥堵。

    B) 它非常有助于缓解交通拥堵。

    C) 它急剧减少了交通事故的发生。

    D) 它有利于那些正在学习开车的人。

【答案及分析】A。根据题干关键词 navigation apps 定位到原文第三段。该段指出，当所有人都使用同一个导航系统时，会出现新的问题，即交通拥堵会延伸至辅路。A 项符合原文，故选 A 项。

54. What does the author say about technology?

    A) Its consequences are usually difficult to assess.

    B) It seldom delivers all the benefits as promised.

    C) It depends on the required knowledge for application.

    D) Its benefits are guaranteed by collective wisdom.

54. 关于科技，作者说了什么？

    A) 它的结果通常很难评估。

    B) 它很少像承诺的一样实现所有好处。

    C) 它依赖于应用程序所需的知识。

    D) 它的好处得到了集体智慧的保证。

【答案及分析】B。根据题干关键词 technology 定位到原文第四段第二句，该句指出，The first is that the promises of technology will never be realised as fully as we hope（第一，科技的承诺永远不会像我们所期待的那样完全实现）。B 项是原文的同义表达，故选 B 项。

55. What key message does the author try to convey in the passage?

    A) The consequences of technological innovation need not be exaggerated.

    B) There is always a price to pay to develop technology for a better world.

    C) Technological innovation should be properly regulated.

    D) The culture of Silicon Valley ought not to be emulated.

55. 作者想在文中传达的关键信息是什么？
   A）科技创新的结果不需要被夸大。
   B）为了世界更美好而开发技术总是要付出代价的。
   C）科技创新应该被适当管控。
   D）硅谷的文化不应该被模仿。

【答案及分析】C。根据题干关键词 in the passage 定位到整篇文章。整篇文章都在讲述汽车技术带来的不利影响，最后一段最后一句指出，What traffic teaches us is that reckless and uncontrolled change is as likely to harm us as it is to benefit us, and that thoughtful regulation is necessary for a better future.（交通现状告诉我们，莽撞和不加控制的改变在给我们带来好处的同时也会带来伤害，经过深思熟虑的监管对于更美好的未来十分必要。）后半句是整篇文章的升华，表达了作者写这篇文章的真实意图。C 项"科技创新应该被适当管控"符合文意，故选 C 项。

Part Ⅳ　Translation

参考译文

Qinghai is a province in northwest China, with an average altitude of more than 3,000 meters. Most of its areas are covered by mountains and plateaus. The name of this province is originated from Qinghai Lake which is the largest saltwater lake in China. Known as "China's most beautiful lake", Qinghai Lake is one of the most popular tourist attractions and a paradise for photographers and artists.

Qinghai boasts magnificent mountains and rivers, and possesses abundant resources on its vast territory. It is rich in oil and natural gas reserves. Driven by the oil and natural gas industries, the economy of many of its cities have achieved substantial development. Qinghai is especially famous for its rich water resources, and it is the birthplace of China's three major rivers, which are the Yangtze Rive, the Yellow River and the Lancang River. So it plays a significant role in China's water ecosystem.

难词总结

province /ˈprɒvɪns/ n. 省份
saltwater lake 咸水湖
photographer /fəˈtɒɡrəfə(r)/ n. 摄影师
magnificent /mæɡˈnɪfɪs(ə)nt/ a. 壮丽的；宏伟的

altitude /ˈæltɪtjuːd/ n. 海拔
tourist attraction 旅游景点
boast /bəʊst/ v. 有（值得自豪的东西）
reserve /rɪˈzɜːv/ n. 储备；贮存

译点释义

1. 第一句中有三个意群，翻译时可适当断句。"青海是中国西北部的一个省份"可作为主句，"平均海拔 3 000 米以上"可处理为 with 的复合结构。考虑到句子太长，"大部分地区为高山和高原"可以独立成句。"海拔"的单词为 altitude，"高原"的单词为 plateau。
2. 第二句比较简单，"得名于"可以翻译为 The name of... is originated from，或者译为 It is named after..."全国最大的咸水湖青海湖"中的修饰成分可以处理为定语从句，放在 Qinghai Lake 的后面。

3. 第三句比较长，翻译时可将第一个意群处理为过去分词短语作状语，"旅游景点"的表达为 tourist attraction，"天堂"的单词为 paradise。

4. 第四句虽然很短，但包含的内容不少，"山川壮丽，地大物博"不好翻译，需要理解成白话文再翻译，即"有壮丽的山和河流，在其宽广的地域上有丰富的资源"，可译为 boasts magnificent mountains and rivers, and possesses abundant resources on its vast territory。

5. 第五句中包含两个分句，可以分开翻译。"石油和天然气储量丰富"可译为 rich in oil and natural gas reserves。后半句较长，句子主干为"省内许多城市的经济得到了长足发展"，直接翻译即可，"长足发展"可译为 substantial development。"在石油和天然气工业带动下"可处理为过去分词短语作状语，译为 Driven by the oil and natural gas industries。

6. 第六句结构较复杂，可适当断句，前两个分句译作一句，第三个分句单独成句。"以……而闻名"的表达为 be famous for 或 be known for，"发源地"的单词为 birthplace。"发挥着重要作用"可译为 plays a significant role。

未得到监考教师指令前，不得翻阅该试题册！

2021年6月大学英语六级考试真题（第二套）

Part Ⅰ　　　　　　　　　　Writing　　　　　　　　　　(30 minutes)

（请于正式开考后半小时内完成该部分，之后将进行听力考试）

Directions: *For this part, you are allowed 30 minutes to write an essay based on the chart below. You should start your essay with a brief description of the graph and comment on **China's achievements in urbanization**. You should write at least **150** words but no more than **200** words.*

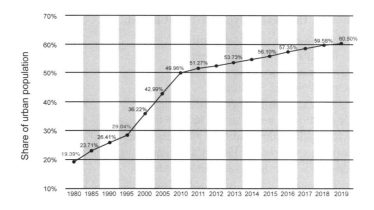

Part Ⅱ　　　　　　　Listening Comprehension　　　　　　(30 minutes)

Section A

Directions: *In this section, you will hear two long conversations. At the end of each conversation, you will hear four questions. Both the conversation and the questions will be spoken only once. After you hear a question, you must choose the best answer from the four choices marked A), B), C) and D). Then mark the corresponding letter on **Answer Sheet 1** with a single line through the centre.*

Questions 1 to 4 are based on the conversation you have just heard.

1. A) Weird.　　　　　B) Efficient.　　　　　C) Tolerant.　　　　　D) Toxic.
2. A) They are arrogant.　　　　　　　　　C) They are ambitious.
   B) They are ignorant.　　　　　　　　　D) They are accommodating.
3. A) They can think big.　　　　　　　　　C) They can break conventions.
   B) They can air their views.　　　　　　D) They can work flexible hours.
4. A) It can alter people's mindsets.　　　　C) It enables people to learn and grow.
   B) It can lead to new discoveries.　　　　D) It is conducive to critical thinking.

Questions 5 to 8 are based on the conversation you have just heard.

5. A) He kept looking for the best place to stay.
   B) He met many tourists from other countries.
   C) He had a great time sightseeing and relaxing.
   D) He managed to visit a different city each day.
6. A) Prioritize what is essential to their best advantage.
   B) Stretch out the process in search of the optimal.
   C) Deliberate the consequences that may occur.
   D) Take all relevant factors into consideration.
7. A) Time pressure.
   B) Tight budget.
   C) Modern technology.
   D) Fierce competition.
8. A) Research as many different options as possible.
   B) Avoid going over the same options repeatedly.
   C) Focus on what is practical.
   D) Trust their gut instinct.

Section B

Directions: *In this section, you will hear two passages. At the end of each passage, you will hear three or four questions. Both the passage and the questions will be spoken only once. After you hear a question, you must choose the best answer from the four choices marked A), B), C) and D). Then mark the corresponding letter on* **Answer Sheet 1** *with a single line through the centre.*

Questions 9 to 11 are based on the passage you have just heard.

9. A) It is beneficial to poor as well as rich communities.
   B) It is conducive to children's future development.
   C) It is welcome to parents but not to children.
   D) It is not of much help to younger children.
10. A) It may put some students in remote areas at a disadvantage.
    B) It gives the majority of students ready access to their teachers.
    C) It effectively improves the learning quality of students in rural areas.
    D) It can bridge the learning gap between kids of different backgrounds.
11. A) Diligent students tend to do their homework independently.
    B) The focus of homework should always be on school subjects.
    C) Doing homework exerts a positive effect on kids' personality development.
    D) The benefits of doing homework vary widely from individual to individual.

Questions 12 to 15 are based on the passage you have just heard.

12. A) It was something he apologized for later.
    B) It was ridiculed by the *New York Times*.
    C) It was a forty-nine-year plan.
    D) It was considered visionary.
13. A) It was of great significance to rocket science.
    B) It was completed in the state of New Mexico.
    C) It was somehow delayed about 12 minutes.
    D) It failed due to a sudden change of weather.
14. A) A laboratory and test range was already set up there.
    B) Its climate was ideal for year-round rocket launching.
    C) A weather expert invited him to go there for his mission.
    D) Its remote valleys were appealing to him and his family.
15. A) He won an award from the US government for his work.
    B) He gained recognition from rocket scientists worldwide.
    C) He was granted over 200 patents in rocket technology.
    D) He boosted the military strength of the United States.

Section C

Directions: *In this section, you will hear three recordings of lectures or talks followed by three or four questions. The recordings will be played only once. After you hear a question, you must choose* the best answer from the four choices marked A), B), C) and D). Then mark the corresponding letter on **Answer Sheet 1** with a single line through the centre.

Questions 16 to 18 are based on the recording you have just heard.

16. A) It requires entrepreneurial experience.
    B) It is usually financially rewarding.
    C) It can be quite frustrating.
    D) It can be rather risky.
17. A) It contributes to rapid business expansion.
    B) It inspires willingness to make sacrifices.
    C) It reduces conflict among team members.
    D) It encourages creation and innovation.
18. A) They have unrealistic expectations.
    B) They often work without any pay.
    C) Few can find willing investors.
    D) Many are idealistic dreamers.

Questions 19 to 21 are based on the recording you have just heard.

19. A) They have better dietary habits.
    B) They bear fewer social responsibilities.
    C) They are born with a stronger ability to socialize.
    D) They are better able to survive or handle disease.
20. A) They have a limited reproductive ability.
    B) They depend on adequate sleep to thrive.
    C) They keep dividing throughout one's life.
    D) They strengthen with regular exercise.
21. A) The process of aging can ultimately be brought under control.
    B) Improved health care for the elderly will contribute to longevity.
    C) Prevention of heart disease and stroke will increase life expectancy.
    D) The resolution of age-related diseases will solve the mystery of aging.

Questions 22 to 25 are based on the recording you have just heard.

22. A) They are reluctant to follow instructions.
    B) They fail to answer emails promptly.
    C) They cannot understand directives.
    D) They do not show due respect.
23. A) They have not been trained to follow the rules.
    B) They are not satisfied with the management.
    C) They want to avoid unnecessary losses.
    D) They find their voice go unheeded.
24. A) When they are on good terms with their managers.
    B) When they find their job goals easily attainable.
    C) When they find their supervisors helpful.
    D) When they are financially motivated.
25. A) They are a useless tool for managers to change employee behavior.
    B) They prove to be a good means for managers to give instructions.
    C) They should be reserved for urgent communication.
    D) They are seldom used for sharing confidential data.

Part III   Reading Comprehension   (40 minutes)

Section A

Directions: *In this section, there is a passage with ten blanks. You are required to select one word for each blank from a list of choices given in a word bank following the passage. Read the passage through carefully before making your choices. Each choice in the bank is identified by a letter. Please mark the corresponding letter for each item on **Answer Sheet 2** with a single line through the centre. You may not use any of the words in the bank more than once.*

A new study had drawn a bleak picture of cultural inclusiveness reflected in the children's literature available in Australia. Dr. Helen Adam from Edith Cowan University's School of Education __26__ the cultural diversity of children's books. She examined the books __27__ in the kindergarten rooms of four day-care centers in Western Australia. Just 18 percent of 2,413 books in the total collection contained any __28__ of non-white people. Minority cultures were often featured in stereotypical or tokenistic ways, for example, by __29__ Asian culture with chopsticks and traditional dress. Characters that did represent a minority culture usually had __30__ roles in the books. The main characters were mostly Caucasian. This causes concern as it can lead to an impression that whiteness is of greater value.

Dr. Adam said children formed impressions about "difference" and identity from a very young age. Evidence has shown they develop own-race __31__ from as young as three months of age. The books we share with young children can be a valuable opportunity to develop children's understanding of themselves and others. Books can also allow children to see diversity. They discover both similarities and differences between themselves and others. This can help develop understanding, acceptance and __32__ of diversity.

Census data has shown Australians come from more than 200 countries. They speak over 300 languages at home. Additionally, Australians belong to more than 100 different religious groups. They also work in more than 1,000 different occupations. "Australia is a multicultural society. The current __33__ promotion of white middle-class ideas and lifestyles risks __34__ children from minority groups. This can give white middle-class children a sense of __35__ or privilege," Dr. Adam said.

A) alienating	I) representation
B) appreciation	J) safeguarded
C) bias	K) secondary
D) fraud	L) superiority
E) housed	M) temperament
F) investigated	N) tentative
G) overwhelming	O) threshold
H) portraying	

Section B

Directions: *In this section, you are going to read a passage with ten statements attached to it. Each statement contains information given in one of the paragraphs. Identify the paragraph from which the information is derived. You may choose a paragraph more than once. Each paragraph is marked with a letter. Answer the questions by marking the corresponding letter on **Answer Sheet 2**.*

How Marconi Gave Us the Wireless World

[A] A hundred years before iconic figures like Bill Gates and Steve Jobs permeated our lives, an Irish-Italian inventor laid the foundation of the communication explosion of the 21st century. Guglielmo Marconi was arguably the first truly global figure in modern communication. Not only was he the first to communicate globally, he was the first to think globally about communication. Marconi may not have been the greatest inventor of his time, but more than anyone else, he brought about a fundamental shift in the way we communicate.

[B] Today's globally networked media and communication system has its origins in the 19th century, when, for the first time, messages were sent electronically across great distances. The telegraph, the telephone, and radio were the obvious predecessors of the Internet, iPods, and mobile phones. What made the link from then to now was the development of wireless communication. Marconi was the first to develop and perfect this system, using the recently-discovered "airwaves" that make up the electromagnetic spectrum.

[C] Between 1896, when he applied for his first patent in England at the age of 22, and his death in Italy in 1937, Marconi was at the center of every major innovation in electronic communication. He was also a skilled and sophisticated organizer, an entrepreneurial innovator, who mastered the use of corporate strategy, media relations, government lobbying, international diplomacy, patents, and prosecution. Marconi was really interested in only one thing: the extension of mobile, personal, long-distance communication to the ends of the earth (and beyond, if we can believe some reports). Some like to refer to him as a genius, but if there was any genius to Marconi it was this vision.

[D] In 1901 he succeeded in signalling across the Atlantic, from the west coast of England to Newfoundland, despite the claims of science that it could not be done. In 1924 he convinced the British government to encircle the world with a chain of wireless stations using the latest technology that he had devised, shortwave radio. There are some who say Marconi lost his edge when commercial broadcasting came along; he didn't see that radio could or should be used to *frivolous* (无聊的) ends. In one of his last public speeches, a radio broadcast to the United States in March 1937, he deplored that broadcasting had become a one-way means of communication and foresaw it moving in another direction, toward communication as a means of exchange. That was visionary genius.

[E] Marconi's career was devoted to making wireless communication happen cheaply, efficiently, smoothly, and with an elegance that would appear to be intuitive and uncomplicated to the user — user-friendly, if you will. There is a direct connection from Marconi to today's social media, search engines, and program streaming that can best be summed up by an admittedly provocative exclamation: the 20th century did not exist. In a sense, Marconi's vision jumped from his time to our own.

[F] Marconi invented the idea of global communication — or, more straightforwardly, globally networked, mobile, wireless communication. Initially, this was wireless Morse code *telegraphy* (电报通讯), the principal communication technology of his day. Marconi was the first to develop a practical method for wireless telegraphy using radio waves. He borrowed technical details from many sources, but what set him apart was a self-confident vision of the paradigm-shifting power of communication technology on the one hand, and, on the other, of the steps that needed to be taken to consolidate his own position as a player in that field. Tracing Marconi's lifeline leads us into the story of modern communication itself. There were other important figures, but Marconi towered over them all in reach, power, and influence, as well as in the grip he had on the popular imagination of his time. Marconi was quite simply the central figure in the emergence of a modern understanding of communication.

[G] In his lifetime, Marconi foresaw the development of television and the fax machine, GPS, radar, and the portable hand-held telephone. Two months before he died, newspapers were reporting that he was working on a "death ray," and that he had "killed a rat with an intricate device at a distance of three feet." By then, anything Marconi said or did was newsworthy. Stock prices rose or sank according to his pronouncements. If Marconi said he thought it might rain, there was likely to be a run on umbrellas.

[H] Marconi's biography is also a story about choices and the motivations behind them. At one level, Marconi could be fiercely autonomous and independent of the constraints of his own social class. On another scale, he was a perpetual outsider. Wherever he went, he was never "of" the group; he was always the "other," considered foreign in Britain, British in Italy, and "not American" in the United States. At the same time, he also suffered tremendously from a need for acceptance that drove, and sometimes tarnished, every one of his relationships.

[I] Marconi placed a permanent stamp on the way we live. He was the first person to imagine a practical application for the wireless spectrum, and to develop it successfully into a *global* communication system — in both terms of the word; that is, worldwide and all-inclusive. He was able to do this because of a combination of factors — most important, timing and opportunity — but the single-mindedness and determination with which he carried out his self-imposed mission was fundamentally character-based; millions of Marconi's contemporaries had the same class, gender, race, and colonial privilege as he, but only a handful did anything with it. Marconi needed to achieve the goal that was set in his mind as an adolescent; by the time he reached adulthood, he understood, intuitively, that in order to have an impact he had to both develop an independent economic base and align himself with political power. Disciplined, uncritical loyalty to political power became his compass for the choice he had to make.

[J] At the same time, Marconi was uncompromisingly independent intellectually. Shortly after Marconi's death, the nuclear physicist Enrico Fermi — soon to be the developer of the Manhattan Project — wrote that Marconi proved that theory and experimentation were complementary features of progress. "Experience can rarely, unless guided by a theoretical concept, arrive at results of any great significance... on the other hand, an excessive trust in theoretical conviction would have prevented Marconi from persisting in experiments which were destined to bring about a revolution in the technique of radio-communications." In other words,

Marconi had the advantage of not being burdened by preconceived assumptions.

[K] The most controversial aspect of Marconi's life — and the reason why there has been no satisfying biography of Marconi until now — was his uncritical embrace of Benito Mussolini. At first this was not problematic for him. But as the *regressive* (倒退的) nature of Mussolini's regime became clear, he began to suffer a crisis of conscience. However, after a lifetime of moving within the circles of power, he was unable to break with authority, and served Mussolini faithfully (as president of Italy's national research council and royal academy, as well as a member of the Fascist Grand Council) until the day he died — conveniently — in 1937, shortly before he would have had to take a stand in the conflict that consumed a world that he had, in part, created.

36. Marconi was central to our present-day understanding of communication.
37. As an adult, Marconi had an intuition that he had to be loyal to politicians in order to be influential.
38. Marconi disapproved of the use of wireless communication for commercial broadcasting.
39. Marconi's example demonstrates that theoretical concepts and experiments complement each other in making progress in science and technology.
40. Marconi's real interests lay in the development of worldwide wireless communication.
41. Marconi spent his whole life making wireless communication simple to use.
42. Because of his long-time connection with people in power, Marconi was unable to cut himself off from the fascist regime in Italy.
43. In his later years, Marconi exerted a tremendous influence on all aspects of people's life.
44. What connected the 19th century and our present time was the development of wireless communication.
45. Despite his autonomy, Marconi felt alienated and suffered from a lack of acceptance.

Section C

Directions: *There are 2 passages in this section. Each passage is followed by some questions or unfinished statements. For each of them there are four choices marked A), B), C) and D). You should decide on the best choice and mark the corresponding letter on **Answer Sheet 2** with a single line through the centre.*

Passage One

Questions 46 to 50 are based on the following passage.

Humans are fascinated by the source of their failings and virtues. This preoccupation inevitably leads to an old debate: whether nature or nurture moulds us more. A revolution in genetics has poised this as a modern political question about the character of our society: if personalities are hard-wired into our genes, what can governments do to help us? It feels morally questionable, yet claims of genetic selection by intelligence are making headlines.

This is down to "*hereditarian*" (遗传论的) science and a recent paper claimed "differences in exam performance between pupils attending selective and non-selective schools mirror the genetic differences between them". With such an assertion, the work was predictably greeted by a lot of absurd claims about "genetics determining academic success". What the research revealed was the rather less surprising result: the educational benefits of selective schools largely disappear once pupils' inborn ability and socio-economic background were taken into account. It is a glimpse of the blindingly obvious — and there's nothing to back strongly either a hereditary or environmental argument.

Yet the paper does say children are "unintentionally genetically selected" by the school system. Central to hereditarian science is a tall claim: that identifiable variations in genetic sequences can predict an individual's aptness to learn, reason and solve problems. This is problematic on many levels. A teacher could not seriously tell a parent their child has a low genetic tendency to study when external factors clearly exist. Unlike-minded academics say the inheritability of human traits is scientifically unsound. At best there is a weak statistical association and not a causal link between DNA and intelligence. Yet sophisticated statistics are used to create an intimidatory atmosphere of scientific certainty.

While there's an undoubted genetic basis to individual difference, it is wrong to think that socially defined groups can be genetically accounted for. The fixation on genes as destiny is surely false too. Medical predictability can rarely be based on DNA alone; the environment matters too. Something as complex as intellect is likely to be affected by many factors beyond genes. If hereditarians want to advance their cause it will require more balanced interpretation and not just acts of advocacy.

Genetic selection is a way of exerting influence over others, "the ultimate collective control of human destinies", as writer H.G.Wells put it. Knowledge becomes power and power requires a sense of responsibility. In understanding cognitive ability, we must not elevate discrimination to a science: allowing people to climb the ladder of life only as far as their cells might suggest. This will need a more sceptical eye on the science. As technology progresses, we all have a duty to make sure that we shape a future that we would want to find ourselves in.

46. What did a recent research paper claim?
    A) The type of school students attend makes a difference to their future.
    B) Genetic differences between students are far greater than supposed.
    C) The advantages of selective schools are too obvious to ignore.
    D) Students' academic performance is determined by their genes.
47. What does the author think of the recent research?
    A) Its result was questionable.   C) Its influence was rather negligible.
    B) Its implication was positive.   D) Its conclusions were enlightening.
48. What does the author say about the relationship between DNA and intelligence?
    A) It is one of scientific certainty.   C) It is subject to interpretation of statistics.
    B) It is not one of cause and effect.   D) It is not fully examined by gene scientists.
49. What do hereditarians need to do to make their claims convincing?
    A) Take all relevant factors into account in interpreting their data.
    B) Conduct their research using more sophisticated technology.
    C) Gather gene data from people of all social classes.
    D) Cooperate with social scientists in their research.
50. What does the author warn against in the passage?
    A) Exaggerating the power of technology in shaping the world.
    B) Losing sight of professional ethics in conducting research.
    C) Misunderstanding the findings of human cognition research.
    D) Promoting discrimination in the name of science.

Passage Two

Questions 51 to 55 are based on the following passage.

Nicola Sturgeon's speech last Tuesday setting out the Scottish government's legislative programme for the year ahead confirmed what was already pretty clear. Scottish councils are set to be the first in the UK with the power to levy charges on visitors, with Edinburgh likely to lead the way.

Tourist taxes are not new. The Himalayan Kingdom of Bhutan has a longstanding policy of charging visitors a daily fee. France's tax on overnight stays was introduced to assist *thermal spa* (温泉) towns to develop, and around half of French local authorities use it today.

But such levies are on the rise. Moves by Barcelona and Venice to deal with the phenomenon of "over-tourism" through the use of charges have recently gained prominence. Japan and Greece are among the countries to have recently introduced tourist taxes.

That the UK lags behind is due to our weak, by international standards, local government, as well as the opposition to taxes and regulation of our aggressively pro-market ruling party. Some UK cities have lobbied without success for the power to levy a charge on visitors. Such levies are no universal remedy as the amounts raised would be tiny compared with what has been taken away by central government since

2010. Still, it is to be hoped that the Scottish government's bold move will prompt others to act. There is no reason why visitors to the UK, or domestic tourists on holiday in hotspots such as Cornwall, should be exempt from taxation — particularly when vital local services including waste collection, park maintenance and arts and culture spending are under unprecedented strain.

On the contrary, compelling tourists to make a financial contribution to the places they visit beyond their personal consumption should be part of a wider cultural shift. Westerners with disposable incomes have often behaved as if they have a right to go wherever they choose with little regard for the consequences. Just as the environmental harm caused by aviation and other transport must come under far greater scrutiny, the social cost of tourism must also be confronted. This includes the impact of short-term lets on housing costs and quality of life for residents. Several European capitals, including Paris and Berlin, are leading a campaign for tougher regulation by the European Union. It also includes the impact of overcrowding, litter and the kinds of behaviour associated with noisy parties.

There is no "one size fits all" solution to this problem. The existence of new revenue streams for some but not all councils is complicated, and businesses are often opposed, fearing higher costs will make them uncompetitive. But those places that want them must be given the chance to make tourist taxes work.

51. What do we learn from Nicola Sturgeon's speech?
    A) The UK is set to adjust its policy on taxation.
    B) Tourists will have to pay a tax to visit Scotland.
    C) The UK will take new measures to boost tourism.
    D) Edinburgh contributes most to Scotland's tourism.
52. How come the UK has been slow in imposing the tourist tax?
    A) Its government wants to attract more tourists.
    B) The tax is unlikely to add much to its revenue.
    C) Its ruling party is opposed to taxes and regulation.
    D) It takes time for local governments to reach consensus.
53. Both international and domestic visitors in the UK should pay tourist tax so as to _____.
    A) elevate its tourism to international standards
    B) improve the welfare of its maintenance workers
    C) promote its cultural exchange with other nations
    D) ease its financial burden of providing local services
54. What does the author say about Western tourists?
    A) They don't seem to care about the social cost of tourism.
    B) They don't seem to mind paying for additional services.
    C) They deem travel an important part of their life.
    D) They subject the effects of tourism to scrutiny.
55. What are UK people's opinions about the levy of tourist tax?
    A) Supportive.   B) Skeptical.   C) Divided.   D) Unclear.

Part IV   Translation   (30 minutes)

Directions: *For this part, you are allowed 30 minutes to translate a passage from Chinese into English. You should write your answer on **Answer Sheet 2**.*

云南是位于中国西南的一个省，平均海拔1 500米。云南历史悠久，风景秀丽，气候宜人。云南生态环境优越，生物多种多样，被誉为野生动植物的天堂。云南还有多种矿藏和充足的水资源，为全省经济的可持续发展提供了有利条件。

云南居住着25个少数民族，他们大多有自己的语言、习俗和宗教。云南独特的自然景色和丰富的民族文化使其成为中国最受欢迎的旅游目的地之一，每年都吸引着大批国内外游客前往观光旅游。

2021年6月大学英语六级考试真题解析
（第二套）

Part Ⅰ Writing

成文构思

通过审题可知，该图表展示了1980年至2019年中国城市化的发展成果，我们可以从图表中清楚地看到，近四十年来中国城市化的程度呈逐渐上升的趋势。可按照如下思路行文：

第一段：指出中国城市化程度逐渐上升这一现象；
第二段：主体部分，分析中国城市化程度升高的原因；
第三段：总结，表明作者的观点。

参考范文及译文

  The chart shows the progress of urbanization in China from 1980 to 2019. According to the data, the proportion of the urban population has been increasing gradually from 19.39% to 60.50%.

  What **brings about** the steady growth of China's urbanization? The main reasons accounting for this phenomenon can be listed as follows. First and foremost, since the **reform and opening up** in 1978, China has gone through rapid growth of economy, which lays a solid foundation for its urbanization. And it conforms to objective law. What's more, the government attaches great importance to urbanization. In order to improve the well-being of its people and promote the **sustainable** development of the country, China has taken various measures to boost urbanization. As a result, people in cities and towns enjoy higher salaries and more satisfactory lives. Thus, people in rural areas are attracted to work in cities and they have earned more **disposable** income, which they could not have imagined in the past.

  In conclusion, China's urbanization enables people to enjoy better living conditions, and we should **cherish** the achievements and continue to deepen urbanization.

  图表显示了1980年到2019年中国城市化的进程。数据显示，城市人口的比例从19.39%逐渐上升到了60.50%。

  是什么促进了中国城市化的持续加深？形成这一现象的主要原因如下。首先，自1978年改革开放以来，中国经济快速增长，这为其城市化奠定了坚实的基础。并且这符合客观规律。此外，政府非常重视城市化。为改善民生、促进可持续发展，中国采取了多种措施来推动城市化，这使城镇居民的收入提高，生活水平也有所提高。因此，农村地区的人们被吸引到城市工作，他们获得了更多的可支配收入，这是他们过去无法想象的。

  综上所述，中国的城市化使人们享受到更好的生活条件，我们应该珍惜城市化的成果，并继续深化城市化。

词句点拨

bring about 带来

sustainable /səˈsteɪnəbl/ a. 可持续的

cherish /ˈtʃerɪʃ/ v. 珍惜；珍爱

reform and opening up 改革开放

disposable /dɪˈspəʊzəbl/ a. 可自由支配的

1. The chart shows... According to the data...

   图表显示了……数据显示……

2. What brings about the steady growth of...? The main reasons accounting for this phenomenon can be listed as follows.

   是什么促进了……的持续加深？形成这一现象的主要原因如下。

3. In order to improve... China has taken various measures to boost...

   为改善……中国采取了多种措施来推动……

Part Ⅱ　Listening Comprehension

Section A

Questions 1 to 4 are based on the conversation you have just heard.

听力原文及译文

M: How are you enjoying your new job?

W: So far so good. I don't miss having managers who deliver blunt, harsh feedback in the name of efficiency.

M: From the way you described your last company, no wonder they had a problem with high staff turnover.

W: Yeah, I couldn't wait to get out of there once my contract expired. (1) <u>The problem with a company culture that prizes directness above all else is that it creates a toxic culture of brilliant jerks that drives people out and erodes itself from within.</u>

M: (2) <u>My company's managers tend to be accommodating and kind, overlooking mistakes or issues so as not to hurt feelings.</u> Issues often get ignored there until they build up and reach a crisis point.

W: That's not surprising. My new company seems to employ a feedback policy that combines compassion and directness. (3) <u>Employees have the power to speak up, give feedback, disagree and discuss problems in real time.</u> It seems to help us to course correct, improve and meet challenges while also building teams that collaborate and care for one another.

M: But that would be based on an atmosphere of mutual trust, wouldn't it? Otherwise, people might interpret feedback as some kind of personal attack.

W: True. Without an atmosphere of trust, feedback can create stress and self-doubt. But I think when we get feedback from someone we trust, we understand that the feedback isn't some kind of personal attack. It's actually a kind of support, because it's offered in the spirit of helping us improve. I think sometimes people need to shift their mindsets around how they receive feedback.

M: Yes. (4) Constructive feedback, after all, is how we learn and grow. It's the basis for healthy parenting, lasting friendships, career development, and so much more. If we shelter our children, friends and colleagues from information that might enrich and enhance their lives, we're not being caring. We're actually doing harm to them.

W: That's exactly right.

男：你觉得你的新工作怎么样？

女：到目前为止还好。我并不怀念那些以效率之名提供直接又苛刻的反馈的管理者。

男：从你对上一家公司的描述来看，难怪他们有员工流动率高的问题。

女：是啊，合同一到期我就迫不及待地想离开那里。（1）崇尚"坦率至上"的企业文化的问题在于，它创造了一种"有毒"的文化，在这种文化下都是聪明的混蛋，把员工赶出去，并从内部腐蚀自己。

男：（2）我公司的经理们往往很乐于助人和友善，忽略错误或问题，以免伤害感情。问题经常被忽视，直到它们日积月累，达到造成危机的地步。

女：这并不奇怪。我的新公司似乎采用了一种既富有同情心又直接的反馈政策。（3）员工有权畅所欲言，给予反馈，提出异议并实时讨论问题。这样似乎帮助我们纠正错误，提高自我和迎接挑战，同时也使团队成员相互协作、相互关心。

男：但那是建立在相互信任的基础上的，不是吗？否则，人们可能会将反馈理解为某种人身攻击。

女：是的。没有信任的氛围，反馈会给人造成压力，让人产生自我怀疑。但我认为，当我们从我们信任的人那里得到反馈时，我们会明白，这些反馈并不是某种人身攻击。这实际上是一种支持，因为它是本着帮助我们进步的精神提供的。我认为有时候人们需要改变他们接受反馈的思维模式。

男：是的。（4）毕竟，建设性的反馈是我们学习和成长的方式。它是健康育儿、维持友谊、发展职业等诸多方面的基础。如果我们保护我们的孩子、朋友和同事，不让他们接触那些可能会丰富和改善他们生活的信息，我们就不是在关心他们。实际上，我们是在伤害他们。

女：完全正确。

难词总结

blunt /blʌnt/ *a.* 直言的；钝的

erode /ɪˈrəʊd/ *v.* 侵蚀；腐蚀

mindset /ˈmaɪndset/ *n.* 观念模式；思维倾向

turnover /ˈtɜːnəʊvə(r)/ *n.* 人事变更率

accommodating /əˈkɒmədeɪtɪŋ/ *a.* 乐于助人的

题目精析

1. How does the woman describe her previous company's culture?

   A) Weird.   C) Tolerant.
   B) Efficient.   D) Toxic.

1. 这位女士如何描述她上一家公司的文化？

   A）奇怪的。   C）包容的。
   B）高效的。   D）有毒的。

【答案及分析】D。本题考查女士对上一家公司文化的看法。音频中女士提到，The problem with a company culture that prizes directness above all else is that it creates a toxic culture of brilliant jerks that drives people out and erodes itself from within.（崇尚"坦率至上"的企业文化的问题在于，它创造了一种"有毒"的文化，在这种文化下都是聪明的混蛋，把员工赶出去，并从内部腐蚀自己。）D 项 Toxic 是原词复现，故选 D 项。

2. What does the man say about his company's managers?

A) They are arrogant.　　　　　　　　C) They are ambitious.

B) They are ignorant.　　　　　　　　D) They are accommodating.

2. 这位男士如何评价他公司的经理们？

A）他们很傲慢。　　　　　　　　　　C）他们野心勃勃。

B）他们很无知。　　　　　　　　　　D）他们很乐于助人。

【答案及分析】D。本题考查男士对他公司经理们的看法。音频中男士提到，My company's managers tend to be accommodating and kind, overlooking mistakes or issues so as not to hurt feelings.（我公司的经理们往往很乐于助人和友善，忽略错误或问题，以免伤害感情。）D 项中的 accommodating 是原词复现，故选 D 项。

3. What does the woman say the employees in her new company can do?

A) They can think big.　　　　　　　　C) They can break conventions.

B) They can air their views.　　　　　　D) They can work flexible hours.

3. 女士说她新公司的员工可以做什么？

A）他们可以大胆设想。　　　　　　　C）他们可以打破传统。

B）他们可以发表观点。　　　　　　　D）他们可以弹性工作。

【答案及分析】B。本题考查女士所在的新公司的员工可以做的事情。音频中女士提到，Employees have the power to speak up, give feedback, disagree and discuss problems in real time.（员工有权畅所欲言，给予反馈，提出异议并实时讨论问题。）B 项中的 air their views 是音频中 speak up 的同义表达，故选 B 项。

4. What does the man say about constructive feedback?

A) It can alter people's mindsets.　　　　C) It enables people to learn and grow.

B) It can lead to new discoveries.　　　　D) It is conducive to critical thinking.

4. 男士如何评价建设性的反馈？

A）它可以改变人们的思维模式。　　　C）它使人们学习和成长。

B）它可以带来新的发现。　　　　　　D）它有利于批判性思维。

【答案及分析】C。本题考查男士对建设性反馈的看法。音频中男士提到，Constructive feedback, after all, is how we learn and grow.（毕竟，建设性的反馈是我们学习和成长的方式。）C 项中的 learn and grow 为原词复现，故选 C 项。

Questions 5 to 8 are based on the conversation you have just heard.

听力原文及译文

W: How was your holiday? Not too many other tourists around, were there?

M: No, very few, relatively. (5) But I found myself moving from one accommodation to another, trying to find the perfect place. It made me realize that indecision is a big problem for me. Instead of relaxing, I was looking for the best spot.

W: It seems you suffer from "fear of better options". I've read about it. It describes this loop of indecision as part of our programming. (6) Essentially, we have this tendency to keep stretching out the decision-making process. Because as human beings, we are hardwired to optimize. We have always looked to get the best things we can as a sort of survival of the fittest. Optimizing isn't the problem, but rather the process that we go through.

M: Well, that makes me feel better. (7-1) But I think thanks to technology, we can make comparisons more easily and have more access to choice and customization. We can now see what we could have, how we might get it and what others have that we might want. We keep looking over and returning to the same options, again and again.

W: Yes. (7-2) Fear of better options offers little benefit. It's an ailment of abundance. You must have choices to have that fear of missing out on better options.

M: Yes. I need to note when I'm worrying about inconsequential things, I guess. If I'm spending too much time worrying over what to have for lunch, I'm robbing myself of the energy to focus on the things that matter.

W: Exactly. But for more important matters, I think gut instinct might be overrated. When you have 30 odd options, trusting your gut is not practical. (8) What you need to do is research, have a process, invest time exploring your options, and eliminate as many things as you can. The most toxic part of decision making is going over the same options, time and time again.

女：假期过得怎么样？周围没有太多其他游客，是吗？

男：是的，相对来说很少。（5）但我发现自己总是从一个住处搬到另一个住处，试图找到一个完美的地方。这让我意识到犹豫不决对我来说是个大问题。我是在寻找最佳的落脚点，而不是放松自己。

女：看来你"害怕更好的选择"。我读过相关的内容。它将这种犹豫不决的循环描述为我们程序的一部分。（6）本质上，我们有不断延长决策过程的倾向。因为作为人类，我们天生擅长优化。我们一直寻求我们所能得到的最好的东西，这应该算作一种适者生存。优化不是问题，我们经历的过程才是问题所在。

男：嗯，这让我感觉好多了。（7-1）但我认为多亏了技术，我们可以更容易地进行比较，有更多的机会进行选择和定制。我们现在可以看到我们能拥有什么，我们如何得到它，以及其他人拥有什么我们可能想要得到的东西。我们一遍又一遍地寻找，不断回到同样的选择。

女：是的。（7-2）对更好选择的恐惧没有什么好处。这是选择过多带来的苦恼。你必须有选择，才会害怕错过更好的选择。

男：是的。我想，当我担心无关紧要的事情时，我就需要注意了。如果我花太多时间担心午饭吃什么，我就剥夺了自己关注重要事情的精力。

女：就是这样。但更重要的是，我认为直觉可能被高估了。当你有30多个选择时，相信自己的直觉是不现实的。（8）你需要做的是研究，经历一个过程，花时间探究你的选择，并尽可能多地排除一些事情。做决定这件事最有害的部分就是一次又一次地纠结同样的选择。

难词总结

indecision /ˌɪndɪˈsɪʒn/ n. 无决断力；优柔寡断
be hardwired to 基本固定的
ailment /ˈeɪlmənt/ n. 轻病；小恙
stretch out 伸出；平躺
optimize /ˈɒptɪmaɪz/ v. 使最优化；充分利用
eliminate /ɪˈlɪmɪneɪt/ v. 排除；清除

题目精析

5. What does the man say about his holiday?

    A) He kept looking for the best place to stay.
    B) He met many tourists from other countries.
    C) He had a great time sightseeing and relaxing.
    D) He managed to visit a different city each day.

5. 关于假期，男士说了什么？

    A）他一直在寻找最好的住处。
    B）他遇到了很多来自其他国家的游客。
    C）他在观光和放松的时候玩得很开心。
    D）他每天都去一个不同的城市。

【答案及分析】A。本题考查男士假期中发生的事情。音频中男士提到，But I found myself moving from one accommodation to another, trying to find the perfect place.（但我发现自己总是从一个住处搬到另一个住处，试图找到一个完美的地方。）A 项中的 looking for the best place 是音频中 trying to find the perfect place 的同义表达，故选 A 项。

6. What does the woman say people tend to do when making decisions?

    A) Prioritize what is essential to their best advantage.
    B) Stretch out the process in search of the optimal.
    C) Deliberate the consequences that may occur.
    D) Take all relevant factors into consideration.

6. 女士说人们在做决定时往往会做什么？

    A）优先考虑对他们最有利的事情。
    B）在寻找最佳选项的过程中延长决策过程。
    C）认真考虑可能出现的结果。
    D）考虑所有相关的因素。

【答案及分析】B。本题考查女士对人们做决定时的倾向的看法。音频中女士提到，Essentially, we have this tendency to keep stretching out the decision-making process. Because as human beings, we are hardwired to optimize.（本质上，我们有不断延长决策过程的倾向。因为作为人类，我们天生擅长优化。）B 项中的 Stretch out 是原词复现，the process 指代音频中的 the decision-making process，optimal 对应音频中的 optimize，故选 B 项。

7. What has made decision making increasingly difficult?

    A) Time pressure.
    B) Tight budget.
    C) Modern technology.
    D) Fierce competition.

7. 是什么让决策日益困难？

    A）时间压力。
    C）现代科技。

B）紧缩的预算。 D）激烈的竞争。

【答案及分析】C。本题考查决策日益困难的原因。音频中提到，But I think thanks to technology, we can make comparisons more easily and have more access to choice and customization.（但我认为多亏了技术，我们可以更容易地进行比较，有更多的机会进行选择和定制。）也提到，Fear of better options offers little benefit. It's an ailment of abundance. You must have choices to have that fear of missing out on better options.（对更好选择的恐惧没有什么好处。这是选择过多带来的苦恼。你必须有选择，才会害怕错过更好的选择。）由此可知，技术使人们拥有了更多选择的机会，而选择过多导致人们害怕做决定，难以做决定，故选 C 项。

8. According to the woman, what should people do when making important decisions?

A) Research as many different options as possible.   C) Focus on what is practical.

B) Avoid going over the same options repeatedly.   D) Trust their gut instinct.

8. 根据女士的说法，人们在做重要决定时应该做什么？

A）尽可能多地研究不同的选择。   C）专注于实际的事情。

B）避免重复纠结同样的选择。   D）相信他们的直觉。

【答案及分析】B。本题考查女士对人们做重要决定时应该采取的做法的看法。音频中提到，What you need to do is research, have a process, invest time exploring your options, and eliminate as many things as you can. The most toxic part of decision making is going over the same options, time and time again.（你需要做的是研究，经历一个过程，花时间探究你的选择，并尽可能多地排除一些事情。做决定这件事最有害的部分就是一次又一次地纠结同样的选择。）B 项中的 going over the same options 是原词复现，repeatedly 是音频中 time and time again 的同义表达，重复纠结同样的选择是做决定过程中最有害的部分，应该尽力避免，故选 B 项。

Section B

Questions 9 to 11 are based on the passage you have just heard.

听力原文及译文

　　The role of homework in classrooms is not a new debate. Many parents and teachers are ardent supporters of homework. But do all students benefit from homework? (9) A 2006 research paper suggested some correlation between the amount of homework done by a student and future academic achievement for middle and high school students. But not so much for younger kids. A Stanford study in 2014 suggested the same was true for students in California's affluent communities. The findings challenged the idea that homework was inherently good. The researchers concluded that there was an upper limit to the correlation between homework and achievement, suggesting that high school students shouldn't be doing more than two hours of homework a night. And the most valuable kind of homework for elementary level children was simply assigned free reading.

　　The topic gets more complicated when we talk about the divide between rural and urban communities. (10) Studies found that in remote areas, the poor quality or lack of Internet access can put students at a disadvantage because 70% of teachers in these areas assign homework that requires Internet access. But one in three households doesn't have Internet. Experts assert homework requiring the Internet isn't fair.

While the debate continues about the effect of homework on academic achievements, there are studies focusing on other benefits of homework. (11) A study in Germany found that homework could have an effect on students' personalities, suggesting that doing homework might help kids to become more conscientious and independent learners.

家庭作业在课堂上的作用并不是一个新的争论话题。许多父母和老师都是家庭作业的热情支持者。但是所有学生都能从家庭作业中获益吗？(9)2006年的一篇研究论文表明，初高中生的家庭作业量与未来的学业成绩之间存在一定的相关性，但对年幼的孩子来说就没有那么强的相关性了。斯坦福大学2014年的一项研究表明，加利福尼亚州富裕社区的学生情况也是如此。这些研究发现对"家庭作业本质上是好的"这一观点提出了质疑。研究人员得出结论，家庭作业和学业成绩之间的相关性有上限，并建议高中生每晚做家庭作业的时间不应超过2小时。对小学阶段的孩子来说，最有价值的家庭作业就是自由阅读。

当我们谈到农村和城市社区之间的差距时，这个话题变得更加复杂。(10)研究发现，在偏远地区，互联网质量差或联不上网会使学生处于不利地位，因为这些地区70%的教师布置的作业需要联网完成。但三分之一的家庭没有互联网。专家认为，需要上网完成的家庭作业是不公平的。

在关于家庭作业对学习成绩的影响的争论继续时，有研究关注家庭作业的其他好处。(11)德国的一项研究发现，家庭作业可能会对学生的个性产生影响，这表明做家庭作业可能有助于孩子们成为更认真、更独立的学习者。

难词总结

ardent /ˈɑːdnt/ a. 热烈的；激情的
correlation /ˌkɒrəˈleɪʃn/ n. 相互关系；相关

inherently /ɪnˈhɪərəntli; ɪnˈherəntli/ ad. 固有地；内在地
conscientious /ˌkɒnʃiˈenʃəs/ a. 勤勉认真的

题目精析

9. What did the 2006 research find about homework?

   A) It is beneficial to poor as well as rich communities.

   B) It is conducive to children's future development.

   C) It is welcome to parents but not to children.

   D) It is not of much help to younger children.

9. 关于家庭作业，2006年的调查发现了什么？

   A）它对穷人和富人社区都有好处。

   B）它有利于孩子未来的发展。

   C）它受父母欢迎，但不受孩子欢迎。

   D）它对年幼的孩子没有多大帮助。

【答案及分析】D. 本题考查2006年关于家庭作业的调查的结果。音频中提到，A 2006 research paper suggested some correlation between the amount of homework done by a student and future academic achievement for middle and high school students. But not so much for younger kids.（2006 年的一篇研究论文表明，初高中生的家庭作业量与未来的学业成绩之间存在一定的相关性。但对年幼的孩子来说就没有那么强的相关性了。）D 项 It is not of much help to younger children 是 But not so much for younger kids 的同义表达，故选 D 项。

10. What do experts think of homework requiring Internet access?

    A) It may put some students in remote areas at a disadvantage.

    B) It gives the majority of students ready access to their teachers.

    C) It effectively improves the learning quality of students in rural areas.

    D) It can bridge the learning gap between kids of different backgrounds.

10. 专家如何看待需要联网才能做的作业？

    A）这可能会对一些偏远地区的学生不利。

    B）这让大多数学生可以随时联系到他们的老师。

    C）这有效地提高了农村地区学生的学习能力。

    D）这可以消除不同背景的孩子之间的学习差距。

【答案及分析】A。本题考查专家对需要联网才能做的作业的看法。音频中提到，Studies found that in remote areas, the poor quality or lack of Internet access can put students at a disadvantage because 70% of teachers in these areas assign homework that requires Internet access. But one in three households doesn't have Internet. Experts assert homework requiring the Internet isn't fair.（研究发现，在偏远地区，互联网质量差或联不上网会使学生处于不利地位，因为这些地区 70% 的教师布置的作业需要联网完成。但三分之一的家庭没有互联网。专家认为，需要上网完成的家庭作业是不公平的。）A 项是对该部分的概括总结，其中，in remote areas 和 at a disadvantage 都是原词复现，故选 A 项。

11. What conclusion could be drawn from the study in Germany?

    A) Diligent students tend to do their homework independently.

    B) The focus of homework should always be on school subjects.

    C) Doing homework exerts a positive effect on kids' personality development.

    D) The benefits of doing homework vary widely from individual to individual.

11. 从德国的研究中可以得出什么结论？

    A）勤奋的学生往往独立完成作业。

    B）家庭作业的重点应该始终放在学校科目上。

    C）做家庭作业对孩子的个性发展有积极作用。

    D）做家庭作业的好处因人而异。

【答案及分析】C。本题考查德国一项研究的结论。音频中提到，A study in Germany found that homework could have an effect on students' personalities, suggesting that doing homework might help kids to become more conscientious and independent learners.（德国的一项研究发现，家庭作业可能会对学生的个性产生影响，这表明做家庭作业可能有助于孩子们成为更认真、更独立的学习者。）C 项是对该部分的概括总结，其中，Doing homework 和 personality 是原词复现，exerts a positive effect on 是音频中 have an effect on 和 help 的同义表达，故选 C 项。

Questions 12 to 15 are based on the passage you have just heard.

听力原文及译文

Robert Goddard, an American born in 1882, is widely regarded as the world's first rocket scientist. At age 27, Goddard published his first book in which he hypothesized that a rocket launched from earth could reach the moon. Like many visionaries, the young scientist encountered numerous skeptics. (12) In January, 1920, the *New York Times* ridiculed Goddard's theory that rockets could be utilized for space exploration. 49 years later, Apollo 11 reached the moon, and the famed newspaper published an apology to Goddard. (13) Goddard launched his first rocket from an aunt's farm in his native Massachusetts in March 1926. His maiden rocket voyage lasted a mere three seconds. It scaled an altitude of only 12 meters. Nonetheless, it was a milestone in rocket science.

(14) Goddard later consulted with a weather expert and determined that the climate of New Mexico was ideal for year-round rocket launches. In 1930, Goddard and his family relocated there to a remote valley in the southwest of the country. There he established a laboratory and test range. However, the ambitious scientist received negligible support from the government.

For four years, wealthy businessman Daniel Guggenheim provided Goddard with an annual $25,000 grant to pursue his dreams. Other rocket enthusiasts also raised funds for him. Over time, Goddard's rockets grew more sophisticated and included the installation of instruments. In spite of his many successes, Goddard was never able to interest the US military in rocket-propelled weapons. (15) He was granted over 200 patents and continued to pioneer rocket technology until his death in 1945.

罗伯特·戈达德，美国人，出生于1882年，被公认为世界上第一位火箭科学家。27岁时，戈达德出版了他的第一本书，在书中他假设从地球发射的火箭可以到达月球。像许多有远见的人一样，这位年轻的科学家遇到了许多怀疑论者。(12) 1920年1月，《纽约时报》嘲笑了戈达德提出的可以用火箭进行太空探索的理论。49年后，阿波罗11号到达月球，这家著名的报纸发表了对戈达德的道歉声明。(13) 1926年3月，戈达德在家乡马萨诸塞州一个姑姑的农场发射了他的第一枚火箭。他的首次火箭航行仅持续了3秒。所到达的高度只有12米。尽管如此，这也是火箭科学的一个里程碑。

（14）戈达德后来咨询了一位气象专家，确定新墨西哥州的气候全年都适合发射火箭。1930年，戈达德和他的家人搬到了新墨西哥州西南部的一个偏远山谷。他在那里建立了一个实验室和试验场。然而，这位雄心勃勃的科学家从政府得到的支持却微不足道。

四年来，富有的商人丹尼尔·古根海姆每年为戈达德提供25 000美元的资助，让他去追求梦想。其他火箭爱好者也为他筹集资金。随着时间的推移，戈达德的火箭变得越来越复杂，包括了仪器的安装。尽管戈达德取得了许多成功，但他始终无法使美国军方对火箭推进的武器产生兴趣。（15）他获得了200多项专利，并继续开拓火箭技术，直到1945年去世为止。

难词总结

hypothesize /haɪˈpɒθəsaɪz/ v. 假设；假定
skeptic /ˈskeptɪk/ n. 怀疑论者

visionary /ˈvɪʒənri/ n. 有远见卓识的人
scale /skeɪl/ v. 攀登；到达……顶点

negligible /ˈneglɪdʒəbl/ *a.* 微不足道的；不重要的　　enthusiast /ɪnˈθjuːziæst/ *n.* 爱好者

题目精析

12. What do we learn about Goddard's idea of using rockets for space exploration?
    A) It was something he apologized for later.　　C) It was a forty-nine-year plan.
    B) It was ridiculed by the *New York Times*.　　D) It was considered visionary.

12. 关于戈达德提出的用火箭进行太空探索的想法，我们了解到什么？
    A）他后来为此道歉了。　　C）它是一个长达49年的计划。
    B）它遭到了《纽约时报》的嘲笑。　　D）它被视为有远见的。

【答案及分析】B。本题考查戈达德用火箭进行太空探索这一想法的相关内容。音频中提到，In January, 1920, the *New York Times* ridiculed Goddard's theory that rockets could be utilized for space exploration.（1920年1月，《纽约时报》嘲笑了戈达德提出的可以用火箭进行太空探索的理论。）B项中的 ridiculed 和 the *New York Times* 是原词复现，故选B项。

13. What does the passage say about Goddard's first rocket launch?
    A) It was of great significance to rocket science.　　C) It was somehow delayed about 12 minutes.
    B) It was completed in the state of New Mexico.　　D) It failed due to a sudden change of weather.

13. 关于戈达德的第一次火箭发射，文章中说了什么？
    A）它对火箭科学有重大意义。　　C）它不知为什么延迟了12分钟。
    B）它是在新墨西哥州完成的。　　D）它因为天气突变失败了。

【答案及分析】A。本题考查戈达德第一次火箭发射的相关内容。音频中提到，Goddard launched his first rocket from an aunt's farm in his native Massachusetts in March 1926. His maiden rocket voyage lasted a mere three seconds. It scaled an altitude of only 12 meters. Nonetheless, it was a milestone in rocket science.（1926年3月，戈达德在家乡马萨诸塞州一个姑姑的农场发射了他的第一枚火箭。他的首次火箭航行仅持续了3秒。所到达的高度只有12米。尽管如此，这也是火箭科学的一个里程碑。）B、C项与音频内容不符，故排除；音频中并未提及发射失败的原因，故D项排除；A项 It was of great significance to rocket science 是音频中 it was a milestone in rocket science 的同义表达，故选A项。

14. Why did Goddard move to New Mexico?
    A) A laboratory and test range was already set up there.
    B) Its climate was ideal for year-round rocket launching.
    C) A weather expert invited him to go there for his mission.
    D) Its remote valleys were appealing to him and his family.

14. 为什么戈达德搬到了新墨西哥州？
    A）那里已经建立了实验室和试验场。
    B）那里的气候全年都适合火箭发射。
    C）一位气象专家邀请他去那里完成任务。
    D）偏远的山谷吸引了他和他的家人。

【答案及分析】B。本题考查戈达德搬到新墨西哥州的原因。音频中提到，Goddard later consulted with a weather expert and determined that the climate of New Mexico was ideal for year-round rocket launches. In 1930, Goddard and his family relocated there to a remote valley in the southwest of the country.（戈达德后来咨询了一位气象专家，确定新墨西哥州的气候全年都适合发射火箭。1930 年，戈达德和他的家人搬到了新墨西哥州西南部的一个偏远山谷。）B 项 Its climate was ideal for year-round rocket launching 是音频中 the climate of New Mexico was ideal for year-round rocket launches 的同义表达，故选 B 项。

15. What does the passage say about Goddard's achievements?

　　A) He won an award from the US government for his work.

　　B) He gained recognition from rocket scientists worldwide.

　　C) He was granted over 200 patents in rocket technology.

　　D) He boosted the military strength of the United States.

15. 关于戈达德的成就，文章中说了什么？

　　A）他的工作获得了美国政府的嘉奖。

　　B）他得到了全世界火箭科学家的认可。

　　C）他获得了 200 多项火箭技术的专利。

　　D）他增强了美国的军事力量。

【答案及分析】C。本题考查戈达德的成就。音频最后提到，He was granted over 200 patents and continued to pioneer rocket technology until his death in 1945.（他获得了 200 多项专利，并继续开拓火箭技术，直到 1945 年去世为止。）C 项中的 He was granted over 200 patents 和 rocket technology 是原词复现，故选 C 项。

Section C

Questions 16 to 18 are based on the recording you have just heard.

听力原文及译文

　　(16) Working for a new venture comes with a lot of risks — that is, instability, unclear responsibilities and the need to be a master of all trades. But the primary benefit is usually the passion and excitement associated with playing a role in a promising new company. The person to thank for that passion and excitement is almost always the entrepreneur. There's something about the founder's energy and enthusiasm that infects the rest of the team. The willingness to take risks may inspire others to be more courageous. The optimism and positivity may motivate people to focus less on trivial and unimportant matters. The celebration of milestones may prompt staff to be more grateful about their own accomplishments and privileges. What becomes set in the firm's culture is a contagious collection of affirmative and positive emotions which are usually shared among the team.

　　(17) Science has already done a good job of proving the results that follow. These include better processes, greater team cohesion, reduced conflict and sharper alertness. But what is yet to be demonstrated is whether the founders' passion leads to increased team performance. This was recently tested in research which analyzed the teams of 73 new companies across a range of industries such as IT, medicine and energy. The CEOs were

consulted once again years after the initial analysis, and most shared their firm's performance reports, so that their success could be more objectively measured.

Entrepreneurial teams generally progress through three phases. The first is inventing a product or service. The second is founding the venture to sell that product or service. And the third is developing the firm so it continues to grow. The research has discovered that when the team is passionate about the third phase — developing a firm — there's a clear link to performance. But the first phase — a passion for invention — is not a reliable indicator that the firm will still be open for business a few years later. Likewise, the second — a passion for founding the venture — doesn't necessarily translate into great success. The solution to great team performance stems from a willingness to recruit others who could direct their passion towards the third phase of entrepreneurialism — developing the business.

Employing more staff can, in itself, be a risk for an entrepreneur, as is paying them big dollars to attract them. (18) On many occasions, the entrepreneurs reported not paying themselves a wage at all initially in order to cover salaries and expenses.

（16）为一家新的企业工作会带来很多风险——不稳定、职责不明确，以及需要精通各领域的工作。但最主要的好处通常在于，在一家前途光明的新公司中发挥作用所带来的激情和兴奋。而感谢那种激情和兴奋的人几乎总是企业家。创始人的精力和热情会感染团队的其他成员。愿意冒险的精神可能会激励别人变得更勇敢。乐观和积极可以激励人们少关注琐碎和不重要的事情。庆祝里程碑式的成就可能会促使员工更加感激自己的成就和特权。在公司文化中形成的是一种具有感染力的肯定和积极情绪的集合，这些情绪通常在团队中共享。

（17）科学已经很好地证明了随之而来的结果。这包括流程优化、团队凝聚力增强、冲突减少和警觉性更敏锐。但还有待证明的是，创始人的热情是否会提高团队绩效。这在最近的一项研究中得到了验证，该研究分析了来自信息技术、医药和能源等一系列行业的73家新公司的团队。在初始分析的几年后，研究者再次咨询了首席执行官们，大多数人分享了他们公司的业绩报告，以便研究者更客观地衡量他们的成功。

创业团队的发展通常经历三个阶段。第一阶段是发明一种产品或服务。第二阶段是建立企业，销售该产品或服务。第三阶段是发展企业，让它继续壮大。研究发现，当团队对第三阶段——发展企业——充满热情时，这种热情与绩效有明显的联系。但是第一阶段——对发明的热情——并不是一个表明公司在几年后还会继续营业的可靠指标。同样，第二阶段——对创业的热情——并不一定会转化为巨大的成功。要想实现优秀的团队绩效，就需要愿意招募那些能够将自己的热情引向创业的第三阶段——发展企业——的人。

雇用更多的员工本身对企业家来说是一种风险，就像支付高薪来吸引他们一样。（18）在很多情况下，创业者报告说，为了支付工资和开销，他们最初根本没有给自己发工资。

难词总结

venture /ˈventʃə(r)/ n. 企业；商业
team cohesion 团队凝聚力

infect /ɪnˈfekt/ v. 使感染；传染
initially /ɪˈnɪʃəli/ ad. 开始；最初；起初

题目精析

16. What does the speaker say about working for a new venture?

A) It requires entrepreneurial experience.　　C) It can be quite frustrating.
B) It is usually financially rewarding.　　D) It can be rather risky.

16. 关于为一家新企业工作，说话者说了什么？

A）这需要创业经验。　　C）这可能非常令人沮丧。
B）这通常有很高的报酬。　　D）这可能相当冒险。

【答案及分析】D。本题考查为一家新企业工作的相关情况。音频开头提到，Working for a new venture comes with a lot of risks — that is, instability, unclear responsibilities and the need to be a master of all trades.（为一家新的企业工作会带来很多风险——不稳定、职责不明确，以及需要精通各领域的工作。）D 项 It can be rather risky 是音频中 comes with a lot of risks 的同义表达，故选 D 项。

17. What has science demonstrated regarding the positive culture of a new venture?

A) It contributes to rapid business expansion.　　C) It reduces conflict among team members.
B) It inspires willingness to make sacrifices.　　D) It encourages creation and innovation.

17. 关于一家新企业的积极文化，科学证明了什么？

A）它有助于业务迅速扩张。　　C）它减少团队成员之间的冲突。
B）它激发人们做贡献的意愿。　　D）它鼓励创造和创新。

【答案及分析】C。本题考查关于新企业的积极文化的科学结论。音频中提到，Science has already done a good job of proving the results that follow. These include better processes, greater team cohesion, reduced conflict and sharper alertness.（科学已经很好地证明了随之而来的结果。这包括流程优化、团队凝聚力增强、冲突减少和警觉性更敏锐。）C 项中的 reduces conflict 是原词复现，故选 C 项。

18. What does the speaker say about entrepreneurs at the initial stage of a new venture?

A) They have unrealistic expectations.　　C) Few can find willing investors.
B) They often work without any pay.　　D) Many are idealistic dreamers.

18. 关于创业初期的创业者，说话者说了什么？

A）他们有不切实际的期望。　　C）很少有人能找到愿意投资的人。
B）他们经常无偿工作。　　D）很多都是理想主义的梦想家。

【答案及分析】B。本题考查创业初期的创业者的相关内容。音频最后提到，On many occasions, the entrepreneurs reported not paying themselves a wage at all initially in order to cover salaries and expenses.（在很多情况下，创业者报告说，为了支付工资和开销，他们最初根本没有给自己发工资。）B 项中的 work without any pay 是音频中 not paying themselves a wage at all 的同义表达，故选 B 项。

Questions 19 to 21 are based on the recording you have just heard.

听力原文及译文

Aging is a curious thing, and people's desire to beat it and death has become an industry worth hundreds of billions of dollars. Despite the huge investment into research, aging remains somewhat obscure, although there are certain things researchers do understand. They know that women tend to have longer life spans, living on average six years longer than men. (19) No one is really certain of the reason for this, although the speculation centers around the idea that women are more capable of surviving or handling disease than men. For virtually every disease, the effects are greater on men than they are on women. Some suggest that women's immune systems benefit from their tendency to prioritize and nurture social connections. But for me, this explanation is hardly convincing.

Researchers also know to an extent what causes aging. For 60 years, it was believed that cells would continue to divide forever. (20) It was only uncovered in relatively recent times that older people's cells divide a smaller number of times than younger people's. Only cancer cells, in fact, are capable of dividing forever. Human cells have a limited reproductive ability. To an extent, we can postpone the eventual stop of cells' dividing through nutrition, exercise, good sleep and even relaxation techniques, but we cannot stop the aging process. And researchers are yet to answer the ultimate question of aging: why does the body ultimately fall to pieces? In the opinion of some of the world's best scientific minds on the subject, part of the reason we don't yet have any answer is because many researchers are looking in the wrong direction. (21) Many public health policymakers believe that the resolution of age-associated disease will tell us something fundamental about the aging process, but, say some top scientists, that's completely erroneous. They point out, when the diseases of childhood were eliminated... this did not provide any insight into childhood development.

In the same way, the idea that the resolution of age-associated diseases like heart disease and stroke will inform us about aging is not based on sound science or logic. At best, if the major causes of death in developed countries were eliminated, this would only add a decade to average life expectancy. But while there is money available to be spent on it, the search to understand the secrets of aging will be ongoing.

衰老是一件奇怪的事情，人们对战胜衰老和死亡的渴望已经成为一个价值数千亿美元的产业。尽管在研究上投入了巨大的资金，但衰老问题仍然有些不明确，尽管研究人员确实了解了一些事情。他们知道女性往往寿命更长，平均寿命比男性长6年。（19）没有人确切地知道其中的原因，尽管推测都集中在女性比男性更有能力生存或应对疾病这一观点上。几乎每一种疾病对男性的影响都大于女性。一些人认为，女性的免疫系统受益于她们优先考虑和培养社会关系的倾向。但对我来说，这种解释很难令人信服。

研究人员也在一定程度上了解导致衰老的原因。60年来，人们一直认为细胞会永远分裂下去。（20）直到最近人们才发现，老年人的细胞分裂次数比年轻人的要少。事实上，只有癌细胞能够永远分裂。人类细胞的繁殖能力有限。在某种程度上，我们可以通过营养、锻炼、良好的睡眠甚至放松技巧来推迟细胞分裂的最终停止，但我们无法阻止衰老的过程。研究人员还没有回答关于衰老的终极问题：为什么身体最终会分解？世界上一些最优秀的科学家认为，我们还没有得出任何答案的部分原因在于许多研究人员找错了方向。（21）许多公共卫生决策者认为，解决与衰老有关的疾病会让我们了解关于衰老过程的一些基本信息，但是，一些顶级科学家说，这是完全错误的。他们指出，当我们战胜儿童疾病时……这并没有为儿童的发展提供任何见解。

同样，认为解决与年龄有关的疾病（如心脏病和中风）会让我们了解衰老的想法，也不是基于健全的科学或逻辑。如果发达国家的主要死亡原因被消除，这充其量只会使平均预期寿命增加10年。

但是，在有资金用于这方面研究的同时，对衰老秘密的探索仍将继续进行。

难词总结

obscure /əbˈskjʊə(r)/ *a.* 鲜为人知的；费解的　　speculation /spekjuˈleɪʃn/ *n.* 推测；猜测

erroneous /ɪˈrəʊniəs/ *a.* 错误的

题目精析

19. What do we learn about the possible reason why women tend to live longer?

　　A) They have better dietary habits.　　C) They are born with a stronger ability to socialize.

　　B) They bear fewer social responsibilities.　　D) They are better able to survive or handle disease.

19. 关于女性往往更长寿的可能的原因，我们了解到什么？

　　A）她们的饮食习惯更好。　　C）她们生来就有更强的社交能力。

　　B）她们的社会责任更少。　　D）她们能更好地生存或应对疾病。

【答案及分析】D。本题考查女性更长寿的可能原因。音频中提到，No one is really certain of the reason for this, although the speculation centers around the idea that women are more capable of surviving or handling disease than men.（没有人确切地知道其中的原因，尽管推测都集中在女性比男性更有能力生存或应对疾病这一观点上。）D 项中的 are better able 是音频中 are more capable 的同义表达，故选 D 项。

20. What is the recent discovery about human cells?

　　A) They have a limited reproductive ability.　　C) They keep dividing throughout one's life.

　　B) They depend on adequate sleep to thrive.　　D) They strengthen with regular exercise.

20. 关于人类细胞的最新发现是什么？

　　A）它们的繁殖能力有限。　　C）它们在人的一生中不断分裂。

　　B）它们依靠充足的睡眠来茁壮成长。　　D）它们通过定期锻炼得到加强。

【答案及分析】A。本题考查关于人类细胞的最新发现。音频中提到，It was only uncovered in relatively recent times that older people's cells divide a smaller number of times than younger people's. Only cancer cells, in fact, are capable of dividing forever. Human cells have a limited reproductive ability.（直到最近人们才发现，老年人的细胞分裂次数比年轻人的要少。事实上，只有癌细胞能够永远分裂。人类细胞的繁殖能力有限。）A 项中的 have a limited reproductive ability 为原词复现，故选 A 项。

21. What do many public health policymakers believe?

　　A) The process of aging can ultimately be brought under control.

　　B) Improved health care for the elderly will contribute to longevity.

　　C) Prevention of heart disease and stroke will increase life expectancy.

　　D) The resolution of age-related diseases will solve the mystery of aging.

21. 很多公共卫生决策者的观点是什么？

　　A）衰老的过程最终会得到控制。

　　B）改善老年人的医疗保健将有助于长寿。

　　C）防止心脏病和中风会增加预期寿命。

　　D）解决与衰老有关的疾病将解开衰老的秘密。

【答案及分析】D。本题考查公共卫生决策者的观点。音频中提到，Many public health policymakers believe that the resolution of age-associated disease will tell us something fundamental about the aging process, but, say some top scientists, that's completely erroneous.（许多公共卫生决策者认为，解决与衰老有关的疾病会让我们了解关于衰老过程的一些基本信息，但是，一些顶级科学家说，这是完全错误的。）D 项 The resolution of age-related diseases will solve the mystery of aging 是音频中 the resolution of age-associated disease will tell us something fundamental about the aging process 的同义表达，故选 D 项。

Questions 22 to 25 are based on the recording you have just heard.

听力原文及译文

Good afternoon. In today's talk, we'll discuss how managers can get their staff to do what they are asked. (22) Much to their frustration, managers often struggle to get their staff to comply with even simple instructions. Often they blame their employees "they don't read emails" "they don't listen" "they don't care" ... that kind of thing. But according to recent research conducted in Australia, it looks like it's not the employees' fault but the managers'. It's easy to understand why people sometimes disobey procedures intentionally. (23) Occasionally, it's because they're pressured to finish in a short time. At other times, they may disagree with the spirit of the procedure — the effort demanded, the time consumed, the lack of potential effectiveness. And every now and then, they just don't want to, maybe deliberately or out of stubbornness.

So apart from that, what else gets in the way of procedural compliance? The research scholars surveyed 152 blue-collar workers from two separate sites in the mining industry. They asked the workers a range of procedure-related questions, such as whether they found the procedures useful, how confident they felt in their job, how comfortable they were to speak up in the workplace, and how closely they followed any new procedures set by their managers. They were also asked to rate the extent to which they perceive their supervisors to be helpful. That last statement was the most instructive because, as the researchers found, (24) there was a remarkably strong correlation between how helpful supervisors were perceived to be, and how likely their employees were to follow their directors.

Supervisors' helping behavior was found to be motivational in nature. It increased employees' perception of the likelihood of success in the attainment of job goals, and therefore fostered a willingness to dedicate their effort and ability to their work.

In short, managers should be ongoing role models for the change. As the saying goes, "Do as I do, not as I say." To affect behavioral change, what's most required is interaction and involvement — the human touch — and, naturally, processes that add value. Although procedures are designed to guide and support employees' work, employees, it seems, can't always be expected to comply with procedures that are not seen as useful. And of course, managers shouldn't keep resending emails. (25) They are an effective tool for the sharing of data and report, but they're a hopeless tool if what a manager's desiring is a change in behavior.

下午好。在今天的谈话中，我们将讨论经理们如何让他们的员工按照要求去做。（22）令经理们非

25

常沮丧的是，即使是简单的指示，他们往往也难以让员工遵守。他们经常责怪员工"他们不看邮件""他们不听话""他们不用心"……诸如此类的话。但根据澳大利亚最近的一项研究，这似乎不是员工的错，而是经理们的错。我们很容易理解为什么人们有时会故意违反程序。(23)有时是因为迫于压力要在短时间内完成工作。在其他时候，他们可能不认同程序所传达的精神——所需要的努力、所消耗的时间，以及潜在有效性的缺乏。有时，他们只是不想这么做，可能是故意的，也可能是固执己见。

那么除此之外，还有什么会妨碍员工遵守程序呢？研究学者调查了152名蓝领工人，他们来自采矿业两个不同的工作地点。研究人员向工人询问了一系列与程序相关的问题，例如他们是否觉得这些程序有用，他们对自己的工作有多大的信心，他们在工作场所有多大的发言权，以及他们在多大程度上遵循了经理制定的新程序。他们也被要求评估他们认为的主管对自己有帮助的程度。研究人员发现，最后一项最有启发性，(24)员工认为的主管对自己有帮助的程度与他们听从雇主指示的可能性之间存在显著的强相关性。

研究发现，主管的帮助行为具有鼓舞性。它增加了员工对成功实现工作目标的可能性的认识，因此培养了他们为工作付出努力和能力的意愿。

简而言之，经理们应该持续成为变革的榜样。俗话说："照我做的去做，不要照我说的去做。"为了影响行为的改变，最需要的是互动和参与——人的接触——当然，还有增加价值的过程。虽然程序的设计是为了指导和支持员工的工作，但似乎不能总是期望员工遵守那些被认为无用的程序。当然，经理们不应该一直重复发送电子邮件。(25)电子邮件是共享数据和报告的有效工具，但如果经理们想要的是行为上的改变，它们就毫无用处了。

难词总结

frustration /frʌˈstreɪʃn/ *n.* 懊恼；沮丧

compliance /kəmˈplaɪəns/ *n.* 服从；遵从

comply with 遵守

题目精析

22. Why are managers often frustrated with their employees?

  A) They are reluctant to follow instructions. C) They cannot understand directives.

  B) They fail to answer emails promptly. D) They do not show due respect.

22. 为什么经理们经常因为他们的员工感到沮丧？

  A）他们不愿意听从指示。 C）他们不能理解指示。

  B）他们不能及时回复电子邮件。 D）他们没有表现出应有的尊重。

【答案及分析】A。本题考查经理们经常因为他们的员工感到沮丧的原因。音频开头提到，Much to their frustration, managers often struggle to get their staff to comply with even simple instructions.（令经理们非常沮丧的是，即使是简单的指示，他们往往也难以让员工遵守。）A项中的 follow instructions 是音频中 comply with even simple instructions 的同义表达，故选 A 项。

23. Why do employees sometimes disobey procedures intentionally?

  A) They have not been trained to follow the rules. C) They want to avoid unnecessary losses.

  B) They are not satisfied with the management. D) They find their voice go unheeded.

23. 为什么员工有时候会故意不遵守程序?

   A) 他们没有接受过要遵守规则的训练。
   C) 他们想避免不必要的损失。
   B) 他们对管理不满意。
   D) 他们发现自己的声音被忽视了。

   【答案及分析】B。本题考查员工有时候故意不遵守程序的原因。音频中提到，Occasionally, it's because they're pressured to finish in a short time. At other times, they may disagree with the spirit of the procedure — the effort demanded, the time consumed, the lack of potential effectiveness. And every now and then, they just don't want to, maybe deliberately or out of stubbornness.（有时是因为迫于压力要在短时间内完成工作。在其他时候，他们可能不认同程序所传达的精神——所需要的努力、所消耗的时间，以及潜在有效性的缺乏。有时，他们只是不想这么做，可能是故意的，也可能是固执己见。）该部分列出了员工有时候不遵守程序的原因，即时间压力大，不认同程序所传达的精神，以及出于故意或固执己见。B 项 They are not satisfied with the management 是对此的概括总结，故选 B 项。

24. When are employees more likely to follow instructions according to the researchers?

   A) When they are on good terms with their managers.
   C) When they find their supervisors helpful.
   B) When they find their job goals easily attainable.
   D) When they are financially motivated.

24. 根据研究人员的调查，员工什么时候更有可能听从指示?

   A) 当他们和自己的经理关系良好时。
   C) 当他们发现主管对自己有帮助时。
   B) 当他们发现自己的目标易于达成时。
   D) 当他们有经济动机时。

   【答案及分析】C。本题考查员工何时更有可能听从指示。音频中提到，there was a remarkably strong correlation between how helpful supervisors were perceived to be, and how likely their employees were to follow their directors（员工认为的主管对自己有帮助的程度与他们听从雇主指示的可能性之间存在显著的强相关性）。C 项中的 supervisors 和 helpful 都是原词复现，故选 C 项。

25. What does the speaker say about emails?

   A) They are a useless tool for managers to change employee behavior.
   B) They prove to be a good means for managers to give instructions.
   C) They should be reserved for urgent communication.
   D) They are seldom used for sharing confidential data.

25. 关于电子邮件，说话者说了什么?

   A) 它们是经理们改变员工行为的无用的工具。
   B) 它们被证明是经理们下达指示的好途径。
   C) 它们应该留作紧急沟通之用。
   D) 它们几乎不被用于共享机密数据。

   【答案及分析】A。本题考查说话者对电子邮件的看法。音频中提到，They are an effective tool for the sharing of data and report, but they're a hopeless tool if what a manager's desiring is a change in behavior.（电子邮件是共享数据和报告的有效工具，但如果经理们想要的是行为上的改变，它们就毫无用处了。）A 项 They are a useless tool for managers to change employee behavior 是音频中 they're a hopeless tool if what a manager's desiring is a change in behavior 的同义表达，故选 A 项。

Part Ⅲ　Reading Comprehension

Section A

全文翻译

一项新的研究描绘了澳大利亚现有的儿童文学作品所反映的文化包容性较弱的状况。埃迪斯科文大学教育学院的海伦·亚当博士调查了儿童书籍的文化多样性。她评估了西澳大利亚州四个日托中心几间幼儿园房间里收藏的书。一共 2 413 本书，其中只有18%的书包含对有色人种的描述。少数民族文化往往以刻板的或象征性的方式表现出来，例如，用筷子和传统服装来描绘亚洲文化。代表少数民族文化的人物在书中通常是次要角色，而主要角色大多是白人。这引起了人们的担忧，因为它会给人留下白人更重要的印象。

亚当博士说，孩子们在很小的时候就形成了对"差异"和身份的印象。有证据表明，他们从3个月大的时候就开始产生对自己种族的偏爱。我们向幼儿分享的书籍可能是培养孩子了解自己和他人的宝贵机会。书籍也可以让孩子们看到多样性。他们发现自己和他人之间的相似点和不同点。这有助于培养对多样性的理解、接受和欣赏。

人口普查数据显示，澳大利亚人来自200多个国家。他们在家里说的语言超过300种。此外，澳大利亚人分属于100多个不同的宗教团体。他们从事的职业有1 000多种。"澳大利亚是一个有着多元文化的社会。目前对白人中产阶级思想和生活方式的大力宣传，可能会使孩子们与少数民族群体疏远。这可能会给白人中产阶级的孩子一种优越感或特权感。"亚当博士说。

难词总结

bleak /bliːk/ *a.* 不乐观的；暗淡的
stereotypical /ˌsteriəˈtɪpɪkl/ *a.* 模式化的；成见的
Caucasian /kɔːˈkeɪziən; kɔːˈkeɪʒn/ *n.* 白种人
representation /ˌreprɪzenˈteɪʃn/ *n.* 表现；描述
inclusiveness /ɪnˈkluːsɪvnəs/ *n.* 包容
tokenistic /ˌtəʊkəˈnɪstɪk/ *a.* 象征性的
alienate /ˈeɪliəneɪt/ *v.* 使疏远

题目精析

26. F。由 Dr. Helen Adam from Edith Cowan University's School of Education ＿＿＿ the cultural diversity of children's books 可知，空格前后都是名词，空格处应填谓语动词，C、E、F、J 项均可作谓语动词。C 项 bias（使有偏见）、E 项 housed（收藏；给……提供住宿；）、J 项 safeguarded（保护）代入文中不符合文意，故排除。F 项 investigated（调查）代入后意为"埃迪斯科文大学教育学院的海伦·亚当博士调查了儿童书籍的文化多样性"，符合语义和逻辑，故选 F 项。

27. E。由 She examined the books ＿＿＿ in the kindergarten rooms 可知，空格前 She examined the books 句子主干完整，books 是名词，空格后是介词短语，所以空格处应填入形容词、副词或非谓语动词作修饰语。E 项 housed（收藏；给……提供住宿；）代入后意为"她评估了幼儿园房间里收藏的书"，符合语义和逻辑，故选 E 项。

28. I。由 Just 18 percent of 2,413 books in the total collection contained any _____ of non-white people 可知，空格前是不定代词 any，空格后是介词短语作后置定语，因此空格处应填名词。B、C、D、I、L、M、O 项都是名词，只有 I 项 representation（描述；代表）代入后符合语义，意为"一共 2 413 本书，其中只有 18% 的书包含对有色人种的描述"，故选 I 项。

29. H。由 by _____ Asian culture with chopsticks and traditional dress 可知，by 后面缺动名词，故空格处应填动名词。A、G、H 项符合语法要求，H 项 portraying（描绘）代入后意为"用筷子和传统服装来描绘亚洲文化"，符合语义和逻辑，故选 H 项。

30. K。由 had _____ roles in the books 可知，空格前是谓语动词，空格后是名词，因此空格处需要填入一个形容词来修饰 roles，G、K、N 项都是形容词。根据空格前的 a minority culture（少数民族文化）和下一句 The main characters were mostly Caucasian（主要角色大多是白人）的对比可知，代表少数民族文化的角色是次要的从属地位，K 项 secondary（次要的）代入后符合语义和逻辑，故选 K 项。

31. C。由 they develop own-race _____ from... 可知，空格处需要填入一个名词，B、C、D、L、M、O 项都是名词。根据上一句可知，孩子们在很小的时候就形成了对"差异"和身份的印象，空格所在句是对上一句的佐证，因此空格所填词也与"差异"有关。只有 C 项 bias（偏爱；偏见）代入后符合语义和逻辑，意为"他们从……开始产生对自己种族的偏爱"，故选 C 项。

32. B。由 develop understanding, acceptance and _____ of diversity 可知，此处需要填入一个名词，与 understanding 和 acceptance 并列，一起作 develop 的宾语。B、D、L、M、O 项都是名词，B 项 appreciation（欣赏）代入后意为"培养对多样性的理解、接受和欣赏"，符合文意，故选 B 项。

33. G。由 The current _____ promotion of... 可知，空格处需要填入一个形容词，修饰 promotion，G、N 项均为形容词。N 项 tentative（不确定的）代入后不符合文意，故排除；G 项 overwhelming（巨大的；压倒性的）代入后意为"对……的大力宣传"，符合语义和逻辑，故选 G 项。

34. A。由 ...promotion... risks _____ children from minority groups 可知，空格前有主语 promotion 和谓语 risks，因此空格所在部分为宾语。risk 作动词时，后面需接 sth. 或 doing sth.，空格后是名词，故空格处应填入动名词，A 项 alienating（使疏远）符合语法要求，代入文中意为"可能会使孩子们与少数民族群体疏远"，符合语义和逻辑，故选 A 项。

35. L。由 a sense of _____ or privilege 可知，空格处需要填入一个名词，且该名词与 privilege 是并列关系，意思相近。D、L、M、O 项都是名词，只有 L 项 superiority（优越；优势）代入文中符合文意，意为"一种优越感或特权感"，故选 L 项。

Section B

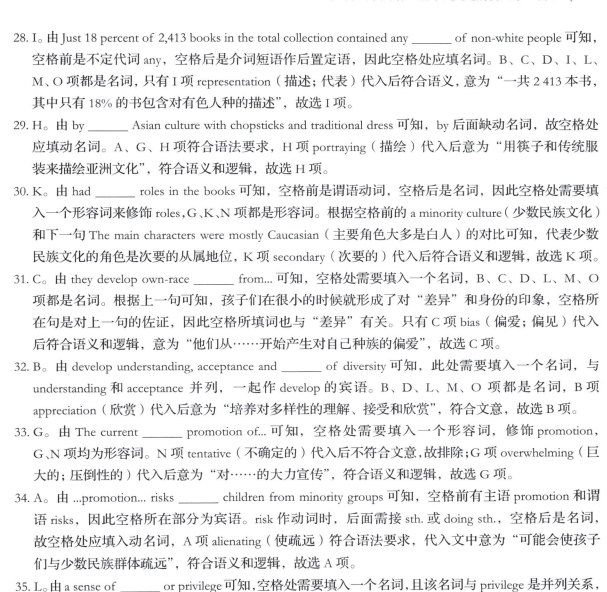

全文翻译

马可尼如何给我们带来无线通信的世界

[A] 在像比尔·盖茨和史蒂夫·乔布斯这样的标志性人物全面影响我们的生活之前的 100 年，一位爱尔兰裔意大利籍的发明家为 21 世纪的通信爆炸奠定了基础。伽利尔摩·马可尼可以说是现代通信领域第一个真正具有全球影响力的人物。他不仅是第一个进行全球通信的人，也是第一个从全

球性角度对通信进行思考的人。马可尼也许不是他那个时代最伟大的发明家，但他比任何人都更深刻地改变了我们交流的方式。

[B] 今天全球联网的媒体和通信系统起源于19世纪，当时信息第一次通过电子方式远距离传送。电报、电话和收音机显然是互联网、iPod音乐播放器和移动电话的前身。无线通信的发展将那个时候和现在联系在一起。马可尼是第一个开发和完善无线通信系统的人，他利用了最近发现的构成电磁波谱的"无线电波"。

[C] 1896年，22岁的马可尼在英国申请了他的第一个专利，1937年他在意大利去世，在此期间，马可尼一直是电子通信领域每一项重大创新的中心人物。他也是一个技术老练、经验丰富的组织者，一个具有创业精神的创新者，他精通企业战略、媒体关系、政府游说、国际外交、专利和起诉的使用。马可尼真正感兴趣的只有一件事：将移动的、个人的、长距离的通信延伸到地球的尽头（甚至更远，如果我们相信一些报道的话）。有些人喜欢称他为天才，但如果说马可尼有什么天赋的话，那就是他的远见。

[D] 1901年，尽管科学上声称这是不可能做到的，但他成功地让信号横跨大西洋，从英格兰西海岸传到了纽芬兰。1924年，他说服英国政府使用他发明的最新技术——短波无线电，在全球建立了一系列无线电台。有人说，商业广播出现后，马可尼失去了优势；他认为无线电不能也不应该用于满足无聊的目的。1937年3月，在他的最后一次向美国广播的公开演讲中，他公开谴责广播已经成为一种单向的通信方式，并预见广播将朝着另一个方向发展，即通信将成为一种交流手段。这是有远见卓识的天才。

[E] 马可尼的职业生涯致力于使无线通信变得廉价、高效、顺畅，并以一种简洁的方式表现出来，对用户来说直观简明——或者说对用户友好，如果你愿意的话。马可尼与今天的社交媒体、搜索引擎和节目流媒体之间存在着直接的联系，用一个无可否认的具有煽动性的感叹来最好地总结：20世纪并不存在。在某种意义上，马可尼的视野从他的时代跳到了我们的时代。

[F] 马可尼发明了全球通信的概念，或者更直接地说，是全球联网、移动、无线通信。最初，这是无线莫尔斯电码电报，是他那个时代的主要通信技术。马可尼是第一个利用无线电波开发无线电报实用方法的人。他借鉴了许多方面的技术细节。但使他与众不同的是，一方面，他对通信技术的模式变革力量很自信，另一方面，他对巩固自己在该领域的地位所需要采取的步骤有把握。追溯马可尼的生平将我们带入现代通讯本身的故事。还有其他重要人物，但马可尼在影响范围、权力和影响力方面，以及在他对当时大众想象力的掌控方面，都超过了他们。在现代通信概念出现的过程中，马可尼显然是一个中心人物。

[G] 在他的一生中，马可尼预见了电视、传真机、全球定位系统、雷达和便携式手持电话的发展。在他去世的前两个月，报纸报道说他正在研究"死亡射线"，还说他"隔着三英尺的距离用一个复杂的装置杀死了一只老鼠"。那时，马可尼所说所做的一切都是有新闻价值的。股票价格的涨跌取决于他的声明。如果马可尼说他认为可能会下雨，那么很可能会出现抢购雨伞的局面。

[H] 马可尼的传记也是一个关于选择及其背后动机的故事。在某个方面，马可尼可以非常独立，不受自己社会阶层的限制。另一方面，他是一个永远的局外人。无论他走到哪里，他从来都不是这个群体的"一员"；他总是"另一个人"，在英国被视为外国人，在意大利被视为英国人，而在美国

被视为"非美国人"。与此同时，他也需要被认可，他因此深受其害，这种需求驱使着他的每一段关系，有时甚至玷污了他的每一段关系。

[I] 马可尼给我们的生活方式烙上了永久的印记。他是第一个设想无线频谱的实际应用，并成功地将其发展成全球通信系统（这包含了该词两个层面的意思，即在全世界范围内和包罗万象）的人。他之所以能做到这一点，有很多因素——最重要的是时机和机遇——但他在执行自己强加的使命时表现出的专一和决心，基本上是基于他的性格；在与马可尼同时代的人中，有数百万人拥有与他相同的阶级、性别、种族和殖民特权，但只有少数人能真正利用这些特权。马可尼需要实现他青少年时期心中设定的目标；当他长大成人的时候，他直觉地明白，为了产生影响，他必须发展独立的经济基础，并与政治权力结盟。对政治权力有纪律的、不加批判的忠诚在他必须做出选择时为他指明了方向。

[J] 同时，马可尼在智力上是毫不妥协的独立。马可尼去世后不久，即将成为曼哈顿计划开发者的核物理学家恩里科·费米写道，马可尼证明了理论和实验是进步的互补特征。"除非在理论概念的指导下，否则经验很少能得出任何重大的结果……另一方面，对理论的过度信任会使马可尼无法坚持实验，而实验注定会带来无线通信技术的革命。"换句话说，马可尼的优势是不受先入为主的假设的影响。

[K] 马可尼一生中最具争议的方面是他对贝尼托·墨索里尼不加批判地拥护，这也是马可尼至今为止没有令人满意的传记的原因。起初，这对他来说不是问题。但随着墨索里尼政权倒退的本质变得清晰，他开始遭受良心的谴责。然而，由于一生都在不同的权力圈子内活动，他无法与权势分裂，于是忠诚地为墨索里尼服务（担任意大利国家研究委员会主席和皇家科学院的主席，并且是法西斯大委员会的成员），直到他适时地在1937年的一天去世。如果他还没有去世，那么很快他将不得不在这场冲突中表明立场，而这场冲突摧毁了在一定程度上是由他创造的世界。

难词总结

explosion /ɪkˈspləʊʒn/ n. 爆炸；突增
entrepreneurial /ˌɒntrəprəˈnɜːriəl/ a. 具有创业素质的
signal /ˈsɪɡnəl/ v. 发信号；发暗号
intuitive /ɪnˈtjuːɪtɪv/ a. 直觉的
intricate /ˈɪntrɪkət/ a. 错综复杂的
conviction /kənˈvɪkʃn/ n. 深信；坚信

airwaves /ˈeəweɪvz/ n. 无线电波
prosecution /ˌprɒsɪˈkjuːʃn/ n.（被）起诉，检举
visionary /ˈvɪʒənri/ a. 有远见卓识的
provocative /prəˈvɒkətɪv/ a. 挑衅的；煽动性的
tarnish /ˈtɑːnɪʃ/ v. 败坏，损坏（名声等）

题目精析

36. Marconi was central to our present-day understanding of communication.

36. 马可尼对我们理解现代通信至关重要。

【答案及分析】F. 根据题干中的 central to 和 present-day understanding of communication 可以定位到F段。最后一句指出，Marconi was quite simply the central figure in the emergence of a modern understanding of communication.（在现代通信概念出现的过程中，马可尼显然是一个中心人物。）题干中的

central to 对应原文中的 the central figure，present-day understanding of communication 对应原文中的 a modern understanding of communication，故选 F 项。

37. As an adult, Marconi had an intuition that he had to be loyal to politicians in order to be influential.

37. 作为成年人，马可尼一直有一种直觉，即他必须对政治家们忠诚，以获得影响力。

【答案及分析】I。根据题干中的 adult、intuition 和 be loyal to politicians 可以定位到 I 段。倒数第二句指出，... by the time he reached adulthood, he understood, intuitively, that in order to have an impact he had to both develop an independent economic base and align himself with political power.（……当他长大成人的时候，他直觉地明白，为了产生影响，他必须发展独立的经济基础，并与政治权力结盟。）题干中的 adult 是原文中 adulthood 的同义表达，intuition 对应原文中的 intuitively，be loyal to politicians 是原文中 align himself with political power 的同义表达，故选 I 项。

38. Marconi disapproved of the use of wireless communication for commercial broadcasting.

38. 马可尼不同意将无线通信用于商业广播。

【答案及分析】D。根据题干中的 disapproved 和 the use of wireless communication for commercial broadcasting 可以定位到 D 段。第三句指出，There are some who say Marconi lost his edge when commercial broadcasting came along; he didn't see that radio could or should be used to frivolous ends.（有人说，商业广播出现后，马可尼失去了优势；他认为无线电不能也不应该用于满足无聊的目的。）题干中的 disapproved 是原文中 didn't see 的同义表达；原文中的 frivolous ends 指的就是 commercial broadcasting，所以题干中的 the use of wireless communication for commercial broadcasting 对应原文中的 radio could or should be used to frivolous ends，故选 D 项。

39. Marconi's example demonstrates that theoretical concepts and experiments complement each other in making progress in science and technology.

39. 马可尼的例子表明，理论概念和实验在使科学和技术进步方面互相补充。

【答案及分析】J。根据题干中的 theoretical concepts and experiments、complement each other、progress 可以定位到 J 段。第二句指出，... Marconi proved that theory and experimentation were complementary features of progress.（……马可尼证明了理论和实验是进步的互补特征。）题干中的 theoretical concepts and experiments 是原文中 theory and experimentation 的同义表达，complement each other 是原文中 were complementary features 的同义表达，progress 为原词复现，故选 J 项。

40. Marconi's real interests lay in the development of worldwide wireless communication.

40. 马可尼的真正兴趣是在全球范围内发展无线通信。

【答案及分析】C。根据题干中的 real interests、the development of worldwide wireless communication 可以定位到 C 段。倒数第二句指出，Marconi was really interested in only one thing: the extension of mobile, personal, long-distance communication to the ends of the earth (and beyond, if we can believe some reports).［马可尼真正感兴趣的只有一件事：将移动的、个人的、长距离的通信延伸到地球的尽头（甚至更远，如果我们相信一些报道的话）。］题干中的 real interests 是原文中 really interested 的同义表达，the development of worldwide wireless communication 对应原文中的 the extension of mobile, personal, long-distance communication to the ends of the earth，故选 C 项。

41. Marconi spent his whole life making wireless communication simple to use.

41. 马可尼毕生都致力于使无线通信易于应用。

【答案及分析】E。根据题干中的 spent his whole life、simple to use 可以定位到 E 段。第一句指出，Marconi's career was devoted to making wireless communication happen cheaply, efficiently, smoothly, and with an elegance that would appear to be intuitive and uncomplicated to the user — user-friendly, if you will.（马可尼的职业生涯致力于使无线通信变得廉价、高效、顺畅，并以一种简洁的方式表现出来，对用户来说直观简明——或者说对用户友好，如果你愿意的话。）题干中的 spent his whole life 是原文中 Marconi's career was devoted to 的同义表达，simple to use 是原文中 uncomplicated to the user 的同义表达，故选 E 项。

42. Because of his long-time connection with people in power, Marconi was unable to cut himself off from the fascist regime in Italy.

42. 因为马可尼长期与有权势的人交往，所以他无法摆脱与意大利的法西斯主义政权的关系。

【答案及分析】K。根据题干中的 long-time、connection with people in power 和 unable to cut himself off from the fascist regime 可以定位到 K 段。最后一句指出，However, after a lifetime of moving within the circles of power, he was unable to break with authority, and served Mussolini faithfully...（然而，由于一生都在不同的权力圈子内活动，他无法与权势分裂，于是忠诚地为墨索里尼服务……）题干中的 long-time 是原文中 lifetime 的同义表达，connection with people in power 是原文中 moving within the circles of power 的同义表达，unable to cut himself off from the fascist regime 是原文中 unable to break with authority 的同义表达，故选 K 项。

43. In his later years, Marconi exerted a tremendous influence on all aspects of people's life.

43. 在晚年，马可尼对人们生活的各个方面都产生了巨大的影响。

【答案及分析】G。根据题干中的 In his later years、exerted a tremendous influence on all aspects of people's life 可以定位到 G 段。第二、三句指出，Two months before he died, newspapers were reporting that he was working on a "death ray," and that he had "killed a rat with an intricate device at a distance of three feet." By then, anything Marconi said or did was newsworthy.（在他去世的前两个月，报纸报道说他正在研究"死亡射线"，还说他"隔着三英尺的距离用一个复杂的装置杀死了一只老鼠"。那时，马可尼所说所做的一切都是有新闻价值的。）题干中的 In his later years 对应原文中的 Two months before he died，exerted a tremendous influence on all aspects of people's life 是原文中 anything Marconi said or did was newsworthy 的同义表达，故选 G 项。

44. What connected the 19th century and our present time was the development of wireless communication.

44. 连接 19 世纪和当今时代的是无线通信的发展。

【答案及分析】B。根据题干中的 connected the 19th century and our present time、the development of wireless communication 可以定位到 B 段。倒数第二句指出，What made the link from then to now was the development of wireless communication.（无线通信的发展将那个时候和现在联系在一起。）题干中的 connected the 19th century and our present time 是原文中 made the link from then to now 的同义表达，the development of wireless communication 是原词复现，故选 B 项。

45. Despite his autonomy, Marconi felt alienated and suffered from a lack of acceptance.

45. 尽管马可尼具有自主性，但他还是感到一种疏离，并因缺乏认可而饱受折磨。

【答案及分析】H。根据题干中的 autonomy、alienated、suffered 和 a lack of acceptance 可以定位到 H 段。该段指出，At one level, Marconi could be fiercely autonomous... On another scale, he was a perpetual outsider... At the same time, he also suffered tremendously from a need for acceptance...（在某个方面，马可尼可以非常独立……另一方面，他是一个永远的局外人……与此同时，他也需要被认可，他因此深受其害……）题干中的 autonomy 对应原文中的 autonomous，alienated 是原文中 perpetual outsider 的同义表达，suffered 是原词复现，a lack of acceptance 是原文中 a need for acceptance 的同义表达，故选 H 项。

Section C

Passage One

全文翻译

人们总是对自己优缺点的来源着迷。这种关注必然是老生常谈：是先天还是后天更能塑造我们的个性。遗传学上的一场革命使这成为一个关于我们社会特征的现代政治问题：如果个性是基因决定的，那么政府能做些什么来帮助我们呢？这在道德上是有问题的，然而按照智力进行遗传选择的说法却成了头版头条。

这源于"遗传决定论"学说，最近的一篇论文声称，"在精英学校和普通学校就读的学生在考试成绩方面的差异反映了他们之间的遗传差异。"不出所料，因为这样的论断，这项研究受到许多关于"基因决定学术成功"的荒谬说法的拥护。这项研究揭示了一个不那么令人惊讶的结果：一旦考虑到学生天生的能力和社会经济背景，精英学校的教育优势在很大程度上就消失了。这十分明显——没有任何东西能为遗传决定论或环境决定论提供强有力的支撑。

然而，这篇论文确实指出，孩子们被学校系统"在无意中进行了基因选择"。遗传科学的核心是一个夸张的论断：可识别的基因序列变异可以预测一个人学习、推理和解决问题的能力。这在许多层面上都存在问题。当外部因素明显存在时，教师不能严肃地告诉家长，他们孩子的学习遗传倾向较低。有学者持不同观点，他们说，人类特征的可遗传性在科学上是不可靠的。DNA 和智力之间充其量只有微弱的统计学联系，而不是因果关系。然而，复杂的统计数据却被用来创造一种令人生畏的科学确定性的氛围。

虽然个体差异有着无可置疑的遗传基础，但认为可以通过遗传来解释社会定义上的群体是错误的。把基因视为命运的观点当然也是错误的。医学的可预测性几乎不能仅仅基于 DNA；环境也很重要。像智力这样复杂的事物可能受到基因之外的许多因素的影响。如果遗传主义者想要推进他们的事业，就需要更公正的解释，而不仅仅是拥护他们的观点。

正如作家 H.G. 威尔斯所言，遗传选择是对他人施加影响的一种方式，是"人类命运的最终集体控制"。知识成为力量，而力量需要责任感。在理解认知能力的过程中，我们绝不能将歧视提升到科学的高度：只允许人们按照细胞暗示的程度攀爬生命的阶梯。这需要对科学持更加怀疑的眼光。随着技术的进步，我们都有责任确保我们塑造一个我们希望置身其中的未来。

难词总结

preoccupation /pri͵ɒkjuˈpeɪʃn/ n. 思虑；全神贯注
inborn /͵ɪnˈbɔːn/ a. 天生的
intimidatory /ɪnˈtɪmɪ͵deɪtəri/ a. 恐吓的；威胁的

poise /pɔɪz/ v. 保持（某种姿势）；抓紧
blindingly obvious 十分明显

题目精析

46. What did a recent research paper claim?
  A) The type of school students attend makes a difference to their future.
  B) Genetic differences between students are far greater than supposed.
  C) The advantages of selective schools are too obvious to ignore.
  D) Students' academic performance is determined by their genes.

46. 近期的一篇研究论文声称什么？
  A）学生就读的学校的类型影响他们的未来。
  B）学生之间的基因差异比想象中更大。
  C）精英学校的优势显而易见，不容忽视。
  D）学生的学业成绩由他们的基因决定。

【答案及分析】D。根据题干中的 a recent research paper 定位到第二段。第一句指出，This is down to "hereditarian" science and a recent paper claimed "differences in exam performance between pupils attending selective and non-selective schools mirror the genetic differences between them". （这源于"遗传决定论"学说，近期的一篇论文声称，"在精英学校和普通学校就读的学生在考试成绩方面的差异反映了他们之间的遗传差异。"）D 项是对该句的概括总结，其中，Students' academic performance 是原文中 exam performance between pupils 的同义表达，is determined by their genes 是原文中 mirror the genetic differences 的同义表达，故选 D 项。

47. What does the author think of the recent research?
  A) Its result was questionable.   C) Its influence was rather negligible.
  B) Its implication was positive.   D) Its conclusions were enlightening.

47. 作者如何看待近期的研究？
  A）它的结果是值得怀疑的。   C）它的影响完全不值一提。
  B）它的含义是积极的。   D）它的结论具有启发性。

【答案及分析】A。根据题干中的 the recent research 定位到第二段。最后一句指出，It is a glimpse of the blindingly obvious — and there's nothing to back strongly either a hereditary or environmental argument. （这十分明显——没有任何东西能为遗传决定论或环境决定论提供强有力的支撑。）由此可知，作者对此持怀疑态度，故选 A 项。

48. What does the author say about the relationship between DNA and intelligence?
  A) It is one of scientific certainty.   C) It is subject to interpretation of statistics.
  B) It is not one of cause and effect.   D) It is not fully examined by gene scientists.

48. 关于DNA和智力之间的关系，作者说了什么？

A) 这是一种科学确定性。　　　　　C) 这取决于对统计数据的解读。

B) 这不是因果关系。　　　　　　　D) 这并未被基因科学家全面检测。

【答案及分析】B。根据题干中的 the relationship between DNA and intelligence 定位到第三段。倒数第二句指出，At best there is a weak statistical association and not a causal link between DNA and intelligence.（DNA和智力之间充其量只有微弱的统计学联系，而不是因果关系。）B项中的 not one of cause and effect 是原文中 not a causal link 的同义表达，故选B项。

49. What do hereditarians need to do to make their claims convincing?

A) Take all relevant factors into account in interpreting their data.

B) Conduct their research using more sophisticated technology.

C) Gather gene data from people of all social classes.

D) Cooperate with social scientists in their research.

49. 遗传主义者需要做什么来使他们的声明更令人信服？

A) 在解读数据时考虑所有相关因素。

B) 使用更先进的技术进行他们的研究。

C) 从各社会阶层人群中收集基因数据。

D) 和社会科学家合作开展研究。

【答案及分析】A。根据题干中的 hereditarians 和 claims 定位到第四段。最后一句指出，If hereditarians want to advance their cause it will require more balanced interpretation and not just acts of advocacy.（如果遗传主义者想要推进他们的事业，就需要更公正的解释，而不仅仅是拥护他们的观点。）想要更有说服力便需要更公正，即考虑全面，A项符合文意，故选A项。

50. What does the author warn against in the passage?

A) Exaggerating the power of technology in shaping the world.

B) Losing sight of professional ethics in conducting research.

C) Misunderstanding the findings of human cognition research.

D) Promoting discrimination in the name of science.

50. 作者在文章中针对什么发出了警告？

A) 夸大技术在塑造世界方面的力量。

B) 在开展研究的过程中忽视职业道德。

C) 误解人类认知研究的发现。

D) 以科学的名义宣扬歧视。

【答案及分析】D。根据选项中的关键词 technology、cognition 和 discrimination 定位到最后一段。第三句指出，In understanding cognitive ability, we must not elevate discrimination to a science: allowing people to climb the ladder of life only as far as their cells might suggest.（在理解认知能力的过程中，我们绝不能将歧视提升到科学的高度：只允许人们按照细胞暗示的程度攀爬生命的阶梯。）D项 Promoting discrimination in the name of science 是原文中 elevate discrimination to a science 的同义表达，故选D项。

Passage Two

全文翻译

尼古拉·斯特金上周二发表的演讲阐述了苏格兰政府未来一年的立法计划，证实了一个已经相当明确的事实。苏格兰议会将成为英国第一个有权向游客收费的地方议会，爱丁堡可能会开先河。

征收旅游税并不是什么新鲜事。喜马拉雅山下的不丹王国有一项长期的政策，即每天向游客征税。法国引入"过夜税"是为了帮助温泉小镇发展，如今法国有大约一半的地方政府都在采用这项税收。

但这类税收正在增长。最近，巴塞罗那和威尼斯通过收费来解决"过度旅游"现象的举措备受关注。日本和希腊最近加入了征收旅游税的国家行列。

按照国际标准，英国之所以落后，是因为英国的地方政府实力薄弱，执政党激进地支持市场，反对税收和监管。一些英国城市进行了游说，要求获得向游客征税的权力，但没有成功。这类税收并不是"万能灵药"，因为与2010年以来中央政府征收的税额相比，这类税额微不足道。尽管如此，人们还是希望苏格兰政府的大胆举措会促使其他地方采取行动。去英国旅游的游客，或者去康沃尔等热门景区度假的国内游客，都没有理由免征旅游税——尤其是在垃圾回收、公园维护和艺术文化支出等重要的当地服务面临前所未有的压力的情况下。

相反，游客必须在自身消费的基础之上为观光地做出经济贡献这一观念应该是更广泛的文化转变的一部分。拥有可支配收入的西方人往往表现得好像他们有权去任何他们想去的地方，几乎不考虑后果。正如必须更严格地审查航空和其他交通工具所造成的环境危害一样，我们也必须正视旅游业的社会成本。其中包括短期出租对居民住房成本和生活质量的影响。包括巴黎和柏林在内的几个欧洲国家的首都正在领导一场运动，要求欧盟实施更严格的监管。社会成本还包括过度拥挤、垃圾和与吵闹的聚会相关的各种行为的影响。

解决这个问题不能"一刀切"。对于一些议会，但不是所有地方议会，新收入来源的存在是很复杂的，而且企业经常持反对态度，担心更高的成本会使他们失去竞争力。但必须给那些想要征收旅游税的地方机会，让这项税收发挥作用。

难词总结

legislative /ˈledʒɪslətɪv/ *a.* 立法的
thermal /ˈθɜːml/ *a.* 热的
unprecedented /ʌnˈpresɪdentɪd/ *a.* 前所未有的
one size fits all 一刀切

levy /ˈlevi/ *v.* 征税
exempt /ɪɡˈzempt/ *v.* 免除
aviation /ˌeɪviˈeɪʃn/ *n.* 航空

题目精析

51. What do we learn from Nicola Sturgeon's speech?

   A) The UK is set to adjust its policy on taxation.
   B) Tourists will have to pay a tax to visit Scotland.
   C) The UK will take new measures to boost tourism.
   D) Edinburgh contributes most to Scotland's tourism.

51. 我们从尼古拉·斯特金的演讲中了解到什么？

　　A）英国决定调整税收政策。

　　B）游客去苏格兰旅游需要缴税。

　　C）英国会采取新措施来促进旅游业发展。

　　D）爱丁堡对苏格兰的旅游业贡献最大。

【答案及分析】B。根据题干中的 Nicola Sturgeon's speech 可以定位到第一段。第一句指出，Nicola Sturgeon's speech last Tuesday setting out the Scottish government's legislative programme for the year ahead confirmed what was already pretty clear.（尼古拉·斯特金上周二发表的演讲阐述了苏格兰政府未来一年的立法计划，证实了一个已经相当明确的事实。）该事实即在下句，Scottish councils are set to be the first in the UK with the power to levy charges on visitors, with Edinburgh likely to lead the way.（苏格兰议会将成为英国第一个有权向游客收费的地方议会，爱丁堡可能会开先河。）B 项 Tourists will have to pay a tax to visit Scotland 是该句的同义表达，其中，pay a tax to visit 是原文中 levy charges on visitors 的同义表达，故选 B 项。

52. How come the UK has been slow in imposing the tourist tax?

　　A) Its government wants to attract more tourists.

　　B) The tax is unlikely to add much to its revenue.

　　C) Its ruling party is opposed to taxes and regulation.

　　D) It takes time for local governments to reach consensus.

52. 为什么英国在征收旅游税上进度缓慢？

　　A）英国政府想吸引更多的游客。

　　B）该税收不太可能大幅增加英国的税收收入。

　　C）英国执政党反对税收和监管。

　　D）地方政府达成一致意见需要时间。

【答案及分析】C。根据题干中的 slow in imposing the tourist tax 可以定位到第四段。第一句指出，That the UK lags behind is due to our weak, by international standards, local government, as well as the opposition to taxes and regulation of our aggressively pro-market ruling party.（按照国际标准，英国之所以落后，是因为英国的地方政府实力薄弱，执政党激进地支持市场，反对税收和监管。）C 项中的 ruling party 是原词复现，is opposed to taxes and regulation 对应原文中的 the opposition to taxes and regulation，故选 C 项。

53. Both international and domestic visitors in the UK should pay tourist tax so as to _____.

　　A) elevate its tourism to international standards

　　B) improve the welfare of its maintenance workers

　　C) promote its cultural exchange with other nations

　　D) ease its financial burden of providing local services

53. 英国国内外的游客应该支付旅游税，以便 _____。

　　A）将英国旅游业提升至国际标准

B）提高英国维修工人的福利

C）推动与其他国家的文化交流

D）缓解英国提供当地服务的财政负担

【答案及分析】D。根据题干中的 international and domestic visitors 定位到第四段。最后一句指出，There is no reason why visitors to the UK, or domestic tourists on holiday in hotspots such as Cornwall, should be exempt from taxation — particularly when vital local services including waste collection, park maintenance and arts and culture spending are under unprecedented strain.（去英国旅游的游客，或者去康沃尔等热门景区度假的国内游客，都没有理由免征旅游税——尤其是在垃圾回收、公园维护和艺术文化支出等重要的当地服务面临前所未有的压力的情况下。）D 项是对该句的概括总结，其中，burden 是原文中 strain 的同义表达，local services 是原词复现，故选 D 项。

54. What does the author say about Western tourists?

　　A) They don't seem to care about the social cost of tourism.

　　B) They don't seem to mind paying for additional services.

　　C) They deem travel an important part of their life.

　　D) They subject the effects of tourism to scrutiny.

54. 关于西方游客，作者说了什么？

　　A）他们看起来并不关心旅游业的社会成本。

　　B）他们看起来并不介意为额外的服务付费。

　　C）他们认为旅行是生活中重要的一部分。

　　D）他们严格审查旅游业的影响。

【答案及分析】A。根据题干中的 Western tourists 定位到倒数第二段。第二句指出，Westerners with disposable incomes have often behaved as if they have a right to go wherever they choose with little regard for the consequences.（拥有可支配收入的西方人往往表现得好像他们有权去任何他们想去的地方，几乎不考虑后果。）A 项中的 don't seem to care about the social cost of tourism 是原文中 with little regard for the consequences 的同义表达，故选 A 项。

55. What are UK people's opinions about the levy of tourist tax?

　　A) Supportive.　　　　　　　　　　C) Divided.

　　B) Skeptical.　　　　　　　　　　　D) Unclear.

55. 英国人对征收旅游税是什么看法？

　　A）支持的。　　　　　　　　　　　C）有分歧的。

　　B）怀疑的。　　　　　　　　　　　D）不清楚的。

【答案及分析】C。根据题干中的 UK people's opinions 可知本题考查观点态度。最后一段第一句指出，There is no "one size fits all" solution to this problem.（解决这个问题不能"一刀切"。）第二句给出一种态度，businesses are often opposed（企业经常持反对态度）；第三句给出另一种态度，But those places that want them must be given the chance to make tourist taxes work.（但必须给那些想要征收旅游税的地方机会，让这项税收发挥作用。）综上可以看出，英国人有支持态度也有反对态度，出现了分歧，故选 C 项。

Part IV Translation

参考译文

　　Located in the southwest of China, Yunnan is a province with an average altitude of 1,500 meters. Yunnan features a long history, picturesque landscapes and pleasant climate. Yunnan is known as a paradise for wildlife thanks to its superior ecological environment and diverse species. Yunnan also boasts abundant mineral resources and adequate water resources, which provide favorable conditions for the sustainable development of the whole province's economy.

　　Yunnan is home to 25 ethnic minorities, most of whom have their own languages, customs and religions. Its unique natural scenery and rich ethnic culture make it one of the most popular tourist destinations in China, attracting a large number of tourists from home and abroad every year.

难词总结

altitude /ˈæltɪtjuːd/ n. 海拔
ecological /ˌiːkəˈlɒdʒɪkl/ a. 生态的
favorable /ˈfeɪvərəbl/ a. 有利的

feature /ˈfiːtʃə(r)/ v. 以……为特点
boast /bəʊst/ v. 有（值得自豪的东西）

译点释义

1. 第一段第一句中，"云南是位于中国西南的一个省"可作为主句，"平均海拔 1 500 米"可处理为介词短语作后置定语。
2. 第一段第二句"云南历史悠久，风景秀丽，气候宜人"说的是云南所具有的特点，谓语动词可用 features，表示"以……为特点（或特征）"，不同的特点之间用 and 连接。
3. 第一段第三句中，"生态环境优越，生物多种多样"是"被誉为野生动植物的天堂"的原因，因此翻译时应体现出因果关系。"生态环境优越，生物多种多样"可译为 superior ecological environment and diverse species。
4. 第一段第四句中的"多种"和"充足"翻译时应选用不同的形容词，体现语言的多样性。"为全省经济的可持续发展提供了有利条件"可处理为从句，也可处理为状语。
5. 第二段第一句中，"云南居住着 25 个少数民族"可译为主句，"他们大多有自己的语言、习俗和宗教"可译为从句，因为"他们"指的就是"25 个少数民族"。
6. 最后一句虽然句子较长，但不难翻译。"每年都吸引着大批国内外游客前往观光旅游"可译为动名词短语作状语，表示一种结果。"国内外游客"可译为 tourists from home and abroad。

未得到监考教师指令前，不得翻阅该试题册！

2021年6月大学英语六级考试真题（第三套）

Part I　　　　　　　　　Writing　　　　　　　　　(30 minutes)

（请于正式开考后半小时内完成该部分，之后将进行听力考试）

Directions: *For this part, you are allowed 30 minutes to write an essay based on the chart below. You should start your essay with a brief description of the chart and comment on **China's achievements in higher education**. You should write at least **150** words but no more than **200** words.*

Gross enrolment ratio in higher education in China (1990-2019)

Year	1990	1995	2000	2001	2002	2003	2004	2005	2006	2007	2008	2009	2010	2011	2012	2013	2014	2015	2016	2017	2018	2019
Ratio	3.4%	6.68%	11%	13.3%	15%	17%	19%	21%	22%	23%	23.3%	24.2%	26.5%	26.95%	30%	34.5%	37.5%	40%	42.7%	45.7%	48.1%	51.6%

Source: Ministry of Education

Part II　　　　　　　Listening Comprehension　　　　　　　(30 minutes)

说明：由于2021年6月六级考试全国共考了两套听力，本套真题听力与前两套内容相同，只是选项顺序不同，因此在本套真题中不再重复出现。

Part III　　　　　　　Reading Comprehension　　　　　　　(40 minutes)

Section A

Directions: *In this section, there is a passage with ten blanks. You are required to select one word for each blank from a list of choices given in a word bank following the passage. Read the passage through carefully before making your choices. Each choice in the bank is identified by a letter. Please mark the corresponding letter for each item on **Answer Sheet 2** with a single line through the centre. You may not use any of the words in the bank more than once.*

At 43, I've reached the stage where women are warned to watch out for the creeping sadness of middle age. We're served up an endless stream of advice on "how to survive your 40s", as if we're in the endurance stage of a slow limp toward __26__. This is the age women start to become "invisible" — our value, attractiveness and power supposedly __27__ by the vanishing of youth. But I don't feel like I'm fading into __28__. I feel more seen than I ever have, and for the first time in my life, I have a clear-eyed view of myself that is __29__, compassionate and accepting.

When I look in the mirror, I'm proud of who I am — even those "broken" parts that for so long seemed impossible to love. So when advertisers try to sell me ways to "turn back the clock", I have to __30__ a laugh. I wouldn't go back to the crippling self-consciousness of my youth if you paid me. This hard-won sense of self-acceptance is one of the joys of being an older woman. But it's a narrative often __31__ out by the shame that marketers rely on to peddle us their diet pills, miracle face creams and breathable yoga pants — as if self-love is a __32__ commodity.

For some women I know, this sense of trust and self-belief later in life gave them the courage to leave dysfunctional relationships or __33__ on new career paths. Others talked about enjoying their own company, of growth through __34__, deepening bonds of friendships, the ability to be more compassionate, less judgmental and to listen more and appreciate the small pleasures. Life past 40 is far from smooth sailing, but it's so much more than the reductive __35__ we see in women's magazines and on the Hollywood big screen.

A) adversity	I) neglected
B) authentic	J) obscurity
C) convey	K) outlines
D) depictions	L) prevalent
E) diminished	M) purchasable
F) drowned	N) submit
G) embark	O) suppress
H) fragility	

Section B

Directions: *In this section, you are going to read a passage with ten statements attached to it. Each statement contains information given in one of the paragraphs. Identify the paragraph from which the information is derived. You may choose a paragraph more than once. Each paragraph is marked with a letter. Answer the questions by marking the corresponding letter on **Answer Sheet 2**.*

What Are the Ethics of CGI Actors — And Will They Replace Real Ones?

[A] Digital humans are coming to a screen near you. As *computer-generated imagery* (CGI) has become cheaper and more sophisticated, the film industry can now convincingly recreate people on screen — even actors who have been dead for decades. The technology's ability to effectively keep celebrities alive beyond the grave is raising questions about public legacies and image rights.

[B] Late in 2019, it was announced that US actor James Dean, who died in 1955, will star in a Vietnam War film scheduled for release later this year. In the film, which will be called *Finding Jack*, Dean will be recreated on screen with CGI based on old *footage* (影片镜头) and photographs, with another actor voicing him. The news was met with excitement by those keen to see Dean digitally brought back to life for only his fourth film, but it also drew sharp criticism. "This is puppeteering the dead for their fame alone," actress Zelda Williams wrote on Twitter. "It sets such an awful precedent for the future of performance." Her father, Robin Williams, who died in 2014, was keen to avoid the same fate. Before his death, he filed a deed protecting the use of his image until 2039, preventing others from recreating him using CGI to appear in a film, TV show or as a *hologram* (全息影像).

[C] The James Dean film is a way to keep the actor's image relevant for younger generations, says Mark Roesler of CMG Worldwide, the firm that represents Dean's estate. "I think this is the beginning of an entire wave," says Travis Cloyd, CEO of Worldwide XR, one of the companies behind the digital recreation of Dean. "Moving into the future, we want James Dean to be brought into different gaming environments, or different virtual reality environments, or augmented reality environments," he says.

[D] Other actors have been revived, with the permission of their estates, for advertising purposes: for example, a 2011 advertisement for Dior featured contemporary actress Charlize Theron alongside iconic 20th-century stars Marilyn Monroe, Grace Kelly and Marlene Dietrich. Later, Audrey Hepburn was digitally recreated for a chocolate commercial in 2013. In the same year, a CGI Bruce Lee appeared in a Chinese-language ad for a whisky brand, which offended many fans because Lee was widely known not to drink alcohol at all. "In the last five years, it's become more affordable and more achievable in a whole movie," says Tim Webber at UK visual effects firm Framestore, the company behind the Hepburn chocolate ad. Framestore used body doubles with resemblance to Hepburn's facial structure and body shape as a framework for manual animation. The process was extremely difficult and expensive, says Webber, but the technology has moved on.

[E] Now, a person can be animated from scratch. "If they're alive today, you can put them in scanning rigs, you can get every detail of their body analysed very carefully and that makes it much easier, whereas working from available photographs is tricky," says Webber, who won an Academy Award for his visual effects work on the 2013 film *Gravity*. "I also see a lot of actors today who will have the desire to take advantage of this technology: to have their likeness captured and stored for future content," says Cloyd. "They foresee this being something that could give their estates and give their families the ability to make money from their likeness when they're gone."

[F] A hidden hazard of digitally recreating a *deceased* (已故的) celebrity is the risk of damaging their legacy. "We have to respect the security and the integrity of rights holders," says John Canning at Digital Domain, a US firm that created a hologram *rapper* (说唱艺人) Tupac Shakur, which appeared at the Coachella music festival in 2012, 15 years after his death.

[G] Legally, a person's rights to control the commercial use of their name and image beyond their death differ between and even within countries. In certain US states, for example, these rights are treated similarly to property rights, and are transferable to a person's heirs. In California, under the Celebrities Rights Act, the personality rights for a celebrity last for 70 years after their death. "We've got a societal debate going on about access to our public commons, as it were, about famous faces," says Lilian Edwards at Newcastle University, UK. Should the public be allowed to use or reproduce images of famous people, given how iconic they are? And what is in the best interest of a deceased person's legacy may conflict with the desires of their family or the public, says Edwards.

[H] A recreation, however lifelike, will never be indistinguishable from a real actor, says Webber. "When we are bringing someone back, representing someone who is no longer alive on the screen, what we are doing is extremely sophisticated digital make-up," he says. "A performance is a lot more than a physical resemblance."

[I] As it becomes easier to digitally recreate celebrities and to entirely manufacture on-screen identities, could this kind of technology put actors out of jobs? "I think actors are worried about this," says Edwards. "But I think it will take a very long time." This is partly because of the risk that viewers find virtual humans scary. Edwards cites widespread backlash to the digital recreation of Carrie Fisher as a young Princess Leia in *Rogue One*, a trick later repeated in the recent *Star Wars*: *The Rise of Skywalker*, which was filmed after Fisher's death in 2016. "People didn't like it," she says. "They discovered the *uncanny valley*(诡异谷)."

[J] This refers to the idea that when objects trying to resemble humans aren't quite perfect, they can make viewers feel uneasy because they fall somewhere between obviously non-human and fully human. "That's always a danger when you're doing anything human or human-like," says Webber. "There're a thousand things that could go wrong with a computer-generated facial performance, and any one of those could make it fall into the uncanny valley," he says. "Your brain just knows there's something wrong." The problem often arises around the eyes or mouth, says Webber. "They're the areas that you look at when you're talking to someone."

[K] An unfamiliar digital human that has been created through CGI will also face the same challenge as an unknown actor: they don't have the appeal of an established name. "You have to spend substantial capital in creating awareness around their likeness and making sure people are familiar with who they are," says Cloyd. This is now starting to happen. "The way you pre-sell a movie in a foreign market is based on relevant talent," he says. "I think we're a long way away from having virtual beings that have the ability to pre-sell content."

[L] Webber expects that we will see more digital humans on screen. "It's happening because it can happen," he says. Referring to a line from *Jurassic Park*(侏罗纪公园), he adds: "People are too busy thinking about what they can do to think about whether they should do it."

36. There is an ongoing debate among the public as to whether the images of deceased celebrities should be recreated.

37. The CGI technology allows the image of the deceased James Dean to be presented to young people in new settings.

38. It is very likely that the CGI-recreated image of a deceased celebrity will fail to match the real actor especially in facial expressions.

39. The use of digital technology can bring images of deceased celebrities back to the screen.

40. Recreating a deceased famous actor or actress may violate their legitimate rights.

41. More CGI-recreated images of deceased celebrities are expected to appear on screen.

42. The image of James Dean will be recreated on screen with his voice dubbed by someone else.
43. However advanced the CGI technology is, the recreated image will differ in a way from the real actor.
44. A lot of actors today are likely to make use of the CGI technology to have their images stored for the benefit of their families.
45. Some actors are concerned that they may lose jobs because of the CGI technology.

Section C

Directions: *There are 2 passages in this section. Each passage is followed by some questions or unfinished statements. For each of them there are four choices marked A), B), C) and D). You should decide on the best choice and mark the corresponding letter on **Answer Sheet 2** with a single line through the centre.*

Passage One

Questions 46 to 50 are based on the following passage.

You can't see it, smell it, or hear it, and people disagree on how precisely to define it, or where exactly it comes from. It isn't a school subject or an academic discipline, but it can be learned. It is a quality that is required of artists, but it is also present in the lives of scientists and entrepreneurs. All of us benefit from it and we thrive mentally and spiritually when we are able to wield it. It is a delicate thing, easily stamped out; in fact, it flourishes most fully when people are playful and childlike. Meanwhile, it works best in conjunction with deep knowledge and expertise.

This mysterious — but teachable — quality is creativity, the subject of a recently-published report by Durham Commission on Creativity and Education. The report concludes that creativity should not inhabit the school curriculum only as it relates to drama, music, art and other obviously creative subjects, but that creative thinking ought to run through all of school life, *infusing* (充满) the way humanities and natural sciences are learned.

The authors, who focus on education in England, offer a number of sensible recommendations, some of which are an attempt to alleviate the uninspiring and fact-based approach to education that has crept into policy in recent years. When children are regarded as vessels to be filled with facts, creativity does not prosper; nor does it when teachers' sole objective is coaching children towards exams. One suggestion from the commission is a network of teacher-led "creativity collaboratives", along the lines of existing maths *hubs* (中心), with the aim of supporting teaching for creativity through the school curriculum.

Nevertheless, it is arts subjects through which creativity can most obviously be fostered. The value placed on them by the independent education sector is clear. One only has to look at the remarkable arts facilities at Britain's top private schools to comprehend this. But in the state sector the excessive focus on English, maths and science threatens to crush arts subjects; meanwhile, reduced school budgets mean diminishing extracurricular activities. There has been a 28.1% decline in students taking creative subjects at high schools since 2014, though happily, art and design have seen a recent increase.

This discrepancy between state and private is a matter of social justice. It is simply wrong and unfair that most children have a fraction of the access to choirs, orchestras, art studios and drama that their more privileged peers enjoy. As lives are affected by any number of looming challenges — climate crisis, automation in the workplace — humans are going to need creative thinking more than ever. For all of our sakes, creativity in education, and for all, must become a priority.

46. What do we learn from the passage about creativity?
    A) It develops best when people are spiritually prepared.
    B) It is most often wielded by scientists and entrepreneurs.
    C) It is founded on scientific knowledge and analytical skills.
    D) It contributes to intellectual growth but can easily be killed.

47. What is the conclusion of a recently-published report?
    A) Natural sciences should be learned the way humanities courses are.
    B) Cultivation of creativity should permeate the entire school curriculum.
    C) Art courses should be made compulsory for all students.
    D) Students should learn more obviously creative subjects.

48. What does the report say is detrimental to the fostering of creativity?
    A) Alleviation of pressure.   C) Test-oriented teaching.
    B) Teacher-led school activities.   D) Independent learning.

49. What do we learn about the private schools in the UK?
    A) They encourage extracurricular activities.
    B) They attach great importance to arts education.
    C) They prioritize arts subjects over maths and sciences.
    D) They cater to students from different family backgrounds.

50. What should be done to meet the future challenges?
    A) Increasing government investment in school education.
    B) Narrowing the existing gap between the rich and the poor.
    C) Providing all children with equal access to arts education.
    D) Focusing on meeting the needs of under-privileged students.

Passage Two

Questions 51 to 55 are based on the following passage.

Emulating your conversation partner's actions is a common human behavior classified as "mirroring" and has been known and studied by psychologists for years. We all tend to subconsciously copy gestures of people we like. But why do we act like this?

As a rule, mirroring means that conversationalists enjoy their communication and that there's a certain level of agreement between them. The topic of discussion is equally interesting for both and they know their interests meet.

Repeating someone's behavior is typical of talented communicators, not always because the person is sympathetic, but because there is a goal to be achieved. This way new idols have been brought to the stage:

politicians, celebrities, and other big names. Popular culture makes people want to look popular, and act and speak like popular people.

Nowadays celebrities steal lyrics from each other and struggle with copyright violation accusations or straightforwardly claim themselves to be the authors, even though all the work was done by other people.

Among celebrities, it's trendy nowadays to use their own speech writers as politicians do. The so-called "ghostwriting" can take various forms: books, articles, autobiographies, and even social media posts.

Who is a true *copycat* (抄袭者) and who gets copycatted? Sometimes, it is a hard nut to crack without an expert's help. But new authorship defending methods based on identifying individual writing patterns are already here. Their aim is to protect intellectual property. Using scientific methods, some of them can define authorship with 85% accuracy.

Writing is not an easy craft to master. If you want to write like a professional without *plagiarism* (抄袭), there are a few lessons to learn and the first one is: "Copy from one, it's plagiarism; copy from two, it's research." The correct interpretation of this statement is not about copying, but rather about creating your own style. When you study an author's writing style, don't stop on a single one, but explore numerous styles instead. Examine types of sentences they use, pay attention to their metaphors, and focus on stories you feel you could write a pretty cool *sequel* (续篇) to.

Imitation is rather paradoxical. As an integral part of learning, it brings about positive changes, making people develop and grow. However, it may do a lot of harm. Copying someone's thoughts, ideas or inventions is completely unacceptable. It infringes on intellectual property rights of others.

Still, many things we do are about copying others one way or another. So if you want to compliment someone on the work they have done and imitate it, just make sure you do it the right way to avoid committing plagiarism.

51. What do people tend to do while engaging in a conversation?

   A) Repeat what their partners say one way or another.

   B) Focus as much as possible on topics of mutual interest.

   C) Imitate their partners' gestures without their knowing it.

   D) Observe carefully how their partners make use of gestures.

52. When does mirroring usually take place in a conversation?

   A) When both sides are sympathetic with each other.

   B) When both sides have a lot of things in common.

   C) When both sides make interesting contributions.

   D) When both sides try to seek common ground.

53. What do we learn about popular culture?

   A) It encourages people to imitate.   C) It acquaints young people with their idols.

   B) It appeals mostly to big names.   D) It can change people's mode of cognition.

54. Why is the saying "copy from two, it's research" a lesson to learn?

   A) It facilitates the creation of one's own writing style.

   B) It helps to protect one's intellectual property rights.

C) It fosters correct interpretation of professional writing.

D) It enables one to write intriguing sequels to famous stories.

55. Why does the author say imitation is rather paradoxical?

A) It is liable to different interpretations.　　C) It can give rise to endless disputes.

B) It is by and large a necessary evil.　　D) It may do harm as well as good.

Part Ⅳ　　　　　　　Translation　　　　　　　(30 minutes)

Directions: *For this part, you are allowed 30 minutes to translate a passage from Chinese into English. You should write your answer on **Answer Sheet 2**.*

海南是中国仅次于台湾的第二大岛,是位于中国最南端的省份。海南岛风景秀丽,气候宜人,阳光充足,生物多样,温泉密布,海水清澈,大部分海滩几乎全年都是游泳和日光浴的理想场所,因而被誉为中国的四季花园和度假胜地,每年都吸引了大批中外游客。

海南1988年建省以来,旅游业、服务业、高新技术产业飞速发展,是中国唯一的省级经济特区。在中央政府和全国人民的大力支持下,海南将建成中国最大的自由贸易试验区。

2021年6月大学英语六级考试真题解析
（第三套）

Part Ⅰ　Writing

成文构思

本文是一篇议论文，主题是"中国高等教育取得显著成果"，可按照以下思路进行写作。
第一段：描述图表，**指出主题**"中国高等教育取得了显著成果"。
第二段：**分析原因**，可以从经济发展、对高等教育的重视程度和就业市场更激烈的竞争等方面出发。
第三段：**总结**，呼应主题，并指出这是一种好的趋势，应该持续下去。

参考范文及译文

　　From the bar chart, we can see clearly that the gross **enrolment** ratio in higher education in China has witnessed a **constant** increase from 1990 to 2019. It rocketed from only 3.4% to 51.6%, which is quite an extraordinary achievement. What's more, the increasing speed **accelerated** from 2011.

　　There are several factors behind such trend. To begin with, China's economy has seen huge development in the past decade, which makes it possible for much more **households** to **afford** their children's college tuition. In addition, China has paid more attention to higher education, so there is more annual budget on it. Thus, there is an increasing number of universities which can recruit more **undergraduates**. Finally, the competition in job market is much fiercer, so people who want to find a satisfactory job have to go to college and get a higher degree.

　　The achievement in China's higher education is encouraging because it means a higher quality of Chinese people. Obviously, such trend should and will continue in the future.

　　从柱状图中，我们可以清楚地看到，从1990年到2019年，我国高等教育入学率在不断上升，从3.4%猛增至51.6%，这是一项了不起的成就。此外，从2011年开始，增长速度有所加快。

　　这种趋势背后有几个因素。首先，中国经济在过去十年获得了巨大的发展，这使得更多的家庭能够负担孩子的大学学费。此外，中国更加重视高等教育，每年有了更多的教育预算。因此，越来越多的大学可以招收更多的本科生。最后，就业市场的竞争更加激烈，所以想要找到一份满意的工作的人必须上大学并获得更高的学位。

　　中国高等教育取得的成就令人鼓舞，因为这意味着中国人民的素质更高了。显然，这种趋势在未来应该且会继续下去。

词句点拨

enrolment /ɪnˈrəʊlmənt/ n. 入学人数；登记
accelerate /əkˈseləreɪt/ v. 加快，加速
afford /əˈfɔːd/ v. 承担得起
constant /ˈkɒnstənt/ a. 持续不断的
household /ˈhaʊshəʊld/ n. 家庭
undergraduate /ˌʌndəˈɡrædʒuət/ n. 大学本科生

1. From the bar chart, we can see clearly that...
   从柱状图中，我们可以清楚地看到……

2. It rocketed from... to..., which is quite an extraordinary achievement.
   它从……猛增至……，这是一项了不起的成就。

3. There are several factors behind such trend.
   这种趋势背后有几个因素。

4. Obviously, such trend should and will continue in the future.
   显然，这种趋势在未来应该且会继续下去。

Part II　Listening Comprehension

说明：由于 2021 年 6 月六级考试全国共考了两套听力，本套真题听力与前两套内容相同，只是选项顺序不同，因此在本套真题中不再重复出现。

Part III　Reading Comprehension

Section A

全文翻译

　　43岁时，我已经到了一个阶段，在这个阶段，人们警告女性小心人到中年时产生的令人毛骨悚然的悲伤感。我们收到无数有关"如何在40多岁存活下来"的建议，仿佛我们正处在缓慢且艰难地走向脆弱的考验耐力的阶段。这是女性开始变得"不起眼"的年龄段——据说我们的价值、吸引力和能力会随着青春的消逝而消失。但我并未感觉自己正变得默默无闻。我感觉自己比以往更能被看见了，并且人生中首次，我对真实、富有同情心且易于接受的自己有了更清晰的认识。

　　当我看向镜子中的自己时，我为自己感到自豪——甚至是那些长久以来看似不可能被人喜欢的"破碎的"部分。因此，当广告商努力向我推销"时光倒流"的方法时，我不得不忍住讥笑。即使你给我钱，我也不要回到我那青春时代自我意识不健全的时光。这种难得的自我接受意识是成为一名年长女性的喜悦之一。但这种说法经常被一种羞耻感淹没。营销者依赖这种羞耻感向我们贩卖他们的减肥药、神奇的面霜以及透气的瑜伽裤——似乎自爱是一种可以购买的商品。

　　对于一些我认识的女性，生命后一阶段的这种信任感和自信让她们有勇气结束异常的关系或开始新的职业旅程。其他女性则表示，她们享受自己的陪伴、通过苦难获得的成长以及友谊的加深，有能力

更加感同身受、更少地去评头论足而更多地去倾听，以及享受小乐趣。40岁之后的生活远非一帆风顺，但也比我们在女性杂志和好莱坞电影中看到的简化的描述更好。

难词总结

creeping /ˈkri:pɪŋ/ *a.* 令人毛骨悚然的
supposedly /səˈpəʊzɪdli/ *ad.* 据说，据传
clear-eyed /ˈklɪərˈaid/ *a.* 头脑清晰的
reductive /rɪˈdʌktɪv/ *a.* 简化论的

invisible /ɪnˈvɪzəbl/ *a.* 不为人注意的，看不见的
vanish /ˈvænɪʃ/ *v.* 消失
crippling /ˈkrɪplɪŋ/ *a.* 严重损害健康的

题目精析

26. **H**。根据句子结构可知，空格处需要填入一个名词，作介词 toward 的宾语。所给选项中 A 项 adversity（困境，逆境）、D 项 depictions（描述）、H 项 fragility（脆弱；虚弱）、J 项 obscurity（无名；默默无闻）和 K 项 outlines（轮廓；概要）符合语法要求，空格所在句意为：我们收到无数有关"如何在40多岁存活下来"的建议，仿佛我们正处在缓慢且艰难地走向_____的考验耐力的阶段。根据前半句可知，"我们"应该很脆弱，fragility 符合文意，故选 H 项。

27. **E**。根据句子结构可知，空格处需要填入一个过去分词作后置定语，修饰 our value, attractiveness and power。所给选项中 E 项 diminished（减弱，降低）、F 项 drowned（淹没）和 I 项 neglected（忽略）符合语法要求。根据常识可知，人们认为女性在40多岁时，价值、吸引力和能力会下降，diminished 代入后符合语义，故选 E 项。

28. **J**。根据句子结构可知，空格处需要填入一个名词，作介词 into 的宾语，所给选项中 A 项 adversity（困境，逆境）、D 项 depictions（描述）、J 项 obscurity（无名；默默无闻）和 K 项 outlines（轮廓；概要）符合语法要求。空格所在句意为：但我并未感觉自己正变得_____。根据下文 I feel more seen than I ever have（我感觉自己比以往更能被看见了）可知，空格所在句应该表示"但我并未感觉自己正变得默默无闻。"obscurity 代入后符合语义，故选 J 项。

29. **B**。根据句子结构可知，空格处需要填入一个形容词，与后面的两个形容词 compassionate 和 accepting 一起充当表语，B 项 authentic（真实的）、E 项 diminished（减少的）、I 项 neglected（被忽略的）、L 项 prevalent（盛行的，普遍的）和 M 项 purchasable（可购买的）符合语法要求。此处的表语形容作者自己，根据后面的并列表语"富有同情心的"和"易于接受的"可知，空格处应填入形容人且表示褒义的词，authentic 代入后最符合语境，故选 B 项。

30. **O**。根据句子结构可知，空格处需要填入一个动词原形，C 项 convey（传达）、G 项 embark（开始）、N 项 submit（提交）和 O 项 suppress（抑制）符合语法要求。结合上文提到的为自己感到自豪可知，在广告商兜售"时光倒流"的方法时，"我"不得不抑制自己的讥笑，suppress 符合语义，故选 O 项。

31. **F**。根据句子结构可知，空格处需要填入一个过去分词，与 out by the shame 一起作后置定语，修饰 narrative。所给选项中还剩 F 项 drowned（淹没）和 I 项 neglected（忽略）符合语法要求。上文提到，"这种难得的自我接受意识是成为一名年长女性的喜悦之一"，空格所在句的 But 引出转折，结合空格后提到商家依靠这种羞耻感兜售商品可知，上文提到的这种说法经常会被这种羞耻感所

掩盖，F 项符合语境，故选 F 项。

32. M。根据句子结构可知，空格处需要填入一个可数名词单数或形容词，修饰 commodity。所给选项中还剩 A 项 adversity（困境，逆境）、E 项 diminished（减少的）、I 项 neglected（被忽略的）、L 项 prevalent（盛行的，普遍的）和 M 项 purchasable（可购买的）符合语法要求。根据其所修饰的单词 commodity（商品）可知，purchasable 符合语义，故选 M 项。

33. G。根据句子结构可知，空格处需要填入一个动词原形，与 leave 并列。所给选项中还剩 C 项 convey（传达）、G 项 embark（开始）和 N 项 submit（提交）符合语法要求。or 连接两个并列的成分，第一个并列成分意为"结束异常的关系"，故空格所在部分也表示一种积极的做法，embark on 意为"开始"，代入后符合语境，故选 G 项。

34. A。根据句子结构可知，空格处需要填入一个名词，作介词 through 的宾语。所给选项中还剩 A 项 adversity（困境，逆境）、D 项 depictions（描述）和 K 项 outlines（轮廓；概要）符合语法要求。根据语义可知，此处的意思应为"通过苦难获得的成长"，adversity 代入原文后符合语境，故选 A 项。

35. D。根据句子结构可知，空格处需要填入一个名词。剩下的选项中只有 D 项 depictions（描述）和 K 项 outlines（轮廓；概要）符合语法要求。reductive 意为"简化论的"，depictions 与其搭配意为"简化的描述"，代入后符合语义，故选 D 项。

Section B

全文翻译

计算机合成图像演员的道德原则是什么——它们将取代真正的演员吗？

[A] 数字人类正出现在你周围的荧屏上。随着计算机合成图像的成本变得更低，且更加精密，电影产业现在能够自信地在荧屏上再现人类，甚至包括那些已经去世几十年的演员。这项拥有使已故名人重现能力的技术正在引发有关公共遗产和肖像权的问题。

[B] 2019 年年末，据宣布，死于 1955 年的演员詹姆斯·迪恩将出演计划于今年晚些时候上映的越南战争电影——《寻找杰克》。在这部电影中，将根据旧时的影片镜头和照片，使用计算机合成图像技术在荧屏上重现迪恩，并让另一个演员为其配音。这一消息令那些渴望看到通过数字化技术使迪恩在他仅有的第四部电影中重生的人十分激动，但是它也引发了剧烈的批评。"这仅仅是为了死者的名气而操纵他们，"女演员泽尔妲·威廉斯在推特上写道，"这为未来的演出行业开了一个如此糟糕的先例。"她的父亲罗宾·威廉斯于 2014 年去世，他强烈希望避免相同的命运。在他去世之前，他提交了一份在 2039 年之前保护其肖像使用的契约，阻止其他人在电影、电视节目或全息影像中使用计算机合成图像技术重现其肖像。

[C] 代理迪恩遗产的 CMG Worldwide 公司的马克·罗斯勒表示，詹姆斯·迪恩的电影是保持该演员在更年轻一代中的意义的一种方式。Worldwide XR 是用数字化技术重现迪恩的公司之一，该公司的首席执行官特拉维斯·克洛伊德说："我认为这是一场浪潮的开端。在未来，我们希望詹姆斯·迪恩会被带到不同的游戏环境、虚拟现实环境或增强现实的环境中。"

[D] 在其遗产允许的情况下，其他演员也被复活了，用于广告宣传。例如，当代女演员查理兹·塞隆和20世纪偶像级明星玛丽莲·梦露、格蕾丝·凯丽以及玛琳·黛德丽一起出演了迪奥2011年的一则广告。后来，通过数字化技术重现的奥黛丽·赫本出演了2013年的一支巧克力广告。同年，通过计算机合成图像技术制作的李小龙形象出现在了一个威士忌品牌的中文广告中，这得罪了许多粉丝，因为众所周知，李小龙根本不喝酒。制作赫本巧克力广告的英国视觉效果公司Framestore的蒂姆·韦伯说："在过去的五年中，在整部电影中使用计算机合成图像变得更加便宜和可行了。"Framestore使用与赫本面部结构及体型相似的替身作为手工动画的框架。韦伯说，这一过程极其困难，成本也很高，但是技术有所进步。

[E] 现在可以从零做起，将一个人制成动画。"如果是活人，你可以让他们进入扫描台，你可以非常仔细地分析他们身体的每个细节，使制作更加容易，但是根据可用的照片来制作则有点难。"韦伯说道。他在2013年凭借其作品《地心引力》中的视觉效果获得了奥斯卡金像奖。"我还看到如今有很多演员想要利用这项技术：将他们的肖像捕捉并保留下来，以备将来使用，"克洛伊德表示，"他们预测这可以成为他们的遗产，在他们去世之后，这可以使他们的家人利用他们的肖像赚钱。"

[F] 数字化再现已故名人的一大隐患是破坏他们的遗产。"我们必须尊重权利持有人的安全性和完整性。"Digital Domain公司的约翰·坎宁说道。这家美国公司制作了15年前逝世的说唱艺人图派克·夏库尔的全息影像，并使其出现在了2012年科切拉音乐节上。

[G] 从法律上来说，一个人对其去世后名字和肖像的商业使用控制权在不同国家有不同规定，甚至在同一个国家的不同地区也有所不同。例如，在美国一些特定的州，对这些权利的规定和财产权类似，可以转给继承者。在加利福尼亚州，根据《名人权利法案》，名人的人格权可以延续至其去世后70年。英国纽卡斯尔大学的莉莲·爱德华兹说："我们正在进行一场关于公共资源获取的社会辩论，例如名人的面孔。"考虑到名人的代表性，公众应该被允许使用或复制名人的形象吗？爱德华兹表示，对逝世者遗产最有利的部分可能与他家人或公众的利益相冲突。

[H] 韦伯说，重建的形象，无论有多么逼真，都不可能和一个真正的演员没有区别。"当我们在荧屏上重现某个人的形象来代替已经去世的人时，我们所做的是极其精密的数码编造，"他说，"一场表演远不止外表上的相似。"

[I] 随着数字重现名人以及完全制作屏幕上的人物变得越来越容易，这种技术会使演员失业吗？"我认为演员们很担心这点，"爱德华兹说，"但是我认为这需要花费很长时间。"部分原因在于存在观众认为虚拟人物令人害怕的风险。爱德华兹提到，通过数字化技术重现的凯丽·费雪在《侠盗一号》中扮演一位年轻的公主，这引发了广泛的反对。这一技术在最近的《星球大战：天行者的崛起》中被再次运用，这部电影是在费雪2016年去世之后拍摄的。"人们对此并不喜欢，"她说，"他们发现其中存在着诡异谷效应。"

[J] 这指的是当试图使重现的对象与人类相似，但效果并不完美时，这些重现的对象便会使观看者感到不舒服，因为它们明显介于非人类和人类这两者之间。"当你做任何人类或仿人类的事情时，那总是危险的，"韦伯说道，"计算机合成的面部表情可能会漏洞百出，其中任何一个漏洞都会使其陷入诡异谷效应，"他说，"你的大脑就是知道哪里出了问题。"问题通常出现在眼睛或嘴巴部分，韦伯表示。"这些是你在和一个人交谈时会看的地方。"

[K] 通过计算机合成图像创造的一个不为人们所熟悉的数字人物也将和一个不知名演员一样面临同样的困难：他们没有已经成名的人那样的吸引力。"你不得不花大量的资本在它们的肖像上创造认知度，并确保人们熟悉它们是谁。"克洛伊德说。这个现在正在实现。"你在一个国外市场预售一部电影基于相关的才能，"他说，"我认为我们距离制作出有能力预售内容的虚拟人物还有很远的距离。"

[L] 韦伯预测我们将在荧屏上看到更多数字人物。"这正在发生，因为这可以发生。"他说。他引用《侏罗纪公园》中的一句台词，补充道："人们忙着思考他们有能力做什么，以至于没有时间思考他们是否应该这样做。"

难词总结

sophisticated /səˈfɪstɪkeɪtɪd/ a. 精密的；复杂巧妙的
release /rɪˈliːs/ n. 上映；发布
relevant /ˈreləvənt/ a. 有意义的；相关的
permission /pəˈmɪʃn/ n. 同意，许可
from scratch 从零开始；白手起家
indistinguishable /ˌɪndɪˈstɪŋɡwɪʃəbl/ a. 难以区别的

schedule /ˈʃedjuːl/ v. 安排，预定
puppeteer /ˌpʌpɪˈtɪə(r)/ v. 操纵
augment /ɔːɡˈment/ v. 增加；加强
body double 替身演员

题目精析

36. There is an ongoing debate among the public as to whether the images of deceased celebrities should be recreated.

36. 关于是否应该重现已故名人的形象，公众中一直存在争议。

【答案及分析】G。根据题干中的 ongoing debate 定位到 G 段。定位句指出，We've got a societal debate going on about access to our public commons, as it were, about famous faces...（我们正在进行一场关于公共资源获取的社会辩论，例如名人的面孔……）题干是该部分内容的同义表达，故选 G 项。

37. The CGI technology allows the image of the deceased James Dean to be presented to young people in new settings.

37. 计算机合成图像技术使得已故的詹姆斯·迪恩的形象在新的情境下被展示给年轻人。

【答案及分析】C。根据题干中的 deceased James Dean 和 young people 定位到 C 段。定位句指出，The James Dean film is a way to keep the actor's image relevant for younger generations（詹姆斯·迪恩的电影是保持该演员在更年轻一代中的意义的一种方式……）题干是原文的同义表达，题干中的 be presented to young people 对应原文中的 keep... relevant for younger generations，故选 C 项。

38. It is very likely that the CGI-recreated image of a deceased celebrity will fail to match the real actor especially in facial expressions.

38. 很有可能，已故名人的计算机合成图像无法匹配真人演员，尤其是在面部表情方面。

【答案及分析】J。根据题干中的 fail to match 和 facial expressions 定位到 J 段。定位句指出，"Your brain just knows there's something wrong." The problem often arises around the eyes or mouth...（"你的大脑就是知道哪里出了问题。"问题通常出现在眼睛或嘴巴部分……）题干中的 fail to match 对应原

文中的 something wrong，题干中的 facial expressions 对应原文中的 eyes or mouth，故选 J 项。

39. The use of digital technology can bring images of deceased celebrities back to the screen.

39. 使用数码技术可以使已故名人的形象重回荧屏。

【答案及分析】A。根据题干中的 digital technology 和 back to the screen 定位到 A 段。定位句指出，...the film industry can now convincingly recreate people on screen — even actors who have been dead for decades.（……电影产业现在能够自信地在荧屏上重现人类，甚至包括那些已经去世几十年的演员。）题干中的 bring images of deceased celebrities back to screen 是原文中 recreate people on screen 的同义表达，故选 A 项。

40. Recreating a deceased famous actor or actress may violate their legitimate rights.

40. 重现已故的著名男演员或女演员的形象可能会侵犯他们的合法权利。

【答案及分析】F。根据题干中的 violate their legitimate rights 定位到 F 段。定位句指出，A hidden hazard of digitally recreating a deceased celebrity is the risk of damaging their legacy.（数字化再现已故名人的一大隐患是破坏他们的遗产。）题干中的 Recreating a deceased famous actor or actress 是原文中 recreating a deceased celebrity 的同义表达，violate their legitimate rights 是原文中 damaging their legacy 的同义表达，故选 F 项。

41. More CGI-recreated images of deceased celebrities are expected to appear on screen.

41. 预计荧屏上将出现更多计算机合成图像制作的已故名人的形象。

【答案及分析】L。根据题干中的 More CGI-recreated images 和 expected 定位到 L 段。定位句指出，Webber expects that we will see more digital humans on screen.（韦伯预测我们将在荧屏上看到更多数字人物。）题干是 L 段该句的同义表达，故选 L 项。

42. The image of James Dean will be recreated on screen with his voice dubbed by someone else.

42. 詹姆斯·迪恩的形象将在荧屏上重现，且会有其他人给他配音。

【答案及分析】B。根据题干中的 James Dean 和 voice 定位到 B 段。定位句指出，...Dean will be recreated on screen with CGI based on old footage and photographs, with another actor voicing him.（……将根据旧时的影片镜头和照片，使用计算机合成图像技术在荧屏上重现迪恩，并让另一个演员为其配音。）题干中的 James Dean will be recreated on screen 是原词复现，with his voice dubbed by someone else 是原文中 with another actor voicing him 的同义表达，故选 B 项。

43. However advanced the CGI technology is, the recreated image will differ in a way from the real actor.

43. 无论计算机合成图像技术多么先进，重现的形象总会在某些方面与真人演员不同。

【答案及分析】H。根据题干中的 differ 和 real actor 定位到 H 段。定位句指出，A recreation, however lifelike, will never be indistinguishable from a real actor...（重建的形象，无论有多么逼真，都不可能和一个真正的演员没有区别……）题干是该句的同义表达，题干中的 However advanced 对应原文中的 however lifelike，题干中的 differ... from the real actor 对应原文中的 never be indistinguishable from a real actor，故选 H 项。

44. A lot of actors today are likely to make use of the CGI technology to have their images stored for the benefit of their families.

44. 为了家人的利益，如今很多演员可能会利用计算机合成图像技术将他们的肖像留存下来。

【答案及分析】E。根据题干中的 A lot of actors today、make use of the CGI technology 和 families 定位到 E 段。定位句指出，"I also see a lot of actors today who will have the desire to take advantage of this technology...," says Cloyd. "They foresee this being something that could give their estates and give their families the ability to make money from their likeness when they're gone."（"我还看到如今有很多演员想要利用这项技术……，"克洛伊德表示，"他们预测这可以成为他们的遗产，在他们去世之后，这可以使他们的家人利用他们的肖像赚钱。"）题干是对原文这部分内容的总结，故选 E 项。

45. Some actors are concerned that they may lose jobs because of the CGI technology

45. 一些演员担心他们可能会因为计算机合成图像技术而失去工作。

【答案及分析】I。根据题干中的 concerned 和 lose jobs 定位到 I 段。定位句指出，As it becomes easier to digitally recreate celebrities and to entirely manufacture on-screen identities, could this kind of technology put actors out of jobs? "I think actors are worried about this,"...（随着数字重现名人以及完全制作屏幕上的人物变得越来越容易，这种技术会使演员失业吗？"我认为演员们很担心这点，"……）题干中的 are concerned 是原文中 are worried 的同义表达，题干中的 lose jobs 是原文中 out of jobs 的同义表达，故选 I 项。

Section C

Passage One

> **全文翻译**

　　看不见，闻不到，也听不见，对于如何准确地定义它以及它到底从何而来，人们各持己见。它不是学校的一门科目，也不是一门学科，但它是可以习得的。它是一项艺术家被要求具备的品质，但它也存在于科学家和企业家的生活中。它对我们所有人都有益处，当我们能够运用它时，我们的智力和精神都能得到发展。它是很脆弱的东西，很容易被破坏；事实上，当人们嬉戏以及充满童真时，它能得到最充分的发展。同时，在深厚的知识储备和专业技能的加持下，它能得到最好的发挥。

　　这个神秘但可教的品质就是创造力，杜伦创新与教育委员会最近发布的一项报告就是以此为主题。该报告指出，不应该只有当学校课程与戏剧、音乐、艺术，以及其他创造性明显的科目有关时，才将创造力融入其中，创造性思维应该存在于学校生活的方方面面，学习人文学科和自然科学的方式也应该充满创造性。

　　该报告的作者们专注于英国教育，他们提供了一些合理的建议，其中一些建议是为了缓和近几年逐渐渗透到教育政策中的没有激励性且只以事实为基础的教育方式。当孩子们被当作填满事实的容器时，创造力无法得到发展；当老师的唯一目的是训练孩子考试时，创造力也无法得到发展。该委员会的一个建议是，通过学校课程，以支持培养创造力为目的，按照现有数学为枢纽的思路，打造教师主导的"创造力协作"网络。

　　然而，通过艺术课程，创造力明显可以得到最充分的发展。私立学校对艺术课的重视很明显。人们只需要看英国顶尖私立学校非凡的艺术设施就能理解这一点。但是在公立学校，对于英语、数学和科学的过度关注可能会破坏艺术课程；与此同时，学校预算的减少意味着课外活动的减少。从2014年开始，参与创造性课程的高中生数量减少了28.1%，尽管值得高兴的是最近参与艺术和设计课程的学生有所增加。

公立学校和私立学校之间的这一差异有关社会公正。大多数孩子能够接触到的合唱团、管弦乐队、艺术工作室和戏剧只有比他们更有特权的同龄人的一小部分，这就是不对且不公平的事情。随着生活被许多迫在眉睫的困难——气候危机、工作场所的自动化——所影响，人们将比以往更加需要创造力。为了我们所有人的利益，对所有人来说，在教育中培养创造性应该被放在首位。

难词总结

precisely /prɪˈsaɪsli/ a. 精确地
stamp out 扑灭；杜绝
sensible /ˈsensəbl/ a. 合理的；理智的
vessel /ˈvesl/ n. 容器；血管
discrepancy /dɪˈskrepənsi/ n. 差异

wield /wiːld/ v. 使用；运用
expertise /ˌekspɜːˈtiːz/ n. 专门技能，专长
alleviate /əˈliːvieɪt/ v. 减轻，缓和
foster /ˈfɒstə(r)/ v. 培养，促进
privileged /ˈprɪvəlɪdʒd/ a. 享有特权的

题目精析

46. What do we learn from the passage about creativity?

　　A) It develops best when people are spiritually prepared.

　　B) It is most often wielded by scientists and entrepreneurs.

　　C) It is founded on scientific knowledge and analytical skills.

　　D) It contributes to intellectual growth but can easily be killed.

46. 关于创造力，我们从这篇文章中了解到什么？

　　A）当人们在精神上准备好时，它能发展得最好。

　　B）最经常用到它的是科学家和企业家。

　　C）它以科学知识和分析技能为基础。

　　D）它能促进智力发展，但能很容易被抹杀。

【答案及分析】D。根据题干关键词 from the passage 定位到整篇文章。第一段第五句提到，It is a delicate thing, easily stamped out; in fact, it flourishes most fully when people are playful and childlike.（它是很脆弱的东西，很容易被破坏；事实上，当人们嬉戏以及充满童真时，它能得到最充分的发展。）可知 A 项错误。第一段第三句提到，It is a quality that is required of artists, but it is also present in the lives of scientists and entrepreneurs.（它是一项艺术家被要求具备的品质，但它也存在于科学家和企业家的生活中。）可知 B 项错误。C 项利用第一段最后一句中的 it works best in conjunction with deep knowledge and expertise（在深厚的知识储备和专业技能的加持下，它能得到最好的发挥）设置陷阱，但与原文内容不符。根据第一段第四句和第五句 All of us benefit from it and we thrive mentally and spiritually when we are able to wield it. It is a delicate thing, easily stamped out...（它对我们所有人都有益处，

当我们能够运用它时，我们的智力和精神都能得到发展。它是很脆弱的东西，很容易被破坏……）可知 D 项正确，故选 D 项。

47. What is the conclusion of a recently-published report?

   A) Natural sciences should be learned the way humanities courses are.

   B) Cultivation of creativity should permeate the entire school curriculum.

   C) Art courses should be made compulsory for all students.

   D) Students should learn more obviously creative subjects.

47. 最近发表的一份报告得出的结论是什么？

   A）应该像学习人文学科一样学习自然科学。

   B）创造力的培养应该渗透至整个学校课程。

   C）应该强制所有学生学习艺术课程。

   D）学生应该学习更多创造性明显的课程。

【答案及分析】B。根据题干关键词 conclusion 和 recently-published report 定位到原文第二段第二句。该句提到，The report concludes that creativity should not inhibit the school curriculum only as it relates to drama, music, art and other obviously creative subjects, but that creative thinking ought to run through all of school life...（该报告指出，不应该只当学校课程与戏剧、音乐、艺术，以及其他创造性明显的科目有关时，才将创造力融入其中，创造性思维应该存在于学校生活的方方面面……）B 项是对该内容的总结，符合文意，故选 B 项。

48. What does the report say is detrimental to the fostering of creativity?

   A) Alleviation of pressure.   C) Test-oriented teaching.

   B) Teacher-led school activities.   D) Independent learning.

48. 报告中说什么对创造力的培养有害？

   A）缓解压力。   C）以考试为导向的教学。

   B）老师主导的学校活动。   D）自主学习。

【答案及分析】C。根据题干关键词 detrimental 和 fostering of creativity 定位到原文第三段第二句，该句指出，When children are regarded as vessels to be filled with facts, creativity does not prosper; nor does it when teachers' sole objective is coaching children towards exams.（当孩子们被当作填满事实的容器时，创造力无法得到发展；当老师的唯一目的是训练孩子考试时，创造力也无法得到发展。）A、B、D 三项文中均未提及，C 项符合文意。故选 C 项。

49. What do we learn about the private schools in the UK?

   A) They encourage extracurricular activities.

   B) They attach great importance to arts education.

   C) They prioritize arts subjects over maths and sciences.

   D) They cater to students from different family backgrounds.

49. 关于英国的私立学校，我们了解到什么？

   A）它们鼓励课外活动。

B）它们看重艺术教育。

C）它们对艺术科目的重视程度高于数学和科学。

D）它们为来自不同家庭背景的学生服务。

【答案及分析】B。根据题干关键词 private schools in the UK 定位到原文第四段第二句，该句指出，The value placed on them by the independent education sector is clear.（私立学校对艺术课的重视很明显。）B 项"它们看重艺术教育"符合文意，故选 B 项。

50. What should be done to meet the future challenges?

A) Increasing government investment in school education.

B) Narrowing the existing gap between the rich and the poor.

C) Providing all children with equal access to arts education.

D) Focusing on meeting the needs of under-privileged students.

50. 为了应对未来的挑战，我们应该做什么？

A）增加政府对学校教育的投资。

B）缩小富人和穷人之间已有的差距。

C）向所有孩子提供相同的艺术教育机会。

D）关注满足弱势学生的需求。

【答案及分析】C。根据题干关键词 future challenges 定位到原文最后一段最后两句。这两句指出，As lives are affected by any number of looming challenges — climate crisis, automation in the workplace — humans are going to need creative thinking more than ever. For all of our sakes, creativity in education, and for all, must become a priority.（随着生活被许多迫在眉睫的困难——气候危机、工作场所的自动化——所影响，人们将比以往更加需要创造力。为了我们所有人的利益，对所有人来说，在教育中培养创造性应该被放在首位。）A 项中的"增加政府投资"和 B 项中的"缩小差距"文中均未提及，C 项符合文意，D 项不全面，故选 C 项。

Passage Two

全文翻译

模仿你谈话对象的动作是一种常见的人类行为，被归类为"镜像"规则，科学家已经了解并研究了多年。我们都倾向于潜意识地模仿我们所喜欢的人的动作。但是我们为什么会这样呢？

作为一项规则，镜像意味着谈话者们享受他们的交流，并且在他们之间存在一定程度的共识。讨论的话题对双方来说都是有趣的，他们知道他们趣味相投。

重复某人的行为是交流天才的典型特征，并不总是因为一个人有共情能力，而是因为他们有要达成的目标。通过这种方式，新的偶像被带上了舞台：政治家、明星，以及其他一些大人物。流行文化使人们想要看起来很受欢迎，并且像受欢迎的人一样行动和说话。

现在的明星彼此之间相互抄袭歌词，与侵犯版权的指控作斗争或直接声称自己就是作者，即使所有工作都是别人做的。

如今，在明星中，像政治家一样使用自己的演讲稿作者是一种趋势。所谓的"代笔"有多种形式：书籍、文章、自传，甚至是社交媒体上的帖子。

谁是真正的抄袭者？谁又被抄袭了？有时，没有专家的帮助便很难解决这一问题。但是新的基于识别个人写作模式的著作权保护方法早已存在。他们的目标是保护知识产权。使用科学的方法，其中一些在定义著作权时准确率可以达到85%。

写作不是一项可以轻易掌握的技艺。如果你想像专业人士一样在不抄袭的情况下写作，则需要借鉴几点经验，第一点是："模仿一本书是抄袭，模仿两本书就是研究。"对这一说法的正确解释不是关于模仿，而是关于创造你自己的风格。当你学习一位作家的写作风格时，不要止于一个作家，而是要探索数个不同的风格。观察他们使用的句子类型，关注他们运用的象征，将注意力集中在你觉得自己可以续写出相当优秀的续篇的故事上。

模仿相当矛盾。作为学习的必要组成部分，它能带来积极的改变，让人有所成长。然而，它可能有许多危害。模仿某人的思想、想法或发明是完全不能接受的。这侵犯了他人的著作权。

但是，我们所做的很多事情都是在以某种方式模仿他人。因此，如果你想称赞某人的作品，或者模仿他们的作品，你只要确保自己采用了正确的方式，避免出现抄袭的情况即可。

难词总结

emulate /ˈemjuleɪt/ v. 模仿
sympathetic /ˌsɪmpəˈθetɪk/ a. 有同情心的
ghostwrite /ˈɡəʊstraɪt/ v. 代写，代笔
compliment /ˈkɒmplɪmənt/ v. 称赞

subconsciously /ˌsʌbˈkɒnʃəsli/ ad. 潜意识地
violation /ˌvaɪəˈleɪʃn/ n. 违反；侵犯
metaphor /ˈmetəfə(r); ˈmetəfɔː(r)/ n. 象征；隐喻

题目精析

51. What do people tend to do while engaging in a conversation?

    A) Repeat what their partners say one way or another.

    B) Focus as much as possible on topics of mutual interest.

    C) Imitate their partners' gestures without their knowing it.

    D) Observe carefully how their partners make use of gestures.

51. 当人们交流时，他们倾向于做什么？

    A）以某种方式重复他们同伴的话。

    B）尽量集中在有共同兴趣的话题上。

    C）在无意识的情况下模仿他们同伴的动作。

    D）仔细观察他们的同伴如何使用动作。

【答案及分析】C。根据题干关键词in a conversation定位到原文第一段第一句和第三句。这两句指出，Emulating your conversation partner's actions is a common human behavior... We all tend to subconsciously copy gestures of people we like.（模仿你谈话对象的动作是一种常见的人类行为……我们都倾向于潜意识地模仿我们所喜欢的人的动作。）C项中的Imitate是原文中Emulating的同义表达，without their knowing it 对应原文中的 subconsciously，C 项符合文意，故选 C 项。

52. When does mirroring usually take place in a conversation?

   A) When both sides are sympathetic with each other.

   B) When both sides have a lot of things in common.

   C) When both sides make interesting contributions.

   D) When both sides try to seek common ground.

52. 镜像通常发生在对话的什么时候？

   A）当双方都对彼此共情的时候。

   B）当双方有很多共同特点的时候。

   C）当双方都做出有趣贡献的时候。

   D）当双方都在努力寻找共同点的时候。

   【答案及分析】B。根据题干关键词 mirroring 和 conversation 定位到原文第二段第一句。该句指出，As a rule, mirroring means that conversationalists enjoy their communication and that there's a certain level of agreement between them.（作为一项规则，镜像意味着谈话者们享受他们的交流，并且在他们之间存在一定程度的共识。）B 项中的 things in common 是原文中 agreement 的同义表达，B 项正确。A 项利用 sympathetic 设置陷阱，但原文第三段第一句中提到，重复某人的行为不总是因为一个人有共情能力，A 项错误。C 项利用 interesting 设置陷阱，但是 contributions 属于无中生有。D 项中的 seek common ground 文中未提及。故选 B 项。

53. What do we learn about popular culture?

   A) It encourages people to imitate.   C) It acquaints young people with their idols.

   B) It appeals mostly to big names.   D) It can change people's mode of cognition.

53. 我们对流行文化有什么了解？

   A）它鼓励人们模仿。   C）它使年轻人了解他们的偶像。

   B）它对大人物最有吸引力。   D）它可以改变人们的思维模式。

   【答案及分析】A。根据题干关键词 popular culture 定位到原文第三段最后一句。该句指出，Popular culture makes people want to look popular, and act and speak like popular people.（流行文化使人们想要看起来很受欢迎，并且像受欢迎的人一样行动和说话。）即流行文化会促进人们模仿受欢迎的人。A 项符合原文，故选 A 项。

54. Why is the saying "copy from two, it's research" a lesson to learn?

   A) It facilitates the creation of one's own writing style.

   B) It helps to protect one's intellectual property rights.

   C) It fosters correct interpretation of professional writing.

   D) It enables one to write intriguing sequels to famous stories.

54. 为什么格言"模仿两本书就是研究"是需要借鉴的经验？

   A）它有助于创造个人的写作风格。

   B）它有助于保护个人的知识产权。

C）它形成了职业写作的正确解释。

D）它让人能够给一个著名的故事写有趣的续篇。

【答案及分析】A。根据题干关键词 "copy from two, it's research" 定位到原文第七段第二句和第三句，第二句提到了这句格言，第三句指出，The correct interpretation of this statement is not about copying, but rather about creating your own style.（对这一说法的正确解释不是关于模仿，而是关于创造你自己的风格。）A 项中的 creation of one's own writing style 是原文中 creating your own style 的同义表达，符合文意，故选 A 项。

55. Why does the author say imitation is rather paradoxical?

　　A) It is liable to different interpretations.　　C) It can give rise to endless disputes.

　　B) It is by and large a necessary evil.　　D) It may do harm as well as good.

55. 作者为什么说模仿相当矛盾？

　　A）它可能有多种解释。　　C）它会引发永无止境的争吵。

　　B）总的来说，它是不可避免的灾祸。　　D）它可能既有好处也有坏处。

【答案及分析】D。根据题干关键词 imitation 和 paradoxical 定位到倒数第二段第二、三句。这两句指出，As an integral part of learning, it brings about positive changes, making people develop and grow. However, it may do a lot of harm.（作为学习的必要组成部分，它能带来积极的改变，让人有所成长。然而，它可能有许多危害。）即模仿相当矛盾的原因是它既有好处也有坏处，D 项符合文意，故选 D 项。

Part Ⅳ　Translation

【参考译文】

　　Hainan is the second biggest island next only to Taiwan and it is the southernmost province in China. Hainan has beautiful scenery, pleasant climate, sufficient sunlight and biological diversity, dense hot springs and clear seawater. Most of its beaches are ideal places for swimming and sunbathing almost all year round. Thus, it is known as China's four-seasonal garden and holiday paradise, attracting lost of domestic and overseas tourists every year.

　　Since the establishment of Hainan Province in 1988, it has witnessed high-speed development in tourism, service industry and high-tech industry, making it the only provincial-level special economic zone in China. With the strong support of the central government and people across the country, Hainan will be built into the biggest pilot free trade zone in China.

【难词总结】

southernmost /ˈsʌðənməʊst/ a. 最南的

sufficient /səˈfɪʃ(ə)nt/ a. 充足的

diversity /daɪˈvɜːsəti/ n. 多样性

witness /ˈwɪtnəs/ v. 经历；见证

scenery /ˈsiːnəri/ n. 风景

biological /ˌbaɪəˈlɒdʒɪk(ə)l/ a. 生物的，生物学的

sunbathe /ˈsʌnbeɪð/ v. 沐日光浴

pilot free trade zone 自由贸易试验区

1. 第一句中有两个意群，可以处理为 and 连接的并列句。第一个分句中的主干为"海南岛是第二大岛"，直接翻译即可，"仅次于台湾"可译为 next only to Taiwan。第二个分句结构简单，"最南端的省份"可译为 the southernmost province。

2. 第二句句子很长，涉及的内容很多，需要适当断句。"海南岛风景秀丽……海水清澈"可处理为并列的结构，翻译为 Hainan has beautiful scenery, pleasant climate, sufficient sunlight and biological diversity, dense hot springs and clear seawater。"大部分海滩几乎全年都是游泳和日光浴的理想场所"可以单独成句，"日光浴"的表达为 sunbathing。后面两个分句可处理为一句，"四季花园"的表达为 four-seasonal garden，"度假胜地"可译为 holiday resort 或 holiday paradise，"每年都吸引了大批中外游客"可处理为现在分词短语作状语的结构，"中外游客"可译为 tourists from home and abroad 或者 domestic and overseas tourists。

3. 第三句中的"海南1988年建省以来"可译为时间状语从句，后面两个分句之间存在一定程度上的因果关系，所以可以将"是中国唯一的省级经济特区"处理为"旅游业、服务业、高新技术产业飞速发展"的结果状语。"省级经济特区"的表达为 provincial-level special economic zone。

4. 第四句结构比较简单，"在……的大力支持下"可处理为 with 结构，即 with the strong support of...。注意主句中的"海南将建成"不是 Hainan will build，而是"海南将被建成"，应该译为 Hainan will be built into。"自由贸易试验区"的表达为 pilot free trade zone。

未得到监考教师指令前，不得翻阅该试题册！

2020年12月大学英语六级考试真题（第一套）

Part Ⅰ　　　　　　　　　　Writing　　　　　　　　　　（30 minutes）
（请于正式开考后半小时内完成该部分，之后将进行听力考试）

Directions: *For this part, you are allowed 30 minutes to write an essay on **why students should be encouraged to develop the ability to meet challenges**. You should write at least **150** words but no more than **200** words.*

Part Ⅱ　　　　Listening Comprehension　　　　（30 minutes）

Section A

Directions: *In this section, you will hear two long conversations. At the end of each conversation, you will hear four questions. Both the conversation and the questions will be spoken only once. After you hear a question, you must choose the best answer from the four choices marked A), B), C) and D). Then mark the corresponding letter on **Answer Sheet 1** with a single line through the centre.*

Questions 1 to 4 are based on the conversation you have just heard.

1. A) She has not received any letter from the man.
   B) Her claim has been completely disregarded.
   C) She has failed to reach the manager again.
   D) Her house has not been repaired in time.
2. A) Their caravan was washed away by the flood.
   B) The ground floor of their cottage was flooded.
   C) Their entire house was destroyed by the flood.
   D) The roof of their cottage collapsed in the flood.
3. A) The woman's failure to pay her house insurance in time.
   B) The woman's inaccurate description of the whole incident.
   C) The woman's ignorance of the insurance company's policy.
   D) The woman's misreading of the insurance company's letter.
4. A) Revise the terms and conditions of the contract.
   B) Consult her lawyer about the insurance policy.
   C) Talk to the manager of Safe House Insurance.
   D) File a lawsuit against the insurance company.

Questions 5 to 8 are based on the conversation you have just heard.

5. A) They are both worried about the negative impact of technology.
   B) They differ greatly in their knowledge of modern technology.
   C) They disagree about the future of AI technology.
   D) They work in different fields of AI technology.
6. A) Stimulating and motivating.
   B) Simply writing AI software.
   C) More demanding and requiring special training.
   D) Less time-consuming and focusing on creation.
7. A) Old people would be taken care of solely by unfeeling robots.
   B) Humans would be tired of communicating with one another.
   C) Digital life could replace human civilization.
   D) There could be jobs nobody wants to do.

8. A) It will be smarter than human beings.　　C) It will take away humans' jobs altogether.
   B) Chips will be inserted in human brains.　　D) Life will become like a science fiction film.

Section B

Directions: *In this section, you will hear two passages. At the end of each passage, you will hear three or four questions. Both the passage and the questions will be spoken only once. After you hear a question, you must choose the best answer from the four choices marked A), B), C) and D). Then mark the corresponding letter on **Answer Sheet 1** with a single line through the centre.*

Questions 9 to 11 are based on the passage you have just heard.

9. A) Try to earn as much money as possible.　　C) Save one-fifth of their net monthly income.
   B) Invest shrewdly in lucrative businesses.　　D) Restrain themselves from high-risk investments.
10. A) Cut 20% of their daily spending.　　C) Try to stick to their initial plan.
    B) Ask a close friend for advice.　　D) Start by doing something small.
11. A) A proper mindset.　　C) An optimistic attitude.
    B) An ambitious plan.　　D) A keen interest.

Questions 12 to 15 are based on the passage you have just heard.

12. A) She found her outfit inappropriate.　　C) She often checked herself in a mirror.
    B) She was uninterested in advertising.　　D) She was unhappy with fashion trends.
13. A) To save the expenses on clothing.　　C) To meet the expectations of fashion-conscious clients.
    B) To keep up with the current trends.　　D) To save the trouble of choosing a unique outfit every day.
14. A) It boosts one's confidence when looking for employment.
    B) It matters a lot in jobs involving interaction with others.
    C) It helps people succeed in whatever they are doing.
    D) It enhances people's ability to work independently.
15. A) Design their own uniform to appear unique.　　C) Do whatever is possible to look smart.
    B) Fight the ever-changing trends in fashion.　　D) Wear classic pieces to impress their clients.

Section C

Directions: *In this section, you will hear three recordings of lectures or talks followed by three or four questions. The recordings will be played only once. After you hear a question, you must choose the best answer from the four choices marked A), B), C) and D). Then mark the corresponding letter on **Answer Sheet 1** with a single line through the centre.*

Questions 16 to 18 are based on the recording you have just heard.

16. A) Their failure to accumulate wealth.　　C) The deterioration of the environment.
    B) Their obsession with consumption.　　D) The ever-increasing costs of housing.
17. A) Things that we cherish most.　　C) Things that cost less money.
    B) Things that boost efficiency.　　D) Things that are rare to find.
18. A) They are mostly durable.　　C) They serve multiple purposes.
    B) They are easily disposable.　　D) They benefit the environment.

Questions 19 to 21 are based on the recording you have just heard.

19. A) All respondents were afraid of making a high expense claim.
    B) A number of respondents gave an average answer of 400 miles.
    C) Most of the respondents got compensated for driving 384 miles.
    D) Over 10% of the respondents lied about the distance they drove.
20. A) They endeavored to actually be honest.　　C) They cared about other people's claims.

B) They wanted to protect their reputation. D) They responded to colleagues' suspicion.
21. A) They seem positive. C) They seem intuitive.
    B) They are illustrative. D) They are conclusive.

Questions 22 to 25 are based on the recording you have just heard.

22. A) Older people's aversion to new music. C) Insights into the features of good music.
    B) Older people's changing musical tastes. D) Deterioration in the quality of new music.
23. A) They seldom listen to songs released in their teens.
    B) They can make subtle distinctions about music.
    C) They find all music sounds the same.
    D) They no longer listen to new music.
24. A) The more you experience something, the better you'll appreciate it.
    B) The more you experience something, the longer you'll remember it.
    C) The more you are exposed to something, the deeper you'll understand it.
    D) The more you are exposed to something, the more familiar it'll be to you.
25. A) Teenagers are much more sensitive. C) Teenagers' memories are more lasting.
    B) Teenagers are much more sentimental. D) Teenagers' emotions are more intense.

Part III   Reading Comprehension   (40 minutes)

Section A

Directions: *In this section, there is a passage with ten blanks. You are required to select one word for each blank from a list of choices given in a word bank following the passage. Read the passage through carefully before making your choices. Each choice in the bank is identified by a letter. Please mark the corresponding letter for each item on **Answer Sheet 2** with a single line through the centre. You may not use any of the words in the bank more than once.*

The idea of taxing things that are bad for society has a powerful allure. It offers the possibility of a double benefit— __26__ harmful activities, while also providing the government with revenue.

Take sin taxes. Taxes on alcohol make it more expensive to get drunk, which reduces excessive drinking and __27__ driving. At the same time, they provide state and local governments with billions of dollars of revenue. Tobacco taxes, which generate more than twice as much, have proven __28__ in the decline of smoking, which has saved millions of lives.

Taxes can also be an important tool for environmental protection, and many economists say taxing carbon would be the best way to reduce greenhouse gas emissions. Economic theory says that unlike income or sales taxes, carbon taxes can actually increase economic efficiency; because companies that __29__ carbon dioxide into the sky don't pay the costs of the climate change they cause, carbon taxes would restore the proper __30__ to the market.

In reality, carbon taxes alone won't be enough to halt global warming, but they would be a useful part of any climate plan. What's more, the revenue from this tax, which would __31__ be hundreds of billions of dollars per year, could be handed out to citizens as a __32__ or used to fund green infrastructure projects.

Similarly, a wealth tax has been put forward as a way to reduce inequality while raising revenue. The revenue from this tax, which some experts __33__ will be over $4 trillion per decade, would be designated for housing, child care, health care and other government benefits. If you believe, as many do, that wealth inequality is __34__ bad, then these taxes improve society while also __35__ government *coffers*(金库).

A) discouraging	I) initially
B) dividend	J) instrumental
C) emotional	K) merging
D) fragments	L) predict
E) impaired	M) probably
F) imprisoned	N) pump
G) incentives	O) swelling
H) inherently	

Section B

Directions: *In this section, you are going to read a passage with ten statements attached to it. Each statement contains information given in one of the paragraphs. Identify the paragraph from which the information is derived. You may choose a paragraph more than once. Each paragraph is marked with a letter. Answer the questions by marking the corresponding letter on* **Answer Sheet 2**.

The Challenges for Artificial Intelligence in Agriculture

[A] A group of corn farmers stands huddled around an *agronomist*（农学家）and his computer on the side of an irrigation machine in central South Africa. The agronomist has just flown over the field with a hybrid unmanned aerial vehicle (UAV) that takes off and lands using propellers yet maintains distance and speed for scanning vast hectares of land through the use of its fixed wings.

[B] The UAV is fitted with a four spectral band precision sensor that conducts onboard processing immediately after the flight, allowing farmers and field staff to address, almost immediately, any crop abnormalities that the sensor may have recorded, making the data collection truly real-time.

[C] In this instance, the farmers and agronomist are looking to specialized software to give them an accurate plant population count. It's been 10 days since the corn emerged and the farmer wants to determine if there are any parts of the field that require replanting due to a lack of emergence or wind damage, which can be severe in the early stages of the summer rainy season.

[D] At this growth stage of the plant's development, the farmer has another 10 days to conduct any replanting before the majority of his fertilizer and chemical applications need to occur. Once these have been applied, it becomes economically unviable to take corrective action, making any further collected data historical and useful only to inform future practices for the season to come.

[E] The software completes its processing in under 15 minutes producing a plant population count map. It's difficult to grasp just how impressive this is, without understanding that just over a year ago it would have taken three to five days to process the exact same data set, illustrating the advancements that have been achieved in precision agriculture and remote sensing in recent years. With the software having been developed in the United States on the same variety of crops in seemingly similar conditions, the agronomist feels confident that the software will produce a near accurate result.

[F] As the map appears on the screen, the agronomist's face begins to drop. Having walked through the planted rows before the flight to gain a physical understanding of the situation on the ground, he knows the instant he sees the data on his screen that the plant count is not correct, and so do the farmers, even with their limited understanding of how to read remote sensing maps.

[G] Hypothetically, it is possible for machines to learn to solve any problem on earth relating to the physical interaction of all things within a defined or contained environment by using artificial intelligence and machine learning.

[H] Remote sensors enable *algorithms*（算法）to interpret a field's environment as statistical data that can be understood and useful to farmers for decision-making. Algorithms process the data, adapting and learning based on the data received. The more inputs and statistical information collected, the better the algorithm will be at predicting a range of outcomes. And the aim is that farmers can use this artificial intelligence to achieve their goal of a better harvest through making better decisions in the field.

[I] In 2011, IBM, through its R&D Headquarters in Haifa, Israel, launched an agricultural cloud-computing project. The project, in collaboration with a number of specialized IT and agricultural partners, had one goal in mind—to take a variety of academic and physical data sources from an agricultural environment and turn these into automatic predictive solutions for farmers that would assist them in making real-time decisions in the field.

[J] Interviews with some of the IBM project team members at the time revealed that the team believed it was entirely possible to "algorithm" agriculture, meaning that algorithms could solve any problem in the world. Earlier that year, IBM's cognitive learning system, Watson, competed in the game Jeopardy against former winners Brad Rutter and Ken Jennings with astonishing results. Several years later, Watson went on to produce ground-breaking achievements in the field of medicine.

[K] So why did the project have such success in medicine but not agriculture? Because it is one of the most difficult fields to contain for the purpose of statistical quantification. Even within a single field, conditions are always changing from one section to the next. There's unpredictable weather, changes in soil quality, and the ever-present possibility that pests and diseases may pay a visit. Growers may feel their prospects are good for an upcoming harvest, but until that day arrives, the outcome will always be uncertain.

[L] By comparison, our bodies are a contained environment. Agriculture takes place in nature, among ecosystems of interacting organisms and activity, and crop production takes place within that ecosystem environment. But these ecosystems are not contained. They are subject to climatic occurrences such as weather systems, which impact upon hemispheres as a whole, and from continent to continent. Therefore, understanding how to manage an agricultural environment means taking literally many hundreds if not thousands of factors into account.

[M] What may occur with the same seed and fertilizer program in the United States' Midwest region is almost certainly unrelated to what may occur with the same seed and fertilizer program in Australia or South Africa. A few factors that could impact on variation would typically include the measurement of rain per unit of a crop planted, soil type, patterns of soil degradation, daylight hours, temperature and so forth.

[N] So the problem with deploying machine learning and artificial intelligence in agriculture is not that scientists lack the capacity to develop programs and protocols to begin to address the biggest of growers' concerns; the problem is that in most cases, no two environments will be exactly alike, which makes the testing, validation and successful rollout of such technologies much more laborious than in most other industries.

[O] Practically, to say that AI and Machine Learning can be developed to solve all problems related to our physical environment is to basically say that we have a complete understanding of all aspects of the interaction of physical or material activity on the planet. After all, it is only through our understanding of "the nature of things" that protocols and processes are designed for the rational capabilities of cognitive systems to take place. And, although AI and Machine Learning are teaching us many things about how to understand our environment, we are still far from being able to predict critical outcomes in fields like agriculture purely through the cognitive ability of machines.

[P] Backed by the venture capital community, which is now investing billions of dollars in the sector, most agricultural technology startups today are pushed to complete development as quickly as possible and then encouraged to flood the market as quickly as possible with their products.

[Q] This usually results in a failure of a product, which leads to skepticism from the market and delivers a blow to the integrity of Machine Learning technology. In most cases, the problem is not that the technology does not work, the problem is that industry has not taken the time to respect that agriculture is one of the most uncontained environments to manage. For technology to truly make an impact on agriculture, more effort, skills, and funding is needed to test these technologies in farmers' fields.

[R] There is huge potential for artificial intelligence and machine learning to revolutionize agriculture by integrating these technologies into critical markets on a global scale. Only then can it make a difference to the grower, where it really counts.

36. Farmers will not profit from replanting once they have applied most of the fertilizer and other chemicals to their fields.
37. Agriculture differs from the medical science of the human body in that its environment is not a contained one.
38. The agronomist is sure that he will obtain a near accurate count of plant population with his software.
39. The application of artificial intelligence to agriculture is much more challenging than to most other industries.
40. Even the farmers know the data provided by the UAV is not correct.
41. The pressure for quick results leads to product failure, which, in turn, arouses doubts about the applicability of AI technology to agriculture.
42. Remote sensors are aimed to help farmers improve decision-making to increase yields.
43. The farmer expects the software to tell him whether he will have to replant any parts of his farm fields.
44. Agriculture proves very difficult to quantify because of the constantly changing conditions involved.
45. The same seed and fertilizer program may yield completely different outcomes in different places.

Section C

Directions: *There are 2 passages in this section. Each passage is followed by some questions or unfinished statements. For each of them there are four choices marked A), B), C) and D). You should decide on the best choice and mark the corresponding letter on **Answer Sheet 2** with a single line through the centre.*

Passage One

Questions 46 to 50 are based on the following passage.

What is the place of art in a culture of inattention? Recent visitors to the Louvre report that tourists can now spend only a minute in front of the Mona Lisa before being asked to move on. Much of that time, for some of them, is spent taking photographs not even of the painting but of themselves with the painting in the background.

One view is that we have democratised tourism and gallery-going so much that we have made it effectively impossible to appreciate what we've travelled to see. In this oversubscribed society, experience becomes a commodity like any other. There are queues to climb Mt. Jolmo Lungma as well as to see famous paintings. Leisure, thus conceived, is hard labour, and returning to work becomes a well-earned break from the ordeal.

What gets lost in this industrialised haste is the quality of looking. Consider an extreme example, the late philosopher Richard Wollheim. When he visited the Louvre he could spend as much as four hours sitting before a painting. The first hour, he claimed, was necessary for misperceptions to be eliminated. It was only then that the picture would begin to disclose itself. This seems unthinkable today, but it is still possible to organise. Even in the busiest museums there are many rooms and many pictures worth hours of contemplation which the crowds largely ignore. Sometimes the largest crowds are partly the products of bad management; the Mona Lisa is such a hurried experience today partly because the museum is being reorganised. The Uffizi in Florence, another site of cultural pilgrimage, has cut its entry queues down to seven minutes by clever management. And there are some forms of art, those designed to be spectacles as well as objects of contemplation, which can work perfectly well in the face of huge crowds.

Olafur Eliasson's current Tate Modern show, for instance, might seem nothing more than an entertainment, overrun as it is with kids *romping*（喧闹地玩耍）in fog rooms and spray mist installations. But it's more than that: where Eliasson is at his most entertaining, he is at his most serious too, and his disorienting installations bring home the reality of the destructive effects we are having on the planet—not least what we are doing to the glaciers of Eliasson's beloved Iceland.

Marcel Proust, another lover of the Louvre, wrote: "It is only through art that we can escape from ourselves and know how another person sees the universe, whose landscapes would otherwise have remained as unknown as any on the noon." If any art remains worth seeing, it must lead us to such escapes. But a minute in front of a painting in a hurried crowd won't do that.

46. What does the scene at the Louvre demonstrate according to the author?
    A) The enormous appeal of a great piece of artistic work to tourists.
    B) The near impossibility of appreciating art in an age of mass tourism.
    C) The ever-growing commercial value of long-cherished artistic works.
    D) The real difficulty in getting a glimpse at a masterpiece amid a crowd.
47. Why did the late philosopher Richard Wollheim spend four hours before a picture?
    A) It takes time to appreciate a piece of art fully.
    B) It is quite common to misinterpret artistic works.
    C) The longer people contemplate a picture, the more likely they will enjoy it.
    D) The more time one spends before a painting, the more valuable one finds it.
48. What does the case of the Uffizi in Florence show?
    A) Art works in museums should be better taken care of.
    B) Sites of cultural pilgrimage are always flooded with visitors.
    C) Good management is key to handling large crowds of visitors.
    D) Large crowds of visitors cause management problems for museums.
49. What do we learn from Olafur Eliasson's current Tate Modern show?
    A) Children learn to appreciate art works most effectively while they are playing.
    B) It is possible to combine entertainment with appreciation of serious art.
    C) Art works about the environment appeal most to young children.
    D) Some forms of art can accommodate huge crowds of visitors.
50. What can art do according to Marcel Proust?
    A) Enable us to live a much fuller life.
    B) Allow us to escape the harsh reality.
    C) Help us to see the world from a different perspective.
    D) Urge us to explore the unknown domain of the universe.

Passage Two

Questions 51 to 55 are based on the following passage.

Every five years, the government tries to tell Americans what to put in their bellies. Eat more vegetables. Dial back the fats. It's all based on the best available science for leading a healthy life. But the best available science also has a lot to say about what those food choices do to the environment, and some researchers are annoyed that new dietary recommendations of the USDA (United States Department of Agriculture) released yesterday seem to utterly ignore that fact.

Broadly, the 2016–2020 dietary recommendations aim for balance: More vegetables, leaner meats and far less sugar.

But Americans consume more calories per capita than almost any other country in the world. So the things Americans eat have a huge impact on climate change. Soil tilling releases carbon dioxide, and delivery vehicles emit exhaust. The government's dietary guidelines could have done a lot to lower that climate cost. Not just because of their position of authority: The guidelines drive billions of dollars of food production through federal programs like school lunches and nutrition assistance for the needy.

On its own, plant and animal agriculture contributes 9 percent of all the country's greenhouse gas emissions. That's not counting the fuel burned in transportation, processing, refrigeration, and other waypoints between farm and belly. Red meats are among the biggest and most notorious emitters, but trucking a salad from California to Minnesota in January also carries a significant burden. And greenhouse gas emissions aren't the whole story. Food production is the largest user of fresh water, largest contributor to the loss of biodiversity, and a major contributor to using up natural resources.

All of these points and more showed up in the Dietary Guidelines Advisory Committee's scientific report, released last February. Miriam Nelson chaired the subcommittee in charge of sustainability for the report, and is disappointed that eating less meat and buying local food aren't in the final product. "Especially if you consider that eating less meal, especially red and processed, has health benefits, " she says.

So what happened? The official response is that sustainability falls too far outside the guidelines' official scope, which is to provide "nutritional and dietary information."

Possibly the agencies in charge of drafting the decisions are too close to the industries they are supposed to regulate. On one hand, the USDA is compiling dietary advice. On the other, their clients are US agriculture companies.

The line about keeping the guidelines' scope to nutrition and diet doesn't ring quite right with researchers. David Wallinga, for example, says, "In previous guidelines, they've always been concerned with things like food security—which is presumably the mission of the USDA. You absolutely need to be worried about climate impacts and future sustainability if you want secure food in the future."

51. Why are some researchers irritated at the USDA's 2016–2020 Dietary Guidelines?
    A) It ignores the harmful effect of red meat and processed food on health.
    B) Too much emphasis is given to eating less meat and buying local food.
    C) The dietary recommendations are not based on medical science.
    D) It takes no notice of the potential impact on the environment.
52. Why does the author say the USDA could have contributed a lot to lowering the climate cost through its dietary guidelines?
    A) It has the capacity and the financial resources to do so.
    B) Its researchers have already submitted relevant proposals.
    C) Its agencies in charge of drafting the guidelines have the expertise.
    D) It can raise students' environmental awareness through its programs.
53. What do we learn from the Dietary Guidelines Advisory Committee's scientific report?
    A) Food is easily contaminated from farm to belly.
    B) Greenhouse effect is an issue still under debate.
    C) Modern agriculture has increased food diversity.
    D) Farming consumes most of our natural resources.
54. What may account for the neglect of sustainability in the USDA's Dietary Guidelines according to the author?
    A) Its exclusive concern with Americans' food safety.
    B) Its sole responsibility for providing dietary advice.
    C) Its close ties with the agriculture companies.
    D) Its alleged failure to regulate the industries.
55. What should the USDA do to achieve food security according to David Wallinga?
    A) Give top priority to things like nutrition and food security.
    B) Endeavor to ensure the sustainable development of agriculture.
    C) Fulfill its mission by closely cooperating with the industries.
    D) Study the long-term impact of climate change on food production.

Part Ⅳ　　　　　　　　　Translation　　　　　　　　(30 minutes)

Directions: *For this part, you are allowed 30 minutes to translate a passage from Chinese into English. You should write your answer on **Answer Sheet 2**.*

北京大兴国际机场位于天安门广场以南46公里处，于2019年9月30日投入使用。该巨型工程于2014年开工建设，高峰时工地上有4万多工人。航站楼设计紧凑，可以允许最大数量的飞机直接停靠在最靠近航站楼中心的位置，这给乘客提供了极大的方便。航站楼共有82个登机口，但乘客通过安检后，只需不到8分钟就能抵达任何一个登机口。机场的设计可确保每小时300架次起降。机场年客运量2040年将达到1亿人次，有望成为世界上最繁忙的机场。

2020年12月大学英语六级考试真题解析
（第一套）

Part Ⅰ　Writing

成文构思

本文是一篇议论文，话题是"为什么应该鼓励学生培养面对挑战的能力"，可按照以下思路进行写作。
第一段：**引出话题**，提出"鼓励学生培养面对挑战的能力很重要"这一观点。
第二段：**分析原因**，可从当前的个人学习和未来的职业发展两个方面进行分析。本段是全文的中心段落。
第三段：**总结**，进一步呼应文章主题。

参考范文及译文

In this constantly changing society, the ability to meet challenges has become **indispensable** among students. That is to say, we students should take a positive action independently in response to a difficult situation.

There stand at least two reasons that can **account for** my perspectives. First, if students could endure hardship and setback, the ever-growing academic pressure will never lead to feelings of depression and exhaustion among them. For example, if a student easily gives up while having difficulties in studies, he or she will never make any considerable progress, which could even cause serious psychological problems. Besides, it is of **vital** importance for students to get fully prepared before they graduate and go to work, such as forming a **determined** and strong-willed character. Accepting the present challenges bravely can build their character, which has a powerful influence on their future job performance and career **prospects**.

From what has been mentioned above, we can draw the conclusion that students should be educated to **cultivate** the awareness that personal progress can be achieved through facing and then overcoming challenges.

　　在这个日新月异的社会，应对挑战的能力对于学生来说是不可或缺的。也就是说，我们学生应该独立地采取积极行动来应对困境。
　　至少有两个原因可以说明我的观点。首先，如果学生能够忍受艰难和挫折，那么不断增长的学业压力就不会让他们感到沮丧和疲惫不堪。例如，如果一个学生在学习上遇到困难便轻易放弃，那么他或她永远不会取得任何显著的进步，这甚至会引起严重的心理问题。此外，对于学生来说，在毕业后进入职场之前做好充分的准备是至关重要的，比如说形成有决心、意志坚定的性格。勇敢地接受当前的挑战能塑造他们的性格，这对他们以后的工作表现和职业前景有着强大的影响力。
　　综上所述，我们可以得出结论：我们应该教育学生培养一种意识，即个人可以通过面对并克服挑战取得进步。

词句点拨

indispensable /ˌɪndɪˈspensəbl/ a. 不可或缺的
vital /ˈvaɪtl/ a. 至关重要的
prospect /ˈprɒspekt/ n. 前途；前景

account for 是……的说明（或原因）
determined /dɪˈtɜːmɪnd/ a. 坚定的
cultivate /ˈkʌltɪveɪt/ v. 培养

1. There stand at least... reasons that can account for my perspectives.
   至少有……个原因可以说明我的观点。

2. Besides, it is of vital importance for... to get fully prepared before...
   此外，对于……来说，在……之前做好充分的准备是至关重要的。

3. From what has been mentioned above, we can draw the conclusion that... should be educated to cultivate the awareness that...
   综上所述，我们可以得出结论：我们应该教育……培养一种意识，即……

Part II Listening Comprehension

Section A

Questions 1 to 4 are based on the conversation you have just heard.

听力原文及译文

M: Good morning, Safe House Insurance. My name is Paul. How can I help you today?

W: Morning. I wouldn't say that it's a good from where I am standing. This is Ms. Wilson, and this is the third time I've called this week since receiving your letter about our insurance claim. (1) <u>I'm getting a little fed up with my calls about my claim being completely disregarded.</u>

M: Ms. Wilson, thank you for calling back. Can I take some details to help me look at your claim?

W: It's Ms. May Wilson of 15 South Sea Road in Cornwall. And the details are that our village was extensively flooded two months ago. (2) <u>The entire ground floor of our cottage was submerged in water.</u> And five of us have been living in a caravan ever since. You people are still withholding the money we are entitled to over a bizarre technical detail and it's not acceptable, Paul.

M: Ms. Wilson, according to the notes on your account, (3) <u>the bizarre technical detail that you mentioned refers to the fact that you hadn't paid house insurance the month before the incident.</u>

W: That money left our account. And now that you should be paying out, you are suddenly saying that you didn't receive it on time. I'm really skeptical about this claim.

M: The contract does say that any mispayment in a year will affect the terms and conditions of the insurance contract and may affect claims. Of course, I can pass you on to my manager to talk to you more about this.

W: I've already spoken to him and you can tell him (4) <u>I'm furious now, and that your company has a lawsuit on its hands. You will be hearing from my lawyer.</u> Goodbye!

男：早上好，这里是房屋安全保险，我是保罗。今天有什么我可以帮助您的吗？

女：早上好。我认为我要说的可不是件好事。我是威尔森太太，自从收到你们关于我们保险索赔的信以后，这已经是我本周第三次给你们打电话了。（1）你们完全无视了我打电话要求索赔一事，这让我感到有些厌烦。

男：威尔森太太，感谢您的回电。我能了解一下具体情况以便查看您的索赔吗？

女：我是住在康沃尔市南海路15号的梅·威尔森太太。具体情况就是我们村两个月前遭遇了严重的洪灾。（2）我们的小屋的一楼全部被淹了。从那以后我们五个人就一直住在一辆拖车里。而你们公司却因为一个奇怪的技术细节扣留了我们有权得到的钱。这令人无法接受，保罗。

男：威尔森太太，根据您账号上的记录，（3）您提到的这个奇怪的技术细节是您在事故发生前一个月未支付房屋保险金。

女：我们已经用账户支付了那笔钱。现在你们应该付钱给我，可你们却突然说没有按时收到钱。我对这种说法持怀疑态度。

男：合同上确实有提到，一年内任何不按时缴费的行为将影响保险合同上的条款和条件，且可能影响索赔。当然，我可以把您的电话转接给我的经理，他会再跟您谈谈这件事情。

女：我已经和他谈过了。你告诉他，（4）我现在十分愤怒，你们公司就等着被起诉吧。你们将收到我的律师函。再见！

难词总结

be fed up with 对……感到厌烦
caravan /ˈkærəvæn/ n. 旅行拖车
lawsuit /ˈlɔːsuːt/ n. 诉讼；起诉

submerge /səbˈmɜːdʒ/ v.（使）浸没，淹没
bizarre /bɪˈzɑː(r)/ a. 怪异的

题目精析

1. What is the woman complaining about?
    A) She has not received any letter from the man.
    B) Her claim has been completely disregarded.
    C) She has failed to reach the manager again.
    D) Her house has not been repaired in time.
1. 这位女士正在抱怨什么？
    A）她没有收到这位男士寄的信。
    B）她要求索赔一事被完全无视了。
    C）她又没联系到经理。
    D）她的房子没有被及时修缮。

【答案及分析】B。本题问女士抱怨的内容。音频中提到，I'm getting a little fed up with my calls about my claim being completely disregarded.（你们完全无视了我打电话要求索赔一事，这让我感到有些厌烦。）B项与音频内容相符，结合后面的音频内容可知本段对话围绕保险索赔展开，故选B项。

2. What is the problem the woman's family encountered?
    A) Their caravan was washed away by the flood.
    B) The ground floor of their cottage was flooded.
    C) Their entire house was destroyed by the flood.
    D) The roof of their cottage collapsed in the flood.
2. 这位女士的家庭遭遇了什么困难？
    A）他们的拖车被洪水冲走了。
    C）他们的整栋房子都被洪水毁坏了。

B）他们的小屋的一楼被淹了。　　　　　D）他们小屋的房顶在洪水中坍塌了。

【答案及分析】B。本题问女士的家庭遭遇的困难。音频中提到，The entire ground floor of our cottage was submerged in water.（我们的小屋的一楼全部被淹了。）B项与音频内容相符，其中 was flooded 是音频中 was submerged in water 的同义表达，故选 B 项。

3. What has caused the so-called bizarre technical detail according to the man?

    A) The woman's failure to pay her house insurance in time.

    B) The woman's inaccurate description of the whole incident.

    C) The woman's ignorance of the insurance company's policy.

    D) The woman's misreading of the insurance company's letter.

3. 根据这位男士的说法，是什么导致了所谓的奇怪的技术细节？

    A）这位女士未及时支付房屋保险金。

    B）这位女士未准确描述整个事件。

    C）这位女士对保险公司的政策置之不理。

    D）这位女士误解了保险公司的信。

【答案及分析】A。本题问导致奇怪的技术细节的原因。音频中提到，the bizarre technical detail that you mentioned refers to the fact that you hadn't paid house insurance the month before the incident（您提到的这个奇怪的技术细节是您在事故发生前一个月未支付房屋保险金），A项与音频内容相符，其中 failure to pay her house insurance 是音频中 hadn't paid house insurance 的同义表达。故选 A 项。

4. What does the woman say she will do at the end of the conversation?

    A) Revise the terms and conditions of the contract.

    B) Consult her lawyer about the insurance policy.

    C) Talk to the manager of Safe House Insurance.

    D) File a lawsuit against the insurance company.

4. 在对话结束时，这位女士说她会做什么？

    A）修订合同的条款和条件。

    B）向律师咨询保险单一事。

    C）和房屋安全保险公司的经理谈话。

    D）向该保险公司提起诉讼。

【答案及分析】D。本题问女士会采取的措施。音频中提到，I'm furious now, and that your company has a lawsuit on its hands. You will be hearing from my lawyer.（我现在十分愤怒，你们公司就等着被起诉吧。你们将收到我的律师函。）D项与音频内容相符，是音频中 your company has a lawsuit on its hands 的同义表达，故选 D 项。

Questions 5 to 8 are based on the conversation you have just heard.

听力原文及译文

W: How do you feel about the future of the artificial intelligence? (5-1) Personally, I feel quite optimistic about it.

M: (5-2) AI? I'm not so optimistic actually. In fact, it's something we should be concerned about.

W: Well, it will help us humans understand ourselves better. And when we have a better understanding of ourselves, we can improve the world.

M: Well, one thing is for sure, technology is evolving faster than our ability to understand it. And in the future, AI will make jobs kind of pointless.

W: (6) I think artificial intelligence will actually help create new kinds of jobs, which would require less of our time and allow us to be centered on creative tasks.

M: I doubt that very much. Probably the last job that will remain will be writing AI software. And then eventually, AI will just write its own software.

W: At that time, we are going to have a lot of jobs which nobody will want to do. So we will need artificial intelligence for the robots to take care of the old guys like us.

M: I don't know. (7) There's a risk that human civilization could be replaced by a superior type of digital life. AI will be able to completely simulate a person in every way possible. In fact, some people think we're in the simulation right now.

W: That's impossible. Humans can't even make a mosquito. Computers only have chips. People have brains. And that's where the wisdom comes from.

M: (8) Once it's fully developed, AI will become tired of trying to communicate with humans as we would be much slower thinkers in comparison.

W: Well, I'm not so sure. A computer is a computer, and a computer is just a toy.

M: Computers can easily communicate incredibly fast. So the computer will just get impatient talking to humans. It'll be barely getting any information out.

W: Well, I believe there's a benevolent future with AI. I also think you watch too many science fiction films.

女：你认为人工智能的前景怎么样？（5-1）就我个人而言，我对此很乐观。

男：（5-2）人工智能？其实我没有那么乐观。事实上，这是一件我们应该担心的事。

女：嗯，它会帮助我们人类更好地了解自己。当我们对自己有了更好的了解时，我们就可以让世界更美好。

男：嗯，有一点可以确定，那就是科技的发展速度超过了我们了解它的速度。将来，人工智能会让工作变得有点儿没有意义。

女：（6）我认为人工智能实际上会帮助创造新的工作岗位，这些工作岗位会节省我们的时间，并让我们专注于创造性的工作。

男：我对此深感怀疑。或许最后剩下的工作会是编写人工智能软件。最终，人工智能会编写自己的软件。

女：到那时，我们会有许多没有人愿意从事的工作。因此，我们会需要人工智能机器人来照顾我们这些老人。

男：我不知道。（7）人类文明面临着可能被更高级的数字化生活取代的风险。人工智能将能够通过一切可行的方式完全模仿一个人。事实上，有些人认为我们现在就处于（被人工智能）模仿的状态中。

女：那是不可能的。人类现在甚至连一只蚊子都做不出来。计算机只有芯片，而人类有大脑，这才是智慧的来源。

男：（8）人工智能一旦得到充分发展就会厌倦于设法与人类交流，因为相比之下，人的思考速度会比人工智能慢得多。
女：嗯，我没这么确定。计算机就是计算机，只是一个玩具而已。
男：计算机的交流速度快得令人难以置信。因此，计算机在与人类交谈时会变得不耐烦。从人类身上它几乎得不到任何信息。
女：嗯，我认为人工智能有一个美好的未来。另外，我觉得你看太多科幻电影了。

难词总结

concerned /kənˈsɜːnd/ a. 担心的；忧虑的
superior /suːˈpɪəriə(r)/ a. 更好的
incredibly /ɪnˈkredəbli/ ad. 难以置信地；极其
pointless /ˈpɔɪntləs/ a. 毫无意义的
mosquito /məˈskiːtəʊ/ n. 蚊子

题目精析

5. What do we learn about the speakers from the conversation?
   A) They are both worried about the negative impact of technology.
   B) They differ greatly in their knowledge of modern technology.
   C) They disagree about the future of AI technology.
   D) They work in different fields of AI technology.

5. 从对话中我们可以了解到说话者的什么信息？
   A）他们都担心科技带来的负面影响。
   B）他们对于现代科技的了解大不相同。
   C）他们对人工智能技术的未来持不同看法。
   D）他们在不同的人工智能技术领域工作。

【答案及分析】C。本题问说话双方对人工智能的看法。音频中女士提到，Personally, I feel quite optimistic about it.（就我个人而言，我对此很乐观。）男士提到，AI? I'm not so optimistic actually.（人工智能？其实我没那么乐观。）可知双方对人工智能的未来持不同看法，C项与音频内容相符，故选C项。

6. What will new kinds of jobs be like according to the woman?
   A) Stimulating and motivating.
   B) Simply writing AI software.
   C) More demanding and requiring special training.
   D) Less time-consuming and focusing on creation.

6. 女士认为新的工作岗位会是什么样的？
   A）振奋人心、有激励性。
   B）仅编写人工智能软件。
   C）要求更高，且需要特殊培训。
   D）耗时更少，专注于创造。

【答案及分析】D。本题问女士对新的工作岗位的看法。音频中提到，I think artificial intelligence will actually help create new kinds of jobs, which would require less of our time and allow us to be centered on creative tasks.（我认为人工智能实际上会帮助创造新的工作岗位，这些工作岗位会节省我们的时间，并让我们专注于创造性的工作。）D项与音频内容相符，其中Less time-consuming是音频中require less of our time 的同义表达，focusing on creation 是音频中 to be centered on creative tasks 的同义表达，故选 D 项。

7. What is the risk the man anticipates?

   A) Old people would be taken care of solely by unfeeling robots.
   B) Humans would be tired of communicating with one another.
   C) Digital life could replace human civilization.
   D) There could be jobs nobody wants to do.

7. 男士预料的风险是什么？

   A）老年人将只能由没有感情的机器人照料。
   B）人类会对与其他人交流感到厌倦。
   C）数字化生活会取代人类文明。
   D）可能会有没人想从事的工作。

【答案及分析】C。本题问男士对人工智能带来的风险的预料。音频中提到，There's a risk that human civilization could be replaced by a superior type of digital life.（人类文明面临着可能被更高级的数字化生活取代的风险。）C 项是音频内容的同义表达，故选 C 项。

8. What is the man's concern about AI technology?

   A) It will be smarter than human beings.
   B) Chips will be inserted in human brains.
   C) It will take away humans' jobs altogether.
   D) Life will become like a science fiction film.

8. 男士对人工智能技术的担忧是什么？

   A）它将比人类更聪明。
   B）芯片将被植入人类的大脑。
   C）它会把人类的全部工作岗位都夺走。
   D）生活会变得和科幻电影一样。

【答案及分析】A。本题问男士对人工智能技术的担忧。音频中提到，Once it's fully developed, AI will become tired of trying to communicate with humans as we would be much slower thinkers in comparison.（人工智能一旦得到充分发展就会厌倦于设法与人类交流，因为相比之下，人的思考速度会比人工智能慢得多。）A 项是音频内容的同义表达，故选 A 项。

Section B

Questions 9 to 11 are based on the passage you have just heard.

【听力原文及译文】

  To achieve financial security, how much you save is always more important than the amount you earn or how shrewdly you invest. (9) If you're under 30 years old, your goal should be to save 20% of your monthly income after tax deductions. This is irrespective of how much you earn. Approximately 50% should be reserved for essentials like food and accommodation. The remaining 30% is for recreation and entertainment, but for many young people, it'll be difficult to designate such a large proportion of their income for savings.

(10) If you find it hard to save any money at all, start by cutting all unnecessary spending. Allocate a tiny amount of 1 or 2 percent for savings and gradually increase that amount. Always keep that 20% goal in mind. Prevent yourself from becoming complacent. It can be challenging to stick to such a strict plan, but if you adopt the right mindset, you should be able to make it work for you.

So what should you be doing with the money that you are saving? Some must be kept easily accessible in case you need some cash in an emergency. The largest proportion should be invested in retirement plans, either through your employer or privately. And you can keep some money for high-risk but potentially lucrative investments. Dividends can be reinvested or used to purchase something you like. (11) By following this plan, you should hopefully be able to enjoy your life now and still be financially secure in the future.

为了获得经济保障，你存多少钱往往比你赚多少钱或者你进行多么精明的投资更重要。（9）如果你还不到30岁，那么你的目标应该是把每月税后收入的20%存起来。这与你赚多少钱没有关系。应该预留50%左右的收入用作生活必需品的开销，如食物和住宿。剩下的30%用作休闲娱乐，但是，对许多年轻人来说，将这么一大部分收入作为存款是很难的。

（10）如果你觉得很难存下钱，那么你可以从削减一切不必要的开支做起。划出1%或2%的收入作为存款，然后逐渐增加这一数额。永远记住20%的存款目标。防止自己变得自满。坚持这样一个严格的计划是有挑战性的，但是如果你摆正心态，你就能够让它为你效力。

那么，你应该如何处理自己存下来的钱呢？一部分钱应该存放在容易取的地方，以防你需要部分现金救急。无论是通过雇主还是自己，最大比例的钱都应该用于投资退休计划。你还可以将一部分钱用于风险高但潜在获利丰厚的投资项目。股息可用于再次投资或购买你喜欢的东西。（11）按照这个计划，你应该有希望能够享受当下的生活，同时未来仍有经济保障。

难词总结

shrewdly /ˈʃruːdli/ ad. 精明干练地
irrespective /ˌɪrɪˈspektɪv/ a. 不考虑的；不顾的
stick to 坚持；紧跟

deduction /dɪˈdʌkʃn/ n. 扣除（额）；推理
complacent /kəmˈpleɪsnt/ a. 自满的
lucrative /ˈluːkrətɪv/ a. 获利多的

题目精析

9. What are people under 30 advised to do to achieve financial security?

   A) Try to earn as much money as possible.   C) Save one-fifth of their net monthly income.

   B) Invest shrewdly in lucrative businesses.   D) Restrain themselves from high-risk investments.

9. 30岁以下的人被建议做些什么来获得经济保障？

   A）尽可能多赚些钱。   C）每月存下五分之一的纯收入。

   B）精明地投资获利丰厚的生意。   D）阻止自己进行高风险投资。

【答案及分析】C。本题问 30 岁以下的人获得经济保障的方法。音频中提到，If you're under 30 years old, your goal should be to save 20% of your monthly income after tax deductions.（如果你还不到 30 岁，那么你的目标应该是把每月税后收入的 20% 存起来。）C 项 Save one-fifth of their net monthly income 是音频中 save 20% of your monthly income after tax deductions 的同义表达，故选 C 项。

10. What should people do if they find it difficult to follow this speaker's advice on their financial plan?

    A) Cut 20% of their daily spending.　　C) Try to stick to their initial plan.
    B) Ask a close friend for advice.　　　D) Start by doing something small.

10. 如果人们觉得遵循说话者关于财务计划的建议很难，那么他们应该怎么做？

    A）削减 20% 的日常支出。　　C）努力坚持最初的计划。
    B）向关系亲密的朋友寻求建议。　　D）从小事做起。

【答案及分析】D。本题问如何实施说话者提出的财务计划。音频中提到，If you find it hard to save any money at all, start by cutting all unnecessary spending. Allocate a tiny amount of 1 or 2 percent for savings and gradually increase that amount.（如果你觉得很难存下钱，那么你可以从削减一切不必要的开支做起。划出 1% 或 2% 的收入作为存款，然后逐渐增加这一数额。）D 项是音频中 Allocate a tiny amount of 1 or 2 percent for savings 的同义表达，故选 D 项。

11. What does the speaker think is important for achieving financial security?

    A) A proper mindset.　　　　C) An optimistic attitude.
    B) An ambitious plan.　　　　D) A keen interest.

11. 在说话者看来，什么对于获得经济保障很重要？

    A）一种良好的心态。　　　C）一种乐观的态度。
    B）一个雄心勃勃的计划。　　D）一种浓厚的兴趣。

【答案及分析】B。本题问获得经济保障的重要前提。音频中提到，By following this plan, you should hopefully be able to enjoy your life now and still be financially secure in the future.（按照这个计划，你应该有希望能够享受当下的生活，同时未来仍有经济保障。）B 项中的 plan 是原词复现，且整段音频内容围绕着存钱计划展开，故选 B 项。

Questions 12 to 15 are based on the passage you have just heard.

听力原文及译文

I work in advertising and I like to keep up with current trends mainly because I'm aware that we live in an image-obsessed world. However, (12) when I first started my job, occasionally, I'd catch a glimpse of myself in the lifts and find myself thinking that I looked a total mess.

Was I being held back by my choice of clothing? The sure answer is yes, especially when clients are quick to judge you on your style rather than your work. (13) But no one can be unique with their outfit every day. I mean, that's why uniforms were invented. So here's what I did. I created my own uniform. To do this, I chose an appropriate outfit. Then I bought multiple items of the same style in different shapes. Now, I never worry about what I'm wearing in the morning even if I do get a bit tired of just wearing the same classic pieces.

Overall, when it comes to work, you have to ask yourself: (14-1) Will looking smarter enhance my ability to do my job? For some, this question may not be an issue at all, especially if you work remotely and rarely see your colleagues or clients face to face. (14-2) But if your job involves interacting with other people, the answer to this is often yes. (15) So rather than finding the system, I think we should just do whatever helps us to achieve our goals at work. If that means playing it safe with your image, then let's face it. It's probably worth it.

  我从事广告行业的工作。我喜欢跟上当前的潮流，主要原因是我意识到我们生活在一个注重形象的世界里。然而,（12）当我刚参加工作时，我偶尔会在电梯里瞥一眼自己，觉得我自己看起来一团糟。

  是我对于衣着的选择阻碍了我吗？答案是肯定的，尤其是当客户快速通过你的穿衣风格而不是你的工作对你进行评价的时候。（13）但是，没有人每天都能穿得与众不同。我的意思是，这就是制服被发明的原因。因此，以下便是我所做的。我设计了自己的制服。为此，我选择了一套合适的衣服。然后我买了许多风格相同但样式不同的单品。现在，我早上从不操心穿什么，即便我对只穿同样的经典款式感到有点厌倦。

  总之，当提到工作时，你必须问自己:（14-1）穿着更讲究能否提升我的工作能力？对于一些人来说，这可能根本不是个问题，尤其是在从事远程工作，很少需要与同事或客户面对面交流时。（14-2）但是如果你的工作涉及与人沟通互动，那么答案通常是肯定的。（15）因此，我认为我们应该做一切有助于实现工作目标的事，而不是寻找方法。如果这意味着确保你的形象不出差错，那就让我们面对它吧。这也许是值得的。

难词总结

obsessed /əbˈsest/ *a.* 对……痴迷的　　　　catch a glimpse of 瞥见
outfit /ˈaʊtfɪt/ *n.* 全套服装　　　　　　　remotely /rɪˈməʊtli/ *ad.* 远程地；偏僻地

题目精析

12. What do we learn about the speaker when she first started her job?

  A) She found her outfit inappropriate.　　C) She often checked herself in a mirror.
  B) She was uninterested in advertising.　　D) She was unhappy with fashion trends.

12. 关于说话者刚开始参加工作时的信息，我们了解到的是什么？

  A）她觉得自己的套装不合适。　　　　C）她时常照镜子打量自己。
  B）她对广告行业不感兴趣。　　　　　D）她对流行趋势不满意。

【答案及分析】A。本题问关于说话者刚开始参加工作时的信息。音频中提到，when I first started my job, occasionally, I'd catch a glimpse of myself in the lifts and find myself thinking that I looked a total mess（当我刚参加工作时，我偶尔会在电梯里瞥一眼自己，觉得我自己看起来一团糟）。结合后面的内容可知，说话者这里谈论的是着装问题。A项中的 found her outfit inappropriate 是音频中 thinking that I looked a total mess 的同义表达，故选 A 项。

13. Why were uniforms invented according to the speaker?

  A) To save the expenses on clothing.
  B) To keep up with the current trends.

C) To meet the expectations of fashion-conscious clients.

D) To save the trouble of choosing a unique outfit every day.

13. 说话者认为制服被发明的原因是什么？

   A）为了节省服装成本。

   B）为了跟上当前的潮流。

   C）为了满足赶时髦的客户的期待。

   D）为了省去每天挑选独特的套装的麻烦。

   【答案及分析】D。本题问制服被发明的原因。音频中提到，But no one can be unique with their outfit every day. I mean, that's why uniforms were invented.（但是，没有人每天都能穿得与众不同。我的意思是，这就是制服被发明的原因。）D 项中的 choosing a unique outfit every day 是音频中 unique with their outfit every day 的同义表达，故选 D 项。

14. What does the speaker say about looking smarter?

   A) It boosts one's confidence when looking for employment.

   B) It matters a lot in jobs involving interaction with others.

   C) It helps people succeed in whatever they are doing.

   D) It enhances people's ability to work independently.

14. 关于穿着更讲究一事，说话者有什么看法？

   A）它增强人在求职时的信心。

   B）它在需要与人沟通互动的工作中很重要。

   C）它帮助人们无论做什么都能成功。

   D）它增强人们独立工作的能力。

   【答案及分析】B。本题问说话者对穿着更讲究一事的看法。音频中提到，Will looking smarter enhance my ability to do my job?（穿着更讲究能否提升我的工作能力？）。紧接着又提到，But if your job involves interacting with other people, the answer to this is often yes.（但是如果你的工作涉及与人沟通互动，那么答案通常是肯定的。）可知 B 项是音频内容的同义表达，故选 B 项。

15. What does the speaker advise people to do in an image-obsessed world?

   A) Design their own uniform to appear unique.   C) Do whatever is possible to look smart.

   B) Fight the ever-changing trends in fashion.   D) Wear classic pieces to impress their clients.

15. 说话者建议人们在这个注重形象的世界里做什么？

   A）设计自己的制服以显得与众不同。   C）尽一切可能让自己显得穿着讲究。

   B）反对不断变化的流行趋势。   D）穿经典款式以给客户留下深刻印象。

   【答案及分析】C。本题问人们在这个注重形象的世界里能采取的措施。音频中提到，So rather than finding the system, I think we should just do whatever helps us to achieve our goals at work.（因此，我认为我们应该做一切有助于实现工作目标的事，而不是寻找方法。）C 项中的 Do whatever 是原词复现，结合前面关于穿着讲究能否提升工作能力的探讨，可知 C 项为音频内容的同义表达，故选 C 项。

Section C

Questions 16 to 18 are based on the recording you have just heard.

听力原文及译文

  Did you know that Americans have approximately three times the amount of space we had 50 years ago? Therefore, you'd think we'd have sufficient room for all of our possessions. On the contrary, the personal storage business is now a growing industry. We've got triple the space, (16-1) but we've become such enthusiastic consumers that we require even more. (16-2) This phenomenon has resulted in significant credit card debt, enormous environmental footprints, and perhaps not coincidentally, our happiness levels have failed to increase over the same half century.

  I'm here to suggest an alternative that having less might actually be a preferable decision. Many of us have experienced, at some stage, the pleasure of possessing less. I propose that less stuff and less space can not only help you economize, but also simplify your life. I recently started an innovative project to discover some creative solutions that offered me everything I required. By purchasing an apartment that was 40 square meters instead of 60, I immediately saved $200,000. Smaller space leads to reduced utility bills and also a smaller carbon footprint, because it's designed around an edited collection of possessions limited to my favorite stuff. I'm really excited to live there.

  How can we live more basically? Firstly, we must ruthlessly cut the unnecessary objects out of our lives. To stem consumption, we should think before we buy and ask ourselves, "Will it truly make me happier?" (17) Obviously, we should possess some great stuff, but we want belongings that we're going to love for years. Secondly, we require space efficiency. We want appliances that are designed for use most of the time, not for occasional use. Why own a six-burner stove when you rarely use even three burners? (18) Finally, we need multifunctional spaces and housewares.

  I combined a movable wall with transforming furniture to get more out of my limited space. Consider my coffee table. It increases in size to accommodate 10. My office is tucked away, easily hidden. My bed simply pops out of the wall. For guests, I can relocate the movable wall and utilize the foldable guest beds I installed.

  I'm not saying we should all live in tiny apartments, but consider the benefits of an edited life. When you return home and walk through your front door, take a moment to ask yourselves, "Could I do with a little live editing? Would that give me more freedom and more time?"

  你知道如今美国人拥有的空间大约是50年前的三倍吗？因此，你会认为我们将有足够的房间来放置我们的所有个人物品。相反，如今个人贮存业务是一个快速发展的行业。我们有了三倍的空间，（16-1）但是我们成了狂热的消费者，以至于我们甚至需要更多空间。（16-2）这个现象导致了巨额的信用卡欠款和巨大的环境足迹，而且我们的幸福指数在过去的半个世纪里并未增长，这也许并非巧合。

  在这里我要提出另一种选择，即少拥有一些东西事实上可能是更好的决定。许多人在某些时候都经历过少拥有一些东西的乐趣。我建议物品少一些，空间小一些，这不仅能帮助节省开支，还能简化生活。最近，我开始了一项创新的项目，以便发掘一些有创造力的解决方法，给我提供我需要的一切。

通过买 40 平方米而不是 60 平方米的公寓，我立即节省了 20 万美元。更小的空间有利于节省物业费，还能减少碳足迹，因为公寓的设计基于简化个人物品（仅存放最喜爱的物品）的理念。住在那儿真的令我很激动。

我们如何才能更简单地生活呢？首先，我们必须坚决舍弃生活中的非必需品。为了抑制消费，我们在买东西前应该考虑一下，问问自己："这真的会令我更开心吗？"（17）显然，我们应该拥有一些极好的物品，但是我们需要的是自己会爱惜多年的东西。其次，我们需要空间利用率。我们需要的家电是大多数时候都能用到的，而不是偶尔才用到的。如果你甚至连三个炉灶都很少用到，那么又为何要买带六个炉灶的炉子呢？（18）最后，我们需要多功能的空间和家庭用品。

我将活动墙和改造家具相结合，使有限的空间得到了更充分的利用。想想我的咖啡桌。它的尺寸可以增加到能容纳 10 个人。我的办公室能够很容易就被隐藏起来。我的床可以直接从墙上弹下来。如果有访客，我便可以调整活动墙的位置，使用我安装的折叠式客人专用床。

我并不是说所有人都应该住到小公寓里去，而是我们应该想想简单生活的好处。当你回到家中，穿过正门时，花点时间问问自己："我能否让生活简化一些？那会给我更多的自由和时间吗？"

难词总结

possession /pəˈzeʃn/ n. 个人财产；私人物品；拥有
credit card 信用卡
coincidentally /kəʊˌɪnsɪˈdentəli/ ad. 巧合地；同时地
preferable /ˈprefrəbl/ a. 更好的；更合适的
utility bill 物业账单

triple /ˈtrɪpl/ a. 三倍的
footprint /ˈfʊtprɪnt/ n. 足迹；脚印
alternative /ɔːlˈtɜːnətɪv/ n. 可供选择的事物
innovative /ˈɪnəveɪtɪv/ a. 革新的；创新的
ruthlessly /ˈruːθləsli/ ad. 坚决地；无情地

题目精析

16. What has prevented American's happiness levels from increasing?

    A) Their failure to accumulate wealth.   C) The deterioration of the environment.
    B) Their obsession with consumption.   D) The ever-increasing costs of housing.

16. 是什么阻碍了美国人幸福指数的增长？

    A）他们未能积累财富。   C）环境恶化。
    B）他们沉迷于消费。   D）住房成本日益增加。

【答案及分析】B。本题问阻碍美国人幸福指数增长的因素。音频中提到，but we've become such enthusiastic consumers that we require even more（但是我们成了狂热的消费者，以至于我们甚至需要更多空间）。B 项中的 obsession with consumption 是音频中 enthusiastic consumers 的同义表达。下文提到，This phenomenon has resulted in... our happiness levels have failed to increase over the same half century.（这个现象导致了……我们的幸福指数在过去的半个世纪里并未增长。）This phenomenon 即上文提到的 we've become such enthusiastic consumers，故选 B 项。

17. What things should we possess according to the speaker?

    A) Things that we cherish most.   C) Things that cost less money.

B) Things that boost efficiency.　　　　　　　　D) Things that are rare to find.

17. 说话者认为什么物品是我们应该拥有的？

　　A）我们最珍爱的东西。　　　　　　　　C）价格更低的东西。

　　B）能提升效率的东西。　　　　　　　　D）罕见的东西。

【答案及分析】A。本题问我们应该拥有的物品类型。音频中提到，Obviously, we should possess some great stuff, but we want belongings that we're going to love for years.（显然，我们应该拥有一些极好的物品，但是我们需要的是自己会爱惜多年的东西。）A项 Things that we cherish most 是音频中 belongings that we're going to love for years 的同义表达，故选 A 项。

18. What do we learn about the items in the speaker's home?

　　A) They are mostly durable.　　　　　　C) They serve multiple purposes.

　　B) They are easily disposable.　　　　　D) They benefit the environment.

18. 关于说话者家中的物品，我们了解到什么？

　　A）它们大多都很耐用。　　　　　　　　C）它们的用途多样。

　　B）它们能轻易地被丢弃。　　　　　　　D）它们对环境有益。

【答案及分析】C。本题问说话者家中物品的特点。音频中提到，Finally, we need multifunctional spaces and housewares.（最后，我们需要多功能的空间和家庭用品。）C 项中的 multiple purposes 是音频中 multifunctional 的同义表达，故选 C 项。

Questions 19 to 21 are based on the recording you have just heard.

听力原文及译文

　　Now, believe it or not, people sometimes lie in order to maintain a good, honest reputation—even if it hurts them to do so. At least, this is what a team of scientists is suggesting, with evidence to prove it.

　　Picture this scenario: You often drive for work and can be compensated for up to 400 miles per month. Most people at your company drive about 300 miles each month. But this month you drove 400 miles. How many miles do you think you'd claim in your expense report? The scientists asked this exact question as part of the study we're discussing today. With surprising results, they found that 12% of respondents reported the distance they drove as less than the actual figure, giving an average answer of 384 miles. (19) In other words, they lied about the number of miles, even though they would forfeit money they were owed.

　　The researchers believe this was to seem honest, with the assumption being that others would be suspicious of a high expense claim. But why would people fabricate numbers to their own detriment? (20) The researchers explained that many people care a great deal about their reputation and how they'll be judged by others. If they care enough, their concern about appearing honest and not losing the respect of others may be greater than their desire to actually be honest.

　　The researchers assert that the findings suggest that when people obtain very favorable outcomes, they anticipate other people's suspicious reactions and prefer lying and appearing honest to telling the truth and appearing as selfish liars.

So why is this research important? Well, experts generally agree there are two main types of lie—selfish lies and lies that are meant to benefit others. The first, as you may predict, is for selfish gain, such as submitting a fraudulent claim to an insurance company. While the second involves lying to help others or not offend others, for example, telling a friend whose outfit you don't like that they look great.

But the researchers are suggesting a third type of lying: lying to maintain a good reputation. Now, this hypothesis is new and some skeptics argue that this isn't a whole new category of lie, (21) but the findings seem intuitive to me. After all, one of the main motivations for lying is to increase our worth in the eyes of others, so it seems highly likely that people will lie to seem honest.

如今，无论你信不信，有时人们会通过撒谎来维持良好而正直的声誉，即便这样做会对他们造成损害。至少，这是一个科学家团队说的，而且有证据可以证明。

设想一下这个场景：你经常开车上班，每月最多可获得400英里的车程补贴。你所在的公司里大多数人每月的驾驶里程大约是300英里。但本月你的驾驶里程是400英里。你认为你会在报销单上申报多少英里呢？科学家们提出了同样的问题，作为今天我们讨论的研究的一部分。结果令人惊讶，科学家们发现，12%的调查对象上报的驾驶里程比实际里程低，平均为384英里。（19）也就是说，他们谎报了英里数，即使他们会失去自己应得的钱。

研究人员认为，这样做是为了让自己显得诚实，这基于其他人会对高额报销费用产生疑虑的假设。但是为什么人们会编造有损于自己的里程数呢？（20）研究人员解释道，许多人都十分在乎自己的声誉以及别人是如何评价自己的。如果他们十分在乎，那么比起真正想要变得诚实的渴望，他们更在乎能让自己显得诚实且不失去其他人的尊重。

研究人员坚称，这些发现表明，当人们获得十分有利的结果时，他们预料别人会起疑，倾向于撒谎，从而让自己显得诚实，而不是说出真相，使自己表现得像自私的骗子。

那么，为什么这个研究很重要呢？嗯，专家们普遍认可谎言有两种主要类型——自私的谎言和旨在令他人获益的谎言。如你所料，第一种是为了获取私利，如向保险公司骗保。而第二种则是为了帮助他人或不冒犯他人而撒谎，比如说，即便有朋友穿了你不喜欢的衣服，可你还是说他们看起来很不错。

但是，研究人员表示还有第三种类型的谎言：为了维持良好的声誉而撒谎。如今，这一假设是新提出来的，一些对此持怀疑态度的人认为，这并不能算作一个全新的谎言类型，（21）但对我来说，这个研究结果似乎凭直觉就能得出来。毕竟，撒谎的一个主要动机是提高我们在他人眼中的价值。因此，人们很可能会为了让自己显得诚实而撒谎。

难词总结

scenario /səˈnɑːriəʊ/ n. 设想；方案
forfeit /ˈfɔːfɪt/ v. 自愿放弃；丧失
detriment /ˈdetrɪmənt/ n. 伤害；损害
fraudulent /ˈfrɔːdjələnt/ a. 欺骗的；欺诈的

respondent /rɪˈspɒndənt/ n. 调查对象
be suspicious of 怀疑
anticipate /ænˈtɪsɪpeɪt/ v. 预料；预期
skeptic /ˈskeptɪk/ n. 持怀疑态度的人

题目精析

19. What did the team of scientists find in this study?

   A) All respondents were afraid of making a high expense claim.

   B) A number of respondents gave an average answer of 400 miles.

   C) Most of the respondents got compensated for driving 384 miles.

   D) Over 10% of the respondents lied about the distance they drove.

19. 该科学家团队在这次研究中发现了什么？

   A）所有调查对象都害怕报销高额费用。

   B）许多调查对象上报的平均驾驶里程为 400 英里。

   C）大多数调查对象获得了 384 英里的车程补贴。

   D）超过 10% 的调查对象谎报了他们的驾驶里程。

【答案及分析】D。本题问这次研究的发现。音频中提到，In other words, they lied about the number of miles, even though they would forfeit money they were owed.（也就是说，他们谎报了英里数，即使他们会失去自己应得的钱。）这里的 they 指上文提到的 12% of respondents。D 项中的 lied about 是原词复现，the distance they drove 是音频中 the number of miles 的同义表达，故选 D 项。

20. Why would people fabricate numbers to their own detriment according to the researchers?

   A) They endeavored to actually be honest.   C) They cared about other people's claims.

   B) They wanted to protect their reputation.   D) They responded to colleagues' suspicion.

20. 根据研究人员所说，为什么人们会编造有损于自己的里程数呢？

   A）他们努力做到真正的诚实。   C）他们关心其他人的报销。

   B）他们想维护自己的声誉。   D）他们对同事的怀疑做出了反应。

【答案及分析】B。本题问人们谎报里程数的原因。音频中提到，The researchers explained that many people care a great deal about their reputation and how they'll be judged by others.（研究人员解释道，许多人都十分在乎自己的声誉以及别人是如何评价自己的。）B 项是音频内容的同义表达，故选 B 项。

21. What does the speaker think of the researchers' findings?

   A) They seem positive.   C) They seem intuitive.

   B) They are illustrative.   D) They are conclusive.

21. 说话者如何看待研究人员的研究结果？

   A）它们似乎是积极的。   C）它们似乎能通过直觉得出。

   B）它们具备说明性。   D）它们不容置疑。

【答案及分析】C。本题问说话者对研究结果的看法。音频中提到，but the findings seem intuitive to me（但对我来说，这个研究结果似乎凭直觉就能得出来）。C 项中的 intuitive 是原词复现，故选 C 项。

Questions 22 to 25 are based on the recording you have just heard.

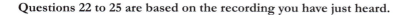

(22) Why do old people dislike new music? As I've grown older, I often hear people of my age say things like "They just don't make good music like they used to." Why does this happen? Luckily, psychology can give us some insights into this puzzle. Musical tastes begin to crystallize as early as age 13 or 14. By the time we're in our early 20s, these tastes get locked into place pretty firmly.

(23) In fact, studies have found that by the time we turn 33, most of us have stopped listening to new music. Meanwhile, popular songs released when you're in your early teens are likely to remain quite popular among your age group through the rest of your life.

There could be a biological explanation for this as there is evidence that the brain's ability to make subtle distinctions between different chords, rhythms and melodies deteriorates with age. So to older people, newer, less familiar songs might all "sound the same." But there may be some simpler reasons for older people's aversion to new music. (24) One of the most researched laws of social psychology is something called "the mere exposure effect", which, in essence, means that the more we're exposed to something, the more we tend to like it. This happens with people we know, the advertisements we see, and the songs we listen to. When you're in your early teens, you probably spend a fair amount of time listening to music or watching music videos. Your favorite songs and artists become familiar, comforting parts of your routine. For many people over 30, job and family obligations increase, so there's less time to spend discovering new music. Instead, many will simply listen to old, familiar favorites from that period of their lives when they had more free time.

Of course, those teen years weren't necessarily carefree. They're famously confusing, which is why so many TV shows and movies revolve around high school turmoil.

(25) Psychology research has shown that the emotions that we experience as teens seem more intense than those that come later. And we also know that intense emotions are associated with stronger memories and preferences. Both of these might explain why the songs we listened to during this period become so memorable and beloved. So there's nothing wrong with your parents because they don't like your music. Rather it's all part of the natural order of things.

（22）为什么上了年纪的人不喜欢新音乐？当我年纪越来越大，我经常听见我的同龄人说"他们现在制作的音乐没以前好了"。为什么会这样呢？幸运的是，心理学能够帮助我们了解这一疑问。音乐喜好早在十三四岁时便开始形成。等我们到了20岁初期，这些音乐喜好便相当固定了。

（23）实际上，研究发现，大多数人到了33岁时便不再听新音乐了。与此同时，在你十多岁时流行的音乐以后可能在你的年龄群体中仍然十分流行。

生物学能解释这一点。因为有证据表明大脑对不同的和弦、节奏和旋律进行细微区分的能力会随着时间而退化。因此，对于老年人来说，不那么熟悉的新歌可能听起来都一样。但是，老年人可能出于一些更简单的原因讨厌新音乐。（24）社会心理学中被研究得最多的定律之一是"曝光效应"，即我们与某个事物接触得越多，往往就越喜欢它。这一现象会发生在我们认识的人身上，也会发生在我们看到的广告和我们听到的歌上。十多岁的你可能会花很多时间听音乐或看音乐视频。你最喜爱的歌曲和艺术家成了你日常生活中熟悉而令人宽慰的一部分。对于许多30岁以上的人来说，工作和家庭义务增加，因此他们没有那么多时间来发现新音乐。相反，许多人仅仅会听一些自己最熟悉、最喜爱的老歌，而这些歌都属于那个他们拥有更多的自由时间的年代。

当然，青少年时期不一定就是无忧无虑的。这段时期是出了名的令人迷茫，这就是为什么这么多的电视剧和电影都以高中时期的焦灼为题材。

（25）心理学研究表明，我们在青少年时期体验到的情感似乎比之后的更强烈。我们也明白，强烈的情感与更深刻的记忆和偏好有关。这些都能解释为什么我们在这一时期听到的音乐会如此难忘和深受喜爱。所以你的父母不喜欢你的音乐并没有错。相反，这都是自然规律的一部分。

难词总结

crystallize /ˈkrɪstəlaɪz/ v. 使成形；具体化
chord /kɔːd/ n. 和弦
turmoil /ˈtɜːmɔɪl/ n. 焦虑；混乱

make a distinction 区分
deteriorate /dɪˈtɪəriəreɪt/ v. 退化；恶化

题目精析

22. What does the speaker mainly discuss in this talk?
    A) Older people's aversion to new music.
    B) Older people's changing musical tastes.
    C) Insights into the features of good music.
    D) Deterioration in the quality of new music.

22. 在这篇讲话中，说话者主要探讨了什么？
    A）年纪较大的人对新音乐的厌恶。
    B）年纪较大的人音乐喜好的转变。
    C）对优质音乐特征的了解。
    D）新音乐的质量下降。

【答案及分析】A。本题问本篇讲话的主题。音频第一句便提到，Why do old people dislike new music？（为什么上了年纪的人不喜欢新音乐？）下文围绕这一话题展开，A项中的 aversion 是音频中 dislike 的同义表达，故选A项。

23. What have studies found about most people by the time they turn 33?
    A) They seldom listen to songs released in their teens.
    B) They can make subtle distinctions about music.
    C) They find all music sounds the same.
    D) They no longer listen to new music.

23. 研究发现大多数人到33岁时会怎么样？
    A）他们很少听他们十几岁时听的歌。
    B）他们能对音乐进行细微的区分。
    C）他们发现所有音乐听起来都一样。
    D）他们不再听新音乐。

【答案及分析】D。本题问大多数33岁的人在音乐方面的情况。音频中提到，In fact, studies have found that by the time we turn 33, most of us have stopped listening to new music.（实际上，研究发现，

大多数人到了 33 岁时便不再听新音乐了。）D 项中的 no longer listen to new music 是音频中 have stopped listening to new music 的同义表达，故选 D 项。

24. What do we learn from one of the most researched laws of social psychology?

   A) The more you experience something, the better you'll appreciate it.
   B) The more you experience something, the longer you'll remember it.
   C) The more you are exposed to something, the deeper you'll understand it.
   D) The more you are exposed to something, the more familiar it'll be to you.

24. 关于社会心理学中被研究得最多的定律之一，我们了解到的是什么？

   A）你经历某件事越多，你就越喜欢它。
   B）你经历某件事越多，你就记得它越久。
   C）你与某个事物接触得越多，你对它的理解就越深刻。
   D）你与某个事物接触得越多，你就越熟悉它。

【答案及分析】A。本题问社会心理学中被研究得最多的定律之一。音频中提到，One of the most researched laws of social psychology... means that the more we're exposed to something, the more we tend to like it.（社会心理学中被研究得最多的定律之一……即我们与某个事物接触得越多，往往就越喜欢它。）A 项中的 the better you'll appreciate it 是音频中 the more we tend to like it 的同义表达，故选 A 项。

25. What might explain the fact that songs people listen to in their teen years are memorable and beloved?

   A) Teenagers are much more sensitive.　　C) Teenagers' memories are more lasting.
   B) Teenagers are much more sentimental.　　D) Teenagers' emotions are more intense.

25. 什么可以解释人们在青少年时期听到的歌令人难忘且深受人们喜爱这一事实？

   A）青少年敏感得多。　　C）青少年的记忆更持久。
   B）青少年多愁善感得多。　　D）青少年的情感更强烈。

【答案及分析】D。本题问人们喜爱青少年时期听到的歌曲的原因。音频中提到，Psychology research has shown that the emotions that we experience as teens seem more intense than those that come later. And we also know that intense emotions are associated with stronger memories and preferences.（心理学研究表明，我们在青少年时期体验到的情感似乎比之后的更强烈。我们也明白，强烈的情感与更深刻的记忆和偏好有关。）D 项与音频内容相符，音频中虽然也提到了 memories，但只是客观地阐述情感与记忆之间的关系，并不能由此推断出 C 项，故选 D 项。

Part Ⅲ　Reading Comprehension

Section A

【全文翻译】

　　对危害社会的物品征税的想法具有很强的吸引力。这可能是一举两得——既阻止了有害行为，又给政府提供了财政收入。

以烟酒税为例。对酒征税意味着要花更多的钱才能喝醉，这减少了酗酒行为和危险驾驶行为。与此同时，它们给州政府和地方政府提供了数十亿美元的财政收入。烟草税带来的财政收入是酒税的两倍，其在降低吸烟率方面发挥了作用，拯救了数百万人。

征税也能成为保护环境的重要手段。许多经济学家提到，对碳排放征税会是降低温室气体排放的最佳途径。经济学理论提到，与所得税或销售税不同，碳排放税能够从实际上增加经济效益，因为往空气中排放二氧化碳的公司没有为它们造成的气候变化买单，而碳排放税会恢复恰当的市场激励机制。

事实上，仅碳排放税一项还不足以阻止全球变暖，但它会是在任何气候计划中都有用处的一部分。此外，该项税收收入平均每年可能是数千亿美元，这笔钱可以作为红利分发给市民，或被用来赞助环保基础设施项目。

同样，财产税的推行在减少不平等的同时增加了财政收入。一些专家预计，该项税收每十年带来的收入将超过四万亿美元，这笔钱可以用在住房、儿童保育、医疗保健和其他政府福利上。如果你和许多人一样，认为不平等从根源上来说就是有害的，那么这些税收可以在改善社会的同时充实国库。

难词总结

revenue /ˈrevənjuː/ *n.* 财政收入；税收收入
dividend /ˈdɪvɪdend/ *n.* 红利；股息
incentive /ɪnˈsentɪv/ *n.* 激励；刺激
designate /ˈdezɪɡneɪt/ *v.* 指定；指派
impaired /ɪmˈpeəd/ *a.* 受损的；损坏的

题目精析

26. A。根据句子结构可知，空格处与后面的现在分词 providing 并列，补充说明上文中提到的 double benefit。所给选项中只有 A 项 discouraging（阻止）、K 项 merging（合并）和 O 项 swelling（增加；膨胀）符合语法要求。结合语境可知此处讲的是益处，故只有 discouraging 符合语境，故选 A 项。

27. E。根据句子结构可知，空格处修饰名词 driving。所给选项中只有 C 项 emotional（情感的）、E 项 impaired（受损的）、F 项 imprisoned（被监禁的）和 J 项 instrumental（起作用的）符合语法要求。结合上文可知 impaired 符合语境，impaired driving 意为"危险驾驶"，故选 E 项。

28. J。根据句子结构可知，空格所在句缺表语，空格处修饰主语 Tobacco taxes。所给选项中只剩 C 项 emotional（情感的）、F 项 imprisoned（被监禁的）和 J 项 instrumental（起作用的）符合语法要求。结合语境可知此处讲的是烟草税带来的益处，instrumental 符合语境，故选 J 项。

29. N。根据句子结构可知，空格处需要填入一个谓语动词，主语是第三人称复数，结合下文提到的 don't pay 可知时态为一般现在时，所给选项中只有 L 项 predict（预言，预计）和 N 项 pump（抽送）符合语法要求。pump carbon dioxide 意为"排放二氧化碳"，符合语境，故选 N 项。

30. G。根据句子结构可知，空格处需要填入一个名词，作 restore 的宾语，且由 proper 修饰。所给选项中只剩 B 项 dividend（红利）、D 项 fragments（碎片；片段）、G 项 incentives（激励；鼓励）、J 项 instrumental（器乐曲）和 O 项 swelling（肿胀处；膨胀）符合语法要求。结合上文提到的对企业征收碳排放税，可知此处指建立市场激励机制，以控制碳排放。故选 G 项。

31. M。根据句子结构可知，空格所在句主干完整，故空格处需要填入一个副词。所给选项中只有 H 项 inherently（内在地，固有的）、I 项 initially（开始，最初）和 M 项 probably（很可能；大概）符合语法要求。结合语境可知此处是预估碳排放税每年将带来的财政收入，probably 符合语境，故选 M 项。

32. B。根据句子结构可知，空格处需要填入一个可数名词单数，且以辅音音素开头。所给选项中只剩 B 项 dividend（红利）和 O 项 swelling（肿胀处；膨胀）符合语法要求，dividend 代入原文后符合语境，故选 B 项。

33. L。根据句子结构可知，空格处需要填入一个谓语动词，主语是第三人称复数 experts，时态为一般现在时态。所给选项中只剩 L 项 predict（预言，预计）符合语法要求和语境，故选 L 项。

34. H。根据句子结构可知，空格所在句主干完整，故空格处需要填入一个副词。所给选项中只剩 H 项 inherently（内在地，固有的）和 I 项 initially（开始，最初）符合语法要求。根据常识可知社会不平等从本质上来说是不好的，inherently 代入原文后符合语境，故选 H 项。

35. O。根据句子结构可知，空格处需要填入一个动词，主语是第三人称复数 taxes。while 引导时间状语从句，主从句的主语一致，故 while 后可省略主语和 be 动词，直接加现在分词，所给选项中只剩 K 项 merging（合并）和 O 项 swelling（增加；膨胀）符合语法要求。swell government coffers 意为"充实国库"，符合语境，故选 O 项。

Section B

全文翻译

人工智能在农业领域的挑战

[A] 在南非中部，一群种植玉米的农民围着一位农学家和他的电脑挤成一团，在他们的旁边还有一台用来灌溉的机器。这位农学家刚刚操控一架混合动力无人机飞越了玉米地。这架无人机利用螺旋桨实现起飞和着陆，同时利用其固定机翼保持飞行高度和速度，对大片田地进行扫描。

[B] 这架无人机上安装了一个四光谱波段精密传感器，可在飞行结束后立即进行机载处理，使农民和现场工作人员几乎能立刻处理传感器可能记录到的异常情况，实现了实时数据收集。

[C] 在这个例子中，农民和农学家正指望通过专用的软件获取精确的植株数量。玉米 10 天前就出苗了，农民想确定地里是否有未出苗或遭受了风害的区域需要补种，这一情况在夏天的雨季开始时会十分严重。

[D] 在玉米生长的这一阶段，农民还有 10 天的时间补种，之后便要使用大量的肥料和化学制品。一旦使用了这些东西，采取纠正措施从经济上来说便不可行了。这会使得所有进一步收集的数据都成为历史数据，只对下一个播种季节有借鉴意义。

[E] 这一软件不到 15 分钟便完成了数据处理，生成了一张植株数量图。如果不知道仅在一年多以前，加工这样一组数据需要 3~5 天的时间，便很难明白现在的速度是多么令人赞叹。这展示了近年来精准农业和遥感领域取得的成就。美国在相似的条件下通过同种作物测试研发了这款软件，农学

家确信这款软件能生成一个近乎精确的结果。

[F] 当植株数量图出现在屏幕上时，农学家脸色一沉。在启动无人机前，他走过了一排排的玉米苗，以便了解田地的实际情况。一看到屏幕上的数据，他便明白植株数量不对。尽管农民们不太读得懂遥感地图，但他们也看出了问题。

[G] 从假设上来说，通过利用人工智能和机器学习，机器有可能学会解决地球上一切与处在被界定或被封闭的环境中的所有事物的物理交互有关的难题。

[H] 遥感使得算法能够将田地环境解读成统计数据，这些数据能被看懂，并有助于农民做出决策。算法处理数据，根据接收到的数据进行调整与学习。收集到的输入信息和统计信息越多，算法在预测一系列结果时就能表现得越好。其目的是让农民能够使用人工智能在田间做出更好的决策，以实现他们获得更好的收成的目标。

[I] 2011年，美国国际商用机器公司（IBM）通过其在以色列海法的研发总部推出了一项农业云计算项目。该项目与一些信息技术和农业领域的专业人员合作，牢记一个目标——从农业环境中获取各种学术和物理数据来源，然后将这些数据来源转化成自动的预测解决方案，提供给农民，帮助他们在田间做出实时决策。

[J] 当时，对IBM项目团队内一些成员的采访表明，该团队相信"算法"农业是完全有可能的，这意味着算法能够解决世界上的所有问题。那年早些时候，IBM的认知学习系统"沃森"在游戏《危险边缘》中挑战前任冠军布拉德·拉特和肯·詹宁斯，并获得了令人惊讶的成绩。几年后，"沃森"继续在医疗领域取得了突破性的成就。

[K] 那么为何该项目在医疗领域而不是在农业领域取得了这样的成就呢？因为农业是最难以实现统计定量化的领域之一。即使是在单块田地里，不同地段的环境也总在不停地变化。天气难以预测，土壤质量会变化，害虫和疾病随时有可能来袭。种植者可能会觉得大丰收指日可待，但在那一天来临前，结果总是未知的。

[L] 相比之下，我们的身体是一个封闭的环境。农业发生在自然环境中。生物和活动在这个生态系统中相互作用，而作物生长便发生在这个生态系统环境中。但这些生态系统并不是封闭的，它们受气候变化（如影响整个半球和各大洲的天气系统）的影响。因此，了解如何管理农业环境意味着要考虑成百上千种因素。

[M] 几乎可以肯定的是，同样的种子和施肥项目在美国中西部地区可能发生的情况与其在澳大利亚或南非可能发生的情况之间没有关联。一些导致该差别的因素通常包括每单位种植作物的降雨量、土壤类型、土壤退化模式、日照时间、温度，等等。

[N] 因此，在农业领域利用机器学习和人工智能时面临的问题并不是科学家在开发程序和制订科学实验计划方面能力不足，不能解决种植者面临的最大的问题，而是在大多数情况下，不会有两个完全相同的环境，这使得在农业领域测试、验证和成功推出此类技术比在大多数其他行业要费时费力得多。

[O] 实际上，要是说开发人工智能和机器学习能够解决所有与我们的物理环境相关的问题，基本上也就是说我们对地球上的物理或物质活动的各个方面都有一个全面的了解。毕竟，只有通过我们对"事物本质"的了解，科学实验计划和进程才会被设计，从而发挥认知系统的理性功能。而且，尽管人工智能和机器学习教给我们许多与如何了解我们所处环境有关的事情，但是我们仍远不能

仅通过机器的认知能力来预测农业等领域的重要结果。

[P] 目前，创投界在这一领域投入数十亿美元。创投界的支持促使如今大多数新创办的农业科技企业尽快完成发展，并鼓励它们尽快将产品推向市场。

[Q] 这通常会导致产品推行失败，从而招致市场的怀疑，并对机器学习技术的完整性造成打击。在大多数情况下，问题不在于技术不行，而在于工业界没有花时间认识到农业是需要进行管理的最开放的环境之一。为了让技术真正对农业产生影响，需要更多的尝试、技能和资金，从而在农民的田地里测试这些技术。

[R] 通过将这些技术和全球的重要市场合为一体，人工智能和机器学习有着改革农业的巨大潜力。只有那样，它才能对种植者产生影响，这才是它真正重要的地方。

难词总结

huddle /ˈhʌdl/ v. 挤在一起
propeller /prəˈpelə(r)/ n. 螺旋桨
unviable /ʌnˈvaɪəbl/ a. 行不通的；不能成功的
quantification /ˌkwɒntɪfɪˈkeɪʃn/ n. 定量；量化
deploy /dɪˈplɔɪ/ v. 有效地利用；调动

unmanned aerial vehicle (UAV) 无人驾驶飞行器
be fitted with 配备有……
hypothetically /ˌhaɪpəˈθetɪkli/ ad. 假设地；假想地
degradation /ˌdeɡrəˈdeɪʃn/ n. 恶化；衰退

题目精析

36. Farmers will not profit from replanting once they have applied most of the fertilizer and other chemicals to their fields.

36. 一旦农民在田地里使用了大量的肥料和其他化学制品，他们将不会从补种中获益。

【答案及分析】D。根据题干中的 Farmers、replanting 和 fertilizer and other chemicals 定位到 D 段。定位句指出，the farmer has another 10 days to conduct any replanting before the majority of his fertilizer and chemical applications need to occur. Once these have been applied, it becomes economically unviable to take corrective action（农民还有 10 天的时间补种，之后便要使用大量的肥料和化学制品。一旦使用了这些东西，采取纠正措施从经济上来说便不可行了）。题干是原文的同义表达，故选 D 项。

37. Agriculture differs from the medical science of the human body in that its environment is not a contained one.

37. 农业与人体医学的不同点在于，农业环境是开放的。

【答案及分析】L。根据题干中的 human body 和 contained 定位到 L 段。定位句指出，By comparison, our bodies are a contained environment. Agriculture takes place in nature... But these ecosystems are not contained.（相比之下，我们的身体是一个封闭的环境。农业发生在自然环境中……但这些生态系统并不是封闭的。）题干是原文的同义表达，故选 L 项。

38. The agronomist is sure that he will obtain a near accurate count of plant population with his software.

38. 农学家确信他会利用他的软件获取一个近乎精确的植株数量。

【答案及分析】E。根据题干中的 agronomist、a near accurate count 和 software 定位到 E 段。定位句

指出，The software completes its processing in under 15 minutes producing a plant population count map... the agronomist feels confident that the software will produce a near accurate result.（这一软件不到15分钟便完成了数据处理，生成了一张植株数量图……农学家确信这款软件能生成一个近乎精确的结果。）题干是原文的同义表达，其中 is sure 是原文中 feels confident 的同义表达，故选 E 项。

39. The application of artificial intelligence to agriculture is much more challenging than to most other industries.

39. 将人工智能应用到农业领域比将其应用到大多数其他行业更具挑战性。

【答案及分析】N。根据题干中的 application of artificial intelligence、agriculture、challenging 和 other industries 定位到 N 段。定位句指出，So the problem with deploying... artificial intelligence in agriculture... is that in most cases, no two environments will be exactly alike, which makes the testing, validation and successful rollout of such technologies much more laborious than in most other industries.（因此，在农业领域利用……人工智能时面临的问题……是在大多数情况下，不会有两个完全相同的环境，这使得在农业领域测试、验证和成功推出此类技术比在大多数其他行业要费时费力得多。）题干是原文的同义表达，其中 application 是原文中 deploying 的同义表达，challenging 是原文中 laborious 的同义表达。故选 N 项。

40. Even the farmers know the data provided by the UAV is not correct.

40. 即便是农民也知道无人机提供的数据不对。

【答案及分析】F。根据题干中的 farmers、data、UAV 和 not correct 定位到 F 段。定位句指出，the agronomist... knows... that the plant count is not correct, so do the farmers（农学家……明白……植株数量不对，农民们也看出了问题）。题干是原文的同义表达，故选 F 项。

41. The pressure for quick results leads to product failure, which, in turn, arouses doubts about the applicability of AI technology to agriculture.

41. 急于求成的压力导致了产品的失败，而这反过来又引起了对人工智能在农业领域适用性的怀疑。

【答案及分析】Q。根据题干中的 product failure、doubts 和 applicability of AI technology to agriculture 定位到 Q 段。定位句指出，This usually results in a failure of a product, which leads to skepticism from the market（这通常会导致产品推行失败，从而招致市场的怀疑）。此处的 This 指上文提到的 "农业科技企业快速把产品推向市场"，题干是原文的同义表达，其中 arouses doubts 是原文中 leads to skepticism 的同义表达。故选 Q 项。

42. Remote sensors are aimed to help farmers improve decision-making to increase yields.

42. 遥感旨在帮助农民做出更好的决策，以提高产量。

【答案及分析】H。根据题干中的 Remote sensors、decision-making 和 yields 定位到 H 段。定位句指出，And the aim is that farmers can use this artificial intelligence to achieve their goal of a better harvest through making better decisions in the field.（其目的是让农民能够使用人工智能在田间做出更好的决策，以实现他们获得更好的收成的目标。）题干是原文的同义表达，其中 improve decision-making 是原文中 making better decisions 的同义表达，increase yields 是原文中 achieve their goal of a better harvest 的同义表达。故选 H 项。

43. The farmer expects the software to tell him whether he will have to replant any parts of his farm fields.

43. 农民指望这款软件告诉自己地里是否有任何区域需要补种。

【答案及分析】C。根据题干中的 farmer、software 和 replant any parts of his farm fields 定位到 C 段。定位句指出，the farmer wants to determine if there are any parts of the field that require replanting（农民想确定地里是否有区域需要补种）。题干是原文的同义表达，故选 C 项。

44. Agriculture proves very difficult to quantify because of the constantly changing conditions involved.
44. 农业很难实现定量化，因为涉及的环境不断地在变化。

【答案及分析】K。根据题干中的 Agriculture、quantify、constantly changing 和 conditions 定位到 K 段。定位句指出，So why did the project have such success in medicine but not agriculture? Because it is one of the most difficult fields to contain for the purpose of statistical quantification... conditions are always changing from one section to the next.（那么为何该项目在医疗领域而不是在农业领域取得了这样的成就呢？因为农业是最难以实现统计定量化的领域之一……不同地段的环境也总在不停地变化。）题干是原文的同义表达，其中 constantly changing 是原文中 are always changing 的同义表达。故选 K 项。

45. The same seed and fertilizer program may yield completely different outcomes in different places.
45. 同样的种子和施肥项目在不同的地方可能会产生完全不同的结果。

【答案及分析】M。根据题干中的 The same seed and fertilizer program 和 different places 定位到 M 段。定位句指出，What may occur with the same seed and fertilizer program in the United States' Midwest region is almost certainly unrelated to what may occur with the same seed and fertilizer program in Australia or South Africa.（几乎可以肯定的是，同样的种子和施肥项目在美国中西部地区可能发生的情况与其在澳大利亚或南非可能发生的情况之间没有关联。）题干是原文的同义表达，其中 completely different 是原文中 almost certainly unrelated 的同义表达。故选 M 项。

Section C

Passage One

全文翻译

　　在缺乏注意力的文化中，艺术有着什么样的地位呢？近期参观卢浮宫的游客表示，如今游客在《蒙娜丽莎》前只能停留一分钟，随后便会被要求继续往前参观（别的作品）。一些游客会把大部分时间用来拍照。他们拍的甚至不是画，而是以画为背景，拍他们自己。

　　一种观点是，旅游业和美术馆游览已十分大众化，因此我们实际上已不可能去欣赏我们旅行时所看到的事物。在这个人满为患的社会里，体验像其他东西一样成了商品。人们排着队去攀登珠穆朗玛峰，也排着队去欣赏有名的画作。因此，休闲被视为苦役，而返回工作岗位成了历经折磨后理应获得的休息。

　　在这种产业化的仓促中，失去的是欣赏的质量。已故哲学家理查德·沃尔海姆是一个极端的例子。当他参观卢浮宫的时候，他可以花上四个小时的时间坐在某幅画前。他声称，第一个小时对于消除误解来说是有必要的。只有到那时画作才会开始显露自身。这在今天似乎是不可思议的，但仍有可能做到。即使是最繁忙的博物馆也有值得人们观赏数小时的展厅和画作，而这些基本上都被人们忽略了。有时候，游客爆满在一定程度上是由于管理不善。如今，欣赏《蒙娜丽莎》成了如此仓促的体验，部分原因是博物馆正在重组。佛罗伦萨的乌菲齐博物馆也是一个文化圣地，通过巧妙的管理，其排队入场的时间被缩短至七分钟。还有一些艺术形式被设计成奇观以及引人沉思的对象，完美地展示在大批游客面前。

　　例如，目前奥拉维尔·埃利亚松在泰特现代美术馆的展览可能看起来只是一场娱乐活动，因为到处都是在雾室和喷雾装置之间嬉戏喧闹的孩子。但事实不止如此：埃利亚松最有趣的地方也是他最严肃的地方，他那些令人失去方向感的装置让我们认识到我们正对地球造成毁灭性影响这一事实——尤其是我们正对埃利亚松钟爱的冰岛的冰川造成破坏。

　　马塞尔·普鲁斯特是另一位卢浮宫爱好者，他写道："只有通过艺术我们才能实现自我超脱，才能了解别人是如何看待这个宇宙的，否则宇宙的风景就会像月球上的风景一样不为人知。"值得观赏的艺术一定是能够引领我们实现这种超脱的。但在匆忙的人群中，在画作前停留一分钟是无法做到这一点的。

难词总结

democratise /dɪˈmɒkrətaɪz/ v. 使大众化　　oversubscribed /ˌəʊvəsəbˈskraɪbd/ a. 供不应求的
ordeal /ɔːˈdiːl/ n. 磨难；折磨　　disclose /dɪsˈkləʊz/ v. 使显露；揭露
contemplation /ˌkɒntəmˈpleɪʃn/ n. 凝视；沉思　　spectacle /ˈspektəkl/ n. 奇观
disorient /dɪsˈɔːrient/ v. 使……失去方向感；使……迷惑

题目精析

46. What does the scene at the Louvre demonstrate according to the author?

　　A) The enormous appeal of a great piece of artistic work to tourists.
　　B) The near impossibility of appreciating art in an age of mass tourism.
　　C) The ever-growing commercial value of long-cherished artistic works.
　　D) The real difficulty in getting a glimpse at a masterpiece amid a crowd.

46. 作者认为卢浮宫的场景说明了什么？

　　A）一件伟大的艺术作品对游客的巨大吸引力。
　　B）在大众旅游时代，了解艺术几乎是不可能的。
　　C）长期受到珍视的艺术品的商业价值不断增长。
　　D）在人群中瞥一眼杰作真的很困难。

【答案及分析】B。根据题干关键词 the scene at the Louvre 定位到原文第一段第二句。该句描绘的场景是游客在《蒙娜丽莎》前只能停留一分钟。第二段第一句提到，One view is that we have democratised tourism and gallery-going so much that we have made it effectively impossible to appreciate what we've travelled to see.（一种观点是，旅游业和美术馆游览已十分大众化，因此我们实际上已不可能去欣赏我们旅行时所看到的事物。）B 项是原文的同义表达，故选 B 项。

47. Why did the late philosopher Richard Wollheim spend four hours before a picture?

A) It takes time to appreciate a piece of art fully.

B) It is quite common to misinterpret artistic works.

C) The longer people contemplate a picture, the more likely they will enjoy it.

D) The more time one spends before a painting, the more valuable one finds it.

47. 为什么已故哲学家理查德·沃尔海姆要在一幅作品前停留四个小时？

A）全面地了解一幅艺术作品需要时间。

B）曲解艺术作品十分普遍。

C）人们凝视一幅画越久，就越有可能喜欢这幅画。

D）人们在一幅画前停留的时间越久，就会发现它越有价值。

【答案及分析】A。根据题干关键词 philosopher Richard Wollheim 和 spend four hours before a picture 定位到原文第三段第二句和第三句。根据下文提到的 The first hour... was necessary for misperceptions to be eliminated（第一个小时对于消除误解来说是有必要的）和 It was only then that the picture would begin to disclose itself（只有到那时画作才会开始显露自身），可知 A 项符合原文。原文有提到"误解艺术作品"，但并未提到这一现象十分普遍，故排除 B 项。C、D 两项文中未提及，均排除。故选 A 项。

48. What does the case of the Uffizi in Florence show?

A) Art works in museums should be better taken care of.

B) Sites of cultural pilgrimage are always flooded with visitors.

C) Good management is key to handling large crowds of visitors.

D) Large crowds of visitors cause management problems for museums.

48. 佛罗伦萨的乌菲齐博物馆的例子说明了什么？

A）博物馆的艺术作品应该得到更好的保护。

B）游客总是涌入文化圣地。

C）好的管理是应对大批游客的关键。

D）大批游客给博物馆造成了管理问题。

【答案及分析】C。根据题干关键词 the Uffizi in Florence 定位到原文第三段倒数第二句，该句提到乌菲齐博物馆通过巧妙的管理控制了游客排队入场的时间，与上文提到的卢浮宫因管理不善而导致游客体验感不佳形成对比，由此可推断出好的管理是应对大批游客的关键，故选 C 项。

49. What do we learn from Olafur Eliasson's current Tate Modern show?

A) Children learn to appreciate art works most effectively while they are playing.

B) It is possible to combine entertainment with appreciation of serious art.

C) Art works about the environment appeal most to young children.

D) Some forms of art can accommodate huge crowds of visitors.

49. 我们能从奥拉维尔·埃利亚松在泰特现代美术馆的展览中了解到什么？

A）孩子们在玩耍的时候能最有效地学会欣赏艺术作品。

B）把娱乐和欣赏严肃艺术结合起来是有可能的。

C）与环境有关的艺术作品最能吸引孩子们。

D）一些艺术形式能容纳大批游客。

【答案及分析】B。根据题干关键词 Olafur Eliasson's current Tate Modern show 定位到原文第四段第一句，该句提到了展览的娱乐性的一面。第四段第二句提到了展览的严肃的一面，即提升人们保护环境的意识，根据本句中的 where Eliasson is at his most entertaining, he is at his most serious too（埃利亚松最有趣的地方也是他最严肃的地方）可知 B 项符合原文，故选 B 项。

50. What can art do according to Marcel Proust?

   A) Enable us to live a much fuller life.

   B) Allow us to escape the harsh reality.

   C) Help us to see the world from a different perspective.

   D) Urge us to explore the unknown domain of the universe.

50. 马塞尔·普鲁斯特认为艺术能做些什么？

   A）使我们能够过上非常充实的生活。

   B）让我们逃离残酷的现实。

   C）帮助我们从一个不同的角度看待世界。

   D）敦促我们探索宇宙的未知领域。

【答案及分析】C。根据题干关键词 Marcel Proust 定位到原文第五段第一句。根据本句中的 It is only through art that we can escape from ourselves and know how another person sees the universe（只有通过艺术我们才能实现自我超脱，才能了解别人是如何看待这个宇宙的），可知 C 项是原文中 know how another person sees the universe 的同义表达，其余三项原文并未提及，故选 C 项。

Passage Two

全文翻译

每隔五年，美国政府便会设法告诉人们应该吃些什么。多吃蔬菜，减少脂肪摄入，一切都是以当下最好的健康生活科学为基础。但当下最好的科学也提到了许多那些食物选择给环境带来的影响。美国农业部昨日发布的新饮食建议似乎完全忽视了这一事实，这令部分研究人员感到恼火。

大致来说，2016 至 2020 年的饮食建议以均衡为目标：多吃蔬菜和瘦肉，少吃糖。

但是美国的人均卡路里消耗量几乎比世界上任何一个国家都要多。所以美国人吃的食物对气候变化有很大影响。土壤耕作释放二氧化碳，运输车辆排放废气。政府的饮食指南本可以大大降低气候成本。这不仅仅是因为其权威性：这些指导方针还通过校园午餐和为贫困人群提供营养援助等联邦政府项目，推动了数十亿美元的食品生产。

就其本身而言，种植业和畜牧业的温室气体排放量占全国总量的 9%。这还不包括运输、加工、冷藏和其他将食物从农场送入我们腹中的路径点所消耗的燃料。其中，红肉是最大、最臭名昭著的温室气体排放源。但是，在一月份用卡车将沙拉从加利福尼亚州运到明尼苏达州也会（给环境）带来巨大的压力。温室气体排放并不是问题的全部。食品生产消耗了最多的淡水，是造成生物多样性缺失的最大因素，也是消耗自然资源的主要因素。

所有这些观点及更多相关信息都出现在美国饮食指引建议协会于去年二月份发布的科学报告中。米瑞安·尼尔森担任负责报告可持续性的小组委员会的主席。少吃肉和购买当地食物未出现在最终的报告中，这让她感到失望。她说："尤其是如果你认为少吃肉，特别是红肉和加工肉，对健康有益时。"

所以到底是怎么一回事呢？官方的回复是可持续性远远超出了指导方针的官方范围，即提供"营养和饮食信息"。

也许负责起草该决策的机构和应该受它们监管的行业走得太近。一方面，美国农业部正在编写饮食建议。另一方面，它们的客户是美国农业公司。

研究人员认为，将指导方针的范围限定在营养和饮食层面的理念是不太正确的。例如，大卫·沃利加说："在之前的指导方针中，它们一般关心的是诸如食品安全之类的事情，这大概是美国农业部的职责。如果你想要在未来确保食品安全，那么你绝对需要担心气候影响和未来的可持续性。"

难词总结

per capita /pə ˈkæpɪtə/ *a.* 人均的；每人的
notorious /nəʊˈtɔːriəs/ *a.* 臭名昭著的
presumably /prɪˈzjuːməbli/ *ad.* 很可能；大概

exhaust /ɪɡˈzɔːst/ *n.* 废气
contributor /kənˈtrɪbjətə(r)/ *n.* 促成因素；作出贡献者

题目精析

51. Why are some researchers irritated at the USDA's 2016-2020 Dietary Guidelines?

    A) It ignores the harmful effect of red meat and processed food on health.

    B) Too much emphasis is given to eating less meat and buying local food.

    C) The dietary recommendations are not based on medical science.

    D) It takes no notice of the potential impact on the environment.

51. 为什么一些研究人员对美国农业部 2016 至 2020 年的饮食指南感到恼火？

    A）它忽视了红肉和加工食物对健康的害处。

    B）它过多地强调了少吃肉和购买当地食物。

    C）饮食建议没有以医学为依据。

    D）它忽视了环境受到的潜在影响。

    【答案及分析】D。根据题干关键词 some researchers irritated 和 USDA 定位到原文第一段最后一句。该句指出，some researchers are annoyed that new dietary recommendations of the USDA... seem to utterly ignore that fact（美国农业部……的新饮食建议似乎完全忽视了这一事实，这令部分研究人员感到恼火）。结合上文可知此处的 fact 指 the best available science also has a lot to say about what those food choices do to the environment（当下最好的科学也提到了许多那些食物选择给环境带来的影响），D 项符合原文，故选 D 项。

52. Why does the author say the USDA could have contributed a lot to lowering the climate cost through its

dietary guidelines?

A) It has the capacity and the financial resources to do so.

B) Its researchers have already submitted relevant proposals.

C) Its agencies in charge of drafting the guidelines have the expertise.

D) It can raise students' environmental awareness through its programs.

52. 为什么作者提到美国农业部本可以通过其饮食指南大大降低气候成本？

A）它有能力和财政资源这样做。

B）它的研究人员已经提交了相关提案。

C）它负责起草指南的机构有这样的专长。

D）它能够通过其项目提高学生的环境意识。

【答案及分析】A。根据题干关键词 lowering the climate cost through its dietary guidelines 定位到原文第三段第四句。该句提到了政府的饮食指南本可以大大降低气候成本。下文分析了两点原因，即 Not just because of their position of authority: The guidelines drive billions of dollars of food production through federal programs（这不仅仅是因为其权威性：这些指导方针还通过联邦政府项目，推动了数十亿美元的食品生产），A 项中的 capacity 和 financial resources 与原文相符，故选 A 项。

53. What do we learn from the Dietary Guidelines Advisory Committee's scientific report?

A) Food is easily contaminated from farm to belly.

B) Greenhouse effect is an issue still under debate.

C) Modern agriculture has increased food diversity.

D) Farming consumes most of our natural resources.

53. 我们能从美国饮食指引建议协会的科学报告中了解到什么？

A）食物在从农场送入我们腹中的过程中容易被污染。

B）温室效应仍是一个处在争议中的问题。

C）现代农业增加了食品多样性。

D）农业消耗了大多数自然资源。

【答案及分析】D。根据题干关键词 Dietary Guidelines Advisory Committee's scientific report 定位到原文第五段第一句。该句指出，All of these points and more showed up in the Dietary Guidelines Advisory Committee's scientific report（所有这些观点及更多相关信息都出现在美国饮食指引建议协会的科学报告中）。结合上文可知此处的 these points 指第四段中提到的观点，其中 D 项与第四段中的 plant and animal agriculture contributes 9 percent of all the country's greenhouse gas emissions（种植业和畜牧业的温室气体排放量占全国总量的 9%）和 Food production is the largest user of fresh water, largest contributor to the loss of biodiversity, and a major contributor to using up natural resources（食品生产消耗了最多的淡水，是造成生物多样性缺失的最大因素，也是消耗自然资源的主要因素）相符，故选 D 项。

54. What may account for the neglect of sustainability in the USDA's Dietary Guidelines according to the author?

A) Its exclusive concern with Americans' food safety.

B) Its sole responsibility for providing dietary advice.

C) Its close ties with the agriculture companies.

D) Its alleged failure to regulate the industries.

54. 作者认为美国农业部的饮食指南忽视可持续性的原因是什么？

A）它只关心美国人的食品安全。

B）它只负责提供饮食建议。

C）它与农业公司有着紧密的联系。

D）它被指控未能监管行业。

【答案及分析】C。根据题干关键词 the neglect of sustainability in the USDA's Dietary Guidelines 定位到原文第五段第二句，该句指出了美国农业部的饮食指南忽视可持续性这一现象，下文分析了原因。第六段中的 The official response is that sustainability falls too far outside the guidelines' official scope（官方的回复是可持续性远远超出了指导方针的官方范围）是美国农业部给出的答案。第七段中的 the agencies in charge of drafting the decisions are too close to the industries they are supposed to regulate（负责起草该决策的机构和应该受它们监管的行业走得太近）是作者的推断。C 项是第七段内容的同义表达，故选 C 项。

55. What should the USDA do to achieve food security according to David Wallinga?

A) Give top priority to things like nutrition and food security.

B) Endeavor to ensure the sustainable development of agriculture.

C) Fulfill its mission by closely cooperating with the industries.

D) Study the long-term impact of climate change on food production.

55. 大卫·沃利加认为，美国农业部应该做些什么以实现食品安全？

A）优先考虑营养和食品安全等问题。

B）努力确保农业可持续发展。

C）与行业紧密合作，履行其职责。

D）研究气候变化对食品生产的长期影响。

【答案及分析】B。根据题干关键词 David Wallinga 定位到原文最后一段第二句。大卫·沃利加提到，You absolutely need to be worried about climate impacts and future sustainability if you want secure food in the future.（如果你想要在未来确保食品安全，那么你绝对需要担心气候影响和未来的可持续性。）B 项中的 the sustainable development of agriculture 对应原文中的 future sustainability。原文有提到 climate impacts（气候影响），但并未提气候变化对食品生产的长期影响，也未提到要对此进行研究，故排除 D 项。A、C 两项原文均未提及，故选 B 项。

Part IV Translation

参考译文

Located 46 kilometers to the south of Tian'anmen Square, Beijing Daxing International Airport went into service on September 30, 2019. The construction of this huge project started in 2014, with over 40 thousand workers on the construction site during its peak time. The compact design of the terminal building allows a maximum number of aircraft to land directly on the position closest to the central of the terminal building, bringing great convenience to passengers. After going through the security check, passengers can get to any one of the 82 boarding gates in the terminal building within eight minutes. The airport is designed to ensure 300 takeoffs and landings per hour. Being able to convey 100 million passengers per year by 2040, Beijing Daxing International Airport is expected to be the busiest airport in the world.

难词总结

compact /kəmˈpækt/ *a.* 紧凑的；袖珍的　　the terminal building 航站楼
aircraft /ˈeəkrɑːft/ *n.* 飞机；航空器　　takeoff /ˈteɪkɒf/ *n.* （飞机）起飞
convey /kənˈveɪ/ *v.* 运送；输送

译点释义

1. 第一句中包含两个动词"位于"和"投入使用"，参考译文将其中一个动词处理成非谓语，仅保留一个谓语动词。"位于天安门广场以南46公里处"可以译为非谓语动词词组 Located 46 kilometers to the south of Tian'anmen Square。

2. 第二句中的"高峰时工地上有4万多工人"可以译为 with over 40 thousand workers on the construction site during its peak time，作伴随状语。

3. 第三句中的"航站楼设计紧凑"可以译为名词短语 The compact design of the terminal building，作为句子的主语。使用固定搭配 allow sb. to do sth. 翻译"可以允许最大数量的飞机直接停靠在最靠近航站楼中心的位置"。"这给乘客提供了极大的方便"可以译为非谓语动词词组 bringing great convenience to passengers。

4. 第四句中的"航站楼共有82个登机口"可以译为名词短语 the 82 boarding gates in the terminal building。

5. 第五句中的"每小时300架次起降"可以译为 300 takeoffs and landings per hour。

6. 第六句翻译时要注意动作"有望成为"的发出者是"北京大兴国际机场"，翻译时需要注意。"机场年客运量2040年将达到1亿人次"可以译为 Being able to convey 100 million passengers per year by 2040，其逻辑主语也是"北京大兴国际机场"。

未得到监考教师指令前，不得翻阅该试题册！

2020年12月大学英语六级考试真题（第二套）

Part I　　　　　　　　Writing　　　　　　　　(30 minutes)
（请于正式开考后半小时内完成该部分，之后将进行听力考试）

Directions: *For this part, you are allowed 30 minutes to write an essay on **why students should be encouraged to develop effective communication skills**. You should write at least **150** words but no more than **200** words.*

Part II　　　　Listening Comprehension　　　　(30 minutes)

Section A

Directions: *In this section, you will hear two long conversations. At the end of each conversation, you will hear four questions. Both the conversation and the questions will be spoken only once. After you hear a question, you must choose the best answer from the four choices marked A), B), C) and D). Then mark the corresponding letter on **Answer Sheet 1** with a single line through the centre.*

Questions 1 to 4 are based on the conversation you have just heard.

1. A) A driving test.　　　B) A video game.　　C) Traffic routes.　　　　　　D) Cargo logistics.
2. A) He found it instructive and realistic.　　C) He was really drawn to its other versions.
   B) He bought it when touring Europe.　　　D) He introduced it to his brother last year.
3. A) Traveling all over the country.　　　　　C) The details in the driving simulator.
   B) Driving from one city to another.　　　　D) The key role of the logistics industry.
4. A) Clearer road signs.　　　　　　　　　　C) Stricter traffic rules.
   B) More people driving safely.　　　　　　　D) More self-driving trucks on the road.

Questions 5 to 8 are based on the conversation you have just heard.

5. A) It isn't so enjoyable as he expected.　　　C) It doesn't enable him to earn as much money as he used to.
   B) It isn't so motivating as he believed.　　　D) It doesn't seem to offer as much freedom as he anticipated.
6. A) Not all of them care about their employees' behaviors.
   B) Few of them are aware of their employees' feelings.
   C) Few of them offer praise and reward to their employees.
   D) Not all of them know how to motivate their employees.
7. A) Job satisfaction.　　B) Self-awareness.　　C) Autonomy.　　　　　D) Money.
8. A) The importance of cultivating close relationships with clients.
   B) The need for getting recommendations from their managers.
   C) The advantages of permanent full-time employment.
   D) The way to explore employees' interests and talents.

Section B

Directions: *In this section, you will hear two passages. At the end of each passage, you will hear three or*

1

four questions. Both the passage and the questions will be spoken only once. After you hear a question, you must choose the best answer from the four choices marked A), B), C) and D). Then mark the corresponding letter on **Answer Sheet 1** with a single line through the centre.

Questions 9 to 11 are based on the passage you have just heard.

9. A) Consumers visualize their activities in different weather.
　B) Good weather triggers consumers' desire to go shopping.
　C) Weather conditions influence consumers' buying behavior.
　D) Consumers' mental states change with the prices of goods.
10. A) Active consumption.　　　　　　　　　　C) Individual association.
　　B) Direct correlation.　　　　　　　　　　　D) Mental visualization.
11. A) Enabling them to simplify their mathematical formulas.
　　B) Helping them determine what to sell and at what price.
　　C) Enabling them to sell their products at a higher price.
　　D) Helping them advertise a greater variety of products.

Questions 12 to 15 are based on the passage you have just heard.

12. A) A naturally ventilated office is more comfortable.
　　B) A cool office will boost employees' productivity.
　　C) Office air-conditioning should follow guidebooks.
　　D) Air-conditioning improves ventilation in the office.
13. A) People in their comfort zone of temperature are more satisfied with their productivity.
　　B) People in different countries vary in their tolerance to uncomfortable temperatures.
　　C) Twenty-two degrees is the optimal temperature for office workers.
　　D) There is a range of temperatures for people to feel comfortable.
14. A) It will have no negative impact on work.　　C) It will sharply decrease work efficiency.
　　B) It will be immediately noticeable.　　　　　D) It will cause a lot of discomfort.
15. A) They tend to favor lower temperatures.　　C) They are not bothered by temperature extremes.
　　B) They suffer from rapid temperature changes.　D) They become less sensitive to high temperatures.

Section C

Directions: *In this section, you will hear three recordings of lectures or talks followed by three or four questions. The recordings will be played only once. After you hear a question, you must choose the best answer from the four choices marked A), B), C) and D). Then mark the corresponding letter on **Answer Sheet 1** with a single line through the centre.*

Questions 16 to 18 are based on the recording you have just heard.

16. A) It overlooked the possibility that emotions may be controlled.
　　B) It ignored the fact that emotions are personal and subjective.
　　C) It classified emotions simply as either positive or negative.
　　D) It measured positive and negative emotions independently.
17. A) Sitting alone without doing anything seemed really distressing.
　　B) Solitude adversely affected the participants' mental well-being.
　　C) Sitting alone for 15 minutes made the participants restless.
　　D) Solitude had a reductive effect on high-arousal emotions.
18. A) It proved hard to depict objectively.　　　C) It helped increase low-arousal emotions.
　　B) It went hand in hand with sadness.　　　D) It tended to intensify negative emotions.

Questions 19 to 21 are based on the recording you have just heard.

19. A) It uses up much less energy than it does in deep thinking.
　　B) It remains inactive without burning calories noticeably.

C) It continues to burn up calories to help us stay in shape.
D) It consumes almost a quarter of the body's total energy.
20. A) Much of the consumption has nothing to do with conscious activities.
    B) It has something to do with the difficulty of the activities in question.
    C) Energy usage devoted to active learning accounts for a big part of it.
    D) A significant amount of it is for performing difficult cognitive tasks.
21. A) It is believed to remain basically constant.   C) It is conducive to relieving mental exhaustion.
    B) It is a prerequisite for any mental activity.   D) It is thought to be related to food consumption.

Questions 22 to 25 are based on the recording you have just heard.

22. A) Job candidates rarely take it seriously.
    B) Job seekers tend to have a ready answer.
    C) Job seekers often feel at a loss where to start in answering it.
    D) Job candidates can respond freely due to its open-ended nature.
23. A) Follow their career coaches' guidelines.   C) Do their best to impress the interviewer.
    B) Strive to take control of their narrative.   D) Repeat the information on their résumé.
24. A) To reflect on their past achievements as well as failures.
    B) To produce examples for different interview questions.
    C) To discuss important details they are going to present.
    D) To identify a broad general strength to elaborate on.
25. A) Getting acquainted with the human resources personnel.
    B) Finding out why the company provides the job opening.
    C) Figuring out what benefits the company is able to offer them.
    D) Tailoring their expectations to the company's long-term goal.

Part III   Reading Comprehension   (40 minutes)

Section A

Directions: *In this section, there is a passage with ten blanks. You are required to select one word for each blank from a list of choices given in a word bank following the passage. Read the passage through carefully before making your choices. Each choice in the bank is identified by a letter. Please mark the corresponding letter for each item on **Answer Sheet 2** with a single line through the centre. You may not use any of the words in the bank more than once.*

Virtually every activity that entails or facilitates in-person human interaction seems to be in the midst of a total meltdown as the *coronavirus*（冠状病毒）outbreak erases Americans' desire to travel. Amtrak says bookings are down 50 precent and cancelations are up 300 percent. Hotels in San Francisco are experiencing __26__ rates between 70 and 80 percent. Broadway goes dark on Thursday night. Universities, now emptying their campuses, have never tried online learning on this __27__. White-collar companies like Amazon, Apple, and the New York Times are asking employees to work from home for the __28__ future.

But what happens after the coronavirus?

In some ways, the answer is: All the old normal stuff. The *pandemic*（大流行病）will take lives, __29__ economies and destroy routines, but it will pass. Americans will never stop going to basketball games. They won't stop going on vacation. They'll meet to do business. No decentralizing technology so far—not telephones, not television, and not the internet—has dented that human desire to shake hands, despite technologists' __30__ to the contrary.

Yet there are real reasons to think that things will not return to the way they were last week. Small __31__ create small societal shifts; big ones change things for good. The New York transit strike of 1980 is __32__ with prompting several long-term changes in the city, including bus and bike lanes, and women wearing sports shoes to work. The Spanish flu pandemic of 1918 prompted the development of national health care in Europe.

Here and now, this might not even be a question of __33__ . It's not clear that the cruise industry will __34__ . Or that public transit won't go broke without __35__ assistance. The infrastructure might not even be in place to do what we were doing in 2019.

A) credentials	I) scale
B) credited	J) strangle
C) cumulative	K) subtle
D) disruptions	L) summoned
E) federal	M) survive
F) foreseeable	N) vacancy
G) predictions	O) wedge
H) preference	

Section B

Directions: *In this section, you are going to read a passage with ten statements attached to it. Each statement contains information given in one of the paragraphs. Identify the paragraph from which the information is derived. You may choose a paragraph more than once. Each paragraph is marked with a letter. Answer the questions by marking the corresponding letter on* **Answer Sheet 2**.

Slow Hope

[A] Our world is full of—mostly untold—stories of slow hope, driven by the idea that change is possible. They are "slow" in their unfolding, and they are slow because they come with setbacks.

[B] At the beginning of time—so goes the myth—humans suffered, shivering in the cold and dark until the titan (巨人) Prometheus stole fire from the gods. Just as in the myth, technology—first fire and stone tools, and later farming, the steam engine and industry, fossil fuels, chemicals and nuclear power—has allowed us to alter and control the natural world. The myth also reminds us that these advances have come at a price: as a punishment for Prometheus' crime, the gods created Pandora, and they gave her a box filled with evils and curses. When Pandora's box was opened, it unleashed swarms of diseases and disasters upon humankind.

[C] Today we can no longer ignore the ecological curses that we have released in our search for warmth and comfort. In engineering and exploiting and transforming our habitat, we have opened tens of thousands of Pandora's boxes. In recent decades, environmental threats have expanded beyond regional boundaries to have global reach and, most hauntingly, are multiplying at a dizzying rate. On a regular basis, we are reminded that we are running out of time. Year after year, faster and faster, consumption outpaces the biological capacity of our planet. Stories of accelerated catastrophe multiply. We fear the breakdown of the electric grid, the end of non-renewable resources, the expansion of deserts, the loss of islands, and the pollution of our air and water.

[D] Acceleration is the signature of our time. Populations and economic activity grew slowly for much of human history. For thousands of years and well into early modern times, world economies saw no growth at all, but from around the mid-19th century and again, in particular, since the mid-20th, the real GDP has increased at an enormous speed, and so has human consumption. In the Middle Ages, households in Central Europe might have owned fewer than 30 objects on average; in 1900, this number had increased to 400, and in 2020 to 15,000. The acceleration of human production, consumption and travel has changed the animate and inanimate spheres. It has echoed through natural processes on which humans depend. Species extinction, deforestation, damming of rivers, occurrence of floods, the depletion of ozone, the degradation of ocean systems and many other areas are all experiencing acceleration, If represented graphically, the curve for all these changes looks rather like that well-known hockey stick: with little change over *millennia*（数千年）and a dramatic upswing over the past decades.

[E] Some of today's narratives about the future seem to suggest that we too, like Prometheus, will be saved by a new Hercules, a divine engineer, someone who will mastermind, manoeuvre and manipulate our planet. They suggest that geoengineering, cold fusion or faster-than-light spaceships might transcend once and for all the terrestrial constraints of rising temperatures, lack of energy, scarcity of food, lack of space, mountains of waste, polluted water—you name it.

[F] Yet, if we envisage our salvation to come from a *deus ex machina*（解围之神）, from a divine engineer or a tech solutionist who will miraculously conjure up a new source of energy or another cure-all with revolutionary potency, we might be looking in the wrong place. The fact that we now imagine our planet as a whole does not mean that the "rescue" of our planet will come with one big global stroke of genius and technology. It will more likely come by many small acts. Global heating and environmental degradation are not technological problems. They are highly political issues that are informed by powerful interests. Moreover, if history is a guide, then we can assume that any major transformations will once again be followed by a huge set of unintended consequences. So what do we do?

[G] This much is clear: we need to find ways that help us flatten the hockey-stick curves that reflect our ever-faster pace of ecological destruction and social acceleration. If we acknowledge that human manipulation of the Earth has been a destructive force, we can also imagine that human endeavours can help us build a less destructive world in the centuries to come. We might keep making mistakes. But we will also keep learning from our mistakes.

[H] To counter the fears of disaster, we need to identify stories, visions and actions that work quietly towards a more hopeful future. Instead of one big narrative, a story of unexpected rescue by a larger-than-life hero, we need multiple stories: we need stories, not only of what Rob Nixon of Princeton University has called the "slow violence" of environmental degradation (that is, the damage that is often invisible at first and develops slowly and gradually), but also stories of what I call "slow hope".

[I] We need an acknowledgement of our present ecological plight but also a language of positive change, visions of a better future. In *The Principle of Hope* (1954—1959), Ernst Bloch, one of the leading philosophers of the future, wrote that "the most tragic form of loss... is the loss of the capacity to imagine that things could be different". We need to identify visions and paths that will help us imagine a different, more just and more ecological world. Hope, for Bloch, has its starting point in fear, in uncertainty, and in crisis: it is a creative force that goes hand in hand with *utopian*（乌托邦的）"wishful images". It can be found in cultural products of the past—in fairy tales, in fiction, in architecture, in music, in the movie—in products of the human mind that contain "the outlines of a better world". What makes us "authentic" as humans are visions of our "potential". In other words: living in hope makes us human.

[J] The power of small, grassroots movements to make changes that spread beyond their place of origin can be seen with the Slow Food movement, which began in Italy in the 1980s. The rise of fast-food restaurants after the Second World War produced a society full of cheap, industrially made foodstuffs. Under the leadership of Carlo Petrini, the Slow Food movement began in Piedmont, a region of Italy with a long history of poverty, violence and resistance to oppression. The movement transformed it into a region hospitable to traditional food cultures—based on native plants and breeds of animals. Today, Slow Food operates in more than 160 countries, poor and rich. It has given rise to thousands of projects around the globe, representing democratic politics, food sovereignty, biodiversity and sustainable agriculture.

[K] The *unscrupulous*（无所顾忌的）commodification of food and the destruction of foodstuffs will continue to devastate soils, livelihoods and ecologies. Slow Food cannot undo the irresistible developments of the global food economy, but it can upset its theorists, it can "speak differently" , and it can allow people and their local food traditions and environments to flourish. Even in the United States—the fast-food nation—small farms and urban gardens are on the rise. The US Department of Agriculture provides an Urban Agriculture Toolkit and, according to a recent report, American *millennials*（千禧一代）are changing their diets. In 2017, 6 per cent of US consumers claimed to be strictly vegetarian, up from 1 per cent in 2014. As more people realise that "eating is an agricultural act", as the US poet and environmental activist Wendell Berry put it in 1989, slow hope advances.

36. It seems some people today dream that a cutting-edge new technology might save them from the present ecological disaster.
37. According to one great thinker, it is most unfortunate if we lose the ability to think differently.
38. Urgent attention should be paid to the ecological problems we have created in our pursuit of a comfortable life.
39. Even in the fast-food nation America, the number of vegetarians is on the rise.
40. The deterioration of the ecological system is accelerating because of the dramatic increase of human production and consumption.
41. It is obvious that solutions must be found to curb the fast worsening environment and social acceleration.
42. Many people believe changing the world is possible, though it may take time and involve setbacks.
43. It might be wrong to expect that our world would be saved at one stroke with some miraculous technology.
44. It is human nature to cherish hopes for a better world.
45. Technology has given us humans the power to change the natural world, but we have paid a price for the change.

Section C

Directions: *There are 2 passages in this section. Each passage is followed by some questions or unfinished statements. For each of them there are four choices marked A), B), C) and D). You should decide on the best choice and mark the corresponding letter on **Answer Sheet 2** with a single line through the centre.*

Passage One

Questions 46 to 50 are based on the following passage.

Vegetarians would prefer not to be compelled to eat meat. Yet the reverse *compulsion*（强迫）is hidden in the proposals for a new plant-based "planetary diet". Nowhere is this more visible than in India.

Earlier this year, the EAT-Lancet Commission released its global report on nutrition and called for a global shift to a more plant-based diet and for "substantially reducing consumption of animal source foods." In countries like India, that call could become a tool to aggravate an already tense political situation and stress already undernourished populations.

The EAT report presumes that "traditional diets" in countries like India include little red meat, which might be consumed only on special occasions or as minor ingredients in mixed dishes.

In India, however, there is a vast difference between what people would wish to consume and what they have to consume because of innumerable barriers around class, religion, culture, cost, geography, etc. Policymakers in India have traditionally pushed for a cereal-heavy "vegetarian diet" on a meat-eating population as a way of providing the cheapest sources of food.

Currently, under an aggressive Hindu nationalist government, Muslims, Christians, disadvantaged classes and indigenous communities are being compelled to give up their traditional foods.

None of these concerns seem to have been appreciated by the EAT-Lancet Commission's representative, Brent Loken, who said "India has got such a great example" in sourcing protein from plants.

But how much of a model for the world is India's vegetarianism? In the Global Hunger Index 2019, the country ranks 102nd out of 117. Data from the National Family Health Survey indicate that only 10 percent of infants of 6 to 23 months are adequately fed.

Which is why calls for a plant-based diet modeled on India risk offering another whip with which to beat already vulnerable communities in developing countries.

A diet directed at the affluent West fails to recognize that in low-income countries undernourished children are known to benefit from the consumption of milk and other animal source foods, improving cognitive functions, while reducing the prevalence of nutritional deficiencies as well as mortality.

EAT-Lancet claimed its intention was to "spark conversations" among all Indian stakeholders. Yet vocal critics of the food processing industry and food fortification strategies have been left out of the debate. But the most conspicuous omission may well be the absence of India's farmers.

The government, however, seems to have given the report a thumbs-up. Rather than addressing chronic hunger and malnutrition through an improved access to wholesome and nutrient-dense foods, the government is opening the door for company-dependent solutions, ignoring the environmental and economic cost, which will destroy local food systems. It's a model full of danger for future generations.

46. What is more visible in India than anywhere else according to the passage?
    A) People's positive views on the proposals for a "planetary diet".
    B) People's reluctance to be compelled to eat plant-based food.
    C) People's preferences for the kind of food they consume.
    D) People's unwillingness to give up their eating habits.
47. What would the EAT-Lancet Commission's report do to many people in countries like India?
    A) Radically change their dietary habits.   C) Make them even more undernourished.
    B) Keep them further away from politics.   D) Substantially reduce their food choice.
48. What do we learn from the passage about food consumption in India?
    A) People's diet will not change due to the EAT-Lancet report.
    B) Many people simply do not have access to foods they prefer.
    C) There is a growing popularity of a cereal-heavy vegetarian diet.
    D) Policymakers help remove the barriers to people's choice of food.
49. What does the passage say about a plant-based diet modeled on India?
    A) It may benefit populations whose traditional diet is meat-based.
    B) It may be another blow to the economy in developing countries.
    C) It may help narrow the gap between the rich and poor countries.
    D) It may worsen the nourishment problem in low-income countries.
50. How does the Indian government respond to the EAT-Lancet Commission's proposals?
    A) It accepts them at the expense of the long-term interests of its people.
    B) It intends them to spark conversations among all Indian stakeholders.
    C) It gives them approval regardless of opposition from nutrition experts.
    D) It welcomes them as a tool to address chronic hunger and malnutrition.

Passage Two

Questions 51 to 55 are based on the following passage.

Back in 1964, in his book *Games People Play*, psychiatrist Eric Berne described a pattern of conversation he called "Why Don't You—Yes But", which remains one of the most irritating aspects of everyday social life. The person adopting the strategy is usually a chronic complainer. Something is terrible about their relationship, job, or other situation, and they moan about it ceaselessly, but find some excuse to dismiss any solution that's proposed. The reason, of course, is that on some level they don't want a solution; they want to be validated in their position that the world is out to get them. If they can "win" the game—dismissing every suggestion until their *interlocutor* (对话者) gives up in annoyance—they get to feel pleasurably *righteous* (正当的) in their resentments and excused from any obligation to change.

Part of the trouble here is the so-called responsibility/fault *fallacy* (谬误). When you're feeling hard done by—taken for granted by your partner, say, or obliged to work for a half-witted boss—it's easy to become attached to the position that it's not your job to address the matter, and that doing so would be an admission of fault. But there's a confusion here. For example, if I were to discover a newborn at my front door, it wouldn't be my fault, but it most certainly would be my responsibility. There would be choices to make, and no possibility of avoiding them, since trying to ignore the matter would be a choice. The point is that what goes for the baby on the doorstep is true in all cases: even if the other person is 100% in the wrong, there's nothing to be gained, long-term, from using this as a justification to evade responsibility.

   Should you find yourself on the receiving end of this kind of complaining, there's an ingenious way to shut it down—which is to agree with it, ardently. Psychotherapist Lori Gottlieb describes this as "over-validation". For one thing, you'll be spared further moaning, since the other person's motivation was to confirm her beliefs, and now you're confirming them. But for another, as Gottlieb notes, people confronted with over-validation often hear their complaints afresh and start arguing back. The notion that they're utterly powerless suddenly seems unrealistic—not to mention rather annoying—so they're prompted instead to generate ideas about how they might change things.

   "And then, sometimes, something magical might happen," Gottlieb writes. The other person "might realise she's not as trapped as you are saying she is, or as she feels." Which illustrates the irony of the responsibility/fault fallacy: evading responsibility feels comfortable, but turns out to be a prison; whereas assuming responsibility feels unpleasant, but ends up being freeing.

51. What is characteristic of a chronic complainer, according to psychiatrist Eric Berne?
   A) They only feel angry about their ill treatment and resent whoever tries to help.
   B) They are chronically unhappy and ceaselessly find fault with people around them.
   C) They constantly dismiss others' proposals while taking no responsibility for tackling the problem.
   D) They lack the knowledge and basic skills required for successful conversations with their interlocutors.

52. What does the author try to illustrate with the example of the newborn on one's doorstep?
   A) People tend to think that one should not be held responsible for others' mistakes.
   B) It is easy to become attached to the position of overlooking one's own fault.
   C) People are often at a loss when confronted with a number of choices.
   D) A distinction should be drawn between responsibility and fault.

53. What does the author advise people to do to chronic complainers?
   A) Stop them from going further by agreeing with them.
   B) Listen to their complaints ardently and sympathetically.
   C) Ask them to validate their beliefs with further evidence.
   D) Persuade them to clarify the confusion they have caused.

54. What happens when chronic complainers receive over-validation?
   A) They are motivated to find ingenious ways to persuade their interlocutor.
   B) They are prompted to come up with ideas for making possible changes.
   C) They are stimulated to make more complaints.
   D) They are encouraged to start arguing back.

55. How can one stop being a chronic complainer according to the author?
   A) Analysing the so-called responsibility/fault fallacy.
   B) Avoiding hazardous traps in everyday social life.
   C) Assuming responsibility to free oneself.
   D) Awaiting something magical to happen.

Part Ⅳ   Translation   (30 minutes)

Directions: *For this part, you are allowed 30 minutes to translate a passage from Chinese into English. You should write your answer on **Answer Sheet 2**.*

   港珠澳大桥（Hong Kong-Zhuhai-Macau Bridge）全长55公里，是我国一项不同寻常的工程壮举。大桥将三个城市连接起来，是世界上最长的跨海桥梁和隧道系统。大桥将三个城市之间的旅行时间从3小时缩短到30分钟。这座跨度巨大的钢筋混凝土大桥充分证明中国有能力建造创纪录的巨型建筑。它将助推区域一体化，促进经济增长。大桥是中国发展自己的大湾区总体规划的关键。中国希望将大湾区建成在技术创新和经济繁荣上能与旧金山、纽约和东京的湾区相媲美的地区。

2020年12月大学英语六级考试真题解析
（第二套）

Part Ⅰ Writing

成文构思

通过审题可知，题目要求写一篇关于"为什么要鼓励学生培养有效的沟通技巧"的议论文，具体写作思路可参考如下：

第一段：**点明主题**——对于学生来说，培养有效的沟通技巧具有非常重要的意义；
第二段：**主体部分，分点阐述**有效沟通技巧的重要性；
第三段：**总结**，提出提高沟通技巧的方法。

参考范文及译文

No man is an island. Anytime and anywhere, students **engage with** different **interpersonal** communication. It is of great significance for students to develop effective communication skills.

First of all, effective communication skill is the tool for **clearing up** misunderstandings. A man with effective communication skills will make his ideas and thoughts well expressed. Therefore, misunderstandings are to be avoided. Secondly, effective communication skill is a helper of improving efficiency which **is synonymous with** success in a fast-speed society. With effective communication skills, a man will be good at building a harmonious interpersonal relationship with other people, and solving problems in an efficient and **flexible** way. Thirdly, a man with effective communication skills usually has the ability to make friends with various people. In this way, he will more or less get some help in his life or his work.

From what has been shown above, effective communication skills are the skill that students need to acquire. To develop effective communication skills, students are encouraged to speak more in public and learn how to communicate with others.

没有人是一座孤岛。无论何时何地，学生都会接触到不同的人际交流。对于学生来说，培养有效的沟通技巧具有非常重要的意义。

首先，有效的沟通技巧是消除误会的工具。一个拥有有效沟通技巧的人，能够使他的观点和想法得到很好的表达，因此，误会得以避免。第二，有效的沟通技巧有助于提高效率，而效率在快节奏的社会里等同于成功。有了有效的沟通技巧，一个人就会善于与其他人建立和谐的人际关系，并以高效而灵活的方式解决问题。第三，一个具有有效沟通技巧的人通常有能力与各种人交朋友。这样一来，他或多或少会在生活或工作中得到一些帮助。

综上所述，有效的沟通技巧是学生需要掌握的技能。为了培养有效的沟通技巧，鼓励学生们在公共场合多发言，学习如何与他人沟通。

词句点拨

engage with 参加；(使)从事
clear up 清理；收拾
flexible /ˈfleksəbl/ a. 灵活的

interpersonal /ˌɪntəˈpɜːsənl/ a. 人际关系的；人际的
be synonymous with 与……同义

1. It is of great significance for... to...
   对于……来说，……具有非常重要的意义。

2. ...is a helper of improving efficiency which is synonymous with success in a fast-speed society.
   ……有助于提高效率，而效率在快节奏的社会里等同于成功。

3. From what has been shown above, ...are the skill that students need to acquire.
   综上所述，……是学生需要掌握的技能。

Part II   Listening Comprehension

Section A

Questions 1 to 4 are based on the conversation you have just heard.

听力原文及译文

W: (1) This is unbelievable, unlike any video game I've ever played before. It's so boring yet so relaxing at the same time. How did you hear about this driving simulator?

M: (2) My brother introduced it to me last year. I was surprised to find how educational and realistic it was. It is called Euro Truck Simulator but they have other versions as well for American and so on. I was really drawn to the scenery. The routes go through parts of the country you don't normally see as a tourist.

W: Yeah, I can see that. It seems so simple, just transporting cargo from point A to point B, driving from one city to another. (3) But I really appreciate all the details that go into the game. It's even giving me a new appreciation for the logistics industry and traffic on the road.

M: I completely agree. My brother also introduced me to some videos of someone that streams the games online. It was fascinating to watch really. This guy drove very carefully, obeyed all the road signs and traffic rules, such a contrast to most violent games.

W: Honestly, playing has inspired me to look into the industry more. I've read articles about how self-driving trucks may soon be available and could greatly impact cargo logistics. Considering all that goes into driving these larger vehicles, it's amazing that we could soon have that kind of technology.

M: Ah, I've gone one step further. I registered to take a safe driving course to improve my real-life driving skills. In a way, I feel like I have a head start compared to other students in the class. Playing this video game has given me some maneuvering practice already.

W: I am not sure how accurate the video game is compared to real life situations. (4) But if it results in more drivers looking both ways before entering an intersection, I'd say that's a positive outcome.

女：(1) 这真是太不可思议了，完全不像我以往玩过的电子游戏。它很无聊，但同时又让人很放松。你是如何知道这款驾驶模拟器的呀？

男：(2) 去年我哥哥推荐给我的。我很惊讶地发现它既有教育意义，又很逼真。它叫作"欧洲卡车模拟"，但也有美国版本和其他版本。我是真的被里面的景色给吸引住了。里面的线路穿过了你一般作为游客时不常见的地区。

女：是的，我也发现了。它看上去简单，只是将货物从 A 点运到 B 点，从一个城市开车去另一个城市。(3) 但是我真的很欣赏游戏中涉及的所有细节。它甚至让我对物流业和道路交通有了新的理解。

男：我完全赞同。我的哥哥也给我推荐了一些别人在线玩游戏的视频。观看的视频真的很赞！这个人开车非常小心，遵守所有的道路标识和交通规则，和大多数暴力游戏截然不同。

女：老实说，玩游戏激励我要更深入地了解这个行业。我读过一些文章，这些文章提到自动驾驶卡车可能即将问世，可能会对货运物流产生极大的影响。考虑到驾驶这些大型车辆要做的一切准备，我们不久就能拥有这项技术真的是太棒了。

男：啊，我领先了一步。我注册了安全驾驶的课程，以提升我的真实驾驶技术。在某种程度上，我感觉自己已经领先于班上的其他同学了。玩这款电子游戏已经让我有了一些操作的实践经验。

女：我不确定相比现实场景，这款电子游戏到底有多准确。(4) 但是如果能让更多的司机在进入十字路口时注意两边的路况，那么我想说这是积极的结果。

难词总结

simulator /ˈsɪmjuleɪtə(r)/ n. 模拟装置；模拟器
be drawn to 被……所吸引
cargo logistics 货运物流
realistic /ˌriːəˈlɪstɪk/ a. 现实的；实际的
stream /striːm/ v. 流播；流动
intersection /ˌɪntəˈsekʃn/ n. 十字路口；交叉路口

题目精析

1. What are the speakers mainly talking about?
   A) A driving test.　　B) A video game.　　C) Traffic routes.　　D) Cargo logistics.

1. 说话者主要在谈论什么？
   A）一次驾照考试。　B）一款电子游戏。　C）交通路线。　　D）货运物流。

【答案及分析】B。本题问音频中谈论的内容是什么。音频开头便提到，This is unbelievable, unlike any video game I've ever played before.（这真是太不可思议了，完全不像我以往玩过的电子游戏。）由此可知 B 项符合题目要求，video game 是原词复现，故 B 项正确。

2. What does the man say about the driving simulator?
   A) He found it instructive and realistic.　　C) He was really drawn to its other versions.
   B) He bought it when touring Europe.　　　D) He introduced it to his brother last year.

2. 这位男士关于驾驶模拟器有何说法？
   A）他发现它具有教育意义，很逼真。　　C）他被其他版本深深吸引。
   B）他是在欧洲旅游时购买的。　　　　　D）他去年把它推荐给了他的哥哥。

【答案及分析】A。本题问音频中的男士对驾驶模拟器的说法。音频中提到，My brother introduced it

to me last year. I was surprised to find how educational and realistic it was.（去年我哥哥推荐给我的。我很惊讶地发现它既有教育意义，又很逼真。）A 项中的 instructive 是 educational 的同义表达，realistic 是原词复现，故 A 项正确。

3. What does the woman say she really appreciates?

  A) Traveling all over the country.　　　　C) The details in the driving simulator.

  B) Driving from one city to another.　　　　D) The key role of the logistics industry.

3. 这位女士说她对什么很欣赏？

  A）周游全国。　　　　　　　　　　　　C）驾驶模拟器的细节。

  B）从一个城市开车去另一个城市。　　　　D）物流业的重要作用。

【答案及分析】C。本题问音频中的女士欣赏什么。音频中提到，But I really appreciate all the details that go into the game.（但是我真的很欣赏游戏中涉及的所有细节。）C 项 The details in the driving simulator 是音频中 the details that go into the game 的同义表达，故 C 项正确。

4. What outcome did this woman expect from the driving simulator?

  A) Clearer road signs.　　　　　　　　　C) Stricter traffic rules.

  B) More people driving safely.　　　　　　D) More self-driving trucks on the road.

4. 这位女士期待驾驶模拟器能产生什么效果？

  A）更清楚的道路标识。　　　　　　　　C）更严格的交通规则。

  B）更多人安全驾驶。　　　　　　　　　D）道路上有更多的自动驾驶卡车。

【答案及分析】B。本题问音频中的女士期待驾驶模拟器产生的效果。音频中提到，But if it results in more drivers looking both ways before entering an intersection, I'd say that's a positive outcome.（但是如果能让更多的司机在进入十字路口时注意两边的路况，那么我想说这是积极的结果。）也就是说，女士希望通过使用这款游戏能够让人们更加注重安全驾驶，故 B 项正确。

Questions 5 to 8 are based on the conversation you have just heard.

听力原文及译文

W: How do you like being self-employed?

M: (5) There are obvious benefits, though I don't seem to have the freedom I anticipated, as I just don't seem able to decline work offers. And working alone, there have been times when I've found that money alone provides insufficient motivation. Have you experienced the same since you began working for yourself?

W: Sometimes, yes. Unlike the rest of the workforce who have managers to prompt motivation whenever they're feeling lazy or bored, we self-employed workers perform our jobs without a manager to lift our spirits. There's no one around to offer praise or initiate collaboration, no one to make greater use of our interests and talents.

M: That's a fact. Not every manager behaves with such awareness and care, of course. (6) And certainly not all managers have a clue how to motivate people. Still, having a manager nearby at least indicates there's an opportunity. They'll be decent enough to look out for you when your energy and focus begin to deplete.

W: (7-1) The motivator I value most is autonomy. I've learned not to sacrifice my prized autonomy by working all hours of the day and by saying yes to every client request.

M: (7-2) Yes, I need to remind myself that I selected this lifestyle for the independence. I don't miss aspects of permanent full-time employment I disliked, such as the office politics, job insecurity, inflexible hours and so on. I wouldn't mind a bit more in the form of praise though, praise which is on the record.

W: That'll come with time. Relatedness is inevitably cultivated via human interaction engaging with clients, getting written testimony and recommendations, staying in contact with clients afterwards. These are things you'll find will come in due course and provide you with motivation.

M: (8) You're right. That's an area I do need to put some more effort into—building closer relationships with those who engage my services and skills.

女：你觉得自主创业怎么样？

男：（5）还是有一些明显的好处的，尽管我似乎没有预期的那么自由，因为我似乎无法拒绝工作邀请。独自工作时，有时我发现，光靠钱无法提供足够的动力。自从你开始为自己工作以来，是否有同样的经历呢？

女：有时我也有这种感觉。和其他的从业人员不一样，当他们感到懒散或无聊时会有经理来激励他们，而我们自主创业者在没有经理鼓励时也要完成自己的工作。周围没有人表扬，没有人发起合作，没有人能充分发挥我们的兴趣和才能。

男：确实如此。当然，不是所有经理都能有这样的意识和关切。（6）当然也不是所有经理都知道该如何激励员工。但是有位经理在身边至少说明有机会。当你的精力和注意力开始耗尽时，他们会适当地留意你。

女：（7-1）我最看重的激励因素就是自主性。我学会了如何能不必牺牲我珍视的自主性，方法就是全天候工作和满足客户的每一项需求。

男：（7-2）是的，我需要提醒自己，选择这种生活方式的目的就是自主性。我不会怀念我所讨厌的固定全职工作的一些方面，比如办公室政治，工作不稳定，时间缺乏弹性等。但是我不介意公开多说点赞扬的话。

女：这是早晚的事。我们不可避免地会通过人际互动来培养人际关系，与客户来往，获取书面证明和建议，事后与客户保持联系。你会发现这些东西将适时出现，并为你提供动力。

男：（8）你说得对。自主创业的确需要我投入更多的精力，与那些使用我的服务和技能的人建立更加紧密的关系。

难词总结

anticipate /ænˈtɪsɪpeɪt/ v. 预期；期盼
prompt /prɒmpt/ v. 促使；激起
autonomy /ɔːˈtɒnəmi/ n. 自主；自治
in due course 在适当的时候；及时地

insufficient /ˌɪnsəˈfɪʃnt/ a. 不充分的；不足的
deplete /dɪˈpliːt/ v. 耗尽
testimony /ˈtestɪməni/ n. 证明；证据

题目精析

5. What does the man say about his life of being self-employed?
   A) It isn't so enjoyable as he expected.
   B) It isn't so motivating as he believed.

C) It doesn't enable him to earn as much money as he used to.

D) It doesn't seem to offer as much freedom as he anticipated.

5. 男士如何评价自己的自主创业生活？

A）没有他期望的那样快乐。

B）没有他认为的那样鼓舞人心。

C）不能让他挣到和往常一样多的钱。

D）似乎没有他期待的那么自由。

【答案及分析】D。本题问男士对自己自主创业生活的评价。音频开头时女士问男士觉得自主创业怎么样，接着男士回答，There are obvious benefits, though I don't seem to have the freedom I anticipated（还是有一些明显的好处的，尽管我似乎没有预期的那么自由）。D 项中的 doesn't seem to offer as much freedom as he anticipated 是音频中 don't seem to have the freedom I anticipated 的同义表达，freedom 和 anticipated 都是原词复现，故 D 项正确。

6. What did the man say about the manager?

A) Not all of them care about their employees' behaviors.

B) Few of them are aware of their employees' feelings.

C) Few of them offer praise and reward to their employees.

D) Not all of them know how to motivate their employees.

6. 这位男士对于经理有何评价？

A）他们并不是全都关心员工的行为。

B）他们很少有人能在意员工的感受。

C）他们很少有人会赞扬和奖励员工。

D）他们并不是全都知道如何激励员工。

【答案及分析】D。本题问男士对于经理的评价。音频中提到，And certainly not all managers have a clue how to motivate people.（当然也不是所有经理都知道该如何激励员工。）D 项中的 know 是音频中 have a clue 的同义表达，how to motivate their employees 是 how to motivate people 的同义表达，故 D 项正确。

7. What do both speakers value most about self-employment?

A) Job satisfaction.　　B) Self-awareness.　　C) Autonomy.　　D) Money.

7. 两位说话者关于自主创业最看重的是什么？

A）工作满意度。　　B）自我意识。　　C）自主性。　　D）金钱。

【答案及分析】C。本题问两位说话者在自主创业中最看重什么。音频中女士提到，The motivator I value most is autonomy.（我最看重的激励因素就是自主性。）男士接下来表示同意女士的观点，提到 Yes, I need to remind myself that I selected this lifestyle for the independence.（是的，我需要提醒自己，选择这种生活方式的目的就是自主性。）autonomy 为原词复现，且是 independence 的同义表达，由此可知两位说话者关于自主创业都最看重自主性，故 C 项正确。

8. What point does the man agree with the woman?

A) The importance of cultivating close relationships with clients.

B) The need for getting recommendations from their managers.

C) The advantages of permanent full-time employment.

D) The way to explore employees' interests and talents.

8. 男士赞同女士的什么观点？
   A）与客户建立紧密关系的重要性。
   B）从经理那获得推荐的必要性。
   C）固定全职工作的好处。
   D）发掘员工兴趣和才能的方式。

【答案及分析】A。本题问男士赞同女士的什么观点。音频中女士说到与客户交流会使人在适当的时候获得工作动力，随后男士表示赞同，提到 You're right. That's an area I do need to put some more effort into——building closer relationships with those who engage my services and skills.（你说得对。自主创业的确需要我投入更多的精力，与那些使用我的服务和技能的人建立更加紧密的关系。）cultivating close relationships 和 building closer relationships 是同义表达，clients 指的就是 those who engage my services and skills，故 A 项正确。

Section B

Questions 9 to 11 are based on the passage you have just heard.

【听力原文及译文】

　　Weather is a constant force in our lives, but there's little marketing research on how it affects businesses.

　　(9) Now a new study reveals how sunny and snowy conditions influence consumer behavior. Those weather conditions trigger consumers to mentally visualize using products associated with the respective weather. This leads to consumers placing a higher value on those products. That is, they're willing to pay more money for them. But the correlation is only found with products related to being outside. How does this work? Researchers give the example of the beach towel. On a sunny day, consumers who see that product are not just looking at the towel itself. (10) They are likely imagining themselves lying on the towel in the sun. This mental picture of using the towel increases the value of the product in the consumers' mind.

　　Researchers put forward the following hypothesis to explain their findings. They think the mental picture works in sunshine and snow, because these weather conditions have a positive association with outside activities. The effect is not seen with rainy weather. Researchers assert this is because there aren't many activities that are enabled by rain. Most products associated with rain, like umbrellas, are only used for protection from the weather and not for any activities. Researchers believe that companies that sell a wide array of products online can benefit most from the insights this study provides. (11) Online sellers often use complex mathematical formulas to determine what products to feature and how to price these products. Incorporating more data about weather would allow them to make better decisions. This could bolster sales.

　　在我们的生活中，天气是一种持久的力量，但是很少有关于天气是如何影响商业的市场研究。（9）现在，一项新的研究揭示了晴天和雪天是如何影响消费者行为的。这些天气状况会触发消费者在脑海中想象与各种天气有关的产品的画面。这会导致消费者更加重视这些产品。也就是说，他们愿意为这些产品支付更多的钱。但是这种相关性仅存在于一些与户外活动有关的产品上。这种相关性是如何起作用的呢？研究人员以沙滩浴巾为例：在阳光明媚的一天，看到产品的消费者看到的不仅是浴巾本身。（10）他们很可能想象自己躺在浴巾上晒太阳的画面。这种想象使用浴巾的画面在消费者心中提升了产品的价值。

研究人员提出了下列假设来解释他们的发现。他们认为这种意识图像会在晴天和雪天起作用，因为这些天气状况和户外活动有着正向关系。这种效果在雨天是没有的。研究人员断定，这是因为下雨天能够进行的活动不多。大多数与下雨有关的产品，比如雨伞，都仅用于挡雨，而不见用于任何活动。研究人员认为，这项研究提供的见解能够使得在网上销售多种产品的公司获益最大。（11）网上卖家常常使用复杂的数学公式来确定产品的特点以及如何给这些产品定价。参考更多有关天气的数据能够使得商家做出更好的决定。这可以促进销售。

难词总结

affect /əˈfekt/ v. 影响；侵袭
associated with 与……有关系；与……相联系
hypothesis /haɪˈpɒθəsɪs/ n. 假说；猜测
formula /ˈfɔːmjələ/ n. 公式；方程式
bolster /ˈbəʊlstə(r)/ v. 改善；加强

trigger /ˈtrɪɡə(r)/ v. 触发；发动
correlation /ˌkɒrəˈleɪʃn/ n. 关联；相关
a wide array of 各种各样的；大量的
incorporate /ɪnˈkɔːpəreɪt/ v. 包含；使并入

题目精析

9. What do we learn about the findings of the new study?
   A) Consumers visualize their activities in different weather.
   B) Good weather triggers consumers' desire to go shopping.
   C) Weather conditions influence consumers' buying behavior.
   D) Consumers' mental states change with the prices of goods.

9. 关于这项新研究的发现，我们能获得什么信息？
   A）消费者会想象他们在不同天气中的活动。
   B）好天气会触发消费者购物的欲望。
   C）天气状况影响消费者的购物行为。
   D）消费者的心理状态会随着产品价格的变化而变化。

【答案及分析】C。本题问新研究的发现。音频中提到，Now a new study reveals how sunny and snowy conditions influence consumer behavior.（现在，一项新的研究揭示了晴天和雪天是如何影响消费者行为的。）C项中的Weather conditions对应音频中的sunny and snowy conditions，influence和behavior为原词复现，故C项正确。

10. What does the passage say may increase the value of products for consumers?
    A) Active consumption.   C) Individual association.
    B) Direct correlation.   D) Mental visualization.

10. 这篇文章说什么可能提升产品在消费者心中的价值？
    A）积极消费。   C）个人联系。
    B）直接关联。   D）心理想象。

【答案及分析】D。本题问什么能提升产品在消费者心中的价值。音频中提到，They are likely imagining themselves lying on the towel in the sun. This mental picture of using the towel increases the value of the product in the consumers' mind.（他们很可能想象自己躺在浴巾上晒太阳的画面。这种想象使

用浴巾的画面在消费者心中提升了产品的价值。）D 项 Mental visualization 是音频中 mental picture 的同义表达，故 D 项正确。

11. How can the findings of the new study benefit online sellers according to the researchers?
    A) Enabling them to simplify their mathematical formulas.
    B) Helping them determine what to sell and at what price.
    C) Enabling them to sell their products at a higher price.
    D) Helping them advertise a greater variety of products.

11. 研究人员称这项新研究的发现将如何使网上卖家受益？
    A）让他们能够简化自己的数学公式。
    B）帮助他们决定销售的产品和价格。
    C）让他们能以更高的价格销售产品。
    D）帮助他们宣传更多种类的产品。

【答案及分析】B。本题问新研究的发现将如何使网上卖家受益。音频中提到，Online sellers often use complex mathematical formulas to determine what products to feature and how to price these products. Incorporating more data about weather would allow them to make better decisions. This could bolster sales.（网上卖家常常使用复杂的数学公式来确定产品的特点以及如何给这些产品定价。参考更多有关天气的数据能够使得商家做出更好的决定。这可以促进销售。）B 项中的 determine what to sell and at what price 是音频中 determine what products to feature and how to price these products 的同义表达，故 B 项正确。

Questions 12 to 15 are based on the passage you have just heard.

听力原文及译文

Setting the office air conditioning at about 22 ℃ has become standard practice across the world. Numerous guidebooks across the world on heating, ventilation and air conditioning claim office performance peaks at 22 degrees. Many people indeed find relief from soaring summer temperatures in air-conditioned offices. (12) But recent studies have challenged the accepted wisdom that a cool office is more productive. The reality is more complex.

Researchers conducted a review of all studies relating to air-conditioning and productivity. (13) They found that 22 degrees was probably a little chilly, even at the height of summer. For a person dressed in typical summer clothing, an optimal range would be between 23 and 26 degrees. And people can even tolerate temperatures beyond this comfort zone, as long as they can adjust their clothing and expectations. In fact, even on very hot days, it makes sense to turn the air-conditioning up. People often chase just one optimum temperature. And this is understandable when people feel hot. (14) But there is a range of at least 3 to 4 degrees, which does not have any adverse impact. Another issue related to this is that people can become psychologically dependent on air conditioning. (15) If they are used to the environment which is air conditioned, they tend to prefer lower temperatures. But the studies found that almost all humans became accustomed to the new temperature. It was only at the extreme ends of the temperature range where people's productivity suffered. This range was above 26 degrees and below 19 degrees.

将办公室空调的温度设定在22℃已经成为全世界的标准做法。全球许多取暖、通风和空调设备的使用手册都表明，办公效率在温度为22℃时达到峰值。有空调的办公室确实能让许多人从气温飙升的夏日里得到解脱。(12)<u>但是，最近的研究对"在凉爽的办公室里工作效率更高"这一公认的观点提出了异议。</u>现实情况要复杂得多。

　　研究人员对所有有关空调和工作效率的研究进行了综述。(13)<u>他们发现即使是在盛夏，22℃还是会有点偏冷。</u>对于一个身着典型夏装的人来说，适宜温度在23℃~26℃。而且只要人们可以调整自己的穿着和期望，甚至可以承受超出这个舒适区的温度。事实上，即使是在非常炎热的日子里，把空调温度调高也是说得通的。人们往往追求一个舒适温度。当人们觉得酷暑难耐时，这是可以理解的。(14)<u>但是仅有3℃~4℃的温差不会产生任何负面影响。</u>与此相关的另一个问题是，人们可能会对空调产生心理依赖。(15)<u>如果他们习惯于空调环境，那么他们往往会喜欢偏低的温度。</u>但是这些研究发现，几乎所有人都习惯于新的温度。只有超过了温度范围的极端值，人们的工作效率才会受到影响。这个范围在26℃以上及19℃以下。

难词总结

numerous /ˈnjuːmərəs/ *a.* 许多的；众多的
peak /piːk/ *v.* 达到峰值；达到最高值
chilly /ˈtʃɪli/ *a.* 寒冷的；阴冷的
tolerate /ˈtɒləreɪt/ *v.* 容忍；允许
become accustomed to 习惯于

ventilation /ˌventɪˈleɪʃn/ *n.* 通风；通风系统
soaring /ˈsɔːrɪŋ/ *a.* 猛增的
optimal /ˈɒptɪməl/ *a.* 最佳的；最优的
adverse /ˈædvɜːs/ *a.* 不利的；有害的

题目精析

12. What is the accepted wisdom concerning the office environment?
　　A) A naturally ventilated office is more comfortable.
　　B) A cool office will boost employees' productivity.
　　C) Office air-conditioning should follow guidebooks.
　　D) Air-conditioning improves ventilation in the office.

12. 关于办公室环境，公认的观点是什么？
　　A）自然通风的办公室要更加舒适。
　　B）凉爽的办公室能够提高员工的工作效率。
　　C）办公室空调应遵守指南使用。
　　D）空调能够改善办公室的通风环境。

【答案及分析】B。本题问关于办公室环境的公认观点。音频中提到，But recent studies have challenged the accepted wisdom that a cool office is more productive.（但是，最近的研究对"在凉爽的办公室里工作效率更高"这一公认的观点提出了异议。）B项中的 A cool office 为原词复现，boost employees' productivity 是音频中 more productive 的同义表达，故 B 项正确。

13. What did researchers find from the review of all studies relating to air conditioning and productivity?
　　A) People in their comfort zone of temperature are more satisfied with their productivity.
　　B) People in different countries vary in their tolerance to uncomfortable temperatures.

C) Twenty-two degrees is the optimal temperature for office workers.

D) There is a range of temperatures for people to feel comfortable.

13. 对所有与空调和工作效率有关的研究进行综述后，研究人员发现了什么？

　　A) 处于温度舒适区的人更满意自己的工作效率。

　　B) 不同国家的人对于不舒适温度的忍耐力不同。

　　C) 对于上班族来说，最佳温度是22℃。

　　D) 有一个让人们感到舒适的温度范围。

【答案及分析】D。本题问研究人员的发现。音频中提到，They found that 22 degrees was probably a little chilly... an optimal range would be between 23 and 26 degrees.（他们发现……22℃还是会有点偏冷……适宜温度在23℃~26℃。）D项中的a range of temperatures指的就是音频中的between 23 and 26 degrees，故D项正确。

14. What do we learn about using a little less air conditioning during hot weather?

　　A) It will have no negative impact on work.　　C) It will sharply decrease work efficiency.

　　B) It will be immediately noticeable.　　D) It will cause a lot of discomfort.

14. 关于在炎热的天气里少用空调，我们能了解到什么？

　　A) 它对工作没有负面影响。　　C) 它将大幅降低工作效率。

　　B) 它将立即被人注意到。　　D) 它会造成很多不适。

【答案及分析】A。本题问在炎热天气里少用空调的信息。音频中提到，But there is a range of at least 3 to 4 degrees, which does not have any adverse impact.（但是仅有3℃~4℃的温差不会产生任何负面影响。）A项是音频中which does not have any adverse impact的同义表达，故A项正确。

15. What happens when people are used to an air-conditioned environment?

　　A) They tend to favor lower temperatures.　　C) They are not bothered by temperature extremes.

　　B) They suffer from rapid temperature changes.　　D) They become less sensitive to high temperatures.

15. 当人们习惯于空调环境时会发生什么？

　　A) 他们倾向于偏爱较低的温度。　　C) 他们不受极端温度的影响。

　　B) 他们受到温度快速变化的影响。　　D) 他们对高温不那么敏感。

【答案及分析】A。本题问人们习惯于空调环境时会发生的情况。音频中提到，If they are used to the environment which is air conditioned, they tend to prefer lower temperatures.（如果他们习惯于空调环境，那么他们往往会喜欢偏低的温度。）A项They tend to favor lower temperatures是音频中they tend to prefer lower temperatures的同义表达，故A项正确。

Section C

Questions 16 to 18 are based on the recording you have just heard.

听力原文及译文

　　Psychology research has tended to portray solitude as negative experience. Studies conducted in the 1970s and 1990s suggested that people felt less happy when alone as compared to being with others. However, a new paper shows an alternative view of solitude, one in which solitude can be positive.

　　Let's start by looking at the earlier research. It had a couple of shortcomings. First it measured emotion on a scale from positive to negative, overlooking the possibility that our positive and negative emotions can fluctuate independently. (16) Also, it categorized emotions as simply positive or negative. It didn't consider that emotions arouse us to different degrees and that both positive and negative emotions can arouse us a lot or a little. That is, whether positive or negative, emotions can be either high-arousal or low-arousal. High-arousal emotions include excitement on the positive side or anger on the negative side; while low-arousal ones include feeling calm on the positive side or lonely on the negative.

This new research attempted to overcome these shortcomings. Researchers began with a simple study. They asked participants to spend 15 minutes sitting alone without engaging in any activity and measured how this solitude influences their emotional state. This experiment specifically aimed to determine the effect of solitude on high-arousal emotions. It looked at positive emotions such as being excited or interested and negative emotions including being scared or distressed. (17) The results were clear: after fifteen minutes of solitude, the participants showed reductions in both types of emotion.

(18-1) A second study measured the effects of solitude on low-arousal emotions. These included both positive and negative emotions such as feeling calm, relaxed, sad or lonely. (18-2) That experiment found that all of these emotions were increased by time alone. Thus, it seems past depictions of solitude were wrong. It doesn't have a simple, emotional effect that can be characterized as good or bad. Rather, it changes the intensity of our inner experience. It amplifies quieter emotions but it diminishes the intensity of stronger feelings.

It's worth clarifying that these findings relate to relatively brief periods of solitude. This is distinct from prolonged loneliness. Research has demonstrated that the latter is correlated with an assortment of negative physical and psychological effects. How can people benefit from being alone? The findings here suggest that people can use solitude to regulate their emotions. Solitude can help us become quiet after excitement, calm after an angry episode or simply feel at peace.

心理学研究倾向于将独处描述为一种消极的体验。20世纪70年代和90年代的研究表明，相比于有人陪伴，人们独处时会不那么开心。然而，一篇新的论文展示了另外一种关于独处的观点，即独处也可以是积极的。

我们先来看看早期的研究，它有许多不足之处。首先，它用积极和消极的尺度来衡量情绪，却忽视了积极情绪和消极情绪可能各自会出现波动的情况。(16)并且，它将情绪简单归为积极和消极两类。它没有考虑到情绪在每个人身上的表现程度不同，以及积极情绪和消极情绪都可能或多或少地造成情绪波动。也就是说，不管是积极情绪还是消极情绪，情绪都可能是高唤醒或低唤醒的。高唤醒情绪包括积极情绪中的激动和消极情绪中的愤怒；而低唤醒情绪包括积极情绪中的平静和消极情绪中的孤独。

这项新的研究试图克服这些不足。研究人员从一项简单的研究开始。他们要求参与者单独静坐15分钟，不参与任何活动，然后测量这种独处如何影响他们的情绪状态。这项实验的具体目标是确定独处对高唤醒情绪的影响。它研究了激动、感兴趣等积极情绪，和恐惧、忧虑等消极情绪。(17)结果显示：经过15分钟的独处之后，参与者的这两种情绪都呈降低趋势。

（18-1)第二次实验评估了独处对低唤醒情绪的影响。这包括了积极情绪和消极情绪，如平静、放松、悲伤或孤独。(18-2)实验发现，随着时间推移，这些情绪全都增强了。因此，过去关于独处的描述似乎是错误的，它对情绪的影响不能简单地被归类为有利或是有弊。相反，它改变了我们内心体验的强度。它增强了更平静的情绪，却减弱了强烈情绪的强度。

值得澄清的一点是，这些发现涉及的是相对短暂的独处。这与长期的独处有着很大区别。研究表明，长期的独处与各种各样消极的生理和心理影响有关。人要如何才能从独处中受益呢？这些发现表明人们可利用独处来调节自己的情绪。独处可以帮助我们在激动后恢复平静，在愤怒过后保持冷静，或只是简单地觉得平和。

难词总结

solitude /ˈsɒlɪtjuːd/ *n.* 独处；独居
shortcoming /ˈʃɔːtkʌmɪŋ/ *n.* 缺点；短处
fluctuate /ˈflʌktʃueɪt/ *v.* 波动；起伏不定
specifically /spəˈsɪfɪkli/ *ad.* 明确地；具体地
diminish /dɪˈmɪnɪʃ/ *v.* 减少；(使) 减弱

alternative /ɔːlˈtɜːnətɪv/ *a.* 可供替代的
overlook /ˌəʊvəˈlʊk/ *v.* 忽略；不予理会
arouse /əˈraʊz/ *v.* 激起；引起
amplify /ˈæmplɪfaɪ/ *v.* 放大；增强
assortment /əˈsɔːtmənt/ *n.* 各种各样，混合

题目精析

16. What is one of the criticisms directed at the early research on solitude?

    A) It overlooked the possibility that emotions may be controlled.

    B) It ignored the fact that emotions are personal and subjective.

    C) It classified emotions simply as either positive or negative.

    D) It measured positive and negative emotions independently.

16. 下列哪一项批评针对的是早期关于独处的研究？

    A）它忽视了情绪可以被控制的可能性。

    B）它忽视了情绪个人化且带有主观性的事实。

    C）它将情绪简单地归类为积极情绪和消极情绪。

    D）它分开评估积极情绪和消极情绪。

【答案及分析】C。本题问针对早期关于独处的研究的批评。音频中提到，Also, it categorized emotions as simply positive or negative.（并且，它将情绪简单归为积极和消极两类。）C 项 It classified emotions simply as either positive or negative 是音频中 it categorized emotions as simply positive or negative 的同义表达，故 C 项正确。

17. What do we learn about the results of the new research?

    A) Sitting alone without doing anything seemed really distressing.

    B) Solitude adversely affected the participants' mental well-being.

    C) Sitting alone for 15 minutes made the participants restless.

    D) Solitude had a reductive effect on high-arousal emotions.

17. 关于新研究的结果，我们能了解到什么？

    A）独自坐着什么都不干真的很痛苦。

    B）独处对参与者的心理健康产生了负面影响。

    C）单独坐 15 分钟使得参与者坐立难安。

D）独处可以减弱高唤醒情绪。

【答案及分析】D。本题问新研究的结果。音频中提到，The results were clear: after fifteen minutes of solitude, the participants showed reductions in both types of emotion.（结果显示：经过15分钟的独处之后，参与者的这两种情绪都呈降低趋势。）D项中的reductive是音频中reductions的同义表达，结合上文可知，音频中both types of emotion指的就是高唤醒情绪中的积极情绪和消极情绪，故D项正确。

18. What does the second experiment in the new research find about solitude?
    A) It proved hard to depict objectively.   C) It helped increase low-arousal emotions.
    B) It went hand in hand with sadness.   D) It tended to intensify negative emotions.

18. 关于独处，新研究中的第二项实验发现了什么？
    A）证明很难对其进行客观描述。   C）它能帮助增强低唤醒情绪。
    B）它与悲伤密切相关。   D）它往往能强化负面情绪。

【答案及分析】C。本题问第二项关于独处的实验的发现。音频中提到，A second study measured the effects of solitude on low-arousal emotions.（第二次实验评估了独处对低唤醒情绪的影响。）紧接着下文提到了实验结果，That experiment found that all of these emotions were increased by time alone.（实验发现，随着时间推移，这些情绪全都增强了。）C项是音频中all of these emotions were increased的同义表达，故C项正确。

Questions 19 to 21 are based on the recording you have just heard.

听力原文及译文

In 1984, the World Chess Championship was called off abruptly, due to the withered frame of a player who was competing for the title. He wasn't alone in experiencing the extreme physical effects of the game. Elite players can reportedly burn up to an absurd 6,000 calories in one day. Does that mean that thinking harder is a simple route to losing weight? (19) Well, when the body is at rest, we know that the brain uses up a startling 20% to 25% of the body's overall energy. This level of utilization actually makes the brain the most energy-expensive organ in the body, and yet it makes up only 2% of the body's weight overall.

So the more we put this organ to work, the more calories we'll burn? Technically, the answer is yes, for cognitively difficult tasks. What counts as a "difficult" mental task varies between individuals. But generally, it could be described as something that the brain cannot solve easily using previously learned routines, or tasks that change the conditions continuously. However, deep thinking will not burn off the calories gained from eating a sugary snack. Because in relation to the brain's huge overall energy usage, which is devoted to a multitude of tasks, the energy required just to think harder is actually comparatively tiny. (20) We are unconscious of most of what uses up the brain's energy. A lot of that activity is unrelated to conscious activities like learning how to sing or play the guitar.

The brain is able to allocate blood and thus energy to particular regions that are being active at that point, (21) but the overall energy availability in the brain is thought to be constant. So, while there might be significant increases in energy use at localized regions of the brain when we perform difficult cognitive tasks, when it comes to the whole brain's energy budget overall, these activities don't significantly alter it.

So why did the chess champion grow too skinny to compete in his chess competition? The general consensus is that it mostly comes down to stress and reduced food consumption, not mental exhaustion. Keeping your body pumped up for action for long periods of time is very energy demanding. If you can't eat as often or as much as you can or would normally— then you might lose weight.

　　1984年，世界国际象棋锦标赛被突然叫停，原因是一位争夺冠军的棋手身形过于瘦削。他不是唯一一个经受比赛对身体的极端影响的人。据报道，精英棋手一天可以消耗高达6 000卡路里的热量。这意味着努力思考是减肥的捷径吗？（19）<u>嗯，当身体处于休息状态时，我们知道大脑会消耗掉全身能量的20%~25%，这相当惊人。</u>实际上，这种消耗水平使得大脑成为全身最耗能量的器官，然而大脑仅占身体总重量的2%。

　　所以大脑工作得越多，我们消耗的卡路里就越多吗？严格意义上来讲，针对认知困难的任务，回答是肯定的。对"困难的"心理任务的定义因人而异。但是通常来说，可以将它描述为大脑不能用以前学到的常规方法轻松解决的事情，或者是条件不断发生变化的任务。但是，深度思考不能消耗吃含糖零食摄入的卡路里。因为与大脑执行多项任务时总体消耗的巨大能量相比，努力思考所需的能量实际上相对较少。（20）<u>我们无法意识到是什么活动消耗了大脑的大部分能量。许多消耗活动都与有意识的活动无关，如学习唱歌或是弹吉他。</u>

　　大脑能够指挥血液运输，进而将能量分配至特定的活跃区域，（21）<u>但是大脑整体能量的可用性是不变的</u>。所以，当我们执行有难度的认知任务时，尽管大脑局部区域的能量消耗会明显增多，但就整个大脑的能量预算来说，这些活动并不会显著改变这一数字。

　　那么这位象棋冠军为什么会瘦到无法参加象棋比赛呢？普遍的共识是因为压力过大，食物摄取减少，而不是心理疲惫。让你的身体长时间保持活跃的状态是十分需要能量的。如果你不能像往常一样保持饮食规律或饭量，那么你的体重可能就会下降。

难词总结

withered /ˈwɪðəd/ a. 干枯的；枯槁的
utilization /ˌjuːtəlaɪˈzeɪʃn/ n. 利用，使用
be unconscious of 未意识到；不知道
significantly /sɪɡˈnɪfɪkəntli/ ad. 显著地；明显地
consensus /kənˈsensəs/ n. 共识；一致的意见
pump up 打气；热切期望；用泵把……抽上来

startling /ˈstɑːtlɪŋ/ a. 令人吃惊的
previously /ˈpriːviəsli/ ad. 先前地；以前地
allocate /ˈæləkeɪt/ v. 分配；拨；划
alter /ˈɔːltə(r)/ v. 改变；更改
exhaustion /ɪɡˈzɔːstʃən/ n. 筋疲力尽；疲惫不堪

题目精析

19. What do we learn about the brain when the body is at rest?

    A) It uses up much less energy than it does in deep thinking.
    B) It remains inactive without burning calories noticeably.
    C) It continues to burn up calories to help us stay in shape.
    D) It consumes almost a quarter of the body's total energy.

19. 当身体处于休息状态时，关于大脑我们能了解到什么？

　　A）它比处于深度思考时消耗的能量要少得多。

　　B）它保持不活跃状态，没有明显燃烧卡路里。

　　C）它持续燃烧卡路里来帮助我们保持身材。

　　D）它几乎消耗人体四分之一的能量。

　　【答案及分析】D。本题问身体休息时大脑的状态是什么样的。音频中提到，Well, when the body is at rest, we know that the brain uses up a startling 20% to 25% of the body's overall energy.（嗯，当身体处于休息状态时，我们知道大脑会消耗掉全身能量的 20%~25%，这相当惊人。）D 项中的 almost a quarter of the body's total energy 和音频中的 20% to 25% of the body's overall energy 是同义表达，故 D 项正确。

20. What does the speaker say about the consumption of the brain's energy?

　　A) Much of the consumption has nothing to do with conscious activities.

　　B) It has something to do with the difficulty of the activities in question.

　　C) Energy usage devoted to active learning accounts for a big part of it.

　　D) A significant amount of it is for performing difficult cognitive tasks.

20. 关于大脑能量的消耗，说话者的看法是什么？

　　A）大部分的能量消耗都与有意识的活动无关。

　　B）它与讨论的活动的难度有关。

　　C）主动学习消耗的能量占比很大。

　　D）有很大一部分被用于执行有难度的认知任务。

　　【答案及分析】A。本题问说话者关于大脑能量消耗的看法。音频中提到，We are unconscious of most of what uses up the brain's energy. A lot of that activity is unrelated to conscious activities like learning how to sing or play the guitar.（我们无法意识到是什么活动消耗了大脑的大部分能量。许多消耗活动都与有意识的活动无关，如学习唱歌或是弹吉他。）A 项中的 has nothing to do with 与 is unrelated to 为同义表达，conscious activities 为原词复现，故 A 项正确。

21. What do we learn about the overall energy availability in the brain?

　　A) It is believed to remain basically constant.　　C) It is conducive to relieving mental exhaustion.

　　B) It is a prerequisite for any mental activity.　　D) It is thought to be related to food consumption.

21. 关于大脑能量的可用性，我们能了解到什么？

　　A）它被认为基本上保持不变。　　C）它有助于缓解心理疲惫。

　　B）它是任何心理活动的先决条件。　　D）它被认为与摄入食物有关。

　　【答案及分析】A。本题问关于大脑能量的可用性的信息。音频中提到，but the overall energy availability in the brain is thought to be constant.（但是大脑整体能量的可用性是不变的）。constant 是原词复现，故 A 项正确。

Questions 22 to 25 are based on the recording you have just heard.

"Tell me about yourself" may seem like an easy job interview question. (22) But the open-ended nature of this question often leaves job seekers at a loss where to start. This common question is actually a critical test of a job candidate's communication skills, so it's important not to give an unprepared response or mess it up. "Tell me about yourself" is often the first question professional career coaches prepare people for when they give interview guidance. It's the opportunity for the candidate to take control of the narrative and tell their story in a way that really matters to the audience. It takes hard work and extensive preparation to answer this question well. (23) When a person goes to a job interview, their interviewer has presumably read the résumé, so they don't need to repeat the information. But that' what most people will do, as it's their instinct to recite things that are already on the résumé.

It's important for job seekers to do their homework on two crucial aspects. Firstly, they're not just telling someone the facts about themselves. They are telling a story, and stories take work to create. Coming up with a good story means getting reflective about what made their career accomplishments—something they're proud of, and what strengths those accomplishments highlight. Candidates should not pick a broad, general strength to elaborate on, such as "I'm smart", "I work hard" and "I get things done". (24) To come up with multiple career accomplishments or examples for different interview questions, job seekers should talk with others, especially people who know them—partners, friends or co-workers, who will bring up different stories from the ones they remember.

(25) Secondly, candidates should know what's at stake for the company with this job opening. What they really are asking you is "Tell me why you're going to help me." If the person is a prepared candidate, they should have already figured out those things. They've read the job description and researched the company on the Internet. What job applicants ought to be looking for is what the company is up to, what they are trying to accomplish, and what is preventing them from accomplishing those things.

How long should it take to answer? Around a minute. That's about right for most people's attention spans. Under a minute could seem rushed, while over two minutes will start to feel more like a speech. But the length of the answer is not an exact science, and candidates need to keep their career story focused and tailored to their audience.

"介绍一下你自己"似乎是工作面试时一个简单的问题。（22）但是这个问题的开放性常常让求职者不知从何开始。这一常见问题实际上是对求职者沟通能力的重要考验，所以不要毫无准备，也不要随意搞砸，这是相当重要的。职业规划师在给人进行面试指导时，"介绍一下你自己"通常是他们让学员准备的第一个问题。对于求职者来说，这是一个机会，能够让他们自己把控叙事节奏，以一种对听众真正重要的方式说出自己的故事。要想答好这个问题，需要努力练习，做好充分准备。（23）当求职者参加工作面试时，面试官可能已经提前浏览过简历，所以他们不必重复已有的信息。但大多数人还是会这么做，因为背诵简历上的信息是他们的本能。

对于求职者来说，在以下两个关键方面做好功课是十分重要的。第一，他们不仅仅是在告诉别人关于自己的事实。他们正在讲故事，而创造故事是需要费点功夫的。想出一个好故事意味着要回顾是什么使他们取得了职业成就，也就是值得他们自豪的事情，以及这些成就突出了哪些优势。求职者不能挑选比较宽泛、笼统的优势进行详述，如"我很聪明""我工作努力""我完成了任务"等。（24）为了想出多项职业成就或事例以应对不同的面试问题，求职者应该与其他人谈一谈，尤其是认识的人——伴侣、朋友或同事，他们能够想出一些他们记得的不同的故事。

（25）第二，求职者应该了解这个职位空缺对于公司有什么影响。面试官真正想问你的是"告诉我为什么你能帮助我"。如果求职者做好了万全的准备，那么他们对这些事情应该已经相当清楚了。他们已经阅读了职位说明，在网上研究过这家公司。求职者应该调查这家公司的业务是什么，致力于达成什么样的目标，以及实现目标的阻碍是什么。

回答这个问题需要多长时间呢？大约一分钟。刚好是大多数人的注意力持续时间。少于一分钟会显得过于仓促，而超过两分钟则会更像是一场演讲。但是回答多长时间并不是一项精准的科学数据，求职者需要让自己的职业故事有重点，为听众"订制"故事。

难词总结

open-ended /ˌəʊpən ˈendɪd/ a. 开放式的；无限制的
mess up 搞糟；陷入困境
instinct /ˈɪnstɪŋkt/ n. 天性；本能
come up with 提出；想出

at a loss 困惑不解；亏本
presumably /prɪˈzjuːməblɪ/ ad. 可能；大概
recite /rɪˈsaɪt/ v. 背诵；吟诵
span /spæn/ n. 持续时间；范围

题目精析

22. What does the speaker say about the job interview question "tell me about yourself"?

   A) Job candidates rarely take it seriously.

   B) Job seekers tend to have a ready answer.

   C) Job seekers often feel at a loss where to start in answering it.

   D) Job candidates can respond freely due to its open-ended nature.

22. 关于面试问题"介绍一下你自己"，说话者是如何看待的？

   A）求职者几乎不会认真对待这个问题。

   B）求职者往往会准备好答案。

   C）求职者往往不知所措，不知从何开始说起。

   D）因为这是一个开放性问题，所以求职者可以自由回答。

   【答案及分析】C。本题问说话者如何看待"介绍一下你自己"这个面试问题。音频中提到，But the open-ended nature of this question often leaves job seekers at a loss where to start.（但是这个问题的开放性常常让求职者不知从何开始。）C项为音频的同义表达，at a loss where to start 为原词复现，故 C 项正确。

23. What will most people do when they come to an interview?

   A) Follow their career coaches' guidelines.

   B) Strive to take control of their narrative.

   C) Do their best to impress the interviewer.

   D) Repeat the information on their résumé.

23. 面试时，大部分人会怎么做？

   A）遵循职业规划师的指导。

   B）努力控制叙事节奏。

   C）尽最大努力让面试官印象深刻。

   D）重复简历上的信息。

   【答案及分析】D。本题问面试时大部分人的做法。音频中提到，When a person goes to a job interview, their interviewer has presumably read the résumé, so they don't need to repeat the information. But that's what most people will do（当求职者参加工作面试时，面试官可能已经提前浏览过简历，所以他们不必重复已有的信息。但大多数人还是会这么做）。that's what most people will do 中的 that 指

代的就是 repeat the information，D 项中的 Repeat the information 为原词复现，故 D 项正确。

24. Why should job seeker talk with partners, friends and co-workers?

A) To reflect on their past achievements as well as failures.

B) To produce examples for different interview questions.

C) To discuss important details they are going to present.

D) To identify a broad general strength to elaborate on.

24. 为什么求职者应该与伴侣、朋友或是同事交谈？

A）为了反思过去的成就和失败。

B）为了给应对不同的面试问题提供事例。

C）为了讨论将要介绍的重要细节。

D）为了确定要详述的宽泛、笼统的优势。

【答案及分析】B。本题问求职者要与身边的人交谈的原因。音频中提到，To come up with multiple career accomplishments or examples for different interview questions, job seekers should talk with others, especially people who know them—partners, friends or co-workers（为了想出多项职业成就或事例以应对不同的面试问题，求职者应该与其他人谈一谈，尤其是认识的人——伴侣、朋友或同事）。B 项是音频的同义表达，B 项中的 examples for different interview questions 为原词复现，故 B 项正确。

25. What other important preparations should job seekers make before an interview?

A) Getting acquainted with the human resources personnel.

B) Finding out why the company provides the job opening.

C) Figuring out what benefits the company is able to offer them.

D) Tailoring their expectations to the company's long-term goal.

25. 面试前，求职者还应该做哪些重要的准备？

A）熟悉人力资源专员。

B）了解公司为什么会有空缺职位。

C）了解公司能够给他们提供什么好处。

D）根据公司的长期目标调整期望。

【答案及分析】B。本题问求职者在面试前应该做的重要准备。音频中提到，Secondly, candidates should know what's at stake for the company with this job opening.（第二，求职者应该了解这个职位空缺对于公司有什么影响。）B 项为音频的同义表达，job opening 为原词复现，故 B 项正确。

Part Ⅲ Reading Comprehension

Section A

【全文翻译】

　　几乎每一项需要或促进人际互动的活动都完全处于崩溃的状态中，因为冠状病毒的暴发扼杀了美国人出游的欲望。美国铁路公司说，预订量下降了 50%，取消量上涨了 300%。旧金山的酒店空置率也在 70% 至 80% 之间。周四晚上的百老汇一片黑暗。各大学在忙着清空校园，之前从未尝试过这么大规模的线上学习。亚马逊、苹果、《纽约时报》等白领公司要求员工在可预见的将来居家办公。

但是冠状病毒暴发之后发生了什么呢？

在某种程度上，答案是：一切照常。疫情夺走生命，抑制经济，打乱日常活动，但它终究会过去的。美国人永远不会停止观看篮球比赛，不会停止度假。他们会见面做生意。迄今为止，还没有任何一项使人分散的技术——如电话、电视、互联网——降低了人类握手的欲望，尽管技术专家的预测恰恰与此相反。

然而，我们也有理由相信事情不会回到像上周那样的状态。小的混乱会造成小的社会转变；大的混乱则会使事情永久改变。1980 年纽约的公交罢工被认为促使该市发生了一些长期变化，包括公交车道、自行车道，以及女性穿运动鞋上班。1918 年的西班牙流感推动了欧洲国家卫生保健的发展。

此时此刻，这甚至可能不是一个偏好的问题。游轮产业能否生存尚不清楚，也不清楚没有联邦政府的援助，公共交通产业会不会破产。现在的基础设施甚至可能没有到位，无法让我们做 2019 年正在做的事情。

难词总结

virtually /ˈvɜːtʃuəli/ ad. 几乎；差不多
facilitate /fəˈsɪlɪteɪt/ v. 促进；促使
meltdown /ˈmeltdaʊn/ n.（公司、机构或系统的）崩溃；情绪突然失控
erase /ɪˈreɪz/ v. 消除；消灭
dent /dent/ v. 损害，伤害；使凹陷
societal /səˈsaɪətl/ a. 社会的
in place 适当；在恰当的位置

题目精析

26. **N**。由 Hotels in San Francisco are experiencing _____ rates between 70 and 80 percent 可知空格处为 rates 的前置定语，起修饰作用，所以空格处需为形容词或名词，且作前置定语的名词需为单数形式。在所给选项中，C、E、F、K 项为形容词，H、I、N、O 项为名词单数。将所给选项代入句中，只有 N 项 vacancy（空缺）符合句意，与 rates 搭配意为"空置率"，故选 N 项。

27. **I**。由 Universities, now emptying their campuses, have never tried online learning on this _____ 可知空格处作介词 on 的逻辑宾语，且因空格前面为 this，故空格处为名词单数。在所给选项中，H、I、N、O 项符合语法要求，I 项 scale（规模，范围）代入文章后符合语义，意为"这种规模"，故选 I 项。

28. **F**。由 to work from home for the _____ future 可知空格处为 future 的前置定语，起修饰作用，可以填入形容词，在所给选项中，C、E、F、K 项为形容词，符合语法要求。此处的语境是要求员工之后在家办公，由此可知 F 项 foreseeable（可预见的）符合语义，意为"可预见的未来"，故选 F 项。

29. **J**。由 The pandemic will take lives, _____ economies and destroy routines 可知空格处为动词，与 economies 构成动宾短语，且和 take、destroy 并列，为动词原形。在所给选项中，I、J、M、O 项符合语法要求，但只有 J 项（抑制；扼杀）符合语义，代入文章后意为"抑制经济"，故选 J 项。

30. **G**。由 despite technologists' _____ to the contrary 可知空格处为名词。在所给选项中，A、D、G、H、I、N、O 项符合语法要求。上文提到：迄今为止，还没有任何一项使人分散的技术——如电话、电视、互联网——降低了人类握手的欲望，可知这种情况与技术专家的预测相反，G 项 predictions（预测）符合语义，故选 G 项。

31. **D**。由 Small _____ create small societal shifts 可知空格处为名词，且为复数形式，因为 create 为动词原形。在所给选项中，A、D、G 项符合语法要求。下文举例提到纽约的公交罢工事件，这是一件带有负面影响的事件，所以空格处所填名词也应带有负面感情色彩。D 项 disruptions（扰乱；妨碍）符合文章语义，故选 D 项。

32. **B**。由 The New York transit strike of 1980 is _____ with prompting several long-term changes in the city 可知空格处为动词的分词形式或形容词。在所给选项中，B、C、E、F、K、L 项符合语法要求。其中只有 B 项 credited 可与 be 动词和 with 搭配，构成短语 be credited with，意为"被认为……"，符合文章语义，故选 B 项。

33. **H**。由 this might not even be a question of _____ 可知空格处为名词，作介词 of 的逻辑宾语。在所给选项中，A、D、G、H、I、N、O 项符合语法要求。上文将一些社会事件分为 Small disruptions（小的混乱）和 big ones（大的混乱），由此可知空格处讨论的是在二者中进行一个偏向性的选择，即选择将这次的冠状病毒归为哪一类。H 项 preference 意为"偏好；喜爱"，符合文章语义，故选 H 项。

34. **M**。由 It's not clear that the cruise industry will _____ 可知空格处为动词原形，且空格后面没有宾语，所以该动词为不及物动词。在所给选项中，只有 M 项 survive（幸存；存活）符合语法要求，代入文章后意为"游轮产业能否生存尚不清楚"，符合文章语义，故选 M 项。

35. **E**。由 Or that public transit won't go broke without _____ assistance 可知空格处为形容词或名词，修饰 assistance。在所给选项中，C、E、F、K 项为形容词，A、D、G、H、I、N、O 项为名词，符合语法要求。本句的主语是 public transit（公共交通），且下文提到 infrastructure（基础设施），这些都与国家或政府有关，E 项 federal（联邦政府的；联邦制的）代入文章后意为"也不清楚没有联邦政府的援助，公共交通产业会不会破产"，符合文章语义，故选 E 项。

Section B

全文翻译

缓慢的希望

[A] 受"改变是可能的"这一观点的推动，我们的世界充满了几乎不为人知的关于缓慢的希望的故事。它们进展"缓慢"，而之所以缓慢，是因为它们伴随着挫折而生。

[B] 神话故事说，人类一开始就受苦受难，在寒冷和黑暗中瑟瑟发抖，直到巨人普罗米修斯从众神那儿盗来火种。正如神话所述，科技——首先是火和石器，然后是农耕、蒸汽机和工业、化石燃料、化学制品和核能——让我们能够改变和控制自然世界。神话也提醒我们，这些进步要付出代价：为了惩罚普罗米修斯的罪行，众神创造了潘多拉，并且给了潘多拉一个装满邪恶和诅咒的盒子。当潘多拉的盒子被打开时，就会向人类释放无数的疾病和灾难。

[C] 如今，我们不能再忽视那些为寻求温暖和舒适所释放出的生态诅咒。在设计、开发和改造栖息地的时候，我们已经打开了数以万计的潘多拉魔盒。最近几十年来，环境威胁已经超出区域界线，在全球蔓延，而最令人忧心的是，这些威胁的增长速率令人咋舌。我们经常被提醒，时间所剩无几。年复一年，速度越来越快，消耗超过了这个星球的生物容量。灾难加速的事件成倍增长。我们担

心电网崩溃，不可再生能源枯竭，沙漠扩张，岛屿消失，空气和水污染。

[D] 加速是我们这个时代的标志。在人类历史的长河中，人口和经济活动增长缓慢。几千年来，直到近代早期，世界经济一直都没有增长，但是大约从19世纪中叶开始，尤其是20世纪中叶以来，实际国内生产总值（GDP）和人类消耗都在以惊人的速度增长。中世纪时期，中欧家庭平均拥有的物品可能少于30件；1900年，这一数字上升到了400；2020年则达到了15 000。人类生产、消费和旅行的加快已经改变了有生命和无生命的范畴。它对人类赖以生存的自然进程也产生了影响。物种灭绝、森林砍伐、河流修坝、洪水暴发、臭氧损耗、海洋系统退化和许多其他领域都在加速。如果用图形表示的话，所有这些变化呈现的曲线将会像著名的曲棍球棒（效应）：这些数据数千年来几乎没有变化，却在过去几十年里急剧上升。

[E] 当今关于未来的一些叙述表明：我们也像普罗米修斯一样，需要一个新的大力神赫拉克勒斯，一位神圣的工程师，一位能够策划、安排和操控地球的人的拯救。他们认为地球工程、冷聚变和超光速宇宙飞船可能能够彻底冲破你能想到的地球上的所有限制——气温上升、能源匮乏、粮食短缺、空间不足、垃圾成山、水污染等。

[F] 但是，如果我们将自己的救赎寄托在一位解围之神、一位神圣的工程师或一位技术解决者身上，希望他们能凭空奇迹般地创造出一种新能源或另外一种革命性的万灵药，那我们可能就找错地方了。我们将自己的星球想象成一个整体这一事实，并不意味着"拯救"星球将随着全球人才的增加和技术的崛起而来。它更有可能是通多许多小的行动才得以实现。全球升温和环境退化并不是技术性问题，而是受到强大利益集团影响的高度政治性问题。此外，如果以史为鉴，那么我们可以假设，任何重大的转变都将带来一系列意想不到的后果。那我们该怎么办呢？

[G] 这一点相当清楚：我们要找到方法，帮助我们拉平那条反映生态急速恶化、社会步伐加快的曲棍球棒曲线。如果我们意识到人类对地球的操控是一种破坏性的力量，那我们也可以想象在未来几个世纪里，人类的努力可以帮助我们建立一个破坏性较小的世界。我们可能会一直犯错，但我们也将从错误中吸取教训。

[H] 为了对抗对灾难的恐惧，我们需要确定能够悄悄走向更有希望的未来的故事、愿景和行动。我们不需要一个宏大的叙事视角，一个富有传奇色彩的英雄意外拯救的故事，我们需要各种各样的故事——我们需要的不仅仅是普林斯顿大学罗博·尼克松所说的环境退化的"慢暴力"（即破坏往往在刚开始时是隐身的状态，然后缓慢、逐渐地发展）的故事，还需要我所说的"缓慢的希望"的故事。

[I] 我们需要承认当前的生态困境，也需要一种积极变革的表达方式，憧憬更加美好的未来。在《希望的原理》（1954—1959）一书中，主要的未来哲学家之一恩斯特·布洛赫写道："最悲惨的损失形式……是无法想象事物会变得不同"。我们需要确定能够帮助我们想象一个不同的、更公正和更生态的世界的愿景和途径。对布洛赫来说，希望始于恐惧、不确定和危机：它是一种能够与乌托邦式的"理想愿景"同行的创造性力量。在童话、小说、建筑、音乐、电影等过去的文化产品和在包含"美好世界的轮廓"的反映人类思想的产品中，都能找到希望的身影。人类之所以真实，是因为能够想象自己的"潜力"。换句话说：生活在希望中使得我们成为人类。

[J] 引起改变的小规模基层运动的力量扩大到了发源地之外，这在开始于20世纪80年代的意大利"慢食运动"中得到体现。"二战"后，快餐店的兴起打造了一个充斥着廉价工业食品的社会。在卡罗·佩特里尼的带领下，慢食运动在意大利的皮埃蒙特开始了，这个地区的贫困、暴力和反抗压迫的历

史由来已久。基于本地植物和动物品种，这项运动将皮埃蒙特改造成了一个适宜传统饮食文化发展的地区。如今，慢食运动在160多个或贫穷、或富有的国家展开，在全球范围内衍生了成百上千个项目，代表了民主政治、粮食主权、生物多样性和可持续农业。

[K] 无所顾忌的粮食商品化和粮食的破坏将继续破坏土壤、生计和生态。虽然慢食运动无法逆转全球食品经济发展势不可挡的局面，但它能让理论家们惴惴不安，能"发出不同的声音"，能让居民以及当地的饮食传统和环境蓬勃发展。即使是在美国这样的快餐国家，小型农场和都市花园也在增加。美国农业部门提供了一个都市农业工具包，并且最近的一份报告显示，美国的千禧一代正在改变自己的饮食习惯。2017年，美国有6%的消费者声称自己是严格的素食主义者，高于2014年的1%。正如美国诗人和环保活动家文德尔·贝利1989年提出的那样，随着越来越多的人意识到"吃是一种农业行为"，缓慢的希望便有了进展。

难词总结

unfold /ʌnˈfəʊld/ v.（使）展开；逐渐显现
shiver /ˈʃɪvə(r)/ v. 颤抖；哆嗦
swarms of 大群
multiply /ˈmʌltɪplaɪ/ v. 成倍增加；乘
outpace /ˌaʊtˈpeɪs/ v.（在速度上）超过
signature /ˈsɪɡnətʃə(r)/ n. 显著特征；签名
sphere /sfɪə(r)/ n. 范围；领域；球体
deforestation /ˌdiːˌfɒrɪˈsteɪʃn/ n. 毁林；滥伐森林
mastermind /ˈmɑːstəmaɪnd/ v. 策划，操纵
manipulate /məˈnɪpjuleɪt/ v. 操纵；影响
terrestrial /təˈrestriəl/ a. 陆地的；陆栖的
salvation /sælˈveɪʃn/ n. 解救；救赎
counter /ˈkaʊntə(r)/ v. 抵制；反驳
irresistible /ˌɪrɪˈzɪstəbl/ a. 不可遏制的；无法抵制的

setback /ˈsetbæk/ n. 挫折；阻碍
unleash /ʌnˈliːʃ/ v. 突然释放；发泄
hauntingly /ˈhɔːntɪŋli/ ad. 萦绕于心头地；难以忘怀地
dizzying /ˈdɪziɪŋ/ a. 使人眩晕的；使人头昏眼花的
catastrophe /kəˈtæstrəfi/ n. 灾难；灾祸
enormous /ɪˈnɔːməs/ a. 巨大的；庞大的
echo through 响彻；回荡
dramatic /drəˈmætɪk/ a. 突然的；令人吃惊的
manoeuvre /məˈnuːvə(r)/ v. 操纵；控制
transcend /trænˈsend/ v. 超越（通常的界限）
envisage /ɪnˈvɪzɪdʒ/ v. 想象；设想；展望
conjure up 使在脑海中显现；用魔法召唤
hospitable /hɒˈspɪtəbl/ a. 适宜的；热情友好的
flourish /ˈflʌrɪʃ/ v. 繁荣；昌盛

题目精析

36. It seems some people today dream that a cutting-edge new technology might save them from the present ecological disaster.

36. 如今人们似乎梦想有一种前沿的新技术能将他们从当前的生态灾难中解救出来。

【答案及分析】E。根据题干中的 a cutting-edge new technology 和 save them from the present ecological disaster 可以定位到 E 段。定位句指出，They suggest that geoengineering, cold fusion or faster-than-light spaceships might transcend once and for all the terrestrial constraints... mountains of waste, polluted water——you name it.（他们认为地球工程、冷聚变和超光速宇宙飞船可能能够彻底冲破你能想到的地球上的所有限制……垃圾成山、水污染等。）题干是定位句的同义转述。题干中的 a cutting-edge new technology 对应原文中的 geoengineering, cold fusion or faster-than-light spaceships；save them from the present ecological disaster 和 transcend once and for all the terrestrial constraints 为同义表达，故选 E 项。

37. According to one great thinker, it is most unfortunate if we lose the ability to think differently.

37. 一位伟大的思想家认为，最不幸的事情是失去用不同方式思考的能力。

【答案及分析】I。根据题干中的 one great thinker 和 the ability to think differently 可以定位到 I 段。定位句指出，Ernst Bloch, one of the leading philosophers of the future, wrote that "the most tragic form of loss... is the loss of the capacity to imagine that things could be different".（主要的未来哲学家之一恩斯特·布洛赫写道："最悲惨的损失形式……是无法想象事物会变得不同"。）题干中的 one great thinker 对应原文中的 one of the leading philosophers，most unfortunate 对应 the most tragic form of loss，lose the ability to think differently 是 is the loss of the capacity to imagine that things could be different 的同义表达，故选 I 项。

38. Urgent attention should be paid to the ecological problems we have created in our pursuit of a comfortable life.

38. 我们在追求舒适生活的过程中所制造的生态问题急需得到关注。

【答案及分析】C。根据题干中的 ecological problems 和 in our pursuit of a comfortable life 可以定位到 C 段。定位句指出，Today we can no longer ignore the ecological curses that we have released in our search for warmth and comfort.（如今，我们不能再忽视那些为寻求温暖和舒适所释放出的生态诅咒。）题干是定位句的同义转述。题干中的 ecological problems 对应原文中的 ecological curses，in our pursuit of a comfortable life 对应 in our search for warmth and comfort，故选 C 项。

39. Even in the fast-food nation America, the number of vegetarians is on the rise.

39. 即使是在美国这样的快餐国家，素食主义者的数量也在增加。

【答案及分析】K。根据题干中的 fast-food nation America、vegetarians、on the rise 可以定位至 K 段。定位内容为 Even in the United States—the fast-food nation（即使是在美国这样的快餐国家）和 In 2017, 6 per cent of US consumers claimed to be strictly vegetarian, up from 1 per cent in 2014（2017 年，美国有 6% 的消费者声称自己是严格的素食主义者，高于 2014 年的 1%）。题干中的 fast-food nation 和 vegetarians 为原词复现，on the rise 是 up from 1 per cent in 2014 的同义表达，故选 K 项。

40. The deterioration of the ecological system is accelerating because of the dramatic increase of human production and consumption.

40. 因为人类生产和消费活动的剧烈增加，生态系统加速恶化。

【答案及分析】D。根据题干中的 The deterioration of the ecological system is accelerating 和 the dramatic increase of human production and consumption 可以定位到 D 段。定位句指出，The acceleration of human production, consumption and travel has changed the animate and inanimate spheres.（人类生产、消费和旅行的加快已经改变了有生命和无生命的范畴。）题干中的 human production 和 consumption 为原词复现，且定位句的后面指出物种灭绝、森林砍伐、河流修坝等生态问题恶化加速，故选 D 项。

41. It is obvious that solutions must be found to curb the fast worsening environment and social acceleration.

41. 很明显，我们必须要找到解决方案，来遏制环境恶化加剧和社会的加快发展。

【答案及分析】G。根据题干中 solutions、curb the fast worsening environment and social acceleration 可以定位到 G 段。定位句指出，This much is clear: we need to find ways that help us flatten the hockey-stick curves that reflect our ever-faster pace of ecological destruction and social acceleration.（这一点相当清楚：我们要找到方法，帮助我们拉平那条反映生态急速恶化、社会步伐加快的曲棍球棒曲线。）

题干中的 It is obvious 是原文中 This much is clear 的同义表达，solutions must be found 是 need to find ways 的同义表达，the fast worsening environment and social acceleration 是 ever-faster pace of ecological destruction and social acceleration 的同义表达，故选 G 项。

42. Many people believe changing the world is possible, though it may take time and involve setbacks.

42. 许多人相信改变世界是可能的，尽管这需要时间，也会遇到挫折。

【答案及分析】A。根据题干中的 changing the world is possible 和 setbacks 可以定位到 A 段。定位句指出，Our world is... driven by the idea that change is possible... they are slow because they come with setbacks.（受"改变是可能的"这一观点的推动，我们的世界……而之所以缓慢，是因为它们伴随着挫折而生。）题干是定位句的同义转述，changing the world is possible 是原文中 change is possible 的同义表达，setbacks 为原词复现，故选 A 项。

43. It might be wrong to expect that our world would be saved at one stroke with some miraculous technology.

43. 期待用奇迹般的技术一下就能拯救世界的想法可能是错误的。

【答案及分析】F。根据题干中的 wrong、our world would be saved 和 one stroke with some miraculous technology 可以定位到 F 段。定位句指出，Yet, if we envisage our salvation... we might be looking in the wrong place... the "rescue" of our planet will come with one big global stroke of genius and technology.（但是，如果我们将自己的救赎寄托在……那我们可能就找错地方了……"拯救"星球将随着全球人才的增加和技术的崛起而来。）题干是定位句的同义转述，题干中的 It might be wrong 是原文中 looking in the wrong place 的同义表达，one stroke with some miraculous technology 对应原文中的 one big global stroke of genius and technology，故选 F 项。

44. It is human nature to cherish hopes for a better world.

44. 珍惜对更美好的世界的希望是人的本性。

【答案及分析】I。根据题干中的 human nature、hopes for a better world 可以定位到 I 段。定位句指出，It can be found... in products of the human mind that contain "the outlines of a better world". What makes us "authentic" as humans are visions of our "potential." In other words: living in hope makes us human.（……在包含"美好世界的轮廓"的反映人类思想的产品中，都能找到希望的身影。人类之所以真实，是因为能够想象自己的"潜力"。换句话说：生活在希望中使得我们成为人类。）题干中的 hopes for a better world 对应定位句中的 the outlines of a better world 和 living in hope，human nature 是定位句中 What makes us "authentic" as humans 的同义表达，故选 I 项。

45. Technology has given us humans the power to change the natural world, but we have paid a price for the change.

45. 科技给予了人类改变自然世界的力量，但人类也为此付出了代价。

【答案及分析】B。根据题干中的 Technology、change the natural world 和 have paid a price 可以定位到 B 段。定位句指出，technology... has allowed us to alter and control the natural world. The myth also reminds us that these advances have come at a price（科技……让我们能够改变和控制自然世界。神话也提醒我们，这些进步要付出代价）。题干中的 Technology 为原词复现，has given us humans the power to change the natural world 是定位句中 has allowed us to alter and control the natural world 的同义表达，have paid a price 是 have come at a price 的同义表达，故选 B 项。

Section C

Passage One

全文翻译

　　素质主义者通常讨厌被人强迫吃肉。然而,一项新的基于植物的"星球饮食"提议则隐晦地透露出强迫人们吃素的信息。这一点在印度最为明显。

　　今年年初,EAT-柳叶刀委员会发布了全球营养报告,呼吁全球转向多以植物为基础的饮食,"大量减少动物源食品的摄入"。在印度这类国家,这种呼吁可能会成为一种工具,加剧原本已经紧张的政治局面,增加本就营养不良的人群的压力。

　　EAT报告推测,在诸如印度这类国家的传统饮食中,红肉的量很少,他们只在一些特殊的场合食用红肉,或将红肉作为混合菜的配菜。

　　但是在印度,由于受到阶级、宗教、文化、成本、地理等无数因素的阻碍,印度人民想要吃的食物和不得不吃的食物之间有着巨大的差异。印度的政策制定者一贯向食肉人群推行以谷物为主的素食主义饮食,以此提供最廉价的食物来源。

　　如今,在印度教民族主义政府的激进统治下,穆斯林、基督教徒、劣势阶层和土著居民都被迫放弃自己的传统饮食。

　　这些担忧似乎完全没有受到 EAT-柳叶刀委员会代表布伦特·洛肯的认可,他说印度在从植物中摄取蛋白质方面堪当模范。

　　但是,印度的素食主义对世界能起多大的模范作用呢?2019年的全球饥饿指数显示,印度在117个国家中排行第102。全国家庭健康调查的数据表明,仅有10%的6~23个月大的婴儿得到充足的喂养。

　　这就是呼吁效仿印度以植物为基础的饮食,会给发展中国家本就脆弱的人群造成另一重击的原因。

　　针对富裕的西方国家的饮食未能认识到,在低收入国家,营养不良的儿童可以从牛奶和其他动物源食品中获益,在改善认知功能的同时降低营养不良的概率和死亡率。

　　EAT-柳叶刀委员会称其目的是在印度所有利益相关者之间"引发对话"。然而,对食品加工业和食品强化战略直言不讳的批评家却缺席了此次辩论,最明显的疏漏可能就是印度农民代表的缺席了。

　　然而,政府对于此项报告似乎很是赞同。政府没有改善有益健康、营养丰富的食品的获取途径,进而解决长期的饥饿和营养不良的问题,反而开门迎接依赖企业的解决方案,忽略环境和经济成本,这将破坏当地的食品体系。对后代而言,这是一种充满危险的模式。

难词总结

compel /kəmˈpel/ v. 强迫,迫使
substantially /səbˈstænʃəli/ ad. 大大地;基本上
tense /tens/ a. (气氛或局势)令人紧张的
aggressive /əˈɡresɪv/ a. 挑衅的;侵略的

reverse /rɪˈvɜːs/ a. 相反的;反向的
aggravate /ˈæɡrəveɪt/ v. 使严重;使恶化
undernourished /ˌʌndəˈnʌrɪʃt/ a. 营养不良的
indigenous /ɪnˈdɪdʒənəs/ a. 本地的;当地的

stakeholder /ˈsteɪkhəʊldə(r)/ n. 利益相关者
conspicuous /kənˈspɪkjuəs/ a. 易见的；明显的
chronic /ˈkrɒnɪk/ a. 长期的；慢性的
wholesome /ˈhəʊlsəm/ a. 有益健康的；有道德的

fortification /ˌfɔːtɪfɪˈkeɪʃn/ n. 强化；防御工事
omission /əˈmɪʃn/ n. 省略；删除
malnutrition /ˌmælnjuˈtrɪʃn/ n. 营养不良

题目精析

46. What is more visible in India than anywhere else according to the passage?

    A) People's positive views on the proposals for a "planetary diet".

    B) People's reluctance to be compelled to eat plant-based food.

    C) People's preferences for the kind of food they consume.

    D) People's unwillingness to give up their eating habits.

46. 根据这篇文章，什么在印度比在其他任何地方都要更为明显？

    A）人们积极看待"星球饮食"建议。

    B）人们不愿被迫吃素食。

    C）人们偏好吃某一种食物。

    D）人们不愿放弃自己的饮食习惯。

    【答案及分析】B。根据题干中的 more visible in India than anywhere else 可定位到第一段最后一句。该句指出，Nowhere is this more visible than in India.（这一点在印度最为明显。）句子中的 this 指代上文的内容，Vegetarians would prefer not to be compelled to eat meat. Yet the reverse compulsion is hidden in the proposals for a new plant-based "planetary diet".（素质主义者通常讨厌被人强迫吃肉。然而，一项新的基于植物的"星球饮食"提议则隐晦地透露出强迫人们吃素的信息。）这里需要理解 reverse compulsion（反向强迫）指的是"被迫吃素"，与被迫吃肉正好相反。B 项中的 reluctance to be compelled to eat plant-based food 对应原文中的 reverse compulsion，故 B 项正确。

47. What would the EAT-Lancet Commission's report do to many people in countries like India?

    A) Radically change their dietary habits. C) Make them even more undernourished.

    B) Keep them further away from politics. D) Substantially reduce their food choice.

47. EAT-柳叶刀委员会的报告可能会对像印度这类国家中的许多人造成什么影响？

    A）从根本上改变他们的饮食习惯。 C）使得他们更加营养不良。

    B）让他们远离政治。 D）大大地减少他们的食物选择。

    【答案及分析】C。根据题干中的 the EAT-Lancet Commission's report 和 in countries like India 可以定位到第二段。最后一句提到，In countries like India, that call could become a tool to aggravate an already tense political situation and stress already undernourished populations.（在印度这类国家，这种呼吁可能会成为一种工具，加剧原本已经紧张的政治局面，增加本就营养不良的人群的压力。）C 项是原文中 stress already undernourished populations 的同义表达，故 C 项正确。

48. What do we learn from the passage about food consumption in India?

    A) People's diet will not change due to the EAT-Lancet report.

    B) Many people simply do not have access to foods they prefer.

C) There is a growing popularity of a cereal-heavy vegetarian diet.

D) Policymakers help remove the barriers to peoples choice of food.

48. 从这篇文章中，我们可以了解到关于印度饮食消费的什么信息？

A）因为 EAT- 柳叶刀委员会报告的发布，人们不会改变饮食习惯。

B）许多人根本不能获取他们喜欢的食品。

C）以谷物为主的素食主义饮食越来越受欢迎。

D）政策制定者帮助人们清除食品选择的障碍。

【答案及分析】B。根据题干中的 food consumption in India 可以定位到第四段第一句。该句提到，In India, however, there is a vast difference between what people would wish to consume and what they have to consume（印度人民想要吃的食物和不得不吃的食物之间有着巨大的差异）。且第五段还提到，indigenous communities are being compelled to give up their traditional foods（土著居民都被迫放弃自己的传统饮食）。由此可知，有许多人民根本无法获取自己喜欢的食物，故 B 项正确。

49. What does the passage say about a plant-based diet modeled on India?

A) It may benefit populations whose traditional diet is meat-based.

B) It may be another blow to the economy in developing countries.

C) It may help narrow the gap between the rich and poor countries.

D) It may worsen the nourishment problem in low-income countries.

49. 关于以印度为模范的植物性饮食，这篇文章说了什么？

A）它可能对以肉食为基础的传统性饮食人群有益。

B）它可能是对发展中国家经济的另一重击。

C）它可能帮助缩小富裕国家和贫困国家之间的差距。

D）它可能会恶化低收入国家的营养问题。

【答案及分析】D。根据题干中的 a plant-based diet modeled on India 可以定位到第八段。该段提到，a plant-based diet modeled on India risk offering another ship with which to beat already vulnerable communities in developing countries（效仿印度以植物为基础的饮食，会给发展中国家本就脆弱的人群造成另一重击）。接着第九段提到，in low-income countries undernourished children are known to benefit from the consumption of milk and other animal source foods（在低收入国家，营养不良的儿童可以从牛奶和其他动物源食品中获益）。由此可知，以植物为基础的饮食会使得低收入国家或发展中国家的营养不良问题更加严重，故 D 项正确。

50. How does the Indian government respond to the EAT-Lancet Commission's proposals?

A) It accepts them at the expense of the long-term interests of its people.

B) It intends them to spark conversations among all Indian stakeholders.

C) It gives them approval regardless of opposition from nutrition experts.

D) It welcomes them as a tool to address chronic hunger and malnutrition.

50. 关于 EAT- 柳叶刀委员会的提议，印度政府做何反应？

A）它以国民的长期利益为代价接受该项提议。

B）它想要在印度的所有利益相关者之间引发对话。

C）它不顾营养专家的反对批准了这些提议。
D）它表示欢迎使用这些提议作为解决长期饥饿和营养不良的工具。

【答案及分析】A。根据题干中的 Indian government respond to the EAT-Lancet Commission's proposals 可以定位到最后一段。该段指出，The government, however, seems to have given the report a thumbs-up... ignoring the environmental and economic cost, which will destroy local food systems（然而，政府对于此项报告似乎很是赞同……忽略环境和经济成本，这将破坏当地的食品体系）。A 项是对该段的总结概括，其中，accepts them 对应原文中的 given the report a thumbs-up，故 A 项正确。

Passage two

全文翻译

早在 1964 年，精神病学家埃里克·伯恩在他的著作《人间游戏》中描述了一种他称之为"你为什么不呢——是的，但是"的对话模式。在日常生活中，这仍然是最令人恼火的方面之一。通常是习惯性抱怨的人采用这种策略。他们的人际、工作或是其他情况糟糕时，他们会无休止地抱怨，却又找借口拒绝他人提议的任何解决方案。当然，其原因从某种程度来看是他们并不想要解决方案；他们希望自己的处境——全世界都在挑他们的毛病——得到认可。如果他们能"赢得"这场游戏——驳回每一条建议，直到他们的对话者怒火中烧，最后放弃——他们就会在怨恨中感到理所应当，不需要履行任何做出改变的义务。

这里的部分问题是所谓的责任/过错谬误。当你感到为难时，比如被你的搭档视为理所应当，或者被迫为一个愚蠢至极的老板工作，你很容易就陷入这样的情境中：解决问题不是你的职责，否则就是在承认自己的错误。但这里有一处混淆。比如，如果我在家门口发现一个新生儿，这不是我的错，但它肯定是我的责任。我们可以做选择，但绝无可能去避开它们，因为试图忽略这件事本身就是一个选择。关键是，发生在家门口婴儿身上的事在任何情况下都是真实的：即使完全是对方错了，从长远来看，用这个作为逃避责任的理由也不会有任何好处。

如果你发现自己正在接收这种抱怨，有一种巧妙的方法可以阻断抱怨，即热情地表示同意。心理治疗师洛瑞·戈特利布将其描述为"过度认可"。一方面，你能幸免于抱怨，因为对方抱怨是为了确认自己的想法，而现在你正在确认。但另一方面，戈特利布指出，面对过度认可的人经常会重新审视他们的抱怨，然后开始反驳。那种认为他们完全无能为力的想法突然变得不切实际——更不用说让人恼火了——所以他们反而被激发产生关于如何改变事物的想法。

戈特利布写道："然后，有时一些神奇的事情可能发生。"对方"可能意识到自己并不像你所说的那样或她自己感觉到的那样被困住了"。这阐释了责任/过错谬误的讽刺意味：逃避责任感觉很舒服，但结果是一座监狱；而承担责任让人不愉快，但最终会得到解脱。

难词总结

psychiatrist /saɪˈkaɪətrɪst/ n. 精神病学家；精神科医生
dismiss /dɪsˈmɪs/ v. 对……不屑一顾；解散
take for granted 认为……理所应当

ceaselessly /ˈsiːsləsli/ ad. 不停地
resentment /rɪˈzentmənt/ n. 怨恨；愤恨
half-witted /ˌhɑːf ˈwɪtɪd/ a. 愚蠢至极的

justification /ˌdʒʌstɪfɪˈkeɪʃn/ n. 正当理由
ardently /ˈɑːdntli/ ad. 热烈地；热心地
generate /ˈdʒenəreɪt/ v. 产生；引起
evade /ɪˈveɪd/ v. 逃避；躲开
afresh /əˈfreʃ/ ad. 从头；重新

题目精析

51. What is characteristic of a chronic complainer, according to psychiatrist Eric Berne?

A) They only feel angry about their ill treatment and resent whoever tries to help.

B) They are chronically unhappy and ceaselessly find fault with people around them.

C) They constantly dismiss others' proposals while taking no responsibility for tackling the problem.

D) They lack the knowledge and basic skills required for successful conversations with their interlocutors.

51. 根据精神病学家埃里克·伯恩的说法，习惯抱怨的人有什么特点？

A）他们只对自己受到的虐待感到愤怒，憎恨那些任何试图帮助他们的人。

B）他们长期不快乐，不停地在周边人身上挑毛病。

C）他们不断地拒绝他人的建议，不承担解决问题的责任。

D）他们缺少与对话者成功交流所需的知识与技能。

【答案及分析】C。根据题干中的 a chronic complainer 和 psychiatrist Eric Berne 可以定位到第一段。本段提到了习惯抱怨的人的特点：find some excuse to dismiss any solution that's proposed（找借口拒绝他人提议的任何解决方案）和 excused from any obligation to change（不需要履行任何做出改变的义务）。C 项是对这两个特点的总结，dismiss others' proposals 是原文中 dismiss any solution that's proposed 的同义表达，taking no responsibility for tackling the problem 是原文中 excused from any obligation to change 的同义表达，故 C 项正确。

52. What does the author try to illustrate with the example of the newborn on one's doorstep?

A) People tend to think that one should not be held responsible for others' mistakes.

B) It is easy to become attached to the position of overlooking one's own fault.

C) People are often at a loss when confronted with a number of choices.

D) A distinction should be drawn between responsibility and fault.

52. 以家门口的新生儿举例，作者是想阐释什么？

A）人们往往认为一个人不应该为他人的错误负责。

B）人们容易陷入忽视自身错误的处境。

C）人们在面临很多选择时往往会不知所措。

D）应该要区分责任和过错。

【答案及分析】D。根据题干中的 the newborn on one's doorstep 可以定位到第二段。本题考查该项示例的作用，例子的前一句指出，But there's a confusion here.（但这里有一处混淆。）这处混淆就是本段首句提到的"责任/过错谬误"。由此可知，作者举新生婴儿的例子是用来说明责任和过错的区别，故 D 项正确。

53. What does the author advise people to do to chronic complainers?

A) Stop them from going further by agreeing with them.

B) Listen to their complaints ardently and sympathetically.

C) Ask them to validate their beliefs with further evidence.

D) Persuade them to clarify the confusion they have caused.

53. 作者建议人们如何应对习惯抱怨的人？

A) 同意他们的意见，进而阻止他们继续抱怨。

B) 热情并同情地倾听他们的抱怨。

C) 让他们用更多的证据来验证自己的想法。

D) 说服他们区分他们自己造成的混淆。

【答案及分析】A。根据题干中的 advise people to do to chronic complainers 定位到第三段第一句。该句指出，Should you find yourself on the receiving end of this kind of complaining, there's an ingenious way to shut it down—which is to agree with it, ardently.（如果你发现自己正在接收这种抱怨，有一种巧妙的方法可以阻断抱怨，即热情地表示同意。）A 项是该句中 to shut it down—which is to agree with it, ardently 的同义表达，A 项中的 agreeing with 为原词复现，故 A 项正确。

54. What happens when chronic complainers receive over-validation?

A) They are motivated to find ingenious ways to persuade their interlocutor.

B) They are prompted to come up with ideas for making possible changes.

C) They are stimulated to make more complaints.

D) They are encouraged to start arguing back.

54. 当习惯抱怨的人受到过度认可时会发生什么情况？

A) 他们被激励去寻找说服对话者的巧妙方式。

B) 他们被激励去思考做出可能的改变。

C) 他们被鼓励去做出更多的抱怨。

D) 他们被鼓励去开始反驳。

【答案及分析】B。根据题干中的 chronic complainers receive over-validation 定位到第三段。其中第四、第五句提到，people confronted with over-validation often hear their complaints afresh and start arguing back... they're prompted instead to generate ideas about how they might change things（面对过度认可的人经常会重新审视他们的抱怨，然后开始反驳……他们反而被激发产生关于如何改变事物的想法）。B 项为该句的同义表达，故 B 项正确。

55. How can one stop being a chronic complainer according to the author?

A) Analysing the so-called responsibility/fault fallacy.　　C) Assuming responsibility to free oneself.

B) Avoiding hazardous traps in everyday social life.　　D) Awaiting something magical to happen.

55. 作者认为怎样才能避免成为一个习惯抱怨的人？

A) 分析所谓的责任/过错谬误。　　C) 承担责任，以解放自己。

B) 避免日常社交生活中的危险陷阱。　　D) 等待一些神奇的事情发生。

【答案及分析】C。根据题干中的 stop being a chronic complainer according to the author 可以定位到最后一段。最后一句提到，evading responsibility feels comfortable, but turns out to be a prison; whereas assuming responsibility feels unpleasant, but ends up being freeing（逃避责任感觉很舒服，但结果是一

座监狱；而承担责任让人不愉快，但最终会得到解脱）。也就是说，应承担责任，解放自己。C 项是原文中 assuming responsibility feels unpleasant, but ends up being freeing 的同义表达，故 C 项正确。

Part IV Translation

参考译文

　　The Hong Kong-Zhuhai-Macau Bridge, with the total length of 55 km, is an extraordinary engineering feat of our country. Connecting three cities, the bridge is the longest sea-crossing and tunnel system in the world, which shortens the travel time among the three cities from 3 hours to 30 minutes. This huge-span reinforced concrete bridge fully proved that China has the ability to build record-breaking huge construction. It will prompt regional integration and economic growth. The bridge is the key to developing China's overall plan for the Great Bay Area. China wishes to build the Great Bay Area into an area that can rival the bay areas of San Francisco, New York and Tokyo in regard to technological innovation and economic prosperity.

难词总结

feat /fiːt/ *n.* 功绩；壮举
reinforced /riːɪnˈfɔːst/ *a.* 加固的；增强的
in regard to 关于

shorten /ˈʃɔːtn/ *v.* （使）变短；缩短
rival /ˈraɪvl/ *v.* 与……相匹敌；配得上

译点释义

1. 第一句中的"全长 55 公里"可以借助介词短语译为 with the total length of 55 km，"工程壮举"可以译为 engineering feat。
2. 第二句中的"将三个城市连接起来"可以译为 Connecting three cities，使句式简洁。第二句和第三句联系紧密，可以将第三句处理成 which 引导的非限制性定语从句。
3. 第四句中的"钢筋混凝土大桥"可以译为 reinforced concrete bridge。
4. 第五句中的"区域一体化"可以译为 regional integration。
5. 第六句中的"大湾区"可以译为 the Great Bay Area。
6. 第七句中的"将……建成……"可以译为 build... into...，"与……相媲美"可以借助动词 rival。

未得到监考教师指令前，不得翻阅该试题册！

2020年12月大学英语六级考试真题（第三套）

Part Ⅰ　　　　　　　　　Writing　　　　　　　　　(30 minutes)

（请于正式开考后半小时内完成该部分，之后将进行听力考试）

Directions: *For this part, you are allowed 30 minutes to write an essay on* **why students should be encouraged to develop creativity.** *You should write at least* **150** *words but no more than* **200** *words.*

Part Ⅱ　　　　　Listening Comprehension　　　　　(30 minutes)

说明：由于2020年12月六级考试全国共考了两套听力，本套真题听力与前两套内容相同，只是选项顺序不同，因此在本套真题中不再重复出现。

Part Ⅲ　　　　　Reading Comprehension　　　　　(40 minutes)

Section A

Directions: *In this section, there is a passage with ten blanks. You are required to select one word for each blank from a list of choices given in a word bank following the passage. Read the passage through carefully before making your choices. Each choice in the bank is identified by a letter. Please mark the corresponding letter for each item on* **Answer Sheet 2** *with a single line through the centre. You may not use any of the words in the bank more than once.*

Social distancing is putting people out of work, canceling school and tanking the stock market. It has been __26__ by fear, and it is creating even more fear as money problems and uncertainty grow. However, at its core is love, and a sacrifice to protect those most __27__ to the *coronavirus'*（冠状病毒）effects — the elderly, people with compromised immune systems, and those whose life-saving resources would be used up by a __28__ epidemic.

Americans make life-saving decisions every day as a matter of course. We cut food into bite-sized pieces, we wear seatbelts, and we take care not to exceed the speed limit. But social distancing is __29__ in that it is completely self-sacrificing. Those who will benefit may be the elderly relatives of the __30__ person we didn't pass in Starbucks, on the subway, or in the elevator.

Social distancing is millions of people making hundreds of sacrifices to keep the elderly alive. It doesn't include the __31__ to run from society or make an excuse to avoid one's obligations — such as life-saving medical work or the parental obligation to buy groceries. What it does include is applying love through caution. And in doing so, it offers an __32__ opportunity for those who care about the elderly to find new ways to love them.

If we're not __33__ as much in our normal work or school, we have extra time to call parents and grandparents. We can also ask elderly relatives how to best support them __34__ and use our sacrifices as an

1

opportunity to bring us, our community and the world ___35___.

A) amazing	I) sentimentally
B) closer	J) spiritually
C) driven	K) temptations
D) engaged	L) thriftier
E) malignant	M) tickled
F) oppressing	N) unique
G) premises	O) vulnerable
H) random	

Section B

Directions: *In this section, you are going to read a passage with ten statements attached to it. Each statement contains information given in one of the paragraphs. Identify the paragraph from which the information is derived. You may choose a paragraph more than once. Each paragraph is marked with a letter. Answer the questions by marking the corresponding letter on **Answer Sheet 2**.*

Why lifelong learning is the international passport to success

[A] Picture yourself at a college graduation day, with a fresh *cohort* (一群) of students about to set sail for new horizons. What are they thinking while they throw their caps in the air? What is it with this thin sheet of paper that makes it so precious? It's not only the proof of acquired knowledge but plays into the reputation game of where you were trained. Being a graduate from Harvard Law School carries that extra glamour, doesn't it? Yet take a closer look, and the diploma is the perfect ending to the modern tragedy of education.

[B] Why? Because universities and curricula are designed along the three unities of French classical tragedy: time, action, and place. Students meet at the university campus (unity of place) for classes (unity of action) during their 20s (unity of time). This classical model has traditionally produced prestigious universities, but it is now challenged by the digitalisation of society — which allows everybody who is connected to the internet to access learning — and by the need to acquire skills in step with a fast-changing world. Universities must realise that learning in your 20s won't be enough. If technological diffusion and implementation develop faster, workers will have to constantly refresh their skills.

[C] The university model needs to evolve. It must equip students with the right skills and knowledge to compete in a world "where value will be derived largely from human interaction and the ability to invent and interpret things that machines cannot", as the English futurist Richard Watson puts it. By teaching foundational knowledge and up-to-date skills, universities will provide students with the future-proof skills of lifelong learning, not just get them "job-ready".

[D] Some universities already play a critical role in lifelong learning as they want to keep the value of their diplomas. This new role comes with a huge set of challenges, and needs largely to be invented. One way to start this transformation process could be to go beyond the "five-year diploma model" to adapt curricula to lifelong learning. We call this model the lifelong passport.

[E] The Bachelor's degree could be your passport to lifelong learning. For the first few years, student would "learn to learn" and get endowed with reasoning skills that remain with them for the rest of their lives. For instance, physics allows you to observe and rationalise the world, but also to intergrate observations into models and, sometimes, models into theories or laws that can be used to make predictions. Mathematics is the language used to formulate the laws of physics or economy, and to make rigorous computations that turn into predictions. These two disciplines naturally form the foundational pillars of education in technical universities.

[F] Recent advances in computational methods and data science push us into rethinking science and engineering. Computers increasingly become principal actors in leveraging data to formulate questions, which requires radically new ways of reasoning. Therefore, a new discipline blending computer science, programming, statistics and machine learning should be added to the traditional foundational topics of mathematics and physics. These three pillars would allow you to keep learning complex technical subjects all your life because *numeracy*(计算)is the foundation upon which everything else is eventually built.

[G] According to this new model, the Master of Science (MSc) would become the first stamp in the lifelong learning journey. The MSc curriculum should prepare students for their professional career by allowing them to focus on acquiring practical skills through projects.

[H] Those projects are then interwoven with fast-paced technical *modules*(模块)learned "on-the-fly" and "at will" depending on the nature of the project. If, for instance, your project is developing an integrated circuit, you will have to take a module on advanced concepts in microelectronics. The most critical skills will be developed before the project even starts, in the form of *boot camps*(短期强化训练), while the rest can be fostered along with the project, putting them to immediate use and thus providing a rich learning context.

[I] In addition to technical capabilities, the very nature of projects develops social and entrepreneurial skills, such as design thinking, initiative taking, team leading, activity reporting or resource planning. Not only will those skills be actually integrated into the curriculum but they will be very important to have in the future because they are difficult to automate.

[J] After the MSc diploma is earned, there would be many more stamps of lifelong learning over the years. If universities decide to engage in this learning model, they will have to cope with many organisational challenges that might shake their unity of place and action. First, the number of students would be unpredictable. If all of a university's *alumni*(往届毕业生)were to become students again, the student body would be much bigger than it is now, and it could become unsustainable for the campus in terms of both size and resources. Second, freshly graduated students would mix with professionally experienced ones. This would change the classroom dynamics, perhaps for the best. Project-based learning with a mixed team reflects the reality of the professional world and could therefore be a better preparation for it.

[K] Sound like science fiction? In many countries, part-time studying is not exceptional: on average across OECD countries, part-time students in 2016 represented 20 per cent of enrolment in tertiary education. In many countries, this share is higher and can exceed 40 per cent in Australia, New Zealand and Sweden.

[L] If lifelong learning were to become a priority and the new norm, diplomas, just like passports, could be revalidated periodically. A time-determined revalidation would ease administration for everybody. Universities as well as employers and employees would know when they have to retrain. For instance, graduates from the year 2000 would have to come back in 2005.

[M] This could fix the main organisational challenges for the university, but not for the learners, due to lack of time, family obligations or funds. Here, online learning might be an option because it allows you to save your "travel time", but it has its limits. So far, none of the major employers associated with online learning platforms such as Coursera and Udacity has committed to hire or even interview graduates of their new online programmes.

[N] Even if time were not an issue, who will pay for lifelong learning? That's the eternal debate: should it be the learner's responsibility, that of his employer, or of the state? For example, in Massachusetts, the healthcare professions require continuing education credits, which are carefully evidenced and documented. Yet the same state's lawyers don't require continuing legal education, although most lawyers do participate in it informally. One explanation is that technology is less of a factor in law than it is in healthcare.

[O] Europe has many scenarios, but the French and Swiss ones are interesting to compare. In France, every individual has a right to lifelong learning organised via a personal learning account that is credited as you work. In Switzerland, lifelong learning is a personal responsibility and not a government one. However, employers and the state encourage continuing education either by funding parts of it or by allowing employees to attend it.

[P] Universities have a fundamental role to play in this journey, and higher education is in for a change. Just like classical theatre, the old university model produced talent and value for society. We are not advocating its abolition but rather calling for the adaptation of its characteristics to meet the needs of today.

36. Students should develop the key skills before they start a project.
37. By acquiring reasoning skills in the first few years of college, students can lay a foundation for lifelong learning.
38. The easy access to learning and rapid technological changes have brought the traditional model of education under challenge.
39. Unbelievable as it may seem, part-time students constitute a considerable portion of the student body in many universities across the world.
40. Some social and managerial skills, which are not easily automated, will be of great importance to students' future careers.
41. A new model of college education should provide students with the knowledge and skills that will make them more inventive and capable of lifelong learning.
42. A mixed student body may change the classroom dynamics and benefit learning.
43. The question of who will bear the cost of lifelong learning is a topic of constant debate.
44. To the traditional subjects of math and physics should be added a new discipline which combines computer science with statistics and other components.
45. Students who are burdened with family duties might choose to take online courses.

Section C

Directions: *There are 2 passages in this section. Each passage is followed by some questions or unfinished statements. For each of them there are four choices marked A), B), C) and D). You should decide on the best choice and mark the corresponding letter on **Answer Sheet 2** with a single line through the centre.*

Passage One

Questions 46 to 50 are based on the following passage.

Why does social media trigger feelings of loneliness and inadequacy? Because instead of being real life, it is, for the most part, impression management, a way of marketing yourself, carefully choosing and filtering the pictures and words to put your best face forward.

Online "friends" made through social media do not follow the normal psychological progression of an interpersonal relationship. You share neither physical time nor emotional conversations over the Internet. You simply communicate photographs and catchy posts to a diverse group of people whom you have "friended" or "followed" based on an accidental interaction. This is not to say that your social media friends can't be real friends. They absolutely can, but the two are not synonymous. Generally speaking, there are no unfiltered comments or casually taken photos on our social media pages. And, rightfully so, because it wouldn't feel safe to be completely authentic and vulnerable with some of our "friends" whom we don't actually know or with whom trust has yet to be built.

Social media can certainly be an escape from the daily grind, but we must be cautioned against the negative effects, such as addiction, on a person's overall psychological well-being.

As humans, we yearn for social connection. *Scrolling*（滚动）through pages of pictures and comments, however, does not provide the same degree of fulfillment as face to face interactions do. Also, we tend to idealize others' lives and compare our downfalls to their greatest accomplishments, ending in feelings of loneliness and inadequacy.

Social media can lead people on the unhealthy quest for perfection. Some people begin to attend certain events or travel to different places so that they can snap that "perfect" photo. They begin to seek validation through the number of people who "like" their posts. In order for it to play a psychological healthy role in your social life, social media should supplement an already healthy social network. Pictures and posts should be byproducts of life's treasured moments and fun times, not the planned and calculated image that one is putting out into cyberspace in an attempt to fill insecurities or unmet needs.

Ultimately, social media has increased our ability to connect with various types of people all over the globe. It has opened doors for businesses and allowed us to stay connected to people whom we may not otherwise get to follow. However, social media should feel like a fun experience, not one that contributes to negative thoughts and feelings. If the latter is the case, increasing face to face time with trusted friends, and minimizing time scrolling online, will prove to be a reminder that your social network is much more rewarding than any "like" "follow" or "share" can be.

46. What does the author imply social media may do to our life?
    A) It may facilitate our interpersonal relationships.
    B) It may filter our negative impressions of others.
    C) It may make us feel isolated and incompetent.
    D) It may render us vulnerable and inauthentic.
47. Why do people post comments selectively on social media?
    A) They do not find all their online friends trustworthy.
    B) They want to avoid offending any of their audience.
    C) They do not want to lose their followers.
    D) They are eager to boost their popularity.
48. What are humans inclined to do according to the passage?
    A) Exaggerate their life's accomplishments.   C) Paint a rosy picture of other people's lives.
    B) Strive for perfection regardless of the cost.   D) Learn lessons from other people's downfalls.
49. What is the author's view of pictures and posts on social media?
    A) They should record the memorable moments in people's lives.
    B) They should be carefully edited so as to present the best image.
    C) They should be shown in a way that meets one's security needs.
    D) They should keep people from the unhealthy quest for perfection.
50. What does the author advise people to do when they find their online experience unconstructive?

A) Use social media to increase their ability to connect with various types of people.
B) Stay connected to those whom they may not otherwise get to know and befriend.
C) Try to prevent negative thoughts and feelings from getting into the online pages.
D) Strengthen ties with real-life friends instead of caring about their online image.

Passage Two

Questions 51 to 55 are based on the following passage.

Imagine that an alien species landed on Earth and, through their mere presence, those aliens caused our art to vanish, our music to homogenize, and our technological know-how to disappear. That is effectively what humans have been doing to our closest relatives — *chimps*（大猩猩）.

Back in 1999, a team of scientists led by Andrew Whiten showed that chimps from different parts of Africa behave very differently from one another. Some groups would get each other's attention by rapping branches with their *knuckles*（指关节）, while others did it by loudly ripping leaves with their teeth. The team identified 39 of these traditions that are practiced by some communities but not others — a pattern that, at the time, hadn't been seen in any animal except humans. It was evidence, the team said, that chimps have their own cultures.

It took a long time to convince skeptics that such cultures exist, but now we have plenty of examples of animals learning local traditions from one another.

But just when many scientists have come to accept the existence of animal cultures, many of those cultures might vanish. Ammie Kalan and her colleagues have shown, through years of intensive fieldwork, that the very presence of humans has eroded the diversity of chimp behavior. Where we flourish, their cultures wither. It is a bitterly ironic thing to learn on the 20th anniversary of Whiten's classic study.

"It's amazing to think that just 60 years ago, we knew next to nothing of the behavior of our sister species in the wild," Whiten says. "But now, just as we are truly getting to know our *primate*（灵长类） cousins, the actions of humans are closing the window on all we have discovered."

"Sometimes in the rush to conserve the specie, I think we forget about the individuals," says Cat Hobaiter, a professor at the University of St. Andrews. "Each population, each community, even each generation of chimps is unique. An event might only have a small impact on the total population of chimps, but it may wipe out an entire community — an entire culture. No matter what we do to restore habitat or support population growth, we may never be able to restore that culture."

No one knows whether the destruction of chimp culture is getting worse. Few places have tracked chimp behavior over long periods, and those that have are also more likely to have protected their animals from human influence.

Obviously conservationists need to think about saving species in a completely new way — by preserving animal traditions as well as bodies and genes. "Instead of focusing only on the conservation of genetically based entities like species, we now need to also consider culturally based entities, " says Andrew Whiten.

51. What does the author say we humans have been doing to chimps?
    A) Ruining their culture.
    B) Accelerating their extinction.
    C) Treating them as alien species.
    D) Homogenizing their living habits.
52. What is the finding of Andrew Whiten's team?
    A) Chimps demonstrate highly developed skills of communication.
    B) Chimps rely heavily upon their body language to communicate.
    C) Chimps behave in ways quite similar to those of human beings.

D) Different chimp groups differ in their way of communication.

53. What did Ammie Kalan and her colleagues find through their intensive fieldwork?
    A) Whiten's classic study has little impact on the diversity of chimp behavior.
    B) Chimp behavior becomes less varied with the increase of human activity.
    C) Chimps alter their culture to quickly adapt to the changed environment.
    D) It might already be too late to prevent animal cultures from extinction.
54. What does Cat Hobaiter think we should do for chimp conservation?
    A) Try to understand our sister species' behavior in the wild.
    B) Make efforts to preserve each individual chimp community.
    C) Study the unique characteristics of each generation of chimps.
    D) Endeavor to restore chimp habitats to expand its total population.
55. What does the author suggest conservationists do?
    A) Focus entirely on culturally-based entities rather than genetically-based ones.
    B) Place more stress on animal traditions than on their physical conservation.
    C) Conserve animal species in a novel and all-round way.
    D) Explore the cultures of species before they vanish.

Part IV   Translation   (30 minutes)

Directions: *For this part, you are allowed 30 minutes to translate a passage from Chinese into English. You should write your answer on **Answer Sheet 2**.*

青藏铁路是世界上最高最长的高原铁路,全长1 956千米,其中有960千米在海拔4 000多米之上,是连接西藏和中国其他地区的第一条铁路。由于铁路穿越世界上最脆弱的生态系统,在建设期间和建成后都采取了生态保护措施,以确保其成为一条"绿色铁路"。青藏铁路大大缩短了去西藏的旅行时间。更重要的是,它极大地促进了西藏的经济发展,改善了当地居民的生活。铁路开通后,愈来愈多的人选择乘火车前往西藏,这样还有机会欣赏沿线的美景。

2020年12月大学英语六级考试真题解析
（第三套）

Part I Writing

成文构思

通过审题可知，题目要求写一篇关于"为什么要鼓励学生培养创造力"的议论文。可按照如下思路行文：

第一段：**点明主题**，随着经济发展，人们越来越注意到创造力的重要性；

第二段：**主体部分**，培养学生的创造力对个人、对社会、对国家都有益；

第三段：**总结**，学生应该培养创造力；社会和国家应该鼓励创新。

参考范文及译文

With the social and economic development, people **are more aware of** the importance of creativity, **especially** for students.

The reasons why students should develop creativity are as follows. First of all, creativity enables students to seize the chance and improve themselves. It is creativity that makes students more competitive when they graduate and apply for a job. Besides, excellent **innovative** students can be **deemed** a valuable and effective driving force to a prosperous and developed society. The more creative students are there in the society, the more **vibrant** the society will be. In addition, it is well-known that creativity is critical to our country. Only with more innovative people will China be a global leader in innovation.

In conclusion, creativity plays an important role in students' life and the development of the society as well as our country. So students should enhance their creativity, apart from which the society and the country should **take steps** to encourage innovation.

随着社会和经济的发展，人们越来越意识到创造力的重要性，尤其对学生更重要。

学生应该培养创造力的原因如下。首先，创造力能让学生抓住机会，提高自我。正是创造力使学生在毕业求职时更具竞争力。其次，优秀的有创造力的学生可以被视为社会繁荣和发展的宝贵而有效的驱动力。社会中有创造力的学生越多，社会就越有活力。此外，众所周知，创造力对我们的国家至关重要。只有拥有更多的创新型人才，中国才能成为全球创新的领导者。

总之，创造力在学生的生活、在社会和国家的发展中扮演着重要的角色。因此，学生应该提高他们的创造力，并且社会和国家应该采取措施鼓励创新。

词句点拨

be aware of 意识到
innovative /ˈɪnəveɪtɪv, ˈɪnəvətɪv/ a. 创新的；有创新精神的
vibrant /ˈvaɪbrənt/ a. 充满生机的；生气勃勃的
especially /ɪˈspeʃəli/ ad. 尤其；特别
deem /diːm/ v. 认为；视为
take steps 采取措施

1. With the social and ecomonic development, people are more aware of the importance of..., especially for...
   随着社会和经济的发展，人们越来越意识到……的重要性，尤其对……更重要。
2. The reasons why students should develop... are as follows.
   学生应该培养……的原因如下。
3. It is... that makes students more competitive when they graduate and apply for a job.
   正是……使学生在毕业求职时更具竞争力。
4. Only with more... people will China be a global leader in...
   只有拥有更多的……人才，中国才能成为全球……的领导者。

Part II Listening Comprehension

说明：由于2020年12月六级考试全国共考了两套听力，本套真题听力与前两套内容相同，只是选项顺序不同，因此在本套真题中不再重复出现。

Part III Reading Comprehension

Section A

全文翻译

扩大社交距离正在使人们失业、学校停课、股市暴跌。它由恐惧驱动，随着资金问题和不确定性的增加，它正在制造更多的恐惧。然而，其核心是爱，以及为了保护那些最容易受到冠状病毒影响的人而做出的牺牲，其中包括老年人、免疫系统受损的人和那些救生资源将被恶性流行病耗尽的人。

美国人每天都理所当然地做出拯救生命的决定。我们把食物切成一口就能吃下的大小，系上安全带，小心不要超过限速。但扩大社交距离的独特之处在于，它是完全的自我牺牲。受益人可能是我们在星巴克、地铁或电梯里不曾碰到的任何人的年长的亲戚。

扩大社交距离是数百万人为了让老人活下去而做出了数百种牺牲。它不包括逃离社会的诱惑，也不包括找借口逃避义务的诱惑——比如挽救生命的医疗工作或父母购买食品杂货的义务。它所包含的是谨慎地践行爱。通过这样做，它为那些关心老人的人提供了一个奇妙的机会，让他们找到新的方式来关爱老人。

如果我们没有在正常的工作或学习中投入很多的时间和精力，我们就有额外的时间给父母和祖父母打电话。我们也可以询问年长的亲戚如何在精神上给予他们最好的支持，并以我们的牺牲为机会，让我们、我们的社区和世界联系得更加紧密。

难词总结

distance /ˈdɪstəns/ v. 拉开距离；与……疏远
parental /pəˈrentl/ a. 父母的；双亲的
malignant /məˈlɪɡnənt/ a. 恶性的
sentimentally /ˌsentɪˈmentəli/ ad. 富有情感地

epidemic /ˌepɪˈdemɪk/ n. 流行病；蔓延
obligation /ˌɒblɪˈɡeɪʃn/ n. 义务
premise /ˈpremɪs/ n. 前提；假定
vulnerable /ˈvʌlnərəbl/ a. 脆弱的，易受……伤害的

题目精析

26. **C**。由 It has been _____ by fear 可知，空格前是 be 动词，空格后是 by，因此空格处应填入动词的过去分词，构成被动语态。C、D、M 项都是过去分词，但 D 项 engaged（从事；参与）、M 项 tickled（呵痒；使高兴）代入文中不符合语义，只有 C 项 driven（驱动）代入后符合文意，意为"它由恐惧驱动"，故选 C 项。

27. **O**。由 and a sacrifice to protect those most _____ to the coronavirus' effects 可知，most _____ to the coronavirus' effects 是 those 的后置定语，most 是最高级，因此空格处应填入形容词原级，且与 to 搭配。A、D、E、H、N、O 项都是形容词原级，但只有 O 项 vulnerable（脆弱的，易受……伤害的）与 to 搭配且代入后符合文意，意为"以及为了保护那些最容易受到冠状病毒影响的人而做出的牺牲"，故选 O 项。

28. **E**。由 whose life-saving resources would be used up by a _____ epidemic 可知，空格前是不定冠词 a，空格后是名词 epidemic，因此空格处应填入形容词。A、B、D、E、H、L、N 项均符合语法结构，但只有 E 项 malignant（恶性的）代入后符合文意，意为"那些救生资源将被恶性流行病耗尽的人"，故选 E 项。

29. **N**。由 But social distancing is _____ in that it is completely self-sacrificing 可知，空格前是 be 动词，因此空格处应填入形容词、分词或不可数名词作表语。A、B、D、F、H、L、M、N 项均符合语法结构，但只有 N 项 unique（独特的）代入后符合文意，意为"但扩大社交距离的独特之处在于，它是完全的自我牺牲"，故选 N 项。

30. **H**。由 the elderly relatives of the _____ person we didn't pass in Starbucks... 可知，空格前是定冠词 the，空格后是名词 person，因此空格处应填入形容词，A、B、D、H、L 项均符合语法结构。根据 person 后的定语从句 we didn't pass in Starbucks 可知，这是我们日常生活场景中不会碰到的人，具有随机性，H 项 random（任意的）代入文中符合文意，意为"我们在星巴克……不曾碰到的任何人的年长的亲戚"，故选 H 项。

31. **K**。由 It doesn't include the _____ to run from society or make an excuse... 可知，空格前是动词 include

和定冠词 the，因此空格处应填名词。G、K 项都是名词，G 项 premises（前提；假定）代入后不符合语义和逻辑，K 项 temptations（诱惑）代入后符合文意，意为"它不包括逃离社会的诱惑，也不包括找借口……"，故选 K 项。

32. A。由 it offers an _____ opportunity for those 可知，空格前是不定冠词 an，空格后是名词 opportunity，因此空格处应填以元音音素开头的形容词。A、D 项符合语法结构，A 项 amazing（令人惊喜的）代入后符合文意，意为"它为那些人提供了一个奇妙的机会"；D 项 engaged（忙于；被占用的）代入后不符合语义和逻辑，故排除。故选 A 项。

33. D。由 If we're not _____ as much in our normal work or school 可知，空格前是 be 动词，空格后是状语，因此空格处应填入形容词或分词作表语。B、D、F、L、M 项符合语法结构，但只有 D 项 engaged（忙于；被占用的）代入后符合文意，意为"如果我们没有在正常的工作或学习中投入很多的时间和精力"，故选 D 项。

34. J。由 We can also ask elderly relatives how to best support them _____ 可知，空格所在句主干完整，且有 best 最高级限定，因此空格处应填副词原级。I、J 项符合语法结构，I 项 sentimentally（富有情感地）代入后不符合语义和逻辑，J 项 spiritually（在精神上）代入后符合文意，意为"我们也可以询问年长的亲戚如何在精神上给予他们最好的支持"，故选 J 项。

35. B。由 bring us, our community and the world _____ 可知，空格所在部分意为"让我们、我们的社区和世界_____"，B 项 closer（更紧密的）代入后可作宾语补足语，意为"让我们、我们的社区和世界联系得更加紧密"，符合语义和逻辑，故选 B 项。

Section B

全文翻译

为什么终身学习是成功的"国际通行证"

[A] 想象你自己在大学毕业那一天，和新的一群即将启航开拓新领域的学生在一起。当他们把帽子扔向空中时，他们在想什么？到底是什么使这张纸（毕业证）如此珍贵？它不仅是所获得知识的证明，还在"你从哪所学校毕业？"的名誉游戏中发挥重要作用。成为哈佛大学法学院的毕业生会有额外的魅力，不是吗？但仔细一看，文凭是现代教育悲剧的完美结局。

[B] 为什么？因为大学和课程都是按照法国古典悲剧的三一律来设计的：时间、情节和地点。学生们在 20 多岁时（时间统一）聚集在大学校园里（地点统一）上课（情节统一）。在传统上，这一经典模式造就了许多著名的大学，但现在它受到了社会数字化的挑战——社会数字化允许每个人通过互联网来学习，每个人都需要获得技能来跟上快速变化的世界，这也对该模式带来了挑战。大学必须意识到，仅仅在 20 多岁学习是不够的。如果技术的传播和实施发展得更快，员工将必须不断更新他们的技能。

[C] 大学模式需要逐步发展。正如英国未来学家理查德·沃森所言，"这个世界的价值主要源于人与人之间的互动，以及拥有机器不具备的发明和解释事物的能力"，大学必须让学生具备适当的技能和知识，以便在这个世界中竞争。通过教授基础知识和最新技能，大学将为学生提供不会过时的终身学习技能，而不仅仅是让他们"做好就业准备"。

[D] 有些大学已经在终身学习中扮演了重要的角色，因为他们想保持他们学校文凭的价值。这个新角色伴随着一系列巨大的挑战，在很大程度上需要创新。开始这一转变过程的一种方法可能是超越"五年制文凭模式"，使课程适应终身学习。我们称这种模式为"终身通行证"。

[E] 学士学位可以成为你终身学习的通行证。在最初的几年里，学生们将"学会学习"，并获得伴随他们余生的推理能力。例如，物理学不但让你观察世界，合理地解释世界，而且让你把观察结果整合成模型，有时，还将模型整合成理论或定律，用来预测。数学是一种语言，用来阐明物理或经济定律，并进行严格的计算以得出预测。这两门学科自然形成了技术大学教育的重要支柱。

[F] 计算方法和数据科学的最新进展促使我们重新思考科学和工程学。计算机越来越成为利用数据来提出问题的主要角色，这需要全新的推理方法。因此，在数学和物理的传统基础课题中应加入一门融合了计算机科学、编程、统计学和机器学习的新学科。这三个支柱学科将使你终身都能学习复杂的技术科目，因为计算能力是其他一切学科最终建立的基础。

[G] 根据这个新模式，理学硕士将成为终身学习之旅的第一个印章。理学硕士课程应该让学生专注于通过项目来获取实践技能，以此为职业生涯做准备。

[H] 然后，根据项目的性质，将这些项目与"实时"和"随意"学习的快节奏技术模块相互交织。例如，如果你的项目是开发集成电路，你就必须学习一个关于微电子学先进概念的模块。甚至在项目开始之前，最关键的技能将以短期强化训练的形式开发出来，而其余的技能可以随着项目的进程一起培养，现学现用，从而提供丰富的学习环境。

[I] 除了技术能力，项目本身也会培养社交技能和创业技能，如设计思维、主动性、团队领导、活动报告或资源规划。这些技能不仅会真正融入课程中，而且在未来会变得非常重要，因为它们很难实现自动化。

[J] 在获得理学硕士学位后，学生在多年内会有更多的终身学习印章。如果大学决定采用这种学习模式，他们将不得不应对许多组织方式上的挑战，这些挑战可能动摇地点统一和情节统一。首先，学生的数量是不可预测的。如果一所大学的所有往届毕业生都重新成为学生，学生群体将比现在大得多，校园在规模和资源上都可能无法维持。其次，刚毕业的学生会和有专业经验的学生混在一起。这将改变课堂上的互动，也许产生最好的结果。和混合团队进行以项目为基础的学习反映了职场的现实，因此可以为职场做更好的准备。

[K] 听起来像科幻小说吗？在许多国家，非全日制学习并不罕见：在经合组织成员国，2016年非全日制学生平均占高等教育招生人数的20%。在许多国家，这一比例更高，在澳大利亚、新西兰和瑞典可能超过40%。

[L] 如果终身学习成为当务之急，并且成为新的规范，那么文凭就像护照一样，可以定期重新验证。

在一段时间内重新验证将简化每个人的管理。大学以及雇主和雇员都知道他们什么时候需要再培训。例如，2000年的毕业生必须在2005年回来接受再培训。

[M] 终身学习可以解决大学面临的主要的组织方式上的挑战，但因为缺乏时间、家庭义务或资金，它不能解决学习者的问题。此时，在线学习可能是一个选择，因为它可以节省你的"通勤时间"，但它有其局限性。迄今为止，在与Coursera和Udacity等在线学习平台相关的主要雇主中，没有一家承诺招聘甚至面试他们新开设的在线课程的毕业生。

[N] 即使时间不是问题，谁来为终身学习买单呢？这是一个永恒的争论：这应该是学习者的责任、雇主的责任，还是国家的责任呢？例如，在马萨诸塞州，医疗保健专业需要继续教育的学分，这些学分需要经过仔细的证明和记录。然而，同一个州的律师不需要继续接受法律教育，尽管大多数律师确实非正式地接受了继续教育。一种解释是，技术在法律中的影响比在医疗保健中的影响要小。

[O] 欧洲各国情况各异，但法国和瑞士的情况比照来看很有趣。在法国，每个人都有权利通过个人学习账户进行终身学习，在你学习时，会给你计入学分。在瑞士，终身学习是个人的责任而不是政府的责任。然而，雇主和国家通过提供部分教育资金或允许雇员参加继续教育来鼓励继续教育。

[P] 在这一过程中，大学扮演着重要的角色，高等教育正在发生变化。就像古典戏剧一样，旧的大学模式为社会培养了人才，创造了价值。我们不是提倡废除它，而是呼吁调整它的特点，以满足当今的需要。

难词总结

diploma /dɪˈpləʊmə/ *n.* 文凭
digitalisation /ˌdɪdʒɪtəlaɪˈzeɪʃən/ *n.* 数字化
implementation /ˌɪmplɪmenˈteɪʃn/ *n.* 实施；执行
rigorous /ˈrɪɡərəs/ *a.* 谨慎的；细致的
tertiary education 高等教育
advocate /ˈædvəkeɪt/ *v.* 提倡；支持；拥护

prestigious /preˈstɪdʒəs/ *a.* 有威望的；声誉高的
diffusion /dɪˈfjuːʒn/ *n.* 扩散；弥漫
future-proof /ˈfjuːtʃə pruːf/ *a.* 不会过时的
exceptional /ɪkˈsepʃənl/ *a.* 罕见的；杰出的
revalidate /ˌriːˈvælɪdeɪt/ *v.* 使重新生效
abolition /ˌæbəˈlɪʃn/ *n.* 废除，废止

题目精析

36. Students should develop the key skills before they start a project.

36. 在开始项目之前，学生应该培养关键技能。

【答案及分析】H。根据题干中的 the key skills 和 before they start a project 定位到 H 段。定位句指出，The most critical skills will be developed before the project even starts（甚至在项目开始之前，最关键的技能将以短期强化训练的形式开发出来）。题干是该句的同义表达，其中 the key skills 是原文中 The most critical skills 的同义表达，before they start a project 是原文中 before the project even starts 的同义表达，故选 H 项。

37. By acquiring reasoning skills in the first few years of college, students can lay a foundation for lifelong

learning.

37. 通过前几年在大学学习推理技能，学生能为终身学习打下基础。

【答案及分析】E。根据题干中的 acquiring reasoning skills 和 lay a foundation for lifelong learning 定位到 E 段。定位句指出，For the first few years, students would "learn to learn" and get endowed with reasoning skills that remain with them for the rest of their lives.（在最初的几年里，学生们将"学会学习"，并获得伴随他们余生的推理能力。）其中，题干中的 in the first few years 是原文中 For the first few years 的同义表达，acquiring reasoning skills 是原文中 get endowed with reasoning skills 的同义表达，lay a foundation for lifelong learning 是原文中 remain with them for the rest of their lives 的同义表达，故选 E 项。

38. The easy access to learning and rapid technological changes have brought the traditional model of education under challenge.

38. 便捷的学习方式和快速的技术变革使传统的教育模式面临挑战。

【答案及分析】B。根据题干中的 the traditional model of education under challenge 定位到 B 段。定位句指出，This classical model has traditionally produced prestigious universities, but it is now challenged by the digitalisation of society — which allows everybody who is connected to the internet to access learning — and by the need to acquire skills in step with a fast-changing world.（在传统上，这一经典模式造就了许多著名的大学，但现在它受到了社会数字化的挑战——社会数字化允许每个人通过互联网来学习，每个人都需要获得技能来跟上快速变化的世界，这也对该模式带来了挑战。）题干是该句的同义表达，其中，题干中的 The easy access to learning 是原文中 which allows everybody who is connected to the internet to access learning 的同义表达，rapid technological changes 是原文中 a fast-changing world 的同义表达，the traditional model of education 对应原文中的 This classical model，故选 B 项。

39. Unbelievable as it may seem, part-time students constitute a considerable portion of the student body in many universities across the world.

39. 虽然看起来令人难以置信，但是非全日制学生在全世界很多大学的学生群体中占比相当大。

【答案及分析】K。根据题干中的 part-time students 和 a considerable portion 定位到 K 段。定位句指出，Sound like science fiction? In many countries, part-time studying is not exceptional: on average across OECD countries, part-time students in 2016 represented 20 per cent of enrolment in tertiary education. In many countries, this share is higher and can exceed 40 per cent in Australia, New Zealand and Sweden.（听起来像科幻小说吗？在许多国家，非全日制学习并不罕见：在经合组织成员国，2016 年非全日制学生平均占高等教育招生人数的 20%。在许多国家，这一比例更高，在澳大利亚、新西兰和瑞典可能超过 40%。）其中，题干中的 Unbelievable as it may seem 是原文中 Sound like science fiction 的同义表达，part-time students 是原词复现，同时对应原文中的 part-time studying，a considerable portion 对应原文中的 20 per cent 和 can exceed 40 per cent，across the world 对应原文中的 In many countries、across OECD countries 和 in Australia, New Zealand and Sweden，故选 K 项。

40. Some social and managerial skills, which are not easily automated, will be of great importance to students' future careers.

40. 一些不容易自动化的社交和管理技能对学生未来的职业非常重要。

【答案及分析】I。根据题干中的 social and managerial skills 和 not easily automated 定位到 I 段。定位句指出，the very nature of projects develops social and entrepreneurial skills... Not only will those skills be actually integrated into the curriculum but they will be very important to have in the future because they are difficult to automate.（项目本身也会培养社交技能和创业技能……这些技能不仅会真正融入课程中，而且在未来会变得非常重要，因为它们很难实现自动化。）其中，题干中的 social and managerial skills 是原文中 social and entrepreneurial skills 的同义表达，同时对应原文中的 those skills，which are not easily automated 是原文中 they are difficult to automate 的同义表达，will be of great importance to students' future careers 是原文中 will be very important to have in the future 的同义表达，故选 I 项。

41. A new model of college education should provide students with the knowledge and skills that will make them more inventive and capable of lifelong learning.

41. 一种新的大学教育模式应该为学生提供知识和技能，使学生更具创造力和终身学习的能力。

【答案及分析】C。根据题干中的 A new model of college education 和 inventive and capable of lifelong learning 定位到 C 段。定位句指出，The university model needs to evolve. It must equip students with the right skills and knowledge... By teaching foundational knowledge and up-to-date skills, universities will provide students with the future-proof skills of lifelong learning（大学模式需要逐步发展。大学必须让学生具备适当的技能和知识……通过教授基础知识和最新技能，大学将为学生提供不会过时的终身学习技能）。其中，题干中的 A new model of college education 是原文中 The university model needs to evolve 的同义表达，should provide students with the knowledge and skills 是原文中 must equip students with the right skills and knowledge 的同义表达，同时对应原文中的 foundational knowledge and up-to-date skills，capable of lifelong learning 是原文中 the future-proof skills of lifelong learning 的同义表达，故选 C 项。

42. A mixed student body may change the classroom dynamics and benefit learning.

42. 混合的学生群体可能改变课堂上的互动，并且有利于学习。

【答案及分析】J。根据题干中的 A mixed student body 和 change the classroom dynamics 定位到 J 段。定位句指出，Second, freshly graduated students would mix with professionally experienced ones. This would change the classroom dynamics, perhaps for the best.（其次，刚毕业的学生会和有专业经验的学生混在一起。这将改变课堂上的互动，也许产生最好的结果。）其中，题干中的 A mixed student body 是对原文中 freshly graduated students would mix with professionally experienced ones 的总结，change the classroom dynamics 是原词复现，benefit learning 对应原文中的 for the best，故选 J 项。

43. The question of who will bear the cost of lifelong learning is a topic of constant debate.

43. 谁来承担终身学习的费用是一个争论不休的话题。

【答案及分析】N。根据题干中的 bear the cost of lifelong learning 和 constant debate 定位到 N 段。定位句指出，Even if time were not an issue, who will pay for lifelong learning? That's the eternal debate: should it be the learner's responsibility, that of his employer, or of the state?（即使时间不是问题,谁来为终身学习买单呢？这是一个永恒的争论：这应该是学习者的责任、雇主的责任、还是国家的责任呢？）其中，题干中的 bear the cost of lifelong learning 是原文中 pay for lifelong learning 的同义表达，constant debate 是原

文中 the eternal debate 的同义表达，故选 N 项。

44. To the traditional subjects of math and physics should be added a new discipline which combines computer science with statistics and other components.

44. 在数学和物理的传统科目上应加入一门将计算机科学、统计学和其他内容相结合的新学科。

【答案及分析】F。根据题干中的 the traditional subjects of math and physics 和 added a new discipline 定位到 F 段。定位句指出，Therefore, a new discipline blending computer science, programming, statistics and machine learning should be added to the traditional foundational topics of mathematics and physics.（因此，在数学和物理的传统基础课题中应加入一门融合了计算机科学、编程、统计学和机器学习的新学科。）其中，题干中的 the traditional subjects of math and physics 是原文中 the traditional foundational topics of mathematics and physics 的同义表达，should be added、a new discipline 是原词复现，combines computer science with statistics and other components 是原文中 blending computer science, programming, statistics and machine learning 的同义表达，故选 F 项。

45. Students who are burdened with family duties might choose to take online courses.

45. 有家庭负担的学生可以选择学习在线课程。

【答案及分析】M。根据题干中的 family duties 和 online courses 定位到 M 段。定位句指出，but not for the learners, due to lack of time, family obligations or funds. Here, online learning might be an option（但因为缺乏时间、家庭义务或资金，它不能解决学习者的问题。此时，在线学习可能是一个选择）。其中，题干中的 family duties 是原文中 family obligations 的同义表达，might choose to take online courses 是原文中 online learning might be an option 的同义表达，故选 M 项。

Section C

Passage One

全文翻译

为什么社交媒体会引发孤独感和自卑感？因为它不是真实的生活，它在很大程度上是一种印象管理，一种营销自己的方式，仔细挑选和筛选图片和文字，把你最好的一面展现出来。

通过社交媒体结交的网友并不遵循人际关系的正常心理发展过程。在互联网上，你们既不共度时间，也不进行情感交流。你只是简单地向一群不同的人发送照片和有吸引力的帖子，而这些人是你在偶然的互动中加了"好友"或"关注"的。这并不是说你在社交媒体上交的朋友就不能成为真正的朋友。他们绝对可以，但这两者不是等同的概念。一般来说，在我们的社交媒体主页上没有未经筛选的评论或随意拍摄的照片。而且，这是有道理的，因为在我们并不真正认识或还没有建立信任的一些"朋友"面前，展示完全真实和脆弱的自己会让我们感到不安全。

社交媒体当然可以作为逃避日常工作的出口，但我们必须警惕沉迷社交网络等对一个人的整体心理健康产生的负面影响，比如上瘾。

作为人类，我们渴望社会联系。然而，浏览一页页的图片和评论并不能提供像面对面交流那么多的满足感。同时，我们倾向于将他人的生活理想化，将自己的失败与他人最大的成就相比较，最终以孤独感和自卑感告终。

社交媒体会导致人们病态地追求完美。有些人开始参加某些活动或到不同的地方旅行，以便他们可以抓拍"完美"的照片。他们开始通过"点赞"他们帖子的人数来寻求认可。为了让社交媒体在社会生活中发挥有利于心理健康的作用，它应该补充完善一个已经相对健康的社交网络。照片和帖子应该是生活中珍贵时刻和快乐时光的副产品，而不是某人为了弥补不安全感或满足需求而在网络空间上发布的精心计划、设计的形象。

最终，社交媒体提高了我们与世界各地形形色色的人联系的能力。它为企业打开了大门，让我们与那些我们在现实生活中不会关注的人保持联系。然而，社交媒体应该给人一种有趣的体验，而不是一种助长消极想法和情绪的体验。如果出现后者的情况，增加与信任的朋友面对面交流的时间，最大限度地减少上网浏览的时间，这将提醒我们，你的社交圈比任何"点赞""关注"或"分享"都更有回报。

难词总结

inadequacy /ɪnˈædɪkwəsi/ *n.* 缺乏信心；不充分
psychological /ˌsaɪkəˈlɒdʒɪkl/ *a.* 心理的；心理学的
synonymous /sɪˈnɒnɪməs/ *a.* 同义的
caution /ˈkɔːʃn/ *v.* 警告；告诫；提醒

filter /ˈfɪltə(r)/ *v.* 筛选；过滤
catchy /ˈkætʃi/ *a.* 引人注意的
authentic /ɔːˈθentɪk/ *a.* 真正的；真实的
downfall /ˈdaʊnfɔːl/ *n.* 衰落；衰败

题目精析

46. What does the author imply social media may do to our life?

   A) It may facilitate our interpersonal relationships.

   B) It may filter our negative impressions of others.

   C) It may make us feel isolated and incompetent.

   D) It may render us vulnerable and inauthentic.

46. 作者暗示社交媒体可能对我们的生活产生什么影响？

   A）它可能会促进我们的人际关系。

   B）它可能会美化我们对他人的负面印象。

   C）它可能会让我们感到孤独和无力。

   D）它可能会使我们变得脆弱，脱离现实。

【答案及分析】C。根据题干关键词 imply 和 social media may do to our life 定位到第一段。第一句指出，Why does social media trigger feelings of loneliness and inadequacy？（为什么社交媒体会引发孤独感和自卑感？）C 项是该句的同义表达，其中，isolated 对应原文中的 loneliness，incompetent 对应原文中的 inadequacy，故选 C 项。

47. Why do people post comments selectively on social media?

　　A) They do not find all their online friends trustworthy.

　　B) They want to avoid offending any of their audience.

　　C) They do not want to lose their followers.

　　D) They are eager to boost their popularity.

47. 为什么人们在社交媒体上有选择性地发表评论？

　　A）他们并不认为所有网友都值得信赖。

　　B）他们试图避免冒犯任何一位观众。

　　C）他们不想要失去关注他们的人。

　　D）他们渴望大受欢迎。

　　【答案及分析】A。根据题干关键词 post comments selectively 定位到第二段。倒数第二句指出，Generally speaking, there are no unfiltered comments or casually taken photos on our social media pages.（一般来说，在我们的社交媒体主页上没有未经筛选的评论或随意拍摄的照片。）这是结论，下一句做出解释，because it wouldn't feel safe to be completely authentic and vulnerable with some of our "friends" whom we don't actually know or with whom trust has yet to be built（因为在我们并不真正认识或还没有建立信任的一些"朋友"面前，展示完全真实和脆弱的自己会让我们感到不安全）。A 项是原文中 with whom trust has yet to be built 的同义表达，故选 A 项。

48. What are humans inclined to do according to the passage?

　　A) Exaggerate their life's accomplishments.

　　B) Strive for perfection regardless of the cost.

　　C) Paint a rosy picture of other people's lives.

　　D) Learn lessons from other people's downfalls.

48. 根据文章，人们倾向于做什么？

　　A）夸大他们人生的成就。

　　B）追求完美，不计代价。

　　C）把他人的生活勾勒得很美好。

　　D）从他人的失败中吸取教训。

　　【答案及分析】C。根据题干关键词 humans inclined to do 定位到第四段。最后一句指出，Also, we tend to idealize others' lives and compare our downfalls to their greatest accomplishments, ending in feelings of loneliness and inadequacy.（同时，我们倾向于将他人的生活理想化，将自己的失败与他人最大的成就相比较，最终以孤独感和自卑感告终。）C 项是原文中 idealize others' lives 的同义表达，故选 C 项。

49. What is the author's view of pictures and posts on social media?

　　A) They should record the memorable moments in people's lives.

　　B) They should be carefully edited so as to present the best image.

　　C) They should be shown in a way that meets one's security needs.

D) They should keep people from the unhealthy quest for perfection.

49. 作者对社交媒体上的照片和帖子是什么看法？

A）它们应该记录人们生活中的难忘瞬间。

B）它们应该经过仔细编辑以展示最佳形象。

C）它们的展示方式应该满足人们的安全需求。

D）它们应该阻止人们病态地追求完美。

【答案及分析】A。根据题干关键词 pictures and posts on social media 定位到第五段。最后一句指出，Pictures and posts should be byproducts of life's treasured moments and fun times（照片和帖子应该是生活中珍贵时刻和快乐时光的副产品）。A 项中的 the memorable moments in people's lives 是原文中 life's treasured moments and fun times 的同义表达，故选 A 项。

50. What does the author advise people to do when they find their online experience unconstructive?

A) Use social media to increase their ability to connect with various types of people.

B) Stay connected to those whom they may not otherwise get to know and befriend.

C) Try to prevent negative thoughts and feelings from getting into the online pages.

D) Strengthen ties with real-life friends instead of caring about their online image.

50. 当人们发现自己的上网体验没有建设性作用时，作者建议人们做什么？

A）利用社交媒体增强与不同人交往的能力。

B）与那些本不可能认识和结交的人保持联系。

C）尽力不在网上传播负面想法，宣泄负面情绪。

D）加强与现实中朋友的联系，而不是关注他们网络上的形象。

【答案及分析】D。根据题干关键词 find their online experience unconstructive 定位到最后一段。最后两句指出，However, social media should feel like a fun experience, not one that contributes to negative thoughts and feelings. If the latter is the case, increasing face to face time with trusted friends, and minimizing time scrolling online, will prove to be a reminder that your social network is much more rewarding than any "like" "follow" or "share" can be.（然而，社交媒体应该给人一种有趣的体验，而不是一种助长消极想法和情绪的体验。如果出现后者的情况，增加与信任的朋友面对面交流的时间，最大限度地减少上网浏览的时间，这将提醒我们，你的社交圈比任何"点赞""关注"或"分享"都更有回报。）D 项中的 Strengthen ties with real-life friends 是原文中 increasing face to face time with trusted friends 的同义表达，instead of caring about their online image 是原文中 minimizing time scrolling online 的同义表达，故选 D 项。

Passage Two

【全文翻译】

想象一下，一个外星物种降落在地球上，仅仅通过它们的存在，这些外星物种就导致我们的艺术消亡，使我们的音乐同质化，让我们的技术知识消失。这实际上是人类对我们的近亲——黑猩猩——所做的事情。

早在1999年，由安德鲁·怀顿领导的一组科学家就发现，来自非洲不同地区的黑猩猩彼此之间的行为差异很大。有的群体会用指关节敲击树枝来引起对方的注意，而另一些群体会通过用牙齿大声撕咬树叶来引起对方的注意。研究小组确定了其中39种传统，这些传统存在于某些群体中，而在其他群体中没有——当时除了人类，这种模式没有在任何动物群体中出现过。研究小组说，这证明黑猩猩有自己的文化。

人们花了很长时间才让怀疑者相信这种文化的存在，但现在我们有很多动物互相学习当地传统的例子。

但就在许多科学家开始接受动物文化的存在时，很多动物文化可能会消失。艾米·卡兰和她的同事通过多年深入的实地研究发现，人类的存在已经侵蚀了黑猩猩行为的多样性。在我们繁荣的地方，它们的文化衰落了。在怀顿的经典研究发布20周年之际得知这个事实，是一件非常讽刺的事情。

"想到就在60年前，我们对我们的近亲（黑猩猩）在野外的行为几乎一无所知，这真是令人惊讶，"怀顿说。"但是现在，当我们真正了解我们的灵长类近亲（黑猩猩）时，人类的行为正在关闭我们所发现的一切的窗口。"

"有时急于保护整个物种，我认为我们忘记了个体，"圣安德鲁斯大学的教授卡特·霍贝特说。"每个种群，每个群体，甚至每一代黑猩猩都是独一无二的。一个事件可能只对黑猩猩整个种群产生很小的影响，但它可能会摧毁整个群体——整个文化。无论我们采取什么措施来恢复栖息地或支持种群数量增长，我们都可能永远无法恢复这种文化。"

没有人知道黑猩猩文化的破坏是否日益加重。很少有地方长期追踪黑猩猩的行为，这么做的地方也更有可能保护动物免受人类影响。

显然，环保主义者需要考虑以一种全新的方式来拯救物种——通过保护动物的传统、身体和基因。"我们不能只注意保护物种等基于遗传的实体，还需要考虑基于文化的实体。"安德鲁·怀顿说。

难词总结

homogenize /həˈmɒdʒənaɪz/ v. 使同样
intensive /ɪnˈtensɪv/ a. 集中的；集约的
bitterly /ˈbɪtəli/ ad. 极其；非常
conservationist /ˌkɒnsəˈveɪʃənɪst/ n. 环境保护主义者

rap /ræp/ v. 敲击；击打
fieldwork /ˈfiːldwɜːk/ n. 实地研究；野外考察
restore /rɪˈstɔː(r)/ v. 恢复；使复原
entity /ˈentəti/ n. 实体

题目精析

51. What does the author say we humans have been doing to chimps?

    A) Ruining their culture.   C) Treating them as alien species.

    B) Accelerating their extinction.   D) Homogenizing their living habits.

51. 作者说一直以来我们人类是如何对待黑猩猩的？

A）摧毁它们的文化。　　C）将它们视作外来物种。
B）加速它们的灭绝。　　D）同化它们的生活习惯。

【答案及分析】A。根据题干关键词 we humans have been doing to chimps 定位到第一段最后一句。题干是该句中 what humans have been doing to our closest relatives——chimps 的同义表达。前一句是具体做法，该句指出，through their mere presence, those aliens caused our art to vanish, our music to homogenize, and our technological know-how to disappear（仅仅通过它们的存在，这些外星物种就导致我们的艺术消亡，使我们的音乐同质化，让我们的技术知识消失）。A 项 Ruining their culture 是对该句的概括，故选 A 项。

52. What is the finding of Andrew Whiten's team?

　　A) Chimps demonstrate highly developed skills of communication.

　　B) Chimps rely heavily upon their body language to communicate.

　　C) Chimps behave in ways quite similar to those of human beings.

　　D) Different chimp groups differ in their way of communication.

52. 安德鲁·怀顿的团队发现了什么？

　　A）大猩猩表现出高度发达的沟通技巧。

　　B）大猩猩主要依赖身体语言来交流。

　　C）大猩猩的行为方式和人类十分相似。

　　D）不同的黑猩猩群体之间交流方式不同。

【答案及分析】D。根据题干关键词 the finding of Andrew Whiten's team 定位到第二段。第一句指出，Back in 1999, a team of scientists led by Andrew Whiten showed that chimps from different parts of Africa behave very differently from one another.（早在 1999 年，由安德鲁·怀顿领导的一组科学家就发现，来自非洲不同地区的黑猩猩彼此之间的行为差异很大。）D 项中的 Different chimp groups 是原文中 chimps from different parts of Africa 的同义表达，differ in their way of communication 是原文中 behave very differently from one another 的同义表达，故选 D 项。

53. What did Ammie Kalan and her colleagues find through their intensive fieldwork?

　　A) Whiten's classic study has little impact on the diversity of chimp behavior.

　　B) Chimp behavior becomes less varied with the increase of human activity.

　　C) Chimps alter their culture to quickly adapt to the changed environment.

　　D) It might already be too late to prevent animal cultures from extinction.

53. 艾米·卡兰和她的同事们在深入的实地研究中发现了什么？

　　A）怀顿的经典研究对黑猩猩行为多样性的影响不大。

　　B）随着人类活动的增多，黑猩猩的行为多样性变少。

　　C）黑猩猩改变自己的文化以快速适应变化的环境。

　　D）阻止动物文化灭绝可能已经太晚了。

【答案及分析】B。根据题干关键词 Ammie Kalan and her colleagues 和 find through their intensive fieldwork

定位到第四段。第二句指出，Ammie Kalan and her colleagues have shown, through years of intensive fieldwork, that the very presence of humans has eroded the diversity of chimp behavior.（艾米·卡兰和她的同事通过多年深入的实地研究发现，人类的存在已经侵蚀了黑猩猩行为的多样性。）B 项中的 Chimp behavior becomes less varied 是原文中 eroded the diversity of chimp behavior 的同义表达，the increase of human activity 对应原文中的 the very presence of humans，故选 B 项。

54. What does Cat Hobaiter think we should do for chimp conservation?

  A) Try to understand our sister species' behavior in the wild.

  B) Make efforts to preserve each individual chimp community.

  C) Study the unique characteristics of each generation of chimps.

  D) Endeavor to restore chimp habitats to expand its total population.

54. 卡特·霍贝特认为我们应该如何保护黑猩猩？

  A）尽力了解我们的近亲（黑猩猩）在野外的表现。

  B）努力保护每一个黑猩猩群体。

  C）研究每一代黑猩猩的独特特征。

  D）努力恢复黑猩猩的栖息地，扩大其总数量。

【答案及分析】B。根据题干关键词 Cat Hobaiter 定位到第六段。前两句指出，"Sometimes in the rush to conserve the species, I think we forget about the individuals," says Cat Hobaiter, a professor at the University of St. Andrews. "Each population, each community, even each generation of chimps is unique…"（"有时急于保护整个物种，我认为我们忘记了个体，"圣安德鲁斯大学的教授卡特·霍贝特说。"每个种群，每个群体，甚至每一代黑猩猩都是独一无二的……"）B 项是对该句的总结概括，其中，each individual chimp community 对应原文中的 each community，故选 B 项。

55. What does the author suggest conservationists do?

  A) Focus entirely on culturally-based entities rather than genetically-based ones.

  B) Place more stress on animal traditions than on their physical conservation.

  C) Conserve animal species in a novel and all-round way.

  D) Explore the cultures of species before they vanish.

55. 作者建议环保主义者做什么？

  A）完全关注基于文化的实体，而不是基于基因的实体。

  B）相比于对动物实体的保护，更要重视保护动物传统。

  C）以新颖、全面的方式保护动物物种。

  D）在物种消失前探索它们的文化。

【答案及分析】C。根据题干关键词 the author suggest conservationists do 定位到文章最后一段。第一句指出，Obviously conservationists need to think about saving species in a completely new way — by preserving animal traditions as well as bodies and genes.（显然，环保主义者需要考虑以一种全新的方式来拯救物种——通过保护动物的传统、身体和基因。）C 项中的 Conserve animal species 是原文中

saving species 的同义表达，in a novel and all-round way 是原文中 in a completely new way 的同义表达，故选 C 项。

Part Ⅳ Translation

参考译文

  The 1,956-kilometer Qinghai-Tibet Railway, with 960 kilometers above the altitude of 4,000 meters, is the highest and longest plateau railroad in the world and the first railway to connect Tibet with other areas of China. As the railroad crosses the most fragile ecosystem in the world, measures to protect ecology have been taken during and after construction to ensure that it becomes a "green railroad". The Qinghai-Tibet Railway has sharply shortened the travel time between other areas of China and Tibet, and, more importantly, it has considerably facilitated the economic development of Tibet and improved the lives of local residents. After its operation, an increasing number of people have chosen to travel to Tibet by train, so that they can get the opportunity to admire the beautiful scenery along the route.

难词总结

plateau /ˈplætəʊ/ n. 高原
ecosystem /ˈiːkəʊsɪstəm/ n. 生态系统
considerably /kənˈsɪdərəbli/ ad. 相当多地；非常
operation /ˌɒpəˈreɪʃn/ n. 运转；运行

fragile /ˈfrædʒaɪl/ a. 脆弱的；易碎的
construction /kənˈstrʌkʃn/ n. 建造；建筑
facilitate /fəˈsɪlɪteɪt/ v. 促进；促使；使便利

译点释义

1. 第一句"青藏铁路是……，全长……，其中有 960 千米……，是连接……的第一条铁路"，句子较长，不能将这 4 个分句全都翻译成完整的句子，应该对句子进行适当的排列组合。可以将主句定为"青藏铁路是……，是连接……"，用 and 连接两个并列表语；"全长……"可以译为定语 The 1,956-kilometer Qinghai-Tibet Railway；"其中有 960 千米……"可以译为独立主格结构 with 960 kilometers above the altitude of 4,000 meters。

2. 第二句中，"最脆弱的生态系统"可以译为 the most fragile ecosystem；"在建设期间和建成后都采取了生态保护措施"一句没有施加动作的主语，因此可以处理成被动语态 measures to protect ecology have been taken during and after construction。

3. 第三句"青藏铁路大大缩短了……"和第四句"更重要的是，它极大地促进了……"之间的逻辑关系比较紧密，都属于青藏铁路建成的意义，属于递进关系，所以可以将这两部分内容翻译成一句。

4. 最后一句中，"铁路开通后"可以译为介词短语 After its operation；"这样还有机会欣赏沿线的美景"可以译为目的状语从句 so that they can get the opportunity to admire the beautiful scenery along the route。

大学英语六级真题

刷题卷

目 录

2020年9月大学英语六级考试真题（第一套）..1

2020年9月大学英语六级考试真题（第二套）..11

2020年7月大学英语六级考试真题（组合卷）..19

2019年12月大学英语六级考试真题（第一套）..29

2019年12月大学英语六级考试真题（第二套）..39

2019年12月大学英语六级考试真题（第三套）..48

未得到监考教师指令前，不得翻阅该试题册！

2020年9月大学英语六级考试真题（第一套）

Part Ⅰ　　　　　　　　　Writing　　　　　　　　　(30 minutes)

（请于正式开考后半小时内完成该部分，之后将进行听力考试）

Directions: *For this part, you are allowed 30 minutes to write an essay on the saying **What is worth doing is worth doing well**. You should write at least **150** words but no more than **200** words.*

Part Ⅱ　　　　　　Listening Comprehension　　　　　(30 minutes)

Section A

Directions: *In this section, you will hear two long conversations. At the end of each conversation, you will hear four questions. Both the conversation and the questions will be spoken only once. After you hear a question, you must choose the best answer from the four choices marked A), B), C) and D). Then mark the corresponding letter on **Answer Sheet 1** with a single line through the centre.*

Questions 1 to 4 are based on the conversation you have just heard.

1. A) She can devote all her life to pursuing her passion.
   B) Her accumulated expertise helps her to achieve her goals.
   C) She can spread her academic ideas on a weekly TV show.
   D) Her research findings are widely acclaimed in the world.
2. A) Provision of guidance for nuclear labs in Europe.　　C) Overseeing two research groups at Oxford.
   B) Touring the globe to attend science TV shows.　　　D) Science education and scientific research.
3. A) A better understanding of a subject.　　　　　　　C) A broader knowledge of related fields.
   B) A stronger will to meet challenges.　　　　　　　D) A closer relationship with young people.
4. A) By applying the latest research methods.　　　　　C) By building upon previous discoveries.
   B) By making full use of the existing data.　　　　　　D) By utilizing more powerful computers.

Questions 5 to 8 are based on the conversation you have just heard.

5. A) They can predict future events.　　　　　　　　　C) They have cultural connotations.
   B) They have no special meanings.　　　　　　　　　D) They cannot be easily explained.
6. A) It was canceled due to bad weather.　　　　　　　C) She dreamed of a plane crash.
   B) She overslept and missed the flight.　　　　　　　D) It was postponed to the following day.
7. A) They can be affected by people's childhood experiences.

1

B) They may sometimes seem ridiculous to a rational mind.

C) They usually result from people's unpleasant memories.

D) They can have an impact as great as rational thinking.

8. A) They call for scientific methods to interpret.   C) They reflect their complicated emotions.

   B) They mirror their long-cherished wishes.   D) They are often related to irrational feelings.

Section B

Directions: *In this section, you will hear two passages. At the end of each passage, you will hear three or four questions. Both the passage and the questions will be spoken only once. After you hear a question, you must choose the best answer from the four choices marked A), B), C) and D). Then mark the corresponding letter on **Answer Sheet 1** with a single line through the centre.*

Questions 9 to 11 are based on the passage you have just heard.

9. A) Radio waves.   B) Sound waves.   C) Robots.   D) Satellites.
10. A) It may be freezing fast beneath the glacier.   C) It may have certain rare minerals in it.
    B) It may have micro-organisms living in it.   D) It may be as deep as four kilometers.
11. A) Help understand life in freezing conditions.   C) Provide information about other planets.
    B) Help find new sources of fresh water.   D) Shed light on possible life in outer space.

Questions 12 to 15 are based on the passage you have just heard.

12. A) He found there had been little research on their language.
    B) He was trying to preserve the languages of the Indian tribes.
    C) His contact with a social worker had greatly aroused his interest in the tribe.
    D) His meeting with Gonzalez had made him eager to learn more about the tribe.
13. A) He taught Copeland to speak the Tarahumaras language.
    B) He persuaded the Tarahumaras to accept Copeland's gifts.
    C) He recommended one of his best friends as an interpreter.
    D) He acted as an intermediary between Copeland and the villagers.
14. A) Unpredictable.   B) Unjustifiable.   C) Laborious.   D) Tedious.
15. A) Their appreciation of help from the outsiders.   C) Their readiness to adapt to technology.
    B) Their sense of sharing and caring.   D) Their belief in creating wealth for themselves.

Section C

Directions: *In this section, you will hear three recordings of lectures or talks followed by three or four questions. The recordings will be played only once. After you hear a question, you must choose the best answer from the four choices marked A), B), C) and D). Then mark the corresponding letter on **Answer Sheet 1** with a single line through the centre.*

Questions 16 to 18 are based on the recording you have just heard.

16. A) They tend to be silenced into submission.   C) They will feel proud of being pioneers.

B) They find it hard to defend themselves. D) They will feel somewhat encouraged.

17. A) One who advocates violence in effecting change.
    B) One who craves for relentless transformations.
    C) One who acts in the interests of the oppressed.
    D) One who rebels against the existing social order.

18. A) They tried to effect social change by force. C) They served as a driving force for progress.
    B) They disrupted the nation's social stability. D) They did more harm than good to humanity.

Questions 19 to 21 are based on the recording you have just heard.

19. A) Few of us can ignore changes in our immediate environment.
    B) It is impossible for us to be immune from outside influence.
    C) Few of us can remain unaware of what happens around us.
    D) It is important for us to keep in touch with our own world.

20. A) Make up his mind to start all over again. C) Try to find a more exciting job somewhere else.
    B) Stop making unfair judgements of others. D) Recognise the negative impact of his coworkers.

21. A) They are quite susceptible to suicide. C) They suffer a great deal from ill health.
    B) They improve people's quality of life. D) They help people solve mental problems.

Questions 22 to 25 are based on the recording you have just heard.

22. A) Few people can identify its texture. C) Its real value is open to interpretation.
    B) Few people can describe it precisely. D) Its importance is often over-estimated.

23. A) It has never seen any change. C) It is a well-protected government secret.
    B) It has much to do with color. D) It is a subject of study by many forgers.

24. A) People had little faith in paper money. C) It predicted their value would increase.
    B) They could last longer in circulation. D) They were more difficult to counterfeit.

25. A) The stabilization of the dollar value. C) A gold standard for American currency.
    B) The issuing of government securities. D) A steady appreciation of the U. S. dollar.

Part Ⅲ   Reading Comprehension   (40 minutes)

Section A

Directions: *In this section, there is a passage with ten blanks. You are required to select one word for each blank from a list of choices given in a word bank following the passage. Read the passage through carefully before making your choices. Each choice in the bank is identified by a letter. Please mark the corresponding letter for each item on **Answer Sheet 2** with a single line through the centre. You may not use any of the words in the bank more than once.*

Overall, men are more likely than women to make excuses. Several studies suggest that men feel the need to appear competent in all __26__, while women worry only about the skills in which they've invested __27__. Ask a man and a woman to go diving for the first time, and the woman is likely to jump in, while the man is likely to say he's not feeling too well.

Ironically, it is often success that leads people to flirt with failure. Praise won for __28__ a skill suddenly puts one in the position of having everything to lose. Rather than putting their reputation on the line again, many successful people develop a handicap—drinking, __29__, depression—that allows them to keep their status no matter what the future brings. An advertising executive __30__ for depression shortly after winning an award put it this way: "Without my depression, I'd be a failure now; with it, I'm a success 'on hold.'"

In fact, the people most likely to become chronic excuse makers are those __31__ with success. Such people are so afraid of being __32__ a failure at anything that they constantly develop one handicap or another in order to explain away failure.

Though self-handicapping can be an effective way of coping with performance anxiety now and then, in the end, researchers say, it will lead to __33__. In the long run, excuse makers fail to live up to their true __34__ and lose the status they care so much about. And despite their protests to the __35__, they have only themselves to blame.

A) contrary	I) momentum
B) fatigue	J) obsessed
C) heavily	K) potential
D) heaving	L) realms
E) hospitalized	M) reciprocal
F) labeled	N) ruin
G) legacies	O) viciously
H) mastering	

Section B

Directions: *In this section, you are going to read a passage with ten statements attached to it. Each statement contains information given in one of the paragraphs. Identify the paragraph from which the information is derived. You may choose a paragraph more than once. Each paragraph is marked with a letter. Answer the questions by marking the corresponding letter on **Answer Sheet 2**.*

Six Potential Brain Benefits of Bilingual Education

[A] Brains, brains, brains. People are fascinated by brain research. And yet it can be hard to point to places where our education system is really making use of the latest *neuroscience*（神经科学）findings. But there is one happy link where research is meeting practice: *bilingual*（双语的）education. "In the last 20 years or so, there's been a virtual explosion of research on bilingualism," says Judith Kroll, a professor at the University of California, Riverside.

[B] Again and again, researchers have found, "bilingualism is an experience that shapes our brain for life," in the words of Gigi Luk, an associate professor at Harvard's Graduate School of Education. At the same time, one of the hottest trends in public schooling is what's often called dual-language or two-way immersion programs.

[C] Traditional programs for English-language learners, or ELLs, focus on assimilating students into English as quickly as possible. Dual-language classrooms, by contrast, provide instruction across subjects to both English natives and English learners, in both English and a target language. The goal is functional bilingualism and biliteracy for all students by middle school. New York City, North Carolina, Delaware, Utah, Oregon and Washington state are among the places expanding dual-language classrooms.

[D] The trend flies in the face of some of the culture wars of two decades ago, when advocates insisted on "English first" education. Most famously, California passed Proposition 227 in 1998. It was intended to sharply reduce the amount of time that English-language learners spent in bilingual settings. Proposition 58, passed by California voters on November 8, largely reversed that decision, paving the way for a huge expansion of bilingual education in the state that has the largest population of English-language learners.

[E] Some of the insistence on English-first was founded on research produced decades ago, in which bilingual students underperformed *monolingual*（单语的）English speakers and had lower IQ scores. Today's scholars, like Ellen Bialystok at York University in Toronto, say that research was "deeply flawed." "Earlier research looked at socially disadvantaged groups," agrees Antonella Sorace at the University of Edinburgh in Scotland. "This has been completely contradicted by recent research" that compares groups more similar to each other.

[F] So what does recent research say about the potential benefits of bilingual education? It turns out that, in many ways, the real trick to speaking two languages consists in managing not to speak one of those languages at a given moment—which is fundamentally a feat of paying attention. Saying "Goodbye" to mom and then "*Guten tag*" to your teacher, or managing to ask for a *crayola roja* instead of a red *crayon*（蜡笔）, requires skills called "inhibition" and "task switching." These skills are subsets of an ability called executive function.

[G] People who speak two languages often outperform monolinguals on general measures of executive function. "Bilinguals can pay focused attention without being distracted and also improve in the ability to switch from one task to another," says Sorace.

[H] Do these same advantages benefit a child who begins learning a second language in kindergarten instead of as a baby? We don't yet know. Patterns of language learning and language use are complex. But Gigi Luk at Harvard cites at least one brain-imaging study on adolescents that shows similar changes in brain structure when compared with those who are bilingual from birth, even when they didn't begin practicing a second language in earnest before late childhood.

[I] Young children being raised bilingual have to follow social cues to figure out which language to use with which person and in what setting. As a result, says Sorace, bilingual children as young as age 3 have demonstrated a head start on tests of perspective-taking and theory of mind—both of which are fundamental social and emotional skills.

[J] About 10 percent of students in the Portland, Oregon public schools are assigned by lottery to dual-language classrooms that offer instruction in Spanish, Japanese or Mandarin, alongside English. Jennifer Steele at American University conducted a four-year, randomized trial and found that these dual-language students outperformed their peers in English-reading skills by a full school-year's worth of learning by the end of middle school. Because the effects are found in reading, not in math or science where there were few differences, Steele suggests that learning two languages makes students more aware of how language works in general.

[K] The research of Gigi Luk at Harvard offers a slightly different explanation. She has recently done a small study looking at a group of 100 fourth-graders in Massachusetts who had similar reading scores on a standard test, but very different language experiences. Some were foreign-language dominant and others were English natives. Here's what's interesting. The students who were dominant in a foreign language weren't yet comfortably bilingual; they were just starting to learn English. Therefore, by definition, they had a much weaker English vocabulary than the native speakers. Yet they were just as good at interpreting a text. "This is very surprising," Luk says. "You would expect the reading comprehension performance to mirror the vocabulary—it's a cornerstone of comprehension."

[L] How did the foreign-language dominant speakers manage this feat? Well, Luk found, they also scored higher on tests of executive functioning. So, even though they didn't have huge mental dictionaries to draw on, they may have been great puzzle-solvers, taking into account higher-level concepts such as whether a single sentence made sense within an overall story line. They got to the same results as the monolinguals, by a different path.

[M] American public school classrooms as a whole are becoming more segregated by race and class. Dual-language programs can be an exception. Because they are composed of native English speakers deliberately placed together with recent immigrants, they tend to be more ethnically and economically balanced. And there is some evidence that this helps kids of all backgrounds gain comfort with diversity and different cultures.

[N] Several of the researchers also pointed out that, in bilingual education, non-English-dominant students and their families tend to feel that their home language is heard and valued, compared with a classroom where the home language is left at the door in favor of English. This can improve students' sense of belonging and increase parents' involvement in their children's education, including behaviors like reading to children. "Many parents fear their language is an obstacle, a problem, and if they abandon it their child will integrate better," says Antonella Sorace of the University of Edinburgh. "We tell them they're not doing their child a favor by giving up their language."

[O] One theme that was striking in speaking to all these researchers was just how strongly they advocated for dual-language classrooms. Thomas and Collier have advised many school systems on how to expand their dual-language programs, and Sorace runs "Bilingualism Matters," an international network of researchers who promote bilingual education projects. This type of advocacy among scientists is unusual; even more so because the "bilingual advantage hypothesis" is being challenged once again.

[P] A review of studies published last year found that cognitive advantages failed to appear in 83 percent of published studies, though in a separate analysis, the sum of effects was still significantly positive. One potential explanation offered by the researchers is that advantages that are measurable in the very young and very old tend to fade when testing young adults at the peak of their cognitive powers. And, they countered that no negative effects of bilingual education have been found. So, even if the advantages are small, they are still worth it. Not to mention one obvious, outstanding fact: "Bilingual children can speak two languages!"

36. A study found that there are similar changes in brain structure between those who are bilingual from birth and those who start learning a second language later.
37. Unlike traditional monolingual programs, bilingual classrooms aim at developing students' ability to use two languages by middle school.
38. A study showed that dual-language students did significantly better than their peers in reading English texts.
39. About twenty years ago, bilingual practice was strongly discouraged, especially in California.
40. Ethnically and economically balanced bilingual classrooms are found to be helpful for kids to get used to social and cultural diversity.
41. Researchers now claim that earlier research on bilingual education was seriously flawed.
42. According to a researcher, dual-language experiences exert a lifelong influence on one's brain.
43. Advocates of bilingual education argued that it produces positive effects though they may be limited.
44. Bilingual speakers often do better than monolinguals in completing certain tasks because they can concentrate better on what they are doing.
45. When their native language is used, parents can become more involved in their children's education.

Section C

Directions: *There are 2 passages in this section. Each passage is followed by some questions or unfinished statements. For each of them there are four choices marked A), B), C) and D). You should decide on the best choice and mark the corresponding letter on **Answer Sheet 2** with a single line through the centre.*

Passage One

Questions 46 to 50 are based on the following passage.

It is not controversial to say that an unhealthy diet causes bad health. Nor are the basic elements of healthy eating disputed. Obesity raises susceptibility to cancer, and Britain is the sixth most obese country on Earth. That is a public health emergency. But naming the problem is the easy part. No one disputes the costs in quality of life and depleted health budgets of an obese population, but the quest for solutions gets diverted by ideological arguments around responsibility and choice. And the water is muddied by lobbying from the industries that profit from consumption of obesity-inducing products.

Historical precedent suggests that science and politics can overcome resistance from businesses that pollute and poison but it takes time, and success often starts small. So it is heartening to note that a programme in Leeds has achieved a reduction in childhood obesity, becoming the first UK city to reverse a fattening trend. The best results were among younger children and in more deprived areas. When 28% of English children aged two to 15 are obese, a national shift on the scale achieved by Leeds would lengthen hundreds of thousands of lives. A significant factor in the Leeds experience appears to be a scheme called HENRY, which helps parents reward behaviours that prevent obesity in children.

Many members of parliament are uncomfortable even with their own government's anti-obesity strategy, since it involves a "sugar tax" and a ban on the sale of energy drinks to under-16s. Bans and taxes can be blunt instruments, but their harshest critics can rarely suggest better methods. These critics just oppose regulation itself.

The relationship between poor health and inequality is too pronounced for governments to be passive about large-scale intervention. People living in the most deprived areas are four times more prone to die from avoidable causes than counterparts in more affluent places. As the structural nature of public health problems becomes harder to ignore, the complaint about overprotective government loses potency.

In fact, the polarised debate over public health interventions should have been abandoned long ago. Government action works when individuals are motivated to respond. Individuals need governments that expand access to good choices. The HENRY programme was delivered in part through children's centres. Closing such centres and cutting council budgets doesn't magically increase reserves of individual self-reliance. The function of a well-designed state intervention is not to deprive people of liberty but to build social capacity and infrastructure that helps people take responsibility for their wellbeing. The obesity crisis will not have a solution devised by left or right ideology—but experience indicates that the private sector needs the incentive of regulation before it starts taking public health emergencies seriously.

46. Why is the obesity problem in Britain so difficult to solve?
    A) Government health budgets are depleted.
    B) People disagree as to who should do what.
    C) Individuals are not ready to take their responsibilities.
    D) Industry lobbying makes it hard to get healthy foods.

47. What can we learn from the past experience in tackling public health emergencies?
    A) Governments have a role to play.
    B) Public health is a scientific issue.
    C) Priority should be given to deprived regions.
    D) Businesses' responsibility should be stressed.

48. What does the author imply about some critics of bans and taxes concerning unhealthy drinks?
    A) They are not aware of the consequences of obesity.
    B) They have not come up with anything more constructive.
    C) They are uncomfortable with parliament's anti-obesity debate.
    D) They have their own motives in opposing government regulation.

49. Why does the author stress the relationship between poor health and inequality?
    A) To demonstrate the dilemma of people living in deprived areas.
    B) To bring to light the root cause of widespread obesity in Britain.
    C) To highlight the area deserving the most attention from the public.
    D) To justify government intervention in solving the obesity problem.

50. When will government action be effective?
    A) When the polarised debate is abandoned.
    B) When ideological differences are resolved.
    C) When individuals have the incentive to act accordingly.
    D) When the private sector realises the severity of the crisis.

Passage Two

Questions 51 to 55 are based on the following passage.

Home to virgin reefs, rare sharks and vast numbers of exotic fish, the Coral Sea is a unique haven of biodiversity off the northeastern coast of Australia. If a proposal by the Australian government goes ahead, the region will also become the world's largest marine protected area, with restrictions or bans on fishing, mining and marine farming.

The Coral Sea reserve would cover almost 990,000 square kilometres and stretch as far as 1,100 kilometres from the coast. Unveiled recently by environment minister Tony Burke, the proposal would be the last in a series of proposed marine reserves around Australia's coast.

But the scheme is attracting criticism from scientists and conservation groups, who argue that the government hasn't gone far enough in protecting the Coral Sea, or in other marine reserves in the coastal network.

Hugh Possingham, director of the Centre of Excellence for Environmental Decisions at the University of Queensland, points out that little more than half of the Coral Sea reserve is proposed as "no take" area, in which all fishing would be banned. The world's largest existing marine reserve, established last year by the British government in the Indian Ocean, spans 554,000 km^2 and is a no-take zone throughout. An alliance of campaigning conversation groups argues that more of the Coral Sea should receive this level of protection.

"I would like to have seen more protection for coral reefs," says Terry Hughes, director of the Centre of Excellence for Coral Reef Studies at James Cook University in Queensland. "More than 20 of them would be outside the no-take area and vulnerable to catch-and-release fishing".

As *Nature* went to press, the Australian government had not responded to specific criticisms of the plan. But Robin Beaman, a marine geologist at James Cook University, says that the reserve does "broadly protect the range of habitats" in the sea. "I can testify to the huge effort that government agencies and other organisations have put into trying to understand the ecological values of this vast area," he says.

Reserves proposed earlier this year for Australia's southwestern and northwestern coastal regions have also been criticised for failing to give habitats adequate protection. In August, 173 marine scientists signed an open letter to the government saying they were "greatly concerned" that the proposals for the southwestern region had not been based on the "core science principles" of reserves—the protected regions were not, for instance, representative of all the habitats in the region, they said.

Critics say that the southwestern reserve offers the greatest protection to the offshore areas where commercial opportunities are fewest and where there is little threat to the environment, a contention also levelled at the Coral Sea plan.

51. What do we learn from the passage about the Coral Sea?
    A) It is exceptionally rich in marine life.
    B) It is the biggest marine protected area.
    C) It remains largely undisturbed by humans.
    D) It is a unique haven of endangered species.

52. What does the Australian government plan to do according to Tony Burke?
    A) Make a new proposal to protect the Coral Sea.
    B) Revise its conservation plan owing to criticisms.
    C) Upgrade the established reserves to protect marine life.
    D) Complete the series of marine reserves around its coast.

53. What is scientists' argument about the Coral Sea proposal?
    A) The government has not done enough for marine protection.
    B) It will not improve the marine reserves along Australia's coast.
    C) The government has not consulted them in drawing up the proposal.

D) It is not based on sufficient investigations into the ecological system.

54. What does marine geologist Robin Beaman say about the Coral Sea plan?

    A) It can compare with the British government's effort in the Indian Ocean.

    B) It will result in the establishment of the world's largest marine reserve.

    C) It will ensure the sustainability of the fishing industry around the coast.

    D) It is a tremendous joint effort to protect the range of marine habitats.

55. What do critics think of the Coral Sea plan?

    A) It will do more harm than good to the environment.

    B) It will adversely affect Australia's fishing industry.

    C) It will protect regions that actually require little protection.

    D) It will win little support from environmental organisations.

Part Ⅳ Translation (30 minutes)

Directions: *For this part, you are allowed 30 minutes to translate a passage from Chinese into English. You should write your answer on **Answer Sheet 2**.*

《西游记》(*Journey to the West*)也许是中国文学四大经典小说中最具影响力的一部,当然也是在国外最广为人知的一部小说。这部小说描绘了著名僧侣玄奘在三个随从的陪同下穿越中国西部地区前往印度取经(Buddhist scripture)的艰难历程。虽然故事的主题基于佛教,但这部小说采用了大量中国民间故事和神话的素材,创造了各种栩栩如生的人物和动物形象。其中最著名的是孙悟空,他与各种各样的妖魔作斗争的故事几乎为每个中国孩子所熟知。

答案速查

Part Ⅱ Listening Comprehension

Section A 1. A 2. D 3. A 4. B 5. B 6. C 7. D 8. C

Section B 9. A 10. B 11. D 12. A 13. D 14. C 15. B

Section C 16. A 17. D 18. C 19. B 20. D 21. A 22. B 23. C 24. A 25. C

Part Ⅲ Reading Comprehension

Section A 26. L 27. C 28. H 29. B 30. E 31. J 32. F 33. N 34. K 35. A

Section B 36. H 37. C 38. J 39. D 40. M 41. E 42. B 43. P 44. G 45. N

Section C 46. B 47. A 48. B 49. D 50. C 51. A 52. D 53. A 54. D 55. C

未得到监考教师指令前，不得翻阅该试题册！

2020年9月大学英语六级考试真题（第二套）

Part I   Writing   (30 minutes)

（请于正式开考后半小时内完成该部分，之后将进行听力考试）

Directions: *For this part, you are allowed 30 minutes to write an essay on the saying **Wealth of the mind is the only true wealth**. You should write at least **150** words but no more than **200** words.*

Part II   Listening Comprehension   (30 minutes)

说明：由于2020年9月六级考试全国共考了一套听力，本套真题听力与前一套内容相同，只是选项顺序不同，因此在本套真题中不再重复出现。

Part III   Reading Comprehension   (40 minutes)

Section A

Directions: *In this section, there is a passage with ten blanks. You are required to select one word for each blank from a list of choices given in a word bank following the passage. Read the passage through carefully before making your choices. Each choice in the bank is identified by a letter. Please mark the corresponding letter for each item on **Answer Sheet 2** with a single line through the centre. You may not use any of the words in the bank more than once.*

It was perhaps when my parents—who also happen to be my housemates—left to go travelling for a couple of months recently that it __26__ on me why I had not yet left the family home.

It wasn't that I relied on them for __27__ reasons, or to keep my life in order, or to ease the chaos of the home. These days, I rely on them for their company.

I missed coming home and talking about my day at work, and I missed being able to read their faces and sense how their day was. I missed having unique __28__ into tiny details that make a life.

While the conversation about young adults staying longer at home is __29__ by talk of laziness, of dependence, of an inability for young people to pull themselves together, __30__ do we talk of the way, in my case at least, my relationship with my parents has __31__ strengthened the longer we have lived together.

Over the years the power dynamic has changed and is no longer defined by one being the giver and another, the taker. So, what does this say for our relationships within the family home?

According to psychologist Sabina Read, there are "some very positive possible __32__ when adult children share the family home", noting the "parent-child relationship may indeed strengthen and mature" in the process.

But, she notes, a strong __33__ doesn't simply come with time. "The many changing factors of the relationship need to be acknowledged, rather than hoping that the mere passage of time will __34__ connect parents to their adult children. It's important to acknowledge that the relationship parameters have changed to avoid falling back into __35__ from the teen years."

A) bond	I) magically
B) contemplated	J) outcomes
C) dawned	K) patterns
D) hierarchy	L) rarely
E) insight	M) saturated
F) legislative	N) stereotypes
G) leverage	O) undoubtedly
H) logistical	

Section B

Directions: *In this section, you are going to read a passage with ten statements attached to it. Each statement contains information given in one of the paragraphs. Identify the paragraph from which the information is derived. You may choose a paragraph more than once. Each paragraph is marked with a letter. Answer the questions by marking the corresponding letter on **Answer Sheet 2**.*

How Telemedicine Is Transforming Healthcare

[A] After years of big promises, telemedicine is finally living up to its potential. Driven by faster internet connections, *ubiquitous*（无处不在的）smartphones and changing insurance standards, more health providers are turning to electronic communications to do their jobs—and it's dramatically changing the delivery of healthcare.

[B] Doctors are linking up with patients by phone, email and *webcam*（网络摄像头）. They're also consulting with each other electronically—sometimes to make split-second decisions on heart attacks and strokes. Patients, meanwhile, are using new devices to relay their blood pressure, heart rate and other vital signs to their doctors so they can manage chronic conditions at home. Telemedicine also allows for better care in places where medical expertise is hard to come by. Five to 10 times a day, Doctors Without Borders relays questions about tough cases from its physicians in Niger, South Sudan and elsewhere to its network of 280 experts around the world, and back again via the internet.

[C] As a measure of how rapidly telemedicine is spreading, consider: More than 15 million Americans received some kind of medical care remotely last year, according to the American Telemedicine Association, a trade group, which expects those numbers to grow by 30% this year.

[D] None of this is to say that telemedicine has found its way into all corners of medicine. A recent survey of 500 *tech-savvy*（精通技术的）consumers found that 39% hadn't heard of telemedicine, and of those who haven't used it, 42% said they preferred in-person doctor visits. In a poll of 1,500 family physicians, only 15% had used it in their practices—but 90% said they would if it were appropriately *reimbursed*（补偿）.

[E] What's more, for all the rapid growth, significant questions and challenges remain. Rules defining and regulating telemedicine differ widely from state to state. Physicians groups are issuing different guidelines about what care they consider appropriate to deliver and in what form.

[F] Some critics also question whether the quality of care is keeping up with the rapid expansion of telemedicine. And there's the question of what services physicians should be paid for: Insurance coverage varies from health plan to health plan, and a big federal plan covers only a narrow range of services. Telemedicine's future will depend on how—and whether—regulators, providers, payers and patients can address these challenges. Here's a closer look at some of these issues:

[G] Do patients trade quality for convenience? The fastest-growing services in telemedicine connect consumers with clinicians they've never met for a phone, video or email visit—on-demand, 24/7. Typically, these are for nonemergency issues such as colds, flu, ear-aches and skin rashes, and they cost around $45, compared with approximately $100 at a doctor's office, $160 at an urgent-care clinic or $750 and up at an emergency room.

[H] Many health plans and employers have rushed to offer the services and promote them as a convenient way for plan members to get medical care without leaving home or work. Nearly three-quarters of large employers will offer virtual doctor visits as a benefit to employees this year, up from 48% last year. Web companies such as Teladoc and American Well are expected to host some 1.2 million such virtual doctor visits this year, up 20% from last year, according to the American Telemedicine Association.

[I] But critics worry that such services may be sacrificing quality for convenience. Consulting a random doctor patients will never meet, they say, further fragments the health-care system, and even minor issues such as *upper respiratory*（上呼吸道的）infections can't be thoroughly evaluated by a doctor who can't listen to your heart or feel your swollen glands. In a recent study, researchers posing as patients with skin problems sought help from 16 telemedicine sites—with unsettling results. In 62 encounters, fewer than one-third disclosed clinicians' credential or let patients choose; only 32% discussed potential side effects of prescribed medications. Several sites misdiagnosed serious conditions, largely because they failed to ask basic follow-up questions, the researchers said. "Telemedicine holds enormous promise, but these sites are just not ready for prime time," says Jack Resneck, the study's lead author.

[J] The American Telemedicine Association and other organizations have started *accreditation*（鉴定）programs to identify top-quality telemedicine sites. The American Medical Association this month approved new ethical guidelines for telemedicine, calling for participating doctors to recognize the limitations of such services and ensure that they have sufficient information to make clinical recommendations.

[K] Who pays for the services? While employers and health plans have been eager to cover virtual urgent-care visits, insurers have been far less willing to pay for telemedicine when doctors use phone, email or video to consult with existing patients about continuing issues. "It's very hard to get paid unless you physically see the patient," says Peter Rasmussen, medical director of distance health at the Cleveland Clinic. Some 32 states have passed "*parity*"（等同的）laws requiring private insurers to reimburse doctors for services delivered remotely if the same service would be covered in person, though not necessarily at the same rate or frequency. Medicare lags further behind. The federal health plan for the elderly covers a small number of telemedicine services—only for beneficiaries in rural areas and only when the services are received in a hospital, doctor's office or clinic.

[L] Bills to expand Medicare coverage of telemedicine have *bipartisan*（两党的）support in Congress. Opponents worry that such expansion would be costly for taxpayers, but advocates say it would save money in the long run.

[M] Experts say more hospitals are likely to invest in telemedicine systems as they move away from fee-for-service payments and into managed-care-type contracts that give them a set fee to provide care for patients and allow them to keep any savings they achieve.

[N] Is the state-by-state regulatory system outdated? Historically, regulation of medicine has been left to individual states. But some industry members contend that having 50 different sets of rules, licensing fees and even definitions of "medical practice" makes less sense in the era of telemedicine and is hampering its growth. Currently, doctors must have a valid license in the state where the patient is located to provide medical care, which means virtual-visit companies can match users only with locally licensed clinicians. It also causes administrative *hassles*（麻烦）for world-class medical centers that attract patients from across the country. At the Mayo Clinic, doctors who treat out-of-state patients can follow up with them via phone, email or web chats when they return home, but they can only discuss the conditions they treated in person. "If the patient wants to talk about a new problem, the doctor has to be licensed in that state to discuss it. If not, the patient should talk to his primary-care physician about it," says Steve Ommen, who runs Mayo's Connected Care program.

[O] To date, 17 states have joined a compact that will allow a doctor licensed in one member state to quickly obtain a license in another. While welcoming the move, some telemedicine advocates would prefer states to automatically honor one another's licenses, as they do with drivers' licenses. But states aren't likely to surrender control of medical practice, and most are considering new regulations. This year, more than 200 telemedicine-related bills have been introduced in 42 states, many regarding what services Medicaid will cover and whether payers should reimburse for remote patient monitoring. "A lot of states are still trying to define telemedicine," says Lisa Robbin, chief advocacy officer for the Federation of State Medical Boards.

36. An overwhelming majority of family physicians are willing to use telemedicine if they are duly paid.

37. Many employers are eager to provide telemedicine service as a benefit to their employees because of its convenience.

38. Different states have markedly different regulations for telemedicine.

39. With telemedicine, patients in regions short of professional medical service are able to receive better medical care.

40. Unlike employers and health plans, insurers have been rather reluctant to pay for some telemedicine services.

41. Some supporters of telemedicine hope states will accept each other's medical practice licenses as valid.

42. The fastest growing area for telemedicine services is for lesser health problems.

43. As telemedicine spreads quickly, some of its opponents doubt whether its service quality can be guaranteed.

44. The results obtained by researchers who pretended to be patients seeking help from telemedicine providers are disturbing.

45. Some people argue that the fact that different states have different regulations concerning medical services hinders the development of telemedicine.

Section C

Directions: *There are 2 passages in this section. Each passage is followed by some questions or unfinished statements. For each of them there are four choices marked A), B), C) and D). You should decide on the best choice and mark the corresponding letter on **Answer Sheet 2** with a single line through the centre.*

Passage One

Questions 46 to 50 are based on the following passage.

Danielle Steel, the 71-year-old romance novelist is notoriously productive, having published 179 books at a rate of up to seven a year. But a passing reference in a recent profile by *Glamour* magazine to her 20-hour workdays prompted an outpouring of admiration.

Steel has given that 20-hour figure when describing her "exhausting" process in the past: "I start the book and don't leave my desk until the first draft is finished." She goes from bed, to desk, to bath, to bed, avoiding all contact aside from phone calls with her nine children. "I don't comb my hair for weeks," she says. Meals are brought to her desk, where she types until her fingers swell and her nails bleed.

The business news website *Quartz* held Steel up as an inspiration, writing that if only we all followed her "actually extremely liberating" example of industrious sleeplessness, we would be quick to see results.

Well, indeed. With research results showing the cumulative effects of sleep loss and its impact on productivity, doubt has been voiced about the accuracy of Steel's self-assessment. Her output may be undeniable, but sceptics have suggested that she is guilty of erasing the role of *ghostwriters* (代笔人) at worst, gross exaggeration at best.

Steel says working 20 hours a day is "pretty brutal physically." But is it even possible? "No," says Maryanne Taylor of the Sleep Works. While you could work that long, the impact on productivity would make it hardly worthwhile. If Steel was routinely sleeping for four hours a night, she would be drastically underestimating the negative impact, says Alison Gardiner, founder of the sleep improvement programme Sleepstation. "It's akin to being drunk."

It's possible that Steel is exaggerating the demands of her schedule. Self-imposed sleeplessness has "become a bit of a status symbol", says Taylor, a misguided measure to prove how powerful and productive you are. Margaret Thatcher was also said to get by on four hours a night, while the 130-hour work weeks endured by tech heads has been held up as key to their success.

That is starting to change with increased awareness of the importance of sleep for mental health. "People are starting to realise that sleep should not be something that you fit in between everything else," says Taylor.

But it is possible—if statistically extremely unlikely—that Steel could be born a "short sleeper" with an unusual body clock, says sleep expert Dr. Sophie Bostock. "It's probably present in fewer than 1% of the population."

Even if Steel does happen to be among that tiny minority, says Bostock, it's "pretty irresponsible" to suggest that 20-hour days are simply a question of discipline for the rest of us.

46. What do we learn from the passage about *Glamour* magazine readers?

   A) They are intrigued by the exotic romance in Danielle Steel's novels.

   B) They are amazed by the number of books written by Danielle Steel.

   C) They are deeply impressed by Danielle Steel's daily work schedule.

   D) They are highly motivated by Danielle Steel's unusual productivity.

47. What did the business news website *Quartz* say about Danielle Steel?

   A) She could serve as an example of industriousness.

   B) She proved we could liberate ourselves from sleep.

   C) She could be an inspiration to novelists all over the world.

   D) She showed we could get all our work done without sleep.

48. What do sceptics think of Danielle Steel's work schedule claims?

   A) They are questionable.   C) They are irresistible.

   B) They are alterable.   D) They are verifiable.

49. What does Maryanne Taylor think of self-imposed sleeplessness?

   A) It may turn out to be key to a successful career.

   B) It may be practiced only by certain tech heads.

   C) It may symbolise one's importance and success.

   D) It may well serve as a measure of self-discipline.

50. How does Dr. Sophie Bostock look at the 20-hour daily work schedule?

   A) One should not adopt it without consulting a sleep expert.

   B) The general public should not be encouraged to follow it.

   C) One must be duly self-disciplined to adhere to it.

   D) The majority must adjust their body clock for it.

Passage Two

Questions 51 to 55 are based on the following passage.

Organic agriculture is a relatively untapped resource for feeding the Earth's population, especially in the face of climate change and other global challenges. That's the conclusion I reached in reviewing 40 years of science comparing the long-term prospects of organic and conventional farming.

The review study, "Organic Agriculture in the 21st Century," is featured as the cover story for the February issue of the journal *Nature Plants*. It is the first to compare organic and conventional agriculture across the main goals of sustainability identified by the National Academy of Sciences: productivity, economics, and environment.

Critics have long argued that organic agriculture is inefficient, requiring more land to yield the same amount of food. It's true that organic farming produces lower yields, averaging 10 to 20 percent less than conventional. Advocates contend that the environmental advantages of organic agriculture far outweigh the lower yields, and that increasing research and breeding resources for organic systems would reduce the yield gap. Sometimes excluded from these arguments is the fact that we already produce enough food to more than feed the world's 7.4 billion people but do not provide adequate access to all individuals.

In some cases, organic yields can be higher than conventional. For example, in severe drought conditions, which are expected to increase with climate change in many areas, organic farms can produce as good, if not better, yields because of the higher water-holding capacity of organically farmed soils.

What science does tell us is that mainstream conventional farming systems have provided growing supplies of food and other products but often at the expense of other sustainability goals.

Conventional agriculture may produce more food, but it often comes at a cost to the environment. Biodiversity loss, environmental degradation, and severe impacts on ecosystem services have not only accompanied conventional farming systems but have often extended well beyond their field boundaries. With organic agriculture, environmental costs tend to be lower and the benefits greater.

Overall, organic farms tend to store more soil carbon, have better soil quality, and reduce soil erosion compared to their conventional counterparts. Organic agriculture also creates less soil and water pollution and lower greenhouse gas emissions. And it's more energy-efficient because it doesn't rely on synthetic fertilizers or pesticides.

Organic agriculture is also associated with greater biodiversity of plants, animals, insects and microorganisms as well as genetic diversity. Biodiversity increases the services that nature provides and improves the ability of farming systems to adapt to changing conditions.

Despite lower yields, organic agriculture is more profitable for farmers because consumers are willing to pay more. Higher prices, called price premiums, can be justified as a way to compensate farmers for providing ecosystem services and avoiding environmental damage or external costs.

51. What do we learn from the conclusion of the author's review study?
    A) More resources should be tapped for feeding the world's population.
    B) Organic farming may be exploited to solve the global food problem.
    C) The long-term prospects of organic farming are yet to be explored.
    D) Organic farming is at least as promising as conventional farming.

52. What is the critics' argument against organic farming?
    A) It cannot meet the need for food.
    B) It cannot increase farm yields.
    C) It is not really practical.
    D) It is not that productive.

53. What does the author think should be taken into account in arguing about organic farming?
    A) Growth in world population.
    B) Deterioration in soil fertility.
    C) Inequality in food distribution.
    D) Advance in farming technology.

54. What does science tell us about conventional farming?
    A) It will not be able to meet global food demand.
    B) It is not conducive to sustainable development.
    C) It will eventually give way to organic farming.
    D) It is going mainstream throughout the world.

55. Why does the author think higher prices of organic farm produce are justifiable?
    A) They give farmers going organic a big competitive edge.
    B) They motivate farmers to upgrade farming technology.
    C) Organic farming costs more than conventional farming.
    D) Organic farming does long-term good to the ecosystem.

Part IV　　　　　　　　　Translation　　　　　　　　(30 minutes)

Directions: *For this part, you are allowed 30 minutes to translate a passage from Chinese into English. You should write your answer on **Answer Sheet 2**.*

　　《水浒传》(*Water Margin*)是中国文学四大经典小说之一。这部小说基于历史人物宋江及其伙伴反抗封建帝王的故事,数百年来一直深受中国读者的喜爱。

　　毫不夸张地说,几乎每个中国人都熟悉小说中的一些主要人物。这部小说中的精彩故事在茶馆、戏剧舞台、广播电视、电影屏幕和无数家庭中反复讲述。事实上,这部小说的影响已经远远超出了国界。越来越多的外国读者也感到这部小说里的故事生动感人、趣味盎然。

答案速查

Part Ⅱ　Listening Comprehension　（略）

Part Ⅲ　Reading Comprehension

Section A　26. C　27. H　28. E　29. M　30. L　31. O　32. J　33. A　34. I　35. K

Section B　36. D　37. H　38. E　39. B　40. K　41. O　42. G　43. F　44. I　45. N

Section C　46. C　47. A　48. A　49. C　50. B　51. B　52. D　53. C　54. B　55. D

未得到监考教师指令前，不得翻阅该试题册！

2020年7月大学英语六级考试真题（组合卷）

Part Ⅰ Writing (30 minutes)

（请于正式开考后半小时内完成该部分，之后将进行听力考试）

Directions: *For this part, you are allowed 30 minutes to write an essay commenting on the saying* **"The best preparation for tomorrow is doing your best today."** *You can give an example or two to illustrate your point of view. You should write at least* **150** *words but no more than* **200** *words.*

Part Ⅱ Listening Comprehension (30 minutes)

Section A

APP 扫码，听音频

Directions: *In this section, you will hear two long conversations. At the end of each conversation, you will hear four questions. Both the conversation and the questions will be spoken only once. After you hear a question, you must choose the best answer from the four choices marked A), B), C) and D). Then mark the corresponding letter on* **Answer Sheet 1** *with a single line through the centre.*

Questions 1 to 4 are based on the conversation you have just heard.

1. A) She is a great athlete.
   B) She has a three-year-old child.
   C) She comes to talk about Olympic Games.
   D) She enjoys reading new books.

2. A) How athletes excel in the past twenty years.
   B) How athletes have challenged their physical abilities.
   C) How comparisons are made between athletes.
   D) How technology has helped athletes scale new heights.

3. A) Our bodies. B) Our scientific knowledge. C) Our thoughts. D) Our ambitions.

4. A) It can be harmful to some athletes' physical health.
   B) Athletes may become too dependent on technological progress.
   C) It may give an unfair advantage to some athletes.
   D) Scientific knowledge can help athletes cheat in competitions.

Questions 5 to 8 are based on the conversation you have just heard.

5. A) Variety. B) Flexibility. C) Sensitivity. D) Family support.

说明：本套试卷的写作、听力及音频和翻译与 2020 年 7 月真题一致。其他试题根据命题规律、考点分布等信息编写或精选往年同等难度真题组合而成。

6. A) Importing all kinds of goods over the years.   C) Exchanging furniture for foods.
   B) Making trades between China and Italy.   D) Using the same container back and forth.
7. A) Warehouses.   B) Cargo containers.   C) Production lines.   D) Business offices.
8. A) Higher prices.   B) More demand.   C) Lower import duties.   D) Rapid growth.

Section B

Directions: *In this section, you will hear two passages. At the end of each passage, you will hear three or four questions. Both the passage and the questions will be spoken only once. After you hear a question, you must choose the best answer from the four choices marked A), B), C) and D). Then mark the corresponding letter on* **Answer Sheet 1** *with a single line through the centre.*

Questions 9 to 11 are based on the passage you have just heard.

9. A) It helps employees reduce their stress.   C) It breaks the boundary of hierarchy.
   B) It distinguishes offices from prisons.   D) It reveals the dislike among employees.
10. A) Productive employees excel at all tasks they perform.
    B) Routine production work cannot make employees satisfied.
    C) Employees perform better after a happy weekend.
    D) Humor can help workers excel at routine tasks.
11. A) Put bizarre expressions on the notes.   C) Beat each other during the breaks.
    B) Take the boss doll apart as long as they reassemble it.   D) Exchange stress-reducing items with each other.

Questions 12 to 15 are based on the passage you have just heard.

12. A) The recent finding of a changed gene in obese mice.
    B) The new development of genes and hormones.
    C) The similarity between human genes and mouse genes.
    D) The influence of genes on individual organism.
13. A) It only works when the organism has sufficient fatty tissues.
    B) How and when the gene has changed is still unknown.
    C) It is named after the geneticist Rockefeller.
    D) It renders mice unable to sense when to stop eating.
14. A) People of different weight have different obesity genes.
    B) Our weight is totally determined by genes.
    C) People are born with a tendency to have a certain weight.
    D) Weight and height are closely related.
15. A) Lack of physical activities among all Americans.   C) The belief that weight cannot be controlled.
    B) The abundant provision of rich foods.   D) The change of food sources.

Section C

Directions: *In this section, you will hear three recordings of lectures or talks followed by three or four questions. The recordings will be played only once. After you hear a question, you must choose* the best answer from the four choices marked A), B), C) and D). Then mark the corresponding letter on **Answer Sheet 1** with a single line through the centre.

Questions 16 to 18 are based on the recording you have just heard.

16. A) Similarity in interests.　　　　　　　C) Compassion.
    B) Openness.　　　　　　　　　　　　D) Mental stimulation.
17. A) Pleasure.　　B) Company.　　　　　C) Popularity.　　　D) Emotional factors.
18. A) Inequality.　　　　　　　　　　　　C) Feelings of betrayal.
    B) Poor communication.　　　　　　　　D) Lack of frankness.

Questions 19 to 21 are based on the recording you have just heard.

19. A) In the deserted fields.　　　　　　　C) In the biology department of big universities.
    B) In the dinosaur pit in Utah.　　　　　D) At museums of natural history in large cities.
20. A) It is so far the largest amount of dinosaur skeletons ever found.
    B) Some natural disaster killed a whole herd of dinosaurs in the area.
    C) The finding of the bones can help discover the cause of dinosaur extinction.
    D) The uniqueness of the deposit makes it a monument in the study of dinosaurs.
21. A) They floated down an eastward flowing river.　　C) Dinosaurs went to their grave before they died.
    B) Some of the dinosaurs died of dryness.　　　　　D) They were preserved well by the sand.

Questions 22 to 25 are based on the recording you have just heard.

22. A) Developing new styles of living at a too fast pace.　C) Failing to care for parents in the traditional way.
    B) Showing less respect to the elder generation.　　　D) Lacking financial and mental independence.
23. A) They don't have the urge to be with friends and relatives.
    B) They have no choice but to live alone.
    C) They prefer different lifestyles due to their different ethnic backgrounds.
    D) They have a sense of independence and autonomy.
24. A) Many mothers don't want to become grandmothers.
    B) There have been extended families in most parts of the world.
    C) Small family units with only parents and children are over-emphasized.
    D) Parents and grandparents should stay out of the children's way.
25. A) Save enough money to pay for the nursing homes.　C) Accept the existence of the generation gap.
    B) Avoid being a burden to their children.　　　　　　D) Understand the real need of their children.

Part Ⅲ　　　　Reading Comprehension　　　(40 minutes)

Section A

Directions: *In this section, there is a passage with ten blanks. You are required to select one word for each blank from a list of choices given in a word bank following the passage. Read the passage through carefully before making your choices. Each choice in the bank is identified by a letter.*

*Please mark the corresponding letter for each item on **Answer Sheet 2** with a single line through the centre. You may not use any of the words in the bank more than once.*

Questions 26 to 35 are based on the following passage.

According to a report from the Harvard School of Public Health, many everyday products, including some bug sprays and cleaning fluids, could lead to an increased risk of brain and behavioral disorders in children. The developing brain, the report says, is particularly __26__ to the toxic effects of certain chemicals these products may contain, and the damage they cause can be __27__.

The official policy, however, is still evolving. Health and environmental __28__ have long urged U.S. government agencies to __29__ the use of some of the 11 chemicals the report cites and called for more studies on their long-term effects. In 2001, for example, the Environmental Protection Agency __30__ the type and amount of lead that could be present in paint and soil in homes and child-care __31__, after concerns were raised about lead poisoning. The agency is now __32__ the toxic effects of some of the chemicals in the latest report.

But the threshold for regulation is high. Because children's brain and behavioral disorders, like hyperactivity and lower grades, can also be linked to social and genetic factors, it's tough to pin them on exposure to specific chemicals with solid __33__ evidence, which is what the EPA requires. Even the Harvard study did not prove a direct __34__ but noted strong associations between exposure and risk of behavioral issues.

Nonetheless, it's smart to __35__ caution. While it may be impossible to prevent kids from drinking tap water that may contain trace amounts of chemicals, keeping kids away from lawns recently sprayed with chemicals and freshly dry-cleaned clothes can't hurt.

A) advocates
B) compact
C) correlation
D) exercise
E) facilities
F) interaction
G) investigating
H) overwhelmed
I) particles
J) permanent
K) restricted
L) simulating
M) statistical
N) tighten
O) vulnerable

Section B

Directions: *In this section, you are going to read a passage with ten statements attached to it. Each statement contains information given in one of the paragraphs. Identify the paragraph from which the information is derived. You may choose a paragraph more than once. Each paragraph is marked with a letter. Answer the questions by marking the corresponding letter on **Answer Sheet 2**.*

The Impossibility of Rapid Energy Transitions

[A] Politicians are fond of promising rapid energy transitions. Whether it is a transition from imported to domestic oil or from coal-powered electricity production to natural-gas power plants, politicians love to talk big. Unfortunately for them (and often the taxpayers), our energy systems are a bit like an aircraft carrier: they are unbelievably expensive, they are built to last for a very long time, they have a huge amount of inertia (meaning it takes a lot of energy to set them moving), and they have a lot of momentum once they are set in motion. No matter how hard you try, you can't turn something that large on a *dime*（10美分硬币）, or even a few thousand dimes.

[B] In physics, moving objects have two characteristics relevant to understanding the dynamics of energy systems: inertia and momentum. Inertia is the resistance of objects to efforts to change their state of motion. If you try to push a *boulder*（大圆石）, it pushes you back. Once you have started the boulder rolling, it develops momentum, which is defined by its mass and velocity. Momentum is said to be "conserved," that is, once you build it up, it has to go somewhere. So a heavy object, like a football player moving at a high speed, has a lot of momentum—that is, once he is moving, it is hard to change his state of motion. If you want to change his course, you have only a few choices: you can stop him, transferring (possibly painfully) some of his *kinetic energy*（动能）to your own body, or you can approach alongside and slowly apply pressure to gradually alter his course.

[C] But there are other kinds of momentum as well. After all, we don't speak only of objects or people as having momentum; we speak of entire systems having momentum. Whether it's a sports team or a presidential campaign, everybody relishes having the big momentum, because it makes them harder to stop or change direction.

[D] One kind of momentum is technological momentum. When a technology is deployed, its impacts reach far beyond itself. Consider the *incandescent*（白炽灯的）bulb, an object currently hated by many environmentalists and energy-efficiency advocates. The incandescent light bulb, invented by Thomas Edison, which came to be the symbol of inspiration, has been developed into hundreds, if not thousands, of forms. Today, a visit to a lighting store reveals a stunning array of choices. There are standard-shaped bulbs, flame-shaped bulbs, colored globe-shaped bulbs, and more. It is quite easy, with all that choice, to change a light bulb.

[E] But the momentum of incandescent lighting does not stop there. All of those specialized bulbs led to the building of specialized light fixtures, from the desk lamp you study by, to the ugly but beloved hand-painted Chinese lamp you inherited from your grandmother, to the ceiling fixture in your closet, to the light in your oven or refrigerator, and to the light that the dentist points at you. It is easy to change a light bulb, sure, but it is harder to change the bulb and its fixture.

[F] And there is more to the story, because not only are the devices that house incandescent bulbs shaped to their underlying characteristics, but rooms and entire buildings have been designed in accordance with how incandescent lighting reflects off walls and windows.

[G] As lighting expert Howard Brandston points out, "Generally, there are no bad light sources, only bad applications." There are some very commendable characteristics of the CFL [compact *fluorescent*（荧光的）light bulb], yet the selection of any light source remains inseparable from the *luminaire*（照明装置）that houses it, along with the space in which both are installed, and lighting requirements that need to be satisfied. The lamp, the fixture, and the room, all three must work in concert for the true benefits of end-users. If the CFL should be used for lighting a particular space, or an object within that space, the fixture must be designed to work with that lamp, and that fixture with the room. It is a *symbiotic*（共生的）

relationship. A CFL cannot be simply installed in an incandescent fixture and then expected to produce a visual appearance that is more than washed out, foggy, and dim. The whole fixture must be replaced—light source and luminaire—and this is never an inexpensive proposition.

[H] And Brandston knows a thing or two about lighting, being the man who illuminated the Statue of Liberty.

[I] Another type of momentum we have to think about when planning for changes in our energy systems is labor-pool momentum. It is one thing to say that we are going to shift 30 percent of our electricity supply from, say, coal to nuclear power in 20 years. But it is another thing to have a supply of trained talent that could let you carry out this promise. That is because the engineers, designers, regulators, operators, and all of the other skilled people needed for the new energy industry are specialists who have to be trained first (or retrained, if they are the ones being laid off in some related industry), and education, like any other complicated endeavor, takes time. And not only do our prospective new energy workers have to be trained, they have to be trained in the right sequence. One needs the designers, and perhaps the regulators, before the builders and operators, and each group of workers in training has to know there is work waiting beyond graduation. In some cases, colleges and universities might have to change their training programs, adding another layer of difficulty.

[J] By far the biggest type of momentum that comes into play when it comes to changing our energy systems is economic momentum. The major components of our energy systems, such as fuel production, refining, electrical generation and distribution, are costly installations that have lengthy life spans. They have to operate for long periods of time before the costs of development have been recovered. When investors put up money to build, say, a nuclear power plant, they expect to earn that money back over the planned life of the plant, which is typically between 40 and 60 years. Some coal power plants in the United States have operated for more than 70 years! The oldest continuously operated commercial hydro-electric plant in the United States is on New York's Hudson River, and it went into commercial service in 1898.

[K] As Vaclav Smil points out, "All the forecasts, plans, and anticipations cited above have failed so miserably because their authors and promoters thought the transitions they hoped to implement would proceed unlike all previous energy transitions, and that their progress could be accelerated in an unprecedented manner."

[L] When you hear people speaking of making a rapid transition toward any type of energy, whether it is a switch from coal to nuclear power, or a switch from gasoline-powered cars to electric cars, or even a switch from an incandescent to a fluorescent light, understanding energy system inertia and momentum can help you decide whether their plans are feasible.

36. Not only moving objects and people but all systems have momentum.
37. Changing the current energy system requires the systematic training of professionals and skilled labor.
38. Changing a light bulb is easier than changing the fixture housing it.
39. Efforts to accelerate the current energy transitions didn't succeed as expected.
40. To change the light source is costly because you have to change the whole fixture.
41. Energy systems, like an aircraft carrier set in motion, have huge momentum.
42. The problem with lighting, if it arises, often doesn't lie in light sources but in their applications.
43. The biggest obstacle to energy transition is that the present energy system is too expensive to replace.

44. The application of a technology can impact areas beyond itself.
45. Physical characteristics of moving objects help explain the dynamics of energy systems.

Section C

Directions: *There are 2 passages in this section. Each passage is followed by some questions or unfinished statements. For each of them there are four choices marked A), B), C) and D). You should decide on the best choice and mark the corresponding letter on **Answer Sheet 2** with a single line through the centre.*

Passage One

Questions 46 to 50 are based on the following passage.

One hundred years ago, "Colored" was the typical way of referring to Americans of African descent. Twenty years later, it was purposefully dropped to make way for "Negro." By the late 1960s, that term was overtaken by "Black." And then, at a press conference in Chicago in 1988, Jesse Jackson declared that "African American" was the term to embrace. This one was chosen because it echoed the labels of groups, such as "Italian Americans" and "Irish Americans," that had already been freed of widespread discrimination.

A century's worth of calculated name changes point to the fact that naming any group is a politically freighted exercise. A 2001 study cataloged all the ways in which the term "Black" carried *connotations* (含义) that were more negative than those of "African American."

But if it was known that "Black" people were viewed differently from "African Americans," researchers, until now, hadn't identified what that gap in perception was derived from. A recent study, conducted by Emory University's Erika Hall, found that "Black" people are viewed more negatively than "African Americans" because of a perceived difference in socioeconomic status. As a result, "Black" people are thought of as less competent and as having colder personalities.

The study's most striking findings shed light on the racial biases permeating the professional world. Even seemingly harmless details on a résumé, it appears, can tap into recruiters' biases. A job application might mention affiliations with groups such as the "Wisconsin Association of African-American Lawyers" or the "National Black Employees Association," the names of which apparently have consequences, and are also beyond their members' control.

In one of the study's experiments, subjects were given a brief description of a man from Chicago with the last name Williams. To one group, he was identified as "African-American," and another was told he was "Black." With little else to go on, they were asked to estimate Mr. Williams's salary, professional standing, and educational background.

The "African-American" group estimated that he earned about $37,000 a year and had a two-year college degree. The "Black" group, on the other hand, put his salary at about $29,000, and guessed that he had only "some" college experience. Nearly three-quarters of the first group guessed that Mr. Williams worked at a managerial level, while only 38.5 percent of the second group thought so.

Hall's findings suggest there's an argument to be made for electing to use "African American," though one can't help but get the sense that it's a decision that papers over the urgency of continued progress.

Perhaps a new phrase is needed, one that can bring everyone one big step closer to realizing Du Bois's original, idealistic hope: "It's not the name—it's the Thing that counts."

46. Why did Jesse Jackson embrace the term "African American" for people of African descent?

    A) It is free from racial biases.　　　　C) It is in the interest of common Americans.

    B) It represents social progress.　　　　D) It follows the standard naming practice.

47. What does the author say about the naming of an ethnic group?

    A) It advances with the times.　　　　C) It merits intensive study.

    B) It is based on racial roots.　　　　D) It is politically sensitive.

48. What do Erika Hall's findings indicate?

    A) Racial biases are widespread in the professional world.

    B) Many applicants don't attend to details on their résumés.

    C) Job seekers should all be careful about their affiliations.

    D) Most recruiters are unable to control their racial biases.

49. What does Erika Hall find in her experiment about a man with the last name Williams?

    A) African Americans fare better than many other ethnic groups.

    B) Black people's socioeconomic status in America remains low.

    C) People's conception of a person has much to do with the way he or she is labeled.

    D) One's professional standing and income are related to their educational background.

50. What is Dr. Du Bois's ideal?

    A) All Americans enjoy equal rights.

    B) A person is judged by their worth.

    C) A new term is created to address African Americans.

    D) All ethnic groups share the nation's continued progress.

Passage Two

Questions 51 to 55 are based on the following passage.

　　Across the board, American colleges and universities are not doing a very good job of preparing their students for the workplace or their post-graduation lives. This was made clear by the work of two sociologists, Richard Arum and Josipa Roksa. In 2011 they released a landmark study titled "Academically Adrift," which documented the lack of intellectual growth experienced by many people enrolled in college. In particular, Arum and Roksa found, college students were not developing the critical thinking, analytic reasoning and other higher-level skills that are necessary to thrive in today's knowledge-based economy and to lead our nation in a time of complex challenges and dynamic change.

　　Arum and Roksa placed the blame for students' lack of learning on a watered-down college curriculum and lowered undergraduate work standards. Although going to college is supposed to be a full-time job, students spent, on average, only 12 to 14 hours a week studying and many were skating through their semesters without doing a significant amount of reading and writing. Students who take more challenging classes and spend more time studying do learn more. But the priorities of many undergraduates are with extracurricular activities, playing sports, and partying and socializing.

　　Laura Hamilton, the author of a study on parents who pay for college, will argue in a forthcoming book that college administrations are overly concerned with the social and athletic activities of their students. In Paying for the Party, Hamilton describes what she calls the "party pathway," which eases many students through college, helped along by various clubs that send students into the party scene and a host of easier majors. By sanctioning this watered-down version of college, universities are "catering to the social and educational needs of wealthy students at the expense of others" who won't enjoy the financial backing or social connections of richer students once they graduate.

　　These students need to build skills and knowledge during college if they are to use their degrees as a stepping-stone to middle-class mobility. But more privileged students must not waste this opportunity either. As recent graduates can testify, the job market isn't kind to candidates who can't demonstrate genuine competence, along with a well-cultivated willingness to work hard. Nor is the global economy forgiving of an American workforce with increasingly weak literacy, math and science abilities. College graduates will still fare better than those with only a high school education, of course. But a university degree unaccompanied by a gain in knowledge or skills is an empty achievement indeed. For students who have been coasting through college, and for American universities that have been demanding less work, offering more attractions and charging higher tuition, the party may soon be over.

51. What is Arum and Roksa's finding about higher education in America?
    A) It aims at stimulating the intellectual curiosity of college students.
    B) It fails to prepare students to face the challenges of modern times.
    C) It has experienced dramatic changes in recent years.
    D) It has tried hard to satisfy students' various needs.
52. What is responsible for the students' lack of higher-level skills?
    A) The diluted college curriculum.   C) The absence of rigorous discipline.
    B) The boring classroom activities.   D) The outdated educational approach.
53. What does Laura Hamilton say about college administrations?
    A) They fail to give adequate help to the needy students.
    B) They tend to offer too many less challenging courses.
    C) They seem to be out of touch with society.
    D) They prioritize non-academic activities.
54. What can be learned about the socially and financially privileged students?
    A) They tend to have a sense of superiority over their peers.
    B) They can afford to choose easier majors in order to enjoy themselves.
    C) They spend a lot of time building strong connections with businesses.
    D) They can climb the social ladder even without a degree.
55. What does the author suggest in the last paragraph?
    A) American higher education has lost its global competitiveness.
    B) People should not expect too much from American higher education.

C) The current situation in American higher education may not last long.
D) It will take a long time to change the current trend in higher education.

Part IV Translation (30 minutes)

Directions: *For this part, you are allowed 30 minutes to translate a passage from Chinese into English. You should write your answer on **Answer Sheet 2**.*

《三国演义》写于14世纪,是中国著名的历史小说。这部小说以三国时期的历史为基础,描写了从二世纪下半叶到三世纪下半叶魏、蜀、吴之间的战争。小说描写了近千个人物和无数的历史事件。虽然这些人物和事件是有历史根据的,但它们都在不同程度上被戏剧化和扩大了。《三国演义》是公认的文学名著。面世以来,对中国一代又一代人产生了持续而久远的影响,吸引了一代又一代读者,对中国历史产生了广泛而深远的影响。

答案速查

Part II Listening Comprehension
Section A 1. A 2. D 3. B 4. C 5. B 6. D 7. A 8. C
Section B 9. A 10. D 11. B 12. A 13. D 14. C 15. B
Section C 16. A 17. D 18. C 19. D 20. B 21. A 22. C 23. D 24. B 25. B

Part III Reading Comprehension
Section A 26. O 27. J 28. A 29. N 30. K 31. E 32. G 33. M 34. C 35. D
Section B 36. C 37. I 38. E 39. K 40. G 41. A 42. G 43. J 44. D 45. B
Section C 46. A 47. D 48. A 49. C 50. A 51. B 52. A 53. D 54. B 55. C

未得到监考教师指令前，不得翻阅该试题册！

2019年12月大学英语六级考试真题（第一套）

Part I　　　　　　　　Writing　　　　　　　　(30 minutes)

（请于正式开考后半小时内完成该部分，之后将进行听力考试）

Directions: *For this part, you are allowed 30 minutes to write an essay on* **the importance of having a sense of family responsibility**. *You should write at least* **150** *words but no more than* **200** *words.*

Part II　　　　　　Listening Comprehension　　　　　(30 minutes)

Section A

Directions: *In this section, you will hear two long conversations. At the end of each conversation, you will hear four questions. Both the conversation and the questions will be spoken only once. After you hear a question, you must choose the best answer from the four choices marked A), B), C) and D). Then mark the corresponding letter on* **Answer Sheet 1** *with a single line through the centre.*

APP 扫码，听音频

Questions 1 to 4 are based on the conversation you have just heard.

1. A) Magazine reporter.　　B) Fashion designer.　　C) Website designer.　　D) Features editor.
2. A) Designing sports clothing.　　　　　　　　　C) Answering daily emails.
   B) Consulting fashion experts.　　　　　　　　 D) Interviewing job-seekers.
3. A) It is challenging.　　B) It is fascinating.　　C) It is tiresome.　　D) It is fashionable.
4. A) Her persistence.　　B) Her experience.　　C) Her competence.　　D) Her confidence.

Questions 5 to 8 are based on the conversation you have just heard.

5. A) It is enjoyable.　　　　　　　　　　　　　C) It is divorced from real life.
   B) It is educational.　　　　　　　　　　　　　D) It is adapted from a drama.
6. A) All the roles are played by famous actors and actresses.
   B) It is based on the real-life experiences of some celebrities.
   C) Its plots and events reveal a lot about Frankie's actual life.
   D) It is written, directed, edited and produced by Frankie himself.
7. A) Go to the theater and enjoy it.　　　　　　C) Watch it with the man.
   B) Recommend it to her friends.　　　　　　　D) Download and watch it.
8. A) It has drawn criticisms from scientists.　　　C) It is a ridiculous piece of satire.
   B) It has been showing for over a decade.　　　D) It is against common sense.

Section B

Directions: *In this section, you will hear two passages. At the end of each passage, you will hear three or four questions. Both the passage and the questions will be spoken only once. After you hear a question, you must choose the best answer from the four choices marked A), B), C) and D). Then mark the corresponding letter on **Answer Sheet 1** with a single line through the centre.*

Questions 9 to 11 are based on the passage you have just heard.

9. A) They are likely to get injured when moving too fast.
   B) They believe in team spirit for good performance.
   C) They need to keep moving to avoid getting hurt.
   D) They have to learn how to avoid body contact.

10. A) They do not have many years to live after retirement.
    B) They tend to live a longer life with early retirement.
    C) They do not start enjoying life until full retirement.
    D) They keep themselves busy even after retirement.

11. A) It prevents us from worrying.
    B) It slows down our aging process.
    C) It enables us to accomplish more in life.
    D) It provides us with more chances to learn.

Questions 12 to 15 are based on the passage you have just heard.

12. A) It tends to dwell upon their joyous experiences.
    B) It wanders for almost half of their waking time.
    C) It has trouble concentrating after a brain injury.
    D) It tends to be affected by their negative feelings.

13. A) To find how happiness relates to daydreaming.
    B) To observe how one's mind affects one's behavior.
    C) To see why daydreaming impacts what one is doing.
    D) To study the relation between health and daydreaming.

14. A) It helps them make good decisions.
    B) It helps them tap their potentials.
    C) It contributes to their creativity.
    D) It contributes to clear thinking.

15. A) Subjects with clear goals in mind outperformed those without clear goals.
    B) The difference in performance between the two groups was insignificant.
    C) Non-daydreamers were more focused on their tasks than daydreamers.
    D) Daydreamers did better than non-daydreamers in task performance.

Section C

Directions: *In this section, you will hear three recordings of lectures or talks followed by three or four questions. The recordings will be played only once. After you hear a question, you must choose the best answer from the four choices marked A), B), C) and D). Then mark the corresponding letter on **Answer Sheet 1** with a single line through the centre.*

Questions 16 to 18 are based on the recording you have just heard.

16. A) They are the oldest buildings in Europe.
    C) They are renovated to attract tourists.

B) They are part of the Christian tradition.   D) They are in worsening condition.

17. A) They have a history of 14 centuries.   C) They are without foundations.
    B) They are 40 metres tall on average.   D) They consist of several storeys.

18. A) Wood was harmonious with nature.   C) Timber was abundant in Scandinavia.
    B) Wooden buildings kept the cold out.   D) The Vikings liked wooden structures.

Questions 19 to 21 are based on the recording you have just heard.

19. A) Similarities between human babies and baby animals.
    B) Cognitive features of different newly born mammals.
    C) Adults' influence on children.
    D) Abilities of human babies.

20. A) They can distinguish a happy tune from a sad one.
    B) They love happy melodies more than sad ones.
    C) They fall asleep easily while listening to music.
    D) They are already sensitive to beats and rhythms.

21. A) Infants' facial expressions.   C) Babies' interaction with adults.
    B) Babies' emotions.   D) Infants' behaviors.

Questions 22 to 25 are based on the recording you have just heard.

22. A) It may harm the culture of today's workplace.   C) It may result in unwillingness to take risks.
    B) It may hinder individual career advancement.   D) It may put too much pressure on team members.

23. A) They can hardly give expression to their original views.
    B) They can become less motivated to do projects of their own.
    C) They may find it hard to get their contributions recognized.
    D) They may eventually lose their confidence and creativity.

24. A) They can enlarge their professional circle.   C) They can make the best use of their expertise.
    B) They can get chances to engage in research.   D) They can complete the project more easily.

25. A) It may cause lots of arguments in a team.   C) It may give rise to a lot of unnecessary expenses.
    B) It may prevent making a timely decision.   D) It may deprive a team of business opportunities.

Part Ⅲ   Reading Comprehension   (40 minutes)

Section A

Directions: *In this section, there is a passage with ten blanks. You are required to select one word for each blank from a list of choices given in a word bank following the passage. Read the passage through carefully before making your choices. Each choice in the bank is identified by a letter. Please mark the corresponding letter for each item on* **Answer Sheet 2** *with a single line through the centre. You may not use any of the words in the bank more than once.*

When considering risk factors associated with serious chronic diseases, we often think about health indicators such as cholesterol, blood pressure, and body weight. But poor diet and physical inactivity also each increase the risk of heart disease and have a role to play in the development of some cancers. Perhaps worse, the __26__ effects of an unhealthy diet and insufficient exercise are not limited to your body. Recent research has also shown that __27__ in a high-fat and high-sugar diet may have negative effects on your brain, causing learning and memory __28__.

Studies have found obesity is associated with impairments in cognitive functioning, as __29__ by a range of learning and memory tests, such as the ability to remember a list of words presented some minutes or hours earlier. There is also a growing body of evidence that diet-induced cognitive impairments can emerge __30__ —within weeks or even days. For example, one study found healthy adults __31__ to a high-fat diet for five days showed impaired attention, memory, and mood compared with a low-fat diet control group. Another study also found eating a high-fat and high-sugar breakfast each day for as little as four days resulted in problems with learning and memory __32__ to those observed in overweight and obese individuals.

Body weight was not hugely different between the groups eating a healthy diet and those on high fat and sugar diets. So this shows negative __33__ of poor dietary intake can occur even when body weight has not changed __34__. Thus, body weight is not always the best indicator of health and a thin person still needs to eat well and exercise __35__.

A) assessed	I) excelling
B) assigned	J) indulging
C) consequences	K) loopholes
D) conspicuously	L) rapidly
E) deficits	M) redundant
F) designated	N) regularly
G) detrimental	O) similar
H) digestion	

Section B

Directions: *In this section, you are going to read a passage with ten statements attached to it. Each statement contains information given in one of the paragraphs. Identify the paragraph from which the information is derived. You may choose a paragraph more than once. Each paragraph is marked with a letter. Answer the questions by marking the corresponding letter on* **Answer Sheet 2**.

Increased Screen Time and Wellbeing Decline in Youth

[A] Have young people never had it so good? Or do they face more challenges than any previous generation? Our current era in the West is one of high wealth. This means minors enjoy material benefits and legal protections that would have been the envy of those living in the past. But there is an increasing suspicion that all is not well for our youth. And one of the most popular explanations, among some experts and the popular media, is that excessive "screen time" is to blame. (This refers to all the attention young people devote to their phones, tablets and laptops.) However, this is a contentious theory and such claims have been treated skeptically by some scholars based on their reading of the relevant data.

[B] Now a new study has provided another contribution to the debate, uncovering strong evidence that adolescent wellbeing in the United States really is experiencing a decline and arguing that the most likely cause is the electronic riches we have given them. The background to this is that from the 1960s into the early 2000s, measures of average wellbeing went up in the US. This was especially true for younger people. It reflected the fact that these decades saw a climb in general standards of living and avoidance of mass societal traumas like full-scale war or economic deprivation. However, the "screen time" hypothesis, advanced by researchers such as Jean Twenge, is that electronic devices and excessive time spent online may have reversed these trends in recent years, causing problems for young people's psychological health.

[C] To investigate, Twenge and her colleagues dived into the "Monitoring the Future" dataset based on annual surveys of American school students from grades 8, 10, and 12 that started in 1991. In total, 1.1 million young people answered various questions related to their wellbeing. Twenge's team's analysis of the answers confirmed the earlier, well-established wellbeing climb, with scores rising across the 1990s, and into the later 2000s. This was found across measures like self-esteem, life satisfaction, happiness and satisfaction with individual domains like job, neighborhood, or friends. But around 2012 these measures started to decline. This continued through 2016, the most recent year for which data is available.

[D] Twenge and her colleagues wanted to understand why this change in average wellbeing occurred. However, it is very hard to demonstrate causes using non-experimental data such as this. In fact, when Twenge previously used this data to suggest a screen time effect, some commentators were quick to raise this problem. They argued that her causal-sounding claims rested on correlational data, and that she had not adequately accounted for other potential causal factors. This time around, Twenge and her team make a point of saying that they are not trying to establish causes as such, but that they are assessing the plausibility of potential causes.

[E] First, they explain that if a given variable is playing a role in affecting wellbeing, then we should expect any change in that variable to correlate with the observed changes in wellbeing. If not, it is not plausible that the variable is a causal factor. So the researchers looked at time spent in a number of activities that could plausibly be driving the wellbeing decline. Less sport, and fewer meetings with peers correlated with lower wellbeing, as did less time reading print media (newspapers) and, surprisingly, less time doing homework. (This last finding would appear to contradict another popular hypothesis that it is our burdening of students with assignment that is causing all the problems.) In addition, more TV watching and more electronic communication both correlated with lower wellbeing. All these effects held true for measures of happiness, life satisfaction and self-esteem, with the effects stronger in the 8th and 10th-graders.

[F] Next, Twenge's team dug a little deeper into the data on screen time. They found that adolescents who spent a very small amount of time on digital devices—a couple of hours a week—had the highest wellbeing. Their wellbeing was even higher than those who never used such devices. However, higher doses of screen time were clearly associated with lower happiness. Those spending 10 — 19 hours per week on their devices were 41 percent more likely to be unhappy than lower-frequency users. Those who used such devices 40 hours a week or more (one in ten teenagers) were twice as likely to be unhappy. The data was slightly complicated by the fact that there was a tendency for kids who were social in the real world to also use more online communication, but by bracketing out different cases it became clear that the real-world sociality component correlated with greater wellbeing, whereas greater time on screens or online only correlated with poorer wellbeing.

[G] So far, so plausible. But the next question is, are the drops in average wellbeing happening at the same time as trends toward increased electronic device usage? It looks like it—after all, 2012 was the tipping point when more than half of Americans began owning smartphones. Twenge and her colleagues also found that across the key years of 2013–16, wellbeing was indeed lowest in years where adolescents spent more time online, on social media, and reading news online, and when more youth in the United States had smartphones. And in a second analysis, they found that where technology went, dips in wellbeing followed. For instance, years with a larger increase in online usage were followed by years with lower wellbeing, rather than the other way around. This does not prove causality, but is consistent with it. Meanwhile, TV use did not show this tracking. TV might make you less happy, but this is not what seems to be driving the recent declines in young people's average happiness.

[H] A similar but reversed pattern was found for the activities associated with greater wellbeing. For example, years when people spent more time with friends were better years for wellbeing (and followed by better years). Sadly, the data also showed face-to-face socializing and sports activity had declined over the period covered by the survey.

[I] There is another explanation that Twenge and her colleagues wanted to address: the impact of the great recession of 2007–2009, which hit a great number of American families and might be affecting adolescents. The dataset they used did not include economic data, so instead the researchers looked at whether the 2013–16 wellbeing decline was tracking economic indicators. They found some evidence that some crude measures, like income inequality, correlated with changes in wellbeing, but economic measures with a more direct impact, like family income and unemployment rates (which put families into difficulties), had no relationship with wellbeing. The researchers also note the recession hit some years before we see the beginning of the wellbeing drop, and before the steepest wellbeing decline, which occurred in 2013.

[J] The researchers conclude that electronic communication was the only adolescent activity that increased at the same time psychological wellbeing declined. I suspect that some experts in the field will be keen to address alternative explanations, such as unassessed variables playing a role in the wellbeing decline. But the new work does go further than previous research and suggests that screen time should still be considered a potential barrier to young people's flourishing.

36. The year when most Americans began using smartphones was identified as a turning point in young Americans' level of happiness.
37. Scores in various wellbeing measures began to go downward among young Americans in recent years.
38. Unfortunately, activities involving direct contact with people, which contributed to better wellbeing, were found to be on the decline.
39. In response to past critics, Twenge and her co-researchers stress they are not trying to prove that the use of digital devices reduces young people's wellbeing.

40. In the last few decades of the 20th century, living standards went up and economic depressions were largely averted in the US.
41. Contrary to popular belief, doing homework might add to students' wellbeing.
42. The author believes the researchers' new study has gone a step further regarding the impact of screen time on wellbeing.
43. The researchers found that extended screen time makes young people less happy.
44. Data reveals that economic inequality rather than family income might affect people's wellbeing.
45. Too much screen time is widely believed to be the cause of unhappiness among today's young people.

Section C

Directions: *There are 2 passages in this section. Each passage is followed by some questions or unfinished statements. For each of them there are four choices marked A), B), C) and D). You should decide on the best choice and mark the corresponding letter on **Answer Sheet 2** with a single line through the centre.*

Passage One

Questions 46 to 50 are based on the following passage.

"The dangerous thing about lying is people don't understand how the act changes us," says Dan Ariely, behavioural psychologist at Duke University. Psychologists have documented children lying as early as the age of two. Some experts even consider lying a developmental milestone, like crawling and walking, because it requires sophisticated planning, attention and the ability to see a situation from someone else's perspective to manipulate them. But, for most people, lying gets limited as we develop a sense of morality and the ability to self-regulate.

Harvard cognitive neuroscientist Joshua Greene says, for most of us, lying takes work. In studies, he gave subjects a chance to deceive for monetary gain while examining their brains in a functional MRI machine, which maps blood flow to active parts of the brain. Some people told the truth instantly and instinctively. But others opted to lie, and they showed increased activity in their frontal *parietal*(颅腔壁的) control network, which is involved in difficult or complex thinking. This suggests that they were deciding between truth and dishonesty—and ultimately opting for the latter. For a follow-up analysis, he found that people whose *neural*(神经的) reward centres were more active when they won money were also more likely to be among the group of liars—suggesting that lying may have to do with the inability to resist temptation.

External conditions also matter in terms of when and how often we lie. We are more likely to lie, research shows, when we are able to rationalise it, when we are stressed and fatigued or see others being dishonest. And we are less likely to lie when we have moral reminders or when we think others are watching. "We as a society need to understand that, when we don't punish lying, we increase the probability it will happen again," Ariely says.

In a 2016 study published in the journal *Nature Neuroscience*, Ariely and colleagues showed how dishonesty alters people's brains, making it easier to tell lies in the future. When people uttered a falsehood, the scientists noticed a burst of activity in their amygdala. The amygdala is a crucial part of the brain that produces fear, anxiety and emotional responses—including that sinking, guilty feeling you get when you lie. But when scientists had their subjects play a game in which they won money by deceiving their partner, they noticed the negative signals from the amygdala began to decrease. Not only that, but when people faced no consequences for dishonesty, their falsehoods tended to get even more sensational. This means that if you give people multiple opportunities to lie for their own benefit, they start with little lies which get bigger over time.

46. Why do some experts consider lying a milestone in a child's development?
    A) It shows they have the ability to view complex situations from different angles.
    B) It indicates they have an ability more remarkable than crawling and walking.
    C) It represents their ability to actively interact with people around them.
    D) It involves the coordination of both their mental and physical abilities.

47. Why does the Harvard neuroscientist say that lying takes work?
    A) It is hard to choose from several options.   C) It requires speedy blood flow into one's brain.
    B) It is difficult to sound natural or plausible.   D) It involves lots of sophisticated mental activity.

48. Under what circumstances do people tend to lie?
    A) When they become too emotional.   C) When the temptation is too strong.
    B) When they face too much peer pressure.   D) When the consequences are not imminent.

49. When are people less likely to lie?
    A) When they are worn out and stressed.   C) When they think in a rational way.
    B) When they are under watchful eyes.   D) When they have a clear conscience.

50. What does the author say will happen when a liar does not get punished?
    A) They may feel justified.   C) They will become complacent.
    B) They will tell bigger lies.   D) They may mix lies and truths.

Passage Two

Questions 51 to 55 are based on the following passage.

Here's how the Pacific Northwest is preparing for "The Big One". It's the mother of all disaster drills for what could be the worst disaster in American history. California has spent years preparing for "The Big One"—the inevitable earthquake that will undoubtedly unleash all kinds of havoc along the famous San Andreas *fault*（断层）. But what if the fault that runs along the Pacific Northwest delivers a gigantic earthquake of its own? If the people of the Cascadia region have anything to do with it, they won't be caught unawares.

The region is engaged in a multi-day earthquake-and-*tsunami*（海啸）drill involving around 20,000 people. The Cascadia Rising drill gives area residents and emergency responders a chance to practice what to do in case of a 9.0-magnitude earthquake and tsunami along one of the nation's dangerous—and underestimated—faults.

The Cascadia Earthquake Zone is big enough to compete with San Andreas (it's been called the most dangerous fault in America), but it's much lesser known than its California cousin. Nearly 700 miles long, the earthquake zone is located by the North American Plate off the coast of Pacific British Columbia, Washington, Oregon and Northern California.

Cascadia is what's known as a "megathrust" fault. Megathrusts are created in earthquake zones—land plate boundaries where two plates converge. In the areas where one plate is beneath another, stress builds up over time. During a megathrust event, all of that stress releases and some of the world's most powerful earthquakes occur. Remember the 9.1 earthquake and tsunami in the Indian Ocean off Sumatra in 2004? It was caused by a megathrust event as the India plate moved beneath the Burma micro-plate.

The last time a major earthquake occurred along the Cascadia fault was in 1700, so officials worry that another event could occur any time. To prevent that event from becoming a catastrophe, first responders will join members of the public in rehearsals that involve communication, evacuation, search and rescue, and other scenarios.

Thousands of casualties are expected if a 9.0 earthquake were to occur. First, the earthquake would shake metropolitan areas including Seattle and Portland. This could trigger a tsunami that would create havoc along the coast. Not all casualties can necessarily be prevented—but by coordinating across local, state, and even national borders, officials hope that the worst-case scenario can be averted. On the exercised website, officials explain that the report they prepare during this rehearsal will inform disaster management for years to come.

For hundreds of thousands of Cascadia residents, "The Big One" isn't a question of if, only when. And it's never too early to get ready for the inevitable.

51. What does "The Big One" refer to?
    A) A gigantic geological fault.
    B) A large-scale exercise to prepare for disasters.
    C) A massive natural catastrophe.
    D) A huge tsunami on the California coast.

52. What is the purpose of the Cascadia Rising drill?
    A) To prepare people for a major earthquake and tsunami.
    B) To increase residents' awareness of imminent disasters.
    C) To teach people how to adapt to post-disaster life.
    D) To cope with the aftermath of a possible earthquake.

53. What happens in case of a megathrust earthquake according to the passage?
    A) Two plates merge into one.
    B) Boundaries blur between plates.
    C) A variety of forces converge.
    D) Enormous stress is released.

54. What do the officials hope to achieve through the drills?
    A) Coordinating various disaster-relief efforts.
    B) Reducing casualties in the event of a disaster.
    C) Minimizing property loss caused by disasters.
    D) Establishing disaster and emergency management.

55. What does the author say about "The Big One"?
    A) Whether it will occur remains to be seen.
    B) How it will arrive is too early to predict.
    C) Its occurrence is just a matter of time.
    D) It keeps haunting Cascadia residents.

Part IV Translation (30 minutes)

Directions: *For this part, you are allowed 30 minutes to translate a passage from Chinese into English. You should write your answer on **Answer Sheet 2**.*

牡丹（peony）花色艳丽，形象高雅，象征着和平与繁荣，因而在中国被称为"花中之王"。中国许多地方都培育和种植牡丹。千百年来，创作了许多诗歌和绘画赞美牡丹。唐代时期，牡丹在皇家园林普遍种植并被誉为国花，因而特别风行。十世纪时，洛阳古城成为牡丹栽培中心，而且这一地位一直保持到今天。现在，成千上万的国内外游客蜂拥到洛阳参加一年一度的牡丹节，欣赏洛阳牡丹的独特之美，同时探索九朝古都的历史。

答案速查

Part Ⅱ　Listening Comprehension
Section A　1. D　2. C　3. B　4. A　5. A　6. D　7. D　8. B
Section B　9. C　10. A　11. A　12. B　13. A　14. C　15. D
Section C　16. D　17. C　18. C　19. D　20. A　21. B　22. B　23. C　24. A　25. B

Part Ⅲ　Reading Comprehension
Section A　26. G　27. J　28. E　29. A　30. L　31. B　32. O　33. C　34. D　35. N
Section B　36. G　37. C　38. H　39. D　40. B　41. E　42. J　43. F　44. I　45. A
Section C　46. A　47. D　48. B　49. B　50. B　51. C　52. A　53. D　54. B　55. C

未得到监考教师指令前，不得翻阅该试题册！

2019年12月大学英语六级考试真题（第二套）

Part Ⅰ　　　　　　　　　Writing　　　　　　　　　(30 minutes)

（请于正式开考后半小时内完成该部分，之后将进行听力考试）

Directions: *For this part, you are allowed 30 minutes to write an essay on* **the importance of having a sense of social responsibility**. *You should write at least* **150** *words but no more than* **200** *words.*

Part Ⅱ　　　　　　Listening Comprehension　　　　　(30 minutes)

Section A

Directions: *In this section, you will hear two long conversations. At the end of each conversation, you will hear four questions. Both the conversation and the questions will be spoken only once. After you hear a question, you must choose the best answer from the four choices marked A), B), C) and D). Then mark the corresponding letter on* **Answer Sheet 1** *with a single line through the centre.*

Questions 1 to 4 are based on the conversation you have just heard.

1. A) It focuses exclusively on jazz.
   B) It sponsors major jazz concerts.
   C) It has several branches in London.
   D) It displays albums by new music talents.

2. A) It originated with cowboys.
   B) Its market has now shrunk.
   C) Its listeners are mostly young people.
   D) It remains as widespread as hip hop music.

3. A) Its definition is varied and complicated.
   B) It is still going through experimentation.
   C) It is frequently accompanied by singing.
   D) Its style has remained largely unchanged.

4. A) Learn to play them.
   B) Take music lessons.
   C) Listen to them yourself.
   D) Consult jazz musicians.

Questions 5 to 8 are based on the conversation you have just heard.

5. A) She paid her mortgage.
   B) She called on the man.
   C) She made a business plan.
   D) She went to the bank.

6. A) Her previous debt hadn't been cleared yet.
   B) Her credit history was considered poor.
   C) She had apparently asked for too much.
   D) She didn't pay her mortgage in time.

7. A) Pay a debt long overdue.
   B) Buy a piece of property.
   C) Start her own business.
   D) Check her credit history.

8. A) Seek advice from an expert about fundraising.
   C) Build up her own finances step by step.

B) Ask for smaller loans from different lenders.   D) Revise her business proposal carefully.

Section B

Directions: *In this section, you will hear two passages. At the end of each passage, you will hear three or four questions. Both the passage and the questions will be spoken only once. After you hear a question, you must choose the best answer from the four choices marked A), B), C) and D). Then mark the corresponding letter on **Answer Sheet 1** with a single line through the centre.*

Questions 9 to 11 are based on the passage you have just heard.

9. A) It is profitable and environmentally friendly.   C) It is small and unconventional.
   B) It is well located and completely automated.   D) It is fertile and productive.
10. A) Their urge to make farming more enjoyable.   C) Their hope to revitalize traditional farming.
    B) Their desire to improve farming equipment.   D) Their wish to set a new farming standard.
11. A) It saves a lot of electricity.   C) It causes hardly any pollution.
    B) It needs little maintenance.   D) It loosens soil while weeding.

Questions 12 to 15 are based on the passage you have just heard.

12. A) It has turned certain insects into a new food source.
    B) It has started to expand business outside the UK.
    C) It has imported some exotic foods from overseas.
    D) It has joined hands with Sainsbury's to sell pet insects.
13. A) It was really unforgettable.   C) It hurt his throat slightly.
    B) It was a pleasant surprise.   D) It made him feel strange.
14. A) They are more tasty than beef, chicken or pork.
    B) They are more nutritious than soups and salads.
    C) They contain more protein than conventional meats.
    D) They will soon gain popularity throughout the world.
15. A) It is environmentally friendly.   C) It requires new technology.
    B) It is a promising industry.   D) It saves huge amounts of labour.

Section C

Directions: *In this section, you will hear three recordings of lectures or talks followed by three or four questions. The recordings will be played only once. After you hear a question, you must choose the best answer from the four choices marked A), B), C) and D). Then mark the corresponding letter on **Answer Sheet 1** with a single line through the centre.*

Questions 16 to 18 are based on the recording you have just heard.

16. A) To categorize different types of learners.   C) To understand the mechanism of the human brain.
    B) To find out what students prefer to learn.   D) To see if they are inherent traits affecting learning.
17. A) It was defective.   C) It was original in design.
    B) It was misguided.   D) It was thought-provoking.
18. A) Auditory aids are as important as visual aids.

B) Visual aids are helpful to all types of learners.
C) Reading plain texts is more effective than viewing pictures.
D) Scientific concepts are hard to understand without visual aids.

Questions 19 to 21 are based on the recording you have just heard.

19. A) Not playing a role in a workplace revolution.   C) Not earning enough money to provide for the family.
    B) Not benefiting from free-market capitalism.   D) Not spending enough time on family life and leisure.
20. A) People would be working only fifteen hours a week now.
    B) The balance of power in the workplace would change.
    C) Technological advances would create many new jobs.
    D) Most workers could afford to have a house of their own.
21. A) Loss of workers' personal dignity.   C) Deterioration of workers' mental health.
    B) Deprivation of workers' creativity.   D) Unequal distribution of working hours.

Questions 22 to 25 are based on the recording you have just heard.

22. A) It is the worst managed airport in German history.
    B) It is now the biggest and busiest airport in Europe.
    C) It has become something of a joke among Germans.
    D) It has become a typical symbol of German efficiency.
23. A) The city's airports are outdated.   C) The city wanted to boost its economy.
    B) The city had just been reunified.   D) The city wanted to attract more tourists.
24. A) The municipal government kept changing hands.   C) Shortage of funding delayed its construction.
    B) The construction firm breached the contract.   D) Problems of different kinds kept popping up.
25. A) Tourism industry in Berlin suffers.   C) Huge maintenance costs accumulate.
    B) All kinds of equipment gets rusted.   D) Complaints by local residents increase.

Part III　　　　　Reading Comprehension　　　(40 minutes)

Section A

Directions: *In this section, there is a passage with ten blanks. You are required to select one word for each blank from a list of choices given in a word bank following the passage. Read the passage through carefully before making your choices. Each choice in the bank is identified by a letter. Please mark the corresponding letter for each item on **Answer Sheet 2** with a single line through the centre. You may not use any of the words in the bank more than once.*

　　The persistent haze over many of our cities is a reminder of the polluted air that we breathe. Over 80% of the world's urban population is breathing air that fails to meet World Health Organisation guidelines, and an estimated 4.5 million people died __26__ from outdoor air pollution in 2015.

　　Globally, urban populations are expected to double in the next 40 years, and an extra 2 billion people will need new places to live, as well as services and ways to move around their cities. What is more important, the decisions that we make now about the design of our cities will __27__ the everyday lives and health of the coming generations. So what would a smog-free, or at least low-pollution, city be like?

Traffic has become __28__ with air pollution, and many countries intend to ban the sale of new petrol and diesel cars in the next two decades. But simply __29__ to electric cars will not mean pollution-free cities. The level of emissions they cause will depend on how the electricity to run them is __30__, while brakes, tyres and roads all create tiny airborne __31__ as they wear out.

Across the developed world, car use is in decline as more people move to city centres, while young people especially are __32__ for other means of travel. Researchers are already asking if motor vehicle use has reached its __33__ and will decline, but transport planners have yet to catch up with this __34__, instead of laying new roads to tackle traffic jams. As users of London's orbital M25 motorway will know, new roads rapidly fill with more traffic. In the US, studies have shown that doubling the size of a road can __35__ double the traffic, taking us back to the starting point.

A) alternate	I) particles
B) crown	J) peak
C) determine	K) prematurely
D) generated	L) simply
E) locating	M) switching
F) merged	N) synonymous
G) miniatures	O) trend
H) opting	

Section B

Directions: *In this section, you are going to read a passage with ten statements attached to it. Each statement contains information given in one of the paragraphs. Identify the paragraph from which the information is derived. You may choose a paragraph more than once. Each paragraph is marked with a letter. Answer the questions by marking the corresponding letter on* ***Answer Sheet 2***.

How much protein do you really need?

[A] The marketing is tempting: Get stronger muscles and healthier bodies with minimal effort by adding protein powder to your morning shake or juice drink. Or grab a protein bar at lunch or for a quick snack. Today, you can find protein supplements everywhere—online or at the pharmacy, grocery store or health food store. They come in powders, pills and bars. With more than $12 billion in sales this year, the industry is booming and, according to the market research company, Grand View Research, is on track to sell billions more by 2025. But do we really need all this supplemental protein? It depends. There are pros, cons and some other things to consider.

[B] For starters, protein is critical for every cell in our body. It helps build nails, hair, bones and muscles. It can also help you feel fuller longer than eating foods without protein. And, unlike nutrients that are found only in a few foods, protein is present in all foods. "The typical American diet is a lot higher in protein than a lot of us think," says registered dietitian Angela Pipitone. "It's in foods many of us expect, such as beef, chicken and other types of meat and dairy. But it's also in foods that may not come immediately to mind like vegetables, fruit, beans and grains."

[C] The U. S. government's recommended daily allowance (RDA) for the average adult is 50 to 60 grams of protein a day. This may sound like a lot, but Pipitone says: "We get bits of protein here and there and that really adds up throughout the day." Take, for example, breakfast. If you eat two eggs topped with a little bit of cheese and an orange on the side, you already have 22 grams of protein. Each egg gives you 7 grams, the cheese gives you about 6 grams and the orange—about 2 grams. Add a lunch of chicken, rice and *broccoli*（西兰花）, and you are already over the recommended 50 grams. "You can get enough protein and meet the RDA before you even get to dinner," says Pipitone.

[D] So if it's so easy to get your protein in food, why add more in the form of powders, snack bars or a boost at your local juice bar? No need to, says Pipitone, because, in fact, most of us already get enough protein in our diet. "Whole foods are always the best option rather than adding supplements," she says, noting the FDA does not regulate supplements as rigorously as foods or drugs. So there could be less protein, more sugar and some additives you wouldn't expect, such as *caffeine*（咖啡因）.

[E] If you are considering a supplement, read the list of ingredients, she says, although this is not always reliable. "I've seen very expensive protein supplements that claim to be high quality but they might not really be beneficial for the average healthy adult," she says. "It could just be a waste of money."

[F] But there are certain situations that do warrant extra protein. "Anytime you're repairing or building muscle," Pipitone says, such as if you're an extreme endurance athlete, training for a marathon, or you're a body builder. If you're moderately exercising for 150 minutes a week, as the Centers for Disease Control and Prevention recommends, or less than that, you're probably not an extreme athlete. Extreme athletes expend lots of energy breaking down and repairing and building muscles. Protein can give them the edge they need to speed that process.

[G] Vegans can benefit from protein supplements since they do not eat animal-based protein sources like meat, dairy or eggs. And, for someone always on-the-go who may not have time for a meal, a protein snack bar can be a good option for occasional meal replacement. Also, individuals recovering from surgery or an injury can also benefit from extra protein. So, too, can older people. At around age 60, "muscles really start to break down," says Kathryn Starr, an aging researcher, "and because of that, the protein needs of an older adult actually increase."

[H] In fact, along with her colleague Connie Bales, Starr recently conducted a small study that found that adding extra protein foods to the diet of obese older individuals who were trying to lose weight strengthened their muscles. Participants in the study were separated into two groups—one group was asked to eat 30 grams of protein per meal in the form of whole foods. That meant they were eating 90 grams of protein a day. The other group—the control group—was put on a typical low-calorie diet with about 50 to 60 grams of protein a day. After six months, researchers found the high protein group had significantly improved their muscle function—almost twice as much as the control group. "They were able to walk faster, had improved balance, and were also able to get up out of a chair faster than the control group," Starr says. All 67 participants were over 60 years of age, and both groups lost about the same amount of weight.

[I] Starr is now looking into whether high-protein diets also improve the quality of the muscle itself in seniors. She's using CT scans to measure muscle size and fat, and comparing seniors on a high-protein diet with those on regular diets. She says her findings should be available in a couple of months.

[J] In the meantime, 70-year-old Corliss Keith, who was in the high protein group in Starr's latest study, says she feels a big difference. "I feel excellent," she says. "I feel like I have a different body, I have more energy, I'm stronger." She says she is able to take Zumba exercise classes three times a week, work out on the *treadmill* (跑步机), and take long, brisk walks. Keith also lost more than 15 pounds. "I'm a fashionable person, so now I'm back in my 3-inch heels," she says.

[K] As people age, Starr says muscle strength is key to helping them stay strong and continue living on their own in their own home. "I feel very much alive now," says Keith. "I feel like I could stay by myself until I'm 100."

[L] But can people overdo protein? Pipitone says you do have to be careful. Other researchers say too much protein can cause *cramps* (痉挛), headaches, and fatigue. Dehydration is also a risk when you eat too much protein. Pipitone says if you increase protein, you also have to increase your fluid intake. "I always tell people to make sure they're drinking enough fluids," which for the average person is 60 to 70 ounces a day, which translates into eight 8-ounce glasses of water or liquid per day.

[M] There have been some indications that extra protein makes the kidneys work harder, which could be problematic for individuals with a history of kidney disease and for them, the supplements may increase the risk of kidney stones, she says.

[N] Bottom line, if you think you need more protein in your diet, consider these questions: Are you an extreme athlete; are you recovering from injury or surgery; or are you 60 years or older? If so, adding high protein foods like eggs and meat products to your diet can be beneficial. And, if you're not sure, it is always a good idea to check with your primary care provider.

36. It is quite easy for one to take in the recommended amount of protein.
37. Pipitone claims that healthy adults need not spend money on protein supplements.
38. The protein supplement business is found to be thriving.
39. Protein can speed the repairing of damaged muscles.
40. Protein supplements may overburden some internal organ, thus leading to its malfunctioning.
41. Older adults need to take in more protein to keep their muscles strong.
42. Protein is found in more foods than people might realize.
43. Additional protein was found to help strengthen the muscles of overweight seniors seeking weight loss.
44. Pipitone believes that whole foods provide the best source of protein.
45. People are advised to drink more liquid when they take in more protein.

Section C

Directions: *There are 2 passages in this section. Each passage is followed by some questions or unfinished statements. For each of them there are four choices marked A), B), C) and D). You should decide on the best choice and mark the corresponding letter on **Answer Sheet 2** with a single line through the centre.*

Passage One

Questions 46 to 50 are based on the following passage.

Last year, a child was born at a hospital in the UK with her heart outside her body. Few babies survive this rare condition, and those who do must endure numerous operations and are likely to have complex needs. When her mother was interviewed, three weeks after her daughter's birth, she was asked if she was prepared for what might be a *daunting* (令人生畏的) task caring for her. She answered without hesitation that, as far as she was concerned, this would be a "privilege".

Rarely has there been a better example of the power of attitude, one of our most powerful psychological tools. Our attitudes allow us to turn mistakes into opportunities, and loss into the chance for new beginnings. An attitude is a settled way of thinking, feeling and/or behaving towards particular objects, people, events or ideologies. We use our attitudes to filter, interpret and react to the world around us. You weren't born with attitudes; rather they are all learned, and this happens in a number of ways.

The most powerful influences occur during early childhood and include both what happened to you directly, and what those around you did and said in your presence. As you acquire a distinctive identity, your attitudes are further refined by the behavior of those with whom you identify—your family, those of your gender and culture, and the people you admire, even though you may not know them personally. Friendships and other important relationships become increasingly important, particularly during adolescence. About that same time and throughout adulthood, the information you receive, especially when ideas are repeated in association with goals and achievements you find attractive, also refines your attitudes.

Many people assume that our attitudes are internally consistent, that is, the way you think and feel about someone or something predicts your behavior towards them. However, many studies have found that feelings and thoughts don't necessarily predict behavior. In general, your attitudes will be internally consistent only when the behavior is easy, and when those around you hold similar beliefs. That's why, for example, many say they believe in the benefits of recycling or exercise, but don't behave in line with their views, because it takes awareness, effort and courage to go beyond merely stating that you believe something is a good idea.

One of the most effective ways to change an attitude is to start behaving as if you already feel and think the way you'd prefer to. Take some time to reflect on your attitudes, to think about what you believe and why. Is there anything you consider a burden rather than a privilege? If so, start behaving—right now——as if the latter is the case.

46. What do we learn from the passage about attitude?
    A) It shapes our beliefs and ideologies.
    B) It improves our psychological wellbeing.
    C) It determines how we respond to our immediate environment.
    D) It changes the way we think, feel and interact with one another.
47. What can contribute to the refinement of one's attitude, according to the passage?
    A) Their idols' behaviors.
    B) Their educational level.
    C) Their contact with the opposite gender.
    D) Their interaction with different cultures.
48. What do many studies find about people's feelings and thoughts?
    A) They may not suggest how a person is going to behave.
    B) They are in a way consistent with a person's mentality.
    C) They may not find expression in interpersonal relations.
    D) They are in line with a person's behavior no matter what.
49. How come many people don't do what they believe is good?
    A) They can't afford the time.
    B) They have no idea how to.
    C) They are hypocritical.
    D) They lack willpower.
50. What is proposed as a strategy to change attitude?

A) Changing things that require one's immediate attention.
B) Starting to act in a way that embodies one's aspirations.
C) Adjusting one's behavior gradually over a period of time.
D) Considering ways of reducing one's psychological burdens.

Passage Two

Questions 51 to 55 are based on the following passage.

Industrial fishing for *krill*（磷虾）in the unspoilt waters around Antarctica is threatening the future of one of the world's last great wildernesses, according to a new report.

The study by Greenpeace analysed the movements of krill fishing vessels in the region and found they were increasingly operating "in the immediate vicinity of penguin colonies and whale-feeding grounds". It also highlights incidents of fishing boats being involved in groundings, oil spills and accidents, which posed a serious threat to the Antarctic ecosystem.

The report, published on Tuesday, comes amid growing concern about the impact of fishing and climate change on the Antarctic. A global campaign has been launched to create a network of ocean sanctuaries to protect the seas in the region and Greenpeace is calling for an immediate halt to fishing in areas being considered for sanctuary status.

Frida Bengtsson from Greenpeace's Protect the Antarctic campaign said: "If the krill industry wants to show it's a responsible player, then it should be voluntarily getting out of any area which is being proposed as an ocean sanctuary, and should instead be backing the protection of these huge tracts of the Antarctic."

A global campaign has been launched to turn a huge tract of Antarctic seas into ocean sanctuaries, protecting wildlife and banning not just krill fishing, but all fishing. One was created in the Ross Sea in 2016, another reserve is being proposed in a vast area of the Weddell Sea, and a third sanctuary is under consideration in the area west of the Antarctic Peninsula—a key krill fishing area.

The Commission for the Conservation of Antarctic Marine Living Resources (CCAMLR) manages the seas around Antarctica. It will decide on the Weddell Sea sanctuary proposal at a conference in Australia in October, although a decision on the peninsula sanctuary is not expected until later.

Keith Reid, a science manager at CCAMLR, said that the organisation sought "a balance between protection, conservation and sustainable fishing in the Southern Ocean." He said although more fishing was taking place nearer penguin colonies it was often happening later in the season when these colonies were empty.

"The creation of a system of marine protected areas is a key part of ongoing scientific and policy discussions in CCAMLR," he added. "Our long-term operation in the region depends on a healthy and thriving Antarctic marine ecosystem, which is why we have always had an open dialogue with the environmental non-governmental organisations. We strongly intend to continue this dialogue, including talks with Greenpeace, to discuss improvements based on the latest scientific data. We are not the ones to decide on the establishment of marine protected areas, but we hope to contribute positively with our knowledge and experience."

51. What does Greenpeace's study find about krill fishing?
A) It caused a great many penguins and whales to migrate.
B) It was depriving penguins and whales of their habitats.
C) It was carried out too close to the habitats of penguins and whales.

D) It posed an unprecedented threat to the wildlife around Antarctica.

52. For what purpose has a global campaign been launched?

   A) To reduce the impact of climate change on Antarctica.

   B) To establish conservation areas in the Antarctic region.

   C) To regulate krill fishing operations in the Antarctic seas.

   D) To publicise the concern about the impact of krill fishing.

53. What is Greenpeace's recommendation to the krill industry?

   A) Opting to operate away from the suggested conservation areas.

   B) Volunteering to protect the endangered species in the Antarctic.

   C) Refraining from krill fishing throughout the breeding season.

   D) Showing its sense of responsibility by leading the global campaign.

54. What did CCAMLR aim to do according to its science manager?

   A) Raise public awareness of the vulnerability of Antarctic species.

   B) Ban all commercial fishing operations in the Southern Ocean.

   C) Keep the penguin colonies from all fishing interference.

   D) Sustain fishing without damaging the Antarctic ecosystem.

55. How does CCAMLR define its role in the conservation of the Antarctic environment?

   A) A coordinator in policy discussions.   C) A provider of the needed expertise.

   B) An authority on big data analysis.   D) An initiator of marine sanctuaries.

Part IV Translation (30 minutes)

Directions: *For this part, you are allowed 30 minutes to translate a passage from Chinese into English. You should write your answer on **Answer Sheet 2**.*

荷花(lotus flower)是中国的名花之一,深受人们喜爱。中国许多地方的湖泊和池塘都适宜荷花生长。荷花色彩鲜艳,夏日清晨绽放,夜晚闭合,花期长达两三个月,吸引来自各地的游客前往观赏。荷花具有多种功能,既能绿化水面,又能美化庭园,还可净化水质、减少污染、改善环境。荷花迎骄阳而不惧,出污泥而不染,象征纯洁、高雅,常常用来比喻人的高尚品德,历来是诗人画家创作的重要题材。荷花盛开的地方也是许多摄影爱好者经常光顾之地。

答案速查

Part II Listening Comprehension

Section A 1. A 2. B 3. A 4. C 5. D 6. B 7. C 8. B

Section B 9. C 10. D 11. D 12. A 13. B 14. C 15. A

Section C 16. D 17. A 18. B 19. D 20. A 21. C 22. C 23. B 24. D 25. C

Part III Reading Comprehension

Section A 26. K 27. C 28. N 29. M 30. D 31. I 32. H 33. J 34. O 35. L

Section B 36. C 37. E 38. A 39. F 40. M 41. G 42. B 43. H 44. D 45. L

Section C 46. C 47. A 48. A 49. D 50. B 51. C 52. B 53. A 54. D 55. C

未得到监考教师指令前，不得翻阅该试题册！

2019年12月大学英语六级考试真题（第三套）

Part Ⅰ　　　　　　　　　　Writing　　　　　　　　　　(30 minutes)

（请于正式开考后半小时内完成该部分，之后将进行听力考试）

Directions: *For this part, you are allowed 30 minutes to write an essay on* **the importance of having a sense of community responsibility**. *You should write at least* **150** *words but no more than* **200** *words.*

Part Ⅱ　　　　Listening Comprehension　　　　(30 minutes)

说明：由于2019年12月六级考试全国共考了两套听力，本套真题听力与前两套内容相同，只是选项顺序不同，因此在本套真题中不再重复出现。

Part Ⅲ　　　　Reading Comprehension　　　　(40 minutes)

Section A

Directions: *In this section, there is a passage with ten blanks. You are required to select one word for each blank from a list of choices given in a word bank following the passage. Read the passage through carefully before making your choices. Each choice in the bank is identified by a letter. Please mark the corresponding letter for each item on* **Answer Sheet 2** *with a single line through the centre. You may not use any of the words in the bank more than once.*

The number of devices you can talk to is multiplying—first it was your phone, then your car, and now you can tell your kitchen appliances what to do. But even without gadgets that understand our spoken commands, research suggests that, as bizarre as it sounds, under certain __26__, people regularly ascribe human traits to everyday objects.

Sometimes we see things as human because we are __27__. In one experiment, people who reported feeling isolated were more likely than others to attribute __28__ to various gadgets. In turn, feeling close to objects can __29__ loneliness. When college students were reminded of a time they had been __30__ in a social setting, they compensated by exaggerating their number of friends—unless they were first given tasks that caused them to interact with their phone as if it had human qualities. According to the researchers, the participants' phones __31__ substituted for real friends.

At other times, we personify products in an effort to understand them. One study found that three in four respondents yelled at their computer. Further, the more their computer gave them problems, the more likely the respondents were to report that it had its own "beliefs and 32 ."

So how do people assign traits to an object? In part, we rely on looks. On humans, wide faces are 33 with dominance. Similarly, people rated cars, clocks, and watches with wide faces as more dominant-looking than narrow-faced ones, and preferred them—especially in 34 situations. An analysis of car sales in Germany found that cars with *grilles*（护栅）that were upturned like smiles sold best. The purchasers saw this 35 as increasing a car's friendliness.

A) alleviate
B) apparently
C) arrogant
D) associated
E) circumstances
F) competitive
G) conceded
H) consciousness
I) desires
J) excluded
K) feature
L) lonely
M) separate
N) spectacularly
O) warrant

Section B

Directions: *In this section, you are going to read a passage with ten statements attached to it. Each statement contains information given in one of the paragraphs. Identify the paragraph from which the information is derived. You may choose a paragraph more than once. Each paragraph is marked with a letter. Answer the questions by marking the corresponding letter on* **Answer Sheet 2**.

Why More Farmers Are Switching to Grass-Fed Meat and Dairy

[A] Though he didn't come from a farming family, from a young age Tim Joseph was fascinated by the idea of living off the land. Reading magazines like *The Stockman Grass Farmer* and *Graze*, he got hooked on the idea of grass-fed agriculture. The idea that all energy and wealth comes from the sun really intrigued him. He thought the shorter the distance between the sun and the end product, the higher the profit to the farmer.

[B] Joseph wanted to put this theory to the test. In 2009, he and his wife Laura launched Maple Hill Creamery, an organic, all grass-fed yogurt company in northern New York. He quickly learned what the market has demonstrated: Demand for grass-fed products currently exceeds supply. Grass-fed beef is enjoying a 25–30% annual growth rate. Sales of grass-fed yogurt and *kefir*（发酵乳饮品）, on the other hand, have in the last year increased by over 38%. This is in comparison with a drop of just under 1% in the total yogurt and kefir market, according to natural and organic market research company SPINS. Joseph's top priority became getting his hands on enough grass-fed milk to keep customers satisfied, since his own 64-cow herd wasn't going to suffice.

[C] His first partnership was with Paul and Phyllis Amburgh, owners of the Dharma Lea farm in New York. The Amburghs, too, were true believers in grass-fed. In addition to supplying milk from their own 85-head herd, they began to help other farmers in the area convert from conventional to certified organic and grass-fed in order to enter the Maple Hill supply chain. Since 2010, the couple has helped 125 small dairy farms convert to grass-fed, with more than 80% of those farms coming on board during the last two years.

[D] All this conversion has helped Maple Hill grow 40–50% every year since it began, with no end in sight. Joseph has learned that a farmer has to have a certain mindset to successfully convert. But convincing open-minded dairy people is actually not that hard, when you look at the economics. Grass-fed milk can fetch up to 2.5 times the price of conventional milk. Another factor is the squeeze that conventional dairy farmers have felt as the price of grain they feed their cows has gone up, tightening their profit margins. By replacing expensive grain feed with regenerative management practices, grass-fed farmers are insulated from jumps in the price of feed. These practices include grazing animals on grasses grown from the pastureland's natural seed bank, and fertilized by the cows' own fertilizer.

[E] Champions of this type of regenerative grazing also point to its animal welfare, climate and health benefits: Grass-fed animals live longer out of confinement. Grazing herds stimulate microbial (微生物的) activity in the soil, helping to capture water and separate carbon. And grass-fed dairy and meat have been shown to be higher in certain nutrients and healthy fats.

[F] In the grass-fed system, farmers are also not subject to the wildly fluctuating milk prices of the international commodity market. The unpredictability of global demand and the lag-time it takes to add more cows to a herd to meet demand can result in events like the recent cheese surplus. Going grass-fed is a safe refuge, a way for family-scale farms to stay viable. Usually a farmer will get to the point where financially, what they're doing is not working. That's when they call Maple Hill. If the farm is well managed and has enough land, and the desire to convert is sincere, a relationship can begin. Through regular regional educational meetings, a large annual meeting, individual farm visits and thousands of phone calls, the Amburghs pass on the principles of pasture management. Maple Hill signs a contract pledging to buy the farmer's milk at a guaranteed base price, plus quality premiums and incentives for higher protein, butter-fat and other solids.

[G] While Maple Hill's conversion program is unusually hands-on and comprehensive, it's just one of a growing number of businesses committed to slowly changing the way America farms. Joseph calls sharing his knowledge network through peer-to-peer learning a core piece of the company's culture. Last summer, Massachusetts grass-fed beef advocate John Smith launched Big Picture Beef, a network of small grass-fed beef farms in New England and New York that is projected to bring to market 2,500 head of cattle from 125 producers this year. Early indications are that Smith will have no shortage of farm members. Since he began to informally announce the network at farming conferences and on social media, he's received a steady stream of inquiries from interested farmers.

[H] Smith says he'll provide services ranging from formal seminars to on-farm workshops on holistic (整体的) management, to one-on-one hand-holding and an almost 24/7 phone hotline for farmers who are converting. In exchange, he guarantees an above-market price for each animal and a calf-to-customer electronic ear tag ID system like that used in the European Union.

[I] Though advocates portray grass-fed products as a win-win situation for all, they do have downsides. Price, for one, is an issue. Joseph says his products are priced 10–20% above organic versions, but depending on the product chosen, compared to non-organic conventional yogurt, consumers could pay a premium of 30–50% or more for grass-fed. As for the meat, Smith says his grass-fed hamburger will be priced 20–25% over the conventional alternative. But a look at the prices on online grocer Fresh Direct suggests a grass-fed premium of anywhere from 35–60%.

[J] And not every farmer has the option of going grass-fed. For both beef and dairy production, it requires, at least in the beginning, more pastureland. Grass-fed beef production tends to be more labor-intensive as well. But Smith counters that if you factor in the hidden cost of government corn subsidies, environment degradation, and decreased human health and animal welfare, grass-fed is the more cost-effective model. "The sun provides the lowest cost of production and the cheapest meat," he says.

[K] Another grass-fed booster spurring farmers to convert is EPIC, which makes meat-based protein bars. Founders Taylor Collins and his wife, Katie Forrest, used to be endurance athletes; now they're advocates of grass-fed meat. Soon after launching EPIC'S most successful product—the Bison Bacon Cranberry Bar—Collins and Forrest found they'd exhausted their sources for *bison*（北美野牛）raised exclusively on pasture. When they started researching the supply chain, they learned that only 2–3% of all bison is actually grass-fed. The rest is feed-lot confined and fed grain and corn.

[L] But after General Mills bought EPIC in 2016, Collins and Forrest suddenly had the resources they needed to expand their supply chain. So the company teamed up with Wisconsin-based rancher Northstar Bison. EPIC fronted the money for the purchase of $2.5 million worth of young bison that will be raised according to its grass-fed protocols, with a guaranteed purchase price. The message to young people who might not otherwise be able to afford to break into the business is, "'You can purchase this $3 million piece of land here, because I'm guaranteeing you today you'll have 1,000 bison on it.' We're bringing new blood into the old, conventional farming ecosystem, which is really cool to see," Collins explains.

36. Farmers going grass-fed are not affected by the ever-changing milk prices of the global market.
37. Over the years, Tim Joseph's partners have helped many dairy farmers to switch to grass-fed.
38. One advocate believes that many other benefits should be taken into consideration when we assess the cost-effectiveness of grass-fed farming.
39. Many dairy farmers were persuaded to switch to grass-fed when they saw its advantage in terms of profits.
40. Tim Joseph's grass-fed program is only one example of how American farming practice is changing.
41. Tim Joseph was fascinated by the notion that sunlight brings energy and wealth to mankind.
42. One problem with grass-fed products is that they are usually more expensive than conventional ones.
43. Grass-fed products have proved to be healthier and more nutritious.
44. When Tim Joseph started his business, he found grass-fed products fell short of demand.
45. A snack bar producer discovered that the supply of purely grass-fed bison meat was scarce.

Section C

Directions: *There are 2 passages in this section. Each passage is followed by some questions or unfinished statements. For each of them there are four choices marked A), B), C) and D). You should decide on the best choice and mark the corresponding letter on **Answer Sheet 2** with a single line through the centre.*

Passage One

Questions 46 to 50 are based on the following passage.

Schools are not just a *microcosm*（缩影）of society; they mediate it too. The best seek to alleviate the external pressures on their pupils while equipping them better to understand and handle the world outside—at once sheltering them and broadening their horizons. This is ambitious in any circumstances, and in a divided and unequal society the two ideals can clash *outright*(直接地).

Trips that many adults would consider the adventure of a lifetime—treks in Borneo, a sports tour to Barbados—appear to have become almost routine at some state schools. Parents are being asked for thousands of pounds. Though schools cannot profit from these trips, the companies that arrange them do. Meanwhile, pupils arrive at school hungry because their families can't afford breakfast. The Child Poverty Action Group says nine out of 30 in every classroom fall below the poverty line. The discrepancy is startlingly apparent. Introducing a fundraising requirement for students does not help, as better-off children can tap up richer aunts and neighbours.

Probing the rock pools of a local beach or practising French on a language exchange can fire children's passions, boost their skills and open their eyes to life's possibilities. Educational outings help bright but disadvantaged students to get better scores in A-level tests. In this globalised age, there is a good case for international travel, and some parents say they can manage the cost of a school trip abroad more easily than a family holiday. Even in the face of immense and mounting financial pressures, some schools have shown remarkable determination and ingenuity in ensuring that all their pupils are able to take up opportunities that may be truly life-changing. They should be applauded. Methods such as whole-school fundraising, with the *proceeds*(收益)pooled, can help to extend opportunities and fuel community spirit.

But £3,000 trips cannot be justified when the average income for families with children is just over £30,000. Such initiatives close doors for many pupils. Some parents pull their children out of school because of expensive field trips. Even parents who can see that a trip is little more than a party or celebration may well feel guilt that their child is left behind.

The Department for Education's guidance says schools can charge only for board and lodging if the trip is part of the syllabus, and that students receiving government aid are exempt from these costs. However, many schools seem to ignore the advice; and it does not cover the kind of glamorous, exotic trips, which are becoming increasingly common. Schools cannot be expected to bring together communities single-handed. But the least we should expect is that they do not foster divisions and exclude those who are already disadvantaged.

46. What does the author say best schools should do?
    A) Prepare students to both challenge and change the divided unequal society.
    B) Protect students from social pressures and enable them to face the world.
    C) Motivate students to develop their physical as well as intellectual abilities.
    D) Encourage students to be ambitious and help them to achieve their goals.

47. What does the author think about school field trips?
    A) They enable students from different backgrounds to mix with each other.
    B) They widen the gap between privileged and disadvantaged students.
    C) They give the disadvantaged students a chance to see the world.
    D) They only benefit students with rich relatives and neighbours.

48. What does the author suggest can help build community spirit?
    A) Events aiming to improve community services.　　C) Events that require mutual understanding.
    B) Activities that help to fuel students' ingenuity.　　D) Activities involving all students on campus.

49. What do we learn about low-income parents regarding school field trips?
    A) They want their children to participate even though they don't see much benefit.

B) They don't want their kids to participate but find it hard to keep them from going.
C) They don't want their kids to miss any chance to broaden their horizons despite the cost.
D) They want their children to experience adventures but they don't want them to run risks.

50. What is the author's expectation of schools?
    A) Bringing a community together with ingenuity.
    B) Resolving the existing discrepancies in society.
    C) Avoiding creating new gaps among students.
    D) Giving poor students preferential treatment.

Passage Two

Questions 51 to 55 are based on the following passage.

Rising temperatures and overfishing in the *pristine*（未受污染的）waters around the Antarctic could see king penguin populations pushed to the brink of extinction by the end of the century, according to a new study. The study's report states that as global warming transforms the environment in the world's last great wilderness, 70 percent of king penguins could either disappear or be forced to find new breeding grounds.

Co-author Celine Le Bohec, from the University of Strasbourg in France, warned: "If there're no actions aimed at halting or controlling global warming, and the pace of the current human-induced changes such as climate change and overfishing stays the same, the species may soon disappear." The findings come amid growing concern over the future of the Antarctic. Earlier this month a separate study found that a combination of climate change and industrial fishing is threatening the *krill*（磷虾）population in Antarctic waters, with a potentially disastrous impact on whales, seals and penguins. But today's report is the starkest warning yet of the potentially devastating impact of climate change and human exploitation on the Antarctic's delicate ecosystems.

Le Bohec said: "Unless current greenhouse gas emissions drop, 70 percent of king penguins—1.1 million breeding pairs—will be forced to relocate their breeding grounds, or face extinction by 2100." King penguins are the second-largest type of penguin and only breed on specific isolated islands in the Southern Ocean where there is no ice cover and easy access to the sea. As the ocean warms, a body of water called the Antarctic Polar Front—an upward movement of nutrient-rich sea that supports a huge abundance of marine life—is being pushed further south. This means that king penguins, which feed on fish and krill in this body of water, have to travel further to their feeding grounds, leaving their hungry chicks for longer. And as the distance between their breeding grounds and their food grows, entire colonies could be wiped out.

Le Bohec said: "The plight of the king penguin should serve as a warning about the future of the entire marine environment in the Antarctic. Penguins, like other seabirds and marine mammals, occupy higher levels in the food chain and they are what we call bio-indicators of their ecosystems." Penguins are sensitive indicators of changes in marine ecosystems. As such, they are key species for understanding and predicting impacts of global change on Antarctic and sub-Antarctic marine ecosystems. The report found that although some king penguins may be able to relocate to new breeding grounds closer to their retreating food source, suitable new habitats would be scarce. Only a handful of islands in the Southern Ocean are suitable for sustaining large breeding colonies.

51. What will happen by 2100, according to a new study?
    A) King penguins in the Antarctic will be on the verge of dying out.
    B) Sea water will rise to a much higher level around the Antarctic.
    C) The melting ice cover will destroy the great Antarctic wilderness.

D) The pristine waters around the Antarctic will disappear forever.

52. What do we learn from the findings of a separate study?
    A) Shrinking krill population and rising temperatures could force Antarctic whales to migrate.
    B) Human activities have accelerated climate change in the Antarctic region in recent years.
    C) Industrial fishing and climate change could be fatal to certain Antarctic species.
    D) Krill fishing in the Antarctic has worsened the pollution of the pristine waters.

53. What does the passage say about king penguins?
    A) They will turn out to be the second-largest species of birds to become extinct.
    B) Many of them will have to migrate to isolated islands in the Southern Ocean.
    C) They feed primarily on only a few kinds of krill in the Antarctic Polar Front.
    D) The majority of them may have to find new breeding grounds in the future.

54. What happens when sea levels rise in the Antarctic?
    A) Many baby king penguins can't have food in time.
    B) Many king penguins could no longer live on krill.
    C) Whales will invade king penguins' breeding grounds.
    D) Whales will have to travel long distances to find food.

55. What do we learn about the Southern Ocean?
    A) The king penguins there are reluctant to leave for new breeding grounds.
    B) Its conservation is key to the sustainable propagation of Antarctic species.
    C) It is most likely to become the ultimate retreat for species like the king penguin.
    D) Only a few of its islands can serve as huge breeding grounds for king penguins.

Part Ⅳ　　　　　　　　Translation　　　　　　　　(30 minutes)

Directions: *For this part, you are allowed 30 minutes to translate a passage from Chinese into English. You should write your answer on **Answer Sheet 2**.*

梅花（plum blossom）位居中国十大名花之首，源于中国南方，已有三千多年的栽培和种植历史。隆冬时节，五颜六色的梅花不畏严寒，迎着风雪傲然绽放。在中国传统文化中，梅花象征着坚强、纯洁、高雅，激励人们不畏艰难、砥砺前行。自古以来，许多诗人和画家从梅花中获取灵感，创作了无数不朽的作品。普通大众也都喜爱梅花，春节期间常用于家庭装饰。南京市已将梅花定为市花，每年举办梅花节，成千上万的人冒着严寒到梅花山踏雪赏梅。

答案速查

Part Ⅱ　Listening Comprehension　（略）
Part Ⅲ　Reading Comprehension
Section A　26. E　27. L　28. H　29. A　30. J　31. B　32. I　33. D　34. F　35. K
Section B　36. F　37. C　38. J　39. D　40. G　41. A　42. I　43. E　44. B　45. K
Section C　46. B　47. B　48. D　49. A　50. C　51. A　52. C　53. D　54. A　55. D